探史求新

——庆祝郭书春先生八十华诞文集

80

哈尔滨工业大学出版社
HARBIN INSTITUTE OF TECHNOLOGY PRESS

▲中国科学院自然科学史研究所在北京九爷府旧址

▲篇首油画系郭书春之侄郭晓军所绘

▲ 中国科学院自然科学史研究所新址

探史求新

庆祝郭书春先生八十华诞文集

郭书春，1941年生，山东省胶州市人，中国科学院自然科学史研究所研究员。1964年8月山东大学数学系毕业后，分配到新建设杂志社工作，随即去山东海阳参加"四清"和劳动学习。1965年12月调至中国科学院中国自然科学史研究室（自然科学史研究所的前身）工作。1992年起享受政府特殊津贴。1993年被国家学位委员会批准为博士生导师。2019年被评为国际科学史研究院通讯院士。曾任自然科学史研究所学术委员会副主任、工会主席、古代数学天文学史研究室主任、全国数学史学会理事长。

他长期从事数学史研究，发表论文100余篇，著有《汇校〈九章算术〉》及其增补版、《九章算术新校》、《古代世界数学泰斗刘徽》、《译注〈九章算术〉》、中法双语评注本《九章算术》（合作）、汉英对照本《九章算术》（合作）、汉英对照本《四元玉鉴》（合作）、《九章算术译注》等学术著作30余种。主持编纂《中国科学技术典籍通汇·数学卷》《中华科技五千年》《李俨钱宝琮科学史全集》《中国科学技术史·数学卷》《中国科学技术史·辞典卷》《中华大典·数学典》等大型著作，主编科普读物《大众科学技术史丛书》。主编的《李俨钱宝琮科学史全集》获"第4届国家图书奖荣誉奖"，主编的《中国科学技术史·数学卷》获"第四届郭沫若中国历史学奖一等奖"，与林力娜（Karine Chemla）合著的 *LES NEUF CHAPITRES: Le Classique mathématique de la Chine ancienne et ses commentaires*（中法双语评注本《九章算术》）获法兰西学士院"平山郁夫奖"。

他共指导和培养了9名博士、硕士研究生。目前正主持国家社科基金重大项目"刘徽李淳风贾宪杨辉注《九章算术》的研究与英译"和国家出版署2021—2035出版规划课题"中国古代数学典籍汇编"。

探史求新
庆祝郭书春先生八十华诞文集

▲1955年2月郭书春的长兄郭集亭、五哥郭常春带病危的母亲去青岛山东大学附属医院看病后所照

▲1956年10月郭书春与父亲、五哥郭常春在青岛

▲1988年郭书春的二哥郭新春

▲1968年5月郭书春与三哥郭淑元、五哥郭常春在北京

探史求新
庆祝郭书春先生八十华诞文集

▲ 2000年7月郭书春与四哥郭阳春、五哥郭常春、侄子郭金铭、侄女郭小宁在父母的墓前致哀

▲ 1969年郭书春夫妇在天安门广场

▲ 2000年8月郭书春夫妇在故乡山东青岛胶州墨河岸边

▲ 2005年4月郭书春夫妇在胶州东埠村已废弃的故居前

探史求新
庆祝郭书春先生八十华诞文集

▲2007年3月23日郭书春夫妇在北海公园仿膳饭庄为孙女王巽庆祝7岁生日

▲2017年5月郭书春在山东胶州艾山郑玄洞前（郑玄是与胶州相邻的高密人，通《九章算术》）

◀2021年郭书春孙女王巽在加州大学伯克利学院毕业到耶鲁大学读研究生之前回国度假，左起夫人王玉芝，女儿郭健，郭书春，孙女王巽，姑爷王文嘉

▲1985年郭书春在巴黎凯旋门

探史求新
庆祝郭书春先生八十华诞文集

◀ 郭书春与林力娜、詹嘉玲、韩琦及郎元等聚餐（1993年9月8日）

郭书春与部分弟子、再传弟子参加中国科学院自然科学史研究所建所60周年学术研讨会（左起朱一文、郭金海、郭书春、田淼、邹大海、陈巍、牛腾）▶

◀ 2019年6月7日"端午节"中国科学院自然科学史研究所门前合影（左起陈建平、张柏春、道本周、郭书春、王玉芝、邹大海、郭金海）

探史求新
庆祝郭书春先生八十华诞文集

▲ 一次关于《九章算术》的科普视频

▲ 1999年8月郭书春与高中部分同班同学回母校青岛第一中学参加75周年校庆

▲ 郭书春协助河北省组建祖冲之研究会（左第二人起冯立昇、郭书春、林群、祖绍春、乔京城、张泽）

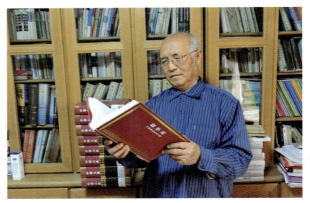

▲ 郭书春主持编纂的《中华大典·数学典》于2018年出版，含4个分典，9册，1490余万字

探史求新

庆祝郭书春先生八十华诞文集

▲ 2019年10月郭书春与郭金海参观中国科学院院史展览，在李俨(下)、钱宝琮(上)二老照片前留影

▲ 2020年12月郭书春在首届珠心算发展高端论坛上发言

▲ 2021年3月23日郭书春参加中国珠算博物馆布展大纲专家论证会

探史求新
庆祝郭书春先生八十华诞文集

◀ 张文台题辞

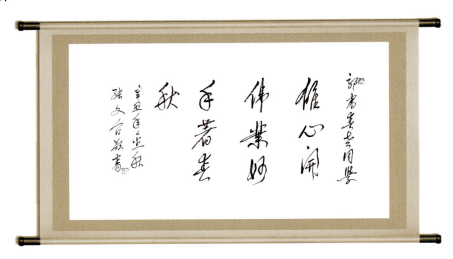

释文：
郭书春老同学
雄心开伟业，妙手著春秋
辛丑年金秋张文台敬书

　　张文台，郭书春在山东省青岛市胶州毛家沟小学的同学，中国共产党第十五、十六届中央委员，中国人民解放军上将，曾任济南军区政委、总后勤部政委。

◀ 郭成春手书——龙蹚肇岁　麟笔书春

　　郭成春（1917—1987），郭书春长兄，长期从事教学工作，后务农。

杜石然贺联

值此新春到来之际，又值吾弟八十华诞，谨以传统春联以及前贤名作移花接木，借花献佛，得对联一副为吾弟寿。联曰：

羲经开泰　汉唐千余年　算经十书校点　周髀　缉古　五经　五曹　记事提要　含英咀华　沉浸浓郁
麟笔书春　华诞八十载　九章算术解读　方田　方程　粟米　勾股　纂言勾玄　爬罗剔抉　刮垢磨光

见笑，见笑。愚兄杜石然拜手恭贺并祝阖家春节健康快乐

杜石然，中国科学院自然科学史研究所研究员、博士生导师、著名数学史家、中国科学史家。

李文林手书——九章之星

李文林，著名数学史家，中国科学院数学研究所原党委书记、副所长，中国数学会秘书长，全国数学史学会理事长。

◀ 袁向东贺书春好友八十寿诞

贺书春好友八十寿诞
——袁向东

四十春秋艰辛路，
一路小跑伙伴多；
今朝八十体尚健，
老骥伏枥志未休。

袁向东，著名数学史家，中国科学院数学与系统科学研究院研究员。

◀ 姜丽魁——赠郭书春君

赠郭书春君
——姜丽魁

读书破万卷，史籍逢春天。
笔耕五十载，著文立新篇。
专著留青史，普物惠少年。
论语治天下，数史鉴科研。

姜丽魁，郭书春高中、大学同学，天津师范大学计算机学院教授。

探史求新
庆祝郭书春先生八十华诞文集

◀ 胡云复题辞

胡云复，郭书春夫人王玉芝在北京师范大学历史系的同学。著名书法家，师从启功。

◀ 张泽贺郭先生八十华诞——临江仙

临江仙
(贺郭先生八十华诞)
——张泽

曾与元首留客饮，
津贴大奖相逢。
忽惊朝杖笑如童。
秉烛午夜，
健步舞东风。

九章算术文远韵，
等身著作丰功。
胶州海域起蛟龙，
山青水阔，
百岁运如鸿。

张泽，河北祖冲之中学前校长，河北祖冲之研究会副会长兼秘书长。

探史求新
庆祝郭书春先生八十华诞文集

◀ 萧灿诗　陈松长书

释文：

郭老吾前辈，德行迈等伦。
童颜开八秩，椽笔敌千钧。
数学书新史，九章探异珍。
惟南将献寿，松鹤映青春。

湖南萧灿作，松长书，以贺书春先生八十华诞。
壬寅正月廿七日，时长沙阳光灿烂，一片早春气象也。
（上印文："陈松长"，下印文"斯是斋"）

萧灿，湖南大学建筑学院教授。
陈松长，湖南大学岳麓书院副院长。

编者简介

邹大海，理学硕士，2006年起任中国科学院自然史研究所研究员，2010年起任博士生导师。曾任研究所编辑部主任、学位评定委员会副主任、《自然科学史研究》副主编、中国数学会理事。现任《自然科学史研究》主编、中国科学院自然科学史研究所学位评定委员会主任、国际科学史研究院通讯院士、中国数学会数学史分会副理事长、湖北省社会科学院科技史研究中心主任、研究员，河北省祖冲之研究会副理事长。主要研究中国数学史和中国早期科学思想史。发表论文《墨家名家的不可分量思想与运动观》《睡虎地秦简与先秦数学》《从出土简牍文献看中国早期的正负数概念》《中国上古时代数学门类均输新探》等40余篇，专著《中国数学的兴起与先秦数学》(2001)、《中国数学在奠基时期的形态、创造与发展》(2022)和工具书《中国近现代科学技术史论著目录》(主编，2006)等。

郭金海，天津人，中国科学院自然科学史研究所研究员、博士生导师。2003年毕业于中国科学院自然科学史研究所，获理学博士学位。主要研究中国数学史、中国近现代科技史、中国科学院院史。发表学术论文50余篇；著有《中国近代中学数学教科书研究》《现代数学在中国的奠基：全面抗战前的大学数学系及其数学传播活动》《院士制度在中国的创立与重建》(获"第三届科史哲青年著作奖")及其英文版 *The Establishment and Reconstruction of the Academician System in China*；访问整理有《席泽宗口述自传》；合作访问整理有《徐利治访谈录》《有话可说——丁石孙访谈录》；整理有《四元玉鉴(汉英对照本)》；参与撰著《中国科学院教育发展史》《中国科学技术史·数学卷》。现任中国科学院自然科学史研究所学术委员会委员、中国数学史学会常务理事、中国数学会理事、《中国科技史杂志》编委、中国科学院院史咨询专家组成员。

田淼，中国科学院自然科学史研究所研究员，博士生导师。1989年考入天津师范大学数学系跟随李兆华老师学习数学史。1994年至1997年就读于中国科学院自然科学史研究所，在郭书春老师指导下完成博士论文《清末书院的数学教育》。以跨文化传统的科学技术交流与比较为主要研究方向。曾在柏林工业大学、巴黎第七大学做博士后研究，并在德国马普学会科学史研究所、法国科研中心、英国剑桥李约瑟研究所任访问学者，在德国海德堡大学、纽伦堡－爱尔兰根大学任客座教授等职。现任自然科学史研究所世界科技史研究室主任、学术委员会委员，并兼任欧洲科学基金会评审、国家语言文字委员会外语中文译写规范部际联席会议专家委员会委员、全国科学技术名词审定委员会委员、*Chinese Annals of History of Science and Technology* 编委、《自然科学史研究》编委、《中国大百科全书》（第三版）科技史卷编委等职。出版《中国数学的西化历程》《传播与会通——〈奇器图说〉研究与校注》（合著）、《科技革命与意大利现代化》（合著）、《科技革命与中国现代化》（合著）等专著及中外文论文三十余篇。

前　言

郭书春先生是我国享有国际声誉的中国数学史家。1941年出生于山东省胶州市胶西东埠村的一个农民家庭。1949—1953年8月在原籍读小学，1953年9月—1959年7月就读于青岛第一中学，1959年9月—1964年8月就读于山东大学数学系，1964年8月毕业分配到哲学社会科学部（今中国社会科学院）新建设杂志社。1965年12月调至中国科学院中国自然科学史研究室（自然科学史研究所的前身），中国数学史学科奠基人之一钱宝琮先生和研究室领导希望他从事世界数学史研究，但不久后"文化大革命"爆发，研究室的主管部门——哲学社会科学部彻底停止了业务工作，先生和研究室的同事都未能在科研业务上开展工作，但他偷偷自学了法语。1978年，神州大地迎来科学的春天，中国科技史研究事业焕发勃勃生机。先生因未学过英语，感到做世界数学史研究力不从心，但他克服因中国数学史研究"贫矿论"而造成的畏难情绪，下定决心研究《九章算术》及其刘徽注原著，遂走上中国数学史研究之路。先生先后于1978、1986、1991年晋升为助理研究员、副研究员、研究员，1992年成为享受政府特殊津贴专家，1993年被国家学位委员会批准为博士生导师，2019年当选为国际科学史研究院通讯院士。

1978年迄今，先生共发表论文100余篇，著有学术著作近30种（含合作），主编学术著作10余种（含合作），硕果累累。先生关于《九章算术》和刘徽的研究极具创新性，取得国内外瞩目的成就。由于先生的这项工作，20世纪八九十年代海峡两岸、国内外数学史界出现了《九章算术》和刘徽研究的高潮。先生因为自己理科出身，文史知识先天不足的弱点，恶补了版本学和校勘学的知识，校雠了《九章算术》约20个不同的版本，纠正了前人大量错校，在吴文俊、李学勤、严敦杰等学者的支持下，完成汇校《九章算术》，将《九章算术》的校勘推进到一个新的阶段。先生与法国国家科学研究中心林力娜（Karine Chemla）教授合著的 *LES NEUF CHAPITRES：Le Classique mathématique de la Chine ancienne et ses commentaires*（中法双语评注本《九章算术》）于2004年在巴黎出版，不到一年便重印，

2006年获法兰西学士院"平山郁夫奖"。此书现已成为国际学界了解和研究《九章算术》的重要文献。先生在先秦数学与秦汉数学简牍研究、祖冲之和《算经十书》研究、宋元明清数学研究等方面，也颇有建树。

除了出众的数学史研究能力外，先生还具有很强的学术组织和领导能力。《中国科学技术典籍通汇·数学卷》《中华科技五千年》《李俨钱宝琮科学史全集》《中国科学技术史·数学卷》《中国科学技术史·辞典卷》《中华大典·数学典》《大众科学技术史丛书》等大型著作或丛书都是由他主持编纂的。其中，《李俨钱宝琮科学史全集》和《中国科学技术史·数学卷》获得我国学界的高度评价，分别获"第四届国家图书奖荣誉奖"（1999年）、第四届"郭沫若中国历史学一等奖"（2012年）。他撰写或主编的学术著作大多数被重印，有的11年间重印或修订出版9次。1994年先生当选为全国数学史学会副理事长，继而于1998年当选为理事长，多次组织数学史学术会议，为推进我国数学史界的学术交流和数学史学科建设做出了重要贡献。他还为河北省祖冲之研究会、祖冲之科技园的筹建和发展做出了重要贡献，并支持位于四川省安岳县的秦九韶纪念馆的布展工作。

先生也是一位出色的数学史教育家。20世纪90年代以来，经先生指导（包括与其他导师共同指导）获得博士、硕士学位的研究生共9人（按时间先后）：邹大海、田淼、傅海伦、乌云其其格、段耀勇、郭金海、朱一文、郑振初、祝捷。1998年，先生荣获"中国科学院优秀教师"称号。此外，先生还指导过两位外国学生。第一位是法国的林力娜（Karine Chemla）。1981年，林力娜到中国科学院自然科学史研究所学习中国数学史，先生是其主要教师。第二位是日本进修生莲沼澄子（原名小林澄子，婚后改为现名）。先生指导她学习《九章算术》。此外，先生指导过到自然科学史研究所进修的陈建平（Jian-Ping Jeff Chen）博士学习中国数学史。先生退休后曾应邀到中国科学技术大学科技史与科技考古系、中山大学哲学系和名师讲坛讲授中国数学史课，传播相关知识和治学理念、方法，为这些机构的人才培养也贡献了力量。

2021年是先生的八十华诞。为了庆祝这个重要的值得纪念的寿辰，先生的研究生发起编纂这本文集。征稿始于2021年元月，历时一年多稿子齐备。先生的同仁、挚友美国道本周（Joseph W. Dauben，国际数学史学会前主席）教授、陈建平教授，丹麦华道安（Donald B. Wagner）教授、英国古克礼（Christopher Cullen，李约瑟研究所前所长）教授、法国詹嘉玲（Catherine Jami）教授、林力娜教授、日本森本光生教授、小川束教授、莲沼澄子女士，韩国洪性士（Hong Sung Sa）教授（韩国数学史学会前理事长）、洪英喜（Hong Young Hee）教授等都从海外发来大作。大陆同仁、挚友代钦教授、邓亮博士、冯立昇教授、高红成教授、郭世荣教授和吴东铭博士、韩琦教授、华觉明研究员、纪志刚教授、李兆华教授、刘邦凡教授、刘芹英教授、罗见今教授、吕变庭教授、乔希民教授、曲安京教授、王青建教授、王荣彬研究员和许微微女士、徐传胜教授、徐泽林教授和田春芝博士、杨国选先生、俞晓群先生、张一杰先生、周瀚光教授（按姓氏拼音为序；文章如合作，则按第一作者姓氏排序，第二作者排于第一作者之后),以及先生指导的学生段耀勇、傅海伦、郑振初(中国香港)、朱一文,再传弟子陈巍等,中国台湾的洪万生教授、李国伟教授、孙文先先生(中国台湾九章出版社社长)等都贡献了大作。先生的同学张文台上将、姜丽魁教授,师兄杜石然研究员,好友李文林研究员、袁向东研究员、胡云复教授、张泽校长、萧灿教授和陈松长教授都慷慨赠诗题字。

创新是科技史研究事业发展的重要驱动力,是一代代专业研究者的崇高追求。因此,文集取名"探史求新"。文集分"学术论文""回忆与评价""访谈录"三部分。"学术论文"收录论文27篇,内容涉及中国数学史、中国天文学史、数学思想与数学起源、日本数学史、朝鲜数学史等研究领域。"回忆与评价"收录文章15篇,包括对先生的回忆和为《郭书春数学史自选集》写的序、书评等,从中可见先生指导学生、参加学术活动,与同仁、挚友交往的点点滴滴,反映学界对先生研究工作的认识与评价。"访谈录"收录两篇对先生的访谈录,展现了先生的人生历程与学术生涯。文章的编次大体按照类别和时代排列。文集正文前载有郭书春先生的部分生活和工作照片,同学、友人的题辞,正文后附录"郭书春论著目录(1978年至今)"。

文集的出版得到国家社会科学基金重大项目"刘徽、李淳风、贾宪、杨辉注《九章筭术》研究与英译"(批准号16ZDA212)的资助。中国科学院自然科学史研究所,哈尔滨工业大学出版社刘培杰先生、张永芹女士、李广鑫女士、聂兆慈女士为文集的编辑和出版给予了大力支持,付出了宝贵的时间和精力。在文集的征稿、编辑和校对过程中,中国科学院自然科学史研究所硕士研究生袁瑞小姐、博士研究生夏庆卓先生先后做了大量的联络、沟通和编务工作。

在文集即将付梓之际,谨向为文集出版做出贡献的个人、单位致以诚挚的感谢。同时,我们也借此机会向多年来在学习、工作和生活上指导、关心我们的郭书春先生表示衷心的感谢。衷心祝愿先生身体健康,阖家幸福,老骥伏枥,宝刀不老,继续为中国数学史和科学史研究事业贡献力量,继续引领和指导学生和后辈们在科学史研究的道路上前进。

编　者
2022年4月于中国科学院自然科学史研究所
2022年7月修订

目 录

第一部分　学术论文

耿寿昌，一位不该低估的中国古代科学家（邹大海） ········· 3

Canon and commentary in ancient China: An outlook based on mathematical sources（Karine Chemla 林力娜） ········· 26

Jiuzhang Suanshu and Equations（HONG Sung Sa 洪性士　HONG Young Hee 洪英喜） ········· 60

"Incorrect corrections" by ancient editors —— a challenge in Chinese mathematical philology（Donald B. Wagner 华道安） ········· 70

《透簾细草》中有关元代丝织生产的几个问题初探（吕变庭　马晴晴） ········· 96

由《测圆海镜》扩展"边径线"数学内容（郑振初） ········· 111

从圭窦形谈起:《测量全义》初探（洪万生） ········· 130

Ferdinand Verbiest and the 'Muslim astronomical system' of Wu Mingxuan, 1669（Christopher Cullen 古克礼　Catherine Jami 詹嘉玲） ········· 148

梅文鼎历算著作刊印的背景及其人际网络（韩琦） ········· 188

方中通交友"六君子"考述（纪志刚） ········· 195

河图洛书与中国传统数学的历史关联——以方中通《数度衍》为中心（朱一文） ········· 203

李善兰《椭圆正术解》注记（李兆华） ········· 214

"微积溯源":晚清传入微积分的拉格朗日代数分析风格（高红成） ········· 223

贵荣关于零比零的讨论——兼论微积分理论在中国的早期传播（田淼） ········· 234

清末数学教科书之兴起（代钦） ········· 242

晚清汉译日本中学数学教科书研究（郭金海） ········· 259

《中西数学名词合璧表》初探（邓亮） ········· 277

中算史内容的现代发掘与应用举隅（罗见今） ········· 286

《大衍历议》所论《鲁历》及其上元积年（王荣彬，许微微） ········· 298

中国传统数学有无证明须看如何理解证明(李国伟) …… 306
理解极限精确定义的另一条进路:来自中国古代数学的智慧(段耀勇) …… 311
物质参与理论视野下的数学起源研究新进展(陈巍) …… 320
《大成算经》中"数"的处理(森本光生) …… 333
算额文化地理学(小川束) …… 338
和算对中算的继承与创新
　　——以关孝和的内插法和建部贤弘的累约术为例(曲安京) …… 344
论川边信一对《周髀算经》的校勘与注解工作(徐泽林,田春芝) …… 362
围绕《几何原本》形成的朝鲜研究学术圈——以朝鲜学者徐浩修为中心(郭世荣,吴东铭) …… 373

第二部分　回忆与评价

Congratulating Professor Guo Shuchun on the Occasion of His 80th Birthday(Joseph W. Dauben 道本周) …… 387
My Gratitude to Professor Guo Shuchun, an Influential Figure in My Accidental Career(Jian-Ping Jeff Chen 陈建平) …… 426
跟郭老师和师母的相遇对我来说是宝物(莲沼澄子) …… 431
九章在台湾(孙文先) …… 433
《郭书春数学史自选集》序(华觉明) …… 435
书写中国数学史研究的春天——《郭书春数学史自选集》读后(周瀚光) …… 437
老师与老乡(王青建) …… 440
郭书春先生(俞晓群) …… 444
我和著名科学史家郭书春先生结识的岁月(杨国选) …… 450
献给郭书春先生80岁寿诞(刘芹英) …… 454
郭先生助我数学教育教学成长二三事(乔希民) …… 458
学为师表言身教　奖掖后学为人梯(徐传胜) …… 461
铭记教诲,感念师恩(傅海伦) …… 469
郭书春先生指导我学习中国数学史(刘邦凡) …… 475
郭书春先生在中山大学(张一杰) …… 482

第三部分　访谈录

走进中国数学史——郭书春教授访谈录(冯立昇提问,郭书春作答) …… 487
我的早期经历与数学史研究工作——郭书春先生访谈录(郭书春口述,郭金海访问整理) …… 494

附　录

郭书春论著目录(1978年至今) …… 500

第一部分
学术论文

耿寿昌,一位不该低估的中国古代科学家

邹大海 (中国科学院自然科学史研究所)

摘要 可能由于史书中没有耿寿昌的专传,他自撰的著作也已失传,而公元3世纪刘徽所记关于张苍与他编纂《九章算术》的史实又受到怀疑,学术界对耿寿昌往往过于轻视。本文对耿寿昌的生平事迹、为官业绩和在数学与天文学上的工作进行了较为全面而系统的梳理和考证。文章通过将出土材料和传世文献相结合,同时引进概率方法,证明《汉书》对新莽以前史实的叙述用到的"斛"主要源于历史实际而非由"石"误写而成,耿寿昌有喜欢用"斛"的偏好,进而证明耿寿昌确实是《九章》的编定者。文章指出,耿寿昌在整理《九章》时具有恢复古旧经典的强烈意识,而很少加入新型的算题;他统一了《九章》中的度量衡,其中包括将石、斛泾渭分明地进行区分,分别用来表示重量和体积(容积);他也对《九章》的数学表达方式、写作的格式和内容的归类与组织进行了规范和统一,对文本的表述进行了修饰。耿寿昌自撰的著作皆已散佚无存,但他精心编定的《九章》成为中国数学史上最重要的经典,足以使他列入最具影响力的数学家名单而无愧,理应受到学术界的重视。

关键词 耿寿昌;《九章算术》;汉代漕运;常平仓;计量制度;概率方法;中国古代科学家;杜陵

一、引言

耿寿昌是活跃于公元前一世纪70年代至40年代的数学家、天文学家、理财家和高级官员。刘徽《九章算术注序》记载,张苍和耿寿昌收集它在先秦的祖本的遗文,进行整理和删补而形成了流传至今的数学经典《九章算术》(以下简称《九章》)。那么,作为两个编纂者中的后一位,耿寿昌实际是《九章》的定稿人(后世流传过程中可能有所改变,这是另一个问题),其重要性是不宜低估的。可惜其事迹尚无学者做系统的梳理。不论是1959年中国科学院中国自然科学史研究室编写的《中国古代科学家》及其以后的修订本,还是1992年出版的杜石然主编的《中国古代科学家传记》(上、下),抑或是1998年金秋鹏主编的《中国科学技术史·人物卷》,都没有把他列为传主。李俨搜集了正史、扬雄《法言》中有关耿寿昌的史料,辑入《中国古代数学史料》中[1],其《中国数学大纲》(修订本)只是根据这些史料做了一篇百余字的简传[2]。一些经济史的著作谈到他在经济上的贡献[3],也未对其生平和学术做系统的爬梳。

不少学者在刘徽所记张苍和耿寿昌之外,还把其他数学家纳入《九章》编者的名单中,特别是根据现存《汉书·艺文志》没有著录它而把其成书推到西汉末年刘歆所编《七略》之后,从而把晚于耿寿昌的数学家纳入《九章》编纂者的名单中。孙文青认为,西汉晚期的许商、杜忠在张、耿的基础上形成见于《汉书·艺文志》的《许商算术》和《杜忠算术》,东汉马续约在公元110年左右又在此二书基础上形成《九章》[4]。李迪则除了许、杜,还把西汉中期的桑弘羊、西汉末年的刘歆加入《九章》编纂者的名单中,并认

---

[1] 李俨:《中国古代数学史料》(第二版),上海:上海科学技术出版社,1963年,第44—45页。
[2] 李俨:《中国数学大纲》(修订本)上册,北京:科学出版社,1958年,第31页。
[3] 如胡寄窗和王迺琮等都讲到耿寿昌的常平仓制度,见胡寄窗:《中国经济思想史》中册,上海:上海人民出版社,1963年,第128—130页;王迺琮、张华、郑振华:《先秦两汉经济思想史略》,北京:海洋出版社,1991年,第267—271页。
[4] 孙文青:《九章算术源流考》,《女师大学术季刊》,1931年第2卷第1期第1—60页。

为刘歆是最后的编定者⁵,那自然就不会有马续了。把许、杜等人加入之后,耿寿昌在《九章》编纂中起的作用就没那么重要了。李迪、查永平在后来的著作中将耿寿昌生、卒年分别取为公元前100年、公元前30年,在"学科及成就"栏中只列了"天文学"、"数学"、"'象浑天仪',可能是造浑天仪"三项。与此同时,他们针对许商和杜忠分别列有《许商算术》和《杜忠算术》⁶,这就将耿寿昌对《九章》的贡献看得无关紧要了。钱宝琮基本上采用孙文青的看法,不同的是在马续与《九章》的关系问题上有矛盾心态,甚至对张苍、耿寿昌是否参与《九章》的编纂也持怀疑态度。一方面,他认为马续研究《九章》在公元90年左右,而《九章》成于公元50—100年之间。可是,按前一估计则《九章》成书的时间下限不可能晚到公元100年。另一方面,他又说"孙文青以为马续就是《九章算术》的编纂者,证据虽不够充分,但这是很可能的",这就又否定了自己前面的说法了。他认为张苍、耿寿昌虽然以善于计算闻名,但"未必有删补《算术》的事实",而刘徽"不提许商、杜忠是他一时的疏漏"。⁷ 这甚至有把张苍、耿寿昌从《九章》编纂者的名单中剔除的偏向了。这些对耿寿昌在《九章》编纂上贡献的评估,特别是影响巨大的钱宝琮《中国数学史》对张苍、耿寿昌整理删补《九章》的否定倾向,大概也是一些科学家传记作者忽视耿寿昌的重要原因之一。

郭书春未在张、耿之外添加其他编纂者,认为他们的工作有以下几项:(1)把汉代"发展起来的以解勾股形为主的勾股知识编入第九卷并改'旁要'为勾股"。(2)对先秦遗文进行整理,包括梳理术文、润色文字和补充例题,认为衰分章三乡算问题是补入的。(3)将一些适应当时需要的算术问题加以"收集、加工,分别编入第三卷和第六卷"。他认为这些工作中,张苍和耿寿昌的具体所为"无从考察",但他还是猜想性地做了一定区分:

> 大体说来,张苍应以抢救幸免于秦火和战乱的先秦遗文并加工整理为主;耿寿昌应以增补卷三、卷六、卷九及其他各章的某些题目为主。⁸

照此说来,他认为汉代补入的问题,由耿寿昌补入的可能性要大得多。他还提到,耿寿昌"在大司农中丞任内,总结收集人们实际生产、生活中的数学问题,加以发展、提高,增补了《九章算术》"。⁹

笔者曾利用考古材料与传世文献结合,推论"《九章算术》中石和斛分工,分别表示重量和体积(容积)很可能是耿寿昌所为"¹⁰,耿寿昌在整理、删补《九章》时"具有恢复原有经典的强烈意识",可能很少补入全新类型的算题¹¹。笔者的研究表明,《九章》的编者确有耿寿昌,而且找不出他之后其他数学家参与编纂的证据,因此本文拟对耿寿昌的生平事迹做系统梳理,利用更丰富的史料,引进概率方法,对他在《九章》编纂中的工作再做申论,并进而对他在中国数学史上的地位做新的定位。

二、耿寿昌的生平

在正史中没有耿寿昌的专门传记,但有其事迹的零星记载,可据以大致描述其生平(所据文献及其出处根据本文叙述方便在合适的地方给出)。

文献中没有明确记载耿寿昌的里籍,但《宋史·礼志》记载,大观三年(公元1109年)"礼部、太常寺请以文宣王为先师,兖、邹、荆三国公配享,十哲从祀。自昔著名算数者画像两庑,请加赐五等爵,随所封

---

⁵ 李迪:《〈九章算术〉是在官简基础上形成的数学专著》,《数学史研究文集》第六辑,呼和浩特:内蒙古大学出版社、中国台北:九章出版社,1998年,第1—7页。

⁶ 李迪、查永平:《中国历代科技人物生卒年表》,北京:科学出版社,2002年,第3页。

⁷ 钱宝琮主编:《中国数学史》,北京:科学出版社,1982年,第32—33页。

⁸ 郭书春:《古代世界数学泰斗刘徽》,济南:山东科学技术出版社,2013年,第97—98页。

⁹ 郭书春主编:《中国科学技术史·数学卷》,北京:科学出版社,2010年,第94页。

¹⁰ 邹大海:《秦汉量制与〈九章算术〉成书年代新探——基于文物考古材料的研究》,《自然科学史研究》,2017年第36卷第3期,第293—315页。

¹¹ 邹大海:《中国上古时代数学门类均输新探》,《自然科学史研究》,2020年第39卷第4期,第395—424页。

以定其服"。由张邦昌拟定这些著名数学家的爵位封号,皇帝下诏批准,其中"耿寿昌安定伯"。[12] 安定为地名。西汉时有一郡三县名安定。安定郡,"武帝元鼎三年置",治所在高平县。辖 21 县,其中有安定县。又钜(巨)鹿郡,治所在钜鹿县。辖 20 县,其中一县名安定,是宣帝时封给刘贤(武帝子燕刺王刘旦的儿子)的侯国。又交趾郡,治所在羸陵。辖 10 县,其中亦有一县名安定。[13] 交趾郡的安定县在今越南境内,太靠南了,与熟悉北方的耿寿昌有关的可能性很低。安定郡范围太大,所以耿寿昌所封安定伯的"安定"可能指钜鹿郡或安定郡下的安定县。《汉书》中的耿姓人物中,只有两个带有地名。《汉书·王商传》提到"前频阳耿定上书言商与父傅通,及女弟淫乱"[14],说明耿定是频阳人。频阳(今陕西富平)为左冯翊的 24 县之一[15],西汉无其他称为频阳的郡或县。《汉书·百官公卿表下》记载,元寿元年(公元前 2 年)"陈留太守茂陵耿丰为少府,二年为复土将军"[16],说明耿丰为茂陵人。茂陵是汉武帝的陵寝,武帝时置有茂陵县(今陕西兴平),它是右扶风 21 县之一[17],西汉无其他称为茂陵的郡或县。右扶风、左冯翊均属三辅,前者与安定郡接壤,后者也与安定郡距离很近。茂陵、频阳与安定郡的安定县直线距离都不到 180 公里,前两者在西汉都有耿姓人,那么如果后者有耿姓人也不奇怪。《汉书》中记载皇帝巡幸安定(可能指郡或县)次数较多,安定郡下的安定县(治所在今甘肃泾川县北五里水泉寺村[18])距离京师很近,有较大可能是耿寿昌的里籍或生长地。这与他很熟悉京师附近郡的产粮情况从而提出改革漕运的建议是相符的。不过,《后汉书·耿弇传》说"耿弇字伯昭,扶风茂陵人也。其先武帝时,以吏二千石自钜鹿徙焉"。李贤等注:"武帝时,徙吏二千石高赀富人及豪杰并兼之家于诸陵也。"[19]说明耿弇的祖先这支耿姓人本来是从巨鹿县(亦可能指巨鹿郡)迁来,可能是巨富商人捐资为官,在武帝时迁到茂陵。那么,巨鹿郡的安定县可能有耿姓,而耿寿昌来自这个安定县(治所在今河北省辛集市东北旧城镇西七里)[20]也是可能的。《辛集市志》说辛集市"原名束鹿县","西汉时,县地先后置贳、鄡、安定、乐信、西梁五个侯国,后改为县。武帝时,贳、鄡、安定、乐信四县属冀州钜鹿郡,西梁县属信都国。"[21]按前一句,则先有安定侯国,那么后一句说的似乎只是四县所在区域(而不是四个行政县)在武帝时属于钜鹿郡。按后一句,则先在武帝时有安定县,此县在宣帝时成为封给刘贤的侯国,那么前一句说的便是此侯国后来又成为一个县。不知在成为侯国之前到底有没有安定县。如果按前一种理解,则耿寿昌不太可能是此安定县人,因为他时代更早;如果按后一种理解,则存在耿寿昌是此安定县人的可能性。或许汉武帝时代迁到茂陵的耿氏族人之后又有分化,有一支迁到左冯翊的频阳,也有一支迁到安定郡的安定县,耿寿昌属于这后一支。

耿寿昌的生卒年不详,其早年事迹亦不清楚。从后面证实他编定了《九章算术》,又靠着数学才能受到宣帝重用来看,他可能年少时就得到了张苍收集整理的《九章算术》未完成本,或家传此本,并勤加研习,从而培养了高超的数学能力。史籍明确提到他的史事中,最早的明确年份是西汉宣帝神爵元年(公元前 61 年),时任大司农中丞。大司农是中央掌管国家财政经济的长官(部门),掌管全国赋税收入和财政开支,兼理各地仓储、水利、官府农业、工商业的经营,调运货物,管理物价等。大司农下有两丞,秩千石。大司农中丞是大司农的主要属官,协助大司农总署曹事,相当于副职。耿寿昌也以大司农中丞的身份出现在宣帝五凤年间(公元前 57—公元前 53 年)和甘露二年(公元前 52 年)的史事中。史籍中还提到大司农中丞耿寿昌为宣帝主持建造杜陵,而元帝初元元年(公元前 48 年)汉宣帝安葬于此,如果没有

---

[12] 脱脱等撰:《宋史》,北京:中华书局,1977 年,第 2551—2552 页。
[13] 班固撰:《汉书》,北京:中华书局,1964 年,第 1575、1615、2759、1629 页。
[14] 班固撰:《汉书》,北京:中华书局,1964 年,第 3372 页。
[15] 班固撰:《汉书》,北京:中华书局,1964 年,第 1545 页。
[16] 班固撰:《汉书》,北京:中华书局,1964 年,第 848—849 页。
[17] 班固撰:《汉书》,北京:中华书局,1964 年,第 1546—1547 页。
[18] 史为乐主编:《中国历史地名大辞典(增订本)》,北京:中国社会科学出版社,2017 年,第 1191 页。
[19] 范晔撰:《后汉书》,北京:中华书局,第 703 页。
[20] 史为乐主编:《中国历史地名大辞典(增订本)》,北京:中国社会科学出版社,第 1191 页。
[21] 辛集市地方志编纂委员会编纂:《辛集市志》,北京:中国书籍出版社,1996 年,第 74 页。

意外的话，耿寿昌也应该负责此事。史籍中没有提到他还担任过其他职务，很可能他在当上大司农中丞之后长期担任此职，未再升迁。但他曾获得关内侯的爵位，算是得到了皇帝的特别恩宠。

《汉书·食货志》提到"宣帝即位，用吏多选贤良，百姓安土，……，农人少利。时大司农中丞耿寿昌以善为算，能商功利得幸于上，五凤中奏言：……"[22]。从宣帝即位（公元前74年）到五凤元年（公元前57年）有17年的间隔，从上述引文看不出耿寿昌"得幸于上"和入仕的具体时间，其他文献也没有明确的记载，但我们可以推算一个大致的时间。

公元前87年武帝去世，霍光等五位顾命大臣拥立不到8岁的刘弗陵登基，是为昭帝。几年后霍光独揽朝政，昭帝形同傀儡。公元前74年昭帝21岁时去世，没有子嗣，权倾朝野的大司马大将军霍光先立其侄子昌邑王刘贺，27日后又将他废去。之后霍光重新迎立了刘病已，是为宣帝。刘病已是武帝的曾孙，废太子刘据的孙子。刘据坐巫蛊之狱几乎满门抄斩，廷尉监邴吉冒险救下几个月大的刘病已。刘病已的生活环境几经转折，饱尝民间疾苦。宣帝汲取昭帝和刘贺的经验教训，在霍光的阴影下小心翼翼行事。本始元年（公元前73年）"大将军光稽首归政，上谦让委任焉"，宣帝听凭霍光处理政事，直到地节二年（公元前68年）霍光去世，"上始视政事"，终于熬到头可以自己做主。地节四年（公元前66年）霍光子霍禹、霍云等谋反，霍家几乎被满门抄斩。至此，宣帝行事再无羁绊，可完全按自己的意志行事。元康二年，宣帝注意到其名病已太容易让臣民触犯其名讳，遂改名为询。从公元前68年以后的几年，宣帝整顿吏治，选拔人才。[23] 可见宣帝即位之初为避免与霍光发生冲突，政事悉听霍光，并不自作主张。霍光去世特别是铲除霍家之后，宣帝才得以扬其天威。《食货志》所说宣帝"用吏多选贤良"应该在这段时间，耿寿昌的快速迁升也应该在这段时间。[24] 至晚在神爵元年（公元前61年）他已做到大司农中丞，这是相当于财政部副部长的高官。那么他此前必有相当长的为官时间，而他始任大司农中丞的时间也可能早于此年。

《汉书·宣帝纪》说"元康元年春，以杜东原上为初陵，更名杜县为杜陵。徙丞相、将军、列侯、吏二千石、訾百万者杜陵"。[25] 这是公元前65年的事。前面提到耿寿昌造杜陵，很可能他在这一年或之后不久就主持其事，他开始担任大司农中丞亦可能就在此时。一个较合理的假设是耿寿昌生于公元前100年前后，在昭帝时代（公元前87—前74年）已经步入仕途。从公元前68年以来，随着宣帝亲政，改革吏治，耿寿昌凭借数学能力获得较快迁升，大约在公元前65年或至晚到公元前61年已担任大司农中丞，时年40岁左右。在史籍中，耿寿昌在汉元帝时期除与杜陵有关外，再无其他事迹，因此可假设此后他生活了10年左右，再取整数，可估计他约于公元前40年左右去世，享年60岁左右。耿寿昌的活动应该经历西汉昭帝时代（公元前87年—公元前74年）的后期、宣帝时代（公元前74年—公元前48年）的全部和元帝时代（公元前48年—公元前33年）的前几年。

三、耿寿昌的政绩

耿寿昌为官的主要贡献有三项：一是参与赵充国与羌人作战时的后勤供给工作；二是经济工作，包括解决京师粮食的供应和提高海租，开设常平仓；三是建造杜陵。

1. 军事后勤供给工作

神爵元年（公元前61年）赵充国奉命靖边。他拟采用"罢骑兵屯田，以待其敝"的对策。正好宣帝派

---

[22] 班固撰：《汉书》，北京：中华书局，1964年，第1141页。
[23] 班固撰：《汉书》，北京：中华书局，1964年，第235—259页。
[24] 《册府元龟》说："耿寿昌，宣帝时为大司农丞。以善算为算工，得幸于上"（王钦若等编纂，周勋初等校订，《册府元龟》（校订本）第十册，南京：凤凰出版社，2006年，第10116页）。《太平御览》也有类似的说法。这是说，耿寿昌因为善于数学而担任算工，受到宣帝的宠信，之后才担任了大农司丞。算工可能是官府聘用的佐吏，主要从事计算工作。那么，耿寿昌是凭借出色的数学才能由佐吏转入官僚系统的。但也有可能这一说法是对《汉书》所说耿寿昌"以善为算、能商功利得幸于上"想象的结果，他可能本来就是官员，只是由于数学能力好并用来解决很多问题而受到重用。
[25] 班固撰：《汉书》，北京：中华书局，1964年，第253页。

人送来了让他进兵的玺书,他的儿子、时任中郎将的赵卬害怕了,让人劝谏父亲遵从上谕进兵。赵充国很不以为然,他发了一通感叹:

> 是何言之不忠也!本用吾言,羌虏得至是邪?往者举可先行羌者,吾举辛武贤,丞相御史复白遣义渠安国,竟沮败羌。金城、湟中谷斛八钱,吾谓耿中丞,籴二百万斛谷,羌人不敢动矣。耿中丞请籴百万斛,乃得四十万斛耳。义渠再使,且费其半。失此二册,羌人故敢为逆。失之毫厘,差以千里,是既然矣。今兵久不决,四夷卒有动摇,相因而起,虽有知者不能善其后,羌独足忧邪!吾固以死守之,明主可为忠言。[26]

赵充国指责他儿子派来的人所说的话不是忠言。他说,如果当初按他的意见行事,就不会造成现在的局面。他坚持认为,根据现在的形势,就必须死守。他提到之前两个失策之处,一是用人失当,用了丞相御史推荐的义渠安国而没有用他推荐的辛武贤;二是粮食问题。因为有粮食问题,所以他需要屯田。在讲以前的粮食问题时,他提到了"耿中丞",服虔注曰:"耿寿昌也,为司农中丞。"他让耿寿昌在金城、湟中谷价只有一斛八钱的情况下籴谷 200 万斛,耿寿昌请求只买 100 万斛,而最后能落实的只有 40 万斛。义渠安国再次出使的时候耗费了一半,造成粮食补给的困难。可见,耿寿昌参与了此次战事的后勤补给工作,只是具体的细节知之不多。后来耿寿昌想法解决京师的粮食漕运、提高海税和开设常平仓的想法,可能与此次经历的教训有关。

2. 经济工作

《汉书·食货志》云:

> 宣帝即位,用吏多选贤良,百姓安土,岁数丰穰,谷至石五钱,农人少利。时大司农中丞耿寿昌以善为算、能商功利得幸于上,五凤中奏言:"故事,岁漕关东谷四百万斛以给京师,用卒六万人。宜籴三辅、弘农、河东、上党、太原郡谷足供京师,可以省关东漕卒过半。"又白增海租三倍,天子皆从其计。御史大夫萧望之奏言:"故御史属徐宫,家在东莱,言往年加海租,鱼不出,长老皆言武帝时县官常自渔,海鱼不出,后复予民,鱼乃出。夫阴阳之感,物类相应,万事尽然。今寿昌欲近籴漕关内之谷,筑仓治船,费直二万万余,有动众之功,恐生旱气,民被其灾。寿昌习于商功分铢之事,其深计远虑,诚未足任,宜且如故。"上不听。漕事果便,寿昌遂白令边郡皆筑仓,以谷贱时增其贾而籴,以利农,谷贵时减贾而粜,名曰常平仓。民便之。上乃下诏,赐寿昌爵关内侯。[27]

这里提到"商功利"和"商功分铢",颜师古注前者曰:"商,度也。""商"应包含测量、计算两方面的意思。"商功利"可能读为"商功、利",包括"商功"和"商利"两个方面。"功"应该指各种工作量。《九章》第 5 章的题名叫"商功",该章涉及城墙、河堤、粮堆和其他立体的体积算法、沟堑、仓库、墓道、墓穴、水池等的容积的算法,以及相应的人工计算。这里的"商功"应该包括这些内容,但范围可能更广。"商利"应该是讲通过计算的方法经营财物获得相应的利润。"分铢"可能是借用字面上的含义——对铢这么轻的东西进行分割,来说明对小的数量进行精确计算。这段文字说明,宣帝即位以后(实际应该指公元前 68 年亲政以后),选拔任用了贤良之臣为官。耿寿昌应该就是其中的一个。他有很强的数学才能,善于商功、商利,正是凭借这种用数学知识解决实际问题的能力而受到宣帝的宠信。在五凤年间(公元前 57—公元前 53 年)耿寿昌曾给皇帝上书,指出过去每年从关东漕运 400 万斛谷到京师,需要用卒 6 万,人力耗费巨大。他提出了直接从三辅、弘农、河东等京师附近的地区籴谷供给京师,可节省超过一半的劳力。这

---

[26] 班固撰:《汉书》,北京:中华书局,1964 年,第 2984 页。
[27] 班固撰:《汉书》,北京:中华书局,1964 年,第 1141 页。

不仅解决了京师粮食的供应问题,而且大幅度降低了成本。

他提出增加海租3倍,以提高财政收入。这样的建议受到了位高权重的御史大夫萧望之的反对。关于提高海租,萧望之称,据过去御史的属官徐宫讲,徐的家乡东莱在往年增加海租的时候,鱼都不出来;而当地的长老还说,武帝时代官府自己去捕鱼,海鱼也不出来,后来把捕鱼权交付给百姓,鱼才出来。萧望之还利用阴阳感应的学说,进行了解释。对于改革漕运,萧氏反对的理由是修建仓库、打造船只就要耗费2亿余钱之巨,耿寿昌的做法会劳师动众,产生旱气,从而使百姓受灾。萧氏从维护百姓利益的角度说事,站在了道德的制高点,然后他又从个人能力的角度去批评耿寿昌:寿昌虽然对于商功、分铢之类具体细小之事很在行,但在大事情上实在没有能力深谋远虑,所以应该把他的建议搁置起来,悉仍旧贯。

萧望之阴阳感应、产生旱气之类的说法,在现代从科学的角度来看很奇怪,不过在当时倒也是常见的理由,只是古人对这类理由常在信、疑与不信之间摆动,而且因人因事而异。最终宣帝没有听从萧望之的反对意见而全面接受了耿寿昌的建议。后来的结果证明按耿寿昌的意见去做,向京师漕运粮食的事情进展很顺利。

耿寿昌又提出,要令边境的郡都修筑粮仓,在粮食价格低时提高价格买入囤积,提高农民的积极性;在粮食价高时降低价格卖出,平抑粮价,称之为常平仓。常平仓的设立,有利于市场粮价的稳定,也可以提升官府形象,受到了百姓的称赞。

耿寿昌设常平仓的事,在《汉书》其他篇中也有提及。《汉书·宣帝纪》载五凤四年"大司农中丞耿寿昌奏设常平仓,以给北边,省转漕。赐爵关内侯。"[28]《汉书·萧望之传》载五凤三年(公元前55年)萧望之接替丙吉担任御史大夫,当时"匈奴大乱",许多谈论国事的人主张"因其坏乱举兵灭之"。宣帝派"中朝大司马车骑将军韩增、诸吏富平侯张延寿、光禄勋杨恽、太仆戴长乐问望之计策",萧望之引《春秋》所载晋国士匄领军侵齐,中途听闻齐侯去世,士匄不但没有进攻反而领军退还,"君子大其不伐丧,以为恩足以服孝子,谊足以动诸侯"的故事,根据"前单于慕化乡善称弟,遣使请求和亲","不幸为贼臣所杀"的情况,提出要善意对待匈奴的相反策略,为宣帝所采。《汉书》说"是时大司农中丞耿寿昌奏设常平仓,上善之,望之非寿昌。"萧望之上书称"百姓或乏困,盗贼未止",二千石以下官员"多材下不任职","三公非其人,则三光为之不明,今首岁日月少光,咎在臣等"。宣帝认为萧望之的意图在于批评年老的丞相丙吉,派好几位大臣诘问他。萧望之脱去帽子答辩,让宣帝很不高兴。[29] 这两条文献关于耿寿昌设常平仓的事有一年的差距,可能他关于设常平仓的上奏在五凤三年(公元前55年),实施则在次年(公元前54年)。

宣帝对耿寿昌在经济方面的作为很满意,赏赐他关内侯的爵位。

3. 建造杜陵

宣帝的陵墓杜陵始建于公元前65年。耿寿昌主持建造杜陵,事见《汉书·傅常郑甘陈段传》。此篇记载,解万年和陈汤讨论修建皇陵的事,提到:"大司农中丞耿寿昌造杜陵,赐爵关内侯,将作大匠乘马延年以劳苦秩中二千石。"[30]这说明耿寿昌主持修造了杜陵,并且因此获赐关内侯的爵位。史籍没有提到其他人造杜陵,因此很可能耿寿昌开始主持杜陵建造的时间就在公元前65年。据上面所引《汉书》中《宣帝纪》和《食货志》,耿寿昌获赐关内侯的原因都是他在经济方面的出色工作,而未说是因为建造杜陵的缘故。由于解、陈是在成帝(公元前33年—公元前7年在位)时代建陵,时间上晚了两朝皇帝,又是以此作为他们自己应该得到奖赏的根据,所以我们认为应以《食货志》和《宣帝纪》的记载为确。不论如何,即使主持修造杜陵是耿寿昌获赐关内侯的原因,也不会是唯一原因甚至不是主要原因。《汉书·元帝

---

[28] 班固撰:《汉书》,北京:中华书局,1964年,第268页。
[29] 班固撰:《汉书》,北京:中华书局,1964年,第3279—3280页。
[30] 班固撰:《汉书》,北京:中华书局,1964年,第3023—3024页。

纪》说"初元元年春正月辛丑,孝宣皇帝葬杜陵"。[31] 初元元年正月辛丑在公元前48年2月6日,距离皇帝去世的时间不到一个整月,可见杜陵此前已经造修好了。修造皇陵是很复杂的事,耿寿昌的数学才能在其中应发挥了不可忽视的作用。

四、作为天文学家的耿寿昌

耿寿昌也是天文学家。《扬子法言》卷十云:"或问浑天。曰:落下闳营之,鲜于妄人度之,耿中丞象之,几乎!几乎!莫之能违也。"[32] 可见对于宇宙结构,耿寿昌持浑天说,还做过浑象(演示每日星空旋转、四季星空变化的仪器),演示效果很好。《后汉书·律历志》记贾逵论曰:"甘露二年(公元前52年),大司农中丞耿寿昌奏:以图仪度日月行,考验天运状,日月行至牵牛、东井,日过〔一〕度,月行十五度;至娄、角,日行一度,月行十三度。赤道使然,此前世所共知也。如言黄道有验,合天,日无前却,弦望不差一日,比用赤道密近,宜施用。上中多臣校。"[33] 天文学史家认为其中的圆仪即浑仪,这份奏书反映了耿寿昌"在天文学史上是颇有造诣的人物"[34]。奏文中提到日月运行的情况和数据。大概因为这个缘故,同时在文献中又找不到西汉时期与"耿昌"相合的其他人物,所以《汉书·艺文志》著录的著作"耿昌月行帛图二百三十二卷"和"耿昌月行度二卷"两种,史学家都认为就是指耿寿昌的著作,而"耿昌"应为"耿寿昌"之脱讹。[35] 遗憾的是,这两种著作都未见于《隋书·经籍志》及以后目录学著作的著录,遑论保留至今。大概它们都在隋代就失传了。耿寿昌善于数学,他的上奏提到日、月运行的度数和"用黄道有验""比用赤道密近",可见他认为采用黄道坐标系有优越性,这也同时说明他的天文工作发挥了其数学才能。

五、作为数学家的耿寿昌

三国时魏国刘徽为《九章》做注,在景元四年(公元263年)的序言中说:

> 周公制礼而有九数,九数之流,则《九章》是矣。往者暴秦焚书,经术散坏。自时厥后,汉北平侯张苍、大司农中丞耿寿昌皆以善算命世。苍等因旧文之遗残,各称删补。故校其目则与古或异,而所论者多近语也。[36]

刘徽讲述了《九章》的形成过程:西周初年周公制定礼乐典章制度的时候,已经形成了"九数",这个"九数"的流传便是一部《九章》。由于秦始皇焚书而导致这部《九章》受到了损坏。此后,汉初的北平侯张苍、昭帝至元帝时代的大司农中丞耿寿昌都以善于数学而闻名于世,经过"(张)苍等"的抢救、删补整理,使《九章》得以流传后世。因此,它的篇目与古代的有所差异,而论述中有很多近代的语言。

按照这个历史叙述,刘徽所用的《九章》最后成书于"(张)苍等"。"等"字本身的理解比较灵活,可以代表省去具体名字的一个人,也可以代表多个人。"苍等"句之前,刘徽只提到张苍和耿寿昌两个具体人

---

[31] 班固撰:《汉书》,北京:中华书局,1964年,第279页。
[32] 汪荣宝撰:《法言义疏》,北京:中华书局,320页。
[33] 范晔撰:《后汉书》,北京:中华书局,1973年,第3029页。
[34] 陈美东:《中国科学技术史·天文学卷》,北京:科学出版社,2003年,第143–144页。原文的"图仪",陈美东引作"圆仪"。可能"图"为"圆"之误。
[35] 如李俨根据《艺文志》,说"耿(寿)昌《月行帛图》二百三十二卷,《月行度》二卷",括补了"寿"字。见李俨:《中国数学大纲》(修订本)上册,北京:科学出版社,1958年,第31页。
[36] 郭书春汇校:《九章算术新校》,合肥:中国科学技术大学出版社,2014年,第3页。

名,而《史记》《汉书》所载以善于数学闻名的,在耿寿昌前后还有桑弘羊、乘马延年、许商等,其官阶更高[37],有的名气也更大,许商和杜忠还有数学著作著录于《汉书·艺文志》流传至今的版本,刘徽却偏没有提他们,说明刘徽认为这些人与《九章》的编纂没有关系。从行文方式看,刘徽提张、耿时没有把他们只是作为代表的意思,之后马上说"苍等因旧文之遗残,各称删补",因此只能认为"苍等"就代表张苍和耿寿昌两人,不再有其他人。也就是说,在刘徽看来,耿寿昌是《九章》的最后编定者。

如前所述,《九章》不见于现存《汉书·艺文志》的著录,有的学者据此认为《九章》在西汉耿寿昌时代还未成书,钱宝琮甚至倾向于张苍、耿寿昌没有参与这部书的编纂("未必有删补《算术》的事实")。对此,20世纪80年代以来学界关于《九章》的成书逐渐向刘徽的记载回归,因而也就承认耿寿昌是《九章》的两个主要编纂者之一。不过多数学者的回归,不是基于直接而充分的证据,而是由于对史料的重新梳理和张家山汉简中出现了"均输律"残简,否定了以前用于将《九章》拉后的旧证据,从而导致了对刘徽记载的信仰。笔者曾指出《汉书·艺文志》的著录与否不可作为一书是否成于西汉末年以前的决定性证据,它甚至在唐初就已非其旧。笔者还分析了《九章》中计量制度的特点与出土文献的关系[38],从而为刘徽的说法提供了正面证据。下面在此基础上再做申论,论述耿寿昌确实参与了《九章》的编纂,并说明他具体做了什么工作,有什么特点,以补刘徽所未及。

1.《九章》的计量方式说明其成书于新莽以前

从先秦至东汉的常用单位中,石既是最大的重量单位(120斤),又是最大的体积(容量)单位(通常为10斗;特定范围内有其他量值,详下。比石大的单位还有秅、籔等,但不常用)。《九章》则与此不同,书中石、斛分工明确,最大的重量单位只用石,最大的体积(容量)单位只用斛,两者泾渭分明。

新莽时代第一年(公元9年)颁行了铜嘉量,将一套单位龠、合、升、斗、斛的五种容器合铸为一器,有人以为斛是从这才开始作为量制单位的。汉代的简牍中有表示10斗的体积(容积)单位斛,绝大多数含"斛"的简上并没有书写纪年,但有少量简含有新莽或东汉的年号,一些学者没发现更早的年号,于是认定斛是新莽时代才开始使用的。例如森鹿三认为同一出土地点的简应该是同时代的,以此为原则,他根据从同一地点出土的其他简的年代,判断不含纪年的含"斛"简也属于这一时代;或者根据一枚含"斛"简上有他们认定的新莽简标志性文字如"禄"、"二十"(不作"廿"或"卄")、"三十"(不作"卅"或"丗")、"四十"(不作"卌"或"䎙")来判定它为新莽简。于是含有"斛"字,也被当成是判断文献属于新莽时代或之后的一条标准。这样的看法,曾较为普遍地为学术界所接受。

笔者近年来对单位"斛"的使用做了系统的考察[39],指出:没有任何古文献说过"斛"的使用始于新莽时代;相反,除《九章》外,从先秦至西汉的传世文献中"斛"一直在使用,早于新莽时代的就有很多,如《管子》《庄子》《荀子》《仪礼》《韩非子》《淮南子》《史记》等。而文物考古材料中,先秦的铜器上已有"斛"的使用;在含有表示一石的"斛"的简牍里,明确带有新莽以前年号的有武威汉简一枚,上书"河平□[年]四月三日,诸文学弟子出谷五千余斛"[40],时间最晚为公元前25年,比新莽时代早30多年。另外,《汉书·律历志》记载,新莽时代的度量衡制度是在新莽以前的元始年间(公元1—6年)先征召全国一大批学者,在刘歆领导下共同制定的,所以含有"斛"的新量制方案早于新莽时代,其中很多要素则来自征召来的学者,既然此前已有"斛"使用,则新量制中的"斛"也应来自民间。这些充分说明"斛"的使用远早于新莽时

---

[37] 司马彪《后汉书志·百官三》:"大司农二千石。本注曰:掌诸钱谷金帛诸货币。郡国四时上月旦见钱谷簿,其逋未毕,各具别之。边郡诸官请调度者,皆为报给,损多益寡,取相给足。丞一人,比千石。部丞一人,六百石。本注曰:部丞主帑藏。"见范晔撰:《后汉书》,北京:中华书局,1973年,第3590页。所以耿寿昌秩禄为比千石。桑弘羊做过大司农、御史大夫,为九卿之一;乘马延年做过将作大匠,中二千石;许商做过光禄勋、大司农、将作大匠,九卿之一,还曾任成帝的老师。他们都比耿寿昌的地位要高。

[38] 关于《九章》成书问题最系统也是最新的研究,见邹大海:《秦汉量制与〈九章算术〉成书年代新探》,《自然科学史研究》,2017年第36卷第3期,第293—315页。

[39] 邹大海:《秦汉量制与〈九章算术〉成书年代新探》。

[40] 甘肃省博物馆、中国科学院考古研究所编著:《武威汉简》,北京:中华书局,2005年,第136页。

代,那么由"斛"的使用来判定《九章》成于新莽或之后,就失去了证据。

不仅如此,被作为新莽简标志性文字的"禄"、"二十"、"三十"、"四十"也见于更早的简牍中。如"禄"见于《居延新简》E.P.T40:87号简:"●临木部绥和二年七月吏受禄☒"[41],其中绥和二年为公元前7年,早于新莽十多年;而上述几个数字表示法则在清华大学藏战国竹简《算表》都已多次出现[42],郭店楚简《缁衣》篇末第四十七号简有表示全文总章数的文字"二十又三",上海博物馆藏战国楚竹书《容成氏》第39号简上有"衹三十岜而能之"[43],信阳楚简第2-06号简有"箕四十又四▬,……四十簋……",第2-22号简有"小囊糗四十又八▬"[44]。那么,说含有这些文字的简牍必定在新莽时代或更晚,就靠不住了;而由这些文字为中介来判定含"斛"简的年代,就更不可靠了。

实际上,新莽时代的量制单位,除上述铜嘉量规定的五个单位龠、合、升、斗、斛外,还有圭、撮,4圭=1撮,5撮=1龠[45]。这些单位中已知有斗、升和龠出现在秦简中,斛出现在武威汉简中,合出现在刘向《说苑》(公元前17年)中[46],都明确在新莽时代以前。[47] 所以,在新莽时代推行的量制,其时代标志主要在于是一套而不在于是单个的单位。从这个意义上讲,《九章》反而不会晚到新莽或之后,甚至要早于公元前17年的《说苑》。因为《九章》只用到斛、斗、升,甚至在需要用合、龠、撮、圭等以避免分数的时候,仍宁愿使用升的分数来表示。如"粟米"章第3题的答案是"繫米二斗一升五分升之三"[48],若采用新莽容量(体积)单位系统,其数量应分别为"二斗一升六合";第4题的答案为"为御米三斗三升五十分升之九",若采用新莽的五量系统,答案应"三斗三升一合一龠五分龠之三";如采用新莽七量系统,则答案应立"三斗三升一合一龠三撮"[49]。因此,从容量制度进行考察,结论指向的是《九章》成书早于新莽时代。[50]

2. 汉简中极可能有耿寿昌时代"斛"的用例

汉简中有多个用例含有"斛"字,指向汉宣帝的时代。如居延汉简77.24号简作"☒为大斛二斗六升☒",同一地点出土有3枚简含有纪年[51],最早的在公元前62年,最晚的在公元前56年,其时间跨度正好全在耿寿昌活跃的时间内。这枚含"斛"的简很可能就是这一时期的。

在《肩水关金汉简》中,出自探方T5的第6号简正面记有"小斛三",出土于此地点的简牍有122枚,内含有纪年者5枚[52],时间跨度为24年,最早为公元前73年,最晚为公元前50年,皆宣帝年号。此含"斛"简很可能是宣帝时代的。

---

[41] 甘肃省文物考古研究所、甘肃省博物馆、文化部古文献研究室、中国社会科学院历史研究所编:《居延新简 甲渠候官与第四燧》,北京:文物出版社,1990年,第91页。

[42] 李学勤主编:《清华大学藏战国竹简(肆)》,上海:中西书局,2016年,《放大图版》,第61—71页;《释文 注释》,第140—142页。

[43] 马承源主编:《上海博物馆藏战国楚竹书(二)》,上海:上海古籍出版社,2002年,第280页。

[44] 河南省文物研究所:《信阳楚墓》,北京:文物出版社,1986年,第129—130页,图版一二〇、一二六。

[45] 丘光明编著:《中国历代度量衡考》,北京:科学出版社,1992年,第224—227、244—245页。

[46] 刘向《说苑》"辨物"篇说:"千二百黍为一龠,十龠为一合,十合为一升,十升为一斗,十斗为一石"(见刘向著,赵善诒疏证:《说苑疏证》,上海:华东师范大学出版社,1985年,第534页),《汉书·律历志》与此非常相似,但以"斛"代替"石",而以二龠为合。

[47] 邹大海:《秦汉量制与〈九章算术〉成书年代新探》。

[48] 郭书春汇校:《汇校九章算术》(增补版),沈阳:辽宁教育出版社,2004年,第71页。

[49] 李继闵已注意到《九章》用分数的升而不用合和龠。见李继闵:《〈九章算术〉的形成与先秦至西汉时期的儒法斗争》,《数学学报》,1975年第18卷第4期,第223—230页。

[50] 邹大海:《秦汉量制与〈九章算术〉成书年代新探》。

[51] 谢桂华、李均明、朱国炤:《居延汉简释文合校》,北京:中华书局,1987年,第136—140页。

[52] 甘肃简牍保护研究中心、甘肃省文物考古研究所、甘肃省博物馆、中国文化遗产研究院古文献研究室、中国社会科学院简帛研究中心编:《肩水金关汉简(壹)》中册,上海:中西书局,2011年,第104—118页。

在探方 T22 中，简 131A 记有"三斛虞季受"。此探方总计 157 个编号简，内有 11 枚含有纪年[53]，时间跨度从公元前 81 年至公元前 20 年。其中，最早的昭帝时代简有 3 枚，之后的宣帝时代简数量最多，有 4 枚（最晚者公元前 56 年），元帝（公元前 40、36 年）和成帝时代简各有 2 枚。约 73% 的纪年简能与耿寿昌的时代相及。所以这枚含"斛"简是耿寿昌所处时代的可能性较大。

探方 T26 中 229 号简正面记有"最凡千八百，粟十斛，梁三斛"，其中的"斛"明显与"石"相当。该探方有 17 枚简含有明确纪年[54]，在公元前 79 年至公元前 24 年之间，最晚者也比新莽早 30 多年，有 12 枚属于昭帝和宣帝时期，2 枚在元帝初元二年（公元前 47 年），约有 82% 的简纪年与耿寿昌的时代相及。[55] 所以这枚含"斛"的简是耿寿昌时代的可能性很大。

探方 T5 中 6 号简正面记有"小斛三"，同出的纪年简 5 枚[56]，时间跨度为 24 年，最早为公元前 73 年，最晚为公元前 50 年，皆宣帝年号。因此，这枚含"斛"的简极有可能是耿寿昌时代的。

在《居延新简》中，探方 T58 的第 124 号简记有"出粟四斛"。此探方共有纪年简 11 枚，时间从公元前 67 年至公元前 10 年，最晚的也比王莽时代早近 20 年。其中宣帝时代简 9 枚，约占总数的 82%，肯定属于耿寿昌活动的时代；元帝时代简（公元前 38 年）占 1 枚，也与耿寿昌的活动时间接近。所以这枚含"斛"的简非常有可能是耿寿昌时代的。

1986 年地湾出土的汉简中，86EDHT:45 号简记有"出麦一斛九斗三升少"，同出的简中带有纪年的有 10 枚，最早为昭帝始元七年（公元前 80 年，2 枚），最晚为元帝初元二年（公元前 47 年，1 枚，简的两面有纪年，另一面早一年）。其他纪年分别为：本始三年（公元前 71 年）[57]、本始四年（公元前 70 年，3 枚）、同一简上的本始五年（公元前 69 年，即地节元年）及地节二年（原简上有"十月尽十二月"，故在公元前 68 年至公元前 67 年），地节四年（公元前 66 年）、地节五年（公元前 65 年）[58]，均属宣帝年代。因此，这枚含"斛"的简极有可能属于耿寿昌时代。

上述含"斛"的简，都很可能与耿寿昌同时代，说明《九章》对"斛"的使用，与刘徽关于耿寿昌是《九章》编定者的记载是相符的。下面结合《汉书》的记载，可以推定，耿寿昌有使用"斛"的偏好。

3. 耿寿昌对"斛"的偏好

《汉书》同时用"石"和"斛"作为体积（容积）单位名。在"斛"的用例中，有些对应的史实发生在新莽以前。杨哲峰认为这是史书作者未加分辨而把新莽以后"斛"的观念带入新莽以前史实中的结果。有很多学者未对众多新莽以前的文献做考察，就认定"斛"是新莽才开始作体积（容积）单位的。这与杨哲峰的看法是相通的。如果只有到新莽才开始使用"斛"，则其他早期文献中有"斛"的使用，那自然就是后来将"石"改成"斛"的结果了。这些意见其实是想当然的。下面通过对《汉书》的用例做统计分析来证明这种想当然的观点是不可信的。

---

[53] 甘肃简牍保护研究中心、甘肃省文物考古研究所、甘肃省博物馆、中国文化遗产研究院古文献研究室、中国社会科学院简帛研究中心编：《肩水金关汉简（贰）》中册，上海：中西书局，2012 年，第 94—112 页。

[54] 甘肃简牍保护研究中心、甘肃省文物考古研究所、甘肃省博物馆、中国文化遗产研究院古文献研究室、中国社会科学院简帛研究中心编：《肩水金关汉简（叁）》中册，上海：中西书局，2013 年，第 68—106 页。

[55] 另有 3 枚简纪年文字保存不全，但可以大体判断年代。221 号简有"初元年八月乙丑朔"，"初"前缺字，据月朔推断应是太初元年（公元前 104 年 9 月 16 日）；239 号简有"凤四年十二月"，"凤"前缺字，与其他纪年简字体对照看，知可能是五凤四年（公元前 54 年）；111 号简有"始二年正月丁亥朔"，"始"前缺字，据月朔推断应是本始二年（公元前 72 年）或永始二年（公元前 15 年），与其他纪年简字体对照看，知可能是本始二年。加上这 3 枚简，时间下限不变，时间上限要提早 20 多年。耿寿昌时代的简有 16 枚，占 80%。

[56] 甘肃简牍保护研究中心、甘肃省文物考古研究所、甘肃省博物馆、中国文化遗产研究院古文献研究室、中国社会科学院简帛研究中心编：《肩水金关汉简（壹）》中册，上海：中西书局，2011 年，第 104—118 页。

[57] 此简编号为 86EDHT:91，其正面写有纪年"□始三年二月"，首字残坏，但与其他有纪年的竹简上的字体对照，可推定年号为"本始"。

[58] 甘肃省博物馆、甘肃省文物考古研究所、出土文献与中国古代文明研究协同创新中心中国人民大学分中心编：《地湾汉简》，上海：中西书局，2017 年，第 148—160 页。

(1)《汉书》中"斛"的用例主要反映史实发生时的情况。

我们首先看《汉书》中"斛"的用例。其《律历志》描述了刘歆主持的计量单位系统,它不能反映"斛"的实际应用,故排除此篇,得到《汉书》含单位"斛"的文字有18段,现将它们按史实发生的时间顺序引录如表1。

表1 《汉书》中"斛"作为体积(容积)单位的应用情况

序号	出处与原文	时间
1	《高帝纪》:(汉王二年)六月,汉王还栎阳。……关中大饥,米斛万钱,人相食。(第38页)[59]	高帝汉王二年(公元前205年),楚汉战争时期[60]
2	《彭越传》:汉三年,越常往来为汉游兵击楚,绝其粮于梁。……越复下昌邑旁二十余城,得粟十余万斛,以给汉食。(第1880页)	高帝汉王三年(公元前204年),楚汉战争时期
3	《食货志》:武帝末年,悔征伐之事,……以赵过为搜粟都尉。过能为代田,一晦三甽。……一岁之收常过缦田晦一斛以上,善者倍之。……过试以离宫卒田其宫壖地,课得谷皆多其旁田晦一斛以上。(第1138—1139页)	武帝末年(公元前90年左右至公元前87年)
4	《匈奴传》:其明年,单于遣使遗汉书云:"……今欲与汉闿大关,取汉女为妻,岁给遗我蘖酒万石,稷米五千斛,杂缯万匹,它如故约,则边不相盗矣。"(第3780页)	武帝征和四年(公元前89年,参考《李广利传》和《武帝本纪》确定时间)
5	《龚胜传》:自昭帝时,涿郡韩福以德行征至京师,赐策书束帛遣归。诏曰:"朕闵劳以官职之事,其务修孝弟以教乡里。……长吏以时存问,常以岁八月赐羊一头、酒二斛。不幸死者,赐复衾一,祠以中牢。"(第3083页)	昭帝元凤元年(公元前80年,据《昭帝纪》确定时间)
6	《赵充国传》:是岁,神爵元年春也。……天子下其书充国,令与校尉以下吏士知羌事者博议。充国及长史董通年以为"武贤欲轻引万骑,分为两道出张掖,回远千里。以一马自佗负三十日食,为米二斛四斗、麦八斛,又有衣装兵器,难以追逐。……"。(第2973、2978页)	宣帝神爵元年(公元前61年)
7	《赵充国传》:充国叹曰:"是何言之不忠也!……金城、湟中谷斛八钱,吾谓耿中丞,籴二百万斛谷,羌人不敢动矣。耿中丞请籴百万斛,乃得四十万斛耳。……"(第2984页)	宣帝神爵元年(公元前61年)
8	《赵充国传》:(赵充国)遂上屯田奏曰:"臣闻兵者,……,不可不慎。臣所将吏士马牛食,月用粮谷十九万九千六百三十斛,盐千六百九十三斛,茭藳二十五万二百八十六石。……"(第2984—2985页)	宣帝神爵元年或之后不久(公元前61年或之后不久)
9	《赵充国传》:(赵充国屯田奏:)"……愿罢骑兵,留弛刑应募,及淮阳、汝南步兵与吏士私从者,合凡万二百八十一人,用谷月二万七千三百六十三斛,盐三百八斛,分屯要害处。……"(第2986页)	宣帝神爵元年或之后不久(公元前61年或之后不久)
10	《食货志》:宣帝即位,用吏多选贤良……,五凤中奏言:"故事,岁漕关东谷四百万斛以给京师,……。"(第1143页)	宣帝五凤年间(公元前57年—公元前53年)
11	《匈奴传》:"明年(指甘露元年的次年,公元前52年),呼韩邪单于款五原塞,愿朝三年正月。……诏忠等留卫单于,助诛不服,又转边谷米糒,前后三万四千斛,给赡其食。(第3798页)	甘露二年(公元前52年)
12	《匈奴传》:元帝初即位,呼韩邪单于复上书,言民众困乏。汉诏云中、五原郡转谷二万斛以给焉。(第3800页)	元帝即位年(公元前48年)

---

59 为避免烦琐,现于引文后直接括注它在中华书局标点本《汉书》中的页码,不一一出注。表2同此。

60 表1和表2中的史实,只有少量段落带有时间。绝大多数段落的时间,系笔者根据上下文或段落中涉及的人与事在《汉书》其他地方或《史记》中的时间考定。

续表1

序号	出处与原文	时间
13	《西南夷两粤朝鲜传》：大将军凤于是荐金城司马陈立为牂柯太守。……钩町王禹、漏卧侯俞震恐，入粟千斛、牛羊劳吏士。立还归郡，兴妻父翁指与兴子郯务收余兵，迫胁旁二十二邑反。（第3845页）	汉成帝河平年间（公元前28—公元前24年）
14	《食货志》：羲和鲁匡言："名山大泽，……一酿用麤米二斛、曲一斛，得成酒六斛六斗。各以其市月朔米曲三斛，并计其贾而参分之，以其一为酒一斛之平。"（第1182页）	王莽即真（由摄真转为正式做皇帝）之年（公元9年）
15	《郊祀志》：莽篡位二年，兴神仙事，……又种五梁禾于殿中，各顺色置其方面，先囅鹤髓、毒冒、犀玉二十余物渍种，计粟斛成一金，言此黄帝谷仙之术也。（第1270页）	新莽二年（公元10年）
16	《匈奴传》：莽将严尤谏曰："臣闻匈奴为害，所从来久矣，……今天下遭阳九之阸，比年饥馑，西北边尤甚。……计一人三百日食，用糒十八斛，非牛力不能胜；牛又当自赍食，加二十斛，重矣。（第3824页）	新莽始建国三年（公元11年）
17	《王莽传》：（王莽即真三年）五月，莽下吏禄制度，……四辅公卿大夫士，下至舆僚，凡十五等。僚禄一岁六十六斛，稍以差增，上至四辅而为万斛云。（第4142页）	王莽即真三年（公元11年）
18	《王莽传》：（地皇元年）……是月，大雨六十余日。令民入米六百斛为郎，其郎吏增秩赐爵至附城。（第4162页）	新莽地皇元年（公元20年）

《汉书》中"石"可以表示石头、姓，也可以作重量单位和体积（容积）单位。我们只统计它作为体积（容积）单位的用例。需要说明的是，汉代官吏按俸禄用"若干石"来命名其级别，其本义与谷子的体积有关，但它固化以后不仅不能反映"石"的应用，而且与实际的数量也较大的出入，排除此种用例后，得到含"石"文字42段，亦按史事发生的时间顺序引录如表2。

表2 《汉书》中"石"作为体积（容积）单位的应用情况

序号	出处与原文	时间
1	《西域传》：大宛左右以蒲陶为酒，富人藏酒至万余石，久者至数十岁不败。（第3894页）	介绍大宛国，时间在张骞之后，无法确定较窄的时间段
2	《食货志》：地方百里之增减，辄为粟百八十万石矣。……今一夫挟五口，治田百晦，岁晦一石半，为粟百五十石，除十一之税十五石，余百三十五石。食，人月一石半，五人终岁为粟九十石，余有四十五石。石三十，为钱千三百五十，除社闾尝新春秋之祠，用钱三百，余千五十。……是故善平籴者，必谨观岁有上中下孰。上孰其收自四，余四百石；中孰自三，余三百石；下孰自倍，余百石。小饥则收百石，中饥七十石，大饥三十石。……行之魏国，国以富强。（第1124—1125页）	战国时魏国李悝"尽地力之教"（公元前5世纪）
3	《赵充国传》：臣所将吏士马牛食，月用粮谷十九万九千六百三十斛，盐千六百九十三斛，茭藁二十五万二百八十六石。（第2985页）	神爵元年（公元前61年）或之后不久
4	《货殖传》：楚汉相距荥阳，民不得耕种，米石至万，而豪桀金玉尽归任氏，任氏以此起富。（第3693页）	楚汉战争时期，公元前205年至公元前204年
5	《食货志》：汉兴，……，米至石万钱，马至四百金。（第1152—1153页）	楚汉战争开始至结束后的三五年内（约公元前205年至公元前197年）
6	《食货志》：汉兴，接秦之敝，……凡米石五千，人相食，死者过半。……漕转关东粟以给中都官，岁不过数十万石。（第1127页）	楚汉战争开始至结束后的三五年内（约公元前205年至公元前197年）

续表2

序号	出处与原文	时间
7	《文帝纪》:年八十已上,赐米人月一石,肉二十斤,酒五斗。(第113页)	文帝元年三月(公元前179年)
8	《贾谊传》:(贾谊的上疏):……矫伪者出几十万石粟,赋六百余万钱,乘传而行郡国,……。(第2244页)	文帝时贾谊任长沙王傅三年时的前后两三年内(约公元前176年前后两三年)
9	《食货志》:其能耕者不过百晦,百晦之收不过百石。……于是文帝从错之言,令民入粟边,六百石爵上造,稍增至四千石为五大夫,万二千石为大庶长,各以多少级数为差。(第1134页)	文帝十四年(公元前165年)左右
10	《爰盎传》:从史适在守盎校为司马,乃悉以其装齎买二石醇醪,会天寒,士卒饥渴,饮醉西南陬卒,卒皆卧。(第2274页)	景帝时,晁错被诛至爰盎死前,公元前152年左右
11	《东方朔传》:上笑曰:"使先生自责,乃反自誉!"复赐酒一石,肉百斤,归遗细君。(第2846页。)	武帝继位后不久,约公元前140年左右
12	《主父偃传》:又使天下飞刍挽粟,起于黄、腄、琅邪负海之郡,转输北河,率三十钟而致一石。(第2800页)	武帝元光元年(公元前134年)或之后不久
13	《沟洫志》:后河东守番系言:"漕从山东西,岁百余万石,更底柱之艰,……,今溉田之,度可得谷二百万石以上。……"。(第1680页)	武帝元光年间(公元前134至公元前129年之间)
14	《食货志》:时又通西南夷道,作者数万人,千里负担馈饟,率十余钟致一石,散币于邛僰以辑之。(第1158页)	武帝时卫青出击匈奴时期(公元前127年前后)
15	《武帝纪》:诏曰:"朕闻咎繇对禹,……曰:'……八十以上米,人三石。有冤失职,使者以闻。'"。(第174页)	武帝元狩四年(公元前122年)
16	《沟洫志》:其后严熊言:"临晋民愿穿洛以溉重泉以东万余顷故恶地,诚即得水,可令亩十石。"(第1681页)	武帝时张汤任御史大夫期间(公元前118年前后)
17	《食货志》:始令吏得入谷补官,郎至六百石。(第1168页)	武帝元鼎二年(公元前115年),据《史记·孝武本纪》定
18	《食货志》:官益杂置多,徒奴婢众,而下河漕度四百万石,及官自籴乃足。(第1173页)	武帝元鼎三年(公元前114年),据《史记·孝武本纪》定
19	《食货志》:它郡各输急处,而诸农各致粟,山东漕益岁六百万石。一岁之中,太仓、甘泉仓满。(第1175页)	武帝元封元年(公元前110年)
20	《武帝纪》:赦所过徒,赐孤独高年米,人四石。还,作甘泉通天台、长安飞廉馆。(第193页)	武帝元封二年(公元前109年)
21	《匈奴传》:其秋,匈奴大入云中、定襄、五原、朔方,杀略数千人,败数二千石而去,行坏光禄所筑亭障。(第3776页)	武帝太初三年(公元前102年)
22	《沟洫志》:举臿为云,决渠为雨。泾水一石,其泥数斗。且溉且粪,长我禾黍。(第1685页)	武帝太始二年(公元前95年)
23	《匈奴传》:单于遣使遗汉书云:"……今欲与汉闿大关,取汉女为妻,岁给遗我糵酒万石,稷米五千斛,杂缯万匹,它如故约,则边不相盗矣。"(第3780页)	武帝太始二年(公元前95年)
24	《昭帝纪》:诏曰:"朕闵百姓未赡,前年减漕三百万石。颇省乘舆马及苑马,以补边郡三辅传马。……"(第228页)	昭帝元凤二年(公元前79年)
25	《王吉传》:王贺虽不遵道,然犹知敬礼吉,乃下令曰:"……使谒者千秋赐中尉牛肉五百斤,酒五石,脯五束。"(第3061页)	昭帝去世前几年之内(公元前76年前后)

续表2

序号	出处与原文	时间
26	《武五子传》：既即位，后王梦青蝇之矢积西阶东，可五六石，以屋版瓦覆，发视之，青蝇矢也。（第2766页）	昭帝去世之年（公元前74年）
27	《食货志》：宣帝即位，用吏多选贤良，百姓安土，岁数丰穰，谷至石五钱，农人少利。	宣帝亲政（公元前68年）后数年
28	《宣帝纪》：比年丰，谷石五钱。（第259页）	宣帝元康四年（公元前62年）
29	《赵充国传》：(宣帝责问赵充国的诏书说)……边兵少，民守保不得田作。今张掖以东粟石百余，刍稿束数十。转输并起，百姓烦扰。（第2979—2980页）	神爵元年（公元前61年）
30	《于定国传》：定国食酒至数石不乱，冬月请治谳，饮酒益精明。（第3043页）	宣帝中期及或以前（公元前60年前后）
31	《韩延寿传》：延寿不忍距逆，人人为饮，计饮酒石余。（第3216页）	宣帝五凤二年（公元前58年）左右
32	《食货志》：元帝即位，天下大水，关东郡十一尤甚。二年，齐地饥，谷石三百余，民多饿死，琅邪郡人相食。（第1142页）	元帝初元二年（公元前47年）
33	《冯奉世》：永光二年秋，……，是时岁比不登，京师谷石二百余，边郡四百，关东五百。四方饥馑，朝廷方以为忧，而遭羌变。（第3296页）	元帝永光二年（公元前42年）
34	《孝成许皇后传》：(许皇后上疏：)故时酒肉有所赐外家，辄上表乃决。又故杜陵梁美人岁时遗酒一石，肉百斤耳。（第3977页）	成帝建始元年（公元前32年），梁美人在宣帝时期（公元前74年至公元前48年）
35	《匡衡传》：衡遣从史之僮，收取所还田租谷千余石入衡家。（第3346页）	成帝建始二年（公元前31年）或之后不久
36	《翟方进传》：使尚书令赐君上尊酒十石，养牛一，君审处焉。（第3423页）	成帝绥和二年（公元前7年）
37	《平当传》：(平帝给平当的诏书)：上报曰："……使尚书令谭赐君养牛一，上尊酒十石。君其勉致医药以自持。"（第3051页）	平帝元始元年（公元1年）
38	《平帝纪》：遣使者捕蝗，民捕蝗诣吏，以石斗受钱。天下民赀不满二万，及被灾之郡不满十万，勿租税。（第353页）	平帝元始二年（公元2年）
39	《食货志》：请法古，令官作酒，以二千五百石为一均，率开一卢以卖，雠五十为准。（第1182页）	新莽始建国元年（公元9年）
40	《沟洫志》：王莽时，……。大司马史长安张戎言："水性就下，行疾则自刮除成空而稍深。河水重浊，号为一石水而六斗泥。……"（第1697页）	新莽始建国三年（公元11年）
41	《食货志》：(王莽)末年，……。北边及青徐地人相食，雒阳以东米石二千。（第1145页）	王莽末年（约公元20—23年）
42	《王莽传》：今洛阳以东，米石二千。（第4172页）	新莽地皇二年（公元21年）

从表1可以看出，在西汉至新莽朝（公元前206—公元23年）的近230年间，"斛"的使用很不均匀。在公元前205年和公元前204年各有1段，而公元前203至公元前93年的110年间，"斛"的用例一个

都没有。这是很特殊的现象,笔者曾根据这一不均匀性现象推论不可能这些"斛"全由"石"误写而成[61],这种看法有一定道理,但证据还不够充分,因为如果这个时段内"石"也很少,那么没有由"石"误成的"斛"也很自然。所以,下面将"斛"与"石"的使用情况做对比,用概率方法来分析问题。

《汉书》中"石"用作体积和容积的计量单位的共有42段。其中第1段描述战国时代的魏国李悝的"尽地力之教";第2段描述大宛国的情况,无法确定其所处较窄的时间段。第3段中粮谷和盐的数量单位为斛,而茭藁的数量单位为石,似乎这个"石"应该是重量单位。不过,在秦简中有对茭藁的单位石的描述,可以看出它不是重量单位,也不是简单的体积单位,而是根据种类不同规定一石的立方尺数,比一石对应的尺数大很多,所以它是一个以体积核算的单位而不是简单的体积单位。[62] 而张家山247号墓出土的《算数书》"传马"条中刍稿的数量在用石的同时又用斗;同墓出土的《二年律令》"金布律"则在用石的同时还用斤和钧。[63] 无论如何,表中第3段的"石"不会是一般意义的体积(容积)单位。为与"斛"的使用做对比,我们把第1~3段排除。

余下的39条,有一半稍多可以确定到年份,其余的可确定误差在1~5年之间。对于公元前206年汉国建立到公元23年新莽覆灭的近230年间,如果按10年划分(公元前9至公元前1年只有9年),除公元前189年至公元前180年、公元前89年至公元前80年、公元前29年至公元前20年、公元前19年至公元前10年没有含"石"段落分布,公元前199年至公元前190年可能没有含"石"段落分布外,其他每个10年都有分布。特别是没有含"斛"段落分布的连续110年间,有第5~23段共19个含"石"段落[64],其中只有惠帝到吕后的约20年没有含"石"段落,其他每个10年都有。新莽以前西汉的215年间,《汉书》中的含"斛"段落有13个,含"石"段落有35个,总共48个,此数据样本足够大,可以用来计算可能的概率。如果《汉书》中新莽以前的"斛"都是由"石"误写而成的,那就意味着"石"误为"斛"的概率为:$13 \div (13+35) = 0.27$,那么这110年间每个含"石"落段都没有被误写成"斛"的概率为$(1-0.27)^{19} = 0.25\%$,即400分之1。这么低概率的事件发生了,说明关于《汉书》中新莽以前的"斛"全是由"石"误写而成的假设是几乎不能成立的,我们应该摒弃这种想当然的假设,承认《汉书》所据在新莽以前的史料中就有"斛"的使用。

我们来看在48个"石"中有几个被误作"斛"的概率下,会使公元前203年至公元前93年间19个段落的"石"都不误成"斛"的概率不小于10%。可设取48个段落的"石"有x个被误作"斛"的概率时,会使这一时期19个段落的"石"都不误成"斛"的概率不小于10%,则$(1-x \div 48)^{19} \geq 0.1$,$x \leq 48(1-\sqrt[19]{0.1})$,取整数解得$x=1,2,3,4,5$。

《汉书》所叙史实在耿寿昌活动的昭帝后期至元帝早期(公元前80年—公元前41年),共有"石"的用例10段,"斛"的用例8段,如果当初都作"石",意味着18段中有8段的"石"在后来误成了"斛",这种可能性的大小可以这样考虑:

上面已经证明,新莽以前的史料中就有"斛"的使用,而且《汉书》对新莽以前史实的叙述中由"石"误成"斛"的概率不应高于5/48。我们取最高的5/48时(这对本文的结论是不利的),会导致耿寿昌时代18段的"石"有8段被误作"斛"的概率为:$C_{18}^{8}(1-5 \div 48)^{10} \times (5 \div 48)^{8} = 0.02\%$,这是低到几乎不可能发生的概率。因此,《汉书》中耿寿昌时代的"斛"至少有一部分是原来就有的。设x为这一时期含"斛"

---

[61] 邹大海:《秦汉量制与〈九章算术〉成书年代新探——基于文物考古材料的研究》。

[62] 邹大海:《从出土文献看秦汉计量单位石的变迁》,in *RIMS Kôkyûroku Bessatsu B50: Study of the History of Mathematics August 27~30, 2012*, edited by Tsukane Ogawa, Research Institute for Mathematical Sciences, Kyoto University, June, 2014, pp.137-156.

[63] 张家山汉墓竹简整理小组编著:《张家山汉墓竹简二四七号墓 释文修订本》,北京:文物出版社,2006年,第139、66页。

[64] 第6—23条明显属于这110年间,容易有疑问的是第5条"汉兴,……,米至石万钱,马至匹百金",它陈述楚汉战争以来战争造成的破坏导致"米至石万钱",这应该是指一段时间,而且战争越往后就越困难,所以至少应该包括公元前202年楚汉战争刚结束的时候,故此条应列入这110年之内。

的 8 个段落中史实发生时就用"斛"的段落数,则此种情况发生的概率 $P(x)$ 可按如下公式计算:$P(x)=$
$C_{18-x}^{8-x}(1-5\div48)^{10}\times(5\div48)^{8-x}$。现将 $x=1,2,\cdots,7$ 时的概率计算结果列如表 3。

表 3　《汉书》中耿寿昌时代"斛"的使用源于史实发生时代的概率表

史实发生时用"斛"的段落数(x)	史实发生时用"石",在《汉书》中被误成"斛"的段落数($8-x$)	情况发生的概率 $P(x)=C_{18-x}^{8-x}(1-5\div48)^{10}\times(5\div48)^{8-x}$
1	7	$C_{17}^{7}(1-5\div48)^{10}\times(5\div48)^{7}=0.09\%$
2	6	$C_{16}^{6}(1-5\div48)^{10}\times(5\div48)^{6}=0.34\%$
3	5	$C_{15}^{5}(1-5\div48)^{10}\times(5\div48)^{5}=1.23\%$
4	4	$C_{14}^{4}(1-5\div48)^{10}\times(5\div48)^{4}=3.92\%$
5	3	$C_{13}^{3}(1-5\div48)^{10}\times(5\div48)^{3}=10.76\%$
6	2	$C_{12}^{2}(1-5\div48)^{10}\times(5\div48)^{2}=23.83\%$
7	1	$C_{11}^{1}(1-5\div48)^{10}\times(5\div48)^{1}=38.14\%$

从表 3 可以看出,史实发生时用"斛"的段落数越高,导致《汉书》中耿寿昌时代"石"的用例有 10 段、"斛"的用例有 8 段这一实际结果的可能性越大,但即使"斛"的用例 8 段中有 7 段继承自史实发生时的实际,其概率也只有不到 40%,所以这 8 段的"斛"都不由"石"误成的可能性较大,而这 8 段中原来用"斛"不高于 5 段的可能性都在 11% 以下,所以可以断言,《汉书》耿寿昌时代的含"斛"段落主要反映了史实发生时代的实际用法。这与出土简牍所反映的情况是一致的。

(2)耿寿昌有对"斛"的偏好。

《汉书》中"斛"的用例有一个值得注意的现象,就是耿寿昌时代含"斛"的 8 段文字有 4 段出自《赵充国传》,文中的叙述表明赵充国与耿寿昌有较密切的关系。文中只有一处用"石"(表 2 第 29 条),出自皇帝给他的敕书,而赵充国和耿寿昌两人都只用"斛"。前引《汉书·食货志》中提到:

宣帝即位,用吏多选贤良,……谷至石五钱,农人少利。时大司农中丞耿寿昌……,五凤中奏言:"故事,岁漕关东谷四百万斛以给京师。"……

元帝即位,……。二年,齐地饥,谷石三百余,民多饿死,琅邪郡人相食。

《食货志》叙述宣帝时事时用石作为谷的单位("谷至石五钱"),而引用的耿寿昌在五凤年间的奏书则用斛作为谷的单位("岁漕关东谷四百万斛以给京师"),到叙述元帝时水灾导致饥荒、物价飞涨时却又仍用石作为谷的单位。《汉书》中没有耿寿昌用"石"为体积(容量)单位的例证,而此书中《赵充国传》和《食货志》两篇则都表明,耿寿昌有喜欢用斛代替石的偏好。

4.《九章》斛、石区分是耿寿昌所为

在出土的秦代、西汉(包括新朝)至东汉简牍中,石一直同时作重量单位和体积(容量)单位。这说明用石和斛分别作重量和体积(容积)单位,不是一部作品成于新莽或之后的反映,而只是《九章》一书的特色,而这一特色正好与《汉书》反映的耿寿昌对"斛"的偏好巧合,也与出土简牍中耿寿昌活跃的时代(包括五凤年间)有"斛"的较多用例相合。另一方面,出土文献中"斛"的使用在张苍时代也很少见,故可断言,对石、斛的使用区别对待,正是耿寿昌所为。

5.《九章》中斛的多值制之渊源

(1)《九章》中斛的多值制。

除通用的尺(指立方尺)、寸(立方寸)外,《九章》表示液体、颗粒物及粉末的体积和带空腔物体的容积只有斛、斗、升三个单位,从升到斗都采用 10 进;从斗到斛,也采用 10 进,但第 5 章有几个例外,值得讨论。此章第 23 题"委粟平地"、第 24 题"委菽依垣"和第 25 题"委米依垣内角",把粟谷、菽(大豆)和米分别往平地、靠墙壁和围墙内角撒落,理想状态下分别形成圆锥形粟谷堆、半圆锥形大豆堆和 1/4 圆锥形的米堆。三题都是已知按尺计量的"下周"(下底圆周长或下底圆弧长)和"高",求其体积。按各自的体积公式求出以(立方)尺计量的体积之后,《九章》还要化为以斛计量的体积。这时,针对三种粮食,《九章》明确表示相应的斛采用这样的体积标准:

> 程:粟一斛,积二尺七寸。其米一斛,积一尺六寸五分寸之一。其菽、荅、麻、麦一斛,皆二尺四寸十分寸之三。[65]

这里的"二尺七寸"、"一尺六寸五分寸之一"和"二尺四寸十分寸之三"分别相当于现代的 2 700 立方寸、1 620 立方寸和 2 430 立方寸,分别等于 $16\frac{2}{3}$ 斗、15 斗和 10 斗。第 27 题是由长方体仓库的广、袤和它能盛粟的斛数,求它的高;第 28 题是由圆柱体仓库的高和它能盛米的斛数,求它的底面周长。经过校算,可知这两个问题中粟的斛和米的斛也分别采用上述的标准。在这 5 个算题中,不同粮食的斛标准不同,是一个非常特殊的现象,在其他汉代的传世文献中没有见过这样的用例。但如果对比出土秦汉简牍中的计量制度,则容易看出其中的端倪。

(2) 秦至汉初石、桶的多值制。

在秦简和西汉初年的简牍中,石作为体积(容量)单位通常为 10 斗,但在政府仓储部门的粮食管理事务中,采用了一种特殊的单位制度,笔者称为多值石制。它根据粮食种类的不同,采用不同的体积标准:

① 对于粟类(粟、粱、禾、黍,还应包括稷)谷子,1 石 = 16 斗;
② 对于稻谷,1 石 = 20 斗;
③ 对于各种米,1 石 = 10 斗;
④ 对于菽(叔)、荅、麦、麻,1 石 = 15 斗。[66]

同时,在秦简中还发现有一种多值桶(简文作"甬")制,除把上述"石"换成"桶"外,完全相同。[67]

(3) 西汉中期至东汉的大石、小石制。

在西汉中期至东汉时期的简牍中,石作体积(容量)单位仍是 10 斗。不过这一时期,存在着一种大石、小石制。与多值石制中不同粮食种类的石采用相同量值的下级单位斗、升不同,大石、小石采用不同量值的下级单位,但同级单位保持相同的量值比,而大石与其下级单位的斗、升采用十进制,小石与其下级单位的斗、升也采用十进制。也就是说:

① 3 大石 = 5 小石;3(大)斗 = 5(小)斗;3(大)升 = 5(小)升。
② 1 大石 = 10(大)斗,1(大)斗 = 10(大)升;
    1 小石 = 10(小)斗,1(小)斗 = 10(小)升。

小石采用多值制中米的标准,也就是以 10 斗为一石的普遍标准。大石以多值制中粟类谷子的一石为标准。小石的斗、升分别继承了早先斗、升的量值标准,而大石的斗、升则分别增大到原来斗、升标准的 $\frac{5}{3}$ 倍。同时,尽管大石和小石分别取早先粟类谷子和由之舂出的粝米一石的数量为标准,但它们所能度量的范围已不再分别限于米和粟类的粮食。[68]

---

[65] 郭书春汇校:《九章算术新校》,第 175 页。

[66] 邹大海:《关于〈算数书〉、秦律和上古粮米计量单位的几个问题》,《内蒙古师范大学学报(自然科学汉文版)》第 38 卷第 5 期,2009 年 9 月,第 508—515 页;邹大海:《从出土文献看秦汉计量单位石的变迁》,RIMS Kôkyûroku Bessatsu B50: Study of the History of Mathematics August 27~30, 2012, edited by Tsukane Ogawa, Research Institute for Mathematical Sciences, Kyoto University, June 2014, pp.137—156.

[67] 邹大海:《关于秦汉计量单位石、桶的几个问题》,《中国史研究》,2019 年第 1 期,第 57—76 页。

[68] 邹大海:《从出土文献看秦汉计量单位石的变迁》;邹大海:《关于秦汉计量单位石、桶的几个问题》。

另外,西汉中后期至东汉还有少量的大斛、小斛用例,当为大石、小石制的替换。

(4)《九章》斛的多值制是耿寿昌对石、桶多值制做替换的结果。

通过对比容易断言,《九章》这 5 个问题所用斛的标准,正好与秦至汉初石或桶的多值制标准相同(只要把石或桶换成斛即可),而与耿寿昌时代至东汉的大石、小石(或大斛、小斛)制区别很大。考虑到《九章》其他问题中的斛全部统一为 10 斗,而多值制只行用于西汉早期及以前,可以断定,这 5 个问题不可能是耿寿昌或其后补入的。它们的原型一定是汉初或以前甚至是先秦时期的算题,只是那时采用了以"石"或"桶"作为单位名的法律标准。耿寿昌在整理《九章》时,让斛、石分工分别表示体积(容量)单位、重量单位,本来是以 10 斗为斛的,但这样不仅会导致原题的答案要改变,而且特别关键的是要改变所引法律的标准,所以他干脆只用"斛"简单替换"石"或"桶"而未对数据做修改,于是形成了极为罕见的多值斛制。

6. 耿寿昌基于恢复古旧经典强烈意识的《九章》整理工作

上述《九章》中 5 个问题的情况很可能说明,耿寿昌在整理《九章》时对原题的保真度较高,并不随便改写。

不仅如此,耿寿昌在整理《九章》时,增补的问题也应该很少,特别是很少有新的类型。这从以下几点可以看出来。

首先,从单位制度看,耿寿昌时代有大石、小石制,也有少量的大斛、小斛,但这些在《九章》中没有反映。上述 5 个问题,如果用大斛、小斛,则可以对应粟、米两种数据,只需要调整一种(菽、荅、麻、麦)数据,不用很麻烦即可与同时代通行的制度相合,但还需要改变原来所引程中的数据,所以整理者宁愿只做简单的替换,从而形成在其时代和以前的现实中并不存在的多值斛制,这说明他在整理时尽量做很少的改动,并没有将带有他所在时代标志的计量制度的新算题补入《九章》之中。

其次,耿寿昌改革漕运,从京师附近的郡采购粮食以节省运费;提出增加海租以提高财政收入;又设常平仓,在市面上谷价低时政府以较高的价格买进,市面上谷价高时政府以较低的价格卖出,以稳定粮价。如果他整理《九章》时补入他同时代所面临的数学问题,那么以这三类工作为背景的算题是他的首选项,因为这种算题与《九章》已有针对政府工作的算题在风格上是协调的。可是,不管是有关从京师附近地区买粮食以节省运费的算题,或是增加海租的算题,还是有关政府高价买进、低价卖出以稳定粮价的算题,在《九章》中都一个也没有。

其三,耿寿昌为宣帝建造杜陵。《九章》中确有两个与墓有关的算题。一个计算"羡除"的容积,"羡除"即墓道。它的下广六尺(1.38 米),上广一丈(2.3 米),深三尺(0.69 米);末广八尺(1.84 米),无深;袤七尺(1.61 米)。杜陵没有被正式挖掘,但做过勘探。"陵墓四面正中各有一条""大小、形制基本相同"的墓道,"封土以外部分的墓道长 20 米、宽约 8 米,墓道口距地表深约 3~4 米,接近封土边的墓道距今地表深约 20 米。"[69] 显然,《九章》此题的墓道规格与帝陵完全无关。另一个算题计算"冥谷"的容积。"冥谷"即墓坑。它的上广二丈(4.6 米),袤七丈(16.1 米),下广八尺(1.84 米),袤四丈(9.2 米),深六丈五尺(14.95 米)。杜陵墓坑有多大不得而知,从墓道看,其规模肯定远比此题中冥谷的数据大。这从马王堆三号墓的数据与《九章》冥谷的对比可以推知。它的墓主是长沙王丞相軑侯利苍的一个儿子,地位不高。其墓坑是带墓道的长方形竖穴,深 17.7 米,墓口南北长 16.3 米,东西宽 15.45 米,墓底长 5.8 米,宽 5.05 米。[70] 此墓坑与《九章》冥谷的高和平均长度相差不大,但冥谷的宽远小于马王堆三号墓,前者的容积不到后者的 1/3。帝王的墓坑当然要远大于马王堆三号墓,更大于《九章算术》的冥谷。特别是"冥谷"下广才 1.84 米,显然不可能以杜陵为原型。可以断言,耿寿昌没有往《九章》中补入以他主持的杜陵建造工作为背景的算题。

---

69 中国社会科学院考古研究所编:《汉杜陵陵园遗址》,北京:科学出版社,1993 年,第 6 页。
70 湖南省博物馆、中国科学院考古研究所:《长沙马王堆二、三号汉墓发掘简报》,《文物》,1974 年第 7 期,第 39—48 转 63 页。

其四,前面提到耿寿昌发挥他的数学才能,制作过天文仪器浑象,计算过日、月运行的度数,写过天文著作,可是《九章》中一个天文计算的问题都没有。可见他的天文工作没有影响到他编纂《九章》的内容。

以上证据充分说明,耿寿昌把对《九章》的整理与他将数学用于解决他从事的多项实际工作,区分得非常清楚,其目的在于恢复被损坏的古旧经典,而非阐发自己在数学上的贡献。这在其他章中也有反映。

《九章》"均输"章有28个算题,另有一个今本《九章》佚失而为王孝通所引的"犬追兔"问题。其中,前4个算题考虑多指标下如何公平摊派赋税,它们的现实背景和数学结构都很接近,属于同一类,被认为是"均输"算题;其他的算题则被认为不是"均输"问题,而只是被编入"均输"章的杂题。20世纪80年代以前学术界普遍认为,经济上的"均输"是汉武帝之后产生的,数学上的"均输"不能早于此时。80年代张家山西汉初年墓出土"均输律"以后,学术界仍认为只有前4题是均输问题,但它们可以更早。对于其他算题,有的学者认为是后来增补的。但笔者的考察发现情况不是这么简单。前4题其实应该用此章第3、4两题提到的"均赋"来概括,而"均输"的含义则包括了"均赋"而范围更广。在经济上,从先秦到西汉,除包括让赋税的分配公平的"均赋"外,"均输"至少还包括先秦和秦代少府下之"均输"官的事务,这种事务成为"均输"章第9题在先秦或秦代的蓝本之现实背景。不仅如此,作为《九章》中数学门类的"均输",其含义除涵盖第1~4、9题外,还能统括此章其他算题(含王孝通所引的"犬追兔"问题),这些算题中的绝大部分都能在秦至西汉初年的竹简算书中找到类似的算题。这说明"均输"章的算题主要来自《九章》在先秦或秦代的祖本,张苍和耿寿昌特别是后者很少补入新的算题,尤其是很少补入新型的算题。[71] 这种情况不限于"均输"章。比如"衰分"章第5题是:

> 今有北乡算八千七百五十八,西乡算七千二百三十六,南乡算八千三百五十六,凡三乡发徭三百七十八人。欲以算数多少衰出之,问各几何?
>
> 答曰:
> 北乡遣一百三十五人一万二千一百七十五分人之一万一千六百三十七。
> 西乡遣一百一十二人一万二千一百七十五分人之四千四。
> 南乡遣一百二十九人一万二千一百七十五分人之八千七百九。
> 术曰:各置算数为列衰,副并为法;以所发徭人数乘未并者,各自为实,实如法得一人。[72]

此问题容易被认为是耿寿昌增补的,其实不然。类似的算题见于秦简《数》:

> 凡三乡,其一乡卒千人,一乡七百人,一乡五百人,今上归千人,欲以人数衰之,问几可(何)归几可(何)?曰:千者归四〔百〕五十四人有(又)二千二百分人千二百·七百者归三百一十八人有(又)二千二百分人四百·五百归二百廿七人有(又)二千二百分人六百。
> 其述(术)曰:同三乡卒,以为法,各以乡卒乘千人为实,如法一人。[73]

"筭(算)"是算赋的单位名。算赋是针对成年劳动力征收的人头税,起征或免征年龄以及一算的多少在不同时期可能有所不同。常见的征收算赋的年龄是15至56岁,一算为120钱。"算"的数目在《九章》这个问题中是成年劳动力的人数。汉代在高帝四年八月(公元前203年)开始征收算赋,但这只是汉代

---

[71] 邹大海:《中国上古时代数学门类均输新探》。
[72] 郭书春汇校:《九章算术新校》,第100页。
[73] 萧灿:《岳麓书院藏秦简〈数〉研究》,北京:中国社会科学出版社,2015年,第88页。为简便起见,此处引文采用校勘后的结果,并将重文号恢复成所指代的字,同时删去重文号。

之始,秦代实际已有算赋。[74] 可以看出,两个算题的现实背景和算法都很相似:都是徭役问题,都是三个乡各有一个基本数(前者是算数;后来是已在服徭役的人数),已知一个总数(前者是要征发的徭役总人数,后者是要从在服徭役者中遣返的总人数),要在三个乡之间进行分配(前者求要从每个乡征发的徭役数,后者求从每个乡在服徭役者中遣返的人数)。两题算法都是比例分配法,都具有一般性,但前者没有具体数字,后者有一处具体数字。《数》表明,《九章》此题很可能是早已有之的,并非耿寿昌所补。当然,他可能做过文字加工。

正是由于耿寿昌对《九章》的整理具有恢复旧有经典的强烈意识,而绝非视为自己的撰作,所以他很少往《九章》里补入以他的时代和他的工作为背景的算题。

另一个值得注意的情节是,从问题和算法的结构上看,《九章》各章之间的界限是非常清楚的。第一、四、五、七至九章的每一章都容易与其他章的内容区分开来。比较容易让人产生误解的是第二章"粟米"、第三章"衰分"和第六章"均输",它们都讲比例问题和算法。这几章内有的算题与章名的对应关系不明显,初看之下在归类上具有随意性,读者容易觉得此书的编排方式不合理,缺乏一致性。其实不然。如前所述,"均输"章的算题本来就可以用"均输"一名来统摄。下面看另两章。

"粟米"章之首是各种粮食及加工品的换算表,称为"粟米之法",然后才是"今有术",即正比例算法。此章之名"粟米"应来源于这张换算表的名称。接下来有三类算题:第一类是"粟米之法"中取两种物品的换算,直接用今有术(正比例算法)解决。第二类是若干钱买若干物,求每物的单价,本来可以直接用除法求解,这比用今有术简单,但《九章》用经率术"以所求率乘钱数为实,所买率为法,实如法而一",它显然还是归结为"今有术",甚至没有提到"所求率"为1,1乘以钱数相当于不乘。第三类是其率术和反其率术问题,形式上的确很特殊,但不难发现,这类算题其实是第二类的扩展;其率术问题也是求单价,只是因为单价为分数,而作者想要整数答案,于是把问题设置为求相差1的两个单价;反其率术则求一钱能买多少物品,答案也是相差1的两个数据。可见,第三类问题是从第二类延伸而来的。因此,"粟米"章的问题保持着其内在的一致性,不存在其他类型的问题误入此章的情况。

"衰分"章有四类问题。章首为"衰分术"即比例分配算法,之后有7个这类算题,这是第一类。然后是"返衰术",是按倒数比例进行分配的算法,之后有2个这类例题,这是第二类。这两类都与章名"衰分"很切合,可以称为"衰分本术"类问题。第三类是第10～19题,它们都具有这样的结构,已知甲物的数量为A,对应于乙物的数量为B,求甲物的数量为a时,对应于乙物的数量是多少。这明显是正比例问题,按今有术求解,从算法上看,确实应该放在"粟米"章。但是,这些问题都和"粟米之法"无关,在算法上比该章经率术问题要复杂,由于"粟米"章本来就不以"今有术"这个方法命名,所以把这10个算题放入"粟米"章也不见得就很贴切。另一个问题是"粟米"章已有46题,而"衰分"章只有20题,如果把此章的这10个题放入"粟米"章,则两章体量相差过于悬殊。考虑到这10个问题比"粟米"章的第二类问题要复杂,把它们置于"衰分"章而不是"粟米"章也是有其内在逻辑的。第四类问题只有此章最末的第20题。它是说,贷1 000钱的月息为30钱,已知贷了750钱,9日归还,求利息。此问题也不是"衰分"问题,而是更复杂但可化为按正比例算法求解的问题,其比例关系是:将所贷钱数与日数相乘,乘积与息钱成正比。这个问题可以说是第三类的延伸。因此,把它放在第三章里也有一定道理。

值得注意的是"均输"章的第7题与"衰分"章的最后一题有相似性,前者是说,雇人运盐2斛走100里,给40钱;如果运盐1斛7斗3升又3分之1升,走80里,问应该给多少工钱。这里,盐的体积和运送的距离之乘积,与工钱数成正比,是解决此问题的关键。这两个问题在算法结构上是相同的,从这点上看,应该把它们归到同一章才合理。但是,汉代常常把盐、铁的经营与"均输"作为一起讨论的话题,所以编者把第7题置于"均输"章而不是"衰分"章大概不是出于偶然而是有意为之的。从这一角度看,"衰分"章的息钱问题置于"均输"章才是最合理的。不过,《九章》问题的归类,也不全是根据算法结构来安排的,它被置于"衰分"章,可能还是由于上面提到的编者觉得它为该章第三类问题的延伸。当然,这里存在考虑不周的问题,但我们不宜假设古人对每个地方都考虑得很周密。

---

[74] 邹大海:《中国数学的兴起与先秦数学》,济南:河北科学技术出版社,2001年,第147—148页。

关于比例问题和算法的三章中,"粟米"章最简单,"衰分"章次之,"均输"章最复杂,除典型的算题外,其他非典型算题的安排也是有规律可寻的:一方面,编者按算法上从易至难的顺序把它们安排到三章中去;另一方面,在同一章内则是大体按现实背景或相关性,基于以类相从的思想进行归类和编排。

在秦简《数》、汉简《算数书》中,数学知识的表达形态和书写格式是多种多样的,而《九章》则相当统一。后来的《孙子算经》和《张丘建算经》也基本上采用了《九章》统一性的表达方式。所以,《九章》统一性的数学表达方式固然可能有一部分源自其在先秦或秦代的祖本,但由于秦火之后的散坏,汉代早期收集的材料有可能经过改写,或将不属于《九章》祖本的材料误为《九章》的,或有意补充新的材料,因此到耿寿昌手里的版本,其表达方式应该仍是多样化的。而上面的讨论表明,耿寿昌对计量单位的使用做过规范,那么他对其他数学表达方式以及书写格式做统一性处理,也在情理之中。另一方面,既然秦火之后《九章》散坏,则收集来的零散内容就不可能在篇章的归属和前后次序上都很清楚,有的算题、算法和数量标准也会不完整,存在讹误,所以整理者必须根据自己的理解,把本身无明确归属标识的材料编入相应的篇章中去,并按一定次序和方式进行编排、校勘和删补,同时根据对表达方式、度量单位、书写格式进行规范化和整齐化所导致的数量转化做相应的修改。张苍做过这样的工作,耿寿昌也应该做过这样的工作。此外,虽然耿寿昌编纂《九章》时注重对经典的恢复,但还是要为当代服务,所以他也应采用当代的语言对文本进行修饰,对照《九章》与出土算书的行文可知刘徽说《九章》"所论者多近语",确非虚言。

耿寿昌以数学能力及其应用受到皇帝的宠信,他改革漕运满足京师粮食供应、为赵充国守卫边疆做后勤工作特别是筹措军粮、设常平仓、造杜陵等政绩都得力于此。既然他著有天文著作,那么他也可能写作过自己的数学著作,可惜的是不论是他自撰的天文著作还是数学著作都没有流传下来。

结语

综上所述,耿寿昌应该是安定(在今甘肃泾川县或今河北辛集市)人,生于公元前 100 年前后,可能年少时就研习过张苍的《九章算术》未完成本,培养了很高的数学才能。他在汉昭帝时期步入仕途。随着宣帝对吏治的整顿和人才的选拔,耿寿昌以优秀的数学水平和善于运用数学方法解决问题的能力而受到重用。他很可能在公元前 65 年开始主持宣帝陵杜陵的建造,大约在此年或至迟在公元前 61 年开始担任大农司中丞。公元前 61 年,耿寿昌为赵充国靖边做后勤供应与保障工作。在五凤年间,他改革了过去通过漕运从关东向京师运送粮食的做法,直接从京师附近地区采购粮食,节省了大量的运费。他又提出增加海租,提高了财政收入。他设立了常平仓,平抑物价,既有益于百姓生活安定,也有助于政治稳定。公元前 48 年他负责宣帝安葬于杜陵的土木工程事宜。耿寿昌可能终其一生只做到了大司农中丞的职位,但他还是以其出色的工作获得了关内侯的爵位。他可能以此身份卒于公元前 40 年左右。

耿寿昌是天文学家,制造过天文仪器,利用黄道计算过日、月运行的度数,著有《月行帛图》232 卷、《月行度》2 卷,但均已失传。

耿寿昌是数学家,他很可能也写过自己的数学著作,但没有流传下来。

耿寿昌在张苍的基础上整理删补《九章》,至少做了以下几个方面的工作:

(1)统一了全书的计量单位,特别是对表示重量的石和表示体积(容量)的斛做了区分。

(2)对全书的数学表达方式以及书写格式做了统一化、规范化的处理,对全书的算题、算法及常数标准等进行了精心的组织与编排,并对文本进行了校勘、删补和文字上的修饰,对数据进行了算校。

(3)在恢复过去经典的强烈意识下,谨慎地删补了少量算题和算法,补入的算题和算法往往与旧有材料属于同种类型。

耿寿昌在恢复古旧经典的强烈意识下所做的精心整理,达到了预期的目的,由他定稿的《九章》后来成为中国传统数学最重要的经典,是此后近两千年中国数学的发展在问题、方法和思想上的源泉。这种成功能在很大程度上弥补他自撰著作佚失的缺憾。虽然没有证据表明耿寿昌在科学原创性上有多么伟大的成就,但他对《九章》的定稿工作,足以使他值得被列入中国科学史特别是数学史上最重要学者的名单,理应受到更大的重视。

说明：1991 年，笔者有幸考入中国科学院自然科学史研究所，在郭书春先生门下攻读硕士学位，毕业后留研究所在先生身边工作，时常受教。记得刚来不久，先生跟我说做学问有两种方式，一种是一开始就努力往深里做，后来逐渐加快速度；另一种是一开始就求快但做得浅，后来再慢慢往深里做。据他的观察，前一种成功的多。他用农村犁田做比喻解释说，做学问就像犁田，一开始就往深里犁，会很慢，犁不动，但是一旦犁动了，也能快起来；如果一开始求快犁得浅，后面往往就深不下去。先生又说，人的能力有大有小，做学问主要是要迈出自己坚实的一步。我们没有李、钱二老的才能，做不出他们那么大的学问，迈不了一大步不要紧，关键是这一步要是自己迈的，不能抄来抄去。先生还说，学生要超过老师，否则老师不如不带学生自己做好了。如今 30 年过去了，先生的教诲言犹在耳，但学问没能做大，有负先生教诲。所幸每写一篇论文，自问能算是自己迈出的一小步，也可聊以自慰。现在的这篇小文是在先生基础上做的一点小工作，作为对先生八十华诞的献礼，希望尚能达到"自己迈的一小步"的要求。

本文的主要观点曾于 2021 年 7 月 28 日凌晨在第 26 届国际科学技术大会分组会"Evolution of mathematics in China: major figures, anonymous contributors, and the giants among them"（网上在线会议）上以"耿寿昌与《九章算术》编纂新证（New Arguments on the Relation Between Geng Shouchang and the Compilation of the *Nine Chapters on Mathematical Procedures*）"为题报告过。

基金项目：中国科学院战略研究专项"中国科技传统及其现实意义研究"（项目编号 GHJ-ZLZX-2021-17-2）。

Geng Shouchang, an Underestimated Scientist in Ancient China

Zou Dahai

(Institute for the History of Natural Sciences, Chinese Academy of Sciences, Beijing 100190)

Abstract There is no special biography of Geng Shouchang in the ancient historical books, the works written by him have also been lost, and the historical fact recorded by Liu Hui of the 3rd century CE that Zhang Cang and Geng Shouchang compiled the *Nine Chapters on Mathematical Procedures* have been doubted by modern historians of sciences as well. All these might lead to that Geng Shouchang's status in the history of science in China has been underestimated by historians of science. This paper will comprehensively and systematically discuss Geng Shouchang's life story, official activities and work in mathematics and astronomy. By combining the unearthed materials with the handed down documents, and introducing the method of probability, it proves that most of the occurrences of unit "*hu* 斛" in the *Hanshu* (*History of Han dynasty*) used to describe the historical facts earlier than the Xin dynasty of Wang Mang originated from the times when the corresponding historical facts occurred, not from miswriting of the unit "*shi* 石", then it proves that Geng Shouchang is indeed the final editor of the *Nine Chapters*, he had a strong intention of restoring the ancient classic when compiling the *Nine Chapters*, and rarely added new types of math problems; he unified the measurement units in the *Nine Chapters*, including the distinction between the unit *shi* and the unit *hu* which were respectively used to represent weight and volume (capacity). He not only standardized and unified the classification and organization of the *Nine Chapters*, but modified its expressions. Though Geng Shouchang's self-authored works have all been lost, the *Nine Chapters* that he carefully compiled has become the most important classic in the history of mathematics in China, this is enough for him to be included in the list of the most influential mathematicians, and he deserves more attention of historians of sciences.

Keywords Geng Shouchang; *Nine Chapters on Mathematical Procedures*; water transportation of grain to the capital; ever normal granary; measurement system; method of probability; ancient Chinese scientist; tomb of Emperor Xuan of Han dynasty

作者简介：邹大海，湖南新化人。1991年在中国科学院自然科学史研究所师从郭书春先生攻读硕士学位，1994年获理学硕士学位，旋即留所工作。2006年起任研究员，2010年起任博士生导师。现兼任研究所学位评定委员会主任，《自然科学史研究》主编，国际科学史研究院（International Academy of the History of Science）通讯院士，中国数学会数学史分会副理事长，湖北省社会科学院科技史研究中心主任、研究员，河北省祖冲之研究会副理事长。曾兼任中国数学会理事（2012—2015），自然科学史研究所编辑部主任（2015年10月—2016年9月）、《自然科学史研究》副主编（2016—2019年3月）。主要研究中国数学史和中国早期科学思想史，在利用出土材料研究中国数学史方面较有心得。撰有专著《中国数学的兴起与先秦数学》（2001）、《中国数学在奠基时期的形态、创造与发展：以若干典型案例为中心的研究》（2022），发表专题论文数十篇。

Canon and commentary in ancient China: An outlook based on mathematical sources

Karine Chemla 林力娜

Some decades after the unification of the Chinese Empire, the compilation of a mathematical book, *The Nine Chapters on Mathematical Procedures* (*Jiuzhang Suanshu*《九章算术》)(hereafter *The Nine Chapters*), that was to have a singular fate in China began. A few centuries after its completion in the first century BCE or CE,[1] the book came to be referred to as a 'Canon' (*jing* 经), and even, later on during the Song dynasty, as the most important of all mathematical Canons.

However insignificant this fact may seem, it raises important issues. For centuries, Chinese readers thus perceived the book as belonging to a specific set of scriptures, all designated by the technical term *jing*. What did it mean for a book to be perceived as a Canon? How was it read accordingly? What kind of attitude, of expectation, did this fact induce in the readers? These are the questions that constitute the scope of this essay. They are much too broad to be exhaustively addressed within a few pages. I shall therefore restrict myself to tackling them from a specific angle, hoping to demonstrate thereby how fruitful they could be for different directions of research.

In fact, in his *Scripture, Canon and Commentary. A Comparison of Confucian and Western Exegesis*, John Henderson treated these questions extensively, mainly with reference to the Confucian Canons. As scripture, these texts have all been the object of traditions of commentary, and, in an attempt to capture how readers perceived them, Henderson observed the attitudes and expectations manifested by commentators towards the Confucian Canons. For fundamental reasons, to which I return in conclusion, his survey offers an appropriate background for identifying which attitudes towards *The Nine Chapters* documented in our historical sources could stem from perceiving the book as a 'Canon.' To begin with, as we will see, the commentaries on *The Nine Chapters* reveal attitudes toward the text and beliefs similar to those described by Henderson. Two issues appear to me to be at stake when reconsidering these questions with respect to a mathematical text.

The first one relates to the history of texts. Despite pioneering research about perceptions of Can-

---

[1] Diverging views about the completion of *The Nine Chapters* are still under discussion today. I have argued elsewhere in favour of dating the completion of the compilation to the first century CE. (See my introduction to chapter 6, in [Chemla and Guo Shuchun 郭书春, 2004, 475—478]. In Chapter B of [Chemla and Guo Shuchun 郭书春, 2004, 43—56], Guo Shuchun presents the evolution of scholars' views on this issue through history). For further detail about the status of the book as a Canon, see below.

ons and modes of reading them as well as about traditions of commentary,[2] we are far from a comprehensive understanding of the properties attributed to this category of texts and the approaches to them developed by readers throughout Chinese history. What is at stake, in this respect, with *The Nine Chapters* is to consider how our understanding of these matters could benefit from considering the case of mathematical Canons. More generally, virtually all scholarly disciplines identified some texts as being Canons, and research on this type of text has so far hardly begun to take into account Canons in scholarly disciplines. This article is an invitation to fill this gap. The key issue, in my view, is hence to determine how considering the Canons elaborated within the context of specific fields of knowledge such as mathematics can improve our understanding of the phenomenon of canonicity in general. Could it be that, in these specific contexts, we are in a better position to describe modes of reading or to account for attitudes and expectations? In this article, I aim to illustrate why I believe so.

The second issue connects with the history of mathematics more specifically. Being essentially composed of problems and procedures of computation for solving them, *The Nine Chapters* has been read, quite anachronistically in my view, as a collection of recipes or a kind of exercise book.[3] This approach, common among contemporary historians of mathematics, can hardly account for the properties Chinese readers attributed to the book in the past. This should sound as a warning that — at least if we want to understand why the book has been perceived as a Canon — such an approach should be reconsidered. The questions raised above stem from the belief that our reading of *The Nine Chapters* can gain from situating the book — as ancient readers regularly did — more adequately within the category of Canons.

With these two agenda in mind, in a first part, I shall introduce one recurring expectation towards *The Nine Chapters* that appears to derive from the fact that it was approached as a Canon, namely, that at different moments in history, readers who left evidence of how they approached the book betray their assumption that it should encompass the whole of mathematics, which, in ancient China, essentially meant all mathematical procedures. Below, we shall examine more closely in three cases what form these statements of completeness took with respect to mathematics. How is it possible to believe that a collection of problems and procedures of computation could be all-encompassing? How are we to understand what, at first sight, appears to be an extravagant claim? One way to deal with these questions is to consider that these statements are mere rhetoric, designed to enhance the status of the Canon. However, I believe that, before deciding on this issue and discarding these claims

---

[2] [Henderson, 1991] aimed at exploring the assumptions on Canons shared by commentators, not only in Chinese history, but in a comparative perspective. In contrast, Rudolf Wagner developed a project devoted to commentaries as writings *per se*, in their variety. In [Wagner, 2000], he particularly concentrates on Wang Bi's commentary on the *Daodejing*《道德经》, and, incidentally, on the *Yijing*《易经》. Wagner thereby extends the type of Canon examined beyond the strict circle of the Confucian scripture. His focus lies in describing ways in which Wang Bi as a commentator interprets the Canons and how his philosophy takes shape as commentary. It is interesting to note that aspects of representations of how the Canon makes sense are common to this case and to ours (see for instance [Wagner, 2000, 166]).

[3] Compare [Martzloff, 1987], 116 (quotation by Zeng Guofan 曾国藩), 119 (quotation by Michael Loewe), 122, 124 ([Martzloff, 1997, 128, 131, 132—133, 134]). It should be stressed that we have no evidence regarding the reasons why *The Nine Chapters* was compiled. The fact that seven centuries later, it was used as a textbook in the Tang "School of Mathematics (*Suan Xue* 算学)" does not tell us anything about its first uses. Nor does it exhaust the meanings different readers attributed to the book. What is more, the fact that in the "School of Mathematics," the Canon served as a textbook does not imply that in this context it was perceived and used as an exercise book.

as intellectually insignificant, we should first at least try to understand them. The essential point for me is that, in the case of mathematics, one can argue for a precise interpretation of these claims. This is the aim of the second part of the article. With respect to *The Nine Chapters*, I shall offer an interpretation of the expectation that the book encompasses all of mathematics. To this end, I shall describe modes of reading the text and practicing mathematics that seem to have been put into play in relation to this belief. This may help us understand the meaning of this kind of statement more generally, as regards other Canons, at least in the eyes of the exegetes who put forward such views.

We can address such questions because our sources provide evidence enabling us to observe the practices of Chinese readers over quite a long time span. Indeed, as was usually the case for Canons, commentaries were composed on *The Nine Chapters*, some being chosen through tradition to be handed down together with the text of the Canon itself. These commentaries reveal attitudes and beliefs regarding the Canon. They display ways in which the scripture was interpreted and they reveal hypotheses underlying the exegesis. The commentaries will provide the source materials that will serve as the basis for tackling our questions. In fact, no extant edition of *The Nine Chapters* survived that did not include the commentaries completed by Liu Hui 刘徽 in 263 and those composed by a group under Li Chunfeng's 李淳风 supervision and presented to the throne in 656. I shall designate the latter as 'Li Chunfeng's comments.' Incidentally, the first known source that refers to *The Nine Chapters* as a 'Canon (*jing*)' is Liu Hui's preface to his own commentary. [4]

Several centuries appear to have passed with nothing known to have been written about *The Nine Chapters* until a revival of interest during the Song dynasty. After what the available evidence shows as an interruption. In 1084, the Department of the Imperial Library (*Mishu sheng* 秘书省) printed an edition of the Canon with its two traditional commentaries; the reprint of this edition by Bao Huanzhi 鲍澣之 around 1213 is the earliest extant edition known today. [5] In relation to this, new commentaries were composed, such as Jia Xian's 贾宪 *Detailed Procedures of Huangdi's Canon of The Nine Chapters on Mathematics* (*Huangdi Jiuzhang Suanjing Xicao*《黄帝九章算经细草》), in the first half of the eleventh century, printed by Rong Qi 荣棨 in 1148, and Yang Hui's 杨辉 *Mathematical Methods Explaining in Detail The Nine Chapters* (*Xiangjie Jiuzhang Suanfa*《详解九章算法》) in 1261. [6] Through these editions and commentaries, over a time span of almost 1000 years, the historian can thus observe specific readers who made explicit their expectations towards, and their interpre-

---

[4] [Chemla and Guo Shuchun 郭书春, 2004, 126−129]. For the text of *The Nine Chapters* and its earliest commentaries, I shall refer systematically to our critical edition and translation into French published in the latter. The critical edition contained in [Qian Baocong 钱宝琮, 1963] presents the Canon within the context of *The Ten Canons of Mathematics*, that is, within the context in which Li Chunfeng's commentary was composed. The interpretation of the sentence in question, which is translated in excerpt (1) below, can be contested. In order not to overload the main text with technicalities, I discuss in Appendix 1 the evidenceregarding this point, on which my conclusions disagree with those of present-day historiography.

[5] These editions of *The Nine Chapters* were produced within the context of larger enterprises for editing the mathematical textbooks used in the "School of Mathematics", including *The Ten Canons of Mathematics*. Bao Huanzhi apparently added postfaces to some of these works. Two of them, including that to *The Nine Chapters*, are dated from the same date of 1200. Two others are signed 1212 and 1213. This seems to indicate that *The Nine Chapters* was among the first of all the Canons to be prepared for this edition. I am glad to be able to express my thanks to Professor Huang Yi-Long 黄一农, who helped me clarify this issue. On Bao Huanzhi's edition, see [Chemla, 2010a].

[6] On these Song commentaries, see [Guo Shuchun 郭书春, 1988] and [Zhou Xiaohan 周霄汉, 2018].

tation of, *The Nine Chapters*. Let us hence start by observing some features of their approach to the Canon.

The commentators' expectations of the Canon

When observing the attitudes towards *The Nine Chapters* manifested by the commentators, the striking fact one is confronted with is that, although Liu Hui, Li Chunfeng and Yang Hui operated at very different time periods and although their commentaries present important differences, they share similar and yet surprising expectations towards the book that seem to relate to its status as a Canon. To bring this point to light, let us concentrate on declarations made by each of them. If, at first sight, they appear somewhat obscure, they should become progressively clearer as I develop an interpretation of the key elements that they introduce and that are all essential for my argument. In this first part, therefore, I suggest that the reader concentrate on the aspects of the declarations related to the completeness of *The Nine Chapters*. The other elements of the quotations will be progressively addressed and clarified as the argument unfolds.

Liu Hui's conception of mathematics

The first declaration, by Liu Hui, occurs in his preface to his commentary, when he describes how he conceives of the genesis of the text of *The Nine Chapters* and his own commentary. He writes:[7]

> (1) In times past there was Baoxi, who, first, drew the eight trigrams to enter into communication with the capacities of clairvoyance and illumination, to classify the essentials of the myriad things, and then created the procedure of the multiplication table so that it be in concordance with the mutations of the six lines (of the hexagrams). Huangdi metamorphosed them [by working at the level of] the unfathomable, increased [their extension] by elongating them, and hence established the structure of the calendar, tuned the musical tubes, and used them to inquire into the source of the Way (*dao*). Hence the essential and minute *qi* of the two exemplars and of the four models could model themselves on them. 昔在包牺氏始画八卦，以通神明之德，以类万物之情，作九九之术，以合六爻之变。暨于黄帝神而化之，引而伸之，于是建历纪，协律吕，用稽道原，然后两仪四象精微之气可得而效焉。

---

[7] See [Chemla and Guo Shuchun 郭书春, 2004, 126–129]. In the following footnotes, I shall give only sketchy indications to explain some of the main features of the preface. For many points or statements that cannot be developed here — in particular the many references the first paragraph makes to one of the key Confucian canonical texts, that is, the *Canon of Changes* (*Yijing* 易经)—, I refer the reader to my footnotes to the preface as well as to my glossary of mathematical terms published in [Chemla and Guo Shuchun 郭书春, 2004], in which I discuss all the terms, whose Chinese pronunciation is mentioned here, and their philosophical implications. See also [Chemla, 2008]. In what follows, I number the passages quoted so as to refer the reader back to them more conveniently. Note that, in the translations given below, I use squared brackets to designate elements that are not explicit in the text, but that express my interpretation of the text. By contrast, round brackets insert transcriptions of the Chinese terms translated into pinyin or 'explanations.'

Records tell that Li Shou created mathematics [8] (...). It is only when the Duke of Zhou established the Rites that [we know that] the nine parts of mathematics existed. The <u>development</u> (*liu*) of these nine parts, this is precisely what *The Nine Chapters* is. [9] Formerly, the cruel Qin burnt the books. [10] The procedures of the <u>Canon</u> got <u>scattered and damaged</u>. After that time, the Bei Ping Marquis Zhang Cang [11] and the Assistant of the Grand Minister of Agriculture, Geng Shouchang, [12] both acquired a universal reputation for their excellence in mathematics. On the basis of scraps of the old text (*wen*) that were handed down, Zhang Cang and others made both <u>excisions</u> (*shan*) [13] and completions. This is why, when one examines its sections, in places they differ from the ancient ones and what is discussed is much in modern terms. 记称隶首作数（……）周公制礼而有九数，九数之流，则《九章》是矣。往者暴秦焚书，经术散坏。自时厥后，汉北平侯张苍、大司农中丞耿寿昌皆以善算命世。苍等因旧文之遗残，各称删补。故校其目则与古或异，而所论者多近语也。

As a child, I studied *The Nine Chapters*; as an adult, I again looked at it in detail. I observed the dividing of Yin and Yang, [14] synthesized the <u>source of mathematical procedures</u>. Having spent much time <u>to fathom its depths</u>, I managed to <u>understand its meaning/inten-</u>

---

[8] Li Shou is said by late sources to have been a minister to the first Emperor Huangdi, a figure of legend, and to have created mathematics. When in the next quoted sentence, Liu Hui mentions the Duke of Zhou and the differentiation of mathematics into nine branches, he speaks of known history and the foundation of Zhou dynasty in the eleventh century BCE.

[9] The idea that the book derives from a 'development' recurs with the following commentator, Li Chunfeng, in the seventh century; see below. On this part of the translation, see footnote 13, in [Chemla and Guo Shuchun 郭书春, 2004, 752].

[10] Liu Hui attributes the interruption of what had been, in his view, until that point, a smooth transmission of the text of *The Nine Chapters* to the burning of books ordered by the Emperor Qin shi huangdi who unified the Chinese empire in 221 BCE. On the next sentence, see the discussion in Appendix 1.

[11] Zhang Cang 张苍 was a civil servant who held quite important positions in the administration of the Han Empire from its beginnings. His domains of expertise included mathematics, astronomy, bookkeeping, management of finance and exegesis of some Confucian Canons. See Guo Shuchun, chapter B in [Chemla and Guo Shuchun 郭书春, 2004].

[12] Like Zhang Cang 张苍, but later, in the first century BCE, Geng Shouchang 耿寿昌 was a civil servant who contributed to the administration of finance and to settling astronomical questions. See Guo Shuchun, chapter B in [Chemla and Guo Shuchun 郭书春, 2004].

[13] This operation of expurgating inauthentic material that had accumulated in the documents during the process of transmission characterizes the way in which the tradition from at least the Han dynasty onwards conceived of Confucius as editor of Canons; see [Henderson, 1991, 26ff]. In the first piece of literary criticism devoted to Canons (*Wenxin diaolong* 文心雕龙, chapter 'Revering the Canons (*Zong jing* 宗经)'), at the turn of the sixth century, Liu Xie 刘勰 refers to Confucius's editing with the same word: *shan* 删. On this point, see [Owen, 1992], pp. 194–195. In other words, Liu Hui's preface here compares the Han editors' textual work on *The Nine Chapters* with Confucius' editing of Canons. The exact same parallel recurs in a commentary placed at the beginning of Chapter 8, when a commentator makes clear that he expects that, for certain specific procedures, the authors of *The Nine Chapters* would use "abstract expressions *kongyan* 空言," instead of what is elsewhere referred to as "accomplishments *shi* 事". Indeed, these are precisely the two types of formulation that Han scholars ascribed to Confucius as an editor of the *Spring and Autumn Annals* (*Chunqiu* 春秋). On this point, see [Chemla, 2021].

[14] For an interpretation on this specific cosmological statement, see [Chemla, 2010b].

tion (*yi*).[15] This is why I dared (...) compose a commentary on it. 徽幼习《九章》,长再详览,观阴阳之割裂,总算术之根源,探赜之暇,遂悟其意,是以敢(……)为之作注。

The accomplishments (*shi*) and their categories (*lei*) develop in relation to one another, but they each have that to which they return/amount (*gui*).[16] Therefore, the reason why, although they divide into branches, they share the same stem is that they emerge from only one of their ends (*duan*). Furthermore, if the internal constitutions (*li*)[17] are analyzed with statements (*ci*) and if the bodies are dissected with figures (*tu*), [one sees that *The Nine Chapters*, as restored during the Han dynasty,] gets close to, though made simple, being able to encompass and, though bringing into communication, not being confusing. (...) Al-

---

[15] As is suggested by the development on this term below, this may also be understood in the plural: 'its meanings/intentions.' Alternatively, if the anaphora refers to the mathematical procedures, this can also be interpreted as 'their meaning/intentions.' We will come back to this point.

[16] One can also interpret this as 'The categories of the accomplishments develop in relation to each other.' In this context, 'accomplishment' probably refers to the mathematical problems contained in *The Nine Chapters* and the procedures developed in relation to the problems, as well as refers to mathematical objects. This passage, essential for delivering Liu Hui's conception of mathematical reality, requires a delicate interpretation. Here is, in my view, a plausible interpretation on the basis of other occurrences of the key terms in his commentary (*lei* 类 'category/class,' *shi* 事 'accomplishments,' *gui* 归 'return/amount to'). With respect to objects, fractions provide a good illustration of how to understand the passage, if one relies on the commentary on the procedure for adding up fractions (after problem I.9). A fraction can be given in two ways: a set of parts (two of three parts for 2/3) or a pair of numbers — numerator and denominator. Basically, a fraction represents a quantity that is expressed on the basis of its structuration into parts. Stating that fractional quantities belong to the same class or category implies that they share the same denominator or are structured with parts of the same size. A given fractional quantity can change category by transformation. Such is the case when one systematically cuts its parts into finer parts (four of six parts, instead of two of three parts), or conversely gathers its parts into coarser ones (two of three parts, instead of four of six parts), or when, correspondingly, one multiplies (2/3 becoming 4/6) or divides (4/6 becoming 2/3) its numerator and denominator by a same number. Expressing the fractional quantity requires that a particular category be adopted. The possibility of transforming fractions and thereby changing their categories is the essential property that allows computing with them and bringing them together, since computing requires that categories of the various fractions involved in the operation be transformed into the same category. In this sense, 'the categories of the realizations (or the realizations and their categories) develop with respect to each other.' However, as quantities, all previous fractions return/amount to the same. Such is, in my view, the set of facts covered by the passage, when considered with respect to fractions. A similar interpretation can be developed for geometrical bodies on the basis of Li Chunfeng's commentary on the extraction of the spherical root (after problem 4.24). Moreover, mathematical problems are also understood as having categories and forming classes defined on the basis of the procedures attached to them. Rephrasing a procedure may change the category, the class to which the problem belongs, with each formulation revealing connections with other problems from a given perspective. We shall analyze below examples of such connections and the mathematical practices attached to the reformulation of procedures. However, beyond reformulation, procedures performing the same task or evaluating the same entities, 'amount/return to the same'. Moreover, as will become clear in what follows, through reformulation, unification can be carried out between procedures that appeared at first sight to be distinct. They are thereby revealed as having derived from the same root before they differentiated into distinct computations. This is why Liu Hui can speak of a 'source' or a 'stem' for mathematical procedures, out of which the procedures develop in distinct categories, relative to each other. To sum up, all mathematical realities can be transformed, according to modalities that need to be analyzed, in relation to the realities with which they interact, or to those with which they are compared or can be unified, and hence they can change 'category'. These transformations are deemed essential to the practice of mathematics, in that they bring different realities into communication or unify them. However, throughout these transformations, that 'to which they amount' does not change. The concepts *lei* 类 and *suogui* 所归 form, I believe, a contrasting pair.

[17] See below.

though one speaks of 'the nine parts of mathematics (*shu*),' they have the capacity to exhaust the subtle (*xian*) and to penetrate the minute (*wei*), to fathom what knows no bounds (what has no location—the *shen*). 事类相推,各有攸归,故枝条虽分而同本干知,发其一端而已。又所析理以辞,解体用图,庶亦约而能周,通而不黩(……);虽曰九数,其能穷纤入微,探测无方(……)。(My emphasis)

Let us, at this point, leave aside several aspects of this difficult text to concentrate on only some remarks. Note, first, that Liu Hui considers *The Nine Chapters* from the perspective of the ability of the Canon to encompass mathematics (they 'get close to, though made simple, being able to encompass...'). More generally, the commentator stresses the unlimited potentiality of the 'nine parts of mathematics,' which, in his view, developed into *The Nine Chapters*, contrasting it with the moderation of its size. If one may note a nuance in Liu Hui's assertion of the comprehensiveness of the Canon ('they get close to being able to encompass'), in my view, it is directed at Zhang Cang's and the other Han editors' inability to adequately restore the Canon, which had been damaged during the Qin burning of books.[18] This interpretation is supported by the second part of Liu Hui's preface, where, after having introduced a problem and evoked some procedures of *The Nine Chapters*, he states:

(2) But [in *The Nine Chapters*] there is nothing of the category (*lei*) of (...I skip the problem Liu Hui introduced here...).[19] Therefore the procedures made by Zhang Cang and the others do not yet suffice to exhaust extensively all mathematics (*bo jin qun shu*).[20] Within the nine parts of mathematics, I investigated the one named 'double difference'. I examined (*yuan*) its essential points (*zhiqu*) so as to make them extend to/be efficient for (*shi*) this [problem]. 无有(……)之类。然则苍等为术犹未足以博尽群数也。徽寻九数有重差之名,原其指趣乃所以施于此也。

(...The statement of procedures solving problems of this class follows...) I elaborated the 'double difference' and wrote a commentary on it so as to explore the meaning/intention (*yi*) of the ancients. I joined it after [the chapter] 'base and height' (i.e., the last chapter). 辄造《重差》,并为注解,以究古人之意,缀于《勾股》之下。(My emphasis)

As one can see here, again, the expectation made explicit is that the restored Canon should 'exhaust all mathematics.' The blame for the failure of *The Nine Chapters* to do so is put on its Han editors, including Zhang Cang, and not on the Classic itself. This interpretation is, in its turn, supported immediately afterwards by the way in which Liu Hui expounds his method for dealing with what he feels is a lacuna that must be filled. To this end, he does not claim to have invented the procedures he introduces in his preface. On the contrary, in a way that recalls his description of how the Han edi-

---

[18] On the idea that the preface describes the compilation of *The Nine Chapters* as a process of recovery of a lost scripture, see [Chemla, 2008].

[19] The category of a problem is defined by a procedure solving it, see [Chemla, 1997]. As is clear from the next statement, Liu Hui states here that the Canon as restored during the Han dynasty fails to provide the means to solve the given problem.

[20] Evidence that *shu* 数 can refer to mathematics or the parts composing mathematics is provided in my glossary, in [Chemla and Guo Shuchun 郭书春, 2004, 984–986].

tors proceeded, he shows how he obtained these procedures through 'investigating,' in a certain way, one procedure found in 'the nine parts of mathematics.' He therefore maintains that, for the purpose of filling the gaps in The Nine Chapters, he is using what he stated in (1) to be its source: the 'nine parts of mathematics.' It is interesting to note, in this respect, that Liu Hui's last sentence in (2) seems to indicate that he conceives of himself as continuing the work of editing the text of the Canon, based on the pieces of scripture available and guided by the assumption that The Nine Chapters should be complete. We shall come back below to his account of how he relies on a given procedure to derive means to fill up the lacunae.

Other elements in these excerpts are worth stressing. According to my interpretation of quotation (1), the commentary seems to be conceived as the exercise bringing to light the capacity of the Canon to fully encompass mathematics. More precisely, it is the analysis of the 'internal constitutions,' or *li*'s (理), and the dissections of the bodies that bring to light the properties of the Canon that are emphasized, i.e., that it 'get close to, though made simple, being able to encompass.'

In addition to this, Liu Hui makes explicit that what prompted the writing of his commentary was having reached an understanding of the 'meaning(s)' or the 'intention(s)' (*yi* 意) of The Nine Chapters, or of its procedures. In the same vein, in passage (2), he again describes his commentary as aiming at 'exploring the meaning (*yi* 意)' of the ancients. One may be tempted to interpret this term quite loosely. However, since understanding the *yi* appears to be an essential goal in his exegesis, I suggest, at least in the beginning, not jumping to a lax conclusion, but rather attempting to determine whether this term might not refer to something more specific.[21] We shall come back to interpreting these terms below.

Lastly, let us stress that, in the same lines of his preface where he introduces the theme of the completeness of the Canon, Liu Hui also alludes to an architecture of mathematical 'accomplishments' as deriving, by a process of differentiation, from a unique stem.[22]

Two features emerge from this declaration that will prove essential for us. First, the Canon is expected to be all-encompassing. Secondly, a structuring of mathematical procedures is sketched, in which various mathematical realities differentiated from a common stem.

Li Chunfeng's approach to the completeness of the Canon

Interestingly enough, a comparable combination of elements is to be found in a declaration by the seventh-century commentator Li Chunfeng, who also reveals his belief that The Nine Chapters somehow encompassed all mathematical procedures. This passage contains several components that will be elucidated below, but first, let us quote it to compare its overall idea with what we just saw. This de-

---

[21] The fact that we are dealing with a text devoted to mathematics will prove here to be quite helpful in this respect. In fact, I argue below that, even though Liu Hui uses here quite a general term, in the context of mathematics, *yi* 意 takes up a more precise denotation that I will discuss. The way in which the term is used in the commentary shows that the nature of the *yi* 意 Liu Hui is after takes a specific form. If this is the case, it is easy to understand why the study of Canons produced by the scholarly disciplines could contribute to the study of canonicity in general. This does not mean, however, that this 'meaning' would be unique and straightforward, as is demonstrated by the fact that the task of exegesis went on for centuries in China. About different interpretations of the *yi* 意 in different contexts in seventh-century China, see [Chemla and Zhu Yiwen 朱一文, 2022].

[22] [Guo Shuchun 郭书春, 1992, 301-320] is devoted to analyzing the structure of mathematics meant by Liu Hui. His results are synthesized on p. 318.

claration, included in the 'Monograph on the musical scale and the calendar (*Lülizhi* 律历志)' of the *History of the Sui Dynasty* (*Suishu* 隋书), authored by Li Chunfeng,[23] reads as follows:

> (3) As for what is called *lü*,[24] there are <u>nine [parts of mathematics] that flow from them</u>: the first is called 'rectangular fields' (... Li Chunfeng lists here the titles of all chapters of *The Nine Chapters* and Liu Hui's commentary on his interpretation of the main purpose of these chapters).... <u>They</u> (i.e., the nine parts of mathematics) <u>all multiply to disaggregate</u> (*san*) them (i.e., the *lü*'s), <u>divide to assemble</u> (*ju*) them, <u>homogenize</u> (*qi*) and <u>equalize</u> (*tong*) to make them communicate (*tong*), apply the [procedure] of '<u>suppose</u>' (i.e., the rule of three) to link (*guan*) them together, <u>hence</u> the <u>methods</u> of the mathematical procedures are <u>exhausted by these</u>. 夫所谓率者,有九流焉:一曰方田,以御田畴界域。二曰粟米,以御交质变易。三曰衰分,以御贵贱廪税。四曰少广,以御积幂方圆。五曰商功,以御功程积实。六曰均输,以御远近劳费。七盈朒,以御隐杂互见。八曰方程,以御错柔正负。九曰勾股,以御高深广远。<u>皆乘以散之</u>,<u>除以聚之</u>,<u>齐同以通之</u>,<u>今有以贯之</u>。<u>则算数之方</u>,<u>尽于斯矣</u>。(My emphasis)

Li Chunfeng thus also both asserts that the Canon is complete in a sense ('... the <u>methods</u> of the mathematical procedures are <u>exhausted</u>...') and describes an architecture of mathematical knowledge, essentially revolving around mathematical procedures. The articulation between these two elements is worth stressing. The statement regarding the comprehensiveness of the Canon appears as a conclusion and is based on the architecture described. The reasoning underlying the assertion can be sketched as follows: the nine chapters of the Canon have a common origin — *lü* 率, a concept to which we shall come back — and their procedures all make use of the same and limited set of fundamental operations applied to such entities. If, from this notation, Li Chunfeng can *deduce* that, more generally, these also 'exhaust the methods of the mathematical procedures,' this implies that he assumes that the property established for *The Nine Chapters* extends to the whole of mathematics. This deduction hence presupposes a precise conception of *how* the Canon encompasses all mathematical procedures. This articulation, which is quite concrete and elaborate, apparently supports our assumption that the belief in the comprehensiveness of the Canon is not vague and superficial, but that we should be able to account for how the Canon could be perceived as all-encompassing. This indicates the direction we will pursue.

Yang Hui's perception of the Canon

In addition, statements from the Song and Yuan dynasties (960—1368) are clear-cut in expressing the same expectation. For instance, the thirteenth-century commentator Yang Hui asserts:

---

[23] [Yang Jialuo (ed.) 杨家骆主编, 1977, vol. 3, 1859].

[24] This term, which I leave untranslated, qualifies quantities that are defined only with respect to each other. *The Nine Chapters* introduces the concept for describing the rule of three. The quantities that govern how to exchange the considered entities are designated as *lü*. The terms of a ratio can be designated as *lü*. If, for instance, one considers that the diameter of a circle is to its circumference as 1 to 3, the quantities are said to form, respectively, a *lü* of the diameter and a *lü* of the circumference. The commentators qualify as *lü* a greater variety of such sets of quantities, such as, for instance, the coefficients of a linear equation. For greater detail, see [Guo Shuchun 郭书春, 1984, Li Jimin 李继闵, 1982] [Li Jimin 李继闵, 1990].

(4) Everyone who studies mathematics (*suan*) considers the method for multiplication as capital. Every time one puts [the terms] of the method [on the calculating surface], one wants its result to be appropriate; if one determines the positions, so that one makes the numbers correspond to each other adequately, one wants it to be not false. In the case when, by division, one does not exhaust (the dividend), one takes the divisor as denominator and the dividend (i. e. , that which, in the end, remains in the position of the dividend) as numerator (i. e. , as becomes clearer below, division is considered from the point of view of what makes it the exact inverse of multiplication). If they are too complex (i. e. , if numerator and denominator have a common divisor), one simplifies them; if, in return, one makes the parts communicate (i. e. , one multiplies the integral part of the quotient by the denominator and adds the result to the numerator), then one returns to the origin (*huanyuan*). Such are the fundamental tools of multiplication and division (... A list of fundamental situations and operations contained in each of *The Nine Chapters* follows,[25] which all amount to diverse uses of multiplication and division…). These are what exhausts the inner constitution (*li*) of mathematical methods. *The Nine Chapters by Huangdi* is complete and subtle; it encompasses all situations (*qing*). It was undeniably written by a Sage. 夫习算者，以乘法为主。凡布置法者，欲其得宜；定位呼数，欲其不错。除不尽者，以法为分母，实为分子，繁者约之，复通分而还源，此乘除之规绳也。题有分者，随母通之；母不同者，齐子并之；田不匠者，折并直之；数皆求者，互乘换之；差等除实，别而衰之；叠垒积者（……）此算法之尽理也。黄帝九章备全奥妙，包括群情，谓非圣贤之书不可也。(My emphasis) [Guo Shuchun 郭书春, 1990, 493]

It is remarkable that this declaration presents a structure quite similar to Li Chunfeng's and includes similar elements to establish the exhaustiveness of *The Nine Chapters*. An architecture of mathematical knowledge is unfolded from a base consisting of multiplication and division. From this base, a list of fundamental operations that are the essence of the various chapters of the Canon is derived. This leads Yang Hui to assert the completeness of the Canon. The emphasis placed by Yang Hui on the 'inner constitution of mathematical methods' echoes Liu Hui's preface. In addition, as in Li Chunfeng's case, Yang Hui's conclusion proceeds from identifying the fundamental operations at play in the procedures of the Canon to asserting that they 'exhaust the inner constitution of mathematical methods.' Hence, the way in which the completeness of the Canon is approached is similar, which confirms that this is the direction to be explored to account for this belief. The recurrence of the same arguments makes it all the more difficult to discard such statements as meaningless.

Recapitulating

In conclusion, even if their declarations display differences, the three commentators concur in believing that *The Nine Chapters* does, or should, encompass all mathematical procedures. In contrast to Li Chunfeng and Yang Hui, who both assert the completeness without restraint, Liu Hui's statement is less affirmative. However, as I have argued, his restriction seemingly regards the text of the Canon as having been edited by previous generations and, in his view, the genuine Canon should be

---

[25] I keep for another paper a detailed analysis of this architecture of mathematical operations. In relation to his commentary, Yang Hui produces a reclassification of the procedures of the Canon, which ought to be confronted with the architecture he outlines in his preface.

comprehensive. Hence, the nature of the expectation remains the same.

Note that, if the commentators believed *The Nine Chapters* encompassed mathematical reality, it is no wonder that their mathematical activity would be to compose a commentary on the Canon.

More importantly, the essential point here is that, as John Henderson (1991, pp. 100 ff.) has shown, this feature constitutes a common expectation that Chinese commentators regularly exhibited with respect to Confucian Canons. One early expression of this belief can be found in the canonical corpus itself, for instance in the 'Great Commentary' (*Xici dazhuan* 系辞大传), which states with respect to the *Canon of Changes* (*Yijing* 易经): 'The *Changes* (*Yi*) is broad, great and all-encompassing. There are in it the Way of heaven, the Way of man, and the Way of earth. 易之为书也，广大悉备，有天道焉，有人道焉，有地道焉。'[26] The corresponding expectation encountered with respect to *The Nine Chapters* therefore probably expresses that the book was perceived as a Canon, comparable to, among others, the Confucian ones. We do have evidence that such a comparison was made by some actors themselves. One of the clearest such expressions can be found in a passage by the thirteenth-century commentator, Yang Hui, who is himself quoting the preface composed by Rong Qi when he had Jia Xian's (eleventh-century) commentary printed in 1148. Yang Hui states: 'When the government instituted the examinations in mathematics to select officials, they chose *The Nine Chapters* to be the most important of the mathematical Canons, since, indeed, it is like the six Canons of the Confucians, the (*Canon of*) *Difficulties* 难(经) and the *Basic* (*Questions*) (素问) of the medical schools, the *Book of Master Sun* of military art! 国家尝设算科取士，选"九章"以为算经之首，盖犹儒者之六经，医家之"难""素"，兵法之"孙子"欤！' [Guo Shuchun 郭书春, 1990, 495]. This piece of evidence, incidentally, legitimates the idea that we may study attitudes towards *The Nine Chapters* to contribute to a historical inquiry into canonicity more broadly.[27]

In other words, placing *The Nine Chapters* against the backdrop of other Canons, in particular of Confucian Canons, provides a context for the expectation that it be all-encompassing. This does not, however, yield an interpretation for this expectation. This is what we can set out to do, for the case of mathematics, by relying on the three assertions made by our commentators.

A second point, common to our three commentators, deserves some attention: they all describe an architecture of mathematical reality in connection to stating the comprehensiveness of the Canon. The commentators also display different conceptions of the architecture of mathematical procedures and of how *The Nine Chapters* encompasses mathematics. Liu Hui's assertion that mathematical 'accomplishments' 'share the same stem' may be interpreted as expressing views that are close to Li Chunfeng's. Indeed, in his commentary on the addition of fractions,[28] Liu Hui states:

(5) Multiply to disaggregate them, simplify to assemble them, homogenize and equalize to make them communicate, how could those not be the key points (*gangji*) of computations/mathematics (*suan*)? 乘以散之，约以聚之，齐同以通之，此其算之纲纪乎？

---

[26] *Xici*, *xia* 系辞，下, chap. 10. Trans. quoted in [Henderson, 1991, 101].

[27] [Sivin, 1995, 191—192] alludes to the fact that the medical Canons were also considered by some of their readers as all-encompassing. We hope that further research may cast light on the ways in which their exegetes interpreted the medical Canons to reach this conclusion. This, too, would allow the phenomenon of canonicity to be dealt with from a comparative perspective.

[28] This passage, mentioned earlier, occurs after problem 9 of chapter 1. See [Chemla, 1991].

Without yet discussing the meaning of this assertion, one can notice that it focuses on three of the four fundamental operations that lie at the core of Li Chunfeng's declaration quoted above (3). These operations, according to Liu Hui's description of the architecture of mathematics, may therefore relate to the stem from which the procedures 'diverge into branches.' In fact, when considering his entire commentary, this is a plausible interpretation.[29] As a result, the architectures described by our two commentators would partially coincide. Two main differences can be noticed, though. First, Li Chunfeng diagnoses that a fourth fundamental operation, the 'rule of three,' should be added to the list of key points suggested by Liu Hui. Moreover, the architecture described by the seventh-century commentator not only consists of a list of operations to which all procedures can be reduced, but it also involves a source — the concept of *lü* — from which *The Nine Chapters* develops and to which the key operations are applied. Yet, beyond these differences, both architectures share fundamental features.

In contrast to the other commentators, Yang Hui (4) claims that a pair of opposing but complementary operations, namely, multiplication and division, is at the basis of mathematics. From this pair, the other fundamental operations at play in the various chapters of the Canon are derived, which then serve to encompass all mathematical procedures, in a sense still to be made clear.

Despite the divergences, it remains common to our three commentators that their formulation of the expectation of completeness always went along with making explicit a conception of an architecture of mathematical procedures. Furthermore, the various architectures described share the feature of displaying how mathematics develops from a limited list of fundamental operations and how these can be exhibited by commenting on the Canon.

These facts raise several questions, which are meaningful for 'Canons' as a type of text, beyond the case of *The Nine Chapters*. First of all, how are we to interpret that a book may be all-encompassing? I hope, at this point, to have convinced the reader that there are reasons to persist in attempting to understand this assertion. The whole purpose of the article is to offer an interpretation by relying on evidence found in mathematical writings. We leave it to further research on Canons to assess how general this interpretation may be. Another related question also requires some elucidation. In our case, more specifically, how does the belief in the all-encompassing nature of the Canon relate to providing a description of the structure of mathematics that shares the features outlined above? Dealing with the issues will lead us to the main questions addressed in this essay: How can we approach in a historical way the topic of how books having the status of 'Canons' were read? How does the kind of exegesis carried out by our commentators connect with these issues? In what follows, I shall address these questions briefly, relying mainly on the commentary ascribed to Liu Hui.

Modes of reading the Canon

A glimpse at the canon

As already noted, the expectation that a book is all-encompassing, that it contains all mathematical procedures, may disconcert a modern reader. This astonishment may become even deeper when skimming through *The Nine Chapters*. In fact, the Canon is composed of 246 particular problems, their numerical answers and algorithms that solve them. Let us quote some examples of these, to give

---

[29] [Guo Shuchun 郭书春, 1992], especially pp. 315 ff, offers a different interpretation, placing the notion of measure at the root of the tree of mathematics.

an idea of the whole.

The ninth chapter, 'Base and Height' (gougu), which is devoted to the right triangle, opens as follows:[30]

(6) SUPPOSE THAT THE BASE IS WORTH 3 CHI AND THE HEIGHT 4 CHI. ONE ASKS HOW MUCH THE HYPOTENUSE MAKES.

ANSWER: 5 CHI

今有句三尺,股四尺,问为弦几何。

答曰:五尺。

(…[31])

PROCEDURE OF THE BASE AND THE HEIGHT:
BASE AND HEIGHT BEING EACH MULTIPLIED BY ITSELF, ONE ADDS (THE RESULTS) AND DIVIDES THIS BY SQUARE ROOT EXTRACTION, WHICH GIVES THE HYPOTENUSE (…).

勾股(……)术曰:句、股各自乘,并,而开方除之,即弦。(……)

We recognize here, in the form of a procedure, what, in ancient China, corresponded to the 'Pythagorean theorem.' This problem is specific as regards its data, but the situation it involves is abstract. However, most of the other problems are specific in both respects, as is illustrated by the following example:[32]

(7) SUPPOSE THAT A GOOD WALKER WALKS 100 BU WHILE A BAD WALKER WALKS 60 BU. IF, NOW, THE BAD WALKER FIRST WALKS 100 BU, BEFORE THE GOOD WALKER [STARTS] PURSUING HIM, ONE ASKS IN HOW MANY BU HE WILL CATCH HIM UP.

ANSWER: 250 BU.

今有善行者行一百步,不善行者行六十步。今不善行者先行一百步,善行者追之。问几何步及之。

答曰:二百五十步。

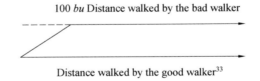

100 bu Distance walked by the bad walker

Distance walked by the good walker[33]

The algorithm given to solve this problem is expressed in terms relating to the described situation and uses concrete numbers:[34]

(7b) PROCEDURE: ONE PLACES (ON THE CALCULATING SURFACE) THE 100 BU OF THE GOOD WALKER, AND

---

[30] See [Chemla and Guo Shuchun 郭书春, 2004, 704—705], problem 1 of chapter 9. Throughout the paper, I quote the Canon *in capital letters* so as to distinguish its text from that of the commentaries.

[31] I skip two problems and procedures similar to the first one, which allowed practitioners to determine the third side of a right triangle, given any two sides.

[32] See [Chemla and Guo Shuchun 郭书春, 2004, 517—519], problem 12 of chapter 6.

[33] I add this diagram and the following to help the reader. They do not belong to the original text.

[34] We come back to its correctness below.

SUBTRACTS FROM IT THE 60 BU OF THE BAD WALKER; THERE REMAINS 40 BU, WHICH IS TAKEN AS DIVISOR. ONE MULTIPLIES, BY THE 100 BU OF THE GOOD WALKER, THE 100 BU THAT THE BAD WALKER HAD FIRST WALKED, WHICH MAKES THE DIVIDEND. DIVIDING THE DIVIDEND BY THE DIVISOR GIVES THE RESULT IN BU.

术曰：置善行者一百步，减不善行者六十步，余四十步，以为法。以善行者之一百步乘不善行者先行一百步，为实。实如法得一步。

Understanding how 246 such problems and procedures for solving them could be conceived of as encompassing all mathematical procedures is the challenge confronting us.

Observing how commentators read *The Nine Chapters* and how they approached mathematics will provide some clues. This implies that, if we do not take these precautions, and if we anachronistically read the Canon as a set of problems and algorithms, we run the danger of completely missing the significance of *The Nine Chapters* for its Chinese readers of the past.

The commentaries attest to several distinct modes of reading that were put into play and that, each in a different way, further developed the text of *The Nine Chapters* beyond its simple appearance. I have already dealt with some of them elsewhere, and I shall simply summarize some results here.

Reading a problem

A first mode of reading illustrates how one item can be taken to stand for a multitude. Indeed, it can be shown that, as one may expect, the commentators did not read a problem as a particular case, but as a paradigm — in the grammatical sense of the word — that stood for a whole category of problems. Interestingly enough, a commentary ascribed to Liu Hui explicitly relates this reading of problems to the way in which, according to the *Analects*, Confucius expects his disciples to develop his teachings: 'The Master said: (...) If I hold up a corner and a man cannot come back to me with the other three, I do not continue the lesson. 子曰：(……)举一隅不以三隅反，则不复也。'[35] Accordingly, the commentator refers to describing a method within the context of a problem as 'holding up a corner.'

In our case, it can be shown more precisely that it is the procedure given to solve a problem that provides the basis for determining the class of problems the given problem stands for.[36] The class consists of all the similar problems that one procedure can solve. It does happen, though, that the procedure given by *The Nine Chapters* is not as general as it could be, and hence that the problem does not

---

[35] [Waley, 1938 [1988], 124], Book VII, § 8. See [Chemla and Guo Shuchun 郭书春, 2004, 222] for the quotation of the statement. [Wagner, 1978a] has expressed doubts regarding the actual author of parts of the commentary attributed to Liu Hui. He has argued that parts of the commentary that ancient editions featured as ascribed to Liu Hui had in fact originally been composed by Li Chunfeng et al. for their subcommentary, and were subsequently included in Liu Hui's commentary by mistake. Wagner was followed by other scholars, in particular [Guo Shirong 郭世荣, 1993]. I have summarized their doubts and explained why I shared them in [Chemla and Guo Shuchun 郭书春, 2004, 472–473]. In fact, I have doubts regarding whether this passage from the commentary must really be attributed to Liu Hui as the ancient editions suggest it. My reasons for considering that it was probably originally part of the subcommentary include the position of the piece of commentary in which it occurs, the terminology this piece of commentary uses, the kind of mathematical understanding to which it refers, the ideas it presents, and in particular the use of the term *lü* 率 (see below). These doubts do not affect the argument I develop here.

[36] See [Chemla, 1997, 96–97]. Note that, in passage (2) quoted above, Liu Hui mentions looking for a problem in the Canon that would belong to the same category as the problem he wants to solve. He concludes that the procedures gathered by Zhang Cang and others do not suffice, which reveals the relation between the procedure and the category.

stand for as large a class as it could. Liu Hui indicates such cases and reformulates a more general algorithm in his commentary. This reveals that the commentator expects that a procedure will be general and that a problem will stand for a class. This interest in the generality of a procedure, as we shall see, extends quite far. Moreover, such examples show that Liu Hui, seemingly, does not manifest any undue awe towards *The Nine Chapters*, despite its status, and, in this case, simply indicates its limitations. Furthermore, let us stress that Liu Hui does not seem to particularly value formulating an *abstract* procedure that would *apply* to various particular cases. Instead, he prizes the *generality* of an algorithm that *circulates* from problem to problem as far as possible. This fits with his reading the Canon as expressing the general in terms of the paradigmatic.

Reading the arrangement of problems in the Canon

Observing Liu Hui's commentary reveals a second technique that is put into play when reading the Canon. The commentator appears to read meanings into the way in which the sequences of problems were organized within *The Nine Chapters*. This can be argued in several ways with regard to Chapter 8 'Measures in Square' (*Fangcheng*), which deals with systems of *n* linear equations with *n* unknowns. Liu Hui's commentary progressively extends the range of systems to which the basic algorithm can be applied by filling the gaps between the successive problems of the Canon. He hence appears to 'interpret' the arrangement of the sequence of problems. Moreover, in this case, his interpretation of Chapter 8 can be shown to develop from understanding the terms of the first problem in two distinct ways, a concrete interpretation and a formal one. [37]

Chapter 9 also provides an example where the commentator appears to read a meaning in the arrangement of the problems. We mentioned above the first and abstract problem (6) with which this chapter devoted to the right triangle opens. The rest of the chapter consists of a sequence of seemingly more concrete problems. The commentary ascribed to Liu Hui comments on the title 'Procedure of the Base and the Height' as follows:

(8)(…)(Base, height, hypotenuse and the procedure linking these terms) are about to be extended (*shi*) to all the algorithms, this is why this procedure is set out first so as to make their origin (*yuan*) appear. 将以施于诸率,故先具此术以见其原也。(My emphasis) [38]

This comment is interesting in several respects. Let us stress several key points. First, the commentator's point aims at *explaining* the position of the first set of problems and procedures in the chapter: he reads a meaning, an intention, in its being placed at the beginning of the chapter.

Secondly, the way in which this location in the chapter is justified is most interesting, and it takes us closer to essential aspects of the commentary. The 'procedure of the base and the height,' an algorithm amounting to what we call the Pythagorean theorem, with its terms that define the shape of the right triangle, are described as the 'origin' of the subsequent algorithms in the chapter. This relates to the fact that, in the comments accounting for the correctness of the algorithms, the commentators bring to light that each of the procedures for solving a problem in Chapter 9 involves, in one way or another, the sides of right triangles and the 'procedure of the base and the height.' There-

---

[37] [Chemla, 2000].

[38] Should this part of the commentary be ascribed to Liu Hui or to Li Chunfeng? For the same reasons as those developed in footnote 35, in my view, the answer is unclear.

fore, a first connection appears between 'going back to their origin,' to the source of the procedures—a recurring theme in Liu's preface, where we read in (1): 'I ... synthesized the source of mathematical procedures'—and proving the correctness of the procedures by revealing that a general algorithm and its terms have been put into play.

Moreover, the relationship between this fundamental procedure as well as the geometric terms attached to it and the subsequent procedures is described as an 'extension,' in the sense that the procedure's use extends to resolving the situations listed in the rest of the chapter. We recognize the interest in the circulation of procedures, or in generality, mentioned above. This remark by the commentator thus reveals a second connection between the fact that a procedure, with the terms it involves, is the 'origin' of others and its capacity to 'spread' widely. In the commentator's understanding, putting the 'procedure of the base and the height' at the beginning of the chapter amounts to highlighting these facts.

It is interesting that a similar connection between 'going upstream' towards the 'essential points' or the 'origin' of a procedure and being able to increase the efficiency of the essential points further can be noticed in Liu Hui's preface (2). We recall that when the commentator was describing how he investigated a given procedure to find out how to extend it to solve the remaining problems, he wrote: 'I examined (yuan) its essential points (zhiqu) so as to make them extend to/be efficient for (shi) this [problem]. 原其指趣乃所以施于此也。'

At this point, if we recapitulate what we have observed, the assumption emerges that 'synthesizing the source of mathematical procedures' and finding out their 'essential points' may relate to exhibiting some general procedures underlying particular mathematical procedures of the Canon and playing a part in the account of the correctness.

Could this assumption be that to which Liu Hui refers, when, twice in his preface, he speaks of his commentary as offering an understanding of 'the meaning(s)' or 'the intention(s) (yi)' of the Ancients or the Canon? I believe it may be so for several reasons. And, in order to capture from yet another angle Liu Hui's ways of reading *The Nine Chapters*, I suggest turning now to what his own commentary tells us of his conception of the '*yi*' of the Canon, a term which seems central in his own representation of his approach to the text.

Elucidating the nature of the *yi* of the Canon

Let us start from an occurrence of the term that is highly revealing of both an assumption the commentator makes with respect to *The Nine Chapters* and the mathematical practice related to inquiring into the 'meaning/intention (*yi*)' of the Canon or its procedures. The context is the procedure given for the 'extraction of the spherical root,' in which the diameter of a given spherical volume must be determined. The Canon reads as follows:[39]

(9) SUPPOSE AGAIN ONE HAS A NUMBER-PRODUCT (JI)[40] OF 1,644,866,437,500 CHI. ONE ASKS HOW MUCH THE DIAMETER OF THE SPHERE MAKES.

ANSWER: 14,300 CHI.

PROCEDURE FOR EXTRACTING THE SPHERICAL ROOT:

---

[39] [Chemla and Guo Shuchun 郭书春, 2004, 378—381], problem 24 of chapter 4. I refer the reader to [Wagner, 1978b], where the whole commentary is treated in detail and translated.

[40] *Ji* 积 designates a number that is considered to have been yielded by a multiplication.

ONE PUTS THE QUANTITY OF *CHI* OF THE NUMBER-PRODUCT, MULTIPLIES IT BY 16, AND DIVIDES IT BY 9. TO DIVIDE WHAT IS OBTAINED BY EXTRACTION OF THE CUBE ROOT GIVES THE DIAMETER OF THE SPHERE.

又有积一万六千四百四十八亿六千六百四十三万七千五百尺,问为立圆径几何。

答曰:一万四千三百尺。(……)

开立圆术曰:置积尺数,以十六乘之,九而一。所得,开立方除之,即立圆径。

In the opening section of his commentary, Liu Hui formulates a reasoning that may have produced the procedure. Let us follow it, before drawing some conclusions. First, Liu Hui identifies that the procedure 'probably (*gai*)' rests on taking the ratio of the circumference of a circle to its diameter as 3 to 1. These values are used throughout *The Nine Chapters*. Liu Hui qualifies them as *lü*—the very concept placed by Li Chunfeng, in (3), at the origin of mathematical procedures. By this designation, the commentator indicates that they can be multiplied or divided by a number without affecting the ability of the new pair of quantities to express the relationship between the circumference and the diameter. More generally, as already alluded to, Liu Hui will qualify as *lü* any set of values sharing this property. Afterwards, he goes on:

(10) If one hence supposes that the surface (*mi*) of the circle fills 3/4 of the surface (*mi*) of the square, the circular cylinder thus also fills 3/4 of the cube.

If, furthermore, one supposes that, the cylinder being represented by the *lü* of the square, 12, what represents the *lü* of the sphere is 9, then, in addition to this, the sphere fills 3/4 of the circular cylinder.

(A computation on fractions to multiply 3/4 by 3/4 follows...)

Therefore the sphere fills 9/16 of the cube. This is why, when one multiplies its volume by 16 and divides by 9, one obtains the volume of the cube.

The diameter of the sphere and the side of the cube are equal, hence, if one divides this by extraction of the cube root, one obtains the diameter.

But this meaning/reasoning (*yi*) is wrong. How to prove (*yan*)[41] this? (My emphasis)

令圆幂居方幂四分之三,圆围居立方亦四分之三。更令圆围为方率十二,为九率九,丸居圆围又四分之三也。(……),故丸居立方十六分之九也。故以十六乘积,九而一,得立方之积。丸径与立方等,故开立方而除,得径也。然此意非也。何以验之?

The most important fact here is that, in a first part of his commentary following this problem, Liu Hui develops a reasoning that accounts for the procedure given by the Canon to solve it, and concludes that this '*yi*' is wrong, a fact that he sets out to prove. Let us sum up the idea of the reasoning just quoted. It runs as follows: the procedure amounts, Liu Hui shows, to giving the sphere as 9/16 of the circumscribed cube. If the ratio of the circumference to the diameter is 3 to 1, the inscribed cylinder fills 3/4 of the cube. Then, if the sphere is taken as filling 3/4 of the cylinder, the coefficient of 9/16, expressing the relationship of the sphere to the cube, is obtained. Based on this, the procedure for extracting the spherical root comes from inverting this ratio: multiplying the volume of the sphere by 16 and dividing by 9 yields the volume of the circumscribed cube, whose side equals the

---

[41] In Liu Hui's commentary and in later mathematical texts, *yan* refers to a kind of proof characterized by its use of visual auxiliaries, 'figure (*tu* 图)' or 'blocks (*qi* 棊),' as is the case here [Chemla, 1997, 120—121]).

diameter of the sphere. Extracting the cube root yields the sought-after value.

This is the *yi* that is said to be wrong, and, in order to criticize it, Liu Hui points out that the solid of whose volume the sphere occupies 3/4 is not the cylinder, but the intersection of two cylinders, both inscribed in the cube, with perpendicular axes. However, he laments being unable to push the reasoning forward and establish the relationship between the volumes of this solid and the cube.

This passage is interesting for us in several respects. In the first place, Liu Hui seems to rely on the context of *The Nine Chapters* as well as on the form of the procedure to formulate the reasoning that yielded the procedure. In fact, his argument exploits the structure of the coefficient 9/16 put into play by the procedure and proceeds from interpreting geometrically that it is the square of 3/4. The essential point for me here is that Liu Hui refers to this whole reasoning that the authors of the procedure may have used to yield the procedure and to account for its correctness with the term '*yi* 意'. This constitutes, in my view, a main clue regarding how he conceives of the nature of the *yi*, this 'meaning' or 'intention,' whose contour we attempt to grasp in this context. The *yi* of the Canon, or of the procedures — the understanding of which has elicited the composition of Liu Hui's commentary, he claims in (1) — could hence have taken the form of a reasoning that yielded the procedure recorded in the Canon. As a consequence, this would imply that Liu Hui assumes there are proofs 'meant' in the statement of the procedures of the Canon, and his commentary makes them explicit.[42] This fits with his conception of a commentary as 'exploring the meaning (*yi*) of the ancients' (passage 2). Li Chunfeng's commentary attests to the same use of the term *yi*, to refer to a reasoning. After having quoted, in his comments on the same problem, the alternative procedure elaborated by Zu Gengzhi for extracting the 'spherical root,' Li Chunfeng introduces the proof that establishes the correctness of the procedure with the question: 'What is its meaning [*yi*]?'.

However, to go back to Liu Hui, another conclusion can be drawn from the spherical root passage quoted above. In this case, after having brought to light a '*yi*,' Liu Hui discards it by proving its mathematical inadequacy. It is difficult for me to determine whether he discards what he conceives of as being here 'the *yi*' attributed to the Canon, or whether he rejects this first interpretation of the Canon. I would be tempted to opt for the first explanation, which would have important consequences as regards our understanding of the practice of exegesis in this case. Whatever the case, it is interesting that we see mathematical reasoning intervening in two ways for the exegesis. First, interpreting the Canon requires writing down a would-be proof. Second, accepting it as *yi* also supposes that reasoning be put into play.

This example illustrates quite adequately some general points concerning proof as carried out in the context of the commentaries to *The Nine Chapters*. Let us stress them, since this will prove useful in what follows.

The deduction quoted above and formulated to account for the 'procedure for extracting the spherical root' combines a geometrical reasoning and the writing of the procedure that yields the sought-after result. Let us observe how they correspond to each other. A first geometrical argument shows how, under an assumption corresponding to taking π as 3, with a rule of three, one obtains the volume of the cylinder on the basis of the volume of the cube — by multiplying it by 3/4. A second

---

[42] [Chemla, 1991] gives arguments in favour of this hypothesis. As we argue in greater detail below, this interpretation of the nature of the *yi* in the context of mathematics accords with most of its occurrences in the commentary, but not all.

geometrical argument reveals the assumption hidden in asserting that the application of a second rule of three yields the volume of the sphere, that is, that the latter would be 3/4 of that of the circumscribed cylinder. These two steps constitute the decomposition of the 'procedure for extracting the spherical root' into building blocks, whose intention can be made clear in terms of the geometrical situation. The third step of the reasoning consists of reworking the sequence of building blocks established in the first steps, so as to fuse them into a more compact, but equivalent, procedure: multiplying 3/4 by 3/4 provides the fraction 9/16 that allows one to go directly, under the same assumptions, from the circumscribed cube to the sphere. This corresponds to rewriting the succession of two rules of three, whose meaning has been established, into a sequence that is closer to the procedure given in the Canon. This rewriting takes a sequence of operations and transforms it into another sequence of operations using what are known to be valid operations. The meaning of the two numbers 9 and 16 is thereby brought to light geometrically. At this point, Liu Hui has shown how to go from the cube to the sphere. The procedure of the Canon requires the inverse transformation. By applying another valid operation — inverting — to the obtained procedure, Liu Hui obtains the procedure that relies on the volume of the sphere to yield that of the circumscribed cube. A last geometrical argument shows how, by appending a cube root extraction to the previous list of operations, one obtains the desired result, the diameter of the sphere. Bringing together the sequence of operations that have been progressively elaborated shows that Liu Hui has attained the procedure of the Canon whose correctness was to be proved, and that he has established that it actually computes the expected result. The correctness of the procedure given by *The Nine Chapters* is thereby established, under the assumptions made explicit during the reasoning.

To recapitulate, the reasoning involves shaping a procedure, the meanings or intentions of which can be made explicit geometrically, step by step. This requires articulating building blocks in a valid way. It also consists of again using various valid operations to gradually transform the procedure that, under an assumption revealed in the second geometrical step, had been shown to yield the correct result into the procedure whose correctness was to be established.[43] It is the whole process that shapes the procedure of the Canon, which Liu Hui refers to as *yi*, before bringing to light why the assumptions made do not hold true.

Another argument supports this interpretation of *yi*. As we saw, the process involves interpreting the results of some operations geometrically. In proving algorithms that evaluate geometrical magnitudes, Liu Hui regularly makes use of 'figures (*tu* 图)' for plane geometry or 'blocks (*qi* 棊)' for spatial geometry. As we saw in (1), he introduced the *tu* as a major tool for his commentary: '(...) and if the bodies are dissected (*jie*) with figures (...)'. When, while proving the correctness of the algorithm of cube root extraction — a passage that comes immediately before the 'procedure for extracting the spherical root' —, Liu Hui first introduces the second type of visual auxiliary, the blocks, he justifies it by both quoting the 'Great Commentary' (*Xici dazhuan*) on the *Canon of Changes* (*Yijing*) and referring to his preface: "Speech cannot exhaust the meaning" (*yi*) (*yan bu jin yi*),[44] hence to dissect/analyze (*jie*) this [volume], one must use blocks, this is the only way to get

---

[43] This component of the proofs can be interpreted a kind of 'algebraic proof within an algorithmic context,' see [Chemla, 1997/1998].

[44] *Xici, shang*, 系辞, 上, chap. 12. In the introduction of chapter 4 and the footnotes to the translation in [Chemla and Guo Shuchun 郭书春, 2004], the reader can find more detail about this proof of the correctness of the algorithm for extracting cube roots.

to understanding [the procedure]. "言不尽意"解此要当以棊,乃得明耳。In fact, this statement concludes his proof of the correctness of the algorithm for cube root extraction, in which he has used solid blocks to decompose the cube and interpret the results or the 'intentions' of the successive prescribed operations. Among the many links that this statement reveals in Liu Hui's thought, let us stress two.

Blocks were just used by Liu Hui to formulate a proof establishing the correctness of a procedure. The commentator thus connects the introduction of the blocks, in addition to words, with making the 'meaning (*yi*)' explicit. Moreover, the production of the proof, with words and blocks, is given as aiming at 'understanding' this part of the Canon. Both points confirm the link we established between looking for the *yi* and producing proofs.

These elements of interpretation of the term *yi*, the 'meaning' or the 'intention' that the commentators seek to explore, are confirmed by another interesting occurrence of the word *yi* in Liu Hui's commentary.[45] To explain this point with some detail, we need to develop a brief analysis of the problem quoted above, in passage (7). It is solved by a procedure (7b), whose correctness the commentator establishes. Let us quote it again:

(7b) PROCEDURE: ONE PLACES (ON THE CALCULATING SURFACE) THE 100 *BU* OF THE GOOD WALKER, AND SUBTRACTS FROM IT THE 60 *BU* OF THE BAD WALKER; **THERE REMAINS 40 *BU***, WHICH IS TAKEN AS DIVISOR. ONE MULTIPLIES, **BY THE 100 *BU* OF THE GOOD WALKER, THE 100 *BU* THAT THE BAD WALKER HAD FIRST WALKED**, WHICH MAKES THE DIVIDEND. DIVIDING THE DIVIDEND BY THE DIVISOR GIVES THE RESULT IN *BU*.

术曰:置善行者一百步,减不善行者六十步,**余四十步**,以为法。**以善行者之一百步乘不善行者先行一百步**,为实。实如法得一步。

(MY EMPHASIS)

Liu Hui's account of the correctness of the procedure proceeds by bringing to light how, in fact, it amounts to a rule of three. To this end, Liu Hui interprets each of the values used in the general terms that form the scheme of the rule of three, which *The Nine Chapters* calls the 'procedure of Suppose 今有术'.[46] In the Canon, the description of the rule of three brings into play three quantities, to which specific and abstract names are attached: the '*lü* of what one has 所有率' and the '*lü* of what one seeks 所求率' designate the known values that govern the exchange between the quantity of the thing that is possessed — the 'quantity of what one has 所有数' — and the quantity of the thing into which it is transformed, i. e. , the unknown. As already alluded to, qualifying some of these data as *lü* indicates that they possess the property that they can be simultaneously transformed in the same way.

Let us sketch how, by simply naming the values involved, Liu Hui accounts for the procedure (7b). The commentator designates the quantity of 40 *bu*, obtained as the difference between the distances simultaneously described by the good and the bad walkers, as the '*lü* of what the bad walker first walked.' In relation to this, the distance of 100 *bu* described by the good walker is called the '*lü* of the pursuit and the catch-up.' In fact, the third value in the procedure (7b) is the distance first walked by the bad walker. It hence corresponds to the 'quantity of what one has,' in contrast to the

---

[45] See [Chemla, 2004], for a detailed analysis of the passage alluded to here. The text is to be found in [Chemla and Guo Shuchun 郭书春, 2004, 516—519].

[46] See the opening section of Chapter 2 [Chemla and Guo Shuchun 郭书春, 2004, 222—225].

unknown, which is the distance along which the good walker pursues and, in the end, catches up to the bad one. Distributing these names amounts to formulating a proportion, which captures the reasoning that accounts for the correctness of the procedure. It corresponds to stating that the desired distance is described by the good walker during the same time as that necessary to describe the 100 *bu* first walked by the bad walker at a speed corresponding to the difference between the speeds of the two walkers. The essential point around which this proof revolves is the interpretation, in terms of the situation considered by the problem, of the difference in relation to the distance first walked.

In other words, Liu Hui formulates a reasoning that explains what the algorithm carries out, and he *simultaneously* highlights that, in fact, the algorithm formally amounts to putting into play a rule of three. The articulation between interpreting the computations with respect to the situation considered and bringing to light a more general algorithm underlying the examined procedure is an essential characteristic of the proofs as carried out by the commentator. We shall find the same combination in the problem that immediately follows this one in the Canon, in relation to a quite telling occurrence of the term *yi*, whose nature we strive to elucidate.

The following problem in *The Nine Chapters* is different, although the situation described is of the same type. Moreover, accordingly, the algorithm given to solve it differs from the previous one. Let us sketch the problem and algorithm, concentrating on only the elements useful for our discussion here.[47]

(7c) SUPPOSE THAT A BAD WALKER FIRST WALKS 10 LI AND THAT A GOOD WALKER, PURSUING HIM FOR 100 LI, HIS ADVANCE ON THE BAD WALKER THEN REACHES 20 LI. ONE ASKS IN HOW MANY LI THE GOOD WALKER HAD REACHED THE BAD ONE.

今有不善行者先行一十里,善行者追之一百里,先至不善行者二十里。问善行者几何里及之。

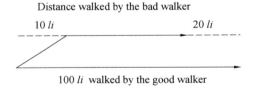

(7d) PROCEDURE: ONE PLACES (ON THE CALCULATING SURFACE) THE 10 LI THAT THE BAD WALKER HAD FIRST WALKED AND ONE **INCREASES** THIS BY THE ADVANCE OF 20 LI TAKEN BY THE GOOD WALKER, WHICH IS TAKEN AS DIVISOR. ONE MULTIPLIES, BY THE 10 LI THAT THE BAD WALKER HAD FIRST WALKED, THE 100 LI OF THE GOOD WALKER, WHICH MAKES THE DIVIDEND. DIVIDING THE DIVIDEND BY THE DIVISOR GIVES THE RESULT IN LI.

术曰:置不善行者先行一十里,以善行者先至二十里**增**之,为法。以不善行者**先行一十里**乘**善行者一百里**,为实。实如法得一里。(MY EMPHASIS)

In this case too, Liu Hui accounts for the correctness of the procedure by highlighting how it brings into play a rule of three. Moreover, he does so in the same way, i. e., by adequately naming, and thereby interpreting step by step, the values in the procedure of *The Nine Chapters*. However, if we compare how he distributes the names in both cases (7b & 7d), an interesting phenomenon appears. In fact, Liu Hui gives the values in the latter procedure the same names as those in the former

---

[47] [Chemla, 2004] provides greater detail on this problem 13 of chapter 6 [Chemla and Guo Shuchun 郭书春, 2004, 518—520].

problem. As a consequence, the value obtained by summing the 10 *li* and the 20 *li* is again called the '*lü* of what was first walked.' In relation to this, the value of 10 *li* that enters in the computation of the 'dividend' appears to be the 'quantity of what one has.' Moreover, Liu Hui calls the 100 *li* described by the good walker the '*lü* of the pursuit and the catch-up.' As previously, the names point to a reasoning that accounts for the correctness of the algorithm. The name chosen for the sum of 10 *li* and 20 *li* brings to light that, like the 100 *bu* in the former problem, the value represents the difference between the lengths of two paths described by the good and the bad walker over the same period of time. The procedure hence appears to state that the sought-after distance is described by the good walker over the same time period as that necessary to describe the 10 *li* first walked by the bad walker at a speed corresponding to the difference between the speeds of both walkers.

In conclusion, Liu Hui again expounds a reasoning showing why this procedure works and highlighting that it too has the structure of a rule of three. However, what is most striking is that the two reasonings exhibited bring to light the fact that, despite superficial differences, both procedures share essential characteristics. They make use of similar features in both situations in the same way. In other words, Liu Hui comments on both procedures from an angle that was chosen to disclose that the same reasoning applies to both and that they both constitute an extension of the same general procedure: the rule of three.

The essential point, now, for us is that the commentator concludes the development relating to the latter procedure by stating: 'Its *yi* is like the one for the previous procedure 其意如上术也.' From this assertion, several points can be made. First, it is again clear that, in Liu Hui's view, the two procedures have a *yi*, 'a meaning,' which he has made explicit. Moreover, this *yi* again takes the shape of a reasoning that accounts for the correctness of the procedure. This is what can be deduced from what is being compared and declared to be similar. Last but not least, the procedures appear to be different. It is only at the level of their 'meaning/*yi*' that their likeness is exhibited and stated.

To sum up, in all these instances, Liu Hui seems to assume that the *yi*(s) of *The Nine Chapters* — the understanding of which, his preface explains, was what prompted the writing of the commentary — can take the form of the reasonings that produced the various algorithms. As a consequence, making reasonings explicit constitutes one of the mathematical practices relating to inquiring into the 'meaning/intention (*yi*)' of the Canon. This agrees with what can be found in Liu Hui's and Li Chunfeng's commentaries: after virtually every procedure of the Canon, they formulate proofs of their correctness. Incidentally, this also agrees with the more general use of the term *yi* throughout the commentaries. *Yi* refers to the 'meaning,' the 'intention' of an operation or a subprocedure, in the sense of an interpretation of that which is being computed, formulated in terms of the situation. The overall reasoning that accounts for a procedure requires elucidating and articulating the 'meaning' of its subprocedures. Making these *yi*s explicit proves to be an essential aspect in the proof of algorithms. The global *yi* for a procedure hence derives from a combination of these more local ones.[48]

Inquiring into the *yi* and exhibiting fundamental procedures

The previous two examples allow us to go one step further towards answering the questions with which we started by revealing a crucial fact: writing down proofs, or, in other words, exhibiting the

---

[48] This is illustrated by the reasoning accounting for the 'procedure for extracting the spherical root,' as described above.

yi, leads to establishing connections between procedures that, at first sight, seem unrelated. Indeed, the fact that, on the basis of the proofs, unseen connections between procedures can be unveiled appears to be an important motivation for inquiring into the *yi*.

The relation exhibited between the two problems above establishes a link between them at two levels. First, at the level of the situations that the procedures solve, the proofs of their correctness bring to light that the reasonings make use of intermediaries that have the same meaning and they use them in the same way. From a *semantic* point of view, the procedures thus appear to rely on the same strategy.

Secondly, at a more *formal* level, the proofs simultaneously highlight that both procedures are instantiations, 'extensions,' of a more general algorithm — the rule of three. In other words, the procedures appear to share the same strategy at the level of the procedure's form as well.[49] Moreover, this connects them with the variety of procedures that the commentators show also formally amount to putting into play rules of three. Such a situation evokes the relationship of the procedures in Chapter 9 to the 'procedure of the base and the height,' with which the chapter begins.

This is the very point where we can go back to the questions addressed in this article. In fact, a link is established here between what is brought to light by the proof and relates to the *yi*, on one hand, and Li Chunfeng's declaration (3)on the other hand. Indeed, the rule of three that the proofs reveal is at play in various procedures happens to be one of the four fundamental operations that the seventh-century commentator lists. What is striking here is that if we now turn to the other operations that appear in the same list and in Liu Hui's list (5), i. e., multiplication, division, homogenization and equalization, we realize that these operations present themselves in proofs too, and for some of them, such as homogenization, <u>only in proofs</u>. Furthermore, in the proofs, they play exactly the same part as we indicated for the rule of three.

Let us outline the case of homogenization and equalization to sketch this point.[50] While proving the correctness of different procedures, Liu Hui regularly interprets the 'meaning' or the 'intention' (*yi*) of their main operations as 'equalizing 同' (*tong*) some quantities and, in correlation with this, 'making' other quantities 'homogeneous 齐' (*qi*). The main example is to be found in his commentary on the procedure for adding up fractions, in the very context of which, as we saw, Liu Hui made his declaration (5). The algorithm described by the Canon to add up fractions (say, for example, 2/3 and 5/7, or, with modern symbolism a/b and a'/b') prescribes multiplying the denominators by each other, which, in the example, yields 21 (in modern terms, bb'). It further prescribes multiplying each numerator by the denominator that does not correspond to it: in the example, 2 (a) becomes 14 (ab') and 5 (a') becomes 15 ($a'b$). The result is thus given as $14+15$ ($ab'+a'b$)to be divided by 21 (in modern terms, bb'). Liu Hui suggests calling the first operation — which computes aa' — equalizing, and the second ones homogenizing. In relation to the designations chosen, he brings to light that 'multiplying the denominators by each other' <u>equalizes</u> the denominators of all the fractions involved. In addition, he shows that 'multiplying each numerator by the denominator that does not correspond to it' — the computation of ba' and ab' — makes each numerator <u>homogeneous</u> with the new denominator, which is why one can now add them. The commentator had indicated previously why such operations on fractions were valid. While highlighting why and how the procedure yields the sought-af-

---

[49] On this concept, see [Chemla and Guo Shuchun 郭书春, 2004, 28—31].

[50] For a more detailed treatment of these operations seen from this angle, see: [Chemla, 1991, Chemla, 2000].

ter result, Liu Hui shows that it brings into play an 'equalization' and 'homogenizations.' This would remain unnoticed, were it not that, in (5), Liu Hui designates them as 'key points in mathematics' when they first occur and, in relation to this, demonstrates that the same operations are at play when he accounts for the correctness of other procedures. For instance, in Chapter 8, the Canon describes an algorithm to solve systems of n simultaneous linear equations with n unknowns. Let us sketch it briefly and hence in somewhat less detail than may be necessary for full accuracy.[51] If the system to be solved is

$$ax+by=c$$
$$a'x+b'y=c'$$

the procedure given in The Nine Chapters amounts to transforming the equations into

$$aa'x+ba'y=ca'$$
$$aa'x+ab'y=ac'$$

so as to obtain y with the equation

$$(ab'-a'b)y=ac'-a'c$$

Liu Hui recognizes here that the procedure proceeds by <u>equalizing</u> the coefficients of x and by <u>homogenizing</u> the other terms of the equations. Again, he has previously accounted for the validity of these operations on equations. By introducing these two designations, the commentator operates at two levels. On the one hand, he indicates the reason why the algorithm works, i.e., why, in fact, there is elimination. However, on the other hand, he discloses a formal strategy at play in the algorithm: equalizing some quantities and homogenizing others. This reveals a connection between the procedures for solving systems of equations and for adding fractions. Equalizing and homogenizing are exhibited in several other contexts. However, these two examples suffice to illustrate what is at stake in all cases.

The interpretation in terms of 'equalization' and 'homogenization' allows Liu Hui to establish that these different procedures are correct. The quantities that are made equal differ in each of these contexts, and the reasons why, once the values are equalized, the procedure can be shown to be correct, differ. However, at the formal level, as in the previous example with the rule of three, the proofs reveal an operational pattern common to all of them. Proofs bring to light that, to yield the desired result, the procedures follow the same formal strategy in the way they rely on the situation in which they operate. This is expressed by the recurrence of the pair of operations 'equalize and homogenize.' As a consequence, in the same way as above, through proofs, Liu Hui unveils links between procedures of The Nine Chapters that, at first sight, seemed unrelated. Procedures given by the Canon and apparently unconnected are revealed, through the proof, as being mere instantiations, or 'extensions,' of the same fundamental procedures. These essential procedures can be understood as the 'origin' or the 'essential points'[52] of the procedures given by the Canon. They represent a quest for the highest generality possible for procedures, which is meaningful for both the history of mathematics and the history of a philosophical reflection on mathematics.

In a similar way, we observe that multiplication and division, often by virtue of their relation of opposition, are regularly exhibited to be at play in the way in which a procedure correctly operates.

---

[51] Compare [Chemla, 2000], or [Chemla and Guo Shuchun 郭书春, 2004], for a more accurate account.

[52] A remark is in order here. The fact that 'the procedure of the base and the height' is not included in the list of fundamental operations seems to indicate that, even though it constitutes the source of the procedures of Chapter 9, its level of generality cannot compare to the procedures that the commentators include in their declarations.

They enter the list of formal strategies available to yield a procedure.[53] In my view, this is what primarily justifies that they be compared to the rule of three or to the procedure of 'equalization and homogenization.'

It is highly interesting that the commentators specifically reserved another term, *yi*' 义, to designate, for a procedure, the kind of 'meaning' that comes from bringing to light the fundamental operation underlying it. One hence regularly reads that a procedure has the '*yi*' of the rule of three (*qitong zhi yi* it should be *yi*' 今有之义).[54]

To sum up, our commentators' practice of proof can be characterized as follows: through accounting for the correctness of the procedures, the proofs bring to light that the various procedures ultimately put into play a limited number of formal strategies or, in other terms, fundamental operations. These fundamental operations can all present themselves in the different steps we distinguished in the proof — in the building blocks that enter in the making of a procedure, as well as in the way they are combined and rewritten.

In this way, the proofs reduce what *The Nine Chapters* gave as a diversity of procedures. And, a crucial connection emerges between the search for the *yi*, as carried out through proving, and the fundamental operations entering the architectures of mathematical knowledge described by our commentators: the limited number of formal strategies that are brought to light by the proofs are the very operations selected to enter into Liu Hui's and Li Chunfeng's lists of fundamental procedures. Note that these operations can be identified through writing down the proofs not separately, but as a whole, and through continuously confronting them as we did above. We provided evidence that clearly demonstrates that Liu Hui compared procedures on the basis of their *yi*.

Also note the convergence between what comes out here through confronting the proofs and the meaning the commentator read, as we saw above, in the organization of Chapter 9: the identification of general operations whose efficiency extends as widely as possible appears to be a concern that permeates his reading of the Canon throughout. In my view, this is precisely what makes *The Nine Chapters* a *canonical* work.[55]

Interpreting the commentators' fundamental declarations

At this point, we are in a position to offer an interpretation of the declarations of our commentators and to elucidate the expectation that *The Nine Chapters* may be all-encompassing. Moreover, we can also suggest how this expectation relates to describing an architecture of mathematical knowledge.

Let us start with Li Chunfeng's statement (3). The previous interpretation of the link between the nature of the commentators' proofs and the emergence of fundamental operations fits with the structure and the wording of his declaration (3). All the procedures of *The Nine Chapters*, he claims, make use of four fundamental operations — this, in my view, is what writing down the proofs, or exhibiting the *yi* of the Canon as he and his predecessor did, brings to light. Li Chunfeng lists the general procedures that he considers to be fundamental based on the proofs made explicit for the whole

---

[53] [Chemla, 1997/1998] illustrates this point.

[54] It is interesting to note that this interpretation of *yi*' agrees with Fung Yu-lan's 冯友兰 interpretation of Wang Bi's 王弼 use of the term, in relation to *li* 理 and *yi* 意 ([Fung Yu-lan, 1952—1953 [1973]], vol. 2, 185—187], quoted on the basis of the 1973 reprint).

[55] I thank the anonymous referee of the *British Journal for the History of Science* for having emphasized this point.

Canon.

Li Chunfeng extends this: he *deduces* that these fundamental procedures exhaust the methods of all mathematical procedures. Notice that, although his target clearly encompasses all mathematical algorithms, his claim does not bear on the procedures themselves, but on their 'methods.' I suggest that, by this term, Li Chunfeng refers to the overall procedure that, as I explained above in the case of the extraction of the spherical root, constitutes the reasoning producing, i.e., accounting for, the algorithm. The 'method' would include the steps of exhibiting the building blocks to be combined to reach the result, as well as of articulating and rewriting them to yield the algorithm that carries out the envisioned task. We shall see below other pieces of evidence supporting this interpretation.

Li's claim could hence be understood as follows: the proofs carried out by the commentators within the framework of *The Nine Chapters* bring to light all the fundamental procedures that could appear in the proof, or in the shaping, of any mathematical algorithm. This leads me to an interpretation of the expectation that the Canon is complete. *The Nine Chapters* would be all-encompassing in the sense that its procedures point to all the fundamental operations needed in the production of mathematical algorithms. Moreover, the algorithms indicate the fundamental operations, in the sense that proving their correctness, while bringing the proofs into confrontation with each other, brings the general operations to light. In other words, borrowed from Liu Hui's preface (1), *The Nine Chapters* allows 'synthesizing the source of mathematical procedures.'

This interpretation would explain *why* the statement of comprehensiveness is always articulated upon the description of an architecture of mathematics. Any commentator, by means of proofs and comparing proofs, establishes a list of the fundamental operations indirectly indicated by the Canon and common to several of its algorithms. The operations constitute the basis of the structure of mathematical knowledge, which explains why these architectures all display the same features. In addition to this, Li Chunfeng distinguishes himself by placing at the root of the structure a kind of object, the *lü*, which he identifies as that which explains the efficiency of the fundamental operations.[56]

The Canon would indicate these fundamental operations by displaying some of the diverse and paradigmatic manifestations they can take. Moreover, the Canon would indicate how the basic patterns present themselves and combine in a diversity of situations — a syntagmatic dimension, if we will — showing how their efficiency can be extended to virtually any situation. For example, adding up fractions and solving systems of simultaneous linear equations, when compared, reveal the fundamental pattern of equalizing and homogenizing. However, a detailed comparison would show that the algorithms differ in the ways they use the fundamental patterns.

The task of the commentator would then be to understand how these manifestations reveal the basic patterns involved in the shaping of mathematical procedures, the 'source' from which all mathematics flow. Interestingly, the fundamental operations that constitute the core of the commentators' most fundamental declarations about *The Nine Chapters* are considered as expressing the *yi*' 义 of procedures, a word traditionally associated with the 'significance' of a canon. It is highly revealing, in this respect, that the commentators diverge in their lists of fundamental operations. This shows that there is not a unique way of conceiving of this list. However, this also discloses that, despite divergences, commentators carry out the same task through their exegesis.

If we understand that bringing to light how the fundamental operations are at play in a given pro-

---

[56] About Li Chunfeng's choice of *lü* as the basis of the architecture, compare [Chemla, 2004].

cedure amounts to exhibiting its *li* 理, its 'inner constitution,' its basic structure, then we can interpret Liu Hui's preface (1) and Yang Hui's statement (4) in similar ways.[57]

In the case of Yang Hui, this interpretation is straightforward. If the 'stem' from which, according to Liu Hui's declaration (1), mathematical procedures diverge is understood as consisting of the list of fundamental operations (5), then we can interpret in the same way that he moves from 'analyzing the *li*' of the procedures to considering *The Nine Chapters* as all-encompassing. In Liu Hui's view, the 'meaning/*yi*' of the procedures would reveal that their *li* consists of articulating only the same limited number of fundamental operations and combining them according to the same principles. Therefore, stating that the Canon is complete would amount to believing that any mathematical procedure could be produced with the same building blocks and syntagmatic principles.

This line of interpretation receives confirmation from a statement included in the postface to *The Nine Chapters* by the 1213 editor of the Tang collection *The Ten Canons of Mathematics*, Bao Huanzhi 鲍澣之. He states:

> (11) Among the books of mathematical procedures, there are altogether ten schools. One can only consider *The Nine Chapters* as being the head of the Canons. With the methods of its nine parts of mathematics (*jiu shu*), there is nothing which is not complete. Although the procedures established by the various schools present variation, when one looks for the original meaning (*yi*), they all come from it [*The Nine Chapters*]. 算数之书凡数十家，独以"九章"为经之首，以其九数之法无所不备。诸家立术虽有变通，推其本意，皆自此出……[Guo Shuchun 郭书春, 1990, 491] (My emphasis)

If we follow Bao Huanzhi, *The Nine Chapters* is not all-encompassing in the sense that the Canon would contain all mathematical procedures. Bao explicitly refers to procedures that may not be included in it. However, when it comes to their original meaning — an expression that combines the idea of 'source' and that of *yi*, two ideas whose connection has already been noted —, then the original meaning should necessarily fall within the scope of *The Nine Chapters*. One may understand that, when inquiring into the reasoning that leads to establishing, or yielding the procedure, the procedure thereby would either appear as an instantiation of a general fundamental operation or amount to a combination of fundamental operations that can derived in a way from the Canon. The proofs of the procedures then would reveal how, in fact, they fall within the scope of the Canon.

CONCLUSION

Let us summarize the main points made in this article. I have argued that the commentators' explicit attempt to explore the *yi*, the 'meaning/intention' of the Canon, led them to systematically formulate proofs of the correctness of the procedures it contained. However, the practice of mathematical proof put into play in relation to exegesis was quite specific. Such proofs seem to have been

---

[57] It is quite interesting that the description of the task required of candidates for State examinations in mathematics, according to the *Xin Tang shu* 新唐书, made use of such terms as *li* 理 and *yi*' 义 (for an interpretation, see [Siu and Volkov, 1999]). The requirement could be understood in a more precise way, if we agree on interpreting these terms as I suggest. This would support Alexei Volkov's thesis that the composition and selection of commentaries may have related to specific modes of mathematical education. In [Chemla and Zhu Yiwen 朱一文, 2022], we offer an interpretation along these lines.

the tool for inquiring at a formal level into connections between apparently unrelated procedures of *The Nine Chapters*. These connections appear to have brought to light fundamental procedures shared by the algorithms of the Canon. This was the main means the commentators used to identify fundamental algorithms from which all the procedures of the Canon derive and whose efficiency would extend the farthest.

Such a practice of exegesis reveals the commentators' conception of how the Canon expresses its meaning. I tried to show that the commentators agreed in the following respect: in their view, *The Nine Chapters* displays a variety of procedures that, although simple, are rich enough, when confronting their proofs, to indicate the 'origin,' the 'essential points,' and how they can extend to virtually any situation. The Canon reveals its source through a variety of procedures that derive from this source.

This may explain how exegesis led the commentators to describe a structure of the world of mathematical procedures in which all procedures are understood to flow from a limited number of fundamental and very general operations. Although this modality of architecture shares the outer shape of a tree with an axiomatico-deductive structure, it is clear that the principles through which the trees are shaped differ fundamentally.

This may also help us understand the ways in which the Canon could be expected to be all-encompassing. *The Nine Chapters* was believed to highlight the fundamental operations for producing any procedure. In Bao Huanzhi's terms, even if a procedure appeared to exceed the scope of the Canon, looking at its 'original meaning' would reveal how, in fact, by extension or combination of fundamental operations, it still fell within the range of *The Nine Chapters*. The specific practice of proof carried out by the commentators may hence appear to be the essential element linking the statement of the completeness of the Canon and the conceptions of the architecture of mathematical reality.

A claim of this kind might incite us to believe that the exegetes who commented on *The Nine Chapters* had ideas about canonicity that were specific to mathematics, and that their representations about how the Canon should be read were too idiosyncratic to be useful beyond the domain of mathematics. However, as I have pointed out above, several clues indicate that the commentators perceived *The Nine Chapters* as comparable to Confucian Canons, and considered that some of the editorial acts that produced the text of this Canon were identical to those Confucius implemented as an editor of Confucian Canons. For instance, Liu Hui's preface refers to the Han editors by stating that "Zhang Cang and others made both excisions (*shan*) and completions", and thereby referring to how, from at least the Han dynasty onwards, Confucius' editing of Canons was perceived. Another commentary formulates the expectation that a certain type of procedure (the "universal/commanding procedures *dushu* 都术") should be expressed using "abstract expressions," whereas commentators referred to procedures attached to problems using the term "accomplishment *shi* 事." This pair of terms designates precisely the two types of formulation between which, for Han scholars, Confucius sought a balance in his editing of the historical chronicle *Spring and Autumns Annals* (see footnote 13). This is not all. For commentators, the choice of composing *The Nine Chapters* in the form of mathematical problems and related procedures was consistent with Confucius' practice, made clear in the *Analects*, of "hold[ing] up a corner" and waiting until would-be disciples "come back to [him] with the other three." Moreover, among the many quotations that commentators on *The Nine Chapters* make from the 'Great Commentary' on the *Canon of Changes* (*Yijing* 易经), one is meant to justify the use of visual auxiliaries. All of these clues suggest, then, that if the commentators on *The Nine Chapters*, like the exegetes on the Confucians Canons, had the same expectation that the Canon be all-encompassing, it is no mere coincidence. For these commentators, these Canons were of the same nature and should be read in the same way. We thus have reasons to believe that the commentaries on *The Nine Chapters* reflect their authors' understanding of how a Canon of this kind should be approached. In this essay, we have focused on a single feature of their interpretation: we have shown how these commentaries allowed us to interpret their belief that *The Nine Chapters* was all-encompassing. How can this description help us understand this same belief with respect to Confucian Canons? This is the task that now lies before us.

Appendix 1:

What is our earliest evidence regarding the status of *The Nine Chapters* as a 'Canon (*jing*)'?

Present-day historiography of mathematics in China generally holds the view that it was only in 656, and not before, that *The Nine Chapters* acquired the status of a '*jing*.' According to this view, this change in status occurred when *The Nine Chapters* was included in the collection *The Ten Canons of Mathematics*, a compilation with commentary by Li Chunfeng and his assistants; the project had been imperially commissioned and, in 656, was presented to the throne. It was within this context that the commentary by Li Chunfeng on *The Nine Chapters* was composed, as part of the subcommentary that he and his assistants wrote on the set of ten Canons and some of their earlier commentaries. Immediately after the production of this collection, the Canons were used as textbooks for teaching mathematics in the College of Mathematics within the State University.[58] It is hence regularly assumed that the Canons were compiled to be used as textbooks in the University.

To be sure, there is clear evidence showing that these books were used for teaching. It is also beyond doubt that within the collection *The Ten Canons*, the title of *The Nine Chapters on Mathematical Procedures* was modified into *The Canon of the Nine Chapters of Mathematics* (*Jiuzhang suan jing*). In the same way, the title of the oldest book included in the collection, *The Gnomon of the Zhou* (*Zhoubi*), whose composition historians date to the first century either BCE or CE, was also changed into *The Mathematical Canon of the Gnomon of the Zhou* (*Zhoubi suanjing*). However, there are reasons to distinguish the fact that the books were considered '*Canons* (*jing*)' from the fact that their title was changed to stress this fact. Although the title was changed for the 656 edition, my first claim is that there is evidence showing that these two oldest texts included in the compilation were designated as *jing* long before this date (point 1).[59] My second claim is that we must also distinguish the fact that the Canons were used in the University from the idea that making a set of Canons was motivated only by the need for textbooks for the University (point 2).

Since there is considerable confusion on this question, I shall attempt to clarify the matter, starting with my second point. As is shown in [Siu and Volkov, 1999], the ten Canons were not the only textbooks used in the university to teach mathematics. In addition, two other books were used that *did not belong to the collection*. Let us leave aside the one that is no longer extant, and concentrate on

---

[58] See [Siu and Volkov, 1999].

[59] More generally, it is clear that the title of the most important of all Canons, that is, the Confucian Canons, did not always include the term *jing* 经.

the second one, the *Memoir on the Procedures of Numbering* (*Shushu jiyi* 数术记遗). Its composition is attributed to Xu Yue 徐岳 around 220 CE, and Zhen Luan 甄鸾 (fl. ca. 560) wrote a commentary on it.[60] However, according to the extant evidence, there is *no commentary by Li Chunfeng* on it. The facts that, on the one hand, it was not part of the collection and that, on the other hand, *no commentary* on it by Li Chunfeng exists reinforce each other and imply that at the very time when the collection *The Ten Canons of Mathematics* was compiled, there was a distinction between belonging to the set of Canons and being a textbook in the University. In other words, we cannot equate being a Canon with being a textbook. Something more is indicated by granting a book the status of a Canon than simply designating it as teaching material.

Let me now turn to my first point and discuss the evidence I found showing that the two oldest Canons, *The Gnomon of the Zhou* and *The Nine Chapters*, were perceived as *jing* earlier than 656. I consider the earliest occurrence of the term *jing* in relation to *The Nine Chapters* to be a sentence in Liu Hui's preface, which reads: 'the procedures of the Canon got scattered and damaged 经术散坏 *jing shu san huai*' (see excerpt 1). This claim can be contested, because the common understanding of the expression *jingshu* is the study of the Confucian classics. However, within the context of mathematics, *shu* designates a 'procedure,' as is the case in the title: *The Nine Chapters on Mathematical Procedures*. Such procedures form the core of this mathematical writing. Moreover, as can be seen in quotation (1), in the context in which the sentence occurs, the previous and the following sentences both relate to mathematics. Further, the problem discussed soon afterwards in the preface is that raised by the restoring of *The Nine Chapters* from pieces of old text. Lastly, from a semantic point of view, I think that the combination of verbs 'scatter' and 'damage,' which follows the expression, is better suited to something material than to the study of the Classics. As a result, I find it more plausible that in the commentator's preface the expression refers to 'the procedures of the Canon'. However, if that were my only piece of evidence, the argument would possibly not be strong enough. To this I can add evidence of two kinds.

First, the preface of another one of the *The Ten Canons*, the *Mathematical Canon Continuing the Ancients* (*Jigu suanjing*), refers twice to *The Nine Chapters* with the term *jing*.[61] The author, Wang Xiaotong, refers to Liu Hui, whose preface he quotes. Like his predecessor, he considers that the scripture, which he compares to the *Canon of Changes* (*Yijing*), has suffered from damage and that its gaps must be filled up. This provides us with evidence that *The Nine Chapters* was considered a *jing* before 656.

At the same time, it is important that we can find two clear and early references to the other book from the beginning of the Common Era, *The Gnomon of the Zhou*, that designate it as *jing*. The first

---

[60] On the attribution and the content, see [Volkov, 1994]. In the thirteenth century, the book had already been lost, when Bao Huanzhi, the thirteenth-century editor of *The Ten Canons of Mathematics*, found a copy in a Taoist temple. As he explains in his postface (Song edition, pp. 10–1), in relation to the fact that the book was used in the Tang University together with the Canons, he made the decision to include it in his reprint of *The Ten Canons*. Incidentally, Bao Huanzhi's postface is extremely clear on the fact that in his view, the ten Canons are books that are of a nature different from Xu Yue's *Memoir*. Following in the same tradition, [Qian Baocong 钱宝琮, 1963, vol. 2, 535–548], includes an edition of the *Memoir on the Procedures of Numbering*.

[61] See the critical edition in [Qian Baocong 钱宝琮, 1963, vol. 2, 493–527]. The text of the preface is on pp. 493–4. In his introduction to the text (p. 487), Qian argues that, even though the book was composed much earlier, the preface must have been completed some time after 626.

occurrence is to be found in the preface from its third-century commentator Zhao Shuang.[62] The second one occurs in the second layer of commentary on the same book by Zhen Luan (fl. ca. 560), who refers to what he is commenting on with the term *jing*.[63]

As mentioned in the introduction, this essay would like to suggest that we ought to investigate what this designation meant, without assuming that the answer will be the same for all books and all readers. It falls outside of our scope to fulfil the entire program. Let me stress that such a program cannot always be developed: for some of the mathematical Canons, we do not have substantial enough evidence of how earlier readers approached them to inquire into the question. Yet, despite such limitations, I urge that we refrain from anachronistic approaches to these texts. Moreover, it is clear that in the case of *The Gnomon of the Zhou*, the evidence of its status as a Canon is abundant, and I hope to be able to devote a publication to it in the future.

CNRS & Université Paris Cité,
SPHERE-REHSEIS, UMR 7219, CNRS, F-75205, France
chemla@univ-paris-diderot.fr

Acknowledgements

I have been working on this essay for more than twenty years now. It is hence appropriate that I publish it in honor of Prof. Guo Shuchun 郭书春, who forty years ago was one of my professors in the history of mathematics and with whom I have had a twenty-year collaboration on *The Nine Chapters* and its commentaries. This essay derives from a talk presented at a workshop organized by Professor Kim Yung Sik on the topic 'Critical Problems in the History of East Asian Science' and held at the Dibner Institute November 16-18, 2001. It is my pleasure to thank Professor Kim Yung Sik for having invited me to take part in the workshop and also for his remarks on a first version of this article. I am also grateful for the comments Sir Professor Geoffrey Lloyd sent me, which helped clarify some points that had remained obscure. I extend my thanks to all the participants in the workshop and to Bruno Belhoste for the discussions that helped me improve my understanding of the problem tackled in this essay. A second version, which I completed during the stay I made at the Max Planck Institut für Wissenschaftsgeschichte, in the summer 2007, has appeared as an online preprint of the Institute (2008, 46 p., http://www.mpiwg-berlin.mpg.de/Preprints/P344.PDF) and has also been submitted to *British Journal for the History of Science*. In this process, I benefited from remarks by Alexei Volkov and Kelaine Vargas, whom I am delighted to thank here. In 2010, the article has been accepted by *British Journal for the History of Science* and I have pleasure in thanking wholeheartedly one of the referees for his or her incredibly helpful comments. However, I wanted to think further on my argument and that required more time than the journal could give me. Last, but not least, I warn the reader that this article addresses various readerships, including sinologists and historians of science. Both communities might find some of the arguments too lengthy for their own use. I apologize for any impatience caused to the reader, for the too many details given in cases that would seem to some to require none.

---

[62] We refer to the critical edition of *The Gnomon of the Zhou* in [Qian Baocong 钱宝琮, 1963, vol. 1, 11-80]. In the preface by Zhao Shuang, one reads: 'I relied on the Canon (*jing*) to make figures 依经为图.' [Qian Baocong 钱宝琮, 1963, vol. 1, 11].

[63] [Qian Baocong 钱宝琮, 1963, vol. 1, 39]. See the entry '*jing* 经 Canon' in my glossary published in [Chemla and Guo Shuchun 郭书春, 2004, 942].

Bibliography

Chemla, K., 1991. Theoretical Aspects of the Chinese Algorithmic Tradition (First to Third Century). Historia Scientiarum. 42, 75-98 + errata in the following issue.

Chemla, K., 1997. Qu'est-ce qu'un problème dans la tradition mathématique de la Chine ancienne? Quelques indices glanés dans les commentaires rédigés entre le IIIe et le VIIe siècles au classique Han *Les neuf chapitres* sur les procédures mathématiques. In: Chemla, K. (Ed.), La valeur de l'exemple. Extrême-Orient, Extrême-Occident. Presses Universitaires de Vincennes, Saint-Denis, pp. 91-126.

Chemla, K., 1997/1998. Fractions and irrationals between algorithm and proof in ancient China. Studies in History of Medicine and Science. New Series. 15, 31-54.

Chemla, K., 2000. Les problèmes comme champ d'interprétation des algorithmes dans les *Neuf chapitres sur les procédures mathématiques* et leurs commentaires. De la résolution des systèmes d'équations linéaires. Oriens Occidens. Sciences Mathématiques et Philosophie de l'Antiquité à l'Age Classique, 189-234.

Chemla, K., 2004. Algorithmes et histoire de la démonstration. In: Morelon, R., and Hasnaoui, A. (Eds.), De Zénon d'Elée à Poincaré. Recueil d'études en hommage à Roshdi Rashed. Peeters, Leuven, pp. 175-204.

Chemla, K., 2008. Antiquity in the shape of a Canon. Views on antiquity from the outlook of mathematics. In: Kuhn, D., and Stahl, H. (Eds.), Perceptions of Antiquity in Chinese Civilization. Edition Forum, Heidelberg, pp. 191-208. See a version at: http://halshs.ccsd.cnrs.fr/halshs-00010369/.

Chemla, K., 2010a. A Chinese Canon in Mathematics and its two Layers of Commentaries: Reading a collection of texts as shaped by actors. In: Bretelle-Establet, F. (Ed.), Looking at it from Asia: the processes that shaped the sources of history of science. Springer, Dordrecht, pp. 169-210.

Chemla, K., 2010b. Mathematics, Nature and Cosmological Inquiry in Traditional China. In: Dux, G., and Vogel, H.-U. (Eds.), Concepts of Nature in Traditional China: Comparative Approaches. Brill, Leiden, pp. 255-284.

Chemla, K., 2021. Writing abstractly in mathematical texts from early imperial China. In: Csikszentmihalyi, M., and Nylan, M. (Eds.), Technical Arts in the Han Histories. Tables and Treatises in the *Shiji* and *Hanshu*. State University of New York Press, Albany, New York, pp. 307-338.

Chemla, K., and Guo Shuchun 郭书春, 2004. Les neuf chapitres. Le Classique mathématique de la Chine ancienne et ses commentaires. Dunod, Paris.

Chemla, K., and Zhu Yiwen 朱一文, 2022. Contrasting commentaries and contrasting subcommentaries on mathematical and Confucian canons. Intentions and Mathematical Practices. In: Chemla, K. C., and Most, G. W. (Eds.), Mathematical Commentaries in the Ancient World: A Global Perspective. Cambridge University Press, Cambridge, pp. 278－433.

Fung Yu-lan, 1952-1953 [1973]. A History of Chinese Philosophy (tr. Derk Bodde). Princeton University Press, Princeton.

Guo Shirong 郭世荣, 1993. Lüe lun Li Chunfeng deng dui "Jiu zhang" ji qi Liu Hui zhu de zhu 略论李淳风等对《九章》及其刘徽注的注 (Sketchy discussion of Li Chunfeng et al.'s commentary on *The Nine Chapters* and Liu Hui's corresponding commentary). In: Wu Wenjun 吴文俊, Bai Shangshu 白尚恕, Shen Kangshen 沈康身, and Li Di 李迪 (Eds.), Liu Hui yanjiu 刘徽研究 (Research on Liu

Hui). Shaanxi renmin jiaoyu chubanshe & Jiuzhang chubanshe, Xi'an, pp. 364-373.

Guo Shuchun 郭书春, 1984. Jiuzhang suanshu he Liu Hui zhu zhong zhi *lü* gainian ji qi yingyong shixi《九章算术》和刘徽注中之率概念及其应用试析(Analysis of the concept of *lü* and its uses in *The Nine Chapters on Mathematical Procedures* and Liu Hui's commentary)(in Chinese). Kejishi Jikan 科技史集刊(Journal for the history of science and technology). 11, 21-36.

Guo Shuchun 郭书春, 1988. 贾宪《黄帝九章算经细草》初探.《详解九章算法》结构试析(Jia Xian *Huangdi jiu zhang suanjing xicao* chu tan. *Xiangjie jiuzhang suanfa* jiegou shixi)(First Exploration on Jia Xian's *Detailed Procedures for Mathematical Classic in Nine Chapters of the Yellow Emperor*. Tentative Analysis of the Structure of the *Mathematical Methods Explaining in Detail The Nine Chapters*). 自然科学史研究(Ziran Kexueshi Yanjiu)(Studies in the History of Natural Sciences). 7, 328-334.

Guo Shuchun 郭书春, 1990. Hui jiao Jiu zhang suan shu 汇校九章算术. Liaoning jiaoyu chubanshe 辽宁教育出版社, Shenyang 沈阳.

Guo Shuchun 郭书春, 1992. Gudai shijie shuxue taidou Liu Hui 古代世界数学泰斗刘徽(Liu Hui, a leading figure of ancient world mathematics). Shandong kexue jishu chubanshe, Jinan.

Henderson, J. B., 1991. Scripture, Canon and Commentary. A Comparison of Confucian and Western Exegesis. Princeton University Press, Princeton.

Li Jimin 李继闵, 1982. "Jiuzhang suanshu" zhong de *bilü* lilun "九章算术"中的比率理论(The theory of ratios in *The Nine Chapters on mathematical procedures*). In: WU Wenjun (Ed.), "Jiuzhang suanshu" yu Liu Hui 九章算术与刘徽(*The Nine Chapters on mathematical procedures* and Liu Hui). Beijing Shifan Daxue Chubanshe 北京师范大学出版社, Beijing 北京, pp. 228-245.

Li Jimin 李继闵, 1990. Dongfang shuxue dianji Jiuzhang suanshu ji qi Liu Hui zhu yanjiu 东方数学典籍——《九章算术》及其刘徽注研究(Research on the Oriental mathematical Classic *The Nine Chapters on Mathematical Procedures* and on its Commentary by Liu Hui). 陕西人民教育出版社 Shaanxi renmin jiaoyu chubanshe, 西安 Xi'an.

Martzloff, J.-C., 1987. Histoire des mathématiques chinoises. Masson, Paris.

Martzloff, J.-C., 1997. A History of Chinese Mathematics. Springer, Berlin ; New York.

Owen, S., 1992. Readings in Chinese Literary Thought. Council on East Asian Studies, Harvard University Press, Cambridge (Mass.).

Qian Baocong 钱宝琮, 1963. Suanjing shishu 算经十书(Qian Baocong jiaodian 钱宝琮校点)(Critical punctuated edition of The Ten Canonical Texts of Mathematics). Zhonghua shuju 中华书局, Beijing 北京.

Siu, M.-K., and Volkov, A., 1999. Official Curriculum in Traditional Chinese Mathematics: How did Candidates Pass the Examinations? Historia Scientiarum. 9, 85-99.

Sivin, N., 1995. Text and experience in classical Chinese medicine. In: Bates, D. (Ed.), Knowledge and the scholarly medical traditions. Cambridge University Press, Cambridge (UK), pp. 177-204.

Volkov, A., 1994. Large numbers and counting rods. Extrême-Orient, Extrême-Occident. 16, 71-92.

Wagner, D. B., 1978a. Doubts concerning the attribution of Liu Hui's commentary on "Chiu-chang suan-shu". Acta Orientalia. Societates Orientales Danica Fennica Norvegica Svecica. 39, 199-212. See a version at: http://donwagner.dk/LiuHui/LiuHui.pdf.

Wagner, D. B., 1978b. Liu Hui and Tsu Keng-Chih on the volume of a sphere. Chinese Science. 3, 59-79. See a version at: http://donwagner.dk/SPHERE/SPHERE.html.

Wagner, R., 2000. The Craft of a Chinese Commentator. Wang Bi on the Laozi. State University of New York Press, New York.

Waley, A., 1938 [1988]. The Analects of Confucius. George Allen and Unwin [Second edition: Unwin Hyman], London.

Yang Jialuo (ed.) 杨家骆主编, 1977. Zhongguo tianwen lifa shiliao 中国天文历法史料 (Historical Material on Chinese Astronomy and Calendar). Dingwen shuju 鼎文书局, Taipei 台北.

Zhou Xiaohan 周霄汉, 2018. Elements of Continuity between Mathematical Writings from the Song-Yuan (13th-14th century) Dynasties and the Ming Dynasty (15th century): Comparing Yang Hui's Mathematical Methods (1261 CE) and Wu Jing's Great Compendium (1450 C.E.), University Paris Diderot, Paris.

Jiuzhang Suanshu and Equations

HONG Sung Sa 洪性士[*]　　HONG Young Hee 洪英喜[**]

Dedicated to our teacher and friend, Guo Shuchun
on the occasion of his 80th birthday

Abstract *Jiuzhang Suanshu* with Liu Hui's commentary gives rise to the most important foundation for the development of East Asian mathematics. After Yang Hui's *Xiangjie Jiuzhang Suanfa* (1261), *Jiuzhang Suanshu* was almost forgotten but its structures have been retained. Guo Shuchun published three editions of *Jiuzhang Suanshu* with complete corrections (九章算术 汇校) among others. We first discuss Guo's *Jiuzhang Suanshu* which gave important influences on our formative stage of the study of history of East Asian mathematics. We also deal with Yang Hui's structural approach in *Xiangjie Jiuzhang Suanfa*, and the theory of equations originated from *Shaoguang* and *Gougu* and solidated in the Song-Jin-Yuan Dynasties. In the Ming-Qing Dynasties, it was almost disappeared until the late 18th century. We discuss its revival in the 19th century through Li Rui's contributions. Finally, we review a short history of equations in the Joseon Dynasty, which is based on *Suanxue Qimeng*.

Keywords *Jiuzhang Suanshu*, Yang Hui, *Xiangjie Jiuzhang Suanfa*, polynomial equations, Li Rui, theory of equations in the Joseon Dynasty.

MSC: 01A13, 01A25, 01A55

Ⅰ. Introduction

Jiuzhang Suanshu（九章算术）sets the ordered field Q of rational numbers as the basic mathematical object which has been retained throughout the history of East Asian mathematics until the end of 19th century. Indeed, the structure of positive rationals was discussed in the first chapter *Fangtian* （方田）and then extended to Q in the eighth chapter *Fangcheng*（方程）. The latter deals with the systems of linear equations, and solves them by eliminations, now known as Gauss-Jordan elimination. *Jiuzhang Suanshu* reveals mathematical structures by solving word problems of daily affairs. Evaluating the square and cube roots in the fourth chapter *Shaoguang*（少广）, *Jiuzhang Suanshu* introduces an inception of higher degree polynomial equations and their solutions but deals just one general quadratic equation in the last chapter *Gougu*（勾股）.

The extant *Jiuzhang Suanshu* is one with comprehensive commentary by Liu Hui（刘徽）in the third century. Indeed, Liu Hui added his own contributions. Among others, he did compute an approximation of π in the first chapter *Fangtian* using the Pythagorean theorem and square roots dealt in chapters *Gougu* and *Shaoguang*, respectively.

---

[*] HONG Sung Sa: Sogang Univ., Seoul, Korea E-mail: sshong@sogang.ac.kr
[**] HONG Young Hee: Sookmyung Women's Univ., Seoul, Korea E-mail: yhhong@sookmyung.ac.kr

In the formative stage of our research on the history of the East Asian mathematics, we read Guo Shuchun's *Jiuzhang Suanshu* with commentaries[1] dealing with the single book for the first time among other comprehensive books of the history. The book gave us a new insight for our study. Thus, we take *Jiuzhang Suanshu* for the wonderful occasion, Guo's 80th birthday. We first recall academic and personal relations with Guo Shuchun and then deal with *Jiuzhang Suanshu*, in particular its influences to the development of history of equations in the East Asian mathematics.

The reader may find all the Chinese sources of this paper in *Zhongguo Kexue Jishu Dianji Tonghui Shuxuejuan*（中国科学技术典籍通汇 数学卷，1993）[2] and they are not numbered as an individual reference.

II. *Jiuzhang Suanshu* and Yang Hui

Before establishing diplomatic relation with China in 1992, the academic sources for the study of sinology were brought into Korea from Taiwan. We should mention the series *Guoxue Jiben Congshu*（国学基本丛书）and *Siku Quanshu Wenyuange*（四库全书 文渊阁）published by Taiwan Shangwu Yinshuguan（台湾商务印书馆）. We also note that works of Yang Hui（杨辉）, including his *Xiangjie Jiuzhang Suanfa*（详解九章算法，1261）were quoted in *Xuxiu Siku Quanshu*（续修 四库全书）published in Shanghai Guji Chubanshe（上海古籍出版社）.

In the beginning of the 21st century, a bookstore dealing with Chinese books was opened in Seoul, where we could buy *Zhongguo Lidai Suanxue Jicheng*（中国历代算学集成）[3] and Guo Shuchun's *Jiuzhang Suanshu* with his Huijiao（汇校，1990）. We could collect later his *Jiuzhang Suanshu*, translation and annotation（九章筭术，译注）[4] and *Zhongguo Kexue Jishu Dianji Tonghui Shuxuejuan*. Having these books and collections, we could begin our study based on the original Chinese texts including mathematics influenced by the Western mathematics.

In 2012, we first met Guo Shuchun at a conference in Xi'an and became immediately good friends. Since then, we met each other every year in China or Korea. He has been so generous to give us his books, *Zhongguo Kexue Jishushi Shuxuejuan*（中国科学技术史数学卷，2010）[5], *Jiuzhang Suanshu*, the new correction（九章算术，新校）[6], his *Shuxueshi Zixuanji*（数学史 自选集）[7]. As soon as I told him our study of *Siyuan yujian*（四元玉鉴）in Joseon mathematics, he sent us its English translation, *Jade Mirror of the Four Unknowns*（四元玉鉴，2006）[8]. Through his collections of the original texts and his contributions about them, our research became much more improved.

We now return to *Jiuzhang Suanshu* in China. We take *Xiangjie Jiuzhang Suanfa* as mentioned above. *Xiangjie Jiuzhang Suanfa* contains chapters, *Yingbuzu*（盈不足）, *Fangcheng*（方程）, *Gougu*（勾股）, *Shanggong*（商功）and *Junshu*（均输）along this order. Yang Hui discussed commentaries along mathematical structures but free from the order of *Jiuzhang Suanshu*. But the first four chap-

---

1 郭书春汇校:《〈九章算术〉汇校本》，辽宁教育出版社，1990.
2 郭书春主编:《中国科学技术典籍通汇·数学卷》，河南教育出版社，1993.
3 靖玉树 编勘:《中国历代算学集成》，山东人民出版社，1994.
4 郭书春译注:《九章算术译注》，上海古籍出版社，2009.
5 郭书春主编:《中国科学技术史·数学卷》，科学出版社，2010.
6 郭书春汇校:《九章算术新校》，中国科学技术大学出版社，2014.
7 郭书春:《郭书春数学史自选集》，山东科学技术出版社，2018.
8 郭书春今译，陈在新 英译，郭金海 整理:《四元玉鉴（*Jade Mirror of the Four Unknowns*）》汉英文对照本，辽宁教育出版社，2006.

ters, *Fangtian*（方田）, *Sumi*（粟米）, *Cuifen*（衰分） and *Shaoguang*（少广） were missing in his *Xiangjie Jiuzhang Suanfa*. In these four chapters, mathematical structures of the nonnegative rational numbers were discussed. Thus, it might be somewhat difficult for the beginners to understand his terminologies.

Yang Hui added *Xiangjie Jiuzhang Suanfa Zuanlei*（详解九章算法 纂类） as an appendix. He first revealed a short history of *Jiuzhang Suanshu* in *Zuanlei*, and claimed that the fundamental mathematical structures in *Jiuzhang Suanshu* are divided into *chengchu*（乘除, 41）, *chulü*（除率, 9）, *helü*（合率, 20）, *huhuan*（互换, 63）, *cuifen*（衰分, 18）, *leiji*（累积, 27）, *yingbuzu*（盈不足, 11）, *fangcheng*（方程, 19） and *gougu*（勾股, 38）, where the numbers in the parenthesis indicate those of problems in *Jiuzhang Suanshu*. We note that the gougu consists of 13 problems in *Shaoguang*, 1 in Shanggong and 24 in *Gougu* of *Jiuzhang Suanshu*. One can find the distributions of the others in *Zhongguo Kexue Jishu Dianji Tonghui Shuxuejuan*.

Along his view on the above mathematical structures, Yang Hui rearranged problems of *Jiuzhang Suanshu* as follows:

Chengchu, *Huhuan*, *Helü*, *Fenlü*（分率）, *Cuifen*, *Leiji*, *Yingbuzu*, *Fangcheng*, *Gougu*.

He began the new classifications with the following sentence:

类题以物理分章 有题法又互之讹 今将二百四十六问 分别门例使后学亦可周知也

In the above quote, he claimed that he did indeed arrange chapters along *wuli*（物理）, namely mathematical structures. Guo Shuchun also points out as follows:

但毕竟是《九章算术》成书后千余年间第一次突破其分类格局，是个创举

Quoting the data in Yang Hui's classifications, we compare his ones with those in *Jiuzhang Suanshu*. Each one was first indicated by numbers of problems（问）in the chapter of *Jiuzhang Suanshu*, and numbers of solving methods（法）.

Chengchu (38; 14 *Fangtian*: 1; 1 *Sumi*),

Huhuan (31 *Sumi*: 11 *Cuifen*: 11 *Junshu*: *Yingbuzu*; 2),

Helü (11 *Shaoguang*: 8 *Junshu*: 1 *Yingbuzu*; 3),

Fenlü (17 *Sumi*, 6 *Yingbuzu*: *guijian*（贵贱）, *fenlü*, 反其率),

Cuifen (9 each *Cuifen* and *Junshu*: 2 each),

Leiji (27 *Shanggong*: 18),

Yingbuzu (11 *Yingbuzu*: 5),

Fangcheng (18 *Fangcheng*, 2 *Junshu*: 4),

Gougu (13 *Shaoguang*, 24 *Gougu*: 2 each *pingfang zengcheng*（平方增乘）,

lifang fenzi（立方分子）, and *pangyao*（旁要）, and 12 *gougu*).

The chapter *Shaoguang* includes the problems of square and cube roots and leads to an origin of theory of polynomial equations in the East Asian mathematics. Yang Hui excluded it as a chapter in his *Xiangjie Jiuzhang Suanfa Zuanlei* as indicated above. One can find small but mostly important remnants of *Xiangjie Jiuzhang Suanfa* in *Yongle Dadian*（永乐大典, 1408）. It quotes 11 items from *Xiangjie Jiuzhang Suanfa*, and they are all concerned with problems in *Shaoguang*. Except the first one on problem 5 in *Shaoguang*, they deal with extractions of square and cube roots. The first one, *kaifang zuofa benyuan*（开方作法本源） is the famous triangle of binomial expansions by Jia Xian（贾

宪, fl. 11th century) in his *Huangdi Jiuzhang Suanjing Xicao*（黄帝九章算经细草）, which led to the *zengcheng kaifangfa*（增乘开方法）for solutions of polynomial equations. Using this, Yang Hui explained solutions of square and cube roots. Finally, he added the extraction of a quartic root, not found in *Jiuzhang Suanshu*. We note that *kaifang zuofa benyuan* indicates that *zengcheng kaifangfa* is independent from the Ruffini-Horner method based on synthetic divisions.

Yang Hui also published *Yang Hui Suanfa*（杨辉算法, 1274－1275）. We quote his view on *Jiuzhang Suanshu* as follows:

九章二百四十六问固是不出乘除开方三术 但下法布置尤宜徧历
如互乘互换维乘列衰方程 并列图于卷首
九章二百四十六问 除习过乘除诸分开方 自余方田 粟米只须一日
下徧衰分功在立衰 少广全类合分 商功皆是折变 均输取用衰分互乘
每一章作三日演习 盈不足 方程 勾股用法颇难 每一章演习更将
九章篡类消类庶知用算门例而九章之义尽矣

Before the above view on *Jiuzhang Suanshu*, Yang Hui discussed his view on the solutions of polynomial equations as follows:

开方乃算法中大节目 勾股 旁要演段 锁积多用 例有七体
一曰开平方 二曰积平圆 三曰开立方 四曰开立圆 五曰开分子方
六曰开三乘以上方 七曰带从开方 并载少广 勾股二章
作一日学一法 用两月演习题目 须讨论用法之源 庶久而无失忘矣

The above quote indicates that Yang Hui may change his view on the theory of equations. He didn't include the construction of equations by *tianyuanshu*（天元术）in *Yang Hui Suanfa*. Furthermore, he might not have *Shushu Jiuzhang*（数书九章, 1247）of Qin Jiushao（1202－1261）. Yang Hui deals with quadratic equations with linear terms in *Tianmu Bilei Chengchu Jiefa*（田亩比类乘除捷法）and their solutions, called *daizong kaifang*（带从开方）. We recall that Qin Jiushao applies the *zengcheng kaifangfa* to equations of the form $p(x)=0$ although his constructions of equations are of the form $q(x)=c$, $x|q(x)$ with a non-zero constant c in *Shushu Jiuzhang*. Along the extractions of square and cube roots in *Shaoguang*, Yang Hui obtained a general quadratic equations of the form $q(x)=c$ mentioned above for various plane figures including rectangles and circles and solved them along extractions of roots. He also solves a general quartic equation for a *hutian*（弧田）, or *hushitian*（弧矢田）

$$-5x^4+52x^3+128x^2=4,096$$

with a solution 4.

III. Li Rui's Algebra

Yang Hui's mathematics was transmitted to *Jiuzhang Suanfa Bilei Daquan*（九章算法比类大全, 1450）of Wu Jing（吴敬）. Wu Jing quoted *kaifang zuofa benyuan* mentioned above, which was again quoted by Cheng Dawei（程大位, 1533－1606）in his *Suanfa Tongzong*（算法统宗, 1592）. Mathematicians in the Ming Dynasty（1368－1644）did not pay any attention to the mathematics developed in the previous Yuan Dynasty（1271－1368）. *Suanxue Qimeng*（算学启蒙, 1299）and *Siyuan Yujian*（四元玉鉴, 1303）of Zhu Shijie（朱世杰）have been completely forgotten in China until the 19th century except quotes by Mei Juecheng（梅毂成,1681－1763）. Since the Western mathematics along with its astronomy was introduced in the 17th century, the most important development of the Song-Yuan Dynasties has been almost, if not completely, forgotten until the 19th century. For the construction of polynomial equations, one may refer to commentaries on Li Ye's *Ceyuan Haijing*（测圆海镜,1248）and *Yigu Yanduan*（益古演段,1259）made by Li Rui（李锐,1769－1817）in 1784 and 1786, respectively.

Zhang Dunren（张敦仁,1754－1834）published *Jigu Suanjing Xicao*（缉古算经细草,1813）. Using *tianyuanshu*, Zhang Dunren constructed equations dealt in *Jigu Suanjing*（656）of Wang Xiaotong（王孝通）. In the mean time, Chinese mathematicians noticed the reappearing *Siyuan Yujian* and pay their attentions to it. Consequently, they found the Song-Jin-Yuan mathematics, in particular the theory of equations is much more advanced than that brought in to China by the Jesuit mathematicians in the 17th century.

In this section, we show that Li Rui did understand the relations between solutions of polynomial equations and their factorizations. Furthermore, his algebraic approach to solve right triangles is much better than the geometric one in *Shuli Jingyun*（数理精蕴,1723）. Li Rui wrote books, *Kaifangshuo*（开方说）and *Gougu Suanshu Xicao*（勾股算术细草,1806）. Unlike his commentaries mentioned above, Li Rui acknowledged the structures of *zengcheng kaifangfa* applied to equations of $p(x)=0$ rather than those of $q(x)=c$ where $x|q(x)$ and $c>0$. Thus, he first classified equations of the form $q(x)-c=0$ and then applied *zengcheng kaifangfa* as that in *Shushu Jiuzhang*. He began with linear equations and dealt with equations with multiple solutions including negative ones and quadratic equations without any real solutions.

Li Rui includes three quadratic equations without real solutions in the final three problems in the first book（上卷）. In the last problem, he exhibits the precise reason for the equation not to have a real solution as follows.

实一百四十五负 方二十四正 隅一负

Using *chushang*（初商）10, Li has the equation for *cishang*（次商）by *zengcheng kaifangfa*

$$-y^2+4y-5=0$$

He takes *cishang* $2=\frac{4}{2}$ and has the equation for the *cicishang*（次次商）

$$-z^2-1=0$$

which has no real solution. Thus he concludes that the equation has no real solution, but Li Rui has essentially the exact complex solutions $(10+2)\pm i=12\pm i$.

The square roots were introduced in *Jiuzhang Suanshu* to find a side of a square with its area, they have never thought about the equation $x^2=a$ with a negative a. It was already introduced in *Jiuzhang Suanshu* that products of two negative numbers are positive. Li Rui is presumably the first East Asian mathematician to notice the equation $x^2+1=0$, which has trivially no real solution.

Furthermore, the above process, namely eliminations of linear term of a quadratic equation implies that solutions of quadratic equations involve essenially square roots, or quadratic formula.

We now discuss Li Rui's concept of factorizations of polynomials.

Problem 6 in the Second book（中卷）

实一万四千四十负　方二千八百三十八正　廉一百五十一负　隅一正
开立方得第一数九第二数一十二第三数一百三十

For the modern readers, we describe the problem as
$$x^3 - 151x^2 + 2,838x - 14,040 = 0$$
Applying *zengcheng kaifangfa* to the equation, he obtained a solution $x = 9$ and the factorization
$$x^3 - 151x^2 + 2,838x - 14,040 = (x-9)(x^2 - 142x + 1,560)$$
We recall that factorizations of polynomials in *tianyuanshu* have never introduced in the East Asian mathematics. We assume that the readers are familiar with *tianyuanshu* and *zengcheng kaifangfa*. The above notion appears in the first stage of the *kaifangfa* for a solution. He didn't pursue the next stages to have an equation for *cishang*.

Li Rui surprisingly solves the equation $x^2 - 142x + 1,560 = 0$ for other solutions of the original equation. Applying the *kaifangfa* to the quadratic equation, he has a solution 12 and claims that it is another solution of the original cubic equation. It is trivial for the present mathematicians but it is not the case for the East Asian mathematicians before the mid 19th century. For this, he obtains *chushang*（初商）10 and then *cishang*（次商）2. For *chushang* 10 of the quadratic equation, he obtains
$$x^2 - 142x + 1,560 = (x-10)^2 - 122(x-10) + 240$$
For *cishang* 2, he has
$$y^2 - 122y + 240 = (y-2)(y-120)$$
where $y = x - 10$.

Thus, Li Rui claims that 12 is solution for the quadratic equation and hence another solution of the original cubic equation. Furthermore, 120 is another solution for y, $120 + 10 = 130$ is also a solution of the original equation as well. We point out that Li includes the process of solving $y - 120 = 0$.

Furthermore, he adds *zengcheng kaifangfa* process for the solution 130 for the same equation. Indeed, for a *chushang* 100, he has the equation for *cishang*
$$y^3 + 149y^2 + 2,638y - 240,240 = 0$$
where $y = x - 100$, and then for *chushang* 30, he has the factorization by *zengcheng kaifangfa*
$$y^3 + 149y^2 + 2,638y - 240,240 = (y-30)(y^2 + 179y + 8,008)$$
and hence a solution $(100 + 30) = 130$.

Solving the equation $y^2 + 179y + 8,008 = 0$, he has -88 for another *cishang* and concludes that he has another solution $100 - 88 = 12$ for the original equation.

For the quadratic equation $y^2 + 179y + 8,008 = 0$ and its *cishang* -8, he has the factorization
$$y^2 + 19y + 88 = (y+8)(y+11)$$
so that he has another *cishang* -11. Here he solves the equation $y + 11 = 0$ as before. Thus, he concludes $(100 - 80) - 11 = 9$ being a solution for the original cubic equation.

Li Rui should have a proper concept of factorizations of an equation and its solutions. In the above problem, he tries to exhibits their structure for solutions with a single or multiple digits together. Also see [9].

Since a quadratic equation was introduced in the chapter *Gougu*, Wang Xiatong constructed four

---

[9] HONG Sung Sa, HONG Young Hee, KIM Chang Il, Zengcheng Kaifangfa and Zeros of Polynomials. *Journal for History of Mathematics*, 33(6)(2020), 303–314.

cubic equations and two quadratic equations in his *Jigu Suanjing* mentioned above. Li Ye introduced terminology for sums and differences of sides of a right triangle in his *Ceyuan Haijing* and Yang Hui called them five sums（五和）and five differences（五较）in his *Xiangjie Jiuzhang Suanfa*. Using these, Zhu Shijie introduced his tianyuanshu to solve them in the chapter *Fangcheng Zhengfumen* of his *Suanxue Qimeng*, and then used extensively gougushu to construct equations in his *Siyuan Yujian*. Mei Wending（梅文鼎，1633－1721）completed *Gougu Chanwei*（勾股阐微）with Yang Zuomei（杨作枚）on solving right triangles word problems, shortly solving right triangles. Mei solved the problems by geometric figures. They were quoted in Book 12, *Gougu* in *Shuli Jingyun*. It divides into *Gouguxian hejiao xiangqiufa*（勾股弦和较相求法）, *Gouguji yu gouguxian hejiao xiangqiufa*（勾股积与勾股弦和较相求法）and *Zhenggou gu bili*（正勾股比例）. The three sections consist of 35, 9 and 9 problems, respectively.

Instead of *tianyuanshu*, *jiegenfang bili*（借根方比例）was introduced in the Book 31 of *Shuli Jingyun* to represent polynomials. Using this, they also construct equations. The equations for gougu problems were also constructed by *jiegenfang*. They obtained 12 quadratic equations in the chapter *Mianlei*（面类）and a cubic equation in *Tilei*（体类）for the *xiangqiufa* without referring to the geometric figures. Li Rui also completed *Gougu Suanshu Xicao*（勾股算术细草，1807）. He dealt with 26 items. They were chosen in the above three sections in *Shuli Jingyun*, but have different dimensions, i.e. the Pythagorean triples. Instead of *jiegenfang*, Li constructed equations by *tianyuanshu* and solved them by *zengcheng kaifangfa* described in his *Kaifangshuo*.

He begins with the basic 3 items for the Pythagorean theorem. For the remaining 23 items, he constructed equations by *tianyuanshu* with gou as the *tianyuan*, whose processes are called cao（草）, and then included the proofs by geometric diagrams in *Shuli Jingyun*, called jie（解）. He obtained linear equations in the item 4－7 and quadratic equations in the remaining items.

In the item 18－20 and 22, he discussed problems with the same conditions but different dimensions, indeed, 4, 2, 2, 4 cases in the items, respectively. For the *tianyuanshu*, the processes are exactly duplicates with substituting the given dimensions. But, Li described the different jie arising from the dimensions. He tries to show that *tianyuanshu* can be applied universally but the methods in *Shuli Jingyun* are not the case. We recall his inclination to *Shuli Jingyun* in his commentaries as mentioned above.

For solutions of equations in *Gougu Suanshu* Xicao, there are 10 cases with *two positive* solutions. They are item 8, 11, 16, 17, 18－2, 20, 20－1, 21, 22－2, and 24. We note that negative solutions do not make any sense for the lengths of three sides of a right triangle. For the three sides gou, gu and xian, a, b, c of a right triangle, Li assumed $0 < a < b < c$ as the usual convention. Except the item 20－1, the other positive solutions are unacceptable, for they violate the assumption. For the item 20－1, he indicates two solutions (198, 336, 390) and (240, 252, 348). The item may indicate that *Kaifanshuo* was written before *Gougu Suanshu Xicao*.

By his two books, *Kaifangshuo* and *Gougu Suanshu Xicao*, Li Rui could recover the fundamental structures of theory of equations up to the Song Dynasty.

Luo Shilin（罗士琳，1784－1853）published the commentary of *Siyuan Yujian*（四元玉鉴细草，1835）, and Shen Qinpei（沈钦裴）also wrote the *xicao*. *Suanxue Qimeng* was republished in 1660 by a Joseon official Kim Si-jin（金始振，1618－1667）, which was found in China by Luo Shilin. He then republished it with corections in China. Thus, the mathematics in the Yuan Dynasty could also be recovered in China.

IV. Equations in the Joseon Dynasty

Since *Yang Hui Suanfa* and *Suanxue Qimeng* were brought into Joseon by the fourth king Sejong（世宗，1397－1450, r. 1417－1450）to improve the calendar system, they became a major reference books for Joseon mathematicians throughout the Dynasty (1392－1910). *Suanxue Qimeng* was reprinted in 1660 as mentioned above, which revived the *tianyuanshu* in the circle of her mathematicians. Among others, Hong Jeong-ha（洪正夏，1684－1723）is prominent, if not the most prominent, and wrote *Guil jib*（九一集，1713－1724）[10]. It comprises eight chapters and an appendix. His main concern is the theory of equations based on *tianyuanshu* and *zengcheng kaifangfa*. Indeed, they were dealt in five chapters, *Gucheok haeunmun*（毬只解隐门）, *Bubyeong toetamun*（缶瓶堆垛门）, *Changdon jeogsogmun*（仓囤积粟门）, *Gugo hoeunmun*（勾股互隐门）and three chapters *Gaebang gagsulmun*（开方各术门，上，中，下）. One can easily discern that the above chapters were used to construct equations in the East Asian mathematics books.

Jia Xian's triangle was introduced in to Joseon by *Suanfa Tongzong*（算法统宗，1592）, where its author Cheng Dawei（程大位，1533－1602）quoted one in Wu Jing's book. Hong Jeong-ha introduced the synthetic multiplications and then obtained the mathematical structure of *zengcheng kaifangfa* (see[11] for the detail). Since Hong Jeong-ha is familiar with the constructions of equations in the chapter *Kaifang shisuomen*（开方释锁门）, Hong's equations are all of the type $p(x)=0$ and he applied *zengcheng kaifangfa* to the equation $p(x)=0$. For the extractions of roots, he changed it to the equation $x^n - a = 0$. We point out that Zhu Shijie applied *zengcheng kaifangfa* to $x^n = a$ in his book. Except multiple solutions including negative solutions, his theory of equations was complete in the 18th century unlike that in China.

Furthermore, Hong Jeong-ha also solved right triangles in *Gugo hoeunmun*, altogether 78 problems using the traditional methods and *tianyuanshu* (see[12]).

His friend, Yu Su-seog（刘寿锡）also left a book, *Gugo Sulyo*（勾股述要）, which contains 223 problems with short comments（术）. By his comments, we can easily assume that he solved them by *tianyuanshu* and *zengcheng kaifangfa* (see[13]). In 1646, *Xiyang Xinfa Lishu*（西洋新法历书）was brought into Joseon, and *Tianxue Chuhan*（天学初函，1628）in the last decade of the 17th century. Joseon scholars could not appreciate them because of the new geometric approach. *Shuli Jingyun* was imported in 1730 and it became a main reference for officers in Gwansang-gam（观象监）. In the 19th century, Chinese mathematical classics from *Jiuzhang Suanshu* to Song-Jin-Yuan books were first imported into Joseon. The latter include books written by Qin Jiushao, Li Ye. Moreover, Luo Shilin's *Siyuan Yujian Xicao* was also brought into Joseon. Thus, Joseon mathematicians paid attentions again to the traditional Chinese mathematics.

We first discuss Jeong Yag-yong（丁若镛，1762－1836）. He is one of the most famous scholar and writer in the Joseon Dynasty. Along his books on *Silhak*（实学）, he also wrote a mathematics

---

[10] 洪正夏：《九一集》(1724)，

[11] HONG Sung Sa, HONG Young Hee, KIM Young Wook, Hong JeongHa's *Tianyuanshu* and *Zengcheng Kaifangfa*, *Journal for History of Mathematics*, 27(3)(2014), 155－164.

[12] HONG Sung Sa, HONG Young Hee, KIM Chang Il, *Gou Gu Shu* in the 18th century, *The Korean Journal for History of Mathematics*, 20(4)(2007), 1－20.

[13] HONG Sung Sa, HONG Young Hee, KIM Chang Il, *Gou Gu Shu* in the 19th century, *The Korean Journal for History of Mathematics*, 21(2)(2008), 1－18.

book, *Gugo Wonlyu*(勾股源流), consisting of 4 chapters. The first chapter is called *Gouguxian Hejiao Xiangqiufa* as in *Shuli Jingyun*. The next three chapters *Gugohyen Myeogjeog Sang-gubeob*, or *Gouguxian Miji Xiangquifa*(勾股弦幂积相求法)in Chinese are in fact its main body. The first part deals with five sums and five differences and their relations, but he used the title in *Shuli Jingyun*. The second part concerns homogeneous polynomials of degree 2 about *gou*, *gu*, *xian* and their five sums and five differences. Using expansions and *factorizations*, Jeong Yag-yong obtained identities, altogether 1,547 items. We note that the polynomials in *Gugo Wonlyu* are of three variables, namely *gou* (a), *gu* (b), *xian* (c) with $a^2+b^2=c^2$. Although he did not apply the identities to solve right triangles, it is really astonishing for him to study the algebraic structures of multivariable polynomials. See [14][15] for the detail.

Finally, we discuss Lee Sang-hyeog (李尚爀, 1810－?) who is one of the most prominent mathematician in the Joseon Dynasty along with Hong Jeong-ha. He is related to Hong Jeong-ha by marriages for generations. Lee's great-great grandfather is Hong Jeong-ha's brother in law and his father is the son-in-law of Hong Jeong-ha's nephew. As mentioned in Lee's postscript to republication of *Guil Jib* (1868), *Guil Jib* had been a major reference in his family.

Lee Sang-hyeog also had a unusual supporter and collaborator, Nam Byeong-gil (南秉吉, 1820－1860) despite their difference in social status.

Lee's first publication is *Chageunbang Mong-gu* (借根方蒙求, 1854) which deals with construction of equations for problems in *Shuli Jingyun* by *jiegenfang bilei*. In the next year, he wrote *Sansul Gwan-gyeon* (算术管见, 1855), where he took *tianyuanshu* instead of *jiegenfang*.

His final work is *Igsan* (翼算, 1868). It divides into two parts, *Jeongburon* (正负论)[16] and *Toetaseol* (堆垛说)[17]. Lee discussed the theory of equations in the first part and the theory of finite series in the second one. He built his theory of equations based on *Jiuzhang Suanshu*, Qin Jiushao, Li Ye, Guo Shoujing (郭守敬, 1231－1316), Zhu Shijie, Gu Yingxiang (顾应祥, 1483－1565), Tang Shunzhi (唐顺之, 1507－1560), Mei Wending, Jiao Xun (焦循, 1763－1820). Lee Sang-hyeog tried to build a theory of equations, where his equations mean linear ones, system of linear ones, polynomial equations and system of polynomial equations up to four unknowns. Since his equations are constructed for word problems as the above mentioned scholars did, solutions should be positive. Thus, his equations should have both positive and negative terms so that his title is *Jeongburon*. He also discussed their solutions by *zengcheng kaifangfa* for the equations of a type $p(x)=0$. He mentioned the clumsy processes for solutions of equations in *Shuli Jingyun* which are influenced by Mei's *Shaoguang Shiyi* (少广拾遗, 1692)(see[18]).

In *Toetaseol*, Lee's main reference is *Siyuan Yujian*, where Zhu Shijie used the theory of finite series for constructions of equations. Before *Siyuan Yujian*, finite series were evaluated by geometrical figures. Since difference sequnces were introduced in the 7th century, Wang Xun (王恂, 1235－

---

[14] HONG Sung Sa, HONG Young Hee, LEE Seung On, Mathematical Structures of Jeong Yag-yong's *Gugo Wonlyu*, *Journal for History of Mathematics*, 28(6)(2015), 301-310.

[15] HONG Sung Sa, HONG Young Hee, LEE Seung On, Mathematical Structures of Polynomials in Jeong Yag-yong's *Gugo Wonlyu*, *Journal for History of Mathematics*, 29(5)(2016), 257-266.

[16] 洪性士 译注:《翼算 上编, 正负论》, 教友社, 2006.

[17] 洪性士 译注:《翼算 下编, 堆垛说》, 教友社, 2006.

[18] HONG SungSa, Solving equations in the early 18th century East Asia, *Advanced Studies in Pure Mathematics: Mathematics of Takebe Katahiro and History of Mathematics in East Asia*, 79(2018), 175-192.

1281) and Guo Shoujing also used the difference sequences in *Shoushili*（授时历，1281）. Zhu Shijie also used extensively difference sequences in *Siyuan Yujian* but did not include any explanations about them as for other problems. Based on the Jiaxian's triangles, Lee Sang-hyeog tried to give commentaries for the mathematical strutures of series in *Siyuan Yujian* in his *Toetaseol*. He introduced also some extensions and used them for construction of equations[19].

Along with *Sanhag Seubyu*（算学拾遗）of Jo Hui-sun（赵羲纯）(see[20] for his contributions), the study of traditional mathematics in the Joseon Dynasty came to an end.

V. Conclusions

Jiuzhang Suanshu begins with the mathematical structure of rational numbers. Using the field of rational numbers, one can solve all the word problems relating to linear equations, including systems of linear equations. Thus, they can solve the word problems of the nine chapters except *Shaoguang* and *Gougu* chapters, which lead to higher degree polynomial equations. Indeed, the extractions of square and cuber roots imply the theory of equations and their solutions as shown in *tianyuanshu* and *zengcheng kaifangfa* later. Frequent changes of Chinese dynasties, the development of Chinese mathematics were rather intermittent, but they always pay attentions to the theory of equations as shown by the theory of the Song-Jin-Yuan development. By the development in the 19th century, they did finally clarify the theory although it is rather too late.

Unlike the Chinese dynasties, the Joseon Dynasty has a long history of more than 500 years, although it experienced devastating foreign invasions. Based on *Suanxue Qimeng*, Joseon mathematicians did establish their own development. Although *Jiuzhang* was introduced to Joseon in the 19th century, they could retain the Liu Hui's *Jiuzhang Suanshu* by *Yang Hui Suanfa*.

We could understand the fundamental structure of East Asian mathematics through Guo Shuchun's comprehensive research on *Jiuzhang Suanshu* and others. We would like to extend our deep gratitude for his kind supports and encouragements for our research.

---

[19] HONG Sung Sa, 朝鲜算学堆垛术. *The Korean Journal for History of Mathematics*, 19(2)(2006), 1-24.

[20] HONG Sung Sa, HONG Young Hee, LEE Seung On, *Siyuan Yujian* in the Joseon Mathematics, *Journal for History of Mathematics* 30(4)(2017), 203-219.

"Incorrect corrections" by ancient editors——a challenge in Chinese mathematical philology

Donald B. Wagner 华道安

Nordic Institute of Asian Studies, Copenhagen 北欧亚洲研究所, www.nias.ku.dk
Department of Archaeology, Sichuan University 四川大学历史文化学院考古学系
Home address: Jernbanegade 9B, DK－3600 Frederikssund, Denmark

www.donwagner.dk, dwag@alum.mit.edu
28 January 2021

Abstract Corruptions of ancient scientific texts stem not only from banal scribal errors, but also from mistaken emendations by well-intentioned early editors. This article considers mathematical examples in three Chinese texts of the Song-Yuan period: *Hefang tongyi* 河防通议, *Mengxi bitan* 梦溪笔谈, and *Shushu jiuzhang* 数书九章.

For Professor Guo Shuchun — Thank you for your friendship, and thank you for your years of research and many publications.

Scholars have long been aware of *scribal errors* in ancient texts, and generations of philologists have developed sophisticated ways of dealing with them. In mathematical texts in particular, the mathematical context is very often a sure guide in identifying this simple type of error.

But historians of Chinese science and technology must also take seriously the possibility of more complex corruptions of their texts, in which an ancient editor, encountering a text that he does not understand, incorrectly 'corrects' the text to make 'sense' to him. Many ancient Chinese technical texts were difficult to read even in their own time. These became increasingly difficult as the centuries passed between then and now; scribes and editors preparing new editions must often have had difficulties in dealing with them, and most often these later editions are all that we have today. I have pointed out several possible examples of this type of problem in my study of ancient Chinese ferrous metallurgy [Wagner 2008, 51 n. g; 52 n. n; 217; 274 n. 126; 346].

In this article I take up three examples of 'incorrect corrections' in mathematical texts of the Song and Yuan periods. In dealing with editor-introduced textual errors, the proper procedure would seem to be: (1) propose a hypothesis as to the intention of the original text, and argue for its historical plausibility; (2) propose a hypothetical course of events that produced, from this, the text as it now appears, suggest how the editor may have interpreted it, and argue for the historical plausibility of the hypothesis. Both requirements are difficult, and will often be impossible, but in these three cases I believe I am able to give plausible hypotheses to explain obvious errors.

In some earlier studies I have referred to this challenge as that of 'the ignorant editor'. Colleagues and friends, some themselves editors, have objected to this perceived slur, so I now refer neutrally to 'incorrect corrections'.

1. Construction of a canal in *Hefang tongyi*

Hefang tongyi 河防通议, 'Comprehensive discussion of Yellow River conservancy', was edited by Shakeshi 沙克什 (1278—1351, also called Shansi 赡思), a man of Arabic ancestry employed by the Yuan state in posts concerned with river conservancy. In its present form it consists of six 'sections' (*men* 门), divided into a total of 68 'headings' (*mu* 目). The first five sections concern practical engineering and administration, while the last, 'Calculation' (*Suanfa men* 算法门), concerns the mathematical techniques needed for this work.[1]

The complex history of the text has been studied by Guo Shuchun (1997).[2] Shakeshi had at hand two versions of a *Hefang tongyi* by Shen Li 沈立, completed shortly after 1048. These he called the 'Directorate version' (*jian ben* 监本) and the 'Kaifeng version' (*Bian ben* 汴本). (The Directorate version had previously been in the possession of the Directorate of Waterways, *Dushui jian* 都水监, of the Jin 金 dynasty.) He writes in his preface that both versions were badly organized and difficult to consult; therefore, 'I have removed redundancies, corrected errors, reduced the number of sections, and organized it in categories.'

Shakeshi's book was completed and printed in 1321. There seems to be no way of knowing whether other editions were printed. It was copied into the great Ming encyclopedia *Yongle dadian* 永乐大典 (completed 1408), and this copy was copied into the Qing collectaneum *Siku quanshu* 四库全书 (completed 1782). All extant versions are ultimately based on the *Siku quanshu* version; no earlier version is now extant. This version, however, contains many banal scribal errors which are corrected in the *Shoushan'ge congshu* 守山阁丛书 and *Congshu jicheng* 丛书集成 editions. (All three editions are available on-line at www.scribd.com/collections/3809180/.)

Comments in smaller characters are scattered throughout the text, and these occasionally include clues to their origin. Some clearly originate in the Directorate version, and some — those which explicitly compare the Directorate version with the Kaifeng version — are clearly by Shakeshi. Some refer to events after 1321, and must therefore be by some later editor, perhaps the *Yongle dadian* or *Siku quanshu* editors. The few comments in the 'Calculation' section do not happen to provide such clues, and may originate from any of these three sources.

1.1. Calculations for the construction of a canal

Many of the 27 problems in the 'Calculation' section are quite simple, and several give incorrect methods and answers. The problem we are concerned with here is the last and most complex, which concerns the distribution of work among several groups of workers. The Chinese text is reproduced in Figure 13, and a translation is given in Appendix 1.

The problem concerns the construction of a canal, shown here in Figure 1.

One group of labourers is to excavate part of it, *IJKLHEFG*, called the 'cut'. The dimensions and volume of the whole canal are given, together with the volume of the cut. The dimensions of the cut are required.

This is a simplified version of a practical problem in construction administration: the available la-

---

[1] The best discussion of the 'Calculation' section that I am aware of is that of Guo Shuchun [1997]. It has also been discussed by Yabuuchi Kiyoshi [1965], Guo Tao [1994], and three others, cited by him, whose publications have not been available to me. None deals with the 'confusion' noted by Guo Shuchun.

[2] Other interpretations of Shakeshi's preface are possible, but here I follow Guo Shuchun.

bour determines the volume to be excavated, and the labourers must be told how far they are to dig, x in Figure 1.

The given dimensions are:

$l = 500$ *bu* 步 ('paces') $= 2,500$ *chi* 尺 ('feet') ≈ 780 metres

$a_1 = 1,040$ *chi*

$a_2 = 890$ *chi*

$b_1 = 1,000$ *chi*

$b_2 = 850$ *chi*

$d = 1$ *zhang* 丈 $= 10$ *chi*

The text relates the two volumes to numbers of 'labour units' (*gong* 功), which seem to correspond to man-days. By the particular administrative norm invoked in the text, one labour unit corresponds to 40 cubic *chi* of the canal, and the volumes of the canal and the cut are:

$V = 590,625$ labour units $\times 40$ chi^3/labour unit $= 23,625,000$ chi^3

$W = 144,450$ labour units $\times 40$ chi^3/labour unit $= 5,778,000$ chi^3

The answers given are:

$x = 120$ *bu*

$a_3 = 926$ *chi*

$b_3 = 886$ *chi*

The text does not state explicitly whether the work starts at the western or the eastern end of the canal, but these answers indicate that the cut is at the western end, for they satisfy equations derived by consideration of similar triangles,

$$\frac{a_3 - a_2}{a_1 - a_2} = \frac{b_3 - b_2}{b_1 - b_2} \tag{1}$$

However, the answers appear to be incorrect, for calculation of the volume of the cut from these dimensions gives

$$\frac{dx}{4}(a_2 + a_3 + b_2 + b_3) = \frac{1}{4} \times 10 \times 600 \times (890 + 926 + 850 + 886)$$

$$= 5,328,000 \ chi^3$$

$$\neq W = 5,778,000 \ chi^3 \tag{2}$$

The text arrives at the given answers using the classical Chinese algebra of polynomials known as *Tianyuan yi* 天元一. Briefly, a column of numbers on the counting board represents what we would call the coefficients of a polynomial equation (see e. g. Mei Rongzhao [1966]; Chemla [1982]; Martzloff [1997, 143—149]; Yabuuchi [1965, 303—304]). The manipulations described in the text result in a column of numbers represented by 'counting rods' (*chou* 筹) on the 'counting board':

15   一 ⅢⅠ

94,500   Ⅲ ≡ ⅢⅠ ○ ○

11,556,000 一 Ⅰ ≡ ⅢⅠ ⊥ ○ ○ ○

which is equivalent to the equation

$$15x^2 + 94,500x = 11,556,000 \tag{3}$$

A root of this equation is found using the ancient Chinese version of Horner's Method (see e. g. Wagner [2017]),

$$x = 120 \ bu$$

The derivation of (3) uses a concept seen several times in the chapter, the *ting* 停, a solid which has the same volume as a given solid, but whose volume is easier to calculate. (I am not aware of any other Chinese mathematical text that uses this word with this meaning.) In this case the *ting* is shown in Figure 2.

The widths at the two ends of the *ting* are calculated:

$$c_1 = \frac{a_1+b_1}{2} = \frac{1,040+1,000}{2} = 1,020 \ chi \tag{4}$$

$$c_2 = \frac{a_2+b_2}{2} = \frac{890+850}{2} = 870 \ chi \tag{5}$$

The rate of change of the width of the *ting* along its length from west to east is then

$$K = \frac{c_1-c_2}{l} = \frac{1,020-870 \ chi}{500 \ bu} = 0.3 \ chi/bu \tag{6}$$

Let $x=$ the length of the cut in *bu*. Then the width of the *ting* at the cut is

$$c_3 = Kx + c_2 = 0.3x + 870 \ chi \tag{7}$$

Then, including a conversion of *bu* to *chi*, twice the volume of the cut of the *ting* is

$$dx(c_3+c_1) \times 5 \ chi/bu = 2W \ [!?] \tag{9}$$

$$15x^2 + 94,500x = 2W = 11,556,000 \ chi^3 \tag{10}$$

This equation has one positive root, $x=120 \ bu$. The breadth of the *ting* at the cut is then calculated, in a curiously roundabout way:

$$c_3 = 2\frac{W}{dx} - c_1 = 2 \times \frac{5,778,000 \ chi^3}{120 \ bu \times 5 \ \frac{chi}{bu} \times 10 \ chi} - 1,020 \ chi = 906 \ chi \tag{11}$$

This quantity could have been calculated more simply, using (7):

$$c_3 = \frac{x}{l}(c_1-c_2) + c_2 = \frac{120 \ bu}{500 \ bu} \times (1,020 \ chi - 870 \ chi) = 906 \ chi \tag{12}$$

Calculating further,

$$a_3 = \frac{1}{2}(2c_3 + \Delta) = 926 \ chi \tag{13}$$

$$b_3 = \frac{1}{2}(2c_3 - \Delta) = 886 \ chi \tag{14}$$

where $\Delta = a_1 - b_1 = a_2 - b_2 = 40 \ chi$.

Using (13) and (14) requires that the difference between widths is the same, Δ, throughout the length of the canal. If instead a_3 and b_3 had been calculated using (1), this requirement would not have been necessary.

1.2. 'Confusion'

'*Attentive readers have undoubtedly been able to see that this reasoning is confused.*' [Guo Shuchun, 1997, 229]. Equation (9) is not correct: we should expect c_2 rather than c_1 here.

Guo Shuchun's solution of this confusion assumes that it was the original author who was confused, and that, since (9) and (11) include references to c_1, the cut proceeded from the eastern end of the canal rather than the western. Correcting equation (9), he arrives at the equations for this situation, corresponding to (9) and (10),

$$dx(2c_1 - Kx) \times 5 \ chi/bu = 2W$$

$$-15x^2 + 102,000x = 11,556,000 \ chi^3$$

and the answers,

$$x \approx 115.25 \ bu$$

$$a_3 \approx 1,005.38 \ chi$$

$$b_3 \approx 965.38 \ chi$$

If we follow Guo Shuchun's reasoning, but assume that the cut proceeded from west to east (as I have argued above, equation (1)), rather than east to west, the calculation requires correction of three equations, (9), (10), and (11):

$$dx(c_3+c_2) \times 5 \frac{chi}{bu} = 2W \qquad (9')$$

$$15x^2 + 87{,}000x = 11{,}556{,}000 \qquad (10')$$

$$x \approx 129.917 \ bu$$

$$c_3 = \frac{2W}{dx} - c_2 \approx \frac{11{,}556{,}000 \ chi^3}{129.917 \ bu \times 5 \frac{chi}{bu} \times 10 \ chi} - 870 \ chi \approx 909.98 \ chi \qquad (11')$$

Then, using (13) and (14),

$$a_3 = \frac{1}{2}(2c_3 + \Delta) \approx 229.98 \ chi$$

$$b_3 = \frac{1}{2}(2c_3 - \Delta) \approx 189.98 \ chi$$

1.3. An alternative hypothesis

A third possibility, which I ask my friend Guo Shuchun to consider, is that the original text gave a correct calculation, that a scribal error corrupted it, and that a later editor, perhaps Shakeshi himself, attempting to make sense of the corrupt text, corrupted it further.

Under this assumption it is a reasonable inference that the given answers have not been corrupted, for they satisfy equation (1). This also indicates that the work proceeded from west to east, as shown in Figures 1 and 2. Then the volume of the cut was $W^* = 5{,}328{,}000 \ chi^3$ (equation (2)), and therefore the number of work units assigned was given in the original text as $5{,}328{,}000/40 = 133{,}200$ rather than the 144,450 of the present text. Therefore, in two places in the text (noted in the translation, Appendix 1), the phrase *da kuo* 大阔, 'larger breadth' (c_1) must be taken to be an error for *xiao kuo* 小阔, 'smaller breadth' (c_2). Then correcting equations (9)–(11) and the given intermediate results gives the following calculation:

$$dx(c_3+c_2) \times 5 \ chi/bu = 2W^* \qquad (9'')$$

$$15x^2 + 87{,}000x = 10{,}656{,}000 \ chi^3 \qquad (10'')$$

This has one positive root,

$$x = 120 \ bu$$

And

$$c_3 = 2\frac{W^*}{xd} - c_2 = 2 \times \frac{5{,}328{,}000 \ chi^3}{120 \ bu \times 5 \frac{chi}{bu} \times 10 \ chi} - 870 \ chi = 906 \ chi \qquad (11'')$$

Finally, using either (1) or the method in the text, (13) and (14),

$$a_3 = 926 \ chi$$

$$b_3 = 886 \ chi$$

These are the answers given in the text.

How may the text have reached its present state? My hypothesis is that the original text gave the number of work units as 133,200 and gave a calculation equivalent to (9″)–(11″). At some point in its history a scribal error crept in: a substitution of *dakuo* 大阔, 'larger breadth', for *xiaokuo* 小阔, 'smaller breadth', in the statement of (9″). This amounts to changing (9″) to (9).

The editor discovers that the given answers do not satisfy (10):

$$15\times(120)^2+94,500\times120=11,556,000\neq2\times40\times133,200$$

He therefore changes the number of work units to $144,450=11,556,000/(2\times40)$. Now the root of the equation is the given answer, $x=120$ *bu*.

He then calculates c_3, a_3, and b_3, and discovers that (11″) and (13)−(14) do not result in the given answers. But he finds that subtracting c_1 instead of c_2 in (11″) does result in the given answers. He therefore changes *xiaokuo* to *dakuo* in the statement of (11″), turning it into (11).

1.4. Correct results from an incorrect calculation

The fact that a correct c_3 comes out of a calculation containing three errors has an interesting explanation. From (6) and (9), and for simplicity letting x be measured in *chi* rather than *bu*,

$$2W=dKx^2+dx(c_1+c_2)=d(c_1-c_2)\frac{x^2}{l}+dx(c_1+c_2)$$

Considering similar triangles in the same way as in (1),

$$\frac{c_3-c_2}{c_1-c_2}=\frac{x}{l}$$

So that

$$c_1-c_2=\frac{l}{x}(c_3-c_2)$$
$$2W=dx(c_3-c_2)+dx(c_1+c_2)=dx(c_3+c_1)$$

Then the calculation (11) gives

$$\frac{2W}{dx}-c_1=(c_3+c_1)-c_1=c_3$$

So whatever volume W^{**} is chosen for W, the solution x^{**} of (9), entered into (11), will give the same value of c_3. This would not be the case if c_3 were calculated using the simpler calculation, (12).

2. Arc measurement in Mengxi bitan

Histories of Chinese mathematics generally state that Shen Gua 沈括 (1031−1095) in his book of jottings *Mengxi bitan* 梦溪笔谈 ('Dream Brook essays')[3] gave this approximation for the length of an arc of a circle:

$$s\approx b+\frac{2h^2}{d} \quad (17)$$

where (see Figure 3) h is the sagitta, b is the chord, and d is the diameter of the circle. This is historically plausible, for (17) is equivalent to an approximation for the area of a circle segment in the *Jiuzhang suanshu* 九章算术 ('Arithmetic in nine chapters', perhaps 1st century CE),[4]

$$S\approx\frac{bh+h^2}{2} \quad (18)$$

A derivation of (17) from (18) proceeds by observing that the area of the circle section $OAQB$, $\frac{sd}{4}$, is equal to the sum of the areas of the segment AQB and the triangle OAB. The approximation (17) is also equivalent to a proto-trigonometric formula in the 13th-century calendrical text *Shou shi li*

---

[3] On Shen Gua and his book see especially Sivin [1995]; also Holzman [1958].
[4] Guo Shuchun [2009, 65−68]; Chemla and Guo [2004, 141; 191−193; 773].

授时历 ('Canon of the season-granting system'),⁵ and was explicitly used by Zhu Shijie 朱世杰 in a book published in 1303, *Siyuan yujian* 四元玉鉴 (Guo Shuchun et al. [2006, 508−511]; Hoe [1977, 297−298]).

However, this is not precisely the formula given in Shen Gua's text. There is a phrase in the text which must be removed to obtain (17); but a comment in smaller characters includes this phrase and gives a very odd interpretation.

All modern studies of *Mengxi bitan* assume that the comments in smaller characters scattered through the text are by Shen Gua himself, but I shall argue here that at least this comment was added by someone else. I conjecture that the original text, including the elided phrase, gave a more complex formula than (17), that some later edition of the book contained a corrupted version of this formula, and that someone published this corrupted version with a comment that attempted to make sense of it.

2.1. The text

The text in question is in chapter 18, 'Arts' (*Jiyi* 技艺) of *Mengxi bitan*. It is reproduced in Figure 4 from the earliest extant version, dated 1305 [*Yuan kan Mengxi bitan*, 1975, 18, 4−7; cf. Hu Daojing [1962, 574−587, § 301]. The raised line, p. 4, line 4, indicates the start of a paragraph; this paragraph continues to the last line of p. 7. None of the versions included in Hu Daojing's critical edition (which are all later than this one) has any important differences from this version.

The paragraph starts with an introduction in a form often seen in Shen Gua's book, with first a statement of what is known or commonly thought on a topic, then the introduction of something new:

> In the arts of calculation, the methods for calculating volumes in [cubic] *chi* 尺 ['feet'], for example ... [list of geometric forms], are complete for all object forms. There remains the technique for 'volumes with interstices' [*xi ji* 隙积]. ... (p. 4, lines 4−6)

The text goes on to give methods for calculating the volumes of several geometric forms, then gives a method for 'volumes with interstices', i.e. stacked spheres or similar objects. This is equivalent to a method for summation of a finite series, but treated as a geometric rather than an algebraic problem.⁶

After this, on page 6, line 5, comes what may originally have been the start of a new paragraph:

> Of methods of measuring *mu* 亩 ['acres', i.e., calculating areas], the square, the round, the crooked, and the straight have been perfected. There remains the technique of 'assembling a circle' [*hui yuan* 会圆]. Since a circular field can be 'broken' [*zhe* 折], it should be possible to assemble [*hui* 会] [the pieces] and restore [*fu* 复] the circle. Among the ancient methods there is only the method of 'splitting the circle in the middle' [? *zhong po yuan* 中破圆] to break it, in which the error can be as much as threefold. I have devised a different technique for breaking and assembling [*zhe hui zhi shu* 折会之术]. (p. 6, lines 5−8)

---

⁵ $h^4 + (d^2 - 2sd)h^2 - d^3h + s^2d^2 \approx 0$, h being approximated, given s and d, by Horner's method [Sivin, 2009, 66−67]. A derivation is given by Martzloff [1997, 328−329].

⁶ Martzloff [1997, 16 fn. 17] gives a very brief summary of the method. Andréa Bréard [1999, 100−118; 357−360] (note also [1998; 2008]) gives a full translation of the main text of the paragraph and analyzes this first part in detail, but does not deal with the difficulties discussed here. Translations are also given by Fu Zong and Li Lunzu [1974] and Hu Daojing et al. [2008, 531−537]; neither deals with these difficulties.

This passage concerns areas, and has no relation to the preceding text on volumes, so the fact that it is not a separate paragraph (does not start on a new line with the initial character raised) may perhaps be a scribal error. (But note the 'two categories' mentioned further on in the text.) Further, it has no relation to what follows. We should expect an explanation of what 'breaking and assembling' means, and how it is done, but neither breaking nor assembling nor areas are mentioned again. Clearly something has been dropped out of the text here, and there appears to be no way of determining with any certainty what Shen Gua meant by *hui yuan*.

Then, without introduction, follows a method for approximating the length of an arc. See Figure 3: first b is calculated, given d and h, using the Pythagorean theorem:

> Lay out the diameter [d] of the circular field and halve it; let this be the hypotenuse [of a right triangle]. Then from the halved diameter subtract [*jian* 减] 'the value of the cut' [*suo ge shu* 所割数, i.e. the sagitta, h], and let the difference be the leg [*gu* 股, the longer leg of the triangle]. Multiply each by itself and subtract [*chu* 除!][7] the [squared] leg from the [squared] hypotenuse. Extract the square root [*kaifang chu* 开方除] of the difference to make the base [*gou* 勾, the shorter leg of the triangle]. Double this to make the 'direct diameter' [*zhi jing* 直径, i.e. the chord, b] of the 'cut field' [*ge tian* 割田, the circle segment]. (p. 6, line 8—p. 7, line 1)

This calculation is

$$b = 2\sqrt{\left(\frac{d}{2}\right)^2 - \left(\frac{d}{2} - h\right)^2} \tag{19}$$

which is correct. Then the length of the arc is calculated:

> Multiply the 'value of the cut' [h] by itself, **shift one place** [*tui yi wei* 退一位, i.e., divide by 10], and double it. Then divide [*chu* 除] the result by the diameter [d] and add the 'direct diameter' [b] to make the arc [s] of the 'cut field'. (p. 7, lines 1—3)

If one chooses to ignore the very odd 'shift one place', this calculation is equivalent to (17). After this follows a statement whose meaning is not clear, but may perhaps be a reference to some process of successive approximations (Bréard [1999, 100—118; 357—360; note also [1998; 2008]):

> If it is cut again [*zai ge* 再割], [the calculation] is the same. Subtracting the previous 'value of the cut' [h] gives the 'value of the second cut' [*zai ge zhi shu* 再割之数]. (p. 7, lines 3—4)

Then there is a comment in smaller characters which will be translated and discussed directly below. The text in large characters then concludes:

---

[7] Shortly before this, the word used for 'subtract' is *jian* 减. *Chu* 除 is occasionally seen in classical Chinese mathematical texts, as here, with the meaning 'subtract', but its more usual mathematical meanings are 'divide' and 'extract a root'. It is a surprise to see the word used with the meaning 'subtract' here, since it is used twice shortly after, respectively with the meanings 'extract a square root' and 'divide'.

> These two categories are precise techniques which the ancient writers did not reach. My idle ambition lies in this. (p. 7, lines 9—10)

'These two categories' may be 'volumes with interstices' and 'assembling a circle', or the phrase may refer to something in a missing part of the original text.

2.1.1. The comment

The comment gives a concrete example, with $d=10$ bu and $h=2$ bu. First the chord b is calculated from d and h:

> Suppose there is a circular field with diameter [$d=$] 10 bu, and one wishes to cut [ge 割] [$h=$] 2 bu. Letting the halved diameter be the hypotenuse, 5 bu, and multiplying this by itself gives 25. Subtracting the amount cut, [$h=$] 2 bu, from the halved diameter, letting the difference, 3 bu, be the leg, and multiplying this by itself, gives 9. Subtracting this from [the square] outside the hypotenuse [xian wai 弦外, i.e. the square on the hypotenuse, 25 bu^2], one has 16. Extracting the square root gives 4 bu, which is the base. Doubling this makes [$b=8$ bu $=$] the 'direct diameter' of the cut [the chord of the segment]. (p. 7, lines 4—6)

This calculation follows (19) above,

$$b=2\sqrt{\left(\frac{10\ bu}{2}\right)^2-\left(\frac{10\ bu}{2}-2\ bu\right)^2}=8\ bu$$

So far there have been no difficulties, but from here on the comment is very difficult to explain:

> Multiplying the 'value of the cut', [$h=$] 2 bu, by itself gives 4, and doubling this gives 8. **Shifting upward one place** [tui shang yi wei 退上一位[8]] gives 4 chi 尺. (p. 7, lines 6—7)

The calculation described here gives:

$$\frac{2\times(2\ bu)^2}{10}=0.8\ bu^2$$

but the result is stated to be 4 chi. It is likely that this value was arrived at in an attempt to convert square bu to square chi by multiplying by 5 chi/bu instead of the correct 25 chi^2/bu^2.

The rest is mere nonsense:

> This [4 chi] is to be divided by the diameter [d], but in this case the diameter, 10 [bu], is an excessive value [ying shu 盈数], and it is not possible to divide, so one simply uses 4 chi. Adding this to the 'direct diameter' [b] gives the arc [s] of the cut [the circle segment]. One obtains in all the diameter of the circle [yuan jing 圆径, sic! i.e. the arc of the segment, s $\approx$], 8 bu 4 chi. (p. 7, lines 7—8)

---

[8] The text has bei 倍, 'double, multiple', which, following Hu Daojing [1962, 575], I take to be a scribal error for wei 位. The characters are graphically similar, the comment refers directly to a parallel sentence in the main text with wei, and the result of the calculation appears in fact to be a division by 10.

The commentator seems to believe that, in a division, if the divisor is greater than the dividend, the quotient equals the dividend. This erroneous calculation fortuitously gives the same result as using (17) would give:

$$s \approx b + \frac{2h^2}{d} = 8\ bu + \frac{2 \times (2\ bu)^2}{10\ bu} = 8.8\ bu = 8\ bu + 4\ chi$$

The comment concludes:

> If one cuts again, this method is also followed. If the diameter is 20 *bu*, to calculate the value of the arc, one should halve it and then, as stated, 'divide by the diameter of the circle'. (p. 7, lines 8—9)

What this might mean is not at all clear to me, and I suspect that it may be further nonsense.

2.2. A hypothesis

It is unlikely that the astronomer and polymath Shen Gua wrote the strange comment translated here. It is more plausible that a later editor wrote it in order to make a kind of sense of a corrupted version of an original text by Shen Gua.

The most common assumption is that the original text gave the formula (17), and that the corruption consisted of the insertion of the phrase 'shift one place'. The comment then attempts to make sense of the corrupted text. Some strange corruptions have occurred in ancient texts, but the insertion of an entirely irrelevant phrase, not found elsewhere in the book, is surely not a very probable scribal error.

I shall suggest another hypothesis to explain Shen Gua's text. The extant part of the text is explicitly a calculation of the length of an arc, and a possible explanation of the problematic phrase 'shift one place' is that it was originally part of a more complex formula. I propose that this formula may have been equivalent to

$$s \approx b + \frac{2h^2}{d} + 0.2h \tag{20}$$

which is (17) with the addition of the term $0.2h$.[9] This is a much better approximation. See Figure 5: using (17), the maximum error is 5.42%; using (20), the maximum error is 1.86%, and for most of the range of h the error is less than 1%.

An ancient Chinese mathematical writer could have expressed multiplication by 0.2 in a number of ways, but one obvious way would be to write 'shift one place and double it', and this exact phrase does in fact occur in the text: *tui yi wei bei zhi* 退一位倍之. It is therefore plausible that Shen Gua's original formula might have been equivalent to (20).

There is no historical evidence that a formula like (20) was ever used in ancient China (or anywhere else), and this is a serious argument against the hypothesis. Nevertheless, it was not a difficult formula to discover.

Using modern software it was of course simple to graph the absolute error of (17) against h and

---

[9] This is reminiscent of Shen Gua's use, in the first part, of a known formula plus a corrective term to obtain a new result. Bréard 1998: 116; 1999: 153; 2008: 82.

observe that the curve lies close to a straight line with slope -0.2 (see Figure 6). Would and could Shen Gua have sought and found the same fact?

First, it is interesting to note that Zhu Shijie 朱世杰 in 1303 used an improvement of (18), the formula in *Jiuzhang suanshu* for the area of a circle segment, by the addition of a corrective term.[10] It is plausible, therefore, that Shen Gua, a bit more than two centuries before this, may similarly have been interested in improving the related approximation (17).

Chinese astronomers were accustomed to fitting linear, quadratic, and cubic relations to empirical data; in fact Shen Gua appears to mention such an interpolation in one of his jottings.[11] If he had sufficient data on the lengths of arcs in relation to chords and sagittae he would have been able to discover (3) quite easily. Such data could have been acquired empirically, for example by directly measuring arcs of a large circular object: a cartwheel 1 metre in diameter would have allowed sufficient precision. Or Shen Gua could have calculated the lengths of several arcs to any desired precision using Liu Hui's method of inscribed polygons (Guo Shuchun [2009, 64–66]; Chemla and Guo [2004, 148–149; 193]).

The mention of 'cutting again' in Shen Gua's text suggests that the original text might in some way have been concerned with successive approximations: the same phrase is used by Liu Hui in his calculation of π (Guo Shuchun [2009, 45–53]; Chemla and Guo [2004, 145–148; 176–184]). In that case it is important to note that if Shen Gua used (20) in, for example, a calculation of π by successive approximations, he would not have obtained good results. As can be seen in Figure 5, for very small arcs the error using (20) is much larger than the error using (17).

3. The area of a banana leaf in *Shushu jiuzhang*

The mathematician Qin Jiushao 秦九韶 (ca. 1202–1261) in his *Shushu jiuzhang* 数书九章[12] gives an incorrect and very odd approximation formula for the area of 'a field shaped like a banana leaf'. It seems that hardly anyone, ancient or modern, has attempted to explain the formula. The only attempt to deal with it that I know of is by Qian Baocong [1966, 84–85], described further below. Libbrecht [1973, 108–109] gives a short account of Qian Baocong's suggestion, but goes no further.

These scholars worked long before interactive mathematical software became widely available and made extensive experimentation possible. After a great deal of experimentation I propose below an explanation of Qin Jiushao's formula.

The term *jiaoyetian* 蕉叶田, 'banana leaf field', does not to my knowledge occur anywhere else in extant classical Chinese mathematical texts. Judging from Qin Jiushao's own illustration, seen in Figure 14 below, it seems certain that the term refers to the intersection of two circles of equal radius, Figure 7.

---

[10] $S \approx \frac{1}{2}h(h+b) + \frac{(\pi-3)b^2}{8}$, which Zhu Shijie uses with two different values of π (Guo Shuchun et al. [2006, 594–597]; Hoe [1977, 295–296; 1978: 149]; Martzloff [1997, 327 (note typographical error)]). The added term is an exact expression for the error of the *Jiuzhang suanshu* approximation in the case of a semicircle, $b = \frac{h}{2}$.

[11] *Yuankan Mengxi bitan* [1975, 7: 19–22]; Hu Daojing [1962: 304–305, § 128]; Hu Daojing et al. [2008, 210–215]; Li Yan [1957, 77]. See also e.g. Qian Baocong [1964, 103–107].

[12] Libbrecht [1973, 2] translates this book title as 'Mathematical treatise in nine sections'.

3.1. Qin Jiushao's approximation

Qin Jiushao's text is reproduced in Figure 14 and translated in Appendix 2. His approximation of the area of the 'banana leaf field' extracts the positive root of the quadratic equation (see Figure 7),

$$x^2 + \left[\left(\frac{c}{2}\right)^2 - \left(\frac{b}{2}\right)^2\right] x = 10(b+c)^3 \tag{21}$$

after which the area approximation is

$$A_{\text{Qin}} = \frac{x}{2} \tag{22}$$

The text gives the full numerical working for a particular case, and from this it is clear that the text of the formula is not corrupt; it is exactly as Qin Jiushao intended, and the text has been understood correctly.

The formula is not at all a good approximation, as we shall see further below, and (21) is dimensionally inconsistent.

3.2. The approximation in the *Jiuzhang suanshu*

The approximation for the area of a circle segment in the *Jiuzhang suanshu*, equation (18) above, gives the area of one-half of the banana leaf, so that an approximation for the area of the banana leaf is

$$A_{JZSS} = \frac{2bc + b^2}{4}$$

3.3. The accuracy of the two approximations

The particular case calculated in the text has $b = 34$ *bu* 步 ('paces') and $c = 576$ *bu*. The result is

$$A_{\text{Qin}} = 10,871 \frac{5,213}{63,070} \ bu^2 \approx 10,871.1 \ bu^2$$

The approximation of the *Jiuzhang suanshu* gives

$$A_{JZSS} = 10,081 \ bu^2$$

So that in this particular case the two approximations are close to each other. The exact value of the area is

$$A = \frac{2bc(b^2 - c^2) + (b^2 + c^2)\sin^{-1}\frac{2bc}{b^2+c^2}}{8b^2} = 13,065.1 \ bu^2$$

and the error percentages of the two approximations are in this case respectively 17% and 23%.

Plotting the values of A, A_{Qin}, and A_{JZSS} for $c = 576$ and the full range of b gives the curves shown in Figure 8. It can be seen immediately that the moderate accuracy of A_{Qin} for this particular case is fortuitous. The formula does not in fact give a useful approximation for the area.

Going further, Figure 9 plots the error percentages of the two approximations for various values of c.

3.4. Qian Baocong's modification of Qin Jiushao's formula

Qian Baocong [1966, 84—85] observes that if the constant term in (21) is changed to $\frac{10}{4}\left(\frac{b+c}{2}\right)^4$, a correct result would be obtained in the case $b = c$ (a circle with diameter c) and $\pi \approx \sqrt{10}$. However, Figures 10 and 11 show that the resulting equation,

$$x^2 + \left[\left(\frac{c}{2}\right)^2 - \left(\frac{b}{2}\right)^2\right]x = \frac{5}{32}(b+c)^4$$

$$A_{\text{Qian}} = \frac{x}{2}$$

is moderately accurate for $b > 0.4c$, but is not in general a useful approximation.

3.5. A hypothesis

Extensive experimentation with variations on Qin Jiushao's formula has led me to this approximation:

$$x^2 + \left[c^2 - \left(\frac{b}{2}\right)^2\right]x = b\left(\frac{b}{2}+c\right)^3 \tag{24}$$

$$A_{\text{new}} = \frac{x}{2} \tag{25}$$

which can be seen to be similar to (21)—(22). This is a fair approximation, as can be seen in Figure 12.

Note the interesting similarity between Figure 12 and the curves for A and A_{JZSS} in Figure 8. It turned out, to my amazement, that in fact A_{new} is *equivalent* to A_{JZSS}. It can be derived from A_{JZSS} as follows.

$$A \approx A_{\text{JZSS}} = \frac{b^2 + 2bc}{4} = \frac{1}{2}b\left(\frac{b}{2}+c\right)$$

$$A\left(\frac{b}{2}+c\right) \approx \frac{1}{2}b\left(\frac{b}{2}+c\right)^2$$

$$bA + 2cA \approx b\left(\frac{b}{2}+c\right)^2$$

Using $2c = b + 2(c - \frac{b}{2})$,

$$2bA + 2(c-\frac{b}{2})A \approx b\left(\frac{b}{2}+c\right)^2$$

Multiplying by $\frac{b}{2}+c$,

$$2bA\left(\frac{b}{2}+c\right) + 2\left[c^2 - \left(\frac{b}{2}\right)^2\right]A \approx b\left(\frac{b}{2}+c\right)^3$$

Again using the *Jiuzhang suanshu* approximation, $4A \approx 2b(\frac{b}{2}+c)$.

$$4A^2 + 2\left[c^2 - \left(\frac{b}{2}\right)^2\right]A \approx b\left(\frac{b}{2}+c\right)^3$$

And this is equivalent to (24)—(25).

The algebraic manipulations shown here would not have been impossible for a mathematician of the Song period. Quite another question is why he would have developed this more complicated formula, which gives exactly the same result as the *Jiuzhang suanshu* formula. He may have believed it to be more accurate, or he may simply have wished to 'show off' with a more complicated calculation.[13]

We can imagine that the original text, by a hypothetical mathematician *Jia* 甲, may have been something like this, equivalent to (24)－(25):

术曰:以长并半广,再自乘,又广乘之,为实。半广、长各自乘,所得相减,余为从方,一为从隅,开平方,半之,得积。

Somehow it ended up in Qin Jiushao's book with the first *ban* 半, 'half', moved to a later position and the second *guang* 广, 'breadth', changed to *shi* 十, 'ten':

术曰:以长并 广,再自乘,又十乘之,为实。半广、半长各自乘,所得相减,余为从方,一为从隅,开平方,半之,得积。

As to the sequence of events by which the first was transformed to the second, numerous scenarios can be imagined. Here is one. There might well have been an expectation that the breadth and height, b and c, would be treated symmetrically, leading a later mathematician or scribe, *Yi* 乙, to a text that amounts to

$$x^2 + \left[\left(\frac{c}{2}\right)^2 - \left(\frac{b}{2}\right)^2\right]x = b(b+c)^3$$

$$A_{Yi} = \frac{x}{2}$$

But when Qin Jiushao (or an intermediate writer, *Bing* 丙) received this text and applied the calculation to the case $b=34$ *bu*, $c=576$ *bu*, he obtained the result $A_{Yi}=27,878$ *bu*^{2}, which is far from $A_{JZSS}=10,081$ *bu*^{2}. In dealing with this problem he focused, for whatever reason, on the multiplication by the breadth in the linear term of the equation. Experimenting, he found that substituting a constant 10 for the breadth, b, gave the result $A_{Qin}=10,871$ *bu*, which is close to A_{JZSS}. He therefore emended the text to what we see in Qin Jiushao's book, amounting to the calculation

$$x^2 + \left[\left(\frac{c}{2}\right)^2 - \left(\frac{b}{2}\right)^2\right]x = 10(b+c)^3$$

$$A_{Qin} = \frac{x}{2}$$

but did not test the formula for other values of the breadth and length.

4. Closing remarks

If nothing else, I hope I have convinced readers that reference to 'incorrect corrections' may occasionally be necessary when attempting to explain passages in classical Chinese mathematical texts. There will be readers, I am sure, who feel that my explanations in these three particular cases are too lengthy and convoluted to be convincing. I can only ask them to provide better explanations for the

---

[13] An example of an unnecessarily complicated calculation in Qin Jiushao's book is a formula requiring numerical solution of a tenth-degree polynomial that can be immediately reduced to fifth degree, and is in fact equivalent to a cubic. Bai Shangshu [1966, 296－299]; Libbrecht [1973, 134－140].

challenges we encounter in these texts.

A reviewer of one of my books makes the accusation that my collaborator and I 'suspect an "ignorant editor" whenever comprehension problems in Chinese syntax arise.' This is not true and not fair, in fact a lie, but it does highlight a potential danger. A loose appeal to 'incorrect corrections' can explain away any problem, just as von Däniken's 'ancient astronauts' can explain away the Egyptian pyramids, the Delhi pillar, and much more.[14] To be useful and convincing, such an explanation must include rigorous arguments concerning the text, the mathematics, and the historical plausibility of the two hypotheses: the proposed original text and the series of textual changes that led to the text as we have it today. Readers will judge whether I have lived up to these requirements in the three cases taken up here.

Appendix 1: Translation of the *Hefang tongyi* text

The *Siku quanshu* text is reproduced in Figure 13. The text includes representations of the setup on the counting board, but these are obviously corrupted and will be ignored here. I have placed philological comments in footnotes and mathematical comments indented in the translation.

In the following see Figure 1.

Suppose a canal is to be opened. The straight length is $[l=]$ 500 *bu*. At the eastern end, the upper breadth is $[a_1=]$ 1,040 *chi* and the lower breadth is $[b_1=]$ 1,000 *chi*. At the western end, the upper breadth is $[a_2=]$ 890 *chi*, and the lower breadth is $[b_2=]$ 850 *chi*. The depth is the same [throughout], $[d=]$ 1 *zhang*. The total volume is $[V=]$ 23,625,000 [cubic] *chi*.

Note that 1 *zhang* 丈 = 2 *bu* 步 = 10 *chi* 尺 ≈ 3.1 metres.

The given total volume of the canal is correct:

$$V = \frac{1}{4} dl(a_1 + b_1 + a_2 + b_2) = \frac{1}{4} \times 10 \ chi \times 500 \ bu \times 5 \ chi/bu$$
$$\times (1,040 + 1,000 + 890 + 850 \ chi) = 23,625,000 \ chi^3$$

One labour unit [*gong* 功], when taking earth at 100 *bu*, is 40 [cubic] *chi*, and it is calculated that 590,625 labour units [will be used].

$$\frac{23,625,000 \ chi^3}{40 \ chi^3/\text{labour unit}} = 590,625 \text{ labour units}$$

It is desired to assign 144,450 labour units. What are the length and breadth of the cut [*jie* 截]?

The 'cut' is *IJKLHEFG* in Figure 1.

Here my hypothesis suggests that the original text had 133,200 work units, and a later editor changed this to 144,450.

---

[14] Erich von Däniken's *Chariots of the gods*, published in 1966, attempted to explain many ancient accomplishments as the work of visitors from outer space.

Answer: The length of the cut is $[x=]$ 120 *bu* and the breadth of the cut is $[c_3=]$ 906 *chi*.

The dimension c_3 is shown in Figure 2.

(The upper breadth of the cut is $[a_3=]$ 926 *chi*, and the lower breadth of the cut is $[b_3=]$ 886 *chi*.)[15]

Method: Lay out the upper and lower breadths at the eastern end $[a_1, b_1]$, add them together, and halve, obtaining $[c_1=]$ 1,020 *chi*, which is the larger breadth of the *ting* 停.

The *ting* is shown in Figure 2.

Further lay out the upper and lower breadths at the western end $[a_2, b_2]$, add them together, and halve, obtaining $[c_2=]$ 870 *chi*, which is the smaller breadth of the *ting*. Subtract this from the larger breadth of the *ting*; the remainder, 150 *chi*, is the difference between the breadths. Divide this by the straight length, $[l=]$ 500 *bu*, obtaining $[K=]$ 3 *cun*, which is the difference per *bu*.

$$c_1 = \frac{a_1+b_1}{2} = \frac{1,040+1,000}{2} = 1,020 \ chi$$

$$c_2 = \frac{a_2+b_2}{2} = \frac{890+850}{2} = 870 \ chi$$

$$K = \frac{c_1-c_2}{l} = \frac{1,020-870 \ chi}{500 \ bu} = 0.3 \ chi/bu$$

Let the *tianyuan* 天元 be $[x=]$ the length of the cut.[16]

This corresponds to letting the length of the cut be the unknown in a polynomial equation.

Multiply by the difference per *bu* $[K]$; this is the difference in breadths at the place where the cut stops.

$$Kx = c_3 - c_2$$

Add the smaller breadth of the *ting* $[c_2]$; this is $[c_3=]$ the breadth of the *ting* at the place of the cut.[17]

$$c_3 = Kx + c_2 = 0.3x + 870 \ chi$$

Add the larger breadth $[c_1]$ of the *ting*; these are the breadths at the two ends of the cut of the *ting*.[18]

$$c_3 + c_1 = Kx + c_1 + c_2 = 0.3x + 1,890 \ chi$$

My hypothesis suggests that *dakuo* 大阔, 'larger breadth' (c_1), is a scribal error for *xiaokuo* 小阔, 'smaller breadth' (c_2), in an earlier version of the text.

15　Comment in smaller characters in the text.
16　Excising one occurrence of *tian* 天.
17　Ignoring *gong* 共 and adding *kuo* 阔 after *ting* 停.
18　Reading *jie* 截 for *cang* 藏.

Multiply by [$d=$] the depth, 1 *zhang*; this makes twice the volume per *chi*.
$$d(c_3+c_1)=dKx+d(c_1+c_2)=3x+18,900\ chi^2$$
Multiply by 5 to make the twice the volume per *bu*.
$$d(Kx+c_1+c_2)\times 5\ chi/bu=(15\ chi^3/bu^2)x+94,500\ chi^3/bu$$
[Move this to the left].[19]

Multiply by the *yuanyi* 元一 [the unknown in the equation], [$x=$] the length of the cut. This makes twice the volume of the cut.
$$2W=dx(Kx+c_1+c_2)\times 5\ chi/bu=(15\ chi^3/bu^2)x^2+(94,500\ chi^3/bu)x$$
Convert the original labour units [assigned to] the cut to a volume [W] and multiply by 2, obtaining 11,556,000 [cubic] *chi*.[20]
$$2W=144,450\ \text{labour units}\times 40\ chi^3/\text{labour unit}\times 2=11,556,000\ chi^3$$
Combine [*xiang xiao* 相消] this with what was moved to the left,[21] obtaining 11,556,000 [cubic] *chi* as the *shi* 实 [the constant term of the equation], 94,500 [cubic] *chi* [per *bu*] [as the linear coefficient], and 15 as the *zongyu* 从隅 [the quadratic coefficient].

The equation is
$$(15\ chi^3/bu^2)x^2+(94,500\ chi^3/bu)x=11,556,000\ chi^3$$
This has one positive root, $x=120\ bu$.

Extract the square root, obtaining [$x=$] 120 *bu*; this is the length of the cut.

Set up the labour units of the cut and convert to a volume, obtaining [$W=$] 5,778,000 [cubic] *chi*.
$$W=144,450\ \text{labour units}\times 40\ chi^3/\text{labour unit}=5,778,000\ chi^3$$
Divide this by the length of the cut [x] converted to *chi*, obtaining 9,630 *chi*.
$$\frac{W}{x}=\frac{5,778,000\ chi^3}{120\ bu\times 5\ chi/bu}=9,630\ chi^2$$
Divide this by the depth, [$d=$] 1 *zhang*...[22] Double this and subtract the larger breadth of the *ting*, [$c_1=$] 1,020 *chi*. The remainder, 906 *chi*, is [$c_3=$] the breadth of the *ting* at the cut.
$$c_3=2d\frac{W}{x}-c_1=2\times\frac{9,630\ chi^2}{10\ chi}-1,020\ chi=906\ chi$$
My hypothesis suggests that an earlier text had here *xiaokuo* 小阔, 'smaller breadth' (c_1), and an editor changed this to *dakuo* 大阔, 'larger breadth' (c_2).

Double this, obtaining 1,812 *chi*...[23] Subtract the difference between the upper and lower breadth, [$\Delta=$] 40 *chi*; halve the remainder, obtaining 886 *chi*; this is the lower breadth of the cut. Add again 40 *chi*, obtaining 926 *chi*; this is the upper breadth of the cut.
$$\Delta=a_3-b_3=40\ chi$$
$$b_3=\frac{1}{2}(2c_3-\Delta)=886\ chi$$

---

[19] Necessary addition by the translator, see fn. 21 below.

[20] Reading *gui* 归 for *sao* 埽. Cf. the parallel usage in lines 7 and 9 on the same page.

[21] See fn. 21 above.

[22] Excising *wei ting jie kuo* 为停截阔, 'this is the breadth of the *ting* at the cut', which is not correct.

[23] Excising *bing shang xia jie kuo* 并上下截阔, 'add together the upper and lower breadths of the cut'. The result just obtained is this sum.

$$a_3 = b_3 + \Delta = 926 \ chi$$

In accordance with what was asked.

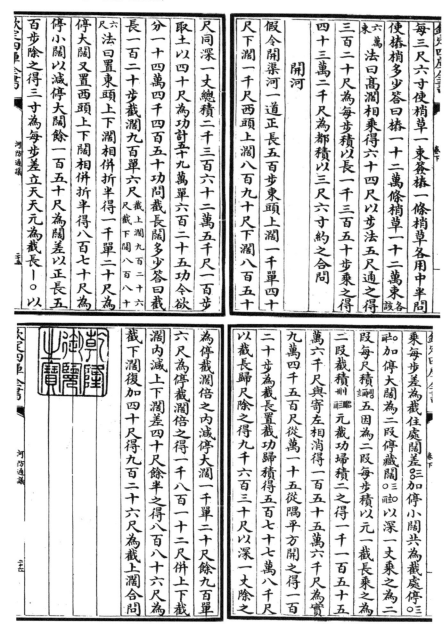

Figure 13 Text of Problem 27 in *Hefang tongyi*, reproduced from the *Siku quanshu* 四库全书 edition, *xia* 下, 24a-25b. www.scribd.com/document/105589337

Appendix 2: Translation of Qin Jiushao's text

The *Yijiatang congshu* text is reproduced in Figure 14.

In the following see Figure 7.

A field shaped like a banana leaf has central length $[c=]$ 576 *bu* and central breadth $[b=]$ 34 *bu*. The circumference is not known. What is the area in *mu*?

Answer: The area of the field is 45 *mu* 亩 1 *jiao* 角 $11\frac{5,213}{63,070}$ [square] *bu*.[24]

One *mu* is equal to 240 square *bu*, and one jiao is 60 square *bu*.

$$45\,mu \times 240\,bu^2/mu + 1\,jiao \times 60\,bu^2/jiao + 11\frac{5,213}{63,070}bu^2 \approx 10,871.08\,bu^2$$

Method: Multiply the sum of the breadth [*b*] and the length [*c*] twice by itself. Further multiply this by 10 to make the *shi* 实 [the constant term of the quadratic equation to be solved].

$$shi = 10(b+c)^3$$

Halve the breadth [*b*]; halve the length [*c*]; multiply each by itself. Subtract the one from the other; this is the *zongfang* 从方 [the linear coefficient].

$$zongfang = \left(\frac{c}{2}\right)^2 - \left(\frac{b}{2}\right)^2$$

Let the *zongyu* 从隅 [the quadratic coefficient] be 1.

$$zongyu = 1$$

Extract the square root and halve it to obtain the area.

$$x^2 + \left[\left(\frac{c}{2}\right)^2 - \left(\frac{b}{2}\right)^2\right]x = 10(b+c)^3$$

$$A_{Qin} = \frac{x}{2}$$

Working: Adding the length, [*c* =] 576 *bu*, and the breadth, [*b* =] 34 *bu*, gives 610. Multiplying this twice by itself gives 226,981,000 [cubic] *bu*. Shifting up one position, that is, multiplying by 10, gives 2,269,810,000 [cubic] *bu*, obtaining this number to be the shi.

$$shi = (576+34)^3 \times 10 = 2,269,810,000\,bu^3$$

Setting up the length, [*c* =] 576, and halving it gives 288. Multiplying this by itself gives 82,944, at the top [of the counting board]. Further setting up the breadth, [*b* =] 34 *bu*, and halving it gives 17. Multiplying this by itself gives 289. Subtracting this from the top, the difference is 82,655, and this is the *zongfang*.

$$zongfang = \left(\frac{576}{2}\right)^2 - \left(\frac{34}{2}\right)^2 = 82,655\,bu^2$$

Letting the *zongyu* be 1

The equation to be solved numerically is then

$$x^2 + 82,655x = 2,269,810,000$$

and extracting the square root gives 21,742 *bu* with a remainder of 10,426 [*bu*²].

The numbers on the counting board are now

the integral part of *x*	21,742
remainder (*shi*)	10,426
zongfang	126,139
zongyu	1

representing the equation

$$y^2 + 126,139y = 10,426$$

in which $y = x - 21,742$ is the fractional part of *x*.

---

[24] The fraction is printed in smaller characters.

Entering the *shang sheng yu* 商生隅 into the *fang*, and further adding the [single] rod of the [*zong*]*yu* [*yusuan* 隅算] gives 126,140 as the denominator.

I do not fully understand the terminology here, but clearly the calculation is
$$\text{denominator} = zongfang + zongyu = 126,139 + 1 = 126,140$$
and the numerator is the remainder of the *shi*, 10,426. This is an application of Qin Jiushao's usual approximation for the fractional part of a root of a polynomial [Libbrecht 1973, 198]:
If $0 < y < 1$ and
$$P(y) = \sum_{i=0}^{n} p_i y^i = 0$$
then
$$y \approx \frac{-p_0}{\sum_{i=1}^{n} p_i}$$

This is equivalent to the assumption that P is approximately linear in the interval $(0,1)$.

So $x \approx 21,742 \frac{10,426}{126,140} = 21,742.082,654,2$, which corresponds well to the exact root, $21,742.082,654,8$.

Halving both the remainder and [*shi* =] the area result of the root extraction gives the final result, $[A = x/2 =] 10,871 \frac{5,213}{63,070}$.

Here the intention is to calculate $A = x/2$, but an error creeps in. The correct result is $A = 10,871 \frac{5,213}{126,140}$, but the calculation mistakenly halves the denominator as well as the numerator, obtaining $10,871 \frac{5,213}{63,070}$.

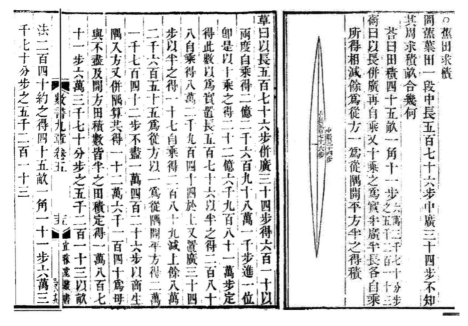

Figure 14 Text of Qin Jiushao's 'banana leaf' problem, reproduced
from the *Yijiatang congshu* 宜稼堂丛书 edition, 5, 14b-15b.
ctext.org/library.pl?if=en&file=83425&page=70

Dividing by the *mu* factor, 240 [bu^2/mu] and simplifying gives 45 *mu*, 1 *jiao*, $11\frac{5,213}{63,070}$ [square] *bu*.

References

All URLs in this article were confirmed in January 2021.

Bai Shangshu 白尚恕, 1966. Qin Jiushao cewang jiu wen zaoshu zhi tantao 秦九韶测望九问造术之探讨 (Qin Jiushao's methodology in nine problems of distant measurement). In: Qian Baocong et al. (eds.), Song Yuan shuxue shi lunwenji 宋元数学史论文集 (Essays on the history of mathematics in the Song and Yuan periods, 960－1368 CE). Kexue Chubanshe, Beijing, pp. 290-303.

Bréard, Andrea, 1998. Shen Gua's cuts. Taiwanese journal for philosophy and history of science 10, 141-162.

——, 1999. Re-Kreation eines mathematischen Konzeptes im chinesischen Diskurs: 'Reihen' vom 1. bis 19. Jahrhundert. Franz Steiner Verlag, Stuttgart.

——, 2008. A summation algorithm from 11th century China: Possible relations between structure and argument. In: A. Beckmann, C. Dimitracopoulos and B. Löwe (eds.), Logic and theory of algorithms. Berlin/Heidelberg: Springer, pp. 77-83. www.springer.com/gp/book/9783540694052

Chemla, Karine, 1982. Étude du livre 《Reflets des mesures du cercle sur la mer》. Dissertation, University of Paris XIII.

Chemla, Karine, and Guo Shuchun, 2004. Les neuf chapitres: Le classique mathématique de la Chine ancienne et ses commentaires. Dunod, Paris.

Fu Zong 傅宗 and Li Lunzu 李伦祖, 1974. Xijishu he huiyuanshu－Shen Gua《Mengxi bitan》pingzhu yize 隙积术和会圆术—《梦溪笔谈》评注一则 (The methods of 'volumes of interstices' and 'assembling a circle'－note on a jotting of Shen Gua). Xibei Shifan Daxue xuebao (Ziran kexue ban) 西北大学学报(自然科学版) (Journal of Northwestern Normal University [Natural science edition]) 1974.4, 17-22.

Guo Shuchun 郭书春, 1997. 《Hefang tongyi－Suanfa men》chutan《河防通议·算法门》初探 (Notes on the mathematical chapter of *Hefang tongyi*). Ziran kexue shi yanjiu 自然科学史研究 ('Studies in the history of natural sciences') 16.3, 223-232. English abstract, pp. 231-232.

Guo Shuchun 郭书春 (ed.), 2009. Jiuzhang suanshu yizhu 九章算术译注 (critical edition of *Jiuzhang suanshu*). In: Zhongguo gudai keji mingzhu yizhu congshu 中国古代科技名著译注丛书. Shanghai Guji Chubanshe, Shanghai.

Guo Shuchun 郭书春, Ch'en Tsai Hsin 陈在新, and Guo Jinhai 郭金海, 2006. Jade mirror of the four unknowns, 2 vols. In: Library of Chinese classics, Chinese-English 大中华文库　英汉对照. Liaoning Education Press, Shenyang. 'Translated into Modern Chinese by Guo Shuchun; translated into English by Ch'en Tsai Hsin; revised and supplemented by Guo Jinhai.'

Guo Tao 郭涛, 1994. Shuxue zai gudai shuili gongcheng zhong de yingyong－《Hefang tongyi · Suanfa》de zhushi yu fenxi 数学在古代水利工程中的应用—《河防通议·算法》的注释与分析 (The use of mathematics in ancient water-control engineering: analysis of the mathematical chapter of *Hefang tongyi*). Nongye kaogu 农业考古 ('Agricultural archaeology') 1994.1, 271-278, 285.

Hoe, John, 1977, Les systèmes d'équations polynômes dans le *Siyuan yujian* (1303). In: Mémoires de l'Institut des Hautes Études Chinoises, vol. 6. Presses Universitaires de France, Paris.

Hoe, J., 1978, The jade mirror of the four unknowns－some reflections. Mathematical chronicle 7, 125-156. www.thebookshelf.auckland.ac.nz/docs/Maths/PDF/mathschron007-015.pdf

Holzman, Donald, 1958. Shen Kua and his *Meng-ch'i pi-t'an*. T'oung Pao 46.3/5, 260-292. www.jstor.org/stable/20185477

Hu Daojing 胡道静 (ed.), 1962. Mengxi bitan jiaozheng 梦溪笔谈校证 (Critical edition of 'Dream Brook essays'). Shanghai. Facsimile reprint, Shanghai Guji Chubanshe, Shanghai, 1987.

Hu Daojing 胡道静, Jin Liangnian 金良年, Hu Xiaojing 胡小静, Wang Hong 王宏, and Zhao Zheng 赵峥, 2008. Brush talks from Dream Brook, 2 vols. In: Library of Chinese classics, Chinese-English 大中华文库 英汉对照. Sichuan Renmin Chubanshe, Chengdu/Shenzhen. 'Translated into modern Chinese by Hu Daojing, Jin Liangnian and Hu Xiaojing; translated into English by Wang Hong and Zhao Zheng.'

Li Yan 李俨, 1957. Zhong suanjia de neichafa yanjiu 中算家的内插法研究 (Studies of the use of interpolation by Chinese mathematicians). Liaoning Jiaoyu Chubanshe, Beijing.

Libbrecht, Ulrich, 1973. Chinese mathematics in the thirteenth century: The Shu-shu chiu-chang of Ch'in Chiu-shao. In: M.I.T. East Asian science series, vol. 1. M.I.T. Press, Cambridge, Mass. & London. Facsimile reprint, Dover, Mineola, 2005.

Martzloff, Jean-Claude, 1997. A history of Chinese mathematics. Translated by S.S. Wilson. Berlin/Heidelberg, Springer-Verlag. 'Corrected second printing', 2006. Original: Histoire des mathémathiques chinoises, Masson, Paris, 1987.

Mei Rongzhao 梅荣照, 1966, Li Ye ji qi shuxue zhuzuo 李冶及其数学著作 (Li Ye and his mathematical works). In: Qian Baocong 钱宝琮 (ed.), Song Yuan shuxue shi lunwenji 宋元数学史论文集 (Essays on the history of mathematics in the Song and Yuan periods, 960-1368 CE). Kexue Chubanshe, Beijing, pp. 104-148.

Qian Baocong 钱宝琮, 1964. Zhongguo shuxue shi 中国数学史 (The history of Chinese mathematics). Kexue Chubanshe, Beijing. Facsimile reprint, 1981.

——, 1966. Qin Jiushao《Shushu jiuzhang》yanjiu 秦九韶《数书九章》研究. In: Qian Baocong et al. (eds.), Song Yuan shuxueshi lunwenji 宋元数学史论文集 (Essays on the history of mathematics in the Song and Yuan periods, 960-1368 CE). Kexue Chubanshe, Beijing, pp. 60-103.

Sivin, Nathan, 1995. Shen Kua. In: Nathan Sivin, Science in ancient China: Researches and reflections. Variorum, Aldershot, pp. 1-53.

——, 2009. Granting the seasons: The Chinese astronomical reform of 1280, with a study of its many dimensions and a translation of its records. In: Sources and studies in the history of mathematics and physical sciences. Springer, New York.

Wagner, Donald B., 2008. Science and civilisation in China, vol. 5, part 11: Ferrous metallurgy. Cambridge University Press, Cambridge.

——, 2017. The classical Chinese version of Horner's method: Technical considerations. donwagner.dk/horner/horner.html

Yabuuchi Kiyoshi 薮内清, 1965. Kabō tsūgi ni tsuite 河防通议について (On the *Hefang tongyi*). Seikatsu bunka kenkyū 生活文化研究 13, 297-304.

Yuankan Mengxi bitan 元刊梦溪笔谈, 1975. (Facsimile reprint of a Yuan-period edition of 'Dream Brook essays'). Wenwu Chubanshe, Beijing.

Figure captions

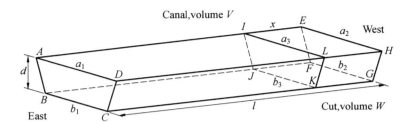

Figure 1 Canal, diagram for Problem 27 of *Hefang tongyi*

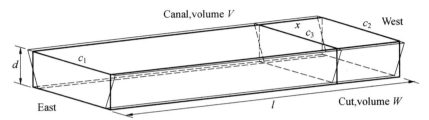

Figure 2 *Ting* 停, geometric construction equivalent to the canal in Figure 1

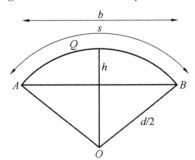

Figure 3 Diagram for the calculation in *Mengxi bitan*

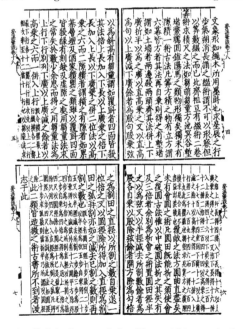

Figure 4 Original text of the *Mengxi bitan* calculation, reproduced from *Yuankan Mengxi bitan* [1975, 18, 4-7]

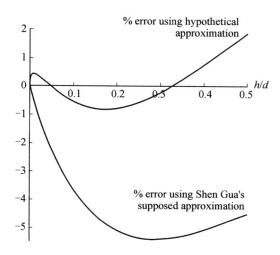

Figure 5 Comparison of error percentages in the two approximations (17) and (20)

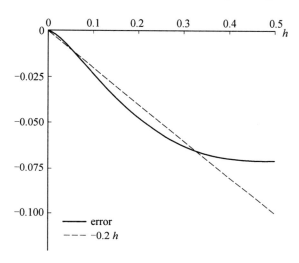

Figure 6 Absolute error using approximation (17) with $d=1$ and b calculated from d and h

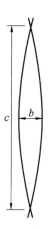

Figure 7 Intersection of two circles with equal radii, presumed to be Qin Jiushao's 'banana leaf'

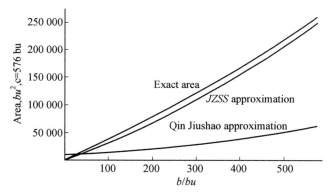

Figure 8 Comparison of Qin Jiushao's approximation, A_{Qin}, with that of the *Jiuzhang suanshu*, A_{JZSS}, and the exact area of the 'banana leaf field' with $c=576\ bu$

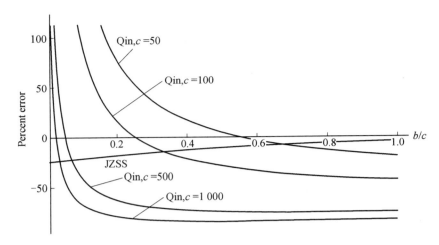

Figure 9 Comparison of the error of the two approximations for various values of c. The curve for A_{JZSS} is the same for all values of c. The error percentage of A_{Qin} is not invariant under scaling because it is not dimensionally consistent

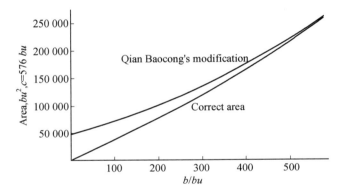

Figure 10 Comparison of Qian Baocong's modification of Qin Jiushao's approximation, A_{Qian}, with the exact value of the area

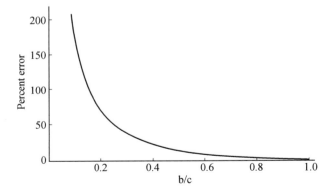

Figure 11 Percentage error of A_{Qian}

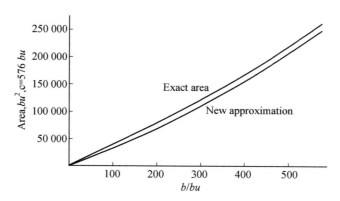

Figure 12　Comparison of the proposed formula, A_{new}, with the exact area of the 'banana leaf field', A, with $c=576\ bu$

《透簾細草》中有關元代絲織生產的幾個問題初探

呂變庭　馬晴晴　（河北大學宋史研究中心）

摘要　《透簾細草》入算的絲織算題較多，可惜對這些絲織算題的史學價值迄今學界尚未給予足夠重視。從《透簾細草》所擇取的典型絲織算題看，它不僅反映了元代中期絲綢織造的繁榮狀況，而且對元代綢絹的織染工藝、價格、匹絹用絲量、折耗等都有專門題例進行描述，具有較強的史料性。尤其通過《透簾細草》和其他元代算書相互參照，我們能夠初步釐清元代絲織物匹重、用絲、匹長及幅面之間的數量關係，而這也是元代算書相對其他文獻來說它們本身所具有的獨特史料價值。

關鍵詞　透簾細草　絲織生產　元代

元代無名氏所撰《透簾細草》計71題，其中有關紡織生產方面的算題26道，約占總題量的37％。如果再進一步細分，則26道算題包括"今有麻"算題2道，"今有生絲"算題1道，"今有絲"算題7道，"今有絹"算題11道，"今有綾"算題1道，"今有布"算題1道，"今有羅"算題1道，其他算題1道。內容涉及從生絲到熟絲的繅練、絲帛的染色、絲織品的交易、稅賦、價格，以及兵士的軍服織造問題等，為研究元代紡織生產保存了不可多得的史料。誠如李迪先生所言："任何一個數學史問題都和歷史緊密相關，離開整個中國歷史的數學史問題是不存在的。"[1]可惜目前學界除鄒大海先生外[2]，尚無人對《透簾細草》做這方面的專門研究，故本文不揣譾陋，擬就《透簾細草》中有關元代絲織生產的幾個問題略述管見，希冀引起同道的重視。

一、元代蠶絲生產的基本狀況

元代的農業生產雖然遭受到一定程度的破壞，但絲織生產就總體而言是向前發展的。據研究，《王禎農書》關於水力大紡車的記述，在西方工業革命之前居於世界紡織機械的領先地位。另從《元史·食貨志》的記載看，元朝"科差"分"絲料"和"包銀"兩類。其中"絲料"總數統計如下：

中統四年（1263年），絲七十一萬二千一百七十一斤。

至元二年（1265年），絲九十八萬六千九百一十二斤。

至元三年（1266年），絲一百五萬三千二百二十六斤。

至元四年（1267年），絲一百九萬六千四百八十九斤。

天曆元年（1328年），絲一百九萬八千八百四十三斤，絹三十萬五百三十匹，綿七萬二千一十五斤，布二十一萬一千二百二十三匹。[3]

上述史料盡管不全，但"絲料"以"絲"和"絹"為大宗，似可從《透簾細草》中整個紡織類算題的內容得到印證，因為《透簾細草》中整個紡織類算題的分布，屬絹類和絲類算題最多，由此表明《透簾細草》不是書齋裡推演出來的東西，而是以元代社會經濟生活的客觀現實為其背景。按《元史》戶籍科差條例規定，

本文為2020年度國家社會科學基金重大項目《17—20世紀國外學者研究中國宋元數理科學的歷史考察和文獻整理》（項目號：20&ZD228）的階段性成果。

1　李迪：《中國數學史中的未解決問題》，吳文俊主編. 中國數學史論文集 3［M］. 濟南：山東教育出版社，1987年，第22頁。

2　鄒大海：《〈透簾細草〉提要》，《中國科學技術典籍通彙》第1冊，鄭州：河南教育出版社，1995年，第1281頁。

3　（明）宋濂等：《元史》卷93《食貨一·科差》，北京：中華書局，1975年，第2363頁。

"元管户"即元成宗元贞元年(1295年)和元仁宗皇庆元年(1312年)括户时入籍的人户,"交参户"即历次籍户时新收之户,"协济户"即穷困之户,"漏籍户"即因各种原因所遗漏的人户,为科"丝"(以户为单位)亦即"财用所出"的主要对象。其中"元管户"又分为"丝银全科户""减半科(丝)户""止纳系官五户丝户"以及"止纳系官丝户"四类,每类民户所负担的科丝数量多少不一。依《元史·食货志一》所载:

> 元管户内,丝银全科系官户,每户输系官丝一斤六两四钱。全科系官五户丝户,每户输系官丝一斤,五户丝六两四钱。减半科户,每户输系官丝八两,五户丝三两二钱。止纳系官丝户,若上都、隆兴、西京等十路,十户十斤者,每户输一斤,大都以南等路十户十四斤者。每户输一斤六两四钱。止纳系官五户丝户,每户输系官丝一斤,五户丝六两四钱。交参户内丝银户,每户输系官丝一斤六两四钱。漏籍户内止纳丝户,每户输丝之数与交参丝户同。协济户内丝银户,每良输系官丝十两二钱。止纳丝户,每户输系官之数与丝户同。摊丝户,每户科摊丝四斤。储也贝八速儿所管户,每户科细丝,其数与摊丝同。[4]

文中的"系官丝"是指输于官府用来供国家支用的丝料,而投下"五户丝"则是指输于官府用来供贵族功臣支用的丝料。二者的比例若"以十分论之",则大致为"纳官者七分(即系官丝),投下(即五户丝)得其三焉"。[5] 据统计,世祖至元七年(1270年)元代民户为192万余户,到至元三十年(1293年)则增至14002700余户。[6] 高树林经过对有元一代的民户进行细致考察后认为,"元朝民户户计数量最多,占全国总户数的80%左右,是元朝诸色户计中最基本的户计"。[7] 其中延祐六年(1319年)统计的五户丝有238787户,分拨丝料总计94222斤。[8] 由于元代要求民户"每丁岁植桑枣二十株,或附宅地植桑二十株",[9] 后又"分农民为三等,上户地十一亩,中户五亩,下户二亩或一亩,皆筑垣墙围之,以时收采桑椹,依法种植",[10] 因而出现了"民间丝绸生产的普遍化"[11]发展状况。与其他民户"科丝"不同,对于丝银全科系官户来说,元代"户籍科差条例"规定:"每户科丝二十二两四钱,二户计算丝二斤一十二两八钱,其二斤即系纳官正丝,内正丝、色丝各半。外将每户剩余六两四钱攒至五户满二斤数目,付本位下支用,谓之二五户丝。"[12] 文中的"正丝"指的是素丝或白丝,也就是用来织绸缎的生丝,而《透簾细草》所有"今有丝"算题中出现的"丝"都是指生丝。我们知道,生丝是桑蚕茧经过缫丝后的产品,由于此时还含有约20%的丝胶成分,故质感光泽柔和,弹力坚韧。仅从元代的地方志记载来看,正丝应以浙江、江苏和广东所产最负盛名,科丝量也最多。以集庆路和湖州路为例,据统计至正年间(1341—1368年)湖州路夏税丝79 964斤,其中乌程县17 122斤,归安县12 504斤,长兴州20 372斤,武康县8 754斤,安吉县15 207斤,德清县5 962斤;集庆路夏税丝49 984斤,其中江宁县5 542斤,上元县12 515斤,句容县11 609斤,溧水州13 075斤,溧阳州7 243斤。[13] 考《透簾细草》算题中所涉及的生丝量有超过1 200斤者,这些数字虽不尽可信,但也能比较委婉地说明这些算题是以南方丝产地为基础来编选的。尤其是元代丝绸之路密如蛛网,已经覆盖了亚、非大洲的主要贸易站点,[14] 而这种远洋贸易路线的空前拓展实与国内蚕

---

[4] (明)宋濂等:《元史》卷93《食货一·科差》,北京:中华书局,1975年,第2361—2362页。
[5] (元)王恽:《秋涧集》卷80《中堂事记》,见顾宏义《金元日记丛编》,上海:上海书店出版社,2013年,第98页。
[6] 周继中、陈金陵编著:《中国古代史简编》下册,中国逻辑与语言函授大学,内部教材,19082年,第104页。
[7] 高树林:《古代社会经济史探》,保定:河北大学出版社,2011年,第262页。
[8] 吴宏岐:《元代农业地理》,西安:西安地图出版社,1997年,第146页。
[9] (民国)何绍忞撰:《新元史》卷69《食货志二》,长春:吉林人民出版社,1995年,第1589页。
[10] (明)宋濂等:《元史》卷93《食货一·农桑》,北京:中华书局,1975年,第2356页。
[11] 范金民:《元代江南丝绸业述论》,《南京大学学报》2019年第3期,第43页。
[12] (元)王恽:《秋涧集》卷80《中堂事记》,见顾宏义《金元日记丛编》,上海:上海书店出版社,2013年,第98页。
[13] 参见吴宏岐:《元代农业地理》,西安:西安地图出版社,1997年,第149页。
[14] 崔京生:《海洋志》,北京:中国青年出版社,2012年,第189页。

丝生产的繁荣景象分不开。当然,也与元代"庞大的官营织造体系"[15]分不开。如题云:"今有丝一千二百三十二斤六两,共直钱一四百二十六贯五百九十七文三分。问一两直钱多少?答曰:七十二文三分五厘。"[16]而元代另外一部《算法全能集》则载有这样两道算题:"今有绢四十四万七百九十一匹,计用车五百三十三辆装载,今只装了三百四十八车,外有一百八十五车听候装载,问各该绢几何?答曰:见装该绢二十八万七千七百九十六匹,听候该绢一十五万二千九百九十五匹。"[17]此题内容恰与《马可波罗行记》所讲的下述史料相互佐证:当时大都城"百物输入之众,有如川流之不息,仅丝一项,每日入城者,计有千车(原注:每车所载不过五百公斤,则每日入城之丝平均有五十万公斤,每年共有十八万吨)。用此丝制作不少金锦绸绢,及其他数种物品"。[18]如果按照"每一十一两六铢(丝),织绢一匹(该四丈二尺)"[19]计算,则"四十四万七百九十一匹"绢,至少需用丝 440 791 匹×11.25 两 = 4 958 898.75 两÷16 两 ≈ 309 931 斤。同理,"今有罗三千三百匹,每匹四十二尺,出关税之,每十匹合税罗一尺"[20]算题,文中所织造的"三千三百匹"罗,则至少需用丝 2 320 斤。由此可见,从《透帘细草》到《算法全能集》,元代的蚕丝生产量较大,是一个丝绸织造的繁荣发展期。

二、算题所反映的元代织染绸绢状况

绢是一种比较简单的平纹丝织物,其纹理平实耐用,因而是一种实用衣料。据考,在距今 4700 余年的浙江吴兴钱山漾新石器文化遗址中,首次出土了经纬交织的绢片。[21]之后,关于中国从夏商到隋唐绢织物的发展,日本学者佐藤武敏在《中国古代绢织物史研究》一书中有详论,不赘。在我国,最早以绢入题的算书当推成书于东晋或南北朝初期[22]的《孙子算经》。然而,若论对《透帘细草》丝绢选题的影响,则莫过于北魏成书的《张丘建算经》。《张丘建算经》载有这样一道算题:"今有绢一匹买紫草三十斤,染绢二丈五尺。今有绢七匹,欲减买紫草,还自染余绢。问减绢、买紫草各几何?答曰:减绢四匹一丈二尺十三分尺之四,买草一百二十九三两一十三分两之九。"[23]这里除了进行专业的数学计算方法和技能训练外,还涉及我国古代丝绢织染过程中的一些工艺问题。例如春秋时期的齐国非常崇尚紫色,"一国尽服紫",于是出现了"五素(即素色绸绢)不得一紫(即紫色绸绢)"[24]的现象。此"一紫"就是用紫草素(即乙酰紫草醌)作媒染剂所染成的紫色绸绢,所以郭璞释《尔雅》"茈(紫)草"云"可以染紫"。[25]但自然界中的紫草资源十分稀少,它难以满足当时等级社会对"染紫"绸绢的客观需要,如《魏书·高祖纪下》曾记载:太和十年(486 年)夏四月,"辛酉朔,始制五等公服",[26]遂开后世"品色衣"之先河。这样便造成了北魏时期"绢一匹买紫草三十斤"的交易现象,自此以后百官公服皆以紫色为贵。《隋书·礼仪志》明确规定:"五品以上,通著紫袍,六品以下,兼用绯绿。"[27]《元史·舆服志》谓"百官公服":"一品紫,大独科花,径五寸。二品小独科花,径三寸。三品散答花,径二寸,无枝叶。四品、五品小杂花,径一寸五分。六品、七品

---

[15] 赵丰主编:《中国丝绸通史 THE GENERAL HISTORY OF CHINESE SILK》,苏州:苏州大学出版社,2005 年,第 327 页。

[16] (元)佚名:《透帘细草》,《中国科学技术典籍通汇》第 1 册,郑州:河南教育出版社,1995 年,第 1294 页。

[17] (元)贾亨:《算法全能集》,《中国科学技术典籍通汇》第 1 册,郑州:河南教育出版社,1995 年,第 1325 页。

[18] (意)马可波罗撰;冯承钧译:《马可波罗行记》第 2 卷第 94 章《汗八里城之贸易发达户口繁盛》,上海:上海书店出版社,2000 年,第 236 页。

[19] 同上,第 1336 页。

[20] 同上,第 1326 页。

[21] 高汉玉:《从出土文物追溯蚕丝业的起源》,《蚕桑通报》1981 年第 1 期,第 17—24 页。

[22] 骆祖英编著:《数学史教学导论》,杭州:浙江教育出版社,1996 年,第 67 页。

[23] (北魏)张丘建:《张丘建算经》卷上,郭书春、刘钝校点:《算经十书(二)》,沈阳:辽宁教育出版社,1998 年,第 11 页。

[24] (周)韩非:《韩非子》卷 11《外储说左上》,《百子全书》第 2 册,长沙:岳麓书社,1993 年,第 1728 页。

[25] 无名氏撰;郭璞注:《尔雅》,杭州:浙江古籍出版社,2011 年,第 53 页。

[26] (北齐)魏收撰:《魏书》卷 7《高祖纪》,北京:中华书局,1974 年,第 161 页。

[27] 《隋书》卷 12《礼仪志》,北京:中华书局,1973 年,第 279 页。

绯罗小杂花,径一寸。八品、九品绿罗,无文。"[28] 紫草本来就稀少,加之元代对紫草的需求量又大。因此,《透帘细草》所讲的以下算题内容应当是可信的。题云:

今有绢一丈一尺买紫草四斤,染绢二丈九尺。今共有绢四十二匹三丈六尺,今欲减绢买紫草,还自染余绢。问染得紫绢多少?答曰:三十一匹三尺。[29]

按:北魏一尺约合今30.9厘米,元代一尺约合今31.68厘米,[30]元代一尺比北魏一尺多约0.78厘米。已知我国古代一匹等于四丈(即40尺),算得"一匹买紫草三十斤"中的"一匹"约为40尺×30.9厘米=1 236厘米=12.36米。又北魏一斤约合今224克,元代一斤约合今600克,则30斤×224克=6 720克=13.44斤,即1米绢可买约1.1斤紫草。同理,已知元代一匹等于四十二尺,即1丈为10.5尺,算得"今有绢一丈一尺买紫草四斤"中的"一匹"约为10.6尺×31.68厘米=335.808厘米=3.358 08米,又4斤×600克=2 400克=4.8斤,即1米绢可买约1.4斤紫草。这表明绢本身的价值,元代较北魏有所提高。据考,北魏"孝文太和十九年(495年)初铸钱时,绢每匹二百钱,至孝庄帝时,涨至每匹三百钱"。[31]换算为今值,则12.36米绢价可得200钱或300钱,即每米值约16.2文钱,或24.3文钱。至于元代的绢价,《透帘细草》载有多道以绢价为内容的算题。

1. "今有绢一尺,直钱二十八文。问一匹长四丈二尺,直钱多少?答曰:一贯一百七十六文。"

2. "今有绢一百二十九匹二丈六尺,每尺价钱三十二文二分五厘。问计钱多少?答曰:一百七十五贯五百六十九文。"

3. "今有绢一匹长四十尺(按:1米绢可买约1.5斤紫草,引者注。),直钱一贯一百六十文。问一尺直钱多少?答曰:二十九文。"

4. "今有绢二十三匹二丈三尺,共直钱二十三贯一百四十二文六分。问一尺直钱多少?答曰:二十三文四分。"[32]

由上述几种价格算得,(1)每匹 3.358 08 米绢价可得 1 176 文钱,即每米值约 350 文钱;(2)$\frac{175\ 569\ \text{文}}{129.56\ \text{匹}} \approx 1\ 355\ \frac{\text{文}}{\text{匹}}$,即每米值约 404 文钱;(3)每匹 3.358 08 米绢价可得 1160 文钱,即每米值约 345 文钱;(4)$\frac{23\ 142\ \text{文}}{23.53\ \text{匹}} \approx 984\ \frac{\text{文}}{\text{匹}}$,即每米值约 293 文钱。按最低绢价计算,元代较北魏至少增长了 11 倍。

那么,织造一匹绢究竟需要多少蚕丝?

这或许是一个不太专业的问题,但却是一个比较重要的问题。南宋洪迈在《容斋三笔》"纳绸绢尺度"条下说:"周显德三年(956年)。敕,旧制织造绝绸、织布、绫罗、锦绮、纱縠等。每阔二尺起,来年后并须及二尺五分。宜令诸道州府,来年所纳官绢,每匹须及一十二两,其绝绸只要夹密停匀,不定斤两。其纳官绸绢,依旧长四十二尺,乃知今之税绢,尺度长短阔狭,斤两轻重,颇本于此。"[33]也就是说宋制绢每匹42尺,重12两。换言之,即12两蚕丝织1匹绢。又《宋会要辑稿》载:乾道八年(1172年)二月十二日,"户部言昨徽州乞将本州上供绢,依祖宗旧制,重十一两为一匹输纳,本部欲依本州所申。今来徽州截日终起到乾道七年(1171年)上供八万一千七百六十余匹,系四十二尺为匹,每匹重一十一两一

---

[28] (明)宋濂等:《元史》卷78《舆服志一》,北京:中华书局,1976年,第1939页。

[29] (元)佚名:《透帘细草》,《中国科学技术典籍通汇》第1册,郑州:河南教育出版社,1995年,第1293页。

[30] 其他观点还有:"1元尺=1宋尺=30.78485厘米"(见曾昭安编:《武汉大学讲义——中外数学史》第1编 上,内部资料,1956年,第126页);"1元尺=1宋尺=1.03唐尺=0.95市尺"(见李伯重:《唐代江南农业的发展》,北京:农业出版社,1990年,第12页);元代1官尺等于今39.5厘米—41.2厘米(见郭正中:《三至十四世纪中国的权衡度量》,北京:中国社会科学出版社,1993年,第315—319页);"取其平均值,则每尺约为34.87厘米"(见陈平先:《从元代官印看元代的尺度》,《考古》1997年第8期,第86—90页)等。

[31] 缪钺:《缪钺全集》第1卷《冰茧庵读史存稿》上,石家庄:河北教育出版社,2004年,第254页。

[32] (元)佚名:《透帘细草》,《中国科学技术典籍通汇》第1册,郑州:河南教育出版社,1995年,第1290页。

[33] (南宋)洪迈著;夏祖尧、周洪武校点:《容斋随笔·三笔》卷10《纳绸绢尺度》,长沙:岳麓书社,1998年,第359页。

分,或一十一两半之数。"³⁴ 在宋代,徽州织工能用 11 两或 11.5 两蚕丝织绢 1 匹。此外,《宋史·食货志三》亦载:"自周显德中,令公私织造并须幅广二尺五分,民所输绢匹重十二两,疏薄短狭、涂粉入药者禁之;河北诸州军重十两,各长四十二尺,宋因其旧。"³⁵ 为了防止"涂粉入药",确保织绢的质量。《元典章》规定:"今后选练不(读墩)中丝绵,须要清水夹密,段匹各长五托半以上。依官尺各阔一尺六寸,并无药丝绵中副布匹,方许货卖。如是依前成造低歹物货及买卖之家,一体断罪,其物没官。"³⁶ 依此为背景,《透帘细草》载有下面一道算题:

> 今有织绢一百七十六匹一丈四尺,每匹长四十二尺,用丝一十一两六铢。问都丝多少?答曰:一百二十三斤一十五两一十八铢。³⁷

"每匹长四十二尺,用丝一十一两六铢"算下来应为 $11.25\frac{两}{匹}$,比较接近实际。参照宋朝"河北诸州军重十两,各长四十二尺"之规定,以及徽州"每匹(绢)重一十一两一分,或一十一两半之数"的文献记载,不难看出《透帘细草》中有关丝织类算题的内容应当是取材于南方的丝织生产现实。在古代,为什么会规定"四丈为匹"的制度呢?《淮南子·天文训》解释说:

> 古之为度量,轻重生乎天道。黄钟之律修九寸。物以三生[三三九]三九二十七,故幅广二尺七寸,[古之制也。]音以八相生,故人修八尺,寻自倍,故八尺而为寻。有形则有声。音之数五,以五乘八,五八四十,故四丈而为匹。匹者,中人之度也。一匹而为制。³⁸

如果以"中人之度"为准,那么,宋元时期人们的平均身高一定会增长,这是自然规律。因此,宋元时期出现丝绸"各长四十二尺"的匹制变化,亦在情理之中。据学者研究,"河北地区比其他地区每匹要少 2 两,则因北方气候干燥,织物的回潮率不同所致"。³⁹ 然而,宋人在议论南北方织绢的差别时总是说:"河北绢经纬一等,故无背面;江南绢则经粗而纬细,有背面。"⁴⁰ 明人亦有"唐绢粗而厚,宋绢细而薄,元绢与宋绢相似而稍不匀净"⁴¹ 的比较与鉴赏。其实,综合来看宋代南方织绢的质量与河北织绢不相上下。对此,《齐东野语》"淳绍岁币"条特别讲到:"红娟十二万匹,匹重十两。浙绢八万匹,匹重九两。"⁴² 文中每匹长为 40 宋尺(官尺)。明人曹昭亦说:"元绢类宋绢,有独梭绢,出宣州。有宓机绢,极匀净厚密,是嘉兴府魏唐宓家,故名宓机。"⁴³ 可见,元时南方绢丝毫不逊色于宋绢。

如众所知,在正常情况下,绢幅相等,其重量越重则用丝越多。所以为了减少蚕丝量,社会上便出现了涂粉入药的作假现象。当然,《透帘细草》所取用的"每匹长四十二尺,用丝一十一两六铢"应是当时的生产标准,因而具有一定的客观性和真实性。比如《元典章》"讲究织造缎匹"条下云:"一匹纱(指绢纱,引者注)十两丝,一匹罗一斤丝。"⁴⁴ 与《透帘细草》所取用的织造标准相差无几。

---

34 (清)徐松辑:《宋会要辑稿》食货 64 之 34,刘琳等校点:《宋会要辑稿》第 13 册,上海:上海古籍出版社,2014 年,第 7751 页。

35 (元)脱脱等:《宋史》卷 175《食货上三》,北京:中华书局,1985 年,第 4231—4232 页。

36 中国台湾文海出版社编:《元典章》卷 58《工部一·缎匹》,台北:文海出版社,1974 年,第 788 页。

37 (元)佚名:《透帘细草》,《中国科学技术典籍通汇》第 1 册,郑州:河南教育出版社,1995 年,第 1293 页。

38 (汉)刘安:《淮南子》卷 3《天文训》,长沙:岳麓书社,2015 年,第 27 页。

39 张保丰:《中国丝绸史稿》,上海:学林出版社,1989 年,第 196 页。

40 (南宋)赵希鹄:《洞天清禄集·古画辨》,《文渊阁四库全书》影印本,第 871 册,第 26 页。

41 (明)张应文:《清秘藏》卷上《论古纸绢素》,景印文渊阁四库全书,台北:商务印书馆,1986 年,第 872 册,第 15 页。

42 (宋)周密撰;黄益元校点.:《齐东野语》卷 12《淳绍岁币》,上海:上海古籍出版社,2012 年,第 121 页。

43 (明)曹昭,明)王佐著:《格古要论》卷 5《古画绢素》,北京:金城出版社,2012 年,第 171 页。

44 中国台湾文海出版社编:《元典章》卷 58《工部一·缎匹》,台北:文海出版社,1974 年,第 786 页。

三、元代绸绢的标准匹长问题

如上所述,《透簾细草》算题出现了两种规格的匹长,一种为 40 尺,另一种则为 42 尺。这里需要明确的是以上两种尺度仅仅是大绢的规格,还有一种小绢,可惜算题中没有出现,本文不拟详论。如南宋陈旉《农书》曾载有一种能使农家致富的"小绢":

> 彼中人(指湖州安吉人)惟籍蚕办生事。十口之家养蚕十箔,每箔得茧一十二斤,每一斤取丝一两三分,每五两丝织小绢一匹,每一匹绢易米一硕四斗,绢与米价常相侔也。以此岁计衣食之给,极有准的也。以一月之劳,贤于终岁勤动,且无旱干水溢之苦,岂不优裕也哉。[45]

这种"小绢"匹长多少,没有明说。元末成书的《老乞大》也仅有"小绢一匹三钱"[46]的记载,同样没有明说匹长多少。考明成化《湖州府志》卷 8 载:"绢阔而长者为官绢,今纳贡,又有狭小绢。"[47]此处的"狭小绢"具体匹长多少也不清楚,好在《元典章》有这样一条规定:"诸人所用不得同御用缎匹,理应□等:今既诸局院见造常课例,每匹长二丈四尺,幅阔一尺四寸,亦系诸人服用之物。"[48]另外,《四元玉鉴》内有一道算题云:"今有纱一匹,先截一尺作牙钱,余卖得钱一贯一百七十六文,只云匹长尺价皆以平方开之,二数相并共得十二,问匹长尺价各几何?答曰:匹长二丈五尺,尺价四十九文。"[49]文中所言"每匹长二丈四尺"及"匹长二丈五尺"应系指"狭小绢"的长度。关于这一点可由下面的事实间接证明,如笔者所述,按大绢匹长 42 尺计算,则根据"每五两丝织小绢一匹"和"一匹纱十两丝"两条资料算得,小绢匹长约等于 21 尺,与《元典章》和《四元玉鉴》所说的长度比较接近。在元代,罗的匹长也分大、小。如《丁巨算法》载有两道关于罗匹长度的算题:

第一题:"今有罗二十三匹一丈六尺八寸,每匹价一十二两半。问共多少?答曰:二百九十五两(二八匹法)。"

第二题:"今有罗二十三匹二丈三尺,每匹四十二尺,共卖钞二百三十一两四钱二分六厘。问每尺该钞几何?答曰:二钱三分四厘。"[50]

"匹法二十八尺"和"匹法四十二尺"的分类与绢匹长的分类相近。当然,相对于小绢,大绢的匹长更难把握,不仅情形复杂,而且时人的说法也相互不一致。例如:

《四元玉鉴》:"今有绢一匹,直钱一贯六百六十六文。只云匹长如尺价五百四十四分之四百四十一。问匹长、尺价各多少?答曰:匹长三丈六尺四分尺之三,尺价四十五文三分文之一。"[51]

《丁巨算法》:"今有绢一丈八尺,卖钱五两五钱二分。问一匹长四十二尺,该钞几何?答曰:一十二两八钱八分。"[52]

《算法全能集》:"今有钞一百二十四两五钱四分五厘,买绢每匹长三十八尺,价钞一十一两五钱。问该绢几何?答曰:该绢一十四匹三丈一尺五寸四分。"[53]

《详明算法》"丈尺数长短之法":"忽者,蚕口所出丝也。十忽为丝,十丝为毫,十毫为厘,十厘为分,

---

[45] (南宋)陈旉:《农书》卷下《种桑之法篇第二》,北京:农业出版社,1965 年,第 55 页。
[46] 李泰洙:《<老乞大>四种版本语言研究》附录,北京:语文出版社,2003 年,第 125 页。
[47] (清)汪日桢:《湖蚕述》卷 3《织绢》,济南:山东画报出版社,2004 年,第 306 页。
[48] 中国台湾文海出版社编:《元典章》卷 58《工部一·缎匹》,台北:文海出版社,1974 年,第 790 页。
[49] (元)朱世杰:《四元玉鉴》卷上《端匹互隐》,《中国科学技术典籍通汇》第 1 册,郑州:河南教育出版社,1995 年,第 1219 页。
[50] (元)丁巨:《丁巨算法》,《中国科学技术典籍通汇》第 1 册,郑州:河南教育出版社,1995 年,第 1308 页。
[51] 同上,第 1218 页。
[52] (元)丁巨:《丁巨算法》,《中国科学技术典籍通汇》第 1 册,郑州:河南教育出版社,1995 年,第 1308 页。
[53] (元)贾亨:《算法全能集》,《中国科学技术典籍通汇》第 1 册,郑州:河南教育出版社,1995 年,第 1334—1335 页。

十分为寸,十寸为尺,十尺为丈,四丈为匹,五丈为端。"[54]

《永乐大典算法》:"今有丝一斤八两换绢一匹,即四十尺及将丝九两,贴钱四两得绢二丈,今有钱五两,问买绢得若干?答曰:六尺二寸五分。"[55]

匹长有"三丈六尺四分尺之三""四十二尺""四十尺""三十八尺"四种长度,如果考虑到绢之外的其他丝绸,那么,说法就更多了。例如,《四元玉鉴》内有题云:"今有锦一端一匹,端长自乘,内减匹长。又匹长自乘,内减端长。二余相并,其得三千五百一十六尺,只云端长多于匹长四分之一。问端匹长各多少?答曰:端长四丈八尺,匹长三丈六尺。"[56]又有题云:"今有锦一匹,先卖了三尺,余卖得钱二贯九百七十五文。只云匹长不及尺价四十七文,问匹长尺价各几何?答曰:匹长三丈八尺,尺价八十五文。"[57]举例至此,也许读者会提出疑问,在《四元玉鉴》内为什么会出现这么多以分数为匹长的算题现象?首先,我们不排除朱世杰为了算法本身的需要而有意增加一些分数内容,从而使算题变得较为复杂,且计算难度也相应加大。但是,如果算题内容完全脱离生活实际,就会失去算题本身的价值和意义,在当时也就很难引起习算者的兴趣。所以朱世杰在设计这些算题时必然会以元代的现实生活为基础,如前揭《元典章》"禁治纰薄缎匹"条内要求匠人织造丝绸:"选拣堪中丝绵,须要清水夹密,缎匹各长五托半之上,依官尺阔一尺六寸。"[58] 在此,"缎匹各长五托半之上"就是指大于 $5\frac{1}{2}$ 托且不超过上限的任何数,里面既包括整数又包括分数。此规定可以看作是朱世杰在《四元玉鉴》一书里用心设计以分数为匹长算题的法律依据。

此外,《元典章》"段匹折耗准除"条还载有下面的内容:

> 至元二十三年(1286年)九月,江西行省,近为织造段匹内纻丝(即今天的缎)六托每用正丝四十两,得生净丝三十六两,八托用正丝五十三两,得生净丝四十七两七钱。别无除豁续头剪接折耗还线体例,移准都省咨该送工部照勘到,织造段匹,续头剪接折耗体例,依数准除相应,仰照验:八托每段折一两,六托每段折七钱。[59]

对于"托"这个量词,学界有多种解释。张保丰认为:"在社会上亦有以两手平举的宽度为托者。姑以此解释元代所谓托的长度,即照 6 呎计算。则当时政府规定绢帛的长度为 35.66 市尺,实际上和宋制的匹长仍很相近。"[60]与此不同,也有学者主张"1 托等于 4 官尺",[61]还有学者认为"1 托等于 5 市尺",[62]或云"一托等于五尺,即两手平伸之长度"。[63]其中本文认为 5 尺×31.68 厘米=1.584 米这个数据较为可靠,因为民族学的史料还可以为我们提供旁证。如有学者曾介绍说:在海南岛,"渔船在黑夜行驶或进港时,用长绳曳铁砣投入水中探测深浅,叫'打水托'。一托等于 1.5 米,约为一个双臂直伸之长度"。[64]

事实上,受等级制度的影响,元代的丝绢尺度并不稳定。据《元典章》"禁军民段匹服色等第"条载,

54　(元)安止斋:《详明算法》卷上,《中国科学技术典籍通汇》第 1 册,郑州:河南教育出版社,1995 年,第 1351 页。
55　(明)解缙等纂修:《永乐大典算法》,《中国科学技术典籍通汇》第 1 册,郑州:河南教育出版社,1995 年,第 1405 页。
56　(元)朱世杰:《四元玉鉴》卷上《端匹互隐》,《中国科学技术典籍通汇》第 1 册,郑州:河南教育出版社,1995 年,第 1218 页。
57　同上,第 1219 页。
58　中国台湾文海出版社编:《元典章》卷 58《工部一·缎匹》,台北:文海出版社,1974 年,第 788 页。
59　同上,第 786 页。
60　张保丰:《中国丝绸史稿》,上海:学林出版社,1989 年,第 196 页。
61　刘坚、蒋绍愚:《老乞大》,载《近代汉语语法资料汇编·元代明代卷》,北京:商务印书馆,1995 年,第 282 页。
62　山东省水产厅渔业处、山东省气象服务台编:《海上渔业安全生产常识》,济南:山东人民出版社,1962 年,第 62 页。
63　青海省民间文学研究会翻译整理:《格萨尔》第 4 册,上海:上海文艺出版社,1962 年,第 217 页。
64　广东地名委员会编:《南海诸岛地名资料汇编》,广州:广东省地图出版社,1987 年,第 64 页。

元贞元年(1295年)十二月二十七日,"承奉中书省劄付,准蒙古文译,照得诸路局院造纳缎匹,内诸王百官长八托缎匹,各幅阔一尺四寸;常课长六托缎匹,每幅各阔一尺四寸。照勘得,既是上位用八托、六托段匹,各幅阔一尺四寸五分。"[65]按照一托等于五尺计算,文中的"八托缎匹"长恰好等于40尺,"六托缎匹"长等于30尺。这里,丝绸匹长40尺应是官方通用的标准,与以往朝代的官方标准并无差异。尽管《透簾细草》只有一道算题的绢匹长为40尺,但从旁的相关资料看,匹长40尺确实是官方采用的统一科绢标准。如元代贾亨《算法全能集》载有"官配绢"算题云:

> 今有官配绢一百一十九匹一丈二寸四分,令五等人户从上作四六出之。第一等二十五户,第二等三十户,第三等四十八户,第四等五十户,第五等六十五户。问每户及逐等该绢几何?答曰:第一等户每户一匹二丈,该三十七匹二丈;第二等每户三丈六尺,该二十七匹;第三等户每户二丈一尺六寸,该二十五匹三丈六尺八寸;第四等户每户一丈一尺九寸六分,该一十六匹八尺;第五等每户七尺七寸七分六厘,该一十二匹二丈五尺四寸四分。法曰:置都绢在地,匹数以四十尺通之。[66]

特别有意思的是,我们在《算法全能集》中看到了以下既因循又变革的"端匹"长度现象。

> "端匹"歌曰:"四十为匹五为端,或减还加二尺宽。端匹乘来方见尺,尺求端匹法除看。"[67]
> 今有绢一丈八尺,卖钞五两五钱二分。问一匹长四十二尺,该钞几何? 答曰:该钞一十二两八钱八分。[68]
> 今有钞一百二十六两八钱二分五厘,买布每端长四十八尺,价钞九两五钱。问该布几何? 答曰:该布一十三端一丈六尺八寸。[69]
> 今有钞一百二十四两五钱四分五厘,买绢每匹长三十八尺,价钞一十一两五钱。问该绢几何? 答曰:该绢一十四匹三丈一尺五寸四分。[70]

首先,"四十为匹"体现了元朝对于前代丝绸长度的继承性。如《唐律疏议》"诸造器用之物及绢布之属,有行滥、短狭而卖者"条议曰:"凡造器用之物,谓供公私用,及绢、布、绫、绮之属。'行滥',谓器用之物不牢、不真;'短狭',谓绢匹不充四十尺,布端不满五十尺,幅阔不充一尺八寸之属而卖。各杖六十。"[71]宋代亦复如此,事实上,自从汉代布帛每匹长40尺的定式之后,历朝都无更新,故元代在原则上因循了前朝的这种绢布制度。其次,这种"名实不副"的现象根源于元代现实生活的复杂性和多变性,因此,李俨在《十三、十四世纪中国民间数学》一书中,将《算法全能集》《丁巨算法》《透簾细草》等元代算书都归之于"民间数学"。因此无论《透簾细草》还是《算法全能集》都须立足于元代社会生活的现实,这样就自然使得入算的题材内容更加丰富和多样。为此,贾亨在《算法全能集》"总说五项"之第三项"端匹"条下特别强调:"古者以五十尺为一端,或五十二尺,或四十八尺,皆为一段;四十尺为一匹,或四十二尺,或三十八尺,皆为一匹。"[72]事实上,经过对敦煌遗书中记载绢长度文献的初步统计,当时民间常见的匹

---

[65] 中国台湾文海出版社编:《元典章》卷58《工部一·缎匹》,台北:文海出版社,1974年,第790页。
[66] (元)贾亨:《算法全能集》,《中国科学技术典籍通汇》第1册,郑州:河南教育出版社,1995年,第1331页。
[67] 同上,第1334页。
[68] 同上。
[69] 同上。
[70] 同上,第1334—1335页。
[71] (唐)长孙无忌等著;袁文兴、袁超注译:《唐律疏议注译》卷26《杂律》,兰州:甘肃人民出版社,2017年,第772页。
[72] (元)贾亨:《算法全能集》,《中国科学技术典籍通汇》第1册,郑州:河南教育出版社,1995年,第1318页。

长有 34 尺、29 尺、2 尺、37.5 尺、38 尺、40 尺、30 尺、37.3 尺、34.7 尺、43 尺、38.5 尺、39 尺、37.2 尺、37 尺、41 尺、36 尺、36.6 尺、34 尺、36.4 尺 19 种。[73]因此,民间丝织物长度的这种复杂性和多变性就成为《透帘细草》《四元玉鉴》等元代算书设计丝织类算题的社会现实基础。

四、元代丝织生产的折耗问题

《元典章》"讲究织造缎匹"条对丝织生产的折耗有如下规定:

> 织造缎匹的丝,分付与匠人打络时分,脚乱丝等十分中一分折耗,自前至今数目里除赔有来,尚书省官人每忻都等折算,折耗的不合除破,合追赔织造丝绸用度。[74]

这是官营作坊的标准要求,非常严苛,超过"折耗"标准就由责任工匠包赔。在民间,元代丝织生产的折耗情形就比较复杂了,因为仅见于各种算书中的丝织"折耗"便不下三四种说法。一般而言,丝织生产的折耗主要由两部分组成:一是从生丝练为熟丝及丝绒过程中的折耗,二是从生、熟丝织造出绸绢过程中的折耗。这里,"缎匹"之"缎"包括绸、缎、绢、绫、罗、纱等织物。

对于第一种折耗情形,前面所述丝银全科系官户所科之"色丝",就是一种与生丝相对应的熟丝,而通常区别生、熟丝的主要标准就是看真丝是否脱胶。因生丝精练去胶质后,质地变得十分柔软,且沾染颜色的能力较强,故称作"色丝",或称丝绵,主要用于织作蚕丝被。当然,在生丝精炼脱脂过程中,必然有一定折耗。对此,《透帘细草》编选了一道计算精练生丝的折耗率算题,其题云:"今有生丝五十二斤一十二两,欲练之,每斤折三两。问都练得多少?答曰:四十二斤一十三两七钱半。"[75]又《丁巨算法》亦有算题道:"今有生丝九十六斤一十二两六钱,欲练绒每斤折四两。问练绒并折丝各多少?答曰:绒七十二斤九两四钱半,折丝二十四斤三两一钱半。"[76]不管"练丝"还是"练绒"都是为了方便沾染颜色,这是二者的共性,故白居易有诗云:"择茧缫丝清水煮,拣丝练绒红蓝染。"[77]但练绒更加辛苦而劳累,且折耗率亦高。同样是生丝,练绒"每斤折四两"即约 25% 的折耗率,而练熟丝却是"每斤折三两"即约 19% 的折耗率,差别十分明显。在当时,这些折耗全都需要由丝银全科系官户自己来承担,其负担之重可想而知。明佚名《天水冰山录》载录明世宗籍没严嵩大量丝绢财产里就有"银红练绒缨络女裙绢九匹"。[78]在清代,广储司六库下面设立了许多作坊,其中"花作"就专司"成造各色绫绸纸绢,络丝、练绒"[79]等事。

对于第二种情形,《透帘细草》谓"每匹长四十二尺用丝一十一两六铢"(引文见前),这里"用丝一十一两六铢"应当包括折耗在内,因为"令公私织造,民所输绢匹重十二两"系后周以降历代王朝所遵循的新章程。与此"按匹重计算"相关,同时在质量上还要求织物组织紧密均匀,且无在浆丝上著粉等增重行为。然而在民间严格执行"绢匹重十二两"难度极大,一方面是计量用的杆秤,各地差别较大,有 13.6 两、16 两、18 两、20 两、24 两等区别;[80]另一方面是在不同的气候条件下使用不同的水质练丝,对织物匹重肯定会产生不同影响。因此,《元典章》特别规定"丝绵要清水夹密",对"减克丝料"的不法行为较前代采取了更进一步的限制措施。即使如此,也很难整齐划一为"绢匹重十二两"。以往学界对"丝织生产的折耗"基本上形成了两种意见。一种意见认为"在丝织过程中,原料(即蚕丝)会有所损耗,但不多,兹略

---

[73] 王进玉:《敦煌学和科技史》,兰州:甘肃教育出版社,2011 年,第 141—145 页。
[74] 中国台湾文海出版社编:《元典章》卷 58《工部一·缎匹》,台北:文海出版社,1974 年,第 786 页。
[75] 同上,第 1296 页。
[76] (元)丁巨:《丁巨算法》,《中国科学技术典籍通汇》第 1 册,郑州:河南教育出版社,1995 年,第 1312 页。
[77] (唐)白居易:《白香山诗集》卷 4《红线毯》,上海:世界书局,1935 年,第 39 页。
[78] (明)佚名:《天水冰山录》,中国历史研究社编:《明武宗外纪》,上海:上海书店出版社,1982.年,第 105 页。
[79] 《钦定总管内务府现行则例·广储司》卷 1。
[80] 钱小萍主编:《丝绸织染》,郑州:大象出版社,2005 年,第 541 页。

而不计,故把绢的匹重作为所需蚕丝的重量"。[81]另一种意见则通过分析下面的史料:南宋文思院言"一岁合织绫一千八百匹,用丝三万五千余两,近年止蒙户部支部丝一万五千两或二万两,止可织绫八百余匹",[82]从而得出结论说:"若按上述 3.5 万余两丝织绫 1 800 匹来计算,则匹重将近 20 两,扣除损耗,也起码有十多两重,而当时一般的红娟匹重 10 两,浙绢匹重 9 两。"[83]由此可见,该丝总量=织物匹重+折耗。式中"折耗"绝对不是一个"略而不计"的量,否则,《元典章》就不会做出"十分中一分折耗"的硬性规定。而有学者以清朝织造绸缎为例,认为"一担丝织品耗丝 1.35 担"。[84]可见,织造丝绸的折耗是造成丝绸价格昂贵的主要因素之一。不同织物,折耗率应当有所差异,即使同一种织物,由于蚕丝质量本身,或者技术熟练与否等因素影响,折耗率也有差异。例如,上面所举南宋织绫出现了两种情况:(1)每匹"该丝"约 19.4 两;(2)每匹"该丝"约 19 两或约 25 两。这里特别需要注意的是"该丝"(即用丝量)不等于"匹重",因为用丝量本身要比匹重多,这样的例题除《透簾细草》有载外在元代其他算书中也并不少见。

如《四元玉鉴》:"今有丝二百七十三两,织锦七匹,织绫一匹;又丝二百四十七两,织绫八匹,织绸一匹;又丝二百四十二两,织绸九匹,织锦一匹。其锦匹长自乘内减绫匹,长余又自乘内加绸匹长,共得三十五万八千八百二十九尺,绫匹长不及绸匹长二尺,却多锦匹长一尺。问三色用丝及匹法各长几何?答曰:锦二丈五尺,丝三十五两;绫二丈六尺,丝二十八两;绸二丈八尺,丝二十三两。"[85]

又如《丁巨算法》:"今有纹锦局织暗花二百六十七匹三丈五尺七寸,每匹用净丝一斤三两。问用丝几斤?答曰:三百一十八斤一两一钱五分。"[86]

《算法全能集》:"今有丝一百二十三斤十五两一十八铢,每一十一两六铢织绢一匹。该四丈二尺,问该绢几何?答曰:该绢一百七十六匹一丈四尺。"[87]

《详明算法》:"今有罗六十八匹,用丝一千一百五十六两。问每匹该丝几何?答:一十七两。"[88]

《详明算法》:"今有织绢八十六丈四尺,计用丝三百二十两。问每两该绢几何?答:二尺七寸。"[89]以每斤 16 两和每匹 42 尺计,则每匹该丝约 16 两。

至于织物的匹重,《宋史·食货上三》载:"自周显德中,令公私织造并须幅广二尺五分,民所输绢匹重十二两,疏薄短狭、涂粉入药者禁之;河北诸州军重十两,各长四十二尺。宋因其旧。"[90]诚如前面所言,到元代,丝织物的标准发生了变化,如织物的幅宽"依官尺阔一尺六寸",[91]又"常科例每匹长二丈四尺,幅阔一尺四寸"(文献注引见前)等。尤其是针对各种丝织物的实际折耗官方对旧的用丝标准做出了适当调整:"一匹纱十两丝,一匹罗一斤丝,物料是在先立定的有来。前,省官人每一匹纱交做八两,一匹罗交做十三两。如今,工部官人并管匠头目等说称,比及打络过,折耗了不勾有,依在先的体例里行呵。俺商量来,依着他每的言语行呵。"[92]这种用丝量的调整与织造过程的折耗有关,也就是说按照以前的用丝量,由于折耗本身的减量,"八两"丝织造不出"一匹纱"。同理,"十三两"丝也织造不出"一匹罗"。所以原来的用丝量与调整后的用丝量之间的差额,应当属于"折耗"的部分,即 1 匹纱折耗 2 两,1 匹罗折耗 3 两。为了厘清"该丝"与折耗的关系,我们不妨引证东汉"任城缣(即生绸,引者注)"残帛的内容于

---

[81] 李伯重:《唐代江南农业的发展》,北京:农业出版社,1990 年,第 202 页。
[82] 刘琳等校点:《宋会要辑稿》职官二九,上海:上海古籍出版社,2014 年,第 3787 页。
[83] 周峰主编:《南宋京城杭州》,杭州:浙江人民出版社,1997 年,第 123 页。
[84] 吴慧:《中国经济史若干问题的计量研究》,福州:福建人民出版社,2009 年,第 383 页。
[85] (元)朱世杰:《四元玉鉴》卷下,《中国科学技术典籍通汇》第 1 册,郑州:河南教育出版社,1995 年,第 1260 页。
[86] (元)丁巨:《丁巨算法》,《中国科学技术典籍通汇》第 1 册,郑州:河南教育出版社,1995 年,第 1313 页。
[87] (元)贾亨:《算法全能集》,《中国科学技术典籍通汇》第 1 册,郑州:河南教育出版社,1995 年,第 1336 页。
[88] (元)安止斋:《详明算法》,《中国科学技术典籍通汇》第 1 册,郑州:河南教育出版社,1995 年,第 1370 页。
[89] 同上,第 1367 页。
[90] (元)脱脱等:《宋史》卷 175《食货上三》,北京:中华书局,1986 年,第 4231—4232 页。
[91] 中国台湾文海出版社编:《元典章》卷 58《工部一·缎匹》,台北:文海出版社,1974 年,第 788 页。
[92] 同上,第 786 页。

兹:"任城国亢父缣一匹,幅广二尺二寸,长四丈,重二十五两。值钱六百一十八(文)。"[93]此缣被考证为公元1世纪末的产物,当时1两约合今0.3两,1尺约合今0.712 5市尺,算得"幅广二尺二寸,长四丈"为88平方尺(约为今62.7平方尺),"重二十五两"约为今7.5两,即每平方尺约重今0.12两。而宋元时期1两约合今0.7两,1尺约合今0.921 6市尺,算得丝绢"幅广二尺五分,长四十二尺"为105平方尺(约为今96.768平方尺),"重十二两"约为今8.4两,即每平方尺约重今0.09两。[94]由于古代绢的类别较多,每种绢之间的经纬密度不同,匹重自然有别。例如,"缣"也是绢的一种,[95]但它的特点是"其丝细致,数兼于绢"。[96]又《居延汉简》:"出河内廿两帛八匹一丈三尺四寸大半寸,直二千九百七十八。"[97]这段话的意思是说河内郡所织造的帛匹重20两,每匹帛的平均价值约350钱。[98]有研究者分析了汉代出土的丝绸实物,汉绢平均每平方厘米经线43~46支,纬线33~36支,汉缣平均每平方厘米经线62~80支,纬线35~55支。[99]至于汉代家蚕丝的质量,有资料说汉代为0.02~0.03毫米,而近代广州为0.028毫米,日本为0.027 3毫米。[100]可见,汉代家蚕丝的纤维直径丝毫不逊于近代家蚕丝。元代丝绸亦如汉代,仅从目前出土的部分丝绢实物分析,内蒙古集宁市出土的元代残绢,每平方厘米经纬线为46×38支;甘肃漳县出土的元代黄色绢每平方厘米经纬线为(28~72)×(16~32)支;新疆盐湖古墓出土的元代黄色油绢每平方厘米经纬线为32×28支,蓝色染缬绢每平方厘米经纬线为42×42支,赭红绢每平方厘米经纬线为52×48支等。[101]这些数据尽管还不足以展现汉代和元代整个丝织技术发展水平的全貌,但至少能说明二者在丝绸织造工艺方面相差无几。因此,汉代的丝织折耗率便可以作为我们认识和理解元代丝织生产折耗问题的一个重要参照。按照前面的分析,我们不妨简单地将元代各种织物的折耗情况列表如下(表1)。

表1 元代绸缎匹重与折耗之关系简表

类别 品种	该丝/匹(两)	匹重(两)	匹法(尺)	折耗(两)	文献来源
锦	19,今13.3				《丁巨算法》
	35,今24.5	30.8,今21.56	25,今17.5	4.2,今2.94	《四元玉鉴》
绢	11.25,今7.857	10,今7	42,今38.7072	1.25,今0.875	《算法全能集》
	16,今11.2	12,今8.4	同上	4,今2.8	《详明算法》
	11.25,今7.857	10,今7	同上	1.25,今0.875	《透簾细草》
		今8.4,10,今7	同上		《宋史·食货志》
罗	17,今11.9	14,今9.8	40,今36.864	3,今2.1	《详明算法》
	16,今11.2	13,今9.1	同上	3,今2.1	《元典章》
绫	28,今19.6	24.5,今17.15	26,今23.9616	3.5,今2.45	《四元玉鉴》
	20,今14				
绸	23,今16.1	20,今14	28,今25.8084	3,今2.1	《四元玉鉴》

---

93 罗振玉、王国维:《流沙坠简考释·释二·器物类》,上虞罗氏宸翰楼影印本,1914年,第43—44页。
94 翁礼华著:《中国历代赋税和当前税制改革》附录,北京:中国税务出版社,1998年,第227—229页。
95 (汉)班固:《汉书》卷97上《外戚传上》唐颜师古注[3],北京:中华书局,1983年,第3963页。
96 (汉)刘熙:《释名·释采帛》。
97 谢桂华等:《居延汉简释文合校》,北京:文物出版社,1987年,第496页。
98 汤明燧编:《中国古代社会经济史》,中州书画社,1982年,第129—130页。
99 王震亚:《汉代蚕桑丝织业及丝绸贸易述论》,甘肃省社会科学学会联合会、甘肃省历史学会编:《史学论丛》,兰州:兰州大学出版社,1992年,第42页。
100 夏鼐:《我国古代蚕桑丝绸的历史》,见氏著《夏鼐文集》中,北京:社会科学文献出版社,2000年,第347页。
101 陈炳应主编:《中国少数民族科学技术史丛书·纺织卷》,南宁:广西科学技术出版社,1996年,第601—602页。

续表1

类别\品种	该丝/匹(两)	匹重(两)	匹法(尺)	折耗(两)	文献来源
纱	10,今7			2,今1.4	《元典章》
缎	53,今37.1	46.7,今32.69	40,今36.864	6.3,今4.41	《元典章》
	40,今28	35.3,今24.71	30,今27.648	4.7,今3.29	《元典章》

注：《元典章》规定绸缎按打络丝"十分中一分折耗"加续头剪接"八托每缎折一两"或"六托每缎折七钱"折耗计算。

由于史料匮乏，表中有些内容虽然只能存以缺憾，但大体上看，元代丝织物生产的折耗每匹大约为2两至6.3两不等。

五、元代士兵的部分军服与丝绸消费问题

元代官营丝绸业比较发达，据《元史·百官志》的粗略统计，二部（指工部、兵部）三院（指储政院、将作院和中政院）一府（指内史府），共设有72所作坊，用于织造丝绸。其作坊几乎遍布全国各大中城市，匠户规模空前庞大，工匠众多。不过，详细内容可参见杨玲的博士论文《元代丝织品研究》，兹不赘论。

一般认为，元代大量丝绸除纳失失专供统治阶级消费之外，其他丝织物也有用于士兵支出者。如《透帘细草》有算题云：

今有兵士二千六百二十六人，每人散与皂衫一领，用绸三丈四尺。问计用绸多少？匹法四十二尺。答曰：二千一百二十五匹三丈四尺。[102]

又《丁巨算法》：

今有兵士三千二百五十人，每人给散胖袄一领，用纻丝一丈八尺五寸。问该几？答曰：二千五百五匹五尺。[103]

关于元代的军事后勤问题，丛海平的博士论文《元代军事后勤制度研究》考述甚祥，有兴趣的读者可以参看，本文仅就元代算书中涉及的元代士兵部分军服问题略做阐释。元代军队有中央宿卫军（包括怯薛和侍卫亲军）和地方镇戍军之分，其中"怯薛丹之禁卫一万二千骑"。[104]到元朝后期，由汉人士兵为主体所构成的侍卫亲军总人数已经达到20万至30万之间。[105]地方镇戍军主要由蒙古军、探马赤军、汉军和新附军四部分组成，因镇戍军是针对有丁之家，"无众寡尽签为兵"，[106]并立为军籍，当时"以兵籍系军机重务，汉人不阅其数。虽枢密近臣职专军旅者，惟长官一二人知之。故有国百年，而内外兵数之多寡，人莫有知之者"，[107]故地方镇戍军究竟有多少人数囿于资料所限，难以详知。不过，据陈高华先生的保守估计，元朝先后签点定籍的汉军户至少有30万户。[108]当役军人需要自备鞍马器仗，但"口粮、物料、衣装"

102　（元）佚名：《透帘细草》，《中国科学技术典籍通汇》第1册，郑州：河南教育出版社，1995年，第1292页。
103　（元）丁巨：《丁巨算法》，《中国科学技术典籍通汇》第1册，郑州：河南教育出版社，1995年，第1308页。
104　（意）马可·波罗：《马可波罗行纪》，北京：东方出版社，2011年，第220页。
105　白寿彝总主编；陈得芝主编：《中国通史》13第8卷《中古时代·元时期》上，上海：上海人民出版社，1997年，第959页。
106　（明）宋濂等：《元史》卷98《兵一》，北京：中华书局，1976年，第2508页。
107　同上，第2509页。
108　陈高华：《论元代军户》，见氏著《元史研究论稿》，北京：中华书局，1991年，第130页。

除外。[109]上面所引《透簾細草》和《丁巨算法》讲到的"每人散与皂衫一领"及"每人给散胖袄一领"应当就是指元朝士兵的部分军服。

《元史·舆服志》规定士兵的服装:"襯袍,制用绯锦,武士所以裼裲裆。士卒袍,制以绢絁,绘宝相花。"[110]考宋代的服饰,学界对"皂衫"有两种认识:其一,"皂衫属于袍衫一类";[111]其二,皂衫"是一种窄短的小衫,交领右衽开襟,窄袖紧身,衫长至腰,两侧开胯"。[112]那么,元代的士兵皂衫究竟是"袍衫"还是"黑色短袖单衣"? 这就需要考察做一件"皂衫"需要多少丝绸。《透簾细草》说一领皂衫"用绸三丈四尺",前揭《淮南子·天文训》云"匹者中人之度",按《汉书·食货志》规定"布帛广二尺二寸为幅,长四丈为匹",[113]表明用"长四丈"的布帛可以裁制一件普通人穿着的上衣与下裳相连的"深衣"。[114]经初步换算,[115]西汉"四丈"约为今 40 尺×0.8295 市尺＝33.18 市尺,元代"三丈四尺"约为今 34 尺×0.9216 市尺＝31.3344 市尺。由此不难看出,元代士兵的"皂衫"实为一种"袍衫",或云"质孙(即蒙古语 JISUM 的音译)服"。《元史·舆服志》载:"质孙,汉言一色服也,内庭大宴则服之。冬夏之服不同,然无定制。凡勋戚大臣近侍,赐则服之。下至于乐工卫士,皆有其服。精粗之制,上下之别,虽不同,总谓之质孙云。"[116]其身份主要以衣料和颜色来区别,如"百官质孙,冬之服凡九等,大红纳石一,大红怯绵里一,大红冠素一,桃红、蓝、绿官素各一,紫、黄、鸦青各一。夏之服凡十四等,素纳石失一,聚线宝里纳石失一,枣褐浑金间丝蛤珠一,大红官素带宝里一,大红明珠褡子一,桃红、蓝、绿、银褐各一,高丽鸦青云袖罗一,驼褐、茜红、白毛子各一,鸦青官素带宝里一。"[117]然而,"庶人除不得服赭黄,惟许服暗花纻丝绸绫罗毛毼",[118]"今后汉人、高丽、南人等投充怯薛者,并在禁限"。[119]因此,元代士兵的皂衫亦应是一种上下连衣裳式样的"质孙",采用黑色的丝绸织成。学界一般认为,元代戎服"只有一种本民族的服饰,即质孙服,样式为紧身窄袖的袍服,有交领和方领、长和短两种,长的至膝下,短的仅及膝。还有一种辫线袄与质孙服完全相同,只是下摆宽大、折为密裥。"[120]

至于"胖袄",亦名"缊袍",[121]即"短质孙服"则是采用缎子制成的一种棉上衣,是士兵的冬装。据考,宋朝的士兵"胖袄"穿在铁甲内,以防止磨伤皮肤,胖袄长 4 尺 6 寸,[122]元明要求"凡胖袄长齐膝窄袖"。[123]元代实行军户制,按照元律,"元代蒙古、探马赤、汉军户从军须自备鞍马器仗和日常盘缠。朝廷发给军士每人每月五斗米(相当于宋 7.415 斤)、一斤盐,另每年支给冬夏衣装"。[124]由于元代兵士的"胖袄"是以纻丝为质料,故纻丝的染织(纻丝是先染后织)数量巨大,事实上已经成为各地官营织染局的主流产品,详细情况见表2。

---

109 左言东、徐诚著:《中国古代行政管理概要》,杭州:浙江古籍出版社,1989.年,第356页。
110 (明)宋濂等:《元史》卷78《舆服一》,北京:中华书局,1976年,第1940页。
111 黄能馥、陈娟娟:《中国服饰史》,上海:上海人民出版社,2014年,第316页。
112 陈艳娥绘:《陈艳娥画仕女·案头画范》,北京:人民美术出版社,2010年,第5页。
113 (汉)班固:《汉书》卷24下《食货志下》,北京:中华书局,1983年,第1149页。
114 钱小萍主编:《丝绸织染》,郑州:大象出版社,2005年,第539页。
115 注:汉代布帛幅阔二尺二寸,元代布帛幅宽二尺五寸。
116 (明)宋濂等:《元史》卷78《舆服一》,北京:中华书局,1976年,第1938页。
117 同上。
118 同上,第1943页。
119 同上,第1944页。
120 李楠编著:《中国古代服饰》,北京:中国商业出版社,2015年,第141页。
121 潘吉星著:《天工开物校注及研究》,成都:巴蜀书社,1989年,第333页。
122 杜文玉编著:《图说中国古代兵器与兵书》,北京/西安:世界图书出版公司,2017年,第28页。
123 《明史》卷67《舆服志》,
124 王晓欣:《关于唐、元士兵经济待遇的几个问题》,南开大学历史系《中国史论集》编辑组编:《中国史论集》,天津:天津古籍出版社,1994年,第184页。

表2　诸书所见江南织染局院岁额丝缎简表[125]

局院名称	岁额情况	资料来源
建昌路织染局	岁课生熟段匹2 250段	《雪楼集》
庆元路织染局	岁课六托段匹3 291段	《元祐四明志》
金陵东织染局	额造段4 527匹，纻丝11 502.8两	《至大金陵新志》
溧阳州织染局	至元二十一年进呈段匹1 820段	《至大金陵新志》
句容县生帛局	造办纻丝斜纹495段	《至大金陵新志》
镇江府织染局	额作段匹3561段	《至顺镇江志》
镇江府生帛局	额作段匹1 830段	《至顺镇江志》
丹徒县生帛局	额作段匹510段	《至顺镇江志》
宁国路织染局	岁造生帛三色凡1 601段，至元二十八年添造宁国路丝绸150段	《永乐大典》《徽州府志》
福建织绣提举司	大德元年，减福建提举司岁织段3 000匹，其所织者加文绣，增其岁输衲服200	《元史》

考元成宗元贞元年（1295）正月，刑部"勒令各司县达鲁花赤、局官等造纳胖袄、皮甲"[126]等军备物质，惜有关胖袄生产的各种具体史料比较缺乏，从这层意义来讲，尽管元代算书仅见两道（不包括《透帘细草》抄自《杨辉算法》的那道"兵士三千四百七十四人，每三人支汗衫绢七十尺"[127]算题）有关兵士军服的算题，数量确实不多，但却颇有史学价值，因为它从侧面反映了元代兵士对丝织品的需求，似可与前面的"丝银全科户""减半科（丝）户""止纳系官五户丝户"及"止纳系官丝户"所负担的丝科数量相呼应。

六、余论

元代从窝阔台执政时期开始施行征税之法，其中心目的还是为了解决军用之需。于是，元代在通政院右司下设工房之科，将"常课段匹"作为其六大职能之一。[128]与中原历代王朝的法定计量方法不同，元代规定丝织物的常用标准是"托"，且对官府作坊常课段匹的用色、匹重、匹长及幅面都有严格规定。元代通过对民户所科"丝料"，把全国各地的大量蚕丝和绸绢集中到官府，遂导致官营丝织业的发展，规模空前，一些民间丝织作坊甚至出现了雇佣劳动关系。[129]

那么，如何比较客观地展现元代丝织业发展的历史全貌？学界普遍认为三重证据法的优点不言自明。然而，究竟哪些传世文献可以用来作为研究元代丝织业发展状况的参考史料，学者的认识并不一致。尤其随着"新史学"的兴起，越来越多的学者已经认识到拓宽史料应用范围对于"新史学"研究的重要性。正是在这样的学术背景下，数学社会史应运而生。在已故数学史家李迪看来，"任何一个数学史问题都和历史紧密相关"。[130]与之相应，《九章算术》《数书九章》以及《杨辉算法》中各种算题与其社会经济之间的关系研究备受学界关注，发表的相关成果较多。相较于前朝，元代留下来的算书典籍大约有10种之多，算是保存算书文献比较丰富的一个时代。当然，充分利用这些算书中的资料对于进一步拓

---

[125] 参见魏明孔主编；胡小鹏著：《中国手工业经济通史·宋元卷》，福州：福建人民出版社，2004年，第646－647页。
[126] 方龄贵校注：《通制条格校注》卷27《杂令》，北京：中华书局，2001年，第617页。
[127] （元）佚名：《透帘细草》，《中国科学技术典籍通汇》第1册，郑州：河南教育出版社，1995年，第1289页。
[128] （明）宋濂等：《元史》卷85《百官志一》，北京：中华书局，1976年，第2123页。
[129] 《线装经典》编委会编：《中国通史》，昆明：云南人民出版社，2017年，第285页。
[130] 李迪：《中国数学史中的未解决问题》，见吴文俊主编，济南：山东教育出版社，1987年，《中国数学史论文集》（三），第22页。

展和丰富元代社会经济史的研究内容无疑具有一定的价值和作用。

《透帘细草》涉及元代丝织业内容的算题数量虽然不是最多,但考其史料价值,却不乏可取之处。例如,通过《透帘细草》和其他元代算书相互参照,我们能够初步厘清元代丝织物匹重、用丝、匹长及幅面之间的数量关系,而这也是元代算书相对其他文献来说它们本身所具有的独特史料价值。

附记

高山仰止,由于晚辈的研究领域是宋元数理科技,先生和刘老合校的《算经十书》(1998)便成为晚辈进入学习杨辉算书的门径。先生从早期的《高次方程数值解法和天元术》(1978)到近期的《吴敬〈九章比类〉与贾宪〈九章细草〉比较刍议》(2016),可以看出先生对宋元数学的钟爱。当然,宋元数学的高峰离不开中国传统数学发展的宏阔背景,正是因为这个缘故,先生先后发表了包括《谈谈刘徽的数学教育思想》(1981)、《〈九章算术〉中的整数句段形研究》(1982)、《刘徽〈九章算术注〉中的定义及演绎逻辑试析》(1983)、《〈九章算术〉和刘徽注中之率概念及其应用试析》(1984)、《〈九章算术〉勾股章的校勘和刘徽勾股理论系统初探》(1985)、《试论刘徽的数学理论体系》(1987)等名篇在内的大量学术成果,遂成为中国《九章算术》研究第一人。同时,先生除了自己用外语撰写论文外,还翻译了德国 F. KLEIN、法国 I. Hadamard 等国外名家的论著,可谓学贯中西,汇通古今。说来机缘巧合,2019 年由河北大学、中国科学院自然科学史研究所、中国数学会联合主办,河北大学宋史研究中心等单位联合承办的《纪念祖冲之诞辰 1590 周年国际学术研讨会》在河北大学新校区举行。晚辈有幸结识了先生,先生德高望重,享誉海内外,不仅学问精深,为人也和蔼可亲,十分平易近人。当先生了解到我们新创办的年刊《科学史研究论丛》急需名家大作来为之增色添彩的情况后,随即将其珍藏多年的力作惠赐本刊,令人感动。晚辈初识数学史学界的名流,不免诚惶诚恐,先生却是那么心地宽厚,胸襟广阔,只要晚辈有求于先生,先生总是二话不讲,慷慨相助。想来晚辈与先生才相识几年,然受其泽惠,车载斗量,不可尽数,实无以报答,谨以此文略表晚辈对先生的敬仰和感激之情。今值先生八十寿辰之际,"愿祝南山寿,千秋日月长"。

作者

吕变庭,男,1962 年生,历史学博士,河北大学宋史研究中心教授、博士生导师,研究方向为宋代科技史。

马晴晴,女,1990 年生,河北大学宋史研究中心博士研究生,研究方向为宋元科技史。

通讯地址:河北省保定市莲池区五四东路 180 号

邮箱:zpiyyn@qq.com

邮编:071002

手机:15903122870

由《测圆海镜》扩展"边径线"数学内容

郑振初　（香港教育学院）

一、引言

学生事师郭书春教授，以《测圆海镜》为研究题目。在参考清代各家学者著作时，偶见刘岳云《算学丛话》的文字。

> 余成此书，时在甲戌年，及丁丑于金陵算学局教习生徒，其提调杭州丁乃文以同文馆李先生题见示，有大中垂线、明勾股和求城径一题，因又以垂线方边配合各勾股率，增二卷。后李先生赠算学课艺一部，内无此题，而有大中垂线虚勾股和求城径题，然两题之难易悬殊矣，其合勾股断，勾股即余之高平和高平较，盖是书必添设二勾股率，其理乃备。李先生固早知也。

笔者参考李善兰《九容图表》和杨兆鋆《须曼精庐算学》的边径线内容，尝试理解大中垂线的数学内容，并为"大中垂线，明勾股和求圆径"求解。

《测圆海镜》系统结合了容圆问题，是勾股问题的扩展。由平行于勾股形的勾股两组线段，与弦组成了 15 个相似的三角形。《测圆海镜》以 13 形 13 事的两事寻找圆径方程（表1）。清代李善兰完备了测圆系统，得出十三事的对应。任取这些三角的十三事中二事，都可用天元术推算圆半径。

表1

13形	大	边	底	高	平	大差	小差	极	虚	明	曳	合	断
周界	$[a+b+c]$	$[c+b]$	$[c+a]$	$[b]$	$[c]$	$[c+b-a]$	$[c-b+a]$	$[c]$	$[a+b-c]$	$[c-a]$	$[c-b]$	$[a+b]$	$[b-a]$
13事	和和	大和	小和	股	勾	较和	较较	弦	和较	大差	小差	和	较

李善兰和杨兆鋆在原有的 13 形 13 事，再加上中垂线和容方边两事，把容圆系统推广至"14 形 14 事"和"15 形 15 事"。笔者得出加上中垂线后的"14 形 14 事"最高方程次数为 6，"15 形 15 事"的圆径方程最高次数为 8。

杨兆鋆在卷二十以"边，径，线"的组合提出以下"8 个新勾股形"，见表2。

表2

新 8 形	中垂线形	容方边形	边线和形	边线较形	边径和形	边径较形	线径和形	线径较形

这"新 8 形 8 事"推广了边和线的容圆系统。原有 13 形 13 事再加上新 8 形 8 事，可以推广为"21 形 21 事"。以 21 形 21 事任两事为条件，寻求容圆方程。把原有"测圆问题"抽象化，而且不必有对应图形，也可以用代数解特定几何问题。

笔者以此小文，贺吾师八十华诞。虽无甚高论，想吾师见学生心意，亦不拘也。

二、《测圆海镜》学者研究结果简述

《测圆海镜》是元数学家李冶(1192—1279)的数学著作。李冶为什么写《测圆海镜》？清阮元(1764—1849)以为《测圆海镜》为发挥立天元一之术而作。其实李冶自己表白他的《测圆海镜》是为了阐释洞渊九容，而非为"发挥立天元一之术"而作。[1]

测圆海镜的问题是由实在情况开始的。由一个圆城的出行，找出城径的问题，抽象为一个勾股容圆问题，再由九容问题，变成 13 事勾股形两事找出圆城径的问题。测圆所探究的问题再不是生活上出现的利息、行军、工程问题。容圆问题自成系统，以代数建立高次代数方程解决几何问题。

李冶的解题法，不一定用半径为方程未知数，部分题目是以另一条件作未知数，然后设方程，再由方程答案推算半径。清代学者已统一用半径或直径作为方程未知数。杨兆鋆在其《须曼精庐算学》卷十四的《九容演代》中以二事作条件，找出容圆半径或直径的方程，共有 160 题。

清代陈维祺提出的"泛积"概念，笔者引用这个形式，发展"比例记数"的数学表达式，以检查所有测圆数式。比例记号法数学形式是" $[p](q) = \dfrac{p}{a+b+c} \cdot q$ "。各勾股型的十三事都可以用 $[p](q)$ 来表示。例如明形为 $[c-a]$，勾为 (a)，所以明勾为 $[c-a](a) = \dfrac{c-a}{a+b+c} \cdot a$。又，平形为 $[a]$，大较为 $(c-a)$，所以平大较为 $[a](c-a) = \dfrac{a}{a+b+c} \cdot (c-a)$。并且可以得出"明勾＝平大较"。又例如 $r = \dfrac{ab}{a+b+c}$，用比例记号法可以表示为 $r = [a](b) = [b](a) = [ab]$。由于表达式出于泛积概念，所以满足" $[i](j) = [j](i)$ "，亦即是满足"形事互换"。

《算学课艺》中不少题目是作图解十三事的数式关系。计有英铎"虚勾更弦较等于更勾股较。试作图解"等题。即以几何证明其条目。用以上的代数记号法，虚形是 $[a+b-c]$，虚勾即 $[a+b-c](a)$，更形为 $[c-b]$，更弦即 $[c-b](c)$。更勾股较为 $[c-b](b-a)$。由 $[a+b-c](a) - [c-b](c) = [ab+bc-ac-bb] = [c-b](b-a)$，得出题目结果。

王季同证明了《测圆海镜》的解可透过 4 次方程解决(以"勾股"比例作天元来表述，并且最高为 4 次)。但并没有证明"圆径方程一定不高于 4 次"。笔者之前在老师指导的毕业论文[2]中给出证明，所有测圆的题目都能以圆径作 x，而其方程次数一定不高于 4。

三、李善兰的《九容图表》

李善兰在容圆系统加入径线内容，推广容圆系统。大中垂线形，是以中垂线 $\dfrac{ab}{c}$ 为周界的相似直角三角形。下图为李善兰《九容图表》的图式，李善兰给出 24 条解释图形的名称，其中第(19)至(22)项给出 4 个中垂线关系。用"比例记数"的形式，可以简易证明数式的关系。

---

[1] 郭书春《尊重原始文献避免以讹传讹》自然科学史研究第 26 卷第 3 期(2007 年)438—448.
[2] 《关于测圆海镜及其清代研究的探讨》2013 年 5 月。

表3

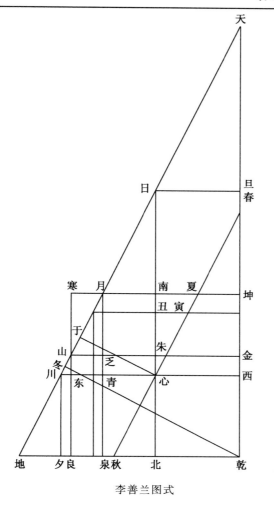

李善兰图式

(1)乾冬大中垂线
(2)心子太中垂线等半径
(3)天金黄广股即股方差
(4)地泉黄长勾即勾方差
(5)天坤大差股即股圆差
(6)地艮小差勾即勾圆差
(7)子地等北地底勾
(8)秋艮等夏坤断勾
(9)天春等日心太股
(10)地秋等心川太勾
(11)日子等天旦高股
(12)秋夕月子等月南明勾
(13)春旦子山等山东更股
(14)月夏夕北等月川平弦
(15)朱青长方等虚勾股积
(16)月山巽心丑寅俱等虚
(17)日心子春心西俱等高
(18)心子川心秋北心夏南俱等平
(19)大中垂线之勾等平中垂线
(20)大中垂线之股等高中垂线
(21)大中垂线之弦等太中垂线
(22)线径较等虚中垂线
(23)更大较乘底大和等于半径方
(24)太弦方减圆径方等于合较方

李善兰并没有证明这些中垂线的关系,以下用数学形式,演示李善兰提出的4条中垂线(表4)。

表4

(19)大中垂线之勾等平中垂线	大中垂线之勾是 $\left[\dfrac{ab}{c}\right](a)$。平形的中垂线是 $[a]\left(\dfrac{ab}{c}\right)$ 所以 $\left[\dfrac{ab}{c}\right]a=[a]\left(\dfrac{ab}{c}\right)$
(20)大中垂线之股等高中垂线 $\left[\dfrac{ab}{c}\right]b=[b]\left(\dfrac{ab}{c}\right)$	(21)大中垂线之弦等太中垂线 $\left[\dfrac{ab}{c}\right]c=[c]\left(\dfrac{ab}{c}\right)$
(22)线径较等虚中垂线	线－径 $=\dfrac{ab}{c}-\dfrac{2ab}{a+b+c}=\dfrac{ab(a+b+c)-2abc}{c(a+b+c)}=\left(\dfrac{a+b-c}{a+b+c}\right)\left(\dfrac{ab}{c}\right)=$ $[a+b-c]\left(\dfrac{ab}{c}\right)=$ 虚中垂线

四、李善兰《九容图表》"勾股边径比例表"

第1组

三事和	倍弦	线	径
边线较	倍边径较	边线和	倍方边

第2组

边	弦	边线较	径
边线和	三事和	线	勾股和

第3组

径	倍勾股和	边径较	径
边线较	倍边	倍线	三事和

第4组

三事和	倍勾股和	边	径
边线较	倍线径较	边线和	倍线

第5组

径	倍弦	线径较	径
边线较	倍方边	线	三事和

第6组

线径较	边径较	倍线减径	径
勾股和	弦	线	边

第7组

二线径较	径	边线较	边
勾股和	弦	勾股和垂线较	较勾股和边径和之

李善兰的比例表没有写出读法,杨兆鋆《须曼精庐算学》卷二十所附的比例表则写出读法,见表5:

表5

①	②	③	④
⑤	⑥	⑦	⑧

"右表凡六方检法左右二纵上下二横东西上下各一交互斜比每方比例六共得比例三十有六"。

所述"左右二纵""上下二横""东西上下各一交互斜比",其关系见表6。

表6

"左右二纵"	"上下二横"	"东西上下各一交互斜比"
$\frac{④}{③}=\frac{⑧}{⑦}, \frac{②}{①}=\frac{⑥}{⑤}$	$\frac{①}{③}=\frac{②}{④}, \frac{⑤}{⑦}=\frac{⑥}{⑧}$	$\frac{①}{⑦}=\frac{②}{⑧}, \frac{③}{⑤}=\frac{④}{⑥}$

以上每样两种,所以两表一组便有6种比例。李善兰的图表共有7组。即是有42种比例数式。能出现这些关系,是因为所有比例表都是以下述比例编成。

表7是以①③⑤⑦这4个数为主体,再而②④⑥⑧是前4个数的倍数k。每组表共有4个等式,每2个等式为一比例式,可得6个比例式。

表7

①	②	③	④
a	ka	b	kb
⑤	⑥	⑦	⑧
c	kc	d	kd

$$\frac{①}{②}=\frac{③}{④}=\frac{⑤}{⑥}=\frac{⑦}{⑧}=k$$

每 2 个等式为一比例式,可得 6 个比例式。

引用杨兆鋆的比例表读法,可以得出各组的数式比例,共 42 条。

第 1 组　比例表

三事和	倍弦	线	径
边线较	倍边径较	边线和	倍方边

(三事和)(径)=(倍弦)(线)。(三事和)(倍边径较)=(倍弦)(边线较)。
(三事和)(倍方边)=(倍弦)(边线和)。(线)(倍边径较)=(径)(边线较)。
(线)(倍方边)=(径)(边线和)。(边线较)(倍方边)=(倍边径较)(边线和)。

第 2 组　比例表

边	弦	边线较	径
边线和	三事和	线	勾股和

(边)(径)=(弦)(边线较)。(边)(三事和)=(弦)(边线和)。
(边)(勾股和)=(弦)(线)。(边线较)(线)=(径)(边线和)。
(边线较)(勾股和)=(径)(线)。(边线和)(勾股和)=(三事和)(线)。

第 3 组　比例表

径	倍勾股和	边径较	径
边线较	倍线	边	三事和

(径)(径)=(倍勾股和)(边径较)。(径)(倍线)=(倍勾股和)(边线较)。
(径)(三事和)=(倍勾股和)(边)。(边径较)(倍线)=(径)(边线较)。
(边径较)(三事和)=(径)(边)。(边线较)(三事和)=(倍线)(边)。

第 4 组　比例表

三事和	倍勾股和	边	径
边线较	倍线径较	边线和	倍线

(三事和)(径)=(倍勾股和)(边)。(三事和)(倍线径较)=(倍勾股和)(边线较)。
(三事和)(倍线)=(倍勾股和)(边线和)。(边)(边线和)=(径)(边线较)。
(边)(倍线)=(径)(边线和)。(边线较)(倍线)=(倍线径较)(边线和)。

第 5 组　比例表

径	倍弦	线径较	径
边线较	倍方边	线	三事和

（径）（径）=（倍弦）（线径较）。（径）（倍方边）=（倍弦）（边线较）。
（径）（三事和）=（倍弦）（线）。（线径较）（倍方边）=（径）（边线较）。
（线径较）（三事和）=（径）（线）。（边线较）（三事和）=（倍方边）（线）。

第 6 组　比例表

线径较	边径较	倍线减径	径
勾股和	弦	线	边

（线径较）（径）=（边径较）（倍线减径）。（线径较）（弦）=（边径较）（勾股和）。
（线径较）（边）=（边径较）（线）。（倍线减径）（弦）=（径）（勾股和）。
（倍线减径）（边）=（径）（线）。（勾股和）（边）=（弦）（线）。

第 7 组　比例组

二线径较	径	边线较	边
勾股和	弦	勾股和垂线较	勾股和边径之较

②×③=①×④⇔（径）×（线）=（二线径较）×（边）
⑥×⑦=⑤×⑧⇔（弦）×（勾股和垂线较）=（勾股和）×（边径和勾股和之较）
②×⑦=①×⑧⇔（径）×（勾股和垂线较）=（二线径较）×（边径和勾股和之较）
③×⑥=④×⑤⇔（线）×（弦）=（边）×（勾股和）
①×⑥=②×⑤⇔（二线径较）×（弦）=（径）×（勾股和）
④×⑦=③×⑧⇔（边）×（勾股和垂线较）=（线）×（边径和勾股和之较）

又李善兰《九容图表》中第七组数字。其中一格"边线较"误。应为"线"[3]。李善兰《九容图表》内的 42 条数式中。有部分是重复的。

例如第 1 组"（倍弦）（线）=（三事和）（径）"等同第 5 组"（倍弦）（线）=（径）（三事和）"。

笔者把第 1 组至第 6 组的 36 个比例式，划去相同部分，得出以下 26 个不重复的比例数式（表 8）。

表 8　李善兰《九容图表》中 26 个不重复的比例数式

（1）	（三事和）（径）=（倍弦）（线）	（14）	（勾股和）（边径较）=（线径较）（弦）
（2）	（三事和）（径）=（倍勾股和）（边）	（15）	（勾股和）（径）=（倍线减径）（弦）
（3）	（三事和）（线）=（边线和）（勾股和）	（16）	（勾股和）（弦）=（线）
（4）	（三事和）（边线较）=（倍线）（边）	（17）	（径）（线径较）=（倍弦）
（5）	（三事和）（边径较）=（径）（边）	（18）	（径）（倍勾股和）=（边径较）
（6）	（三事和）（线径较）=（径）（线）	（19）	（径）（线径较）=（边径较）（倍线减径）
（7）	（三事和）（倍方边）=（倍弦）（边线和）	（20）	（径）（边）=（边线较）（弦）
（8）	（三事和）（倍边径较）=（倍弦）（边线较）	（21）	（径）（线）=（倍线减径）（边）
（9）	（三事和）（倍线径较）=（倍勾股和）（边线较）	（22）*	（径）（边线和）=（线）（倍方边）

---

[3] 《关于测圆海镜及其清代研究的探讨》2013 年 5 月。

续表8

(10)	(边线较)(倍线)=(边线和)(倍线径较)	(23)	(径)(边线和)=(线)(边线较)
(11)	(边线较)(倍方边)=(边线和)(倍边径较)	(24)	(径)(边线较)=(边线和)(边)
(12)	(边线较)(勾股和)=(径)(线)	(25)	(径)(边线较)=(线径较)(倍方边)
(13)	(线径较)(边)=(边径较)(线)	(26)	(径)(边线较)=(线)(倍边径较)

五、李善兰比例表如何推导

李善兰比例表内第 1 至第 6 组所用的比例项目,计有"弦(c),勾股和($a+b$),三事和($a+b+c$),边(E),径(D),线(H),边线和($H+E$),边线较($H-E$),边径较($H-D$),线径较($D-E$)"共 10 项。李善兰是如何推出比例表的?以下是一些猜想,由其中几个和较推出部分比例关系(表 9)。

表 9

①	由边线和可以推出"(边线和)(勾股和)=(线)(三事和)"及"(边线和)(弦)=(边)(三事和)"	数式(3) 数式(7)
②	由边线较可以推出"(边线较)(勾股和)=(线)(径)"及"(边线较)(弦)=(边)(径)"	数式(13) 数式(20)
③	由边径较可以推出"(边线较)(倍勾股和)=(径)(径)"及"(边径较)(三事和)=(边)(径)"	数式(18) 数式(5)
④	由线径较可以推出"(线径较)(三事和)=(线)(径)"及"(线径较)(倍弦)=(径)(径)"	数式(6) 数式(17)

其转变过程如下:

① 边线和 $=\left(\dfrac{ab}{c}+\dfrac{ab}{a+b}\right)=\dfrac{ab(a+b+c)}{c(a+b)}\Rightarrow$

$(H+E)=\dfrac{ab(a+b+c)}{c(a+b)}=\left(\dfrac{ab}{c}\right)\left(\dfrac{a+b+c}{a+b}\right)$,即"(边线和)(勾股和)=(线)(三事和)"$\Rightarrow$

$(H+E)=\dfrac{ab(a+b+c)}{c(a+b)}=\left(\dfrac{1}{c}\right)\left(\dfrac{ab}{a+b}\right)(a+b+c)$,即"(边线和)(弦)=(边)(三事和)"$\Rightarrow$

② 边线较 $=\dfrac{ab}{c}-\dfrac{ab}{a+b}=\dfrac{ab}{c}\cdot\dfrac{a+b-c}{(a+b)}\Rightarrow$

$(H-E)=\dfrac{ab}{c}\left(\dfrac{a+b-c}{a+b}\right)$,即"(边线较)(勾股和)=(线)(径)"$\Rightarrow$

$(H-E)=\dfrac{ab}{c}\left(\dfrac{a+b-c}{a+b}\right)=\left(\dfrac{1}{c}\right)\left(\dfrac{ab}{a+b}\right)(a+b-c)$,即"(边线较)(弦)=(边)(径)"

③ 边径较 $=\dfrac{2ab}{a+b+c}-\dfrac{ab}{a+b}=ab\left(\dfrac{2}{a+b+c}-\dfrac{1}{a+b}\right)=\dfrac{a+b-c}{ab((a+b+c)(a+b))}\Rightarrow$

$(D-E)=ab\left(\dfrac{a+b-c}{(a+b+c)(a+b)}\right)=\left(\dfrac{2ab}{a+b+c}\right)\cdot\dfrac{a+b-c}{2(a+b)}$,即"(边径较)(倍勾股和)=(径)(径)"$\Rightarrow$

$(D-E)=ab\left(\dfrac{a+b-c}{(a+b+c)(a+b)}\right)=\left(\dfrac{ab}{a+b}\right)\cdot\dfrac{a+b-c}{(a+b+c)}$,即"(边径较)(三事和)=(边)(径)"。

④ 线径较 $=\dfrac{ab}{c}-\dfrac{2ab}{a+b+c}=ab\left(\dfrac{1}{c}-\dfrac{2}{a+b+c}\right)=ab\left(\dfrac{a+b+c-2c}{c(a+b+c)}\right)=\left(\dfrac{ab}{c}\right)\left(\dfrac{a+b-c}{a+b+c}\right)\Rightarrow$

$(H-D)=\left(\dfrac{ab}{c}\right)\left(\dfrac{a+b-c}{a+b+c}\right)$,即"(线径较)(三事和)=(线)(径)"$\Rightarrow$

$(H-D)=\left(\dfrac{ab}{c}\right)\left(\dfrac{a+b-c}{a+b+c}\right)=\left(\dfrac{2ab}{a+b+c}\right)\left(\dfrac{a+b-c}{2c}\right)$,即"(线径较)(倍弦)=(径)(径)"。

六、《须曼精庐算学》卷二十比例数式建立方程

杨兆鋆《须曼精庐算学》卷二十解第 5 题至第 7 题,用了以下 5 个比例表的数式建立方程(表 10)。括号内数字对应李善兰 26 条式的数字次序。

表 10

数式	比例式	代数符号
(4)	(倍边)(线)=(边线较)(三事和)	$(2E)H=(H-E)(a+b+c)$
(13)	(边)(线径较)=(线)(边径较)	$E(H-D)=H(D-E)$
(21)	(径)(线)=(边)(倍线减径)	$DH=E(2H-D)$
(22)	(倍边)(线)=(径)(边线和)	$(2E)H=D(E+H)$
(26)	(二线)(边径较)=(径)(边线较)	$(2H)(D-E)=D(H-E)$

例如卷二十第 5 题"今有边径和一百三十,线与边径较较七十四。求方边圆径垂线各若干"。

以"(倍边)(线)=(径)(边线和)"找出方边的方程,

以"(径)(线)=(边)(倍线减径)"找出圆径方程,

以"(二线)(边径较)=(径)(边线较)"找出中垂线方程。

杨兆鋆给出本题三个"边径线"方程,见表 11。

表 11

边方程	$5x^2-[4(边径和)+3(较较)]x+[(边径和)^2+(边径和)(较较)]=0$
径方程	$-5x^2+[6(边径和)-3(较较)]x+[2(边径和)(较较)-2(边径和)^2]=0$
线方程	$-5x^2+[2(边径和)+4(较较)]x-[(边径和)^2-(较较)^2]=0$

又杨兆鋆卷二十第 7 题"今有边径较十。线和和二百一十四。求边径线各若干。"

以"(边)(线径较)=(线)(边径较)"找出方边的方程,

以"(径)(边线较)=(线)(倍边径较)"找出圆径方程,

以"(倍边)(线径较)=(倍线)(边径较)"找出中垂线方程。

杨兆鋆给出本题三个"边径线"方程见表 12。

表 12

边方程	$3x^2-(线和和)x+[(边径较)(线和和)-(边径较)^2]=0$
径方程	$3x^2-[6(边径较)+(线和和)]x+2(边径较)(线和和)-2(边径较)^2=0$
线方程	$3x^2+[4(线和和)-6(边径较)]x+[(边径较)^2-(线和和)^2]=0$

由比例式(22)"(倍边)(线)=(径)(边线和)"及联立方程解题。

由于以上问题的两个条件是"边径线"的线性组合,条件形如 $\alpha D+\beta E+\sigma H=p$ 及 $\delta D+\tau E+\lambda H=q$。

这类问题用变数作转换,可以用联立方程形式解出答案。

$$\begin{cases} \alpha D+\beta E+\sigma H=p & (A) \\ \delta D+\tau E+\lambda H=q & (B) \end{cases}$$

上述第(22)个比例式"(倍边)(线)=(径)(边线和)",即 $(2E)H=D(H+E)$,连接起三个变数,D,E,H。

由此可以轮转找出 $D=\dfrac{2HE}{H+E}, H=\dfrac{DE}{2E-D}, E=\dfrac{DH}{2H-D}$。

解"边径线"这类线性方程组,公式 $D(E+H)=2EH$ 的功能,有如勾股形的公式 $a^2+b^2=c^2$。(表 13)

表 13　卷二十第 5 题，找出"圆径方程，方边方程"

设边为 x	设径为 x
$\begin{cases} E+D=p & (A) \\ H-(D-E)=q & (B) \end{cases}$	$\begin{cases} E=p-D & (A) \\ H=q+D-(p-D) & (B) \end{cases}$
$(A) \Rightarrow D=p-x$	引用数式 $D(E+H)=2EH$，把上面内容代入
$(B) \Rightarrow H+x=q+D \Rightarrow H+x=q+D \Rightarrow H=(p+q-2x)$	$x(E+H)=2EH$
引用数式 $D(E+H)=2EH$，把上面内容代入。	$\Rightarrow x(p-x+q-p+2x)=2(q-p+2x)(p-x)$
$(p-x)[x+(p+q-2x)]=2x(p+q-2x)$	$\Rightarrow 5x^2+3qx-6px+2p(p-q)=0$
$\Rightarrow 5x^2-(4p+3q)x+p(p+q)=0$	

七、引用 Sylvester 定理找圆径方程

为了有系统地解决这类高次方程求解问题，本文引用了 Sylvester 的定理。

Sylvester 给出高次方程组有解的判别式，过程中也建立方程，其结果如下[4]。

Sylvester 定理：

有方程组 $\begin{cases} f(x)=a_3x^3+a_2x^2+a_1x+a_0 \\ g(x)=b_2x^2+b_1x+b_0 \end{cases}$，如要有 x_0，使得 $\begin{cases} f(x_0)=0 \\ g(x_0)=0 \end{cases}$，则必须有

$$\det \begin{vmatrix} b_2 & b_1 & b_0 & 0 & 0 \\ 0 & b_2 & b_1 & b_0 & 0 \\ 0 & 0 & b_2 & b_1 & b_0 \\ a_3 & a_2 & a_1 & a_0 & 0 \\ 0 & a_3 & a_2 & a_1 & a_0 \end{vmatrix} = 0。$$

这是方程组有共同解的条件。

八、《算学课艺》和"14 形 14 事"

《算学课艺》部分题目，也在测圆 13 事的基础上，加上中垂线或容方边为条件。

例如赓善的这一题"有虚勾股和有大中垂线，求圆径"，解题过程不难。赓善给出的方程是 $2r^2-2(大中垂线)r+(虚勾股和)(大中垂线)=0$。

回到文首刘岳云《算学丛话》提及的题目"已知大中垂线，明勾股和，求圆径"。也归类为"14 形 14 事"的题目。即是有大中垂线 $\frac{ab}{c}=p$，明和 $=[c-a](b+a)=q$，求 r。

由 $\begin{cases} \dfrac{ab}{c}=p & (A) \\ [c-a](b+a)=q & (B) \end{cases}$，把 a,b,c 用 r 及 $t=\tan\dfrac{\theta}{2}$ 表示。

因为 $a=\left(\dfrac{1-t}{t}\right)r, b=\dfrac{2}{(1-t)}r, c=\dfrac{1+t^2}{t(1-t)}r$，故

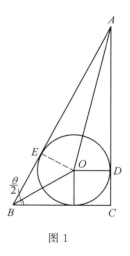

图 1

---

[4] Sylvester's Dialytic Method Elimination，见 Leonard Eugene Dickson，First Coursein the Theory of Equations，John Wiley & Sons, Inc. 1922。Sylvester 定理通用于一般的情况，即是 m 次方程和 n 次方程。这里只以 3 次和 2 次做演示。

$$\frac{ab}{c}=\frac{2(1+t)}{1+t^2}r,\ [c-a]=\frac{2t(1-t^2+2t)}{2(1+t)(1-t)}r\Rightarrow\begin{cases}\dfrac{2(1+t)}{1+t^2}r=p & \text{(A)}\\ \left(\dfrac{t}{1-t^2}\right)(1+2t-t^2)r=q & \text{(B)}\end{cases}$$

这是两个二元二次方程(t 为高次,r 为 1 次),引用 Sylvester 定理。把(B)式用(A)除,得

$$\left[\left(\frac{t}{1-t^2}\right)(1+2t-t^2)\right]r\Big/\left[\frac{2(1+t)}{1+t^2}r\right]=\frac{q}{p}$$

$$\Rightarrow\frac{t(1+2t-t^2)(1+t^2)}{2(1+t)(1-t^2)}=\frac{q}{p}\quad\text{(C)}$$

$$\Rightarrow pt(1+2t-t^2)(1+t^2)=2q(1+t)(1-t^2)$$

$$\Rightarrow pt^5-2pt^4-2qt^3-2(q+p)t^2+(2q-p)t+2q=0$$

由(A),$2(1+t)r=p(1+t^2)\Rightarrow pt^2-(2r)t+(p-2r)=0$

$$\det=\begin{vmatrix} p & (-2r) & (p-2r) & 0 & 0 & 0 & 0 \\ 0 & p & (-2r) & (p-2r) & 0 & 0 & 0 \\ 0 & 0 & p & (-2r) & (p-2r) & 0 & 0 \\ 0 & 0 & 0 & p & (-2r) & (p-2r) & 0 \\ 0 & 0 & 0 & 0 & p & (-2r) & (p-2r) \\ p & (-2p) & (-2q) & -2(p+q) & (2q-p) & 2q & 0 \\ 0 & p & (-2q) & (-2p) & (2q-p) & (2q-p) & 2q \end{vmatrix}$$

$$=(-4r^5+10pr^4+(6pq-8p^2)r^3+(2p^3-8p^2q)r^2+(2p^3q-2p^2q^2)r+p^3q^2)32p^2=0$$

此即为圆径方程。由于最后的 2 列没有 r,所以圆径方程不超过 r 的 5 次。

"14 形 14 事"可以有两种情况。

第一种"14 形 14 事"是"原 13 形"加上"容方边"。

第二种"14 形 14 事"是"原 13 形"加上"中垂线"。

更一般可以推广至"15 形 15 事",即是 13 形加上"容方边"和"中垂线"两形为 15 形。

《算学课艺》中还有以下"14 形 14 事"的例子,r 为半径,方程都是 5 次的。

例 1

"有断股弦较,有大中垂线,求圆径"作者贵荣。13 形加上"中垂线"。

$4r^5+6(\text{大中垂线})r^4-[8(\text{大中垂线})^2-2(\text{大中垂线})(\text{断股弦较})]r^3+$
$[2(\text{大中垂线})^3+4(\text{大中垂线})^2(\text{断股弦较})]r^2-$
$[2(\text{大中垂线})^3(\text{断股弦较})+2(\text{大中垂线})^2(\text{断股弦较})^2]r+[(\text{大中垂线})^3(\text{断股弦较})^2]=0$

例 2

"有容方边。有亷勾股较。求圆径"。作者王镇贤。13 形加上"容方边"。

$4r^5-18(\text{容方边})r^4+[16(\text{容方边})^2-2(\text{容方边})(\text{亷勾股较})]r^3-$
$[4(\text{容方边})^3-8(\text{容方边})^2(\text{亷勾股较})]r^2-$
$[4(\text{容方边})^3(\text{亷勾股较})+2(\text{容方边})^2(\text{亷勾股较})^2]r+[(\text{容方边})^3(\text{亷勾股较})^2]=0$

九、"14 形 14 事圆径方程"最高为 6 次

仿照附录的"13 形 13 事"径方程最高次数为 4 的证明,可以证明 14 形 14 事的"径方程的最高次数是 6 次"。按 Sylvester 的解题过程,设 r 为圆半径,而"14 形 14 事"的 6 次方程有百多题。以下选录"14 形 14 事"中,"以断和为一事,另一事为其他中垂线"的圆径次数最高的方程,共有 9 题,方程最高是 6 次。(表 14)

表 14

"14 形 14 事"方程次数最高例子为 6 次，"以断和为一事，不同形中垂线为另一事"。
(1)边中垂线及断和 $r^6-8(边中垂线)r^5+20(边中垂线)^2 r^4-[2(断和)^2(边中垂线)+16(边中垂线)^3]r^3+$ $[5(断和)^2(边中垂线)^2+4(边中垂线)^4]r^2-4(断和)^2(边中垂线)^3 r+(断和)^2(边中垂线)^4=0$
(2)底中垂线及断和 $r^6-8(底中垂线)r^5+20[(底中垂线)^2]r^4-[2(断和)^2(底中垂线)+16(底中垂线)^3]r^3+$ $[5(断和)^2(底中垂线)^2+4(底中垂线)^4]r^2-4(断和)^2(底中垂线)^3 r+(断和)^2(底中垂线)^4=0$
(3)高中垂线及断和 $r^6-4[(高中垂线)^2]r^4-[(断和)^2(高中垂线)^2-4(高中垂线)^4]r^2+(断和)^2(高中垂线)^4=0$
(4)平中垂线及断和 $r^6-4[(平中垂线)^2]r^4-[(断和)^2(平中垂线)^2-4(平中垂线)^4]r^2+(断和)^2(平中垂线)^4=0$
(5)大差中垂线及断和 $-4r^6+16[(大差中垂线)^2]r^4-16[(大差中垂线)^3]r^3+[4(断和)^2(大差中垂线)^2]+$ $4(大差中垂线)^4 r^2-4[(断和)^2(大差中垂线)^3]r+[(断和)^2(大差中垂线)^4]=0$
(6)小差中垂线及断和 $-4r^6+16[(小差中垂线)^2]r^4-16[(小差中垂线)^3]r^3+[4(断和)^2(小差中垂线)^2]+$ $4(小差中垂线)^4 r^2-4[(断和)^2(小差中垂线)^3]r+[(断和)^2(小差中垂线)^4]=0$
(7)虚中垂线及断和 $-4r^6+[16(虚中垂线)^2]r^4+[16(虚中垂线)^3]r^3+$ $[4(断和)^2(虚中垂线)^2+4(虚中垂线)^4]r^2+4(断和)^2(虚中垂线)^3 r+[(断和)^2(虚中垂线)^4]=0$
(8)明中垂线及断和 $r^6-[8(明中垂线)]r^5+[20(明中垂线)^2]r^4-[2(断和)^2(明中垂线)+16(明中垂线)^3]r^3+$ $[5(断和)^2(明中垂线)^2+4(明中垂线)^4]r^2-4(断和)^2(明中垂线)^3 r+[8(断和)^2(明中垂线)^4]=0$
(9)更中垂线及断和 $r^6-[8(更中垂线)]r^5+20(更中垂线)^2 r^4-[2(断和)^2(更中垂线)+16(更中垂线)^3]r^3+$ $[5(断和)^2(更中垂线)^2+4(更中垂线)^4]r^2-4(断和)^2(更中垂线)^3 r+(断和)^2(更中垂线)^4=0$

《须曼精庐算学》卷十九的"14 形 14 事"

杨兆鋆以大中垂线再加上 13 事其中一事，建立解勾股形的方程，共有 5 题。例如卷十九第 3 题，"有弦有中垂线求勾股"，杨兆鋆给出一条方程求勾，及一条方程求股。这两条方程是一样的。

$x^4-[(弦)^2]x^2+[(弦)^2(线)^2]=0$，$x$ 为勾。

$x^4-[(弦)^2]x^2+[(弦)^2(线)^2]=0$，$x$ 为股。

卷十九并未为圆径立方程。

现以 Sylvester 的过程，以大中垂线及大勾股形 13 事中之一事为条件，给出 13 条圆径方程。（表 15）

表 15

十三事	大中垂线及十三事求圆径方程（r 为半径）
(1)勾	$2[(勾)+(中垂线)]r^2-2[(勾)^2+(勾)(中垂线)]r+[(勾)^2(中垂线)]=0$
(2)股	$-2[(股)+(中垂线)]r^2+2[(股)^2+(股)(中垂线)]r-[(股)^2(中垂线)]=0$
(3)弦	$2r^2+2(弦)r-[(弦)(中垂线)]=0$
(4)勾股和	$-2r^2+2[(勾股和)+(中垂线)]r-[(勾股和)^2(中垂线)]=0$
(5)勾股较	$-4r^4-8(中垂线)r^3+4[(勾股较)^2+(中垂线)^2]r^2-4[(勾股较)^2(中垂线)]r+[(勾股较)^2(中垂线)^2]=0$

续表15

十三事	大中垂线及十三事求圆径方程(r 为半径)
(6)勾弦和	$4(勾弦和)r^3+[4(勾弦和)^2+2(勾弦和)(通垂线)+2(中垂线)^2]r^2+\{(勾弦和)[-4(勾弦和)-2(中垂线)](中垂线)\}r+[(勾弦和)^2(中垂线)^2]=0$
(7)勾弦较	$-4r^3-[6(勾弦较)-2(中垂线)]r^2-[2(勾弦较)^2-2(勾弦较)(中垂线)]r+[(勾弦较)^2(中垂线)]=0$
(8)股弦和	$4(股弦和)r^3+[4(股弦和)^2+2(股弦和)(中垂线)+2(中垂线)^2]r-[4(股弦和)^2(中垂线)+2(中垂线)^2]r+[(股弦和)^2(中垂线)^2]=0$
(9)股弦较	$-4r^3-[6(股弦较)-2(中垂线)]r^2-2[(股弦较)^2-(股弦较)(中垂线)]r+[(股弦较)^2(中垂线)]=0$
(10)弦较和	$-4[(弦较和)-(中垂线)]r^2-[2(弦较和)^2]r+[(弦较和)^2(中垂线)]=0$
(11)弦和较	$2r-(弦和较)=0$
(12)弦较较	$4[(弦较较)-(中垂线)]2r+2[(弦较较)^2]r-[(弦较较)^2(中垂线)]=0$
(13)弦和和	$[2(弦和和)+2(中垂线)]r-[(弦和和)(中垂线)]=0$

十、"15 形 15 事的圆径方程"最高为 8 次

"原13事再加上边线两事为15事",由 Sylvester 定理可得圆径方程,理论上方程最高次数为 8 次,笔者找出所有 8 次方程,共有 8 条。由于形事互换的关系,"方边形中垂线"可换为"中垂线形方边",所以这两事和其他一事所得的方程形式是对称的。这些 8 次方程,必定有一事为"中垂方边",或"方边中垂线"。另一事则为"极较,合较,断弦,断和"其中一事。以下列出"15 形 15 事"内所有 8 次的圆径方程。(表16)

表16 "15 形 15 事"内所有 8 次的圆径方程

(1)$x^8-8(中垂方边)^2x^6-2(极较)^2(中垂方边)^2x^4-8(极较)^2(中垂方边)^4x^2+[(极较)^4(中垂方边)^4]=0$
(2)$x^8-8(方边中垂线)^2x^6-2(极较)^2(方边中垂线)^2x^4-8(极较)^2(中垂方边)^4x^2+[(极较)^4(方边中垂线)^4]=0$
(3)$x^8-8(中垂方边)^2x^6-2(合较)^2(中垂方边)^2x^4+4(合较)^2(中垂方边)^4x^2+[(合较)^4(中垂方边)^4]=0$
(4)$x^8-8(方边中垂线)^2x^6-2(合较)^2(方边中垂线)^2x^4-4(合较)^2(中垂方边)^4x^2+[(合较)^4(方边中垂线)^4]=0$
(5)$x^8-8(中垂方边)^2x^6-2(断弦)^2(中垂方边)^2x^4-8(断弦)^2(中垂方边)^4x^2+[(断弦)^4(中垂方边)^4]=0$
(6)$x^8-8(方边中垂线)^2x^6-2(断弦)^2(方边中垂线)^2x^4-8(断弦)^2(方边中垂线)^4x^2+[(断弦)^4(方边中垂线)^4]=0$
(7)$x^8-8(中垂方边)^2x^6-2(断和)^2(中垂方边)^2x^4+4(断和)^2(中垂方边)^4x^2+[(断和)^4(中垂方边)^4]=0$
(8)$x^8-8(方边中垂线)^2x^6-2(断和)^2(方边中垂线)^2x^4+4(断和)^2(方边中垂线)^4x^2+[(断和)^4(方边中垂线)^4]=0$

十一、《须曼精庐算学》卷二十"8 个新勾股形"为"新 8 形 8 事"

杨兆鋆《须曼精庐算学》卷二十的比例表和李善兰的前 12 个表是相同的。以下说明杨兆鋆的图式(表17)。

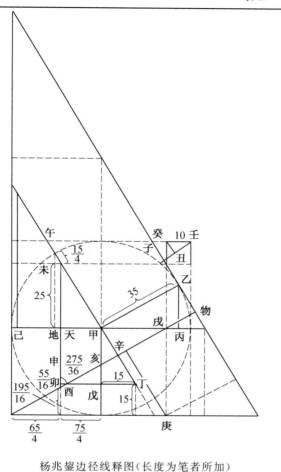

	甲乙丙中垂线勾股 中
	甲丁戊方边勾股 方
	己庚辛边线和勾股 正
	壬癸丑边线较勾股 负即方倍线中倍边
	寅卯丁边径和勾股 右
	申酉卯边径较勾股 左
	辰巳申线径和勾股 前
	午未线径较勾股 后
	壬癸为虚容方边即边径较
	壬子为虚中垂线即边径较
	甲戊亥即断勾股
	寅甲天即虚勾股
	午甲地等甲乙丙庚戊辛
	人戊物等甲丁戊

杨兆鋆边径线释图（长度为笔者所加）

杨兆鋆的"勾股边径线比例表"有如下用数（表18）。

表18

勾	股	弦	容圆直径	容方的边	大中垂线
105	140	175	70	60	84
a	b	c	$D=\dfrac{2ab}{a+b+c}$	$E=\dfrac{ab}{a+b}$	$H=\dfrac{ab}{c}$

卷二十引入边径线释的图式，和8个勾股形，它们是"中垂线，方边，边线和，边线较，边径和，边径较，线径和，线径较"等勾股形。然后再给出"勾股边径线比例表"，共有6组。再有8个条目，其中前4条用几何形式证明4个数式，后4条是4个边径线作条件求勾股形的问题。

杨兆鋆给出的8勾股形，只有前4个勾股形的周界长度合乎数式，后4个形勾股周界则不合。

以下为第1至第4个勾股形的截图。除了周界合乎长度要求，笔者也做了简单证明（表19）。

表 19

①中垂线勾股甲乙丙 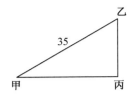	△甲乙丙周界是84,合乎中垂线勾股要求 甲乙丙之弦为半径 即 $[x]c=r=[ab]$,故 $[x]=\left[\dfrac{ab}{c}\right]$
②方边勾股甲丁戊 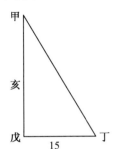	△甲丁戊周界是60,合乎方边勾股要求 甲丁戊为以平之方边为其勾 即 $[a]\left(\dfrac{ab}{a+b}\right)=[y](a)$。得 $[y](a)=\left[\dfrac{ab}{a+b}\right](a)$,故有 $[y]=\left[\dfrac{ab}{a+b}\right]$
③边线和勾股己庚辛 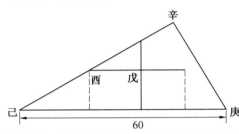	△己庚辛周界是144,数值合乎边线和勾股要求 边线和 $=(E+H)=\dfrac{ab}{a+b}+\dfrac{ab}{c}=\dfrac{ab(a+b+c)}{(a+b)c}=\dfrac{E}{c}(a+b+c)$ 己庚辛之弦为边,即 $[x](c)=\dfrac{ab}{a+b}=E$ 故 $[x]=\dfrac{E}{c}=\dfrac{\dfrac{E}{c}(a+b+c)}{a+b+c}=\left[\dfrac{E}{c}(a+b+c)\right]=[E+H]$
④边线较勾股壬癸丑 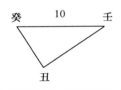	△壬癸丑周界是24,合乎边线较勾股要求 壬癸丑之弦为边线较 即 $[x](c)=D-E=\dfrac{BD}{a+b+c}=\dfrac{BD}{c}\dfrac{c}{a+b+c}=\left(\dfrac{ED}{c}\dfrac{1}{a+b+c}\right)(c)=\left[\dfrac{ED}{c}\right](c)=[H-E](c)$,故 $[x]=[H-E]$

以下4个勾股形(第5个至第8个)不合周界数值要求,其截图及周界数值计算如下(表20)。

表 20

⑤边径和勾股寅卯丁 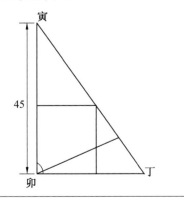	因为寅卯的长度是45 得出△寅卯丁的周界是135,不是130 不合"边径和勾股"的数值130

续表20

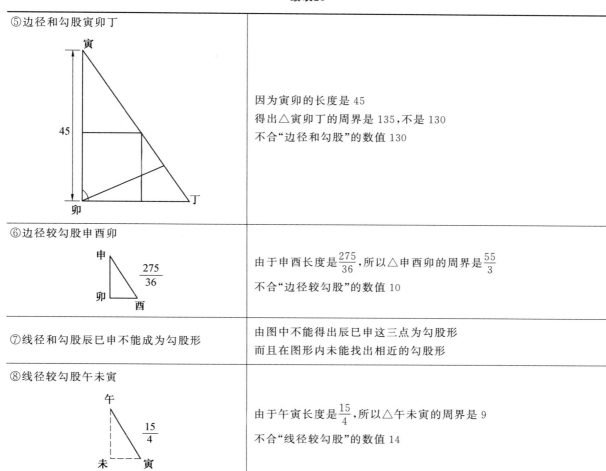

⑤边径和勾股寅卯丁	因为寅卯的长度是 45 得出△寅卯丁的周界是 135,不是 130 不合"边径和勾股"的数值 130
⑥边径较勾股申酉卯	由于申酉长度是 $\frac{275}{36}$,所以△申酉卯的周界是 $\frac{55}{3}$ 不合"边径较勾股"的数值 10
⑦线径和勾股辰巳申不能成为勾股形	由图中不能得出辰巳申这三点为勾股形 而且在图形内未能找出相近的勾股形
⑧线径较勾股午未寅	由于午寅长度是 $\frac{15}{4}$,所以△午未寅的周界是 9 不合"线径较勾股"的数值 14

虽然杨兆鋆所列的 8 个形中,后 4 个形不合勾股形长度要求。这些"边线径勾股形"仍然能以"8 形 8 事"来建立一个容圆系统。因为容圆系统可以抽象建立的,几何图形不出现这些勾股形也可以抽象发展"8 形 8 事"的容圆数学内容。

由杨兆鋆卷二十的"中垂线,方边,边线和,边线较,边径和,边径较,线径和,线径较"的形和事,可以任选两事作圆径方程。例如以大勾股"新 8 形 8 事",便可得 28 条圆径方程(表 21)。

表 21

条号	以大勾股形内"新 8 事"中两事为条件所得的圆径方程。"r 为直径"。
1	$2r-(边径和+边径较)=0$
2	$2r^2-(线径和+3 边径较)r+2(线径和)(边径较)]=0$
3	$-(线径较-边径较)r+2(线径较)(边径较)=0$
4	$r+[(中垂线)-(线径和)]=0$
5	$-r^2+(3 边+线径和)r-2[(边)(线径和)]=0$
6	$-2r^2+[4(线径和)-3(边径和)]r-[2(线径和)^2-2(线径和)(边线和)]=0$
7	$-4r^2+[6(线径和)-3(边线较)]r-[2(线径和)^2-2(线径和)(边线较)]=0$
8	$-4r^2+[3(线径和)+3(边径和)]r-2[(线径和)(边径和)]=0$
9	$2r-[(线径和)-(线径较)]=0$
10	$-r+[(中垂线)-(线径较)]=0$

续表21

条号	以大勾股形内"新8事"中两事为条件所得的圆径方程。"r为直径"。
11	$-r^2+[(容方边)-(线径较)]r+[2(容方边)(线径较)]=0$
12	$-2r^2-[4(线径较)-(边线和)]r-[2(线径较)^2-2(线径较)(边线和)]=0$
13	$2-[(线径较)-(边线较)]r-[2(线径较)^2-2(线径较)(边线较)]=0$
14	$-2r^2-3[(线径较)-(边线和)]r+[2(线径较)(边线和)]=0$
15	$[2(边径较)-(边线较)]r-[2(边径较)^2-2(边径较)(边线较)]=0$
16	$2-(边线和)r+[(边线和)^2-(边线较)^2]=0$
17	$4r^2-[6(边径和)+3(边线较)]r+[2(边径和)^2+2(边径和)(边线较)]=0$
18	$2r^2-[4(边径和)-3(边线和)]r+[2(边径和)^2-2(边径和)(边线和)]=0$
19	$r+[(边)-(边径和)]=0$
20	$r-[(边)+(边径较)]=0$
21	$-[2(边)+(边线较)]r+[2(边)^2+2(边)(边线较)]=0$
22	$(边线和)r+[2(边)^2-2(边)(边线和)]=0$
23	$r^2-[(中垂线)+(边径较)]r+[2(中垂线)(边径较)]=0$
24	$r^2-[3(中垂线)+(边径和)]r+[2(中垂线)(边径和)]=0$
25	$-[2(中垂线)-(边线较)]r+[2(中垂线)^2-2(中垂线)(边线较)]=0$
26	$(边线和)r+[2(中垂线)^2-2(中垂线)(边线和)]=0$
27	$[(边)+(中垂线)]r-2[(边)(中垂线)]=0$
28	$2r^2-[4(边径较)+(边线和)]r+[2(边径较)^2+2(边径较)(边线和)]=0$

再推展下去,原有13事和新的8事可以扩展为"21形21事"。任选其中两事,都可以建立圆径方程。这已经完全抽象,不必以某两个图形上的长度为条件而得出圆径方程。不需在图形上找出"线径和勾股形"对应的勾股形,仍能抽象以"线径和勾股形"的21事中任何两事作为容圆问题的条件,解决容圆的问题。

十二、"21形21事"的圆径方程

本文前述已给出"15形15事"的方程例子。结合卷二十,原则上可以推广出两事均为"21形21事",得出容圆方程。"21形21事"方程数量庞大,现分为三个部分给出方程例子。

第一个部分为每一个"新8勾股形"给出容圆方程例子。

第二部分给出新"新8形原13事"及第三部分以"原13形新8事"为条件的容圆例子。

现给出三类例子如下。

1."21形21事"第一部分例子

为卷二十每一个新勾股形,以"新8形及原13事"的条件,举一些方程例子,说明不必有相对的几何有图形,仍可以抽象得出圆径方程。

(1)中垂线形以"中垂线小和"及"边径较形弦"为条件。

$r^6-3(中垂线形小和)r^5+[2(中垂线形小和)^2]r^4-[4(边径较形弦)^2(中垂线形小和)-16(边径较形弦)(中垂线形小和)^2]r^3+[40(边径较形弦)^2(中垂线形小和)^2-16(边径较形弦)(中垂线形小和)^3]r^2-[96(边径较形弦)^2(中垂线形小和)^3]r+[64(边径较形弦)^2(中垂线形小和)^4]=0$

(2)方边形以"方边形大和"及"线径和形和"为条件。

$r^6-3(边形大和)r^5+[18(边形大和)^2-4(边形大和)(线径和形和)]r^4+[24(边形大和)^2(线径和

形和)+4(边形大和)(线径和形和)^2]r^3-[96(边形大和)^3(线径和形和)+8(边形大和)^2(线径和形和)^2]2r+[64(边形大和)^4(线径和形和)^2]=0

(3)边线和形以"边线和形和"及"边径和形较"为条件。

$4r^6$+76(边线和形和)r^5+[169(边线和形和)^2]r^4+[16(边径和形较)^2(边线和形和)+48(边线和形和)^3]r^3+[88(边径和形较)^2(边线和形和)^2-72(边线和形和)^4]r^2+[16(边径和形较)^4(边线和形和)^2-32(边径和形较)^2(边线和形和)^4]=0

(4)边线较形以"边线较形股"及"边径和形和"为条件。

$-16r^6$+[48(边径和形和)+6(边线较形股)]r^5-[48(边径和形和)^2+34(边径和形和)(边线较形股)-9(边线较形股)^2]r^4+[16(边径和形和)^3+68(边径和形和)^2(边线较形股)-48(边径和形和)(边线较形股)^2]r^3-[56(边径和形和)^3(边线较形股)-88(边径和形和)^2(边线较形股)^2]r^2+[16(边径和形和)^4(边线较形股)-64(边径和形和)^3(边线较形股)^2]r+[16(边径和形和)^4(边线较形股)^2]=0

(5)边径和形以"边径和形小差"及"边线和形大和"为条件。

$8r^6$+[52(边线和形大和)]r^5+[40(边径和形小差)(边线和形大和)-22(边线和形大和)^2]r^4+[12(边径和形小差)^2(边线和大和)+42(边径和小差)(边线和形大和)^2-21(边线和大和)^3]r^3+[4(边径和小差)^3(边线和大和)+28(边径和小差)^2(边线和大和)^2-72(边径和小差)(边线和大和)^3+9(边线和大和)^4]r^2+[20(边径和小差)^3(边线和大和)^2-80(边径和小差)^2(边线和大和)^3+12(边径和小差)(边线和大和)^4]r+[8(边径和小差)^4(边线和大和)^2-48(边径和小差)^3(边线和大和)^3+8(边径和小差)^2(边线和大和)^4]=0

(6)边径较形以"边径较形较"及"边线和形和"为条件。

$-r^6$-2(边线和形和)r^5+[11(边线和形和)^2]r^4-[12(边线和形和)^3]r^3+[4(边径较形较)^2(边线和形和)^2+4(边线和形和)^4]r^2-[16(边径较形较)^2(边线和形和)^3]r+[16(边径较形较)^2(边线和形和)^4]=0

(7)线径和形以"线径和形和"及"边线和形较"为条件。

$-7r^6$+8(线径和形和)r^5-[2(线径和形和)^2+9(线径和形较)^2]r^4-[4(线径和形和)(线径和形较)^2]r^3+[6(线径和形和)^2(线径和形较)^2]r^2-8(线径和形和)^3(线径和形较)^2]r+[8(线径和形和)^4(线径和形较)^2+8(线径和形和)^2(线径和形较)^4]=0

(8)线径较形以"线径较形弦"及"边线和形较"为条件。

$-r^6$+12(线径较形弦)r^5-[4(线径较形弦)^2-(边线和形较)^2]r^4-[8(线径较形弦)^2(边线和形较)^2]r^2+[16(线径较形弦)^4(边线和形较)^2]=0

2. "21形21事"方程例子第二部分"原13形新8事"及"新8形8事"作为两事

所选方程两事,其中是"大形边线和",其另一事为"新8形8事",方程次数全为4次。

(1)"大形边线和"及"边径和形边径和"。

$64r^4$+80(大形边线和)r^3+[12(大形边线和)^2-32(大形边线和)(边径和形边径和)]r^2-[9(大形边线和)^3-4(大形边线和)(边径和形边径和)^2]r+[2(大形边线和)^3(边径和形边径和)]=0

(2)"大形边线和"及"边径和较形边径较"。

$-64r^4$-16(大形边线和)r^3+20[(大形边线和)^2]r^2-[3(大形边线和)^3+8(大形边线和)^2(边径和形边径较)+4(大形边线和)(边径和形边径较)^2]r+[2(大形边线和)^3(边径和形边径较)]=0

(3)"大形边线和"及"边径较形边径较"。

$-64r^4$-16(大形边线和)r^3+20[(大形边线和)^2]r^2-[3(大形边线和)^3+8(大形边线和)^2(边径较形边径较)+4(大形边线和)(边径较形边径较)^2]r+[2(大形边线和)^3(边径较形边径较)]=0

(4)"大形边线和"及"边径较形边径和"。

$-64r^4$-16(大形边线和)r^3+20[(大形边线和)^2]r^2-[3(大形边线和)^3+8(大形边线和)^2(边径较形边径和)+4(大形边线和)(边径较形边径和)^2]r+[2(大形边线和)^3(边径较形边径和)]=0

(5)"大形边线和"及"边径较形边径较"。

$64r^4 - 48(大形边线和)r^3 + [12(大形边线和)^2 + 32(大形边线和)(边径较形边径较)]r^2 - [(大形边线和)^3 + 16(大形边线和)^2(边径较形边径较) - 4(大形边线和)(边径较形边径较)^2]r + [2(大形边线和)^3(边径较形边径较)] = 0$

(6)"大形边线和"及"线径和形线径和"。

$-64r^4 - 80(大形边线和)r^3 - [12(大形边线和)^2 + 32(大形边线和)(线径和形线径和)]r^2 + [9(大形边线和)^3 - 4(大形边线和)(线径和形线径和)^2]r + [2(大形边线和)^3(线径和形线径和)] = 0$

(7)"大形边线和"及"线径和形线径较"。

$-64r^4 - 16(大形边线和)r^3 + [20(大形边线和)^2]r^2 - [3(大形边线和)^3 + 8(大形边线和)^2(线径和形线径较) + 4(大形边线和)(线径和形线径较)^2]r + [2(大形边线和)^3(线径和形线径较)] = 0$

(8)"大形边线和"及"线径较形线径和"。

$-64r^4 - 16(大形边线和)r^3 + 20[(大形边线和)^2]r^2 - [3(大形边线和)^3 + 8(大形边线和)^2(线径较形线径和) + 4(大形边线和)(线径较形线径和)^2]r + [2(大形边线和)^3(线径较形线径和)] = 0$

(9)"大形边线和"及"线径较形线径较"。

$-64r^4 + 48(大形边线和)r^3 - [12(大形边线和)^2 - 32(大形边线和)(线径较形线径较)]r^2 + [(大形边线和)^3 - 16(大形边线和)^2(线径较形线径较) - 4(大形边线和)(线径较形线径较)^2]r + [2(大形边线和)^3(线径较形线径较)] = 0$

3."21形21事"方程例子第三部分"新8形原13事"的容圆方程

以下所选的两事,均为"新8形及原13事"其中一事。由于方程条数太多,现选新8形中的"大中垂形大和"为一事,"新8形原13事"为另一事的最高次方程。

大中垂线形大和为一事,"新8形原13事"为另一事的6次方程

(1)"中垂线形大和"及"边径和形较"。

$r^6 - 23(中垂大和)r^5 + 146[(中垂大和)^2]r^4 - [4(边径和形较)^2(中垂大和) - 24(边径和形较)(中垂大和)^2 + 264(中垂大和)^3]r^3 + [40(边径和形较)^2(中垂大和)^2 - 32(边径和形较)(中垂大和)^3 + 144(中垂大和)^4]r^2 - 96[(边径和形较)^2(中垂大和)^3]r + [64(边径和形较)^2(中垂大和)^4] = 0$

(2)"中垂线形大和"及"边径较形弦"。

$r^6 - 3(中垂大和)r^5 + [2(中垂大和)^2]r^4 - [4(边径较形弦)2(中垂大和) - 16(边径较形弦)(中垂大和)2]r^3 [40(边径较形弦)2(中垂大和)2 - 16(边径较形弦)(中垂大和)3]r^2 - [96(边径较形弦)2(中垂大和)3]r + [64(边径较形弦)2(中垂大和)4] = 0$

(3)"中垂线形大和"及"边径较形和较"。

$r^6 - 6(中垂大和)r^5 + 13(中垂大和)^2 + 2(中垂大和)(边径较形和较)r^4 - [12(中垂大和)3 + 22(中垂大和)2(边径较形和较) + (中垂大和)(边径较形和较)2]r^3 + [4(中垂大和)4 + 36(中垂大和)3(边径较形和较) + 10(中垂大和)2(边径较形和较)2]r^2 - [16(中垂大和)4(边径较形和较) + 24(中垂大和)3(边径较形和较)2]r + [16(中垂大和)4(边径较形和较)2] = 0$

(4)"中垂线形大和"及"边径较形大差"。

$r^6 - 7(中垂大和)r^5 + [18(中垂大和)^2 - 8(中垂大和)(边径较形大差)]r^4 - [20(中垂大和)^3 - 72(中垂大和)^2(边径较形大差) + 4(中垂大和)(边径较形大差)^2]r^3 + [8(中垂大和)^4 - 96(中垂大和)^3(边径较形大差) + 40(中垂大和)^2(边径较形大差)^2]r^2 + [32(中垂大和)^4(边径较形大差) - 96(中垂大和)^3(边径较形大差)^2]r + [64(中垂大和)^4(边径较形大差)^2] = 0$

(5)"中垂线形大和"及"边径较形小差"。

$r^6 - 5(中垂大和)r^5 + [9(中垂大和)^2]r^4 - [7(中垂大和)^3 - 8(中垂大和)^2(边径较形小差) + (中垂大和)(边径较形小差)^2]r^3 + [2(中垂大和)^4 - 16(中垂大和)^3(边径较形小差) + 10(中垂大和)^2(边径较形小差)^2]r^2 + [8(中垂大和)^4(边径较形小差) - 24(中垂大和)^3(边径较形小差)^2]r + [16(中垂大和)^4(边径较形小差)^2] = 0$

(6)"中垂线形大和"及"边径较形较"。

$r^6-11(中垂大和)r^5-[8(边径较形较)(中垂大和)-34(中垂大和)^2]r^4-[4(边径较形较)^2(中垂大和)+40(边径较形较)(中垂大和)^2+40(中垂大和)^3]r^3+[40(边径较形较)^2(中垂大和)^2-32(边径较形较)(中垂大和)^3+16(中垂大和)^4]r^2-96[(边径较形较)^2(中垂大和)^3]r+[64(边径较形较)^2(中垂大和)^4]=0$

(7)"中垂线形大和"及"边径和形小差"。

$r^6-17(中垂大和)r^5+[49(中垂大和)^2-4(中垂大和)(边径和形小差)]r^4-[51(中垂大和)^3-28(中垂大和)^2(边径和形小差)+(中垂大和)(边径和形小差)^2]r^3+[18(中垂大和)^4-48(中垂大和)^3(边径和形小差)+10(中垂大和)^2(边径和形小差)^2]r^2+[24(中垂大和)^4(边径和形小差)-24(中垂大和)^3(边径和形小差)^2]r+[16(中垂大和)^4(边径和形小差)^2]=0$

(8)"中垂线形大和"及"边径和形大差"。

$r^6-19(中垂大和)r^5+[82(中垂大和)^2-16(中垂大和)(边径和形大差)]r^4-[132(中垂大和)^3-136(中垂大和)^2(边径和形大差)+4(中垂大和)(边径和形大差)^2]r^3+[72(中垂大和)^4-224(中垂大和)^3(边径和形大差)+40(中垂大和)^2(边径和形大差)^2]r^2+[96(中垂大和)^4(边径和形大差)-96(中垂大和)^3(边径和形大差)^2]r+[64(中垂大和)^4(边径和形大差)^2]=0$

(9)"中垂线形大和"及"边径和形和较"。

$r^6-18(中垂大和)r^5+[65(中垂大和)^2+6(中垂大和)(边径和形和较)]r^4-[84(中垂大和)^3+50(中垂大和)^2(边径和形和较)+(中垂大和)(边径和形和较)^2]r^3+[36(中垂大和)^4+92(中垂大和)^3(边径和形和较)+10(中垂大和)^2(边径和形和较)^2]r^2-[48(中垂大和)^4(边径和形和较)+24(中垂大和)^3(边径和形和较)^2]r+[16(中垂大和)^4(边径和形和较)^2]=0$

(10)"中垂线形大和"及"边径和形弦"。

$r^6-15(中垂大和)r^5-[8(边径和形弦)(中垂大和)-18(中垂大和)^2]r^4-[4(边径和形弦)^2(中垂大和)-48(边径和形弦)(中垂大和)^2]r^3+[40(边径和形弦)^2(中垂大和)^2-48(边径和形弦)(中垂大和)^3]r^2-96[(边径和形弦)^2(中垂大和)^3]r+[64(边径和形弦)^2(中垂大和)^4]=0$

十三、结语

清代研究《测圆海镜》学者繁多,自翰林阮元以下至李锐等人,为《测圆海镜》校正及补充细草。李善兰以测圆题教于同文馆,刘岳云点评测圆解题之法。刘彝程则不立天元术,以本法解二次方程题。陈维祺整理泛积,王季同证明容圆题的方程最高次数。李镠选题简化所用方程,杨兆鋆则整理所有测圆题目,以自有恒等式解题。晚清时局日新,学者如能有多点时间,谅必能有更多述作。本文略续李善兰及杨兆鋆在"边,径,线"的容圆内容,讨论圆径方程之建立。

学生年前就学郭师,得老师耐心指导,学习此书,不单介绍中国科学院图书馆各藏书内容,并提供大量近代学者相关著作参考[5],百忙中亦带同学生前往国家图书馆研究《测圆海镜》元刻本各章节,尽得各书目参考之便。

今值郭师八十华诞,学生以小文附各学长鸿文骥尾,并祝老师郭书春教授及师母多福多寿,生活如意。

---

5 书目繁多,只记其二者。李俨"《测圆海镜》研究历程考"1955。钱宝琮"有关《测圆海镜》的几个问题"1966。

从圭窦形谈起：《测量全义》初探

洪万生　（中国台湾数学史教育学会）

一、前言

《测量全义》引起我的注意主要因为三个背景：其一，大约四十多年前，我从史学家李俨的《中国算学史》读到作者引自《测量全义》的阿基米德《圆书》。其二，2006年，我曾与多位研究生在《HPM通讯》上共同规划出版一个"海龙公式"专辑（https://math.ntnu.edu.tw/~horng/letter/904.pdf），其中，李建勋曾就罗雅谷的海龙公式深入探讨，并将他的证明较之于梅文鼎的研究，而得到有趣的结论。[1] 其三，我最近深入了解"圭窦形"的语源之机缘。[2]

阿基米德的《圆书》（*Measurement of a Circle/Circle Measurement*）引进与面积公式有关的三个命题，可惜，一直都没有获得中国数学史家应有的注意，尽管前述李俨著作全文照录。不过，这或许可以多少解释中算史家过度"执迷"于刘徽之割圆术"创见"，以致无从觉察此一逼近圆周率近似值之估算，必须以"精确的"圆面积公式为前提。试想如果以圆面积公式（或"圆田术"）"径自相乘，三之，四而一"为依据，来追求圆周率之近似值，那么，此一公式显然无法运用，因为它已经假设了圆周率（近似值）为三。事实上，刘徽"割圆术"的全文是出现在"圆田术"四个公式中的第一个"半周、半径相乘得积步"之下，由于这个公式并未出现圆周率——不像我们今日所熟知的 πr^2（r 为圆之半径），因此，当然可据以推算圆周率之近似值。

此一史实/数学实作（mathematical practice）在《圆书》的映照之下，应该会"透显"出它的深刻意义。不过，显然并非如此。事实上，中算史家是在19世纪80年代之后，才陆续"警觉到"刘徽注"圆田术"的真实（或"贴近"）读法。丹麦汉学家华道安（Donald Wagner）的贡献也应该记上一笔才是，他在1984年与我通信时，曾寄给我一篇论文，其中他就明确地指出上述刘徽注的真实面貌。[3]

回到《测量全义》上。最近，我为了撰写《从圭窦形到抛物线：闲话数学名词的翻译语境》，特别追溯"圭窦形"的源头出处，结果就在《测量全义》找到它的最早汉语"足迹"。不过，本书之编者罗雅谷（Giacomo Rho/Jacques Rho，1593—1638）显然只想"便宜行事地"交代一下，因此，后来在相关的汉译语境中，"圭窦形"被"抛物线"所取代，一点也不令人意外。[4] 本文"从圭窦形谈起"，意在吸引读者眼球，我们的主要目标当然是《测量全义》的文本分析，特别是罗雅谷在撰著此书时，如何"收编"他所谓的"九章等"（或中国传统算书概念、算法及公式）。这个中西算学"交流"的个案似乎还没有赢得（数学）史家应有的关注，且让我在此先起个头，抛砖引玉，希望后来者可以贡献更恰当的历史理解。

因此，本文"初探"的范围就限定在与传统中算"不无互动"的《测量全义》第四～六卷，至于第一～三卷及第七～九卷主题是"平行的"，前者是平面三角学，后者则是球面三角学。根据数学史家的初步研

---

[1] 李建勋，《海龙公式的流变：由徐光启到梅毂成》。

[2] 洪万生，《从圭窦形到抛物线：闲话数学名词的翻译语境》，台湾数学史教育学会年会暨东亚数学史研讨会，1/30/2021，台北：台湾师范大学数学系M202。

[3] 有关这一段重要的插曲，可参考郭书春，《尊重原始文献 避免以讹传讹》。

[4] 这是因为在18世纪50年代，解析几何与（近代）物理学同时传入中国，前者的"抛物线"与后者的"抛射体运动"终于连成一气，而将"圭窦形"送进了历史的灰烬。参考洪万生，《从圭窦形到抛物线：闲话数学名词的翻译语境》。

究，⁵其中公式是针对 15 世纪欧洲数学家玉山若干（Johannes Regiomontanus/Johannes Muller，1436—1476）的相关成果所做的增补。⁶第十卷（也就是最后一卷）介绍测量仪器，由于它与前述平面三角及球面三角一样，其内容主要传自西方的数学与天文学，同时，也缺乏中西之"会通"企图，所以，本文都不打算讨论。

有关本文论述进路，我们还必须再做一个交代。由于清初历算大师梅文鼎深受《测量全义》乃至编入它的《崇祯历书》之影响（内容与形式两方面），因此，当我们针对《测量全义》进行文本分析时，也将援引梅文鼎的相关论述，作为必要的参考点，从而借以更清晰地映照清初中算未来之走向。

二、罗雅谷及其《测量全义》

罗雅谷的生平事迹略见维基百科（正体、简体中文版都出自英文版），仅知他 1593 年出生于米兰，父亲是著名法学家。他在 1614 年加入耶稣会，数学方面的训练似乎颇为到位。1617 年，他在罗马被贝拉明（Cardinal Bellarmino）枢机主教授任神父职。之后，他与多个伙伴被派到东亚地区传教。他先是在印度果阿邦学习神学，后来到澳门传教。1624 年，他随高一志（Alfonso Vagnoni）神父进入中国，居停山西，学习语言与在地知识。1631 年，被传唤至北京历局与徐光启、耶稣会士汤若望、龙华民和邓玉函共事，一起编修《崇祯历书》，以便改革明朝中国历法（大统历）。1638 年，他逝世于北京，享年 45 岁。

罗雅谷在数学及天文学方面的素养，我们只能从一些相关著作的叙述来推测。天文史家金格瑞契（Owen Gingerich）有关哥白尼《天体运行论》(De revolutionibus)（版本）之研究，⁷为我们提供了些许蛛丝马迹。事实上，根据他的研究，《天体运行论》的 1566 年的第二版及 1617 年的第三版，都在 1618 年被带到中国，⁸尽管梵蒂冈教廷早在 1616 年已经下令将该书"扫入"禁书目录。而将 1566 年《天体运行论》第二版带到中国的，正是罗雅谷。可见，罗雅谷对于当时欧洲的天文学研究现况相当熟悉而且颇有"胆识"。这或许也可以解释何以他最后会获邀加入徐光启的历局团队。

事实上，我们从本文讨论的《测量全义》，也可发现他应该受过非常严谨的数学训练，譬如他在该书中，就始终强调"法之所以然也"，而其论证之主要依据或范本，则是利玛窦（Matteo Ricci）、徐光启合译的《几何原本》前六卷（后文简称利徐版），以及其中译母本丁先生（Christopher Clavius）改编版，⁹足见他娴熟这部经典的内容与形式。事实上，我们从本节下文将简要介绍的《测量全义》内容，也可以略窥一二。至于测量之义，可征之于耶稣会士邓玉函（Johann Schreck）所撰之《测天约说》（也收入《崇祯历书》）：¹⁰

> 测法与量法不异，但近小之物寻尺可度者，谓之量法。远而山岳，又远而天象，非寻尺可度，以仪象测知之，谓之测法。其量法如算家之重术，其测法如算家之缀术也。¹¹

5　这些球面三角的内容甚至启发了清初梅文鼎的同一主题之研究。参考郭书春主编，《中国科学技术史：数学卷》，620 页。

6　玉山若干（或约翰·穆勒）的三角学贡献，可以参考毛尔的《毛起来说三角》或 Katz 的《数学史通论》，312—315 页。

7　参考：金格瑞契，《追踪哥白尼》，177 页。

8　1617 年的三版是由金尼阁（Nicholaus Trigault，1577—1628）带入中国，参考同上。

9　在本文中，《几何原本》前六卷所指的，是利、徐二人根据丁先生（Christopher Clavius）的改编本所中译的版本。另外，罗雅谷也参考了未译的后九卷，譬如《测量全义》卷六，页四所引述。《几何原本》(The Elements) 目前被认为只有十三卷（譬如 Heath 版），此处提及卷十四、十五系由后人增补。丁先生改编的版本就有十五卷。

10　根据维基百科 https://en.wikipedia.org/wiki/Johann_Schreck，邓玉函原本在阿特多夫大学（University of Altdorf）习医，毕业后，他成为发明符号法则的法国数学家韦达（François Viète）之助手。韦达于 1603 年去世后，邓玉函转往意大利巴都亚大学（University of Padua）投入伽利略的门下，但继续研习医学。

11　邓玉函，《测天约说》卷上，页一，徐光启编纂、潘鼐汇编，《崇祯历书》(后文简称《崇祯历书》)，1139 页。

在此,邓玉函使用了中算家熟悉的名词如"叀术"及"缀术",[12]显见耶稣会士深知会通中西文化"修辞"(rhetoric)之重要。

根据《测量全义》〈叙目〉,本书(十卷中的)"前九卷属法原,后一卷属法器"。所谓"法原",是指:

> 法之所以然也。凡事不明于所以然,则已然者茫茫不知所来,其当然者,昧昧不知所往。[13]

至于其法原精髓,当然就表现在前九卷。我们先引述全书目录:"第一卷测直线三角形,第二卷测线上,第三卷测线下,第四卷测面上,第五卷测面下,第六卷测体,第七卷测曲线三角形,第八卷测球上大圈,第九卷测星,第十卷仪器图说"。其次,再让我们一起考察罗雅谷如何"遵循"《几何原本》之体例。事实上,第一卷之首开宗明义就是"界说二十三则",譬如

> 第一界:正弧,全圈四分之一。或大焉或小焉。
> 第二界:余弧,正弧之剩分。
> 第三界:通弦者,通弧之相当线,分圈为两分。
> 第四界:圈内线极大过心者,为圈径。
> 等等。[14]

不过,罗雅谷并未提供类如《几何原本》利徐版的"求作"与"公论",[15]而是直接呈现(卷一)十七题的内容。兹以其第九题为例:

> 第九题 三角形。边与边之比例,若各对角之正弦。[16]

按:这是目前我们称之为正弦定律的一个命题。仿《几何原本》体例,罗雅谷在提供"论曰"(证明)之前,先依据插图进行"解曰"(解题);针对这个给定三角形,罗雅谷区分成三种情况,"一言直角形""二言三边等"(亦即等边三角形),"三言三边形不等"。在此,我们仅以第三种情况的"任意三角形"为例,来考察他的"解曰"。参考图1,"以巳以小边,引长于丁,为乙丁,与巳丙等。丙为心,巳为界,作巳庚弧。又乙为心,丁为界,作丁戊弧。末作丁辛、甲巳两垂线至乙丙底。"紧接着,就是他的"论曰":

> 丁辛乙、甲巳乙两直角形之丁辛、甲巳平行。同用乙角,即各边俱相似六卷四[17],则乙丁与乙辛,若乙巳与乙甲。又先设乙丁、巳丙等,是丙巳边与丁辛,若巳丙与甲巳也。夫丁辛为乙角之正弦,甲巳为丙角之正弦,更之,则丙巳边与巳乙边,若乙角正弦之丁辛,与丙角正弦之甲巳也。

---

12 这两个名词俱见秦九韶《数书九章》序,此处应该都指测量方法,尽管秦九韶将前者视为"外算",后者视为"内算"。秦九韶,《数书九章》序,页一;郭书春主编,《中国科学技术典籍通汇》(一),439页。

13 罗雅谷,《测量全义》"叙目"页一,《崇祯历书》1295页。

14 "圈"等同"圆"或"圆周",罗雅谷将这两个名词混用,不知何故?又,正弧是指一个象限内的一段弧,"过弧"则大于一个象限之圆弧。圈径=圆的直径。

15 Clavius 的《几何原本》之"求作"("求作者,不得言不可作")与"公论"("公论者,不可疑")不同于 Heath 版(Heath, 1956),尽管它们(依序)类似后者之设准(postulate)与公理(common notion)。更值得注意的,是 Clavius 将与平行有关的第五设准,转变成为他的改编本之第十一论。将攸关非欧几何学滥觞的第五设准改成"公论",是值得注意的一个"认知"特色,但似乎尚未赢得史家的注意。

16 《测量全义》第一卷第一题"比例等"(比例相等)之说,罗雅谷原注称:"比例等后省曰若",亦即:$a:b=c:d$,这两个比(例)相等,后文就简称为"$a:b$ 若 $c:d$"。

17 这个小字是原注,"六卷四"是指《几何原本》第六卷命题四。

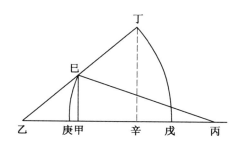

图 1 《测量全义》证明之正弦定律之插图

这个证明及其插图完全袭自玉山若干(或约翰·穆勒或雷格蒙塔努斯)的《论各种三角形》(*De Triangulis Omnimodis*，1463/1533)——被史家 Katz 称之为第一部"纯"三角学的著作，也见证了史家 Grattan-Guinness 所刻画的欧洲 1540—1660 年间是一个"三角学世纪"(the age of trigonometry)。[18] 现在，且让我们引述 Katz 的解说与评论：

> 由于他的正弦是给定半径的圆中的直线，他对三角形 ABG 的正弦定理的证明就需要分别以 B 和 G 为圆心，以相等直线 BD 和 GA 为半径画出两个圆。再从 A 和 D 分别作出 BG 的垂线，依次相交于 K 和 H，雷格蒙塔努斯然后指出，应用相等半径的圆可知，DH 是∠ABG 的正弦，而 AK 是∠AGB 的正弦。因为 BD=GA，∠AGB 的对边为 GA，且∠AGB 的对边为 AB，所以，由三角形 ABK 和 DBH 的相似性可得出要证明的结论。[19]

图 2 是 Katz《数学史通论》所复制的插图，我们可以据以确认罗雅谷所参考的来源。其实，罗雅谷依据《论各种三角形》来改编，是其来有自的，因为雷格蒙塔努斯曾从希腊文翻译托勒密(Ptolemy)的《天文学大成》(*The Almagest*)，并且注意到天文学界需要有一本简洁、有系统的著作，来论述平面、球面三角的边角关系之法则。值得注意的，正如前述，他的体例完全模仿《几何原本》的(定义—公理—命题)逻辑架构，同时，针对各个命题(或定理)，还加上《几何原本》所欠缺的"解释性"(explanatory)实例。还有，史家 Katz 也提醒我们："雷格蒙塔努斯的三角学是以弧的正弦为基础，正弦的定义是二倍弧的半弦，但他也指出，可以把正弦视为依赖于相应的圆心角。"[20]

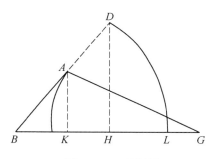

图 2 Katz 复制图

《论各种三角形》所以赢得罗雅谷的青睐，可能是他的"市占率"。根据 Katz 的说明，16 世纪 30 年代之后的一段时间内，出现了大约二十本论三角学的著作，其内容绝大部分都与该书雷同。另一方面，"以雷格蒙塔努斯的著作为典范的 15 世纪三角学(仍)为解决当时的天文学问题提供了必要的数学工

---

18 参考 Grattan-Guinness，The Fontana History of Mathematical Sciences，174-233.
19 引 Katz，《数学史通论》，313 页。《论各种三角形》中的相应原始文本(primary source materials)，可参见李文林，《数学珍宝》，208-210 页。
20 Katz，《数学史通论》，312 页。

具。"[21]

总之,罗雅谷根据、甚至模仿《论各种三角形》的内容与(体例)形式,来编写他自己的《测量全义》,应该极有可能。不过,他在该书第四~六卷中,以其论述为主体,企图"肆应"(accommodate)或"收编"(assimilate)中国传统的"九章筭",倒是值得我们深入探索。紧接着,我们就来处理这个主题。

三、罗雅谷收编"九章筭"

"九章筭"是指哪一本中国算书,目前我们还不得而知,不过,它可能泛指中国算学的概念(及其名词)、方法或公式。我们从罗雅谷在《测量全义》所引述的相关内容,可以推测他应该是在西算的"理论架构"中,收编中国传统算学。这个进路有别于徐光启以降的明清算家,他们都如同徐光启所期许的,"先(以中算)会通(西算)",然后"再(努力)超胜",[22] 其"主体性"显然在明清算家这一边。

现在,我们先考察罗雅谷在《测量全义》的论述架构中,如何"借用"(appropriate)中算用词及方法。由于《测量全义》卷一~卷三、卷七~卷十几乎未引述中国传统算书概念或方法,[23] 因此,我们仅就卷四~卷六进行考察,而这当然也是本文的焦点所在。

在本节中,我将先讨论《测量全义》卷四,再继之以卷六,这是因为这两卷的内容与形式颇有"平行"的风格。事实上,罗雅谷收编"九章筭"中的平面图形、立体图形的"容"积计算公式或方法时,[24] 显然相当受惠于《几何原本》,尤其是利玛窦、徐光启未曾中译的立体几何内容(第十一~十三卷)。至于《测量全义》第五卷,我们将以其中《圜书》及"变形法"的一个案例为主题,依序分述于本文第四、五节。

《测量全义》卷四(测面上)主题是有关三角形、四边形及多边形面积之计算。不过,罗雅谷一开始就引进十三个界说,其中第十界之"亩法"与《九章算术》相同,亦即,一亩等于二百四十(方)步,所相异者,是罗雅谷补上"因次"(dimension)概念,而改称为"方步"。[25] 然而,他的"一方步"却是等于"二十五方尺",亦即,一步=五尺,与明代算家程大位的《算法统宗》(1592)所载相同,[26] 不像秦汉度量衡制度中的"一步=六尺",正如《九章算术》所示。

现在,有关界说(definition),我要特别引述本卷的第四、五界,因为我们在卷六"测体"将可以发现罗雅谷的"平行论述"进路:

第四界 一界之面
一曲线内之形,如圆形在圈界之内。凡有三:一平圆,从心至界,各线俱等。一椭圆,如圆柱而斜刻之,得两面焉。一无法曲线,如桃梨之面。[27]

第五界 二界之面
如两弧或无法之曲线,或一直线一曲线,而形成之有法与否,则视曲线。[28]

---

21 同上,315页。
22 徐光启在他的《历书总目表》中,指出:"臣等愚心,以为欲求超胜,必先会通",《崇祯历书》,1558页。
23 《测量全义》卷二,页十二有"物莫能到,复不能作线与叄直",《崇祯历书》,1324页。卷三有矩尺测量法(《崇祯历书》,1335页),类似《周髀算经》的"用矩之道"。
24 罗雅谷使用"容积"一词既代表面积,也代表体积,由上下文可知其指涉。
25 罗雅谷,《测量全义》卷四,页四,《崇祯历书》,页1354。中国算书如《九章算术》有时会强调面积计算(比如方田术)所得是"积步"。
26 程大位,《算法统宗》,卷三,页二,郭书春主编,《中国科学技术典籍通汇》(二),1264页。
27 罗雅谷,《测量全义》卷四,页一、二,《崇祯历书》,1353页。所谓"无法",最早出处应该是《几何原本》利徐版卷一的第三十三界:"已上方形四种谓之有法四边形。四种之外,他方形,皆谓之无法四边形。"以上四种,是指第二十九界"直角方形"(正方形)、第三十界的"直角形"(长方形)、第三十一界的"斜方形"(菱形),以及第三十二界的"长斜方形"(平行四边形)。
28 罗雅谷,《测量全义》卷四之首,页二~三,《崇祯历书》,1353页。

图3　一界之面(《测量全义》扫描)　　图4　二界之面(《测量全义》扫描)

另一方面,由于第七、八界说涉及多边形概念之(阶层 hierarchy)分类(图5、图6),[29] 我们也将引述如下,方便下文之解说:

第七界　四界之面

方面有五。边角俱等者,正方也。角等、边不等者,长方也。边等、角不等者,斜方也。各对角、对边等者,长斜方也。边角俱不等者,无法之方也。首两种之外,皆属无法,盖有设边,无设角,或大或小,容积因之异焉。欲求其容,须定角之度或中长线也。[30]

第八界　五以上多界之面

边角俱等者,有法之形也。或边或角不等者,皆无法之形也。[31]

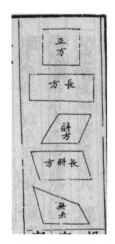 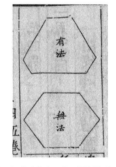

图5　四界之面(《测量全义》扫描)　　图6　五以上多界之面(《测量全义》扫描)[32]

由于《九章算术》卷一"方田章"主题就是面积计算,[33] 所以,我们以之对照"测面上",是一个颇有启发性的比较史学工作,这是因为《几何原本》并未包括面积或体积计算。

《测量全义》卷四"测面上"除了前文提及的十三个界说之外,还包括三个命题,依序为第一题"量四

29　这一做法呼应欧几里得如何遵守亚里士多德有关(数学)定义之规范,亦即概念的"原始属类"与"区别属性"之划分,参考奔特等(Bunt et. al.),《数学起源》,176—179页。

30　罗雅谷,《测量全义》卷四之首,页二～三,《崇祯历书》,1353—1354页。相较于《几何原本》利、徐版的卷一第二十九～三十二界说之叙述(参见前注27),罗雅谷的对应界说显然更为清晰可辨。

31　罗雅谷,《测量全义》卷四之首,页三,《崇祯历书》,1354页。

32　此一扫描图之原图似有谬误,"有法"与"无法"应该互相颠倒才是。

33　由于"计算",当然也一并介绍分数的四则运算,以及约分术等方法。

边形"、第二题"量三边形",以及第三题"量多边形"。此一顺序有违我们的直观,因为,三边形显然比四边形"简单",为何论述之顺序刚好相反?[34]为此,罗雅谷在本卷"第九界"试图提出他的理由:

> 量线用直线,以直线在万线中为最短故。量面用平面、用正方,以平面在万面中为最短,正方之理视万物之理为最准故。[35]

于是,他将正方(形)、长方(形)的面积公式视为已知,所谓的"公量为方"(可公度量(commensurable)单位是正方形),并以正方田、长方田之面积计算为例。紧接着,他也说明"斜方"(亦即平行四边形)面积计算。然后,再以"等边斜方形"(菱形)将"梭田"收编进来,他说(参见图7):

> 若等边斜方形,作两对角线,分元形为四勾股形,两对角线之交为直法。法以两对角线相乘,二而一。[36]

在四边形的单元中,梭田既然有了"归宿",且看罗雅谷如何对待"梯田"(图8):

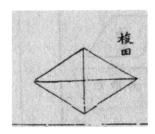 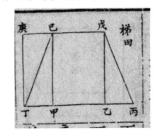

图7　梭田,《测量全义》扫描　　图8　梯田,《测量全义》扫描

四边形有上下不等而在平行线内者,名梯田。旧法:并两广,半之,以中长线乘之。[37]

此处"中长线"是指"从形之一边或一角至对边作垂线",亦即我们今日所谓的高。罗雅谷特别指出:"半之者,损下广以益上广也,此旧法所自出也。"至于"斜田、箕田诸法俱同前。两腰之等与不等,角之等与不等,俱以平行线为本。"[38]显然,无论是"梯田""斜田"或"箕田",它们都以"平行线为本",而让面积公式之证明变得"有所本",同时也有助于他的"反驳"旧法之谬。

兹以"四不等田"为例(参考图九)。先引述罗雅谷的论述如下:

> 旧法:四不等田,东长四十二、西长五十六、南六十四、北五十八。并东西两边,半之;并南北两边,亦半之。两半相乘得二九八九步,为其容。[39]

按:上引"容"是指面积,以下视文本脉络不同,也可能指"体积"。针对这个面积计算,罗雅谷不以为然,"驳曰":

---

[34] 譬如,梅文鼎在他的《平三角举要》中,就在"有形"vs."无形"的脉络中,指出三角形的"优先性":"凡可算者,为有法之形;不可算者,为无法之形。三角者有法之形也。不论长短斜正,皆可求其数,故曰有法。若无法之形,析之成三角则可量,故三角者量法之宗也。"4—463页。

[35] 罗雅谷,《测量全义》卷四之首,页三~四,《崇祯历书》,1354页。

[36] 罗雅谷,《测量全义》卷四之首,页六~七,《崇祯历书》,1355—1356页。

[37] 罗雅谷,《测量全义》卷四之首,页七,《崇祯历书》,页1356。

[38] 同上。

[39] 罗雅谷,《测量全义》卷四之首,页八,《崇祯历书》,页1356。按:"四不等田"最早现身于《五曹算经》。

若甲为直角。试作乙丁对角线,成甲乙丁勾股形。有勾股,以求弦,为七十六又一五三之九四。其积为一三四四。又以乙丙丁形之三边,求其容,得一五三七,并两形积,得二八七一,知法为未合也。[40]

图 9　四不等田,《测量全义》扫描

最后,他"论曰"以纠其谬,指出其关键在于是否为"有法形":

> 两广或两长在平行线内者,并而折半,损有余,补不足,改为方形也。以中长线乘之,则得其容。若四不等,无法形也。损此益彼,一不能为方,一不能为中长线,何缘得合乎?[41]

现在,我们紧接着进入本卷第二题"量三边形"。本题主旨是海龙(Heron)公式:"乙丙丁三边形,有边数,无角数,求实。其法并三边数,半之为实,以每边之数为法,各减之。三较连乘得数,以半总数乘之为实,平方开之,得实。"[42]罗雅谷所提供的证明显然有瑕疵,梅文鼎曾试图改正,也未竟全功,最后,康熙主编的《数理精蕴》总算给出了严密的证明。[43]在中算史上,尽管南宋秦九韶也曾给出与海龙公式等价的"三斜田"面积公式,[44]但却未曾说明如何道出他自己的公式,因此,我们不打算进一步讨论。

本卷第三题主旨是:"量多边形",亦即是:计算五边及更多边形的面积。由于正多边形面积的计算"必先分元形,皆为两边等三角形,故不论几何边俱同法",因此,罗雅谷特别讨论等边三角形面积之计算("旧法三角形"),说明旧法未考虑平方根近似值的"误差"作用,以致于答案略有出入。请参考图 10、他的举例及论证如下:

> 旧法三角形,每面十四。以六乘面,得八十四。以七而一,得十二,为实。半面七为法,乘之,得八四。积也。试用前法,分元形作两勾股形,各形有弦有勾,以求股而求积。得八四又三十之二十八,几为八五,非八四。
>
> 论曰:所以然者,古法正六面七,谓丙乙十四,则丙甲十二,故七六相乘得四十二,为丙乙丁之实八十四矣。不知丙乙十四、乙甲七,各自之相减开方,乃十二有奇也,且七除又七乘,安用之?[45]

40　罗雅谷,《测量全义》卷四之首,页八～九,《崇祯历书》,1356—1357 页。

41　罗雅谷,《测量全义》卷四之首,页九,《崇祯历书》,1357 页。

42　罗雅谷,《测量全义》卷四,页九,《崇祯历书》,1357 页。海龙公式之现代形式如下:令 a, b, c 为三角形的三边,则其面积 $= \sqrt{s(s-a)(s-b)(s-c)}$,其中 $s=(a+b+c)/2$。

43　参考李建勳,《海龙公式的流变:由徐光启到梅瑴成》,或该文所刊的《HPM 通讯》9(4)海龙公式专辑。梅瑴成是梅文鼎的孙子,他时任康熙的算学大臣,是《数理精蕴》的主力编辑之一。

44　朱世杰所给的"三斜田"面积计算则不同,因为他多给了一个"中股长"的条件。参看朱世杰,《算学启蒙》卷中,郭书春主编,《中国科学技术典籍通汇》(一),1149 页。

45　罗雅谷,《测量全义》卷四,页二十四～二十五,《崇祯历书》,1364 页。

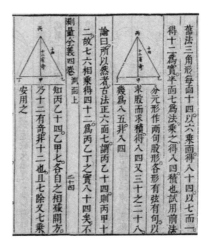

图 10 "正六面七"(《测量全义》扫描)

同理,他也评论"旧法及古法六角形"。不过,他更有兴趣讨论的,应该是本卷最后的"古法八角田"。此一"古法"出处何在,还有待探索。[46] 不过,这个论述显然延续了他在旧法三角形、六边形等计算时,对于平方根近似值的"计较"。我们且先看他所引述的"古法":

> 古法八角田。每面十四,以面五乘得七十,七而一得十,倍之得二十,求一面,得三十四。自之得一一五六为实,面数自之得一九六为法,减之,余九六〇,八角形积也。[47]

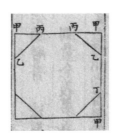

图 11 方五斜七八角田,《测量全义》扫描

上引"每面十四"以"五乘、再七而一",是指 $\frac{14}{\sqrt{2}} \approx \frac{14}{\frac{7}{5}}$,在正方形边为五(所谓"方五")的情况下,以七为其对角线之长(所谓"斜七")。[48] 紧接着,他提供"正法",说明八角田每边 14 的情况下,以其为弦的等腰直角三角形之两腰并不等于 10,而是 $\sqrt{98}$。至于古法答案"所以然者",乃是因为:

> 古法方五斜七,不知方五斜七有奇,不发之根也。彼以甲乙等各勾各股俱为十,则乙丙边与乙丙弦俱十四。不知各率皆是,而独乙丙弦非十四也。故八角形之积实少,而误以为多。[49]

---

46 朱世杰,《算学启蒙》卷中有"方五斜七八角田"题如下:"今有方五斜七八角田一段,只云每面阔二十八步,问为田几何?"郭书春主编,《中国科学技术典籍汇编》(四),1149—1150 页。

47 罗雅谷,《测量全义》卷四之首,页八,《崇祯历书》,页 1364—1365。

48 口诀"方五斜七"最早现身于《孙子算经》,至于"方五斜七八角田"则出现于朱世杰《算学启蒙》(1299)。另外,与此近似值息息相关的"不发之根",则是指开方不尽的无理根如 $\sqrt{2}$。罗雅谷,《测量全义》卷四,页十六,《崇祯历书》,1360 页。

49 罗雅谷,《测量全义》卷四,页二十五~二十六,《崇祯历书》,1365 页。

《测量全义》有关"测面"部分我们就讨论到此为止。在进入"测体"之前,我们有必要提及上文所引述的"正六面七"及"方五斜七"这两个古法的可能出处。正如前述,罗雅谷曾有七年时间(1624—1631)在山西学习语言与"在地学问",又由于利玛窦、李之藻所编译的《同文算指》(1614)直接袭自《算法统宗》的至少有22题之多,[50]因此,罗雅谷研读《算法统宗》的可能性极大,从而进一步"收编己有"似乎也顺理成章。譬如,在《算法统宗》的"方圆定则九图"前三个依序就是"周三径一""方五斜七"及"正六面七",[51]至于作者程大位的相关说明,则完全被罗雅谷所引用。更有趣的,是罗雅谷有关"四不等田"的例子,也符合程大位所说的"四不等田分两段,一为勾股一为斜"。[52]

现在,我们开始进入《测量全义》第六卷"测体",亦即有关体积之计算。罗雅谷首先说明(立)体的意义,以及一些相关的概念之界说(或定义):

> 体者面之积,或实如金木土石等,或空如盘池陶穹等,俱同理同法。其界为面,面居体之周。[53]

紧接着,罗雅谷补了一个自注:"面截面生棱,如线遇线生角也。又棱为两面之共界。"再接着,针对"一面之体""二面之体""三面之体""四面之体""五面之体""六面之体""八面之体""十二面之体",以及"二十面之体"等,他尽可能提供"界说",逐一说明其图形性质。

以"一面之体""二面之体"为例,他所给出的界说依序如下:

> 一面之体如球、如卵。
> 二面之体,如半球、半卵、圆角、圆堆。[54]

图12 《测量全义》扫描

像"一面之体"或"二面之体"这样的概念,他大概只能图示,希望读者可以直观理解。显然,这是罗雅谷"类推"卷四的第四、五界的结果。其实,在平面的案例中,他也很难说明白。

至于他的参考论述涉及《九章算术》卷五"商功章"之立体图形,则有如下三类("立面体""角体"与"斗体"):

---

50 陈敏皓,《〈同文算指〉内容分析》,122—125页。罗雅谷撰著《筹算》时,也曾参考《同文算指》,《崇祯历书》,1527页。
51 程大位,《算法统宗》,郭书春主编,《中国科学技术典籍汇编》(二),1265页。
52 同上,1264页。
53 罗雅谷,《测量全义》卷六,页二,《崇祯历书》,1383页。
54 同上。

第一体名立面体。如正立方、斜立方、多边立体、正立圆体、扁圆体。公法。以高乘底之积,得其容。其高之度,则垂线也。

《几何原本》十二卷七增题曰:两平行面内之体或同高两体,其比例为体与体,若底与底,但取同类相求,以正高为据,不论体势直与不直。[55]

参考图13。罗雅谷在此引述《几何原本》第十二卷第七增题,其进路即清晰地呼应卷四中的"以平行线为本"。其实,他在解说立体图形的性质时,也早已经使用了二、三维的"类比"手法,譬如正立方与正方、斜立方与斜方,等等。

现在,引述"角体"如下:

第二体名角体。底广上锐,如堆垛峰亭之类,其法同也。《几何(原本)》十二卷七题之系曰:同底等高之角体与平行面体(即同高体)之比例,若一比三。[56]

参考图14,这些出自《九章算术》"商功章"如委粟、倚垣等概念,都是角体的例子。针对"角体"与"立面体"之关联,罗雅谷也是运用《九章算术》"商功章"的概念工具如"立方"(立面)、"堑堵""阳马"及"鳖臑",提供他的"论曰"如下:

论曰:角体为立面体三之一者,何也?如正立方体,自上而下,对角平分之,为两堑堵。每一堑堵得正立方二之一。又于堑堵之两方面,自上而下,对角平分之,成大小两分。大者为阳马,得堑堵三之二。小者为鳖臑,得堑堵三分一。则一正立方,分之为堑堵,得二。阳马则三,鳖臑则六。角体者,阳马也,故得立面体三之一也。详见九章算。[57]

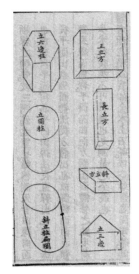 

图13 《几何原本》卷十二立体(《测量全义》扫描)　　图14 《九章算术》"商功章"立体(《测量全义》扫描)

紧接着上述"论曰"及插图(图十四)之后,[58]罗雅谷显然为了计算椭球体积(本卷最后有"量撱圆体

---

[55] 罗雅谷,《测量全义》卷六,页四,《崇祯历书》,1384页。
[56] 罗雅谷,《测量全义》卷六,页五,《崇祯历书》,1384页。
[57] 罗雅谷,《测量全义》卷六,页八,《崇祯历书》,1386页。
[58] 这个插图除了鳖臑之外,另外三个立体已经企图呈现空间视觉效果,这可能是在中国问世的算书最早出现的例子。不过,这四个立体图形并非从最上面的立面逐次切割而成,它们之间缺乏逻辑连结,显示罗雅谷、编辑及刻工等人员插图训练之不足。

之容"),而引进"截角体法"(截圆锥体法)及其五种圆锥截痕:三角形、平圆形、圭窦形(抛物线)、陶丘形(双曲线),以及撱圆形(椭圆形)。由于我已经另文论述此一主题,此处就略而不赘。[59]

《测量全义》内容与"商功"有关的立体,还有下列第三种:

> 第三名斗体。古名方窖、圆窖等。其上下两面不等而相似,盖角体之截分也。引长其棱,即相遇而成全角之体。凡置斗体,大而居下。本角体之截分,角体欲自立,底必在下也,其置裁分亦然。[60]

所谓的"角体",亦即今日所谓的"锥体",至于"斗体"就是截顶的"角体"。(截顶锥体)。罗雅谷在计算"斗体"体积时,先是就已知本角体之高的情况,"先求本角体之容,后求所阙截分之容,相减,余为元体之容",[61]亦即,在锥体高已知时,将未截的锥体之体积,减去截掉的锥体之体积,剩下来的就是所求体积。(参考图15,16)这个公式(算法)或并未现身在《九章算术》"商功章"之中,不过,对于"斗体"图形之形象认识,显然不无助益。

 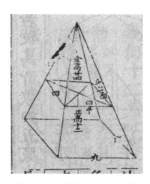

图15 《测量全义》扫描　　图16 《测量全义》扫描

然而,

> 若不知全角体之高,则截体分求之法曰:如甲乙丙丁,斗体之大面也,边各二十四。戊巳庚辛,小面也,边各十八。用垂线截斗体。从戊巳边向下至午未底,分元体为二。从辛庚边向下至申酉底,从庚巳至戊亥,从辛戊至子丑,皆如之。分元体为九。一居中,成立面体。四边四体为堑堵。四隅四体为阳马。各以本法求其容,并为斗体之容。[62]

上述这个"截体分求之法"(参考图17),几乎就是《九章算术》"方亭术"的部分内容之翻版。[63]罗雅谷究竟如何得知?或许他所参考的"九章筭"就包括此内容吧!不过,有了底边是正方形(方亭底面(大面)是正方形)的案例,罗雅谷相当得心应手地将此公式推广到下列情况:"若斗面为多边形而无法,或其棱

59　洪万生,《从圭窦形到抛物线:闲话数学名词的翻译语境》。
60　罗雅谷,《测量全义》卷六,页九,《崇祯历书》,1386页。
61　同上。
62　罗雅谷,《测量全义》卷六,页十,《崇祯历书》,1387页。
63　有关《九章算术》卷五"方亭术",可参考郭书春,《九章算术译注》,177—178页。

不等,亦用此法"。

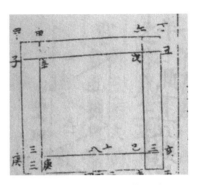

图 17 "方亭"之截体分求

《测量全义》卷六还有五种正多面体的体积计算、"量圆球之容",以及"量椭圆体之容"等等。在此,我们只简略引述其中的"量圆球之容"(球体积计算),他指出:"圆球之全理,见亚奇默德《圆球圆柱书》,并见《几何(原本)》一十四卷。"请参考他的第一题:"球上大平圆之积,为本球圆面积四之一",亦即(半径为 R 的)球面上大圆(great circle)的面积等于球表面积($4\pi R^2$)的四分之一。在中算的脉络中,球表面积的计算涉及《九章算术》卷一"方田章"的"宛田"图形概念,[64]而这当然是中算家(包括刘徽与祖冲之)无从处理的主题。

四、阿基米德《圆书》

《测量全义》卷五"测面下"主题单元依序是"圆面求积"(圆面积公式)、"量撱圆法"[65]"量圈之一分",以及"量面用法"。对照卷四的"测面上"之处理三边形、四边形、五边形及五以上之多边形,卷五主要针对圆面及撱圆面积之计算。当然,为了计算比较复杂的多边形之面积,罗雅谷还引进"变形法"及"截形法",前者我们将在下一节讨论其中一个案例。

在"圆面求积"这个单元中,罗雅谷开宗明义就针对阿基米德的《圆书》提出下列说明:

> 凡圆面积,与其半径线偕半周线作矩内直角形之积等。依此法,则量圆形者,以半径乘半周而已。古高士亚奇默德作《圆书》,[66]内三题洞烛圆形之理。今表而出之,为元本焉。[67]

紧接着,罗雅谷引述那三(个命)题及其证明。在此,仅引述这三题内容及其相关的备注:[68]

第一题 圆形之半径偕其周做勾股形,其容与圆形之积等。
第二题 凡圈周,三倍圈径有奇。此法有二。其一云三倍又七十之十,则朒。其二云三倍又七十一之十,则盈。[69]
第三题 圆容积与径上方形之比例。解曰:一为十一与十四为朒,一为二百二十三与二百八十四为盈。

---

64 "宛田"被认为是一种"球冠形"(spherical cap)。参考郭书春,《九章算术译注》,63页。
65 "撱"字无误。
66 罗雅谷将阿基米德中译为亚奇默德。
67 罗雅谷,《测量全义》卷五,页二,《崇祯历书》,1366页。
68 《圆书》第一题的"现代"版本,可参考李文林主编,《数学珍宝》,147—149页。
69 此处是指圆周率的不等式:$3\frac{10}{71}<\pi<3\frac{10}{70}$,后者就是我们熟悉的 22/7。上界为盈,下界为朒,罗雅谷的说法刚好相反,显然有误。

此外,罗雅谷还给出"今士别立一法"所得的圆周率 π 之精密近似值(二十一位):[70]

$$3.141\ 592\ 653\ 589\ 793\ 238\ 46 < \pi < 3.141\ 592\ 653\ 589\ 793\ 238\ 47$$

但却评论说:"子母之数,积至二十一字,为万亿亿,难可施用",而且也没有说明此一近似值的出处。在本节"圆面求积"最后,罗雅谷给了两个备注,值得引述如下:

> 古设周问积法曰:周自之,十二而一。此犹是径一围三,较之径七围二十二者,尤疏也,故不合。

> 古设径问积法,以径自乘,三之,四而一。如设径一,自之得一,三之得三,四而一,则四之三,为圈之积。全数为径上之方形,则知径上之方,与圈之积为四与三。然前论一四与一一而合。今之四与三,则所谓虚隅二五也。[71]

根据这两个备注,再加上(前文所引)罗雅谷在"圆面求积"(图18)的开场白所指称的"量圆形者,以半径乘半周而已",以及他在"一题之系"(第一命题的系理)中所提及的"若全径偕全周矩内方形,则四倍圈积",[72] 我们可以确信他熟谙《九章算术》的圆田四术:

- 圆田术曰:半周、半径相乘得积步;
- 又术曰:周、径相乘,四而一;
- 又术曰:径自相乘,三之,四而一;
- 又术曰:周自相乘,十二而一。[73]

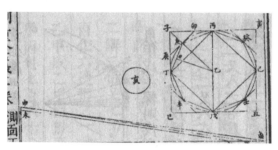

图18 阿基米德"圆面求积"证明用图

只是这些"术"的刘徽注解,如前文提及,他应该无从得知。不过,以阿基米德的《圆书》为立论基础,他显然清晰地掌握了箇中的"法之所以然"之故。

五、"两正方形变为一正方"

在《测量全义》卷五中,罗雅谷也介绍"变形法",并以六题解说之,兹先引述如下:

> 其一:设三角形。求变为等底、等积方形。
> 其二:设一方形、一线。求变为他方形,其边与线等。
> 其三:设矩内形。变为正方形。
> 其四:设多边形。变为正方形。
> 其五:两正方形。变为一正方。

---

[70] 罗雅谷,《测量全义》卷五,页十三,《崇祯历书》,1372页。
[71] 引《测量全义》卷五,页十三,《崇祯历书》,1372页。
[72] 引《测量全义》卷五,页十一,《崇祯历书》,1371页。
[73] 引郭书春,《九章算术译注》,39,58—59,60页。

其六：设矩形。求变为他矩形,其边各有比例。

这六个命题应该都沿袭自《几何原本》或其应用。针对第五个,罗雅谷给了一个注解:

《几何原本》一卷四十七题备论其理,此则用法。[74]

这部几何经典的第一卷命题四十七就是鼎鼎大名的毕氏定理,罗雅谷显然利用其"证法",解决此一作图问题。以下引述他所谓的"用法":

置两正方形。以角相切,令其边为直线,角之外为直角,即成甲勾股虚形。其弦联两元形之各一角,即以为底,作正方形,其积与两元形并积,等。其变法作丙戊庚巳丁矩形,及乙寅线。又截壬形,与子形、庚形等。次截取癸实形,移补丙丁虚形。次取丙子实形,移补甲虚形。次取壬实形,移补庚虚形。次取庚丑实形,移补戊巳虚形。次取戊实形,移补辛虚形,成卯辰午未正方形。[75]

参考图19(罗雅谷原书插图),罗雅谷将给定的两个正方形之一边变成为一个勾股形的勾与股,作出一个"勾股虚形"。接着,再以这个勾股形之弦为边,作一个正方形,他的"所求"就是给定的两个正方形的面积之和,会等于这个新的(大)正方形之面积。为此目的,"变法"先是包括了下列作图:矩形"丙戊庚巳丁"、乙寅线(前述矩形之对角线,又此线与勾股形的弦边垂直)。又作壬形、丑形,以及子形(原已存在)。然后,将癸形"实形""移补"到丙丁"虚形"。[76]将丙子实形"移补"到甲虚形。将壬实形"移补"到庚虚形。将庚丑实形"移补"到戊巳虚形。最后,戊实形"移补"到辛虚形,而成为卯辰午未正方形,得其所求。

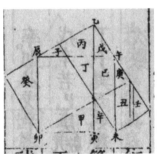

图19 《测量全义》扫描

罗雅谷的上述"证明"之特色,乃是基于《几何原本》的"备论其理"(之启发),于是,所求正方形就可从勾股形的弦边作图出来。不过,上述这个"移补"尽管都基于全等变换,其进路却完全不是欧几里得的本色。欧几里得的证明是找到"勾边正方形+股边正方形"与"弦边正方形"的概念连结关系,而不是像罗雅谷一样,从前者一步一步地"移补"而得到后者。[77]事实上,罗雅谷的进路很难不让我们联想到刘徽

---

74 引罗雅谷《测量全义》卷五,页二十七,《崇祯历书》,1379页。
75 同上。
76 癸形(勾股形)是原先所给定股边正方形之一部分,故称之为"实"形。丙丁形(勾股形)不是一开始就存在,故称之为"虚"形。
77 参考洪万生,《传统中算家论证的个案研究》。罗雅谷的"移补"与刘徽的"出入相补"都结合了程序性知识(procedural knowledge)及概念性知识(conceptual knowledge),不像欧几里得的《几何原本》命题之证明(譬如毕氏定理),是完全概念性面向的知识内容。有关程序性与概念性,可参考 J. Hiebert ed., *Conceptual and Procedural Knowledge: The case of mathematics*. Hillsdale, NJ/London: Lawrence Erlbaum Associates, Publishers, 1986.

的"出入相补"。至于他的想法源头何在,我们还无从得知。可以想见,罗雅谷绝对不可能从欧几里得的证明中,找到关键证明步骤中的"移补"程序,因为欧几里得的进路是概念性(conceptual)而非程序性的(procedural)。[78]

由于南宋版《九章算术》(含刘徽注)在明代失传,因此,罗雅谷所谓的"九章筭"不可能指向《九章算术》,他当然更不可能知道刘徽的注解。同样的情况,当然也适用于明末清初的中国数学家。梅文鼎就是一个绝佳的案例,他对刘徽注究竟有多少理解我们无从得知,尽管他曾看过《九章算术》第一卷"方田章"。[79]不过,也正因为如此,所以当他在自己的《勾股举隅》中,显然引用罗雅谷的插图及主要进路,[80]以证明毕氏定理,他主张所谓的"几何即勾股",似乎因而有了更吸引人的诉求力量。[81]事实上,他在此提供了两个证明。由于第二个证明之插图袭自罗雅谷,请让我们引述其方法如下:

> 甲乙丙勾股形。乙丙弦,其幂戊乙丙丁。甲丙股,其幂甲壬辛丙。甲乙勾,其幂乙庚癸甲。
> 论曰:从甲角作巳甲丑垂线,[82]分弦幂为大小两长方,一为子丙大长方,准股幂;一为戊丑小长方,准勾幂。试移甲丑丙勾股形补巳子丁虚形;又移巳壬甲勾股形补丁丙辛虚形,则子丙大长方即移为甲辛股幂。次移甲丑乙为勾股形补巳子戊虚形,再移巳戊卯勾股形补戊癸寅虚形。末移戊卯甲癸形补癸寅乙庚虚形。则戊丑小长方即移为庚甲勾幂矣。[83]

参考图20(取自梅文鼎原书版),结合上述"论曰",我们可以发现梅文鼎的"移补"进路完全与罗雅谷相反,他是将"弦边正方形"一步一步地"移补"成"勾边正方形+股边正方形"。同时,他在论证时,图形的(直线交点)符号标示以及说理的程序,[84]都远比罗雅谷成熟且高明,不愧为明末清初一代历算大师。

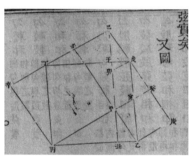

图20 《勾股举隅》扫描

---

[78] 程序性知识诉诸"算则或算法"(algorithm),参考同上。这是因为欧几里得从"弦边正方形"切出两个长方形之后,然后,再证明它们各自等于"勾边正方形"及"股边正方形"。在此过程中,他运用"SAS"全等性质而非等面积图形的"移补"。参考《几何原本》卷一第四十七题。

[79] 1678年,梅文鼎曾在黄虞稷处所见到《九章算术》"方田章",但一生未见全书。参考李迪,《梅文鼎评传》,429页。

[80] 梅文鼎熟悉《崇祯历书》可以征之于他的著作如《勾股举隅》《几何通解》,以及《几何补编》等等。他的《几何补编》自序,就留下忠实的见证:"壬申春月偶见馆童屈篾为灯,诧其为有法之形,乃覆取《测量全义》量体诸率,实考其作法根源。"

[81] 梅文鼎的"几何即勾股"以及其孙子梅毂成后来所提出的"借根方即天元一"(前者代数版),是清初"西学中源"立论的可演示案例,而不是《史记》所"泛称"的"畴人子弟四散,或在夷狄,或在诸夏"。

[82] 梅文鼎自注:"与乙丙弦成十字",此一垂直性质之形容非常形象化。

[83] 引梅文鼎,《勾股举隅》,4—5页,郭书春主编,《中国科学技术典籍通汇》(四)(郑州:河南教育出版社),433—446页。

[84] 这个现象是很奇特的,照理说出身西算背景的罗雅谷,应该会以比较具有"现代性"的手法,来表现"图示"才是。

六、结语

罗雅谷所引述的"九章筭"究竟是一部著作,或是泛指传统中算的概念、方法或公式,由于我们还找不到直接相关的线索,在此无法给出定论。[85] 不过,有一些蛛丝马迹,倒是指向程大位的《算法统宗》(1592年首版问世)。正如前述,《同文算指》(1614)就有多题与《算法统宗》所收相同,利玛窦、李之藻据以编译的这部西算之母本,就是丁先生的 Arithmetica practica(实用算术)。另一方面,罗雅谷在山西居停七年学习语言与"在地知识",他不可能未曾接触《算法统宗》,因为这一部算书非常畅销,到了清初,"海内握算持筹之士,莫不家藏一编,若业制举者之于四子书、五经义,翕然奉以为宗"。[86]

无论如何,罗雅谷编写《测量全义》时,除了在三角学(平面与球面)主题上,主要参考玉山若干的《论各种三角学》之外,在平面与立体的"容"积计算上,则是运用《几何原本》的核心概念,譬如平行,来收编《九章算术》卷一"方田章"、卷五"商功章"的主要公式。即使他可能研读程大位的《算法统宗》,然而,他无从得知刘徽注的成果,则是完全可以确定的事实。

尽管如此,他在证明面积或体积公式时,使用了类似刘徽"以盈补虚"或"出入相补"的"移补"进路,这显然是颇具"中算特色"的方法,足见他在收编时,已经相当可以掌握"在地的"数学风格。另一方面,如果他在处理《测量全义》的面积计算时,确曾参考程大位《算法统宗》,那么,他对于平面图形的收编,就相当节制而有所选择,并以能否纳入定义的概念的阶层(hierarchy of concept)为依归。譬如说,《算法统宗》就收入五个不规则曲线形,依序称之为"五不等田""三圭形""倒顺二圭""六角形",及"八角形"。[87] 针对这些《几何原本》所谓的"无法之形",罗雅谷显然视而不见。还有,即使程大位也纳入下列看来是比较规则的平面图形,如"二圭并弧矢""圭并弧矢""股圭并弧""三弧并一圭",及"二弧并一圭"等等,[88] 不过,由于其中所涉"弧田"(弓形)也是"无法之形",因此,罗雅谷显然也不曾考虑这些图形。

另一方面,罗雅谷也极为关注"不发之根"与圆周率近似值的估计,他常以"驳曰"来指出传统中算"口诀"之谬,再继之以"论曰",为他的"测面"(面积计算理论)提供一个更清晰的图像。至于他所引进的海龙公式尽管证明略有瑕疵,然而,却留给梅文鼎及其孙子梅瑴成一个尚待完成的研究课题。

梅文鼎深受《测量全义》乃至《崇祯历书》之影响,除了本文第五节所讨论的具体案例之外,我们从他的年谱中,也可以找到文献的证据。[89] 其实,他的《平三角举要》更是仿效《测量全义》之论述(体例),我们轻易复按即可掌握大致轮廓。史家刘钝认为这是中国史上第一部三角学教程的著作,也是梅文鼎借助中算勾股术整合(西方)三角学的一个尝试。[90]

不过,无论梅文鼎的"几何即勾股"乃至梅瑴成的"借根方即天元一",如何替后来的"西学中源说"助威,中国传统数学终于是在1600年左右告一段落了。[91] 之后朝向西化或现代化的发展,有一点反讽地,梅文鼎祖孙两人竟然是领头羊。然而,论其端倪,罗雅谷的《测量全义》(包括论证与计算)就像《几何原本》(只包括论证)一样,都是非常关键的(西算)启蒙著作。

---

85 史家王渝生指出:徐光启曾将吴敬的《九章算术比类大全》勾股卷的中算测量法六种,与《测量法义》中的西法进行比较,而撰著《测量异同》,参考王渝生《〈测量异同〉提要》,郭书春主编《中国科学技术典籍通汇:数学卷》(四),页19。因此,如果徐光启曾参考吴敬算书,那么,罗雅谷当然也不无可能。不过,在此我们不打算讨论此一议题。

86 转引李俨、杜石然《中国古代数学简史》,221页。那是1716年,程家后代子孙在清康熙新刻本的序言中,所指出的出版热潮。也就在那个时候,程家还在旧宅对面起造了印刷厂。

87 程大位《算法统宗》,卷三,页十一~十二,郭书春主编《中国科学技术典籍通汇:数学卷》(二),1269页。

88 程大位《算法统宗》,卷三,页十三,郭书春主编《中国科学技术典籍通汇:数学卷》(二),1270页。

89 1675年(康熙十四年),时年四十三岁的梅文鼎再赴南京参加乡试,购得《崇祯历书》(内缺《比例规解》),"穷昼夜不舍",李迪《梅文鼎评传》,428页。

90 刘钝《〈平三角举要〉提要》,郭书春主编《中国科学技术典籍通汇:数学卷》(四),459页。

91 参考苏俊鸿《学术赞助:清代数学发展的一个数学社会史的考察》,洪万生主编《数学的东亚穿越》,171-195页。

参考资料

[1] Grattan-Guinness, Ivor (1997). The Fontana History of Mathematical Sciences. London: FontanaPress.
[2] Heath, Thomas L. (1956). Euclid: Thirteen Books of Elements. New York: Dover Publications, INC.
[3] Martzloff, Jean-Claude (1997). A History of Chinese Mathematics. Berlin/Heidelberg: Springer-Verlag.
[4] 毛尔(Eli Maor)(2000).《毛起来说三角》(Trigonometric Delights),台北:天下文化出版公司。
[5] 李文林主编(2000).《数学珍宝:历史文献精选》,台北:九章出版社。
[6] 李迪(2006).《梅文鼎评传》,南京:南京大学出版社。
[7] 李建勋(2006).〈海龙公式的流变:由徐光启到梅瑴成〉,《HPM通讯》9(4):9-15。
[8] 李俨、杜石然(1976).《中国古代数学简史》,香港:商务印书馆香港分馆。
[9] 金格瑞契(Owen Gingerich)(2007).《追踪哥白尼》(The Book Nobody Read),台北:远流出版公司。
[10] 奔特等(Lucas N. H. Bunt et. al.,)(2019).《数学起源:进入古代数学家的另类思考》(The Historical Roots of Elementary Mathematics),台北:五南出版社。(中译者:黄美伦、林美杏、邱佩瑜、王瑜君、黄俊玮、刘雅茵)
[11] 洪万生(2007).《传统中算家论证的个案研究》,《科学教育学刊》15(4):357-385。
[12] 洪万生(2010).《数学与明代社会:1368-1607》,祝平一主编,《中国史新论:科技与中国社会分册》(南港:中央研究院历史语言研究所/台北:联经出版公司),353-422页。
[13] 洪万生(2021).《从圭窦形到抛物线:闲话数学名词的翻译语境》,发表于2021台湾数学教育学会年会暨东亚数学史研讨会,1/30/2021,台北:台湾师范大学数学系M202。
[14] 程大位(1993).《算法统宗》,郭书春主编,《中国科学技术典籍通汇:数学卷》(二)(郑州:河南教育出版社),1217-1422页。
[15] 陈敏皓(2002).《〈同文算指〉内容分析》,台北:国立台湾师范大学数学研究所硕士论文。
[16] 梅文鼎(1993).《平三角举要》,郭书春主编,《中国科学技术典籍通汇:数学卷》(四)(郑州:河南教育出版社),461-506页。
[17] 郭书春(2007).《尊重原始文献 避免以讹传讹》,《自然科学史研究》26(3):438-448。
[18] 郭书春主编(2010).《中国科学技术史:数学卷》,北京:科学出版社。
[19] 彭君智(2002).《人文社会科学史料典籍研读会之〈测量全义〉道读》,《HPM通讯》5(6):
[20] 罗雅谷(1631/2009).《测量全义》,载徐光启编纂、潘鼐汇编,《崇祯历书》,上海:上海古籍出版社,1295-1464页.
[21] 苏俊鸿(2013).《中国近代数学发展(1607-1905):一个数学社会史的进路》,台北:国立台湾师范大学数学系博士论文。
[22] 苏俊鸿(2018).《学术赞助:清代数学发展的一个数学社会史的考察》,洪万生主编,《数学的东亚穿越》,台北:开学文化出版社,171-195页。

附记:2021/2/19初稿,张秉莹、杨清源协助文献收集,黄美伦协助编辑,都谨此申谢。

Ferdinand Verbiest and the 'Muslim astronomical system' of Wu Mingxuan, 1669

Christopher Cullen* 古克礼

Needham Research Institute, 8 Sylvester Road, Cambridge CB3 9AF, UK

Centre for the Study of China, Korea, and Japan－UMR 8173

(CNRS－EHESS－Université Paris Cité), France

Catherine Jami** 詹嘉玲

CNRS, Centre for the Study of China, Korea, and Japan－UMR 8173, France

Abstract In early 1669, the Jesuit missionary astronomer Ferdinand Verbiest (1623－1688, Nan Huairen 南怀仁 in Chinese) was ordered by the Kangxi emperor (r. 1662－1722) to take part in a test of his abilities to make accurate astronomical predictions, principally those needed to construct a luni-solar calendar of the type used by all literate members of the population of Imperial China, lay or official, for planning their daily activities. He was to do this in competition with the Muslim astronomer Wu Mingxuan 吴明烜. In his account of that competition, Verbiest states repeatedly that Wu based his predictions on the 'Muslim [astronomical] system' (*Hui hui li* 回回历). This essay is an initial investigation of the methods used by Wu Mingxuan to make astronomical calculations, with the aim of finding the extent to which his results really were based on the system to which Verbiest refers. This investigation indicates that Verbiest's characterisation of Wu Mingxuan's methods is incorrect. Wu Mingxuan was in fact using a version of the Ming dynasty's Great Concordance system *Da tong li* 大统历, that had been restored to use by the Astronomical Bureau (*Qin tian jian* 钦天监) after Jesuit astronomers and their Chinese colleagues were deprived of their offices in 1665 as a result of the accusations made by Yang Guangxian 杨光先. The reasons why Verbiest nevertheless described Wu's methods as 'Muslim' are best understood in the context of the Jesuits' struggle to re-establish themselves as astronomical experts at the Qing court.

Ⅰ. The rise, fall and restoration of Jesuit astronomy: retrospect from 1644 to 1668 [1]

In 1644 the Qing dynasty began its rule over the former empire of the Ming dynasty. That same year, they gave responsibility for overseeing the state Astronomical Bureau (*Qin tian jian* 钦天监) to a Jesuit astronomical specialist, Johann Adam Schall von Bell (Tang Ruowang 汤若望, 1592－1666). Thereafter the annual luni-solar calendar that symbolized the dynasty's success in maintaining harmony between the human and the natural orders was produced using the western astronomical methods

---

* cc433@cam.ac.uk

** catherine.jami@ehess.fr

[1] The opening section of this article recapitulates events that are traced in detail with full references and citations of textual evidence in Cullen and Jami (2020); for the wider context see also Jami (2012), particularly chapters 2 and 3.

that the Jesuits had brought to China in the closing years of the Ming.[2] But in 1665 Schall and a number of his Chinese colleagues were sentenced to death after being convicted of serious errors in their work, principally in wrongly deciding the most auspicious time for the funeral of a child of the Shunzhi emperor (r. 1644–1661) and thus allegedly causing the emperor's death.[3] Schall's sentence was later commuted to house arrest, but several of his Chinese colleagues were executed. Jesuit missionaries working in the provinces were exiled to Canton.

The Jesuits' principal accuser, Yang Guangxian 杨光先 (1597–1669) was appointed as Director (*Jian zheng* 监正) of the Astronomical Bureau, and despite his repeated protestations that he lacked the necessary technical astronomical knowledge, the regents who ruled during the emperor's minority insisted on his assuming office, which he finally did in October 1665. Once in office, he ordered the readoption by the Bureau of the Great Concordance astronomical system (*Da tong li* 大统历)[4] which had been the official system of the Ming dynasty, and the Qing dynasty's official calendar was henceforward calculated on this basis rather than using the Jesuit's western methods.[5] His tenure of the Directorship was not widely seen as successful. The staff of the bureau had not used the old system since 1644, and in 1666 Yang was obliged to recruit Wu Mingxuan 吴明烜, the disgraced former director of the Astronomical Bureau's Muslim section (*Hui hui ke* 回回科), which had been abolished during Schall's period in office, in order to have access to the skills in predicting planetary motions, in which the Muslim section had traditionally specialised. Yang did this in the face of complaints from some officials that Wu was a convicted criminal who had escaped a death sentence for misleading the emperor only because he was lucky enough to be covered by a general amnesty to celebrate the recovery of a member of the imperial family from a serious illness.

Yang Guangxian was by his own admission quite unable to carry out calendrical computations, which he therefore entrusted to his subordinates in the Bureau. Instead, he began a project to restore an alleged ancient method known as *hou qi* 候气 'watching for the *qi*', for experimental determination

---

[2] These astronomical methods were set out in the multi-authored collection of explanatory texts, calculation procedures and tables of data compiled under the supervision of Xu Guangqi 徐光启 (1562–1633), the *Chong zhen li shu* 崇祯历书 (Texts on astronomical systems [compiled in] the Chongzhen reign), and submitted to the throne between 1630 and 1635. In 1644 a new version of this collection, which continued to be modified thereafter, was issued by Schall under the title *Xi yang xin fa li shu* 西洋新法历书 (Texts on astronomical systems according to the new western methods). The words *Xi yang* 'western' were later dropped from the title to give *Xin fa li shu* 新法历书 (Texts on astronomical systems according to the new methods). The collated edition of Shi and Chu (2017) includes all the material added to the text under the early Qing.

[3] It was a routine part of the Bureau's work to compile the annotations to the imperially issued annual calendar, indicating which days were favourable or unfavourable for certain activities; see the account of the criticisms levelled against Schall by some of his fellow Jesuits for taking part in such 'superstitious' activities in Jami (2012), 38–40. It was a natural extension of such activities for the Bureau to choose appropriate times for important state activities such as an imperial funeral.

[4] In the texts referred to in this article, the word *li* 历 is used to refer to two things whose names demand different English translations. It may refer to a text in pamphlet form such as the 'People's *li*' *Min li* 民历, promulgated annually by imperial authority and used by all literate households, giving information relating to each day of the lunar months of the year: here the translation 'calendar' is appropriate. Elsewhere, as in 'Great Concordance *li*' (*Da tong li* 大统历) it refers to a complex document specifying the astronomical calculations and tabulated data which, amongst other functions, enable such documents as the annual lunisolar calendar to be produced. Here the words 'system' or 'astronomical system' are more appropriate. On this issue, see the discussion in Cullen (2017), 24.

[5] By the time Yang took office, it was too late for calendars based on the Great Concordance to be produced for Kangxi 5, 1666, and those already calculated under the Jesuits for that year had to be used; see note 84.

of the initial moments of the 24 subdivisions of the seasons of the year.[6] This supposedly worked by constructing pitch pipes whose lengths would enable them to resonate with the different cosmic *qi* 气, associated with each season. These 24 subdivisions, themselves called *qi*, sometimes *jie qi* 节气, were crucial reference points in deciding whether the months were in step with the seasons, or whether an intercalary month needed to be inserted in the calendar to restore their correct relations. Despite devoting considerable time and official funds to his project, Yang was unable to report any success, and by the end of 1668 a number of high ministers, and even the young Kangxi emperor himself (1654—1722, then aged 14, having formally assumed personal rule since August 1667), had begun to display impatience with Yang's procrastination.

Around this time, the emperor became aware of the presence of the group of Jesuits still under house arrest in Beijing, of whom three remained after the death of Schall two years earlier. One of the group, Ferdinand Verbiest (Nan Huairen 南怀仁, 1623—1688), was expert in astronomy and had served as Schall's assistant in the work of the Astronomical Bureau. The others were Lodovico Buglio (Li Leisi 利类思, 1606—1682, the superior of the group), and Gabriel de Magalhães (An Wensi 安文思, 1609—1677). Early in the morning of Christmas Day, 25 December 1668 (Kangxi 7/11/28), a group of four senior officials were sent to the Jesuit residence by the emperor, and asked for comments on the calendar prepared by the Astronomical Bureau for Kangxi 8, 1669,[7] which had been issued a few weeks earlier (see note 14). Verbiest responded with a number of trenchant criticisms which evidently impressed the visitors, since they returned later in the day to convey to the Jesuits a summons to appear at the palace early on 26 December. There, together with Yang Guangxian and Wu Mingxuan, they were closely questioned on astronomical matters, first by high ministers, and then by the emperor himself, who had previously sent a message urging Yang, Wu, and the Jesuits to discuss calendrical matters in a cooperative and non-contentious spirit. Despite this injunction, Yang claimed that the Jesuits were engaged in plotting rebellion against Qing rule, and should therefore play no role in calendrical reform. The emperor rejected as implausible the suggestion that a small number of missionaries could pose any danger to the dynasty, and angrily rebuked Yang as a 'petty and venal person' (*xiao ren* 小人) for having concealed the presence of the Jesuits in Beijing when the emperor had, earlier in the year, issued a call for astronomical experts to be located and sent to the capital.

In contrast, the emperor questioned Verbiest and his colleagues (who were probably the first Europeans with whom he had had any significant contact) with friendly interest. When the emperor asked Verbiest to suggest some test that would enable anybody to see whether the Jesuits' astronomical methods were or were not correct, Verbiest suggested the simple experiment of asking for predictions of the length of the noon shadow of a gnomon of any given length on any day that might be assigned. On the emperor asking Yang and Wu whether this was a fair test, they agreed that it was, and the emperor ordered that the shadow prediction trial should begin the next day, 27 December. When it came to the day itself, Yang and Wu admitted that they were in fact unable to make the re-

---

[6] On this see Huang and Chang (1996). Like many sinologists, we prefer to leave the word *qi* untranslated, since none of the English translations proposed, such as 'pneuma', 'vapor' or 'ether' seem to capture its range of meanings to an adequate degree.

[7] During the Ming and Qing periods, a regnal year began on the first day of the first lunar month, which typically fell during February, or sometimes in late January. Thus, Kangxi 8 began on 1 February 1669, and Kangxi 9 on 21 January 1670. In this article, we give the Gregorian year in which a given regnal year begins, and during which most of its months fall.

quired predictions, and Verbiest alone was tested on that and the two subsequent days. He was held to have completed the trial with a high degree of success.[8]

As a result of Verbiest's criticisms of the official calendar, for which Yang Guangxian was formally responsible even if others had actually produced it, added to his failure in the 'watching for the *qi*' project and his incapacity to meet the shadow prediction challenge, Yang appears to have lost all credit in the emperor's eyes, although he was not formally dismissed until March 1669. Wu Mingxuan, however, was apparently seen by the emperor as a competitor against whom Verbiest still needed to prove himself further, despite Wu's failure in the shadow trial. To see why this was, and what it entailed, we need to look back at events earlier in 1668.

II. Wu Mingxuan as a contender in the project of astronomical reform

As already mentioned, it was Yang Guangxian who had rescued Wu Mingxuan from obscurity and disgrace by bringing him back into the Astronomical Bureau in 1666. But by 1668 it seems that Wu's sense of gratitude was wearing thin, since in August of that year he launched a major attack on the competency of the Bureau as an organization, and thus by implication attacked the management of the Bureau by its Director Yang Guangxian:

> 康熙七年⋯七月⋯壬子。钦天监监副吴明烜疏言、见用古历、不无差谬。如五官正戈继文等所进历、暨回回科七政历三本、互有不同。宜令四科知历之官、详加较正、以求至精。然推历以黄道为验。黄道以浑仪为准。今观象台浑仪损坏、亟宜修整。又地震方向、各有所占。请造滚球铜盘一座。并设台上。仪器备、则占验始为有据。
> 得旨、历法甚为精要。如何而使大备。永远可行。著礼部确议具奏
>
> Kangxi 7 ⋯ 7th month ⋯ (15th day) *renzi*. 49 (22 August 1668):[9]
>
> The memorial of the Deputy Director of the Astronomical Bureau, Wu Mingxuan, states:
>
> The way the old astronomical system [i.e. the Great Concordance system], is being used is not without errors. As for the calendar submitted by the Supervisor of the Five Offices Ge Jiwen and his colleagues,[10] and the three versions of the Planets Calendar of the Muslim section, they are not consistent with one another. It would be appropriate to order those officials of the Four Sections [of the Bureau][11] who understand astronomical systems to go into this in detail and make corrections, in order to arrive at the greatest accuracy.
>
> Now in making predictions with an astronomical system, the ecliptic is the reference, and the ecliptic uses an armillary sphere as its standard. But the armillary sphere on the Ob-

---

[8] A detailed analysis of the calculation methods used by Verbiest to make these predictions, and of the circumstances that led him to adopt them is given in Cullen and Jami(2022).

[9] The number 49, not given in the original, is the number in the 60-day cycle of the sexagenary day labelled *renzi*, added here and elsewhere for the reader's convenience. For a tabulation of the whole cycle, see Cullen (2017), 57, Table 2.3. The day of the month, added here for clarity, is not normally given in the *Shi lu*. All Western dates given in this article are in the Gregorian calendar.

[10] From the context, and what is said in the report of the Board of Rites that follows, it appears that this is not the 'People's Calendar' for general distribution, but the 'Planets Calendar' giving daily positions of the sun moon and planets, that was only circulated to the officials of the capital bureaucracy.

[11] These were the Calendar Section (*Li ke* 历科), the Observatory [Literally 'Celestial signs'] Section (*Tian wen ke* 天文科), the Clepsydra Section (*Lou ke* 漏科), and the Muslim Section (*Hui hui ke* 回回科).

servatory platform is damaged, and it should be repaired as a matter of urgency. Further, the directions of earthquakes all have divinatory significance. I therefore request that there should be made a bronze 'ball-rolling plate',[12] to be set up on the observatory. When the instruments are complete, then for the first time divination will have something to serve as a basis.

A Rescript was received [from the emperor] in response: Astronomical systems are a matter of vital importance. How can their completeness be assured, so that they will work permanently? Let the Board of Rites come to a definite decision on this, and memorialize accordingly.[13]

The concern that this attack caused to the emperor and his advisors is evident from the words of the rescript, which asked in effect how, if the restored 'old system' (the Great Concordance system) was problematic, the dynasty was to find a system that could be guaranteed to work in the long term. The Board of Rites took over a month to reply, an interval which suggests that they had investigated this problem with considerable care:

康熙七年 ··· 八月 ··· 丙申。礼部等衙门、议覆五官正戈继文等、所算七政历、金水二星、差错太甚。主簿陈圭新七政历、未经测验、亦有差错。监副吴明炫之七政历。与天象相近、理应颁行。但陈圭新推算己酉年民历、已经颁行各省、不便更换、止于本年暂用。其七政经纬躔度、月五星凌犯等历、及日月交食。既据吴明炫自认、务求合天。应自康熙九年以后。俱交吴明炫推算。仍令钦天监堂官、公同四科官员每日上台。昼测暑影。以定节气。夜测日月五星。以定行度。四年之内修正。务期合天。著成历书。得旨、著吴明炫将康熙八年历日、七政历日、推算进览。余依议

Kangxi 7 ··· 8th month ··· (30th day) *bingshen*. 33 (5 October 1668):

The Board of Rites and other offices report on their deliberations:

[As for] the Planets Calendar calculated by the Supervisor of the Five Offices Ge Jiwen and others, there are very large errors in relation to the two planets Venus and Mercury. The Planets Calendar of the Recorder Chen Yuxin has not yet been subjected to observational testing, and it may also have errors. The Planets Calendar of the Deputy Director Wu Mingxuan is close to the celestial phenomena, and in principle it ought to be promulgated for use. But the People's Calendar calculated by Chen Yuxin for the *jiyou*. 46 year [Kangxi 8, 1669] has already been promulgated to every province,[14] and since it would be inconvenient to make a change, it should be used for that year only. As for the calendars giving the degrees of the orbits of the planets in celestial longitude and latitude, and the approaches and

---

[12] This device used the direction in which a ball rolled from a central position on a horizontal plate as an indication of the location of the earthquake causing the disturbance.

[13] *Da Qing li chao shi lu* 26, 16b—17a.

[14] This had taken place, as was the custom, in the fourth lunar month to enable provincial officials to print a sufficient number of copies for general distribution to the population on the first day of the tenth month, which in 1668 was 4 November. See the account in Verbiest (1687), ch 8, translated and commented in Verbiest and Golvers (1993), 71—73.

invasions of the moon and five planets[15], together with solar and lunar eclipses, Wu Mingxuan is resigned to having to work to seek agreement with the heavens. It would be proper to order Wu Mingxuan to make calculations for the years from Kangxi 9 [1670] onwards. Accordingly, the chief officers of the Astronomical Bureau, with the officials of the Four Sections, should be ordered to go up to the observatory every day, to measure the [gnomon] shadow during the daytime, in order to determine [the times of] the qi, and at night to observe the (sun)[16] moon and five planets, in order to determine their motions. They should carry out [this work of] revision and correction for four years, with the aim that during that time they will achieve agreement with the heavens, and can then compose [a new] treatise on the astronomical system.

Rescript [from the emperor]: Let Wu Mingxuan take in hand the [People's] Calendar for Kangxi 8 and the Planets Calendar, and submit his calculations for inspection. Let the rest be in accordance with the report.[17]

The internal situation of the Astronomical Bureau revealed here is very striking, and appears to indicate that Yang Guangxian was failing to control his subordinates' activities — a not unexpected state of affairs given his confessed lack of technical understanding. There were apparently several conflicting versions of the Planets Calendar for 1669 in existence, one prepared by Ge Jiwen, another by Chen Yuxin and another prepared by Wu Mingxuan, together with perhaps up to three others from the Muslim section. It is not clear how the Board of Rites had decided that Ge Jiwen's calendar was in error in its predictions for Mercury and Venus, and that Wu Mingxuan's calendar was relatively accurate: it may simply be that Wu had more supporters in the Bureau than Ge. The fact that Chen Yuxin's People's Calendar had already been promulgated to provincial governments may explain why his Planets Calendar was spared serious criticism — although it had not yet been released to the senior officials who would normally receive this document, it would have caused difficulties if a different Planets Calendar had been substituted that was not consistent with those parts of its data (such as the times of luni-solar conjunctions marking the first days of months) that had already been used in the People's Calendar. But although Wu Mingxuan's Planets Calendar was not selected for immediate use in Kangxi 8, 1669, the Board still recommended that he should be given responsibility for the Planets Calendar in subsequent years. The Board also took up Wu's suggestion that the officers of the whole Bureau should cooperate in work to improve the astronomical system — and not only proposed that this work should extend over several years but also laid stress on observation as a basis for the elaboration of a body of theory. Finally, the explicit reference to determining the times of qi by observation may well be intended as a veiled criticism of Yang Guangxian's contention that such observational

---

[15] This last document, *the Ling fan li* 凌犯历, was in principle submitted only to the emperor, in manuscript form. It contained detailed calculations of the close approaches of the moon and five planets to one another, and to astrologically significant stars.

[16] This word is clearly out of place here, since the sun is not observable at night; it has probably slipped in by way of a reminiscence of the conventional phrase *ri yue wu xing* 日月五星.

[17] *Da Qing li chao shi lu*, 26, 25b—26a.

work was unnecessary if his 'watching for the *qi*' method was put into practice.[18]

The emperor's response expressed approval of these proposals, but also revealed his desire to make more immediate progress with astronomical issues by insisting that Wu Mingxuan should go ahead immediately with the production of trial versions of a People's Calendar and a Planets Calendar for Kangxi 8, 1669, so that his abilities could be judged on that basis in advance of his being given responsibility for the calendars that would, if all went according to plan, be prepared for Kangxi 9, 1670. It appears that if Wu succeeded, the emperor was prepared to give him the main responsibility for the project of producing an astronomical system for the dynasty that could be used in the long term. Under those circumstances, it was unlikely that the emperor would abandon these plans purely because of Verbiest's success in predicting gnomon shadows, a matter that was decidedly peripheral to the imperative need for the dynasty to produce a reliable calendar.

So, far from giving Verbiest any responsibility for astronomical matters, or even any reward for his success, the emperor simply set him a heavy task to perform, as set out in the imperial response dated 29 December to the report of the officials who had supervised the shadow trial:

知道了。将吴明烜所造。七政及民历。着南怀仁验看差错之处写出。俟报部之日。尔等议奏钦此。

Acknowledged. Take the Planets and People's Calendars made by Wu Mingxuan, and let Verbiest[19] examine them. If he sees any errors he is to point them out in writing. You shall wait for the day when he reports back, and then you shall deliberate and report.[20]

Verbiest was no doubt well aware of the fact that he was being given an opportunity to prove that he should replace Wu Mingxuan as the person responsible for producing a calendrical system that would be 'capable of working permanently' (*yong yuan ke xing* 永远可行), as the emperor had demanded in his rescript on Wu Mingxuan's memorial of the preceding August. Unsurprisingly he made full use of this opportunity to attack Wu Mingxuan's astronomical competence. It appears that Verbiest spent most of January 1669 on this task. The copy of his memorial to the emperor that he prepared to accompany his detailed report is dated to Kangxi 7/12 (which ran from 2—31 January 1669), but the day of the month is blank. However, in the copy given in the documents collected in *Xi chao ding an* 熙朝定案 (*Cases decided during the [Kang]xi reign*, hereafter abbreviated as *XCDA*), the emperor's rescript in response is dated to Kangxi 7/12/26, 27 January 1669. Given the brevity of the rescript it is likely that the report was received at most a day or two before that date. In his manuscript Latin account, written seven years later, Verbiest tells us that the emperor responded *statim*

---

[18] He had first made this claim during the Jesuit's trial in 1665, when he said that it was not necessary to go up to the observatory to make observations (*fei deng tai guan xiang* 非登台观象), so long as the 'watching for the *qi*' procedure was properly followed: An (2015), 116—117, report of trial proceedings submitted Kangxi 4/1/29, 15 March 1665.

[19] In translating Chinese texts in which Verbiest's Chinese name, Nan Huairen 南怀仁 occurs, we commonly render it as 'Ferdinand Verbiest', 'Verbiest', or when the term is used self-referentially by Verbiest 'I', 'me' 'my' or 'mine' as appropriate.

[20] *CYJL* 6b—7a.

('immediately'). [21] In his rescript, the emperor ordered that the report should be passed to the Deliberative Council *Yi zheng wang da chen hui yi* 议政王大臣会议 for discussion. [22] Two days later, the Deliberative Council, headed by Prince Giyešu, responded by declaring their incapacity to evaluate Verbiest's report, and suggesting a way of proceeding that might satisfactorily resolve the issue between Verbiest and Wu:

> 南怀仁所称吴明炬推算历日种种差错之处。皆系精微。其是非一时据难定议。必须差委测验大臣。同钦天监马祜等。将南怀仁吴明炫推算历日内可以测验之数欸。谁人合天象不合天象之处测看。完日再议具题。

The different kinds of errors and inaccuracies in Wu Mingxuan's calendars set out by Verbiest are all very precise and subtle, and it is difficult to come to any overall conclusion as to whether [Verbiest's criticisms] are correct or not. What should be done is to send some high officials to observe, together with Mahu[23] and his colleagues from the Bureau of Astronomy, so that they can take all the numerical data by Verbiest and Wu Mingxuan capable of being tested by observation, and see whose [predictions] match the heavens and whose do not. When this has been done a further report should be made. [24]

The emperor responded on the same day with a list of twenty names of suitable officials to be delegated to carry out the required observations. These included the Presidents and other senior officials of the Boards of Works, Personnel, Rites, Punishments and War, together with two Censors. It was agreed that observations should take place on the third and eighteenth days of the first month of Kangxi 8 (3 and 18 February 1669), which were the days on which Verbiest had predicted that the two *qi* associated with the first month, Establishment of Spring and Rain Waters, should fall. As well as checking when these events actually occurred, there were also to be observations to check predictions of the positions of Mars and Jupiter on the first occasion and of the Moon on the second occasion. [25]

Verbiest and Wu made their predictions in advance of the dates fixed, and the designated officials attended the subsequent observations by which those predictions were checked. Finally, the officials jointly signed a detailed report on the 22nd day of the month, in which they set out the results of their observational evaluation of the predictions made by Verbiest and Wu Mingxuan, and attested that in every instance Verbiest's predictions were correct and Wu's were wrong. [26] Two days later Giyešu

---

[21] *Xi chao ding an*, 4a-6b, Verbiest (1687), IV, 12 and Golvers and Nicolaidis (2009), 128—129. The collection of memorials and imperial pronouncements in XCDA appears to have been initially assembled in 1669, but continued to be added to and modified in later editions.

[22] This was composed of Manchu princes and ministers, and was the major advisory body for emperors in early Qing. On its role and development see Oxnam (1975), 70—76 and elsewhere.

[23] This is the Manchu who was co-president (*Jian zheng* 监正) of the *Qin tian jian* 钦天监 with Yang Guangxian.

[24] XCDA, 7a—7b.

[25] In both the 1676 manuscript and in *Astronomia Europaea* eleven years later, Verbiest indicates that he and Wu Mingxuan were summoned to a meeting by the Board of Rites (the ministry to which the Astronomical Bureau was then subordinate), at which it was decided what predictions were to be made and tested. He seems to suggest that he had an influential voice in this choice; there is no record of this meeting in Chinese. See Golvers and Nicolaidis (2009), 129—131 and Verbiest and Golvers (1993), 67.

[26] CYJL, 43a—38b.

summarised their report for the emperor in a memorial on behalf of the Deliberative Council, and recommended that Verbiest should be appointed to an office in the Bureau of Astronomy and put in charge of calendrical calculation for the following year, Kangxi 9, 1670. Wu Mingxuan, on the other hand, should be investigated by the Board of Personnel. At this point we shall conclude our narrative and look more closely at the calculations and predictions that have been central to the story.

III. Verbiest's criticism of Wu Mingxuan and the 'Muslim system *Hui hui li* 回回历' in early 1669

On what basis had Wu Mingxuan produced his two calendars for Kangxi 8, and made his predictions for the observational tests of February 1669? As we shall see below, in Verbiest's criticisms of the calendrical writings that Wu Mingxuan had produced, he repeatedly refers to Wu's calculations as resulting from the *Hui hui li* 回回历 'Muslim astronomical system'. Taken with the fact that Wu was indeed a Muslim, and had previously headed the Muslim section of the Astronomical Bureau, it would indeed be no surprise to find that Wu's work actually was based on Muslim astronomical techniques.

Astronomical theory and practice from the Islamicate world, which Dror Weil has characterised as 'Arabo-Persian astronomy', was first introduced into East Asia under the patronage of the Yuan dynasty.[27] The Chinese texts nowadays associated with the title *Hui hui li* originate from the early years of the Ming dynasty (1368—1644), when translations of astronomical texts from the imported system were first produced, and Muslim specialists in their use were given a place in the Astronomical Bureau of the new dynasty. The origins and subsequent history of this material has been studied by a number of scholars, based on detailed descriptions of its methods of calculation in a number of extant sources from the 15th century onwards.[28] The *Hui hui li* is, ultimately, a descendant of the system set out in the second century CE *Almagest* of Ptolemy of Alexandria, transmitted and modified over the centuries by astronomers working in the Islamicate world, before it was finally embodied in a Chinese language version. It may thus be regarded as a distant cousin of Verbiest's methods, which ultimately go back to the same Hellenistic roots, via the modifications of Copernicus and Tycho Brahe, who in turn drew on work by astronomers in the medieval Islamicate world.[29]

But was there any connection between tables and calculation procedures set out in the various extant documents associated with the title *Hui Hui li*, and Wu Mingxuan's Planets and People's Calendars for Kangxi 8, 1669, together with the predictions of lunar and planetary positions he was ordered to submit for observational testing in February 1669?

Verbiest criticises the predictions of Wu Mingxuan's draft People's and Planets calendars at length and in great detail. His report is preserved as part of the document collection relating to his

---

[27] See Weil (2018).

[28] See for instance Yabuuti and van Dalen (1997) and van Dalen and Yano (1998), also Shi (2003). We have made use of these and other sources in our work towards understanding the *Hui hui li*, and are grateful to Benno van Dalen and Shi Yunli for their personal responses to queries, which have been of great assistance.

[29] In his 1676 manuscript Verbiest specifically stated that Wu's methods were 'according to the tables of Ptolemy [*secundum Ptolem<a>ei tabulas*], which he had inherited from his ancestors': Golvers and Nicolaidis (2009), 126—127. This is the only point at which Verbiest refers by implication to the common ancestry of Wu's methods and his own.

conflict with Yang Guangxian and Wu Mingxuan that was assembled, apparently by Verbiest himself in response to an imperial command, under the title *Qin ding xin li ce yan ji lue* 钦定新历测验纪略 (*A summary of observations in accordance with the new astronomical system, imperially commissioned*), abbreviated as *CYJL*. He opens the collection with the following introduction:

> 奉旨查对杨光先吴明烜所造各历，并测念诸差纪略。治理历法极西耶稣会士南怀仁述。
>
> In response to a Rescript commanding him to examine and report on the various calendars produced by Yang Guangxian and Wu Mingxuan, and on their discrepancies with observation, Ferdinand Verbiest from the Far West, member of the Society of Jesus, Managing Calendrical Methods reports as follows.[30]

This text of *CYJL* is thus likely to have been composed at some time after Kangxi 8/3/15 (15 April 1669), the date of the first memorial by Verbiest in which he described himself as 治理历法 'Managing Calendrical Methods', the title used in his opening.[31] It is a fairly lengthy text, taking up 84 single pages counted in the western manner, printed on 42 centre folded sheets in the normal Chinese book design. At three points in the text, the sequence of *CYJL* pages pauses to allow the insertion of pages containing documents taken from the woodblock print of the *Xi chao ding an* (*XCDA*) collection of memorials and other official documents, of which the first version was also assembled in 1669. After each of these three documents (which preserve the *XCDA* pagination and were clearly printed from the *XCDA* woodblocks), the *CYJL* page sequence resumes. These insertions add another 6 folded sheets. Verbiest's discussion of Wu Mingxuan's work on the People's and Planets Calendars for Kangxi 8 takes up pages 11a—28b of the main text.

We do not however have to wait until that point for Verbiest to make it clear on what basis he thinks that Wu Mingxuan performed his calendrical calculations. On the very first page of his report, he states:

> 仁当查对吴明烜所用回回历法诸差者。缘奉特旨。
>
> The reason for my taking responsibility for examining and reporting on all the errors in the Muslim astronomical methods used by Wu Mingxuan was that I received a special edict.[32]

And later:

> 先是杨光先保用大统授时诸历。以为较之回回历法。远天特甚。故康熙七年。奉旨谓历交吴明烜推算。及至仁查对明烜所用回回历法。仍复大谬。与大统授时诸历无异。
>
> The origin [of this affair] was that Yang Guangxian treated the Great Concordance and

---

[30] *CYJL* 1a.

[31] See *XCDA*, no 7, 15a—16a. Although *li fa* usually refers to the methods embodied in astronomical systems, the 'calendrical' rendering reflects the way that Verbiest probably expected his skill-set to be viewed in this context.

[32] *CYJL*, 1a.

Season Granting systems as precious heirlooms.[33] It was considered that compared with the *Hui hui* system methods these erred greatly from [the phenomena seen in] the heavens. Thus in the 7th year of the Kangxi period, a Rescript was issued that the calendar should be handed over to Wu Mingxuan to calculate. When I came to check and report on the methods of the *Hui hui* system, thereupon [I found] further major errors, no different from those in the Great Concordance and Season Granting systems.[34]

Here Verbiest is evidently referring to the events of August and October 1668, Kangxi 7, when Wu Mingxuan criticised the official calendars for the coming year Kangxi 8, which was to begin in early 1669. Wu's memorial was given in full in the preceding section of this article, followed by the memorial of the Board of Rites suggesting that he should be given responsibility for a long-term project of astronomical reform, as well as for calculating the calendars for Kangxi 9, 1670. It will be recalled that while agreeing to this proposal, the emperor demanded that Wu should also produce draft calendars for Kangxi 8. However, if we look again at Wu's memorial of 22 August 1668 cited above, his only reference to the work of the Muslim section was to include it in a note referring to officials whose work was inconsistent:

如五官正戈继文等所进历、暨回回科七政历三本、互有不同。

As for the calendar submitted by the Supervisor of the Five Offices Ge Jiwen and his colleagues, and the three versions of the Planets Calendar of the Muslim section, they are not consistent with one another. (See above for full text)

And Wu's reform project was not to be based solely on the Muslim section, but was inclusive of all qualified persons in the entire Bureau:

宜令四科知历之官、详加较正、以求至精。

It would be appropriate to order those officials of the Four Sections [of the Bureau] who understand astronomical systems to go into this in detail and make corrections, in order to arrive at the greatest accuracy. (See above for full text)

Verbiest himself, when writing for a European readership some years after the events of 1669, indicated that the connection between the 'Muslim system' and Wu Mingxuan's predictions embodied in his two calendars was by no means as straightforward as he had indicated in *CYJL*:

Mahumetanus ille, quàm temerarius in loquendo, tam ignarus in calculando, & rudis in

---

[33] The expression in the text, *bao yong* 保用 literally means 'preserve and use'. The translation given here is based on the role of this expression as a variant of the common phrase *bao yong* 宝用 'treasure and use', found in inscriptions on ancient bronze vessels, in such phrases as *zi sun yong bao yong* 子孙永宝用 'May sons and grandsons treasure and use this for ever': for one example amongst many, see Shaughnessy (1991), 8. The variant form occurs in early texts, such as *Hou Han shu* 23, 817, and is used on a seal of the Qianlong period on a Southern Song dynasty scroll in the British Museum, *Illustrations to the Odes of Chen*, Museum number 1964, 0411, 0.1. Yang Guangxian certainly regarded the Chinese tradition of calendrical astronomy as a precious heritage to be preserved at all costs against foreign encroachments: see his memorial in *XCDA*, no 26, 52a—54b.

[34] *CYJL*, 1a—1b.

Astronomia, sibíque plane inconstans & contrarius, pleraque Calendariis suis sine ordine ponebat, id est Sinica Arabicìs, & Arabica Sinicis miscebat, atque ita Calendarium. Arabico-Sinicum dici poterat.

The Muslim, as bold in speech as he was ignorant in calculating, and unskilled in astronomy, while openly inconsistent and contradictory to himself, put many things into his calendars[35] without any order, that is, he mixed Chinese materials with Arabic and Arabic with Chinese, so that it might be called an Arabic-Chinese calendar.[36]

Moreover, a detailed analysis of the calculations that Wu Mingxuan performed, and Verbiest's criticisms of them, show that it was probably not Wu's intention to attack the Great Concordance system in itself, or to replace it by a new system based on the Muslim tradition, but rather to criticise the way that the Great Concordance system was being applied by the officials of the Astronomical Bureau.[37] To that analysis we now turn.

Ⅳ. Wu Mingxuan's calculations of *qi*

In pages 14a—18a of *CYJL*, Verbiest compares his own and Wu Mingxuan's predictions of the moments of inception of the two *qi* 气 contained in each month of the coming civil year Kangxi 8, 1669. Thus, for the first month, we read:

一正月初四日。戌初一刻。回回历为立春。臣等所推历法。正月初三日。巳初二刻八分为立春。则回回历后天一日零三十八刻有余。

一正月二十日。子正二刻。回回历为雨水。臣等所推历法。正月十八日。卯初三刻二分为雨水。则回回历后天一日零七十四刻有余。

Item: On the 4th day of the 1st month, 1 mark into the first half of [the period] xu (19:00—21:00) [*i.e.* 19:15][38], the Muslim system makes it [the *qi*] Establishment of Spring. The astronomical system calculated by me and my colleagues makes it Establishment of Spring on the 3rd day of the first month, 2 marks into the first half of [the double-hour] si (09:00—11:00) and 8 minutes [*i.e.* 09:38]. So the Muslim system lags behind heaven by 1 day, 38 marks and a fraction.

Item: on the 20th day of the 1st month, 2 marks into the second half of [the period] zi (23:00—01:00) [*i.e.* 00:30], the Muslim system makes it [the *qi*] Rain Waters. The astronomical system calculated by me and my colleagues makes it Rain Waters on the 18th day of the 1st month, 3 marks into the first half of [the period] mao (05:00—07:00) and 2 mi-

---

[35] Despite this translation, a *calendarium* in an astronomical context was considerably more than a simple calendar in the modern sense; see for instance the great variety of astronomical information given in Regiomontanus (1485).

[36] Verbiest (1687), Ⅳ, 12, translated with commentary in Verbiest and Golvers (1993), 65.

[37] Huang (1993), 60, 65, 66 and 68 appears to have been the first modern scholar to make the assumption that Wu Mingxuan's calculations were based on the Muslim system. In this he was followed by Chu (1997), 29. We made the same assumption when referring to Wu's project in Cullen and Jami (2020), 13. But in the light of the analysis discussed in this paper, this view must be abandoned.

[38] An explanation of how these pre-modern Chinese time notations can be translated into the modern 24-hour clock is given below.

nutes [05:47]. So the Muslim system lags behind heaven by 1 day, 74 marks and a fraction.[39]

Although Verbiest consistently refers to his opponent's results as having been calculated according to the *Hui hui li* 回回历 'Muslim system' (and we shall discuss the accuracy of that characterisation later in this article), he does not give any formal title to what he calls "the astronomical system calculated by me and my colleagues". The astronomical system introduced by the Jesuits has sometimes been referred to by modern scholars as the *Shi xian* 时宪 'Timely modelling' system. This is however not strictly accurate. While a full account of this question will require a longer discussion elsewhere, the essential point is that we must distinguish between the official title given to all calendrical publications issued with Qing imperial authority, and the methods by which they were calculated. A document issued by the Board of Rites in the first months of the Qing makes this explicit. It notes that the Ming dynasty used the title *Da tong* 大统 'Great concordance' for its calendars, and that the new dynasty needed to change this for a title of its own. For this reason, it tells us, an order from the regent on Shunzhi 1/7/4 (5 August 1644) had defined the title *Shi xian* for the Qing calendar.[40] However, in referring to the systems used for calculating calendars, the methods used under the Ming dynasty and the methods advocated by Schall are distinguished by the Board as the *jiu fa* 旧法 'old method' and the *xin fa* 新法 'new method'. Accordingly, the title *Shi xian li* 时宪历 'Timely modelling calendar' appears on the cover of all available calendrical documents produced during the period when Schall was in charge, when Yang Guangxian had taken over the bureau, and after Verbiest was given responsibility for calendar production.

Turning to the actual data given by Verbiest, the figures in square brackets in the above translation, e.g. [19:15], represent the time in the modern 24-hour clock equivalent to that given in Chinese. At this point, it is necessary to explain the time units used by Verbiest and his opponent. Both take as their largest unit of time the 'period' *shi* 时, of which there are twelve in a day, so that each period contains two modern hours (nowadays called *xiao shi* 小时 'small periods'), for which reason some scholars refer to a *shi* period as a 'double-hour'. These periods were named using the standard 12-fold sequence of cyclical characters, beginning with *zi* 子 and ending with *hai* 亥. For timekeeping purposes, each two-hour period was divided into halves of one modern hour each, the first designated as *chu* 初 'beginning' and second as *zheng* 正 'regular'; the hour designated as *zi zheng* 子正 began at midnight, so that the first half of the period zi began at 23:00 at the end of the preceding day. In referring to the time 23:00 on a given day, the term *ye zi chu* 夜子初 'the start of the period *zi* in the evening' is commonly used.

For the convenience of the reader, in this discussion, we shall convert periods into modern hours counted from midnight. Both Verbiest and Wu Mingxuan use the *ke* 刻 'mark' (literally 'cut' representing a graduation cut into the indicator rod of a float clepsydra) as their next smaller unit below the period. Verbiest's marks are each worth 1/96 day (a quarter of a modern hour), and the *fen* 分 'parts' into which he divides his marks are each 1/15 mark, a modern minute. In Verbiest's system, each half period (1 hour) is divided into four equal intervals, as shown in Table 1; the *fen* are, like the

---

[39] *CYJL*, 14a—14b.

[40] See Tang (after 1661, 1993 repr.), 10a—11b, 8:863—864. The term *shi xian* 时宪 was drawn from the text of the ancient Book of Documents *Shu jing* 书经, as were the titles *da tong* 大统 and *shou shi* 授时 used under the Ming and Yuan dynasties.

marks *ke*, numbered according to the whole *fen* elapsed at the moment they begin.

Table 1 Subdivisions of the half-period (1 hour) according to Verbiest's system using 96 *ke* in 1 day

	Instant when interval begins	Instant when interval ends
Chu ke 初刻 'beginning of marks'	Start of the hour	15 complete minutes after start of hour
Yi ke 一刻 'one [elapsed] mark'	15 complete minutes after start of hour	30 complete minutes after start of hour
Er ke 二刻 'two [elapsed] marks'	30 complete minutes after start of hour	45 complete minutes after start of hour
San ke 三刻 'three [elapsed] marks'	45 complete minutes after start of hour	60 complete minutes after start of hour.

So to the nearest minute, the latest time period within an hour that can be recorded in Verbiest's terms without using smaller time divisions is *san ke shi si fen* 三刻十四分 'three marks and 14 minutes', a designation which applies to the whole of the last minute of an hour, beginning when $3 \times 15 + 14 = 59$ minutes have elapsed. The start of the next minute is the first instant within the *chu ke* 初刻 'beginning of *ke*' for the next hour. A time specified in Verbiest's system can thus never include *si ke* 四刻 'four marks'.

Wu Mingxuan, on the other hand, follows Chinese tradition in using marks equal to 1/100 day, equal to 14.4 modern minutes each. Each mark was divided into 100 *fen* 分 'parts', each of which was thus 0.144 modern minutes or 8.64 seconds. For all but the most precise purposes, if Wu Mingxuan gives a time in (elapsed) marks within an hour as, say, *er ke* 二刻 'two elapsed marks', the difference from the moment designated by the same expression used by Verbiest is inconsiderable—in this case only 30 min − 28.8 min = 1.2 min, 62 s. Of course, Wu's 'parts' are much smaller than Verbiest's minutes. But there is one significant difference: In Wu's system, when four completed marks have passed, the total time elapsed is only 400 parts. But an hour (or half a 'period') contains more parts than that, since there are $100 \times 100 = 10000$ parts in a day, and

$$10000 \text{ parts}/24 = 416 \frac{2}{3} \text{ parts}$$

As a result, the hour does not end after 4 complete marks have elapsed, since there are still $16 \frac{2}{3}$ hundredth parts of the hour left to expire. We may therefore, relatively rarely, see examples of timing such as that for *qi* 15, 'Great Heat', which Wu gives as 'four marks' in the relevant hour, as he also does for *qi* 19, 'Autumn Equinox'. The fact that Verbiest reproduces Wu's predictions in these cases shows that he has not converted Wu's original figures based on 100 *ke* into his own 96 *ke* system; however, since the differences noted by Verbiest between Wu's predictions and his own are in all cases at least several hours, no question of importance arises. The problem of *fen* conversion need not be considered, since all Wu's predictions are given in periods and *ke* alone.

Predictions such as those given by Wu Mingxuan and Verbiest were not merely technical matters of concern to astronomical specialists. They were crucially important in the construction of the People's Calendar by which all the subjects of the Qing empire, from high officials down to the mass of the population, were expected to regulate their daily lives. That is because the placement of *qi* within a month determines whether the month belongs in the normal sequence of months from 1 to 12, or whether it is an anomalous 'intercalary' month, an extra month inserted in the series without a number of its own, but labelled as 'intercalary Nth month' *run N yue* 闰 N 月, where N is the number of the normal month preceding it, so that the year in question has 13 months rather than 12. The decisive factor is that each normal month must contain a 'medial *qi*' (*zhong qi* 中气), *i.e.* one of the twelve odd-numbered *qi* beginning with winter solstice as number 1. A month that does not contain a medial *qi* is counted as intercalary. Thus if a medial *qi* fell near the midnight separating two months, a small shift in the prediction of that *qi* could change which month was counted as intercalary.[41] Verbiest had already referred to such an issue in the first part of his report in *Ce yan ji lue*. There he stated that, according to his calculations, *qi* number 5 Rain Waters *yu shui* 雨水 fell in the month following the twelfth month of Kangxi 8, which would normally have been designated as the first month of Kangxi 9:

本月二十九日午初二刻六分。
On the 29th day of that month, at 2 marks 6 minutes into the first half of the period *wu* (11:00—13:00) [*i.e.* 11:36].[42]

That month (which contained 30 days) therefore contained a medial *qi*, and was a normal month, being the first month of the next year, Kangxi 9. But, Verbiest notes, Wu Mingxuan made this an intercalary twelfth month, because Wu's time for the *qi* in question was so late compared with Verbiest's that it fell on the first day of the month *after* the month following the twelfth month. As Verbiest notes, the delay was 1 day and 71 marks (41 hours and 45 minutes in Verbiest's units), so that the *qi* in question as determined by Wu fell 21 marks into the first day of the next month, at around 05:15.

A disagreement about the placing of an intercalary month raised issues with an impact far outside the concerns of professional astronomers. If Verbiest was correct, then nor only was Wu Mingxuan's calendar for Kangxi 8 incorrect, but so was the already promulgated official calendar for that year, which also had an intercalary 12th month. It was no doubt because he realised the importance of this issue that Verbiest made it the subject of an experimental test during his observation made during the first lunar month of Kangxi 8, which coincidentally began on 1st February 1669.

Verbiest had already predicted that Rain Waters early in Kangxi 8 would fall on the 18th day of the 1st month (18 February 1669), 3 elapsed marks and 2 minutes into the first half of [the period] *mao* (05:00—07:00) [*i.e.* 05:47]. When on that day his predictions were, he claimed, verified by observation, then since the 'New Western' value used by Verbiest for the interval between *qi* in successive years was then 365 days, 23 marks, 3 minutes and 33 seconds (365d 5h 48m 33s, = 365.24205d),[43] no more than simple addition was needed in order to predict that the Rain Waters of Kangxi 9 should fall on day 29 of the first month (18 February 1669), at a time given by:

05:47 + 5 h 49 min (to the nearest minute) = 11:36, as he had predicted.

In his *Astronomia Europaea*, Verbiest makes the connection with intercalation explicit:

> ... observavi Solis ingressum in signum piscis, à quo tanquam fundamento pendebat illa quaestio, num scilicet mensis ille intercalaris, de qua supra, ex Calendario illo tam Sinico, quàm Arabica expungendus effet: certè expungendum esse altitudo & declinatio Solis, eo die

---

[41] Since Verbiest and Wu did not disagree about the days when months of Kangxi 8 began and ended, the discussion is simpler than it might otherwise have been.

[42] *CYJL*, 11a.

[43] See Shi and Chu (2017), 893.

in meridie observata, clarissimè demonstrabat.

... I observed the entry of the sun into the sign Pisces [longitude 330°, when Rain Waters began according to Jesuit reckoning], on which depended the fundamental question of whether the intercalary month referred to earlier should be deleted from the calendar, [which was] as much Chinese as it was Arabic: the altitude and declination of the sun as observed at noon on that day showed very clearly that it should be deleted.[44]

As Verbiest indicates, a critical observation for him was that of the sun's noon altitude, from which, in combination with the known altitude of the north celestial pole the sun's declination at that instant could be deduced. Hence by the use of a table of obliquity, the celestial longitude of the sun at noon could be found, and compared with the longitude corresponding to Rain Waters (as defined by Verbiest), which was 330°. While this is not the place for a detailed examination of Verbiest's observations, with the apparatus we know Verbiest to have used it should have been possible for him to check the day of entry of the sun into Pisces by a noon observation of the sun's altitude, as well as verifying that his timing of that event within the day was broadly correct. He also used a sextant zeroed on the noon altitude of the celestial equator to determine the declination of the sun directly.[45]

The predictions of both Verbiest and Wu Mingxuan for all 24 *qi* of Kangxi 8 are shown in Table 2, where they occupy the two main central divisions of the table. In each case the Chinese civil month and day of the month appear first, in the columns labelled 'Chinese lunar month, day', followed in the next columns to the right by the month and day of the month in the Gregorian calendar. Next follow three columns showing the units as recorded by Verbiest in his report, followed by the corresponding hour and minute of the day in the 24-hour clock. The next division shows the corresponding predictions of Wu Mingxuan.

---

[44] Verbiest (1687), V, 14 tr. and comm. in Verbiest and Golvers (1993), 68.

[45] In *CYJL* 36b—37a, Verbiest states that the noon altitude of the sun observed on the day in question was 38° 38′, and that the altitude of the pole was 39° 55′. This would imply that the sun's noon declination was 90°−38° 38′−39° 55′ =11° 27′, whereas the declination he gives is 11° 25′, which is in fact the value implied by calculation from the tables in the *XFLS* and the stated timing of the *qi* (see a forthcoming publication). However, since he tells us that the altitude was observed using a quadrant *xiang xian yi* 象限仪 which from *CYJL* fig 5 we know was based on a circle of diameter 5.2 *chi* 尺, and 1 *chi* was 32 cm, the difference of two minutes of arc would only amount to half a millimetre on the quadrant scale, below the limits of visual accuracy. The change in solar declination between the true moment of Rain Waters at 05:47 and noon on the same day would have been about 16 minutes of arc, corresponding to a 4 mm shift on the scale. If we may rely on the illustration in *CYJL*, the smallest division marked on the scale corresponded to 20 minutes, about 5 mm. It would therefore have been possible for Verbiest to verify that his *qi* timing was right to within an hour or so. In this context, it is worth noting that the observational procedure did not involve reading values off a scale, but checking whether the sighting device appeared to align with the sun when the diopter was adjusted to match the line previously marked on the instrument according to Verbiest's calculations. Similar remarks apply to Verbiest's use of a sextant with a 10 *chi* circle radius, which he used to measure declination directly (*CYJL* fig 6).

Table 2 *Qi* predictions for Kangxi 8, 1669

Qi number			Qi dates and from times found using *Hui hui li* solar longitudes at 15° intervals		Qi dates and times predicted by Verbiest, from *CYJL*					Qi dates and times predicted by Wu Mingxuan, from *CYJL*					Interval from Verbiest to Wu Mingxuan predictions
			Gregorian Month Day	Time of day	Chinese Lunar Month Day	Gregorian Month Day		Hours	Marks= Day /96	Mins= Mark /15	Time of day	Chinese Lunar Month Day	Gregorian Month Day		Hours	Marks =Day /100	Parts =Mark /100	Time of day	hours
4	Establishment of spring	立春	Feb	3	9:35	1	3	Feb	3	9	2	8	9:38	1	4	Feb	4	19	1		19:14	−33.60
5	Rain waters	雨水	Feb	18	5:56	1	18	Feb	18	5	3	2	5:47	1	20	Feb	20	0	2		0:29	−42.70
6	Emerging insects	惊蛰	Mar	5	4:57	2	5	Mar	5	5	0	10	5:10	2	6	Mar	7	5	3		5:43	−48.55
7	Spring equinox	春分	Mar	20	7:06	2	19	Mar	20	7	0	10	07:00	2	21	Mar	22	11	0		11:00	−51.83
8	Clear and bright	清明	Apr	4	12:34	3	4	Apr	4	11	3	6	11:51	3	6	Apr	6	16	1		16:14	−52.38
9	Grain rains	谷雨	Apr	19	21:20	3	19	Apr	19	21	1	11	21:26	3	21	Apr	21	21	2		21:29	−48.05
10	Establishment of summer	立夏	May	5	9:09	4	6	May	5	7	2		7:30	4	8	May	7	2	3		2:43	−43.22
11	Grain fills	小满	May	20	23:36	4	21	May	20	23	0		23:00	4	23	May	22	8	0		8:00	−33.00
12	Grain in ear	芒种	Jun	5	16:01	5	7	Jun	5	15	3		15:45	5	8	Jun	6	13	1		13:14	−21.48
13	Summer solstice	夏至	Jun	21	9:41	5	23	Jun	21	9	2		9:30	5	23	Jun	21	18	2		18:29	−8.98
14	Little heat	小暑	Jul	7	3:43	6	10	Jul	7	4	1	7	4:22	6	9	Jul	6	23	3		23:43	4.65
15	Great heat	大暑	Jul	22	21:15	6	25	Jul	22	22	0		22:00	6	25	Jul	22	4	4		4:48	17.03
16	Establishment of autumn	立秋	Aug	7	13:28	7	11	Aug	7	15	0		15:00	7	10	Aug	6	10	0		10:00	29.00
17	Limit of heat	处暑	Aug	23	3:36	7	27	Aug	23	5	1	8	5:23	7	25	Aug	21	15	2		15:29	37.90
18	White dew	白露	Sep	7	15:03	8	13	Sep	7	16	3	8	16:53	8	11	Sep	5	20	3		20:43	44.17
19	Autumn equinox	秋分	Sep	22	23:25	8	29	Sep	23	1		9	1:09	8	27	Sep	21	1	4		1:48	47.18
20	Cold dew	寒露	Oct	8	4:25	9	14	Oct	8	6	0		6:00	9	12	Oct	6	7	0		7:00	47.00
21	Frost-fall	霜降	Oct	23	6:09	9	29	Oct	23	7	2		7:30	9	27	Oct	21	12	1		12:14	43.27
22	Establishment of winter	立冬	Nov	7	4:49	10	14	Nov	7	6	0	5	6:05	10	12	Nov	5	17	2		17:29	36.60
23	Little snow	小雪	Nov	22	0:51	10	29	Nov	22	2	2		2:30	10	27	Nov	20	22	3		22:43	27.78
24	Great snow	大雪	Dec	6	18:55	11	14	Dec	6	20	0		20:00	11	14	Dec	6	4	0		4:00	16.00
25	Winter solstice	冬至	Dec	21	11:45	11	29	Dec	21	12	3		12:45	11	29	Dec	21	9	1		9:14	3.52
26	Little cold	小寒	Jan	5	4:11	12	14	Jan	5	3	3		3:45	12	14	Jan	5	14	2		14:29	−10.73
27	Great cold	大寒	Jan	19	21:08	12	28	Jan	19	21	3		21:45	12	29	Jan	20	19	3		19:43	−21.97

As can be seen from the table, Verbiest only specifies minute in eleven out of the 24 *qi*, and Wu Mingxuan does not specify parts at all.[46] The rightmost column in the table gives the differences be-

---

[46] In this essay we shall concentrate on how Wu Mingxuan's predictions were made, and it will be shown that they can be reproduced precisely by relatively simple calculations. For Verbiest's *qi* predictions, the situation is more complex. One of us (Cullen) has constructed an Excel workbook that follows the step by step instructions for calculation from the tabulated data in the *Xin fa li shu*. The dates of the *qi* in Kangxi 8 thus found match those given by Verbiest, as well as those calculated in Liu (2018—2022) using modern trigonometrical expressions taken from or constructed on the basis of publications such as Chu and Shi (2012). However, neither method succeeds in reproducing Verbiest's stated times of day for the *qi* of that year. This topic will be discussed further in later publications.

tween the two sets of predictions in hours, with a negative value meaning that Wu Mingxuan's predictions are later than Verbiest's, as they were in the example quoted above. Verbiest has earlier in his report insisted that his success in the shadow trial proved that the Jesuits' system represented the true state of the heavens[47]— hence his confident statement above that if Wu Mingxuan's 'Muslim system' made a prediction later than his own, it was 'lagging behind heaven'. While not all the discrepancies Verbiest lists are as large as those noted in the example, in only three cases are they less than ten hours, whether lagging behind 'the heavens' or in advance of them, and in 16 cases they are greater than a day.

Discrepancies of this size cannot be blamed on any essential defect in the historical 'Muslim system' set out the *Hui hui li* texts. The historical texts of the *Hui hui li* make no attempt to predict the moments of inception of the 24 *qi* as equal divisions of time, which are an East Asian reference framework absent from the astronomical systems descended from the Ptolemaic tradition.[48] The same was however true of the European systems used by the Jesuits, which traced their origins to the same roots. But the Jesuits could not ignore the 24 *qi* if they wished to win responsibility for managing the Chinese state calendar; they dealt with the problem by simply redefining the *qi* as equal intervals of solar longitude measured along the ecliptic, or as they put it, calculating the true *qi*, rather than the mean *qi* defined according to Chinese custom as falling at equal intervals of time.[49] Had the practitioners of 'Muslim methods' wished to do likewise, the *Hui hui li* was well able to produce values of solar longitude based on mean ecliptic motion of the sun, corrected to true motion by the addition or subtraction of an 'equation of centre' *tai yang jia jian cha fen* 太阳加减差分 (literally 'solar additive or subtractive difference parts'), whose magnitude, given in tables, depends on the position of the sun in its orbit relative to its apogee, the point where the sun-earth distance is greatest.[50] If therefore Wu Mingxuan had wished to compete with Verbiest in computing *qi* based on the moments when the sun's longitude passed through a multiple of 15° using the 'Muslim system', he could have done so with reasonable success.

Thus, to take two examples, Verbiest complains that Wu Mingxuan's calculations for the *qi* 'Establishment of Spring' *li chun* 立春, and 'Autumn Equinox' *qiu fen* 秋分 are both more than a day wrong (that is, they differ by more than a day from his own predictions). Verbiest takes Establishment of Spring as marking the moment when the sun passes through 315° longitude. Now the longitudes of the sun computed according to the *Hui hui li* for two successive noons when the sun's lon-

---

[47] Given the very slow rate of change of noon solar altitude during the three days of the trial shortly after winter solstice (6.7 minutes of arc from noon on 27 December to noon on 29 December), and the poor precision of shadow observations, Verbiest had a somewhat limited scientific basis for this claim.

[48] See Huang (1993), 61 & 63. Lu Dalong 鲁大龙 also made this point in a comment during a brief presentation of the material of this paper at the online 26th International Congress of History of Science and Technology in July 2021.

[49] See Shi and Chu (2017), 893.

[50] See *Chiljeongsan oepyeon*, 14a-31b.

gitude is near this value are:[51]

1669, 2 February: 314.089°

1669, 3 February: 315.102°

Linear interpolation between these two values suggests that the sun will pass through 315° (corresponding to 'Establishment of Spring') at 09:35 on 3 February; Verbiest's prediction was that this *qi* will occur at 09:38, so the difference is inconsiderable.

For Autumn Equinox (180° longitude), the two successive noon longitudes from *Hui hui li* are:

1669, 22 September: 179.533°

1669, 23 September: 180.515°

which predicts that the sun will pass through 180° at 23:25 on 22 September; Verbiest's prediction is for 01:09 on 23 September, 1 hour 44 mins later. But as Verbiest notes, the actual predictions made by Wu Mingxuan for these two *qi* are respectively more than 33 hours later and 47 hours earlier than his own.

If we compare the complete set of *qi* timings computed using the longitudes predicted by the *Hui hui li* (given in the leftmost division of Table 2) with Verbiest's, there are certainly differences. However, the predicted days are identical, and although the differences in time of day may be as large as two hours, in many cases they are no more than a few minutes. But if the comparison is made with Wu Mingxuan rather than Verbiest, the differences of his predictions from those using the *Hui hui li* are so large — at times as much as two days — that it is clear that whatever Wu Mingxuan was doing, he was not using the *Hui hui li* to make *qi* predictions using equal intervals of longitude in the way that Verbiest had done. Indeed, it is in any case not very likely that he would have attempted to do so, since the Jesuit redefinition of the *qi* as 24 equal shifts in longitude, each one 360°/24 =15°, rather than as equal divisions of the time interval between winter solstices was one of the innovations that their opponents had denounced as a dangerous departure from Chinese tradition.[52] So let us instead try to find a method to reproduce Wu Mingxuan's predictions that would have been less revolutionary than using the *Hui hui li* as described above. Thus, for instance, how do Wu Mingxuan's predictions compare with the *qi* times listed in the official calendar, issued for Kangxi 8 by the Astronomical Bureau under the leadership of Yang Guangxian, and calculated according to the Great Concordance system?[53] The result of the comparison is shown in Table 3.

---

[51] These values have been computed using an Excel workbook developed by Christopher Cullen, incorporating specially created VBA functions, whose structure follows step by step the instructions for calculation and worked examples set out in the 15th century Korean text *Chiljeongsan oepyeon jeongmyonyeon ilsig galyeong* 칠정산외편정묘년일식가령 七政算外篇丁卯年日食假令 (Reckoning [the positions of] of the Seven Governors [sun, moon and five planets], part 2: the example of the solar eclipse in sexagenary year 4 [1447]). (abbr. *CJSOPGY*). The resulting system has been tested using the example of the 1447 eclipse, which it computes precisely as in the original text. As a cross-check, calculations of sun and moon longitudes at noon on the day of spring equinox for 1432 and 1910 made using the workbook agree closely with those made by Shi (2003), 46 'calculated with the methods of the CCSOP [*Chiljeongsan oepyeon*, 1447]', and in general Excel calculations support Shi's conclusion that the *Hui hui li* remained capable of predicting these quantities with an absolute error of less than a degree up to recent times.

[52] See for instance the exchanges recorded in the secret Manchu records of the trial of the Jesuits, where both Schall and Yang Guangxian are questioned on this matter, translated in An (2015), 19−20 as part of a report of proceedings submitted on Kangxi 3/11/11 (27 December 1664); see An (2015), 37 for the date. Yang Guangxian's complaint on this point was first submitted on Shunzhi 17/12/3 (3 January 1661) without any official response; see Chen (2000), 35−38.

[53] The relevant data for Kangxi 8 and all other years discussed in this paper are taken from copies of the Planets Calendars for those years preserved in the National Palace Museum, Taibei. We are grateful to Professor Guan Yuzhen 关瑜桢 and Yang Boshun 杨伯顺 at the University of Science and Technology of China, Hefei, for helping with technical problems in accessing the file format of this material.

Table 3 *Qi* predicted by Wu Mingxuan and the Kangxi 8 Planets Calendar

				Qi dates and times for Kangxi 8 predicted by Wu Mingxuan, as found in *CYJL*						*Qi* dates and times predicted by Kangxi 8 Planets Calendar					
				Chinese Lunar		Gregorian		Hour	Marks= Day/100	Parts= Mark/100	Chinese Lunar		Gregorian		Hour	Marks= Day/100	Parts= Mark/100
				Month	Day	Month	Day				Month	Day	Month	Day			
4	Establishment of spring	立春		1	4	Feb	4	19	1		1	4	Feb	4	19	1	63
5	Rain waters	雨水		1	20	Feb	20	0	2		1	20	Feb	20	0	2	64
6	Emerging insects	惊蛰		2	6	Mar	7	5	3		2	6	Mar	7	5	3	65
7	Spring equinox	春分		2	21	Mar	22	11	0		2	21	Mar	22	11	0	49
8	Clear and bright	清明		3	6	Apr	6	16	1		3	6	Apr	6	16	1	50
9	Grain rains	谷雨		3	21	Apr	21	21	2		3	21	Apr	21	21	2	52
10	Establishment of summer	立夏		4	8	May	7	2	3		4	8	May	7	2	3	53
11	Grain fills	小满		4	23	May	22	8	0		4	23	May	22	8	0	37
12	Grain in ear	芒种		5	8	Jun	6	13	1		5	8	Jun	6	13	1	38
13	Summer solstice	夏至		5	23	Jun	21	18	2		5	23	Jun	21	18	2	39
14	Little heat	小暑		6	9	Jul	6	23	3		6	9	Jul	6	23	3	40
15	Great heat	大暑		6	25	Jul	22	4	4		6	25	Jul	22	5	0	24
16	Establishment of autumn	立秋		7	10	Aug	6	10	0		7	10	Aug	6	10	1	25
17	Limit of heat	处暑		7	25	Aug	21	15	2		7	25	Aug	21	15	2	27
18	White dew	白露		8	11	Sep	5	20	3		8	11	Sep	5	20	3	28
19	Autumn equinox	秋分		8	27	Sep	21	1	4		8	27	Sep	21	2	0	12
20	Cold dew	寒露		9	12	Oct	6	7	0		9	12	Oct	6	7	1	13
21	Frost-fall	霜降		9	27	Oct	21	12	1		9	27	Oct	21	12	2	14
22	Establishment of winter	立冬		10	12	Nov	5	17	2		10	12	Nov	5	17	3	15
23	Little snow	小雪		10	27	Nov	20	22	3		10	27	Nov	20	22	4	16
24	Great snow	大雪		11	14	Dec	6	4	0		11	14	Dec	6	4	1	0
1	Winter solstice	冬至		11	29	Dec	21	9	1		11	29	Dec	21	9	2	2
2	Little cold	小寒		12	14	Jan	5	14	2		12	14	Jan	5	14	3	3
3	Great cold	大寒		12	29	Jan	20	19	3		12	29	Jan	20	19	4	4

One difference is immediately obvious: as already noted, Wu Mingxuan's predictions are made to the nearest mark (1/100 day), without parts, whereas the Planets Calendar values are in every case given to the nearest part (1/100 mark). In two cases, *qi* 23 and 3, parts are given after 4 elapsed marks; in the first case, 16 parts are given, so that only 2/3 part is left before the next hour begins. Wu Mingxuan's hours and marks match those of the Planets Calendar for the first 11 *qi* of the calendar (numbers 4 to 14, beginning the numbering from winter solstice). *Qi* numbers 15 and 16 disagree, however, as do *qi* numbers 19 to 3 of the next cycle. Another point worthy of notice is that where Wu Mingxuan's marks do agree with those of the Planets Calendar, they have not been produced by rounding up marks in accordance with the parts where these are greater than 50 (out of 100), as is the case for *qi* numbers 4, 5, 6, 9 and 10. The parts are simply ignored. We shall return to this point below.

What kinds of calculation lie behind the figures we see here? There is a full specification of the calculation methods of the Great Concordance system in the *Ming shi* 明史.[54] The specified procedure begins by finding the day of the winter solstice that fell in the 11th month of the civil year preceding the year for which we wish to find the dates and times of *qi*. Before we carry out the calculations for Kangxi 8, it will be helpful for comparative purposes if we first carry out the calculation for the preceding year, Kangxi 7, 1668—1669.

In accordance with the Great Concordance system as specified in the *Ming shi*, the process starts by finding the time elapsed since the beginning of the first year with the sexagenary number *jiazi*. 1 during the Hongwu reign period (1368—1398, when the first Ming emperor was on the throne). That year was Hongwu 17, 1384, during which the winter solstice fell on the first day of the 11th month (13 December in the Julian calendar), which was a *jiazi*. 1 day. In fact, however, the process of calculating the calendar for any given civil year begins by finding the winter solstice near the end of the preceding civil year. For Hongwu 17, this fell on the 14th day of the 11th civil month of the preceding year, a *jiwei*. 56 day (14 December 1383).

In the calculations below (Box 1), days are shown at a scale of 10000 — so that the quantity 'Year Cycle' (*sui zhou* 岁周), 3652425, represents 365.2425 days, the interval between one winter solstice and the next, the functional equivalent of the modern 'tropical year'. '*Qi* Correspondence' (*qi ying* 气应), 550375, represents 55.0375 days, the interval between the moment of winter solstice on 14 December and the midnight beginning Hongwu 16/9/24 (20 October 1383), which is the *jiazi*. 1 day preceding the winter solstice. '[Sexagenary] Sequence Factor' (*ji fa* 纪法), 600000, represents 60 days, the length of a completed sexagenary cycle.

Box 1 Finding the winter solstice of 1667 using the Great Concordance system from the *Ming shi*

Text from *Ming shi* 35, 689	Translation of text	Calculation specified
推天正冬至置距洪武甲子积年减一	To predict the winter solstice in the first celestial month. Set out the accumulated years[55] from Hongwu [17] *jiazi*. 1, and subtract 1	Accumulated years: 1384 … 1668 inclusive = 1668−1383=285 years 285−1=284 (Or simply: 1668−1384=284)
以岁周乘之为中积	Multiply it by Year Cycle [3652425] to make Accumulated Medial *Qi*	3652425×284=1037288700
加气应为通积	Add *Qi* Correspondence [550375] to make Overall Accumulation	1037288700+550375=1037839075
满纪法去之，至不满之数,为天正冬至	Cast Out what fills [Sexagenary] Sequence Factor [600000]. When you come to the number that does not fill, that makes the winter solstice in the first celestial month	1037839075−1729×600000=439075
以万为日	Take 10000 for a day	43
命甲子算外，为冬至日辰	Then count off from *jiazi*. 1, and outside the count is the sexagenary day of winter solstice.	*jiazi*. 1+43=*dingwei*. 44

---

54 *Ming shi*, chapter 35.

55 'Accumulated years' is not simply the difference in the year dates, but includes the first year, so that the count begins at 1. By subtracting 1, we simply obtain the difference in the year numbers.

The prediction is thus that the winter solstice near the end of regnal year Kangxi 6, *qi* number 1, which serves to define the starting point for calculating the calendar for Kangxi 7, 1668, will fall on a *dingwei*. 44 day in the 11th civil month of Kangxi 6, i. e. 21 December 1667.

Later in the text we are told how to find the other *qi* of the civil year following this winter solstice. '*Qi* Reckoning' (*qi ce* 气策), 152184.375, is 1/24 of 'Year Cycle', 3652425, and thus represents the constant interval of 15.2184375 days from the beginning of one *qi* to the next.[56]

Box 2 Finding subsequent *qi* from the time of winter solstice

Text from *Ming shi* 35 690	Translation of text	Calculation specified
推各恒气 置天正冬至，加三气策	To predict the regular *qi*, set out the winter solstice and add three times *Qi* Reckoning [152184.375]	439075＋3×152184.375＝895628.125
满纪法去之，即得立春恒日	Cast out what fills [Sexagenary] Sequence Factor [600000], and you get the day of Establishment of Spring [*qi* number 4]	895628.125－600000＝295628.125
以气策累加之，去纪法，即得二十四气恒日	Add *Qi* Reckoning [152184.375] in succession, casting out the [Sexagenary] Sequence Factor [600000], and you obtain the days of all 24 *qi*	

To find the sexagenary day on which each successive *qi* falls, we treat the numbers found here as we did the 439075 that defined winter solstice. Thus the 295628.125 found for Establishment of Spring is a number of days scaled up by 10000, representing 29.5628125 days. Adding the 29 whole days to *jiazi*.1, we find *guisi*.30 as the day of Establishment of Spring. This is the 23th day of the 12th lunar month of Kangxi 6, 5 February 1667.

If we wish to find the first *qi* of the regnal year Kangxi 7 that began in early 1668 (which is number 5, 'Rain Waters' *yu shui* 雨水), we need to add four *Qi* Reckonings to the original quantity found for winter solstice, *qi* number 1:

$$439075＋4×152184.375＝1047812.5$$

Casting out [Sexagenary] Sequence Factor to eliminate repetitions of the 60-day cycle, we obtain:

$$1047812.5－600000＝447812.5$$

This is 44.78125 days, so this *qi* will fall on sexagenary day:

44＋*jiazi*.1＝*wushen*.45, the 9th day of the first month of Kangxi.7, 20 February 1668. The fractional part of the day is 0.78125 days; rather than working in 2-hour 'periods' *shi* 时. we may simply find the number of modern hours directly, multiplying the fractional part of the day by 24 to find:

24 hours/day × 0.78125 days ＝18.75 hours, so we have 18 whole hours

0.75 hour ＝0.03125 days, which is 3 marks and 12 parts.

And so Rain Waters is predicted by the Great Concordance system as falling on Kangxi 7/1/9, 18

---

[56] Here we see that unlike the Jesuit system which reckoned *qi* as falling at equal intervals of solar longitude, the Great Concordance followed the traditional Chinese practice of placing *qi* at equal time intervals.

hours, 3 marks (3/100 day) and 12 parts (12/100 mark) after midnight. In the modern 24-hour clock this is equivalent to 18:45, to the nearest whole minute.

This result and the results of the *qi* calculations for the rest of the year are set out in Table 4, compared with the times given in the Planets Calendar for that year. As we can see, for this year the Kangxi 7 Planets Calendar gives its data in the same style as the predictions of Wu Mingxuan in Kangxi 8: unlike the Kangxi 8 Planets Calendar, after the period (here shown in terms of hours) only whole marks are given, without any indication of parts. What is more, as seemed to be the case with Wu Mingxuan in Kangxi 8, parts are ignored completely, even in a case like *qi* number 8 'Clear and Bright' where calculation yields 10 hours, 1 mark and 98 parts, just 2 parts short of 2 marks. If and only if we adopt this practice, we may say that using the Great Concordance method set out in the *Ming shi* we have successfully reproduced all the official Planets Calendar predictions for the regnal year Kangxi 7, which runs from early 1668 to early 1669.

Table 4 *Qi* in Kangxi 7 Planets Calendar, and calculated using Great Concordance System

					Qi dates and times predicted by Kangxi 7 Planets Calendar				*Qi* times predicted for Kangxi 7 by *Da tong li*, using *Qi* counterpart 550375		
			Chinese Lunar Month Day		Gregorian Month Day		Hour	Marks= Day/100	Parts= Mark/100	Hour	Marks= Day/100	Parts= Mark/100
5	Rain waters	雨水	1	9	Feb	20	18	3		18	3	12
6	Emerging insects	惊蛰	1	24	Mar	6	23	4		23	4	13
7	Spring equinox	春分	2	10	Mar	22	5	0		5	0	97
8	Clear and bright	清明	2	25	Apr	6	10	1		10	1	98
9	Grain rains	谷雨	3	11	Apr	21	15	3		15	3	0
10	Beginning of summer	立夏	3	26	May	6	20	4		20	4	1
11	Grain fills	小满	4	12	May	22	2	0		2	0	85
12	Grain in ear	芒种	4	27	Jun	6	7	1		7	1	86
13	Summer solstice	夏至	5	13	Jun	21	12	2		12	2	87
14	Little heat	小暑	5	28	Jul	6	17	3		17	3	88
15	Great heat	大暑	6	13	Jul	21	23	0		23	0	72
16	Beginning of autumn	立秋	6	29	Aug	6	4	1		4	1	73
17	Limit of heat	处暑	7	14	Aug	21	9	2		9	2	75
18	White dew	白露	7	29	Sep	5	14	3		14	3	76
19	Autumn equinox	秋分	8	15	Sep	20	20	0		20	0	60
20	Cold dew	寒露	9	1	Oct	6	1	1		1	1	61
21	Frost-fall	霜降	9	16	Oct	21	6	2		6	2	62
22	Beginning of winter	立冬	10	2	Nov	5	11	3		11	3	63
23	Little snow	小雪	10	17	Nov	20	17	0		17	0	47
24	Great snow	大雪	11	2	Dec	5	22	1		22	1	48
1	Winter solstice	冬至	11	18	Dec	21	3	2		3	2	50
2	Little cold	小寒	12	4	Jan	5	8	3		8	3	51
3	Great cold	大寒	12	19	Jan	20	14	0		14	0	35

We might expect that the *Ming shi* method would be equally successful in reproducing the *qi* times given in the official Planets Calendar predictions for Kangxi 8. The comparison is shown in Table 5, which also includes Wu Mingxuan's predictions for that year. Surprisingly, the predictions of the *Ming shi* method just described differ in every instance in the parts column from those of the Planets Calendar, in eleven instances in the marks column, and in two cases even in the hours column. On the other hand, the hours and marks of the *Ming shi* method match those of Wu Mingxuan (who gives no parts) in every case. It seems that Wu Mingxuan made his predictions using exactly the same *Ming shi* method as did the official Planets Calendar of Kangxi 7, even to giving hours and marks only, while ignoring partsbut the Planets Calendar of Kangxi 8 is no longer using that method.

There is, however, one small adjustment to the *Ming shi* calculation method that produces perfect concordance between the calculated *qi* times and those given in the Kangxi 8 Planets Calendar. If we work out the time difference between the *Ming shi* results for Kangxi 8 and the *qi* timings given in the Planets Calendar, we see that in every case the Planets Calendar timings are 27 parts later than the *Ming shi* calculation. All that is necessary to eliminate the discrepancy is to increase the value of *Qi* Correspondence, 550375, by 27 to 550402, which amounts to shifting the instant of every *qi* 0.0027 day = 3.888 minutes later. With this exact adjustment, neither more nor less, we find that all the calculations made using the adjusted Great Concordance system produce precise agreement, to the nearest part, with the predictions in the Planets Calendar for that year.

Since the changing value of the *Qi* Correspondence is key to explaining what happened in 1668 – 1669 in relation to the way basic calendrical calculations were carried out, it is helpful to look at the origins of the value of this constant. The Great Concordance system used under the Ming was, as we know, an adaptation of the Yuan dynasty Season Granting system *Shou shi li* 授时历 produced in 1280 by Guo Shoujing 郭守敬 and his collaborators.[57] The basic constants used in the calculations above were common to both systems—Year Cycle [3652425], *Qi* Reckoning [152184.375] and [Sexagenary] Sequence Factor [600000].[58] The origins from which *qi* were reckoned were however different, as a result of which the values of *Qi* Correspondence in the two systems also differed.

Thus, for the Season Granting system, the initial point for *qi* calculations was the winter solstice of late 1280, which was assumed to fall on 14 December 1280 (Julian calendar), at 01:26, 0.06 day after midnight, or 600/10000 day. The day of the solstice was sexagenary day *jiwei*.56, so the interval to the moment of the solstice from the beginning of the preceding *jiazi*.1 day was 55.06 days, or 550600 at a scale of 10000, which is the value of *Qi* Correspondence. As we have explained above, the *Qi* Correspondence value 550375 for the Great Concordance system simply reflects the fact that it counts its *qi* from a different starting point, the winter solstice of 14 December 1383, which fell at 0.0375 of a day after midnight on sexagenary day *jiwei*.56, and hence was 55.0375 days from the midnight beginning Hongwu 16/9/24 (20 October 1383), which is the *jiazi*.1 day preceding the winter solstice, thus giving 550375 for the *Qi* Correspondence to be used. At the beginning of the description of the Great Concordance system, the *Ming shi* explains how to calculate the Great Concordance

---

[57] See the detailed analysis of this work and its background in Sivin (2009).

[58] [Sexagenary] Sequence Factor in the Season Granting system was given in terms of days, 60, rather than in units of 1/10000 day, 60000, but these values are functionally identical.

value for *Qi* Correspondence from the Season Granting value:

Box 3 How to calculate *Qi* Correspondence

Text from *Ming shi* 35, 686	Translation of text	Calculation in text
洪武十七年甲子岁为元。上距至元辛巳一百〇四算。	Hongwu 17, *jiazi*. 1 [1384] is the system origin. Back to Zhiyuan [18] *xinsi*. 18 [1281] is 104 counts	Counting both 1281 and 1384 and all intervening years, we obtain 104.
岁周三百六十五万二千四百二十五分	The Year Cycle is 3 652 425 parts [1 part = 1/10000 day]	This is in effect a value for the length of the tropical year, given at a scale of 10000
置距算一百〇四	Set out the separation count, 104	[See above]
求得中积三亿七千六百一十九万九千七百七十五分	One obtains Accumulated Medial *Qi* 376199775 parts [1 part = 1/10000 day]	3652425×103 [59] $= 376199775$
加辛巳气应五十五万〇六百分,得通积三亿七千六百七十五万〇三百七十五分	Add the *xinsi*. 18 [year, 1281] *Qi* Correspondence [550600], to obtain the Overall Accumulation 376750375 parts	$376199775 + 550600 = 376750375$
满纪法六十去之,余为大统气应。	Cast out what fills [Sexagenary] Sequence Factor 60 [600000 parts], and the remainder is the *Qi* Correspondence for the Great Concordance. (*Ming shi* 35, 686)	$376750375 - 627 \times 600000 = 550375$

This explains how the 550375 value is to be obtained. But what about 550402, the value used in calculating the official calendar for Kangxi 8, 1669? Could this value of *Qi* Correspondence simply be the result of a third change of origin for *qi* calculations? The problem immediately arises that this number can never be the result of a process such as that outlined about, which, since the calculation necessarily involves multiplying Year Cycle [3652425] by some integer, then adding 550600 and subtracting multiples of 600000. Those processes can only result in number that is a multiple of 5, which 550402 is not. A second possibility is that the change might result from a desire to shift predicted times of *qi*, perhaps to accord with what might have been held to have been a more accurate observation of the time of a winter solstice. But the change involved is very small, only 0.0027 day = 3.888 minutes, and we have no indication of related observations and calculations having taken place before early Kangxi 7, 1668, when the calculations for the Kangxi 8, 1669 calendar would have had to have taken place. On the other hand, Wu Mingxuan's memorial in Kangxi 7 certainly indicates that there was at that time considerable dissension in the Astronomical Bureau, which might have been the result of a decision by the Recorder Chen Yuxin to make adjustments to the Great Concordance system in calculating his People's Calendar. It may well have been that change that motivated Wu's state-

---

[59] In the calculation that follows, we need to know the numbers of years (103) between 1281 and 1384, which are those from which the two systems begin their calculations. It is therefore essential, though not stated explicitly, that we should subtract 1 from the inclusively reckoned 'separation count' of 104 before proceeding; if we do not do so, we fail to obtain the result 550375 said to result from the calculation.

ment (quoted above) on 22 August 1668 that 'the way the old astronomical system [i. e. the Great Concordance system], is being used is not without errors' (*jian yong gu fa*, *bu wu cha miu* 见用古法不无差谬). Had there been any such adjustment, it is unlikely that it could have won the support of Yang Guangxian, who had argued that the 'old system' was worthy of adoption in its original form: but his name is not mentioned in this connection, and in any case it does not seem that he was ever involved in such technical matters. At the time of writing, it is not therefore possible to reconstruct with any certainty the thinking that led the staff of the *Qin tian jian* to take the step of changing the *Qi* Correspondence value by 27 as they seem to have done.

V. Wu Mingxuan's calculation of the position of the moon and planets

So far, Verbiest's exposition has used a system of astronomical coordinates equivalent to that still in use today. To follow his discussion of the positions of the moon and planets, we shall need to take into account a somewhat different system, the Chinese system of lodges, *xiu* 宿, by which the circuit of the heavens is divided into 28 unequal intervals, each named after an asterism (a group of stars). The beginning of each lodge is, in principle, defined by a 'determinative star' *ju xing* 距星, which is the star that first crosses the observer's meridian as a lodge rises in the east and moves westwards to its setting. The lodges are normally enumerated in a sequence from west to east, reflecting the order in which they cross the meridian in the course of a day and a night, commonly beginning with the lodge named 'Horn' *Jiao* 角,[60] whose determinative star is Spica, α Virginis — not to be confused with the quite different star named 'Great Horn' *Da jiao* 大角, which is Arcturus, α Bootis. Both stars will be mentioned shortly.

The most ancient usages of the lodge system for quantitative measurements of positions of the sun, moon and planets were equivalent in modern terms to measuring differences in the right ascensions of celestial bodies.[61] Right ascension, as its name implies, was originally conceived in the western tradition to indicate how long it would take for various intervals on the celestial equator to rise above the horizon as the heavens rotate about the celestial axis in the course of a day and a night; it is therefore measured in hours, but can be converted to degrees at the rate 24 hours = 360°. Right ascension is conventionally measured from zero at the spring equinox, where the sun moving on the ecliptic crosses the celestial equator from south to north.

Although right ascension is measured with reference to the celestial equator, the asterisms of the lodges do not however lie neatly along the line of the celestial equator on the celestial sphere; they were in any case defined and used well before the concept of the celestial sphere came into use. By the first century CE, by which time the celestial sphere was widely adopted by astronomers, Jia Kui gave the first time a listing of the extents of the lodges in terms of what we would nowadays call celestial longitude, measured along the ecliptic circle of his armillary instrument.[62] From this time on, and up to the time of the conflict between Verbiest and Wu Mingxuan, when someone tells us that a given celestial body is, for example '3 *du* into lodge X', we need to ask ourselves first whether this is an equatorial or an ecliptic measurement — and then we need to know where the beginning of lodge X is located in terms of (equatorial) right ascension or (ecliptic) longitude.

---

[60] This is now the common pronunciation; the more 'literary' form *jue* is also found.
[61] For a discussion see Cullen (2017), 186—207.
[62] Cullen (2017), 251—255.

Table 5 Qi for Kangxi 8, 1669 as given by Wu Mingxuan, the Planets calendar, and calculated using the Great Concordance System with different values of Qi Correspondence

				Qi dates and times for Kangxi 8 predicted by Wu Mingxuan, as found in CYJL						Qi dates and times predicted by Kangxi 8 Planets alendar						Qi times for Kangxi 8 predicted by Da tong li, using Qi correspondence 550375			Qi times for Kangxi 8 predicted by Da tong li, using Qi correspondence 550402		
				Chinese Lunar		Gregorian		Hour	Marks= Day/100	Parts= Mark/100	Chinese Lunar		Gregorian		Hour	Marks= Day/100	Parts= Mark/100	Hour	Marks= Day/100	Parts= Mark/100	Hour	Marks= Day/100	Parts= Mark/100
				Month	Day	Month	Day				Month	Day	Month	Day									
4	Establishment of spring	立春		1	4	Feb	4	19	1	63	1	4	Feb	4	19	1	63	19	1	36	19	1	63
5	Rain waters	雨水		1	20	Feb	20	0	2	64	1	20	Feb	20	0	2	64	0	2	37	0	2	64
6	Emerging insects	惊蛰		2	6	Mar	7	5	3	65	2	6	Mar	7	5	3	65	5	3	38	5	3	65
7	Spring equinox	春分		2	21	Mar	22	11	0	49	2	21	Mar	22	11	0	49	11	0	22	11	0	49
8	Clear and bright	清明		3	6	Apr	6	16	1	50	3	6	Apr	6	16	1	50	16	1	23	16	1	50
9	Grain rains	谷雨		3	21	Apr	21	21	2	52	3	21	Apr	21	21	2	52	21	2	25	21	2	52
10	Establishment of summer	立夏		4	8	May	7	2	3	53	4	8	May	7	2	3	53	2	3	26	2	3	53
11	Grain fils	小满		4	23	May	22	8	0	37	4	23	May	22	8	0	37	8	0	10	8	0	37
12	Grain in ear	芒种		5	8	Jun	6	13	1	38	5	8	Jun	6	13	1	38	13	1	11	13	1	38
13	Summer solstice	夏至		5	23	Jun	21	18	2	39	5	23	Jun	21	18	2	39	18	2	12	18	2	39
14	Little heat	小暑		6	9	Jul	6	23	3	40	6	9	Jul	6	23	3	40	23	3	13	23	3	40
15	Great heat	大暑		6	25	Jul	22	4	4	24	6	25	Jul	22	4	4	24	4	4	14	5	0	24
16	Establishment of autumn	立秋		7	10	Aug	6	10	0	25	7	10	Aug	6	10	0	25	10	0	98	10	1	25
17	Limit of heat	处暑		7	25	Aug	21	15	2	27	7	25	Aug	21	15	2	27	15	2	0	15	2	27
18	White dew	白露		8	11	Sep	5	20	3	28	8	11	Sep	5	20	3	28	20	3	1	20	3	28
19	Autumn equinox	秋分		8	27	Sep	21	1	0	12	8	27	Sep	21	1	0	12	1	4	2	2	0	12
20	Cold dew	寒露		9	12	Oct	6	7	1	13	9	12	Oct	6	7	1	13	7	0	86	7	1	13
21	Frost-fal	霜降		9	27	Oct	21	12	2	14	9	27	Oct	21	12	2	14	12	1	87	12	2	14
22	Establishment of winter	立冬		10	12	Nov	5	17	3	15	10	12	Nov	5	17	3	15	17	2	88	17	3	15
23	Little snow	小雪		10	27	Nov	20	22	4	16	10	27	Nov	20	22	4	16	22	3	89	22	4	16
24	Great snow	大雪		11	14	Dec	6	4	0	0	11	14	Dec	6	4	0	0	4	0	73	4	1	0
1	Winter solstice	冬至		11	29	Dec	21	9	1	2	11	29	Dec	21	9	2	2	9	1	75	9	2	2
2	Little cold	小寒		12	14	Jan	5	14	2	3	12	14	Jan	5	14	3	3	14	2	76	14	3	3
3	Great cold	大寒		12	29	Jan	20	19	3	4	12	29	Jan	20	19	4	4	19	3	77	19	4	4

To convert such measurements as referred to by Verbiest into modern terms, we may use the convenient tables provided in Jesuit sources such as the *Chong zhen li shu* and its successors. Turning first to the ecliptic (relative to which the separations of stars do not change as the centuries pass), the widths of the lodges are given in the table headed 'The degrees of each lodge on the ecliptic' *Ge xiu huang dao ben du* 各宿黄道本度.[63] The degrees of each lodge are given twice, in the upper register of the table in terms of the western style degrees and minutes used by the Jesuits, with 360° to a complete revolution and 60 minutes to each degree, and below in Chinese *du*, with $365\frac{1}{4}$ *du* to a complete revolution and 100 'parts' *fen* 分 to each *du*. On the page preceding that table is another table listing the *du*, but this time giving 'The accumulated degrees for [the starts of] lodges on the ecliptic' *Huang dao xiu ji du* 黄道宿积度; this is the distance in longitude along the ecliptic from the defined starting point of the spring equinox to the start of the given lodge. Here the two registers contain 'ancient' *gu* 古 and 'modern' *jin* 今 values, which differ because the position of the spring equinox moves slowly round the ecliptic from east to west, completing a circuit in about 26000 years. The 'ancient' values are calculated for the late third millennium BCE, the time when the mythical emperor *Yao* 尧 was traditionally believed to have laid down the first systematic relation between the stars, the seasons, and the lengths of day and night.[64]

Similarly, if we convert equatorial lodge measurements into degrees of right ascension, we may use the two tables 'The degrees of each lodge on the equator' *Chi dao ge xiu du* 赤道各宿度 and 'The accumulated degrees for [the start of] each lodge on the equator' *Chi dao ji xiu du* 赤道积宿度.[65] Both tables include both 'ancient' and 'modern' values; in the first case the modern values are given both in 360° notation and in $365\frac{1}{4}$ *du* notation.

The officials appointed by the emperor to supervise the observational tests reported the answer given by Verbiest to their request for a statement of his observations of the moon on Kangxi 8/1/18 (18 February 1669):

问南怀仁正月十八日。测太阴以何时何仪器为凭。南怀仁供称。正月十八日。角宿离天中之西。二十五度时。即寅正二刻。(见第八图)据明炫黄道算太阴。于本时刻。在翼宿十度二十三分有余。依南怀仁在翼宿一度二十三分。相差九度。依南怀仁所算太阴。于本时刻。在秋分前九度二十七分。而轸宿在秋分后。六度零十分。则彼此相距十五度三十七分。(见第九图)依吴明炫相距不过七度。则差八度三十六分。依怀仁算。大角星在秋分后十九度三十七分。而太阴在秋分前九度二十七分。则彼此相距二十九度四分。依吴明炫相距四十二度二十分。则差十三度十三分。

至期公测太阴。正与南怀仁所定黄赤仪上界限。脗合无差。

We asked Verbiest: On the 18ᵗʰ day of the first month, at what time and in reliance on what instrument did you observe the moon? Verbiest submitted this statement:

On the 18ᵗʰ day of the first month, at the time when the lodge Horn was 25° to the west of the meridian, that is, at 2 marks of the middle of the period *yin* (03:00—05:00) [*i.e.*

---

63 Shi and Chu (2017), 448.
64 On this story and its astronomical implications, see Cullen (2017), 20—27.
65 Shi and Chu (2017), 441—443.

04:30—04:45] (see the 8th diagram)⁶⁶ then according to Wu Mingxuan's calculation of the Moon's [position] on the ecliptic, at that time it was at slightly over 10° 23′ of the lodge Wings. According to my calculation it was at 1° 23′ of the lodge Wings, a difference of 9°. According to my calculation of the Moon's [position], at that time it was 9° 27′ before the autumn equinox, while the lodge Axletree was 6° 10′ after the autumn equinox. So these two points were 15° 37′ apart (see the 9th diagram).⁶⁷ According to Wu Mingxuan they were no more than 7° apart, so the difference was 8° 37′.⁶⁸ According to my calculations, the star Great Horn [Arcturus, alpha Bootis] was 19° 37′ after the autumn equinox, and the moon

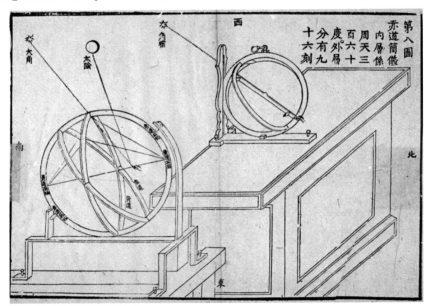

Figure 1: Measuring the position of the moon 1 February 1669 (*Ce yan ji lue*, figure 8). Source: gallica. bnf. fr /Bibliothèque nationale de France, Chinois 4992.

was 9° 27′ before the autumn equinox. So they were 29° 4′ apart. According to Wu Ming-

---

⁶⁶ Shown here as Figure 1. The draughtsman does not seem to have understood exactly how the instruments in question were used, so his drawing fails to represent the situation accurately The moment when the azimuth of Spica (alpha Virginis)the defining star of the lodge Horn (Sun and Kistemaker (1997), 52, Table 3. 1)was 205°, making it 25° to the west of the meridian, was Julian Date 2330698. 367, which corresponds to 4 hours 19 minutes after local midnight at Beijing, 4 minutes into the second mark after the middle of the period *Yin* 寅 (03:00—05:00) — close to the time stated by Verbiest. Julian Date (JD)is a common time reference used by astronomers, representing the time counted in days from Greenwich mean noon on 1 January 4713 BCE.

⁶⁷ Shown here as Figure 2. Unlike the previous figure, this diagram shows the situation fairly accurately. The distance between the Moon's position and gamma Corvi, the defining star of Axletree (Sun and Kistemaker (1997), 52, Table 3. 1)was 15° 39′ of longitude rather than Verbiest's stated 15° 37′.

⁶⁸ For consistency with the previous stated 9° difference of the stated positions of the Moon in Wings, this figure should also have been 9°, making the distance from Wu Mingxuan's lunar position to the start of Axletree 6° 37′, which for some unknown reason has been expressed as 'no more than 7°'.

xuan they were 42° 20′ apart, a difference of 13° 13′.[69] When the time came, all the gentlemen observed the moon, and it was exactly in accordance with the line that I had marked on the ecliptic-equatorial instrument, without the slightest discrepancy.[70]

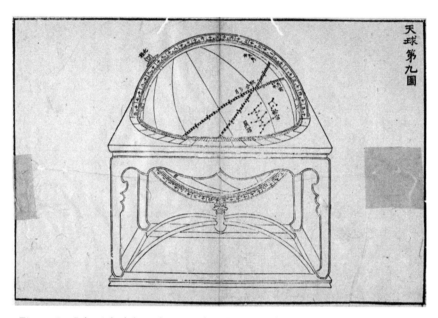

Figure 2: Celestial globe, showing the Moon in relation to the autumn equinox and the stars mentioned in the text (*Ce yan ji lue*, figure 9). Source: gallica. bnf. fr /Bibliothèque nationale de France, Chinois 4992.

Measured on the ecliptic, as stated, the lodge Wings (whose determinative star is α Crateris) begins at longitude 168° 36′ according to the tables referred to above. So the moon's position at 10° 23′ in Wings according to Wu Mingxuan equates to a longitude of:

$$168° 36′ + 10° 23′ = 178° 59′$$

Similarly, Verbiest's position of 1° 23′ in Wings[71] equates to a longitude of 169° 59′, which is 10° 1′ before the autumn equinox at 180°, not 9° 27′ as he states. This appears to show that Verbiest had updated the longitudes of the start of the lodges to account for the effect of precession of the thirty years since the tables were calculated, whether by observation or by recalculation. In February 1669, the longitude of α Crateris was in fact 169.1355° = 169° 8′ rather than the tabulated 168° 36′, so the

---

[69] Since 42° 20′ − 29° 4′ = 13° 16′, the 13′ 十三分 here seems to be a typographical error for 16′ 十六分. The distance between the Moon's position at the stime stated and gamma Corvi, the defining star of Axletree (Sun and Kistemaker (1997), 52, Table 3.1) was 15° 39′ of longitude rather than Verbiest's stated 15° 37′, and the distance between the Moon and the star named Great Horn *Da jiao* 大角, alpha Bootis, see (Sun and Kistemaker (1997), 147, *App.* 1.2), was 29° 9′ in longitude rather than Verbiest's 29° 4′. Following the previous logic, we would have expected Wu Mingxuan's result to be 29° 4′ − 9° = 20° 4′ in longitude. It seems likely that the 42° 20′ figure ascribed to Wu Mingxuan does not represent the difference in longitude between the Moon and alpha Bootis, but is an attempt at finding their angular separation on the celestial sphere, which was 39° at the instant considered. The 3° discrepancy is not surprising, given that we do not know precisely where Wu placed the Moon in relation to the ecliptic (its latitude at the relevant instances was close to 3° 20′) and that Wu would have had to make the measurement manually on the surface of a celestial globe on which the position of the two bodies had been marked.

[70] *CYJL*, 36a—36b.

[71] At the moment of observation stated, the Moon was then at 1° 25′ of Wings in longitude, compared with Verbiest's stated 1° 23′.

longitude corresponding to 1° 23′ in that lodge was 170° 31′, which is 9° 29′ before the autumn equinox—very close to the value that Verbiest states.[72]

Using the Excel workbook for the 'Muslim system' *Hui hui li* (see footnote 51), we obtain for the longitude of the moon:

Noon on 17 February: 162.1°
Noon on 18 February: 174.183 3°
Hence by interpolation, at 04:30 on 18 February: 170.407 3° = 170° 24′

The modern calculated value found using Starry Night Pro using UT +7.8 hours for local mean time Beijing at 04:30 (JD 2330698.36250) on 18 February is 170.4309° = 170° 26′. It was 170.4073° at 04:26:25. It seems that the *Hui hui li* lunar longitude value as represented by the *CJSOPGY* system is very close to the true value.

So the *Hui hui li* predicted distance of the moon before the autumn equinox at the moment specified is

$$180° - 170.4073° = 9.5927° = 9° 36′$$

Verbiest had 9° 27′. So if Wu Mingxuan really had used the *Hui hui li*, his position of the moon would have been only about 9′ closer to the equinox than Verbiest's, rather than 9°, the distance calculated by Verbiest from the difference between his position of the moon at "1° 23′ of the lodge Wings", and Wu Mingxuan's stated position at "slightly over 10° 23′ of the lodge Wings"

So if Wu's position of the Moon at 10° 23′ (10.38° or 10.53 *du*) of the lodge Wings did not come from the Muslim system, where might it have come from? If we consult the official planets calendar for Kangxi 8 (see note 53), we are told that the position of the moon at dawn (*chen du* 晨度) on the 18th day of the first lunar month (18 February) was at Wings 11 *du* 37 *fen* (11.37 *du*). Now the mean motion of the moon in one day is 13.36875 *du*.[73] To get from 11.37 *du* down to 10.53 *du* requires a displacement of 0.84 *du*, for which the time required is:

24 hours × (0.84/13.36875) = 1.508 hours, 1 hour 30 minutes to the nearest minute.

Now sunrise on that day was at 06:51; allowing the conventional value 2.5 marks = 36 minutes back from sunrise to the start of dawn,[74] we get to 06:15, which is 1 hour 45 minutes from 04:30. It seems that Wu Mingxuan is using a longitude for the moon based on essentially the same methods as the Planets Calendar, and certainly not based on the *Hui hui li*.

Finally, let us consider the planetary positions on 3 February that Verbiest gives for Mars and Jupiter as predicted by himself and Wu Mingxuan. Here there are signs of some confusion; in the case of Mars this may be related to the procedural errors by his opponent cited by Verbiest in his 'Remarks at the time of observation' *Ce yan cheng yu* 测验呈语, where he complains

---

[72] In the explanation of the tables referred to above, it is noted that the effect of precession is to shift longitudes by 51 seconds of arc each year: see Shi and Chu (2017), 438. Thus, since the tables were based on calculations made for Chongzhen 1, 1628, then the 32′ difference between 169° 8′ and 168° 36′ would correspond to a time interval of 32 × 60/51 years = 38 years, which would take us up to 1666, the beginning of Verbiest's confinement in Beijing, during which period he might well have passed the time by updating his tables in this way.

[73] See *Ming shi* 35, 698: 月平行度一十三度三十六分八十七秒半.

[74] *Ming shi* 34, 656: 晨分加二百五十分，为日出分。日周一万分，内减晨分为昏分。昏分减二百五十分，为日入分，又减五千分，为半昼分。故立成只列晨昏分，则出入及半昼分皆具，不必尽列也.

在依黄道推算。以赤道测验。

[Wu] makes calculations based on the ecliptic, and then uses the equator for observations.[75]

Thus for Mars, Verbiest says:

依吴明烜七政历。康熙八年正月初三日。火星在室宿十五度五十八分。依南怀仁历法。本日火星在室宿七度五十分。则吴明烜历。先天八度八分。

According to Wu Mingxuan's planets calendar, on Kangxi 8/1/3 [3 February 1669], Mars was in House, at 15° 58′. According to my astronomical system, on that day Mars was in House, at 7° 50′. So Wu Mingxuan's astronomical system was 8° 8′ ahead of heaven.[76]

Now in February 1669 the longitude of the determinative star of House, α Pegasi, was 348.8780° = 348° 53′, so if Verbiest is, as before, using the then current longitude for this star rather than its tabulated value (which was 348° 20′), his longitude for Mars would be 356° 43′ (subtracting the whole revolution).[77] At Beijing dusk (the time specified for the observation), the predicted longitude of Mars using modern planetarium software (Starry Night Pro) was 356.7603° = 356° 47′, extremely close to Verbiest's value.[78] If Wu's value for Mars was indeed an ecliptic value, then it was certainly as wrong as Verbiest says it was — and it was not far from the erroneous values for the position of Mars given by the official Planets Calendar around that time — which were 13 *du* 46 *fen* in House for midnight beginning 3 February, and 14 *du* 23 *fen* in House for the following midnight. Since we have seen that his *qi* predictions were made using a version of the Great Concordance system, the same may be true of his planetary positions. If, however he had accurately predicted the right ascension of Mars, which was 23.815 4 hours = 357.231° = 357° 14′ at Beijing dusk according to modern calculations, then using the tabulated right ascension of the start of House, 341° 34′, Mars would in equatorial terms be 15° 40′, which would be close to the value ascribed to him — which would then indicate something like the confusion referred to by Verbiest, in which equatorial and ecliptic measurements were muddled.[79] But since the *Hui hui li*, which had a common Ptolemaic ancestry with Verbiest's system, calculated planetary positions on the ecliptic, this would be a further point against the likeli-

---

[75] *CYJL*, 16a.
[76] *CYJL*, 34a—34b.
[77] See Shi and Chu (2017), 447.
[78] The tabulation in Argoli (1648), vol 2, 864, gives Pisces 26° 44′, i.e. longitude 356° 44′ on this date at Rome noon, which is close to Beijing dusk. It is known that Verbiest made use of this text in his work around this period: the copy of this text in the Beijing National Library, (inspected by Cullen in May 2017), which has annotations in Verbiest's handwriting, has inked horizontal marks next to the entry rows for the ephemeris data for 27 and 28 December 1668, the first two dates for which Verbiest had to make shadow predictions. Verbiest also mentions Argoli's tables in Verbiest and Golvers (1993), 74 and the original text in Verbiest (1687), VIII, 23.
[79] This point is made in Huang (1993), 65—66.

hood of Wu Mingxuan having used the Muslim system for such calculations.[80]

Turning briefly to the case of Jupiter, we read in Verbiest's account:

> 依吴明烜七政历。正月初三日。木星在昴宿七度十五分。依南怀仁历法。木星在昴宿五度五十四分。则吴明烜历。先天一度二十一分。以日计之。则差有二十三日矣。
>
> According to Wu Mingxuan's Planets Calendar, on [Kangxi 8] 1/3 (3 February 1668), Jupiter was in Mane, at 7° 15′. According to my astronomical system, Jupiter was in Mane at 5° 54′. So Wu Mingxuan's astronomical system was 1° 21′ ahead of heaven. Reckoning in days, the difference is 23 days.[81]

A modern calculation of the longitude of Jupiter at Beijing dusk on 3 February gives 61.5876°, and the observed longitude of 17 Tauri, normally taken as the determinative star of Mane (basically the Pleiades) was then 54.7931°. That would mean Jupiter was 6.7945° = 6° 48′ into Mane,[82] which makes Verbiest's value about a degree wrong, corresponding to a month's movement of the planet. The issue may of course have been a simple error on Verbiest's part — but that would be a little surprising, since he could easily have checked his prediction against Argoli's tables for that date (which we know he consulted; see note 78), which gave a Rome noon (roughly Beijing dusk) longitude of 1°15′ of Gemini or 61° 15′ = 61.25°, which would have been 6° 27′ into Mane using 17 Tauri, rather than the 5° 54′ he predicted.[83] If, however, Verbiest did not observe 17 Tauri, but (mistakenly?) observed 27 Tauri, a star of similar magnitude further to the east of the asterism, then since that had longitude 55.7372°, Jupiter would be reckoned as being at 5° 51′, very close to his stated result. From the official Planets Calendar we may compute that Jupiter would have been close to 6.33 *du* into Mane; Wu Mingxuan differs from that by about a degree. No very clear picture emerges from this comparison — in part no doubt because Jupiter moves much more slowly on the celestial sphere than does Mars, and so the differences involved are much smaller.

Ⅶ. Conclusion

On the basis of the reconstruction of Wu Mingxuan's calculations carried out in this essay, we may say that so far as the prediction of the 24 *qi* is concerned, it appears that he did not use anything that might be called the 'Muslim system' *Hui hui li* 回回历 as represented in the extensive writings setting out its methods. Instead, he simply used the 'Great Concordance system' *Da tong li* 大统历, the Ming dynasty adaptation of the Yuan dynasty 'Season Granting system' *Shou shi li* 授时历.

This was the system that had been abandoned when in 1644 the Qing gave responsibility for leading the Astronomical Bureau to Schall with his 'New Western methods', but which was restored to

---

[80] The Excel version of the *Hui hui li* created by Christopher Cullen (see note 51) has not yet been extended to include planetary longitudes. But examples given in Shi (2003), 46, show that the *Hui hui li* produced values of the longitude of Mars from the mid 15th to the early 20th centuries that were within one or two degrees of the values found from modern methods.

[81] *CYJL*, 34b.

[82] As noted in Huang (1993), 63.

[83] Argoli (1648), vol 2, 864.

use by Yang Guangxian after the Jesuits were removed from office in 1665.[84] What is more, in his predictions for the qi of Kangxi 8, 1669 Wu continued to use the original version of the Great Concordance system as applied by the Astronomical Bureau up to the time when the Kangxi 7 (1668) calendar was calculated. The Bureau itself had, as we have seen, slightly modified the system used to prepare its calendar for Kangxi 8. Wu's prediction of the position of the moon is nearly 9° different from the position predicted by the *Hui hui li*, but close to the position predicted in the official Planets Calendar, based on the Great Concordance system. Moreover, if Wu had made any use of the *Hui hui li* at all we would have expected him to use it for such a prediction, since it is well adapted for this purpose and the Muslim section had long been held to have particular skills in planetary calculations.[85] The figures for Wu's predictions of the positions of Mars and Jupiter appear somewhat confused (as may be Verbiest's prediction for Jupiter), but so far as we can make sense of them, Wu's position of Mars is certainly close to that in the Planets Calendar.

Given this state of affairs, there are two questions that present themselves:

(1) Why did Wu Mingxuan not use the *Hui hui li*?

(2) Why did Verbiest repeatedly assert that Wu was using the *Hui hui li*?

On the first question, one immediate response is that whatever his intentions might have been when he made his proposal for reforming the calculation practices of the bureau in August 1668, Wu Mingxuan was not expecting to have to produce a new system of astronomical calculation on an immediate basis. In this original memorial he set no timescale, but the report by the Board of Rites a month later, which is not likely to have been written without further consultation with him, proposed a four-year programme of observation and revision before a final result could be expected, and it would become possible to 'compose [a new] treatise on the astronomical system'. However, as we have seen, the emperor demanded that Wu should immediately produce drafts of the People's Calendar and Planets Calendar for Kangxi 8, 1669.

If Wu Mingxuan had originally planned to produce a new system for computing the calendar based in some way on the *Hui hui li*,[86] he cannot have been intending to do so within a few months of mak-

---

[84] The removal of the Jesuits in Kangxi 4, 1665, did not lead to the Great Concordance system immediately becoming the basis for all calendrical documents issued for subsequent years. This is evident in the case of the Planets Calendars from the formats adopted in successive years. Because the Great Concordance did not attempt to calculate planetary latitudes, the data for each month in the Planets Calendar calculated using that system only occupied two pages rather than the six-page format used by the Jesuits, which included latitudes. The six-page format with latitudes was still used in the Planets Calendar for Kangxi 5, 1666, which must have been calculated the previous year. The first Planets Calendar generated using the Great Concordance 2-page format was that prepared for Kangxi 6, 1667, and must have been calculated in Kangxi 5, 1666. Similarly, while the last 'Approaches and Invasions' Calendar (*Ling fan li* 凌犯历 see note 15) to bear the signature of Schall (Tang Ruowang 汤若望) and his colleagues is that of Kangxi 4, 1665, the signatures of Mahu and Yang Guangxian do not appear until Kangxi 6, 1667. The *Ling fan li* for the preceding year, Kangxi 5, 1666, bore only the signature of a few officials, headed by Zhang Qichun 张其淳, who had been temporarily promoted to Director from Observatory Manager to fill the gap created by Schall's removal; he was replaced by Yang Guangxian the following year. It must have been calculated using Jesuit methods in the earlier part of Kangxi 4, 1665, although the signatures of those who had prepared it could no longer be shown for political reasons. As with the Planets Calendars, all copies of the Approaches and Invasions Calendars used in this article come from the collections of the National Palace Museum, Taibei: see note 53.

[85] It was for this reason that Yang Guangxian had brought Wu Mingxuan and before him another Muslim Ma Weilong 马惟龙, back into the Astronomical Bureau: see de Magalhães (1666 October), folios 205r and 206v.

[86] See note 37 above.

ing his original proposal. For a start, Wu Mingxuan faced the problem that, as he stated in his memorial, the Astronomical Bureau had three different and inconsistent versions of a planets calendar based on the *Hui hui li*, so his first task would have been to settle on an authoritative interpretation of the *Hui hui li* itself. And once that had been done, although the documents that set out the procedures of the *Hui hui li* enabled its users to make a large number of astronomical calculations, such as those needed to find the longitudes of the sun, moon and planets, and the precise times and circumstances of solar and lunar eclipses, considerable adaptation would have been required to use it as a basis for direct computation of a Chinese style calendar; on this, see the discussion of the 24 *qi* above. The *Hui hui li* was an astronomical system used by Muslim officials of the Astronomical Bureau, not a calendar. There was no 'Muslim calendar' usable in the Chinese context that could have been adopted directly in place of the calendar calculated using the Great Concordance system. Indeed, in order to use the *Hui hui li* for any purpose, the first task to be performed was to transform the Chinese date of interest into a date in the Muslim *hijra* calendar around which the computational machinery of the *Hui hui li* was structured.[87]

The *Hui hui li* had never previously functioned in China as the basis of an alternative official calendar but had always been restricted to supplementing and providing checks and comparisons to certain aspects of the official astronomical system. The Jesuits who worked to compose the texts in the *Chong zhen li shu* had succeeded in creating a system that enabled a Chinese calendar to be produced on a theoretical basis imported from Europe, but that task had taken the work of several astronomical specialists during the years from 1629—1635. As their patron Xu Guangqi 徐光启 (1562—1633) said, they had 'melted their [European] material and substance to cast them into the mould of the Great Concordance' (*rong bi fang zhi cai zhi ru Da tong zhi xing mo* 镕比方之才质入大统之型模).[88] To do the same with the material of the Islamicate astronomical tradition (if that had been what Wu Mingxuan intended) would have been perfectly possible — but it could certainly not have been accomplished in the few months that the emperor allowed Wu for his task of producing calendars for Kangxi 8. And quite apart from the astronomical problems involved, there would have been personal and political problems to resolve before such a new system could be accepted, given that the Director of the Astronomical Bureau, Yang Guangxian, under whom Wu now served as Deputy Director (rather than as head of the Muslim section, the role he had filled earlier in the dynasty), had already fought bitterly to banish what he saw as a "foreign" system in favour of a purely "Chinese" one. Yang would certainly have resisted any attempt to displace the Great Concordance system from use in the Astronomical Bureau.

Given all this, it is not surprising that the drafts of the People's Calendar and Planets Calendar for Kangxi 8, 1669 that Wu submitted in accordance with the emperor's command of early October 1668 appear to have been calculated using the basic methods of the Great Concordance system — though without the change in *Qi* Correspondence that appears to have been adopted by the Astronomi-

---

[87] There are some signs that early in the Ming dynasty Muslim astronomers did produce calendars in the *hijra* system that were designed to meet the religious and cultural needs of the significant Muslim communities established in China. But these were not intended to replace the imperially issued Chinese-style calendars around which all official activities were structured, and which were therefore an essential reference for all the emperor's subjects. See Shi, Li and Li (2013), 161 and Shi (2014), 54. We are grateful to Professor Shi Yunli for helpful email discussions on this and related points (20—23 July 2021).

[88] Jami (2012), 32—34.

cal Bureau in its computations for Kangxi 8. The adoption of that very small change may have been what Wu complained of in his memorial of August 1668 cited above, when he wrote that the use of the Great Concordance system in the Astronomical Bureau at that time was 'not without errors'. The fact that, even without that innovation, Wu did not consider the Great Concordance system to be wholly satisfactory may have been behind his response to the questions put to him on the morning of 26 December 1668 when Wu, Yang Guangxian and the three Jesuits were questioned by high officials in the palace. In his letter of 2 January 1669 Gabriel de Magalhães recorded the following exchange between the officials and Wu Mingxuan on the subject of the calendars he had produced:

> They asked the Moor [Wu Mingxuan] if he would venture to defend his [astronomical system]? He answered, that he had not yet finished making it nor correcting it.
> They asked him further if the calendar that he had made for the 8th year [1669] was good? He answered, that it was adequate.
> "Adequate?" replied one of the four mandarins who had summoned us. "Mind what you say: does it have errors, or does it not have errors?" The Moor replied: "It still has some minor errors that need to be corrected."
> "So," put in another mandarin, "you really dared to give the King [i. e. the emperor] an erroneous calendar as if it was correct?" [89]

We may note that in *Astronomia Europaea*, a text written for a European readership, Verbiest stated explicitly that Wu's calendrical predictions were *tam Sinica quam Arabica* 'as much Chinese as Arabic' — something he never hints at in his writings in Chinese. [90] He was certainly correct in suggesting that Wu was using Chinese methods in his predictions — but what the 'Arabic' elements might have been, he never specifies, perhaps because he could not identify any. Indeed, it is quite possible that Verbiest had never learned anything significant about the *Hui hui li*, which was in effect the hereditary intellectual property of the families that provided the staff of the Muslim section of the Astronomical Bureau, a section which had been shut down years before Verbiest joined the Bureau under Schall. [91] But even assuming that Verbiest was ignorant in this respect, he would surely have noticed the very close resemblance between Wu Mingxuan's *qi* predictions for Kangxi 8, and those already published in the official calendar for that year, which he knew was calculated according to the Chinese system in official use up to 1644, and restored to use by Yang Guangxian after 1665. It is clear from the answers Verbiest gave to the four officials who visited the Jesuits on Christmas morning 1668 that he had not only seen the official calendar for Kangxi 8, which had been made public six weeks earlier, but had studied it in detail. [92] Why then, given all this, did Verbiest constantly refer to Wu as using the *Hui hui li* in all the texts in Chinese that he submitted by way of criticism of Wu's work?

The answer, we suggest, may perhaps be found in the rhetoric of persuasion. By the end of

---

[89] For the source, see, de Magalhães (1669 January 2), 270v, extract translated from Portuguese in Cullen and Jami (2020), 16—17.

[90] Verbiest (1687), V, 16; compare Verbiest and Golvers (1993), 69.

[91] As pointed out in Shi (2003), 35, Chinese astronomers of the Qing period complained that Muslim astronomers concealed the techniques for converting between Chinese dates and the *hijra* dates needed to operate the *Hui hui li*, thereby making the Muslim system inaccessible to them. Verbiest would naturally have shared this handicap.

[92] See Cullen and Jami (2020), 11.

1668, Verbiest knew that Yang Guangxian had lost the confidence of the emperor and his court.[93] He no longer needed to mount any attacks in that direction. His target now had to be Wu Mingxuan, the person whom the emperor was clearly considering in October 1668 as a possible candidate to be entrusted with the calculations needed to prepare an official calendar — which was of course the role he wished to fill himself. It was important, however, to ensure that his attack damaged Wu's personal credibility alone, while doing as little as possible to cause unnecessary offence to others, such as the Han staff of the Astronomical Bureau, or the Han ministers who might still have been sympathetic to Yang Guangxian's project of restoring the use of the Ming dynasty's Great Concordance system. Verbiest certainly did not want to be seen at this stage as an advocate of something 'foreign' attacking a Chinese opponent: in referring to his own calculations, he simply calls them 'the astronomical calculations made by me and my colleagues' *chen deng suo tui li fa* 臣等所推历法, without any characterisation of his methods as 'new' or 'western'. In contrast, he makes continual use of the alienating characterisation of Wu Mingxuan's astronomy as 'Muslim', *Hui hui* 回回. As we have seen, this does not appear to have been an accurate description of the basis on which Wu Mingxuan was making his calculations — unless Verbiest is simply contrasting the *li* of 'me and my colleagues' with the *li* of 'the Muslim' (Wu Mingxuan was of course a Muslim), which would have been somewhat misleading, given the normal reference of the term *Hui hui li*.

But let us recall that the stakes for the Jesuits and for the future of their religion in the Qing empire were very high. As Verbiest put it, the situation was one in which

> … res pro Dei & Religionis nostrae gloria, tam manifeste agebatur …
> … the honour of God and of our Religion was so clearly at stake …[94]

Verbiest makes it clear in his writings for a European readership that it was only by completely discrediting his opponents and competitors in astronomical matters — which necessitated eliminating Wu Mingxuan from consideration — that he was eventually able to ensure that the Jesuits in exile in Canton were allowed to return to their posts throughout the empire. Without that return, the Christian mission in China would have been effectively terminated, leading to the potential consequence (in the eyes of a 17th century Catholic believer) of millions of Chinese souls remaining unredeemed for lack of baptism. That was a outcome that Verbiest must have felt bound to avoid at all costs.

Abbreviations:

CJSOPGY: see *Chiljeongsan oepyeon jeongmyonyeon ilsig galyeong*

CYJL: see *Qin ding xin li ce yan ji lue*

XCDA: see *Xi chao ding an*

Bibliography

Works cited by title

Chiljeongsan oepyeon 칠정산외편 七政算外篇 (*Reckoning [the positions of] of the Seven Governors [sun, moon and five planets], part 2 [the Islamic system]*). (c. 1447). Yi Sunji 李纯之 and Kim Dam 金淡.

Chiljeongsan oepyeon jeongmyonyeon ilsig galyeong 칠정산외편정묘년일식가령 七政算外篇丁卯年日

---

[93] See Cullen and Jami (2020), 12—14 and 19—20.

[94] Verbiest (1687), IV, 11 and Verbiest and Golvers (1993), 64—5.

食假令 (*Reckoning [the positions of] of the Seven Governors [sun, moon and five planets], part 2: the example of the solar eclipse in sexagenary year 4 [1447]*). (c. 1447). Jeong Heumji 郑钦之, Yi Sunji 李纯之 and Kim Dam 金淡.

Chong zhen li shu 崇祯历书 (*Texts on astronomical systems [compiled in] the Chongzhen reign*). (Compiled under the leadership of Xu Guangqi 徐光启 (1562—1633) ed., and submitted to the throne between 1630 and 1635, repr. 2009). ed. Pan Nai 潘鼐, Shanghai, Shanghai guji chubanshe 上海古籍出版社.

Da Qing li chao shi lu 大清历朝实录 (*Veritable records of the successive reigns of the Great Qing dynasty*). (1937). Anon., Xinjing 新京 (Changchun 长春), Da Manzhou di guo guo wu yuan 大满洲帝国国务院.

Hou Han shu 后汉书 (*History of Eastern Han dynasty*). (Main text completed c. 450 CE, monographs by Sima Biao 司马彪 (c. 240-c. 306 CE) added later. Punctuated edition of 1963). Fan Ye 范晔 (398-445 CE), Beijing, Zhonghua Press.

Ming shi 明史 (*History of the Ming dynasty*). (1739; punctuated edition of 1974). Zhang Tingyu 张廷玉 (1672-1755) et al., Beijing, Zhonghua Press.

Qin ding xin li ce yan ji lue 钦定新历测验纪略 (*A summary of observations in accordance with the new astronomical system, imperially commissioned*). (1669). Nan Huairen 南怀仁 (Ferdinand Verbiest).

Xi chao ding an 熙朝定案 (*Cases decided during the [Kang]xi reign*). (after 1669). Nan Huairen 南怀仁 (Ferdinand Verbiest), Rome, National Central Library, 72 C530.1.

Works cited by author

An Shuangcheng 安双成 (2015). *Qing chu xi yang chuan jiao shi Man wen dang an yi ben* 清初西洋传教士满文档案译本 (*Translations of Manchu language memorials relating to western missionaries in early Qing*). Zhengzhou 郑州, Daxiang chubanshe 大象出版社.

Argoli, Andrea (1648). *Exactissimae caelestium motuum ephemerides … ab anno 1641 ad annum 1700*. Patavii, Typis Pauli Frambotti, 3 vols.

Chen Zhanshan 陈占山, Ed., (2000). *Bu de yi, fu er zhong* 不得已, 附二种 ('*I cannot do otherwise*' [by Yang Guangxian 杨光先, 1597—1669] *and two other works*). Hefei, Huangshan shushe 黄山书社.

Chu Longfei 褚龙飞 and Shi Yunli 石云里 (2012). "Chong zhen li shu xi lie li fa zhong de tai yang yun dong li lun《崇祯历书》系列历法中的太阳运动理论 (The Theory of Solar Motions in the Chongzhen Lishu Series)." *Ziran kexueshi yanjiu* 自然科学史研究 **31** (4): 410-427.

Chu, Pingyi (1997). "Scientific dispute in the imperial court: the 1664 calendar case." *Chinese Science* **14**: 7-34.

Cullen, Christopher (2017). *Heavenly Numbers: Astronomy and Authority in Early Imperial China*. Oxford, Oxford University Press.

Cullen, Christopher and Catherine Jami (2020). "Christmas 1668 and after: how Jesuit astronomy was restored to power in Beijing." *Journal for the History of Astronomy* **51** (1): 3-50.

Christopher Cullen and Catherine Jami (2022). "Prediction and politics in Beijing, 1668: A Jesuit astronomer and his technical resources in a time of crisis." *Journal for the History of Astronomy* **53** (4): 422-474.

de Magalhães, Gabriel (1666 October). Letter addressed to the Fathers in Canton, October 1666: Relação em que se conta o succedido na corte de Pe Kim, depois que os Padres della partirão (An account in which is recorded what happened at the court of Beijing, after the Fathers departed from thence) (manuscript). Real Academia de la Historia, Madrid, Jesuitas, ms. Legajo 22, folio 204r-209v.

de Magalhães, Gabriel (1669 January 2). Letter addressed to Luis da Gama, Father Visitor at Macao, 2 January 1669 (manuscript). Archivum Romanum Societatis Iesu, Japonica-Sinica, ms. 162, folio 269-273v.

Golvers, Noël and Efthymios Nicolaidis, Eds., (2009). *Ferdinand Verbiest and Jesuit science in 17th century China: an annotated edition and translation of the Constantinople manuscript (1676)*. Leuven Chinese studies. Athens and Leuven, Institute for Neohellenic Research and Ferdinand Verbiest Institute.

Huang Yi-Long and Chih-ch'eng Chang (1996). "The Evolution and Decline of the Ancient Chinese Practice of Watching for the Ethers." *Chinese Science* (13): 82-106.

Huang Yi-Long 黄一农 (1993). "Qing chu tian zhu jiao yu hui jiao tian wen jia jian de zheng dou 清初天主教与回教天文家间的争斗 (The struggle between Catholic and Muslim astronomers in early Qing)." *Jiuzhou xuekan* 九州学刊 5 (3): 47-69.

Jami, Catherine (2012). *The Emperor's new mathematics: Western learning and imperial authority in China during the Kangxi reign (1662—1722)*. Oxford, Oxford University Press.

Liu, Yuk Tung (2018—2022). "Conversion between Western and Chinese Calendar (722 BCE—2200 CE)." Last accessed February 2022, from https://ytliu0.github.io/ChineseCalendar/index.html?y=1670.

Oxnam, Robert B. (1975). *Ruling from horseback: Manchu politics in the Oboi Regency*, 1661-1669. Chicago, University of Chicago Press.

Regiomontanus, Joannes (1485). *Calendarium*. Venezia, Erhard Ratdolt.

Shaughnessy, Edward L. (1991). *Sources of Western Zhou history: inscribed bronze vessels*/ Berkeley, Oxford, University of California Press.

Shi Yunli (2003). "The Korean Adaptation of the Chinese-Islamic Astronomical Tables." *Archive for History of Exact Sciences* 57 (1): 25-60.

Shi Yunli (2014). "Islamic Astronomy in the Service of Yuan and Ming Monarchs." *Suhayl. International Journal for the History of the Exact and Natural Sciences in Islamic Civilisation* 13: 41-61.

Shi Yunli 石云里 and Chu Longfei 褚龙飞 (2017). *Chong zhen li shu he jiao* 崇祯历书合校 (*Collated edition of the Chong zhen li shu*). Hefei 合肥, Zhongguo kexue jishu daxue chubanshe 中国科学技术大学出版社.

Shi Yunli 石云里, Li Liang 李亮 and Li Huifang 李辉芳 (2013). "Cong 'Xuande shi nian yue wu xing lingfan' kan hui hui li fa zai Ming chao de shi yong 从《宣德十年月五星凌犯》看回回历法在明朝的使用 (The Actual Applications of the Chinese-Islamic System of Calendrical Astronomy in the Ming Dynasty as Seen from the Encroachments of the Moon and the Five Planets in the 10th Year of the Xuande Reign)." *Ziran kexueshi yanjiu* 自然科学史研究 32 (2): 156-164.

Sivin, Nathan (2009). *Granting the Seasons: the Chinese astronomical reform of 1280, with a study of its many dimensions and a translation of its records*. New York, Springer.

Sun, Xiaochun and Jacob Kistemaker (1997). *The Chinese sky during the Han: constellating stars and society*. Leiden; New York, Brill.

Tang Ruowang 汤若望 (Johann Adam Schall von Bell) (after 1661, 1993 repr.). Zou shu 奏疏 (Memorials). *Zhong guo ke xue ji shu dian ji tong hui: tian wen* 中国科学技术典籍通汇:天文 (*Comprehensive collection of classic texts of Chinese science and technology: astronomy*). Bo Shuren

薄树人 et al., Ed. Zhengzhou, Henan jiaoyu chubanshe 河南教育出版社, 8, 857-964.

van Dalen, Benno and Michio Yano (1998). Islamic astronomy in China: two new sources for the Huihui li ("Islamic calendar"). *Highlights of Astronomy*. J Andersen, Ed. **11B**, 697-700.

Verbiest, Ferdinand (1687). *Astronomia Europaea sub imperatore Tartaro Sinico Cám Hý appellato ex umbra in lucem revocata à R. P. Ferdinando Verbiest Flandro-Belga e Societate Jesu*. Dillingen, Joannis Caspari Bencard, per Joannem Federle.

Verbiest, Ferdinand and Noël Golvers (1993). *The Astronomia Europaea of Ferdinand Verbiest, S. J. (Dillingen, 1687): text, translation, notes and commentaries*. Nettetal, Steyler Verlag.

Weil, Dror (2018). The Fourteenth Century Transformation in China's Reception of Arabo-Persian Astronomy. *Knowledge in Translation: Global Patterns of Scientific Exchange, 1000-1800 CE* (Pittsburg: Pittsburg University Press, 2018), 345-370. Patrick Manning and Abigail Owen, Eds. Pittsburg, Pittsburg University Press, 345-370.

Yabuuti, Kiyoshi and Benno van Dalen (1997). "Islamic Astronomy in China during the Yuan and Ming Dynasties." *Historia Scientiarum* **7** (1): 11-43.

梅文鼎历算著作刊印的背景及其人际网络

韩 琦 （浙江大学历史学院）

梅文鼎（1633—1721），字定九，号勿庵，安徽宣城人，清初著名数学家及天文学家，是清代数学史上承先启后的重要人物。他上承明末传入的西方数学，下启乾嘉时期的历算研究，历算之学被誉为"国朝第一"，其著述等身，汇通中西，影响了有清一代数学的发展。梅氏"湛心经术，旁通诸家"，广收博览，藏书万卷。研究历算之余，多有诗文唱和之作，现存《绩学堂诗文钞》共十卷，记述了其学术和思想的历程与师友交往，不仅体现了他对中西历算的理解，还体现了一位通儒对传统学术的思考。梅文鼎曾有"才与不才之间"的自我定位，其为文作诗，都力求以博学取胜，如他所撰的《璇玑玉衡赋》，旁征博引，写成后洛阳纸贵，获得了时人的赞扬。

早在1925年，李俨在《清华学报》上发表了《梅文鼎年谱》。1932年，钱宝琮、商鸿逵分别在《国立浙江大学季刊》和《中法大学月刊》发表了《梅勿庵先生年谱》和《梅定九先生年谱》，后者主要依据了《绩学堂诗文钞》。之后，李俨依据新发现的史料，对年谱多有增补，1955年收入《中算史论丛》第三集。之后，国内对梅文鼎的研究相对较少[1]，直至20世纪80年代开始，才出现了研究梅文鼎的高潮，并召开了纪念梅文鼎的国际会议，涌现了许多成果。[2]

本文根据现存日本、美国和国内梅氏著作的早期刊本，并结合梅文鼎的诗文集、梅瑴成《兼济堂历算书刊缪》和梅氏家谱，并系统查阅了清人文集，对梅文鼎的交友网络，以及康乾时期梅氏历算著作的刊印活动做一全面系统的梳理，希冀说明康熙时代历算书的刊刻，并不完全是梅文鼎的个人行为，而与政治、文化诸因素有着密切的关系，不仅与皇帝、大臣与士人有关，甚至与传教士的活动有关联。

梅文鼎九岁即熟读五经，并随祖父治《易》。顺治十八年（1661），他跟随同里倪正先生学习大统历交食法，对历法颇有领悟，并补其缺漏，著有《历学骈枝》，颇得倪正首肯。康熙五年（1666），他到南京参加乡试，之后在十四至十六年间（1675—1677），又多次游历南京，自购得《崇祯历书》之后，便开始潜心研究西洋历算，并在此时获知穆尼阁（Johannes Nikolaus Smogulecki，1610—1656）和薛凤祚的著作。在秦淮河畔，他广交朋友，吟诗唱和，其中就有方以智之子方中通；此外，他还认识了著名的藏书家黄虞稷，并到黄家看书、抄书，并接触到宋刊本《九章算术》。康熙十九年（1680），他再次到南京，下榻蔡璧（玑先）之观行堂。蔡氏为他刊刻了《筹算》（1678年自序）[3]，此外，康熙十九年，蔡氏还帮助刊刻了《中西算学通初集》一书[4]，这部小册子并不是真正意义的算学著作，而是梅文鼎拟刊书籍的"广告"。

梅文鼎的数学研究大致可以康熙十九年为界。[5]前期的成果主要以《中西算学通初集》为代表，主要

---

[1] 1970年、1973年，日本学者桥本敬造在《东方学报》上先后发表了《梅文鼎的历算学：康熙年间的天文历算学》和《梅文鼎的数学研究》两文，较为详细地分析了梅文鼎的学术生涯、著述活动及其在历算方面的成就。

[2] 研究主要集中于对梅文鼎历算著作的解读，可以刘钝的一些论文为代表，严敦杰的论文、李迪的《梅文鼎传》则全面介绍了梅氏的生平和成就。

[3] 梅瑴成《兼济堂历算书刊缪》指出"此书蔡君玑先于康熙庚申岁刻于江宁"；《宣城梅氏历算丛书辑要》校阅助刻姓氏，则为"康熙二十□年"（"二十"后有空格）。

[4] 2005年9月5日，笔者陪同北京大学郭润涛和法国魏丕信教授到清华大学图书馆看书，并查阅清华大学善本书目所载梅文鼎算书，结果发现著录版本年代有误，目录所列书并非乾隆版，而是康熙年间李光地、金世扬的保定刻本，此外又有蔡璧所刻《中西算学通初集》和梅文鼎自刻《勿庵历算书目》，令我喜出望外，感谢清华大学冯立昇教授陪同进库，此后其学生童鸿钧对《中西算学通初集》进行了研究，他的另外一位学生高峰将《勿庵历算书目》加以系统整理，于2014年出版。

[5] 严敦杰：《梅文鼎的数学和天文学工作》，《自然科学史研究》1989年第2期，页99—107。

包括对《筹算》《笔算》《度算》《比例算》《方程论》《三角法举要》《几何摘要》《勾股测量》和《九数存古》九种书的介绍。据蔡璇《中西算学通》序(1680),可知九种书在此前都已成稿。梅文鼎撰书之主要目的是为了会通中西算学,平息当时中法和西法之争。在自序中,他批评习中法者"株守旧闻,遽斥西儒为异学",同时也批评习西法者鄙薄古法,"张皇过甚",无暇深考中算源流,导致"两家之说遂成隔碍"。梅文鼎后期的研究主要涉及球面三角学和几何学研究,他试图会通中西,其数学研究主要以西法为主,也参考了少数明代数学著作。明末清初传入西方几何学、三角术、对数等,和天文学中的球面天文学知识,以及一些新的推理方法,研究领域得以拓展,但梅文鼎仍保持了传统数学中《九章算术》和勾股的体系。

梅文鼎广为交友,虽在远道,也不耻下问。1687至1688年间,他至杭州,特意拜访了意大利耶稣会士殷铎泽(Prosper Intorcetta,1625—1696),并结交毛际可。1689年,梅文鼎又为访问南怀仁(Ferdinand Verbiest,1623—1688)到北京,遗憾的是南怀仁已在前一年去世。这年可算是他学术生命的转折点,之后的近三年间(1689—1691),恰逢康熙皇帝学习西学的高潮,传授数学的帝师有葡萄牙耶稣会士徐日昇(Tomás Pereira,1645—1708)、比利时耶稣会士安多(Antoine Thomas,1644—1709)、法国耶稣会士张诚(Jean-François Gerbillon,1654—1707)和白晋(Joachim Bouvet,1656—1730)。康熙学习数学的消息引起了文人学士的广泛关注。梅文鼎在京期间,还在1691年初拜访了安多,讨论田亩测量问题。当时,梅文鼎因擅长历算而名闻京城,并应邀参与修订《明史·历志》。他在京约四年间,期间顾祖禹、朱彝尊、阎若璩、万斯同、刘献廷、李光地、陆陇其、黄百家、赵执信、戴名世、徐善、方苞等学者名流争相和他往来。

李光地是清代名重一时的大臣,参与了许多御制著作的编纂,包括《朱子全书》《周易折中》《性理精义》等著作。他尽管没有主持历算著作《律历渊源》,但他培养的一些学生(如梅瑴成、魏廷珍、王兰生)则直接参与了汇编、分校的工作,这与李光地的幕后推动与支持有很大关系。实际上,早在李光地考中进士不久,就与传教士南怀仁有来往,讨论宇宙问题。而李光地热衷历算,则与康熙帝有密切关系。康熙二十八年(1689)二月二十七日,李光地随康熙皇帝第二次南巡,在南京观星台观测老人星,受到了皇帝的考问和责备,受此事件的刺激,回京后他即把梅文鼎迎入馆中[6],并亲自向梅氏学习数学。

1689年底至1691年间,是康熙皇帝热衷数学学习的时期,耶稣会士作为帝师轮流向康熙传授算术、几何学和代数学等内容。[7] 为了迎合康熙帝对数学的兴趣,像朝廷官员急于举荐擅长历算的人才。1691年底,康熙专门派人考察梅文鼎历算水平以及有关日影观测的知识,可能就是缘于李光地的推荐,可惜当时梅氏的表现令康熙帝颇为失望[8],况且他当时刊刻的只有介绍西方数学的《筹算》一书,创见不多,自然很难得到康熙帝的首肯。而在1687年,清代思想家方以智之子方中通《数度衍》二十四卷(1661序)刊成。[9] 此书主要仿九章体系,并参考了《几何原本》《同文算指》《比例规解》等西方数学著作和程大位的《算法统宗》等书,卷首之三中的"几何约"是对《几何原本》前6卷的改编。大约是康熙得知了此书刊印的消息,而方中通当时远在南方,于是有人将身在北京的"明经"、方中通之子方正珠推荐给皇帝。康熙三十一年正月初四日,康熙在乾清宫进行了日影观测,方正珠应邀在场,乘机将《数度衍》进呈皇帝。康熙帝还和他讨论了《九章算术》的一些问题,此事引起了不小的反响,不仅在场官员提及,梅文鼎的安

---

[6] 韩琦:《君主和布衣之间:李光地在康熙时代的活动及其对科学的影响》,《清华学报》(新竹)1996年12月,新26(4),页421—445。收入韩琦:《康熙皇帝·耶稣会士·科学传播》,北京:中国大百科全书出版社,2019。

[7] Isabelle Landry-Deron, *Les leçons de sciences occidentales de l'empereur de Chine Kangxi (1662-1722): Texte des Journaux des Pères Bouvet et Gerbillon.* Paris: EHESS, 1995.

[8] 韩琦:《科学、知识与权力:日影观测与康熙在历法改革中的作用》,《自然科学史研究》2011年第1期,页1—18。

[9] 方中通字位伯,号陪翁,安徽桐城人,自幼受家庭影响,对历算产生兴趣,1652-1653年在南京时,曾随传教士穆尼阁学习数学。参见《数度衍》卷首之三《几何约》,75页,康熙间胡氏继声堂刻本。1687年,方中通在女婿的帮助下,在广东刊刻了《数度衍》一书。

徽朋友朱书在《杜溪文稿》一书中也有专门记述[10]，消息此后也传到了方正珠的老家桐城县。

康熙三十二年，梅文鼎的历算成就虽已博得京城士人与官员的赞赏，但并没有获得皇帝的青睐便黯然离开北京，这一年，他请李光地为《历学疑问》作了序。次年，李光地提督顺天学政，康熙三十七年十二月(1699)，升任直隶巡抚(任期至1705年)，大约在康熙三十八年在保定刊成《历学疑问》。与《历学疑问》刊刻几乎同时，李光地之弟李鼎徵[11]在康熙三十七年着手刊刻《方程论》，次年撰序，在泉州刊印完成。此书是梅文鼎一生中最得意的著作之一，论稿成于康熙十一年冬，全书十三年完成，二十九年潘耒作序。最初阮于岳曾想刊刻，但未能成功。康熙三十八年，梅文鼎访问福建，曾打算拜访李鼎徵，但最后是否见面，尚待确证。但可以肯定的是，梅文鼎确实到了泉州，并参观了开元寺。[12]在康熙三十八年十二月(1700年初)，施闰章之子彦恪还撰写《征刻〈历算全书〉启》，呼吁刊刻梅文鼎的历算著作。可惜的是，目前我们还没有发现李鼎徵《方程论》康熙刊本，但从乾隆元年鹏翮堂版《方程论》中可见，此书有康熙己卯(1699)李鼎徵序、吴云序、康熙庚午(1690)潘耒序、梅文鼎康熙甲寅(1674)序和《方程论》发凡[13]，显然鹏翮堂本参考了李鼎徵的《方程论》刊本。

康熙四十一年(1702)十月，李光地以抚臣扈跸德州，进所刻《历学疑问》三卷。康熙对此书颇为赞赏，并称梅文鼎"此人用力深矣"，将书带回宫中，"仔细看阅"，并做了大量批注，第二年春发还李光地。1704年，李光地为此书新写了"恭记"，记述其事，并再次印刷，从此《历学疑问》被广为传播，成为文坛佳话。而在1702年12月，几乎与《历学疑问》的进呈同时，在安多的指导下，皇三子胤祉主持了自北京至霸州一度经线长度的测量。[14]在这次测量前后，安多编写了《测量高远仪器用法》。受此次测量的影响，康熙在1703年专门写了一篇讨论三角形的文章《御制三角形推算法论》，并于次年用满、汉两种文字刊刻问世，并四处宣传，影响甚广。[15]可见，传教士、大臣和康熙的所作所为，是互有因果关系的。

正是在这样的背景之下，为迎合康熙帝和朝廷之需，时任直隶巡抚的李光地再次邀请梅文鼎至保定传授数学，于是梅文鼎在1703年携孙子毂成北上。李光地的学生(魏廷珍、王兰生、王之锐、陈万策、徐用锡)、其子钟伦和梅毂成均随梅文鼎习算，梅文鼎之弟文鼐与梅文鼎之子以燕也到了保定。在李光地的赞助下，梅文鼎的五种历算书付梓，他的这批学生参与了校对工作。大约受《御制三角形推算法论》一文的刺激，李光地以最快的进度，在1705年春之前刊成《三角法举要》，并择机呈送皇帝，以赢得康熙的欢心。除此书之外，李光地刊刻的梅氏书还有《弧三角举要》《堑堵测量》《环中黍尺》《交食蒙求订补》四种。此外，受李光地的影响，三韩金世扬在保定官署也帮助刊刻了《历学骈枝》和《笔算》，扩大了梅文鼎的影响。康熙时代梅文鼎著作刊刻情况见表1.

10　朱书：《杜溪文稿》卷一，乾隆元年梨云阁刻本，《清代诗文集珍本丛刊》(第183册)，北京：国家图书馆出版社，2017，57—68页。

11　李鼎徵1691年在北京和梅文鼎有交往。

12　刘岩：《大山诗集》卷四，宣统二年寂园丛书铅印本。

13　2012年7月，应日本爱知大学葛谷登教授的邀请访问日本，期间查阅了日本国立公文书馆所藏梅文鼎历算著作，特致谢意。其中有乾隆元年鹏翮堂版《宣城梅氏算法丛书》共六册，吴门(苏州)环川张宗祯(安谷)刊，包括梅文鼎的《方程论》《少广拾遗》《交食蒙求》《交食管见》《冬至考》等五种历算著作，上有"鹏翮堂藏书"红章，又有"姑苏阊门外上塘义慈巷口东首萃秀堂发兑"红印戳。笔者在牛津大学馆亦见鹏翮堂版，为伟烈亚力旧藏。

14　韩琦、潘澍原：《康熙朝经线每度弧长标准的奠立：兼论耶稣会士安多与欧洲测量学在宫廷的传播》，《中国科技史杂志》2019年第3期，290—312页。

15　韩琦：《康熙帝之治术与"西学中源"说新论：〈御制三角形推算法论〉的成书及其背景》，《自然科学史研究》2016年第1期，1—9页。

表1 康熙时代梅文鼎著作刊刻情况一览表

书名	序	刊刻者、刊刻地	校对者
筹算	康熙戊午(1678)梅文鼎自序	蔡璿庚申刻于江宁	
中西算学通	康熙庚申蔡璿序、方中通序、康熙庚申梅文鼎自序	蔡璿庚申刻于江宁	
历学疑问	康熙癸酉李光地序;甲申李光地恭记	李光地刻于保定。康熙壬午(1702)进呈	安溪李光墺广卿、李光型仪卿
方程论	李鼎徵康熙己卯序、吴云序、康熙庚午潘耒序、梅文鼎康熙甲寅序	李鼎徵刻于泉州。年希尧再刻	
三角法举要	刻本康熙乙酉(1705)进呈	李光地刻于保定	受业宿迁徐用锡坛长、安溪李锺伦世得、陈万策对初、景州魏廷珍君璧
弧三角举要	康熙二十三年梅文鼎序	李光地刻于保定	梅以燕正谋、梅瑴成玉汝、受业宿迁徐用锡坛长、安溪李锺伦世得、李鑑世宪、陈万策对初、景州魏廷珍君璧、河间王之锐仲颖、交河王兰生振声
堑堵测量		李光地刻于保定	同上
环中黍尺	康熙三十九年梅文鼎序	李光地刻于保定	同上
交食蒙求订补		李光地刻于保定	同上
历学骈枝	康熙元年梅文鼎序	金世扬刻于保定	梅以燕正谋、梅瑴成玉汝、受业宿迁徐用锡坛长、安溪李锺伦世得、李鑑世宪、陈万策对初、景州魏廷珍君璧、常熟陈汝楫季方、河间王之锐仲颖、交河王兰生振声
笔算	康熙四十五年金世扬序、康熙癸酉梅文鼎自序	金世扬刻于保定。年希尧再刻于金陵	
勿庵历算书目		自刻	
度算释例	年希尧康熙丁酉序	年希尧刻于金陵	
少广拾遗		家刻	
交会管见		家刻	
春秋以来冬至考		家刻	

康熙四十四年(1705)可说是梅文鼎人生最为荣耀的时刻。是年二月,康熙"南巡狩,李光地以抚臣扈从。上问:'汝前道宣城处士梅文鼎者,今焉在?'臣地以'尚留臣署'对。上曰:'朕归时,汝与偕来,朕将面见。'"闰四月,康熙帝一连三天召见梅文鼎于临清州御舟中,"临辞,特赐四大颜字,曰'绩学参微',则是月二十八日也。"[16]当时在场的人除李光地之外,还有督学杨名时、天津道蒋陈锡。[17]接见时,梅文鼎将刚刚刊刻的《三角法举要》进呈康熙,显然是回应康熙的短文《御制三角形推算法论》,目的昭然若揭。此事令梅文鼎声名大噪,一时间文人争相与之结交,并写诗唱和,竭尽恭维赞美之能事。康熙接见梅文鼎,以及庙堂对历算的支持,这一故事在民间广为传播,营造了民间学习历算的风气,甚至可以说乾嘉学派对历算研究的重视,也无疑受到了康熙帝支持历算之事的影响。同年,李光地升任大学士。次年,梅文鼎返回江南,之后的近十年时间,他没有新的著作刊刻。

---

16 梅文鼎:《绩学堂诗文钞》李光地恭记。
17 梅文鼎:《绩学堂诗钞》卷四。

梅文鼎的晚年仍然颇得大臣的宠爱。康熙五十六年(1717)初,年希尧任职金陵藩署,与梅文鼎多有来往,讨论比例规问题,协助梅文鼎刊刻《度算释例》,并重刊《笔算》。年希尧,字允恭,汉军镶黄旗人,康熙五十年升大名道,五十二年任广西按察使司按察使,五十五至五十九年为安徽布政使,五十九年夏被革职,六十一年以布政使衔署广东巡抚,与外国人多有交往。雍正三年,任工部右侍郎,四年任内务府总管,并管理淮安宿迁关务,还曾负责景德镇御窑的烧造。

年希尧对历算颇有兴趣,"以西人测算之切要者,摘录刊布",著有《测算刀圭》三卷(康熙五十七年序刊本),即《三角法摘要》《八线真数表》《八线假数表》;又刊有《对数广运》和《面体比例便览》(雍正十三年序刊本),年氏所著书大体根据康熙时宫廷数学手稿编写而成。《三角法摘要》开头有年希尧康熙五十七年(1718)秋所写序言,可能由梅文鼎代笔。[18]雍正年间,年氏在北京时与传教士郎世宁(Giuseppe Castiglione,1688—1766)多有来往,并刊刻有《视学》。年希尧还约请"监司王公希舜、魏公荔彤同任剞劂,之后才刻完《笔算》《方程论》数种,而年公被议以去"。[19]

大约从康熙五十七年到雍正二年,曾任江苏常镇道和按察使的魏荔彤组织了《兼济堂历算丛书》的刊刻,其子乾敦、士敏、士说参与了丛书的编校工作,但最主要工作则由无锡人杨作枚担任。梅毂成因杨作枚"素好历算之学,尝往来余家,予曾属魏公任以校对",而梅文鼎已刻未刻诸稿则由梅毂成之弟玕成提供。杨作枚对丛书的校对不够认真,错讹不少,加之书中加入了自己的作品(如《割圆八线表根》),为此遭到梅毂成的诟病。值得指出的是,书中个别内容,如《勾股阐微》后所附"通率表",并不是梅文鼎的作品,而应当是蒙养斋算学馆开馆时,梅毂成从内廷抄录的。[20]

雍正元年,《历算丛书》已经大体刊成。到了第二年,正式刊成定本,日本国立公文书馆(原内阁文库)藏有《历算丛书》,扉页题"柏乡魏念庭辑刊""雍正二年镌",上有"兼济堂藏板"红章。[21]从内容看,雍正二年本新增《割圆八线之表》两册,还有杨作枚《三角法会编》(康熙癸巳自序)。现存常见的雍正元年本,在不少地方与雍正二年刻本有差异,目录多有不同[22],特别是校对人员有较大改动,现以《解八线割圆之根》为例,将两个版本的人名对照见表2.

表 2

《历算丛书》雍正二年版	《历算丛书》雍正元年版
锡山杨作枚学山甫著	宣城梅文鼎定九著
柏乡魏荔彤念庭辑	男以燕正谋参
男乾敦一元、士敏仲文、士说崇宽	孙毂成玉汝、玕成肩琳
宣城梅毂成玉汝、玕成肩琳	柏乡魏荔彤念庭辑
毗陵钱松期人岳	男乾敦一元、士敏仲文、士说崇宽同校
锡山华希闵豫原、秦轩然二南	锡山后学杨作枚学山订补
受业武陵胡君福似孙同校	

因为《解八线割圆之根》实际上并非梅文鼎所著,而雍正元年版归于梅氏,令梅毂成颇为不满,于是雍正二年的版本,被改为杨作枚著,并修改了协助校对的人员。魏荔彤在江苏时,与梅文鼎族孙竹峰相

---

18 此序也收入梅文鼎《绩学堂文钞》卷二。
19 梅毂成:《兼济堂历算书刊缪》引,乾隆四年刊本,湖北图书馆藏。日本国立公文书馆藏有抄本。
20 《增删算法统宗》是梅毂成的晚年之作,刊刻后流传很广,此书增加了部分从蒙养斋获得的知识。
21 梅文鼎《历算全书》(雍正二年版)在享保十一年(1726)经海舶东传日本长崎,受到数学家建部贤弘等重视,并命弟子中根元圭誊写一部献给将军,师徒二人还受命翻译此书,献给八代将军德川吉忠,为此得到了幕府的表彰。关于梅文鼎著作在日本的流传,以及雍正元年、二年《历算全书》的内容比较,参见小林龙彦:《德川日本对汉译西洋历算书的受容》,上海:上海交通大学出版社,2019,249页;亦可参见其之前的文章:《关于红叶山文库收藏的梅文鼎著作》,载日文版《科学史研究》,41(2002),26—34页。
22 复旦大学图书馆古籍部所藏两部雍正元年《历算全书》,目录也不尽相同,可见刻版随时在修改。

好,在 1729 年稍前回到北方之前,把书版转让给了梅竹峰。[23]

梅文鼎之孙毂成,字玉汝,号循斋,又号柳下居士。父以燕,早卒,自幼跟祖父文鼎学习天文历算,1703 至 1706 年间,随祖父在保定三年,与陈万策、魏廷珍等时相过从。经陈厚耀推荐[24],康熙五十一年(1712)六月初三日,李光地向江西巡抚郎廷极(1663—1715)之子传旨:"朕近日闻得梅文鼎之孙算法颇好,虽不知学问深浅,命他来京看看。钦此。"于是由郎廷极之子派家人护送进京,又前赴行在(热河)。[25]梅毂成至京后,被赐为举人。1715 年成进士,在畅春园蒙养斋学习,主持《数理精蕴》《钦若历书》的编纂。梅毂成因屡受清廷的恩泽,平步青云,官运亨通,曾任翰林院编修、顺天府府丞、都察院左副都御史、刑部右侍郎等职。雍正乾隆时又参与《历象考成后编》《仪象考成》和《大清国史天文志》的编纂。乾隆帝南巡时,他还于乾隆二十七年二月八日在南京受到接见。

鉴于兼济堂《历算全书》"谬舛盈纸",以及杨作枚在书中加入自己的著作,梅毂成十分不悦。魏荔彤和杨作枚过世后,梅毂成有感于兼济堂的板片曾一度"质他姓,不可得而修改,则传讹沿误,后学何赖焉?"于是在乾隆四年(1739)撰《兼济堂历算书刊缪》,逐条列举校刊错误。在《增删算法统宗》"国朝算学书目"中,他曾再次提及:"因魏公所刻《历算全书》编次缪乱,重为厘正,汰其伪附,去其重复,正其鲁鱼,而为是书。"于是对梅文鼎的著作重新加以校对,在乾隆十年序刊《宣城梅氏历算丛书辑要》六十二卷,收录梅文鼎算书十三种,天文历法著作十种,共六十卷,是为"承学堂"版。[26]并将自己的著作《赤水遗珍》《操缦卮言》各一卷附于丛书之后(卷六十一、六十二)。

现存李光地、金铁山在保定的刻本已十分少见,就笔者所知,日本国立公文书馆藏有《历学全书》,包括《历学疑问》三卷、《历学骈枝》四卷、《堑堵测量》二卷、《环中黍尺》五卷、《弧三角举要》五卷、《笔算》五卷、《三角法举要》五卷、《交食蒙求订补》二卷等八种,此丛书刷印精良,当为初印本。美国华盛顿国会图书馆也藏有上述八种,此外还有《历象本要》(有"明善堂览书画印记",为怡亲王弘晓藏书)[27],由同治皇帝在 1869 年 6 月作为礼物送给美国政府,成为美国国会图书馆最早的中文藏书。在国内,清华大学除缺藏《交食蒙求订补》二卷外,其余所藏八种与美国国会图书馆相同,此外还多《中西算学通初集》和《勿庵历算书目》这两种稀见的康熙刻本,各书均有"安乐堂藏书记"藏书章(皇十三子胤祥藏书)。[28]而李光地在保定所刻的板片,后来"携归安溪,不得流通"[29],归其家族保存,后人曾根据这些板片重新刷印,以《梅氏历学六种》之名出版,扉页题"安溪李氏校刊",包括《历学骈枝》[30]《交食蒙求订补》《环中黍尺》《弧三角举要》《三角法举要》《堑堵测量》。此丛书书板多有缺损,刷印漫患,原为李俨先生旧藏,现藏中国科学院自然科学史研究所图书馆。

明清之际是西学传入中国的关键时期,受杨光先反教案和日影观测事件的影响,康熙重视数学的学

23　乾隆己巳(1746),梅竹峰之子汝培又"命工补缀,复还旧观",再次刷印。咸丰九年,梅氏族裔梅体萱又在苏州得到残缺板片,"促工补刻",书后有跋一则,记录了这段历史。

24　见《文峰梅氏宗谱》,光绪十八年刘坤一序刻本。

25　《宫中档康熙朝奏折》第 3 辑,台北:"国立"故宫博物院,1976 年,822 页。

26　关于"承学堂"之名的来由,梅毂成曾提到:"余小子自幼侍先徵君,南北东西,未离函丈,稍能窃取余绪。后赴召内庭,得读中秘书,蒙圣主仁皇帝耳提面命,遂充蒙养斋《律历渊源》总裁,故于此道略知途径。历事三朝,洊登宪府,屡蒙圣天子殷殷垂训,谓家学不可失,宜传子孙,钦遵不敢忘。"(梅毂成《增删算法统宗》凡例后自识语)乾隆十年承学堂刊本现在十分稀见,不知何故未能广为流通。乾隆二十六年,《梅氏丛书辑要》重新刊刻,亦称"承学堂"版,序言亦为梅毂成所撰,但文字多有所删节,此本是梅氏族人所为还是书贾所刻,待考。咸丰时,因太平天国事起,乾隆二十六年板片被毁;同治十三年,梅文鼎七世孙缵高根据原书重新雕版印刷(颐园刊本)。晚清随着西方石印术的传入和西学研究热潮的兴起,梅氏的历算著作再次受到关注,梅氏丛书以小开本印刷,更便于士子携带,从而促进了数学的普及,现有上海龙文书局、敦怀书屋石印本等传世。

27　此书康熙刻本未署作者,后有 1742 年梅毂成序刊本,作者归于李光地名下。或以为此书原为杨文言所作。

28　北京大学图书馆所藏个别梅文鼎历算著作也有"安乐堂藏书记"章。国家图书馆藏有怡府书目,原为郑振铎先生旧藏,其中收录《中西算学通》《历学疑问》和康熙时代宫廷编纂的历算著作。

29　梅毂成《兼济堂历算书刊缪》引,乾隆四年刊本。

30　据《勿庵历算书目》和《兼济堂历算书刊缪》,《历学骈枝》为金世扬所刻。

习,并将其用于国家的治理。清朝一些大臣受此影响,也开始学习西学,以迎合康熙所好,并支持民间的历算家,李光地对刊印梅文鼎著作的赞助,正是受这一政治氛围的影响。即使在梅文鼎的晚年,仍有朝廷大臣钟情梅氏的历算著作,魏荔彤刊刻兼济堂《梅氏历算全书》是受到上司年希尧的约请,这与金世扬和李光地在保定对梅文鼎著作的刊刻,情况类似,只是地点不同,书籍不同而已。不同的官员在不同的地点,对同一位布衣历算家的支持,背后无疑都受到了皇帝的影响。通过对梅文鼎历算著作刊刻过程的不同时间点的细致分析,可以看出这些书籍的刊印与政治、皇权密切关联。康熙对历算的爱好,以及大臣为了迎合康熙的需求,使得梅文鼎的历算著作得以问世,进而对清代数学的发展产生了深远的影响;同时,也可以看出传教士、皇帝、梅文鼎著作的写作、刊印也息息相关,安多的《测量高远仪器用法》,康熙的《御制三角形推算法论》,乃至梅文鼎的《三角法举要》,都涉及三角的问题,这三种著作在大约两年的时间内先后推出,显然互有影响。李光地赞助刊刻《三角法举要》,梅文鼎进而进呈皇帝,迎合康熙帝的意图十分明显。因此我们不仅要充分掌握中文文献,也要借助西文文献,才能充分理解梅文鼎历算著作刊印背后的复杂的人际网络,并还原历史的真相。

〔附记:此文完稿于2020年春,删减后作为导言收入《梅文鼎全集》。〕

方中通交友"六君子"考述

纪志刚　（上海交通大学科学史与科学文化研究院）

摘要　方中通《中西算学通》序(1680年)记叙了早年研习历算获交的六位友人，即：汤濩、薛凤祚、游艺、揭暄、丘维屏和梅文鼎。后在其著《数度衍》(1687年刊刻)中尊此六人为"六君子"，发愿"以志不忘"。本文通过对"六君子"的生平传记资料的勾陈发掘，可见他们与方家有着极深的学术交往，或受到方以智(方中通之父)所称赞，或拜方以智为师("强半游先君门")，"六君子"之间或书信往来，或互赠序言，展示出明末清初数学社会史的文化生态。更有意义的是，方中通在《中西算学通》序中提出"九章皆勾股"，认为学术之要在于创新："始期能因，继期能创"，并强调"道寓于器，理藏于数"，希冀借九数沟通中西，倡实学以前民用。

关键词　方中通；汤濩；薛凤祚；游艺；揭暄；丘维屏；梅文鼎；《中西算学通》序

1680年(清康熙十九年，庚申)梅文鼎(1633—1721)将其所著《勿庵筹算》《勿庵笔算》《勿庵度算》《比例数解》《三角法举要》《方程论》《几何摘要》《勾股测量》和《九数存古》9种算书汇编为《中西算学通》。[2]友人蔡壡(字玑先，江宁人，生卒年不详)"取而授诸梓，以广其传"。[3]梅文鼎请方中通作序，方中通(1634—1698)慨然应允，写下了《中西算学通》序。方中通在序言中开篇直言治学经历中得交六人：

> 当吾世而言历算之绝学，通得交者六人：汤子圣弘、薛子仪甫、游子子六、揭子子宣、丘子邦士与梅子定九也。[4]

早在1661年(清顺治十八年，辛丑)，方中通就已著成《数度衍》，但是书却延宕至1687年方付梓刊刻。在其书《凡例》中，方中通言道：

> ……校阅诸子不能悉载，同学象数而辩难讨论者，则惟揭子子宣、梅子定九、薛子仪甫、汤子圣弘、游子子六、丘子邦士六君子居多。今皆各有著述，为方内所珍重。通谨书其姓氏，以志不忘云。[5]

这次，方中通则尊汤、薛、游、揭、丘、梅为"六君子"。因此，方中通与此"六君子"的交友，是明末清初数学社会史的一个值得考察的个案。

一、汤、薛、游、揭、丘、梅"六君子"生平简述

本节先作汤、薛、游、揭、丘、梅六人的生平简述，除薛凤祚、梅文鼎外，其余四人在文献中的记载相当

1　基金项目：国家社会科学基金"汉译《几何原本》的版本整理与翻译研究"，批准号：21BZS021。
2　童庆均，冯立昇，梅文鼎《中西算学通》探原，内蒙古师范大学学报（自然科学汉文版），2007，36(6)：716－720页。
3　[清]蔡壡，梅定九《中西算学通》叙，[清]梅文鼎著，韩琦整理，《梅文鼎全集》，第一册，合肥，黄山书社，2020年，第225页。
4　[清]方中通，《中西算学通》序，[清]梅文鼎著，韩琦整理，《梅文鼎全集》，第一册，合肥，黄山书社，2020年，第227页。
5　[清]方中通，《数度衍·凡例》，光绪十六年(1890)太原王氏志古堂成都重校刊本。

简略,亦多陈陈相因。如《清史稿》"畴人"收有薛凤祚、梅文鼎、揭暄(附在方中通下),《畴人传》各编亦未收汤濩、丘维屏。以下对"六君子"的介绍根据多种文献蒐集而成[6],并侧重"六君子"与方家的学术联系。

汤濩,字圣弘(为避讳又称圣宏),生卒年不详。据《六合县志》"文苑·汤濩传"载:

> 汤濩,字圣宏,原籍吴人。居六合,与弟沐俱以诗名。唱和数百首。尤精天文历法。是时言算法者,有宣城梅氏,大兴何氏、王氏,皆未兴,而濩独为之先,亦特立之士。[7]

汤濩于音律亦有研究,《六合县续志稿》"艺文志"记载汤濩有《音声定位图》《言树堂集韵学》。顾炎武(1613—1682,字宁人)曾致函汤濩,请其为所著《音学五书》指正:

> ……拙著《音统》已改名《音学五书》,以鬻产之资,付力臣兄刻之淮上,尚需改定,故未印出,先以序目请正。内诗本音已毕工,又有《下学指南》一帙,便中索之清江,即可得也。《日知录》续已改定为三十卷,前本复有增损,且可勿刻。期于二载之内,南来一奉话言,或有便人至金陵,当令叩宅也。率尔不尽。[8]

顾炎武去世后,汤濩作诗怀念:

怀顾宁人[9]

> 虎头应复让君痴,儒侠僧樵事事宜;
> 千百国风存野记,十三陵树补新诗。
> 因声小悟殊堪喜,姓字频更莫浪疑,
> 怀友句成反自愧,半函烟雨隔秋思。

《六合县续志稿》卷十五"艺文志"中还记载"(汤濩)尤精天文、六书,桐城方以智、山阳张弨往复删订。"可见,汤濩与方以智(161—1671)已有学术交往。梅文鼎亦是汤濩好友。梅氏《绩学堂诗钞》"读栗亭诗有怀东西洞庭"[10]云:

> 我友汤圣弘,昔家太湖里。语我洞庭山,东西接天起。
> 今日诵新诗,选胜一何美。安能续快游,鼓棹乘春水。
> 放歌缥缈颠,濯足渔山趾。坐听胥江涛,泠泠清吾耳。

薛凤祚(1600—1680,字仪甫)号寄斋,山东益都(今淄博市临淄区金岭镇)人。《清史稿》、阮元《畴人传》、钱仪吉《碑集传》均有记载。而清毛永柏等修、刘耀春撰《青州府志》记述为详。录之如下。

> 薛凤祚,字仪甫。近洙子。明生员,少承家学,以孝友谦让闻于乡。定与鹿善继、容城孙奇逢讲学北方。凤祚往从之游,两家学本姚江(即王守仁),尝慨然欲有建树于时。凤祚得其传,又病后之宗姚江者内心性,而外学问,无致用之实。故其学无所不究。而尤以天文名于海内。……凤祚初学历法于魏文魁,主持旧法。及见西洋穆尼阁于江宁,尽得其术。既又从汤道未

---

[6] 有关汤濩、薛凤祚、揭暄、丘维屏等人事迹,可参阅:冯锦荣《方中通及其〈数度衍〉》,《论衡》,1995年2卷1期,第123—204页。

[7] [清]谢延庚等修,[清]贺廷寿等纂:《光绪六合县志》,光绪十年(1884)刊本,现收入《中国地方志集成》之《江苏府县志辑》,第6册,南京:江苏古籍出版社,1991年,第20页上。

[8] [清]顾炎武,《与汤圣弘》,载《传世藏书·集成·别集12顾亭林集》,海口:海南国际新闻出版中心,1996年,第124页。

[9] [民国]陈田辑,《明诗纪事》187卷·辛籤卷三十一,清光绪二十五年(1899)贵阳陈氏听诗斋刻本。

[10] [清]梅文鼎著,韩琦整理,《梅文鼎全集》,第八册,合肥,黄山书社,2020年,第263页。

（即汤若望）游，所学日精。而未尝挟其术而干于时，时亦不能用。河道总督王光裕耳凤祚名，折节下之，用佐治河修守之事，漕河交济之宜，莫不犁然有当。当事卒亦无荐引者，故以著述老。……[11]

据记载，顺治五年（1648），薛凤祚撰述《天学真原》，顺治九年（1652），薛凤祚续译。康熙三年（1664），薛凤祚将当时各家历算方法、实用科学方面的知识及其本人的天文著作汇集为《天学会通》刊行于世。

梅文鼎对薛凤祚给予了很高评价。曾作"寄怀青州薛仪甫先生"四首[12]，诗中有论：

……
君子任名教，而无章句拘。著撰极高深，事理兼陈敷。
当世有同方，千里良非孤。引领青齐间，渺渺瞻长途。
……

游艺，《畴人传》对其生平记述非常简略：

游艺，字子六，建宁人也。著有《天经或问》前集四卷，皆设为问答，以推阐天地之象，大旨以西法为宗。与揭暄相友善，故集中多取其说。[13]

冯锦荣撰写《天经或问提要》，对游艺生平记载比较详细，摘编如下：

游艺，字子六，号岱峰。福建建阳崇化里人。少年丧父，由母亲抚养成人。年轻时从黄道周（1585—1646）问学，留意天学。入清以后，游艺尝任福州府建安县训导，顺治元年至六年（1644—1649）随熊明遇学习天算之学。大约顺治十七年（1660）左右，游艺读桐城方氏《易》学著作，并致书方以智请教《易》理。康熙六年（1667）方以智前往建阳、建宁主持刻印著作之事，游艺追随方氏左右，并执弟子礼，请求方氏为其《天经或问前集》鉴定和赐序。……[14]

今传抄本《天经或问前集》有方以智序。可见，游艺与方家的交往素有渊源。

揭暄（约1610—1702，或作1613—1695），字子宣，江西广昌人。《畴人传》有其传记，甚是简略。《广昌志·文学传》称揭暄"少颖悟，通天人之学。"同时又"有奇气，好论兵，慷慨自认"。清人入关后，率众抵抗于赣、闽之间，辅佐过南明隆武政权（1645—1647）。清顺治十六年（1659）方以智禅游江西，引徒谈经，揭暄始与方氏父子交游论学，并对方以智执弟子礼。揭暄曾为方以智刊《通雅》，校《物理小识》。又与方中通讨论"光影肥瘦""古今岁差"，及天体运行机制等问题，写成《揭方问对》……。著述中影响最大是《璇玑遗述》。[15]

丘维屏（1614—1679），字邦士，江西赣州府宁都县人。《江西通志》记载如下：

维屏少孤，弱冠为明诸生。值国变，避乱翠微峰，同志数人讲习于《易》堂故居。邑之河东多古松，望之苍霭无际，维屏著书其下，号曰松下先生。其学原本六经，通畴人书，旁及泰西之说，了然心目。……[16]

---

[11] ［清］毛永柏等修、刘耀春撰，《青州府志》卷46，人物传·国朝薛凤祚。
[12] ［清］梅文鼎著，韩琦整理，《梅文鼎全集》，第八册，合肥，黄山书社，2020年，第255页。
[13] 冯立昇等，《畴人传合编校注》，郑州：中州古籍出版社，2012年，第321页。
[14] 冯锦荣，《天经或问提要》，载《中国科学技术典籍通汇·天文卷》，第六册，济南：河南教育出版社，1993年，第153页。
[15] 石云里，《璇玑遗述提要》，载《中国科学技术典籍通汇·天文卷》，第六册，济南：河南教育出版社，1993年，第275页。
[16] ［清］刘坤一等修，［清］赵之谦等纂，《江西通志》卷一百六十九·列传，光绪七年（1891）刻本。

清杭世骏(1695—1773)《道古堂集》又称：

> ……。晚尤精泰西算,易数、历法皆不假师授,冥思力索而得之。方以智以僧服来《易》堂,尝与布算,退而谓人曰:"此神人也。"[17]

梅文鼎(1633—1721),字定九,号勿庵,安徽宣城人。梅文鼎九岁熟读五经,随祖父研读《易经》。年轻时习《大统历》,著有《历学骈枝》(1662)。康熙五年(1666)到南京参加乡试,之后在十四至十六年间(1675—1677),多次游历南京,广交朋友,在此期间得交方氏三兄弟[18],结识藏书家黄虞稷,到黄家看书、抄书,得以读到宋刻残本《九章算术》。康熙十九年(1680),梅文鼎再次到南京,下榻蔡玑先之观行堂,正是在这一年,蔡氏为梅文鼎刊刻了《中西算学通初集》。康熙四十四年(1705),康熙在南巡返京途中召见梅文鼎,连续三日在御舟中畅谈天文、数学,特书"绩学参微"予以表彰。"御舟召见"令梅文鼎声名大噪,也推动了民间研习历算的风气。梅文鼎的主要天文与数学著作都被收入《梅勿庵先生历算全书》(1723)和《梅氏丛书辑要》(1759)中。他的诗文则辑录成《绩学堂诗文钞》(1757)刊刻。梅文鼎倾慕方家《易》学渊源,服膺方以智的"易学"造诣,但却"未获浮公(即方以智)法席",深以为憾,写有"浮山大师哀辞"二首。梅文鼎与方氏三兄弟多有书信往来,互致诗文。如梅文鼎《寄方位伯》[19]五首之二:

> 中丞廷尉有渊源,群从于今家学传。
> 握手秦淮先后至,知名皖上兄弟贤。
> 殷勤两月书频及,珍重千秋序一篇。
> 相讯年来将北辙,可能联辔帝城边。

方中通曾祖方大镇(1560—1629)官至廷尉,祖父方孔炤(1590—1655)官至中丞,梅诗"中丞""廷尉"指方中通家学渊源。"序一篇"即指梅文鼎请方中通为其著《中西算学通》作序,正是此篇序言,引出了"六君子"的话题。

二、方中通与"六君子"之交游

方中通称汤、薛、游、揭、丘、梅为"六君子",并发愿"以志不忘",[20]六人对方中通的学术成长产生了很大影响。如方中通在《中西算学通》序的记述:

> 通少嗜象数,初讯《授时》于汤子。已与薛子游泰西穆先生所,适刊其《天步真原》成,语通,喜而交焉。嗣入都,闻之道未汤先生,始知游子精西历,获读《天经或问》,屡书往复辨难,然犹迄今神交,未一见。及省亲旴江,而逢揭子,《写天新语》一书多深湛之思,质测旁征,剖析无留义。丘子则遇于芝山,览所衍《倚数引申图》,论三昼夜,往往悟合。最后得交梅子,交十五年,而会于金陵者四,方慨聚晤之难,顾以视游子与汤子、薛子、揭子、丘子为幸焉。[21]

方中通首先记述他与汤濩的交往,是向汤濩学习《授时历》。前节汤濩传记中已有其"尤精天文"的记载。方以智对汤濩多有赞誉,如其《物理小识》称:

---

17 [清]杭世骏撰,《道古堂集》76卷·文集卷三十一,清乾隆四十一年(1776)刻,光绪十四年(1888)汪曾唯修本。
18 方以智有三子:长子方中德(1632—?),字田伯,号依岩;次子方中通(1634—1698),字位伯(白),晚号陪翁;三子方中履(1638—1689),字素伯,号合山。
19 [清]梅文鼎著,韩琦整理,《梅文鼎全集》,第八册,合肥:黄山书社,2020年,第251页。
20 [清]方中通,《数度衍》,光绪十六年(1890)太原王氏志古堂成都重校刊本。
21 [清]方中通,《中西算学通》序,[清]梅文鼎著,韩琦整理,《梅文鼎全集》,第一册,合肥,黄山书社,2020年,第227页。

> 六合汤圣弘，好读书，知《授时历》，与黄俞邰善。[22]

黄俞邰即方以智的学生黄虞稷(1629—1691)。黄虞稷与江南藏书家丁雄飞(字菡生，1605—?，江宁人)共创"古欢社"，二人尽出家藏秘本，"社员"互通有无，相与问难，参订发明。1678年梅文鼎到南京应乡试时曾到黄虞稷家中翻阅残宋本《九章算术》。[23]方以智称赞汤濩"知《授时历》"，所以方中通向汤濩学习《授时历》的推算方法，当在情理之中。

1645年(顺治二年)波兰传教士穆尼阁(Nikolaus Smogulecki, 1610—1656)抵达澳门，翌年在江南传教。大约1648年，穆尼阁受中国副教区南部传教区之副会长艾儒略(Giulio Aleni, 1582—1649)派遣至南京。据薛凤祚《天步真原·人命部》中记载："壬辰(顺治九年，1652)予来白下(即南京)，暨西儒穆先生闲居讲译，详悉参restaurants，益以愚见。得其理，为旧法所未及者数种。"[24]方中通曾有诗记述他与薛凤祚的相识，继而结交穆尼阁。

> 喜遇薛仪甫同受西洋穆先生历算[25]
> 参差看七政，不解古今疑。
> 共道天问难，谁云日可追。
> 偶因同调至，得与异人期。
> 我欲方平子，山中造浑仪。

穆尼阁对方中通的影响甚大，方中通《几何约》最后有一段注记：

> 西学莫精于象数，象数莫精于几何。余初读，三过而不解。忽秉烛玩之，竟夜而悟。明日质诸穆师，极蒙许可。凡制器尚象、开物成务，以前民用，以利出入，尽乎此矣。故约而记之于此。[26]

方中通的《几何约》对《几何原本》的公理化体系结构进行了比较大的改动，这种逻辑结构上的改动在古今中外诸多《几何原本》阐释著作中可谓绝无仅有。安国风认为"《几何约》中最令人感兴趣的地方是对'基本原理'做了重新编排"。[27]在《几何约》中，或依照方中通对《几何原本》的理解重新进行编排，或基于当时学者对几何学掌握程度做出简化。比如以"名目"替代"界说"，将"公论""求作"划归于"说"，以"论"统摄"命题"，但却"述而不证"。这种做法却得到穆尼阁的赞许("极蒙许可")。方中通早年从汤若望(Johann Adam Schall von Bell, 1592—1666，字道未)处得知游艺："嗣入都，闻之道未汤先生，始知游子精西历。"大约康熙十四年(1675)，游艺撰成《天经或问前集》。前节游艺小传中述及约康熙六年(1667)方以智游建阳、建宁，游艺追随方氏左右，并执弟子礼，请方以智为其《天经或问前集》鉴定和赐序。方中通或从父亲处得读游艺的《天经或问》，便与游艺"屡书往复辨难，然犹迄今神交，未一见"。可见，方中通与游艺多通过书信交往，未曾晤面。

大约1659年，方以智禅游江西，居停广昌(即盱江)时[28]，揭暄慕名拜见，对方以智执弟子礼。方中

---

[22] [清]方以智，《物理小识》卷一，三十五a，汤圣弘，清光绪十年(1884)宁静堂重刻本。
[23] 钱宝琮，《九章算术》提要，载钱宝琮点校，《算经十书》，北京：中华书局，1963年，第87—88页。
[24] 穆尼阁述，[清]薛凤祚译，《天步真原》，清道光年间钱熙祚校刊《守山阁丛书》本。
[25] [清]方中通，《陪集·陪诗》卷一，继声堂藏版，《清代诗文集汇编》133册，上海：上海古籍出版社，2010年，第71页。
[26] [清]方中通，《数度衍·几何约》，卷首之三，靖玉树编勘，《中国历代算学集成》(中)，济南：山东人民出版社，1994年，第2621页。
[27] [荷]安国风著，纪志刚等译，《欧几里得在中国：汉译〈几何原本〉的源流与影响》，南京：江苏人民出版社，2009年，第396页。
[28] 盱江发源于江西省抚州市广昌县驿前镇血木岭，流经广昌、南丰、南城、临川、进贤、南昌，在南昌市滕王阁附近汇入赣江，总长约四百千米。广昌段称盱江，南丰段称盱江及旴江，南城段称盱江。

通与其弟方中履(字素伯,号合山)同赴旴江省亲(《陪集》),得交揭暄("及省亲旴江,而逢揭子")。揭暄与方氏父子交游论学,与方中通讨论"光影肥瘦""古今岁差",及天体运行机制等问题,写成《揭方问对》。不幸的是康熙二十五年(1686)方中通家中遭火,《揭方问对》以及《易经深浅说》《四艺略》《数度衍》卷首第三卷《重学解》等书稿不幸被焚。光绪庚寅(1890)成都志古堂刻本《数度衍·外序》载有揭暄的"序"。

揭暄《璇玑遗述》首刊于康熙十四年(1675),此版今极为罕见。常见有乾隆三十年(1765)刻十卷本,以及光绪二十五年(1899)《刻鹄斋丛书》七卷本。《刻鹄斋丛书》本前有方以智、丘邦士、甘京和方中通等人的序言。方中通在序言中记载了他与揭暄相互问难后的感受:

> ……及遇子宣,以素所疑难者质问子宣,辄为剖析无留意,豁然万里一气,万数一理,万种之动皆由一动,纱出参差,指掌犁然也。[29]

方中通记述他与丘维屏的交往是:"丘子则遇于芝山,览所衍《倚数引申图》,论三昼夜,往往悟合。"寥寥数语,却含义深蕴。"倚数"出自"《易》曰:参天两地而倚数"。丘维屏为"易堂九子"[30],于《易》学造诣颇深。方家世代传《易》,方中通自述"奉余易象本家传",可见家学渊源。方中通与丘维屏在《易》学上有很多共鸣,方有"论三昼夜,往往悟合"。遗憾的是,丘维屏的《倚数引申图》今不见史籍记载。方中通亦有诗赠丘维屏:

> 芝山赠丘邦士[31]
> 绝学惟君好,翩然道貌殊。三才应在抱,六艺始成儒。
> 白业何穷达,苍天任有无。违时还用拙,不礙指为迂。

方中通与梅文鼎结交虽晚,但交往时间最久,面晤次数也最多:"最后得交梅子,交十五年,而会于金陵者四,方慨聚晤之难,顾以视游子与汤子、薛子、揭子、丘子为幸焉。"方中通《中西算学通》序做于康熙十九年(1680),据此推之二人初交当在康熙五年(1666),是年梅文鼎在南京参加乡试。

方以智获知梅文鼎天文历算造诣不凡,晚年向梅文鼎函索其历算著作。梅文鼎对此十分感佩,但未能得晤方以智,深以为憾。梅文鼎《绩学堂诗钞》"浮山大师哀辞"诗前小序称:

> 某晚学未获浮公法席,前年(1671)承自青原致书,征象数之学,时以草稿无副,未敢驰应。又闻精舍方成,将归憩息,私心奉窃喜教有日也。无何讣闻。癸丑(1673)夏,舟舶皖江,望君子之旧庐,亦不能往至,因作短章,用伸哀悼。[32]

[按:方以智号浮山,晚年归隐青原山,1671年自沉于惶恐滩。]

梅文鼎方氏三兄弟方中德、方中通、方中履过往密切,与方中通更是引为历算知己。康熙十一年(1672)梅文鼎《方程论》撰成。梅氏"冀得古书为征而不可得,故不敢出以示人"。只有三两好友"会钞

---

29 [清]方中通,《璇玑遗述》序,载《中国科学技术典籍通汇·天文卷》,第六册,郑州:河南教育出版社,1993年,第287页。

30 "易堂九子"是指明末清初以魏禧为首的九位文学家。魏禧父魏兆凤,于明亡后削发隐居于今距宁都县城西2.5公里远的翠微峰,名其居室曰"易堂"。魏禧(1624—1680)与兄际瑞(1620—1677)、弟礼(1629—1695)以及彭士望(1610—1683)、林时益(1618—1678)、李腾蛟(1609—1668)、丘维屏(1614—1619)、彭任(1624—1708)、曾灿(1625—1688)讲学于此,提倡古文实学,世称"易堂九子"。

31 [清]方中通,《陪集·陪诗》卷三,继声堂藏版,《清代诗文集汇编》133册,上海:上海古籍出版社,2010年,第96页。

32 [清]梅文鼎著,韩琦整理,《梅文鼎全集》,第八册,合肥,黄山书社,2020年,第229页。

副墨",方中通即是其一。日后,梅文鼎撰函"复柬方位伯",诗前小序说道:

> 方子精西学,愚病西儒排古算数,著《方程论》,谓虽利氏(即利玛窦)无以难,故质之方子。[33]

1680年,梅文鼎有诗四首给方中履(字素北,方中通弟),第四首后附有小注:

> 别后晤田伯(即方中德,方中通长兄)于秦淮,因附讯位白(即方中通)。无何以《中西算学叙》邮至,余方病,为之霍然。[34]

正是梅文鼎致函方中通"属为序",引出了方中通的《中西算学通》序。在序言之中,方中通饱含对六位友人的深情追叙,万千感慨凝聚笔端,他说到:

> 今者丘子已逝,游子天南,薛子山左,揭子江右,各数千里,汤子亦数百里,通与梅子相去亦复不近。齿日以增,离合不可必。(方中通《中西算学通》序)

作为给梅著之序,方中通高度赞誉了梅文鼎的数学成就("于前人不传之秘有所发明"),同时也阐述了方中通自己对数学的认识("通因悟九数皆勾股",值得注意的是方中通的这一思想得到梅文鼎的赞同。[35]),更重要的是方中通提出学术之要在于"创新":

> 夫今人学古人为文章,初苦于不似,后苦于不化,其于实学,宁有异乎!始期能因,继期能创。(方中通《中西算学通》序)

兹将方中通《中西算学通》序附于文末,期待"方内实学之士群聚而讲明之,以不负此午会"。(方中通《中西算学通》序)

附:方中通《中西算学通》序[36]

当吾世而言历算之绝学,通得交者六人:汤子圣弘、薛子仪甫、游子子六、揭子子宣、丘子邦士与梅子定九也。通少嗜象数,初讯《授时》于汤子。已与薛子游泰西穆先生所,适刊其《天步真原》成,语通,喜而交焉。嗣入都,闻之道未汤先生,始知游子精西历,获读《天经或问》,屡书[37]往复辨难,然犹迄今神交,未一见。及省亲旴江,而逢揭子,《写天新语》一书多深湛之思,质测旁征,剖析无留义。丘子则遇于芝山,览所衍倚数引申图[38],论三昼夜,往往悟合。最后得交梅子,交十五年,而会于金陵者四,方慨聚晤之难,

---

[33] [清]梅文鼎著,韩琦整理,《梅文鼎全集》,第八册,合肥,黄山书社,2020年,第230页。
[34] [清]梅文鼎著,韩琦整理,《梅文鼎全集》,第八册,合肥,黄山书社,2020年,第251页。
[35] 梅文鼎于《方程论》"余论"中称"吾友桐城方位伯为《九章》出于勾股,盖以此也。"参见[清]梅文鼎著,《方程论》,载《四库全书》文渊阁本,台湾商务印书馆影印,795册,1984年,第65—66页。
[36] 说明:今所见方中通《中西算学通》序有两种版本,一是康熙十九年(1680)《中西算学通初集》本,此为方中通手书致梅文鼎,文后注明"桐城世小弟方中通拜手书于南亩之随厓","南亩"为方中通晚年归隐处。另一种为方中通收入《陪集》,编在《陪古》篇。《陪集》本《中西算学通》序文字与《初集》本稍有差异,且文后未记"手书"等文字。此处所录为《初集》本,《陪集》本的差异文字以脚注给出。又可参阅[清]梅文鼎撰,高峰校注《勿庵历算书目》,长沙:湖南科学技术出版社,2014年,第224—225页。
[37] 屡书,《陪集》作"累书"。
[38] 引申图,《陪集》作"引伸图"。

顾以视游子与汤子、薛子、揭子、丘子为幸焉。梅子探历学之奥,造器立法,合七十余家而著为《历法通考》。不独于前人不传之秘有所发明,能证古今之误而改正之,而其所以精义入神者,盖研极于算术日久耳。且夫九数非小学也,载之《周礼》,故凡天地、人身、礼制、乐律、音韵、兵阵、丘赋以及日用器具,莫不前民用焉,是故七十子皆通六艺。六艺以九数为指归,格物以数度为中节。道寓于器,理藏于数,此固圣人之教也。迨目词章为才人,闻记为博物,遂废置实学,苟非专家深入,徒涉其大纲陈迹,吐之为言,笔之为文,则似乎平子、冲之、一行、康节合为一人,及举一端而求其故,即无以应。嗟乎!实学之失,患在才人不讲,更患在博物君子标其大纲陈迹,而不穷其所以然,令周公、商高之法不尽传于今,中学隐而西学彰。梅子二十年殚力苦心,而成《中西算学通》者,深有感于此耳。吁!学者固当如是乎。通尝侍先君子栾庐合山衍《易》,教以一切征诸河、洛。通因悟九数皆勾股,勾股出于河图,加减乘除出于洛书,诸算无非方圆参两所生,谬为《数度衍》二十五卷[39]。学浅力薄,弃之高阁,业有年所。今读梅子之书,而通书益可终弃矣。夫今人学古人为文章,初苦于不似,后苦于不化,其于实学,宁有异乎!始期能因,继[40]期能创。梅子《筹算》易直为横,《笔算》易横为直,非以因为创乎?悟[41]尺算即勾股[42],为别立《度算》。明方程之和较,而九章复旧[43],非以创为因乎?曰《比例》,曰《三角》,曰《几何摘要》,曰《勾股测量》,亦曰即因即创耳。而以《九数存古》终篇,又何其退让,不欲以创自居耶!蔡子玑先留心实学,为刻《筹算》,其八种将次第成之。梅子书至,属通为序。通不敏,虽受先人遗教,象数微有所窥,顾瞻梅子,愧莫企及。而不能不深有望于梅子诸书之流通,使方内实学之士群聚而讲明之,以不负此午会。惜夫诸子强半游先君门,当时未遇一堂,以穷斯学。今者丘子已逝,游子天南,薛子山左,揭子江右,各数千里,汤子亦数百里,通与梅子相去亦复不近。齿日以增,离合不可必。实学既难其人,有其人有其书,而又必俟之知己之力。鸣乎!刻梅子之书者,独梅子感之已哉。虽然,天下后世之学者,集诸子之书而会观焉,不可谓非一时之盛也。桐城世小弟方中通拜手书于南亩之随寓。[44]

---

[39] 二十五卷,《陪集》作"二十六卷"。
[40] 继,《陪集》作"终"。
[41] 悟,《陪集》作"虑"。
[42] 即勾股,《陪集》作"之歆侧"。
[43] 而九章复旧,《陪集》作"为更立新法"。
[44] 《陪集》无此句。

河图洛书与中国传统数学的历史关联[1]
——以方中通《数度衍》为中心

朱一文（中山大学 哲学系暨逻辑与认知研究所）

摘要 河图洛书不仅是中国古代易学研究的重要内容,同时也与中国传统数学有密切的关联。宋代图书之学兴起,诸儒以黑白点图表示河图洛书,与隶首作数、周公制礼、张苍定章程等经典故事一道,河图洛书生数进入中国数学起源的叙事系统;同时,由河图洛书衍生而来的纵横图成为古代数学著作的一部分。元中叶以降,朱子理学被定于一尊,河图洛书黑白点图取得了在中国传统数学体系的固定位置。明清之际,秉承家学的方中通著《数度衍》,发明"勾股出于河图""加减乘除出于洛书"两说,由此把数学的基础建立在河图洛书黑白点图之上,并重新调整了中西数学体系的结构,开辟了河洛之学在算学领域内的新发展。康熙年间,清廷编撰《数理精蕴》《周易折中》,两书都认为"加减出于河图,乘除出于洛书"。清中叶,江永撰《河洛精蕴》亦用勾股解河图洛书。由此来看,《数度衍》对数学和易学的影响值得进一步研究。

关键词 河图;洛书;中国传统数学;方中通;《数度衍》

河图洛书是古代易学研究的重要议题之一,也是中国重要的文化遗产。一般认为"河图"最先记载在《尚书·顾命》中,《周易·系辞》明确提出"河出图,洛出书,圣人则之"。宋代图书之学兴起以后,将河图洛书与黑白点图联系起来。[2] 由此建立了与数学[3]的紧密联系,河图洛书被宋代算家认为是数学的起源。[4] 与此同时,河图洛书尤其是洛书图与纵横图(即幻方(magic square))密切相关,因此宋代算家们也普遍承认它们是中国传统数学的重要内容。[5]

明代,朱熹理学被定于一尊。一方面,图书之学在象数学派之内继续发展。同义理学派相比,该派以象数法则解释天文、地理、物理、易学和算学,或者引入这些自然科学知识及其成果说明易学中的象数法则。明末之际方孔炤、方以智父子接续完成的《周易时论合编》被认为是总结象数之学的重要著作。[6] 该书反映了方氏家族以《周易》为一切自然原理之基础的信念,凸显出中国古代象数易学与数学并未歧而为二的思维模式。[7] 另一方面,明代算家们也继承了宋代学者的看法,确认了河图洛书、纵横图与数学的关联。

基于这些史实,河图洛书与中国传统数学的关系一直是学术界研究的重要议题。1927年,李俨梳

---

[1] 本文原刊于《哲学研究》2022年第4期,此次收入文集略有改动。本文系国家社科基金重大项目"桐城方氏学派文献整理与研究"(19ZDA030)子课题"方中通著作整理与研究"的阶段性成果。本文在修改的过程中得到刘未沫、潘澍原、张永义、邢益海等朋友的帮助,两位匿名审稿人也提出了有价值的修改意见,好友金檀教授帮助修饰英文摘要,编辑部胡海忠老师进行了极为认真负责的编辑,谨此一并表示感谢。
[2] 朱伯崑:《易学哲学史》第2卷,北京:华夏出版社,1995年,第8—53页。
[3] 在宋代的语境中,"数学"不同于"算学",前者等同于象数学,后者则近于今日之数学(mathematics)。在本文之,"数学"只取今义,不取象数学之义。
[4] 〔宋〕秦九韶:《数书九章》,见《四库提要著录丛书》子部第20册,北京:北京出版社,2010年,第98页。
[5] 〔宋〕杨辉:《续古摘奇算法》,见《中国历代算学集成·上》,济南:山东人民出版社,1994年,第900页。
[6] 朱伯崑:《易学哲学史》第3卷,北京:华夏出版社,1995年,第336—348页。
[7] 李忠达:《〈周易时论合编·图象几表〉的〈易〉数与数学:以〈极数概〉为核心》,《清华学报》2019年第3期:第399页。

理了中算家的纵横图研究。[8]之后,钱宝琮认为宋代理学家的"河图图""洛书图""伏羲八卦次序图""伏羲六十四卦次序图"都是属于数字神秘主义范畴,既不能阻碍,也不能推动数学的发展。[9]何丙郁认为中国古代数学包括现今所称的数学(mathematics)、数字学(包括河图洛书)与术数(包括太乙、壬甲、三式等)。[10]李迪通过梳理丁易东与杨辉的纵横图,认为其数学成果是易学研究的副产品。[11]侯钢梳理了河图洛书的历史发展,探讨了纵横图的易学渊源,并认为两宋时期数学与易学的内容互相渗透。[12]朱伯崑从易学史的角度亦论及焦循易学与数学之关系。[13]

事实上,河图洛书与大衍筮法是与中国传统数学密切相关的两项易学内容。笔者先前通过将秦九韶、邵雍、朱熹的大衍筮法进行分析对比,发现算家与易家的具体操作有相似性但实质内容并无相互渗透,宋代易学与数学始终不断合并与重组,并扩大了传统算学的应用领域。[14]在此研究路径之下,河图洛书之学的历史发展及其与算学的关系仍有进一步的研究空间。而且,一般认为以方孔炤、方以智为代表的象数之学是以河洛之学和先后天易学解释《周易》经传,又将象数之学推向极端,遭到义理学派和考据学派的抨击,导致了王夫之易学和黄宗羲、黄宗炎、毛奇龄、胡渭等人对图书学派和邵雍易学的否定。因此,以方氏为代表的象数之学,亦标志着宋易中象数学派的终结。[15]然而,笔者发现方以智之子方中通所著《数度衍》进一步重构了河图洛书与数学的关系,是方氏易学发展的重要阶段,可以说开启了宋代图书之学在算学之内的新发展。然而,该书长期被认为是数学著作,当代易学家关注不多,数学史家则较少关注其在易学方面的贡献。[16]因此,本文拟先重审明末之前河图洛书与中国传统数学的关系,继而在此基础上分析方中通对两者关系的建构,以推进学界对此议题之研究。

一、明末以前河图洛书与中国数学的关联

我们可以从两个角度思考河图洛书与中国数学的关联:(1)河洛进入中国数学起源叙事系统的过程;(2)河洛纵横图成为中国数学的研究内容。为此我们先简单介绍宋之前关于中国数学起源的经典故事。[17]

魏景元四年(263)刘徽注《九章算术》时说:"昔在庖牺氏始画八卦,以通神明之德,以类万物之情,作九九之术,以合六爻之变。暨于黄帝神而化之,引而伸之,于是建历纪,协律吕,用稽道原,然后两仪四象

---

[8] 李俨:《中算家之纵横图(Magic Squares)研究》,《学艺》1927年第9期。

[9] 钱宝琮:《宋元时期数学与道学的关系》,载钱宝琮编《宋元数学史论文集》,北京:科学出版社,1966年,第233—234页。

[10] 何丙郁:《从科技史观点谈易数》,载《中国科技史论文集》,台北:联经出版事业公司,1995年,第21页。

[11] 李迪:《中国数学通史·宋元卷》,南京:江苏教育出版社,1999年,第162—164页。

[12] 侯钢:《两宋易数及其数学之关系初论》,中国科学院自然科学史研究所博士学位论文,2006年,第5—24页,第99—114页。

[13] 朱伯崑:《易学哲学史》第4卷,北京:华夏出版社,1995年,第360—362页。

[14] 朱一文:《宋代的数学与易学——以〈数书九章〉"蓍卦发微"为中心》,《周易研究》2019年第2期。

[15] 朱伯崑:《易学哲学史》第3卷,北京:华夏出版社,1995年,第348页。

[16] 学术界对方中通《数度衍》的研究主要集中在其数学成就上。参见严敦杰:《方中通〈数度衍〉评述》,《安徽史学》,1960年第1期;郭世荣:《方中通〈数度衍〉所见的约瑟夫问题》,《自然科学史研究》2002年第1期;杨玉星,《清代算学家方中通及其算学研究》,台湾师范大学数学系硕士学位论文,2003年;徐君:《略论方中通"四算"研究及其特点》,《内蒙古师范大学学报(自然科学版)》,2004年第1期;吴文俊主编:《中国数学史大系》第7卷,北京:北京师范大学出版社,2000年,第131—138页。其中严敦杰对方中通《数度衍》"数原"部分进行了初步讨论,参见严敦杰:《方中通〈数度衍〉评述》,《安徽史学》,1960年第1期,第55页。

[17] 侯钢讨论了文献中关于河图洛书的早期记载,并认为"学者们对河图洛书有诸多的猜测,但他们都没有说明、更没有具体记载河图洛书究竟是什么。一直到了宋代,才明确地为河图洛书制作了黑白点的图式。"参见侯钢:《两宋易数及其与数学之关系初论》,中国科学院自然科学史研究所博士学位论文,2006年,第5—6页。据李俨考证,东汉《数术记遗》记载之"九宫算"是最早记载纵横图的数学著作。参见李俨:《中算家之纵横图(Magic Squares)研究》,《学艺》1927年第9期,第2页。

精微之气可得而效焉。《记》称'隶首作数',其详未之闻也。周公制礼而有九数,九数之流,则《九章》是矣。……自时厥后,汉北平侯张苍、大司农中丞耿寿昌皆以善算命世。苍等因旧文之遗残,各称删补。故校其目则与古或异,而所论者多近语也。"[18]刘徽的叙述包含了关于中国数学起源的三个经典故事,即隶首作数、周公制礼、张苍定章程。其中"隶首作数"被广泛记载在历代正史《律历志》之中,"周公制礼"来自于《左传》等古籍,"张苍定章程"来自于《汉书》。[19]在成书不早于北宋末期的《算学源流》中,对中国数学发展的叙述首先引《晋书·律历志》"隶首作算数"的记载,其次引《汉书·律历志》筹算制度,再引《周礼》"九数"郑玄注、贾公彦疏,再引《汉书》"张苍定章程",最后记述唐宋国子监算学制度。[20]《算学源流》可视为中国第一部简明数学史纲,但其中并没有河图洛书的位置。

(一)河图洛书进入中国数学起源叙事系统

宋代图书之学的兴起是河图洛书进入中国数学起源叙事系统的起点,从此之后河图洛书与中国数学建立了紧密的关联。一般认为宋代易学分成象数派与义理派。始于北宋道士陈抟的图书之学是象数易的重要组成部分。按《宋史·朱震传》记载,邵雍和刘牧分别是陈抟所传先天图和河图洛书之终点。[21]两者对建立河图洛书与传统算学的关系都起到十分重要的作用。

刘牧《易数钩隐图》序云:"夫卦者,圣人设之观于象也。象者,形之上应。原其本,则形由象生,象由数设。……今采撮天地奇偶之数,自太极生两仪而下至于复卦,凡五十五位,点之成图。"[22]刘氏又云:"数之所起,起于阴阳。"[23]于是,《易数钩隐图》用黑白点图表示易数图像,其中白点表阳或奇数,黑点表阴或偶数。刘牧河图总计有1、2、3、4、5、6、7、8、9,合为45(图1);其洛书则多一个10,合为55(图2,图3),所谓"九为河图,十为洛书"。邵雍等则与之不同,以"十为河图,九为洛书"。朱熹先采刘牧说法,后听从蔡元定意见,改从邵雍,并将二图刊于《易学启蒙》《周易本义》卷首,明代以后遂成定式。[24]可以发现,刘牧河图(即朱熹洛书)相当于一个三阶幻方,但宋儒等并无揭示其内部数学规律之研究取向。

  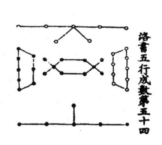

图1 刘牧河图[25]   图2 刘牧洛书生数图[26]   图3 刘牧洛书成数图[27]

邵雍云:"大衍之数,其算法之源乎?是以算数之起,不过乎方圆曲直也。阴无一,阳无十。乘数,生数也。除数,消数也。算法虽多,不出乎此矣。"[28]邵雍的这一看法非常重要,将大衍之数视作算法的源

---

[18] 郭书春汇校:《汇校〈九章算术〉增补版》,沈阳:辽宁教育出版社;台北:九章出版社,2004年,第1页。

[19] 段垒垒从功能论的角度对中国数学起源叙事进行了研究。参见段垒垒:《试论中国传统数学的起源与功能观念的转变》,天津师范大学硕士学位论文,2011年,第12—31页。

[20] [汉]徐岳:《数术记遗》,见《宋刻算经六种》,北京:文物出版社,1980年,第13—18页。

[21] [元]脱脱:《宋史》,北京:中华书局,1977年,第12908页。

[22] [宋]刘牧:《易数钩隐图》,见《正统道藏》第71册,上海涵芬楼影印,1923年,第1页。

[23] [宋]刘牧:《易数钩隐图》,见《正统道藏》第71册,上海涵芬楼影印,1923年,第33页。

[24] 温海明:《朱熹河图洛书说的演变》,《周易研究》2000年第4期,第53页。

[25] [宋]刘牧:《易数钩隐图》,见《正统道藏》第71册,上海涵芬楼影印,1923年,第41页。

[26] [宋]刘牧:《易数钩隐图》,见《正统道藏》第71册,上海涵芬楼影印,1923年,第42页。

[27] [宋]刘牧:《易数钩隐图》,见《正统道藏》第71册,上海涵芬楼影印,1923年,第42页。

[28] [宋]邵雍:《皇极经世》,见《邵雍全集》,上海:上海古籍出版社,1995年,第1195页。

头,直接联系了象数学与算学。[29]朱熹不同意邵雍,他说"康节天资极高,其学只是术数学。后人有聪明能算,亦可以推。"[30]朱熹认为象数学与算学仍有区别,不应将两者联系起来,这代表了一些宋儒的看法。然而,由于儒学与算学的地位悬殊,对算家而言,邵雍的说法显然是更有利的思想资源。因此可以说,邵氏观点为河图洛书进入数学起源叙事系统奠定了思想基础。

从数学史的角度看,宋代也是中国传统算学发展的新阶段。不但取得了许多世界级的数学成就,而且这些成就往往与算学中出现的新文本内容有关,例如天元术的符号表达、秦九韶《数书九章》中的算图连线,由此也取得了数学文本化之成就。[31]就此而言,宋代图书之学黑白点图的出现亦可视为易学文本化之过程,宋儒以之解释河图洛书,大衍筮法等诸多内容,由此建立起算学与易学之间的对应关联。邵雍的论述代表了宋儒将算与数相互联系的观点,使象数学作为算学的基础成为可能。

秦九韶《数书九章》原名《数术》,极力建立算学与《周易》之联系,提升算学之重要性。在此背景之下,秦氏自序云"爰自河图、洛书,闿发秘"[32],把河图洛书纳入数学起源故事。不过,并非当时所有算家都会在谈数学起源时提到河图洛书。金朝李冶《测圆海镜》《益古演段》[33]、南宋杨辉《详解九章算法》《续古摘奇算法》[34]序言都没有提到河图洛书。其原因可能与算家个人对于易学或象数学的取向有关。入元之后,河图洛书进入数学著作逐渐成为常态,与隶首作数、周公制礼、张苍定章程一道成为经典故事。莫若为朱世杰《四元玉鉴》写前序,云:"故《易》一太极也。……河图洛书泄其秘,黄帝九章著之书。"[35]由是把河图洛书置于黄帝之前。《丁巨算法》开篇云:"稽古河图五十有五。一二三四互为七八九六,大衍之数五十。隶首作算数,羲和以闰月定四十成岁。"[36]丁巨进一步在算书中直接给出了河图55的数据。不过,另一本元代算书《详明算法》依然采用隶首、张苍及《汉书·律历志》的说法。[37]

明朝以降,朱熹理学被定于一尊,河图洛书在数学著作中的位置愈加重要。吴敬《九章算法比类大全》序云:"有理而后有象,有象而后有形。昔黄帝使隶首作算数,而其法遂传于世。图书出于河洛,大衍五十有五之数。圣人以之成变化而行鬼神。"[38]宋儒程颐云"有理而后有象,有象而后有数"。[39]因此,吴敬把理学和河图洛书都融入了中国数学起源叙事。之后王文素《算学宝鉴》、程大位《算法统宗》都把河图

---

29 邵雍并云:"《易》之大衍何数也,圣人之倚数也。天数二十五,合之为五十。地数三十,合之为六十。故曰'五位相得而各有合'也。五十者,蓍之数也。六十者,卦数也。五者蓍之小衍也,数五十为大衍也。"[宋]邵雍:《邵雍全集》,上海:上海古籍出版社,1995年,第1191—1192页。由此给了大衍之数一个算术解释。

30 [宋]黎靖德编:《朱子语类》,北京:中华书局,1986年,第2554页。

31 Zhu Yiwen, "On Qin Jiushao's Writing System," *Archive for History of Exact Sciences*, 2020, 74(4).

32 [宋]秦九韶:《数书九章》,见《四库提要著录丛书》子部第20册,北京:北京出版社,2010年,第98页。

33 李冶《测圆海镜》自序云"数一出于自然。吾欲以力强穷之,使隶首复生亦未如之何也。"[金]李冶:《测圆海镜》,见《中国科学技术典籍·数学卷一》,郑州:河南教育出版社,1993年,第730页。显示出其道家的取向。其《益古演段》自序又云:"致使轩辕隶首之术。"[金]李冶:《益古演段》,见《中国科学技术典籍·数学卷一》,郑州:河南教育出版社,1993年,第875页。

34 杨辉《详解九章算法》自序云"黄帝《九章》备全奥妙"。[宋]杨辉:《详解九章算法》,见《中国历代算学集成·上》,济南:山东人民出版社,1994年,第759页。其荣棨序云"夫算者,数也。数之所生,生于道。……爰昔黄帝推天地之道,究万物之始,错综奇数,列为《九章》,立术二百四十有六。"[宋]杨辉:《详解九章算法》,见《中国历代算学集成·上》,济南:山东人民出版社,1994年,第758页。荣棨将道置于黄帝之前,已有河图洛书之意味。其鲍澣之序则云:"《九章算经》九卷,周公之遗书,而汉丞相张苍之所删补者也。……近世民间之本题曰《黄帝九章》,岂以其为隶首之所作,欺名已不当。"[宋]杨辉:《详解九章算法》,见《中国历代算学集成·上》,济南:山东人民出版社,1994年,第759页。杨辉《续古摘奇算法》自序则开篇就谈到黄帝、隶首和周公的故事。[宋]杨辉:《续古摘奇算法》,见《中国历代算学集成·上》,济南:山东人民出版社,1994年,第900页。

35 [元]朱世杰:《四元玉鉴》,见《中国科学技术典籍·数学卷一》,郑州:河南教育出版社,1993年,第1205页。

36 [元]丁巨:《丁巨算法》,见《中国科学技术典籍·数学卷一》,郑州:河南教育出版社,1993年,第1303页。

37 [元]安止斋、何平子:《详明算法》,见《中国科学技术典籍·数学卷一》,郑州:河南教育出版社,1993年,第1349页。

38 [明]吴敬:《九章算法比类大全》,见《中国科学技术典籍·数学卷二》,郑州:河南教育出版社,1993年,第6页。

39 [宋]程颐、程颢:《二程集》,北京:中华书局,1981年,第271页。

洛书黑白点图刊于卷首。柯尚迁《数学通轨》云:"天地之始一气而已,气之运动而自然者为理,有气而后有象,有象而后有数,故数亦理之形。"[40]黄龙吟《算法指南》谈数学起源也沿用了隶首作数、周公制礼故事。[41]

(二)河图洛书纵横图成为中国数学内容

河图洛书与中国传统数学发生关联的另外重要一面是:由其衍生而来的诸多纵横图逐渐成为算学著作的重要内容。中国古代最重要的数学经典《九章算术》并无纵横图内容。东汉徐岳《数术记遗》云"隶首注术乃有多种"[42],依次给出:积算、太乙、两仪、三才、五行、八卦、九宫、运筹、了知、成数、把头、龟算、珠算、记数。其中"九宫算,五行参数,犹如循环"。北周甄鸾注曰:"九宫者,即二、四为肩,六、八为足,左三、右七,戴九、履一,五居中央。五行参数者,设立之法依五行。"[43]该书被列入唐国子监十二部教科书之一,是纵横图在算学著作中的最早记载。一般认为,九数图起源于《礼记·月令》等记载的明堂九室制度,十数图源于《尚书·洪范》五行生数学说。[44]宋儒图书之学把它们与河图洛书结合起来。

杨辉《续古摘奇算法》刊载了15张纵横图:洛书数、河图数、花十六图、五五图、六六图、衍数图、易数图、九九图、百子图、聚五图、聚六图、聚八图、攒九图、八阵图、连环图。其洛书以黑白点表达,总为55;河图以汉字表达,总为45(图4)。这与刘牧看法接近,而与朱熹等不同。其洛书图下云:"天数一三五七九,地数二四六八十,积五十五。求积法曰:并上下数[共一十一],以高数[十]乘之,[得百一十]。折半[得五十五]为天地之数。"[45]给出了1+2+…+10的求和算法。其河图云:"九子斜排,上下对易,左右相更,四维挺出。"[46]则解释了三阶纵横图的构造原理。杨氏又在纵横图下设"换易术""求等术"等构造方法。杨辉《续古摘奇算法》自序说其纵横图来自刘碧涧、丘虚谷等人,但其图下算法解释具有明显的算学取向,似为杨氏所作。由此可见,杨辉对纵横图的解释或是给出求和算法,或是给出构造原理,显示出探索其内部数学规律的研究取向,把邵雍将数与算联系的想法往前推进一步。[47]尽管丁易东《大衍索隐》以河图洛书释大衍之数,也给出多个纵横图,[48]但是其解说往往集中于易学原理而非算法或构造。遂呈现出丁氏属易学研究,杨氏属算学研究之别。

40　[明]柯尚迁:《数学通轨》,见《中国科学技术典籍·数学卷二》,郑州:河南教育出版社,1993年,第1167页。
41　[明]黄龙吟:《算法指南》,见《中国科学技术典籍·数学卷二》,郑州:河南教育出版社,1993年,第1425页。关于明代学者对数学起源的论述,亦可参见金福:《对明代数学思想的几点分析》,载李迪编《数学史研究文集》(第一辑),呼和浩特:内蒙古大学出版社,台北:九章出版社,1990年,第94—96页。
42　[汉]徐岳:《数术记遗》,见《宋刻算经六种》,北京:文物出版社,1980年,第5页。
43　[汉]徐岳:《数术记遗》,见《宋刻算经六种》,北京:文物出版社,1980年,第6页。
44　侯钢:《两宋易数及其与数学之关系初论》,中国科学院自然科学史研究所博士学位论文,2006年,第9—12页。
45　[宋]杨辉:《续古摘奇算法》,见《中国历代算学集成·上》,济南:山东人民出版社,1994年,第900页。[]内原为小字杨辉自注。
46　[宋]杨辉:《续古摘奇算法》,见《中国历代算学集成·上》,济南:山东人民出版社,1994年,第900页。
47　秦九韶《数书九章》首问"蓍卦发微"同样把数(大衍之数)与算(大衍筮法)结合起来,同样推进了邵雍的想法。朱一文:《宋代的数学与易学——以〈数书九章〉"蓍卦发微"为中心》,《周易研究》2019年第2期,第87—88页。
48　关于对丁易东纵横图的研究,参见王荣彬:《丁易东对纵横图的研究》,载李迪编《数学史研究文集》(第一辑),呼和浩特:内蒙古大学出版社,台北:九章出版社,1990年,第74—82页;何丙郁:《纵横图与〈大衍索隐〉》,载《何丙郁中国科技史论文集》,沈阳:辽宁教育出版社,2001年,第256—275页;侯钢:《两宋易数及其与数学之关系初论》,中国科学院自然科学史研究所博士学位论文,2006年,第16—24页。

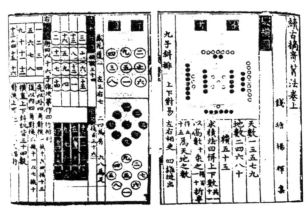

图 4　杨辉《续古摘奇算法》卷上首页[49]

杨辉算书在明代影响很大。王文素《算学宝鉴》自序云受其影响,卷首刊载河图与洛书黑白点图。不过王氏河图总为55、洛书45,采朱子定式。其河图下有"求天数法""求地数法"与"求总积法",延续并扩展了杨辉算法。其洛书下增设"求积法"。之后王氏又给出数张汉字纵横图的求和、构造方法。[50] 程大位《算法统宗》在明末影响很大。其卷首亦刊载河图(55)洛书(45),并延续杨辉给出求和算法和构造方法。之后,程氏给出"伏羲则图作易"之"易有太极""是生两仪""两仪生四象"和"四象生八卦"四图,又有"洛书释数""九宫八卦图""洛书易换数"等内容。并在卷十七"杂法"刊载了多张易数纵横图及其求积、构造方法。[51] 总之,王氏、程氏把黑白点河图洛书置于卷首,显示其与中国数学起源之关联,又把汉字数字表达的纵横图作为新的数学内容刊载于书。这显示出经过宋明约六百年的演变,河图洛书黑白点图与其衍生的纵横图均已在中国传统数学知识体系中获得了稳定的位置。[52]

二、方中通对河图洛书与中国数学关系的建构

明清之际的方氏家族是安徽桐城地区最重要的易学世家。方学渐著有《易蠡》,其子方大镇著有《易意》和《野同录》。大镇之子方孔炤精通易学著有《周易时论》,是为方氏易学的代表作,孔炤之子方以智为此书作跋又加按语,并命方中德、方中通、方中履三子将前后稿整理成书,是为《周易时论合编》,方以智又编《图象几表》置于书前。《周易时论合编》之中,已有大量算学内容渗透进象数学。[53] 在此家学背景之下,方中通早年便对象数学和算学产生了兴趣。

朱伯崑认为《周易时论合编》进一步吸收了元明以来象数之学的成果,并在其基础上做出新的发展,终于完成了象数学派本体论的体系,是总结象数之学的重要著作。又说该书将象数之学推向极端,遭到义理学派和考据学派王夫之、黄宗羲、黄宗炎、毛奇龄、胡渭等人的否定,标志着宋易象数流派的终结。[54] 其实,方中通所撰《数度衍》对河洛象数之学亦有发展。但长期以来,该书被认为是一部数学著作(《四库全书》将之收入子部天文算法类),从而使得学者们不仅忽视了其易学贡献,而且未意识到该书是宋易象

---

[49] [宋]杨辉:《续古摘奇算法》,见《中国历代算学集成·上》,济南:山东人民出版社,1994年,第900页。

[50] [明]王文素:《算学宝鉴》,见《中国科学技术典籍通汇·数学卷二》,郑州:河南教育出版社,1993年,第347—348,352—355页。

[51] [明]程大位:《算法统宗》,见《中国科学技术典籍通汇·数学卷二》,郑州:河南教育出版社,1993年,第1227—1228,1410—1415页。

[52] 学界已有对明代数学与象数神秘主义的关系的研究,参见金福:《对明代数学思想的几点分析》,载李迪编《数学史研究文集》(第一辑),呼和浩特:内蒙古大学出版社,台北:九章出版社,1990年,第98—100页。

[53] 学界已有对此书的易学思想及其与算学的关系的研究,参见张永堂:《方孔炤〈周易时论合编〉一书的主要思想》,《成功大学历史学报》1985年第12期;李忠达:《〈周易时论合编·图象几表〉的〈易〉数与数学:以〈极数概〉为核心》,《清华学报》2019年第3期。

[54] 朱伯崑:《易学哲学史》第3卷,北京:华夏出版社,1995年,第348页。

数之学在算学领域内的新发展。⁵⁵就此而言,该学派在方氏以后并未终结,而是从易学领域转换至算学领域。在易学与数学关系史上,《数度衍》占有十分重要的位置。

《数度衍》的象数学背景十分明显。是书家序"药地老人(即方以智)示"云:"漆园《天下篇》曰:'明于本数,系于末度。'吾谓数自有度。《易》曰:'制数度以议德行',神自无方,准不可乱。舍日无岁,无内无外,秩序变化,原同一时,因其条理而付之中节之谓度。故曰:一在二中,物自献理,谁能惑我。然则数乃质耳,度也者,其大本之时几乎?泥于数则技,通于数则神。汝既知数,即可以此通神明,类万物矣。专精藏密,勉之勉之。"⁵⁶之后,方中德语说明了是书的写作目的和成书过程:"此大人见《数度衍》而勉二弟之语也。弟之所研极者,十余年矣。初大人庐墓合山,重编《时论》时,衍极数以示懋等,弟退即变数十图以进。大人甚喜,因命精数,弟遂发明勾股出于河图,加减乘除出于洛书。既而玩泰西诸书,乃合笔、筹、珠三法而穷差别于《九章》已。三弟得尺算一法,即以贻弟,复数昼夜而尽其变,可谓精矣。方第之著是书,独处一室,废寝食而寒暑不缀。故宜其探赜索隐,钩深制远,莫不具也。"⁵⁷因此,《数度衍》是在《周易时论》的基础上,以"勾股出于河图,加减乘除出于洛书"来重构古代算学知识体系,由此将象数学与算学结合起来。

《数度衍》共8册,分别命之以八卦之名"乾、坤、震、巽、坎、离、艮、兑",对应不同之算学内容。⁵⁸是书"凡例"云:"此书明勾股出于河图,加减乘除出于洛书。知一切不外河洛也。故首言其原。黄钟为数之始,故次律衍。线面体之理,尽于《几何》,故约之。至于历法别有专书。"又云:"西学精矣,中土失传耳。今以西学归《九章》,以《九章》归《周髀》。《周髀》独言勾股而《九章》皆勾股所生。故以勾股为首,少广次之,方田次之,商功次之,差分次之,均输次之,盈朒次之,方程次之,粟布次之。"⁵⁹据此调整了传统算学的《九章算术》结构,并增设了西方数学几何学的内容。⁶⁰这一体系的关键在于建立河图洛书与算学的关系。《数度衍》开篇"数原"就是解释"勾股出于河图,加减乘除出于洛书"。方中通云:

> 九数出于勾股,勾股出于河图,故河图为数之原。《周髀》曰:"勾广三,股修四,径隅五。"天数二十有五,弦之开方也。河图之数五十有五,中五不用,用其五十,合勾自之、股自之、弦自之之数也。勾三,阳数也,居左。和弦而为八,故八与三同位。股四,阴数也,居右。和弦而为九,故九与四同位。弦五,勾股所求之数也,居中。勾弦较得二,居上。股弦较得一,居下。勾弦较与弦和为七,故七与二同位。股弦较与弦和为六,故六与一同位。弦居中,倍为十,而倍之之数不可用。故洛书不用十也。勾股左右,两较上下,四和四围。岂偶然哉!勾不尽于三,而始于三。股不尽于四,而始于四。弦不尽于五,而始于五。较不尽于一、二,而始于一、二。和不尽于六、七、八、九,而始于六、七、八、九。此勾股之原也。⁶¹

方中通解释"勾股出于河图"的总体思路是把河图中1至10这十个数字都与勾股数关联起来,从而说明河图中蕴含了勾股数(图5)。在《周髀算经》勾3(设为a)股4(设为b)弦5(设为c)的基础上,方氏以1为股弦较或勾股较($c-b$或$b-a$),2为勾弦较($c-a$),3、4、5为勾股弦(a、b、c),6为股弦较与弦和

---

⁵⁵ 萧萐父也认为方中通《数度衍》是宋易象数学派的发展,但并未做具体论文。参见萧萐父:《中国哲学史史料源流举要》,武汉:武汉大学出版社,1998年,第90页。萧氏观点系由潘澍原告知,在此表示感谢。
⁵⁶ [清]方中通:《数度衍》,见《中国历代算学集成·中》,济南:山东人民出版社,1994年,第2556页。
⁵⁷ [清]方中通:《数度衍》,见《中国历代算学集成·中》,济南:山东人民出版社,1994年,第2556页。
⁵⁸ 关于各册对应的数学内容,参见郭书春主编:《中国科学技术史·数学卷》,北京:科学出版社,2010年,第637页。
⁵⁹ [清]方中通:《数度衍》,见《中国历代算学集成·中》,济南:山东人民出版社,1994年,第2557页。
⁶⁰ 方中通与当时数学界多有交往。早年受其家学影响,随波兰传教士穆尼阁(Johannes Nikolaus Smogulecki)学习数学,康熙年间则多次与梅文鼎交流。参见郭书春主编:《中国科学技术史·数学卷》,北京:科学出版社,2010年,第637页。
⁶¹ [清]方中通:《数度衍》,见《中国历代算学集成·中》,济南:山东人民出版社,1994年,第2561页。

$(c-b+c)$,7 为勾弦较与弦和或勾股和$(c-a+c$ 或 $a+b)$,8 为勾弦和$(a+c)$,9 为股弦和$(b+c)$,10 为两倍的弦$(2c)$。方氏又按易学传统,以奇数为阳(以白点表示)、偶数为阴(以黑点表示)。这些做法实质把易学的黑白点表数与数学的线段表数等价起来的,可视为杨辉做法的拓展。[62]方氏云:"天数二十五,弦之开方也。"即指 25 为弦平方(c^2),然此处云"开方"是沿用了孔颖达、贾公彦等儒家算法传统的术语,实为平方,与传统算学之"开方"不同。[63]河图总数为 55($1+2+\cdots+10=55$),不用中间的弦 5(方氏并未进一步解释原因),剩下 50 恰为勾方、股方、弦方之和($a^2+b^2+c^2$)。以此"勾股左右,两较上下,四和四围"的方式,勾股数与河图数完全对应起来,方中通认为这不可能是偶然形成的,是为"勾股之原也"。

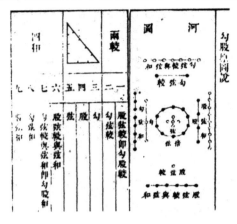

图 5　方中通河图[64]

总体来看,方氏以河图解释勾股数的做法融合了传统算学(《周髀算经》《九章算术》等)、儒家经学研究中的算学传统(如"开方"术语)和宋代图书之学。但又与南宋以降学者仅把河洛视作数学起源不同,方中通给出了具体的数理化联系,因此确可称之为"发明"。从数学史和易学史的角度看,方氏做法的核心是把河洛的黑白点与勾股的线段长度等价起来,从而融合了算学与易学两个相对独立的研究领域,并显示了其对于数学在本质上具有的统一性的认识和理解。

接着,方氏继续阐述加减乘除出于洛书:

> 不用十而用九,河图变为洛书。加减乘除之数皆从洛生,而九数之用备焉。加者,并也。一阴一阳相并,而生阳为用。故一并六为七。七并二为九。九并四为十三,去十不用,所生为三。三并八为十一,去十不用,所生为一。数始于阳,故阳统阴。此加之原也。减者,去也。阴中去阳,则六去一为五,八去三为五。阳中去阴,则九去四为五,七去二为五。边去中存。此减之原也。
>
> 乘者,积也。除者,分也。一无积分,相对而为乘除者,仍为九焉。二与八对,二其八,八其二,所积皆十六。截东南三、四、九之数合矣。二分十六得八,八分十六得二,此二与八之互见也。三与七对,三其七,七其三,所积皆二十一。不用三下之八,七下之六,而一、二、四、五、九之数合矣。三分二十一得七,七分二十一得三,此三与七之互见也。四与六对,四其六,六其四,所积皆二十四。三八亦积二十四,不用三八,而一、二、五、七、九之数合矣。四分二十四得六,六分二十四得四,此四与六之互见也。五宜与十对,而洛书无十,故以中五乘四隅,所积之数,必止于十而无余。五乘二为一十,是为两方之数。[四正四隅两方相对皆十。]五乘四为二十,是为四方之数。[四正合为二十,四隅亦合为二十,两正两隅亦合为二十。]五乘八为四十,

---

[62]　[清]方中通:《数度衍》,见《中国历代算学集成·中》,济南:山东人民出版社,1994 年,第 2561 页。

[63]　朱一文:《从宋代文献看数的表达、用法与本质》,《自然辩证法研究》2020 年第 12 期,第 99-100 页。

[64]　Zhu Yiwen, "Different Cultures of Computation in Seventh Century China from the Viewpoint of Square Root Extraction," *Historia Mathematica*, 2016, 43(1): 23.

是为八方之数。[四正四隅合为四十。]五除十得二,五除二十得四,五除三十得六,五除四十得八。二除十,四除二十,六除三十,八除四十,皆五。即五与十之互见也。洛书无十,而十藏于中矣。足后反无余,不足然后足。此乘除之原也。[65]

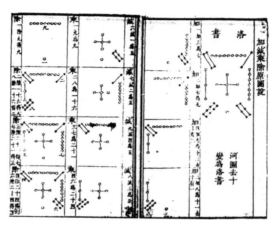

图 6：方中通洛书[66]

方中通解释"加减乘除出于洛书"的总体思路是揭示洛书各数字之间的运算关系,从而说明加减乘除实际已经蕴含在洛书之中。方氏各以四张图解释洛书各数字间的加法和减法关系(图 6)。"加者,并也"。按洛书由底部白点逆时针做加法,则有 $1+6=7$，$7+2=9$，$9+4=13$("去十不用"取 3），$3+8=11$("去十不用"取 1），由此可知洛书除中五外八数构成递进的加法关系,"此加之原也"。"减者,去也"。按洛书由底部顺时针做减法,则有 $6-1=5$，$7-2=5$，$9-4=5$，$8-3=5$,由此可知,洛书除中五外八数两两相减均得中五,"此减之原也"。方氏又以四张图解释洛书各数字间的乘法和除法关系(图 6)。"乘者,积也;除者,分也。"按洛书上下、左右、斜对角各做乘法,则有 $1\times 9=9$，2×8(右上左下两数相乘)$=16=3+4+9$(左上角三数之和),3×7(左中右中二数相乘)$=21=4+9+2+1+5$(不用"三下之八""七下之六",其余数之和),4×6(左上右下两数相乘)$=24=9+2+7+5+1$(不用"三""八",其余数之和)。"五宜与十对,而洛书无十",因此以 $5\times 2=10$(两方之数)$=1+9=3+7=2+8=4+6$,为上下、左右或斜对角两数之和。$5\times 4=20$(四方之数)$=1+3+7+9$(四正之和)$=2+4+6+8$(四隅之和),为四边或四角数之和。$5\times 8=40$(八方之数)$=1+2+3+4+6+7+8+9$(四正四隅之和),为四边与四角之和。除取乘之逆运算: $9\div 1=9$，$16\div 2=8$，$16\div 8=2$，$21\div 3=7$，$21\div 7=3$，$24\div 4=6$，$24\div 6=4$。"此乘除之原也"。

从数学史的角度看,杨辉给出了三阶纵横图的构造原理,方氏进一步揭示了洛书各数字之间运算关系,亦体现了其对运算本质统一性的理解和认识。从运算工具看,明末以来大致有筹算、珠算和西方笔算三种,方氏以黑白点来计算的做法实延续了易学传统。方中通在《数度衍》笔算章末尾提出"洛书算",即"洛书用九,八卦旋中,加减升降,法异理同,九内易位,越十移宫,过去未来用之无穷"。[67]这说明方氏亦继承了汉末《数术记遗》"八卦算"等数术传统,并有所发展。

总之,方中通利用数理化的方式重构了河图与勾股数、洛书与加减乘除运算的关系。在中国传统数学的领域中,数与运算是最基本的知识。方氏将两者的起源推至河图洛书,使后者成为算学之基础。之

65　[清]方中通：《数度衍》,见《中国历代算学集成·中》,济南：山东人民出版社,1994 年,第 2562—2563 页。
66　[清]方中通：《数度衍》,见《中国历代算学集成·中》,济南：山东人民出版社,1994 年,第 2562 页。
67　[清]方中通：《数度衍》,见《中国历代算学集成·中》,济南：山东人民出版社,1994 年,第 2651—2652 页。笔者搜罗文献,未见方中通之前言"洛书算"者,最接近之为《数术记遗》之"八卦算"。由于方氏发明了加减乘除出于洛书的说法,因为笔者推测"洛书算"也很可能是方氏发明,或者是方氏在其他算法的基础上进行的改造。

后,方氏论述"《九章》皆勾股说",把《九章算术》建立在勾股的基础上,并以西学归九章;[68]又论"四算说"云"泰西笔算筹算皆出于九九";并在此后,引出"九九图说",给出多张纵横图(大体沿用程大位《算法统宗》说)。[69]由此确定了纵横图在其算学体系中的位置。

值得注意的是,《数度衍》是一部百科全书式的著作,囊括了当时所有的数学知识(三角学属于历算,故不介绍)。因此,《数度衍》"数原"是从易学数理化的角度将河图洛书置于最基础的地位,并重新调整当时数学知识各分支的位置。依此设定算学为易学之分支——易学论数并产生算,进而以算学论算。方氏学说推进了邵雍"大衍之数,其算法之源乎"[70]的观点,使得图书之学成为算学的切实内容,是河图洛书与中国传统算学关系发展的重要阶段。从易学史的角度看,朱伯崑认为明清之际易学中的两大流派(即象数派和义理派)都各自出现了总结前人的代表性人物。方孔炤、方以智《周易时论合编》对以前的象数之学做一总结;王夫之等则对宋明以来义理学派及其哲学做一总结。[71]据此而言,方中通《数度衍》实为《周易时论合编》之发展。

三、结语

随着宋代图书之学的兴起,河图洛书与中国数学之起源发生关联,并引出算学家的纵横图研究。入明以后,随着朱子理学取得压倒性的地位,河图洛书在中国数学起源叙事系统中的经典地位逐渐被确立,河图洛书黑白点图和纵横图都逐渐成为算书不可或缺的内容。然而,两者与算学的实质关联尚未完全建立。明清之际,桐城方氏学派深研象数易学,方孔炤、方以智之《周易时论合编》已将传统算学纳入易学。方以智之子方中通精研中西数学与象数易学。在《周易时论》之基础上,发明"勾股出于河图""乘除出于洛书"两说。由此把数学的基础建立在河图洛书之上,并重新调整了中西数学各分支的位置。这一做法一方面将宋儒邵雍关联数与算的观点推到一个前所未有的程度,另一方面又开辟了河洛之学在算学领域内的新发展。

从数学史的角度看,方中通《数度衍》重构了传统算学知识体系的结构,把河图洛书黑白点图、纵横图等都放置在基础的位置上,可视为秦九韶、杨辉等人之后继。从易学史的角度看,方氏进一步数理化了宋明以来的图书之学,把算学引入象数易学,可视为朱熹、丁易东等人之发展。于是按照方氏的观点,含有数理解释的河图洛书、纵横图等内容应该同时出现在易学与算学著作中。方氏对数学统一性的认识既沿用了传统算学家的看法,又有所拓展。[72]

清康熙年间,清廷编撰大型算学著作《数理精蕴》和大型易学著作《周易折中》。《数理精蕴》开篇"数理本原"即指出"粤稽上古河出图、洛出书",并云"加减实出于河图,乘除殆出于洛书"。[73]继而刊载河图、洛书黑白点图,阐述其中加减乘除道理。《周易折中·启蒙附论》云"河图加减之源,洛书乘除之源"[74],又刊载多张纵横图揭示数理,此解释与《数理精蕴》相同。与《数度衍》相比,尽管两书并未完全采纳"勾股出于河图,加减乘除出于洛书"之说,但阐明河洛如何成为数学的基础,如何与具体算法相关的做法和思路实与方中通相通。事实上,康熙三十一年(1692),皇帝召见方中通次子方正珠,正珠"进其父中通所

---

68 严敦杰:《方中通〈数度衍〉评述》,《安徽史学》,1960年第1期,第53—54页。
69 [清]方中通:《数度衍》,见《中国历代算学集成·中》,济南:山东人民出版社,1994年,第2563—2567页。
70 [宋]邵雍:《皇极经世》,见《邵雍全集》,上海:上海古籍出版社,1995年,第1195页。
71 朱伯崑:《易学哲学史》第4卷,北京:华夏出版社,1995年,第11—12页。
72 传统算学家往往强调将算学应用于其他领域,以此来取得数学的统一性。参见 Zhu Yiwen, "How do We Understand Mathematical Practices in Non-mathematical Fields? Reflections Inspired by Cases from 12th and 13th Century China," Historia Mathematica, 52: 21. 方氏继承了这一面向,并同时强调其他领域的知识(易学)亦应可以应用于算学,从而形成对称的应用关系。
73 《数理精蕴》,见《中国科学技术典籍通汇·数学卷三》,郑州:河南教育出版社,1993年,第12页。
74 [清]李光地:《周易折中》,北京:九州出版社,2002年,第1098页。

著《数度衍》,并自著《乘除新法》,一时从学者奉为准绳。"[75]《周易折中》以朱熹《周易本义》为纲领而杂采其他易说。[76]康熙皇帝对《周易》的兴趣有多方面的原因,其中易学与算学关联的纵横图是他邀请法国耶稣会士白晋(Joachim Bouvet)研究《周易》的主因。[77]因此,《数理精蕴》《周易折中》等官方著作不乏参用《数度衍》的可能。

清中叶皖派经学家江永撰《河洛精蕴》,被认为是清代汉学家中推崇图书之学的代表作。[78]该书直云:"方圆内外之体象已藏于河图,勾股开方之算术悉具于洛书。"[79]其卷六直以勾股解河洛。因此,虽然一般认为"《数度衍》一书在梅文鼎的大量著作及其影响之下只好为清初第二等的数学著作了,而方中通的工作因此也一直没有被清代后来一些数学家所重视"[80],但其实《数理精蕴》《周易折中》及清代之后的易学、算学研究很可能受到《数度衍》的影响,不过这个问题还需要进一步的确证。

---

[75] 韩琦:《科学、知识与权力——日影观测与康熙在历法改革中的作用》,《自然科学史研究》2011年第1期,第6—7页。

[76] 朱伯崑:《易学哲学史》第4卷,北京:华夏出版社,1995年,第4页。

[77] 韩琦:《易学与科学:康熙、耶稣会士白晋与〈周易折中〉的编撰》,《自然辩证法研究》2019年第7期,第63页。

[78] 朱伯崑:《易学哲学史》第4卷,北京:华夏出版社,1995年,第295页。

[79] [清]江永:《河洛精蕴》,蕴真书屋,1774年,第3页。潘澍原已关注到江永《河洛精蕴》中河图洛书与算学内容的具体关联,将有专论发表。

[80] 严敦杰:《方中通〈数度衍〉评述》,《安徽史学》,1960年第1期,第56—57页。

李善兰《椭圆正术解》注记

李兆华 （天津师范大学数学科学学院）

摘要 徐有壬(1800—1860)《椭圆正术》(成于1840年之前)简化了《历象考成后编》(1742)记载的真近点角与平近点互求的方法。以徐著文字过简，李善兰(1811—1882)著《椭圆正术解》(成于1860年之前)为之注解。本文解释并补充了李善兰的证明，指出徐有壬《椭圆正术》推动了李善兰关于开普勒方程的研究。

关键词 历象考成后编；椭圆正术；椭圆正术解

《历象考成后编》(1742)卷一"椭圆角度与面积相求"节给出"以角求积""以积求角""借积求角""借角求角"四种算法。[1]其中，后三种算法所解决的是同一类问题，故亦可统称为"以积求角"。"以角求积""以积求角"分别对应太阳视运动的有真近点角求平近点角、有平近点角求真近点角的计算。《历象考成后编》认为，地球位于椭圆的一个焦点上，太阳绕地球沿椭圆轨道运动。这是日地位置颠倒的开普勒第一定律。"以角求积""以积求角"与这一设定并未表现出矛盾。《历象考成后编》的计算过程均以具体数值表述，注重计算结果的精确，而计算的主要步骤并非显然。焦循(1763—1820)《释椭》[2](1796)省略具体数值，提炼计算步骤，使之成为比较完整的算法。徐有壬(1800—1860)《椭圆正术》[3](1840年之前成书[4])进一步简化算法，且以比例式表出所求量以便运用对数计算。是书之重点是第一术以角求积、第二术以积求角。李善兰(1811—1882)以徐"法简而密""恐学者骤难悟入"[5]，为之注解，包括图与说，成《椭圆正术解》二卷(约成于1860年之前[6])。其重点在于第一术和第二术的注解。李善兰照录徐著原文，所加注解低一字区别。是书包括徐、李两氏的工作，其第一术与第二术为本文关注之所在。

在中国数学史的研究中，李俨先生首先注意到"椭圆角度与面积相求"四法及徐有壬、李善兰的著作。[7]薄树人先生首先指出，"以积求角"给出开普勒方程的近似解法。[8]近年来，这一课题的研究出现新的进展。在内容诠释、方法分析等方面均有深刻的结果面世。[9,10,11]本文仅就《椭圆正术解》涉及的数学知识做几点注记，以此作为上述诸说的补充。

1　戴进贤、徐懋德，等：《历象考成后编》，《中国科学技术典籍通汇》，天文卷，第7分册，郑州：河南教育出版社，1993年，第998—1021页。

2　焦循：《释椭》。《里堂学算记》，1799(嘉庆四年)刊本。

3　徐有壬：《椭圆正术》。《白芙堂算学丛书》，1872(同治十一年)刊本。

4　韩琦：《务民义斋算学摘要》，《中国科学技术典籍通汇》，数学卷，第5分册，郑州：河南教育出版社，1993年，第647页。

5　李善兰：《椭圆正术解》卷一。《则古昔斋算学》，1867(同治六年)刊本。

6　徐有壬殁于1860年，谥庄愍。《椭圆正术解》小序称徐有壬"徐君青中丞"。李著若成于徐氏殁后，则应称谥号。

7　李俨：《中算家的圆锥曲线说》，《李俨钱宝琮科学史全集》，第7卷，沈阳：辽宁教育出版社，1998年，第492—495页。

8　薄树人：《清代对开普勒方程的研究》，《薄树人文集》，合肥：中国科学技术大学出版社，2003年，第455—466页。

9　冯立昇，牛亚华：《李善兰对椭圆及其应用问题的研究》，李迪主编：《数学史研究文集》，第三辑，呼和浩特：内蒙古大学出版社，台北：九章出版社，1992年，第100—111页。

10　高红成：《李善兰对微积分的理解和运用》，《中国科技史杂志》，第30卷第2期，2009年，第222—230页。

11　高红成：《此算与彼算：圆锥曲线在清代》，广州：广东人民出版社，2018年，第64—73页，第115—128页。

一、"以角求积""以积求角"的数学意义

"以角求积""以积求角"与开普勒第二定律有关。兹仅就其数学意义作一说明。在以下的讨论中，角 α，M 等均为弧度，运算结果化为角度。

如图1，点 O 是椭圆的中心，点 A 是顶点，F_1，F_2 是焦点，大半径 $OA=a$，小半径 $OC=b$，两心差 $OF_1=OF_2=c$。点 P 在椭圆上，$\angle AF_1P=\alpha$，点 G 在大辅圆上，$\angle AOG=M$。

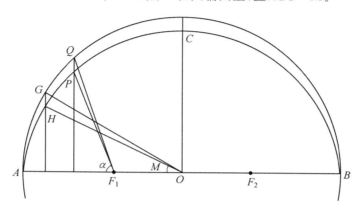

图1 实引角与平引角互求示意图

依《椭圆正术解》，"以角求积""以积求角"分别给出下列两个问题的解法：

(a) 已知 α，面积 $AF_1Q=$ 面积 AOG，求 M。

(b) 已知 M，面积 $AOG=$ 面积 AF_1Q，求 α。

其中，α 称为实引角或实行（真近点角），M 称为平引角或平行（平近点角）。在(a)中，"角""积"分别指 α、面积 AF_1Q。在(b)中，"积""角"分别指面积 AOG、α。

题设面积相等这一条件亦可表示为

$$\text{面积 } AOG = \frac{a}{b} \text{ 面积 } AF_1P$$

$$\text{面积 } AF_1P = \text{面积 } AOH$$

前者相当于平近点角的定义。后者是《历象考成后编》采用的条件。在此条件下，在(a)中，"角""积"分别指 α、面积 AF_1P。在(b)中，"积""角"分别指面积 AOH、α。比较可知，《椭圆正术解》采用的条件可减少计算量。

二、第一术以角求积注记

《椭圆正术解》第一术共分三步完成计算。注记顺序依此。

第一步求借角。李善兰注解求借角图如图2所示。其中，辅助圆系本文添加以便叙述。

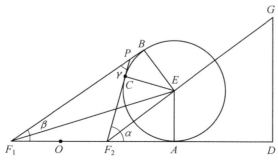

图2 求借角图

在图 2 中，点 O 是椭圆的中心，点 A 是顶点，F_1,F_2 是焦点，$OA=a,OF_1=OF_2=c$，点 P 在椭圆上。α,β,γ 分别是实引角、借角、较角。EF_2,EF_1 分别是 α,β 的角平分线。$EA\perp F_1A$。

徐有壬给出的结果是

$$\frac{a+c}{a-c}=\frac{\tan\frac{\alpha}{2}}{\tan\frac{\beta}{2}} \tag{1}$$

据此，已知 α，可得 β。既得 β，可得 $\gamma=\alpha-\beta$。

李善兰注解给出的推导过程是，在 $\text{Rt}\triangle F_1AE$ 中求得 $EA=(a+c)\tan\frac{\beta}{2}$。延长 F_2A 使得 $F_2D=F_1A=a+c$。在 $\text{Rt}\triangle F_2DG$ 中求得 $GD=(a+c)\tan\frac{\alpha}{2}$。又知 $F_2A=a-c$。由 $\text{Rt}\triangle F_2DG$ 与 $\text{Rt}\triangle F_2AE$ 相似，知 $\frac{F_2D}{F_2A}=\frac{GD}{EA}$。将各值代入即得式(1)。

依李善兰题设条件，EA 应是椭圆顶点 A 的切线。这里引出一个问题：两条角平分线 EF_1,EF_2 与顶点 A 的切线 EA 何以三线共点。一种意见认为，根据椭圆的几何性质，这两条角平分线的交点正落在这条垂线上。[12] 此外，未见具体说明。另一种意见认为，比较直接的解法是运用下述性质：椭圆的相交两切线对同一焦点张等角。同时指出，在当时以及后来有关圆锥曲线的翻译著作中，这一性质未见记载。[13] 这一问题迄今尚无比较一致的意见。本文给出如下的解释以资讨论。参见图 2，作外角 α、内角 β 的角平分线，交点为 E。作 $EA\perp F_1F_2$，交延长线于点 A。以 E 为圆心（旁心），EA 为半径作圆，与 F_1P 的延长线、F_2P 分别切于点 B、点 C。因点 F_1,F_2 是焦点，点 P 在椭圆上，故 $\triangle PF_1F_2$ 的三边和为 $2(a+c)$，又

$$\begin{aligned}F_1A+F_1B&=(F_1F_2+F_2A)+(F_1P+PB)\\&=(F_1F_2+F_2C)+(F_1P+PC)\\&=F_1F_2+F_1P+(F_2C+PC)\\&=F_1F_2+F_1P+F_2P\end{aligned}$$

即

$$2F_1A=2(a+c)$$
$$F_1A=a+c$$

此式说明，垂足 A 恰是椭圆的一个顶点。由是可知，李善兰题设条件合理。

第二步求借积。求借积的注解，李善兰有所修改。修改的结果载于该书卷二之末。所见文献尚未论及此一修改后的方法。李善兰说明了修改的原因：

> 《椭圆正术解》既卒业，吾友华君若汀读之，谓求借积度正弦之图微嫌太繁。因复作图，稍简于前，解之如左。[14]

如图 3，右侧（圆内部分）为李善兰"复作"之图。点 O 是椭圆中心，点 A 是顶点，F_1,F_2 是焦点，$OA=a,OC=b,OF_1=OF_2=c$，点 P 在椭圆上。较角 $\angle F_1PF_2=\gamma$，求借积度（偏近点角）$\angle AOQ$，记为 E。

---

[12] 薄树人：《清代对开普勒方程的研究》，《薄树人文集》，合肥：中国科学技术大学出版社，2003 年，第 463 页，注①。
[13] 高红成：《此算与彼算：圆锥曲线在清代》，广州：广东人民出版社，2018 年，第 66－68 页。
[14] 李善兰：《椭圆正术解》卷二，《则古昔斋算学》同治六年(1867)刊本。

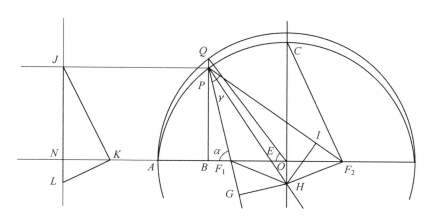

图 3 求借积度图

徐有壬给出的结果是

$$\frac{c}{b}=\frac{\tan\frac{\gamma}{2}}{\sin E} \tag{2}$$

据此，已知 γ，可得 $\sin E, E$。

李善兰注解给出的推导过程是，求出 $\triangle PF_1F_2$ 面积的两个不同的表达式，建立等式。先作 $\angle OF_2H=\frac{\gamma}{2}$，得点 H。联结 HP，李善兰认为 HP 是角 γ 的角平分线。作 HG, HI 分别垂直于角 γ 的两边，有 $\text{Rt}\triangle HGF_1$ 与 $\text{Rt}\triangle HIF_2$ 全等，$\text{Rt}\triangle PGH$ 与 $\text{Rt}\triangle PIH$ 全等。于是

$$2a=PF_1+PF_2=PG+PI=2PI$$
$$PI=a$$

$$\text{面积 } PF_1HF_2=\text{面积 } PGHI=PI\times HI=a^2\tan\frac{\gamma}{2}$$

$$\text{面积 } HF_1F_2=c^2\tan\frac{\gamma}{2}$$

$$\begin{aligned}\text{面积 } PF_1F_2&=\text{面积 } PF_1HF_2-\text{面积 } HF_1F_2\\&=a^2\tan\frac{\gamma}{2}-c^2\tan\frac{\gamma}{2}=(a^2-c^2)\tan\frac{\gamma}{2}\\&=b^2\tan\frac{\gamma}{2}\end{aligned}$$

又

$$\text{面积 } PF_1F_2=\frac{1}{2}F_1F_2\times PB=\frac{1}{2}F_1F_2\times\frac{b}{a}QB=\frac{1}{2}\times 2c\times\frac{b}{a}\times a\sin E=bc\sin E$$

因而

$$b^2\tan\frac{\gamma}{2}=bc\sin E$$
$$b\tan\frac{\gamma}{2}=c\sin E$$

此即式(2)。

李善兰作 $\angle OF_2H=\frac{\gamma}{2}$，得点 H。联结 HP，认为 HP 是角 γ 的角平分线。这是计算过程中的关键一步，而并未说明理由。本文补充说明如下。作 $\triangle PF_1F_2$ 的外接圆，与小半径 OC 所在的直线交于 H。此直线即 F_1F_2 的垂直平分线，必平分 F_1F_2 所对的弧，即点 H 是 $\overset{\frown}{F_1HF_2}$ 的中点。因 P, F_1, H, F_2 四点共圆，同弧或等弧上的圆周角相等，故 $\angle F_1PH=\angle HPF_2=\angle OF_2H=\frac{\gamma}{2}$。李善兰确定点 H，联结 HP

即较角平分线的做法正确。

华蘅芳指出,原有求借积度正弦之图太繁。意见中肯。虽然太繁,但是并无错误。由上述计算可知,当 P, F_1, H, F_2 四点共圆时,有

$$\frac{PB}{OH}=\frac{\text{面积 } PF_1F_2}{\text{面积 } HF_1F_2}=\frac{b^2\tan\frac{\gamma}{2}}{c^2\tan\frac{\gamma}{2}}=\frac{b^2}{c^2}$$

将李善兰未化简之求借积度图中勾股形移至图 3 左侧并保持原有条件不变,得图 3 Rt△JKL,且 PJ∥BN,JN⊥BN,JK∥CF_2,KL⊥JK。因 Rt△COF_2 与 Rt△JKL 相似,故

$$\frac{b}{c}=\frac{CO}{OF_2}=\frac{JK}{KL}, \quad \frac{b^2}{c^2}=\frac{JK^2}{KL^2}=\frac{JN}{NL}$$

综上可知

$$\frac{PB}{OH}=\frac{JN}{NL}$$

因 $JN=PB$,故 $NL=OH$。李善兰原截取 $OH=NL$ 以确定点 H。所截之点 H 恰是 △PF_1F_2 的外接圆与 F_1F_2 的垂直平分线的交点。联结 HP 必为较角的角平分线。其余的计算,并无难点。李善兰注解求借积度之原法原图虽繁不误。

第三步求积差。李善兰注解求积差度图如图 4 所示。其中,平引角 M 系本文添加以便说明角 M 的计算。在图 4 中,点 O 是椭圆的中心,点 A 是顶点,F_1, F_2 是焦点,$OA=a$,$OC=b$,$OF_1=OF_2=c$,点 P 在椭圆上。李善兰称三角形面积 QF_1O 为积差,是借积 AOQ 与面积 AF_1Q 之差,勾股形面积 DOF_1 为盈缩大差。

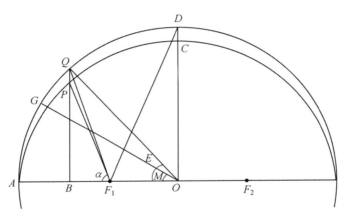

图 4　求积差度图

徐有壬给出的结果是

$$\frac{\text{半径}}{\text{借积度正弦}}=\frac{\text{盈缩大差度}}{\text{积差度}}$$

据此,可得积差度。在"盈缩大差度"之下徐氏有注:"两心差乘半周天度以圆周率除之,得盈缩大差度。"

盈缩大差度的意义是,将勾股形面积 $DOF_1=\frac{1}{2}ac$ 作为大辅圆的扇形面积,所得之扇形角度数。由《椭圆正术解》卷二"依《后编》法求诸用数于后"一节,知徐有壬以《历象考成后编》的数据为依据。《历象考成后编》取圆周率 31 415 926,大半径 $a=10^7$,两心差即 c。故"两心差乘半周天度以圆周率除之"可以表为

$$c\times\frac{180°}{3.141\ 592\ 6\times 10^7}=c\times\frac{180°}{a\pi}=\frac{c}{a}\times\frac{180°}{\pi}$$

注意到 $\frac{1}{2}ac=\frac{1}{2}la$,$l=c$,知扇形弧长等于两心差 c。故 $\frac{c}{a}$ 的意义是大辅圆的扇形角的弧度值,化为

度即 $\dfrac{c}{a} \times \dfrac{180°}{\pi}$。因而，徐有壬的结果即

$$\dfrac{a}{a\sin E} = \dfrac{\dfrac{c}{a} \times \dfrac{180°}{\pi}}{\text{积差度}} \tag{3}$$

$$\text{积差度} = \dfrac{c}{a}\sin E \times \dfrac{180°}{\pi}$$

由式(2)，式(3)得平引角度

$$M = E \times \dfrac{180°}{\pi} - \dfrac{c}{a}\sin E \times \dfrac{180°}{\pi}$$

此即徐有壬所给平引角度。徐氏称为椭圆面积度，意义相同。

盈缩大差度亦可用下法求得。设扇形角为 δ，$\dfrac{1}{2}ac = \dfrac{1}{2}\delta a^2$，则 $\delta = \dfrac{2(\tfrac{1}{2}ac)}{a^2}$，化为度，$\delta = \dfrac{2(\tfrac{1}{2}ac)}{a^2} \times \dfrac{180°}{\pi} = \dfrac{\tfrac{1}{2}ac}{\dfrac{\pi a^2}{360°}}$，即以勾股形面积 DOF_1 除以大辅圆一度之积。

依李善兰注解，徐有壬求积差度之由来如下。参见图4。

$$\dfrac{\text{高}\,DO}{\text{高}\,QB} = \dfrac{\text{面积}\,DOF_1}{\text{面积}\,QF_1O} = \dfrac{\text{面积}\,DOF_1\,\text{化度}}{\text{面积}\,QF_1O\,\text{化度}} = \dfrac{\text{盈缩大差度}}{\text{积差度}}$$

亦即

$$\dfrac{a}{a\sin E} = \dfrac{\tfrac{1}{2}ac}{\text{面积}\,QF_1O} = \dfrac{\dfrac{\tfrac{1}{2}ac}{\dfrac{\pi a^2}{360°}}}{\dfrac{\text{面积}\,QF_1O}{\dfrac{\pi a^2}{360°}}} = \dfrac{\dfrac{c}{a} \times \dfrac{180°}{\pi}}{\text{积差度}}$$

即

$$\dfrac{a}{a\sin E} = \dfrac{\dfrac{c}{a} \times \dfrac{180°}{\pi}}{\text{积差度}}$$

此即式(3)。

参照李善兰注解，求平引角的要点可概括如下。在图4中

$$\text{借积}\,AOQ - \text{积差}\,QF_1O = \text{面积}\,AF_1Q = \text{面积}\,AOG$$

或即

$$\text{面积}\,AOG = \text{借积}\,AOQ - \text{积差}\,QF_1O$$

$$\text{积差}\,QF_1O = \dfrac{1}{2}OF_1 \times QB = \dfrac{1}{2}ac\sin E$$

故

$$\dfrac{1}{2}Ma^2 = \dfrac{1}{2}Ea^2 - \dfrac{1}{2}ac\sin E \tag{4}$$

$$M = E - e\sin E,\ e = \dfrac{c}{a}$$

此即椭圆轨道的开普勒方程。由此得 M，化为度

$$M = (E - e\sin E) \times \dfrac{180°}{\pi}$$

由以上式(1)至式(4)，问题(a)获解。

三、第二术以积求角注记

《椭圆正术解》第二术共分五步完成计算。兹将第一步、第二步、第四步合并说明。

第一步求借角,第二步求借积,第四步求借边。此处借角亦称实引借角。李善兰求实引借角图如图5所示。已知平引角 $\angle AOG = M$,求实引借角 $\angle PF_1B$,记为 α_1。过焦点 F_2 作 OG 的平行线,得点 P。联结 PF_1 即得 α_1。在第一术式(1)中,令 $\beta = M$,求得 α_1。由此得较角 $\gamma = \alpha_1 - M$。一般说来,设 $\angle PF_2F_1 = M$,求得之 α_1,只是实引角的近似值,还需求其修正值。此处过焦点 F_2 作 OG 的平行线得点 P 的方法出自《历象考成后编》"借积求积"之"又法"。[15] 在图5中,若联结 OQ,则 $\angle AOQ$ 为借积度 E。既得 γ,由第一术式(2)可得 $\sin E, E$。

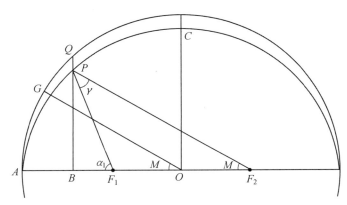

图 5 求实引借角图

此外,在 $\triangle PF_1F_2$ 中,已知 $\gamma, M, F_1F_2 = 2c$,由正弦定理可得借边

$$PF_1 = \frac{2c \times \sin M}{\sin \gamma} \tag{5}$$

第三步求积差。[16] 第一术式(4)亦即

$$\frac{1}{2}Ma^2 - (\frac{1}{2}Ea^2 - \frac{1}{2}ac\sin E) = 0$$

若

$$\frac{1}{2}Ma^2 - (\frac{1}{2}Ea^2 - \frac{1}{2}ac\sin E) = \Delta S \neq 0$$

则说明 $\frac{1}{2}Ma^2$ 还有余积或不足减。以下仅说明 $\Delta S > 0$ 的情形,$\Delta S < 0$ 的情形可以推知。参见图6,设面积 $AOD = \Delta S = \frac{1}{2}\Delta M \times a^2$,上式变为

$$\frac{1}{2}\Delta M \times a^2 = \frac{1}{2}Ma^2 - (\frac{1}{2}Ea^2 - \frac{1}{2}ac\sin E) \tag{6}$$

其中,$\frac{1}{2}Ea^2, \frac{1}{2}ac\sin E$ 分别是实引借角 α_1 相应之借积、积差。由式(6)可得

$$\Delta M = M - (E - \frac{c}{a}\sin E)$$

化为度

$$\Delta M = (M - E + \frac{c}{a}\sin E) \times \frac{180°}{\pi}$$

---

[15] 戴进贤、徐懋德,等:《历象考成后编》.《中国科学技术典籍通汇》,天文卷,第7分册,郑州:河南教育出版社,1993年,第1001页。

[16] "差",徐有壬《椭圆正术》白芙堂算学丛书本作"较"。第三步的重点是求积较。"较"字妥当。

上式即徐有壬所给积较。

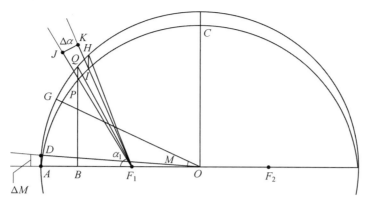

图 6 求角较度图

第五步求实引角。将李善兰本节注解的第二图、第四图简化绘为一图,得图 6。在图 6 中,PF_1 是借边,ΔM 是积较,$\Delta \alpha$ 是角较度(修正值)。徐有壬给出的结果是

$$\frac{借边自乘}{大半径乘小半径}=\frac{积较}{角较度}$$

或即

$$\frac{PF_1^2}{ab}=\frac{\Delta M}{\Delta \alpha} \tag{7}$$

由此可得

$$\Delta \alpha = \frac{ab}{PF_1^2}\Delta M = \frac{ab}{PF_1^2}(M-E+\frac{c}{a}\sin E)\times \frac{180°}{\pi}$$

于是

$$\alpha = \alpha_1 \times \frac{180°}{\pi}+\frac{ab}{PF_1^2}(M-E+\frac{c}{a}\sin E)\times \frac{180°}{\pi}$$

此即徐有壬所给实引角度。

如图 6,面积 $AOD=\Delta S>0$,说明 $\frac{1}{2}Ma^2$ 还有余积,即所得之 α_1 小于实引角。故点 P 应沿椭圆轨道继续移动,设为点 I。点 I 在大辅圆上的对应点为 H,此时

$$面积 QF_1H = 面积 AOD = \Delta S$$

面积 QF_1H 称为平引积较。面积 PF_1I 称为实引积较(小圆角积)。以点 F_1 为圆心,以 a 为半径画弧,与 F_1P、F_1I 的延长线分别交于点 J、点 K,面积 JF_1K 为角较度(大圆角积)。

依李善兰注解,式(7)的推导分为以下三步——

先化平引积较为实引积较:

$$\frac{大半径}{小半径}=\frac{平引积较}{实引积较}$$

次求角较度:

$$\frac{借边自乘}{大半径自乘}=\frac{实引积较(小圆角积)}{角较度(大圆角积)}$$

并两次比例:为一次比例

$$\frac{借边自乘}{大半径乘小半径}=\frac{平引积较}{角较度}$$

参见图 6,各式的意义显然。前式表示面积 QF_1H 与面积 PF_1I 之比。次式表示面积 PF_1I 与面积 JF_1K 之比。后式表示面积 QF_1H 与面积 JF_1K 之比。前式、次式等号两端对应相乘得后式。李善兰指出,小圆角积的两边 PF_1 与 IF_1 不等,以借边 PF_1 作为扇形半径是近似值。"两边之差极微,可勿论焉。"由后式知

$$\frac{PF_1^2}{ab} = \frac{\text{面积 } QF_1H}{\text{面积 } JF_1K} = \frac{\text{面积 } AOD}{\text{面积 } JF_1K} = \frac{\frac{1}{2}\Delta M \times a^2}{\frac{1}{2}\Delta \alpha \times a^2} = \frac{\Delta M}{\Delta \alpha}$$

即

$$\frac{PF_1^2}{ab} = \frac{\Delta M}{\Delta \alpha}$$

此即式(7)。

李善兰注解的推导稍嫌复杂。事实上,由前式

$$\frac{a}{b} = \frac{\text{面积 } QF_1H}{\text{面积 } PF_1I} = \frac{\text{面积 } AOD}{\text{面积 } PF_1I} = \frac{\frac{1}{2}\Delta M \times a^2}{\frac{1}{2}\Delta \alpha \times PF_1^2}$$

由此可得式(7)

$$\frac{PF_1^2}{ab} = \frac{\Delta M}{\Delta \alpha}$$

因而,李善兰注解的次式与后式并非必要,即不必引入"大圆角积"。《椭圆正术解》此法源自《历象考成后编》"借积求积"。[17] 因两书题设面积相等这一条件不同,故李善兰可省去"大圆角积"。《清代对开普勒方程的研究》一文给出式(7)的一个证明,[18] 其依据实即上述之前式,而于李善兰注解则未予置评。

由以上式(1)至式(3)、式(5)至式(7),问题(b)获解。

在《椭圆正术解》中,式(4)和式(6)均为文字叙述,并未列出算式。兹据"总论曰"列出以示两术之依据。李善兰注文以日行盈缩分别说明。本文仅以"行盈"的情况举例,即选定一个焦点,从椭圆大径近顶点起算。除"盈减缩加"之外,"行缩"的计算并无不同。

在《历象考成后编》之前,虽然有零星的椭圆知识传入中国,但是尚不足以提出有研究意义的问题。《历象考成后编》介绍的"椭圆角度与面积相求"四法与历法的精度相关,遂引起算家的关注。徐有壬《椭圆正术》一个明显的特点是算法的简化。其中,从"积"到"度"的简化最为突出。就"以角求积"而言,《历象考成后编》需求借积、分椭圆积、椭圆积差、实行积,再以椭圆一度定积除之得平行度。相比之下,《椭圆正术》先求较角,再求借积度与积差度,相减即得平行度。由上文式(4)、式(6)可知,从"积"到"度"简化的关键是题设面积相等这一条件的简化。虽推证的难度有所增加,但繁重的乘除运算确可避免。李善兰注解的贡献在于抓住数学要点进而阐明立术依据,且补充了必要的预备知识,使得"以角求积"与"以积求角"成为理术完整的算法。在《代微积拾级》十八卷出版(1859)之前,"椭圆角度与面积相求"与"椭圆求周"是圆锥曲线研究的重点。《椭圆正术解》是"椭圆角度与面积相求"研究成果的一个总结。开普勒方程是一个超越方程,用初等数学知识求解这一方程存在误差控制的困难。要使计算结果达到预先指定的精度,运用无穷级数是一有效途径。在《椭圆正术解》之后,李善兰继续研究这一课题,著《椭圆新术》不分卷,《椭圆拾遗》三卷。[19] 其中的成果及意义,参见前揭冯立昇、高红成的论述。

---

17 戴进贤、徐懋德,等:《历象考成后编》。《中国科学技术典籍通汇》,天文卷,第7分卷,郑州:河南教育出版社,1993年,第1009页。

18 薄树人:《清代对开普勒方程的研究》,《薄树人文集》,合肥:中国科学技术大学出版社,2003年,第464页,注①。

19 此二种约成于1860—1863年间。

"微积溯源"：晚清传入微积分的拉格朗日代数分析风格

高红成 （天津师范大学 数学科学学院）

摘要 晚清传入的微积分主要有两个来源：《代微积拾级》(18卷)和《微积溯源》(8卷)。以这两部著作中极限、函数、微分、泰勒展式、积分等几个概念为例分析晚清传入微积分的特点。《拾级》和《溯源》中函数级数表达式直接展开，收敛性和余项均不讨论，涉及的函数均为初等函数，但两书均认为"任何函数"都可以展开成幂级数形式。展开式各项系数主要是高阶微商，即"叠求微系数"，因此晚清常提到的"叠微分之法"一般都指向泰勒展式和麦克劳林公式。积分看成是微分的逆运算(reverse)。这句话也指出微分和积分的关系如同加法与减法、乘法与除法的关系，起到了"微积分基本定理"的作用。很多理论推导的基础就建立在泰勒展式上，如证明曲边梯形面积微分、旋转体的体积微分、表面积微分以及曲线弧长、曲率等。微分就是求展开式线性项的系数，积分是通过系数(导函数)求原函数，微积分运算就是建立在函数的幂级数展开上。微积分只是初等代数的一个推广。从源头上说晚清传入微积分实际上是属于拉格朗日分析代数风格，这个属性与中国传统数学有很好的契合度，很大程度上决定了晚清数学家对微积分的理解。

关键词 晚清；微积分；拉格朗日；代数分析风格

微积分是在晚清传入中国的，可以《代微积拾级》(1859年)和《微积溯源》(1874年)两书出版为标志。《代微积拾级》(后文简称《拾级》)共18卷，伟烈亚力和李善兰合译，英文底本是美国数学家罗密士(Elias Loomis, 1811—1889)著的 *Elements of Analytical Geometry and of the Differential and Integral Calculus* (New York: Harper & Brothers Publishers, 1852)。该书卷1至卷9是"代数几何"，即现在的解析几何，卷10至卷16为微分学基本内容，卷17至18为积分学基本内容。

《微积溯源》(8卷)，傅兰雅和华蘅芳合译，英文底本是《不列颠百科全书》(*Encyclopaedia Britannica*)第8版(1853—1860年)中 Fluxions("流数术")词条，该词条由英国数学家华里司(William Wallace, 1768—1843年)撰写。前4卷论述微分，后4卷论述积分。华蘅芳《微积溯源》的序言中称：

> 余既与西士傅兰雅译毕《代数术》二十五卷，更思求其进境，故又与傅君译此书焉。先是咸丰年间，曾有海宁李壬叔与西士伟烈亚力译出《代微积拾级》一书，流播海内，余素与壬叔相友，得读其书，粗明微积二术之梗概，所以又译此书，盖欲补其所略也。[2]

《微积溯源》(后文简称《溯源》)所介绍的微积分知识比《拾级》丰富，也更为系统。

这两本书所带来的"微积分"方法引起了晚清数学家极大的关注。李善兰曾称有了"微分术"和"积分术""由是一切曲线、曲线所函面、曲面、曲面所函体，昔之所谓无法者今皆有法。一切八线求弧背、弧背求八线、真数求对数、对数求真数，昔之视为至难者，今皆至易。"[3] 他甚至这样对华蘅芳介绍《代微积拾级》：

---

[1] 基金项目：中国博士后科学基金资助项目(编号：2017M621115)。
[2] 华里司原著：《微积溯源》，傅兰雅、华蘅芳合译，上海：江南制造局，1874年，华蘅芳序。
[3] 罗密士原著：《代微积拾级》，伟烈亚力、李善兰合译，上海：墨海书馆，1859年，李善兰序。

此为算学中上乘功夫,此书一出,非特中法几可尽废,即西法之古者亦无所用之矣。[4]

我们知道,在微积分和泰勒公式传入之前,清代中期数学家在研究一些弧矢互求问题中已经形成了自己独特的关于三角函数、对数函数幂级数展开研究传统,已经触及微积分。伟烈亚力曾评述道:

微分、积分为中土算书所未有,然观当代天算家,如董方立氏、项梅侣氏、徐君青氏、戴鄂士氏、顾尚之氏,暨李君秋纫所著各书,其理有甚近微分者,因不用代数式,故或言之甚繁,推之甚难。[5]

按理说,这种处理曲线求积问题更快捷、更具有竞争力的方法应该很快就被晚清数学家所理解和接受,很大程度上可以解决之前传统方法"言之甚繁""推之甚难"的问题,但是,事实上并非如此,甚至"微积分"一度还被忽视或忽略。以李善兰本人为例,他就没有多少练习这一"上乘功夫"的实践。

已有研究表明,当时的学习者几乎都只关心如何利用微积分方法去解决他们以前很难或者无法解决的具体问题,问题主要集中于积分术与曲线求积问题,如微积分方法在长度、面积、体积、三角函数与对数函数幂级数展开等方面的应用[6],夏鸾翔[7]与李善兰[8]可称这方面的代表。中算家们对微积分是有选择性地吸收。为什么有这种选择性呢?本文认为这与晚清传入的微积分的特点有关。这一方面,以往的研究并不多。洪万生曾说《拾级》 a programmed and algorithmic style [9],汪晓勤说《拾级》"通俗易懂"[10],田淼认为《拾级》中"一个一般性的可以将任何函数化为幂级数的公式"自然会引起中算家的关注,同时《拾级》具有程序性和算法性的特点,也使得中算家更容易接受。[11]这些都是简单介绍,没有深入地探讨。本文对照英文底本,结合微积分发展史的研究,对晚清传入微积分的特点进行"溯源"研究。

一、两书中函数、极限、微分、泰勒级数、积分等概念分析

(一)函数概念

《拾级》卷十:"凡此变数中函彼变数,则此为彼之函数。"(原文为:One variable is said to be a function of another variable, when the first is equal to a certain algebraic expression containing the second.)这是function翻译成"函数"的来源,这里的函数基本上指的是包含变量和自变量的代数表达式,"函"有"包含"的意思。

《溯源》第2款:"若有彼此二数皆为变数,此数变,而彼数因此之变而亦变者,则彼数为此数之函数。"(原文为:One quantity is said to be a function of another when they are so related that the latter being supposed to change its value, the former also changes its value。)

按两书之后的举例,函数包括幂函数、指数函数、对数函数、三角函数及其他们通过加减乘除开方运算组成的解析式,可以与当今的"初等函数"对应,但还分代数函数(algebraic function,《拾级》译为"代数函数",《溯源》译为"常函数",平常函数的意思)和超越函数(transcendental function,"越函数"),显函数(explicit function,"阳函数"),隐函数(implicit function,"阴函数")的区别。

---

[4] 华蘅芳:《学算笔谈》,行素轩算稿本,1893,卷五。
[5] 罗密士原著:《代微积拾级》,伟烈亚力、李善兰合译,上海:墨海书馆,1859年,伟烈亚力序。
[6] 汪晓勤:《关于〈代微积拾级〉的一个注记》,《浙江大学学报(理学版)》2001年第4期。
[7] 高红成:《夏鸾翔对二次曲线求积问题的研究:兼论中算家对微积分的早期认识和理解》,《自然科学史研究》2009年第1期。
[8] 高红成:《李善兰对微积分的理解与运用》,《中国科技史杂志》2009年第2期。
[9] Horng, Wann-sheng, Li Shanlan: The impact of Western mathematics in China during the 19th century, The City University of New York, 1991, p.330.
[10] 汪晓勤:《中西科学交流的功臣——伟烈亚力》,北京:科学出版社,2000年,第54页。
[11] 田淼:《中国数学的西化历程》,济南:山东教育出版社,2005年,第189页。

可见,这两书中的"函数"大多数指向解析表达式,结合后来对级数的论述,还包括幂级数。

(二)极限概念

《拾级》中极限概念。微分部分倒是从"极限"开始,《拾级》称"凡变数有限,限者,其数为变数所渐近而永不能到,或必不能过,故谓之限。"(卷十页二)"限"是"极限(limit)"的翻译,原文是:

The limit of a variable quantity is that value which it continually approaches, so as, to differ from it by less than any assignable quantity.[12]

在《微积溯源》中,第3款开始讲极限,也只是例说。如用圆的面积同为圆的外切正多边形的面积、内接正多边形面积的极限,引用《代数术》中的结论说明 $\frac{x}{\sin x}$ 的极限是 1,$(1+\frac{1}{n})^n$ 的极限是 e。

显然,这两书中"极限"定义都是描述性的,并没有用严格的 $\varepsilon-\delta$ 语言。《拾级》底本虽然是1852年出版,但所介绍的微积分并非以极限论为基础。书中对函数的连续性、可导性、级数的收敛性等问题均不讨论。

(三)微分概念及其算法

微分的定义为"变比例的极限"。

《拾级》中"微分之理乃详明函数及自变数两变比例相与之比例"(《拾级》卷十页六),原文是:The object of the Differential Calculus is to determine the ratio between the rate of variation of the independent variable, and that of the function into which it enters. (p118)

微分的定义是"函数与变数之变比例,俱谓之微分,用彳号记之。"(卷十页八至九)原文是:The rate of variable of a function or of any variable quantity is called its differential, and is denoted by the letter d placed before it. (p120)

求微系数(微商、导数)的法则:"一切独变数函数之微系数可类推。法任以长数若干加于自变数,求得函数之同数,以原式减之,又以辛约之,乃令辛为○而求比例之限,所得即微系数。"(《拾级》卷十页十)原文是:

RULE Give to variable any arbitrary increment h, and find the corresponding value of the function; from which subtract its primitive value. Divide the remainder by the increment h, and find the limit of this ratio, by making the increment equal to zero; the result will be the differential coefficient. (p122)

在这里,求微商就是在求得函数与自变量的增量比之后令增量为0的运算,即

$$\frac{u(x+h)-u(x)}{h} \Rightarrow 令 h=0 \Rightarrow \frac{du(x)}{dx} \tag{1}$$

进一步,该书先证明幂函数的增量函数可以展成级数形式,进而推广到任何函数的增量函数 $u(x+h)$ 可以展成 h 的幂级数,在这个基础上认为 $u(x+h)$ 为三部分之和:

> 以戌为天之函数,天变为天⊥辛,则所得函数为三者所合。一,原函数戌;二,原函数之微系数乘辛;三,天辛二元之函数乘辛平方。

用现代数学符号表示即

$$u(x+h) = u(x) + \frac{du(x)}{dx}h + g(x,h)h^2$$

---

[12] Loomis Elias, Elements of Analytical Geometry and of the Differential and Integral Calculus, New York: Harper & Brothers, 1852, p.115.

《溯源》中第 4 款：先通过一些案例，说明函数变比例。之后指出：任意函数 u 是 x 的函数，它的自变量 x 获得一个增量 h（"长数"），则增量函数 u' 可表示为

$$u' = u + ph + qh^2 + rh^3 + sh^4 + \cdots \tag{2}$$

这是一个关键代数式，也是之后推导的出发点，即默认任何函数与其增量函数之间相差增量的幂级数。这样的话，"变比例"为

$$\frac{u'-u}{h} = p + qh + rh^2 + sh^3 + \cdots$$

当 h "小至甚近于 0" 时，"变比例之限"为 p。

第 6 款给出"求微分之公法"，任何函数 u 求微分，就将增量函数 u' 展开式（2）的一次项 ph 中 h 换为 $\mathrm{d}x$ 即 $p\mathrm{d}x$ 即可，即 $\mathrm{d}u = p\mathrm{d}x$。

第 7 款说明第 4 款和第 6 款求微分是一样的，"其法本无异"。

之后在式（2）、第 6 款以及二项式展开式的基础上，推导出函数的和差积商求微分法则以及基本初等函数的微分。

可以看出，这两书中"微分"更多是一种演算、一种算法。在《拾级》中是令"变比例"中增量为 0 的演算，在《溯源》中则是求增量函数幂级数展开式中一次项系数的演算。

（四）泰勒级数及其基础作用

《拾级》卷十一"叠微分"，即高阶微分，此卷第一款和第三款分别介绍了"马格老临公式"和"戴劳公式"，即现今一般译作的麦克劳林（C. Maclaurin,1698—1746）公式和泰勒（B. Taylor,1685—1731）公式，两人的人名当时分别译为"马格老临"和"戴劳"。推导（说理）过程是，以二项式函数的展开式为例例证任何函数 $u(x)$ 可以展成 x 的幂级数形式，然后用待定系数法和逐阶求微商的方法证明这一级数的各次项的系数与高阶微商的关系，从而得到泰勒公式。用现代的数学符号表示如下：

$$u(x) = (u)_{x=0} + \left(\frac{\mathrm{d}u}{\mathrm{d}x}\right)_{x=0} x + \left(\frac{\mathrm{d}^2 u}{\mathrm{d}x^2}\right)_{x=0} \frac{x^2}{1\cdot 2} + \left(\frac{\mathrm{d}^3 u}{\mathrm{d}x^3}\right)_{x=0} \frac{x^3}{1\cdot 2\cdot 3} + \cdots \tag{3}$$

$$u(x+y) = u(x) + \frac{\mathrm{d}u}{\mathrm{d}x} y + \frac{\mathrm{d}^2 u}{\mathrm{d}x^2} \frac{y^2}{1\cdot 2} + \frac{\mathrm{d}^3 u}{\mathrm{d}x^3} \frac{y^3}{1\cdot 2\cdot 3} + \cdots \tag{4}$$

《拾级》这个证明是例证推广，不是严格的证明。

《微积溯源》第 27 款介绍高阶微分的定义，即所谓的"叠微分"。

第 28 款指出，$f(x)$ 任何函数的增量函数 $f(x+h)$ 都可以表示为增量 h 的级数，即

$$f(x+h) = f(x) + ph + qh^2 + rh^3 + sh^4 + \cdots \tag{5}$$

这是欧拉（《溯源》翻译成"尤拉"）的观点，也是之后泰勒公式推导的出发点。之后的几款就是要证明式（5）可以化成泰勒级数。

第 29 和第 30 款两款证明，$f(x+h)$ 按 h 的幂任何展开式中，除特殊的 x 值外，不会包含 h 的分数幂和负幂。

在前两款的基础上，第 31 款证明，$f(x+h)$ 按 h 展开的级数必定是式（5）。这就相当证明了（5）中"任何函数都可以展成增量的幂级数"。紧接着，通过形式论证的方式，考虑 $f(x+h+k)$ 的两种形式的展开，(i) 用 $h+k$ 代替（5）中的 h，相当于 $f[x+(h+k)]$；(ii) 用 $x+k$ 代替（5）中的 x，相当于 $f[(x+k)+h]$。通过比较两个级数的系数之后，得到式（5）中系数 $p,q,r,s,\cdots$ 与高阶微商的关系

$$p = \frac{\mathrm{d}u}{\mathrm{d}x}, q = \frac{1}{1\cdot 2}\frac{\mathrm{d}^2 u}{\mathrm{d}x^2}, r = \frac{1}{1\cdot 2\cdot 3}\frac{\mathrm{d}^3 u}{\mathrm{d}x^3}, s = \frac{1}{1\cdot 2\cdot 3\cdot 4}\frac{\mathrm{d}^4 u}{\mathrm{d}x^4}, \cdots$$

代入到式（5）中，即得到

$$f(x+h) = u + \frac{\mathrm{d}u}{\mathrm{d}x} h + \frac{\mathrm{d}^2 u}{\mathrm{d}x^2} \frac{h^2}{1\cdot 2} + \frac{\mathrm{d}^3 u}{\mathrm{d}x^3} \frac{h^3}{1\cdot 2\cdot 3} + \frac{\mathrm{d}^4 u}{\mathrm{d}x^4} \frac{h^4}{1\cdot 2\cdot 3\cdot 4} + \cdots \tag{6}$$

《溯源》指出这就是"戴劳所设之例"，即泰勒定理（Taylor's theorem），一般称为泰勒公式。

第 28～31 款相当于"证明"了任何函数可以展成幂级数，而且这个级数就是泰勒公式，与高阶微系数（微商）联系起来了。证明细节在此不展开。

第39款,由泰勒公式推导出麦克劳林公式。

同样,《拾级》并没有对式(5)进行证明,而是先讲麦克劳林公式,再讲泰勒公式。《溯源》对于"任何函数可以展成幂级数"这个命题进行了证明,而且还证明这个幂级数就是泰勒级数,然后推导出麦克劳林公式。这个逻辑链十分清晰。这也许就是华蘅芳所说补《拾级》"所略",将 Fluxions 这个词条译成"微积溯源",而不是直接译成"流数术"的原因所在。卢靖在研究《溯源》时注意到了这一点,他在第31款注道:"《拾级》只有戴氏新术,无下款(指第31款)"。

这两部译著采用李善兰和伟烈亚力创建的汉译代数符号,如(6)式当时表示成

$$戌' = 函(天 \perp 辛) = 戌 \perp \frac{彳天}{彳戌}辛 \perp \frac{彳天^{二}}{彳戌^{二}} \times \frac{一 \cdot 二}{辛^{二}} \perp \frac{彳天^{三}}{彳戌^{三}} \times \frac{一 \cdot 二 \cdot 三}{辛^{三}} \perp \frac{彳天^{四}}{彳戌^{四}} \times \frac{一 \cdot 二 \cdot 三 \cdot 四}{辛^{四}} \perp \cdots$$

需要指出的是,《拾级》和《溯源》中级数表达式直接展开,收敛性和余项均不讨论,涉及的函数均为初等函数,但两书均认为"任何函数"都可以展开成幂级数形式。展开式各项系数是高阶微商,即"叠求微系数",因此晚清常提到的"叠微分之法"一般都指向这两个公式。作为示例,书中用这两个公式推导了二项式展开式、指数函数的幂级数、三角函数的幂级数,显示出了很强的程序性和算法特点。

在现代数学中,泰勒公式是现代有限差分的理论基础,其重要意义在于表明充分光滑的函数可以用多项式进行局部逼近,它使得单变量函数幂级数展式在理论上成为可能,具有很强的一般性。[13] 因为《拾级》和《溯源》两书涉及的大都是初等函数,在"充分光滑的函数"范围内。

之后,与微分应用有关的理论推导几乎都建立在泰勒公式上,如推求函数的极值、不定式的极限、曲线的切线与法线、曲率、渐近线等,证明曲边梯形面积微分、旋转体的体积微分、表面积微分,以及曲线弧长、曲率等。

如《拾级》卷十四第九款,推导曲边面积微分的过程。

梯形 $PRR'P'$ 的面积 $= RR' \times \frac{1}{2}(PR + P'R') = \frac{1}{2}h(y+y')$,所以 $\frac{梯形}{h} = \frac{1}{2}(y+y')$,由泰勒公式有,$y' = y + \frac{dy}{dx}h + \frac{d^2y}{dx^2}\frac{h^2}{1 \cdot 2} + \cdots$,

所以,$\frac{1}{2}(y+y') = y + \frac{dy}{dx}\frac{h}{2} + \frac{d^2y}{dx^2}\frac{h^2}{4} + \cdots$

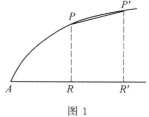

图1

$\frac{梯形}{h} = y + \frac{dy}{dx}\frac{h}{2} + \frac{d^2y}{dx^2}\frac{h^2}{4} + \cdots$,令 $h=0$(相当于求极限,$h \to 0$),可得

$$\frac{ds}{dx} = y, \text{或者 } ds = ydx \tag{7}$$

再如,《溯源》第65款推求次切距,$QR:RP = PB:BS$,即

$$y' - y : h = y : BS$$

$$y' - y = \frac{dy}{dx}h + \frac{d^2y}{dx^2}\frac{h^2}{1 \cdot 2} + \cdots$$

所以

$$\left(\frac{dy}{dx} + \frac{d^2y}{dx^2}\frac{h}{1 \cdot 2} + \cdots\right) : 1 = y : BS$$

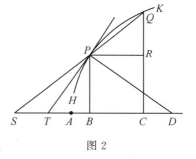

图2

当点 Q 趋近于点 P,BS 趋近于次切距 BT,所以 $\frac{dy}{dx} : 1 = y : BT$,

次切距 $BT = y\frac{dx}{dy}$。

(五)积分概念

至于"积分",《拾级》卷十七"积分"的"总论"称,"积分为微分之还原。其法之要在识别微分所由生

---

[13] 陆晓明,王能超:《泰勒公式通古今:微积分史学习札记之二》,《高等数学研究》1998年第3期。

之函数"。原文是

> The Integral Calculus is thereverse of the differential Calculus, its object being to determine the expression or function from which a given differential has been derived. //The function from which the given differential has been derived, is called its integral. [14]

《溯源》第 99 款,"反流数者,即积分算法也。此法专以任何函数之微分,求其原函数之式。"英文原文是

> The inverse method of fluxions, or integral calculus, treats of the analytic processes by which a function may be found, such, that being differentiated, it shall produce a given differential. This function has been called, by writers on fluxions, the fluent or flowing quantity; and by writers on the differential calculus, the integral of the proposed differential. //To find the integral of a differential is to integrate that differential; and the process by which the integral is found is called integration. [15]

在这两部著作中,积分都看成微分的逆运算(reverse,inverse)。这里的"积分"其实用现今的"不定积分"解释比较合适。在书中,微分和积分的关系如同加法与减法、乘法与除法的关系,这个关系就是"微积分基本定理"。[16]华蘅芳也认识到这一点,他说:"其积分术为微分之还原,犹之开平方为自乘之还原,除法为乘之还原,减法为加之还原也。"[17]积分定义之后,介绍了各种函数的(不定)积分以及运算的技巧,遇到"不可积函数"时则直接运用泰勒公式将其展开成无穷级数,然后逐项积分。

《拾级》的第 18 卷、《微积溯源》的第 7 卷介绍了积分的应用,主要有求面积与体积、曲线弧长,以及旋转曲面的表面积和旋转体的体积,显示了积分术在求积问题上强大的功效。

纵观两书所译介的微积分,都是以微分为中心,积分当成微分的逆运算。泰勒公式(函数的幂级数展开)被当成是运算的基础。利用幂级数,就可把微积分推广到超越函数上,而且可以通过逐项微分和积分来计算"任意"超越函数的导数及原函数,从而得出其微分及积分。

二、19 世纪初微积分的拉格朗日代数分析风格

函数是数学史上一个重要定义,明确的函数定义是从欧拉开始的。[18] 1748 年欧拉《无穷分析引论》出版,提出一个变量的函数是用任何方式由这个变量和数字或常量所构成的一个解析表达式。"解析表达式"表示是与代数运算或超越运算联系的由符号标示的量或者数的表示式。代数运算包括加、减、乘、除、乘方、开方,还可以加上代数方程求解。超越运算包括指数运算、对数运算以及"积分法大量提供的运算",由此他把函数划分为代数函数和超越函数。[19]。前者由变量和常数通过加、减、乘、除、乘幂、开根号,以及一个方程的解析所构成。后者是那些通过指数、对数,以及更一般地,通过积分而定义的。欧拉讨论函数时的一个重要工具是幂级数。他深信,或许除了孤立点上,任何函数和都可以用幂级数来表

---

14 Loomis Elias, Elements of Analytical Geometry and of the Differential and Integral Calculus, New York: Harper & Brothers, 1852, p. 217.

15 William Wallace. Fluxions. Encyclopaedia Britannica, 8th ed., 1853～1860, p. 714.

16 洪万生先生认为这在《拾级》中起到微积分基本定理(the Fundamental Theorem of calculus)的作用(Horng, Wang-Sheng. p335),这是不对的,这里仅仅是证明面积微分的求法。

17 华里司原著:《微积溯源》,傅兰雅、华蘅芳合译,上海:江南制造局,1874 年,华蘅芳序。

18 胡作玄:《近代数学史》,济南:山东教育出版社,2006 年,第 250 页。

19 胡作玄:《近代数学史》,济南:山东教育出版社,2006 年,第 251 页。

示,但他没有给出证明。欧拉的函数概念对后世有着极大的影响,虽然之后有若干修正,但直到柯西1821年出版的《代数分析》还一直用欧拉函数定义。

从微积分发展史的角度而言,泰勒当时也认为,可以用有限差分和极限既可解释牛顿的流数法又可解释莱布尼茨的微分法,流数法的原理全部能从增量的原理直接推导出来。但如何从有限差分过渡到流数,他并不清楚,认为只要把"初始的增量"写成零就行了。因此,他先从有限差分出发,得到格雷戈里-牛顿内插公式,然后令其中的初始增量为零,项数为无穷,既没有考虑级数的收敛性,也没有给出余项的表达式。[20] 即便是牛顿和莱布尼茨,他们当时也都认为微积分是代数的扩展,是"无穷"的代数,或者是类似于无穷级数那样具有无穷多项的代数。[21] 他们之后的半个世纪,拉格朗日在他那部著名的《解析函数的理论,包括微分学的原理,从无穷小量或渐进于零的量、极限或流数的每一种考虑中解脱出来,简化到有限量的代数分析》(一般简称《解析函数论》,1797年)将泰勒公式刻画为微积分的基本定理,并将其作为自己工作的出发点。按拉格朗日的观点,微分就是求展开式线性项的系数(导函数),积分是通过系数(导函数)求原函数,微积分运算就是建立在函数的幂级数展开上。微积分只不过是初等代数的一个推广。[22] 他的目的是把微积分归结为代数,但是他的代数不仅包含多项式,而且特别包含作为多项式的推广的幂级数。欧拉认为,可以把函数 $f(x+h)$ 展成 h 的整数幂或分数幂,而只有当 $f(x)$ 中含根式时才会出现分数幂。拉格朗日把这种情形当作例外而不去管它,认为每个函数都能表示成级数,因此他得出了泰勒展开的余项公式,并在该书中首先得出了微分中值定理。虽然拉格朗日意识到收敛与发散的区别,但是他没有进行细致的研究,尤其是他没有考虑到一般函数未必可微,更谈不上多次可导。

利用幂级数,就可把微积分推广到超越函数上,而且可以通过逐项微分和积分来计算"任意"超越函数的导数及原函数,从而得出其微分及积分。在欧拉和拉格朗日时代,很少有人考虑这样做是否合理,他们连收敛、发散都很少考虑,更不用说一致收敛的概念。[23]

18世纪的数学家,都把积分当成导数或微分的逆。他们从来不问一个积分的存在性,当然在18世纪的大部分应用问题中,积分都能明确地求出来,因而不会发生积分存在与否的问题。[24] 不定积分比定积分更为基本,而定积分只不过是定积分在上限和下限取值之差而已。

拉格朗日的代数化方案就是在泰勒级数法的基础上,通过使微积分变成解析函数理论,从而最终使其成为代数分析的一部分。微积分是关于函数的一种代数形式演算,而函数 $y=f(x)$ 由一个解析表达式给出,并且这个表达式由变量和常数通过解析运算而形成,y 和 x 之间的关系由一系列示意 $f(x)$ 的运算予以揭示。[25]

从本质上看,当时的数学分析与代数学并没有什么不同,实际上都是一种符号演算技术。如果说有什么不同,那就是代数学一般涉及有限的数量,而分析涉及无穷的步骤以及无穷大、无穷小之类的量。17—18世纪的数学分析的研究对象主要是演算(calculus),如微分演算、积分演算、函数演算以及变分演算,后来还有概率演算、算符演算、向量演算、张量演算等。这些演算如同代数学中的四则运算一样,当它们有了基础之后,分析中的主要问题就成为解微分方程了。[26] 经过欧拉、拉格朗日、拉普拉斯及勒让德等人的努力,到19世纪初,微积分已经摆脱掉原来的几何的或力学的语言,形成了以函数为中心、以

---

[20] 朱学贤:《泰勒》,吴文俊主编:《世界著名科学家传记·数学家·III》,北京:科学出版社,1994年,第282—289页。

[21] M. 克莱因著:《古今数学思想》第二册,朱学贤,申又枨,叶其孝等译,上海:上海科学技术出版社,2002年,第26页。

[22] Victor J. Katz 著:《数学史通论》第2版,李文林,邹建成,胥鸣伟译,北京:高等教育出版社,2004年,第456页。

[23] 胡作玄:《近代数学史》,济南:山东教育出版社,2006年,第257页。

[24] M. 克莱因著:《古今数学思想》第二册,朱学贤,申又枨,叶其孝等译,上海:上海科学技术出版社,2002年,第126页。

[25] FRASER C G, Joseph Louis Lagrange's algebraic vision of the calculus,Historia Math,1987,14 (1):38—53;FRASER C G,The calculus as algebraic analysis: some observations on mathematical analysis in the 18—thcentury,Archive for History of Exact Sciences,1989,39(4):317—335.;范广辉,贾小勇:《拉格朗日微积分的代数视角及其评价》,《西北大学学报(自然科学版)》,2010年第3期。

[26] 胡作玄:《近代数学史》,济南:山东教育出版社,2006年,第106页。

代数运算为基础的数学分析系统。无穷的代数方法原则上已成为可解决积分、微分方程的工具。[27]

法国数学家拉克鲁瓦(S. F. Lacroix,1765—1843)的三卷本《论微分与积分》(俗称"大本拉克鲁瓦")第一卷1797年出版了,在前言中宣称,是受到拉格朗日新方法的启示,才决定撰写一本关于微积分的教程,文中将一种具有启发性的方式代替无穷小法来做微积分的基础。但是,在文本中他表现出这一时期的犹豫不决。拉克鲁瓦根据达朗贝尔和吕利耶的极限,阐释拉格朗日的级数方法。[28]为了教学,他将三卷教程写成一卷的缩减本,书名为《微积分导论》(俗称"小本拉克鲁瓦"),1802—1881年出版了九版。他一开始把微分运算建立在一类极限的概念上,这类极限在他确定微商的极限过程定义出来。因此,他指出,如果 $u=ax^2, u_1=a(x+h)^2$,则 $2ax$ 是"比值 $\frac{u_1-u}{h}$ 的极限",或者说当量 h 变小时这个比值均衡地趋向这个值,而且它可按我们选取的程度来靠近这个值。拉克鲁瓦解释说,"微分运算就是求函数和它所依赖的变量变化时产生的增量间比值的极限。"[29]

拉格朗日的幂级数方法对剑桥分析学那些有改革意识的成员颇具吸引力,他们之中包括乔治·皮柯克(G. Peacock,1791—1858),查理·巴贝奇(C. Babbage,1791—1871),赫舍尔(J. Herschel,1792—1871),1816年他们把拉克鲁瓦的《导论》翻译成英文,作为剑桥使用的一本分析教程。译者们对拉克鲁瓦"用达朗贝尔的极限方法取代更为正确和自然的拉格朗日方法"感到失望,他们在译本中前言广而告之,要读者们运用拉格朗日的方法而不用极限方法。[30]皮柯克写了长达24页的注解,详细解释拉格朗日怎样证明任何函数可以展开泰勒级数,并且明确指出泰勒公式是建立微分演算的理论基础(... the name of Taylor's Theorem, and which exhibits the whole theory of the Differential Calculus)[31]。就这样,拉格朗日的代数分析风格的微积分影响到了英美等英语国家。

从以上两部分分析可知,《拾级》《溯源》中的微积分本质上属于拉格朗日代数分析(Lagrange's algebraic analysis)风格。《拾级》的英文书名 Elements of Analytical Geometry and of the Differential and Integral Calculus 翻译成《解析几何与微分积分演算初步》可能更符合书中微积分的内容实质。

二、当时中算家的反应

华蘅芳在《算学笔谈》中以师生对话的形式谈论微积分的理解与学习,其中对泰勒公式(级数)在微分中的地位和作用认识非常到位。他认为"微分之理,必使其新函数能详为级数"[32],对于泰勒级数的用处很是推崇,他说:[33]

> 今且不论微分之用,而先言叠微分之用。用叠微分之法详各种函数为级数,凡代数术中最繁最难之式以叠微分之法驭之,俱属至简至易。又有算学中甚难求之数、不易明之理,如隐分数之同数、函数之极大极小、一切曲线之理及其独异之点,非用叠微分之法不能明。而其叠微分则从微分之法而累次求之者也。

这段话表明华蘅芳认识到把高阶微分与函数级数的关系及其强大作用。

---

[27] 胡作玄:《近代数学史》,济南:山东教育出版社,2006年,第190页。

[28] 卡尔·B. 波耶著:《微积分概念发展史》,唐生译,上海:复旦大学出版社,2007年,第257—258页。

[29] Victor J. Katz著:《数学史通论》第2版,李文林,邹建成,胥鸣伟译,北京:高等教育出版社,2004年,第548—549页。

[30] Advertisement, S. F. Lacroix. An Elementary Treatise on the Differential and Integral Calculus, with an appendix and notes, Cambridge, 1816

[31] Note B, S. F. Lacroix. An Elementary Treatise on the Differential and Integral Calculus, with an appendix and notes, Cambridge, 1816, p. 604.

[32] 华蘅芳:《学算笔谈》卷十,行素轩算稿本,1893年,十六页。

[33] 华蘅芳:《学算笔谈》卷十,行素轩算稿本,1893年,二十~二十二页。

紧接着,以学生的口吻提出,为什么泰勒公式、麦克劳林公式能将"任何函数"展成幂级数?

> 今之习算者于微分之理未能深知灼见,往往亦能从戴氏、马氏之术详各种函数为级数,则试从而问之曰:戴氏、马氏之术均能将代函数、指函数、对函数、圆函数详为级数,其造此公式之时究凭何理?何以能既合于二项例,又合于对数,又合于平圆之各线,又合于平圆弧背也?则其人必不能答矣。

华氏的回答先是指出一切函数都能求微分和高阶微分。

> 则试从而语之曰:微分之理本能赅变数所成之一切函数,则各种代函数、指函数、对函数、圆函数莫不在其赅括之中,故无不能求其微分,亦无不能求其叠次之微分,戴氏、马氏之术为各次微系数所成,则其式之能兼代、指、对、圆四种函数之用,固是微分中分内之事耳,无足为怪也。戴、马二术其理不外乎此。然学者致力于微分,其功候若在将悟未悟之时,则闻此即可恍然大悟;若其功候尚相去悬殊,恐仍不能破其疑团,何也?凡论算学之事,实义易解而虚理难明也,浅近之说易晓,而元妙之语难通也。

然后,华氏引用《溯源》的内容,从欧拉"任何函数可以展成幂级数"和拉格朗日证明这个级数就是泰勒公式,也就是(5)到(6)式的证明。他说:

> 《微积溯源》云戴氏之术其根源亦从尤拉之纪函数之法而生。如令为函(天)为变量之任何函数,以天⊥辛代其天,而令其新函数为函(天⊥辛),则此式可详之为级数函(天)⊥巳辛⊥午辛²⊥未辛³⊥…,其巳、午、未各数为天之他新函数,由原函数而生,皆与辛无涉。因其天为不定之数,故各项中之辛不能有负数、分数为指数。
>
> 此为尤拉所设之例,曾有拉果兰诸证其不误者也。学者何反疑之乎?原其所以致疑之故,盖由于未将"任何函数"四字看清耳。"令函(天)为变量天之任何函数",此句之意乃是兼代函数、指函数、对函数、圆函数而言之,并非专指一种也,则其以天加辛所成之新函数及其详得之级数亦必兼代函、指函、对函、圆函而言之,并非专指一种也。因此四种函数各详之为级数,其第一项皆为原函数,其后各项皆可依辛之正方之数自小而大序之,又皆可巳、午、未用等元代其各方之倍数,是级数虽有四类而其形则归一例也。所以可用一个公式以赅之。
>
> 借径于叠微分而得任何函数之级数。其所以必借于微分者,因微分各有其本形之公微分之式,而其叠次之微分易求也。盖自有此术而微分乃有大用矣。[34]

卢靖《叠微分补草》(稿本),书的正文分为"《拾级》求叠微分""《溯源》叠求微系数""补《拾级》求函数极大极小六题补草"三节。序文一篇,圈点勾划已见用心之专,寥寥数语颇具该书主旨:

> 微积分以叠微分为最切用。凡驭正负整分各方之二项例以及指函数、对函数、圆函数、角函数之级数,求函数之极大、极小,无不由叠求微分与代于戴、马二公式而得。[35]

卢氏稿本书名之下还有一个副标题——"求级数通法"。结合书中的例证,可以看出卢靖关注微积分的焦点在于泰勒公式。

---

[34] 华蘅芳:《学算笔谈》卷十,行素轩算稿本,1893年,二十五页。
[35] 卢靖:《叠微分补草(求级数通法)》,稿本(天津师范大学图书馆藏),1902,卢靖自序。

在南菁书院学习的杨冰[36]曾作文《微积术补代数未尽说》，把微积分当成代数的一个分支，他说：

> 今之学者耳"微积"之名，或诧为神奇，或疑为隐奥，苦无以诱其人也，则告之曰：微积术所以补代数未尽也。夫几何之学，拘于迹象，而不能如积，于是有天元补其未尽；天元之学苦于演数，而不能求公式，于是有代数补其未尽。代数既创，可谓尽矣，然而未定之数，必资于大衍（《代数术》二十一论未定之相等式，与《数书九章》大衍类似为一法），循环之数，或证以连分，驭指数以对数，驭无穷以级数，驭割圆以八线。若此类者，多非代数常法所能解，而皆统于代数，良以代数之名，固无所不赅，微积之于诸法，用虽不同，其为代数之支派一也。[37]

黄启明《微积通诠》"微分明纲"直接就说"微分之术从代数变通而得。"[38]

如前文所述，在微积分和泰勒公式传入之前，清代中期数学家在研究一些弧矢互求问题中已经形成了自己独特的关于三角函数、对数函数幂级数展开研究传统。伟烈亚力曾评述道，这些成果"其理有甚近微分者，因不用代数式，故或言之甚繁，推之甚难。"[39]

如此等等，他们的评论中，其实也把微积分归为代数。

三、结语

传入的具有现代数学特点的泰勒公式和"积分术"不仅具有很强的一般性，还具有很好的程序性和算法特点，这从"叠求微系数"的"叠"字就可看出，优势明显。李善兰在序中称有了"微分术"和"积分术"。

> 由是一切曲线、曲线所函面、曲面、曲面所函体，昔之所谓无法者今皆有法。一切八线求弧背、弧背求八线、真数求对数、对数求真数，昔之视为至难者，今皆至易。呜呼，算术至此，观止矣，蔑以加矣！[40]

总之，从以上分析可以看出，晚清传入的微积分中微分就是求展开式线性项的系数，积分是通过这个系数（其实就是导函数，但两书都没有用这个名词）求原函数，微积分运算就是建立在函数的幂级数展开上。微分与积分是互逆演算，起到了微积分基本定理的作用。微积分只是初等代数的一个推广。级数是无穷项的多项式。从"溯源"上看，晚清传入的微积分实际上是属于拉格朗日代数分析风格，很多方法具有程序性和算法特点，与中国传统数学有很好的契合度，很大程度上影响了晚清数学家对微积分的理解与吸收的程度，以及应用的偏好。

---

[36] 杨冰，字冷仙，江苏东台人，数学家和数学教育家。杨冰自幼聪颖，勤奋好学。年少时，他就聘于仇湖马家舍庞氏家族教授其子弟。1894 年，进入江阴南菁书院深造，师从崔朝庆。1901 年，任江南师范学堂数学教席，随后被派赴日本考察学制，并为日本明治大学数学家长泽龟之助邀请讲学。回国后，执教于江南高等学堂、江南师范学堂、三江师范学堂等校。陈克胜，郭世荣：《中国第一部近代学堂所用的综合科学用表——〈算表合璧〉》，《中国科技史杂志》2012 年第 1 期。

[37] 杨冰：《南菁文钞·微积术补代数未尽说》，高时良、黄仁贤主编：《中国近代教育史资料汇编·洋务运动时期教育》，上海：上海教育出版社，2007 年，第 839 页。

[38] 黄启明：《微积通诠》，广州：菁华阁，1905 年，卷一，一页．

[39] 罗密士原著：《代微积拾级》，伟烈亚力、李善兰合译，上海：墨海书馆，1859 年，伟烈亚力序。

[40] 罗密士原著：《代微积拾级》，伟烈亚力、李善兰合译，上海：墨海书馆，1859 年，李善兰序。

Lagrange's Algebraic Analysis Style of Calculus in the late Qing Dynasty

Gao Hongcheng

There are two main sources of calculus introduced in the late Qing dynasty: Dai weiji Shiji(代微积拾级,1859)and Weiji Suyuan(微积溯源,1873). The former was introduced from Elements of Analytical Geometry, and of the Differential and Integral Calculus (by Elias Loomis, New York: Harper & Brothers,1852), and the latter was from Fluxtions(by Wallace, in Encyclopaedia ,1853). Taking the concepts of limit, differentiation, Taylor expansion and integral in these two works as examples, the characteristics of calculus in the late Qing Dynasty are analyzed. Direct expansion of function series expressions was gave, and the convergence and the remainder were not discussed, and all the functions involved were elementary functions, but the two books all thought that any function can be expanded into power series form. The expansion coefficient is mainly of higher-order derivatives, namely "Dieqiu Weixishu"(叠求微积术), so this method often referred to the Taylor formula and Maclaurin formula in the late Qing Dynasty. Integral is regarded as the reverse operation of differential. It also points out that the relation between differential and integral is like the relation of addition and subtraction, multiplication and division, and plays the role of basic theorem of calculus. The basis of many theoretical derivations is based on the Taylor expansion, such as proving the differential of curved trapezoid area, volume differentiation of rotating bodies, surface area differentiation, curve arc length and curvature, etc. Differential is the coefficient of the linear term of the expansion. The integral is obtained by the coefficient (derivative function), and the calculus is based on the power series expansion of the function. Calculus is considered to be a generalization of elementary algebra. From the source, the introduction of calculus in the late Qing Dynasty actually belongs to the Lagrange's algebraic analysis style, which has a good fit with Chinese traditional mathematics and largely determines the understanding to calculus by mathematicians in the late Qing dynasty.

贵荣关于零比零的讨论
——兼论微积分理论在中国的早期传播

田淼　（中国科学院自然科学史研究所）

摘要　1877年,贵荣在《格致汇编》中以"数学奇题"的方式发表了一篇关于零比零的问题的短文,认为零比零的结果为1,并给出证明。本文指出,零比零问题是微积分理论中的一个重要问题,欧拉也曾给出相同的结论,但在早期微积分研究的语境中,他又给出此问题不同的几何解答,含无穷小的阶的讨论。《代数学》和《微积溯源》中均含以无穷小理论阐释零比零问题的内容,从二书的译者李善兰与傅兰雅对此问题的忽视,本文进一步分析了微积分在中国早期传播的特点。

1877年,贵荣在《格致汇编》中以"数学奇题"的方式发表了一篇关于零比零的问题的短文,从讨论可以看出,贵荣对此问题含意的理解并不正确。有趣的是,我们在欧拉的著作《微分学基础》中也可以看到与贵荣相似又截然本质不同的内容。通过此案例我们还可以进一步认识微积分在中国早期传播的过程及跨国知识传播的特点。

一、贵荣关于零比零问题的讨论

在1877年春的《格致汇编》中,同文馆算学生贵荣发表了一个"算学奇题",其内容为:

设有式 $\frac{0}{0}$,此式或云得0,或云得1,究竟得0得1,试求其证。

解曰: $\frac{0}{1}$ 即 $\frac{1-1}{1}=1-1$; $\frac{0}{0}=1$ 即 $\frac{1-1}{1-1}=1$。

如云 $\frac{0}{0}$ 得0不得1,则是 $\frac{0}{0}$ 等于 $\frac{0}{1}$, $\frac{1-1}{1-1}$ 等于 $\frac{1-1}{1}$ 矣。有是理乎？此一证也。

又解曰: $\frac{1}{1}=1, \frac{2}{2}=1, \frac{3}{3}=1, \frac{10}{10}=1, \frac{100}{100}=1, \frac{1000}{1000}=1, \frac{无穷}{无穷}=1$,即知 $\frac{0}{0}=1$。

如云 $\frac{0}{0}$ 得他数不得1,何以所列各试俱得1耶？以是知子母相同者,其约谓之数必为1,此又一证也。

此后,贵荣还结合《易经》《河图》《洛书》《道德经》中的内容将0和1对应于有无及传统宇宙论中的相关内容做了进一步的论述。本文仅就引文中的数学问题进行分析。

贵荣的论述无疑是错的。从分数计算的角度,分母为零的分数是没有意义的。在微积分中,零比零则涉及微分学的基础理论。贵荣给出的第一个证明为反证法,但在有限与无限之间的转换过程中,该反证法是不成立的。第二个证明为简单归纳法,同样不能推到无限。但贵荣的这篇短文所引发的问题远非仅是提供了一个错误的例证而已。下文中,我们可以看到,首先,这样的错误并非仅出现于贵荣这样

---

[1]　此文的内容是1997年在郭书春老师指导下完成的博士论文《清末书院的数学教育》中的一部分,最近又做了补充与修改。此文为国家"十四五"发展规划重大学术文化工程《(新编)中国通史》纂修工程科学技术史卷阶段性成果(项目编号:E0189001)。谨以此文感谢郭老师的指导,并为郭老师八十寿辰之贺。

图 1 贵荣"算学奇题",《格致汇编》

的清末中国数学学生的课作中,而是困扰着早期微分学研究者的普遍问题。

二、欧拉关于零比零问题的讨论

1748 年,在其《微分学基础》一书中[2],欧拉在对无穷小的讨论中探讨了零比零问题。首先,欧拉称,"无穷小量确实是零"[3],并由此引出问题:那么我们为什么不用 0 来表示无穷小。欧拉称,"两个 0 是彼此相等的,所以,它们之间没有任何区别。然而,我们要通过算术的和几何的两种方式来比较它们,我们首先通过看这些量的商来看出其中的区别"。正是在此这一语境中,欧拉引出了零比零的问题。欧拉直接叙述:"任意两个零的算数比率是相等的"[4],也即零比零等于 1。到这一段,可以说,欧拉的结论与贵荣一致,且其论证比贵荣还要简单。但欧拉的讨论并未止于此处,在对算数的零比零问题给出上述简单地讨论之后,欧拉给出了关于几何的零比零问题的长篇论述:

> 这些事情很明确,即使在一般的算数中,任何人都知道当 0 被其他任何数乘时,其积为 0,即 $n \cdot 0 = 0$。所以 $n:1=0:0$。很明显,几何两个零可以是任何一个几何比例。虽然从算数的角度,这个比例总是相等的。因为两个零的比例可能是任何比率,我们用不同的符号是为了在研究两个零的几何比例时有所区别。在关于无穷小的计算中,我们可以准确地处理两个无穷小量的几何比率。因为这个原因,在这些计算中,除非我们用不同的符号表示量,我们会陷入我们自己无法摆脱的巨大困境[5]。

> 如果我们接受在无穷分析中的符号,$\mathrm{d}x$ 表示一个无穷小的量,那么,$\mathrm{d}x=0$,而且 $a\mathrm{d}x=0$。其中 a 是任意有限量。不仅如此,几何比率 $a\mathrm{d}x:\mathrm{d}x$ 是有限的,也就是 $a:1$。两个无穷小量 $\mathrm{d}x$ 和 $a\mathrm{d}x$ 都等于零,当我们在考虑他们的比率时不能够混淆。类似地,我们要处理无穷小量 $\mathrm{d}x$ 和 $\mathrm{d}y$。虽然这些都等于零,他们的比例并不相等。确实的,微分计算的所有量都与探讨任意这类两个无穷小的量的比例有关。乍看,这样的比例的应用应该很小。但是,它实际上非常巨大,这一点日益明显。

> 由于无穷小实际上是无,很明显,一个有限量不会因为加上或者减去一个无穷小量而增大或者减小。令 a 是一个有限量,令 $\mathrm{d}x$ 是一个无穷小,那么 $a+\mathrm{d}x$ 和 $a-\mathrm{d}x$,或者更一般地,$a\pm$

---

[2] 该书于 1755 年出版。
[3] L. Euler: Institutiones Calculi Differentialis, 1755. 78.
[4] 同上,78—79。
[5] 同上。

$n\mathrm{d}x$ 都等于 a。无论在算术上还是几何上,$a \pm nd$ 和 a 的比例都是相等的。算数率的相等性是很明显的,因为 $n\mathrm{d}x=0$,我们有:

$$a \pm n\mathrm{d}x - a = 0$$

另一方面,几何率也明显相等。因为

$$\frac{a \pm n\mathrm{d}x}{a} = 1$$

由此,我们得到那个著名的法则,在与有限相比时,无穷小消失了,而且,可以被忽略。从这一原因,反对无穷分析的意见,即其缺乏几何严谨性失败,因为除非是无,没有什么是可以被忽略的。于是,以完美的公正我们能够确定在这一崇高的科学中我们保持了完美的在古代书中找到的几何严谨。

由于无穷小量 $\mathrm{d}x$ 实际上等于 0,它的平方 $\mathrm{d}x^2$,立方 $\mathrm{d}x^3$,及任意 $\mathrm{d}x^n$,其中 n 为正指数,都等于 0。于是与有限量相比将消失。然而,即使无穷小量 $\mathrm{d}x^2$ 与 $\mathrm{d}x$ 相比也会消失。无论在算术还是几何意义上,$\mathrm{d}x \pm \mathrm{d}x^2$ 与 $\mathrm{d}x$ 的比率是相等的。在算术上是毫无疑问的,在几何上比较

$$\mathrm{d}x \pm \mathrm{d}x^2 : \mathrm{d}x = \frac{\mathrm{d}x \pm \mathrm{d}x^2}{\mathrm{d}x} = 1 \pm \mathrm{d}x = 1$$

以相似的方式,我们有 $\mathrm{d}x \pm \mathrm{d}x^3 = \mathrm{d}x$ 和一般性的 $\mathrm{d}x \pm \mathrm{d}x^{n+1} = \mathrm{d}x$,其中 n 是正数。确实,几何比率 $\mathrm{d}x \pm \mathrm{d}x^{n+1} : \mathrm{d}x$ 等于 $1 + \mathrm{d}x^n = \mathrm{d}x$,而由于 $\mathrm{d}x^n = 0$,其比率相等。于是,如果我们依照指数的用法,我们将 $\mathrm{d}x$ 称为第一级的无穷小,$\mathrm{d}x^2$ 为第二级,$\mathrm{d}x^3$ 为第三级,如此类推。很明显,那些更高的级会消失[6]。

虽然对于无穷小理论的严谨性尚未建立,但欧拉对于零比零问题的几何论述已经涉及无穷小的阶的问题,他指出,在几何上,零比零可以是任何数值。我们可以轻易指出欧拉论述中的错误,其中最基本的是他认为无穷小是零。实际上,纯粹的零比零的问题是没有意义的。古希腊计算传统中一直努力回避无法得到正有理解的问题,而零是不可以作为分母的。中国传统数学问题多以带有具体数值的实践问题为题面,其结果则仅要求给出符合题意的一个解,这样的条件限定保证了该题至少有一个符合题意的解,在计算过程中也规避了零比零这样没有实践意义的问题。那么,为什么欧拉和贵荣要讨论这样的问题呢?

我们先来看欧拉,上述引文给了我们很多的提示。欧拉考虑的是微分学的基础问题。微分中的 $\mathrm{d}x$ 和 $\mathrm{d}y$ 实际上都是无穷小,欧拉认为无穷小就是零,那么,微积分中最常见的符号 $\mathrm{d}y/\mathrm{d}x$ 就是零比零,于是,零比零便成为欧拉在《微分学基础》涉及无穷的开篇必须要解决的问题。实际上,直到19世纪下半叶微积分严格化之前,关于微积分和代数学的基础性问题一直困扰着欧洲数学家,如何定义和表述无穷小是其中的关键问题。欧拉本人在早期微积分和代数发展中做出了巨大的贡献,但也犯了很多的错误。引文中,割裂算数与几何便是其中一例,但从引文中,我们可以看到他还是在回应对无穷小的质疑[7],并

---

[6] 同上,79–81。

[7] 从引文中这一段"从这一原因,反对无穷分析的意见,即其缺乏几何严谨性失败,因为除非是无,没有什么是可以被忽略的。于是,以完美的公正我们能够确定在这一崇高的科学中我们保持了完美的在古代书中找到的几何严谨"可以看出,欧拉意识到他人对无穷小的质疑,并试图解决无穷分析的严谨性问题。

在这方面做出努力[8]。

至于贵荣,我们很难判断他为什么要讨论这一问题(图2)。贵荣是同文馆算学生,微积分列入了同文馆的算学课程之中。按照1876年同文馆总教习丁韪良(W. A. P. Martin 1827—1916)拟就两种同文馆课程表,学习外语的算学生于第六年学习微积分,不学外语的算学生于第四年学习微积分。虽然此后出版的同文馆《算学课艺》中并不包括微积分内容,但这并不说明同文馆天算馆并未学及微积分。

1883年,总理各国事务衙门"札饬命"总教习丁韪良"将天文馆副教习席淦、杜法孟、贵荣、肄业生胡玉麟、陈寿田、熊方柏、联印等授以格物测算"。丁韪良称:"幸七生曾习算术于海宁李壬叔先生,故入此学较易也。"同年十二月丁氏将其教学内容编为《格物测算》,该书采取问答形式,丁在序言中称:七生"功课日积月累,已成卷帙""七生中有勤于问难而敏于会悟者,可谓起予者矣。是书之成七生亦同其劳焉"[9]。可见此书很有可能即是丁韪良以其与学生的问答及学生课艺编辑而成。《格物测算》中涉及求微分、求积分、求高重微分及利用微积分求曲线长度、曲面面积、旋转体体积等,丁韪良在书中直接应用求微分公式,可以证明上述七名同文馆算学学生都是学过微积分的。书中涉及微积分内容并未超出《代微积拾级》水平,书中多次引用《代微积拾级》中的定理,如卷一第六章有"依《微分》十四卷十一款例"一语,引用《代微积拾级》第十四卷"第十一款,曲线体积之微分等于底面乘母曲线横线之微分"[10]求旋转体体积等。

《代微积拾级》是伟烈亚力(Alexander Wylie,1815—1887)和李善兰(1811—1882)根据美国数学家罗密士(Elias Loomis,1811—1899)所著《解析几何与微积分基础》(*Elements of Analytical geometry and of differential and Integral calculus*,1851)翻译而成的。此书"并非为数学家,或有特殊数学才能或数学爱好的人,而是为有着一般能力的大学生"所写的[11]。全书十八卷,分为三部分,代数几何九卷;微分七卷;积分两卷。"代数几何"主要为平面解析几何知识,讲解如何利用坐标系建立直线、圆、椭圆、双曲线、抛物线、摆线及其他曲线的代数方程式及其解法。利用代数方程解几何问题是中国传统数学中常用的方法。

《代微积拾级》中的微分部分以"函数及自变数两变比例相与之比例"来阐述微分概念。值得注意的是,书中虽然提到极限的概念,但其给出的极限定义并不严谨[12],且所介绍的微积分原理并非是严格建立在极限理论基础上的。书中对函数的连续性、可导性、级数的收敛性等问题均不讨论,直接引入麦克劳林(Maclurian)及泰勒(Taylor)展开式阐释和推导超越函数及曲线弧长、曲线内所包的面积及旋转体

---

[8] 中国传统数学中虽然对于无穷小量并没有专题研究,但刘徽在《九章算术》的第二个圆田题目中的注解中注文"割之弥细,所失弥少,割之又割以至于不可割,则与圆周合体而无所失矣"。(刘徽:"又有圆田一百八十一步"术文注.《九章算经》,宋嘉定六年版. 上海:文物出版社,1980,11a。)其内容为以六边形为起点,通过倍加边数逼近圆周,直至不可割。其"与圆周合体而无所失"一语的含意亦是无穷小是0。(关于刘徽的无限思想,参见:郭书春:刘徽的极限理论. 科学史集刊,第11集. 1984. 38—39。)而古希腊数学中则存在着实无穷与潜无穷的争论,阿基米德在涉及无穷的证明时均采用反证法,避免了无穷小算法问题。荷兰数学家斯蒂文在证明一般三角形重心公式时以平行四边形的阶梯组逼近三角形,称:"通过无穷逼近,我们可以在该三角形中加入这样一个图形,它与该三角形的差小于任意给定的平面图形,无论该形有多小",并由此而得出三角形的重量与逼近图形相等的结论。这段证明被视为微积分"ε−Δ"式定义无穷小的先声。斯蒂文重心定理于1628年通过《奇器图说》译成中文,《奇器图说》中删去了证明。后梅文鼎给出注文,试图通过证明围绕三角形的三条中心的任意小的三角形的面积均相等这样的证据证明该定理。但以重心为支点的是力矩平衡而非重量平衡,此证明从严格意义上并不成立。见:田淼、张柏春:梅文鼎《远西奇器图说录最》注之研究. 中国科技史杂志,27(4):330—339。

[9] 丁韪良:格物测算序. 格物测算. 清末刊本。

[10] 同上。

[11] E. Loomis, Preface, Elements of Analytical geometry and of differential and Integral calculus, 引自:Wann-Sheng Horng, Li Shanlan: The Impact of Western Mathematics in China During the Late 19th Century. 330。

[12] 《代微积拾级》中将根极译为"限"。其中对极限的定义为:"凡变数有限,限者其数为变数所渐近而永不能到,或必不能过。古谓之限"(见:《代微积拾级》.卷10,1a)。这并不是极限的严格定义。《代数学》中引入了严格的"ε−δ"方式的极限定义,但其叙述方式非常烦琐,不易被读者理解。

表面积和体积等其他微分公式,以及函数极值的判定等问题,同样,在解释及利用泰勒展开式时,书中亦未提到函数的收敛性问题。该书并不关注微积分理论问题,也不含关于零比零的讨论。

虽然我们不能确定贵荣在发表他关于$\frac{0}{0}$的短文时是否是已学了微积分,但同文馆的微积分教学参考书《代微积拾级》中并不含关于零比零的内容,那么,我们是不是可以说,相关无穷小理论在当时没有传入中国呢?下文中我们可以看到,答案是否定的。

三、《代数学》与《微积溯源》中对零比零问题的讨论

通过考察,我们发现《代数学》和《微积溯源》中都有关于零比零问题的很详尽的阐释。

《代数学》由伟烈亚力和李善兰合译,于1859年出版的第一部系统介绍符号代数的著作。该书根据英国数学家德摩根(Augustus De Morgan,1806—1871)所著《代数学基础》(*Elements of Algebra*,1835年,第一版)翻译而成[13]。德摩根原著全名为:*Elements of Algebra: Preliminary to the Differential calculus, and fit for the higher class of Schools in which the principles of Arithmetic are taught*,意为:《代数基础:微分学初步适合于学习过算术原理的高级班》。从名称上可以看出,该书即是一部代数学原理性著作,同时,也包括微积分初级知识,德摩根所设计的读者群是已经掌握了算术原理的高级班的学生[14]。《代数学》卷首的"入门例言"第八条特别提及0不可以为分母:

又如$\frac{甲}{0}$,学者每误谓同于甲,而实不然,如问六容几个0,答曰,此问不合理[15]。

此文献说明,《代数学》从一开始便指出了0不可以作分母。也就是说,$\frac{0}{0}$问题是不合理的。但书中仍然讨论了这一问题(图2)。该书中第六章第一节"论限及变数"中讨论了$\frac{0}{0}$问题,与卷首的说法一致,称此问题为不合理之式。此节首论曰:

图2 《代数学》中关于零比零问题的介绍

13　参见:Wann－Sheng Horng. Li Shanlan: The Impact of Western Mathematics in China During the Late 19th Century, A dissertation submitted to the Graduate Faculty in History in partial fulfillment of the requirements for the degree of Doctor of Philosophy, The City University of New York, 1991. 312－315.

14　Augustus De Morgan. Preface. Elements of Algebra: Preliminary to the Differential calculus, and fit for the higher class of Schools in which the principles of Arithmetic are taught.

15　德摩根著. 伟烈亚力,李善兰译.《代数学》. 1859年上海活字版. 卷首. 4b.

前卷曾论,易解之几何,有时变作 $\frac{丙}{0}$、$\frac{0}{0}$、甲 0 诸式。

为了解释这些问题,德摩根讨论了 0 在计算中的特殊性,即,"特解 0 之理",详细地解释了 0 成为分母会造成计算的不确定性。此后,文中又通过对近似相等与相等的讨论引入以极限理论解决此问题的方式。

《代数学》中的相关介绍为:

诸式外,又有数式。如 0^0、$0^{\frac{1}{0}}$、$\left(\frac{1}{0}\right)^0$ 等。设有 $(天-甲)^{天-甲}$ 又 $(天-甲)^{\frac{1}{天-甲}}$ 又 $\left(\frac{1}{天-甲}\right)^{天-甲}$。若不知天=甲,则推时恒遇上三式。故若有式非显几何,则不必问此式之同数,亦不必问此式可有同数否。但当问若渐近于难解之式,则难解之式渐近何同数[16]。

如天=甲,则 $\frac{天^2-甲^2}{天-甲}=\frac{0}{0}$。

若考天渐近于甲,此分数之同数有何变化式?则知其同数渐近于 2 甲。

若天任近于甲,则 $\frac{天^2-甲^2}{天-甲}$。可任近于 2 甲。天无限渐近于甲,则 $\frac{天^2-甲^2}{天-甲}$ 无限渐近于 2 甲。如此,设天=甲,则 $\frac{天^2-甲^2}{天-甲}=\frac{0}{0}=2$ 甲,即 $\frac{0}{0}=2$ 甲。[17]

德摩根此段论述之意即以极限的方式,给出一个 $\frac{0}{0}$ 的特解。

此后,在同书同章第七款,德摩根又称:

若分母分子俱无限损,则分之限或为 0,或有穷,或无穷。即言其分或无限损,或有限,或无限增,此三种若分母分子俱无限损,皆可合于理[18].

德摩根还给出了相关的例证和证明,此处不再详述。据此,我们可以确定地说,《代数学》中 $\frac{0}{0}$ 有详细地论证。

1874 年出版的《微积溯源》中以同样的算例分析了零比零问题。《微积溯源》,8 卷,为爱丁堡大学数学教授华里司(William Wallace,1768—1843)于 19 世纪初为《大英百科全书》第四版写的"流数"(Fluxions)词条[19]。前 4 卷论微分,卷一介绍了一些微积分的基本概念,如函数、变量、极限等,多项式求微分的方法,以及微积分的一些性质;卷二讲解高阶导数及利用泰勒公式和麦克劳林公式求函数展开式的方法;卷三为求函数极大、极小值;卷四为求曲线相切;卷五讲解积分的概念及性质;卷六求虚函数之积分;卷七求曲线面积;卷八讲解含两个未知数的函数的积分[20]。书中以微分的反函数定义积分,且对

---

[16] 此段译文的原文为:In all these cases, when we get a form which is not a direct representation of quantity, we shall not ask "what is the value of that form?" or in any way enter into the question whether it is demonstrable that it has a value or not. But the question we shall always ask is this:"As we approach the supposition which gives the unintelligible form, to what value does the expression which gives the unintelligible form approach?" 可以翻译为:对于所有这些例子,当我们得到一个不能直给表述为量的表述式时,我们不应该问"这个式的值是多少?"或者说,无论如何都不要使我们进入还可以证明它是否有一个值的问题。但是我们总是可以问这样的问题,"当我们渐近这个给定的不可认知的形时,从这个渐近过程中,这个表述式的值是什么"。Augustus De Morgan, Elements of Algebra:Preliminary to the Differential calculus, and fit for the higher class of Schools in which the principles of Arithmetic are taught, London:Taylor and Walton, 1837, 156。通过对比,此段比较准确地翻译了 De Morgan 的原著中"On Limits and Variable Quantities"151—156 页的内容。但对于此段,De Morgan 的原文更为直接和严格,即根本不要问这类不合理之式的值是多少。

[17] 德摩根著. 伟烈亚力,李善兰译.《代数学》. 1859 年上海活字版,卷 6. 4b。

[18] 同上,卷 6,5。

[19] 王扬宗认为,傅兰雅和华蘅芳是根据《大英百科全书》第 8 版译成二书的。见:王扬宗. 傅兰雅与近代中国的科学启蒙。《大英百科全书》第四版的"流数"词条的内容一直保留到第八版。

[20] 华里司著. 傅兰雅,华蘅芳译. 微积溯源. 江南制造局刊本.

定义微分的基本概念极限给予严格的定义。该书卷一第五十五款称：

> 如有分数之式 $\dfrac{\text{天}^2-\text{甲}^2}{\text{天}-\text{甲}}$，此为能隐之分数。因天＝甲，则分母分子皆为0，而其式变为 $\dfrac{0}{0}$ 故也。观此形，宛如其分数之定同数无法可求，然而不难知也。

> 唯因 $\dfrac{\text{天}^2-\text{甲}^2}{\text{天}-\text{甲}}$＝天＋甲，故天＝甲，则其原式之真同数必为甲＋甲＝二甲。由是知原式于天＝甲之时必变为 $\dfrac{0}{0}$ 者，因其分母子有天－甲为公约数，所以天等于甲之时母子能皆变为0。

《微积溯源》中称不定型为隐分数。在上述引文之后，书中又举三例指出 $\dfrac{0}{0}$ 形问题在不同具体情况的不同结果。其下一款以大量篇幅给出以泰勒展开式解 $\dfrac{0}{0}$ 型的具体算法[21]。

至此，我们可以确定地说，《代数学》和《微积溯源》中已给出了关于 $\dfrac{0}{0}$ 问题详尽的解说和计算方法。那么，贵荣在1877年在《格致汇编》中发表的"算学奇题"是不是只能说明该同文馆算学生没有注意到这两部译著里的相关内容而犯的错误呢？此事并非如此简单。

《代数学》的翻译者为李善兰，李善兰于1868年到京师同文馆任算学教习，也即，李善兰是贵荣在同文馆的数学教师，而贵荣称他的"算学奇题"为京师同文馆"算学课作"。《格致汇编》的主编为傅兰雅，傅兰雅是《微积溯源》的翻译，他在仅四年后便在其主编的刊物中发表了与其译作完全相悖的内容，并未在该刊后来的刊本中给予修正。由此，则两位最早在中国传播微积分的人物并没有注意到他们各自译作中的相关内容。而 $\dfrac{0}{0}$ 问题并不简单地是一个算术问题，而是关乎微积分理论的关键问题，二位译者对此问题的忽视表现出的则是对微积分理论的忽视。

我们知道，李善兰对他翻译的《代数学》和《代微积拾级》是非常重视的。华蘅芳记述："访秋纫（李善兰）于墨海书馆，见其方与西士伟烈亚力对译《代数学》《代微积拾级》，尚未告竣。秋纫谓余曰：此书为算学中上乘功夫，此书一出，非特中法几可尽废，即西法之古者亦无所用之矣"[22]。如果李善兰并不关注微积分理论问题，那么是什么使得他如此看重《代数学》和《代微积拾级》呢？为了回答此问题，我们需要从李善兰最早接触伟烈亚力说起。

大约在1852年6—7月份，李善兰来到麦都斯布道的教堂，向他出示了《对数探原》等其自著的数学著作，询问西方是否有同样的研究，伟烈亚力由此请李善兰翻译西方的算学和天文学书籍，《代数学》和《代微积拾级》是二人完成的两部重要数学译作。前文已述，《代微积拾级》并不关注理论问题，书中直接引入马克劳林（Maclurian Colin，1698—1746）及泰勒（Brook Taylor，1685—1737）级数阐释和推导超越函数及曲线弧长、曲线内所包的面积及旋转体表面积和体积等其他微分公式，以及函数极值的判定等问题，卷十八介绍积分应用，主要是如何利用积分求曲线的长、曲面体、旋转体的表面积及旋转体的体积等。从纯粹数学的立场上来说，《代微积拾级》并不能算是一部理论性很强的微积分著作。然而，该书比相对理论性较强的《代数学》引起了中国数学家更大的兴趣。该书出版当年（1859年），冯桂芬与徐有壬便一起研究《代微积拾级》，后冯桂芬与陈旸合著《西算新法直解》阐释《代微积拾级》中的数学方法。华蘅芳亦是由《代微积拾级》和《代数学》学习代数和微积分的，此后，他也是受这两部著作的影响而与傅兰雅合译《代数术》和《微分溯源》的。

泰勒展开式是英国数学家泰勒于1712年给出的现代有限差分的理论基础，利用此公式使得任意单变量函数展为幂级数成为可能。《代微积拾级》中介绍的另一个重要展开式公式——麦克劳林公式可被视作泰勒公式的特殊形式。中国传统数学在有限差分方面有着突出的成果，差分法在中国古代被应用

---

[21] 同上，卷2,41l—43b。
[22] 华蘅芳，论加减乘除开方之用. 学算笔谈. 光绪八年刊本，卷5.3a。

于制订历法。18世纪以来,包括李善兰在内的中国数学家对于三角函数、对数函数的幂级数展开式的研究倾注了很多的心血。所以,《代微积拾级》中的相关内容可以较为容易地为他们所理解。同时,一个一般性的可以将任何函数化为幂级数的公式也自然会引起他们的重视。回到李善兰初次找基督新教传教士询问西方是否有与《对数探源》相似的研究,那么泰勒展开式便是在此方面更为普遍的方法。这也正应了李善兰所说的"此书一出,非特中法几可尽废,即西法之古者亦无所用之矣"一语。实际上,清末虽有多部中国数学家自著的以"微积分"为内容的著作出版,但它们多与泰勒展开式和麦克劳林公式有关[23]。

同样,向中国传播符号代数和微积分的伟烈亚力和傅兰雅都不是专业数学家,微积分的严格化及基础理论在当时的欧洲仍是新知识,《代数学》作者德摩根自己也是在这方面做出成果的数学家。从傅兰雅对 $\frac{0}{0}$ 问题的忽视也可以反映传入微积分学的西方人在此方面也缺乏应有的重视及知识基础。

以此案例,我们可以对微积分理论在清末传播问题有更全面的理解。一个学科或者一种理论的跨国传播通常与接受方的需求与条件有关。当符号代数和微积分传入中国时,中方接受者最易接受的仍是与他们自身研究相关的内容。如符号代数可以解决李善兰研究的传统四元术的一般化问题,泰勒展开式是李善兰、徐有壬等数学家长期致力的幂级数展开式问题的一般性解法。而一些理论问题,如零比零问题及相关微积分理论则被忽视。

贵荣等当时学习数学的学生是以传入的西方近代数学工作为基础开始数学学习的,这使得他们关注一些本身没有实践意义,或者是并非以实践问题为题面的纯数学的数学问题。从这个角度来看,虽然他对 $\frac{0}{0}$ 问题的解答是错误的,但仍然体现出中国数学转向纯数学研究的一个方面。

四、结语

贵荣在《格致汇编》中发表的 $\frac{0}{0}$ 问题研究虽仅短短一页,但从而引发了微积分在19世纪下半叶在中国传播的一些非常有趣的问题,而李善兰与傅兰雅这两位在中国最早传播微积分的人物对微积分理论的忽视则让我们对该学科在中国的早期传播的过程和特点有了更多的理解。不仅如此,此问题也为知识的跨国传播研究提供了宝贵案例。

Abstract In 1877, Guirong, a student of Beijing Tongwenguan published a short article on the ratio between two 0s, and proved that the result is 1. In this paper, I argue that the problem concerning the ratio between 0s is of great importance in the development of calculus theories. Euler gave the same result as Guirong, but in the context of foundation of deferential calculus, he also presented a detailed analysis of the geometrical result of the problem, in which he developed the theory about the order of infinite small. Before the publication of Guirong's article, two Chinese books, both of which translated from European mathematical books already introduced theoretical discussion on the ratio between two 0s into China, but this was neglected by Guirong, and the two translators of the books. From this point, this paper provides further arguments concerning the transmission of calculus in the 19th century China.

---

[23] 参见:田淼. 中国数学的西化历程. 山东:山东教育出版社,2005,182-196.

清末数学教科书之兴起

代钦 （内蒙古师范大学科学技术史研究院）

摘要 自1902年至1912年的清末十年教育大变革过程中，中国中小学数学教科书建设迈入一个崭新阶段，在追求"最新"的理念下，遵照教科书审定制度，基于中国国情，以日本为主，以欧美为辅，大量编译引进中学数学教科书，参照日本小学数学教科书编写中国的笔算、珠算教科书，以满足数学教育发展之急需。小学数学教科书呈现以自编为主、翻译为辅，教科书发展之多样化，珠算与笔算之平衡，中西度量衡取舍之平衡等特点；中学数学教科书呈现"新""多样化""滞后性""国际合作"等特点；在内容处理方面采取内容的"删减与添加""参合与融化"的方法；编排方面采用竖排编写形式、数学符号全部采用中国传统数学符号，横排编写、采用中国传统数学符号，以及完全采用西方编写形式。清末中小学数学教科书一般有"序""例言""弁言""编辑大意"等，其中阐明编写意图、教科书特色、教学要义等事项。教科书的迅速兴起推动了出版企业的蓬勃发展，反之，出版企业的发展也积极地促进了教科书建设。

关键词 清末；中小学数学教育；数学教科书

清末是中国历史上极其特殊的重要时代，是一个巨变的时代，是中国传统文化和西方现代文化碰撞和交融的大变革时期，也是中国传统数学教育走向近代化的转型时期。在这个新旧交替的过渡时期，旧的已经被动摇，但还没有被淘汰；新的已经开始，但还没有完全形成。这一时期数学教育和以往的数学教育及其以后的数学教育有着很多显著的差异和特点。这些特点在数学教科书的内容、形式和编写思想上反映最为突出。在这一变化过程中，1904年颁布的《奏定学堂章程》对数学教科书的转型发展起到了重要的导向作用。在数学教科书的建设中，也反映了国人追求西方新式数学教育的梦想以及接受新事物的矛盾心态。

1902年，管学大臣张百熙所拟订的《钦定学堂章程》（亦称"壬寅学制"），是中国近代教育史上第一个法定学制系统，也是中国新式学校体系诞生的标志。该章程的特点是注重国民教育、实业教育、与科举制度并行、女子教育毫无地位。当时该章程虽然得到一些进步人士的支持，但是由于以荣庆为首的保守派反对，没有得到实施。[1]

1904年，颁布完全模仿日本学制的学堂章程——《奏定学堂章程》（亦称"癸卯学制"）。该章程虽说是由张百熙、张之洞、荣庆三人重新拟订，但实质上反映的仅是张之洞一个人的思想。[2]"癸卯学制"对学校体系、课程设置、学校管理等都做了具体规定。这个章程是中国近代史上最早颁布并经法令正式公布在全国施行的新学制，一直沿用到中华民国成立为止。中国后来学校制度的建立，实际上是在这个学制的基础上演变而来的。这个学制的施行改变了中国长期以来的官学、私学、书院等办学模式，为中国建立现代形式的学校制度奠定了基础。

清末，在兴办中小学教育过程中，有些人对于教科书在教育中的作用已经有了很明确的认识："教科书者，教育之目标，教科图书者，教育之材料。"[3]这种教科书是指国人自编的教科书，这样，教育方为中国教育，国家才有希望。然而，在新学制下，中国中小学所使用的数学教科书以国人编译外国的教科书

---

[1] 代钦.中国の清末の数学教育と日本からの影響について[J].《数学教育研究》（大阪教育大学），1997年(27)：191-198.

[2] 代钦.中国の清末の数学教育と日本からの影響について[J].《数学教育研究》（大阪教育大学），1997年(27)：191-198.

[3] 《教育世界》，第十五号，1901年12月。

为主,其中多数底本取自日本原著或日译西著[4],更有甚者直接使用外文原版教科书。鉴于此,蔡元培在《国化教科书问题》中指出:"'国化教科书'五个字的意义,就是想把我国各学校(偏重高中以上)的各项教科书——社会科学或自然科学的——除外国文而外,都应当使之中国化。再明白点讲,就是除开外国文一项,其余各种学科,都应该来用中国文做的教本。"[5]

在清末数学教科书建设方面,小学数学教科书由国人自编的较多,中学数学教科书几乎都是翻译或编译日本、美国和欧洲的教科书。随着社会的进步,中国中学数学教科书由最初的翻译、编译外国教科书,最终实现了自主创新,使数学教科书具有了自己的特色。中学数学教科书在宏观上呈现出"新""多元化""滞后性"和"国际合作"的特点,以及微观上表现为编写形式上的竖排、横竖混合编排、使用中国传统数学符号、完全横排、内容的"删减与添加"和"参合与融化"等若干特点。其中,竖排、横竖混合编排和采用中国传统数学符号的特点,不仅仅是形式上的问题,而是当时不少中国知识人担心像潮水般涌入中国的西方科学知识淹没自己的传统文化,思想和感情上处于一种矛盾状态。这也反映了部分中国数学教育工作者对西方数学教育的认知的缺失,他们觊觎用中国传统数学的方式表述西方数学的做法,在无形当中阻碍了近代数学教育的顺利发展。清末中国中小数学教科书发展的这一奇特现象与日本迥然不同。日本从明治维新后翻译引进数学教科书时与他们的传统数学的表述方式彻底决裂,完全采用西方数学的符号系统和表达方式,而中国的数学教科书编写者们在自己传统数学和西方近代数学之间徘徊,直至1908年以后这一现象才被彻底改变。在清末中小学数学教科书中一般有序言、例言和编辑大意等内容,这也是一个显著特点,到民国以后这一特点逐渐减弱。

另一方面,清末中小学数学教科书的编写、出版发行都没有国家统一的规划。因此编译教科书时,同一本教科书由不同的学者编译出版的情形也不少。例如,日本藤泽利喜太郎、上野清、菊池大麓等学者的数学教科书有不少中文版本。至于出版社方面,1903年前文明书局处于领先地位,后来成为出版界巨擘的商务印书馆当时并不是独占鳌头,其优势不明显。正如汪家熔所说:"文明书局因为《蒙学读本全书》有七本之多,编得可以……生意好,利润多。……后来的教科书巨擘商务印书馆,开始时也赶不上它。……究其原因,商务印书馆当时知根知底能使用的作者队伍还小:夏瑞芳方面,谢洪赉因为他不久专注于办理'中华基督教青年会'而不再关注世俗出版物;张元济方面,夏曾佑除中国史外,他对其他学科懂得也不多;杜亚泉从日文可以翻译些自然科学,但他自己还办个学社,此外就没有较多人,显然还不能互相配套成系统。商务印书馆能压倒文明书局,是次年吸收日资之后。"[6]因此,清末数学教科书的出版似乎出现"百花齐放,百家争鸣"之景象,但是民国初期,即中华书局成立后这一景象逐渐消失,商务印书馆和中华书局占领了大部分教科书市场份额。

一、清末中小学数学教科书发展之背景

(一)新式教育制度之诞生

1902年颁布的《钦定学堂章程》虽然没有得以实施,但是它的颁布预示着中国学校教育的未来走向。数学教育工作者据以着手翻译和编写学堂数学教科书,这为《奏定学堂章程》颁布后的数学教科书建设奠定了良好的基础。随即颁行的《奏定学堂章程》(图1)对学级的划分,新式教科书的推广使用,都做了更为切实可行的规划。"癸卯学制"规定小学分为初等小学堂和高等小学堂,前者为五年,后者为四年。中学堂为五年,不分初中和高中。其"学科程度章第二之第八节"中制定了教科书审定制度:"凡各科课本,须

图1 《奏定学堂章程》

---

[4] 李兆华.中国近代数学教育史稿[M].济南:山东教育出版社,2005:182.
[5] 高平叔.蔡元培教育论著选[M].北京:人民教育出版社,1991:583.
[6] 汪家熔.民族魂——教科书变迁[M].北京:商务印书馆,2008:23.

用官设编译局编纂,经学务大臣奏定之本,其有自编课本者,须呈经学务大臣审定,始准通用。官设编译局未经出书之前,准由教员按照上列科目,择程度相当,而语无流弊之书,暂时应用。出书之后,即行停止。"[7]由于《奏定学堂章程》颁布施行之际,清政府尚无能力及时推出适合学制的教科书,因此只能通过教科书的审定制度来掌控教科书质量和编订,以应各学校的教学急需。但是初期新教科书的翻译、编写往往无所顾及新学制的要求,数学教育工作者仍按照自己的选择和判断选译、编写。

(二)编译教科书之肇始

《奏定学堂章程》颁布之前,清末已经出现中小学堂水平的数学教科书,这为其后的数学教科书翻译、编译和编写直接或间接地提供了基础。当时,基督教士对新式数学教科书的肇始与发展起到了关键性作用,如传教士狄考文等主张:"教会学校的成败在相当程度上取决于是否拥有好的和适用的教科书"。[8]在对教科书的这种认识下,基督教士编译了如下数学教科书:《算法全书》(ST. PAUL'S COLLEGE, HONGKONG,圣保罗书院,1852年)、《数学启蒙》二卷(英国伟烈亚力撰,上海六先书局藏版,1853年)、《形学备旨》十卷(美国罗密士原撰,美国狄考文选译,邹立文笔述,刘永锡参阅,上海美华书馆,1885年)、《代数备旨》(美狄考文撰,邹立文、生福维笔述,上海美华书馆,1891年)、《八线备旨》四卷(美国罗密士原撰,美潘慎文选译,谢洪赉校录,上海美华书馆,1894年)、《笔算数学》三卷(美国狄考文辑,邹立文述,上海美华书馆,1892年)、《代形合参》三卷附一卷(美国罗密士原撰,美国潘慎文选译,谢洪赉笔述,上海美华书馆,1893年)等。其中,《笔算数学》《代数备旨》《形学备旨》《八线备旨》《代形合参》刊印次数较多,流传较广。与此同时,国人也编写一些数学教科书,如《算学入门》(周广询撰,成都玉元堂刊本三册,1898年)。这些数学教科书的出版,为清末数学名词术语的确立、翻译体例等方面产生了直接影响。这里值得指出的是,并不是说学堂章程颁布施行后,国人就立即使用新的教科书而与过去的上述数学教科书一刀两断。作为过渡阶段,上述数学教科书也被使用一段时间。如《代数备旨》至1907年印行十次,直至1917年才结束印刷[9]。

(三)无组织编写者群体之形成

清末新式教育伊始,数学教科书成为急缺之物。教育工作者们以"教育兴亡,匹夫有责"之精神参与进来数学教科书的编译或编写工作中,形成一个编写数学教科书的群体。这种群体是没有任何组织,从各自的实际情况出发参与数学教科书建设事业。他们中有数学家或数学教育工作者、非数学教育工作的学者或教育工作者、留学生,甚至还有日本学者。如,数学家或数学教育工作者有崔朝庆、顾澄、周达、周藩、黄元吉、马君武、仇毅、赵缭、张修爵、程荫南、何崇礼、陈文等;非数学家或数学教育工作者的学者有谢洪赉、丁福保等;日本学者有西师意、藤森温和等。虽则数学教科书编写者在整体上是无组织的,但也存在有组织的个别群体,可以叫作团队。如商务印书馆编译所、武昌中东书社编译部等,其中前者为由水平较高的学者组成的有一定规模的团队,而后者一般为由留日学生组成的团队,规模相对于前者小。正因为这样,清末数学教科书的内容和形式向多元化发展,也表现为数学教科书的编译、编写等方面的水平参差不齐。

(四)出版事业之勃兴

中国自创办学堂以来,新式的出版事业也逐渐发展,并展开激烈竞争。出版企业的成长是整个商业活动扩张的重要一环,它调动了相关产业的增长,因此新兴学堂的蓬勃发展不是单纯的仅限于教育领域,而对整个社会带来新气象。1897年2月11日,上海一家名为创设商务印书馆的小型印书房正式成立,后来在夏瑞芳、张元济、蔡元培等人的努力下,成为中国出版界之巨擘。1902年,商务印书馆设编译所,开始编辑出版各种教科书。同年,在上海文明书局成立,也开始编印教科书。出版数学教科书的企

7　张之洞等.奏定学堂章程[M].台北:台联国风出版社,1970:374.

8　[美]费正清,刘广京.剑桥中国晚清史1800—1911年(上卷)[M].中国社会科学院历史研究所编译室,译.北京:中国社会科学出版社,2007:561.

9　李迪.中国数学史大系(副卷第二卷中国算学书目汇编)[M].北京:北京师范大学出版社,2000:205.

业还有上海科学会、上海普及书局、教科书编译社、上海东亚公司、武昌中东书社、上海科学书局、山西大学译书院、上海群益社、湖南作民译社、日本东京清国留学生会馆等。这些出版企业的相互竞争客观上促进了数学教科书的发展，同时也为数学教科书建设者提供了实现自己梦想的舞台。

近代数学教科书虽然从 1850 年就开始出现，但到 1904 年以前，没有一套完整的能够供应小学和中学水平学生使用的数学教科书。这反映出当时的教育决策者和教育工作者教科书对普及教育的认识不足。但后来他们逐渐地认识到教科书的重要性："欲使一国之教育日有进步，在多设学校，欲使教育有成效之可睹，在办理学校者之热心，而办理学校者所挟之利器，即教科书是矣。故兴办教育欲收取普及之效，必借有用之教科书。"[10] 在这种认识下，谢洪赉、丁福保、范迪吉、崔朝庆、何崇礼、陈文、程荫南、顾澄、陈幌等积极翻译、编译和编撰教科书，一时不同的出版机构、不同的数学教育工作者争先恐后地翻译、编译教科书，使中小学数学教科书迈入一个新的发展阶段。在争相出版教科书的众多出版机构中，商务印书馆在教科书的出版方面起到引领作用。在 1904 年至 1907 年间，第一套完整的中小学数学教科书问世，即"晚清唯一一套完整的、始终是最重要、最有影响的中小学教科书是商务印书馆的《最新教科书》。……《最新教科书》由各年级、各课程组成。"[11] 这一套中小学数学教科书包括：《最新初等小学用笔算教科书》（徐隽编，商务印书馆，1904 年）、《最新高等小学用笔算教科书》（王兆枏、杜亚泉编，商务印书馆，1905 年）、《最新中学教科书代数学》（William J. Milne 原著，谢洪赉译述，商务印书馆，1905 年）、《最新中学教科书几何学》（William J. Milne 原著，谢洪赉编译，商务印书馆，1906 年）、《最新中学教科书三角术》（美国费烈伯、史德郎原著，谢洪赉译述，商务印书馆，1907 年）等。

二、清末小学数学教科书

清末开始兴办学堂，由于没有系统的学制，数学教科书多用外国传教士编译的教本，如《算法全书》《代数备旨》《形学备旨》《八线备旨》《代形合参》《笔算数学》等。戊戌变法之前，新式学堂虽出现，但比较切实的发展则在 1901 年 8 月 2 日"改书院为学堂上谕"之后。[12] 所谓"除京师已设大学堂应切实整顿外，著各省所有书院，于省城均改设大学堂，各府及直隶州均改设中学堂，各州县均改设小学堂"，[13] 为了适应新式小学堂的兴办，满足新式小学堂对教科书的需求，新式教科书的编纂势在必行。

这时期教科书的发展表现出明显的阶段性：以清政府"新政"为标志，从翻译西洋教科书过渡到翻译日本教科书，形成两次高潮。在引进外国教科书的过程中，中国人逐渐地认识到，必须有自己的教科书。

《奏定学堂章程》的《学务纲要》说明教材来源有三个：学堂自编讲义、私家编纂课本及编译的西方成书，这大致反映了当时教材采用的情形。"癸卯学制"后，则以国人自行编译教科书为主，这一时期自编教科书的主要来源是学堂自编、书坊自编和中央编书机构编书三种，其中多数底本取自日本原著或日译西著[14]，多渠道的教科书编写推动了清末自编小学算术教科书的发展。

（一）学堂自编教科书

学堂是指不同于传统的私塾或书院的具有近代色彩的新式学堂[15]，如南洋公学、无锡三等公学堂、上海澄衷学堂等。由于新式学堂的创办和发展，为满足学校自身教学需要和社会需求，一些有实力、有良好师资的学校开始，以传统蒙学教材为基础，吸收西学内容，开始自编小学教科书。如最先出版的数学教科书是 1901 年由南洋公学师范生编译、南洋公学师范生院出版的《物算教科书》《笔算教科书》。这两种书均为供该校外院（小学）学生学习使用而编的最早的新式算学教科书，开启了我国近代数学教科

---

10 《论限用部编教科书有妨教育之进步》，《申报》，1910 年 3 月 11 日：11—12.
11 汪家熔. 民族魂——教科书变迁 [M]. 北京：商务印书馆，2008：55.
12 李兆华. 中国近代数学教育史稿 [M]. 济南：山东教育出版社，2005：155.
13 陈谷嘉、邓洪波. 改书院为学堂上谕——中国书院史资料（下册）[M]. 杭州：浙江教育出版社，1998：2489.
14 李兆华. 中国近代数学教育史稿 [M]. 济南：山东教育出版社，2005：182.
15 "学堂"一词，清末泛指新兴的学校以与国子监、州府县学等官学相区别. 壬寅学制颁布之后，普遍使用大学堂、高等学堂、中学堂、小学堂的称谓. 至民国元年《普通教育暂行办法》颁行之后，学堂改称学校.

书编纂之先河。

(二)书坊编辑教科书

书坊是指各地的民营出版企业,教育的发展为其崛起提供了经济基础。比较典型的书坊有商务印书馆、文明书局等。在《学部第一次审定初等小学暂用书目表》中,首先审定通过商务印书馆、文明书局的算术教科书。

商务印书馆创建于1897年,它对小学数学教科书的发展做出了重要贡献,具有引领作用。蒋维乔在《编辑小学教科书之回忆》一文中说:"教科书之形式内容,渐臻完善者,当推商务印书馆之《最新教科书》。"该套教科书被认为是晚清唯一一套完整的、始终是重要的、最有影响的中小学教科书。《学部第一次审定初等小学暂用书目表》中数学教科书有徐隽编的《最新初等小学笔算教科书》《最新初等小学笔算教科书教授法》;《学部第一次审定高等小学暂用书目表》中的数学教科书有杜亚泉及王兆楠编的《最新高等小学笔算教科书》、杜综大和杜玓孙编纂的《最新初等小学珠算教科书教授法》、杜玓孙编的《最新初等小学珠算入门(教员)》。总之,《最新教科书》根据学制规定按学年学期编写,并有与之配套的教授书(教授法)等教学参考书,一经出版便势不可挡,大受欢迎,可谓横空出世,独步神州,既取代了其他小学算术教科书,又成为后世小学算术教科书模仿的典范。《最新教科书》是新学制颁布后按学制要求编写的全国最早、最完整的教科书,构建了我国近代数学教科书的基本框架。

(三)清末小学数学教科书特点

从翻译、编写教科书、教科书建设者群体、中国传统数学知识和西方数学知识之间的平衡等方面可以总结出清末小学数学教科书的以下四个特点。

以自编为主,翻译为辅。西学的传播在晚清达到一个高潮。由于新教育的样板是西方教育,在中国没有先例可循,因而人们在创办新教育的过程中只好搬抄西方的教育模式。处于清末内忧外患的时代,许多有识之士都力图借鉴西方先进的文化,大量翻译和引进西方教科书。在此基础之上,自编教科书者大胆借鉴和采纳西方教科书的体例。在借鉴的同时,由于对西方的文化和思维习惯没有做深入的研究和探讨,也忽略了中国传统文化和特有的思维方式,所移植的西方教科书的内容体例很难为学生理解和接受,甚至出现了与学生的思维和习惯相冲突的地方。这一时期学制模仿日本,对小学数学的教学目的、任务和教学要求等方面的规定相当模糊:"教学之目的、任务始终不明确,……更不知教材要服从教学目的"[16]。"旧的教育体系和旧的民族习惯被破坏了,新的教育——根据科学的教育——已经开始……我们必须知道教育制度不能通过模仿得来,必须从思考与实践中得来。西洋教育不能整个搬到中国来,必须斟酌中国国情,做出适当的选择。"[17]

从整体上看,翻译或编译引进中学数学教科书较多,翻译引进小学数学教科书并不多,国人自编的居多。

教科书发展之多样化。清末学堂兴办,教科书奇缺,官方在教科书编写方面力不从心,只好放任各地各学堂自编教科书。在这样的特殊历史条件下,由于清末民间自编教科书具有广泛的群众性,反而促成了教科书民间编写的百花齐放、自由竞争的局面。这种局面在一定程度上使得小学数学教科书多样化,呈现出不同风格、不同特点。首先,从小学教科书编写者情况看,可以大致地分为数学教育工作者和热衷于关心数学教育的非数学教育工作者。如,张景良、徐隽、寿孝天、陈文等为数学教育工作者,而丁福保、杜亚泉等为非数学教育工作者。其次,从小学数学教科书内容体系来讲,参差不齐,有些教科书也没有明确的学习年级等方面的说明。如,丁福保编写的《蒙学笔算教科书》、寿孝天编写的《简易算术课本》等均没有学习阶段的说明。再次,从小学数学教科书内容广度和难度等方面而言,更是千差万别。客观地讲,徐隽、杜亚泉、寿孝天等编写的"最新教科书"内容广度、难度、编排体系等比较符合学堂章程的要求。最后,小学数学教科书方面,有的是按照中国传统书写方式——从右到左竖排形式书写,有的

---

[16] 董远骞,施毓英.俞子夷教育论著选[M].北京:人民教育出版社,1991:2—3.

[17] 费正清、费维恺.剑桥中华民国史[M].北京:中国社会科学出版社,1994:417.

是采用竖排和横排混合形式书写,个别的是采用西方的横排形式书写。

珠算与笔算之平衡。中国新式学校教育是在西方教育的冲击下形成的,在数学教育方面,中学和大学都完全采用西方数学内容,但是小学数学教学内容采纳从西方引进来的笔算数学的同时,也要考虑设置中国传统数学珠算内容的问题。于是出现如何平衡中国传统的珠算内容和西方引进的笔算数学内容的问题。虽然清末教育制度和数学教学内容是模仿日本,而且日本小学数学教育中也有珠算内容,但是中日两国的实际情况不同,因此小学数学中的珠算内容和周教学钟点不能完全模仿日本。在初等小学堂从四年级开始学习珠算,高等小学堂从二年级开始学习珠算,珠算的课时大约占小学数学总课时的三分之一,具体如下:

"奏定初等小学堂章程"规定初等小学学制五年,教学目标要求如下:

> 算术教授要义为:使知日用之计算,与以自谋生计必须之知识,兼使精细其心思。当先就十以内之数示以加减乘除之方,使之熟悉无误,然后渐加其数至万位为止,兼及小数;并宜授以珠算,以便将来寻常实业之用。

"奏定初等小学堂章程"中的数学教学内容和每星期钟点[18]:

第一年　书目之名,实物计算,二十以下之算数,书法,记数法,加减
第二年　百以下之算术,书法,记数法,加减乘除
第三年　常用之加减乘除
第四年　通用之加减乘除,小数之书法,记数法,珠算之加减
第五年　通用之加减乘除,简易之小数,珠算之加减乘除

"奏定高等小学堂章程"中教学目标要求如下:

> 其笔算讲加减乘除、分数小数、比例百分数,至开方开立方而止;珠算讲加减乘除而止。兼讲簿记之学,使知诸账簿之用法,及各种计算表之制式。

"奏定高等小学堂章程"中的数学教学内容和每星期钟点[19]:

第一年　加减乘除,度量衡货币及时刻之计算,简易之小数
第二年　分数,比例,百分数,珠算之加减乘除
第三年　小数,分数,简易之比例,珠算之加减乘除
第四年　比例,百分数,求积,日常簿记,珠算之加减乘除

在"奏定学堂章程"的指导下进行珠算教学急需珠算教科书,于是出现水平各异的珠算教科书,其中水平较高的如下:

> 董瑞椿编《蒙学珠算教科书》(上海文明书局,1903年初版,1906年第九版);杜玠孙编的《最新初等小学珠算入门》(上海商务印书馆,1906年);杜综大、杜玠孙编的《最新初等小学珠算教科书》(上海商务印书馆,1906年);杜就田编《最新初等小学用珠算入门(上、下卷)》(上海

18　张之洞等.奏定学堂章程[Z].台北:台联国风出版社,1970:448—455.
19　张之洞等.奏定学堂章程[Z].台北:台联国风出版社,1970:407.

商务印书馆,1905年初版,1907年第四版,1914年第七版);郑家斌编《最新应用珠算教科书(上、下编)》(粤东编译公司,1907年);学部编译图书局编《初等小学堂珠算教科书》(学部编译图书局,1909年)。

在上述教科书中,前三部是清末学部第一次根据国家统一的教育宗旨、学制课程标准而审定的初等小学教科书。《学部第一次审定教科书书目表》的颁布标志着中国历史上有目的、有计划、有系统的教科书审定工作的正式实施。

珠算是中国人日常生活中普遍使用的数学,学校和社会需求量颇为广泛。珠算教科书的出版远远跟不上实际需要,于是新式学校教育出现前的传统珠算教材也在被广泛使用,如清末和民国初年各种版本的《增删算法统宗》被反复印行,数量可观。

中西度量衡取舍之平衡　度量衡在国家文化中扮演着重要角色,虽然从表面上看,度量衡是一种数量方面的标准,但是它在国家大一统的意识形态中起着杠杆作用。自秦汉时期以来中国的传统度量衡标准已经形成,以实用为主的传统数学教学中度量衡是必修之内容。清末新式数学教育伊始,随着翻译引进西方数学知识,日本度量衡、西方度量衡知识接踵而来,给小学数学教学教科书编写和教学带来如何取舍的难题。诚然,直接翻译的教科书中自然有日本或西方的度量衡知识占据主导地位,但国人自编教科书中一般以中国度量衡知识为主,国人编写个别教科书中有中国度量衡和外国度量衡知识,并给出相关的换算方法。

坚持使用中国度量衡的小学教科书方面,以方楷(1839—1891)编撰之《笔算初阶》(聚文书局,1884年)为典型,《笔算初阶》的"名式略例"中写道:

"凡量物长短之数,名为度,度之单位为丈,丈以下有尺、寸、分、厘、毫、丝、忽、微、纤、沙、尘、埃、渺、漠皆以十进。凡容物多少之数,名为量,量之单位为石,石以下有斗、升、合、勺、撮抄圭、粟皆以十进。凡称物轻重之数,名为衡,衡之单位为两,两以下有钱、分、厘、毫、丝、忽、微、纤、沙、尘、埃、渺、漠皆以十进。十六两为斤。凡度量衡自单位以上,则有十、百、千、万,万以上,有亿、兆、京、垓、秭、穰、沟、涧、正、载、极。凡天文历法之位为宫,宫三十度,宫之下有度,度六十分,度之下有分、秒、微、纤、忽、芒尘皆以六十进。每日有十二时,或为二十四小时,时有八刻,或以小时为四刻,刻,十五分,分,六十秒,秒以下,有微、纤、忽、芒、尘皆以六十进。每田百亩为顷,二百四十方步为亩,二十四方步为分,五尺为步,二尺五寸为跬,三百六十步为里。凡圆形中直线为径,外边为周向有定率,每径一尺,得周三尺一寸分厘五毫九丝二忽,每圆周一得径三寸一分八厘三毫零九忽八微。"

《笔算初阶》中介绍的完全是中国传统度量衡知识。但是后来这一情况发生变化,如杜亚泉编撰之《高等小学用最新笔算教科书》中一般采用国外度量衡单位后再给出换算表。如外国货币和中国银两的换算如下[20]:

日本　圆　　〇.〇二〇一一八四两;英　英镑〇.一九六二二三一两
美　　弗　　〇.〇四〇三二〇九两;法　佛郎〇.〇〇六九七八七两
德　　马克　〇.〇〇九六〇五一两;俄　卢比〇.〇二七四四九九两

在平面图形面积和立体图形体积计算中一般没有采用千米、米、厘米等国外长度单位,仍然使用中国传统的丈、步、尺等单位。在小学数学教科书中普遍使用国际通用度量衡单位是到民国以后才完成的。

20　王兆枬、杜亚泉.高等小学用最新笔算教科书(第四册)[M].上海:商务印书馆,1905:48.

三、清末中学数学教科书发展

(一)清末中学数学制度及相关问题

中学数学教育制度 清末《奏定学堂章程》中规定了中学算学教学目标要求和课程门类。中学数学教科书编撰是遵照章程规定来进行的,尽管个别数学教科书存在超规定现象。《奏定中学堂章程》规定的教学目标要求如下:

> 中学堂学习五年,开设课程有十二科,算学是其中之一。算学教授要义为:先讲算术(外国以数学为各种算法总称,亦犹中国御制《数理精蕴》定名为数之意,而其中以实数计算者为算术,其余则为代数、几何、三角,几何又谓之形学,三角又谓之八线);其笔算讲加减乘除、分数小数、比例百分数,至开方开立方而止;珠算讲加减乘除而止。兼讲簿记之学,使知诸账簿之用法,及各种计算表之制式;次讲平面几何及立体几何初步,兼讲代数。将算学分为算术、代数、几何,各自教授要求如下:凡教算学者,其讲算术,解说务须详明,立法务须简捷,兼详运算之理,并使习熟于速算。其讲代数,贵能简明解释数理之问题;其讲几何,须详于论理,使得应用于测量求积等法。

《奏定中学堂章程》规定中学数学课程为算术、代数、几何、三角和簿记,其中前四门为主科。簿记所占课时很少,每一学年每星期终点为四学时,课程安排如下:

第一年 算术;第二年 算术、代数、几何簿记;第三年 代数、几何;第四年 几何、三角。

分科数学教科书 《奏定中学堂章程》规定的四门主科的教科书是按照分科形式编写的,这是受19世纪欧洲传统数学教育和20世纪初日本数学教育影响之结果。这里需要指出的是,20世纪初欧美国家已经进行数学教育改革,德国进行"以函数为纲"的数学教育改革,英国进行"以应用为主"的数学教育改革,美国进行"以融合为纲"的数学教育改革,融合即为混合之意。从整体上看,欧美国家的这次教育改革倡导的是混合数学教学,于是逐渐摆脱分科编写教科书而走向混合数学教科书的建设。因为,中国清末学习的是日本数学教育,日本学习的是19世纪欧洲传统数学教育,而不是20世纪初的现代数学教育。这就直接导致了日本和中国的分科数学教科书,即算术教科书、几何教科书、代数教科书和三角教科书。极个别的教科书采用"数学教科书""算学教科书"之名,如有叶懋宣编《数学教科书》(上下两册,上海中新活板部,1905年)、商务印书馆编译所编《数学教科书》(上下两册,商务印书馆,1904年初版)等。实际上,这些"数学"命名的教科书即为算术教科书。

分科数学教科书一直延续到1923年民国"新学制"的实施,1923年开始实施初中混合数学教学,1929年开始混合数学和分科数学教学并行,1941年停止混合数学教学。民国时期高中一直实施分科教学。

数学名词术语 人们普遍认为,"从公众看来,教科书是权威的,是准确无误和十分必要的。教师们则需要依靠教科书来安排自己的教学内容。"[21]但是在清末的动荡不安之际彰显中学数学教科书权威的先决条件之一即为数学名词术语的统一问题。清末数学中学教科书中名词术语主要有三个来源:一为中国传统数学之名词术语,如整数、负数、分数、方程、勾股等;二为国人翻译西方数学书时创造的名词术语,如几何、函数等;三为从日本数学书中借用的名词术语,如坐标、定理、命题等。就整体而言,清末数学教科书中的名词术语基本统一,然而这并不是官方认定,而是数学界同仁们约定俗成的结果。有些名词术语并不是一下子被确定下来,经历一段时间甚至很长时间才被确定下来,如函数图象,经历了"界线"(1874年)、"图解"(自1929年以后)后最终成为"图象"[22]。

---

[21] M.阿普尔,L.克丽斯蒂安·史密斯.教科书政治学[M].侯定凯译.上海:华东师范大学出版社,2005:5.
[22] 代钦.中国数学教育史[M].北京:北京师范大学出版社,2018:319.

这里为了使读者更清晰地了解清末中学数学教科书中名词术语起见,对谢洪赉翻译的《最新中学教科书》中的代数学、几何学和三角学的名词术语与现在名词术语进行比较,这对今后数学教科书历史研究有重要参考作用。表1中清末教科书中的名词术语表示为"清末",现在的用"现行"表示。

表1 《最新中学教科书代数学》名词术语对照表

清末	现行	清末	现行	清末	现行
自理	公理	集项劈生法	提公因式法	小公倍	最小公倍数
相似项	同类项	二几何和较相乘	平方差公式	简方程	一次方程
独项式	单项式	二几何和之平方	完全平方公式	平方程	二次方程
覆验	检验	二几何较之平方		立方程	三次方程
命分	分数	劈生	因式分解	同局方程	同解方程
端	种子	互相为质	互为质数	展括弧式	去括号
共生	公约数	相似命分	同分母分数	习问	练习题
质几何	质数	不相似命分	异分母分数	真几何	实数
合几何	合数	乘法特式	乘法公式	幻几何	虚数
		大公生	最大公约数	无定方程	不定方程

表2 《最新中学教科书几何学平面部》名词术语对照表

清末	现行	清末	现行	清末	现行
界说	定义	同理比例	等比	小弧	劣弧
理题	证明题	有法多边形	正多边形	函角	圆周角
作题	作图题	常度	常量	所配	所对
系	推论	变度	变量	合	积
演习	习题	中率	内项	之较	之差
交角	对顶角	外率	外项	等势之轴	对称轴
断线	折线	自理	公理	周界	周长
倚角	邻角	案	总结	公边	公共边
配角	同位角	圆径	直径	斜方形	菱形
正角	直角	尖	顶点	平行方形	平行四边形
		等角三角形	等边三角形	无法四边形	不规则四边形
		相当之件	对应边(角)	等势	对称
		正交	垂直	曲角	钝角

表3 《最新中学教科书几何学立体部》名词术语对照表

清末	现行	清末	现行	清末	现行
界说	定义	断线	折线	常度	常量
理题	证明题	函角	圆周角	变度	变量
作题	作图题	倚角	邻角	合位	轨迹
系	推论	体角	二面角	假设	条件
演习	习题	正角	直角	断语	结论

续表3

清末	现行	清末	现行	清末	现行
等势	对称	曲角	钝角	自理	公理
尖	顶点	交角	对顶角	平行棱体	平行六面体
棱角	顶角	斜方形	菱形	正三角形	直角三角形
旁面	侧面	锋	棱	矩棱体	长方体
旁锋	侧棱	弧角	球面角	直线向平面之倚度	直线与平面所成的角
正棱柱体	直棱柱	弧多边形	球面多边形	直角	平角
有法棱体	正多面体	迈当度数表	单位换算表	教授要言	教授法
球径	直径	极大(小)度	极大(小)值	有法多边形	正多边形
		米［突］	公尺	有法棱柱体	正棱柱
		瓦	公分		
		粉	公寸		

表 4 《最新中学教科书三角术》与现行的名词术语对照表

清末	现行	清末	现行
界说	定义	倚角	邻角
演习	习题	间角	夹角
尖	顶点	有法多边形	正多边形
端	种	三角反函数	反三角函数
正角	直角	覆验	检验
角尖	角顶点	平行方形	平行四边形
曲线代表法	图像法	配角(62,109 页)	
双线函数(86 页)		纳白尔氏对数之底	自然对数底
仰视角	仰角	能敛	收敛
俯视角	俯角	周界	周长
		正三角形	直角三角形
		正弧三角形	球面直角三角形

清末中学数学名词术语到民国以后也保留了绝大部分,根据数学科学研究和数学教育发展需要,科学名词审查会于1938年公布了《算学名词汇编》[23],基本终止了有些数学名词术语不统一的现象。

(二)清末中学数学教科书之特点

清末国人的数学教育思想、制度等方面的特点具体地反映在数学教科书的建设上,可以概括为数学教科书宏观特点和教科书编写特点。

从宏观上看,清末中学数学教科书呈现"新""多元化""滞后性"和"国际合作"等特点。

"新"特点。清末新式教育甫兴,配套的教科书成为奇缺之物。教科书的编译、印刷和发行,成为社会新兴的一个产业。为了吸引人们的眼球,出版者也纷纷标榜各自教科书的新颖、先进。于是一时间,

---

[23] 曹惠群.科学名词汇编[Z].科学名词审查会,1938.

市场上充满了各种《最新教科书》《新体教科书》《新式教科书》《新教科书》《新译教科书》和《新编教科书》，呈现一种"新"特点。就最新中学数学教科书而言，至少有四种，如：(1)武昌中东书社的《最新代数教科书》(1904年)；(2)(上海)昌明公司和(日本东京)清国留学生会馆的《最新平面几何教科书》(1905年)；(3)上海科学书局的《最新中学代数教科书》(1907年)；(4)商务印书馆的《最新中学教科书代数学》(1904年)和《最新中学教科书几何学》(1906年)等。除"最新教科书"外还有十三种"新"教科书。一般来讲，清末的各种"新"教科书的水平很高，有些教科书一直沿用到民国初期，如上海科学书局的《最新中学代数教科书》((日)桦正董著，周藩译，1907年)至1913年已经出版第七版。所谓"新"是相对的，这些"新"教科书到民国时期随着国人自编数学教科书的兴起逐渐地销声匿迹了。

有眼光的出版企业并没有停留在"新"教科书上，在出版"新"教科书的同时，组织编写出版其他数学教科书，而且水平有所提高。如，商务印书馆编译所编写的《中学代数学教科书》(上、下卷，1908年)参考了日本的十一种代数教科书，到1920年已再版十五次。

"多元化"特点。《奏定学堂章程》中虽然有审定教科书的制度，但遵守规定的人和出版企业甚少，他们从各自的立场和需要出发翻译、编写出版教科书，相互之间很少交流和沟通。这就导致了在同一个时期出现多种教科书，更有甚者出现同一种外国教科书的不同翻译本，例如，日本藤泽利喜太郎、上野清、菊池大麓等学者的数学教科书有不少中文版本。虽然教科书的这种多元化现象对出版企业的竞争和发展有推动作用，但是对教师如何选择使用教科书以及如何使教科书与教学计划相适应等问题带来极大的困难，使中学数学教科书市场处于一种无组织状态。

从翻译引进的渠道看，也呈现"多元化"现象。首先，清末的中学数学教科书几乎都是翻译或编译日本和美国的教科书，其中以翻译日本的居多，翻译美英的次之。随着时间的推移，也出现国人自编的数学教科书。其次，清末中学数学教科书在国内翻译出版的同时，留日学生在日本东京翻译出版后输送到国内供使用。例如，日本东京清国留学生会馆、日本东京科学会和东京并木活版所翻译出版了不少中学数学教科书。

从翻译教科书者的职业看，他们并不一定限制在数学教育领域。虽然有周达、崔朝庆等数学家，但也有一些非数学家的人员参与到数学教科书建设中来并做出重要贡献。如谢洪赉是教育家，不是数学家；丁福保也不是数学家，但也编译、编写数学教科书。这可能是当时他们认识到数学在整个教育中的重要性。

"滞后性"特点。20世纪初，欧美掀起数学教育改革运动，如英国的贝利(J. Perry, 1850—1920)运动，以克莱因(F. Klein, 1849—1925)为代表的德国新主义数学运动和美国穆尔(E. H. Moore, 1860—1952)的数学教育改革思想。但中国学习的是欧美传统数学教育，而不是新的数学教育。原因在于《奏定学堂章程》完全接受和模仿了日本明治后期的教育制度，而日本当时的数学教育制度是在崇尚欧洲传统数学教育的藤泽利喜太郎的指导下制定的。"正因为中国数学教育受日本的影响，中国没有受到20世纪初的数学教育改革运动的影响，而与世界潮流背道而驰。"[24]在这种思想背景下，中国翻译出版的数学教科书是在欧美已经停止使用或很少使用了。20世纪初的欧美中学数学教科书中已经有解析几何、函数等内容，但中国清末中学数学教科书中没有这些近代数学内容。从这个意义上看，清末中学数学教科书凸显出"滞后性"特点。另外，"滞后性"表现在教科书内容的设置上。20世纪初在欧美已经摆脱分科数学教育转向混合数学教育，而在中国还沉浸在分科数学教育中。从中国数学教育制度层面上看，这种"滞后性"特点直至1922年"新学制"的颁布才结束。总之，中学数学教科书虽然"定名为最新教科书，实即为最老者"。[25]这种评价与西方现代数学教育思潮相比不足为过。

"国际合作"特点。清末翻译、编写和出版数学教科书活动在作者之间、出版企业之间出现一种"国际合作"的特点。第一，多家出版企业虽然有激烈的竞争，但是在竞争中也有一定的合作。如，高木贞治

24　代钦，李春兰. 中国数学教育史研究进展七十年之回顾与反思[J].《数学教育学报》, 2007(16)3:7.
25　王云五. 王云五文集——岫庐八十自述(上册)[M]. 南昌：江西教育出版社, 2011:229.

著,周藩译《新体中学代数学教科书》是由文明书局、科学书局和群学社合作出版的。第二,出现国际间的合作现象。首先,教科书在日本出版,由国内出版社发行。其次,日本学者为中国翻译中学数学教科书。如日本学者西师意翻译藤泽利喜太郎的《算术教科书》《初等代数学教科书》(译名为《代数学教科书》),而且西师意请英国学者窦乐安为《算术教科书》作序[26]。又如,日本著名数学家寺尾寿主编,日本学者藤森温和编《日清对译算术教科书》[27],是为中国留学生编写的中学数学教科书。再次,中日数学家的合作。如,周达在日访算学时,长泽龟之助和上野清给周达介绍西方和日本数学教科书情况。另外,长泽龟之助还为崔朝庆主办的《数学杂志》(1912年)提供赞助。

四、翻译引进教科书内容的处理

清末,无论是以日本的数学教科书为底本还是欧美的数学教科书为底本进行编译,难能可贵的是,中国学者都能够意识到教科书是因国而异的,不能盲目地直接翻译外国数学教科书,必须将外国教科书内容中国化,并为此付出了实际的行动。

内容的"删减与添加"。清末国人翻译引进外国数学教科书时采用"删减"与"添加"法。翻译时,删减外国原著中某些命题证明、例题解答、习题等不适合于中国国情的内容。例如黄传纶等编译的《最新平面几何教科书》(上下卷)的原著为原滨吉的《平面几何学讲义》(东京金刺芳流堂,1904年),原书为一册,32开本,726页,中译本为上下两册。在编译过程中,中译本采用删减和填补方式。他们删除掉认为不必要的内容,而对只用文字表述,学生理解起来比较困难的内容进行技术处理,增补几何图形。如,原书第三编的绪论在编译本中被删除;原书中对于平行四边形高的定义没有给出几何图形,而编译版中给出了几何图形;同时,原书中的习题较多,如第三编有275道题,而且均附几何图形,编译本中大量删减了习题,只留下六十道题[28]。原书只用文字叙述部分,在编译本中给出文字叙述内容的相应的几何图形(如图2)。

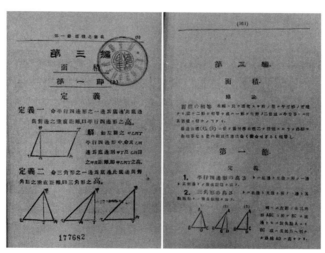

图2 《最新平面几何教科书》《平面几何学讲义》

余焕东、赵缭翻译日本桦正董的《新译算术教科书》(上卷),1906年在翻译的改正版的"凡例"中译者写道:"原书度量衡、钱币、历法皆以日本为主,故详于日本而略于中国。译者详考国制及各省不同者列之为表以备检查……原书例题等均注意其本国教育,与我国无甚关系,其日用诸算尤多,与我国不合,本书改之,总期能合我国之教育为善。"其中关于度量衡方面的编译,在其他人编译的数学教科书中也都

---

[26] [日]藤泽利喜太郎.算术教科书[M].西师意译.上海:山西大学译书院,1904:序.

[27] [日]藤森温和.日清对译算术教科书[M].东京:富山房,1906.

[28] [日]原滨吉.平面几何学讲义[M].东京:金刺芳流堂,1904:280—361;原滨吉.最新平面几何教科书[M].黄传纶,刘采麟,杨清贵编,译.东京:清国留学生会馆,1905:80—96.

注意到这一点。

内容的"参合与融化"。清末,中国数学教育虽然学习模仿日本,但在编写数学教科书方面不完全是这样的。一般来讲,在中小学数学教科书编写过程中,以某一数学教科书为底本,同时参考其他多种数学教科书。另外,在模仿日本的数学教科书编写的同时也学习和参考西方的数学教科书。我们可以从国人编写的中学数学教科书的"凡例""例言"或者"绪言"中查知。例如:余焕东、赵缭编译的《新译算术教科书》(上卷)改正版译者所写的"凡例"中指出:"本书以翻译日本桦正董改订之算术教科书为主,而旁采他书以补所为备。"

武昌中东书社编译的《最新代数学教科书》绪言中指出:"本书同人慨然于因编译部之设首取日人真野氏及宫田氏合编之代数学教科书,悉心译述参考西书数种,以补其引例演式之所为备。寒暑过半,仅乃成之。编译之劳梁溪顾君沛然助力良多,是书之出,总期教者可据为讲义之稿本,而学者亦可藉为独习之用书,故说理极其简明,而立式归于精审。"

程荫南在《新式数学教科书》之"例言"中说:"一、本书以日本著名数学大家泽田吾一所著《中学算术教科书》为蓝本,并采择桦正氏、长泽氏所著之算术各教科书编译而成。删繁就简,化险为夷,以期适于中学教科之用。二、本书算式,概仍原书之旧。唯日本教科书,说理多有未透,间参考东京数学院算术讲义录,及中国现今通行之数学书,以补原书之未遂,故较原书多有出入。"

何崇礼在《中等教育几何教科书》"例言"中提出:"本书以日本长泽龟之助先生所著几何教科书为主,益参以己意,简者详之,繁者约之,晦者明之,缺者补之。斟酌损益,凡历两载,及克成帙,教科用之,庶无遗憾。"

陈文在《中学适用算术教科书》"例言"中说:"本书以日本桦正董所著算术教科书之和文本为主。然其中不宜于我国之处,悉删除之。别搜罗他书以补其缺。最显著者,如诸等法,百分算两编,全由译者自行编辑。此外诸编,改窜增补,亦复不少,并变更例题三百有余。"

谢洪赉在《最新中学教科书代数学》"译例"中提出:"是书以美国纽约师范学校校长宓尔君所著归纳法代数学为原本,参酌我国情形,略为修饰,以合中学程度。"

另外,国人编写的数学教科书有的是参考了几个国家的数学教科书而编写成的,如《大同大学丛书》之二:初级中学适用的《初学代数学》就取材于多个国家的代数教科书。作者在编辑例言中就明确指出:"本编取材,大都取诸美国人温德华氏、郝克斯氏、英国人司密斯氏、郝而那氏、日本人早川氏等所著初等代数学,而于温氏采用尤多。"

可见,清末国人已经意识到自编数学教科书的重要性,在借鉴外国的数学教科书时,唯有按中国的国情引进一些内容加以熔铸,做到取多家所长,补己之短,才能成就出适合国人使用的数学教科书。

除此之外,清末中学数学教科书的装帧、装订、印刷等方面几乎都是采用西方技术和形式。首先,当时西方数学教科书一般是精装本,国人翻译出版时也按照西方原著的版式出版。其次,清末数学教科书的装订和纸张质量非常好,在整体上比后来民国教科书好。再次,清末数学教科书凸版印刷较多。清末个别教科书按中国传统的线装出版,如日本高木贞治著,周藩译的《新体中学代数学教科书》为线装书。

清末数学教科书的"序""例言""编辑大意"特点。清末中小学数学教科书在整体上呈现序言、例言和编辑大意等特点,具体如下:首先,清末中小学多数数学教科书有序言,有的有一则序言,有的有两则序言,更有者三则序言。"序"是中国传统的一种文体,一般为写在著作正文之前的文章,有作者自己写的,多说明写书宗旨和经过。也有请别人写序文的,"为人作序可带来收入,并搭建社会网络,为作家带来名声。"[29]在清末数学教科书中也延续了这一传统。诚然,翻译数学教科书的原书也有序,有的译者把

---

29 李弘祺.中国教育史英文著作评介[M].台北:台湾大学出版社中心,2005:256.

原书的序文全文翻译,有的译者没有翻译原书序文。有的教科书有"弁言",弁言是序言的另一种说法。清末有的数学教科书没有序言,但是有"提要",这就相当于序言,如张景良著《小学笔算新教科书》(1908年)有"学部提要",其指向性比序文更强。

其次,清末一些中小学数学教科书有"例言",它说明教科书体例、实例等典型内容。其中一般相当于内容提要、教与学的注意事项。如董瑞椿编《蒙学珠算教科书》,程荫南《新式数学教科书》,余焕东、赵镠编译的《新译算术教科书》,何崇礼编《中等教育几何教科书》,陈文编《中学适用算术教科书》等教科书均有例言。

再次,清末中小学部分数学教科书有"编辑大意",说明编辑意图、内容范围等。

这些教科书前的文字是了解编纂、编译意图的重要资料,从中可见清末国人已经意识到自编数学教科书的重要性,在借鉴外国的数学教科书时,唯有按中国的国情引进一些内容加以熔铸,做到取多家所长,补己之短,才能成就出适合国人使用的数学教科书。

五、清末中小学数学教科书编排形式的变化

中国传统的文章编排形式为竖排,即从右边开始往左竖排形式编写,这与西方的从上到下的横排形式迥然不同。中国的传统编排方式对于数学或自然科学书籍的编写不方便。但是,中国的不少数学教育工作者一直到清末仍然采用这种传统的竖排形式编写教科书,而对西方的横排编写形式采取拒绝态度。清末,中国数学教科书一般在国内出版,但有些是在日本印刷出版后在国内发行的,凡在日本出版的数学教科书全部采取横排。具体呈现的特点如下:

采取竖排编写形式、数学符号全部是中国传统数学符号。清末,谢洪赉、周达等学者将西方数学教科书按照中国人的习惯翻译编写出版。如谢洪赉翻译的《最新中学教科书代数学》(上海商务印书馆,1905年)和《最新中学教科书几何学》(上海商务印书馆,1906年)就是典型例子。他把原著中的阿拉伯数字和加减符号以外的数学符号全部用中国传统数学符号甲、乙、丙、丁代替,并用竖排形式编写;表示几何图形的顶点、端点等不用 A、B、C 等字母而用汉字(图3,图4)。

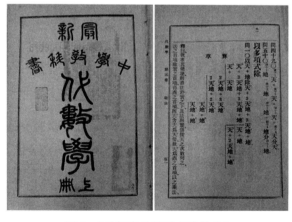 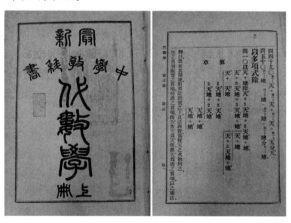

图3 《最新中学教科书代数学》　　　　　图4 《最新中学教科书几何学》

采取横竖混合编排形式、采用西方数学符号。有些数学教科书的文字介绍部分采用竖排形式,数学表达式部分采用竖排和横排的混合编排形式,同时采用西方数学符号。例如,长泽龟之助著,崔朝庆译的《中等平面几何学阶梯》(上海会文学社,1906年)就采用这种形式(图5)。

图 5 《中等平面几何学阶梯》第 21 页、第 32 页

横排编写、采用中国传统数学符号。清末出版的数学教科书也有横排编写的,而采用的数学符号仍然是中国传统的数学符号,如黄传纶等翻译日本原滨吉著的《最新平面几何学教科书》(1906 年)就是其中一个代表(图 6)。

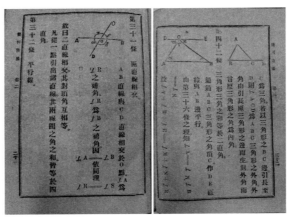

图 6 《最新平面几何学教科书》下卷封面、下卷第 5 页

采用西方数学教科书形式和符号。清末有些数学教科书完全采用西方数学教科书的编排形式及数学符号。特别是在日本印刷出版的数学教科书,如长泽龟之助著,周达翻译的《新几何学教科书(平面)》(上海东亚公司,1906 年,如图 7)。又如日本数学家菊池大麓著,仇毅翻译的《中学校数学教科书几何之部》(群益书社,1907 年,如图 8)。

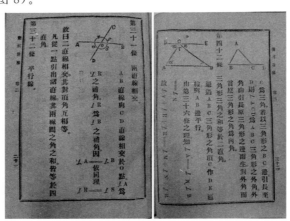

图 7 《新几何学教科书(平面)》封面、第 20 页

关于中学数学教科书采用横排编写的问题,数学教科书编纂者也提出自己的理由。例如:武昌中东书社编译部的《最新代数学教科书》绪言中说:"编既竣,或难之曰:代数用字夙有成式,吾国行文必用直

· 256 ·

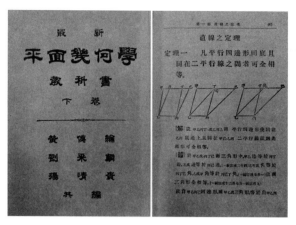

图 8 《中学校数学教科书几何之部》封面、第 121 页

行,是书勿乃反是。则应之曰:吾国事事惟拘于成例,故往往知其良而亦鲜有改之者。横文二十六字,竭一时间之力,而强记之,已无余事,由是进而读西文原书,纵未易明其理,解必可窥其算式,何便如之。至横行体例:(一)便于演式,(二)便于引例,(三)便于分段,眉目清爽,开卷了然,尤足以厌读者之心。"[30]

《新式数学教科书》之"例言"中也明确指出使用横排的优点:"本书仿西文例,皆用横行,非好奇也。缘演算式非横行不便,故书从之。谅从事此道者,必能鉴此微衷。"[31]

另外,陈鼎元、黄元吉等学者也强调按西方数学书形式编写的重要性,在此不赘述。

除此之外,清末中学数学教科书的装帧、装订、印刷等方面多数都已采用西方的技术和形式。首先,当时西方数学教科书一般是精装本,国人翻译出版是也按照西方原著的版式出版。其次,清末数学教科书的装订和纸张品质非常好,在整体上比后来民国教科书好。再次,清末数学教科书凸版印刷较多。个别教科书按中国传统的线装出版。如日本高木贞治著,周藩译的《新体中学代数教科书》为线装本。

六、结语

从清末中小学数学发展历程及其特点看,中国数学家和热心参与数学教育工作的有识之士付出了极大的努力,做出了积极贡献。也有日本长泽龟之助、上野清和西师意等学者对中国数学教科书建设给予了帮助。由各种教科书"书目"可见,清末中小学数学教科书在各学科教科书中数量上居冠,为民国数学教科书发展奠定了坚实的基础,最终使中国数学教育与世界数学教育接轨。一言以蔽之,清末数学教科书建设取得了可喜的成绩。但是我们看到它的优点的同时,也有必要探查其存在的诸多问题。清末或民国时期,学者们已经发现了教科书建设中存在的问题,如著名教育家余家菊(1898—1976)对教科书的教材和形式两个方面存在之问题提出[32]:

(一)在教材方面

1.不合教育宗旨,取材太无主义。2.不合人生需要,太重学术的体制。3.不合时代需要,又多废话,又多胧漏。4.不合地方需要,多抄袭日本的。5.不合科学的新趋势,太陈旧腐败。6.不合科学的精神,太支离,太抽象。

(二)在形式方面

1.文体无生气,板滞的。2.前后无结构,破碎的。3.不合教授法,注入的。4.忽略审美性,像插图的粗糙。5.忽略卫生,像字的太小,纸的太光。

---

30 武昌中东书社编译部.最新代数学教科书[M].东京并木活版所,1904:2.
31 程荫南.新式数学教科书(第六版)[M].中国图书公司,1914:例言.
32 余家菊:《余家菊(景陶)先生教育论文集》,财团法人台北市慧炬出版社,1997:102-103.

这些批评不一定完全贴切，但是基本反映了清末中小学数学教科书中存在的问题，对清末中小学教科书研究具有良好的借鉴作用。

另外，这里指出的一点是，清末翻译、编写的中小学数学教科书，并不是到民国时期就突然停止，不少清末中小学数学教科书在民国期间也被使用一段时期才退出历史舞台，如张景良的《小学笔算新教科书》（四卷）以及上野清、菊池大麓、桦正董等数学家的教科书一直使用到1922年。更有甚者，如查理斯密、温特沃斯的数学教科书直至使用到20世纪30年代。

晚清汉译日本中学数学教科书研究

郭金海[1] （中国科学院自然科学史研究所）

摘要 甲午战争后，随着中国学习日本浪潮的推动，图书编译、教育改革活动的展开，汉译日本中学数学教科书兴起，并成为晚清中学数学教科书的主流。晚清汉译日本中学数学教科书至少有109种，几何类最多，其后相继是代数类、三角类、算术类、解析几何类。各类的底本都有多种著作，呈现出底本多样化的特点。底本作者不乏日本著名数学家和数学教育家。译者多为中国留日学生，也有无留学经历的中国本土学者和日本学者。晚清汉译日本中学数学教科书主要由国人独立翻译和编译，大都模仿底本，采用对文字和公式排版方式、数码、数学符号的西化做法，不乏风靡一时，流传甚广之作，对晚清中学数学教育产生深远的影响。但晚清汉译日本中学数学教科书编译水平参差不齐，有不少未能尽如人意。

关键词 晚清；中学数学教科书；甲午战争；学习日本；癸卯学制

1895年甲午战争败于日本后，中国民族危机加重，晚清政府将学习日本作为国家救亡图存和富国强兵的一条新路。因此，全国很快掀起学习日本的浪潮。而且留学日本和翻译日本书成为由晚清政府推动的事业。国人兴办的图书编译出版社团和机构在中国和日本大量涌现。1900年因八国联军入侵，再次遭受重创，晚清政府推行新政。在20世纪第一个十年，晚清政府以兴学育才为当务之急，采取了兴学堂、颁行"癸卯学制"、废科举等教育改革举措，中学数学教育在中国大规模展开。全国中学堂亟需适于新式教育的中学数学教科书。至1912年2月清朝覆灭，有大量日本中学数学教科书被汉译。

关于晚清汉译日本中学数学教科书，目前有些论著有所涉及。如冯立昇在专著《中日数学关系史》中探讨晚清日本数学教科书的翻译和影响时，对部分汉译日本中学数学教科书做了考察[2]。萨日娜在专著《东西方数学文明的碰撞与交融》中介绍了部分晚清汉译日本中学数学教科书[3]。刘冰楠在博士学位论文《中国中学三角学教科书发展史研究(1902—1949)》中对3部晚清汉译日本中学三角学教科书做了案例研究[4]。张美霞的博士学位论文《清末民国时期中学解析几何学教科书研究》论及部分晚清汉译日本中学解析几何学教科书[5]。张冬莉在博士学位论文《中国数学教科书中勾股定理内容设置变迁研究(1902—1949)》中对两部晚清汉译日本中学几何教科书中的勾股定理内容做了案例研究[6]。

然而，学界迄今对晚清汉译日本中学数学教科书尚无专门的研究。关于这批教科书兴起的背景和

---

[1] 作者简介：郭金海，1974年生，天津人，博士，研究员，研究方向为中国数学史、中国近现代科技史、中国科学院院史，E-mail: gjinhai@ihns.ac.cn。
[2] 冯立昇：《中日数学关系史》，济南：山东教育出版社，2009年，第231—254页。
[3] 萨日娜：《东西方数学文明的碰撞与交融》，上海：上海交通大学出版社，2016年，第317—320页。
[4] 刘冰楠：《中国中学三角学教科书发展史研究(1902—1949)》，呼和浩特：内蒙古师范大学博士学位论文，2015年，第44—60页。
[5] 张美霞：《清末民国时期中学解析几何学教科书研究》，呼和浩特：内蒙古师范大学博士学位论文，2018年，第62—69页。
[6] 张冬莉：《中国数学教科书中勾股定理内容设置变迁研究(1902—1949)》，呼和浩特：内蒙古师范大学博士学位论文，2020年，第22—32页。

这批教科书的整体面貌,基本还没有探讨;关于这批教科书的底本作者和译者、翻译与编译情况、流传与影响的研究,还较为薄弱。而探清这些问题,不仅可以较为深入地还原晚清汉译日本中学数学教科书的历史,可以深入认识日本对晚清中学数学教育的影响,而且可以从侧面展现晚清最后十余年在国家寻求救亡图存和富国强兵之路的大背景下,政府与国人在新式数学教育方面的互动。鉴于此,本文基于原始文献,探讨晚清汉译日本中学数学教科书兴起的背景,考察其种类、底本作者和译者、翻译与编译情况、流传与影响,以求有所创获。

一、晚清汉译日本中学数学教科书兴起的背景

1894年,日本趁朝鲜政府请求晚清政府协助镇压东学党起义之机,乃一面怂恿晚清政府出兵,一面抢派重兵进驻朝鲜。7月25日,日本舰队在牙山口外丰岛海面袭击中国运兵船舰,正式挑起甲午战争,8月1日中日双方正式宣战。这场战争以晚清政府战败,北洋舰队全军覆没,1895年4月17日中日双方签订《马关条约》而告终。[7] 当时晚清政府部分官员和有识之士认识到帝国主义列强对中国瓜分豆剖的形势迫在眉睫,开始将学习日本作为救亡图存、富国强兵的一条新路。甲午战争结束的次年即1896年旧历三月底,晚清政府派遣的首批留日学生13人便抵达日本。[8]

1898年,主要由于日本于明治维新后崛起的经验值得效法,学习日本具有路近、费省、文字相近、收效快速等优点,晚清朝野上下主张学习日本的呼声已高涨。1898年1月,康有为在《进呈日本明治变政考序》中说:"大抵欧、美以三百年而成造成治体,日本效欧、美,以三十年而摹成治体。若以中国之广土众民,近采日本,三年而宏规成,五年而条理备,八年而成效举,十年而霸图定矣。"[9] 同年6月1日,山东道监察御史杨深秀在进呈光绪皇帝的奏折中提出:"我今欲变法而章程未具,诸学无人,虽欲举事,无由措理,非派才俊出洋游学,不足以供变政之用。特泰西语言文字不同,程功之期既远,重洋舟车,饮食昂贵,虚糜之费殊多,故郑重兹事,迟迟未举。臣以为日本变法立学,确有成效,中华欲游学易成,必自日本始。政俗文字同则学之易,舟车饮食贱则费无多。"[10]

晚清重臣张之洞也持有这种主张,并提倡广译日本书。1898年,他在《劝学篇》中指出:"日本,小国耳,何兴之暴也?伊藤、山县、榎本、陆奥诸人,皆二十年前出洋之学生也,愤其国为西洋所胁,率其徒百余人分诣德、法、英诸国,或学政治工商,或学水陆兵法,学成而归,用为将相,政事一变,雄视东方。……各种西学书之要者,日本皆已译之,我取径于东洋,力省效速,则东文之用多。……学西文者,效迟而用博,为少年未仕者计也。译西书者,功近而效速,为中年已仕者计也。若学东洋文,译东洋书,则速而又速者也。是故从洋师不如通洋文,译西书不如译东书。"[11] 同年8月,光绪皇帝下谕旨:"现在讲求新学,风气大开,唯百闻不如一见,自以派人出洋游学为要。至游学之国,西洋不如东洋,诚以路近费省,文字相近,易于通晓。且一切西书均经日本择要翻译,刊有定本,何患不事半功倍。"[12]因此,全国掀起学习日本的热潮,留学日本和翻译日本书成为由晚清政府推动的事业。

当时国内一些有识之士关心日本书的翻译工作,迫切希望晚清政府快速推进这项工作,积极建言献策。如1898年,康有为向光绪皇帝建议在京师设译书局,提出了针对译书局人员有限,日本书难以尽

---

[7] 郑天挺、谭其骧主编:《中国历史大辞典》,上海:上海辞书出版社,2010年,第464页。

[8] 实藤惠秀著,谭汝谦、林启彦译:《中国人留学日本史》,北京:北京大学出版社,2012年,第1页。

[9] 汤志钧编:《康有为政论集》上册,北京:中华书局,1981年,第222—224页。

[10] 《山东道监察御史杨深秀请议游学日本章程片》,陈学恂、田正平编:《中国近代教育史资料汇编:留学教育》,上海:上海教育出版社,2007年,第333页。

[11] 张之洞著,李凤仙评注:《劝学篇》,北京:华夏出版社,2002年版,第87—102页。

[12] 《军机处传知总理各国事务衙门面奉之谕旨片》,陈学恂、田正平编:《中国近代教育史资料汇编:留学教育》,上海:上海教育出版社,2007年,第3页。

译,国人虽多,但重科第的现实情况,调动国人译书积极性的奖励办法。他说:"译日本之书,为我文字者十之八,其成事至少,其费日无多也。请在京师设译书局,妙选通人主之,听其延辟通学,专选日本政治书之佳者,先分科程并译之。不岁月后,日本佳书,可大略皆译也。虽然日本新书无数,专恃官局为人有几,又佳书日出,终不能尽译也,即令各省皆立译局,亦有限矣。窃计中国人多,最重科第,退以荣于乡,进仕于朝,其额至窄,其得至难也。诸生有视科第得失为性命者,仅以策论取之,亦奚益哉?臣愚请下令,士人能译日本书者,皆大赉之,若童生译日本书一种,五万字以上者,若试其学论通者,给附生。附生、增生译日本书三万字以上者,试论通,皆给廪生。廪生则给贡生。凡诸生译日本书过十万字以上者,试其学论通者,给举人。举人给进士。进士给翰林。庶官皆晋一秩。"[13]再如,1900年张謇在《变法评议》中向晚清政府建议"译书分省设局",认为:"今中国为先河后海之谋,宜译东书。即为同种同文之便,亦宜译东书。然各省同时并立学堂,并需课书。若专倚一省,不及供求取之殷,而各省辏兴,亦虑有复沓之弊。谓宜约分门类,就江南(苏州淮南书局并入)、上海、江西、湖北、湖南、山东、四川、浙江、福建、广东十处,原有书局经费,各认若干门,延致通才,分年赶译。"[14]

晚清政府支持设立图书编译机构。1898年,京师大学堂设立译书局,由梁启超办理,管学大臣孙家鼐督率办理[15]。据1902年《京师大学堂译书局章程》,译书局当时"所译各书,以教科为当务之急",而把翻译小学、中学教科书放在首位,具体规定为:"教科书通分二等,一为小学,一为中学,其深远者,俟此二等成书后,再行从事。"[16] 1902年,京师大学堂于上海设立译书分局。其首批译成的书籍均是底本为日文的日本书。[17] 1905年,晚清政府成立学部,专职统管全国教育事务。次年6月,学部设立编纂各级各类学堂教科书的专职机构编译图书局。[18]

不仅如此,甲午战争后,中国"无论士商官吏怦然心动,以为中国之制度远不及欧美之良,而欲自振兴不得不仿西法、读西学、知西史矣。"[19]以梁启超为代表的有识之士大力倡导译书。1897年,梁启超在上海创办大同译书局,"以东文为主,而辅以西文",并大声疾呼:

> "译书真今日之急图哉! 天下识时之士,日日论变法。然欲变士,而学堂功课之书,靡得而读焉。欲变农,而农政之书,靡得而读焉。欲变工,而工艺之书,靡得而读焉。欲变商,而商务之书,靡得而读焉。欲变官,而官制之书,靡得而读焉。欲变兵,而兵谋之书,靡得而读焉。欲变总纲,而宪法之书,靡得而读焉。欲变分目,而章程之书,靡得而读焉。……故及今不速译书,则所谓变法者,尽成空言,而国家将不能收一法之效。"[20]

这反映出梁启超对译书的急迫心情。究其原因,一方面是因为梁启超认识到吸收西方文明对明治维新

---

[13] 《康有为:广译日本书设立京师译书局折(1898)》,黎难秋等:《中国科学翻译史料》,合肥:中国科学技术大学出版社,1996年,第96页。

[14] 《变法平议·译书分省设局》,宋原放主编,汪家熔辑注:《中国出版史料(近代部分)》第2卷,武汉:湖北教育出版社,2004年,第22页。

[15] 《梁启超奏议书局事务折》,北京大学校史研究室编:《北京大学史料》第1卷,北京:北京大学出版社,1993年,第191—193页。

[16] 《京师大学堂译书局章程》,北京大学校史研究室编:《北京大学史料》第1卷,北京:北京大学出版社,1993年,第194页。

[17] 《上海译书分局为开办情形呈报京师大学堂》,北京大学校史研究室编:《北京大学史料》第1卷,北京:北京大学出版社,1993年,第193页。

[18] 关晓红:《晚清学部研究》,广州:广东教育出版社,1993年,第85,377页。

[19] 《论译西学书》,《益闻录》,1897年第1694号,第338页。

[20] 《大同译书局叙例》,梁启超:《梁启超全集》第1册,北京:北京出版社,1999年,第132页。

后日本崛起的重要性,而译书是日本吸收西方文明的一条重要途径;另一方面则是因为中国虽然自明末清初至甲午战争前通过中外人士合译了一些西书,但还难以满足社会变革的需求。

在晚清政府的支持、推动和梁启超等人的倡导下,甲午战争后我国民间图书编译出版机构和社团如雨后春笋,四处兴起。1897年大同译书局成立的当年,维新派就在上海创立译书公会,以"采译泰西东切用书籍为宗旨"[21]。至20世纪初,还有浙江特别译书局、杭州合众译书局、东亚译书局、新民译书局、会文学社[22]、新学会社[23]、农学社[24]等图书编译出版机构和社团陆续成立。自1897年起,也陆续有图书出版机构成立,编译出版教科书和其他图书。如1897年,中国近代重要出版机构——商务印书馆在上海成立,其于1902年成立编译所[25]。编译所成立后,组织翻译了大量国外图书[26];而且,邀请日本教育家伊泽修二担任编辑、教科书籍顾问[27]。1898年,冯镜如与何澄一等在上海创立广智书局,以出版译著作为主要业务之一[28]。1902年文明书局成立,初称文明编译印书局,是我国较早编印系列新式教科书的机构之一[29]。同年,陈子沛、陈子寿兄弟于湖南长沙创设群益书社,1907年于上海设分社,继于1909年在日本东京设分社,1912年迁至上海设总社。群益书社早期以编译出版理科教科书为主[30]。

当时有不少中国留日学生热心创办图书编译出版社团和机构。1900年,中国留日学生在日本东京成立译书汇编社。这是中国留日学生首个翻译出版日本书籍的团体,以翻译大学教材为主。该社共有14名社员,社长戢翼翚是晚清政府派遣的首批13名留日学生之一。[31] 1902年,陆世芬等中国留日学生在东京成立教科书译辑社,"编译东西教科新书,备各省学堂采用。"[32] 据实藤惠秀的研究,教科书译辑社是译书汇编社的分社,专译中学教科书[33]。同年,戢翼翚和日本女教育家下田歌子合作创办作新社,先在东京设发行所,后在上海、北京、扬州等地设分社[34]。1904年,福建省留日学生成立了闽学会[35]。晚清留日学生还成立了上海科学会编译部、湖南编译社等图书编译出版社团。上海科学会编译部总发行所位于上海四马路老巡捕房东首,主要编辑出版中学理科用书[36]。此外,1902年成立于东京的清国留学生

---

[21] 《译书公会章程》,张静庐辑注:《中国近代出版史料二编》,北京:中华书局,1957年,第90页。

[22] 会文学社成立于1903年由汤寿潜与沈霖在上海创办,开始以编译出版教科书为主。参见邹振环:《20世纪上海翻译出版与文化变迁》,南宁:广西教育出版社,2001年,第76页。

[23] 新学会社于1908年由孙锵与江起鲲合资创办,最初开在宁波,后迁至上海。参见石鸥、吴小鸥:《简明中国教科书史》,北京:知识产权出版社,2015年,第39页。

[24] 农学社于1896年由罗振玉与蒋廷黻在上海创办,专门从事对国外农业方面著述的翻译。参见冯志杰:《中国近代翻译史·晚清卷》,北京:九州出版社,2011年,第194—195页。

[25] 李家驹:《商务印书馆与近代知识文化的传播》,北京:商务印书馆,2005年,第45页。

[26] 冯志杰:《中国近代翻译史·晚清卷》,北京:九州出版社,2011年,第193—194页。

[27] 《日本教育家伊泽修二君传略》,《东方杂志》,1904,(11):251。

[28] 许力以主编:《中国出版百科全书》,太原:书海出版社,1997年,第575页;邹振环:《20世纪上海翻译出版与文化变迁》,南宁:广西教育出版社,2001年,第58—67页。

[29] 姚一鸣:《中国旧书局》,北京:金城出版社,2014年,第103—144页。

[30] 邹振环:《清末民初上海群益书社与〈纳氏文法〉的译刊及影响》,复旦大学历史学系、中外现代化进程研究中心编:《中国现代学科的形成》,上海:上海古籍出版社,2007年,第91—100页。

[31] 实藤惠秀著,谭汝谦、林启彦译:《中国人留学日本史》,北京:北京大学出版社,2012年,第179—183页。

[32] 林煌天主编:《中国翻译词典》,武汉:湖北教育出版社,1997年,第329页;实藤惠秀著,谭汝谦、林启彦译:《中国人留学日本史》,北京:北京大学出版社,2012年,第183页。

[33] 实藤惠秀著,谭汝谦、林启彦译:《中国人留学日本史》,北京:北京大学出版社,2012年,第183页。

[34] 张泽贤:《民国出版标记大观续集》,上海:上海远东出版社,2012年,第651页。

[35] 林煌天主编:《中国翻译词典》,武汉:湖北教育出版社,1997年,第495页。

[36] 石鸥、吴小鸥:《简明中国教科书史》,北京:知识产权出版社,2015年,第41页。

会馆[37]是中国留日学生的团体,出版发行中国留日学生编译的图书。

1904年"癸卯学制"颁行后,中学数学教育在晚清大规模展开。但国内中学程度的数学教科书屈指可数,体例也不完全符合教科书的规范。国内流传较广的数学译著,如傅兰雅和华蘅芳合译的《代数术》,知识已较为陈旧。其底本作者华里司(William Wallace)生于1768年,卒于1843年,主要生活于19世纪40年代前的六七十年,书中未涉及18世纪以后的代数学知识。因此,中国亟需新式中学数学教科书。而"癸卯学制"主要是模仿日本学制的产物,规定的中学课程算术、代数、几何、三角,日本中学大都设置[38]。全国包括上海商务印书馆、文明书局、科学书局、群益书社等在内的多家出版机构激烈竞争出版汉译日本中学数学教科书。

鉴于"应编各书,浩博繁难,断非数年所能蒇事,亦断非一局[39]所能独任"[40],晚清政府在"癸卯学制"中主张由京师大学堂译书局、京外官局、民间个人合力编译和编撰教科书,也允许各省中小学堂各学科教员"按照教授详细节目,自编讲义"[41]。按照"癸卯学制"中《学务纲要》的规定,各省中小学堂各学科教员所编讲义在"每一学级终,即将所编讲义汇订成册,由各省咨送学务大臣审定,择其宗旨纯正、说理明显、繁简合法、善于措辞、合于讲授之用者,即准作为暂时通行之本。其私家编纂学堂课本,呈由学务大臣鉴定,确合教科程度者,学堂暂时亦可采用,准著书人自行刊印售卖,予以版权。"[42] 其中,私家指民间个人。

正是在这样的背景下,甲午战争后中国展开一场别开生面的"学战"[43],出现翻译和编译日本中学数学教科书的热潮,汉译日本中学数学教科书由此兴起。

二、晚清汉译日本中学数学教科书的种类、底本作者和译者

1904年颁行的"癸卯学制",规定中学堂"算学"课程分为算术、代数、几何、三角、簿记5门[44]。1909年经学部奏请,中学堂分为文科和实科,实科"算学"课程增加解析几何、"微积初步"。[45]晚清汉译日本中学数学教科书自1896年或稍后开始出版,分为算术、代数、几何、三角、解析几何5类。其门类在"癸卯学制"规定的中学堂"算学"课程科目之内。据笔者亲见和对前人相关书目的调查,晚清汉译日本中学数学教科书至少有109种,如表1。

---

[37] 清国留学生会馆亦称中国留学生会馆。参见刘德有,马兴国主编:《中日文化交流事典》,沈阳:辽宁教育出版社,1992年,第668—669页。

[38] 1901—1902年,李宗棠以安徽省特派官二品顶戴按察使衔湖北道员的身份,游历日本,考察学务。1902年,他这次考察学务的成果之一《考察日本学校记》出版。书中记载的日本中学课程虽然不尽相同,但当时日本中学大都设置算术、代数、几何、三角。参见李宗棠:《李宗棠文集·考察日本学校记》,合肥:黄山书社,2019年,第483—601页。

[39] "一局"指京师大学堂译书局。

[40] 张百熙、荣庆、张之洞纂:《奏定学堂章程》,湖北学务处本。

[41] 张百熙、荣庆、张之洞纂:《奏定学堂章程》,湖北学务处本。

[42] 张百熙、荣庆、张之洞纂:《奏定学堂章程》,湖北学务处本。

[43] "学战"是时人的用语,与"兵战"对应。参见周达:《日本调查算学记》,上海:上海通社,1903年,第1页;徐家璋:《中学教科书数学新编》,东京:清国留学生会馆,1906年,序页。

[44] 张百熙、荣庆、张之洞纂:《奏定学堂章程》,湖北学务处本。

[45] 《学部:奏变通中学堂课程分为文科、实科折》,璩鑫圭,唐良炎编:《中国近代教育史资料汇编——学制演变》,上海:上海教育出版社,1991年,第552—560页。

表 1　晚清汉译日本中学数学教科书书目表

类别	序号	书名	底本作者或机构[46]	译者[47]	出版机构	出版年[48]
算术	1	算术条目及教授法	藤泽利喜太郎	王国维	上海教育世界社	1901
	2	算术教科书	藤泽利喜太郎	（日）西师意	山西大学译书院	1904
	3	中学适用算术教科书	桦正董	陈文	科学会编译部	1905
	4	新式数学教科书	泽田吾一、桦正董、长泽龟之助	程荫南	清国留学生会馆	1905
	5	新译算术教科书	桦正董	余焕东、赵缭	湖南编译社	1906
	6	最新算术教科书	东野十治郎	（日）西师意	东亚公司	1906
	7	近世算术	上野清	徐念慈	商务印书馆	1906
	8	中学教科书数学新编	布施氏[49]、桦正董、三轮桓一郎	徐家璋	清国留学生会馆	1906
	9	新式中等算术教科书	三轮桓一郎	谌兴凡	上海文盛编译书局	1907
	10	中学数学教科书	桦正董、上野清、藤泽利喜太郎、长泽龟之助	曾钧	文明书局	1907
	11	中等算术教科书	田中矢德	崔朝庆	文明书局	1908
	12	订正算术教科书	桦正董	周京	上海科学编辑书局	1908
	13	师范及中学用女子算术教科书	小林盈	吴灼照	上海广智书局	1908
	14	中学校数学教科书：算术之部	桦正董	赵缭、易应崐	群益书社	1908
	15	中学校数学教科书：算术之部问题详解	桦正董	赵缭、易应崐	群益书社	——
	16	算术条目及教授法	藤泽利喜太郎	赵秉良	南洋官书局、会文学社、崇实斋	1908
	17	中学算术新教科书	藤泽利喜太郎	赵秉良	商务印书馆	1911
	18	陈文中等算术详草	桦正董	陈文	上海科学书局	

[46] 本栏仅对非日籍者注明国籍，未注明者均为日籍人员或机构。
[47] 本栏仅对非中国籍者注明国籍，未注明者均为中国籍人士。
[48] 本栏所注一般为初版时间，对未查到初版时间的教科书，标注再版时间；本栏空白者，出版时间不详。
[49] "布施氏"为《中学教科书数学新编》序所述底本作者名，指徐家璋在日本留学时姓为布施的一位日本教师。

续表 1

类别	序号	书名	底本作者或机构	译者	出版机构	出版年
代数	1	初等代数新书	富山房	范迪吉等	会文学社	1903
	2	代数因子分解法	平井善太郎	黄乾元	昌明公司	1904
	3	最新代数学教科书	真野肇、宫田耀之助	权量[50]	中东书社编译部	1904
	4	改订代数学教科书	桦正董	彭世俊、陈尔锡、张藻六	清国留学生会馆	1905
	5	最新中学代数学教科书	桦正董	周藩	上海科学书局	1905
	6	初等代数学解式	宫崎繁太郎	知白	教科书译辑社	1905
	7	普通新代数教科书	上野清	徐虎臣	—	1905
	8	查理斯密小代数学	（英）查理斯密（Charles Smith）著，长泽龟之助英文增补	陈文转译	科学会编译部	1906
	9	初等代数教科书	长泽龟之助	松坪叔子[51]	湖南作民译社	1906
	10	中学适用代数学教科书	长泽龟之助	言焕彰编译，言浃彣补录	群益书社	1906
	11	代数学讲义	奥平浪太郎	施普	东京同文印刷社	1906
	12	最新代数教科书	泽田吾一	张务本、赵宪曾	河北译书社	1906
	13	最近代数学	三木清二	刘晓	点石斋	1906
	14	新体中学代数学教科书	高木贞治	周藩	文明书局、科学书局、群学社[52]	1906
	15	代数因子分解全草	松冈文太郎	顾澄译，李方鸦演草	文明书局	1906
	16	代数学讲义	上野清	周藩	上海科学书局	1907
	17	小代数学	宫本久太郎	李宗鉴	新学会社	1907
	18	代数学教科书	立花赖重	（日）金太仁作	东亚公司	1907
	19	初等代数学教科书	田中矢德	崔朝庆	商务印书馆	1907
	20	代数学教科书	渡边光次	（日）西师意	山西大学译书院	1907
	21	二十世纪新代数学	寺尾寿、吉田好九郎	周京	文明书局	1907
	22	二十世纪新代数学详草	寺尾寿、吉田好九郎	周京	文明书局	1907
	23	新代数学教科书	长泽龟之助	佘恒	东亚公司	1908
	24	中学校数学教科书:代数之部	桦正董	赵缭、易应崐	群益书社	1908
	25	中学校数学教科书:代数之部问题详解	桦正董	赵缭、易应崐	群益书社	—
	26	初等代数学	（英）查理斯密著，长泽龟之助增补	仇毅转译	群益书社	1908
	27	普通教育代数学教科书	上野清、长泽龟之助、高木贞治、查理斯密	陈福咸	上海普及书局	1908
	28	大代数讲义	上野清	王家菼、张廷华	商务印书馆	1908
	29	查理斯密初等代数学	（英）查理斯密	王家菼转译	商务印书馆	1908

50　该书仅注武昌中东书社编译印行，未注明具体编译者。据1909年《教育杂志》所刊《学部审定中学教科书提要》，该书编译者应为权量。参见《学部审定中学教科书提要》，《教育杂志》，1909,1(2):9。

51　松坪叔子为中国人。

52　据代钦的研究，该书由上海文明书局、科学书局、群学社共同出版。参见代钦:《漫话清末中学数学教科书》，《中华读书报》，2012-06-06:14。

续表1

类别	序号	书名	底本作者或机构	译者	出版机构	出版年
几何	1	初等几何学	富山房	范迪吉等译	会文学社	1903
	2	平面几何教科书	田中矢德	薛光瞭	京师译学馆	1905
	3	初等平面几何学	菊池大麓	任允	教科书译辑社	1905
	4	几何学初步教科书	菊池大麓	周藩	上海科学书局	1905
	5	几何学初等教科书	菊池大麓	曾嗾	科学会社	1905
	6	几何学初步	小村氏	顾澄	上海科学书局	1905
	7	新撰几何学教科书：平面之部	林鹤一	邬肇元	新学会社	1905
	8	重译足本几何教科书	林鹤一	彭清鹏	上海普及书局	1906
	9	新几何学教科书：平面	长泽龟之助	周达	东亚公司	1906
	10	几何学教科书	威廉氏	（日）奥平浪太郎、（日）大胁瑛之助译补，黄际遇再译	富山房书局	1906
	11	平面几何讲义录	上野清	叶懋宣、叶树宣	上海群学社	1906
	12	中等教育几何学教科书：平面之部	上野清	仇毅	群益书社	1906
	13	中学教育几何学教科书：平面	长泽龟之助	何崇礼	科学会编译部	1906
	14	中等平面几何学阶梯	长泽龟之助	崔朝庆	会文学社	1906
	15	新几何学教科书：平面	长泽龟之助	曾杰	湖南广雅新译社	1907
	16	新译几何学教科书：平面	桦正董	曾钧	中国图书公司	1907
	17	新译几何学教科书：立体	桦正董	曾钧	中国图书公司	1907
	18	普通教育几何教科书：平面之部	阪井英一	顾澄	理学社	1907
	19	平面几何学讲义	东京数学院	谷钟琦	群益书社	1907
	20	立体几何学讲义	奥平浪太郎	吴灼昭	上海广智书局	1907
	21	初等几何画详解	学海指针社	彭兆龙	清国留学生会馆	1907
	22	新几何学教科书：立体	长泽龟之助	张其祥	东亚公司	1908
	23	几何学教科书：平面	三轮桓一郎	叶懋宣、叶树宣	新学会社	1908
	24	普通教育立体几何教科书	林鹤一	彭清鹏	上海普及书局	1908
	25	中学校数学教科书几何小教科书：平面	菊池大麓	仇毅	群益书社	1908
	26	平面几何学新教科书	菊池大麓	黄元吉	商务印书馆	1908
	27	立体几何学新教科书	菊池大麓	胡豫	商务印书馆	1908
	28	立体几何学教科书	高桥丰夫	胡文藻	宏文馆	1908
	29	实用几何学初步	（法）破鲁倍耳	（日）森外三郎译，华凤章转译	商务印书馆	1908
	30	新式中学用器画	竹下富次郎	阎永辉	阎永辉自行发行	1908
	31	用器画教本	白滨徵	吴应机译绘	旅京江苏学堂	1908
	32	平面新几何学教科书详解	长泽龟之助	文锷	保阳官书局	1908
	33	几何学难题详解：平面部	白井义督	高慎儒	商务印书馆	1908
	34	几何学难题详解：立体部	三木清二	高慎儒	商务印书馆	1909
	35	中等教育几何学教科书：立体之部	上野清	仇毅	群益书社	1909
	36	几何学教科书	生驹万治	（日）金太仁作	东亚公司	1909
	37	用器画教科书几何画法	平濑作五郎	吴应机、吴应权	作新社、商务印书馆	1910
	38	新编初等几何学教科书	本森岩太郎	张廷华	商务印书馆	1911

续表1

类别	序号	书名	底本作者或机构	译者	出版机构	出版年
三角	1	中等教育克依其氏最新平三角法教科书	克依其	（日）原滨吉	上海科学书局	1896[53]
	2	新撰三角法	松村定次郎	范迪吉	会文学社	1903
	3	平面三角法讲义录	上野清	乔冠英	三江师范学堂	1904
	4	初等三角教科书	上野清	蕉缘	上海科学仪器馆	1904
	5	近世平面三角法教科书	远藤又藏	湖南编译社	昌明公司	1905
	6	普通教育平面三角教科书	长泽龟之助	张修爵	上海普及书局	1906
	7	三角法教科书	林鹤一	松坪叔子	湖南作民译社	1906
	8	平面三角法教科书	桦正董	仇毅	群益书社	1907
	9	中等教育平面三角法教科书	远藤又藏	言涣彣、言焕彰	商务印书馆	1907
	10	球面三角法	饭岛正之助	周道章	理学社	1907
	11	球面三角法	长泽龟之助	包荣爵	新学会社	1907
	12	新三角法教科书	长泽龟之助	包荣爵	东亚公司	1907
	13	初等平面三角法	奥平浪太郎	周藩	文明书局	1907
	14	最新平面三角法教科书	原滨吉	无锡译书公会	上海科学书局	1907
	15	最新平面三角法教科书详草	原滨吉	周藩	上海科学书局	1907
	16	新撰平面三角法教科书	（英）凯西（John Casey）	据日译本，顾澄转译	商务印书馆	1908
	17	新编初等三角法教科书	饭岛正之助	周藩	商务印书馆	1908
	18	平面三角法	泽田吾一	赵秉良	南洋官书局	1908
	19	三角法讲义	奥平浪太郎	宋屿	上海广智书局	1908
	20	平面三角法新教科书	菊池大麓，泽田吾一	王永炅	商务印书馆	1909
	21	中等平三角教科书	（英）托德亨特[54]	（日）田中矢德译，崔朝庆转译	商务印书馆	1909
	22	三角法难题详解	白井义督	骆师曾	商务印书馆	1910
解析几何	1	解析几何学教科书	（英）查理斯密	（日）宫本藤吉原译，仇毅转译	群益书社	1908
	2	高等数学解析几何学	长泽龟之助	彭觐圭	北京琉璃厂、第一书局、作新社、普及社	1910

资料来源：表1所列部分图书；冯立昇：《中日数学关系史》，济南：山东教育出版社，2009年，第234—246页；王有朋主编：《中国近代中小学教科书总目》，上海：上海辞书出版社，2010年，第615—685页；毕苑：《建造常识：教科书与近代中国文化转型》，福州：福建教育出版社，2010年，第256—266页；《近代中算著述记》，李俨：《中算史论丛》第2集，北京：中国科学院，1954年，第103—308页；李迪主编：《中国算学书目汇编》，北京：北京师范大学出版社，2000年。

---

53 该书刊有明治二十九年即1896年上野清所写绪言，其出版年在该年或稍后。
54 托德亨特（Isaac Todhunter），英国数学家、科学史家。《中等平三角教科书》序称其"突罕德"。

从表1可见,这109种汉译日本中学数学教科书中几何类教科书最多,有38种,代数类次之,有29种,其后相继是三角类22种、算术类18种,最后是解析几何类2种。这109种教科书中各类的比重反映出时人对日本几何、代数、三角、算术、解析几何类教科书在取向上的细微差异。从表1还可以看出,1904—1909年,即"癸卯学制"颁行的当年及其后5年是晚清汉译日本中学数学教科书出版的高峰期。这折射出在学习日本的热潮下,"癸卯学制"的颁行对时人编译汉译日本中学数学教科书积极性的激发。

在晚清汉译日本中学科学教科书中,数学教科书的引进规模最大。换言之,数学是晚清中学科学教育中引进汉译日本教科书力度最大的学科。据毕苑的统计,1890—1915年汉译日本中小学教科书中,有物理类19种、化学类27种、地理类38种、矿物类9种、博物类5种、植物类20种、动物类20种、生理卫生类14种[55]。而表1所列晚清汉译日本中学科学教科书就有109种。自1607年利玛窦(Matteo Ricci,1552—1610)和徐光启合译的《几何原本》前6卷刊行至1895年的288年间,我国全部数学译著和外国人在中国所撰数学著作有50部左右,没有1部汉译日本著作[56]。由表1可知,1896年或稍后,第一部汉译日本数学教科书《中等教育克依其氏最新平三角法教科书》由上海科学书局出版。自1896年至1911年的16年里,汉译日本中学数学教科书数量约是这288年我国数学译著和外国人在中国所撰数学著作的两倍,也远多于这16年间我国译自欧美的数学著作。当时我国留日学生编译的汉译日本中学数学教科书有不少在日本印刷,但运返中国销售[57]。1912年之后,汉译日本中学数学教科书虽然还有新作出版或旧作再版,但开始走向衰落。

在这109种教科书中,各类的底本都有多种著作,呈现出底本多样化的特点。其中,算术类多用桦正董、藤泽利喜太郎、长泽龟之助等人的著作作为底本,还用到小林盈、三轮桓一郎、田中矢德等人的著作作为底本;代数类多用桦正董、长泽龟之助、上野清等人的著作作为底本,还用到奥平浪太郎、三木清二、高木贞治、宫崎繁太郎、松冈文太郎、真野肇和宫田耀之助、寺尾寿和吉田好九郎等人的著作作为底本;几何类多用菊池大麓、长泽龟之助、上野清、林鹤一、桦正董、三轮桓一郎等人的著作作为底本,还用到阪井英一、高桥丰夫、生驹万治等人的著作作为底本;三角类多用长泽龟之助、上野清、饭岛正之助、远藤又藏、奥平浪太郎等人的著作作为底本,还使用松村定次郎、原滨吉、菊池大麓和泽田吾一等人的著作作为底本。

这些底本作者中,桦正董、藤泽利喜太郎、上野清、长泽龟之助、菊池大麓、林鹤一等都是日本著名数学家和数学教育家。1902年,周达受知新算社嘱托,赴日本调查数学情况,与上野清和长泽龟之助进行过深谈。周达对这两位日本数学家评价颇高:"二君者彼邦畴人中之泰斗,译书等身。彼邦算学界中著述之富,舍二君外,殆无第三人矣。"[58]这些底本作者的教科书在明治后期有不少被日本中学或师范学校使用,有的风行一时,被广泛采用。据1900年日本的一个调查,在46所中学和32所师范学校中,算术教科书使用藤泽利喜太郎的有40所,使用三轮桓一郎的有8所,使用桦正董的有7所,使用长泽龟之助的有6所,使用池田吾一的有6所,使用松冈文太郎的有3所;几何学教科书使用菊池大麓的有67所,使用长泽龟之助的有5所,使用其他教科书的有6所。[59]这个调查结果说明了藤泽利喜太郎、三轮桓一郎、桦正董、长泽龟之助、池田吾一的算术教科书,菊池大麓、长泽龟之助的几何学教科书在当时日本的中学或师范学校都有使用,尤以藤泽利喜太郎的算术教科书、菊池大麓的几何学教科书使用最广。

晚清汉译日本中学数学教科书的译者有中国留日学生、无留学经历的中国本土学者和日本学者,主体是中国留日学生。表1所列教科书译者共73人,其中,少数是日本学者,包括西师意、金太仁作和上

---

55 毕苑:《建造常识:教科书与近代中国文化转型》,福州:福建教育出版社,2010年,第246—284页。
56 笔者据李迪《中国算学书目汇编》统计。参见李迪主编:《中国算学书目汇编》(《中国数学史大系》,副卷第2卷),北京:北京师范大学出版社,2000年,第17—609页。
57 实藤惠秀著,谭汝谦、林启彦译:《中国人留学日本史》,北京:北京大学出版社,2012年,第191页。
58 周达:《日本调查算学记》,上海:上海通社,1903年,第33页。
59 《日本の数学100年史》编集委员会编:《日本の数学100年史》上册,东京:岩波书店,1984,第145页。

野清等;一部分是无留学经历的本土数学家和学者,包括徐念慈、崔朝庆、顾澄、周达、佘恒[60]、王国维等;多数为中国留日学生,包括陈文[61]、赵缭[62]、余焕东[63]、徐家璋[64]、吴灼照[65]、范迪吉[66]、黄乾元[67]、彭世俊[68]、陈尔锡[69]、张藻六[70]、施普[71]、赵宪曾[72]、任允[73]、仇毅[74]、彭清鹏[75]、黄际遇[76]、何崇礼[77]、谷钟琦[78]、张修爵[79]、周道章[80]、王永炅[81]、程荫南[82]、曾杰[83]等。这批留日学生虽然大都并非专攻数学,有的专业是医科(张修爵)、药科(谷钟琦)、路矿(徐家璋),但通晓日文。这是他们翻译或编译汉译日本中学数学教科书的优势。

这批留日学生多为志学之士,翻译和编译日本数学教科书,是为了给国家兴学育才尽力。其中一些人所译之书的底本是其留学时所用的课本。如彭世俊、陈尔锡、张藻六所译《改订代数学教科书》的底本,就是他们留学时所用桦正董的同名教科书上卷[84]。彭世俊、陈尔锡、张藻六在所译该书绪言中说:"迩来普通学教科书译自东西文者颇贡于我国学界。志学之士得以寻其涂辙精微博大,遂各因人之才力而至焉。然则教科书者不啻学海津梁,不可不郑重视之也。桦正董氏代数教科书条理井然,解析详尽,日本中学校几无不以此授徒。吾国人留学东京者率亦肄业此书。某等自课之余,特选译之,欲以饷同志。"[85]

三、晚清汉译日本中学数学教科书的翻译与编译情况

在翻译形式上,晚清汉译日本中学数学教科书主要由国人独立翻译和编译,仅有《算术教科书》《最新算术教科书》《代数学教科书》《几何学教科书》《中等教育克依其氏最新平三角法教科书》等少数教科书由日本学者翻译。这改变了明末清初以降,中国引进的国外科学译著基本都由传教士口译、国人笔述的翻译形式,是中国引进国外科学著作在翻译形式上的一个进步。

---

60 佘恒,字雨东,曾任两江师范学堂算学教习。参见长泽龟之助:《序》,长泽龟之助著,佘恒译:《新代数学教科书》,东京,上海:东亚公司,1908年,目录前1页。
61 陈文编辑:《中学适用算术教科书》,上海:科学会编译部,1909年,第1—2页。
62 许康,许峥编著:《湖南历代科学家传略》,长沙:湖南大学出版社,2012年,第430页。
63 许康,许峥编著:《湖南历代科学家传略》,长沙:湖南大学出版社,2012年,第311页。
64 徐家璋:《中学教科书数学新编》,东京:清国留学生会馆,1906年,序页。
65 李君明编:《东莞文人年表》,广州:广东人民出版社,2015年,第1205页。
66 咏梅:《中日近代物理学交流史研究:1850—1922》,北京:中央民族大学出版社,2013年,第124页。
67 孝南区地方志编纂委员会编:《孝南区志:1990—2008》,武汉:湖北人民出版社,2015年,第715页。
68 饶怀民:《同盟会代理庶务刘揆一传》,长沙:岳麓书社,2018年,第36页。
69 李翠平,寻霖编著:《历代湘潭著作述录(湘乡卷)》,湘潭:湘潭大学出版社,2019年,第162—163页。
70 饶怀民:《同盟会代理庶务刘揆一传》,长沙:岳麓书社,2018年,第36页。
71 周正环主编:《安徽当代先贤诗词选》,芜湖:安徽师范大学出版社,2018年,第329页。
72 刘真主编,王焕琛编著:《留学教育——中国留学教育史料》第2册,台北:"国立"编译馆,1980年,第826页。
73 刘真主编,王焕琛编著:《留学教育——中国留学教育史料》第2册,台北:"国立"编译馆,1980年,第817页。
74 余焕东,赵缭辑译:《新译算术教科书》上卷,东京:湖南编译社,1906年,第2页。
75 《苏州通史》编纂委员会编,李峰主编:《苏州通史·人物卷》下卷,苏州:苏州大学出版社,2019年,第91—92页。
76 饶宗颐:《黄际遇教授传》,陈景熙,林伦伦编著:《黄际遇先生纪念文集》,汕头:汕头大学出版社,2008年,第30页。
77 萨日娜:《东西方数学文明的碰撞与交融》,上海:上海交通大学出版社,2016年,第286页。
78 牛亚华:《清末留日医学生及其对中国近代医学事业的贡献》,《中国科技史料》,2003,24(3):第232页。
79 牛亚华:《清末留日医学生及其对中国近代医学事业的贡献》,《中国科技史料》,2003,24(3):第231页。
80 丛中笑:《王选的故事》,合肥:安徽少年儿童出版社,2015年,第2页。
81 吴家琼:《闽学堂沿革》,福建省政协文史资料委员会编:《文史资料选编》第1卷教育编,福州:福建人民出版社,2000年,第125页。
82 白战存编著:《民国前的鄂东教育》,武汉:武汉大学出版社,1991年,第134页。
83 湖南省革命烈士传编纂委员会编:《三湘英烈传(旧民主主义革命时期)》,第4卷,长沙:国防科技大学出版社,2005年,第325页。
84 桦正董:《改订代数学教科书》上卷,东京:三省堂,1902年。
85 桦正董著,彭世俊,陈尔锡,张藻六译述:《改订代数学教科书》,东京:清国留学生会馆,1905年,绪言页。

对于底本,有些译者是经过慎重选择后决定的。如顾澄所译《新撰平面三角法教科书》为英国几何学家凯西(John Casey)原著,转译自日译本,该日译本的选定就是慎重选择的结果。上海商务印书馆编译所在《新撰平面三角法教科书》序中就说:"此书原著者,英国JOHN CASEY,经日本翻译,已不止一家。如佐之井愿,如东野十治郎,其所译之初等平面三角法,皆即此书。盖三角法之书,行世者虽不少,然或图学者之易解,而不免失于冗长。或文义高尚,力求简约,学者受之,又生困难之感。唯此书体例完善,详略适宜,于学校教科,最为合用。宜其自西徂东,纸贵一时也。无锡顾君澄,现择日本最善之本,重为迻译,于我国教者、学者,其裨益正非浅尠。"[86]

日本数学教科书在明治中期已采用阿拉伯数码和西方数学符号,并采用西方国家通行的文字、公式从左至右横排的形式。据冯立昇的研究,日本数学教科书采用文字、公式横排的方式始自明治二十年(1887年)出版的长泽龟之助所译查理斯密《初等代数学》[87]。晚清汉译日本中学数学教科书普遍以日本明治后期的数学教科书为底本。

对于日本数学教科书数码、数学符号、文字和公式的西化做法,晚清有的汉译日本中学数学教科书没有完全采用,而是采用了文字、公式横竖混排,阿拉伯数码和汉字数字兼用、数学符号中西混合的形式。1908年,上海文明书局出版的崔朝庆编译的《中等算术教科书》即采用这种形式[88]。晚清有的汉译日本中学数学教科书仍为竖排,未用阿拉伯数字,仍沿用伟烈亚力和李善兰等人发明的数学符号。徐虎臣编译的《普通新代数教科书》是其中之一[89]。这反映出中西数学文化碰撞中存在的冲突。

图1 原滨吉编译的《中等教育克依其氏最新平三角法教科书》封面和书页

然而,晚清大量汉译日本中学数学教科书学习日本,采用了对数码、数学符号、文字和公式的西化做法。1896年或稍后,第一部汉译日本数学教科书——上海科学书局出版的原滨吉编译的《中等教育克依其氏最新平三角法教科书》就采用了阿拉伯数码和西方数学符号和文字、公式从左向右横排的方式[90]。1904年中东书社编译部出版的权量编译的《最新代数学教科书》[91],1905年清国留学生会馆出版的彭世俊、陈尔锡和张藻六合译的《改订代数学教科书》[92],1908年上海商务印书馆出版的华凤章转译的

86　顾澄编译:《新撰平面三角法教科书》,上海:商务印书馆,1913年,序页。
87　冯立昇:《中日数学关系史》,济南:山东教育出版社,2009年,第251页。
88　田中矢德编,崔朝庆编译:《中等算术教科书》上下册,上海:文明书局,1908年。
89　张奠宙:《中国近现代数学的发展》,石家庄:河北科学技术出版社,2000年,第15页。
90　该书未印刷编译者姓名。上野清撰写了该书绪言,指出"此编纂原滨吉氏专从事于此,而与曩在本院所编纂之新算术为同种"。据此可知,该书编译者为原滨吉。参见《中等教育克依其氏最新平三角法教科书》,上海:科学书局,1896年(或稍后),绪言页。
91　中东书社编译:《最新代数学教科书》,武昌:中东书社,1904年。
92　桦正董著,彭世俊、陈尔锡、张藻六译:《改订代数学教科书》,东京:清国留学生会馆,1905年。

《实用几何学初步》[93],1909年上海科学会编译部出版的陈文编译的《中学适用算术教科书》[94]等也都是如此。1906年,周达在所译长泽龟之助《新几何学教科书:平面》中不仅采用底本使用的阿拉伯数码、西方数学符号和文字、公式排印方式,而且明确指出:

> "我邦之译西书者并其算式而改之,非善法也。不佞于壬寅东游以后即主张改用西式,曾于《日本调查算学记》中反复言之。尔后数年间,学者译著各书间有采用此议者,可见风气之渐开矣。是编概用西式,自左向右横行,一变从前译籍之面目。学者习用之,自觉其较旧式为便也。"[95]

这段话表明了周达受日本的影响,反对国人翻译西书将文字、公式竖排的方式,反映出汉译日本中学数学教科书采用西化的做法已逐渐被接受。

图 2　周达所译《新几何学教科书:平面》封面和书页

至晚清最后几年,汉译日本中学数学教科书已普遍采用西方通用的数码、数学符号和西方通行的文字、公式排版方式。这不仅促进了中国近代新式中学数学教育与世界接轨,而且对晚清民初中国数学由传统向现代过渡的完成产生了重要影响。

晚清汉译日本中学数学教科书有些也没有完全拘泥于底本,而是做了一些改编。陈文编译的《中学适用算术教科书》具有代表性。该书主要以日本著名数学家桦正董《改订算术教科书》为底本,正文前有正在日本留学的曾汝璟"序"、陈文"例言"、目录,正文包括7编,共35章,附录有"级数及省略计算",并设有包括杂题的"总问",最后给出全书例题、杂题答案。各编内容依次为"整数及小数""诸等法""整数之性质""分数""比例""百分算""开方"。[96]其中,"诸等法"即单位换算法和带单位数值的计算法;"百分算"又名百分法、子母法、折成法[97]。桦正董《改订算术教科书》于1903年由东京三省堂出版[98],出版后在日本"风行一时"[99]。该书出版两年后,即1905年陈文便编译出版了《中学适用算术教科书》。《中学适用算术教科书》采用了《改订算术教科书》的体例,基本采用了该书的框架,大部分内容照译自该书。但对于不适宜中国之处,悉数删除,"搜罗他书以补其缺"[100]。陈文变更了《改订算术教科书》的例题300余

93　森外三郎原译,华凤章译述:《实用几何学初步》,上海:商务印书馆,1908年。

94　该书初版于1905年出版,1909年出版的是第8版。参见陈文编辑:《中学适用算术教科书》,上海:科学会编译部,1909年。

95　长泽龟之助著,周达译:《新几何学教科书:平面》,东京,上海:东亚公司,1913年,第5页。

96　陈文编辑:《中学适用算术教科书》,上海:科学会编译部,1909年。

97　陈稼轩:《实用商业辞典》,上海:商务印书馆,1935年,第287页。

98　桦正董:《改订算术教科书》上下册,东京:三省堂,1903年。

99　《序》,陈文编辑:《中学适用算术教科书》,上海:科学会编译部,1909年,第2页。

100　《例言》,陈文编辑:《中学适用算术教科书》,上海:科学会编译部,1909年,第1页。

道[101]。最显著之处是,陈文对"诸等法""百分算"两编进行了大量的改编。在第2编"诸等法"中,站在中国的角度对于"本国度量衡""外国度量衡、货币"的内容做了大量改编,并将例题中的日本名称、单位改为中国名称、单位,如将"富士山"改为"昆仑山",将"东京到京都"改为"长江到汉口",将"町"改为"顷"等。[102]

客观而言,晚清汉译日本中学数学教科书编译水平参差不齐,有不少并不令人满意。1908年,王家葵在其所译《查理斯密初等代数学》序中指出:"我国旧译西算,自出板于制造局,三十年来无新面目。迩来风气大开,学校林立,教育者咸知斯学之不可忽也。而旧译之书,一鳞一爪,不足以为教科之用。且世界新理日出不穷,徒抱残守阙无以为研究之资。于是海内通人,采集欧美新著争译之,以供学者之用。乃二三年来,旁行象数之数,由东籍转译而出者,其数顿增。然则今日者其为我国数学界上革新之时代乎。所惜者,凡关于象数学之教科书,为现今所刊行,其能满足于人意者殆尠。盖以所据之原本,或非为当世有名之著作,则价值不高。又译笔稍不经意,动多乖谬。或措辞未善,令人读之佶屈聱牙,易致误会。如是者皆不足为完全纯粹之教科书。"[103]从这段话可窥见当时汉译日本中学数学教科书令人满意者少的状况及其原因。

其实,晚清汉译日本中学数学教科书令人满意者少,还有译者完全直译底本,不按照中国习惯对底本进行编译的原因。1906年,东亚公司在日本学者西师意所译东野十治郎的《最新算术教科书》的广告中就说:"算数之书,行于世者,汗牛充栋。其为清朝人译成汉文者亦不鲜少也。顾近出之书,不过以日本现行之课本翻译其文者也。故如诸名数皆套用日本度量衡,且应用问题等亦有颇不适切于清朝人者。岂不斯学之一恨事乎?著者于数学驰名天下久矣。尝在学习院执教鞭者十数年于兹。顷者有鉴于此,用力于拣撰问题,说其理论也,亦务期平易简明。若其度量衡诸目,主取准于清国旧惯,以欲俾清国学生速通数理也。初学者一翻是书,则算数之学自应融会贯通矣。"[104]

由于译者一般都自行其是,晚清汉译日本中学数学教科书中的名词术语,也未统一,较为混乱。译者有的完全移用日本原名,有的则使用中国数学译著中的译名、中国古籍中的译名或创制新名。译者完全移用日本原名,读者对内容难免半懂不懂、莫名其妙。1908年,言焕彣在其弟言焕彰编译的《中学适用代数学教科书》再版"序"中,即指出当时中等代数学教科书译本颇多,但适用的少的一个原因是:"直译和文,语多格格不吐,致读者苦思,莫能解其意"。[105]周达编译《新几何学教科书:平面》时,使用了汉译《几何原本》中的译名,对于自认为《几何原本》中不甚妥帖的译名则另从中国古籍中寻找新名,若中国古籍中没有的则自创新名。如他在该书"译例"中说:"是编正名、定义悉遵《几何原本》,其有旧名未甚妥帖者或新立名义为旧籍所无者,则斟酌一切当之名用之。不尽袭东文原名,致贻生吞活剥之诮也。"[106]

在当时名词术语不统一的情况下,有的汉译日本中学数学教科书则列有中西名词对照表性质的表格。如崔朝庆所译《初等代数学教科书》列有"代数学中西名词合璧表",列出了主要名词术语的英文原名和中文译名。[107]这是规范名词术语的努力,有助于读者理解教科书中的知识内容。

四、晚清汉译日本中学数学教科书的流传与影响

晚清汉译日本中学数学教科书不乏风靡一时,流传甚广之作。陈文编译的《中学适用算术教科书》是其中之一。晚清学部将该书纳入了审定的中学教科书,并对该书做了介绍和高度评价:

---

101 《例言》,陈文编辑:《中学适用算术教科书》,上海:科学会编译部,1909年,第1页。
102 陈文编辑:《中学适用算术教科书》,上海:科学会编译部,1909年,第63—98页;樺正董:《改訂算術教科書》上册,東京:三省堂,1903年,第77—114页。
103 王家葵译述:《查理斯密初等代数学》,上海:商务印书馆,1919年,序言页。
104 东野十治郎著,西师意译:《最新算术教科书》,东京:东亚公司,1906年,广告页。
105 长泽龟之助著,言焕彰编译,言焕彣补录:《中学适用代数学教科书》,上海:群益社,1909年,第1页。
106 长泽龟之助著,周达译:《新几何学教科书:平面》,东京,上海:东亚公司,1913年,第5页。
107 田中矢德著,崔朝庆译辑:《初等代数学教科书》,上海:商务印书馆,1907年,第1—3页。

"自藤泽利喜太郎著《算术条目及教授法》,一矫旧日陵躐无序之弊,编辑教本者翕然宗之,而以桦正董氏《算术教科书》为最擅名。惟其中诸等法、百分算两编,不适吾国学子之用,自非另行编辑不可。而向之从事迻译者,于此处罔甚措意,其于数学进步阻碍实多。译者有鉴于此,特以平日所心得者摘要补入,甚便学者。是书之特色,计有数端:说理清晰,毫无翳障,一也;由浅及深,阶级犁然,二也;所载例题,于科学多有关系,三也。故言中学算术者,当以是书为最完备云。间有误刊之处,具详校勘表中,再版时当详加改正。"[108]

其中指出了陈文编译该书所做有别于底本的工作和该书的特色。《中学适用算术教科书》1905年出版后,多次再版,1912年中华民国成立后仍被使用。1917年该书已出至第26版[109],可见其流传之广。

周达所译《新几何学教科书:平面》也具有代表性。该书以适用于日本中学和师范学校的长泽龟之助的同名教科书为底本[110],1906年由东亚公司出版[111]。底本具有与其他学科相联系、着重应用、几何学中所用理论不单独成编、与用器画相联系等特点[112]。译本依次分为"直线""圆""面积""比例"4编,并设"补习问题",附"几何学不能解问题之一例""几何学与代数学解法之比较"。除部分名词术语外,译本与底本从体例、框架到内容都相同。[113]周达与长泽龟之助是相交多年的朋友,底本是1905年春长泽龟之助送给他并请他译成中文的。周达译成后适有日本之行,与长泽龟之助对译稿进行了商榷和改订。[114]因此,译稿对底本的忠实程度和文辞的畅达程度颇高,做到了严复提出的译事三难中的"信"和"达"[115]。

周达对此也十分自信。他在译本"自序"中说:"长泽氏经历教育界垂二十余年,先后译著教科书无虑十数种,最后乃成此书,其完美可知也。译者谫陋于东西新旧象数之书,亦尝普及而涉猎之。尝慨《几何原本》之不合于教科,而后出之译本又多芜浅而不可用,恒思编一适当之书,以为学者标准。此编固不足以当之。然迻译之际,固汲汲以蕲于信达也。"[116]他在译本的"译例"中还强调:"译者与著者相识有年,宗旨契合。迻译之际,既经审慎周详,书成又与著者重加商榷,则译本中亦可自信无疵累矣。"[117]周达所译该书出版后多次重印,中华民国成立后仍被使用,至1913年已重印16次[118]。

陈文转译自日本的《查理斯密小代数学》亦相当流行。该书以长泽龟之助英文增补的英国数学家查理斯密《初等代数学》(Elementary Algebra)[119]为底本,1906年由上海科学会编译部出版。至1909年,《查理斯密小代数学》出至第12版。[120]中华民国成立后,该书仍被使用,1915年已出至第23版。1932年商务印书馆印行该书国难后第1版,次年即出至第4版。[121]王家荚转译的《查理斯密初等代数学》1908年由上海商务印书馆出版,中华民国成立后也被使用,1919年出至第18版。[122]

---

108 《学部审定中学教科书提要》,《教育杂志》,1909,1(1):8。
109 陈文编辑:《中学适用算术教科书》,上海:科学会编译部,1917年。
110 長澤龜之助編纂:《新幾何学教科書:平面》,東京:日本書籍株式会社,1904年。
111 长泽龟之助著,周达译:《新几何学教科书:平面》,东京,上海:东亚公司,1906年。
112 長澤龜之助編纂:《新幾何学教科書:平面》,東京:日本書籍株式会社,1904年,第5—9页。
113 长泽龟之助著,周达译:《新几何学教科书:平面》,东京,上海:东亚公司,1906年;長澤龜之助編纂:《新幾何学教科書:平面》,東京:日本書籍株式会社,1904年。
114 长泽龟之助著,周达译:《新几何学教科书:平面》,东京,上海:东亚公司,1913年。
115 另一难是"雅"。参见赫胥黎著,严复译:《天演论》,上海:商务印书馆,1933年,第1页。
116 长泽龟之助著,周达译:《新几何学教科书:平面》,东京,上海:东亚公司,1913年,第4页。
117 长泽龟之助著,周达译:《新几何学教科书:平面》,东京,上海:东亚公司,1913年,第6页。
118 长泽龟之助著,周达译:《新几何学教科书:平面》,东京,上海:东亚公司,1913年。
119 该书1886年出版,后由查理斯密增订后于1890年再版,是经典的初等代数学教科书。Charles Smith. *Elementary Algebra*. London: Macmillan and Co., 1886; Charles Smith. *Elementary Algebra*. London: Macmillan and Co. and New York, 1890.
120 陈文译:《查理斯密小代数学》,上海:科学会编译部,1909年。
121 C. Smith著,陈文译述:《查理斯密小代数学》,上海:商务印书馆,1933年。
122 王家荚译述:《查理斯密初等代数学》,上海:商务印书馆,1919年。

再如，黄元吉编译的《平面几何学新教科书》。该书以日本著名数学家菊池大麓《几何学小教科书：平面几何学》为底本编译。译本分为"直线""圆""面积""比及比例"4编，另列"杂问题""附录"；其与底本的体例、框架完全相同，内容基本相同。[123] 1908年3月，《平面几何学新教科书》由商务印书馆出版，同年秋便再版[124]。至1912年10月，该书已出至第9版[125]。除黄元吉编译的这部教科书外，晚清以菊池大麓的几何学教科书为底本的汉译中学数学教科书至少还有5种。这些教科书在晚清中学被不同程度地使用。1907—1912年，郭沫若在四川读中学期间就使用过汉译的菊池大麓的几何学教科书。1955年12月8日，郭沫若在日本早稻田大学以"中日文化的交流"为题的演讲中说："中国为了向日本学习，在派遣大批留学生去日本的同时，又从日本招聘了很多教师到中国来。我们当时又翻译了大量的日本中学用的教科书。我个人来日本以前，在中国的中学所学的《几何学》，就是菊池大麓先生所编纂的。"[126]

在东亚公司出版的教科书中，1906年出版的周达、包荣爵所译《新数学教科书》，1907年出版的包荣爵所译《新三角法教科书》、1908年出版的佘恒所译《新代数学教科书》，均以长泽龟之助的教科书为底本，出版后都较为流行。至1913年，《新数学教科书》和《新代数学教科书》都重印了6次，《新三角法教科书》重印了8次[127]。

晚清汉译日本中学数学教科书是清朝最后16年中学数学教科书的主流，被广泛使用。据1909年刊行的《教育杂志》，清朝学部审定了一批中学教科书（含教学参考书）。其中，数学教科书有12种：(1)曹汝英著《直方大斋数学》（上编4册附卷2册）；(2)余焕东、赵缭辑译《新译算术教科书》（2册），湖南编译社本；(3)陈文编译《中学适用算术教科书》（1册），科学会本；(4)陈榥著《中等算术教科书》（2册），教科书译辑社本；(5)沈羽编《算学自修书》（2册），中国图书公司；(6)权量译《最新代数学教科书》（1册），中东书社本；(7)周藩译《新体中学代数学教科书》（3册），科学书局本；(8)陈文译《查理斯密小代数学》（1册），科学会本；(9)算学研究会编《平面几何学教科书》（1册）、《立体几何学教科书》（1册），昌明公司；(10)曾钧译《新译几何学教科书》（2册）[128]，中国图书公司；(11)谢洪赉译《最新中学教科书几何学：平面部》（1册）、《最新中学教科书几何学：立体部》（1册），商务印书馆本；(12)谢洪赉编译《最新中学教科书三角术》（1册），商务印书馆本[129]。其中，有7种即第(2)、(3)、(6)、(7)、(8)、(9)、(10)种为汉译日本中学数学教科书，占这批教科书的一半以上。这些决定汉译日本中学数学教科书在晚清新式中学数学教育建立过程中担当着重要角色。

晚清部分汉译日本中学数学教科书教学效果较好。当时一位名叫萧屏的数学教师，以长泽龟之助的《几何学初步讲义录》为底本[130]，编译了《中学几何学初步教科书》[131]。译本未出版前，他将其用于教学，取得意想不到的效果。萧屏在该译本序中说："友人购赠日本长泽龟之助氏《几何学初步教科书》[132]。初以其浅，未甚措意。继而译授学生，无不言下顿悟，欣欣有得。再进以稍深之书，则忽然开朗，非复前此之倦而思卧。盖今昔之心理异矣。客春重游鄂渚，承乏蚕业学堂，复以是书讲授，学者亦能怡然了悟，无所扞格。其合于今日学生心理盖无疑义，乃修改一过，付诸剞劂。"[133]

---

123 菊池大麓著，黄元吉译述：《平面几何学新教科书》，上海：商务印书馆，1908年；菊池大麓编纂：《幾何學小教科書：平面幾何學》，東京：大日本圖書株式會社，1899年。

124 菊池大麓著，黄元吉译述：《平面几何学新教科书》，上海：商务印书馆，1908年。

125 菊池大麓著，黄元吉译述：《平面几何学新教科书》，上海：商务印书馆，1912年。

126 实藤惠秀著，谭汝谦、林启彦译：《中国人留学日本史》，北京：北京大学出版社，2012年，第193页。

127 长泽龟之助著，周达译：《新几何学教科书：平面》，东京，上海：东亚公司，1913年，广告页。

128 2册分别为《新译几何学教科书：平面》《新译几何学教科书：立体》。

129 《学部审定中学教科书提要》，《教育杂志》，1909，1(1)：7—8；《学部审定中学教科书提要（续）》，《教育杂志》，1909，1(2)：9—12。

130 長澤龜之助講述：《幾何學初步講義錄》，東京：大日本中學會，出版年不详。

131 该译著于1912年由上海商务印书馆出版。

132 这是萧屏原文，确切的书名为《几何学初步讲义录》。

133 长泽龟之助著，萧屏译述：《中学几何学初步教科书》，上海：商务印书馆，1912年，序言页。

五、结语

甲午战争后,学习日本是晚清朝野上下最认可的一条救亡图存、富国强兵的新路,成为中国的社会热潮。译书尤其翻译日本书得到晚清政府的支持和推动,广大国人积极投入其中,从而图书编译出版机构和社团大量涌现。晚清政府在"癸卯学制"中还主张由京师大学堂译书局、京外官局、民间个人合力编译和编撰教科书,允许各省中小学堂各学科教员"按照教授详细节目,自编讲义"[134]。这有力地促进了晚清社会对国外著作特别是日本书的编译出版活动。

伴随着政府和民间对新式教科书编译和出版工作的共同推进,晚清甲午战争后汉译日本中学数学教科书日益增多。晚清汉译日本中学数学教科书至少有109种。它们主要由国人独立翻译和编译,大都模仿底本,采用对文字和公式排版方式、数码、数学符号的西化做法,不乏风靡一时,流传甚广之作,对晚清中学数学教育产生深远的影响。这些从侧面展现了晚清最后十余年在中国寻求救亡图存和富国强兵之路的大背景下,政府与国人在新式数学教育方面的互动,同时反映出日本对晚清中学数学教育的影响。

晚清汉译日本中学数学教科书的兴起,使中国近代中学数学教科书的引进主流发生从欧美到日本的历史转变。作为主要译者,中国留日学生是晚清汉译日本中学数学教科书兴起的重要内在动力。他们在这一历史转变过程中发挥了不可替代的作用。他们中的一些人选择日本或日本转译自英国数学、教育名家的名作作为底本,是晚清一些汉译日本中学数学教科书流行的重要因素。不过,晚清汉译日本中学数学教科书水平参差不齐,有些版式和符号有新有旧、名词术语较为混乱,有不少未能尽如人意。1912年中华民国成立后,新的教育改革继起,新的中学数学教科书陆续出版,晚清汉译日本中学数学教科书逐渐被淘汰。

---

134 张百熙、荣庆、张之洞纂:《奏定学堂章程》,湖北学务处本。

A Study on the Chinese Translations of Japanese Middle School Mathematical Textbooks in the Late Qing Dynasty

Guo Jinhai

(Institute for the History of Natural Sciences, CAS, Beijing 100190, China)

Abstract With the promotion of the wave of learning from Japan and the launching of activities of book compilation and educational reform after the Sino-Japanese War of 1894—1895, the Chinese translations of Japanese middle school mathematical textbooks sprang up, and became the mainstream of middle school mathematical textbooks in the Late Qing Dynasty. At that time, there were at least 109 Chinese translations of Japanese middle school mathematical textbooks, with the largest number of geometry, followed by algebra, trigonometry, arithmetic and analytic geometry. The Chinese translations of Japanese middle school mathematical textbooks in each of the five branches have multiple original texts, which show the characteristics of diversity of original texts. Some authors of original texts are famous mathematicians and mathematical educators in Japan. Most of the compilers are Chinese students studying in Japan, as well as Chinese scholars without overseas study experience and Japanese scholars. The Chinese translations of Japanese middle school mathematical textbooks in the Late Qing Dynasty were mainly independently compiled by Chinese people. Most of them imitated the original texts and adopted the Westernized practice of typesetting of characters and formulas, numbers, mathematical symbols. Many of them were popular and spread widely. The Chinese translations of Japanese middle school mathematical textbooks had a far-reaching impact on the middle school mathematical education in the Late Qing Dynasty. However, the level of compilation of these Chinese translations was uneven, and many of them were not satisfactory.

Keywords Late Qing Dynasty, middle school mathematical textbooks, the Sino-Japanese War of 1894—1895, learning from Japan, Gui-mao School System

《中西数学名词合璧表》初探

邓亮　（清华大学科学技术史暨古文献研究所）

摘要　《平面三角法》是一种中国学者部分参考日译数学词汇翻译的数学著作，其所附《中西数学名词合璧表》译自长泽龟之助的《解法适用数学辞书》中的第二门《英和学语之部》，是晚清一部较早较完整的数学名词表。

关键词　《平面三角法》；《中西数学名词合璧表》；《解法适用数学辞书》；日译数学名词

晚清时期，近代西方数学的入华传播，大体上可分为两个阶段。第一个阶段是从鸦片战争到洋务运动时期，尤其是19世纪50年代以后，主要特征是西方数学著作的汉译，主要方式是来华西方人口译，中国学者笔述；学科涉及算术、代数学、微积分、平面几何、解析几何、三角学等，促进了中国乃至东亚数学的近代化转变；然而由于译书机构与翻译者各有不同，译名呈现较为混乱的现象。第二个阶段是从甲午战争到辛亥革命时期，尤其是20世纪初实行新学制以后，除了翻译西方数学著作外，日本数学著作汉译或编译逐渐流行，主要方式是中国学者或留学生笔译；涉及学科与之前基本一致，但有若干新知识，对中国数学的近代化转变起到重要推动作用；因为日本数学界已对数学名词做了一定程度上的审查，因此除了一些新词汇外，日译数学名词相对统一。对于晚清民国时期中日数学的交流，已有大量的研究，比如李俨、三上义夫、实藤惠秀、李迪、魏庚人、李兆华、冯立昇、代钦、萨日娜等，此不一一列举。

《平面三角法》，由英国翰卜林斯密士（Hamblin Smith，1829—1901）著，由湖南高等实业学堂学生李国钦、邓彬翻译，1908年由上海群益书社出版。此书译自英文原本，而名词则选择日译名词，所附《中西数学名词合璧表》，是所见较早的一份较全面的数学名词表，有一定特色，因此本文对此做一初步讨论。

一、《平面三角法》之底本

翰卜林斯密士，是一位高产的科学著作编辑者，曾编辑出版数学、物理学、语言学、教会史等著作数十种，其中数学著作主要有：*Elementary Algebra*，*Elements of Geometry*，*Elementary Trigonometry*，*Exercises in Arithmetic*，*A Treatise on Arithmetic*，*A Key to a Treatise on Arithmetic*，*Key to Exercises in Arithmetic*，*Exercises on Algebra*，*A Key to Algebra*，*A Treatise on Elementary Algebra*，*A Key to Elementary Algebra*，*A Key to the exercises in Elements of Geometry*，*A Key to Elementary Trigonometry*，*An Introduction to the study of Geometrical Conic Sections*，*A Shilling Arithmetic for the use of elementary classes and preparatory schools*，*Riders in Euclid*，*Book of Enunciations for Hamblin Smith's Geometry*，*Algebra*，*Trigonometry*，*Statics and Hydrostatics*，*Hamblin Smith's Mathematical Series* 等等[1]，以教科书、习题、考试用书为主，主要涉及算术、代数、几何、平面三角学、圆锥曲线等。

《平面三角法》一书共20编，介绍几何学基础知识、三角函数性质及应用，主要包括定义或例题，每编附有习题。其书目录如下：

---

[1] 数学书目整理自大英图书馆检索结果，多种著作有多个版本。

第一编　线量
第二编　周径之比
第三编　角量
第四编　各种角度之化法
第五编　论方向及"＋"(正)"－"(负)号之用法
第六编　三角函数
第七编　三角函数之号与量因角度之增减而异
第八编　第一象限内各角之函数
第九编　同角度各函数之关系
第十编　异角三角函数之比较
第十一编　三角方程式之解法
第十二编　二角之三角函数
第十三编　倍角与分角之三角函数
第十四编　对数
第十五编　三角函数表及对数表
第十六编　三角形之边与角之函数之关系
第十七编　直角三角形之解法
第十八编　斜三角形之解法
第十九编　距离及高之测法
第二十编　论三角形多边形及圆形之面积
答案
附录　中西数学名词合璧表[2]

对于此书内容，刘冰楠已有一定讨论，对其中的页码、知识点、例题、习题、函数图像、诱导公式等做了数量统计与对比[3]。

对于此书之底本，根据翰卜林斯密士所著之书，推测此书底本应为三角学两种。笔者对 *Elementary Trigonometry* 一书未曾得见，从网络上搜见 *A Key to Elementary Trigonometry*（1904，第六版）。对比之下（图 1，图 2），可见习题部分确有相同之处。由此可知，中译本或是对其 *Elementary Trigonometry* 和 *A Key to Elementary Trigonometry* 两者的合译本，版次不知，有待进一步核实。由于附录之名词表，范围已远超此书三角学内容之范围，应另有来源。

实际上，在此中译本出版之前，翰卜林斯密士之算术书已有翻译，并且他的数学著作也在一定程度上有广泛使用。比如由于新学制的施行，京师大学堂得以重建，其译书局于 1903 年已译成之书中，即包括"罕木楞斯密《算法》1 卷[4]、威理孙《形学》5 卷、洛克《平三角》1 卷"[5]等数学类著作。又如，1907 年拟考选江宁、江苏、安徽、江西等地 10 名男生、3 名女生赴美留学，开列出洋考试科目中数学学科之科目、程度与参考书籍（表 1）。从表中可以看出，出洋考试参考用书均选用英美著作，翰卜林斯密士之著作均在其列。这或许也是李国钦和邓彬合译名词表的原因之一。

2　(英)翰卜林斯密士著，李国钦，邓彬译：《平面三角法 [M]》.上海：群益书社，1908 年.

3　刘冰楠：《中国中学三角学教科书发展史研究(1902－1949)》.内蒙古师范大学，博士论文，2015 年，第 226－227 页.

4　"罕木楞斯密《算法》"，在一些著作中有"罕木楞斯密《算法》""《罕木楞斯密算法》""罕木愣斯密《算法》""罕木愣斯密《算法》""罕木勒斯《密算法》""罕木愣斯密《算法》"等不同说法。

5　张运君：《京师大学堂和近代西方教科书的引进》，《北京大学学报(哲学社会科学版)》，2003 年 3 期。此文引用第一历史档案馆档案"大学堂译书局十二月分报销册"记载"支罕木楞斯密算法，领译费银 300 两。"

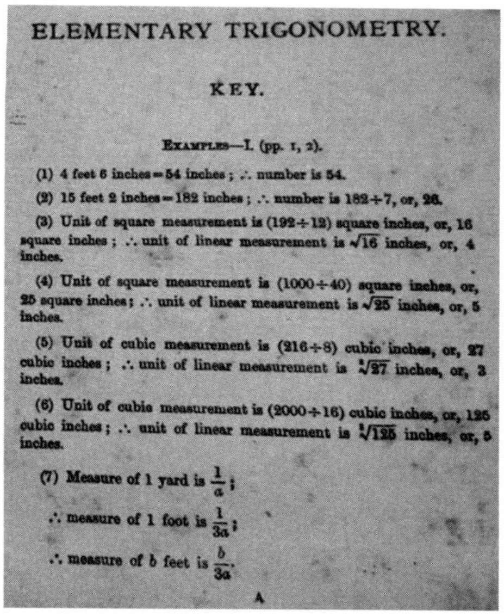

ELEMENTARY TRIGONOMETRY.

KEY.

EXAMPLES—I. (pp. 1, 2).

(1) 4 feet 6 inches = 54 inches ; ∴ number is 54.

(2) 15 feet 2 inches = 182 inches ; ∴ number is 182 ÷ 7, or, 26.

(3) Unit of square measurement is (192 ÷ 12) square inches, or, 16 square inches ; ∴ unit of linear measurement is $\sqrt{16}$ inches, or, 4 inches.

(4) Unit of square measurement is (1000 ÷ 40) square inches, or, 25 square inches ; ∴ unit of linear measurement is $\sqrt{25}$ inches, or, 5 inches.

(5) Unit of cubic measurement is (216 ÷ 8) cubic inches, or, 27 cubic inches ; ∴ unit of linear measurement is $\sqrt[3]{27}$ inches, or, 3 inches.

(6) Unit of cubic measurement is (2000 ÷ 16) cubic inches, or, 125 cubic inches ; ∴ unit of linear measurement is $\sqrt[3]{125}$ inches, or, 5 inches.

(7) Measure of 1 yard is $\frac{1}{a}$;

∴ measure of 1 foot is $\frac{1}{3a}$;

∴ measure of b feet is $\frac{b}{3a}$.

A

图 1 *A Key to Elementary Trigonometry*(1904,第六版),取自孔夫子旧书网

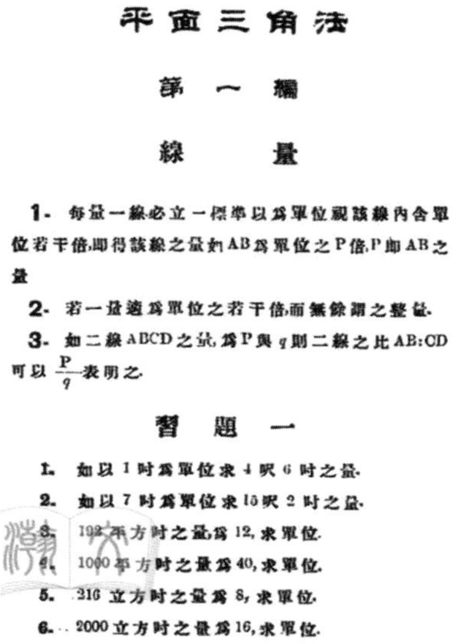

平面三角法

第一編

線量

1. 每量一線必立一標準以爲單位視該線內含單位若干倍,即得該線之量如AB爲單位之P倍,P即AB之量

2. 若一量適爲單位之若干倍,而無餘謂之整量.

3. 如二線ABCD之量,爲P與q則二線之比AB:CD可以$\frac{P}{q}$表明之.

習題一

1. 如以1吋爲單位求4呎6吋之量.

2. 如以7吋爲單位求15呎2吋之量.

3. 192平方吋之量爲12,求單位.

4. 1000平方吋之量爲40,求單位.

5. 216立方吋之量爲8,求單位.

6. 2000立方吋之量爲16,求單位.

图 2 《平面三角法》,取自瀚文民国书库数据库

表 1 《代提学使陈拟出洋考试布告》中数学学科参考书籍 [6]

学科	程度	课本
笔算	全部 Complete	翰卜林斯密士、洛克等本均可用 Hamblim Smith or J. B. Locke
代数术 Elementary Algebra	至双位括弧级数 Binomial theorem series	温特斡思、翰卜林斯密士、察理士密等本均可用 Wentaworth or H. Smith, Charles Smith
几何	平面及浑体	温特斡思、翰卜林斯密士、卫里森等本均可用 Wentaworth, Hamblin Smith or James M. Wilson James
平面三角术 Plane Trigonometry	边角相求对数原理 Solution of Triangle's Logarithmic Series	温特斡思、翰卜林斯密士、洛克等本均可用 Wentaworth, Hamblin Smith or J. B. Locke

二、关于翻译者

对于此书之翻译,时任湖南实业学堂监督的曹典球(1877—1960)在序言中称:

> 李生、邓生肄业湖南高等实业学堂者有年,通晓西文,于自然科学亦有心得,又得名师许君奎垣、李君希易为之疏导烦滞,订其舛误。[7]

由此可知,此书之翻译,还得到许奎垣、李希易之帮助。接下来将对这些人物的生平略做介绍。

李国钦(1887—1961),字炳麟,湖南长沙人,是湖南实业学堂实业教育的成功实践者之一。李氏1903年冬入湖南实业学堂矿科甲班,后升入矿业本科第一班,1910年毕业留校,后入英国伦敦皇家矿业学院,1915年回国在华昌炼锑公司任职,1915年底赴美国纽约筹设办事处,1916年将公司改为华昌贸易公司。经过其艰苦经营,成为矿业巨商,第二次世界大战时入美国籍。除《平面三角法》外,李氏还曾翻译罗斯福自述而成《我怎样改造美国》(1938),发明碳化钨冶炼法以及钛的冶炼新法,与王曾佑合著

6 转录自严复:《代提学使陈拟出洋考试布告》,见王栻主编:《严复集》第2册诗文下,北京:中华书局,1986年,第247—250页。

7 (英)翰卜林斯密士著,李国钦,邓彬译:《平面三角法》,上海:群益书社,1908年,曹典球序。

《钨》(1943)。[8]

邓彬,生卒年不详,湖北江陵人。据1933年《湖南年鉴》记载,常宁水口山铅锌矿局的历任主管长官中,李国钦曾任次长,于民国元年八月到任,应于民国二年八月离任;邓彬任协理,于民国四年八月到任,似于同年十二月离任。[9]可知其毕业后,应在湖南矿业界工作过。此年鉴另一条记录记载,1933年湖南建设厅第三科科长为邓彬(子周)[10]。又据1943年中国矿冶工程学会会员录记载会员的姓名、字号、任职和通信处等信息,其中有"邓彬,子周,资源委员会钨业管理处湖南分处工程师,湖南零陵九号信箱"[11],且候选会员中还有任职于资源委员会锑业管理处的王道纯、周颂两人,毕业于湖南高等实业学堂采冶科。据《常宁县志》记载,资源委员会钨业管理处湖南分处常宁钨矿工程处于1941年在荫田开业。[12]这两条信息中的邓彬,均在湖南任职,且后一条为钨业管理处的工程师,与其学习、工作经历相符,应该是同一个人。

许奎垣(1868—1914),又名兆魁,湖北黄陂人。早年曾得张之洞赏识,受邀担任长沙雅礼书院数学教授,曾任系主任[13],1897年任湖南常德德山书院主讲,制定学算生童课章[14];1897年又受聘至湖南时务学堂任算学教习,此后在时务学堂演变而来求实书院、求实大学堂、湖南高等学堂任算学教习[15];著有《圆锥曲线法》《数理与人生》,未刊[16];曾翻译的数种数学书[17],应为教科书,未见出版。他长期在湖南任教,是清末民初著名数学教育家。

李希易,生卒年不详,李国钦之兄。李氏家贫,偶然间得到一本英文几何教科书,尽管不识英文,无人指导,通过看图自学,无师自通,由此闻名乡里,被聘为数学教员[18],曾先后任教于湖南长郡中学[19]、湖南第一师范学校[20]等。李希易与黄俊、仇棱生为好友,均参加辛亥革命,1917年曾共同与李国钦、李鹏兴、陶幼圃等创办安化华隆茶业公司,由此将湘茶输入美国。[21]其后应赴美,与其兄弟合创李氏基金会。

三、《中西数学名词合璧表》的可能来源

《平面三角法》所附之《中西数学名词合璧表》,共46页,922词条,包含算术、代数、平面几何、解析几何、三角学、微积分等学科,以英文字母排序,但偶有乱序。

对于这一词汇表的来源,经过初步对比1908年(日本明治四十一年)之前的多种日英数学名词对照表,发现此表应是以长泽龟之助《解法适用数学辞书》之中第二门《英和学语之部》(图3,图4),略有删减。

---

8 许康编:《湖南历代科学家传略》,长沙:湖南大学出版社,2012年,第313—316页。
9 湖南省政府秘书处统计室编纂:《湖南年鉴(民国二十二年)》,湖南省政府秘书处,1933年,第786—788页。
10 湖南省政府秘书处统计室编纂:《湖南年鉴(民国二十二年)》,湖南省政府秘书处,1933年,第174页。
11 中国矿冶工程学会:《中国矿冶工程学会会员录》,中国矿冶工程学会,1943年,第40页。
12 常宁县志编纂委员会编:《常宁县志》,北京:社会科学文献出版社,1993年,第155页。
13 陈惠生:《数学英才许奎垣》,见黄陂县政协文史资料委员会:《黄陂文史》第4辑,水利部长江水利委员会测航大队印,1992年,第77—79页。
14 《常德德山书院许奎垣主讲兆魁新定学算生童课章》,见朱有瓛主编:《中国近代学制史料》第一辑(下册).上海:华东师范大学出版社,1986年,第433—435页。
15 许康:《创新之光》,海口:海南出版社,2002年,第120—122页。
16 陈惠生:《数学英才许奎垣》,见黄陂县政协文史资料委员会:《黄陂文史》第4辑,水利部长江水利委员会测航大队印,1992年,第77—79页。
17 贺延年译述:《汉译何鲁陶三氏高中代数学》(下册),商务印书馆,1926第六版,民国五年贺延年自序.
18 上海《中国对外经济贸易丛书》编纂委员会编,王垂芳、陆志濂主编:《世界著名华侨华人企业家列传》,上海:上海科学技术出版社,1996年,第91—92页。
19 李人琢、梁涤青:《中学时代的李富春》,见利广安等编:《纪念李富春》,北京:中国计划出版社,1990年,第148页。
20 《湖南第一师范与校长易培基》,见郭廷以编:《白瑜先生访问记录》,北京:九州出版社,2012年,第79—89页。
21 黄俊:《弈楼诗集》,武汉:华中师范大学出版社,1998年,第94页,第610页。

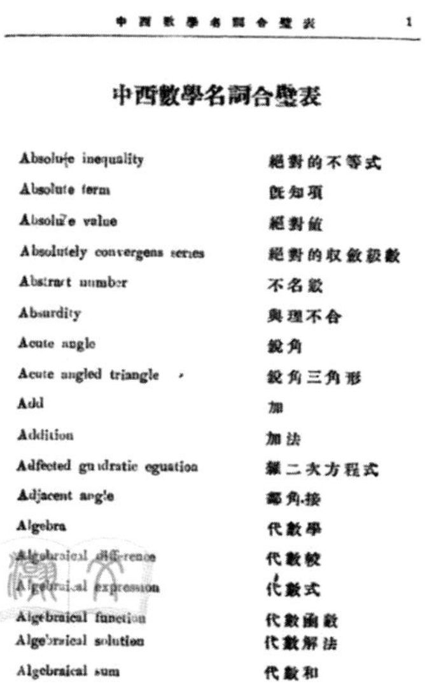

中西数學名詞合璧表 1

中西數學名詞合璧表

Absolute inequality	絕對的不等式
Absolute term	旣知項
Absolute value	絕對値
Absolutely convergens series	絕對的收斂級數
Abstract number	不名數
Absurdity	與理不合
Acute angle	銳角
Acute angled triangle	銳角三角形
Add	加
Addition	加法
Adfected guadratic equation	雜二次方程式
Adjacent angle	鄰角,接
Algebra	代數學
Algebraical difference	代數較
Algebraical expression	代數式
Algebraical function	代數函數
Algebraical solution	代數解法
Algebraical sum	代數和

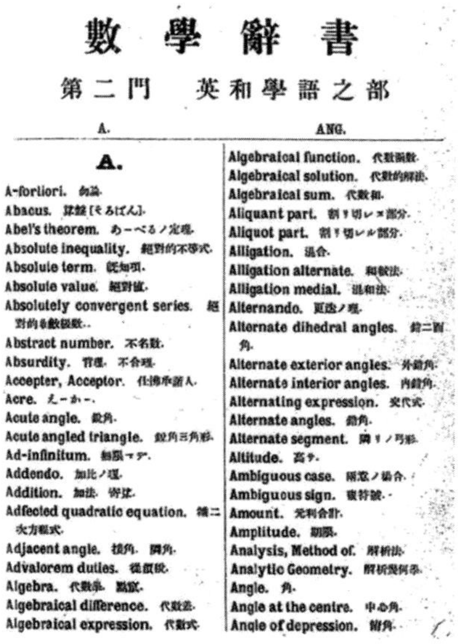

數學辭書

第二門 英和學語之部

A. ANG.

A.

A-fortiori. 勿論.
Abacus. 算盤[そろばん].
Abel's theorem. あーべるノ定理.
Absolute inequality. 絕對的不等式.
Absolute term. 旣知項.
Absolute value. 絕對値.
Absolutely convergent series. 絕對的收斂級數.
Abstract number. 不名數.
Absurdity. 背理. 不合理.
Accepter, Acceptor. 仕拂承諾人.
Acre. えーかー.
Acute angle. 銳角.
Acute angled triangle. 銳角三角形.
Ad-infinitum. 無限マデ.
Addendo. 加比ノ理.
Addition. 加法. 併法.
Adfected quadratic equation. 雜二次方程式.
Adjacent angle. 接角. 鄰角.
Advalorem duties. 從價稅.
Algebra. 代數學. 點竄.
Algebraical difference. 代數差.
Algebraical expression. 代數式.
Algebraical function. 代數函數.
Algebraical solution. 代數的解法.
Algebraical sum. 代數和.
Aliquant part. 割リ切レヌ部分.
Aliquot part. 割リ切レル部分.
Alligation. 混合.
Alligation alternate. 和較法.
Alligation medial. 混和法.
Alternando. 更迭ノ理.
Alternate dihedral angles. 錯二面角.
Alternate exterior angles. 外錯角.
Alternate interior angles. 內錯角.
Alternating expression. 交代式.
Alternate angles. 錯角.
Alternate segment. 錯リノ弓形.
Altitude. 高サ.
Ambiguous case. 兩意ノ場合.
Ambiguous sign. 複符號.
Amount. 元利合計.
Amplitude. 輻限.
Analysis, Method of. 解析法.
Analytic Geometry. 解析幾何學.
Angle. 角.
Angle at the centre. 中心角.
Angle of depression. 俯角.

图 3 《中西数学名词合璧表》,取自瀚文民国书库数据库

图 4 《解法适用数学辞书》第二门《英和学语之部》,取自日本国立国会图书馆

以部分词汇为例(表 2),可见二者的直接承袭关系。

表 2 《中西数学名词合璧表》词汇举例

英文	中文	《解法适用数学辞书》用语
absolute inequality	绝对的不等式	绝对的不等式
absolute term	既知项	既知项
absolute value	绝对值	绝对值
absolutely convergens series	绝对的收敛级数	绝对的收敛级数
abstract number	不名数	不名数
absurdity	与理不合	背理,不合理
acute angle	锐角	锐角
acute angled triangle	锐角三角形	锐角三角形
add	加	—
addition	加法	加法
adfected guadratic equation	杂二次方程式	杂二次方程式
adjacent angle	邻角,接[角]	接角,邻角
algebra	代数学	代数学,点窜
algebraical difference	代数较	代数差
algebraical expression	代数式	代数式
algebraical function	代数函数	代数函数
algebraical solution	代数解法	代数的解法
algebraical sum	代数和	代数和
alternate exterior angles	外错角	外错角
alternate interior angles	内错角	内错角
alternating expression	交代式	交代式

续表2

英文	中文	《解法适用数学辞书》用语
alternate angels	错角	错角
alternate segment	交换弓形	邻リノ弓形
altitude	高	高サ
ambiguous case	两可之意	两意ノ场合
ambiguous sign	复符号	复符号
amount	本利和	元利合计

中译本并非是长泽龟之助原书词汇表的全部翻译,而是略有舍去,主要是含有较多日文假名的词汇,或可说明李国钦和邓彬对日文的掌握程度或许有限;对于一些含有假名的词汇,中译者应是按照英文作音译,比如 Euclid,长泽龟之助以平假名翻译为ゅーくりっど,而中译本则译为"有克里德",但此名词作为人名译为"欧几里得"应已常见;少数词汇的翻译略有改动,如 algebraical difference 一词,日文词为"代数差",中译本者改为"代数较",更符合中国传统用词方法,但在其他翻译的日文数学著作中,常常直接沿用"代数差"。另外,长泽龟之助此辞书所用之词汇,有时也与自己所著的其他书有不同。比如 abstract number 一词,长泽龟之助《中等教育算术书》用词为"无名数",辞书则选择了"不名数",此"不名数"译法或许是参考自藤泽利喜太郎《数学用语英和对译字书》。

长泽龟之助(1860—1927),筑后人,日本民间数学家,一生撰著或翻译数学著作 150 种[22],其中有 20 种教科书和 5 种题解中心辞典被译为中文[23],与中国学者周达、崔朝庆等保持密切交往[24]。其《解法适用数学辞书》,初版于 1905 年(明治三十八年),共分《辞书之部》《英和学语之部》《算术解法之部》《代数学解法之部》《平面几何学解法之部》《立体几何学解法之部》《平面三角法解法之部》《数学小史之部》八门,前有崔朝庆写于光绪乙巳(1905)之序,叙述搜集、利用日本数学书籍,与长泽龟之助的交往等[25]。《解法适用数学辞书》的中译,则在 1923 年由赵燎编译,略加改动,增加了中国数学家传记,以《数学辞典》为名由群益书社出版。其《算术辞典》《代数学辞典》《几何学辞典》《续几何学辞典》《三角法辞典》几种数学辞典,直至 20 世纪三四十年代,方才由薛德炯、吴载耀合译出版。长泽龟之助的辞典与著作的中译本,几经重印,对几代中国学生或数学工作者产生了重要的影响。[26]

大约与《中西数学名词合璧表》的翻译同时或稍晚,清学部编订名词馆审定了数学名词,现存的算学、代数、形学、解析形学、平三角、弧三角中英名词对照表,大约 1 000 条,与《中西数学名词合璧表》的词条书目数目大体相近。然而,与《中西数学名词合璧表》选择日译名词不同,学部审定的名词,多依照旧译名词,部分为严复重新雅驯,对日语词的选用颇为谨慎。[27]

晚清时期,数学译著中还有多种单科名词对照表。比如日本田中矢德著《初等代数学教科书》,由崔朝庆翻译,1907 年上海商务印书馆出版,附有《代数学中西数学名词合璧表》,但仅 44 词条,且译语也有不同[28]。又如马瀛所译长泽龟之助《微分积分学》,1911 年出版,附有《中英名词表》,有 181 个词条[29]。再如佘宾王译《代数问答》,约于 1903 年初版,附有《代数名目华文拉丁文法文合表》,即拉丁文、法文、中

---

[22] 李春兰,代钦:《长泽龟之助对中国近现代数学教育的贡献》,《数学教育学报》,2014 年 2 期。
[23] 徐喜平:《长泽龟之助数学著作在中国的翻译与传播》,《咸阳师范学院学报》,2017 年 2 期。
[24] 冯立昇:《中日数学关系史》,济南:山东教育出版社,2009 年,第 269—293 页。
[25] (日)长泽龟之助:《解法适用数学辞书》,郁文舍,1905 年。
[26] 闫晓民:《〈代数学辞典〉中译本研究》,内蒙古师范大学,2012 年。
[27] 杜良:《编订名词馆与〈数学中英名词对照表〉的编订》,《中国科技术语》,2016 年 3 期。
[28] (日)田中矢德著,崔朝庆译:《初等代数学教科书》,上海商务印书馆,1907 年。
[29] (日)长泽龟之助著,马瀛译:《微分积分学》,商务印书馆,1911 年。

文名词对照表,共 73 个词条。[30]震旦学院翻译的教科书《代数学》,约于 1910 年出版,附有英、法、汉名词表。[31]商务印书馆编译所编译的《中学代数学教科书》,附有新定旧译名词对照表,但未有对应英文名词。[32]其时,也有一些著作,虽未附译中英数学名词对照表,但在正文中有相应英文名词标注。比如《查理斯密大代数学》中定义代数学时称,"代数学(Algebra)仍如数学(Arithmetic)亦论数之学科也。"[33]又如北京大学堂周道章编译的《新代数学》,以脚注的方式给出英文名词。[34]再如马君武所译之《温特渥斯平面几何学》《温特渥斯立体几何学》中,也有大量的随文英文名词。[35]

以下以崔朝庆译《初等代数学教科书》所附代数学名词表中部分名词、马君武《温特渥斯平面几何学》中释名中的部分名词为例,与晚清三种名词表做一对比。

表 3　代数学译名对比举例

英文	崔朝庆	狄考文[36]	李国钦	清学部[37]
Ratio	比	比例,率	比	率
Term	率	率,项	项	项
Antecedent	前率	一头目[语法上]	前项	前项
Consequent	后率	关碍,关系 Consequences	后项	后项
Compound Ratio	复比	—	复比例,又 Compound Proportion	复率
Duplicate Ratio	二倍比	倍比例,二次比例	二乘比	二次权率
Triplicate Ratio	三倍比	三次比例	三乘比	三次权率
Proportional Quantity	比例数	同理比例	比例量	比例几何 Proportional quantities
Extremes	外率	外率 Extremes of proportion	—	外项
Means	内率	中率	中项 Mean	中项
Continued Proportion	连比例	—	连比例	连比例
Mean Proportion	比例中率	连比例中率	比例中项	中比例几何
Inversion	比例反理	反理	一逆×Inverse×	一反×Inverse×
Alternation	比例更理	属理	一错×Alternate×	一互×Alternate×

30　(德)佘宾王(Scherer S. J.)译:《代数问答》,上海土山湾印书馆,1923 年重印第三版。
31　(法)Bourlet 原著,陆翔译:《代数学》,上海土山湾印书馆。所见名词表已缺,仅余一页。
32　商务印书馆编译所编:《中学代数学教科书》,商务印书馆,1906 年。
33　(英)Charles Smith 著,何崇礼,陈文编译:《查理斯密大代数学》,上海广智书局,1905 年,第 1 页。
34　周道章编译:《新代数学》,上海普及书店,1906 年。
35　(美)George A. Wentworth 著,马君武译:《温特渥斯平面几何学》,科学会编译部,1910 年,第 5—6 页。
36　Educational Association of China. Technical terms, English and Chinese. Shanghai: Printed at the Presbyterian Mission Press, 1904.
37　清学部编订名词馆:《数学中英名词对照表》,清学部编订名词馆。

表 4　几何学译名对比举例

英文	马君武	狄考文	李国钦	清学部
Theorem	定理	术,替	定理	定理,求证题
Construction	构图	—	作图	构造,作图亦可
Postulate	假定	可作,求	公法	准作,旧译可作
Problem	推问	—	问题	求作题,成术
Corollary	系言	系	系	系
Scholium	特记	案	—	旁案
Contradictory of a theorem	悖定理	—	—	驳论之定理 Contradictory theorem
Opposite of a theorem	反定理	对 Opposite	对 Opposite	对论之定理 Opposite theorem
Converse of a theorem	逆定理	—	逆 Converse	互论之定理 Converse theorem

四、结语

《中西数学名词合璧表》,节译自长泽龟之助《解法适用数学辞书》中的英和学语之部,虽然只是简单的英汉对照,未有详解的定义或解释,但是所见最早的一份全面的汉译日本数学名词表,无疑仍有一定的史料价值。

对于此名词表的翻译,或许是译者的自觉行为,也可能是群益书社的安排。清末民初时期,翻译、编译、编著了大量的数学教科书,涉及数十家出版社,所用名词依然呈混乱状态,总体上看汉译日本数学著作的词汇相对一致,且已有数种数学辞典出版。由于日文翻译的相对简单,因此选择一种日文数学辞典译为中文,是相对容易实现的事。群益书社,是清末民国时期著名的出版社,1902 年由湘籍留日归国的陈子沛、陈子寿兄弟创办于长沙,后于 1907 年、1909 年在上海、东京开设分社,1912 年在上海成立总社[38],早期翻译出版了大量教科书、参考用书等,其中包括大量翻译、转译的日本数学教科书,比如桦正董、上野清、菊池大麓、泽田吾一、长泽龟之助、宫本藤吉、小林盈、稻垣作太郎等人所编著或翻译的算术、代数学、几何学、三角学教科书,中译者中也有许多湘籍或有在湘求学经历的学生,比如李国钦、邓彬、赵缭、易应崐、仇毅、言涣彰、言涣迓等。

翻译者或出版社对此名词表之译或许带有期待,但它在清末民初可能并未产生太大影响。因为当时大量的西译、日译或编著的数学著作,据刘冰楠研究,1902—1911 年间仅三角学教科书就达 35 种,加之其时众多的留日学生有自主翻译的能力,因此作为《平面三角法》的附录,此词汇表对清末民初数学著作的翻译的帮助应有限。

尽管近代数学知识几乎都是从西方引进,但名词之翻译创造,也部分地体现出传统概念的延续或民族情感。这在日本人确定数学名词上也有体现。日本数学界在江户中后期至明治初期,数学名词也是呈混乱状态,有沿用和算术语者,有翻译新创者,也有选用早期输入的汉译著作中的名词,尤其是墨海书馆、江南制造局的译书,比如《数学启蒙》《代微积拾级》《代数学》《代数术》等[39];至 1877 年东京数学会社成立,进而于 1880 年成立译语会,对数学名词进行了确定,得到较大范围内的接受,促进了数学的发展,但此后新出现词汇的翻译仍然是各行其是;一些名词的确定依然有较大争议,比如 algebra 一词,有汉译词"代数学"和和算词"点竄"之议,最后确定并存。[40]

---

[38] 邹振环:《作为〈新青年〉赞助者的群益书社》,《史学月刊》,2016 年 4 期。
[39] 冯立昇:《中日数学关系史》,济南:山东教育出版社,2009 年,第 220 页。
[40] 萨日娜:《近代日本数学名词术语的确定历程考》,《内蒙古师范大学学报(自然科学汉文版)》,2020 年 5 期。

甲午战争战败之后,学习日本成为更多中国学者的选择。这在数学上也有所体现,比如借鉴日本数学制度,延聘日本数学教师、派遣留学生赴日学习数学、翻译日本数学著作等各种措施。面对中日数学关系的逆转,中国学者也深有感触。正如曹典球在《平面三角法》序言中解释日本数学之所以较中国发展更快的原因,并进而评论李国钦、邓彬之翻译,提出希望,"而课其实效,吾知二生当益勤勉忍耐,克奏成功,为湘学光,为天下实业倡导,而一洗三百年来畴人逊谢东瀛后进之耻也。"[41] 当然,曹典球所称中国数学"三百年来"不如日本,则属夸张之语。

晚清数学名词的翻译与选择,尚有许多值得探讨之处,有待进一步的研究。本文仅对《中西数学名词合璧表》做初步探讨。

后记: 自 1999 年考入中国科学院自然科学史研究所得识郭书春先生始,迄今已 20 余年,得到先生的指点甚多,也有幸参与先生主持的多个项目,获益良多。值郭先生八十寿诞之际,恭祝先生身体健康,诸事顺遂!

---

[41] (英)翰卜林斯密士著,李国钦,邓彬译:《平面三角法》,上海:群益书社,1908 年,曹典球序。

中算史内容的现代发掘与应用举隅

罗见今* （内蒙古师范大学科技史研究院）

摘要 数学史家、数学家和数学教师对中算史的认识和应用各有侧重,把历史的研究同现代的发展联系起来不乏成功的先例。本文举出中算史洛书、六十四卦、朱—范公式、卡塔兰数、幂和公式等8个例子,说明后人如何认识、应用和发展这些传统的题材。

关键词 中算史;组合计数;区组设计;洛书;六十四卦;朱—范公式;卡塔兰数;幂和公式

1 引言

出于数学发展的需要,数学史家、数学家和数学教师对中算史的认识和应用各有侧重,把历史的研究同现代的发展联系起来,不乏成功的先例:吴文俊先生发掘宋元数学,揭示数学机械化的内涵,应用于机器证明,是古为今用的典范,彰显出数学史研究的目的。本文举出中算史8个例子,说明后人从区组设计和组合计数如何认识、应用和发展这些传统的题材。

2 洛书与拉丁方:组合设计应用正交拉丁方构造幻方

20世纪60年代以来兴起的组合数学（combinatorial mathematics, combinatorics）,是伴随着计算机科学而发展的现代数学分支,当年有影响的《组合数学》(1962)在介绍书名时写道:"这是一门起源于古代的数学学科。据传说,中国皇帝禹(约公元前2200年)在一个神龟的背上观察到纵横图(图1)。"[1]这个数字方阵叫"洛书",即3阶幻方。洛书成为现代组合数学起源的标志,在国际上得到公认。

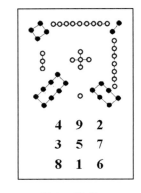

图1 洛书

幻方的一种实数类比叫双随机矩阵,应用它可以找出达到最佳经济效益的多因素配置方案。现代对幻方的研究,有奇数幻方、素数幻方、级数幻方、双重幻方(不仅行、列、对角线的和一定,而且它们的积也一定)[2]、复数幻方、优美幻方等,还向三维发展,讨论幻体的构造。[3]国际上对幻方功能、富兰克林幻方等都有研究。

欧洲在中世纪将扑克牌中A,K,Q,J四种16张排列成方形,使得每横行、每纵列均包含这四种牌,这种方阵即拉丁方。其实这种排法至迟战国时就出现在玄戈占星表上[4](图2)。

在组合数学基本内容区组设计(block design, BD)中,正交拉丁方成为西方的兴趣点之一,例如1960年构造出高阶正交拉丁方,欧拉关于三十六军官问题的猜想不成立[5],轰动一时。而幻方研究一般

---

* 作者简介:罗见今(出生于1942年),河南新野人,内蒙古师大教授、博士生导师。研究方向:数学史、组合数学史、简牍年代学。本文系"中国古代科技文献整理与研究"项目论文(项目号:19JZD042)。

1 Ryser H J. Combinatorial Mathematics [M]. New York: Published by the Math. Assoc. of America, 1962:1.

2 梁培基. 双重幻方[J]. 数学研究与评论,1982(2):14.

3 陈沐天. 幻体的构作[J]. 北京大学学报(自然科学版),1980(3):1—10.

4 罗见今. 睡虎地秦简《日书》玄戈篇构成解析[J]. 自然辩证法通讯. 2015,37(1):65—70.

5 欧拉猜想:对任何非负整数t,$n=4t+2$阶欧拉方不存在。$t=1$时,这就是三十六军官问题;$t=2$时,$n=10$,而10阶欧拉方可构造出,1960年证明了$n=4t+2(t\geqslant 2)$阶欧拉方均存在,因此欧拉猜想不成立。

玄武 青龙 白虎 朱雀 青龙 朱雀 玄武 白虎 朱雀 白虎 青龙 玄武 白虎 玄武 朱雀 青龙	北 东 西 南 东 南 北 西 南 西 东 北 西 北 南 东	NEWS ESNW SWEN WNSE

图 2 玄戈占星表的解读：四象占星四阶拉丁方

却归于代数学。[6]

幻方构造在中国既是一个古老的神秘课题，又是一个现代的研究对象[7]，有较多论著。[8]但一般未从组合数学 BD 的角度提出和解决问题。其实，幻方与拉丁方有密切联系。新近的研究表明，可通过构造两正交 $6m+3$ 阶拉丁方，将其组合而获得 $6m+3$ 阶全对称幻方，说明幻方与正交拉丁方存在内在联系，幻方能够成为 BD 研究的一个新领域。

3 莱布尼兹怎样看卦序与方位：伏羲六十四卦的对称结构

邵雍六十四卦方位图（图 3）中方图的排序在诸本易卦中独树一帜，各卦彰显出数字性质。孙小礼[9]等学者的论文提到莱布尼兹（G. W. Leibniz，1646—1716）在《二进算术》(1679)中建立了二进制的表示及运算，1703 年他给法国科学院提交"关于仅用 0 与 1 两个符号的二进制算术的说明，并附其应用以及据此解释古代中国伏羲图的探讨"。莱布尼兹将阴爻和阳爻与 0 和 1 对等，他是发现这种对等关系的第一人。如果应用数学方法分析易卦的卦序，以此为切入点，用二进制的视角去研究易卦的性质，这正是莱布尼兹方法的要点。要透彻认识易经，二进制数学是一有力的工具。

现将邵雍所绘伏羲六十四卦方位图（图 3）中的方图按逆时针方向旋转 135°，得到一个菱形图（图 4）：63 乾☰在上，0 坤☷在下，左 07 为否☷，右 56 为泰☰。垂直的乾坤轴与水平的否泰轴相交于菱图的中心。然后按莱布尼兹二进制，算出各卦位的卦值，如：

卦位 04 ⇔ 蒙 ⇔ 下卦水☵，上卦山☶ ⇔ 卦数 010001 ⇔ (2,1) ⇔ 卦值 17

卦位 49 ⇔ 革 ⇔ 下卦火☲，上卦泽☱ ⇔ 卦数 101110 ⇔ (5,6) ⇔ 卦值 46

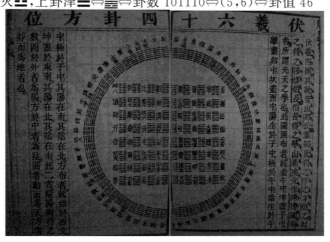

图 3 伏羲六十四卦方位图

---

[6] Gilbert W J. Modern Algebra with Application [M]. New York John Wiley & Sons, 1976. C. -Y. Jean Chan. A construction of regular magic squares of odd order [J]. Linear Algebra and its Applications, 2014(457): 293-302.

[7] 李立. 用第 1 类 4 阶等值全对称幻方砌块构成的 $4n$ 阶全对称幻方 [J]. 数学季刊, 1987(3): 76-81. 李立. $4n$ 阶优化全对称幻方的最快构造方法 [J]. 数学进展, 1988(1): 85-90.

[8] 柳光轩. 幻方的构造与数量 [M]. 杭州: 浙江大学出版社, 2016.

[9] 孙小礼. 莱布尼茨对中国文化的两大发现 [J]. 北京大学学报（哲学社会科学版）. 1995(3).

图 4　邵雍先天图的中心方图将方图旋转后所得菱形图

卦位 39⇔蹇⇔下卦山☶，上卦水☵⇔䷦⇔卦数 001010⇔(1,2)⇔卦值 10

卦位 38⇔睽⇔下卦泽☱，上卦火☲⇔䷥⇔卦数 110101⇔(6,5)⇔卦值 53

今本周易的卦位、卦名、卦值依序为：1 乾 63，2 坤 0，3 屯 34，4 蒙 17，……，64 未济 21。在菱图中，在 63 的位置填入 1，在 0 的位置填入 2，……，在 21 的位置填入 64。然后将 1—2，3—4，…，63—64 连接起来，得到周易卦序的结构图(图 5)，本文称其为邵雍先天二进卦值菱图(简称菱图)。

菱图具有三种基本置换和对应，每种都决定了一个二元组(或有序对)。经过仔细的分析，可以发现图 5 的映射和对应关系，例如，䷐随 38↔25 蛊䷑；䷐随 38↔52 归妹䷵；䷐随 38↔11 渐䷴；离䷝ 45↔18 坎䷜；益䷩ 35↔28 恒䷟；等等。这说明乾坤轴与否泰轴的对等性。用二进卦值表示的邵雍先天菱图具有许多明显的数学性质，用细线将上述三种对应连接起来，就构成直观的、对称的几何图像；对纵、横、斜线两端的数字分别做四则运算，能得到许多相仿而有趣的结果，此不详论。于是，今本周易卦序结构的庐山真面目便清晰、完整地展现在世人面前。[10]

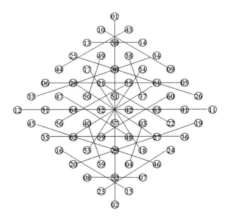

图 5　今本周易卦序结构图邵雍二进卦值菱图的对称性

人们看到，周易的卦序呈现出优美的对称性和完备的均衡性，全部有序对勾画出卦序的结构，展示了深奥的易理意境和高超的构造方法。因此可以提出"易经卦序结构"的概念。卦序可以转换为形象的对称结构意味着什么？这给易理研究提出一个新课题。

---

[10] 罗见今. 周易卦序的对称结构探赜——邵雍先天图的数学解析和应用[C]. 东方学教学理论与实践论文集. 俄罗斯布里亚特：布里亚特国立大学出版社，2014：27-41.

4 徐利治和高尔德如何将朱世杰－范德蒙公式拓展为现代研究

1923年钱宝琮《朱世杰垛积术广义》[11]将《四元玉鉴》中一个垛积恒等式推广，表述成现代形式——卷积型组合恒等式，后来形成了现代计数组合论中使用的术语"the Chu-Vandermonde formula"，即"朱世杰－范德蒙公式"，它是组合计数论的一个基本公式。

朱世杰《四元玉鉴》"茭草形段"第4题给出的关系利用组合与求和符号可表示为

$$\sum_{k=1}^{n}\binom{k+1}{2}\binom{n+2-k}{2}=\sum_{k=1}^{n}\binom{k+3}{4}=\binom{n+4}{5} \tag{1}$$

而《四元玉鉴》"果垛叠藏"第6题可表示为

$$\sum_{k=1}^{n}\binom{k+2}{3}\binom{n+2-k}{2}=\sum_{k=1}^{n}\binom{k+4}{5}=\binom{n+5}{6} \tag{2}$$

将上两式推广，获得

$$\sum_{k=1}^{n}\binom{k+p-1}{p}\binom{n+q-k}{q}=\sum_{k=1}^{n}\binom{k+p+q-1}{p+q}=\binom{n+p+q}{p+q+1} \tag{3}$$

现代科学史学科的奠基人、科学史家乔治·萨顿(G. Sarton)在他的名著《科学史导论》[12]中将钱先生总结的这一公式介绍到西方；1955年李约瑟的《中国的科学与文明》[13]第3卷数学中也引用了这一结果。西方数学家通过这一传播渠道了解到朱世杰的工作。

算法和程序设计技术的先驱者、美国斯坦福大学教授克努特(Donald E. Knuth，中文名高德纳)在他的荣获"图灵奖"的名著《计算机程序设计艺术》[14]中，第59页讲"the Chu-Vandermonde formula"，指明朱世杰的组合公式在先，在第70页还留了一道题目，要求证明"朱－范公式"。在国际组合数学界，"朱－范公式"已成为一个基本公式。

徐利治介绍朱－范公式的现代发展[15]，其中有他和美国高尔德(H. W. Gould)的成果。

二百多年来，朱－范公式已有Rothe(1793)，Gauss，Hagen(1891)，Gould(1956)，Handa和Mohanty(1969)等人的多种扩充，应用甚广。从历史上看，德国数学家高斯(Karl Friedrich Gauss，1777—1855)研究超比例级数时曾将类似的卷积关系推广到复数的情形[16]，被称为"Gauss-Vandermonde公式"。Rothe-Hagen-Gould的卷积型恒等式可写成[17,18]

$$\sum_{k=0}^{n}\frac{x}{x+kz}\binom{x+kz}{k}\frac{y}{y+(n-k)z}\binom{y+(n-k)z}{n-k}=\frac{x+y}{x+y+nz}\binom{x+y+nz}{n} \tag{4}$$

其中，Hagen的恒等式为[19]

---

[11] 钱宝琮.朱世杰垛积术广义[J].学艺.1923，4(7).

[12] Sarton G. Introduction to the History of Science Vol. 3 [M]. Williams Wilkins，1953:701.

[13] Needham J，Wang Ling. Science and Civilization in China，Vol. 3，Mathematics (10) [M]. Series and Progressions. Cambridge at the University Press，1959:138－139.

[14] Knuth D E. The Art of Computer Programming. Vol. 1 Fundamental Algorithms. Third Edition [M].英文影印版.北京:清华大学出版社，2002:53,59,70.

[15] 罗见今.朱世杰－范德蒙公式的发展简介[J].台北:中央研究院数学研究所.数学传播季刊.2008，32(4):66－71.

[16] Graham R L.，Knuth D E.，Patashnik O. Concrete Mathematics [M]. New Jersey: Addison－Wesley，Reading MA，1989:212(in a section on hypergeometric functions).

[17] Hsu F J，Hsu L C.(徐利治). A unified treatment of a class of combinatorial sum [J]. North Holland: Discrete Mathematics. 1991(90):191－197.

[18] Gould H W. Some generalizations of Vandermonde's convolution [J]. Amer. Math. Monthly，1956，(63): 84－91.

[19] Hagen J G. Synopsisder Hoeheren Mathematik. Vol. Ⅰ [M]. Arithmetische und algebraische analyse. Chapter Ⅲ: "Theorie der combinationen". Berlin: Verlag Felix L. Dames，1891:55－68.

$$\sum_{k=0}^{n}\binom{x+kz}{k}\binom{y-kz}{n-k}\frac{x}{x+kz}=\binom{x+y}{n} \tag{5}$$

有多种卷积公式均可由朱－范公式推广而获得,此不一一列举和证明。注意到组合数学界同感兴趣的事实——历来公认为 Rothe-Hagen-Gould 卷积型恒等式是朱－范公式的"非平凡推广"(non-trivial extension),这里却有必要说明,只需利用 Hsu-Gould inversion[20](徐利治－高尔德反演)公式,即可证明式(4)可由朱－范公式推证。这说明式(4)实质上仍与原始的朱－范公式等价,详见文献。[21][22]

5 Chinese Game of Nim:博弈论、图论一个深奥的游戏模型

在古代数学书中数学游戏虽不见记载,但一些特殊的游戏确实包含了深奥的数学内容。我国民间流传一种二人数学游戏,它的规则:有 k 堆物件,每堆物件数量不同,两人轮流从中拿取,每次只能在其中一堆中至少取一个,至多取一堆,最后谁取完谁胜(或负)。$k=3$ 时北方叫作"抓三堆";南方叫作"拧法"或"翻摊";国外称为 Chinese game of Nim[23] 或 Simple game of Nim,或 Fan Tan[24],表明这种游戏源于中国。Nim 游戏从古代流传至今,闪耀着先人智慧之光,现已遍及世界,引起了数学界的兴趣和重视。

Nim 是一个古动词,《牛津英语词典》(*The Oxford English Dictionary*)中说:"nim 大多数应用同后来的动词'拿,取'(take,源出斯堪的纳维亚语)的各种含义相一致,15 世纪之前一直通用"。可知 Nim 作为数学游戏的名称,在西方不迟于 15 世纪。美国人 A. S. 弗兰克尔(A. S. Franker)认为 Nim 是世界上最古老的游戏,它起源于几千年前的东方。[25] 穆尔(E. H. Moore)提出了一种 p 阶 Nim,成为图论 Nim 型对策第三定理的主要例子。[26]

可利用求布尔和来寻找 Nim 的制胜方法:将三堆的数目例如 11,22,29,用二进制表示出来(图 6),规定一种特殊的加法,即 1 加 1 为 0,1 加 0 为 1,0 加 0 仍为 0。叫"点加"或"模 2 加",加出来的和叫作"点和"或"布尔和",这种加法在研究群、环、域的近世代数或逻辑代数中很有用。

如果规定谁取最后 1 个谁输,那么甲方取出的数字一定要保证所余三堆数字的布尔和为 0,轮到乙方来取时,无论他取出多少,只要甲方步步不错(即布尔和总保持为 0),等待乙方的必然是取最后 1 个,失败。

$(11)_{10}=(\cdot 1011)_2$
$(22)_{10}=(10110)_2$
$(29)_{10}=(11101)_2$
$\overline{}$
00000

图 6 二进制的点加

百年来随着数论、近世代数、逻辑代数、特别是对策论、图论和组合数学的发展,当人们用新的眼光观察 Nim 时,它作为一种数学模型,又给人以新的启示。于是 Nim 升格了,一跃而成为一个新的数学名词,开始在数学论文和专著中出现。

在图论中 Nim 受到重视。法国贝尔热(C. Berge)在《图论及其应用》(*The Theory of Graphs and Its Applications*,1962)中开辟第六章介绍"在一个图上的对策",主要就是定义"Nim 型对策",这里的对策,即游戏或博弈(game)。这个图不能有由首尾相接的有向边所组成的圈,不然游戏就有可能无限进行下去。经过严格定义的 Nim 型对策,揭示了 Nim 的特性,扩展了 Nim 的外延,使得一些图的游戏、扑克游戏、数字游戏等都归于这一类。"抓三堆"Nim 就成为一特例。从 Nim 型对策还可引出四个定理,能够保证制胜的结局,此不赘言。

---

[20] Gould H W, Hsu L C(徐利治). Some new inverse series relations [J]. Duke Math. J. 1973,(40):885－891.

[21] Hsu Fangjun, Hsu Leetsch C(徐利治). A unified treatment of a class of combinatorial sum, Discrete Mathematics, North Holland,1991(90):191－197.

[22] Gould H W, Hsu L C(徐利治). Some new inverse series relations [J]. Duke Math. J. 1973,(40):885－891.

[23] 孙泽瀛. 数学方法趣引 [M]. 上海:中国科学图书仪器公司,1955.

[24] Berge C J. The Theory of Graphs and Its Applications [M]. London:Methuen Publishing,1962.

[25] Frankel A S. (Lack of title) [J]. Mathematics Magazine. 1980,53(1):22.

[26] Berge C J. The Theory of Graphs and Its Applications [M]. London:Methuen Publishing,1962.

Nim制胜方案如表1,可视为Nim三元系。拓展的研究表明[27]:与斯坦纳三元系相同。限于篇幅,这里不再对斯坦纳(J. Steiner,1796—1863)三元系进行说明。Nim制胜方案变成了一个区组设计的结果。特别有趣的是,它恰为柯克曼(T. P. Kirkman,1806—1895)在1851年所给出的著名的"十五个女学生问题"的排列方案(只是区组顺序有别)。这当然不仅仅是巧合,中国古代Nim包含深奥的数学道理,在组合数学中具有基本的重要性,它的规则的简明性与它的内涵的深刻性互为表里,自相辉映。

表1 "抓三堆"Nim制胜方案

(0,1,1)	(1,2,3)	(2,4,6)	(3,4,7)	(4,8,12)	(5,8,13)	(6,8,14)	(7,8,15)	…
(0,2,2)	(1,4,5)	(2,5,7)	(3,5,6)	(4,9,13)	(5,9,12)	(6,9,15)	(7,9,14)	…
(0,3,3)	(1,6,7)	(2,8,10)	(3,8,11)	(4,10,14)	(5,10,15)	(6,10,12)	(7,10,13)	…
(0,4,4)	(1,8,9)	(2,9,11)	(3,9,10)	(4,11,15)	(5,11,14)	(6,11,13)	(7,11,12)	…
(0,5,5)	(1,10,11)	(2,12,14)	(3,12,15)	(4,16,20)	(5,16,21)	(6,16,22)	(7,16,23)	…
(0,6,6)	(1,12,13)	(2,13,15)	(3,13,14)	(4,17,21)	(5,17,20)	(6,17,23)	(7,17,22)	…
(0,7,7)	(1,14,15)	(2,16,18)	(3,16,19)	(4,18,22)	(5,18,23)	(6,18,20)	(7,18,21)	…
…	…	…	…	…	…	…	…	

6 明代王文素《算学宝鉴》"三同六变"题与科克曼"女生问题"

王文素(约生于1465年),字尚彬,山西汾州(今汾阳市)人,明代数学家,1524年完成巨著《新集通证古今算学宝鉴》12本42卷,近50万字,所惜当时未能出版。民国年间由北京图书馆于旧书肆中发现一蓝格抄本,收购入藏。1993年,王文素《算学宝鉴》抄本影印版由《中国科学技术典籍通汇·数学卷》[28]刊出。2008年,《算学宝鉴校注》[29]由科学出版社出版,标志着对王文素的研究进入一个新阶段。

《算学宝鉴》中有一问题"三同六变"(图7):"假令二十四老人,长者寿高一百,次者递减一岁,止于七十七。共积总寿二千一百二十有四。卜[30]会三社,八老相令(会)七百八岁,盖因人情逸顺,散而复令(会),更换六次,其积仍均七百有八,此见连用之道。"

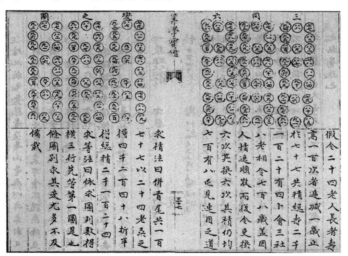

图7 王文素《算学宝鉴》图录"三同六变"图文

该题意即:有$m=2nk=24$位老人聚会,年龄从77岁到100岁,依次相差1岁,共2124岁。$2k=8$人分到一"社"(组,S),共有$n=3$组,每组年龄和皆$p=708$岁;3组为一变局(T)。问能编成多少不同

---

27 罗见今. Nim——从古代的游戏到现代的数学[J]. 上海:自然杂志. 1986,9(1):63—67.
28 [明]王文素. 算学宝鉴[M]//中国科学技术典籍通汇. 数学(2). 郑州:河南教育出版社,1993:337—971.
29 [明]王文素著. 算学宝鉴校注[M]. 刘五然,郭伟,潘有发校注. 北京:科学出版社,2008.
30 卜,占卜。用占卜的方法确定聚会的地址。

组(S)？能构成多少相异局(T)？

他给出的6种答案绘在图7中，最后他说道："其变尤多，不及备载"，明确指出求变局之数很难，这就提出了"王文素问题"，须找出共有多少种方案。

这是一种复杂约束条件下的组合问题，李培业[31]较早认识到它的组合性质。笔者认为，"王文素问题"可分为三类子问题：连续数组、偶数组和奇数组问题（不详论），运用组合方法，可以得到[32]：

组(1)：{78，80，82，88，90，94，96，100}；　　组(10)：{78，82，84，86，90，92，96，100}
组(2)：{78，80，84，88，90，92，96，100}；　　组(11)：{78，80，84，86，90，94，96，100}
组(3)：{78，82，84，88，90，92，94，100}；　　组(12)：{78，80，82，86，92，94，96，100}
组(4)：{78，80，82，84，92，94，98，100}；　　组(13)：{80，82，84，88，90，92，94，98}
组(5)：{78，80，82，86，90，94，98，100}；　　组(14)：{78，82，84，88，90，92，96，98}
组(6)：{78，80，84，86，90，92，98，100}；　　组(15)：{78，80，84，88，90，94，96，98}
组(7)：{78，80，86，88，90，92，96，98}；　　组(16)：{80，82，84，86，90，92，96，98}
组(8)：{78，82，84，88，90，92，94，98}；　　组(17)：{78，82，84，86，90，94，96，98}
组(9)：{80，82，86，88，90，92，94，96}；　　组(18)：{78，80，84，86，92，94，96，98}

当然这不是全部，还可以找到许多连续数组和奇数组。

王文素问题产生于500年前，把一个派生能力很强的数学问题大众化，使之普及，可推衍出形形色色的问题，极具生活情趣，可以使用集合论、计数组合学和设计的方法来解决。

数学史上不乏一些著名组合问题，如约瑟问题、科克曼女生问题、夫妇入座问题等，女生问题也并非一开始就变成了世界著名难题[33]，而是在百余年的认识过程中逐步形成，它与王文素问题形式相似，条件不同，解法相异。王文素问题涉及连续自然数在不同约束条件下适当配置，聚为一些等值数组，构成若干相异数局，属于在组合计数基础上的区组设计。

7 明安图－卡塔兰数：高德纳的评说和拉坎布的证明

卡塔兰(E. C. Catalan,1814—1894)在1838年提出了C_n，后来被称为卡塔兰数(Catalan numbers)[34]，C_n的定义式为

$$C_n = \frac{1}{n}\binom{2n-2}{n-1} \quad (n \geq 1) \tag{6}$$

$n \leq 10$的数列如下：1，1，2，5，14，42，132，429，1 430，4 862，…

1758—1759年，大数学家欧拉(L. Euler)公布了对$n < 23$的正确的C_n值[35]，还给出了表示C_{n+2}的公式。毕纳特(J. Binet,1839)，他获得了C_n的生成函数[36]，卡塔兰数有两个递推公式，在基础论著《组合学导引》[37]中有详细介绍：

$$C_n = \sum_{k=1}^{n-1} C_k C_{n-k} \quad (C_1 = 1, n > 1) \tag{7}$$

$$C_n = \frac{(4n-6)}{n} C_{n-1} \quad (C_1 = 1, n > 1) \tag{8}$$

---

[31] 李珍. 王文素"三同六变"题解[J]. 中国珠算心算协会主办. 珠算. 2000,122(3):2－4. "李珍"是李培业署名.

[32] 罗见今.《算学宝鉴》幻图和"王文素问题"[J]. 上海珠心算. 2015(12):42－48.

[33] 罗见今. 科克曼女生问题[M]. 世界数学名题欣赏丛书. 沈阳:辽宁教育出版社,1990:1－204.

[34] Catalan E. Note sur une equation aux differences [J]. J. Math Pures Appl. 1838,3(1):508－516.

[35] Brown W G. Historical note on a recurrent combinatorial problem [J]. The American Mathematical Monthly. 72,1965:973－977.

[36] Binet J. Reflexions sur le probleme de determiner le nombre de manieres dontune figure rectiligne peutetre partagee en triangles au moyen deses diagonals [J]. J. Math Pures Appl. 1839(4):79－91.

[37] Brualdi R A 著. 李盘林,王天明译. 组合学导引[M]. 武汉:华中工学院出版社,1982.

卡塔兰序列至少有50种组合解释，应用广泛，已成为与斐波那契数（Fibonacci numbers）、斯特灵数（Stirling numbers）类似的一个基本计数函数。在世界数学史上，第一个提出卡塔兰数并有大量研究和应用的，却是清代蒙古族科学家、钦天监监正（国家天文台台长）明安图（1692—1765）。他在《割圆密率捷法》（1839）第三卷（原稿1730年代撰成）中给出

$$C_{n+1} = \sum_{k \geq 0} (-1)^k \binom{n-k}{k+1} C_{n-k} \quad (C_1 = 1, n \geq 1) \tag{9}$$

这是一个数学界未知的公式。在计算中明安图应用了式（3），并得到（$|\alpha| < \pi/2$）

$$\sin 2\alpha = 2\sin \alpha - \sum_{n=1}^{\infty} 4^{1-n} C_n (\sin \alpha)^{2n+1} \tag{10}$$

笔者1988年在《内蒙古大学学报》上发表《明安图是卡塔兰数的首创者》。[38] 算法和程序设计技术的先驱者、斯坦福大学教授Donald E. Knuth（克努特，中文名高德纳）在获图灵奖的名著《计算机程序设计艺术》中，论述了图论中trees（树）的概念，专辟一节回顾卡塔兰数的历史。他说："中国蒙古族数学家明安图1750年前在研究无穷级数时算出了卡塔兰数，但他没有将其同树或别的组合对象联系起来"[39]，引用了笔者1988年的论文。

英国德尔比大学的拉坎布（P. J. Larcombe）博士在此基础上在2001年发表《论卡塔兰序列生成函数：一个历史的透视》[40]，指出明安图的方法是一种生成函数法，并证明了该法的正确性。拉坎布研究明安图所创卡塔兰数的相关论文共发表了14篇。

明安图的成果与卡塔兰数西方早期研究相比，具有独辟蹊径的特点，即对今天的学者来说，也是十分新奇的。由于明安图是卡塔兰数的首创者，早于卡塔兰约100年，李文林主张，C_n应当称为"明安图－卡塔兰数"。

8 戴煦的正切数与欧拉数：区别于西方传统的递推公式

正切数（tangent number）T_n和欧拉数（Euler number）E_n是两种重要计数函数，也是特殊函数和递归函数。西方对正切数的研究在1857年开始，远不及对欧拉数的认识。[41]

戴煦（1805—1860），字鄂士，浙江钱塘（今杭州市）人，晚清著名数学家。在1852年的《外切密率》[42]第四卷中使用具有特色的递归方法，同时获得现今所说的正切数和欧拉数的递推公式（略），成绩斐然。他算出前十个正切数（图8）：

$T_1 = 1$　（原著未列）

$T_2 = 2$　（第一乘法）

$T_3 = 16$　（第二乘法）

$T_4 = 272$　（第三乘法）

$T_5 = 7936$　（第四乘法）

$T_6 = 353792$　（第五乘法）

$T_7 = 22368256$　（第六乘法）

$T_8 = 1903757312$　（第七乘法）

---

[38] 罗见今.明安图是卡塔兰数的首创者[J].内蒙古大学学报.自然科学版.1988,19(2):239-245.

[39] Knuth D E. The Art of Computer Programming, Volume 1, Fundamental Algorithms, Third Edition [M].高德纳.计算机程序设计艺术.第1卷基本算法.第3版(英文影印).北京:清华大学出版社,2002:407.

[40] Larcombe P J, Wilson P D C. On the Generating Function of the Catalan Sequence: A Historical Perspective [J]. Congressus Numerantium(Winnipeg Canada). 2001,(149):97-108.

[41] 罗见今.正切数的数学意义和中西研究史[J].内蒙古师大学报(自然科学版).2008,37(1):120-123.

[42] 戴煦.外切密率第四卷[M].粤雅堂丛书本.1852（咸丰二年）.中国科学技术典籍通汇.数学（五）.求表捷术.河南教育出版社,1993:767-850.

$T_9 = 209865342976$ （第八乘法）

$T_{10} = 29088885112832$（第九乘法）

他已完全掌握了正切数 T_n 的递推规律，得到

$$\tan \alpha = \sum_{n=1}^{\infty} T_n \frac{\alpha^{2n-1}}{(2n-1)!} \tag{11}$$

戴煦同样正确地算出了前十个欧拉数（图略）：

$E_0 = 1$（原著未列）；$E_1 = 1$（第〇乘法）；

$E_2 = 5$（第一乘法）；$E_3 = 61$（第二乘法）；

$E_4 = 1385$（第三乘法）；$E_5 = 50521$（第四乘法）；

$E_6 = 2702765$（第五乘法）；$E_7 = 199360981$（第六乘法）；

$E_8 = 19391512145$（第七乘法）；$E_9 = 2404879675441$（第八乘法）。

于是，他已完全掌握了欧拉数 E_n 的递推规律，从而获得正割幂级数展开式：

$$\sec \alpha = \sum_{n=0}^{\infty} E_n \frac{\alpha^{2n}}{(2n)!} \tag{12}$$

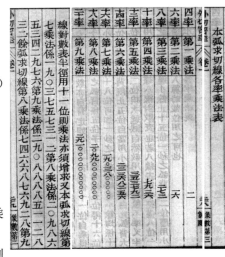

图 8　戴煦求得的正切数（tangent numbers）表

经比较，显而易见，戴煦把 T_n 和 E_n 相提并论，定义酷似，且相补充。他的基本思想是两者相匹配、相"对称"。因而在他的原著中，全部论述和结果都保持这种"对称性"，这与现代数学中将欧拉数同伯努利数（Bernoulli numbers）相提并论的做法是不一样的。

20世纪西方对正切数的文献有：Estanave[43]（1902）研究 $\tan x$，$\sec x$ 展开式系数；Schwartz[44]（1931）应用麦克劳林公式展开 $\tan^p x$；Toscano[45]（1936）给出了有关交错置换和正切数的另一种表述；Entrenger[46]（1966）和 Knuth，Buckholtz[47]（1967）用组合数学计数的观点，通过欧拉数与伯努利数来研究正切数，后者给出正切数前60个数值。

9　李善兰、夏鸾翔、华蘅芳的幂和公式与现代发展

幂和问题具有悠久的历史[48]，晚清算家亦有不凡贡献。限于篇幅，这里只提出部分结果。

李善兰（1811—1882）独创欧拉数（表2），见于《垛积比类》第7表，李氏还给出它的递归定义（略）。据《垛积比类》（1845?）"乘方垛解义"：

$$m^n = \sum_{k=1}^{n} A_{n,k} \binom{m+k-1}{n} \tag{13}$$

---

[43] Estanave. Sur les coefficients des developments en serie de tgx, secx…[J]. Bull S M F. 1902(30)：220—226.

[44] Chwartz. The expansion of tg^{p}x by MacLaurin theorem [J]. Tohoku M J. 1931,(33)：150—152.

[45] Toscano. Sulla derivate di ordine n della funzioe tgx [J]. Tohoku M J. 1936,(42)：144—149.

[46] Entrenger. A combinatorial interpretation of the Euler and Bernoulli numbers [J]. Nieuw Arch. Wisk. 1966, (14)：241—246.

[47] Buckholtz, Knuth. Computation of tangent, Euler and Bernoulli numbers [J]. M Comput. 1967,(21)：663—688.

[48] Luo Jianjin. On the Development of the Formulae for Sums of Powers of Integers [J]. Historia Scintiarum, Vol. 2003,13(2)：100—109.

表 2 欧拉数 $A_{n,k}$ 据《垛积比类》第 7 表

$A_{n,k}$	$k=1$	2	3	4	5	6
$n=1$						
2	1	1				
3	1	4	1			
4	1	11	11	1		
5	1	26	26	26	1	
6	1	57	302	302	57	1

据"乘方垛求积术",求自然数前 m 项 n 次幂和

$$\sum_{r=1}^{m} r^n = \sum_{k=1}^{n} A_{n,k} \binom{m+k}{n+1} \tag{14}$$

即李善兰将幂和分解成 n 类组合之和,每类组合的个数依欧拉数分布。这个幂和公式简洁优美,可求任意次幂和。

夏鸾翔(1823—1864)在《洞方术图解》"单一起根诸乘方诸较图"中创"夏氏数"(表 3),表示出乘方公式:

$$x^n = \sum_{k=0}^{n} X_k^n \binom{x-1}{k} \tag{15}$$

继而获得自然数前 m 项的幂和公式:

$$\sum_{x=1}^{m} x^n = \sum_{k=0}^{n} X_k^n \binom{m}{k+1} \tag{16}$$

即将幂和分解成 $n+1$ 类组合之和,每类组合的个数依夏氏数分布。运用计数函数求幂和的公式中,如以计算量衡量,该式最简,迄今仍是佼佼者。

表 3 夏氏数 X_k^n 据单一起根诸乘方诸较图

X_k^n	$k=0$	1	2	3	4	5	6	7
$n=0$	1							
1	1	1						
2	1	3	2					
3	1	7	12	6				
4	1	15	50	60	24			
5	1	31	180	390	360	120		
6	1	63	602	2 100	3 360	2 520	720	
7	1	127	1 932	10 205	25 200	31 920	20 160	5 040

华蘅芳(1833—1902)《积较术》"诸乘方正元积较表"用现今所说的有限差分法提出一种计数函数"华氏数"(表 4),给出它的递推定义式,将它应用于求乘方以及求幂和:

$$x^n = \sum_{k=1}^{n} h_k^n \binom{x+k-1}{k} \tag{17}$$

$$\sum_{x=1}^{m} x^n = \sum_{k=1}^{n} h_k^n \binom{m+k}{k+1} \tag{18}$$

李善兰从垛积术(和分)、华蘅芳从招差术(差分)各自获得幂和公式,可谓殊途同归。

华氏数具有优秀的性质,将它的定义稍做改变,即将表 4 中的数字取绝对值,针对幂和问题可以建

立起"取盒-放球"模型,给它一个全新的组合解释。[49]

表 4 华氏数 h_k^n 据诸乘方正元积较表

h_k^n	k＝0	1	2	3	4	5	6	7	8
n＝0	1								
1	0	1							
2	0	－1	2						
3	0	1	－6	6					
4	0	－1	14	－36	24				
5	0	1	－30	150	－240	120			
6	0	－1	62	－500	1 560	－1 800	720		
7	0	1	－126	1 806	－8 400	16 800	－15 120	5 040	
8	0	－1	254	－5 796	40 824	－126 000	191 520	－141 120	40 320

幂和问题极富趣味性和挑战性,形成一个专题、一种文化。数学家和爱好者构造各种数论函数孜孜以求。公式的简明性和算法复杂性可一较高下。李善兰、夏鸾翔、华蘅芳的结果具有类似而不同的结构,形式简洁优美,对计数组合论的发展做出令人印象深刻的贡献。

Sum of power of integer 这样一个具有魅惑力的问题不乏现代兴趣,吸引着一些数学家。笔者查阅,仅从 1968 年到 1980 年,J. Riordan,[50] J. L. Paul,[51] S. L. Gupta,[52] M. J. A. Sharkey,[53] H. W. Gould,[54] B. Turner 等人提出或用不同方法证明了这一问题或与它相关的、用组合表达的若干公式。迄今互联网上仍有不少网页涉及,真是代不乏人,盛况空前。

10 结语:几点联想

(1)上古河图洛书、八卦九畴等不符合数学起源的唯生产论,曾被斥之为迷信。在数学书出现之前,音乐、占卜、游戏中内涵潜在的数学,体现排列、配置、排序、对称、集合、映射、对应等的应用,研究商周数学思想无法回避,应当予以正视。

(2)中算以计数见长,长期保持算法倾向、离散性、寓理于算、程序性、机械化的特征。400 年前当西方已进入微积分时代,中算却跌入低潮,停留在离散数学早期,未能进入连续数学时代。当然并非一无是处,在计数理论中还有一些闪光点。

(3)数学原理在本质上保持一致,算法途径古今中外总有差别,因此,东西方对某一对象采用不同数学方法却获得类似的结果,可谓殊途同归,在这一问题上各有千秋。因处于不同历史发展阶段,如用单一坐标予以高下之分,似有"辉格"之嫌。

(4)数学史在数学中的位置决定了它自身的发展目标,因此它不会沦为随意拈来使用的工具。基本史实不可动摇。值得庆幸的是,在大数据时代,人们可以从不同的途径获取真相的各个方面,选择性遗忘仅能维系一时,罔顾事实将成过眼烟云。

49　罗见今.华蘅芳数在幂和问题中的新应用[J].数学研究与评论. 2003,23(4):750－756.
50　Riordan J. Combinatorial Identities [M]. Hoboken:John Wiley & Sons, New York－London－Sydney,1968:160.
51　Paul J L. On the sum of the kth powers of the first n integers [J]. Amer. Math. Monthly. 1971,(78):271－272.
52　Gupta S L. An identity involving the sum of the kth powers of the first n natural numbers [J]. Math. Gaz. 1972,(56):128－129.
53　Sharkey M J A. An identity involving the sums of powers [J]. Math. Gaz. 1973,(57):131－133.
54　Gould H W. Sums of powers integers [M]. Number Theory Class Notes Part I. West Virginia University,1974/1975:3－4.

Examples of Modern Exploration and Application of the Contents in the History of Mathematics in China

Luo Jianjin

(Institute for the History of Science and Technology, Inner Mongolia Normal University, Huhhot 010022)

Abstract Mathematical historians, mathematicians and mathematics teachers have different emphasis on the understanding and application of the history of mathematics. There are many successful precedents in linking the study of history with the development of modern times. This paper gives eight examples of Luoshu; 64 hexagrams; the Chu-Vandermonde formula; Catalan number; formula of sum of power of integer, etc. to illustrate how future generations recognize, apply and develop these traditional themes.

Key Words the history of mathematics in China; enumerative combinatorics; block design; Luoshu; 64 hexagrams; the Chu-Vandermonde formula; Catalan number; formula of sum of power of integer

《大衍历议》所论《鲁历》及其上元积年

王荣彬　（中国民主同盟中央委员会）
许微微　（《今注本二十四史》编辑部）

摘要　唐代僧一行在其《大衍历议》中对《春秋》及《左传》的历日资料进行了大量的核算。本文先梳理古代历算家关于历法与天象"先""后"关系概念，从而辨证了《大衍历议》所记僖公五年、昭公二十年合朔冬至《鲁历》与《周历》先后的文字倒互之误，还原并补充了《大衍历议》关于《鲁历》的核算，确认了张培瑜对《开元占经》所载《鲁历》上元积年的校改。

关键词　《春秋》；《左传》；《大衍历议》；《鲁历》；上元积年

一般认为，中国古代历法经历了观象授时和历法推算等不同发展阶段。中国古历有悠久的历史，远在商周时期就出现了有一定水平的历法，至少在春秋时代已有了较为成熟的历法，战国后期更是相继出现了古六历，使历法进入了推步治历阶段。但先秦历法皆无传，今天已经很难知道其具体内容了。传世的最早历法则是《史记·历书》记载的《历术甲子篇》及太初改历时编制的历法（《太初历》已不传，刘歆据之改编的《三统历》存于《汉书·律历志》）。关于古六历，古今学者做过很多研究，清代人顾观光著《六历通考》，[1] 现代学者张培瑜等有专门的深入研究。[2] 本文仅就《大衍历议》（以下简称《历议》）记载，拟对古六历之一《鲁历》做一点补充探讨。

一、经传历日与古六历

《春秋》是一部春秋时期鲁国史官编写、后经孔子整理的编年史著作，记载了鲁隐公元年（公元前722）至鲁哀公十四年（公元前481）共242年的历史，其中包含丰富的历日资料（包括37次日食、393个历日干支）。《春秋》记事历日所用的历法应是当时鲁国实际行用的历法，是后人研究春秋时期鲁国历法乃至春秋历法的珍贵资料。

由于《春秋》经文言简意深，难以理解，便有了注释《春秋》的"传"，后有亡逸，汉代时有重新编撰整理的《春秋左氏传》《春秋公羊传》《春秋谷梁传》。其中《左传》记载了386个历日干支，且较《春秋》多为新增。尤其是其中的27条朔、晦、闰，除鲁文公六年闰月外，皆为《左传》所特有。《左传》中还有两次日南至记载，经现代研究者核算，皆是当时历算家的实测结果，且误差在2日以内。《左传》不是单纯采用鲁国历法，近代学者梳理发现，其中有用《周历》解说《春秋》历日的痕迹。[3]

我们把《春秋》历日和《左传》历日统称为"经传历日"。由于春秋历法已不见史籍，《春秋》鲁国历法成为人们间接了解春秋历法的重要途径。其实，从汉代开始，人们就不断努力研究鲁国历法了。据不完全统计，先后有20多种鲁国历谱问世。唐代以前对春秋历法做过重要研究的学者主要有刘歆、杜预、姜岌、何承天、祖冲之、僧一行等。清代学者的研究众多，其中以王韬的工作最为重要。[4] 近代的代表成果

---

[1] 顾观光：《六历通考》，《武陵山人遗书》第一册，清光绪十九年刊本。
[2] 参见张培瑜、卢央、徐振韬：《春秋鲁国历法与古六历》，《南京大学学报（哲学社会科学）》1985年第4期，第64—71页。
[3] 参见张培瑜、陈美东、薄树人等：《中国天文学史大系·中国古代历法》，石家庄：河北科学技术出版社，2000年，第177～186页。
[4] 参见王韬：《春秋历学三种》，北京：中华书局，1950年。

则见于张培瑜和陈美东的研究工作。[5]

根据上述前贤的研究,我们知道:春秋鲁国历法不是四分术,所用朔望月长度约为29.531日,大、小月相间,大月30日、小月29日。由特定的周期来安排连大月。虽然置闰的方法尚不规范,但19年7闰法已见端倪。鲁僖公五年(公元前655年)前多建丑,后多建子。春秋各诸侯国的历法与鲁国历法大同小异,在建正问题上各行其是。春秋历法为战国后期古六历的出世奠定了基础。

古六历今已不传,史料仅有零星记载。最早载"六历"之名的是《汉书》,《汉书·律历志》曰:"三代即没,五伯之末,史官丧纪,畴人子弟分散,或在夷狄,故其所记,有《黄帝》《颛顼》《夏》《殷》《周》及《鲁历》。"[6]《汉书·艺文志》亦记有"《黄帝五家历》三十三卷;《颛顼历》二十一卷;《颛顼五星历》十四卷;《日月宿历》十三卷;《夏殷周鲁历》十四卷"。[7]后汉时期,人们对春秋历法已经搞不清楚了,古六历当时也已不见全貌。班固认为《春秋》鲁国历法用《鲁历》,而汉代纬书《春秋命历序》认为用《殷历》,可见汉代时就有《春秋》历日为《鲁历》或《殷历》两种说法了。近代学者认为古六历或经汉代学者的发掘与整理,现今所知的古六历材料,如历元、建正、步法等,或为汉人追改,当称为汉传古六历。[8] 这种汉传古六历在中唐以前应该还有较完整的资料。

后秦姜岌上《三纪甲子元历》时有言:"班固以为《春秋》因《鲁历》。《鲁历》不正,故置闰失其序。《鲁》以闰余一之岁为蔀首,检《春秋》置闰不与此蔀相符也。《命历序》曰:孔子为治《春秋》之故,退修殷之故历,使其数可传于后。如是,《春秋》宜用《殷历》正之。今考其交会,不与《殷历》相应,以《殷历》考《春秋》,月朔多不及其日。"[9]说明姜岌时或可见《鲁历》与《殷历》等。南朝宋齐时,祖冲之还指出"古之六术,并同《四分》",[10]这基本成为学界共识。对于古六历编制年代,晋杜预、南朝宋何承天及祖冲之等都已怀疑其非时王之术。今张培瑜等从古六历合天时间的角度分析,认为:"古六历在战国时期比较合天""《颛顼历》约当前350年前后合天,《殷历》约当前440年,《鲁历》约当前465年,《夏历》(历元雨水)约前470年,《周历》约前230年,《黄帝历》约前200年合天"。"古六历是战国时期(前5至前3世纪)各国先后创制并施行的。"[11]

现将能见到的关于《鲁历》内容具列如下:

《汉书·律历志》:"周道既衰,幽王既丧,天子不能班朔,《鲁历》不正,以闰余一之岁为蔀首。"[12]

《后汉书·律历志》给出古六历上元甲子:"黄帝造历,元起辛卯,而颛顼用乙卯,虞用戊午,夏用丙寅,殷用甲寅,周用丁巳,鲁用庚子。"[13]

唐《开元占经》给出古六历上元甲子及积年(至开元二年甲寅,公元714年),具体为:《黄帝历》上元辛卯,2760863年;《颛顼历》上元乙卯,2761019年;《夏历》上元乙丑,2760589年;《殷历》上元甲寅,2761080年;《周历》上元丁巳,2761137年;[14]《鲁历》上元庚子,2761334年。

既然古六历皆四分术,至少汉传古六历的气朔常数、章蔀纪元法、步法、置闰等都是一致的,所不同

---

[5] 参见张培瑜:《中国先秦史历表》,济南:齐鲁书社,1987年;陈美东:《鲁国历谱及春秋、西周历法》,《自然科学史研究》,第19卷第2期,2000年4月,第124—142页。

[6] 《汉书》卷二一上《律历志上》,北京:中国社会科学出版社,2020年,第1949页。

[7] 《汉书》卷三〇《艺文志上》,北京:中国社会科学出版社,2020年,第3511—3512页。

[8] 参见张培瑜、陈美东、薄树人等:《中国天文学史大系·中国古代历法》,石家庄:河北科学技术出版社,2000年,第206—216页。

[9] 《晋书》卷一八《律历志下》,北京:中国社会科学出版社,1974年,第566页。

[10] 《宋书》卷一三《律历志下》,北京:中国社会科学出版社,2020年,第615页。

[11] 张培瑜、卢央、徐振韬:《春秋鲁国历法与古六历(哲学社会科学)》,《南京大学学报》1985年第4期,第66页。

[12] 《汉书》卷二一上《律历志上》,北京:中国社会科学出版社,2020年,第1964页。原文"鲁历"指"古六历"之《鲁历》,应加书名号。

[13] 《后汉书·律历志下》,北京:中国社会科学出版社,2021年,第5870页。

[14] 按,《四库全书》本《开元占经》原文作"《周历》上元丁巳至今二百七十六万一千一百三十算外"。据推算,"三十"下应脱"七"字。近日见到一残本《开元占经》,只有三卷,其中"三十"恰作"三十七"。参见(唐)瞿昙悉达等奉敕撰,(清)徐有壬校:《大唐开元占经》残三卷,钞本,日本京都大学人文科学研究所藏。

就是历元、建正等，但《鲁历》或许是古六历较为特殊的一种，如《鲁历》的蔀首有"闰余一"。

《历议》对《左传》的两次冬至记录进行了推算，且在《中气议》和《日度议》中有前后相互补益的推算内容，涉及了《鲁历》蔀首气朔不齐与上元等特殊问题，对加深我们关于《鲁历》的认识具有十分重要的意义。下面将对相关问题进行讨论。

二、关于历法先天与后天

由于下文将涉及文字校正，而相关问题又与古代历法中的"先天""后天"概念相联结，故先对其做一辨正。

所谓"先天""后天"，就是历法推算结果和相应天象的先后关系。我们检索了正史的所有《律历志》，发现古代历算家对历法"先天""后天"的表述既没有专门约定，也没有发生概念变化。但"先"字与"后"字，在史志的流传中确有颠倒，现代人的表述中有意无意也出现了一些混乱。

我们从《后汉书》《唐书》和《元史》中分别举出关于"先""后"表述的例证，从而给出"先""后"概念的明确约定。

《后汉书·律历志》："自太初元年始用及《三统历》，施行百有余年，历稍后天。朔先历朔或在晦，月见。"[15] 这两句话实际上说了两件事，皆涉及"先后"概念。

第一句是说，《三统历》自太初元年（前104）行用100多年来，历家通过天象观测验证，发现它已经后天了。因为《三统历》的回归年和朔望月分别大于《四分历》，所以其实质上说的是历法的气余和朔余强，必"久则后天"。[16] 为什么气余和朔余强历法会后天？

这里，需要对"先""后"的含义进行约定，即给"先""后"定义。将天象发生的时间标注在一个由古代向现在再向将来、自左向右的时间轴方向上，则轴的右方为先（参见图1）。或以现在为0，向左为负，向右为正，越向左或越向右，其数值的绝对值越大。假设天象的发生时刻就是现代的理论值，如果历法的推算值小于理论值，则历法后天；大于理论值为先天。

按此约定，所谓历法气余、朔余强，即回归年、朔望月值大于理论值，必然导致其推算天象的结果小于理论值（后天）。这一点其实也不难理解，比方说，有一条10米长的绳子，用古代某种大的尺子量，比如这种尺子1尺=1.01米，则测量这条绳子的得数为$10 \div 1.01 \approx 9.9$（尺）。

同理，如果用气余、朔余强的历法逆推古代的天象，所得的数值的绝对值小，推算结果在时间轴上必将落在古代天象的右方，从而使得历法先天。从杜预到祖冲之，都是用这个原理认识到了古六历"非时王之术"。

如果知道历法气余、朔余弱强的具体量，则可以推算出该历法先天、后天的量。我们今天用现代天文学分析古历推算误差，就是我们有了理论值，从而知道这个气余、朔余弱强的量。其实，祖冲之和僧一行就是在用这个原理分析古历，只是他们估算的气余、朔余的弱强之量在今天看来也有误差。如《历议》曰："古历与近代密率相较，二百年气差一日，三百年朔差一日。推而上之，久益先天；引而下之，久益后天。"[17] 其中"古历"即古六历和汉历，"密率"则指《大衍历》的回归年值。

总之，历取回归年、朔望月值的强弱与历法后天、先天的关系，以及图1所示先后方向的约定，二者是相辅相成的。史料和今人著述中凡出现与之先后关系相反而未做说明的，皆当属先后关系混乱之表述。

第二句则是说，如果"朔"[18] 先于"历朔"，或者"朔"在"晦"，这两种情形下，月亮在"历朔"之日皆可

15　《后汉书·律历志中》，北京：中国社会科学出版社，2021年，第5749页。"朔先历朔或在晦，月见"一句，中华本校勘、标点作"朔先〔于〕历，朔或在晦，月〔或朔〕见"，有害文意，不妥。

16　"久则后天"一词，我们在中华书局"中华经典古籍库"中检索到8次，其中《宋书》所载祖冲之和戴法兴的辩论中出现2次，《大衍历议》出现1次，都是在说《四分历》久则后天。《大衍历议》又曰："刘洪以古历斗分太强，久当后天。"

17　《新唐书》卷二十七上《历志三上》，北京：中华书局，1975年，第612页。

18　此"朔"指日月相合天象，与"历朔"相对，可称之为"真朔"。

见。这就是古代文献中常说的"食二日"或"食晦"。如图1所示,如果日食(真朔)发生在历法的初二,则历法后天了;如果出现"食晦",则历法先天。

图 1　食晦食二日与历法先后天示意图

另外,还有一种先后关系,是指不同历法的推算结果之间的"先""后"关系。如《授时历议》曰:"今按献公十五年戊寅岁正月甲寅朔旦冬至,《授时历》得甲寅,《统天历》得乙卯,后天一日。"[19]可见,历法推算的得数大为"先",或推算所得的相应干支序号大为"先",反之为"后"。

三、《历议》所论《鲁历》

《历议》在其《中气议》与《日度议》中分别用《殷历》《周历》《鲁历》以及《大衍历》等推算《左传》所记载的僖公五年和昭公二十年两次冬至时刻。尤其值得注意的是,僧一行分别针对两次冬至进行了顺推与逆推,反复核算,且两段中皆有《鲁历》参与,所以对于《鲁历》(至少是僧一行所见的《鲁历》)的参数也给予了反复验证。下面,我们将先就《中气议》原文逐步还原僧一行的具体演算过程。《中气议》曰:

> 《春秋传》僖公五年正月辛亥朔日南至,以《周历》推之,入壬子蔀第四章[20],以辛亥一分合朔冬至。《殷历》则壬子蔀首也。昭公二十年二月己丑朔日南至,鲁史失闰,至不在正。左氏记之,以惩司历之罪。《周历》得己丑二分,《殷历》得庚寅一分。……《鲁历》南至又先《周历》四分日之三,而朔后九百四十分日之五十一。故僖公五年辛亥为十二月晦,壬子为正月朔。又推日蚀密于《殷历》,其以闰余一为章首,亦取合于当时也。[21]

《左传》记载僖公五年(前655)和昭公二十年(前522)"朔日南至"的干支分别为辛亥和己丑。但用《周历》推算,僖公五年的合朔冬至为辛亥日一分(四分术一分即0.25日);用《殷历》推算则为壬子日初,且正好在蔀首。而用《鲁历》来推算,冬至在 $46\frac{1}{2}$ 日(日名干支为庚戌,时辰在午时),合朔在 $47\frac{286}{940}$ 日(辛亥日辰时)。演算步骤如下,其得数如图2所示。

其一,用《殷历》推算。据《开元占经》,《殷历》上元积年数为2761080(上元到开元二年,公元714年)。2761080−605×4560=2280=714+1566,则距离开元二年最近的纪首为成汤十三年(前1567)。[22] 1566−654=912=12×76,故僖公五年正月朔为《殷历》入纪912年,亦即第12蔀的蔀首。四分术岁实365.25日×912=333108日,满60去之,余数为48。算外[23]得干支序号49,即壬子。所以说"《殷历》则壬子蔀首"。

其二,用《周历》进行推算。由于《开元占经》所给的《周历》上元积年数大于《殷历》57年,57×365.25日=20819.25日。据之,从《周历》纪首起推算,则有333108+20819.25=353927.25日,满60去之,余数为47.25。算外干支序号48,即辛亥。小余0.25日为四分术的"一分"。

19　《元史》卷五十二《历一》,北京:中华书局,第1138页。
20　所谓"壬子蔀",是指该蔀的蔀首日日名为壬子,这是古历对蔀的传统命名法。
21　《新唐书》卷二七上《历志三上》,北京:中华书局,1975年,第591—592页。原文标点有若干不当者,本文已作更正。
22　因公元纪年没有0年,所以用公元前纪年数入算时数字要减1。公元前1567年的天文纪年即为−1566。
23　"算外"字面意思就是不算在内,由于满60取之的余数是从0开始的,而干支序号从1起算,故推算得数一般需"算外"命名干支。

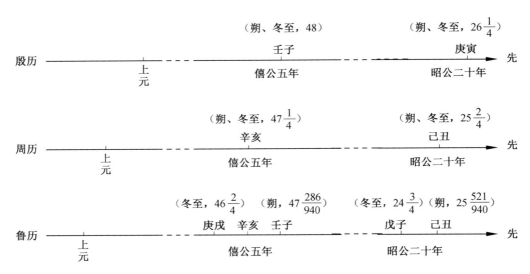

图 2 《殷历》《周历》《鲁历》推算僖公五年、昭公二十年合朔南至时刻示意图

其三,用《鲁历》推算。《开元占经》所记《鲁历》上元积年数有误,我们先取张培瑜校正的数字 2761514 入算,将在下面给出进一步分析。由于 $2761514 = 605 \times 4560 + 2714$,$2714 = 2000 + 714$,则《鲁历》最近的纪首为公元前 2001 年。$(2000 - 654) \times 5.25 = 1346 \times 5.25 = 7066.5 = 7020 + 46.5$。算外得干支序号 47,即庚戌日午时冬至。

从以上对僖公五年的三个推算过程可见,《周历》推《左传》干支吻合,《殷历》先《周历》"四分日之三",而《鲁历》后《周历》"四分日之三",且蔀首气朔不合。

关于昭公二十年记录的推算。自僖公五年至昭公二十年为相隔 133 年,$133 = 7 \times 19$ 年,恰好是 7 章。以《殷历》推算,由 $365.25 \text{ 日} \times 133 = 48578.25 \text{ 日}$,满 60 去之,得 38.25,从壬子起数至第 39(算外)得干支为庚寅$(48 + 38.25 - 60 = 26.25)$,余数 0.25 即加时一分。以《周历》推,即从辛亥起数至第 39,得干支为己丑,而 2 个小余 0.25 相加得余数 0.5,即加时为二分。以《鲁历》推,$38.25 + 46.5 - 60 = 24.75$,算外得干支戊子。同样是《周历》合《传》,《殷历》先《周历》"四分日之三",《鲁历》后《周历》"四分日之三"。

接下来,我们讨论《日度议》文字的推算,《日度议》曰:

> 僖公五年,《周历》、汉历、唐历皆以辛亥南至。后五百五十余岁,至太初元年,《周历》、汉历皆得甲子夜半冬至,唐历皆以辛酉,则汉历后天三日矣。祖冲之、张胄玄促上章岁至太初元年,冲之以癸亥鸡鸣冬至,而胄玄以癸亥日出,欲令合于甲子,而适与《鲁历》相会。自此推僖公五年,《鲁历》以庚戌冬至,而二家皆以甲寅。且僖公登观台以望而书云物,出于表晷天验,非时史亿度。[24]

此段文字大致是说,僖公五年冬至辛亥是当时的实测值,僖公曾登观台视察。太初元年冬至甲子也是当年改历时选取的值,用《周历》、汉历(《太初历》)、唐历(《大衍历》)分别从僖公五年推算到太初元年,《周历》、汉历皆后天三日。另外,祖冲之、张胄玄为了契合历家传统祥瑞观念,各自调整其历法的气余与朔余以合太初元年甲子朔旦冬至,而适与《鲁历》相会(言下之意,以《鲁历》推算也得太初元年冬至为甲子)。从此逆推到僖公五年,则《鲁历》得庚戌冬至,而祖、张二家皆得甲寅。

《大衍历》从僖公五年到太初元年的推算过程为:《大衍历》回归年为 365.2444 日,$(654 - 103) \times 5.2444 = 2889.6644 = 2880 + 9.6644$,辛亥 $+ 9.6644 =$ 辛酉(算外)。

---

[24] 《新唐书》卷二七上《历志三上》,北京:中华书局,1975 年,第 612—613 页。

《大明历》从太初元年逆推到僖公五年:祖冲之的回归年为 365.2428 日,(654－103)×5.2428＝2888.7828＝2880＋8.7828→60－8.7828＝51.2172,干支为甲寅(逆推应取算上)。

《鲁历》从太初元年逆推到僖公五年和昭公二十年则分别为:(654－103)×5.25＝2892.75＝2880＋12.75→60－12.75＝47.25,算上干支为庚戌。(521－103)×5.25＝2194.75＝2160＋34.5→60－34.5＝25.5,算上干支为戊子。但一行没有交代太初元年冬至时刻《鲁历》的小余,考虑到《鲁历》有气朔不齐的特殊安排,故此处推算的小余当不可为凭。

四、《历议》所述《鲁历》《周历》南至先后辨正

《中气议》文字中有这样一句:"《鲁历》南至又先《周历》四分日之三,而朔后九百四十分日之五十一。"这是要说明《鲁历》合朔和冬至不在同一时辰了,冬至先《周历》四分日之三,合朔后《周历》九百四十分日之五十一。但这和前面反复推算的结果不一致,如图 2 所示,此处当是"《鲁历》南至又后《周历》四分日之三,而朔先九百四十分日之五十一","先""后"二字倒互。

其实,对这句话历代学者持多种议论。中华本校勘记曰:"《唐会要》卷四二载傅仁均奏新术七事:'《春秋命历序》云鲁僖公五年壬子朔旦冬至,诸历莫能符合,臣今造历,却推僖公五年春正月壬子朔日冬至则同。'《考异》卷四三据本卷《中气议》及《合朔议》所述推论,以为鲁术推僖公五年冬至应在壬子,此云'庚戌冬至'误。"我们知道,《春秋命历序》所言鲁僖公五年壬子朔旦冬至,是依据《殷历》。钱大昕《二十二史考异》的推算迂回,且僧一行的推算和本文以上补充的反复核算,足以证明钱氏推算有误。[25] 故中华本校勘记的结论自然站不住脚了。王应伟先生发现此处核算不合,[26] 但未说明原因。张培瑜等则认为此处有错误,所给出的校改意见是"《鲁历》南至又先《周历》四分日之三,而朔后此值(四分日之三)又九百四十分之五十一"。[27] 最近,郜积意指出张培瑜等的校改"深嫌不辞,古人无此行文之法"。他认为此后半句当校改为"而朔后[殷历]九百四十分日之五十一""此句省'殷历'二字者,以上下文皆论殷历,故不复出之"。[28] 但按上下文,《殷历》二字承前省略之说亦不通。

实际上,前面所述关于僖公五年和昭公二十年冬至的推算,一行的本意就是要上推下推反复核算验证,我们也特意补充若干演算过程。仅就冬至来看,改庚戌为壬子完全不可取。同理,张培瑜所校改的《鲁历》上元积年数字当是可信的。

为了进一步确认张氏积年数,我们再来分析一下僧一行《中气议》这段文字的论述思路。一行先指出《传》中僖公五年朔日南至为辛亥,《周历》合,《殷历》的干支先一日。但说到昭公二十年时,由于《传》所记月份为二月,故一行接着就分析"鲁史失闻"及其他相关问题(引文中省略号部分内容),然后一行又回头来说前述两次冬至之事,且回头说的这三句话有三层意思。

其一,一行是要说:根据其反复核算,僖公五年的记载中,《鲁历》南至后《周历》南至"四分日之三",朔先"九百四十分日之五十一"。昭公二十年的记载中,《鲁历》南至又后《周历》"四分日之三",朔又先"九百四十分日之五十一"。上文我们所还原冬至推算过程已经证明了《鲁历》这两次冬至确实是皆后

---

[25] 钱大昕考证原文为:"自此推僖公五年,《鲁历》以庚戌冬至。按:鲁术元起庚子,其积年之数未闻,难以布算。据上文《中气议》云《鲁历》南至,又先《周历》四分日之一,而朔后九百四十分日之五十一,故僖公五年辛亥为十二月晦,壬子为正月朔,是鲁术推僖公五年冬至在壬子矣。而此云以庚戌冬至,前后自相矛盾。又《合朔议》云僖公十六年正月戊申朔,与《殷历》《鲁历》合。今算僖公五年,尽十五年,积月一百三十六,(经月一百三十二,闰月四。)积日四千一十六,大余五十六,起壬子算外,得次年天正戊申朔旦。《殷》《鲁》二术,朔晦多同,辛亥南至,《殷》朔后一日,《鲁》必不异至又当在朔后,则此云庚戌冬至,其误明矣。"(《嘉定钱大昕全集·廿二史考异》卷四三《唐书三》,南京:凤凰出版社,2016年,第813页)

[26] 参见王应伟:《中国古历通解》,沈阳:辽宁教育出版社,1998年,第81—82页。

[27] 张培瑜、卢央、徐振韬:《春秋鲁国历法与古六历》,《南京大学学报(哲学社会科学)》1985年第4期,第67—68页。

[28] 郜积意:《经学与历学的贯通——春秋朔闰表与经文历日研究》,《学术月刊》第52卷第1期,2020年1月,第156页。

《周历》，并示意在图2中。

至于《鲁历》的两次合朔与《周历》的先后关系，首先，图2中我们的计算结果有 $\frac{286}{940} > \frac{1}{4}$，$\frac{521}{940} > \frac{2}{4}$。其次，由于《鲁历》与《周历》都是四分术，二者推算的合朔和冬至将同步移动，如果不是《鲁历》气朔不齐，其先后关系是不会变化的。故不妨再仔细分析《历议》的相关论述。上文我们提到过，一行在《日度议》中已经根据他自己的历法取值(密率)，估算出"古历与近代密率相较，二百年气差一日，三百年朔差一日"。若某个时间的合朔冬至(比如太初元年)向古代逆推，则逆推二百年时(大约是古六历的编制年代)，则冬至合天，而朔仍先天半日。再向古代逆推三百年(大约是僖公时代)，冬至后天约一日半，朔仅后天半日。就是说《鲁历》在僖公时代，朔应先气约一日(图2)。由于一行能见到《鲁历》的具体数据，他反复核算而给出的这种结论应该是可信的。

其二，僖公五年《周历》《殷历》皆是蔀首之年，但《鲁历》在此处气朔不齐，故《鲁历》的历谱以辛亥为前一年的十二月晦，壬子为五年正月朔。

其三，《鲁历》章首有"闰余一"，是《鲁历》编制者当年为了更好取合天象，从而牺牲了其历法的整齐性。但一行随即指出，以他所见到的资料，《鲁历》推算日食比《殷历》精密，就是说这种牺牲是值得的。

一行以上对《鲁历》的三点评介，所透露的《鲁历》相关信息，对我们今天了解《鲁历》弥足珍贵。

综上所述，传本《中气议》此"先""后"二字倒互，不应是一行的过失，而是古代某位研读者的错误改动，当改正。

五、《鲁历》上元积年

《后汉书·律历志》言"鲁用庚子"，唐《开元占经》所给《鲁历》上元亦为庚子，积年数为2761334(至开元二年甲寅，公元714年)。其实，若《鲁历》上元积年为2761334，有 $2761334 = 605 \times 605 + 2534$，得其天纪甲子蔀首距开元二年为2534年，即公元前1821年，确为庚子年。

《汉书·律历志》记载《鲁历》"以闰余一之岁为蔀首"，《历议》载《鲁历》"以闰余一为章首"。但以《鲁历》上元庚子、积年2761334，以及"以闰余一之岁为蔀首"进行计算，得出鲁僖公五年入己酉蔀27年，天正丙子朔，小余798；日南至乙丑，小余16(分母32)。与《历议》上述记载不符。即使用《鲁历》上元庚子、积年2761334，以及以蔀首闰余为0进行计算，得鲁僖公五年入己酉蔀27年，天正戊申朔，小余379；日南至乙丑，小余16。也不合。这说明《鲁历》上元庚子、积年2761334有误。张培瑜根据他的缜密推算，改2761334为2761514，以"闰余一之岁为蔀首"推算的结果与《历议》的记述吻合。[29]

清代顾观光撰《六历通考》，改2761334为2764394。[30]顾观光先据《开元占经》所载古六历上元积年，列出入蔀年表，阐述入蔀、冬至、节气、朔望等的推算法，然后考证《汉书·律历志》《后汉书·律历志》《宋书·律历志》《晋书·律历志》《隋书·律历志》《新唐书·历志》等史志中有关古六历的论述，加以评述。顾氏发现，《大衍历》中的《周历》《殷历》《颛顼历》的蔀、章首年名、日名与《开元占经》所载的上元积年核算皆相合。但《开元占经》记载的《鲁历》上元积年数与《历议》的记述不合，他意识到《开元占经》的《鲁历》上元积年应当予以校订。但顾氏的复原以庚子为上元，以闰余为0之岁作蔀首，与文献记载不符。

最近，郜积意先生采顾氏之说并进行了补证，他进而以《鲁历》上元积年为2764394、僖公五年正月壬子朔为基础排算历表，恐有失实。[31]

总之，关于《鲁历》上元积年数，综合张培瑜先生的推算以及本文以上的补充验算与分析，改2761334为2761514是可信的。

---

29 参见张培瑜、卢央、徐振韬：《春秋鲁国历法与古六历》，《南京大学学报(哲学社会科学)》1985年第4期。

30 顾氏原文为："依法推之，当作四千三百九十四"，见《六历通考》，《武陵山人遗书》第一册，清光绪十九年刊本，第1a页。

31 参见郜积意：《经学与历学的贯通——春秋朔闰表与经文历日研究》，《学术月刊》第52卷第1期，2020年1月。

作者简介：

1. 王荣彬，1964 年生，安徽六安人。中国民主同盟中央委员会，博士、研究员，主要研究方向为中国数学史、中国历法史。E-mail：rbwang64@163.com。

2. 许微微，1983 年生，吉林松原人。《今注本二十四史》编辑部，硕士、中级编辑，主要研究方向为秦汉史。E-mail：xuweiwei1119@163.com。

中国传统数学有无证明须看如何理解证明

李国伟　（中国台湾"中央"研究院数学研究所退休研究员）

摘要　以往对于中国古代数学缺乏证明的论调，多以欧几里得《几何原本》组织数学知识的方式为评判标准，造成一种只从规范性视角观察证明的结果。数学证明至少包含思维活动及其产物两个方向，无可避免会承载历史演化的痕迹。本文从讨论旧式评判观点开始，渐次触及当代数学家与数学哲学家对于证明的多元、包容与开放的见解，从而肯定证明并未在中国古算中缺席，尝试对郭书春先生主张中国古算有理论、有推理的立场做一个注脚。

在《应冷静客观地看待祖先的成就》文中，郭书春先生简练地说："学术界还有一种普遍的然而却是十分错误的看法，就是中国古代数学只有成就，没有理论，没有演绎推理。诚然，与古希腊比较，中国古代数学理论研究确实薄弱一些，但绝不是没有理论，没有推理。刘徽全面论证《九章算术》的公式、解法时主要使用了演绎推理，他的数学知识形成了一个完整的理论体系。刘徽和其他数学家还往往采取寓理于算的做法，同样是数学推理，是数学理论的一种表现形式。"[2] 另外在《中国古代数学：不仅重应用，而且有理论》文中，郭先生再次强调："我们经过考察发现，现今形式逻辑教程中关于演绎推理的几种主要形式，刘徽都娴熟地使用过，而且没有任何循环推理。刘徽的数学证明是相当严谨的。说中国古代数学没有演绎逻辑，大约是没有读或者没有读懂刘徽的《九章算术注》。"[3] 郭先生之所以能对刘徽的数学推理、证明与理论体系做出肯定而高度的评价，完全建立在他对《九章算术》及其刘徽注长期、深刻，以及忠实于原典的研究成果之上，从而能发前人所未能发，不受成见遮蔽。

郭先生举证国际上认同中国古代数学缺乏理论，特别是演绎逻辑的例子，包括"三上义夫认为，中国古代数学最大的缺点是缺少严格求证的思想。李约瑟断言，在从实践到纯知识领域的飞跃中，中国数学是未曾参与过的。比利时学者李倍始则宣称："中国中世纪所有数学著作都没有证明。"[4] 三上义夫是研究中国古代数学的先锋，特别以英语写作而导引西方对于中国古代数学的认识。但是受其置身时代条件的限制，能够广泛介绍中国古代数学成就已属不易，很难期望有更深入的评判。至于李约瑟的《中国科学技术史·数学卷》，郭先生曾指出他对中国古代数学成就的阐述并不充分，甚至有不得要领之处。[5] 然而李约瑟这本书却成为西方人士认识中国数学的重要参考书。例如克来恩在他1 200余页皇皇巨著《古今数学思想》的序言里说："我不谈像中国、日本、马雅等文明，是因为他们的成果对于数学思想的主流没有实质的影响。"[6] 他在中国之后还加一注脚，请读者参阅李约瑟"相当好的"《中国科学技术史·数学卷》。李倍始在1973年出版对于秦九韶《数书九章》的研究，成果相当出众，他对于"没有证明"

1　谨以本文恭祝郭书春先生八秩华诞。
2　郭书春：〈应冷静客观地看待祖先的成就〉，《郭书春数学史自选集》下册，济南：山东科技出版社，2018年，第856页。
3　郭书春：〈中国古代数学：不仅重应用，而且有理论〉，《郭书春数学史自选集》下册，济南：山东科技出版社，2018年，第762页。
4　郭书春：〈刘徽《九章算术注》中的定义与演绎逻辑试析〉，《郭书春数学史自选集》上册，济南：山东科技出版社，2018年，第150页。
5　郭书春：〈应冷静客观地看待祖先的成就〉，《郭书春数学史自选集》下册，济南：山东科技出版社，2018年，第856页。
6　Morris Kline, Mathematical Thought from Ancient to Modern Times, New York: Oxford University Press, 1972, p. viii.

的论断,应该是相对于某种有关"证明"的规范所做的结论。

在李倍始之后,华道安于一篇讨论刘徽推导锥体体积的论文结论里说:"刘徽对于《九章算术》陈述的解释,并非基于一套公理系统,因此最好不要称它们为'证明';我把它们叫作'推导',类似于当代工程教科书里,能找到的一些松散的数学推导。"他在论文的摘要里甚至说:"这些解释满足我们所谓证明的许多评断标准。"所以华道安采纳规范"证明"的要件应该会包括"公理系统"。他在结论里接下去说:"刘徽的推导立基于他认为显然为真,却通常未明白说出的预设。……刘徽要求严谨性的标准很高,他从来不会犯循环论证的错误。"[7] 也就是说刘徽论证的结构与使用公理并无显著不同,只是他没有意识到有必要把预设条件一一叙明。所以对于中国古代数学确保获得正确知识的方法上,华道安比李倍始更具包容性,承认"证明"的功能是存在的,只是名字叫"推导"。范·德·瓦尔登是20世纪弘扬抽象代数贡献卓著的数学家,当他援用华道安的论文说明刘徽的方法时,毫无保留地把华道安的"推导"都称为"证明"。[8] 他的做法在我们看来可说呼应郭书春先生对于刘徽注的定性。

1. "证明"的多重意义

证明之始是一种有意向性的认知活动,并不必然以文字记载的方式表示出来。郭书春先生虽然承认没有给任何术文留下推导与证明是《九章算术》的缺点,但他表示:"这不是说当时根本没有推导或论证。《九章算术》的许多解法和公式相当高深,已非经验所能及,没有某种形式的推导是不可能的。"[9] 一段数学文本从给出问题到列举解答之间,也许未着任何文字。例如:《九章算术·方田》第6题,"又有九十一分之四十九。问:约之得几何?答曰:十三分之七。"后续虽然给出一段著名的约分术曰:"可半者半之;不可半者,副置分母、子之数,以少减多,更相减损,求其等也。以等数约之。"但是没有说明为什么会是正确的。从想求取约分的结果,到诉诸于一般性且并非显然的算法,这中间没有用文字表现出来的过程,无论是原作者对自己,或对他可能的读者,都应该有自认为足够说服此法可以获得正确答案的认知经历,否则何必将错误的答案或方法示诸于人?当然有可能自认具说服力的想法,存有漏洞或未能完全达到目标的缺失,但其意向原本在追求正确结果。所以讨论有关"证明"的方方面面时,首先应回归到"证明"这种从事说服结果正确的初始意向。

"证明"这个词其实包含有多重的意义,例如林力娜在讨论刘徽注关于分数加法的论文中,曾经区分了证明的两种意义。一种称为"规范性",意思是针对某一命题,证明是要充分建立其真确性,而且是相对于一套给定的超越历史的规范,例如亚里士多德明白陈述出的那套系统。传统上大量关于证明的议论,主要就是分析这种脉络里的文本质量,或者叙述这类的规范。证明的第二种意义是指一种活动及其产物。当今的数学家撰写与发表证明时,并不会仔细讨论是否符合设定的规范,他们并不在意建立命题的真确性超越任何"合理的"怀疑,"他们作证明是想了解所证明的命题,想知道为什么为真,而不仅仅知道它为真。换句话说,做出证明并非写出证明的唯一动机。"[10]

与李倍始或华道安相比,林力娜对于"证明"的观点更能反映证明的整体面貌,特别是证明活动在认知过程中的意向性。如果从非"规范性"意义角度观察证明,也就是说证明的目的在说服人接受结果是正确的,一个应该会先考虑的问题是,这种说服过程有可能不使用逻辑推理吗?人类在思考上做素朴的推理,是一种普遍的能力,未见什么民族不会做一些因果之间的推理,也没有什么种族与其他种族思考

---

[7] Donald B. Wagner, "An Ancient Chinese Derivation of the Volume of a Pyramid: Liu Hui, Third Century A. D.," Historia Mathematica, vol. 6, no. 2 (May 1979), pp. 164−188.

[8] B. L. van der Waerden, Geometry and Algebra in Ancient Civilizations, Berlin: Springer−Verlag, 1983, pp. 41−42.

[9] 郭书春汇校:《关于〈九章算术〉及其刘徽注——汇校本之导言》,《〈九章算术〉新校》上册,合肥:中国科学技术大学出版社,2014年,第77页。

[10] Karine Chemla, "What is at Stake in Mathematical Proofs from Third−Century China?" Science in Context, vol. 10, no. 2 (Summer 1997), pp. 227−251.

方式截然不同。近年研究数学美感的神经基础的泽奇(Semir Zeki),援引康德对于美的直觉的观点,认为数学公式所以美,是因为它"合理"(make sense)。合什么理呢? 就是大脑天生的逻辑演绎系统,这个系统没有种族与文化的差异性。泽奇又征引罗素的说法:"逻辑的命题可先验性地知晓,不需要钻研真实的世界。"也就是说逻辑命题的根源,立基于先天的脑内概念。[11]因此之故,在证明的认知历程中,某种层次的逻辑功能必不可缺少。而在数学这种因果链明确的知识体系里,想要保证结果正确的推理方式,不可能不使用到演绎逻辑。这种演绎逻辑的应用是一种直觉性的操作,并不必然需先认识到以及述明推导的形式规则。然而当规范性的推导规则给出来后,因为人类推理思维的普遍性,原先直觉的操作也可重新加以组织并表述为符合推导规则的形式。针对刘徽《九章筭术注》,郭书春先生已经执行过这种重组与表述的工作。[12]

2. 证明在西方的辩证发展

其次,暂时把证明限制在"规范性"意义来观察,特别是相对于亚里士多德建立的逻辑体系,及其表现在欧几里得《几何原本》的数学证明范式作为评判的依据。正是对照这样一个限定证明的架构下,中国传统数学以往才经常被判决缺乏证明。但是这个标准在西方数学史上是否就严格遵守呢? 这个标准真的是超越历史不发生变异的吗? 两个问题的答案应该都是否定的,但是西方论者往往把这个标准当作是静态的,忽略它的辩证发展,把一些实质上跨越它的行为,仍然视为可以接受。

最明显的一个例证出现在有关数学分析学的发展上。自从牛顿与莱布尼兹各自发展出微积分,以及接下去17与18世纪数学分析的英雄式发展期,因为涉及无穷小这个古希腊数学家回避的概念,所呈现的证明其实多有违背欧几里得范式的作为,然而数学史家依旧接受它们还是数学证明。至于欧几里得的公理体系,在被认为是保证获得命题真理性的唯一架构两千余年之后,也因为对于数学概念的更加精准的理解,终于被识破其实也是不完备的,从而才有希尔伯特撰写《几何基础》的动机,以严谨的手段重新塑造欧几里得几何。

其实希腊在欧几里得的传统之外,丢番图提供了截然不同的另外一条路径。他的《算术》一书,扬弃把代数问题几何化的希腊传统风格,直接做数字的推算以解决给定的问题。他的推论建立在对于数的直觉理解上,不需要明述一个算术的公理系统。特别地,丢番图使用个别数字来表达计算的过程,可是将这些数字更换为其他数字,计算方法仍然保持有效。这与中国古代数学的风格非常相似,看起来好像是解决了一些特例,其实意涵了足够一般的通用解法。因此当代有学者认为:"在现代数学的脉络里,丢番图的解答可以称之为通性证明(generic proof),这是用来称呼一种演示,就是针对某个类里特定对象做证明,但其实适用到同类所有的对象。"[13]作者在论文结论中更强调,在数学的教学方面,这种使用实例来演示的丢番图方法,会优于一般干瘪的证明。另外,以论述数学本质、实务、与社会影响力著称的贺希于一篇论文中特别强调:"在数学研究里,证明的目的在于说服。检验某个东西算不算是证明,要看它能否说服够资格的裁判。另外一方面在教室里,证明的目的是要解释。在数学教室里开明地使用证明,志在激发学生的理解,而非满足'严谨'或'诚实'的抽象标准。"[14]从上述引用当代数学家关于证明的观点,能够看出对于所谓证明的内涵,不必谨小慎微地只遵循其"规范性"的意义。一方面对于古代不能划归欧几里得范式的表现真理方式,不吝于赋予证明的称呼。另一方面在面对教育的实务操作上,证明更

---

[11] Semir Zeki, Oliver Y. Chén and John Paul Romaya, "The Biological Basis of Mathematical Beauty," Frontiers in Human Neuroscience, vol. 12 (November 2018), Article 467.

[12] 郭书春:〈刘徽《九章筭术注》中的定义与演绎逻辑试析〉,《郭书春数学史自选集》上册,济南:山东科技出版社,2018年,第150—164页。

[13] Cyrus Hettle, "The Symbolic and Mathematical Influence of Diophantus's Arithmetica," Journal of Humanistic Mathematics, vol. 5, no. 1 (January 2015), pp. 139—166.

[14] Reuben Hersh, "Proving Is Convincing and Explaining," Educational Studies in Mathematics, vol. 24, no. 4 (December 1993), pp. 389—399.

可以脱下铁夹克,从说服专家接受真理,软化为解释真理让学生能接受。

3. 一窥当代数学哲学看证明[15]

从当代数学哲学的立场来看,"证明是什么?"这个问题也有不只单一的回答方式,除了诸如形式主义、柏拉图主义、经验主义、维根斯坦式等不同观点外,提森从现象学或认知的角度来理解证明的作用。[16]他认为证明供给了数学经验的证据,他更强调除了通过实际或可能的经验,不会更有其他的"证据"。他认为在实际的数学工作中,证明涉及许多非形式的成分,虽然不失某种未全然形式化的严谨性,但也包含"意义"或语意内涵。学习数学知识时,如果只是机械性地跟着证明里的推导步骤走,并没有真正了解一个定理。当我们想通时才真正"看到"定理的真,也才掌握到提森所谓的证据。证明由这种观点来看,最初必然是一种行动或过程,之后才自身成为一种对象。所以掌握"证据"也就是使数学的意向得以实现。提森的基本看法便是:"证明就是数学意向的实现。"他借用康德的口吻说,"在数学里,缺乏证明的(指向对象的)意向是空洞的,而缺乏意向(即"关于什么",意义或语意内容)的证明是盲目的。"人类认知的功能基本上是一致的,因此数学意向的实现并不会落入一种唯我的、个别的混乱"证据"中。提森对证明的说法,不至于与数学知识的社会性发生矛盾。

提森所依循的现象学就是胡赛尔所开创的哲学学说。已故组合数学大师柔塔曾是麻省理工学院唯一同时是数学与哲学的教授,他写过三篇有关数学的现象学的重要文章:《数学真理的现象学》《数学美的现象学》《数学证明的现象学》。在《数学证明的现象学》一文中,柔塔相当扼要地综述了胡赛尔对于真实描述的规律是如何实施于数学上的:

1. 实在的描述应该把隐藏的特征揭开来。数学家经常口头上传讲的,并不是他们真正实际操作的,他们很不愿意坦白承认自己每日的工作实况。

2. 一些平常清扫到背景里的边缘现象,应该给予应有的重要性。数学家闲聊时会涉及理解、深度、证明的类别、清晰程度,以及许多其他的字眼,严格讨论这些字眼的角色,应该属于数学证明的哲学。

3. 现象学的实在主义要求不能用任何借口,把数学的某些特征贴以心理的、社会的或主观的标签,而从探讨的范围内排斥出去。

4. 任何规范性的预设应该滤除。常常一种对数学证明的描述暗藏了作者对于证明应该是什么样子的要求。虽然很困难甚至包含潜在危险,我们仍然有必要采取严格的描述态度。这种态度有可能导致令人不愉快的发现:例如,可能会体会出没有任何一种特征为所有数学证明所共享。或者可能不得不承认矛盾是数学真实面貌的一部分,是与真理肩并肩共存的。[17]

4. 当代数学家议论证明

这种重视描述性而非规范性的检视方式,用来观察数学界的日常真实运作,会披露更为生动、多样,

---

[15] 本节与下节取材自李国伟:〈证明的流变:一个数学哲学与数学史的综合观察〉,《台湾哲学研究》,(中国台北)第3期,2000年,页1—22。

[16] Richard Tieszen, "What is a Proof?" in M. Detlefsen ed., Proof, Logic and Formalization, London: Routledge, 1992, pp. 57—76.

[17] Gian-Carlo Rota, "The Phenomenology of Mathematical Proof," in F. Palombi ed., Indiscrete Thoughts Boston: Birkhäuser, 1997, p. 135.

甚至有些矛盾的生态环境。1993年，贾飞与奎因两位在《美国数学会会志》上发表了一篇宏文，[18]他们认为获得有关数学结构的信息须通过两阶段：第一阶段发展直觉的洞识，推测将其正当化的途径。第二阶段修正推测并进而加以证明。他们将直觉与思辨阶段的工作叫作"理论数学"，将以证明为核心的阶段叫作"严格数学"。他们要倡议这种区分，主要受到近年来理论物理促进了数学突破性进展的刺激。一些理论物理学家运用数学工具，发展出像弦论、保形场论、拓扑量子场论、量子重力等理论。但要检验这些理论的实验，都超越目前能力所及的范围，因此实验物理学家对这些成果持有相当保留的态度。有趣的是这些结果却刺激数学家开展了许多新的天地，例如用费曼路径积分或量子群表现来理解三维流形上扭结的多项式不变量。这些理论物理学家正是运用揣测与不严格的思辨性方法，创造数学上的突破。这类数学工作可说就是贾飞与奎因所谓的理论数学，然而他们很担心如果没有建立新的工作规范与价值导入稳定健康的发展轨道中，很可能在一阵热闹后，数学家要清扫一大堆虽然宣称是证明，其实是有失严谨的推断，从而使得思辨方法的积极意义遭致抹杀。贾飞与奎因提出了若干补救这种情形的具体建议，因而引起主编向数学界邀集对该文的响应，结果产生了一份非常有意思的记录。在诸多名家的傥论中，曾在1982年获颁菲尔兹奖的瑟斯顿发表了一篇《论证明与数学进步》的文章，[19]他认为贾飞与奎因的"理论数学"所想引人注意的思辨方法，其作用是用来产生问题、制造推测、猜想答案，以及试探什么会是真的。但是他们未曾深究这些行动到底所为何来？我们并不是为了满足某种抽象的生产指标，而要造出一定数量的定义、定理、证明。所有这些作为是要帮助人理解数学，以及更清楚、更有效地思考数学。瑟斯顿在深度申论人如何理解数学之后，他强调数学知识与理解其实是编织在数学共同体的社会与心智的脉络里，文字的记述支持了这种知识的存续，但文字并不是最基础的部分。透过人与人之间理念的交流，数学知识的可靠性获得了保证。数学家检验证明的形式论证，虽然也是一种巩固数学知识的方法，但是数学知识的生命真正来自数学家的思想活动，缜密而批判性的思维交流。瑟斯顿的观点突显了有效发挥证明传达数学知识的作用，真正的重点不在"形式性""逻辑性"，而在于所存身的数学共同体的网络结构。

5. 结语

昔日数学史家或数学家对于中国传统数学缺乏理论体系与证明的见解，其实表现了一种定见，就是视欧几里得《几何原本》为证明的权威范式，只有符合欧式体系的组织与表述方式，才得以认证为合法的数学证明。这种定见其实有几项弱点：(1)西方数学史上某些创造力爆发的阶段，并没有循规蹈矩遵从这个范式；(2)这个范式本身并不完备，而且直到相当近代才补齐它的漏洞；(3)古希腊在几何概念居主导的传统之外，还有其他数学发展的脉络，而其成就为现代数学家接纳应属证明。因此证明的内涵、意义、操作都不是僵化地存身在一个抽象的天地，它有演化与辩证发展的历程。特别是现代数学家看到证明的有效性，其实超出逻辑或形式的规范界线，会深度涉及数学共同体的网络结构。是一种社会性的活动，而非个人纯粹理性的思辨行为。当我们对证明建立了边界更为广阔、内容更为多元的认识后，中国传统数学并不缺乏证明便成为自然的结论。

---

[18] Authur Jaffe and Frank Quinn, "'Theoretical Mathematics': Toward a Cultural Synthesis of Mathematics and Theoretical Physics," Bulletin (New Series) of the American Mathematical Society, vol. 29, no. 1 (July 1993), pp. 1—13.

[19] William Thurston, "On Proof and Progress in Mathematics," Bulletin (New Series) of the American Mathematical Society, vol. 30, no. 2, (April 1994), pp. 161—177.

理解极限精确定义的另一条进路：来自中国古代数学的智慧

段耀勇[1] （中国人民警察大学 智慧警务学院）

摘要 极限给我们带来了一个巨大的悖论。微积分的每一个主要概念——导数、连续性、积分、收敛/发散——都是用极限来定义的。极限是微积分最基本的概念，事实上，极限是使我们把微积分同代数、几何和其他数学区分开来的基本概念。因此，就微积分的有序逻辑发展而言，极限必须放在第一位。其本质涉及无限或者说无穷（无穷大/无穷小）问题，这对人类的智慧而言是一个巨大的挑战。在人类的智力领域，无穷有关问题无处不在，而我们只能用有限的方法和工具来研究它。幸运的是，微积分产生后，伟大的数学家路易·柯西和维尔斯特拉斯给出了极限的精确定义，至此人们才完全掌握和理解了微积分的实质，而中国古代数学所具有的算法特征以及对待无穷的态度，为很好地理解无穷或者对于极限来说提供了另一种视角，在具体教学中也是很好的 HPM 案例。

关键词 微积分；无穷；极限

正如我们所知，在当前的微积分教科书中采用极限、连续性、导数、积分和收敛/发散的顺序，但实际上，历史记录正好相反。几个世纪以来，极限的概念一直与模糊的、有时是哲学的无限概念（无穷大、无穷小的数字和其他数学实体）以及主观的、未定义的几何直觉相混淆。我们现代意义上的"极限"一词是18世纪末19世纪初欧洲启蒙运动的产物，我们现代的定义还不到200年。在此之前，只有极少数情况下严格而正确地使用了极限的概念。

科学史上的诸多事实都显示出无穷概念的巨大重要性和深远影响。实数系的逻辑基础在19世纪末才被建立的事实之所以令人惊奇，正是因为人们在理解无穷这个概念上所遇到的巨大困难造成的，同样原因也阻碍人们对20世纪20年代所发现的最惊心动魄的微观物质理论（量子力学）深刻本质的认识。对无穷（包括无穷大和无穷小）的思考并试图理解它和准确地定义它，是对人类智慧的一个挑战。自古希腊以来，无穷的概念就引起了哲学家和数学家们的注意，但它固有的超越人类有限思维的特征，使得人们对它理解的进展缓慢。希尔伯特曾说过，无穷是一个永恒的谜。正因如此，对这一古老的哲学问题的讨论始终会那样的迷人。直到19世纪，伟大的数学家柯西和维尔斯特拉斯给出极限的精确定义为止，人们都无法治愈这一思维中的症结。反观这段历史，结合中国古代数学中的相关工作和对之的处理方式不难看出，中国古代数学采取了与西方完全不同的方式，充满了东方智慧。

在我们心智中如果承认"一个量是无限可分"的假设，那么分割过程永远也不会终结。这是因为在我们的思维中存在一个"魔鬼"。我们生存在一个无限的环境中，可悲的是我们只能借助有限的手段部分地认识他们。我们的思维是有限的，在处理无限问题时，只能借助"有限"的思维。如恩格斯所言"在数学上，为了达到不确定的、无限的东西，必须从确定有限的东西出发"。可以说，除一些泛泛的形而上的思辨外，至今我们对什么是无限（或无穷）知之甚少。

这个问题不仅困扰过我们的祖先，同样也会困扰我们。随着人类能用语言交流思想，开始了知识的积累，随着书写的发明，知识得以储存。从而使藏书和教育之间互惠互利，印刷术大大提高了知识的增

---

[1] 作者简介：段耀勇（出生于1969年），男，山东济南人，理学博士，中国人民警察大学智慧警务学院教授，主要从事中国数学史、科技战略研究和数学教育研究。文章的重要内容在2004年12月在印度印多尔的国际会议上进行了报告，本文在此基础上进行了修改和完善。

长速度,但同欧洲近代科学兴起之后突然加速增长比较起来是较为缓慢的。知识的增长遵循"复利规律",可令人遗憾的是,人类在智力和道德上并没有得到普遍提高。对很多问题的理解和处理,我们并不比古人高明,对无穷问题的思考和理解就是一例。

1 东西方古代数学与无穷的遭遇

1.1 基于逻辑证明的古希腊数学:从回避到迂回

这个问题可追溯到古希腊。量的可分性显然有两个假定:即一个量无限可分(潜无限)和一个量是由非常多的极微小的不可分的部分组成的。第一个假定,对我们大多数人来说似乎比较合理,但是第二种假定在发现新事物过程中很有用,这就使它表面上的一些荒谬之处显得不那么重要。在古希腊,数学推理的不同学派有的用这个假定,有的则用另一个[1]。

两种假定都会遇到逻辑上的困难,埃利亚的哲学家芝诺在前约 450 年构造了著名的"芝诺悖论"[2],即"二分法悖论""跑步者悖论""飞箭不动悖论"和"运动场悖论",这几个悖论涉及的极限、收敛性等问题直到 19 世纪才获得彻底解决(参考文献[2],446 页)。

比如"跑步者悖论":一名叫阿奇里的善跑者,但是他永远也追不上乌龟,因为当他追到乌龟的出发点时,乌龟已经向前爬行了一小段,他追完这一段,乌龟又向前爬了一段,这样永远重复下去,总也追不上。在"运动场悖论"中,芝诺论证了时间和它的一半相等。对于这些悖论曾有人给出许多解释,要说明它们与普通的直觉的信念想抵触并不难。比如我们直觉信念认为:无限多个正量(即使这些量非常小)之和是无穷大,这正是"跑步者悖论"原因所在;实际上无穷多个无穷小之和是个有限量,不是无穷大[3]。现在我们知道,无限多个正量之和可以是无穷大、常数或无穷小量。比如:"跑步者悖论"中无限多个正量之和为常数,实际上,经无限可分后 A,B 两点间的距离为 l,被我们错误地理解为无穷大的距离,悖论由之产生。

"芝诺悖论"对西方古代数学的影响。自古希腊时期以来,无穷的概念就引起了哲学家和数学家的注意,但它看来是矛盾的性质使得对它的理解进展十分缓慢。西方的数学在毕达哥拉斯学派的影响下,认为万物皆数。用整数和几何图形构建了一个宇宙图式。为了避免直线无限可分中的无穷概念,将"不可公度"这一伟大发现秘而不宣。但是随着这个表征数学史第一次危机"$\sqrt{2}$"问题的出现,希腊人开始重新审视自己的数学,并最终导致放弃了以数为基础的几何。第一次危机使人们不能再依靠图形和直观,而需要更多地依靠推理和逻辑;同时危机还使几何学拒绝了无穷小。此时,西方数学成为以证明为主的证明数学,他们要的是准确的数学,或者说他们的数学推崇准确性。其表现形式为逻辑、演绎的体系。虽然希腊人也讲计算,但他们认为计算是初等的、低级的;是几何证明后的一个应用而已。他们重视演绎和证明,尽管有时(尤其在希腊后期)也搞数值计算,但这只是理论证明后的应用[4]。

西方数学采用反证法对"无穷"进行了迂回处理。由于受到无法解释和理解的无限问题的困扰,同时西方数学逻辑严密的证明的要求,反证法随之出现。它无非是为了解决人类思维中的一个症结——无限思维。在西方证明数学里,极其重视证明过程中逻辑的严密性。因此,第一次数学危机和第二次数学危机都与无限有关,即无理数和无穷小。西方数学家不能给无理数和无穷小以准确的定义,也不能解释与之有关的芝诺悖论。没办法,他们在处理无限的问题上,基于 $A\Rightarrow B \Leftrightarrow \overline{B}\Rightarrow \overline{A}$,借助反证法化无限为有限,再去完成其证明。公元前 5 世纪,早于刘徽的安提丰首先提出割圆术,欧多克斯改造了安提丰的方法,利用穷竭法和反证法为手段化无限为有限,其方法一直为古代西方数学所用。这里欧多克斯在割圆时,借助反证法将一个潜无限问题,化为一个对圆的有限次分割的问题。因此,反证法与极限(无穷问题)开始就结下了不解之缘。

1.2 以算法为中心的中国传统数学:直接计算

穷竭法和反证法并未真正解决无限问题。中国古代数学中并未将无限问题作为一个研究对象。"……刘徽未将求微数的程序进行到底。可见他对于无限,也只是把它作为处理问题的手段和方法,而没有把它本身作为研究对象。刘徽仍未摆脱中国古算讲求实际的传统影响,在他的方法能满足实际需要之后,去探讨无限更深层次的问题的动因就大大减弱了。加之比较成熟的归谬法也没有发展起来…………对于由开方术过程来确认无理数是否存在这样的问题,没有富有成效的归谬法是难以解决的,而归谬法不仅不是中国古代数学的传统,而且还是中国古代哲学思维的薄弱环节。"[5]这里"归谬法"指以反证法为核心,以穷竭法为理论基础的方法。刘徽和当时的思想家们已能熟练地使用归谬法,但是并未解决无限问题严格意义上的反证法,却很鲜见。

关于量可分的两种假定,在中国古代对应着两个命题。"一尺之棰,日取其半,万世不竭"的"尺棰命题"中隐含着一个量无限可分(潜无限)的假定。而"非半弗斫,说在端"的"非半弗斫"命题则认为一个量是有非常多的极微小的不可分部分组成的。古希腊人(我们也一样)会认为,一个量无限可分成的无穷个量之和不可能为定值。也即,古希腊人误认为由此得到的这个无穷级数的和为无穷大,但是这与现实是相悖的。那么,这两种假设孰是孰非?二者都会导致"运动"不能,从而产生悖论。我们分析一下"跑步者"悖论和"飞矢不动"悖论中的"飞矢不动",既然"一个量是有非常多的极微小的不可分部分组成",我们就有理由认为在不可分割的时间 T 时刻上,箭是不动的。

与西方的数学家不同,中国古代的数学家从未受到无限问题的困扰。刘徽在遇到无理数时采用"开方不尽求微数……"。显然,尽管刘徽对"开方不尽"的理解比前人深刻,但中国古代数学重视实际的传统的确是限制了对理论问题做更深层次的探讨。因而,这也阻碍了无理数的发现。刘徽认为只需得到无限接近的一个值就可以;因此,他只关心重要计算方法,而根本不用考虑这个无限问题本身的性质。而且刘徽受《墨经》的影响认为"不可分量可积"[6],刘徽在处理无限问题而作积分时就有了思想依据。对于割圆术(图1),刘徽显然受墨家思想的影响很深,而且刘徽对割圆术的处理也比较符合中国古代数学讲求直观的传统。

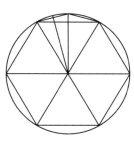

图 1　刘徽割圆术示意图

另外,从墨家的传统来看刘徽的处理也较好理解,实际上刘徽在无限的运用上,其思想和墨、道两家一脉相承[7]。刘徽将道、墨两家的无限思想辩证地统一起来,即无需由于受到无限的困扰,而去寻求化无限为有限的反证法,刘徽解决极限问题,只需求得无限过程下的极限值。刘徽道:"……割之又割,以至于不可割,则与圆周和体而无所失矣……"。这里刘徽对待无限的态度是作一个可操作的程序"割之"的动作。同时这个动作又可无限地做下去,那么在极限过程下正多边形的周长即为圆的周长。这种辩证的极限思想使有关"量的可分性"假定都得到了解释,从某种意义上来说刘徽的极限思想与现代的微积分思想一致[8]。中国的数学家还有什么理由困惑无穷,而去寻求并未真正解决问题的反证法呢?中国传统数学最终经清朝数学家李善兰的努力研究和传承,其"尖锥术"达到了微积分的一些初步结果。西方数学家因不能解决芝诺悖论,因此对于"一个量无限可分(潜无限)"和"一个量是有非常多的极微小的部分组成的"都采取回避的做法,并充分利用逻辑关系,采用反证法把无限转化为有限,进行了迂回式的处理。

2　微积分的建立与极限的精确定义

2.1　牛顿、莱布尼兹与微积分的创立

17 世纪,无穷小量在被遗弃千余年后又被德国天文学家,数学家开普勒捡回,拂去了岁月的尘埃,无穷小量又放出夺目的光彩。他在《新天文学》和《测量酒桶体积的新方法》中系统地阐述了应用无穷小来求曲线所围面积和各种立体的体积的方法,得到了一些前人很难得到的结果。例如:他把圆的面积看作是无穷多个顶点在圆心,底在圆周上的三角形面积的和,球的体积看作是底面为球面面积高为球体半径的圆锥的体积。这给后人创立微积分以灵感和启迪

$$S_{圆} = \sum_{i=1}^{\infty} S_{三角形} = \sum_{i=1}^{\infty} \frac{1}{2} l_{半圆} r = \frac{1}{2} l_{半圆} r, \quad V_{球} = \frac{1}{3} S_{球} r = \frac{1}{3} 4\pi r^2 r = \frac{4}{3} \pi r^3$$

还有很多数学家,也是微积分的先驱者,如卡瓦利里、托里拆利、帕斯卡、沃利斯、费马、笛卡儿,以及巴罗等人深入研究了无穷小量问题,并取得了一些有成效的成果,但他们都没有真正把无穷小量驯服。

原因是他们没有彻底摆脱欧几里得体系的束缚。牛顿、莱布尼兹也概莫能外[9]。

牛顿在《流数术》一书中改变了变量是由无穷小元素组成的看法。他假定：一个量可以无限分割，或者可以（至少在理论上说）使之连续减小，直至它完全消失，达到了称之为"零量"的程度，或者说它们是无限的小，比任何一个指定的量都小。这里，牛顿认为点的连续运动就得到线，他把一个产生中的量称之为流量，其生长率叫流量的流数，一个无限小的时间间隔叫瞬，在这无限小时间间隔内流量增加的无穷小部分叫流量的"瞬"。于是牛顿成功地建立起无穷小的分析数学——微积分。[10]

牛顿从运动变化的量入手，利用无穷小建立了他的新理论。但是，尽管他已注意到无穷、极限的概念，但因不能明确定义他的最终比（无穷小），因此在他的著作中只能回避它。这座空中楼阁，受到了贝克莱主教的猛烈攻击，他称牛顿微积分理论中的无穷小是"消失的鬼魂"，贝克莱的指责可谓切中要害（参考文献[3]的205页）。与牛顿同时代的莱布尼兹独立地发现了微积分理论，尽管他使用了像今天我们所使用的微积分符号，但他和牛顿一样对他理论中的无穷小量解释不清，甚至比牛顿更不注意严格的逻辑性和严密性。微积分这门新学科的基础很不完善，其固有的矛盾在逻辑上确实说不清楚，这场争论导致了"第二次数学危机"。在英国数学家泰勒和麦克劳林采用几何方法为《流数术》辩护，现在看来是走错了方向。而且，麦克劳林采用了与古希腊应对"第一次数学危机"所使用的几何解释路线相同。刘徽在极限方面的工作的"算数化"至少不会遇到无穷小，或者无限问题的羁绊。东方数学的算术化特征正是解决两次数学危机的正确方向。

总之，数学家们的工作并没有解决微积分在逻辑基础上的困难。困扰人类思维的无穷、无限问题；量无限可分假定自身造成的悖论，此时归结为无穷小的精确定义问题。无穷小的问题解决了，人们就解决了量可分的两个假定的调和问题，从而由之导致的"运动不能"悖论才能得以化解。

2.2 从欧多克斯的穷竭法到极限的精确定义

欧多克斯的穷竭法[11]。这种求曲边梯形面积的方法，即为古希腊数学家安提丰（Antiphon）、欧多克斯（Eudoxus）和阿基米德（Archimedes）所使用的"穷竭法"，其基础包含在如下命题中（《几何原本》第十卷，命题1）：

如果从任何一个量中减去不少于其一半的部分，然后在余量中再减去不少于其一半的部分。并且，如果让这个减的过程持续下去，最终总会得到一个余量，使其小于任何一个预先给定的同类型的量。

此命题，我们可称为"穷竭性"，借助欧多克斯-阿基米德公理通过归谬法容易证明其正确性。用现代术语表示它：给定两个量 a 和 b，且 $a>b>0$，如果对于所有 $i=1,2,3,\cdots$，都有 $0\leqslant r_i \leqslant \frac{1}{2}$，对于无论多么小的 b，都有一个数 n 使得 $ar_1r_2r_3\cdots r_n<b$（实际上，这里对这些 r 的限制过分严格，如果 $0<r_i\leqslant k<1$，对于 k 满足要求的任意一个确定的值，结论仍然成立）。我们通过证明《几何原本》卷十二中的命题2："圆的面积必等于其直径上正方形的比"，展示穷竭法的使用方法。该定理本身是希波克拉底最先提出的，但是他的证明方法我们却不得而知。欧多克斯-欧几里得的过程大致如下：设两圆 c 和 C 的直径为 d 和 D，面积分别为 a 和 A，求证 $a:A=d^2:D^2$。采用归谬法证明。假设 $a:A>d^2:D^2$，然后必然有一个量 $a'<a$，使 $a':A>d^2:D^2$ 成立。设 $a'-a=\varepsilon>0$ 为事先指定的量。

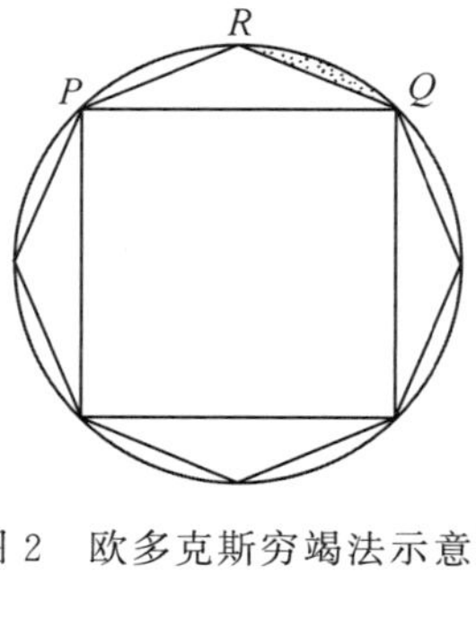

首先我们先证明圆可以被它的内接多边形序列"穷竭"，如图2所示，作圆的内接正方形，则圆与其内接正方形的面积差（我们称其为"剩余面积"）等于弓形 PQR 面积的四倍。接着作出圆内接正八边形，容易证明新的"剩余面积"（阴影区域面积的八倍）小于前一个剩余面积的一半。重复这个过程，作出圆内接 $16,32,64,\cdots$ 边的正多边形，每一步的"剩余面积"都必小于前一次"剩余面积"的一半。因此，我们最终可以达到"剩余面积"小于 ε 的一半。如果 p_n 是这一步时圆内接多边形的面积，则有 $a-p_n<\varepsilon$，又因为 $a'-a=\varepsilon>0$，所以 $p_n>a'$。令 P_n 为圆 C 中所内接相应多边形的面积。《几何原本》卷十二的命题1中，欧几里得证明了结论 $p_n:P_n=d^2:D^2$。据我们最初的假设，将得出

图2 欧多克斯穷竭法示意图

$p_n:P_n=a':A$。已证 $p_n>a'$，因此得出 $P_n>A$。由于多边形 P_n 内接在圆 C 中，因此这导致了矛盾，所以最初的假设 $a:A>d^2:D^2$ 不真。对于另一个假设 $a:A<d^2:D^2$，同理可证。因此，我们证得 $a:A=d^2:D^2$。

《几何原本》第十二卷中的大多数定理，以及第五册中的定理，大都被认为来自欧多克斯。就此，是否可以称他为积分学之父或者之祖父呢？特别是阿基米德向他致敬并指出《几何原本》中卷十二的命题10：圆锥体积等于和它同底同高圆柱体体积的三分之一，第一个严格的证明来自欧多克斯。尽管欧多克斯的方式提供很好的思路，也采用了后来极限精确定义中特别重要的"无论多么小的 b"，但是在本质上并没有解决极限问题。

靠解析几何的帮助，微积分成为 17 世纪最伟大的数学工具。它在解决希腊数学"第一次数学危机"后的诸多很难攻破的问题时很有效(参考文献[3]中的 314 页)。这从微积分在 18 世纪的广泛应用中可见一斑。依靠物理和直观，数学家们通过施展高超的技巧发掘并增进了微积分的威力，从而拓展了无穷级数、微分方程、微分几何和变分法等新领地，基本上构建了当今数学中最广阔的领域——数学分析。18 世纪的数学家们完全陶醉于自己取得的伟大成就，对于失去的严密性大都无动于衷。以证明、演绎和逻辑为特征的希腊数学传统此时丧失殆尽。

尽管"第二次数学危机"中，牛顿-莱布尼兹所创立的微积分倍受攻击，但是它广泛而又惊人的实用性吸引的 17 世纪乃至 18 世纪末的大量的数学家加入到这个领域中来。数学家们苦心经营的微积分大厦毕竟建立在直观的、形式主义的松散的沙土之上。于是从 18 世纪末开始，历时近一个世纪进行了分析的算术化过程，或者说是极限定义的精确化过程。其中，微积分中的许多概念(如：极限、连续性、可微性及可积性等)必须很明白、仔细地被定义出来，当然，核心问题是无穷小这个包含着逻辑悖论、无限思维问题的解决。

第一个试图给予微积分中的无穷小分析以严密性的是 18 世纪第一流的数学家拉格朗日(1736—1813)，他抛弃了牛顿的极限说，从泰勒的定理出发，决定只用代数方法，但由于对级数的收敛性注意不够，他的探索没有成功。接着"算术化之父"波尔查诺首次把 $f'(x)$ 定义为："当 Δx 经由正、负值趋于零时，比 $\dfrac{f(x+\Delta x)-f(x)}{\Delta x}$ 无限接近地趋向的量 $f'(x)$，他强调 $f'(x)$ 不是两个零之商，也不是两个消失的量的比，而是前面指出的比所趋近的一个数"[10]。微分中值定理常被称作波尔查诺定理，尽管他的工作未引起同时代的数学家的足够重视。比如他在 1843 年构造的一个在区间上处处连续但又处处不可导的函数。我们通常认为是 40 年后的维尔斯特拉斯发现的(参考文献[1]中的 352 页)。

最后，无穷小(极限)的精确化经有教师身份的法国的柯西和德国的维尔斯特拉斯两位数学家之手完成。就教师身份而言，可以想见他们在授课中必须自圆自己讲授的内容，或者要应付学生的质疑，故而比其他非教师身份的数学家多了额外的策动。这是时代的要求和历史的必然，微积分的基础摇摇欲坠让诸多数学家的良心惴惴不安，因此几代数学家们都在为数学分析的精确化(给出精确的极限定义)付出诸多艰辛努力，这是最为根本的条件，实际上如果不是柯西和维尔斯特拉斯给出极限的精确定义，一定会有其他数学给出同样的结果。只是，他们二人的教师身份给了他们更多的机会。但是，最为重要的一点是绝对值(其几何意义表示两点间的距离)这个概念的形成给极限的精确定义提供了必要的基础，幸运的是这个概念正是维尔斯特拉斯提出的。1841 年维尔斯特拉斯首先引用"||"为绝对值符号，及后为人们所接受，且沿用至今，成为现今通用之绝对值符号。于实数范围内，此外，他亦指出，复数之绝对值就是它的"模"。到了 1905 年，赫伯特·甘斯以"||"符号表示向量之长度，有时亦称这长度为绝对值。若以向量解释复数，那么"模""长度"及"绝对值"都是一样的。这体现了赫伯特·甘斯符号之合理性，因而沿用至今。

柯西对数学发展最伟大的贡献就在于他对这门学科采用了清楚严谨的论述方式，他专心致志于为微积分中关于无穷小应用的基本原理奠定牢固的基础，以至于被认为是新思想家之首。在极限的定义："当一个变量逐次所取的值无限趋近一个定值，最终使变量的值和该定值之差要多小有多小，这个定值就叫作所有其他值的极限"中，尽管使用了描述性语言"无限趋近""一个变量趋于它的极限"，但是，他的

"当一个变量的数值这样无限地减小,使之收敛到极限零,那么人们就说这个变量为无穷小"的定义澄清了令前人迷惑的无穷小概念,而且把无穷小的概念从行而上学的束缚中解放出来。不难看出,柯西的极限定义仍与时间和运动有牵连。

维尔斯特拉斯进一步将极限和连续性概念加以严密和抽象化,并彻底地摆脱了几何直观。他力求避免例如一个变量趋于一个极限的直观说法,而把分析完全建立在算术基础上。他对极限的定义就是我们熟知的"$\varepsilon-\delta$"("$\varepsilon-N$")语言。"$\varepsilon-\delta$"语言,本质上是一种"邻域"观点。维尔斯特拉斯的最大功绩就在于,他使极限概念完全摆脱了几何的直观,在一般的拓扑空间可以建立[12]。

柯西迈出了第一步,他创造性地用极限定义把微积分学中的定理加以严格系统的证明,使微积分有了较坚实的理论基础。但柯西的工作也存在不足,他用动态的观点定性地描述极限定义显得不够精确。19世纪后期的数学家发现,使柯西产生逻辑矛盾的问题的原因是在奠定微积分基础的极限概念上没有摆脱几何直观,没有建立在纯粹严密的算术基础上。极限需要一个封闭的数域,而当时的有理数域对极限运算不封闭,柯西未能解决。维尔斯特拉斯、戴德金、康托尔各自经过独立深入的研究,都将微积分基础归结为实数理论并分别建立了"有界单调序列""戴德金分割"和"基本序列"的实数体系,并被称为三大实数理论,它们撑起了摇摇欲坠的微积分大厦(参考文献[9]中的149页)。因此,1900年,庞加莱在巴黎举行的"第二届国际数学大会"上自豪地说:"今天在分析中,如果我们不厌其烦地严格的话,就会发现只有三段论或归结于纯数的直觉是不可能欺骗我们的。今天我们可以宣称绝对的严密已经实现了。"[13]

20世纪60年代,罗宾逊提出了一种称为非标准分析的理论,其中无穷小被定义为一个大于零,小于任何正数的数(泊松在此之前已提出极限定义意义下的ε的存在)。虽然这种理论不会得到更多新的结果,但它加深了我们对无穷小的认识。近年来国内众多的专家学者在该研究领域取得了突破性的进展,张景中院士提出了和"ε语言"同样严格但易于被初学者所掌握的"D-语言"的极限定义:(1)D-数列极限定义:若存在恒正递增无界数列$\{D_n\}$,使得对一切n,总有$|a_n-a|<\frac{1}{D_n}$,则$\lim_{n\to\infty}a_n=a$[14]。

3 极限的精确定义是否真正揭示了无限的本质

从东西方不同传统的数学发展历程中,我们不难发现极限概念的思想和描述定义还是易于理解的。东方刘徽割圆时采用了与欧多克斯截然不同的方法解决,摆脱了来自芝诺悖论的困扰(中国春秋战国时期也有类似与无限分割相关的悖论,如"飞矢不动"与"轮不碾地"等等)。因为中国传统数学中并未明确讨论到无穷或极限这个概念,因此研究极限问题时,我们主要以西方传统数学为研究对象。

在《几何原本》第五卷的第四个定义中蕴涵着阿基米德公理:如果我们有两个同类量,那么总能找到较小者的一个倍数,使之大于较大者。可以由之证明穷竭法的基础命题:"如果从任何量中减去一个不小于它的一半的部分,从余部中再减去不小于它的一半的另一部分等等,则最后将留下一个小于任何给定的同类的量"(参考文献[1]中的284页)。而柯西对极限的描述定义,而所谓的"无限接近"以及"当一个变量逐次所取的值无限趋近一个定值,最终使变量的值和该定值之差要多小有多小……"。而且柯西的概念和定义对人们理解经典连续运动中的无穷小和连续性有很大帮助,而且在描述的严格性上大大前进了一步,因此也就更加能够使人们接近运动的内在本质。关于人们还一直在探索无穷的问题,这些探索将大大加深我们对无穷的理解,也将加深我们对运动本身的理解[10]。再看维尔斯特拉斯的算术定义("$\varepsilon-N$"的语言,以开始讨论的跑步者悖论为例:$\lim_{n\to\infty}t_n=k\Leftrightarrow\forall\varepsilon>0,\exists N$,当$n>N$,有$|t_n-k|<\varepsilon$)。

从上述极限定义粗线条的勾画中,我们可以在欧多克斯的穷竭法中发现维尔斯特拉斯的精确定义中ε的影子,在柯西的定义中发现维尔斯特拉斯的精确定义中$|t_n-k|$的表达方式:"变量的值和该定值之差。"因此,从欧多克斯到维尔斯特拉斯的极限定义在形式上是逐步算术化(从而具备可计算特征)的过程,在本质上定义本身并没有回答最初的芝诺"跑步者悖论"和后来"无穷小"的争论。也即在数学里事先假定了极限的存在:即我们可以调和量可分的两种假定,极限过程是个无限可分("尺棰命题"或者潜无限)的过程,同时我们(存在矛盾)又可以达到一个不可分割的点("非半弗斫"命题或实无限)。当然

将这种假定变成可以计算的准确的数学形式，确实并非易事。因为极限的"ε－"定义，术语抽象且符号陌生，其中的辩证关系不易搞清。$\lim\limits_{n\to\infty}t_n=k\Leftrightarrow\forall\varepsilon>0,\exists N,$ 当 $n>N,$ 有 $|t_n-k|<\varepsilon$ 中存在两个极限（$n\to N;t_n\to k$）过程，同时还有一对对称的逻辑符号"$\forall$"和"$\exists$"。这个拥有天使般面容的极限概念中，内含诸多玄机。它美丽的外表掩盖了无穷的"魔鬼"本质，隐藏了2 000余年来人类面对无限的困惑和努力。它美丽的外表下包含着"动与静"的辩证法，包含着从有限到无穷的飞跃，包含着纯洁的数学美。

个体的认识规律会反演数学史的发展历程，因此在教学中，学生自然会提出的一系列问题：既然极限描述性定义简单明白，为什么要搞个"ε－"定义？它与描述性定义有什么不同？数学家怎么会想出这种"古怪而讨厌"的定义？正如R. 柯朗与H. 罗宾所说："初次遇到它时暂时不理解是不足为怪的，遗憾的是某些课本的作者故弄玄虚，他们不做充分的准备，而只是把这个定义直接向读者列出，好像做些解释就有损于数学家的身份似的。"要弄清这些问题，只有翻开数学史，从哲学的角度认识极限法，这样不仅能帮助我们搞清极限的概念，也有助于建立正确的数学观念[15]。特别是在教学中，中国古代数学家的视角和处理方式，当是一个很好的HPM案例。

极限的概念与运动（无限分割）有关，因此极限的概念必须要调和量可分的两种假定，否则就会面临芝诺悖论致使运动不能。既然极限的定义与无穷（无限）有关，我们的思维必须完成从有限到无限的飞跃，这里在我们的心智中既然假设了它的存在，那么我们就坚信一个同样的动作一经开始就会永无止境地进行下去。当然我们还是常常会不假思索地将有限思维领域的诸多法则推广到无限的世界里，这样我们就会犯一些幼稚的错误，毕竟有限与无限之间有一条不可逾越的鸿沟。

4 简短结语

"量可分"的两个假设对应着哲学上的不可知论和可知论的两种观点。我们要认识世界，倘若"一个量无限可分"，我们也只能先视之为"一个量是有非常多的极微小的不可分部分组成"来认识它，随着这个微小部分数量级的减小，我们相信我们会越来越接近要认识的目标的。因为在我们的内心深处坚信一个动作可以无限次地重复，比如自然数列，虽然我们不知道是否存在一个无穷大，但是我们可以无限地接近它。

极限的概念正是这种认识论的具体体现：给定一个动作"$|t_n-k|<\varepsilon$"，就可以重复操作下去。每操作一次即取得一个"N"，随着"N"增大我们会逐渐接近我们的极限。或者称之为一个认识目标，但这个过程会永远地继续下去，永远也不会达到这个目标，这只是一个波浪式前进、螺旋式上升的过程。

回到"二分法悖论"上来，$t_n=\sum\limits_{n=1}^{\infty}t_n=\frac{1}{2}k+\frac{1}{4}k+\frac{1}{8}k+\frac{1}{2^n}k+\cdots=k$，给其描述：只要 n 充分大，t_n 就会无限地接近 k，记作：$\lim\limits_{n\to\infty}t_n=k\Leftrightarrow\forall\varepsilon>0,\exists N,$ 当 $n>N,$ 有 $|t_n-k|<\varepsilon$，这样通过准确的极限的定义，从而给出计算无穷级数和的方法，当然关键是求极限的一些方法。这种以精确的极限定义为基础的数学计算，只是在"量无限可分"的前提下对我们所观察到的"可以到达B点"的一个解释。

极限的精确定义是微积分理论体系的基石，极限的精确定义真的解决了无穷问题所带来的困扰了吗？这仍是一个值得探究的问题。但是正如M. 克莱因对"二分法悖论"的分析：所有无限个时间间隔加在一起等于k，得到k的数学分析完全脱离了物理过程，但结果仍是一致的。并以此说明，人们只有通过引入极限甚至是人造的概念才能建立自然的秩序。也许人类的数学仅仅是一个可行的方案，也许自然本身更为复杂或者并没有什么固有的设计。但是，数学仍不失为一种探索，是表示和掌握自然的一般方法[16]。在数学领域中的极限定义的精确化过程，也是如此。

参考文献

[1] [美] H. 伊夫斯. 欧阳绛译. 数学史概论 [M]. 太原：山西经济出版社，1993:283.

[2] 梁宗巨. 数学历史典故 [M]. 沈阳：辽宁教育出版社，1992:444-445.

[3] 李迪. 中外数学史教程 [Z]. 福州：福建教育出版社，1993:41.

[4] 段耀勇，杨朝明. 反证法的历史沿革 [A]. 武警学院学报 [J]. Vol.19(4). 2003.86－88.

[5] 邹大海.刘徽的无限思想及其解释[A].自然科学史研究[J].14(1).1995.12—21.
[6] 邹大海.《墨经》"次"概念与不可分量[A].自然科学史研究[J]19(3);2000.222—233.
[7] 郭书春.古代世界数学泰斗刘徽[M].济南:山东科技出版社,1992.321.
[8] 段耀勇.浅谈刘徽的"割圆术"与微积分[A].高等数学研究[J].1999.65—66.
[9] 周后卿.对微积分中无穷小思想的认识[A].邵阳学院学报(自然科学)[J].vol.2(5).2003.148.
[10] 高山.无穷研究简史[A].http：//www.oursci.org/ency/math/025.htm.
[11] Stuart Hollingdale. Makers of Mathematics. Dover Publications：New York,pp30—32.
[12] 李经文.极限理论的发展及其历史评价[A].邵阳师范高等专科学校学报[J].vol.23(5).2001.18.
[13] 纪志刚.分析算术化的历史回溯[A].自然辩证法通讯.2003,vol.25(4)
[14] 吴振英,陈湛本.论极限的思想方法[A].广州大学学报(自然科学版)[J].vol.2(5).2003.411.
[15] 刘云章.极限法的哲学思考[A].中学数学教学参考[J].2002(7).1.
[16] M·克莱因.李宏魁(译).数学:确定性的丧失[M].长沙:湖南科学技术出版社,1999.361—62.

The Approach to Understand the Precise Definition of Limit: the Wisdom from Mathematics of Ancient China

Duan Yaoyong

(School of Intelligence Policing, China People's Police University, Langfang, Hebei, 065000.)

Abstract Limits present us with a grand paradox. Every major concept of calculus—derivative, continuity, integral, convergence/divergence—is defined in terms of limits. Limit is the most fundamental concept of calculus; in fact, limit is what distinguishes at the most basic level what we call calculus from algebra, geometry, and the rest of mathematics. Therefore, in terms of the orderly and logical development of calculus, limits must come first. Actually, it's concerning of infinity/infinitesimal. And the intelligence of mankind is always tested and puzzled by the problem of infinite. The infinite named demon is everywhere in the field of human being's intellectuality, while we only possess the limited methods and tools to study it. Fortunately, we have contrived mathematics in which the definition of limit is given by great mathematicians Louis Cauchy and Weierstrass, and what surprises us is that the demon has a seraphic appearance.

Key words calculus; infinitude; limit

物质参与理论视野下的数学起源研究新进展[1]

陈巍　（中国科学院自然科学史研究所）

摘要　在过去一百余年中,哲学、心理学、人类学、考古学等领域对数学起源进行了大量研究,获得众多成果。近年来马拉福瑞斯、奥弗曼等学者运用自认识考古学演化出的物质参与理论(MET),为这一问题的考察提供了新的视野。结合马拉福瑞斯等学者的论述,简述了 MET 思考即物思、成为人类即人类成为、人类进化是创造性的进化等主张,以及奥弗曼以美索不达米亚的陶筹为主要对象的早期数学认知研究。

关键词　物质参与理论；数学起源；创造性物思；陶筹

数学通常被认为需要通过抽象化和逻辑推理导向某类确切结果,包括早期数学在内,绝大多数数学史研究依赖于文本,或可通过若干标准变换为文本的遗物或行为,对其表象进行阐释。由于可利用材料往往处于零星断裂、缺乏充足语境的状态,或只能通过时空错位的现代人类学调查和尺度不同的神经科学获得的间接证据协助建构,关于数学如何起源和最初演化、原始数学呈现出何种面貌、如何认识原始数学与人类思维发展的关系等问题,仍远未得到解决。早在两千多年前,苏格拉底等哲人就对此问题产生浓厚兴趣,自文艺复兴时期以来,哲学家们对包括数学在内的人类心智的性质给出诸多论述。对这类问题从历史方面展开探讨,主要是在 20 世纪人类学、心理学等学科蓬勃发展后兴起的。具备数学、文化人类学、神经生理学、认知考古和发展心理学等众多学科领域背景的学者各显所长,相互借鉴,融会各家方法,将史前的纹样、原始数字等符号与现存原始部落的认知进行参照,并寻找这些行为和认知在心理发展和脑科学中的对应解释。

近十年来,除以上各学科论述方兴未艾之外,在认知考古基础上提出的物质参与理论(material engagement theory,以下简称 MET)又赋予数学起源问题新的视角,显露出对包括史前数学在内诸多科学认知进行创新阐释的潜力。在中国学界,特别是为研究提供出土实物证据和科技分析结果的考古学界,操作链、"精神文化考古"等与史前数学思维亲缘较近的概念都并非主流,在数学史领域,对数学起源的探讨亦不多见[2],新研究方法和视野的纳入对于激活材料丰富但讨论冷清的这个领域或不无裨益。笔者不揣冒昧,尝试通过本文,在概览既往研究方法形成观点的基础上,列举 MET 的研究重心,并简述国外学者运用 MET 来透视数学起源和早期发展的研究,初步揭示该方法对研究中国材料带来的启发潜力,冀以激发同仁关注新理论和新方法并进行移植和修正后,积极进行具体问题的研究。

一、数学起源研究的传统方法

数学思维是多方面的。史前人类掌握的数学知识就复杂程度而论,很难赶得上现代接受过初等数学教育的人,但他们接受计数、进行运算,或者说发展出数学思维的潜在能力,是否与现代人具有一致性,数学思维的基础在于智人大脑的特殊生理构造,还是语言、文化和所在环境的塑造,人类思维中的数学认知与现代能够看到的资料之间是什么样的关系,显然都是关系到数学思维起源的重要问题。此前

---

[1]　本文受中国科学院青年创新促进会项目"古代东西方金银冶炼术比较研究"（项目编号：E1SQCHXM01）支持,以及国家"十四五"发展规划重大学术文化工程《（新编）中国通史》纂修工程科学技术史卷阶段性成果（项目编号：E0189001）。

[2]　邹大海,中国数学的兴起与先秦数学,石家庄:河北科学教育出版社,2001 年,第 1—90 页；郭书春主编,中国科学技术史·数学卷,北京:科学出版社,2010 年,第 1—28 页。

学者运用各学科方法，主要从先验论到建构论这一光谱上选择不同坐标，作为参加争论的立场。

关于数学知识在人类中的普遍存在性，哲学家早有关注。古希腊的柏拉图曾记录苏格拉底对从属于希腊人的一名奴隶加以"催产式"引导，使其认识到正方形的若干性质，苏格拉底进而提出"他的灵魂一定一直拥有这种知识"[3]。17世纪笛卡儿(R. Descartes，1596—1650)认为人因感知到自己思想而存在，进而世界也因自己所感知到的东西而存在，个人意识是知识的唯一来源[4]。18世纪哲学家康德(I. Kant，1724—1804)认为欧氏几何以先验的空间直觉为基础，并以此为出发点论述其先验阐释[5]。胡塞尔(E. Husserl，1859—1938)写于1936年的《几何学起源》一文中则强调几何研究的对象是"绝对的观念对象"，只能用抽象语言表述。作为揭示观念对象的工具，语言揭示观念对象是历史的，与先验主体相联系的[6]。这样，胡塞尔在保留几何认知基础的先验可能性的同时，把它的传承发展与语言挂钩。乔姆斯基(N. Chomsky，1928—　)则认为人类的数字能力本质上是从语言中抽象出来的，消除语言其他特殊功能后，保留离散的无穷性[7]。这些观点虽主要为哲学论述，但也或多或少吸取了当时数学哲学、科学史、心理学成果，并反过来对后几个领域产生很大影响，成为后世学者建立观点的学术铺垫。如布劳威尔(L. E. J. Brouwer，1881—1966)开创的认为数学陈述对应于心理构造而非客观现实的数学直觉主义即可追溯到笛卡儿的影响[8]。

伴随着近代西方殖民扩张脚步，进入各地土著社群开展调查的民族学逐渐兴起。不少西方学者在搜集资料时，会涉及当地人数学认知的情况，并积累起相当多关于原始思维中这一方面的记录。法国学者列维－布留尔(L. Lévy-Bruhl，1857—1939)对原始思维中的计数和运算进行了集中论述。他观察到原始部落并不能把数字与所计量的对象清楚分离，对应数字的词是可变而非固定的，即计数法来源于社会集体表象及与这些表象互渗的自然基础。列维－布留尔还总结了原始思维中盛行的数字神秘主义[9]。处于现代人类学建立明确规范时代前夕的列维－布留尔，其论述所据材料存在许多问题，不过他的观点启发了瑞士心理学家皮亚杰(J. Piaget，1896—1980)。包括数学抽象思维在内的认知发展是皮亚杰等建构主义心理学家所关注的核心领域之一，他们认为随着儿童的成长，基本的认知结构经过组织与适应、失衡与平衡等过程，从童年到青少年时期逐渐完善运算思维[10]。与之相应，从社会角度看，数学也可视为一种文化发明，在数学史上逐步完善。不过，就像受苏格拉底引导的奴隶有可能沾染希腊文化一样，皮亚杰等以现代社会中的儿童为对象所作实验，也存在可能受到其他来源的数学思维暗示的影响。

另一派习性学家则认同认知和知觉范畴先于个体经验而存在，它们能够适应外部环境[11]。对此，21世纪初，S. Dehaene，P. Pica，V. Izard和E. Spelke等几名学者，以生活在亚马逊丛林里、几乎没有机会接触外来数学思维的Mundurukú部落为对象，合作探讨了包括儿童和成年人在内的部落成员的几何和计数能力与部落语言之间的关系。他们先后发表了一系列文章，从实证角度探讨人类数学思维具有普遍存在的先验性和向复杂化发展的建构性的双层性质。他们发现，在缺乏5以上数字词汇的情况下，这个部落能够对超出范围的更大数字做出比较和增补，但无法对大于4或5的数字进行精确算术[12]。该部落的儿童和成人能够自发利用基本几何概念，把点、线、平行线或直角与同类其他对象进行

---

[3] Plato, Meno, W. R. M. Lamb, trans., Cambridge(Mass.)：Harvard University Press, 1952, pp. 305－313.

[4] 笛卡儿，谈谈方法，王太庆译，北京：商务印书馆，2000年，第28－30页。

[5] 康德，纯粹理性批判，蓝公武译，北京：商务印书馆，1997年，第51－56页。

[6] 胡塞尔，欧洲科学的危机与超越论的现象学，王炳文译，北京：商务印书馆，2001年，第427－458页。

[7] N. Chomsky, Language and problems of knowledge, Cambridge(Mass.)：The MIT Press, 1987, p. 169.

[8] L. Brouwer, "Intuitionism and formalism", Bulletin of the American Mathematical Society, 1913, (Nov.)：81－96.

[9] 列维－布留尔，原始思维，丁由译，北京：商务印书馆，1981年，第175－218页。

[10] J. Piaget, The child's conception of number, New York：Routledge, 1952.

[11] I. Eibl－Eibesfeldt, Human ethology, New York：Aldine de Gruyter, 1989, p. 9.

[12] P. Pica, et al., Exact and approximative arithmetic in an Amazonian indigene group, Science, 2004, 306(5695)：499－503.

区分,还能利用几何地图中距离、角度和感觉的关系来定位隐藏物体[13]。在把数字向空间映射方面,部落成员可以把数字词按大小指向一条线段中距端点相应远近的位置,但从数字分布来看,映射呈对数而非线性转换,即划分刻度为10的线段,其中点对应的数字在3和4之间,而非5和6[14]。对于欧几里得几何学的基本观念,如三角形内角和为180°、通过直线外给定一点存在单一平行线,部落成员的得分高于随机结果水平,但这些直觉通常仅限于平面,少数情况下部落成员还可在球面情况下对这些直觉进行灵活调整[15]。经过比较,可发现亚马逊雨林里远离现代文明的原始部落,儿童和成人所拥有的空间和算术能力,与现代文明里未受教育的儿童相差不远。这意味着一些基本的数学观念在原始思维里很可能已经存在了,但它们要进一步发展离不开语言、符号等更抽象的事物。此外,萨林斯(M. Sahlins,1930—2021)基于莫斯的礼物交换总结了对原始社群中等价交换、随亲疏程度和社会等级变动的分配比例,以及种种因素影响下的相对稳定的交易价值与围绕其波动的交易价格[16]。萨林斯揭示的现象在学界很有影响,对研讨史前贸易网络也很有启发,但从考古遗物很难发现贸易品之间的确切比例,故而也难以估量当时人们对比例计算的认知。

发展心理学与人类学相结合的方法为探讨数学起源提供了当代参照,但要发掘历史上原始社会数学发展,还需要对考古遗物进行仔细研究。其中一方面在于人脑进化出适宜数学思维运行的结构,以此作为抽象化思维发展的生理基础。数学的萌芽被视为智人出现前后人类思维加速化转折的突出标志,故智人与进化树上相邻的尼安德特人的大脑差异尤其受到关注。当然,对数字的感知甚至可以追溯到更远,前面提到的亚马逊原始部落对4及以下数字的认知,与包括灵长类在内的部分哺乳动物和鸟类中都不稀见,这被称作"数感"(number sense)[17]。而人类还具有制作工具的能力,与昆虫鸟类筑巢不同,制造石器的技艺必须通过演示练习才能代际传授。这的确要求人类在黑猩猩使用简单工具之上再进一步,在大脑中营造出更加复杂的"预见性反思"图景。从有目标但无规律的石器制造,向在头脑中预设层级化操作,再到对更精细材料的细致加工,既需要对上肢肌肉的灵敏控制,又需要头脑中对操作程序形成记忆的存取。通过对尼安德特人和智人之间大脑差异进行细致比较,发现尽管尼安德特人脑容量略大于智人,但其前后距离较长,影响神经传导和能量利用效率。智人大脑则近于更紧致高效的球形,具有更加突出的额叶、顶叶及小脑[18]。这些部位里,顶叶区参与定向、注意、对刺激的感知、计划基础的感觉运动转换、视觉空间整合、想象、自我意识、工作和长期记忆、数字处理和工具使用,如手指计数和将其用数字形式阐述出来,就与顶叶内沟和角回,以及顶叶相邻区域的活动密切相关[19]。与顶叶隆起相伴随的楔前区增大则有利于认知的专门化。小脑不仅主要控制运动相关的功能,如运动的协调和平衡,而且还与空间处理、工作记忆、语言、社会认知和情感处理有关。这些结构的出现,或可解释为经过长时间跨度的与人类实践互动后神经元再循环(neuronal recycling)这一进化假说的结果[20]。

与史前遗物密切相关的另一方面,在于被视为能够反映史前人类记数行为的遗物的发现。不少遗物上都带有刻痕,或者其尺寸形状带有某些规律。这些遗物是否能视为具有原始计数功能的工具,需要

---

[13] S. Dehaene, et al., "Core knowledge of geometry in an Amazonian indigene group", Science, 2006, 311(5759): 381−384.

[14] S. Dehaene, et al., "Log or linear? distinct intuitions of the number scale in western and Amazonian indigene cultures", Science, 2008(5880), 320: 1217−1220.

[15] V. Izard, et al., "Flexible intuitions of Euclidean geometry in an Amazonian indigene group", PNAS, 2011, 108(24): 9782−9787.

[16] 萨林斯,石器时代经济学,张经纬、郑少雄、张帆译,北京:生活·读书·新知三联书店,2019年,第221−376页。

[17] S. Dehaene, Number sense: how the mind creates mathematics, New York: Oxford University Press, 1997, pp. 13−40.

[18] S. Neubauer, J−J. Hublin, P. Gunz, "The evolution of modern human brain shape", Science Advance, 2018, (4): eaao5961.

[19] M. Amalric, S. Dehaene, "Origins of the brain networks for advanced mathematics in expert mathematicians", PNAS, 2016, 113(18):4909−4917.

[20] S. Dehaene, L. Cohen, "Cultural recycling of cortical maps", Neuron, 2007, 56(2): 384−398.

一些衡量标准。例如刻纹在长度、间距和方向上具有一致性,在器物表面具有能够与装饰功能相区别的分布,标记方式可以和当时已知的自然现象相联系,器物磨损反映的使用与保存状况,以及微痕显示标记是否由同类工具或工艺制作出来等等[21]。不少学者认为发现于南非的莱邦博骨(Lebombo bone)是最早的符合以上多个标准的遗物,其放射性碳同位素测年为距今4.42至4.3万年之间,与数学相关的特征为上面带有29个刻痕,推测可能与月相周期计数有关[22]。另一具有相近载体的遗物是发现于尼罗河源头附近的伊尚戈骨(Ishango bone),年代为距今2.2至2万年之间,它上面的刻痕可划分成不对称的三列,引发研究者做不同的解释[23]。然而,需要注意的是,仅仅根据遗物本身来概括其所含数学信息显然带有极大风险,诸多因素为阐释带来影响效果不同的向量,数学角度仅是提供众多可能阐释中的一种,关于它们数学含义的解释高度依赖于观察者的主观倾向,对于遗物携带的更多歧义性细节则无从解释。例如在显微镜观察下,莱邦博骨一端折断,29或非刻痕总数,这样之前的目的论解释就面临失效的窘境[24]。伊尚戈骨也存在类似情况。再如法国学者马尔沙克把法国La Marche遗址出土距今约1.5万年的带刻痕的旧石器时代鹿角制品上的点与线符号阐释成数字与月相记录[25],德埃里克也论证该物件上发现的标记可被解释为具有形态和空间分布的复杂意指的预设记忆[26],但他们的观点因无法证实或证伪而受到不少质疑,甚至有学者从别的角度说它实际上是一件乐器[27]。

比起侧重于围绕单件遗物展开的论证,苏联学者弗罗洛夫(B. Frolov, 1939—2005)于20世纪70年代初对旧石器时代遗物提供的数学认知线索进行了相当全面的概括。他在《旧石器时代图形中的数字》[28]一书中总结了缺乏文字记录的石器时代先民展现出的数学思维。比较于寻求对特定遗物或对个别部落所做人类学调查的阐述,弗罗洛夫更注重论证原始人头脑中复现事物过程中存在的"预见性反思"对数量概念发展的决定性影响。他论述了原始人可能拥有相当多方面的数学技能,它们很可能是经过数十万年实践,由工具和加工技法带来的结果逐渐演变为具有数学意蕴的表现。这些技能包括制造石器的"标准化"操作、对燃料和食物空间分布的估算、器物装饰性划痕中的带有秩序的平行线条、食物分配和居住场所涉及的平均对应想法、以人整体或部分为单位的长度和面积的度量、最简单的天文观测带来的对空间和时间规律性的觉知、以时空规律节奏衍生的记数分组、拟人人造物所用比例与尺度,以及对诸如5,7这样数字的习惯性使用等等。不过在考古遗物统计中,被认为原始人倾向使用的特殊数字,仍有可能是对特定聚落中特定遗物的孤立解释,在其他语境中缺乏统计上的明显优势,把7作为周期记数并从天文学角度为其溯源,难以排除用以今人眼光去把遗物进行选择过滤。仅可运用少量数字,也或许并非只受到尚未充分发展的语言的限制,还有可能是拥有的同种事物很少多于五六个,以至于重

---

[21] K. Overmann, The material origin of numbers: insights from the archaeology of the ancient Near East, Piscataway: Gorgias Press, 2019, pp. 141—143.

[22] P. Beaumont, "Border Cave—A progress report", South African Journal of Science, 1973, 69: 41—46.

[23] V. Pletser, D. Huylebrouck, "The Ishango artefact: the missing base 12 link", Forma, 1999, 14: 339—346.

[24] P. Beaumont, R. Bednarik, "Tracing the emergence of paleoart in sub-Saharan Africa", Rock Art Research, 2013, 30(1): 33—54.

[25] A. Marshack, "Upper paleolithic notation and symbol", Science, 1972, 178(4063): 817—828. 对其质疑参见 D. Schmandt-Besserat, Before writing, Austin(TX): University of Texas Press, 1992, p. 160.

[26] F. d'Errico, "A new model and its implications for the origin of writing: the La Marche Antler revisited", Cambridge Archaeological Journal, 1995, 5(2): 163—206.

[27] S. de Beaune, "L'art préhistorique, support de mémoire", Les Grands Dossiers des Sciences Humaines, 2008, 11: 22—27, 转引自 O. Schlaudt, "Type and token in the prehistoric origins of numbers", Cambridge Archaeological Journal, 2020, 30(4): 629—646.

[28] Б. Фролов, Числа в графике палеолита, Novosibirsk: Nauka, Sib. otd-nie, 1974. 其文字内容基本被译为英文,见 B. Frolov, "Numbers in paleolithic graphic art and the initial stages in the development of mathematics"[Part 1], Soviet Anthropology and Archeology, 1977, 16(3—4): 142—166; [Part 2], Soviet Anthropology and Archeology, 1978, 17(1): 73—93; [Part 3], Soviet Anthropology and Archeology, 1978, 17(3): 41—74; [Part 4], Soviet Anthropology and Archeology, 1978, 17(4): 61—113.

复计数发展来的抽象化数字也以此为限,进一步影响着同时起到存储数字信息作用的语言规则的发展。

二、物质参与理论的要点

从上节所涉内容,可看到关于数学起源的讨论,目前处于多学科齐头并进的态势,但无论考古学、心理学还是人类学,在方法论上与史前认知之间似乎都或多或少存在难以消弭的张力,近年来活跃的MET 吸收前述各学科成果,从扩大思维边界到物,再聚焦于物来反观于思维或许有助于关注点的腾挪,或有助于更灵活地理解史前数学观念。

谈论MET,有必要先对其发展的直接渊源认知考古进行简介。这个考古学分支领域诞生于20世纪70年代,是对此前十年中坚持严格按照物质证据来解释过去的过程考古学的反响,它从一开始就充分运用发展心理学、进化神经科学等工具,对物质形态的变化所揭示的人类认知复杂化、石器制作技术的发展,以及语言起源等问题展开探讨[29]。英国考古学家伦福儒(C. Renfrew,1937—)是认知考古的主要推动者,20世纪80年代初,他提出一种"认知过程主义"(cognitive processualism),即保留过程主义把客观性置于首位的传统,并融入认知和符号因素,以及强调思想观念是任何社会中活跃的组织力量,考察古人如何思考,甚至可能思考些什么,由于物质文化在构成文化现实中发挥着积极作用,认知行为可以通过考古发现的物质形式得到确认。伦福儒把印度河流域哈拉帕文明的若干重量规则分布的方形石块认定为砝码,从而探讨这里居民的测量实践与定量思想,该研究因具备可验证性而被视为认知考古学最重要的一项早期成果。[30]认知考古学至今仍把人类学、灵长类考古学带来的现代人类与非人类物种行为参照,与心理学、神经影像学实验方法得出的大脑认知功能等信息获取方法作为基础,不仅对旧石器时代的早期认知发展进行考察,还涉足弓箭、陷阱等较复杂但难以从发掘中获得直接证据的技术。

MET 是认知考古进一步向哲学转向的体现。主要倡导者马拉福瑞斯(L. Malafouris)是伦福儒的学生,从21世纪初开始致力于构建这一理论体系,该理论最完整的阐述和应用范例可见于2013年出版的《物品如何塑造思维》一书[31],据谷歌学术搜索显示,该书出版至2022年初还不到十年间,被引用近1500次,在考古学思想和语言学、心理学、哲学等领域都产生较大影响。近年许多论文里,马拉福瑞斯对MET 的要点继续加以提炼和论证,限于篇幅,本文仅引述马拉福瑞斯等学者概括的三个主要方面,而忽略大部分相关理论基础的分析。这三个方面分别是:思考即物思(thinking is thinging)[32];成为人类即人类成为(becoming human is human becoming);人类进化是创造性的进化[33]。前两项从字面看近乎是文字游戏,仔细了解后却不难察觉到其中蕴涵着研究出发点的重大转变。

所谓思考即物思,在《物品如何塑造思维》等书中称作"事物的认知生命"(cognitive life of things),对应于思维边界由此前仅限于大脑,不但扩充到包括手、脚等身体其他部位,更要包容个体以外的文化和物质世界,从而突破"神经中心主义",即由神经科学提供的神经结构及网络扫描结果支配人类思想来

---

[29] K. Overmann, F. Coolidge, eds., Squeezing minds from stones: cognitive archaeology and the evolution of the human mind, New York: Oxford University Press, 2019, pp. 2—5.

[30] C. Renfrew, Towards an archaeology of mind: an inaugural lecture delivered before the University of Cambridge on 30th November 1982, Cambridge: Cambridge University Press, 1982.

[31] L. Malafouris, How things shape the mind: a theory of material engagement, Cambridge (Mass.): The MIT Press, 2013.

[32] Thinging 一词源于海德格尔《论事物》一文:"如果我们让事物从世界化的世界中存在于它的 thinging 中,那么我们就是在把事物当作事物来思考",马拉福瑞斯对这个术语除保留其"聚集"的原始含义外,主要意图为"阐明并提请注意在与物质事物一起思考(和感受)的'实际场合'中实例化的认知生活的具体种类",本文将其与主要指"人思"的 thinking 相对,译为"物思"。参见 M. Heidegger, The thing, in Poetry, language, thought, A. Hofstadter, trans., New York: Harper & Row, 1975, pp. 161—184;L. Malafouris, "Creative thinging: the feeling of and for clay", Pragmatics & Cognition, 2014, 22(1): 140—158.

[33] L. Malafouris, "Making hands and tools: steps to a process archaeology of mind", World Archaeology, 2021, 53(1): 38—55; "How does thinking relate to tool making"?, Adoptive Behavior, 2021, 29(2): 107—121.

源的论述框架。马拉福瑞斯借由导盲棒作为例子入手,论证在人体与外界之间,存在着大脑、身体和文化交融的由物质参与的中间层。以往学者对于这些物质的认识以"人类思维创造事物,事物的形态反映人类思维"的因果性为经典论述方向,仅强调"思考"(thinking)造成结果的一面。MET 则强调大脑并不是独立存在的主体,思考是身体与外界互动融合的结果,是一个由包括人工制品、文化实践和社会制度等各种物质符号持续生产、使用、交换和循环构成的动态定位"过程"。物质并非完全被动地由思维赋予表征,而是积极参与思考的构建(thinging)。例如人类行为技能的熟练性,显然难以仅仅对着空气演练即可获得,而是需要物质的参与。物质本身也不是一成不变的,而是随着长时间积累的渐进变化,逐渐拥有在互动中引起操作者特定行为和心理反应的能力。在这一机制下,物质性成为知识传承者向自己行为和心理输入知识和技能的储存库。

马拉福瑞斯给出了不少例子来演示事物对人类认知的塑造。其中一个是约公元前 1500—1200 年间迈锡尼人使用的泥板,而不是泥板上书写的信息。人们可以在湿润的泥板上书写,泥板的表面会在几小时到一天内迅速干燥,这时上面的文字就不能更改。这意味着人们要么在几小时内迅速写完所有信息,要么把信息存储到小型碎片上再集中使用。这种物质性促使泥板通过强化空间属性来引导注意力和提供给读者更多视觉线索。其后果就是为便于识别和感知以后要刻的信息,通常要用手画出几条贯穿整个碑文宽度的横线。特别是在细长的石板上,文字的第一个字是用大符号写的,段落之间用一到两条空行分开。在设定的空间格式内重复标准公式,对单个条目进行仔细的空间分隔,在连续条目内对词汇和表意项目进行随机格式化,以及总体上系统地使用表意文字作为参考和检索的工具,促进记录和检索技术得到明显发展[34]。这一个例子很容易让我们想到目前正时兴的同样强调书写材料物质性的写本学研究,MET 或可为中国学者研究写本提供另一层面的视角与方法工具[35]。

另一个例子与手斧等旧石器有关。马拉福瑞斯不赞成传统的考古类型学划分,认为分类的整齐性掩盖了实践层面的复杂性和可变性,而过程考古倡导的操作链方法中对认知与实践的分配也是基于现代假设的目的论,这时从 MET 角度进行讨论或有助于推进理解。具体所转化的问题就是:石料敲击者的思维在何处结束,而石器从何处开始?此前学者对这一问题的回答路径是认为石器只不过是人内部思维预先形成的想法或认知过程的产物或外部表征,而这一过程随后在外部物理世界中得以实现。因此考古学家只能利用手斧所提供的任何"外部"和"间接"的残留认知痕迹来产生对过去思维方式的推断。为论证石器可被视为能够改变和扩展人类祖先认知结构的能动的认知中介,马拉福瑞斯首先检视了训练猴子使用单个耙子或长短耙子的组合来取回食物,以及缺乏经验的现代人制作石器时大脑活动的扫描结果,其结果显示人和猴子近似地依赖于脑部顶额的(parieto-frontal)感知—运动和抓握功能,以及与视觉特化有关的背侧顶内沟(dorsal intraparietal sulcus)。在更熟练的石器制作者那里,大脑的前额叶和右脑的贡献则显著增大。马拉福瑞斯对此解读为"在任何关于人类大脑显著扩张的化石证据之前,石器不是人类大脑的成就;相反,它们是人类大脑的一个机会,换句话说,一个积极的物质参与的机会"。

就手斧这类器物来说,此前学者提出过其对称性源于作为屠宰工具效率的适应性手段,或论证它为早期象征符号,或作为古人类审美意识标志等纷繁看法,但这些看法背后都存在一个手斧的对称性是"有意识的刻意"产物。马拉福瑞斯却认为手斧问题的根源并非制作者"意图"的确切内容,而在于人类认知进化中这些意向性状态的实际性质、位置和构成的问题。"人类,而不是其他动物,是如何拥有我们称之为'意向性'的特殊属性的?人类是如何以及何时意识到自己和他人行为的意向性的?"探讨这两个问题需要关注手斧具有何种意向性特征,以及导致手斧出现的意向的内部结构与具体执行等方面。此

---

[34] L. Malafouris, How things shape the mind: a theory of material engagement, Cambridge (Mass.): The MIT Press, 2013, pp. 69—73.

[35] 例如有学者参考马拉福瑞斯和其他写本学研究者观点,对更大范围内地中海东部青铜时代书写实践进行讨论,参见 P. Steele, "Material Entanglements of Writing Practices in the Bronze Age Aegean and Cyprus", Sustainability, 2020, 12: 10671.

前学者的论述里,"意图"已经存在于制造者头脑中,他决定着敲击的顺序、力量、方向和角度,敲击的动作、目标和产品与思维意图是分开的。MET 则把意图转移到敲击石头的定向行动,敲击和剥落有一部分是由石料本身构成的,石料和敲击者身体都是敲击意图的组成部分,并"涉及肢体、物体、视觉子系统和声学子系统(因为成功地移除一个石片会有独特的声音)之间的复杂反馈"。石料的性质决定敲击意图须在行动中发现,这影响到敲击者认识石料性质这一无形知识,并依据接触感觉形成隐性思维,熟练的史前敲击者经过约 200 小时练习,其手指、手腕和前臂的准确抓握等操作能力得以显著增强,手和工具的功能可见性交互促进改变,敲打石料的操作仅需几秒钟即可完成,这对工具的设计和制造过程中的感觉层次产生重要影响。由此意图与行动变得重合,消除了思维与物质之间的界限。[36]

所谓"成为人类即人类成为",指相对于提供一种关于人类起源的观点,关注最终产品的"成为人类"实际只是一个已完成的过去事件,MET 所说的"人类成为"更侧重于过程,它无始无终地持续着。"成为人类"造成遗传上固定的、预先规定的和继承的生物进化与可变的、建构的和社会传播/学习的文化两者之间的割裂,同时它又隐含地假设智人发展有一个不可逆的从前现代到现代性进步的趋势,一旦我们的物种从解剖学、认知学或行为学上达到"现代性",成为的过程即宣告停止,随后学者的关注点从一个局限于自然和生物进化范围内的世界向到文化构建的意义和历史转变的世界过渡或提升,从而为后者提供稳定而统一的人性基础。我们常听到的"用旧石器时代形成的大脑面对信息化时代"即是这类倾向的通俗化说法。然而,即便是在现代社会,人类的演化也从未停止,自然和文化演进的历程不能割裂,在论述中没有必要设置一个固定的分隔点。人类智慧的本质如看作是一种持续成为的模式,仍然受制于深刻的重组。

"人类成为"的生理学理论基础是大脑的再可塑性(metaplasticity)。即我们的大脑和思维由每天与文化实践和物质世界的接触而引起的终生持续变化。这种现象从 20 世纪末以来得到发育神经科学家的大量讨论,促使考古学者开始反思以往大脑在智人出现后即稳定于生物常量的观点。在 MET 中,人类大脑进化的标志,与其说是不断增加的复杂性和模块思维的专业化,更在于允许环境和文化引发的大脑回路结构和功能变化的投射灵活性,而物质世界与思维积极接触对其引发的变化,是理解人类认知的独特特征以及它如何变化的关键。MET 将神经科学中的再可塑概念调整为用来描述大脑和文化之间的主动构成性交织的突现属性[37],即不仅是大脑各区域之间互动性因达到一定阈值的刺激事件发生变化,而且物质文化也与任何其他脑区一样,在人类认知系统中竞争着一席之地,互动性不是与实践或物质世界互动的大脑"内部"结果,而是连续的、与物质世界共存的[38]。

前面提到的迈锡尼文化泥板,以及手斧的例子,都同时显示存在这一阐释的可能性。马拉福瑞斯另以南非布隆伯斯洞窟(Blombos Cave)中石器时代的赭石标记为例论证它与"人类成为",或思维与物质文化各自可塑性之间的关系。[39]鉴于标记在史前遗址中的常见性,这一例证无疑具有示范价值。与之前例子类似,此前学者多从表征角度尝试把标记预设性地解释为抽象符号,它是通过某种运算机制把外界信息在大脑中处理后,再外化出来的呈现,进而作为人类心智发展到一定水平"成为人类"的标志。从这一角度,绘制标记的过程、标记本身都被排除在思维之外。但对于材料,它的表征性功能只是当代解释

---

[36] L. Malafouris, How things shape the mind: a theory of material engagement, Cambridge (Mass.): The MIT Press, 2013, pp. 153—177; L. Malafouris, "Making hands and tools: steps to a process archaeology of mind", World Archaeology, 2021, 53(1): 38—55.

[37] L. Malafouris, "Metaplasticity and the human becoming: principles of neuroarchaeology", Journal of Anthropological Sciences, 2010, 88: 49—72; "Metaplasticity and the primacy of material engagement", Time and Mind, 2015, 8(4): 351—371.

[38] L. Malafouris, How things shape the mind: a theory of material engagement, Cambridge (Mass.): The MIT Press, 2013, pp. 45—53.

[39] L. Malafouris, "Mark making and human becoming", Journal of Archaeological Method and Theory, 2021, 28: 95—119.

者强加上去的,其本身并没有什么内在证据。因此对具体标记做阐释实际意义远小于从它们入手观察原始人对利用标记制作符号的能力发展程度。在 MET 中,赭石既可以研磨成粉状构成图案线条,也可呈片状作为雕刻图案的平面材料,还能充作尖锐笔头在砾岩片上绘画。它既提供了一个表面,也提供了学习画标记、观察和理解线条的媒介,作为一种被感知的对象,是做标记本身,而不是标记的符号解释实际参与到"人类成为"过程中。

马拉福瑞斯建议从我们自己入手来体验标记制作,由此提出两个问题:布隆伯斯洞窟的交叉平行线标记是由什么构成的,以及当我们看到这些标记时,会有什么样的感受。它们似乎可以很容易地由我们在纸上模仿绘制原始标记,并且把成品与原样加以比较后得出一个答案。但这时我们须记得今天的人们自幼学习用笔,以及目的性的摹写,造成结果突出、过程隐去的偏颇。如前文提到思考即物思所说,这里采用 MET 视角可绕开这种偏颇。视觉观察、持笔手势、赭石颜料与显示痕迹融为一个中间空间,它们可视为几乎同时暂时性出现的姿势轨迹,而看似平行的轨迹之间,人的眼睛和手与颜料、颜料与划痕之间通过赭石尺寸、平滑或尖锐性,以及对象平面的表面特征等物质性相互连接和反馈。从图案内容来说,它也不一定带有预设意图,其构成有可能在前一步完成后自然产生下一步的需求,如若干组平行线交叉形成的菱形网格,其横向交点处于同一直线上,就容易促使标记者将这些交点连接,这又将成为下一次落笔的基础。在即兴式创作中,标记本身改变了人类对世界的感知关系,并为创造性的材料参与和材料想象提供了新的机会[40],这种对物质性新功能的发现,与大脑思维的积极接触,向我们展示"人的成为"中的一环。值得一提的是,MET 并不贬低已有的信息获取方法,但要用它获取更强的解释力,显然需要转换未来获取信息侧重的方向。

MET 的第三方面要点是"人类进化是创造性的进化",即人类通过与物质世界的创造性接触而成为人类,人类并不是简单地在生物遗传性上自我重复,而是通过创造性物质参与而构建改造着成为自身的条件,自然与文化因素相互依赖、相互作用的运行和演进促使考古记录呈现出"人类成为"的变化,这种变化的因素被称作"创造性物思"(creative thinging),这一概念特别指定了人类通过与事物和生成形式的原料相互饱和专注参与,来发现物质符号的新品种和能动符号的模式的倾向。马拉福瑞斯将创造性物思之于"人类成为",类比为自然选择之于"成为人类"。通过自然选择进行的适应是"自然选择论者"进化逻辑的产物,被视为生物体对外部环境产生的选择压力的反击或回应方式。适应发生在离散的、预先形成的实体或过程(人类或环境)之间。这反过来又假设这些实体或过程相互作用(适应)但不参与。它们不参与是因为它们的适应是预先存在的。然而,作为过程的创造性物思却不是指人类对环境的行动,而是与环境一起并通过环境的行动,它是参与的,这意味着它关联于跨行为的共同构成,而非相互的因果关系[41]。有机体和环境、身体和世界是耦合的动态系统,其耦合是如此密集,以至于不可能将因果分开。各种各样的生命形式都在改变它们的物质环境。但在"人类成为"中,制造的意义是不同的。我们是智人(Homo faber),不仅仅是因为我们制造东西,而且还因为我们被制造,并通过它们生活[42]。创造性物思不是某种预先赋予的和静态的适应,而是在制造者和材料之间的建设性对话中不断产生和转化。如前所述,人类是可塑的生物,与我们制造的物质形式的可塑性密不可分,人类的认知成为一个未完成的过程,可以进行扩展的重组和修复性的修正,因此,有可能处于一个持续的创造性进化的永久状态。

创造性物思可以很容易从对爵士乐钢琴家演奏时大脑前额叶活动的变化伴随着新皮质感觉运动区(影响音乐表演发生的组织和执行)的广泛激活,以及边缘结构(调节动机和情绪基调)的失活现象中观

---

[40] M. Koukouti, L. Malafouris, "Material imagination: an anthropological perspective", in A. Abraham, ed., The Cambridge handbook of the imagination, Cambridge: Cambridge University Press: pp. 30−46.

[41] J. Dewey, A. Bentley, Knowing and the Known, Boston: Beacon Press,1949, p. 108。转引自 L. Malafouris, "Making hands and tools: steps to a process archaeology of mind", World Archaeology, 2021,53(1):38−55.

[42] D. Ihde, L. Malafouris, "Homo faber revisited: postphenomenology and material engagement theory", Philosophy & Technology, 2019, 32(2): 195−214.

察到。而对于史前事物,马拉福瑞斯举了一个制陶的例子。陶工在发掘材料的可见功能方面有大量即兴创作,并与物质的力量和形成技能相适应,但不迷恋新奇。制陶过程中呈现出的创造性意识的多样性,被称为关于(of)和对于(for)黏土的感觉。它们采取了两种与创造性物思相关的物质意识形式。第一种可看作是材料对意识产生改变作用的表现,关于和对于黏土的感觉都是随着时间和材料的参与而自然发展的,陶工通过对熟练的、中介性行动体验的隐性参与,获得这种对材料可见功能给出情感的、动态的身体微调、记忆和选择性反应的混合体,而陶工也往往把黏土描述为一种温暖的、有生命力的、有灵魂的或有精神作用的材料,因之产生身体运动和大脑区域性活动的回应。他们的感知—行动循环和动作是动态耦合的,并与手头材料的可见功能和物理品质产生共鸣。在创造与调整人和事物相互理解的努力中,创造性可视为一种交易性的关系成就。在第二种主要形式里,陶工具有意图的行为也对黏土起到定向的支配作用,但这种支配也缺乏完全的目的性。陶工的确可以对拥有的技能充满自信,同时机械地复制一些设定好的形式和形状也是他们日常工作的一部分,不过他们仍无法对行为的结果拥有完全把握,在手指与材料间的协商和即兴创作中,陶工如钢琴家一样,呈现出"一种几乎自动的、毫不费力的、但高度集中的意识状态",该状态贯穿制作者和材料之间的创作张力的不同阶段。综合以上两种形式,创造性物思突破了从精神或大脑状态通过身体运动流向外物的因果关系束缚,而是建立了机体和物质之间动态流动的模式。[43]

通过对以上三个要点的概括,我们可以发现 MET 希望做的事甚至可归纳成一句话,即破除人类认知史研究中的"人类中心主义"。人脑不再贵为"万物之灵","万物有灵"立场则获得新生。通过 MET 视野,研究者关注的焦点从人把哪些从外界输入的信息,通过心理计算主义变换成输出符号转交给物,以及通过物质性呈现的结果,以及借助分类和表征等工具不免于现代目的论地寻觅呈现符号的自然原型,来推测古人的心理计算规则,进而树立人类心智发展的里程碑,转换为从物质变动的功能可见性出发,开辟物质与人思之间相交融的互动空间,把具体到物品个例表象的"什么"转化为该物品本身具有的"如何"上来。这样的结果是,研究者舍弃掉了一些实际上难以证明或证伪的问题,而获得给出对遗物与人关系新诠释的潜力。由于立足于多个学科领域的交叉融合,MET 援引了古今多种对象作为例证,但它特别有助于榨取缺乏抽象符号表达的考古资料中残存的关于人类认知发展的宝贵信息。

三、物质参与理论视野下的数学起源研究

前面提到的中石器时代赭石绘图的例子已经对当时人们拥有的图形认知能力有所涉及,在 MET 中,史前数学是一个格外受到关注的领域。马拉福瑞斯在其著作里,已经提到近东地区的早期计数系统。不过,在 MET 视野下进行的早期数学研究,主要是由马拉福瑞斯的学生奥弗曼(K. Overmann)进行的。在其代表作《数字的物质之源》[44]中,奥弗曼从"工具造就思想"观点出发,认为物质形式的变化是行为和心理过程变化的指标。借由 MET,奥弗曼分析了以美索不达米亚陶筹(tokens)为代表的史前数字认知。在回顾了诸如"数感"等能力的演变之后,她研究了美索不达米亚的考古记录中的第一个明确的数字,其中计数的物质形式的作用,以及这种物质形式的变化暗示的可能的考古迹象和更早时期的时间线。

对美索不达米亚早期数学的已有论述几十年来可谓汗牛充栋,亦不乏学者从认知角度论述陶筹在数学符号起源中的位置[45],以至于奥弗曼在向其师祖伦福儒汇报选题时遭到无情训斥。不过奥弗曼在

---

[43] L. Malafouris, "Creative thinging: the feeling of and for clay", Pragmatics and Cognition, 2014, 22(1):140—158.

[44] K. Overmann, The material origin of numbers: insights from the archaeology of the ancient Near East, Piscataway: Gorgias Press, 2019.

[45] 如 D. Schmandt-Besserat, "Before numerals", Visible Language, 1984, 18(1): 48—59; P. Damerow, R. Englund, "Die Zahlzeichensysteme der Archaischen Texte aus Uruk", in M. Green, et al., Archaische Texte aus Uruk, Band 2, Zeichenliste der Archaischen Texte aus Uruk, Berlin: Mann Verlag, 1987, pp. 117—166 等。

马拉福瑞斯的指导下,认为MET重新划定认知的边界以把物质性包容进来,带来基于以往学者取得认识基础上获得新见解的可能性。奥弗曼对MET也做出可与前一节所列互为参照的三点概括,即认知是扩展和相互激活的、物质具有对思维产生影响的中介性以及物质性具有符号学功能或是有意义的。

其中物质的中介性在前文已多有显示,它在改变人类行为时得到显露,但这不意味着中介物必须要有自由意志或意图,也不需要因行动而存在,例如减速带对冲过来的汽车司机有中介性,天然石头产生锋利边缘的能力对石器制造者具有中介性等等。中介性让物质与人类密不可分,而它又由中介者的功能可见性(affordance)引导和制约。后者在前文中也多次出现,指环境提供给中介者的能力,它在中介者与环境的互动中被发现,而不是任何一方的内在属性,而如果一个行动者缺乏利用特定功能可见性的能力,对该物种来说就不是一个可见的功能。当可见功能以物质人工制品的形式出现时,它将对行为产生影响。一个例子是猴子不能使用计算器,但计算器却塑造着财务工作者手与眼之间的连接。在第一节中曾提到"数感",即包括人类在内许多物种不借助物质即可感受到4以下的数量。对于超过4的数量,人类发展出重复,或进一步分组等策略。如第一节所引列维-布留尔等学者观察,在不同场合和物质条件里分组策略并不统一,但手作为代表和操纵数量的设备,用其计数是跨文化存在的普遍现象,而手指计数和它所发生的数字阐述的范围反映了感知数量和认识手指的能力的神经学整合。另一方面,手指计数的顺序可以随文化而定,但逐一增加的视觉效果,还带来了离散计数的顺序认知,这是一种设备隐含的中介性。与手类似具有功能可见性的物质还有身体其他部位逐一触摸形成的顺序、分散的石子或珠子、绳结、刻线的计数棒、果实、草叶乃至猎物身体部位等,它们适宜的数量范围、增减相对难度、保存时效等属性各异,如刻线很难直观显示减法操作,而石器却很容易分成数量变动的组,一些原始部落以身体部位计数会导致缺失特定数字之间的关系而影响数字的线性感受[46]。以上种种演化结果意味着特定材料形式提供的功能可见性促进或限制着数字认知的潜在发展。

物质具有符号功能在前文很少涉及,但它关系到一个论述数学起源的重要方面,就是物质性与在数学认知发展中起到关键作用的语言、数码、表示基数和序数,以及数量关系的词等概念化要素出现和发展的互动。为物质赋名最初是一个随机的暂时性过程,这可以从让儿童排列物体并为它们创造名称的观察中得出。但在声音传导的语言急速消失后,只有以规律顺序出现的名称才能更稳定地保存下来。命名规律则由与物质互动获取的经验塑造,语言通过将有限数量的声音和词语集按规则组合,来表示无限数量,而在诸如意为十加一的数字"十一",其"十性"(ten-ness)源于手指的物质性,这样就不同于乔姆斯基关于数字是语言子集的论点。[47]大脑为提高效率,遵循大量减少内部进行表述,而把这项负担转回给周边世界,也就是让物质承担储存信息的功能,与大脑不断动态互动的是物质形式上的符号化组合方式,物质借此锚定和稳定着大脑所形成的概念。就数字起源而言,这意味着它们既决定于物体的固有总数[48],又受到物体形式营造的稳定感知的影响。对总数计数的操作让数量变得有形、离散和明确,稳定感知则使一些通过图标或典范指示物索引式表述的概念得以萌生,物质总数和稳定感知之间的数量关系和计算过程,由此逐渐演变成数字属性和关系。就像手指计数的显著优势那样,5和10往往是"数感"数量之后最先稳定出现的[49]。它们与数感数量的关系,成为能够表达这种关系的数码的特征,这一特征具有跨文化普遍性,是一种在运算上有意义的半文字。一些死语言的文字可能很难识别,但它所含的数码却更可能得到破译。而计数的物质形式也有助于鉴识社群中是否存在实例化的数字词汇,无论

46　G. Saxe, Cultural development of mathematical ideas, Cambridge: Cambridge University Press, 2012, p. 86.

47　K. Overmann, The material origin of numbers: insights from the archaeology of the ancient Near East, Piscataway: Gorgias Press, 2019, p. 91.

48　奥弗曼借用罗素提出的术语"基数"(cardinality),指代一组物体共享的指定其数量的数字。在一个已拥有数字的文化中,基数是通过从一个人开始依次计数,直到没有更多的人可以计数,来辨别这个群体的成员。

49　少数情况下存在某些手指被排除在计数功能以外,或使用各个指节而非整根手指计数的情况。

能否识别其附着的语音信息。[50]

第一节提到考古学家为辨别遗物是否具有表示和操作这两项数学功能,设置了一系列标准,根据这些标准,数万年前的狒狒骨头和串珠被认为具有原始计数功能。奥弗曼对这些物质装置提出两个马拉福瑞斯式问题,我们为什么要用它们来表示和操作数字?当我们这样做的时候会发生什么?第一个问题在上一段已有解答,第二个问题则是 MET 之前认为物质仅具有被动性的方法难以作答的,实际上从数量思维萌芽的一开始,物质材料形式的融入就与数字阐述紧密结合。最初阶段即上文所说的对物体基数的抽象化,如抑制颜色等多余信息,而保留数量比较关系和分类判断。仅有一个的 1 和表示成对的 2 很可能是最先出现的数字,3 则往往表示为 1 和 2 的结合。如不进一步纳入手指表示的 5 等可用于为更高数量的概念提供支架的物质形式,数量将停留于数感阶段[51],而更频繁收集到物质形式上的数字则逐渐因容易比较和排序而减少离散性。

手指的使用堪称数字发展中的革命。手具有很强的计数功能可见性:手指数量超出数感范围,它位于人的视野之内,在神经层面大脑皮层很大一块区域用于控制手的运动。在数字方面,手具有多种功能。它为数字操作提供了预测功能,操作者越熟悉其手指,越可能在小数字计算的任务中取得良好表现。手指提供了一个虚拟的算具,实际动作存在被心理意图取代的可能性。手还提供了极为便利的比较功能。因此它连接了计算能力的心理、行为和物质层面。人们不但可以通过视觉、本体感觉和互感来体会手指的数量、位置和运动,它还能进一步延伸,作为中介者操作其他物质。这就进入下一层次,即如前文提到的计数棒、绳结等,计数呈线性增加,其符号依数量增加而逐一排列下去。这称为"一维数字"。随着与周期性实物对象相联系的经验增加,相同的符号得到分组,比如计数棒上的刻线出现周期性长短、深浅变化,以增强过多符号中的可辨识性,这时就出现"二维数字"。在演化的下一阶段,人们使用不同物质形式来区别数量级之间的差异,最早出现于距今约 1 万年美索不达米亚一带用黏土烧制的陶筹,可能是最早的这类物品。不同形状的陶筹对应不同级别的数字,如 10 个小圆锥体相当于 1 个小球,6 个小球相当于 1 个大圆锥体。在不同形状大小组合中,还指定了谷物、鱼等对应商品,这既是具有记账功能的价格表,也是物质性对数字认知的进一步固化。这种级间差异性物质形式表达,最终通向了手写数字符号的诞生。[52]

具体到美索不达米亚的情况,这里计数的最早形式与世界许多其他地方近似,也是手指和计数棒(tallies)。在苏美尔人的语言里,6 到 9 是以 5 和其他小数合并的方式表达的,陶筹的数量级间形态变化则显示他们所采用的六十进制是以手指计数为基础的 10,以及常见的周期数字 6 相结合的产物。美索不达米亚数学的另两个源头阿卡德和埃兰数字,则是更常见的十进制。[53]计数棒至今仍是生活中常见的现象,例如在东亚语境里,画"正"字就是计数棒的一种二维数字变体。如第一节所说,计数棒很可能最早在数万年前的非洲即存在,近东一带最早的有可能作为计数棒使用的遗物发现于以色列的凯巴拉洞(Kebara Cave),其年代为距今 6—4.8 万年。其次是距离这里不远的哈约宁洞(HaYonim Cave),年代为距今 3—1 万年。[54]这里都发现了带刻痕的骨头,其中凯巴拉洞的刻痕比较晚的哈约宁洞还要规整些,不过与南非和东非相关遗物类似,这些刻痕的意义还有许多争议。与之同时期的美索不达米亚一

---

[50] K. Overmann, The material origin of numbers: insights from the archaeology of the ancient Near East, Piscataway: Gorgias Press, 2019, pp. 9—24.

[51] 第一节提到的对亚马逊地区原始部落的调查已显示这一点,同时它也表明数字感知与语言发展的可分离性。

[52] K. Overmann, The material origin of numbers: insights from the archaeology of the ancient Near East, Piscataway: Gorgias Press, 2019, pp. 30—42, 85—88; 136—137; K. Overmann, "Constructing a concept of number", Journal of Numerical Cognition, 2018, 4(2): 464—493; K. Overmann, "Finger-counting and numerical structure", Frontiers in Psychology, 2021, 12:723492.

[53] K. Overmann, The material origin of numbers: insights from the archaeology of the ancient Near East, Piscataway: Gorgias Press, 2019, pp. 136—139.

[54] D. Schmandt-Besserat, "The earliest precursor of writing", in P. Heyer, P. Urquhart, eds., Communication in history, New York: Routledge, 2018, pp. 1—10.

带还乏人居住,这片地方计数棒的集中出现是在公元前5000年到青铜时代早期,它可能响应着当时社会物质财富增加带来的记数需求。对这些遗物的研究为数不少,MET主要关注于如何认识它们提供的认知机会,即探讨标记是否拥有与物质形式互动的前提,并以某种形式被它改变。计数棒独立于身体,因此其功能可见性与手指不同,它具有离开身体周围的公共性,可以把所记数量稳定保存一段相当长的时间,印记是累增而非减损式的,因此容易对应于加法而不利于减法,在记录序数方面,计数棒拥有很大的数量空间。前一段提到,计数棒这类装置最初对应于一维数字,不过在上面刻画数字的同时,这些数字有可能与其他具体事物建立对应关系进而从周期和形式上都出现差异,这样它就得以向二维数字过渡。因为从手指直接向二维记号跨越并不容易,计数棒可能填补了这一差距。

陶筹在数字层次上较计数棒更进一步,它在公元前9000年到公元前1000年的美索不达米亚遗址中均有出现,目前已发现数千枚之多。陶筹的形状主要有球体、圆锥体、圆盘体、圆柱体和四面体等,尺寸主要分成大小两种,偶有中间尺寸。大部分学者接受陶筹作为一种记数工具发挥作用。如前所说,陶筹的形状大小代表着不同数量级,而集中到一起的同种陶筹个数代表着级内数量。但是关于其细节还有许多争议,如陶筹与原始楔形文字之间是否存在一一对应关系,它们是否在存在的整个时间跨度内都作为数学符号使用,以及复杂的陶筹组合符号是否是手写数字符号的前身等。不过我们更关心的是如何从MET出发探讨陶筹的物质性对数学认知带来的影响。陶筹作为商品价格标签时,以具有一定形状、大小、顺序和数字关系的特定组合覆盖到黏土上形成印记。通过整理陶筹资料,学者们发现对于不同类型的商品,同种陶筹代表的数量不同。例如在计量谷物时,有一种专用于此的圆盘形陶筹表示1 500升谷物,一个大圆锥体相当于3个圆盘,即4 500升,一个圆盘相当于10个小球,1小球又相当于6个圆柱体,1个圆柱体又可换算为5个小球,这样小球相当于150或5升。而在计算动物和动物产品的系统中,一个大圆锥体的价值是60,它可换算成6个小球,这样每个球相当于10。同种符号在不同环境(如常规六十进制和现场计量行为)中的挪用,是数字系统容量有限的体现,这样就降低了大脑中视觉辨别的压力。拥有松散形态和分组不同形式的陶筹可以解决计数棒等许多一维数字载体缺乏可操作性的问题,不同形状大小陶筹与交易物之间,以及它们自己之间的数量关系,在松散的组织下能够根据需要添加或移除,或用许多次级陶筹来代替一个高数量级陶筹,可操作性的物质性为关系的表达和进一步抽象提供了机会。至于不同语境下陶筹的运用是否可作为具体计算的证明,目前还难以确定。现代人类学调查显示拥有多个赋值的数码可以用颜色等加以区分,尽管我们从陶筹的印记无法看到这一点,不过在一些泥板上发现了与陶筹使用场景有关的文字说明,这将促使学者对抽象性数学符号的发展过程进行更丰富的思考。[55]

如何从MET角度看待陶筹与数字符号和书写之间的关系呢?奥弗曼主张在关注书写的象征性之余,还应看到它拥有的物质形式,也就是思维扩张后被纳入考虑的在页面上移动眼睛、控制产生可读字符所需的精细动作,以及协调手和眼睛的运动等行为,以及符号载体的功能可见性之间形成的互动。与今天用电脑打字形成标准化字符不同,手写文字的形式准确性与产生速度之间的张力是无法忽视的(智能手机的手写输入模式又让这重新凸显出来),这揭示了手写行为的模糊性,而它由此成为精神内容、物质形式和连接两者的行为共同组成的物思地带。用于楔形文字书写的黏土表面特性和书写方式同样影响着文字的制作方式,在泥板上划出线条沟壑,若在附近区域制作新线条,有可能在交叉重叠作用下损坏已有笔画,这就要求书写者把表意转换成简单的线条组合,并在仔细考虑后再下笔。物质可见功能影响下的书写习惯经历了大约15个世纪,到公元前2000年左右的乌尔第三王朝时期才趋于构建完整。与文字不同的是,数字要更简单一些,因为它既可以用表格和记号等非文字形式表示,又不必携带语音

---

55 P. Damerow, Abstraction and representation: Essays on the cultural evolution of thinking, Dordrecht: Kluwer Academic Publishers, 1996, pp. 288－291; K. Overmann, The material origin of numbers: insights from the archaeology of the ancient Near East, Piscataway: Gorgias Press, 2019, pp. 174－178; M. Valério, S. Ferrara, "Numeracy at the dawn of writing: Mesopotamia and beyond", Historia Mathematica, 网络版,2020年12月8日上线,https://www.sciencedirect.com/science/article/pii/S0315086020300665#tbl0040 查阅时间2022年3月20日。

信息。反过来,数字缺乏词序的严格性,把数字颠倒排列依然有意义,这让它缺乏推动书面形式对语言的忠实性所需的品质。由于文字需要更多符号、表达语音的能力,以及表达意图的语法结构,它很难从数字衍生出来。这也反映在神经解剖学中语言和算术分别对应大脑区域的差异上。陶筹在文字最初诞生后与其共存了很长时间,这段时间里手写数字为计数观念带来一些深刻影响。例如陶筹及其印记中用七个小圆锥体来表示 7,它是离散物体的集合,而楔形文字的七则在书写习惯影响下凝集为一个连贯实体。这种简洁表达在乌尔第三王朝时推行的文吏技能训练中更加密集地与日常数学实践产生联系。面积、分数以及乘方等计算的结果因文字的简洁性可被收集进表格,不但使文吏留下深刻记忆,还使更多人有机会拥有熟练地查找和记录中间过程的技能。[56]

通过对 MET 要点的回顾和美索不达米亚早期计数形式的演变,奥弗曼总结道:用于计数的每种物质形式都提供了一定的能力和结构。当一种新的数字表达物质形式出现后,将添加更多样的数字、数字关系和操作关系的算法。与物质的互动也会改变心理和行为,而先前物质形式中所含的数字属性和相应的神经反应往往转变为默认为应知的隐性知识,在未发掘物质参与能力时,我们容易倾向认为自己是针对外界的中介者,从而将物质置于完全被动位置。通过物质对数学起源各环节进行还原,有助于我们认识到尽管数字从最初的数感,到手指等实物计数,再进入一维数字和二维数字,最终出现文字符号的过程具有普遍性和文化特异性。奥弗曼倡导对不同文化的数学起源发展情况进行全面调查,来理解远远超过先前历史叙述的物质对数学认知的心理、行为和语言方面的影响潜力。

四、结语

通过全面搜集阅读马拉福瑞斯和奥弗曼等学者的论述,笔者的总体印象是经过视角转换后,的确打开了一个崭新的研究空间。在已发表的众多论述里,马拉福瑞斯等学者的一项重要任务就是重申和推广 MET 的主要理念,时常用更精炼的术语来迭代之前的表述。他们论述的大量篇幅是综合心理学、人类学、神经科学的哲学化表达,有时会令读者急于了解他们用什么样的实证方法来实践或验证其理念,显然这还是一套有待从实物寻找更多支持论据的理论。在这一方面,马拉福瑞斯做出不少努力,他在不同文章里结合微痕分析、心理实验和工艺实作,给出相对全面的解释,使得其观点不至于完全沦为空洞口号,而拥有更强的说服力。

MET 是西方认知考古学发展的结果,几乎未见有熟悉中国材料的学者加入讨论,但在阅读过程中,笔者不断从他们的论述中联想到中国科技史的各类对应材料,不仅不限于史前起源阶段,而且不限于数学史领域,从而启发笔者提出一些试探性问题。例如对于中国史前常见的玉器、细石器等遗物,如何发掘其物质性,提出较弗罗洛夫所关注问题更新颖全面的见解?以《道德经》中"三生万物"为代表,这里的"三"是否为史前"数感"的孑遗?再如何从算筹和算盘的中介性和功能可见性来论证它们对中国传统数学发展的影响?与美索不达米亚泥板颇有异同之处的甲骨文和金文的载体,其物质性对知识选择性记载与流传构成何种影响?这些初步疑问尚有待日后继续提炼。

近年考古成果层出不穷,与包括数学在内的科学认知有关的遗物不断出土,但面对这些在时间与空间都明显缺乏连续性的残篇断简,我们如何开展对古人心灵认知领域的探索,学者们无论重视程度还是所掌握运用的方法论,在意识上还缺乏自觉性,在具体研究上则时有回避之意。近年来中国学者在科技考古领域取得飞速进展,MET 不排斥甚至较以往的意识研究更加仰仗先进的科技检测和实验方法,但马拉福瑞斯对朴素或自满的科技考古理论并不满意。MET 作为理论框架,对设计和组织研究方案具有明显的指导意义。这也激励科技史学者在虚心了解各学科方法、特长、成果,充分与其他领域学者合作的同时,加速创立本学科独立的综合性研究方法。

---

[56] K. Overmann, The material origin of numbers: insights from the archaeology of the ancient Near East, Piscataway: Gorgias Press, 2019, pp. 196—201.

《大成算经》中"数"的处理

森本光生[1] （日本四日市大学关孝和数学研究所）

前言

郭书春先生与我同年，今2021年迎来伞寿。为祝贺先生80岁生日，计划在中国出版纪念文集，也邀请笔者投稿，深感光荣之至！我参加在中国及东亚各地召开的数学史研讨会，时常见到郭书春先生的温颜，愉快地听他对中国数学史特别是《九章算术》的深刻见解。希望在今后一段时间里，作为数学史研究的先行者给予厚谊和鞭策。

1 《大成算经》概要

宝永末(1711)，传为关孝和、建部贤弘、建部贤明合著的《大成算经》全20卷、约900张(1 800页)的巨著，经建部贤明之手完成了。这本数学书是当时所知的和汉数学及作者们自己创造的数学知识的集大成著作。

本文旨在思考这本鸿篇巨制的数学书中是怎样处理所谓的"数"的。《大成算经》(1711)由卷一至二十的20卷及首篇构成，没有刊行，手抄本传至今日，现在日本图书馆收藏的抄本超过20种(参照[1])。

另外，小松彦三郎对《大成算经》全20卷做了校订，作为京都大学数理解析研究所讲究录[2,3]刊行，可以从京都大学数理解析研究所的网页上下载。

《大成算经》20卷的章节，请参照小川束等人的著作[4]及徐泽林等人的著作[5]。这里只记述与本论题关联的几个地方。

首篇 总括（算数论，基数，大数，小数，异名，度数，量数，衡数，钞数，纵横，正负，上退，用字例）

前集（卷一至卷三）

卷一"五技"（加，减，因乘，归除，定位，商除，开方）

卷二"杂技"（相乘，归除，又（别法），开方）

卷三"变技"

中集（卷四至卷十五）

卷四"三要"

后集（卷十六至卷二十）

本文所讨论的"数"，含在首篇"总括"、卷一"五技"，卷二"杂技"，卷三"变技"，卷四"三要"中。卷一、二、三是对数的演算即加减乘除与开平方进行考察，在卷四"三要"中考察数的本质。这些都含于小松的校订本(其1)。

2 《大成算经》中"数"的处理

《大成算经》中是如何理解"数"的呢？笔者试着把想到的写下来。

(1)从关于数的儒学解释开始（首篇"数学论"）。

(2)但是，从卷一来看，"数"是可以在"算盘"上操作、计算的，根本就没有提出"数是什么"的问题。

---

[1] 日本四日市大学关孝和数学研究所副所长，日本上智大学名誉教授。

加减是最基本的操作,使用口诀将乘除用"算盘"就能完成,这是有关数的技的基础。

用"算盘"可以计算的"数"是指整数、有限小数等。作者认为,虽然很难处理无限小数,但它被理解为有限小数的"极限"。总之,有限小数是"数"。

（3）换句话说,就是在算盘上作为计算对象的东西,即"数"的排列(数向量更容易理解)作为和"数"一样的东西被认识的[2]。天元术中有限小数带系数的1个变量多项式（或方程）,其系数是作为项的数向量在算板上处理的。对于数向量,加法、减法、标量积的代数运算在算板上实行。数向量恰好被当作一般的"数"。

（4）代数运算的结合律、可交换律,最初在《解隐题之法》等书中,是对一般"数"的数向量而记述的。尔后,对用"算盘"计算的数也被意识到了。

江户时代的数学书,是以"问、答、法(解法)"这一中国算书风格来书写的。再者处理一个变量多项式的天元术时有不表示未知变量的限制。加法、乘法交换律这些抽象的概念在此表述和记录上的限制也必须叙述。

在本文中,将逐节介绍《大成算经》中有关"数"的记述,在下节介绍《大成算经》的作者是怎样把抽象的概念通过数值问题提示出来的。

2.1 算数论

首篇"总括"的开头,是汉文写的"算数论"。汉文没有句读标点、没有段落、没有注音释义（这里引用时加上了标点符号）。

算者,数也。数言万物本具之体,算言已显而相为之用也。盖混沌本无极而太极,是众理之肇,动而生一焉。一者阳也,奇也,是数所始,为增,为满。由理论之,则为正,由物名之,则为象,由技言之,则为加也。一数静而生二焉。二者阴也,偶也。是数所成,为损,为干。由理论之,则为负,由物名之,则为形。由技言之,则为减也。（以下略）[2]17

从用汉文撰著来看,可以说《大成算经》的读者对象是武士阶级有教养的人,而一般庶民是不能阅读的。相反,吉田光由的《尘劫记》(1627)是用日文假名文撰写的,预设读者层为在寺子屋学习的一般庶民。与之相比,《大成算经》用汉文撰写数学书的形式也许当时在日本国内也受到了不可忍受的批评。

2.2 首篇"总括"中的数

在首篇"总括"中介绍了如下的数名。

一、二、三、……、九等基数；

一、十、百、千、万、亿、兆等大数；

分、厘、毫、丝等小数。

注：亿为万万与现代相同,但兆为万万亿、京为万万兆、……与现代相异。

在首篇"总括"中还介绍了处理数的工具,即梁上2珠、梁下5珠的算盘。

例如,给出珠算加减法练习题。123456789 在算盘上逐次做加法时,对求 $123456789 \times 9 = 11111111101$ 的珠算拨珠法做了详细说明。随后,说明了从 11111111101 依次减 123456789 的拨珠法。当然第 9 次结果为 0。

2.3 卷一"五技"

卷一"五技"内容如下：

加(3问)

减(3问)

---

2 "算盘"有两个意思,所以在本文中分别说成"算盘"和"算板"。

因乘（释级数，九因式，留头乘式）
归除（九归句诀，九归式，撞除句诀，撞除式）
定位
商除，开方

即在卷一中导入乘法口诀（所谓"九九"）和除法口诀（"二一添作五"等），是丰富的珠算乘除问题。最后是商除法、开平算（平方根，立方根，四乘根）的计算，使用算盘和算筹进行计算。但理论性考察都没有。还有，卷一中的单位只出现"个"。这是卷一对象是"数"的证据吧！

2.4 卷二"杂技"

卷二"杂技"内容如下：

相乘（重乘，更乘，截乘，孤乘，破头乘，掉尾乘，隔位乘，穿乘，损乘，身外加，身前加）
归除（重除，□除，穿除，益除，身外减，身前减）
又（金蝉脱壳，二字法，铺地锦，一笔锦，井字法）
开方（积平圆，开立圆，带从开方，减从开方，益积开方，减积开方，翻积开方，归除开方，损益平方，相应开方）

卷二给出各种杂多的乘法、除法、开平方的问题，还安排了意味有关乘除法交换律、分配律的问题混杂其中。列出长度单位、重量单位、容积单位等，寓意"数"应用的可能性。

2.5 卷三"变技"

卷三"变技"内容如下：

加减第一（加法，减法，兼加减）
乘除第二（乘法，除法，兼乘除）
开方第三（开出总法，三式，十商，适尽方级法，替数）
全商式，变商式，无商式，课商，穷商，通商，叠商，幂商，乘除商，增损商，加减商，报商，反商，适尽方级法（平方，立方，三乘方，四乘方适尽方级相乘法）
替数

卷三的后半部分给出了2次、3次、4次方程的判别式。若没有卷十七行列式（终结式）的知识，判别式是不能求的。用天元术，单变量多项式加减、数积成为可能，意识到了代数构造，关孝和的《解隐题之法》(《大成算经》卷十七）中，以问题的形式，记述了交换律、结合律等。我想卷三受到卷十七强烈的影响。

2.6 关于卷四的"三要"

卷四"三要"在《大成算经》中篇的开端一卷，也是对中篇主题关于"象""形"的总括，并且作为"象""形"的基础，对"数"进行了论述。

最初关注并讨论"三要"的是徐泽林[6]，笔者也感兴趣，发表了其论文的日本译本[7]。尾崎文秋[8]及笔者尝试着将"三要"翻译成了现代日本语[9]。徐泽林的论述也收入其著作[5]，可参照佐佐木力（1947—2020）的书评[10]。

3 代数演算性质的记述方法

卷三加减问题

在卷一、卷二中已经十分详尽地叙述了加减法，为什么在卷三还再次处理加减呢？到底是什么缘故？

第1问如下（以下翻译成现代语引用）：

[第3—1问] 假如有牛三十头，生犊二十四头，育之。问共数。
答曰：共五十四头。

法曰:置牛三十头。加犊二十四头,得共数。或先置犊二十四头,后加牛三十头者,亦同。

解曰:是一次加也。先置牛,乃此。后加犊,乃彼。先置犊,彼后加此者,各共数全同。故曰相并也。若模状者,唯用一条之画分界而释其理也。是以不必每一问注之矣。

问:养牛 30 头,子牛 24 头,共几头?

答:54 头。

法:30 加 24 合计而得。先置 24 再加 30 也相同。[2]99

这个"法"叙述的是加法交换律

$$a+b=b+a$$

当时的数学(和算,中算)中文字变量不发达,所以只能这样用数值问题的解法叙述。在"解"中,a 为此、b 为彼而更抽象地记述着。

第 2 问如下:

[第 3—2 问]假如有客,借本金四百七十五两于东西二邻,及还东利一百二十两,西利九十两。问共金。

答曰,共金六百八十五两。

法曰,缀求者,置本金四百七十五两,加东利一百二十两,得五百九十五两,又加西利九十五两,得共金。或先加西利、后加东利者,亦同。

括求者,置东利一百二十两,加西利九十两,得二百一十两,以之加本金四百七十五两,得共金也。[2]99

问:某人向东、西两家借 475 两。返东家利息 120 两,返西家利息 90 两。共多少钱。

答:共 685 两。

法:475+120=595,595+90=685。

或利息相加 120+90=210,再加本金 475+210=685 也可以。

此"法"叙述的是加法结合律

$$(a+b)+c=a+(b+c)$$

第 3 问如下:

[第 3—3 问]假如有红丝四百二十斤,白丝五十四斤,青丝一百四十斤,黄丝七十斤。问共重。

答曰:共重六百八十四斤。

法曰:缀求者,置红丝四百二十斤,加白丝五十四斤,得四百七十四斤。又加青丝一百四十斤,得六百一十四斤。复加黄丝七十斤,得共重。或先加青丝,后加白黄两丝,或先加黄丝,后加白青两丝者,皆同。

括求者,置白丝五十四斤,加青丝一百四十斤,得一百九十四斤,又加黄丝七十斤,共得二百六十四斤,以之加红丝四百二十斤,得共重也。[2]99

问:有红丝 420 斤,白丝 54 斤,青丝 140 斤,黄丝 70 斤,全部的重量是多少?

答:共重 684 斤。

法:420+54=474,474+140=614,614+70=684。

或 54+140=194,194+70=264。

这个再加红丝,420+264=684,也可以。

此"法"以数值特例显示

$$((a+b)+c)+d=a+((b+c)+d)$$

仅看前三题得出结论也许有些仓促,但我认为作者似乎对抽象的一般理论感兴趣并努力记述它。习惯用现代数学论述的话,第3-3问表示

$$((a+b)+c)+d=a+((b+c)+d)$$

这是画蛇添足的结合律,但我想无暇做那样的斟酌。

参考文献

[1] 森本光生,小川束.《大成算経》の諸写本について.RIMS Kōkyūroku,B73:21～32,2019.

[2] 関孝和,建部賢明,建部賢弘.《大成算経》(小松校訂本.その1).RIMS Kōkyūroku,1858,2013。

[3] 関孝和,建部賢明,建部賢弘.《大成算経》(小松校訂本.その2;その3;その4),RIMS Kōkyūroku,2024;2025;2026,2017。

[4] 小川束,佐藤健一,竹之内脩,森本光生.建部賢弘の数学.共立出版,2008.

[5] 徐泽林,周畅,夏青.建部贤弘的数学思想.科学出版社,2013

[6] 徐泽林.建部贤弘的数学认识论——论《大成算经》中的"三要".自然科学史研究,21(3):232-243,2002.日本語訳:森本光生訳.数学史研究,206号,2010年.

[7] 徐澤林,建部賢弘の数学認識論——《大成算経》の"三要"を論ず(日本語訳:森本光生).数学史研究,206:30～47,2010.

[8] 尾崎文秋.《大成算経》卷之四三要(象形、満干、数)の謎".RIMS Kōkyūroku,1392:186～196,2004.

[9] 森本光生.《大成算経》卷之四三要(読み下し文と現代語訳).RIMS Kōkyūroku,1831:158～223,2013.

[10] 佐々木力.评《建部贤弘的数学思想》.自然科学史研究,32(4):541～547,2013.

算额文化地理学

小川束 （日本四日市大学关孝和数学研究所）

1　引言

很荣幸受到为纪念郭书春先生伞寿的论文集的约稿，感到非常高兴。思案良久，最后决定介绍未在中国出现，而独具日本特色的数学文化内容。记得曾经在北京的一次学术会议上介绍近世[1] 日本数学私塾之一"至诚赞化流"的门人活动时，郭老师说道："在中国没有出现过普通人相互提（数学）问题而乐在其中的习惯。"当时只做了口头报告，借此机会我想谈一谈近世日本独具特色的算额习惯和数学流派门人的地理活动。

本文题目中的"算额文化地理学"，作为一个新概念成为本人算额研究框架的基础，在 2021 年 2 月在京都大学数理解析研究所做了首次报告，后又撰写了相关论文，本文是在两篇论文的基础上进一步深入研究的成果。[1][2]

2　算额

自 17 世纪至 19 世纪前半期，日本传统数学发展的契机来源于《算法统宗》和《算学启蒙》两本著作，在这个意义上可以说日本是中国数学影响波及的一个地区。然而，自关孝和（约 1642—1708）以来，独自高度发展的日本数学与中国数学发展的历程呈现出非常不同的面貌，其发达的数学文化使 19 世纪后半期的日本迅速接受西方数学成为可能，反之对中国数学界也产生了影响[4]。

在近世日本社会，很多普通百姓喜爱数学，也能理解某些数学原理。这为日本传统数学的高度发展奠定了基础，他们中间也诞生了一些著名数学家，但多数人只是享受着数学带给他们的乐趣，并没有留下相关业绩，"算额"作为保留其数学研究的痕迹而留存至今。

所谓算额，按照字面意思就是写有数学问题和答案的算额，18 世纪后期以来盛行将其放置于神社之中。目前有实物留存的有 900 余件，加上一些文献中的记载，共有 2 600 件算额可考证[2]。

图 1 是 1844 年放置在三重县四日市市川岛町的神明神社的算额[3]。如图所示直径为 1 218（分）的大圆和与之外切正方形之间的缝隙里依次放入半圆以下的圆，然后继续在它们和大圆形成的缝隙中放入圆，这时最后一个圆的直径成为 1（分），那么这个圆是第几个圆呢？算额中给出的答案是 16 个，类似问题在当时较为普遍。

这个算额的背面写着 20 年后（即 1864 年）的解答过程。正面问题的作者叫柳川安左卫门，背面的答案则是其门人清水中治给出的答案。由此可知，第一个大圆以下的圆直径的算法。即，若大圆的直径为 R，则后面的圆直径为

$$\frac{R}{28}, \frac{R}{52}, \frac{R}{84}, \frac{R}{124}, \frac{R}{172}, \cdots$$

---

[1]　"近世"一般指 1590 至 1867 年的日本历史时期，有时也指日本历史上的关原大战（1600）至大政奉还（1867）为止的时期，大部分时间跟江户时期（1603—1868）重叠。

[2]　现存日本最早的算额是 1683 年捐献给枥木县佐野市星宫神社的算额。18 世纪后半期，"算额"的供奉习俗迅速兴起。这个最早的算额因遭遇火灾，多数文字无法辨认。算额张数等详细信息请参照文献 [5]。

[3]　小川束"川岛御厨神明社天保十五年的算额研究"（日文原名"川岛御厨神明社天保十五年的算额について"）《四日市大学论集》第 2 卷第 1 号（1989 年）157—166。

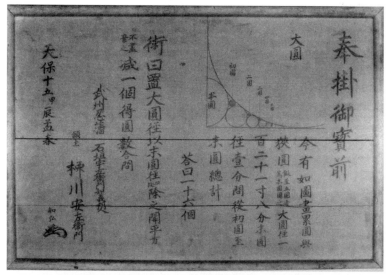

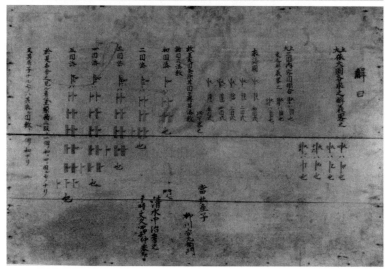

图 1　神明神社 1844 年算额的正面和背面（背面的日期是 1864 年）

（由当时广为人知的和算中的勾股定理"三圆容圆术"公式而得）。

这是一个求此数列的值为 1 的时候是第几项的问题。所以解题一般是求出这个数列的第 n 个式子，然后把式子设为 1，再解方程即可。虽然在算额的正面上没有写此数列，但给出问题的柳川安左卫门当然也知道这个解法。

那么，我们也可能会这样考虑，因分子 R 是共用的，所以求第 n 项的分母就可以了。首先，每一项都能被 4 整除，所以要认为用 4 除 7,13,21,31,43,…，接着计算阶差，得 6,8,10,12,…。

之后再取一次阶差，便得相等的 2,2,2,…。

由此（经过简单的计算）推测第 n 项为 n^2+3n+3。

但在算额背面，其门人清水中治给出的解法，到除以 4 为止的步骤相同，其后就成为

$$7=2(1+2)+1$$
$$13=2(1+2+3)+1$$
$$21=2(1+2+3+4)+1$$
$$31=2(1+2+3+4+5)+1$$
$$43=2(1+2+3+4+5+6)+1$$

经过这样巧妙的变形，第 n 项被预测为 $(n+1)(n+2)+1$。

我们自然想到的获取阶差的方法，其实在当时也是广为人知的。之所以这么说，是因为取阶差的方

法原本在中国的历法中被大量使用,后来传到日本,在关孝和的《括要算法》(1712 年)中已经以扩展的形式进行了记述。因此,很自然地认为给予正面解的柳川安左卫门取了阶差。另一方面,从背面的"清水中治考之"可以看出,清水构思出了与师傅柳川不同的方法,并将其记载在背面。

当然,清水一定知道如何取得阶差的方法。2011 年在川岛町的柳川家发现了《算法点窜指南录》及《天文图解》。在《算法点窜指南录》的末尾发现了"清水晴信"的署名。清水晴信虽然没有留下算额,但很有可能与川岛神明神社的其他算额中留下姓名的清水永信、清水贞信一起属于同一族人。如果清水中治看过当时经常被阅读的教科书《算法点窜指南录》和有关历法的《天文图解》,那么他应该是在熟悉、了解正面柳川解的基础上,用新的想法对公式进行改变,并将其记在算额背面。

当时的和算传统是算额上不写解题方法和计算过程,所以清水中治只能把自己想出的解法以算额的形式发表出来,就写在其背面了。对此和算"传统"做说明的话,算额中的文字均用汉字书写,这是近世日本讲究算法格式的情况下惯用的一种手法[4]。

综上所述,算额的解法是多种多样的。算额一般不写具体解法的细节,因此猜测敬献者如何解答比较困难。正因为如此,后人可以通过被供奉时期的数学发展为依据,推测一些概率较高的解法,这样不至于陷入与事实不符的"时代错误"中[5]。如某些算额上的问题用三角函数或反函数可以容易解答,但却不知当时是否用了类似的方法,最重要的是需要了解当时的解题方法。算额与数学书都是将近世日本数学文化的丰富性流传后世的遗物。为了详细了解近世日本数学文化的构成,需要分析其解题方法加以考察。

上面举例的 1844 年的算额还给出了关于算额研究的另一个问题。在这个算额中,问题的答案如下所述:

"术曰,置大圆径,以末圆径(四段)除之,开平方(不尽弃之),减一个,得圆数,合问",假设大圆的直径为 R,最后一个圆的直径为 r,则将 [ ] 看作高斯符号,可得如下算式

$$\left[\sqrt{\frac{R}{4r}}\right]-1$$

将算额中给出的数值 $R=1\ 218$ 和 $r=1$ 代入,便可得到写在算额上的答案 16。如果正确解答这个问题,那么其答案为

$$\sqrt{\frac{R}{4r}-\frac{3}{4}}-\frac{3}{2}$$

这里代入问题的数值,其值成为 $15.9\cdots$。在求个数的问题中得到的值有尾数,也就是说没有解。关于这一点,原山润一指出该问题的大圆直径是 $1\ 228$。实际上,将这个值代入现在的数学公式,就能得出正确值 16。另一方面,代入算额上的式子也能得出 16。那为什么算额的正面没有给出正确的式子,而写的是去掉尾数的式子呢?关于这一点,很长一段时间人们都无法理解其原因[6]。1801 年供奉于名古屋铃鹿市(毗邻四日市)铃鹿明神社的算额中的算题也许给我们一些提示(图 2)。该算额没有现存实物,只留下了相关记录。

这道题的外圆中有圆,这一点与川岛神明神社的算额不同,但其答案为 15,还有解算题的公式和神明神社的算额类似。现将其重新举例如下:

(川岛神明神社)

"术曰,置大圆径,以末圆径(四段)除之,开平方(不尽弃之),减一个,得圆数,合问。"

(铃鹿明神社)

---

[4] 近世日本人将中国的"四书五经"等文献直接能用日语的发音遵照日语的语法阅读。借用于中国的汉字,没能按照原来中文发音,但是却能很顺畅地阅读和书写。现在日本的大学入学考试中,苏轼等人的文章也被称作"汉文"。

[5] 类似于吴文俊先生所倡导的"古证复原"思想。

[6] 小川束"川岛御厨神明社宽政二年的算额"(日文名"川岛御厨神明社寛政二年の算額")《四日市大学论集》第 2 卷第 2 号(1990)207-215。

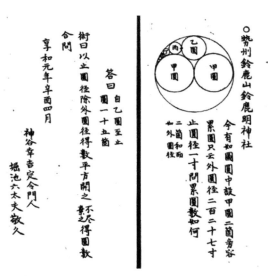

图 2 《赛词神算》卷之三(东北大学冈本记录 0867)11 丁里～12 丁表。

"术曰,以止圆径,除圆径,得数平方开之,得圆数,合问。"

换成现代数学公式为:

(川岛神明神社) $$\left[\sqrt{\frac{R}{4r}}\right]-1$$

(铃鹿明神社) $$\left[\sqrt{\frac{R}{4r}}\right]$$

由此看来,供奉在川岛神明神社的柳川安左卫门或许亲眼目睹过这个算额,并将答案与之相符的形式记录下来。但是,为什么一定要那样做,算额正面问题的答案 1 218 是 1 228 的误写吗? 这些还不是很清楚。就后者的问题而言,很难认为供奉神社的算额有错字。但是,这样做问题不成立也是事实。

过于细致的讨论难免有繁杂之嫌,但通过以上讨论可以了解算额的研究中,若只独立考察算额的个别情况,就无法解决一些问题,有时可通过当时人们的实际生活状况,考察其活动的地理范围,或许可发现一些新的问题。

3 算额奉纳者的地理关系

算额的供奉者能否见到其他算额,跟他当时的活动范围有密切关系。那么可以设想的活动范围应该多大呢? 为此,需了解被供奉的神社所在地以外,还应该知道算额上所记录的供奉者所有人员的姓名,以及他们的门派和老师们的姓名,还有其生活过的地方等,这些都可以作为参考的依据。以前文所述 1844 年的算额为例,我们可以了解以四日市地区为中心的算额供奉者的活动范围。

首先,1844 年算额的供奉者柳川安左卫门是神明神社的人士,居住于川岛町,其老师石垣宇左卫门知义是武州忍藩(士)。所谓武州忍藩归属于四日市北部的忍藩辖区。藩士所居住地位于大矢知村,距离川岛大约 8 公里。虽不知其老师所居住地的确切位置,但可以推测他是到 8 公里以外的地方学习数学。又川岛到铃鹿明神社约有 10 公里,从川岛神明神社往西北方向 15 公里左右的伎留田神社(菇野町切田)中留存一块 1797 年供奉的算额。供奉者为切畑村村长大桥政五郎,其老师的名字叫作森川永兴。1790 年、1844 年、1863 年均有人将算额供奉于川岛的神明神社,其中最早的,即 1790 年算额的供奉者为伊藤永信和广田忠兴,他们的老师也是森川永兴[7]。因此,可以知道森川的两组门人居住在相隔 15 公里左右的地方,他们跟同一个老师学习数学,供奉算额的时间相隔 7 年,也有可能他们相互认识。因为是同一个老师的门派弟子,也许互相有交流,并看过对方的算额。

---

[7] 小川束"川岛御厨神明社宽政 2 年的算额相关 28 种香的问题"(日文名"川岛御厨神明社宽政 2 年の算額における 28 種香の問題")《四日市大学论集》第 1 卷第 1·2 号(1989 年)149—156。

另外，1790 年川岛神明神社算额上有广田忠兴所写的算题，其中写道"江洲日野神社供奉答"。江洲，即为现在的滋贺县，与四日市相隔个铃鹿山脉。广田也许把自己在日野神社看到的算额的问题解答出来后供奉到所住地的神社。川岛和日野之间的距离约有 18 公里，中途需要跨越铃鹿山脉。广田是越过铃鹿山脉到达日野地区，还是沿着当时的道路，即东海道，绕过铃鹿山脉的南部前往日野？他是为了做生意，还是另有要事，就不得而知了。

位于川岛的神明神社和切田的伎留田神社中间另有一所神社，叫作广幡神社（菇野町广幡），其中也留存着两块算额。其中有一块 1812 年奉纳的算额，供奉者村井长影是菇野藩的勘定奉行[8]，他的老师是著名的关流数学家藤田定贞。另一张 1852 年供奉的算额来源于伊藤小兵卫重业，他是桑名的关流人士中川泰职的弟子，当时的年龄为 21 岁（[3]）。菇野和桑名之间的距离大概有 16 公里，虽然广幡神社的供奉者与川岛神明神社或伎留田神社的供奉者之间的关系还不是很清楚，但他们一定都看到了彼此的算额。如果这些算额的供奉年比较靠后，那么他们或许就无法看到彼此的算额了。所以考察算额的历史和地理文化的时候不仅考虑地域上的维度，同时也应该考虑时间上的跨度。

就四日市地区而言，1844 年供奉的算额背后的数学地理文化，大概在半径 8 公里左右的范围之内，那些数学爱好者们由于工作或旅行，需要出远门的时候，得到数学相关的知识并进行交流。另一方面，当时书籍的流通也已盛行，所以从那里获得信息的可能性也比较多了。

4 算额奉纳者的师徒关系

如前所述，森川永兴在川岛有两个弟子，在切田有一个弟子。如果对算额上的信息进行整理，就可以得出师徒之间关系的树状图，因此也就能了解当地数学文化的共时性、随时性及其扩展。如果到留存大量算额的福岛、岩手等地进行数学地理文化的考察，也许会得出更多有趣的数学史的研究结果。

5 算额供奉者的社会地位

在算额上，关于供奉者的社会地位方面的记载往往比较少，但偶尔可通过一些信息了解其社会地位。在上面举的例子中，切畑村大桥政五郎是一位村长，村井长影是菇野藩的勘定奉行，这些信息只能存在于地方的乡土历史资料中。在数学文化的研究视域下，了解供奉者的社会地位也有重要意义。

在海南岛，郭老师与笔者（2016 年 3 月 19 日）

---

8 江户时期的官名。

6 算额文化地理学

综上所述，在算额问题的数学研究中，应同时考虑多个算额之间的关系。又通过对算额相关人员的地理关系、师徒关系以及以乡土历史资料为基础的社会地位的研究，可以进一步揭示近世日本数学文化的空间结构或时间结构。依据已经收集到的算额信息点亮那些留存的算额，启动一轮崭新的综合性的研究，必将看到一个新的研究视角。以此为契机，我暂且将这种研究称之为"算额文化地理学"[9]。

7 结束语

虽说日本和中国离得很近，跟郭书春先生见面的机会却不是很多，但每次见面时都感到十分亲切，令人无比怀念，郭老师就是这样一位让大家尊敬和想念的前辈老师。通过此文向郭老师，及约稿的田森老师、邹大海老师、郭金海老师表示由衷的谢意。

参考文献

[1] 小川束：《算额文化地理学的尝试》（"算額文化地理学の試み"），*RIMS Kôkyûroku Bessatsu*，B85(2021)：1-13。

[2] 小川束：《日本数学史研究的可能性》（"日本数学史研究の可能性"），《现代思想》2021年7月号，22-34页。

[3] 佐佐木一：《菰野町的绘马》（日文原名"こものの絵馬"），《现代文化遗产报告》（日文期刊名"こもの文化財だより"）第12号（1997年）1—16页。

[4] 萨日娜：《日中数学界的近代—西洋数学移入之比较》（日文书名《日中数学界の近代—西洋数学移入の様相》），临川书店，2016年。

[5] 深川英俊：《从例题中了解日本的数学与计算》（日文书名"例題で知る日本の数学と算額"），森北出版，1998年。

（上海交通大学 萨日娜 译）

---

[9] 关于算额的书籍和论文很多，其中也出现了不把算额看作简单的数学问题集，而是将其归入到文化史范畴内探讨的意识。如福岛县和算研究保存会《新·福岛的和算》（1982）中包含了供奉算额的场所和显彰碑的分布、算额年表、供奉者相关信息等。另外，安富有恒《和算岩手现存算额的一切》（日文名"和算岩手の現存算額のすべて"）青磁者（1987）中也记载了现存算额的分布和详细年表。

和算对中算的继承与创新
——以关孝和的内插法和建部贤弘的累约术为例

曲安京 （西北大学科学史高等研究院）

摘要 以和算家的累裁招差法与累约术为例,通过探讨和算家的问题来源,及其处理这些问题时与中算家的不同方法和态度,说明中日两国数学家在数学创造方面的一些异同之处。和算作为继承并发展中国古代数学的一个标本,对于深刻理解机械化的程序算法体系的数学传统,是有益处的。

关键词 和算；内插法；不定分析；关孝和；建部贤弘

日本传统数学（和算）在 17 世纪中叶出现了一大批著名的数学家和数学成果。关孝和（Seki Takakazu,约 1642—1708）及其弟子建部贤弘（Takebe Katahiro,1664—1739）是其代表人物。

和算的成长时期,大体与我国的清代同时,他们是在接受传统中国数学的基础上发展起来的。与清代数学家不同的是,和算家研究的问题,虽然大部分都可以追朔到中算的源头,但是,这些问题,基本上都被和算家抽象为纯粹的数学问题,而且多有创造性的贡献。而与和算家同时代的明清数学家,则在对传统数学的继承与创新方面,相较和算家逊色很多。

比较和算与中算的异同,对于我们理解明清时期复兴中国传统数学的各种努力,特别是对我们理解中国古代数学的机械化程序算法体系的特征,及其在整个数学史长河中的地位,是有重要意义的。

关孝和的累裁招差法与建部贤弘和中根元珪（Nakane Genkei,1662—1733）的累约术,基本上根源于中国传统数理天文学中提出的问题,本文以这两个问题为例,通过复原和算家处理这些问题的思想方法,并比较它们与中国古代算法的异同,以期说明和算家对中国传统数学的机械化程序算法体系的继承与创新。

1 《授时历》的内插法与关孝和的累裁招差法

日本数学家对于内插法的研究,提出了若干种不同的算法,如累裁招差法、混沌招差法等。经过前人的研究,这些算法的具体内容和程序,已经很清楚了。[1]可以肯定的是,和算家构造的这些算法,都是在研究了《天文大成管窥辑要》(1653)中记录的《授时历》(1280)中的三次内插法的基础上发展起来的。

比较有意思的问题是,关孝和的累裁招差术与《授时历》的关系到底是怎样的？尽管已经有若干文章讨论,但是,由于这些研究者未能很好地理解《授时历》内插法的构造思想,因此,尚未见到很好的答案。[2,3]为了比较《授时历》与关孝和算法之构造思想的异同,让我们先简要地回顾一下《授时历》的内插法。

1.1 《授时历》的三次内插法

在《授时历》中,郭守敬创造了三次插值算法。令插值函数为
$$f(x) = ax + bx^2 + cx^3$$

其中,系数 a,b,c 分别被称为定差、平差、立差,因此,人们也称该算法为平立定三差算法。《授时历》三次插值函数 $f(x)$ 的构造原理,《元史》未做交代,目前人们最常引用的材料,即梅文鼎根据《大统历通轨》与《大统历历草》编写的《大统历法原》,收载于《明史历志》（卷33）。[4]根据梅文鼎的记述,我们可以知道《授时历》三次插值函数 $f(x)$ 是按以下的方式构成的：

首先,取 $x_k = kn$ 为插值点,称为"积日",则"积差" $f(x_k)$ 为已知。因为 $f(0) = 0$,所以,令
$$y(x) = \frac{f(x)}{x} = a + bx + cx^2$$

于是,当 $k \geqslant 1$ 时,"日平差"为

$$y_k = \frac{f(x_k)}{x_x}$$

为已知数据。由此可以得到

一差:$\Delta_k = y_{k+1} - y_k$

二差:$\Delta_k^2 = \Delta_{k+1} - \Delta_k$

因为构造的函数 $f(x)$ 是三次插值函数,所以,二差 Δ_k^2 彼此相同,记为 Δ_1^2。根据《明史历志》的记录,插值函数 $f(x)$ 的各项系数分别为:

定差:$a = y_1 - (\Delta_1 - \Delta_1^2)$

平差:$b = \dfrac{(\Delta_1 - \Delta_1^2) - \dfrac{\Delta_1^2}{2}}{n}$

立差:$c = \dfrac{\Delta_1^2}{2n^2}$

我们以《授时历》太阳视运动中心差为例,将《明史历志》记录的冬至前后的差分表的各项数据,照录在表1([4],3595—3596)。根据表1中的数据,按照上面给出的定差 a、平差 b、立差 c 的构成,可以立刻得到《授时历》太阳中心差在冬至前后的插值函数。

表1 《授时历》三差数据(冬至前后太阳时运动的中心差)

段日 k	积日 kn	积差 $f(kn)$	日平差 y_k	一差 Δ_k	二差 Δ_k^2
1	14.82	7058.0250	476.25	−38.45	−1.38
2	29.64	12976.3920	437.80	−39.83	−1.38
3	44.46	17693.7462	397.97	−41.21	−1.38
4	59.28	21148.7328	356.76	−42.59	−1.38
5	74.10	23279.9970	314.17	−43.97	
6	88.92	24026.1840	270.20		

1.2 《授时历》三次内插法是如何构造出来的?

我们已经看到,《授时历》的三次插值函数 $f(x)$ 是通过降阶,构造一般的二次函数 $y(x)$ 而得到的。这个二次函数与刘焯在其《皇极历》(600)中创立的二次内插函数的重要差别是出现了常数项,即定差 a。所以,对于郭守敬来说,构造函数 $y(x)$ 的关键,是要确定"定差"$a = y_0$ 的意义。

由于《明史历志》仅仅说明了《授时历》三次内插函数的系数构成,并没有告诉我们其三次内插法的构造过程,所以,清初以来,就不断有学者试图说明《授时历》的构造方法,可谓众说纷纭。[5,6,7,8]我们根据《天文大成管窥辑要》中记录的一些史料,可以将《授时历》构造三次内插法的方法复原。[9]现概述如下:

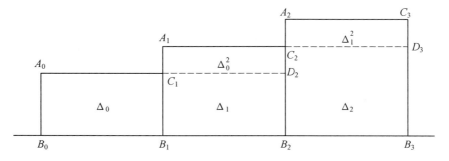

图1 《授时历》三次插值法的构造(1)

根据假设,当 $k \geqslant 1$ 时,已知一差
$$\Delta_k = y_{k+1} - y_k$$
令 $y_0 = a, \Delta_0 = y_1 - y_0, \Delta_0^2 = \Delta_1 - \Delta_0$,如图 1 所示,其中,$\Delta_k = $ 矩形 $A_k B_{k+1}$。根据假设,$\forall k \geqslant 0$,二差
$$\Delta_k^2 = \Delta_{k+1} - \Delta_k$$
彼此相等,是一个常数。由此可知
$$\Delta_0^2 = \Delta_1^2$$
于是,根据定义
$$y_1 - y_0 = \Delta_0 = \Delta_1 - \Delta_0^2 = \Delta_1 - \Delta_1^2$$
即
$$a = y_0 = y_1 - (\Delta_1 - \Delta_1^2)$$
这就是"定差"a 的来源。根据图 1,由于矩形 $A_k B_{k+1} = \Delta_k$,容易看出
$$y_1 = a + \Delta_0$$
$$y_2 = a + \Delta_0 + \Delta_1$$
$$y_3 = a + \Delta_0 + \Delta_1 + \Delta_2$$
根据《天文大成管窥辑要》的提示,[10] 将图 1 的相邻的矩形,"切"成一个大的、等积的梯形,如图 2 所示。令 $B_0 B = x$,记
$$y(x) = a + G_0 B_0 BG = a + G_0 B_0 BF + G_0 FG$$
因为
$$G_0 B_0 B_1 F_1 = \Delta_0 - \frac{\Delta_1^2}{2} = (\Delta_1 - \Delta_1^2) - \frac{\Delta_1^2}{2}$$
而
$$G_0 B_0 B_1 F_1 : n = G_0 B_0 BF : x = b$$
由此即得"平差"
$$b = \frac{(\Delta_1 - \Delta_1^2) - \frac{\Delta_1^2}{2}}{n}$$
又
$$G_0 F_1 G_1 = \frac{\Delta_1^2}{2}$$
而
$$G_0 F_1 G_1 : n^2 = G_0 FG : x^2 = c$$
由此即得"立差"
$$c = \frac{\Delta_1^2}{2n^2}$$

这就是《授时历》三次内插法的构造过程。由此可见,《授时历》算法的关键,是对于定差 a 的推算。在定差确定后,平差 b 和立差 c 可以根据几何图形(图 2),利用相似形的面积关系得出。

1.3《授时历》内插法的一般化

《授时历》三次内插法的构造,借助了几何图形。如果我们允许代数变换的话,根据《授时历》三次内插法的构造思想,可以将其推广到一般的情形,这样就更容易看出其造术思想的本质是什么。设所求函数为
$$f(x) = a_1 x + a_2 x^2 + \cdots + a_n x^n$$
第一步,令
$$y(x) = \frac{f(x)}{x} = a_1 + a_2 x + a_3 x^2 + \cdots + a_n x^{n-1}$$
取 $x_k = km$ 为插值点,若 $k \neq 0$,记

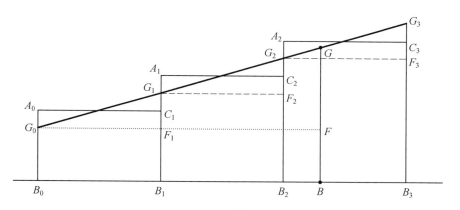

图 2 《授时历》三次插值法的构造(2)

$$y_k = \frac{f(x_k)}{x_k}$$

并且记 $y_0 = a_1, \Delta_k = y_{k+1} - y_k, \Delta_k^2 = \Delta_{k+1} - \Delta_k$,一般地,$\forall k \geqslant 0$,记

$$\Delta_k^r = \Delta_{k+1}^{r-1} - \Delta_k^{r-1}$$

如果存在 p,使得 $\Delta_1^p = \Delta_0^p$,则有

$$a_1 = y_0 = y_1 - \Delta_0 = y_1 - (\Delta_1 - \Delta_0^2) = \cdots = y_1 - \Delta_1 + \Delta_1^2 - \Delta_1^3 + \cdots + (-1)^p \Delta_1^p$$

第二步,令

$$z(x) = \frac{y(x) - a_1}{x} = a_2 + a_3 x + a_4 x^2 + \cdots + a_n x^{n-2}$$

若 $k \neq 0$,记

$$z_k = \frac{y_k - a_1}{x_k}$$

并且记 $z_0 = a_2, \Delta z_k = z_{k+1} - z_k, \Delta^2 z_k = \Delta z_{k+1} - \Delta z_k$,一般地,$\forall k \geqslant 0$,记

$$\Delta^r z_k = \Delta^{r-1} z_{k+1} - \Delta^{r-1} z_k$$

如果存在 q,使得 $\Delta^q z_1 = \Delta^q z_0$,则有

$$a_2 = z_0 = z_1 - \Delta z_0 = z_1 - (\Delta z_1 - \Delta^2 z_0) = \cdots = z_1 - \Delta z_1 + \Delta^2 z_1 - \cdots + (-1)^q \Delta^q z_1$$

第三步,重复上述步骤,令

$$w(x) = \frac{z(x) - a_2}{x} = a_3 + a_4 x + a_5 x^2 + \cdots + a_n x^{n-3}$$

可以得到系数 a_3。如此往复,即可得到函数 $y(x)$ 的所有系数。

1.4 关孝和的累裁招差法

累裁招差法,是关孝和的创造,记录在其《括要算法》中。[11] 根据前人的研究,累裁招差法的程序,已经非常清楚了。(文献[1],148—150 页)与《授时历》一样,关孝和欲构造的插值函数,也是缺少常数项的多项式,形如

$$f(x) = a_1 x + a_2 x^2 + \cdots + a_n x^n$$

并且,关孝和也是令

$$y(x) = \frac{f(x)}{x} = a_1 + a_2 x + a_3 x^2 + \cdots + a_n x^{n-1} \tag{1}$$

并通过确定函数 $y(x)$ 的系数,得到插值函数 $f(x)$。假设 $x = x_k$ 为插值点,记

$$y_k = y(x_k), k = 1, 2, \cdots$$

由此,可以构造一个差分表,如表 2 所示。

表 2　关孝和累裁差分表

k	y_k	Δy_k	$\Delta^2 y_k$	⋯	$\Delta^{n-1} y_k$
1	y_1	$\dfrac{y_2-y_1}{x_2-x_1}$	$\dfrac{\Delta y_2-\Delta y_1}{x_3-x_1}$	⋯	$\dfrac{\Delta^{n-2} y_2-\Delta^{n-2} y_1}{x_n-x_1}$
2	y_2	$\dfrac{y_3-y_2}{x_3-x_2}$	$\dfrac{\Delta y_3-\Delta y_2}{x_4-x_2}$	⋯	⋯
⋯	⋯	⋯	⋯	⋯	
$n-2$	y_{n-2}	$\dfrac{y_{n-1}-y_{n-2}}{x_{n-1}-x_{n-2}}$	$\dfrac{\Delta y_{n-1}-\Delta y_{n-2}}{x_n-x_{n-2}}$	⋯	
$n-1$	y_{n-1}	$\dfrac{y_n-y_{n-1}}{x_n-x_{n-1}}$	⋯⋯		
n	y_n	⋯			
$n+1$	y_{n+1}				

关孝和发现,函数(1)的最高次项的系数一定是:

$$a_n = \Delta^{n-1} y_1 = \frac{\Delta^{n-2} y_2 - \Delta^{n-2} y_1}{x_n - x_1}$$

于是,令

$$z(x) = y(x) - a_n x^{n-1} = a_1 + a_2 x + a_3 x^2 + \cdots + a_{n-1} x^{n-2}$$

则很容易得到

$$z_k = y_k - a_n x_k^{n-1}, k=1,2,3,\cdots$$

根据这些插值 z_k,可以构造一个类似表 2 的差分表(只需将表 2 中的 y 置换为 z),最后得到函数 $z(x)$ 的最高次项的系数 a_{n-1}

$$a_{n-1} = \Delta^{n-2} z_1 = \frac{\Delta^{n-3} z_2 - \Delta^{n-3} z_1}{x_{n-1} - x_1}$$

由此,确定函数(1)的系数 a_{n-1}。重复上述步骤,令

$$w(x) = z(x) - a_{n-1} x^{n-2} = a_1 + a_2 x + a_3 x^2 + \cdots + a_{n-2} x^{n-3}$$

可以确定系数 a_{n-2}。如此往复,即可得到所求函数 $y(x)$ 的所有系数。这就是关孝和的累裁招差法。

1.5 关孝和是如何构造出累裁招差法的?

关孝和在《括要算法》中利用累裁招差法构造了《授时历》平立定三差,并且在《天文大成管窥辑要》中专门撷取了 15 条与历法有关的算法,进行翻译校点,撰成《関订书》,其中就包含了《授时历》内插法的内容。[12]因此,三上义夫认为,关孝和的累裁招差法是在研究《天文大成管窥辑要》记录的《授时历》内插法的基础上创造的,和算史家们也普遍接受了三上义夫的看法。[13]

在和算史家针对关孝和垛积术的大量研究中,基本上倾向于运用现代数学符号,对累裁招差法的构造原理以及关孝和给出的各种"演段"(即具体的算法过程)进行详细的解说。[14,15]这些解说,对于我们理解"什么是累裁招差法"是很有帮助的,不过,要搞清楚"累裁招差法是怎么得到的",似乎还需要进一步的探究。

由于累裁招差法与《授时历》内插法的种种联系,人们很自然地会问:"累裁招差法是《授时历》内插

法的推广吗?"根据上面的讨论可以看到,《授时历》差分表1与累裁招差法的差分表2有着本质的不同。

因此,欲复原累裁招差法的构造思想,关键的问题是,关孝和是如何想到构造差分表2的?

实际上,在《括要算法》的开篇"垛积总术"中,关孝和以"累裁招差之法"为题,明确地阐释了他的算法的构造过程。关孝和说:

> 夫元积之各数参差者,齐之以累裁招差之法求之矣。凡以定积一次相减,各积差得等数者,招平定二差,而依一次相乘之法(古所谓相减相乘之法)求之;到二次相减各积差得等数者,招立平定三差,而依二次相乘之法(古所谓三差之法)求之;到三次相减各积差得等数者,招三乘立平定四差,而依三次相乘之法求之。皆俟各段得等数者,而招诸差率求元积也。(参考文献[1],273页)

根据这段文字可以知道,关孝和非常深刻地认识到,所求插值函数的阶数,与差分表的阶数是密切相关的,即:差分表的阶数,决定了插值函数的阶数。而关孝和得到这个深刻的见解,应该来源于他对于二次差分、三次差分的一种归纳。我们不难复原这个过程如下:

首先,如果假设所求函数为

$$y(x) = a_1 + a_2 x \tag{2}$$

令 $x = x_k$ 为插值点,称为第 k 段的"限数",则已知"定积" y_k 如下:

$$y_k = y(x_k), k = 1, 2, \cdots$$

根据

$$y_2 - y_1 = (a_1 + a_2 x_2) - (a_1 + a_2 x_1) = a_2(x_2 - x_1)$$

立刻得到函数(2)的最高次项的系数,即"平差" a_2

$$a_2 = \frac{y_2 - y_1}{x_2 - x_1} = \Delta y_1 \tag{3}$$

这就是《括要算法》"一次相乘演段"推导"平差"的过程。进一步,若假设所求函数为

$$y(x) = a_1 + a_2 x + a_3 x^2 \tag{4}$$

同样令 $x = x_k$ 为插值点,称为第 k 段的"限数",则已知"定积" y_k 如下

$$y_k = y(x_k), k = 1, 2, \cdots$$

于是有

$$y_2 - y_1 = (a_1 + a_2 x_2 + a_3 x_2^2) - (a_1 + a_2 x_1 + a_3 x_1^2) = a_2(x_2 - x_1) + a_3(x_2^2 - x_1^2)$$

记

$$\Delta y_1 = \frac{y_2 - y_1}{x_2 - x_1} = a_2 + a_3(x_2 + x_1)$$

同理可得

$$\Delta y_2 = \frac{y_3 - y_2}{x_3 - x_2} = a_2 + a_3(x_3 + x_2)$$

根据

$$\Delta y_2 - \Delta y_1 = a_3(x_3 - x_1)$$

立刻得到函数(4)的最高次项的系数,即"立差" a_3

$$a_3 = \frac{\Delta y_2 - \Delta y_1}{x_3 - x_1} = \Delta^2 y_1 \tag{5}$$

这就是《括要算法》"二次相乘演段"推导"立差"的过程。

根据以上的推理,不难归纳出以下的猜想:设所求函数为

$$y(x) = a_1 + a_2 x + a_3 x^2 + \cdots + a_n x^{n-1}$$

令 $x = x_k$ 为插值点,并且记

$$y_k = y(x_k), k = 1, 2, 3, \cdots$$

则根据(3)与(5)的提示,一定可以得到函数 $y(x)$ 的最高次项的系数 a_n

$$a_n = \frac{\Delta^{n-2} y_2 - \Delta^{n-2} y_1}{x_n - x_1} = \Delta^{n-1} y_1$$

由此,即可非常自然地构造出差分表2。

累裁招差法的构造思想由两个部分组成:首先,通过对简单情形的分析、归纳,猜测出一般的过程和结果;然后,完全利用代数变换,构造出一个纯粹的机械化的内插法算法。关孝和之所以能够成功地超越《授时历》的内插法,构造出一个全新的算法,关键的一点是,他能够将内插法的构造,从更加一般的角度抽象成一个纯粹的数学问题,从而利用代数变换,彻底摆脱了对几何图形的依赖。

2 中日内插法之异同

2.1 累裁招差法与《授时历》内插法的构造思想是不同的

《授时历》的内插法,是根据历法问题构造出来的一种算法。关孝和是在研究《天文大成管窥辑要》中记录的这个算法时,创造出来他自己的算法。因此,中日数学家内插法问题的来源是一致的,都是为了构造形如

$$f(x) = a_1 x + a_2 x^2 + \cdots + a_n x^n$$

的插值函数。值得注意的是,这个函数缺少常数项,据此,通过降阶,得到新的插值函数

$$y(x) = \frac{f(x)}{x} = a_1 + a_2 x + a_3 x^2 + \cdots + a_n x^{n-1}$$

然后,依次通过确定函数 $y(x)$ 的系数 a_k 来得到插值函数。

所差异者,《授时历》采用等间距的插值,利用事先给定的差分表,并按照如下次序

$$a_1 \to a_2 \to \cdots \to a_n$$

由低到高,确定函数的系数。关孝和则采用不等间距的插值,每降阶一次,按照相同的方式构造一个差分表,并按照次序

$$a_n \to a_{n-1} \to \cdots \to a_1$$

由高到低,次第确定函数的系数。

郭守敬《授时历》三次内插法的构造,延续了刘焯《皇极历》(600年)二次内插法的传统,始终依赖于几何图形解释所构造函数的数理意义,这个事实说明,郭守敬尚未深刻地认识到内插法的本质,因此,无法自觉地利用代数变换的技巧,也就很难发展完善更加一般的内插法。

关孝和在构造这个算法时,娴熟地利用了代数变换,完全超越了利用几何图形解释算法意义的做法。在算法的构造方面,这是一个深刻的飞跃。由此可以看出,关孝和对于内插法的本质有深刻的认识。

2.2 累裁招差法应该称为"关孝和内插法"

很多研究者称《授时历》或者关孝和的内插法是牛顿内插法,实际上这都是不准确的。牛顿插值函数是

$$f(x) = f(x_0) + \sum_{i=1}^{n} b_i \prod_{k=0}^{i-1} (x - x_k)$$

系数 b_i 按下面的方式次递获得

$$b_i = f_i(x_i) = \frac{f_{i-1}(x_i) - f_{i-1}(x_{i-1})}{x_i - x_{i-1}}$$

其中,$f_0(x) = f(x)$。确定系数的次序为

$$b_1 \to b_2 \to \cdots \to b_n$$

牛顿内插法在形式上,与《授时历》三次内插法和关孝和的累裁招差法显然不同。虽然,《授时历》与关孝和的算法,都采用了降阶的思想,通过逐次确定插值函数的系数,来构造插值函数,这一点与牛顿内插法是类似的。但是,他们采用降阶的方式是不同的。另外,牛顿内插法确定函数的系数是从低向

高,与关孝和相反。

概而言之,累裁招差法本身,堪称一个机械化的、完美的、崭新的算法,与牛顿内插法不同,可以直接称之为"关孝和内插法"。

3 建部贤弘的累约术

和算家的累约术,是处理一次不定不等式或一次同余式的算法。建部贤弘《累约术》的问题表述与解法均为一次不定不等式;中根元珪的《累约拾遗》则用同余式的方式处理相关的问题。

3.1 中日不定分析问题的来源

建部贤弘的《累约术》是一篇12页的短文,由三个问题及其解法组成。[18]他所考虑的主要问题可以表述为如下形式的不定不等式

$$|ax - by - c| < 1 \tag{6}$$

其中 a,b,c 为给定的有理数。中根元珪的《累约拾遗》则是由三个问题和两个历算问题的应用及其解法构成。[16]我们将会看到,中根元珪将所有问题都化为如下的标准的同余形式

$$ax - c \equiv r \pmod{b} \tag{7}$$

其中 $0 < r < d$。不难看出,不定不等式(6)与同余式(7)彼此可以转换。

《累约拾遗》的两个应用,都是根据日本当时行用的中国历法《宣明历》(822年)而设计的问题,可以肯定地说,《累约拾遗》就是为了解决这些历算问题而专门撰著的。

而在中国古代,为了计算上元积年,历法家们发明了所谓的"演纪术"。简单地说,上元,是一种特殊的历元,基本上是所有历法项目的共同起算点,为了计算这个历元,需要求解一个同余式组。可惜的是,在《授时历》(1280年)废除演纪上元之后,明清时期的数学家已经无人知晓推算上元的具体程序。从理论上讲,可以用中国剩余定理解决这个问题,但实际上,中国古代的历法家是按照代入法,依次逐个求解同余式,以获得理想的上元。[17]这个算法,被称为"演纪术"。对于演纪术,只需要知道如下同余式的解法

$$ax \equiv r' \pmod{b} \tag{8}$$

其中 $c < r' < d$。若令 $r = r' - c$,则式(8)立刻转化为中根元珪的同余式(7)。

由此可见,和算家的累约术的问题来源,与中国古代的同余理论类似,大体上都是源自历法中的实际问题。

3.2 建部贤弘的连分数算法

为了得到不定不等式(6)的一对整数解 (x,y),建部贤弘首先考虑 $c = 0$ 的情形。藤原松三郎(1881—1941)曾经对建部贤弘的累约术进行过详细的解读,(见文献[13],21—30页)据此可知,建部贤弘是按照如下的方式处理不定不等式

$$|ax - by| < 1 \tag{9}$$

首先,按照连分数展开,可以得到如下的序列

$$\frac{b}{a} = a_1 + \frac{r_1}{a}, \frac{a}{r_1} = a_2 + \frac{r_2}{r_1}, \frac{r_1}{r_2} = a_3 + \frac{r_3}{r_2}, \cdots, \frac{r_{n-2}}{r_{n-1}} = a_n + \frac{r_n}{r_{n-1}}$$

根据这些展式所得到的商 a_n 与不尽 r_n,可以获得 $\frac{b}{a}$ 的一系列渐近分数 $\frac{p_n}{q_n}$,其算法程序可以用表格表示出来,如表3所示。

根据表3给出的程序,可以得到如下的关系式:

$$ap_n - bq_n = (-1)^n r_n \tag{10}$$

当 $r_n < 1$ 时,就可以得到满足不定不等式(9)的一对整数解:

$$(x, y) = (p_n, q_n)$$

显而易见,建部贤弘给出的求解 (p_n, q_n) 的程序,与按连分数展开求渐近分数的程序是一致的。

表 3　累约术之连分数程序

商	不尽	益段	损段
a_1	$r_1 = b - a\,a_1$	$p_1 = a_1$	$q_1 = 1$
a_2	$r_2 = a - r_1 a_2$	$p_2 = 1 + p_1 a_2$	$q_2 = a_2$
a_3	$r_3 = r_1 - r_2 a_3$	$p_3 = p_1 + p_2 a_3$	$q_3 = q_1 + q_2 a_3$
a_4	$r_4 = r_2 - r_3 a_4$	$p_4 = p_2 + p_3 a_4$	$q_4 = q_2 + q_3 a_4$
…	…	…	…
a_n	$r_n = r_{n-2} - r_{n-1} a_n$	$p_n = p_{n-2} + p_{n-1} a_n$	$q_n = q_{n-2} + q_{n-1} a_n$

《累约术》设计的第一问,专门说明上述程序的应用。原题称:

假如有以一千三百一十八个七三〇六累益之,以五万九千五百九十四个七七〇五累损之,弹个数,问强弱损益段各几何?

答曰:弱益段:四千〇二十二;弱损段:八十九。强益段:五十五万〇〇六十五;强损段:一万二千一百七十二。

根据上述文字,可以列出如下的不定不等式

$$|1\,318.730\,6x - 59\,594.770\,5y| < 1$$

假设 (p_n, q_n) 是一组解,所谓"弱损益段",是指 (p_n, q_n) 满足

$$-1 < ap_n - bq_n < 0$$

"强损益段"是指 (p_n, q_n) 满足

$$0 < ap_n - bq_n < 1$$

《累约术》给出上述问题的演草如表 4 所示。

表 4　《累约术》第一问演草

号 n	商 a_n	不尽 r_n	益段 p_n	损段 q_n
甲 1	45	弱 251.893 5	45	1
乙 2	3	强 59.263 1	226	5
丙 3	4	弱 14.841 1	949	21
丁 4	2	强 14.739 8	3 073	68
戊 5	1	弱 0.101 3	4 022	89
己 6	136	强 0.963 0	550 065	12 172

这个程序中求序列 $\{p_n\}$ 的部分,就是中国数学史上著名的大衍求一术。式(10)也可以表示成

$$ap_n \equiv (-1)^n r_n \pmod{b}$$

当 b, a 都是整数的时候,总是可以得到 $(-1)^n r_n = 1$,此时 $p_n = k$ 就是我们所熟悉的乘率,它使得

$$ak \equiv 1 \pmod{b}$$

据此,可以得到同余式(8)的解。不过,在中国数学史上,我们没有发现求损段序列 $\{q_n\}$ 的程序,因此,关于是否中国古代已经有连分数算法的猜测,始终没有得到肯定。[18,19]

3.3 建部贤弘的累约术是如何构造出来的?

建部贤弘累约术的数学意义,是藤原松三郎首先揭示的,他用现代数学语言对累约术的算法程序进行了详细的解释,这些工作已经写入了日本数学史,而广为人知。(参见文献[1],310—318 页)

我们知道,建部贤弘的累约术,目的在于求解形如式(6)的不定不等式,这个不等式,也可以写为如

下形式的不定方程

$$ax - by - c = r, |r| < 1 \tag{11}$$

其中,$0 < a < b, c$ 为任意给定的有理数。我们感兴趣的是,建部贤弘到底是如何构造出他的累约术的？这是本节所要讨论的主要问题。

前面已经提到,为了求解形如式(11)的不定方程,建部贤弘利用连分数展开的方法,首先构造出了当 $c = 0$ 时的相关算法,并得到关系式(10):

$$ap_n - bq_n = (-1)^n r_n$$

这个结果非常重要。建部贤弘由此出发,构造不定方程(11)的算法程序。首先,由

$$\frac{b+c}{a} = b_1 - \frac{s_1}{a}, s_1 < a$$

可以得到

$$ab_1 - b - c = s_1$$

若令 $x_1 = b_1, y_1 = 1$,上式可以写成如下的形式

$$ax_1 - by_1 - c = s_1 \tag{12}$$

比较(11)与(12),不难知道,如果我们可以找到一系列的 s_n,使之不断地缩小,直至小于 1,则对应的 x_n 与 y_n 就可以满足不定方程(11)。由于序列 $\{r_n\}$ 是逐次递减的,因此,可以利用 r_n 来构造 s_n。所以,令

$$\frac{s_1}{r_1} = b_2 - \frac{s_2}{r_1}, s_2 < r_1$$

由此可得

$$s_2 = r_1 b_2 - s_1$$

根据式(10),可以得到

$$ap_1 b_2 - bq_1 b_2 = -r_1 b_2 \tag{12'}$$

式(12)与(12')相加,可以得到

$$a(x_1 + p_1 b_2) - b(y_1 + q_1 b_2) - c = -(r_1 b_2 - s_1)$$

若令 $x_2 = x_1 + p_1 b_2, y_2 = y_1 + q_1 b_2$,则上式化为

$$ax_2 - by_2 - c = -s_2 \tag{13}$$

同理,由

$$\frac{s_2}{r_2} = b_3 - \frac{s_3}{r_2}, s_3 < r_2$$

可得

$$s_3 = r_2 b_3 - s_2$$

根据式(10),可以得到

$$ap_2 b_3 - bq_2 b_3 = r_2 b_3 \tag{13'}$$

式(13)与(13')相加,可以得到

$$a(x_2 + p_2 b_3) - b(y_2 + q_2 b_3) - c = r_2 b_3 - s_2$$

若令 $x_3 = x_2 + p_2 b_3, y_3 = y_2 + q_2 b_3$,则上式化为

$$ax_3 - by_3 - c = s_3$$

重复上述步骤,可以得到

$$ax_n - by_n - c = (-1)^{n+1} s_n \tag{14}$$

其中

$$x_n = x_{n-1} + p_{n-1} b_n, x_1 = b_1$$
$$y_n = y_{n-1} + q_{n-1} b_n, y_1 = 1$$
$$s_n = r_{n-1} b_n - s_{n-1}, s_1 = ab_1 - (b+c)$$

当 $s_n < 1$ 时,满足式(14)的 (x_n, y_n) 即为不定方程(11)的解。

4 中根元珪的《累约拾遗》

中根元珪的《累约拾遗》由三个问题和两个应用组成。[16] 这些问题,都是用一次同余式的形式给出的。或许因为其最后的两个应用问题与历法有关,而当代的和算史家对此不是很熟悉,所以,有关的和算史研究论述中,很少仔细地讨论这部著作。

4.1 《累约拾遗》的问题

中根元珪《累约拾遗》中设计的三个问题,反映了一次同余式可能出现的几种不同的情况,他们最终都被转化为一种标准的同余形式。

第一问:给定同余式为
$$75.36x + 240.02 \equiv r' \pmod{301.63}$$
其中,$0 < r' < 1$。令原损 $c = 61.61 = 301.63 - 240.02$(原文误为 261.61),则化为定式:
$$75.36x - c \equiv r \pmod{301.63}$$
其中 $0 < r < 1$。这是小数的情形,余数被限定在单位1,与建部贤弘《累约术》设定的问题类似。

第二问:给定同余式为
$$1\,835x + 2\,675 \equiv r' \pmod{8\,400}$$
其中 $170 < r' < 250$。令原损 $c = 5\,895 = 170 - 2\,675 + 8\,400$,许限 $d = 80 = 250 - 170$。则化为定式:
$$1\,835x - c \equiv r \pmod{8\,400}$$
其中 $0 < r < d$。于是,问题被化为整数同余式的一般情形。

第三问:给定同余式为
$$170x + 50 \equiv r' \pmod{952}$$
其中 $10 < r' < 18$。由于等数 $(170, 952) = 34$,所以,上式有解的充分必要条件是:$r' = 16$。令原损 $c = 912 = 10 - 50 + 952$,许限 $d = 8 = 18 - 10$。则化为定式:
$$170x - c \equiv r \pmod{952}$$
其中 $0 < r < d$,实际上,$r = 6$。这也是化为整数同余式的情形,特别之处是,由于余数被唯一确定,因此,这个同余式的小于模 952 的解也是唯一的。

4.2 中根元珪的一次同余式的解法

根据上面的讨论可以看到,中根元珪将余数不定的一次同余的所有问题,都化为标准型:
$$ax - c \equiv r \pmod{b} \tag{15}$$
其中 a 称为累加,b 为累减,通常,$a < b$,c 为原损。令许限 $= d$,余数满足条件:
$$0 < r < d$$
为了求解同余式(15),先考虑 $c = 0$ 的情形:
$$ax \equiv r \pmod{b} \tag{16}$$
其中,$a < b$,$0 < r < d$。对于这个同余式,在前面讨论建部贤弘的算法时已经得到了求解的程序。首先,按照连分数展开,可以得到如下的序列:
$$\frac{b}{a} = a_1 + \frac{r_1}{a}, \frac{a}{r_1} = a_2 + \frac{r_2}{r_1}, \frac{r_1}{r_2} = a_3 + \frac{r_3}{r_2}, \cdots, \frac{r_{n-2}}{r_{n-1}} = a_n + \frac{r_n}{r_{n-1}}$$
由此可以得到一系列的商 a_n 与不尽 r_n,以及益段 p_n。因为中根元珪按同余问题处理,所以,不再考虑损段 q_n。

表 5　干营与支营

干营			
k	商 a_k	不尽 r_k	益段 p_k
甲 1	a_1	$r_1 = b - a a_1$	$p_1 = a_1$
乙 2	a_2	$r_2 = a - r_1 a_2$	$p_2 = 1 + p_1 a_2$
丙 3	a_3	$r_3 = r_1 - r_2 a_3$	$p_3 = p_1 + p_2 a_3$
…	…	…	…
n	a_n	$r_n = r_{n-2} - r_{n-1} a_n$	$p_n = p_{n-2} + p_{n-1} a_n$

支营			
k	商 b_k	不尽 s_k	益段 x_k
子 1	b_1	$s_1 = a b_1 - (b + c)$	$x_1 = b_1$
丑 2	b_2	$s_2 = r_1 b_2 - s_1$	$x_2 = x_1 + p_1 b_2$
寅 3	b_3	$s_3 = r_1 b_3 - s_2$	$x_3 = x_2 + p_2 b_3$
…	…	…	…
n	b_n	$s_n = r_{n-1} b_n - s_{n-1}$	$x_n = x_{n-1} + p_{n-1} b_n$

由此可以将同余式(16)转化为新的同余式

$$a p_n \equiv (-1)^n r_n \pmod{b} \tag{17}$$

这个结果非常重要。中根元珪由此出发，构造同余式(15)的算法程序。首先，由

$$\frac{kb+c}{a} = b_1 - \frac{s_1}{a}, s_1 < a, k = \begin{cases} 0, c > a \\ 1, c < a \end{cases}$$

可得

$$a b_1 - c = s_1 + kb$$

若令 $x_1 = b_1$，上式可以写成如下的同余形式：

$$a x_1 - c \equiv s_1 \pmod{b} \tag{18}$$

比较(15)与(18)，不难知道，如果我们可以找到一系列的 s_n，使之不断地缩小，当 $|s_n| > d$（许限）时，恒取 $s_n > 0$，直至满足

$$0 < (-1)^{n+1} s_n < d$$

则对应的 x_n 就可以满足不定方程(15)。由于序列 $\{r_n\}$ 是逐次递减的，因此，可以利用序列 $\{r_n\}$ 来构造 $\{s_n\}$。所以，令

$$\frac{s_1}{r_1} = b_2 - \frac{s_2}{r_1}, s_2 < r_1$$

可得

$$s_2 = r_1 b_2 - s_1$$

根据式(17)，可以得到

$$a p_1 b_2 \equiv -r_1 b_2 \pmod{b} \tag{18'}$$

(18)与(18′)相加，可以得到

$$a(x_1 + p_1 b_2) - c \equiv -(r_1 b_2 - s_1) \pmod{b}$$

若令 $x_2 = x_1 + p_1 b_2$，则上式化为

$$a x_2 - c \equiv -s_2 \pmod{b} \tag{19}$$

同理，由

$$\frac{s_2}{r_2} = b_3 - \frac{s_3}{r_2}, s_3 < r_2$$

可得
$$s_3 = r_2 b_3 - s_2$$
根据式(17),可以得到
$$a p_2 b_3 \equiv r_2 b_3 \pmod{b} \tag{19'}$$
(19)与(19')相加,可以得到
$$a(x_2 + p_2 b_3) - c \equiv r_2 b_3 - s_2 \pmod{b}$$
若令 $x_3 = x_2 + p_2 b_3$,则上式化为
$$a x_3 - c \equiv s_3 \pmod{b}$$
重复上述步骤,可以得到
$$a x_n - c \equiv (-1)^{n+1} s_n \pmod{b} \tag{20}$$
其中
$$x_n = x_{n-1} + p_{n-1} b_n, x_1 = b_1$$
$$s_n = r_{n-1} b_n - s_{n-1}, s_1 = a b_1 - (kb + c), k = \begin{cases} 0, c > a \\ 1, c < a \end{cases}$$

其中,$|s_n| > d$(许限)时,总是取 $s_n > 0$。当 $0 < (-1)^n s_n < d$ 时,满足式(20)的 x_n 就是同余式(15)的解。不难看出,中根元珪的算法与建部贤弘的算法,在构造思想上是一致的。但是,由于中根元珪用同余式的形式来处理问题,不再单独考虑所谓损段 q_n,因此,简化了相关的计算。

4.3 《累约拾遗》的应用题 I

《累约拾遗》的最后两个问题都是《宣明历》的应用。依笔者之孤陋,似乎未见现代和算史家对此进行研究,因此,让我们稍微做一些讨论。第一个应用问题称:

> 按建仁二年壬戌岁(1202)冬至,在庚午日夜子初一刻强,以辛未为冬至,盖为贺朔旦冬至也。由是观之,每在子初者,属明日也,亦不可知。故考贞观壬午(862)已来常气加时在子初以后者,如左。(贞观壬午(862)距贞享甲子(1684),行《宣明历》。)

通常我们认为夜半(子正)为日界,即一日的分界点。中根元珪发现,建仁二年(1202 年)冬至时刻在庚午日子初一刻强,即 23^h 至 24^h 之间,而历注当年冬至在辛未日,即庚午日之后一天。于是,中根元珪试图通过计算证明,对于 24 节气的时刻,《宣明历》都是以子初(23^h)为日界的。

令 $t = 3\,068\,055/8\,400$(日)表示《宣明历》的回归年常数,$c' = 4\,590/8\,400$(日)为贞观壬午(862 年)的冬至时刻,设贞观壬午冬至后第 x 节气的时刻为 r',则有
$$\frac{t}{24} x + c' \equiv r' \pmod{1}$$
我们试图求解 x,使得
$$\frac{8\,050}{8\,400} = \frac{23}{24} < r' < 1$$
将《宣明历》一节气的长度
$$\frac{t}{24} = 15 \frac{1\,835 + \frac{5}{8}}{8\,400} \text{(日)}$$
代入上面的同余式,稍加整理,可以得到
$$1\,835 \frac{5}{8} x - 3\,460 \equiv r \pmod{8\,400}$$

其中,累加 $a = 1\,835 + \frac{5}{8}$;累损 $b = 8\,400$;等数 $(a, b) = 1 + \frac{7}{8}$。原损 $c = 3\,460 = 8\,050 - 4\,590$;许限 $d = 350 = 8\,400 - 8\,050$。当不尽 $r = (-1)^{n+1} s_n$,满足

时,对应的 $x = x_n$,即为我们所需要的答案。《累约拾遗》中给出的演草如表 6 所示。因为 $c > a$,所以

$$s_1 = ab_1 - c = (1\ 835 + \frac{5}{8}) \times 2 - 3\ 460 = 211 + \frac{2}{8}$$

$$0 < r < d$$

此时,余数 $r = s_1 = 211 + \frac{2}{8} < d$,满足许限 d 设定的条件,对应的解为:$x = 2$,即贞观壬午(862 年)冬至后第二个节气的时刻就发生在 $23^h - 24^h$ 之间。

欲求下一个解,只需对 s_1 加(弱)或减(强)干营的余数 $r_n (n \geqslant 3)$,只要保证结果满足 $0 < r < d = 350$,则相应的 $x + p_n$ 即为所求的结果。例如

$$0 < r = s_1 + r_5 = 271 + \frac{2}{8} < 350$$

所以,$x + p_5 = 2 + 32 = 34$,这个结果的意思是,贞观壬午(862 年)冬至后第 34 个节气的时刻也发生在 23^h 至 24^h 之间。

表 6 《累约拾遗》应用题 I 演草

干营				支营			
n	a_n	r_n	$p_n = p_{n-2} + p_{n-1} a_n$	n	b_n	s_n	x_n
甲 1	4	弱 $1\ 057 + \frac{4}{8}$	$4 = 1 \times 4$	子 1	2	强 $211 + \frac{2}{8}$	$2 = 2$
乙 2	1	强 $778 + \frac{1}{8}$	$5 = 1 + 4 \times 1$				
丙 3	1	弱 $279 + \frac{3}{8}$	$9 = 4 + 5 \times 1$				
丁 4	2	强 $19 + \frac{3}{8}$	$23 = 5 + 9 \times 2$				
戊 5	1	弱 $60 + \frac{0}{8}$	$32 = 9 + 23 \times 1$				

4.4 《累约拾遗》的应用题 II

《累约拾遗》的第二个应用题,也是有关《宣明历》节气的推算。原题称:

> 《宣明》求天正经朔入气,世算历者,唯言视闰余在大雪定数已下为入大雪,已上,为入小雪。而不及言入立冬之数。岂不误乎?今按闰余分二十四万四千六百七十二已上者,皆得入立冬。因考贞观壬午(862)已来逢次限者,如左。[乃起长元五年壬申(1032)至元历元年甲辰(1184),百五十三年之间,逢此限者,九次。尔后五百年有余,不逢此限,宜乎人不知有此数也。]

天正经朔到冬至时刻的时间,称为"闰余"。由于两个平气的长度(约 30.46 日)大于一个朔望月的长度(约 29.53 日),因此,天正经朔时刻,通常在小雪之后。若在小雪与大雪之间,称为"入小雪";在大雪之后,称为"入大雪"。但是,如果采用定气注历,则小雪与大雪定气之和

$$d' = 14\ \frac{5\ 235 + \frac{5}{8}}{8\ 400} + 14\ \frac{4\ 235 + \frac{5}{8}}{8\ 400} \approx \frac{244\ 672}{8\ 400} < 29.53 (日)$$

也就是说,天正经朔时刻,有可能出现在立冬与小雪之间,称为"入立冬"。我们可以建立如下的同余式,来计算贞观壬午(862 年)之后第 x 年的闰余,即当年的天正经朔时刻到冬至时刻的时间 r'

$$tx + c' \equiv r' \pmod{u} \tag{21}$$

其中《宣明历》的常数:回归年 $t = 3\ 068\ 055/8\ 400$(日);朔望月 $u = 248\ 057/8\ 400$(日);$c' =$

94 249/8 400(日),表示贞观壬午(862 年)闰余,称为"元数"。因此,当余数 r' 满足

$$d' < r' < u$$

时,天正经朔时刻应该在立冬与小雪之间,即入立冬。同余式(21)可以简化为

$$(t - 12u)x + c' \equiv r' \pmod{u}$$

其中,$t - 12u = \frac{91\ 371}{8\ 400}$(日)。以 8 400 同乘于上面的同余式,并稍加整理,可以得到同余式

$$91\ 371x - 150\ 423 \equiv r \pmod{248\ 057}$$

其中,累加 $a = 91\ 371$;累损 $b = 248\ 057$;等数 $(a, b) = 1$。原损 $c = 150\ 423 = 244\ 672 - 94\ 249$;许限 $d = 3\ 385 = 248\ 057 - 244\ 672$。当不尽 $r = (-1)^{n+1}s_n$,满足

$$0 < r < d$$

时,对应的 $x = x_n$,即为我们需要的答案。《累约拾遗》给出的演草如表 7 所示。其中

$$s_6 = r_5 b_6 - s_5 = 350 \times 7 - 5\ 563 = -3\ 113$$

所以,余数 $r = -s_6 = 3\ 113 < d$,这是满足许限 d 的最大的余数。相应的解为 $x = x_7 = 170$,即贞观壬午(862 年)之后第 170 年的天正经朔时刻一定在立冬与小雪之间,这一年是长元五年(1032 年)。求下一个解的方法,与上一节讨论的应用题 I 类似。

表 7 《累约拾遗》应用题 II 演草

干营				支营			
n	a_n	r_n	$p_n = p_{n-2} + p_{n-1}a_n$	n	b_n	s_n	$x_n = x_{n-1} + p_{n-1}b_n$
甲 1	2	弱 65 315	$2 = 1 \times 2$	子 1	2	强 32 319	$2 = 2$
乙 2	1	强 26 056	$3 = 1 + 2 \times 1$	丑 2	1	弱 32 996	$4 = 2 + 2 \times 1$
丙 3	2	弱 13 203	$8 = 2 + 3 \times 2$	寅 3	2	强 19 116	$10 = 4 + 3 \times 2$
丁 4	1	强 12 853	$11 = 3 + 8 \times 1$	卯 4	2	弱 7 290	$26 = 10 + 8 \times 2$
戊 5	1	弱 350	$19 = 8 + 11 \times 1$	辰 5	1	强 5 563	$37 = 26 + 11 \times 1$
己 6	28	强 3 053	$543 = 11 + 19 \times 28$	巳 6	7	强 3 113	$170 = 37 + 19 \times 7$
己 6	29	强 2 703	$562 = 11 + 19 \times 29$				

5 中日不定分析的异同

建部贤弘和中根元珪的累约术,分别给出了一次不定方程与同余式的算法,从算法的构造思想来看,两者是相通的。建部贤弘考虑了一般形式的二元一次不定方程

$$ax - by - c = r, |r| < 1$$

中,根元珪考虑了对应的一次同余问题

$$ax - c \equiv r \pmod{b}, 0 < r < d \tag{22}$$

在构造上述问题的解法时,都采用了如下策略:先考虑 $c = 0$ 时的算法,并由此出发,得出一般问题的解法程序。值得一提的是,建部贤弘在处理 $c = 0$ 时的不定方程的时候,应用了连分数展开的算法,并得到了渐近分数列。

中国古代除了百鸡之类的问题以外,很少从不定方程的角度设计问题。通常都将问题化为同余式来处理。在解决同余式的时候,关键的算法是大衍求一术,也就是建部贤弘与中根元珪设计的求益段 p_n 的程序,一直进行到 $(-1)^n r_n = 1$。这个算法中,并未涉及损率 q_n,因此,累约术对于连分数算法的应用是建部贤弘的一项创造。

中根元珪选取的应用问题,都是《宣明历》带来的实际问题,与中国古代利用演纪术推求上元积年的问题类似。利用同余式处理不定方程,可以大大简化算法的复杂性,这是中根元珪对建部贤弘之累约术的发展。

当同余式中余数 r 的选择范围不是很大的时候,利用大衍求一术,直接求得乘率 $k=p_n$,使得 $(-1)^n r_n = 1$,此时
$$ak \equiv 1 (\mod b)$$
由此可以得到同余式(22)的解
$$x \equiv (r+c)k (\mod b) \tag{23}$$

这是中国古代处理此类问题的一般方法。不过,当余数 r 的选择范围很大时,欲根据式(23)得到合适的解,就有点费事。此时,建部贤弘与中根元珪设计的支营的算法就显得很有必要了,这也是和算家对一次不定分析算法的另一项创造。

由于累约术处理的问题,大体上都是单个的不定方程或同余式,因此,与中国剩余定理基本上没有关系。实际上,中国剩余定理是秦九韶的一项数学创造,它的诞生,虽然与历法上元积年的推求有关,但是,却并未真正在历法计算上发挥作用。

另外,值得指出的是,建部贤弘与中根元珪的累约术,都是非常完整的机械化的程序算法。这一点,继承了中国古代处理不定分析问题的算法传统。

6　结论

本文以关孝和的累裁招差术、建部贤弘和中根元珪的累约术为例,讨论了和算家研究这些问题的出发点、研究方式,及其与中国古代数学家的异同之处。根据上面的讨论可以看出,和算家的出发点,都是基于中国传统数理天文学所提出的问题,他们处理这些问题的思想方法与中国古代类似,也是通过设计机械化的程序算法,获得问题的解答。

值得我们深思的是,中算家在设计算法的时候,常常从具体问题出发,依赖于其几何意义的阐述,较少运用代数变换的技巧,因此,不容易洞悉他们所设计的算法的数学本质,由此便很难抽象、归纳出更加一般的程序算法。与此同时,中国传统的数学家,绝大部分都是带着直接为历法服务的功利性的目的来设计算法的,因此,他们的数学创造,常常是有局限的、适可而止的。这一点,中算家的内插法是一个典型的事例:对于中国古代历法家来说,从使用功能的角度看,基于几何图形构造的分段二次内插法(刘焯,600 年),或三次内插法(郭守敬,1280 年),不仅是合理的,而且是充分的。很难,也似乎没有必要在此基础上做出新的创造。

与之形成鲜明对比的是,和算家通常都是比较纯粹的数学家,因此,他们的研究较少急功近利的、实用主义的桎梏,导致他们在探索中国传统数学问题的处理方法时,更加关注解决这些问题的算法的数学本质,从而将现实问题抽象为更为一般的数学问题。例如:

对于内插法,关孝和深刻地认识到,通过给定的 n 个插值点 $x=x_k$,就可以确定如下形式的多项式插值函数
$$y(x) = a_1 + a_2 x + a_3 x^2 + \cdots + a_n x^{n-1}$$
这就是内插法的本质。

对于一次不定分析,建部贤弘总是将问题抽象为如下的数学形式
$$ax - by - c = r, |r| < 1$$
其中 $0 < a < b$,c 为任意给定的有理数。而中根元珪则将问题归结为统一的同余形式
$$ax - c \equiv r (\mod b), 0 < r < d$$
其中 a,b,c,d 都是非负有理数。他们都是从 $c=0$ 的特殊情形出发,构造出上述问题的一般算法程序。

将现实问题抽象为数学问题,是近代科学的一个极为重要的标志。和算家在现实中提取问题,并能超越具体问题的束缚,是和算家在继承中算传统时,能够做出更多深刻的、创造性的数学成就的主要原因,这也是和算对中国数学传统的最为重要的创新。

作为一个纯粹的数学家,秦九韶在《数书九章》中所设计的中国剩余定理和大衍求一术都成功地超越了实际问题的限制。可惜,这样的中国数学家并不多见。

吴文俊先生认为，在数学历史的长河中，应该存在着两种交互出现的数学潮流，其一为公理化的逻辑演绎体系，其二为机械化的程序算法体系。后者的典型代表，就是中国传统数学。对于数学史来说，以算法为特征的中国古典数学，是否可以得到深刻而全面的发展，并在适当时机成为数学发展的主流，是一个引人关注的问题。[20]

和算中的许多问题，来源于中国传统的数学与数理天文学，比较17世纪以来中日两国数学家在数学领域的继承与创新，是非常有趣的题目。

中国古代数学，在14世纪以后，基本上停止了发展。在17世纪（明末清初），西方科学第一次传入中国的时候，一些数学家开始树立复兴传统数学的旗帜。但是，从清代数学家的表现来看，在继承并发扬中国数学传统方面，似乎并不成功，我们很少看到清代的数学家在机械化算法的设计方面，取得令人赞叹的成就。

与此同时，日本明治之前的数学（和算），继承了中国古代数学的传统，并且有深刻的发展和创新。和算家的数学实践证明，中国传统数学的思想方法，在代数变换技巧的辅助下，可以在很大程度上发展出一套完美的机械化的程序算法体系。只要将合适的现实问题转化为合适的数学问题，机械化的程序算法体系是可以大有作为的。

吴文俊先生自己在数学机械化方面的工作是现代数学家继承中国传统数学的一次实践。不过，我们确实希望在没有广泛经受西方近代数学浸淫的文化中，可以找到中国传统数学获得继承和发展的实例。

如果说，在人类数学文明的历史上，以机械化算法为特色的数学思想，确曾主导过数学的潮流，并在计算机的时代，有可能再度成为数学家们关注的焦点，那么，和算家的数学活动，作为中国数学传统得以延续和发展的一个珍贵的化石，或许可以算是我们必须认真对待和算研究的一个重要的理由。

参考文献

[1] 日本学士院编. 明治前日本数学史(2). 东京:临川书店,1979,148—154

[2] 冯立升. 从关孝和的累裁招差法看《授时历》平立定三差法之原. 自然科学史研究,2001,20(2):132—142

[3] 徐泽林. 和算家对招差法的继承与发展. 李迪. 数学史研究. 第七辑. 呼和浩特:内蒙古大学出版社,2001,124—133

[4] 中华书局编. 历代天文律历等志汇编(10). 北京:中华书局,1976,3595—3620

[5] (清)黄宗羲. 授时历故. 嘉业堂丛书本. 1923

[6] 李俨. 中算家的内插法研究. 北京:科学出版社,1957,62—73

[7] 钱宝琮. 中国数学史. 北京:科学出版社,1964,189—197

[8] 曲安京,纪志刚,王荣彬. 中国古代数理天文学探析. 西安:西北大学出版社,1994,185—200,309—321

[9] 曲安京. 中国古代历法中的三次内插法. 自然科学史研究,1996,15(2):131—143

[10] (清)黄鼎. 天文大成管窥辑要(卷12). 云林阁刊本. 1653(顺治十年). 台北:老古文化事业公司影印本,1984,163

[11] 平山谛等编. 関孝和全集·括要算法. 大阪:大阪教育图书株式会社,1974,273—282

[12] 平山谛等编. 関孝和全集·关订书. 大阪:大阪教育图书株式会社,1974,423—464

[13] 土仓保等编. 東洋数学史への招待－藤原松三郎数学史论文集. 仙台:东北大学出版会,2007,57—72

[14] 竹之内修. 関孝和《括要算法·卷元》垛积术. 数理解析研究所讲究录(1546). 京都:京都大学数理解析研究所,2007,157—162

[15] 小川束. 関孝和によるベルヌーィ数の発见. 数理解析研究所讲究录(1583). 京都:京都大学

数理解析研究所,2008,1—18

[16] 建部贤弘. 累约术.(日本)东北大学图书馆藏,冈本文库写 0304

[17] 曲安京. 中国历法与数学. 北京:科学出版社,2005,74—91

[18] 华罗庚. 从祖冲之的圆周率谈起. 华罗庚科普著作选集. 上海:上海教育出版社,1984,47—80

[19] 李继闵. "通其率"考释. 中国数学史论文集(1). 济南:山东教育出版社,1985,24—36

[20] Wu Wentsun, Mathematics Mechanization. Beijing:Science Press & Dorrecht:Kluwer Academic Publishers,2000,1—66

论川边信一对《周髀算经》的校勘与注解工作

徐泽林[1]　（东华大学人文学院）
田春芝　（上海交通大学科学史与科学文化研究院）

摘要　中国古代数理天文学经典《周髀算经》流传历史源远流长，并且流传到周边的汉字文化圈国家，为汉字文化圈各国学者所注解和研究。日本江户时期的川边信一与清代乾嘉时期的戴震生活年代大致相同，在经学范式下分别独自对《周髀算经》进行了校勘和注解。本文对他们的校勘、注解工作进行了比较，认为尽管他们采用的底本不同，但在校勘方面的工作都很出色，在注释方面，川边信一的图解工作更为细致，也敢于对前人的注解提出批评。

关键词　《周髀算经》；校勘；注解；川边信一；戴震

引言

成书于西汉的《周髀算经》是中国古代一部重要的数理天文学经典，自三国时期赵爽为之作注后，在经学学术传统中历代为之校勘、注解不绝，明清时代随着经学考据之学的隆盛，在西方数理天文学的刺激下出现了《周髀算经》文献学研究的高潮，以梅文鼎（1633—1721）、戴震（1724—1777）、顾观光（1799—1862）等人的校勘注解工作为代表。进入20世纪，《周髀算经》也成为现代学术语境下中国科学史研究的热点之一，特别是20世纪60年代之后，随着中国数学史与天文学史研究的深入，再次出现了研究《周髀算经》的高潮，除围绕其中天文、数学问题的诸多专题研究外，也出现了一批文献整理性成果，如钱宝琮（1892—1974）的校点[1]、郭书春与刘钝的校点[2]、江晓原与谢筠的译注[3]、曲安京的新议[4]、程贞一与闻人军的译注[5]等。

在中国文化影响下，《周髀算经》传播于汉字文化圈国家，而且也在这些国家被翻刻、注解和研究。日本江户时代（1603—1867）共出现三种有关《周髀算经》注解的刊本，即川边信一（生卒年不详）的《周髀算经图解》（1785年刊）、石井宽道（生卒年不详）的《周髀算经正解图》（1813年刊）以及筱原善富（生卒年不详）的《周髀算经国字解》（1815年刊）。前者不仅给出许多注解，而且做了大量的校勘工作，后两者是在前者基础上进行注解的。这些日本人注解书至今尚未受到学术界关注，其校勘与注解的成果对我们校勘《周髀算经》并理解其中有关内容具有参考价值。本文探讨川边信一的校勘注解工作，并将其与戴震的校勘注解工作相比较。

一、《周髀算经》传播日本及其在江户时代注解概况

江户时代的汉学，是指江户时代通过汉籍研读来研究中国古典学术思想、学做汉文诗文的学问，即由中国传入的学术的总称，是相对于江户时代日本固有学术与神道的国学以及由荷兰传入的学术——兰学（洋学）而称谓的。江户时代经学发展与其儒学发展紧密联系在一起。德川幕府为确立政权的正统

1　徐泽林，1963年生，东华大学人文学院教授，主要研究方向为东亚数学史。田春芝，上海交通大学科学史与科学文化研究院博士后。基金项目：东华大学中央高校基本科研业务费专项基金项目"中华文明及其现代转型研究"（项目编号：2232019H—02）；国家自然科学基金项目"江户时代日本学者对《授时历》的历理分析与算法改进"（项目编号：11873024）；国家重点文化工程"全球汉籍合璧"工程招标项目"日本馆藏天文历算汉籍编目"（合同编号：HBB201904）。

性且利于政治思想上的统治而大力提倡儒学，因此江户时代的儒学摆脱对佛教禅宗的从属而独立发展。17 世纪初至中叶，朱子学被列为幕府的"官学"后，儒家思想观念对武士与町人等社会阶层都产生了重要影响，同时也促进了经学的发展。儒学家伊藤仁斋[2](1627—1705 年)认为，要想真正掌握汉学精华，就必须了解古典乃至古代的真实面貌，对宋学采取批判态度，主张摈弃朱子学，恢复儒家经典的古义。其古义学派的治学与清初考据学已有了共通之处。仓石武四郎(1897—1975)认为：

学术方面，在徂徕之后出现了皆川淇园和山本北山。他们摇着折中的大旗，与清朝初期的顾炎武、阎若璩等人的主张几乎如出一辙。但经过吉田篁墩、大田锦城，再到松崎慊堂、山梨稻川这一代时，已渐渐显露了乾嘉学派钱大昕、段玉裁的风格了。[6]

江户时代儒学流派林立，著名者有以藤原惺窝(1561—1619)为首的朱子学派、中江藤树(1608—1648)的阳明学派、山崎暗斋(1618—1682)和浅见絅斋(1652—1712)的敬义学派[3]、伊藤仁斋的古学(古义)学派[4]、荻生徂徕(1666—1728)的古文辞学(复古学)派、榊原篁州(1656—1706)和山本北山(1752—1812)的折中学(考证学)派、猪饲敬所(1761—1845)和宇野明霞(1698—1745)的古注学派、德川光圀(1628—1701)的水户学派[5]以及三浦梅园(1723—1789)和二宫尊德(1787—1856)的独立学派等，各学派对汉文经典的研究促进了考据学的发展。伴随汉籍的大量输入，考据学风在日本儒学界大为盛行，日本学者不仅征引清代学者的研究成果，而且对汉籍经典进行全面校勘、训诂、注释与诊解。江户幕府时期(1639—1853)日本民族的自我意识尤为强烈，十分成功地吸收、改造了外来文化，完成了汉学的日本化。

据现存资料考证，《周髀算经》首次传入日本当在 7 世纪大化革新时期，日本模仿唐朝建立律令制国家，颁布的学令中所规定的算学教育与考试使用的教科书包括《周髀算经》[7]。公元 10 世纪以前，《周髀算经》一直在日本使用，但是平安时代、镰仓时代、室町时代乃至战国时期的历史文献中未见有关《周髀算经》的记录。宋刊《周髀算经》是否流播于日本，今无从稽考。从 16 世纪下半叶到 17 世纪上半叶，中国元代与明代的天文算学书主要通过海上走私贸易以及丰臣秀吉(1537—1598)侵略朝鲜期间而流入日本。明刊本《周髀算经》随《秘册汇函》《津逮秘书》丛书流入日本。江户时代的日本汉学家对《周髀算经》也进行了校勘与注解。

二、川边信一对《周髀算经》的校勘与注解

川边信一，生卒年不详，字以清，通称百弥，号南长，尾张名古屋藩藩士，江户中期的汉学家与和算家，学于同为武士的和算家鸟居圆秋(1691—1744)。深受经学、考据学及西学的影响，他有感于明刊本《周髀算经》中的舛误甚多，于天明五年(1785 年)著《周髀算经图解》，这是日本人首次对《周髀算经》进行校勘和注解。

1. 关于《周髀算经图解》的底本

川边信一在《周髀算经图解》中有一案语，明确指出其底本为明刻本。从《周髀算经图解》收录毛晋的校、书末还有毛晋的识语等信息也可断定《秘册汇函》本《周髀算经》乃其工作底本之一。另外，石原正贺(生卒年不详)为《周髀算经图解》所写的跋文如下：

"吾友有川边信一者，自幼覃思算法，研穷不倦，尝得《周髀算经》而览之，惜乎传写有鲁鱼错简而读者惑焉，于是并考明毛晋所辑《津逮秘书》，所载脱简误字亦未得其正也。信一废卷叹

---

[2] 日本江户时代的儒学家，在中国，大约在五十年后才出现了与伊藤仁斋相似的对朱子学批判的观点。
[3] 山崎暗斋，字敬义，著名的朱子学者，他创立的特殊的朱子学派名为"新南学""崎门学派"或"敬义学派"。
[4] 日本江户时代儒学学派别之一。古学者原多为朱子学追随者，后怀疑朱子学，认为与孔子、孟子原意不同，而倡古学，呼吁不依赖后人的注疏，而从孔孟的原著中直接探索儒学的真意。以山鹿素行、伊藤仁斋、荻生徂徕为代表。
[5] 水户，指水户藩的学术，以朱子学为中心，综合国学和神道，倡导尊王和大义。

云：古历之所传，纰缪如此，盖订之。乃倚闲窗，忘寝食，参伍考索，殆剖折其义，故以国字图解之，间亦补脱简、正谬误，校订新成矣。欲锓诸梓便童行，予一见以为古历之法，坐致度数如斯夫，实发古人所未发。正贺感其精核，喜大有辅仁之益，贻之以言耳。天明五年岁次乙巳季夏。"[8]150

在此跋文中，石原正贺称川边"并考"毛晋所辑《津逮秘书》。此外，在《周髀算经图解》的注释中还提到了"另本"，在"算法源流"之后川边又注曰："一本不载此'算学源流'，今因一本。"众所周知，《津逮秘书》本不载"算学源流"，而《秘册汇函》本有载。这些信息也表明，川边信一所谓的"另本"或"一本"，指的是《秘册汇函》本，他校勘的底本应该是《秘册汇函》本《周髀算经》，校勘过程中与《津逮秘书》本《周髀算经》做了对校。

2.《周髀算经图解》中的文献考证工作

日本汉学家与中国历代经学家一样，对古文献进行文字训诂与文献考证。《周髀算经图解》参考了大量的汉籍，主要有：《史记》《汉书·天文志》《汉书·地理志》《法言》《魏书·律历志》《晋书·天文志》《隋书·律历志》《旧唐书·天文志》《宋书·天文志》《宋书·历志》《元史·天文志》《授时历议》《元史·地理志》《孙子算经》《易经》《说文》《尔雅》《书经》《诗经》《论语》《易纬通卦验》《周礼》《大戴礼》《天地万物造化论》《尚书·考灵曜》《灵宪》《律历记候》《淮南子》《吕氏春秋》《河图括地象》《邹子》《释名》《元命包》《梅氏历算全书》《天经或问》等。关于《周髀算经》的源流，川边信一采用《汉书·天文志》《法言》《晋书·天文志》《元史·天文志》等文献的说法，并引用梅文鼎《历算全书》中的论述。如对卷下经文"欲知北极枢，璇玑周四极"，川边注解如下：

云北极璇玑四游也。璇，玉也。玑，操也。极中不动，极枢也。《音义》：极枢者，取其居中而临制四方。《尚书·舜典》：在璇玑玉衡以齐七政。孔安国云：璇，美玉。玑、衡，王者正天文之器，可运转者。马融亦同云：玑，浑天仪可转旋，故曰玑；衡，其中横箇[6]，以璇为玑，以玉为衡，盖贵天象也。《史记·天官书》云：北斗七星，所谓旋玑玉衡，以齐七政。《索隐》曰：《春秋运斗枢》云：斗，第一天枢，第二璇，第三玑，第四权，第五衡，第六开阳，第七摇光。《晋志》云"北斗，魁四星为旋玑，杓三星为玉衡"云云。今命北极游而云璇玑，名北斗之星为旋玑，皆出自《舜典》之"璇玑"、拟运转之象而为其名也。[8]

为解释"璇玑"而征引了六种古书中的说法及两位经学家的注解。在征引的中国文献中，参考最多的是梅文鼎的《历算全书》。由此可见梅氏著作在江户时代的影响。

3. 川边对《周髀算经》的校勘工作

《秘册汇函》与《津逮秘书》本《周髀算经》中的脱字、讹字、衍字、倒字和错简等处较多，《周髀算经图解》对其进行校勘，共出校注229条，其中上卷共117条，下卷共112条。

（1）补脱字

川边补脱字共38处，其中卷上23处，卷下15处。所补脱字多为当补之字。但有些地方的补字也未必准确。如卷上后面在论述夏至之日中光与各处的距离时，明刊本经文如下：

"夏至之日中光，南过冬至之日中光四万八千里；南过人所望见一万六千里；北过周十五万一千里；北过极四万八千里。"[9]

川边认为明刻本脱"夏至日中光"五字，补之如下：

6　"箇"当为"箫"之误。

"夏至之日中光,南过冬至之日中光四万八千里。夏至日中光[7],南过人所望见一万六千里。夏至日中光[8],北过周十五万一千里。夏至日中光[9],北过极四万八千里。"[8]50-51

此处中国历代校勘者皆未校补。这段文字先言夏至日中,日光向南超过冬至之日中的距离,继言夏至日中,日光距离周地一万六千里,后言向北过周十五万一千里,最后言北过极的距离。后三句的主语都是"夏至日中光",既然首句已有,则后三句的主语皆可省略。川边为了保持句式的统一而补字,补字后反使文句拖沓、烦琐。

另外,明刊本中某些脱文,川边和戴震都没有补出,且注解皆不甚准确。如对求日高、日远和邪至日的甄鸾注文:

"求远者,影乘定间,差法而一,所得加表,日之高也。求邪去地者,弦乘定间,差法而一,所得加弦,日邪去地[10]"。[8]32

川边认为:"此文有错误而难算。今改言之:求远者,以表乘定间差,以影而一,所得加表,日之高也。"川边所改的术文依然有误,既然求日远,为何要加表高?戴震也没有给出校注,郭书春与刘钝校勘本、程贞一与闻人军校勘本皆从戴震本,但钱宝琮认为此处有脱文,故补之如下:

"求远者,影乘定间,差法而一,所得加影,日之远也。求高者,表乘定间,差法而一,所得加表,日之高也"。[1]38

正好与下文"求邪去地者,弦乘定间,差法而一,所得加弦,日邪去地"相对应。

校改后,相对应的计算公式如下:

$$日高 = \frac{表高 \times 定间}{影差} \times 表高 \quad (1)$$

$$日远 = \frac{日影 \times 定间}{影差} \times 日影 \quad (2)$$

$$邪至日 = \frac{弦 \times 定间}{影差} \times 弦 \quad (3)$$

依据上下文义和公式可知,钱宝琮所补脱文为是。

(2)改讹字

川边改《秘册记录》本中的讹字共104处,其中《题辞》部分2处,卷上59处,卷下43处。绝大多数的校改是正确的,但有些错字也没有做校改。如卷下"夏至昼极长……阳照九,不覆三"。赵注"《考灵曜》曰:分周天为三十六头,头有十度九十六分之十四……行二十四头。"中的"头"字川边没有校改出来。戴震校曰:"顷,各本讹作头,下同。今据《隋书·天文志》《梁大同十年考周一百八》到依《尚书·考灵曜》昼夜三十六顷之数,因而三之可证头字当为顷,所谓顷刻是也,今并改正。"戴震之后,中国各版本皆从戴校,改"头"为"顷"。

又如卷上勾股圆方图中"既方之外,半之一矩"。戴震校改作"既方其外,半之一矩",认为各本讹作"既方之外,半其一矩",讹舛不可通。进一步说明:"内引径作'既方其外',惟'半之',讹作'半其'耳。据

---

[7] 图解本补"夏至日中,光"五字,四库本和殿本无。
[8] 图解本补"夏至日中,光"五字,四库本和殿本无。
[9] 图解本补"夏至日中,光"五字,四库本和殿本无。
[10] 四库本和殿本作"地也"。

上云折矩以为'勾广三,股修四,径隅五',谓以十二折之,勾三、股四,其弦必五。此盖变上所折之形。令其外,各自成方,则勾实九,股实十六,弦实二十五,合五十,也为一矩。于内减股实,开其余得勾,减勾实,开其余得股。若开此一矩,则得弦。下云'环而共盘,得成三、四、五'是也。弦实二十五,为一矩,并勾实、股实亦二十五,为一矩。故下又云'两矩共长二十有五,是谓积矩。'推究上下文可证'其'字、'之'字互讹,今改正"。由戴震的分析以及赵注可知,戴校是合理的。但川边没有对此做校改。

又如卷上勾股圆方图中,"凡并勾股之实即成弦实,或矩于内,或方于外"。[11]戴震认为:"各本讹作'或矩于内,或方于外',与下云'勾实之矩,股方其里;股实之矩勾实方其里'适相反。据刘徽注《九章算术》云:里者则成方,幂其居表里则成矩幂,可证'外内'二字互讹,今改正"。正如程贞一、闻人军的注释所指出:有的矩方在内部,如内弦图;有的矩方在外部,如外弦图(如图1所示)。但根据戴震的注释和川边有关勾实之矩和股实之矩的图示(如图2所示),股实方在矩形内部。钱宝琮也赞同戴震的校补,只是顺序有所不同,为"或方于内,或矩于外"。可见戴校本的分析似乎更为合理。此处川边也没有校补。

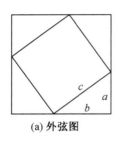 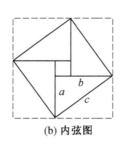 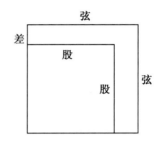

(a) 外弦图　　　　　(b) 内弦图

图1　外弦图和内弦图　　　　　图2　勾实之矩

(3) 删衍字

川边删衍字共23处,其中卷上12处,卷下11处。其中某些所删衍字是中国学者没有注意到的,较为合理。如经文:"三遂为一首,……周天除之,①除积后天分,得一周,即弃之。②其不足除者③,如合朔。"川边认为:此三简,前"经月不及故舍"条后面的文字是错出的衍文。根据上下文分析可知,①②③简皆在求小月、大月及经月的术中,是求月不及故舍之步骤中的最后一步,前后联系性强,算法过程严密,但若在此,其前有文"何以知天三百六十五度四分度之一,而日行一度……十二月十九分月之七为一岁",于是"周天除之"这三简显然与上文没有联系,在此过于突兀,因此其为衍文的可能性较大,由此看来,川边的观点较为合理。但是戴校本和后世中国学者的校勘本都未做出如是评论。

当然,也有一些衍字川边没有校勘出来。如利用竹管测日径的文字:"即取竹空径一寸,长八尺,捕影而视之,空正掩日,而日应空之孔。""以径寸之空视日之影……捕犹索也,掩犹覆也。"明刊本、川边图解本、戴震校本、郭书春与刘钝校本、曲安京新译本、程贞一与闻人军注释本都没有校删"之孔"二字。顾观光《周髀算经校勘记》认为:空即孔,不得云空之孔,疑"之孔"二字衍。钱宝琮校本、江晓原与谢筠注解本都从顾氏所校,认为是衍字而删之。从语句对仗角度看,言"空正掩日,而日应空"较为合理;其次,赵注中已有对径长一寸的"空"的解释,可以看出"空"即"孔",据此分析,"之孔"确为衍字。

(4) 调倒字

川边调整倒字共8处,其中卷上4处,卷下4处。所改不尽正确。兹举几例如下:

卷下求"月后天"度数的术文:"置章月二百三十五,以章岁十九除之,加日行一度,得十三度十分九度之七。"川边认为:刻本"分九"倒,当作"九分"。戴震校本也校改为"九分",程贞一与闻人军注释本、江晓原与谢筠注解本均从之。从古代分数命句式来看,川边与戴震的校改是正确的。

卷下"四章为一蔀,七十六岁……又以一岁之日除蔀日,亦得七十六矣岁",最后"矣岁"二字倒文明显,戴校本倒为"岁矣",后世各本从之。但川边图解本没有校出。

卷下"置周天度数,以十二月十九分月之七除之,得二十九日九百四十分日之四百九十九,则一月之

11　四库本和殿本作"或矩于外,或方于内"。

日数"。最后一句,戴震认为应该倒为"一月日之数",后世各本从之。但川边图解本也没有校改。

卷上商高问与周公对话中"夫天不可阶而升……请问数从安出?"一句,戴震校本做"数安从出",后世各本皆从之。但川边图解本仍从明刻本,没有校改。

(5)调错简

对于《周髀算经》的错简问题,自戴震以来的中国学者没有予以注意。川边共调整错简13处,其中卷上7处,卷下6处。例如,对于荣方与陈子关于周髀测影的对话,明刊本与《永乐大典》本文字如下:

> 此一者,天道之数。周髀长八尺,夏至之日晷一尺六寸。髀者,股也。正晷者,勾也。正南千里勾一尺五寸,正北千里勾一尺七寸,日益表南,晷日益长。候勾六尺,即取竹空径一寸,长八尺,捕影而视之,空正掩日,而日应空之孔,由此观之,率八十寸而径一寸。故以勾为首,以髀为股。从髀至日下六万里而髀无影,从此以上至日则八万里。若求邪至日者,以日下为勾,日高为股,勾股各自乘,并而开方除之,得邪至日,从髀所旁至日所,十万里。以率率之,八十里得径一里,十万里得径千二百五十里。故曰日晷径千二百五十里。法曰:周髀长八尺,勾之损益差千里。故曰:极者,天广袤也。今立表高八尺以望极,其勾一丈三寸,由此观之,则从周北十万里三千里而至极下。荣方曰:周髀者何?陈子曰:古时天子治周此数望之从周,故曰周髀。髀者,表也。[10]7-19

这段文字,中国历代校勘者没有注意其错简问题。川边认为这里多处错简,调整如下:

> 法曰:周髀长八尺,勾之损益差千里。此一者,天道之数。荣方曰:周髀者何?陈子曰:古时天子治周此数望之从周,故曰周髀。髀者,表也。髀者,股也。正晷者,勾也。故以勾为首,以髀为股。周髀长八尺,夏至之日晷一尺六寸,正南千里勾一尺五寸,正北千里勾一尺七寸,日益表南,晷日益长。候勾六尺,从髀至日下六万里而髀无影,从此以上至日则八万里。若求邪至日者,以日下为勾,日高为股,勾股各自乘,并而开方除之,得邪至日,从髀所旁至日所,十万里。即取竹空径一寸,长八尺,捕影而视之,空正掩日,而日应空之孔,由此观之,率八十寸而径一寸。以率率之,八十里得径一里,十万里得径千二百五十里。故曰日晷径千二百五十里。故曰:极者,天广袤也。今立表高八尺以望极,其勾一丈三寸,由此观之,则从周北十万里三千里而至极下。[8]24-42

川边调整后的文脉比较自然也合乎逻辑。承前文陈子首先向荣方介绍勾股测影原理,故首句为"法曰:周髀长八尺,勾之损益差千里。"由此而引出"此一者,天道之数。"问题及其解释,如果两者顺序颠倒,"此一者"无所出,很是突兀。再者,首句提及"周髀"概念,故荣方有所问"周髀者何?",陈子立即答"古时天子治周此数望之从周,故曰周髀。髀者,表也。髀者,股也。正晷者,勾也。故以勾为首,以髀为股。"非常自然。概念解释清楚之后,陈子继续介绍周髀、竹筒测望的计算方法。先是围绕"千里影差一寸"的原理,谈在夏至日利用勾股定理计算出髀至日下六万里、上至日八万里、邪至十万里的方法,然后讲利用竹筒窥日计算出日晷径千二百五十里的方法。首先提出计算方法:勾之损益差千里;然后总结这是"天道之数",为承接上文周髀的含义,引出荣方对于"周髀者何"的提问以及陈子的回答;之后开始介绍如何测日晷并指出正南正北的晷长;接下来讲述如何求得日高、日远以及邪至日十万里;再用竹空得到此时空径与竹长之比,根据相似三角形求邪至日与日径之比恰等于空径与竹长之比,得到比例为$\frac{1}{80}$;最后由前面所求的邪至日长度求得日径。(如图3所示)如此调整,前后联系紧密,逻辑性强。

再如,卷下开始论"日月运行四极":

> 凡日月运行四极之道。极下者,其地高人所居六万里,滂沱四隤而下。天之中央,亦高四

旁六万里。故日光外所照,径八十一万里,周二百四十三万里。故日运行处极北,北方日中,南方夜半;日在极东,东方日中,西方夜半;日在极南,南方日中,北方夜半;日在极西,西方日中,东方夜半。凡此四方者,天地四极四和。昼夜易处,加四时相及。然其阴阳所终,冬夏至所极,皆若一也。天象盖笠,地法覆盘。天离地八万里。冬至之日,虽在外衡,常出极下地上二万里。[10]卷下之一,1-3页

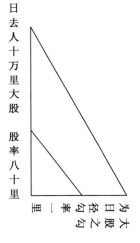

图3 测日高、日远

中国历代校勘者对此处没有意识到错简问题而没有校改,川边则认为此处错简较多,调整如下:

凡日月运行四极之道①。故日光外所照,径八十一万里,周二百四十三万里。故日运行处极北,北方日中,南方夜半;日在极东,东方日中,西方夜半;日在极南,南方日中,北方夜半;日在极西,西方日中,东方夜半②。凡此四方者,③天地四极四和。④昼夜易处,加四时相及。⑤然其阴阳所终,冬夏至所极,皆若一也。⑥天象盖笠,地法覆盘。⑦极下者,其地高人所居六万里,滂沱四隤而下。⑧天之中央,亦高四旁六万里。⑨天离地八万里。冬至之日,虽在外衡,常出极下地上二万里。[8]95-98

川边调整后的语句①②③④⑤⑥几句说明"日月运行四极之道",⑦⑧⑨⑩几句解释盖天模型,层次分明,句句紧扣。明刊本中将第②句插在第⑧句之后,则前后没有联系,有脱节的感觉,欠缺逻辑性。所以笔者认为,川边的调整使行文更加流畅,思路更加清晰。

4. 川边对《周髀算经》的注释工作

《周髀算经图解》以通俗的日文并辅以图示,解释《周髀算经》的经文以及赵爽、甄鸾、李淳风等人的注释。江户时代的汉学家对汉籍的注释有汉文注解与日文注解两种,后者又称作谚解。他们采用这种方式研究、传播汉学,在消化汉学的基础上结合日本本土文化发展汉学。川边信一对《周髀》经文、赵注、李注和鸾注中的某些问题都做了注释与辩证。兹列举其中至今仍存有争议的如下几个问题,我们来看川边的注释。

(1) 对"勾股方圆图注"的注解及其对勾股定理的证明。

对《周髀》经文"既方之[12]外,半之一矩。"川边注道:"既,尽也。勾股弦各自乘,皆方实也。变通及分一矩者,勾方实、股方实各在弦方实中相取所得也。"并给出图4加以说明。

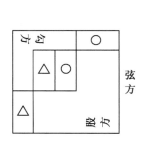 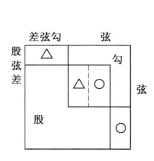 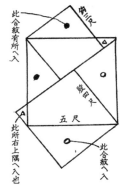 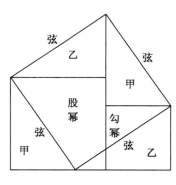

图4 勾股弦方图　　图5 勾实之矩　　图6 村濑义益的图　　图7 关孝和的图

---

[12] 四库本和殿本为"其"。

对于经文"环而共盘,得成三四五。"及赵注"盘,读如盘桓之盘。言取而[13]并减之积,环屈而共盘之谓[14]。开方除之,其[15]一面。故曰'得成三、四、五'也。"与鸾注"以股弦差一乘勾弦差二,得二。倍之为四,开之得二。以股弦差一增之,得三,勾也",川边注释道:"弦实内勾股方实重处,与两差相乘之倍同实也,开之得数加股弦差,为勾,加勾弦差,为股,两差加,成弦也。"(图5)

图4与图5的结构以及所反映的数量关系是一样的,川边用此图证明了勾股定理。如设勾为 a,股为 b,弦为 c,勾弦差与股弦差相乘并加倍之后的面积恰好与勾方和股方重合的面积相等,即 $[a-(c-b)][b-(c-a)]=2(c-a)(c-b)$。将公式左边开方之后便得 $a+b-c$,将其加股弦差 $c-b$ 可得勾,加勾弦差 $c-a$ 可得股。和算中最初给出勾股定理证明的是村濑义益的《算法勿惮改》(约1673年),其证明方法如图6,此图后又出现于《增补算法阙疑抄》。关孝和(约1642—1708)在《规矩要明算法》《解见题之法》中也证明了勾股定理,但采用的是图7。

(2)对日高图与日高图注的注释。

对于日高图的注释和复原,历来也是学者们关注的问题,川边信一对赵注也做了校改:

> 黄甲与黄乙其实正等,以表高乘两表相去,为黄甲[16]之实,以影差为黄甲之广,而一,所得则变得黄甲[17]之袤,上与日齐。按图当加[18]表高,今言八万里者,从表以上复加之。青丙与青己[19]其实正等。黄甲与青丙相连,黄乙与青己相连,其实亦等。皆以影差为广[20]。[8]42

川边校改了两处:一是与戴震补图(图8)相比,在"上天"加了一行"青丙"(图9);二是将"加"改为"如"。第二处校改与"重差公式"不是很吻合,或许在川边的认知中,此日高图旨在解释"日高八万里,距离日下六万里之阳城夏至表无影,以及表距二千里影差二寸"的数量关系,非以等积变换证明"日高术"公式。由此可见,川边对于日高图的注释并不尽善。

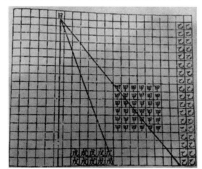 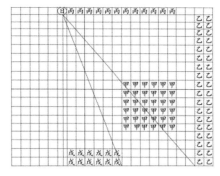

图8 戴震所补之日高图　　　　图9 川边所补之日高图

(3)关于盖天宇宙模型的注释。

经文"天象盖笠,地法覆盘。"及赵爽注"见乃谓之象,形乃谓之法。在上故准盖,在下故拟盘。象法义同,盖盘形等。互文异器,以别尊卑;仰象俯法,名号殊矣。"是叙述盖天说宇宙模型的关键文字。川边注释引用抄录了《历算全书》中的释文。对于经文"极下者,其地高人所居六万里,滂沱四隤而下。"及赵

13　四库本和殿本作"其"。
14　四库本和殿本删"谓"字。
15　四库本和殿本作"得其"。
16　戴震作"乙"。
17　川边注曰:"甲"当作"乙"。戴震作"乙"。
18　川边注曰:"加"当作"如"。
19　川边注曰:"己"当作"戊"。戴震作"巳"。
20　戴震认为此简为衍文。

注"游北极从外衡主[21]极下乃高六万里。而言人所居,盖复尽外衡,滂沱[22]四隤而下,如覆盘也。"以及经文"天之中央亦高四旁六万里"与赵注"四旁,犹四极也。随地穹隆而高,如盖笠。"川边进一步做了注解:"游者,不在常处也。随极游外衡,其在中天也。盖也尽外衡如图。滂沱四隤,覆盘四下也。穹隆,天之势随地也,中央高而如盖笠也。"同时,川边还驳斥了域外天文学的观点,他依然引用《历算全书》的说法:"然佛经所言,则其下为华藏海,而世界生在其中,须弥之顶为诸天而通明,故夜能见星,此则不知有南北二极,而谓地起海中,上连天顶,殆如圆塔圆柱之形,其说难通。"[8]42川边根据梅文鼎的观点,绘制出如图10所示的宇宙模型。现代学者以恰特莱(H. Chatley,1885—1955)、李约瑟(Joseph Needham,1900—1995)[11]、能田忠亮(1901—1989)[12]、钱宝琮[13]、曲安京[14]等为代表的双重球冠模型与川边的见解相同。江晓原站在域外天文学的角度提出天与地为平行平面,在北极下方的大地中央矗立着高6万里、底面直径为2万3千里的上尖下粗的"璇玑",天在北极也并非平面而是柱形向上耸起的,其形状也与地上的"璇玑"一样,[15]这种观点恰恰是川边所否定的。

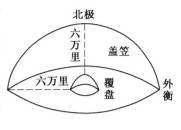

图10 盖天宇宙模型

(4)对黄道的注释

经文"月之道常缘宿,日道亦与[23]宿正"。赵注:"内衡之南[24],外衡之北,圆而成规,以为黄道。二十八宿列焉,日[25]之行也,一出一入,或表或里,五月、二十三分月之二十一[26]道[27]一交,谓之合朔交会及月食相去之数,故曰'缘宿'也。日行黄道以宿为正,故曰'宿正'。于中衡之数与黄道等。"川边注解道:"内衡,夏至之日道径也;外衡,冬至之日道径也。其南北之中分者,为中衡乃黄道也。此黄道二十八宿依附也。日行者,行其黄道,故以宿正躔次,宿度亦依躔次生,故云宿正。月道者,云此以出入黄道表里缘于宿也。"对于经文"南至夏至之日中,北至冬至之夜半;南至冬至之日中,北至夏至之夜半,亦径三十五万七千里,周一百七万一千里。"及赵注"此皆黄道之数,与中衡等",川边又注解道:"内外衡中分为黄道,又自春秋分之日径及冬夏至之日中至夜半,成黄道径,如图11所示。"但是,对于"七衡图"之赵注"黄图画者,黄道也,二十八宿列焉,日月星辰躔焉"。川边却注曰:"若以黄图画为黄道,即日月运行之路线,此七衡图之每衡,皆黄道也。"川边对"黄道"的解释前后出现了不一致,前文认为黄道即是中衡,后文又认为黄道是日月运行的每衡都是黄道。对"黄道"在"七衡图"中的解释,后人依旧莫衷一是。钱宝琮认为:此处的"黄道"是"在内衡之外,外衡之内涂上黄色"的"一个圆环,和球面天文学里的黄道意义不同"。[16]陈遵妫(1901—1991)也称"它是一个圆环,和表示太阳一年内在天球上移动的路径即黄道的意义不同"[17]。曲安京在《黄道与盖天说的七衡图》一文中指出:七衡图注中的黄道,亦应是一个与中衡大小一致的圆圈。即太阳在恒星背景图画上的周年视位移轨迹。[18]

图11 黄道图

三、几点结论

17至19世纪是东亚传统经学昌盛的时期,乾嘉学派以考据为主要治学方法,因它采用汉朝儒生训诂考订的治学方法,与着重于理气心性抽象议论的宋明理学有所不同,所以有"汉学"之称。因乾嘉学派

---

[21] 戴震作"至"。
[22] 川边补"沱"字。
[23] 川边注曰:"与"当作"为"。戴震改作"与"。
[24] 戴震作"内"。
[25] 川边注曰:"日"当作"月"。戴震作"月"。
[26] 四库本和殿本作"二十而一"。
[27] 四库本作"食道",殿本与川边图解本同。

的文风朴实简洁,重证据罗列而少理论发挥,故经学又有"朴学""考据学"之称。经历明末清初以天算、实用技术为主要内容的西学传播与消化吸收之后,中国文人重新思考儒家学术的传统,并试图把历算之学重新纳入儒学正统的框架之内。[19]自王(锡阐)、梅(文鼎)提倡斯学之后,许多古算书渐渐复活,经学大师大率兼治算,[20]进而促进了历算的发展。另外,"定九因治西算而印证以古籍,知吾国亦有固有之算学,因极力提倡以求学问之独立",[21]其著作《历学疑问》和《历学疑问补》完成了天文学领域的"西学中源"说,他在著作中频繁地阐述这一观点,极力证明"谁知欧罗言,乃与周髀同",从而促进了"西学中源"说的盛行。清朝中期,经学家仍然对天文、数学抱有热情,中国传统天算典籍成为他们经学治学的一个独特领域。乾嘉经学大师戴震师从江永(1681—1762),对天文、地理、历史、数学都有研究,著有《原象》《历问》《历古考》《策算》《勾股割圆记》等。进入四库馆之后,利用音韵、文字、训诂等考据学方法对天文、算法、地理、文字声韵等各方面的书籍详加校订。西学的刺激与经学发展是戴震《周髀算经》进行校勘注解工作的文化背景。川边信一及其同时代日本汉学家的经学注解工作,从时间上说与乾嘉学派大约同时,但之间没有直接的联系。江户初期幕府对儒学尊崇及奖励政策,加之对西方基督教文化传播禁止,推动了以经学为核心的汉学的发达,以中国传统学术为基础的天文历算学在武家文化与町人文化环境中获得了史无前例的繁荣昌盛。如果将川边信一的校勘注解工作与戴震的工作进行比较的话,可以得出如下结论:

1. 采用的底本不同,影响校勘的结果

戴震从《永乐大典》中辑出《周髀算经》2卷,李籍撰《周髀算经音义》1卷,据此以校勘明刻本。而川边信一采用《秘册汇函》和《津逮秘书》为底本。底本的不同必然造成了校勘和注解的内容和范围的不同。戴震补脱文147字,改讹舛113字,删衍复18字。旧书内有图5幅,失传三幅,讹舛一幅。川边共出校注229条,补脱字共38处,改讹字共104处,删衍字共23处,调整倒字共8处,共调整错简13处。

2. 校勘形式上的细微差别

在对脱、衍、讹、倒字的处理上,川边信一图解本保持明刻本原貌,将需要改正的内容用夹住或眉注的形式加以说明;对于脱字,则直接补入并在注释中说明,既能最大限度保持经书的原貌又能方便读者阅读。戴震采取在原文中大胆改字并加案语的方式进行注解。

戴震极为重视校勘的体例,例如对于经文"陈子曰:复坐……夏至南万六千里。"戴震作案语:"经文之例,首位一万但称万,一千但称千,一百但称百,一十但称十,省去一字,次位以下不得省,注文则首位亦不省。此书中通例。"文中共有252处对"一"字的处理,都按照此体例。川边信一图解本对"一"字的处理与戴震正相反,但也有多处不合通例。

3. 在注释方面的差别

戴震的主要工作是校勘,在注解方面做得比较少。川边信一在校勘的同时,做了大量的注解工作。其注解包括对经文与历代注解的日文注解(谚解)以及大量的图解。其中篇幅最大的地方就是图解,对于宇宙结构模型、七衡六间、勾股圆方图、重差术、竹空测日径、日高、日远、邪至日、春秋分和冬夏至日道径等都给出了图示解析。这是与戴校本的显著不同之处,便于读者更清晰、直观地阅读。

在对古注的批判方面,戴震没有对前人的注解加以评判。川边则对赵注、李注、甄注都给出评论。例如卷下"故日运行处极北,北方日中,南方夜半;日在极东,东方日中,西方夜半;日在极南,南方日中,北方夜半;日在极西,西方日中,东方夜半。凡此四方者,天地四极四和。四和者,谓之极子、午、卯、酉,得东、西、南、北之中,天地之所合,四时之所交,风雨之所会,阴阳之所和。然则百物阜安,草木蕃庶,故曰四和。"川边信一给出案语:此注为"天地四极四和"许之注,《周礼》所谓"地中"也。经文似有脱字,自"天地之所合"以下,即"太司徒"之文,"四极四和",全云中国之事也。前云"四方昼夜"者,显著错出也。又如,对于"《吕氏》曰[28]:凡四海之内,东西二万八千里,南北二万六千里。"川边指出:"《吕氏春秋》之事,

---

[28] 四库本作"春",殿本同图解本。

委于《音义》。《淮南子》曰：盖四海之内，东西二万八千里，南北二万六千里云云，是非据《吕氏》。《吕氏》之言亦无推算准确之处也。"在图解本中可以经常看到"似不妥也""援错出也""鸾注及寅曰共误""两注皆不洁也"等批判性文字，这表明川边不盲从古人，更具批判精神。

川边信一的校勘与图解不仅使我们了解到日本汉学界对汉籍经典的研究情况，也为当今研究《周髀算经》提供了参考资料。

参考文献

[1] 钱宝琮校.算经十书·周髀算经[M].北京:中华书局,1963

[2] 郭书春,刘钝校.算经十书·周髀算经[M].沈阳:辽宁教育出版社,1998

[3] 江晓原,谢筠译注.周髀算经[M].沈阳:辽宁教育出版社,1996

[4] 曲安京.周髀算经新译[M].西安:陕西人民出版社,2002

[5] 程贞一,闻人军.周髀算经译注[M].上海:上海古籍出版社,2012

[6] [日]仓石五四郎讲述,杜轶文译.日本中国学之发展[M].北京:北京大学出版社,2013:146

[7] 冯立升.中日数学交流史研究[M].济南:山东教育出版社,2009:11

[8] 川边信一著,徐泽林,刘丽芳译注.《周髀算经图解》译注[M].上海:上海交通大学出版社,2015:10。

[9] 周髀算经[M].秘册汇独本,卷上,44-45.

[10] 周髀算经[M].文渊阁四库全书本,卷上之二,7-19.

[11] 李约瑟.中国科学技术史.第四卷天学(第一分册)[M].北京:科学出版社,1975:92－104

[12] [日]能田忠亮.周髀算经の研究[M].京都:东方文化学院京都研究所,1933:55－61

[13] 钱宝琮.周髀算经考[A].钱宝琮科学史论文选集[C].北京:科学出版社,1983:119－142

[14] 曲安京.《周髀算经》的盖天说:别无选择的宇宙结构[J].自然辩证法研究,第13卷第8期(1997):37－40

[15] 江晓原.《周髀算经》盖天宇宙结构[J].自然科学史研究,第15卷第3期(1996):248－253

[16] 钱宝琮.盖天说源流考[A].钱宝琮科学史论文选集[C].北京:科学出版社,1983:377－403

[17] 陈遵妫.中国天文学史[M].上海:上海人民出版社,1980。

[18] 曲安京.黄道与盖天说的七衡图[J].自然辩证法通讯,第16卷第6期(1994):55－60

[19] 韩琦.清初历算与经学关系简论[A].载彭林编:清代经学与文化[C].北京:北京大学出版社,2005:409－418

[20] 戴名世.戴南山先生全集[M].卷3.民国戊午(1918)重刻本:38

[21] 梁启超.中国近三百年学术史[M].上海:东方出版社,1996:158

围绕《几何原本》形成的朝鲜研究学术圈
——以朝鲜学者徐浩修为中心

郭世荣　（内蒙古师范大学　科学技术史研究院）
吴东铭　（南开大学　历史学院）

摘要　利玛窦和徐光启翻译的《几何原本》前六卷，在中国乃至整个东亚产生了重要的影响。从18世纪中期开始，朝鲜有不少人对《几何原本》（以下简称《原本》）感兴趣，数学、儒学、实学、宗教等各领域都有学者研究或学习过《原本》，他们收集、阅读、学习、研究、使用《原本》，还有人撰写了专门著作，形成了较为热烈的局面。

徐浩修（1736—1799）是属于朝鲜最高统治阶层"两班"的高级官员和学者，是朝鲜颇有影响的历算家，他对《原本》的兴趣和他所组织的研究工作对于扩大《原本》在朝鲜的影响具有重要意义。以他为中心形成了一个研究《原本》的学术圈。这个学术圈由各阶层的人员组成，包括徐浩修及其两个儿子徐有本（1762—1822）、徐有榘（1764—1845），其弟徐滢修（1749—1824）、"中人"数学家文光道（1727—1775）、柳琴（1741—1788）、平民学者韩以亨（1742—1789）和金泳（1749—1817）等学者。这些人的社会地位悬殊，但是都对《原本》有浓厚的兴趣，都积极学习研究《原本》。

本文在发掘大量朝鲜原始史料的基础上，从数学社会史和数学文化史的角度考察了上述学者的数学工作，特别是他们对《几何原本》的学习、研究与认识情况。

关键词　《几何原本》；朝鲜数学；徐浩修；数学社会史

意大利传教士利玛窦（Mattio Ricci，1552—1610）和明代科学家徐光启（1562—1633）合译的西方数学名著《几何原本》前六卷（以下简称《原本》）于明万历三十五年（1607年）初版刊刻，这是第一部译成汉文的西方数学著作。从18世纪中期开始，朝鲜数学、儒学、实学、宗教等领域的学者对《原本》产生了很大的热情，他们收集、阅读、学习、使用《原本》，还有人撰写了专门著作，出现了较为热烈的局面。

在朝鲜，以徐浩修（1736—1799）为中心形成了一个研究《原本》的学术圈，包括徐浩修及其两个儿子徐有本（1762—1822）、徐有榘（1764—1845），其弟徐滢修（1749—1824）、文光道（1727—1775）、柳琴（1741—1788）、韩以亨（1742—1789）、金泳（1749—1817）等学者。这些人的社会地位相差很大，既有最高层的"两班"政治家，也有处于社会中层的"中人"数学家，还有平民甚至贫穷潦倒的学者，但是他们对于《原本》却有着共同的兴趣。本文从文化史的角度，探讨以徐浩修为中心的朝鲜学者对《原本》的兴趣、研究与认识。至于《原本》在朝鲜的整体情况，已另有专文介绍。[1]

1　"两班"学者徐浩修与《原本》

朝鲜达城徐氏为名门大族，其社会地位属于统治阶层"两班"。徐家在高丽时代（918—1392）就有人担任官职，进入朝鲜时代（1392—1910），一直有人在王朝中担任要职，"达城徐氏，在近世缙绅家，为最盛，多至大官"。[2]徐浩修的六世祖徐景霌，是朝鲜宣祖国王时期（1567—1608年在位）的驸马，五世祖徐贞履（1599—1664）[3]、曾祖徐文裕（1651—1707）[2]、祖父徐宗玉（1688—1745）[4]、父亲徐命膺（1716—1787）[5]，及徐浩修本人和其子徐有本都是朝廷高官。

徐家在学术上也颇有名声。就历算方面来说，徐命膺曾掌管朝鲜的国家天文历法机构，是懂得历算的官员。他对易学颇有研究，"旁及历象律吕，各究其蕴奥。"[5]指导观象监人员制作了新的天象图以取代旧的盖天图,对历象律吕有自己的论述。[6]

受家学影响,徐浩修对天文历法与数学也颇有研究,他"素娴历象之学",在朝廷官员中,被认为是身怀"专门绝艺"的专家,曾负责观象监的工作,组织编纂《国朝历象考》和《七政步法》等官修著作,"朝廷有星历述作,辄待公裁定"。[7]他"精《周髀》、几何学,推及历象律吕。其书满家,尝谓诸子曰:'此绝学也,吾思以传家。'"[8]他把历算学视为应该世代传下去的学问。他著有《浑盖图说集笺》二卷、《数理精蕴补解》《律吕通义》诸书。其中,《浑盖图说集笺》研究明代利玛窦与李之藻(1565—1630)合译的《浑盖通宪图说》。1790年他作为副使访问北京,与纪昀(1724—1805)、王杰(1725—1805)、翁方纲(1733—1818)、铁保(1752—1824)等多有交流,特别是与后二人讨论了天文历法问题。在交流过程中,徐浩修对传统历法和西法,均有自己的看法。当时翁方纲正在撰写《春秋四家朔闰表》,有一些问题,向徐浩修请教。徐氏将其《浑盖图说集笺》送给铁保与翁方纲,请翁氏写了序言。但他对翁氏的历学水平颇不满意,觉得其"空疏",认为其所表现出来的历算水平较低。[9]《数理精蕴补解》是朝鲜第一部专门研究康熙御制《数理精蕴》的作品,对原著有一定的认识,比如,对全书的整体看法为:"《数理精蕴》四十五篇,旁罗线、面、体之全,而曲尽度、量、衡之用,自九章、八线,以致对数、比例、比例规,非徒言其法,必明其所以然之故,绝无子云之奇僻、尧夫之铺叙,而见者易知、闻者易能,此正实用之书,而济事之具也。"而《补解》就是在《原本》思想的指导下展开的:"《补解》者,衍说、增图、校误,而益讲其所以然之故,羽翼四十五篇之旨。敢曰寒冰而蓝青?只效泰西《几何》增题之例已。"[10]

徐浩修是朝鲜研究《原本》的一个重要人物。他收藏有一部《原本》,是"北京原板吴淞重订者"[11],即徐光启译再版本,是个善本。徐浩修可能是朝鲜最早认真研读《原本》的学者之一,与他一起研讨《原本》的学者是文光道,向他学习《原本》的有其子徐有本、徐有榘和朋友柳琴等。

徐浩修与文光道共同研究了《原本》。《原本》是另一种数学体系,与东方数学传统不同,对中朝数学家来说,不易习读,徐浩修与他的下属数学家文光道共同展开了对《原本》的研究。徐滢修对乃兄的工作十分重视,评价很高,他说:

> 于是几何之书,又东出我国。然文涩而旨奥,亦未有知其妙者。近有文教授光道,独得其宗,与我伯氏参判公,讲明授受,如徐公之于明。[12]

这里所谓的"伯氏参判公"即指徐浩修。他认为,正是文光道与徐浩修共同研究《原本》,才使朝鲜学者开始理解它,这对朝鲜来说,就像徐光启将《原本》译成中文那样重要。当然,当时几何毕竟不是传统正宗学术。所以徐滢修对于乃兄在《原本》上花时间下功夫,并不完全理解:

> 余尝请于公曰:"道者,形而上者也。艺者,形而下者也。君子语上而不语下。公之所好,无乃不择于术乎?"公曰:"然。吾固无不知也。夫道无形而易眩,艺有象而难假。吾非不好道也,所恶名好道而实不道,并与所谓艺者而无得焉尔。"余虽不敢更请,犹未之信。及余从事于道十有余年,卒未窥圣人之藩。而乃公之所造,如彼其卓荦。则未始不叹公之明,而服公之得一体也。[12]

按照传统观念,数学属于"艺"的层面,离"道"很远。"道"为形而上者,"艺"为形而下者,"君子语上而不语下"。因此,这对儒者来说,显然是不务正业。徐浩修的看法正相反,他认为道与艺是统一的,空论道是不可能的,只能引起混乱。而艺是实实在在的有形之事,不可能以假乱真。正所谓"道无形而易眩,艺有象而难假。"他不是不向往"道",而是讨厌"名好道而实不道",反对"与所谓艺者而无得焉尔"的说法。这是颇有见地的见解,也是他研究几何的认识基础。十多年后,徐滢修才体会到乃兄所作所为的意义和价值。正是徐浩修和文光道的研究引起了一批人对《原本》的兴趣。

2 "中人"数学家文光道与《原本》

文光道,字尔五,又字玄度,本贯全罗道南平。他出身于"中人"家族,其父文百龄、祖父文益昌、曾祖父文尚俊,皆供职于司译院。文光道于乾隆十八年(1753)参加癸酉式年试,得了阴阳科"式魁",被选入观象监,后补为三历官、天文学教授,因为精通历法计算而被提升为义盈库主簿,后来任咸兴监牧官,不久后去世。[13,14]

他从学习西学开始其历算研究,初获西方著作时,"闭户精思,独得人所不知,自夫躔离留伏,以至交食凌历,一握筹尽之方。"[13] 他当时"名于数理",是著名的历算家。同时期的另一位著名数学家黄胤锡(1729—1791)在讲朝鲜数学发展历程中提到了文光道,说他研习《数理精蕴》[15],"能明算理",并提到他与徐家的特殊关系:"出入大监宅,被眷久矣。"[16] 这里大监指徐命膺。

文光道是徐命膺和徐浩修父子的下属,也是他们在工作中所倚重的学者。他比徐浩修大9岁,但徐命膺说"文生光道精于历数,从吾儿浩修游",[17] 应该是指他们经常共同研究历算,分享心得。作为上级,徐浩修不仅给他布置研究任务,也经常向他咨询。在朝廷组织编纂《东国文献备考》过程中,文光道提出了重要见解,受到当时朝鲜国王英祖(1724—1776在位)的重视。在徐命膺的影响和指导下,他著成《新法浑天图》,徐命膺还专门撰写了序言[17]。他去世后,徐滢修为他撰写了墓表,评价道:"况君之学,乃圣门六艺之一。而我国云观之能通此艺,惟君一人也乎。"[13]

关于他与徐浩修一起研究《原本》的情况,文献中没有细节说明。可以推断,徐浩修在访问北京时获得了《原本》,回国后与文光道共同研究,因徐氏公务繁重,研究中文氏出力较多。他们对《原本》的研究,在朝鲜产生了很大的影响。不仅使徐家的私塾教师柳琴和徐浩修的儿子们对《原本》产生了兴趣,还有一位叫韩以亨的人也跟随文光道学习了《原本》。

3 布衣学者"几何先生"柳琴

柳琴,字弹素,本名柳琏,字连玉,号窄庵,以布衣终其身。柳琴在学术上"治文艺视第一等,非杜诗、韩文、右军书法,不屑为也"。[18] 对数学、治印、弹琴有特殊兴趣,在朝鲜文人眼中,他属于与众不同的另类学者,但颇有名声。

柳琴虽为布衣,但与大批学者有交往,特别是与徐浩修、徐滢修昆仲交往密切,情谊深厚。1777年柳琴随父亲、谢恩使团成员柳汉相入燕,在北京期间改名。此次赴燕徐浩修为副使。当时,朝鲜国王正祖(1776—1800在位)命令徐氏购买《四库全书》,可该书正在编纂中,徐氏转而购买《古今图书集成》,但他"莫知书所在,惶甚"。柳琴通过关系获知购书渠道,帮了徐浩修大忙。[18] 最终徐氏花银2 150两,购得《古今图书集成》10 000卷5 022册。[19] 柳琴曾在徐家任私塾老师,教过徐有本、徐有榘等徐家子弟,并且与他们终身保持着紧密的联系。徐有榘在柳琴去世后回忆道:

> 余之塾师曰几何子柳弹素。余发鬅鬖覆颅,则从弹素课书,迄今余髭长如当时之发,而弹素之迹,未尝一日不在。余也,至不设主客礼,即促膝谈诗文,闲出书画金石刻,评品鉴赏以为常。[20]

柳氏与徐家的关系如此亲密,以至于师生之间不拘礼仪,常在一起促膝相谈,交流学术,品鉴书画石刻。徐有榘还代替其父撰写了《祭柳君弹素文》。[21]

柳琴与李德懋(1741—1793)、朴齐家(1750—1805)被人视为"石交"朋友[22],与朴趾源(1737—1805)关系也十分密切。这些人常在一起相互切磋,品鉴柳琴的收藏[23],有时甚至夜访柳家。㉑

柳琴为出访北京做了一番准备,其中最重要的是将李德懋、柳得恭(1748—1807)、朴齐家、李书九(1754—1825)四家诗编成《韩客巾衍集》,带到北京与中国文人交流。他在北京结识了李调元(1734—

㉑ 朴齐家有一首《夜访柳连玉》,颇为生动,其诗曰"夜行何跄跄,涧道多低仰。余雪照衣裾,栖禽惊展响。道见一来者,或非我友生。相看久不辨,犹自望其行。苍苍市尽处,惟见一灯低。斗柄当额上,纤月睨笠西。初更逢柳君,四更寻李子。今宵亦云半,如是岁暮矣。灯烬寒渐堕,杯杓犹罗列。耳阒忽有籁,酒醒窗外雪。今夜几人宿,独行桥与陌。已有先我者,雪上有数迹。"参见[24]。

1803)及其从弟李鼎元(1749—1812),还有纪昀(1724—1805)、祝德麟(1742—1798)、翁方纲、潘庭筠(1742—?)、铁保等一批官员和学者。特别是在40天内5次访问李家,"每酒阑诗成,上下千古语,蝉联不知倦,至日昃乃罢。"双方结下深厚友谊。李调元与潘庭筠等对《韩客巾衍集》大加赞赏,作序评论,使李德懋等深为感动。这也在李德懋等与李调元之间架起交往讨论的平台,他们之间书信不断,讨论大量问题,[25]也为李德懋后来赴燕奠定了人脉基础。

柳琴和他的同伴们都特别重视李调元,特别是他本人对李氏十分崇拜。他回国时获赠李调元画像,"归即装以文绡,轴以香木。每岁十一月十三日,则必洁堂帪罗长筵,挂图于座右,而鳞次问答笔帖及赠遗书砚诸物于案上,邀诸同志,相与玩绎,以为欢然。家故贫,不能庀酒肴,则好事者往往助之。于是引满浮白,西向沥一卮而后始饮。饮罢赋长歌一阕,为雨村(李调元)祝嘏。是日即雨村览揆之辰,而李德懋懋官、朴齐家次修,皆弹素石交也。至期二人者未尝不在座焉。"[26]柳琴、李德懋、朴齐家三人年年在李调元生日举行这样的活动,在异国为他庆祝生日,直到柳琴去世。由此足见朝鲜学者对李调元的敬重。有人并不理解,"闻之者或笑之"[22]。

柳琴十分喜欢弹琴,"尤癖于琴,自名曰琴,字以弹素。及其垂老困踣,家奇贫无儋石资,顾独净扫洒峙图籍,哦诗弄弦。以发其侘傺不平之鸣。"[20] 刻章制印也是他的特长,朴趾源对他的刻章技艺有惟妙惟肖的介绍:

> 连玉善刻章。握石承膝,侧肩垂颐,目之所瞬,口之所吹,蚕饮其墨,不绝如丝,聚吻进刀,用力以眉,既而捧腰仰天而欷。懋官过而劳之曰:"子之攻坚也,将以何为?"连玉曰:"夫天下之物,各有其主。有主则有信,故十室之邑,百夫之长,亦有符印。无主乃散,无信乃乱。我得晕石,肤理腻沃,方武一寸,莹然如玉,狮蹲其钮,鞠乳狞吼。镇我文房,绥厥四友。我祖轩辕,氏柳名琏。文明尔雅,鼎鼓乌云。印我书秩,遗我子孙。无忧散佚,百卷其全。"[27]

柳琴不仅刻章技艺精良,而且还把印章视为信义的象征,认为守信很重要,"无信乃乱"。

柳琴特别喜欢数学,其友人异口同声提到这一点。例如:徐有本说:"多才艺,尤精象数之学。"[26]徐有榘称:"弹素治周髀学,明律吕。"[20] 其侄柳得恭记:"又喜周髀之术。构一室扁之曰'几何',潜思其中,推测浑盖,究极而后已。是故人谓之几何先生。几何者,举数质问之词云。"[22] "周髀",本来是中国古代数学著作之名,这里代指数学。柳琴因为喜好研究数学,而给自己的书斋起名为"几何",又称"几何室",因而人们称他为"几何先生"。李德懋曾有《题弹素几何室》诗。[28] "几何"这词正是来源于《几何原本》,徐滢修《几何室记》对此有明确的说明:

> 几何者,泰西之书之名也。泰西之书之名而名朝鲜之人之室,亦已远矣。昔泰西人利玛窦,浮海朝宗于中国,以其几何之书译传于太学士徐公光启。徐公,明之贤大夫也,一见之,知其为羲和冯保之遗也。与友李之藻,讲明授受。以至于梅鼎[定]九、薛凤祚之徒出,而其术益繁衍昌炽矣。……柳琴弹素,又从伯氏学者也,扁其室曰'几何'。征余为记。余谓:朝鲜之去泰西,其远不知几何也。今世之后利氏,其远又不知几何也。然子得以名其室,书之无远也。书者,心之迹也。故曰地相去千里,世相后亦千载,若合符节者,心也。子之于几何,夫既得其术矣,又能善推所为,使心之为本者,无远于尧、舜、禹、汤之传。则吾道之与几何,高下又几何也。吾以是卞几何之说,而进吾子之志。子其勉之![29]

徐滢修在盛赞柳琴积极学习几何的同时,他妙用"几何"一词作为数学学科名词与传统"几何"表示"多少"的双重含义,悟出一个书为心迹、道与几何不相远的道理。不论东西相去多远、古今相去多久,大"道"无异,几何与"道"并无高下。这与中国南宋数学家秦九韶通过数学"进之于道"的思想一脉相通。柳琴不仅掌握了几何,"更能善推所为",由几何进之于道。柳琴学习研究几何,也是受徐浩修的影响。徐滢修"记"所提到的伯氏就是徐浩修。

徐有榘也写了一篇《几何室记》。柳琴研究几何让徐有榘悟出一个道理："疏者达者其学大,精而审者其学小,盖由性之近。而圣人之教之者,亦惟因其性尔。未有能抑其精审而强其为大者也,是以观其学可以知其性,观其性可以知其人。"在当时看来,几何属于"小"的方面,但是柳琴在举世骛"大"之时,却专业于研究"小"学问几何,且对于他人诘难其专注于"道之末"而无动于衷,而且"学之而弗知弗措也,思之而弗得弗措也"。这与徐浩修的对几何的认识完全相同。其"几何室"中"皆天文历数之书",[30]他置身其中,研究历算,快然自得。

4 徐有本、徐有榘与《原本》

徐浩修的儿子徐有本和徐有榘都精通历算。徐有本曾用五年时间专攻历算,他对《数理精蕴》与《原本》均很熟悉。在数学与天文历法方面,他与数学家柳琴、韩以亨、金泳、柳僖(1773—1837)[1]颇有交流。他学习《原本》经历了艰难困苦的过程,他在1808年撰写的《题几何蒙求》中,对此有详细的描述:

> 余始读《几何原本》,如穿铁壁,如络生马,甚或不能以句。凡三读。遇有透不去处,心气为之烦懑,则辄掩卷舍置。或于饭后,或于枕上,宛转沉思,不得则又舍之。平朝又思之,不得则又舍之。而但令存心勿他,时时揭起。则虽至棼错处,未尝不释然而顿悟。[31]

东方数学家初读《原本》,确实困难不少。主要是因为东亚数学与西方数学的思维模式不同,《原本》注重基本概念和在概念基础上的逻辑推导,是一个演绎体系,这与东方数学著作的结构很不相同,东方数学家初习《原本》确实难以适应。徐有本初读《原本》时,十分艰难,甚至连句子都断不开,学习三遍后才有所进展。尽管有烦懑,有困难,但是他坚持不放松,反反复复研读,一心一意,"存心勿他,时时揭起",最终达到释然而顿悟的效果。徐有本把学习《原本》与儒家学习观紧紧相连,把学习《原本》的过程视为对中国先哲孔子、管子语录的注解。他悟到:"人患不思耳。苟能推极吾之良知,不得不措,则天下诚无不可读之书矣,诚无不可穷之理矣。奚特几何之一艺而已哉。"只要肯于思考,善于思考,坚持不懈,没有学不会的东西。基于对《原本》的理解,他"于是或设为问答,或另为解论,汇成一篇",完成了自己的著作《几何蒙求》。[31]这是目前所知朝鲜研究《原本》的第一部著作,可惜不知其书是否还有流传。

李圭景引用了徐有本的《读几何原本杂志》:

> 《读几何原本杂志》,徐左苏山人所传也。首题之"公论""求作"诸条与各卷"界说",乃凡例也,不可不成诵。各题大文,乃正文也,亦可成诵。而义不通,则随看"解曰""法曰",达意而止。"解法"者,训诂也。至于"论",则乃各题所以然之故也。论下或有小注曰"几卷几题"者,乃本题之证题也。论旨之或未通晓,既本证题泛看之致也,更揭本证题。二卷之有碍,亦因一卷之不能融会,更著工于一卷。步步却顾,专务反求,即读此书之第一义谛也。"增题"者,是因本题推广本题之旨者也。"系题"者,不另立题文与解论于章后,而于此系付者也,所以省文也,宜与各题正文一体成诵。几何诸题,不出"公论""求作"二者。每各题之下,"法曰"者,是求作之法也,"解曰"者,是公论之证也。总而论之,蔽一言曰,等大小三字而已。题旨者,犹《易》之意也,图论者,犹《易》之象也。既因其图论而解得题旨,则姑忌之而不系着于图画。只熟讲本题文义,瞭然于心目,则后来推用时,庶无想象线画混淆境界之弊,犹《易》之得意忘象也。"[11][2]

---

[1] 柳僖,早年名儆,号方便子。死后有遗著百余卷,其中历算方面有《观象志》《周髀经章句释》《律吕新书摘解》《乐律管见辨》等,有人汇集成《方便子遗稿》。他最著名的著作是《谚文志》。他在崔锡鼎的《九数略》的书眉上加了很多注解与说明。

[2] 这段记述出自参考文献[11],周振鹤在"朝鲜史料中的徐光启与《几何原本》"一文中全文引录了文献[11],也是该文中唯一涉及《几何原本》的史料。参见文献[32]。

上文应该是《几何蒙求》的一个段落。从这篇《杂志》可以看出,经过艰难的学习过程后,徐有本对《原本》确实有了深刻的理解。其中对《原本》术语的解读及学习方法的论述,不仅体现了他的理解深度,而且揭示出这对于进一步学习《原本》非常有用。

黄胤锡认为《数理精蕴》之《原本》是对利译本的一种编辑[1],徐有本不仅接受了这个观点,而且有所发挥。据李圭景说:

> 胤左苏山人教官有本曰:"此书,中原亦几绝种者。清圣祖康熙命编《数理精蕴》,撮《几何原本》之旨,更著《几何原本》。而仍毁利本。原板不得并行。而《精蕴·几何原本》特体比例等篇,利本所无者。以此利本稀贵,便作禁书,故购得甚难者,有以也。"[11]

徐有本说因为《原本》被撮要编辑入《数理精蕴》,清政府便禁毁利译《原本》。这是他的发挥,不是事实。

徐有榘对数学也不陌生。其父撰写《数理精蕴补解》,序言就是由他代写的,他应该参与了此项工作。他利用自己掌握的数学知识向朝鲜国王纯祖(1800—1834 在位)进呈"拟上经界策",这是一篇很长的奏折,其核心是改革,提出"田制之亟宜更张者二,量法之亟宜讲磨者三,农政之亟宜训励者六"。该折是一篇讲述数学与经济学的文章。文中的田制改革包括"改结负为顷亩法""正尺步以遵古制"。"讲磨"量法包括:"用方田以括隐漏""颁数法以豫肄习""设专司以考勤慢"。其中应用数学来说明自己的见解,在"颁数法以豫肄习"一节中主张由国家颁布相关的计算方法:"臣闻数有九章,方田居其一焉。传曰:方田以御田畴界域。盖以田畴界域之象形,求其亩步之积实。如以广纵而求方、直、圭、棱、梯、斜,以周径而求圆田、碗田、环田是也。然自《孙子筭经》以下,言其法者略而不详。近世新法,如《几何原本》《数理精蕴》诸书,皆不少概及。盖以其粗率而略之也。臣尝用新法勾股三角之法,拟作量田数法十五题,谨开录如后。"[33]不仅考察了《原本》与《数理精蕴》等书,还专门培训相关人员编制了 15 个算题。

5 平民学者金泳与《原本》

金泳,字季涵,金海人,出身平民。他少年时孤贫无依,辗转流落到朝鲜王京,后来发愤读书。偶然读到《原本》,十分喜好,连续数月攻坚学习,终于读通该书。于是开始对天文历算感兴趣,专心于此,强探力索,刻厉自持,经过十五六年的努力,终于成为一名优秀的天文历算家。

起初,金泳不为人所知。他主动与徐浩修联系,获得赞赏,经徐氏的大力宣传,其学识才为世人所了解。戊申年(1788)五月朔,发生日食,金泳获得了展示才能的机会。当时朝鲜观象监官员根据《历象考成后编》推算亏复时刻,得到的两个数据互相抵牾,明显不合理,观象监官员去请教金泳,他给出正确的资料,并认为《历象考成后编》有误,后来观象监呈报清礼部咨询,所得结果与金泳所算相合。这件事使他名声大振。接着,第二年,朝鲜要给孝纯贵嫔举行葬礼,需要精确选定下葬时刻。领观象监事金熤向国王推荐了金泳,并说:"都下有金泳者,晓解历象,请令造仪器,以之测验推步。"金泳因而有机会"承命创铸赤道经纬仪、地平日晷各二坐[座],又编《新法中星》《纪漏筹通义》各一卷以进"。葬礼完成之后,国王正祖力排众议,破例将他这一介平民任命为观象监三历官。后来他迁升司宰监直长、通礼院引仪。[34]

在观象监,金泳成为核心历算家,一切重要学术问题均依赖他完成,凡遇重要天象出现,他必亲自测候。辛未年(1811 年)在历法计算方面遇到了问题,按无中气法置闰,将导致癸酉年(1813 年)冬至在十月晦日,观象监拿不准主意,决定派人到北京咨询,金泳被推荐赴燕与钦天监官员研讨,回国时"购得《万年历》几卷",存在观象监中。他参加了观象监《国朝历象考》和《七政步法》等书的编纂工作,还给丹元子《步天歌》"绘图以明之",印行于世。他在观象监的出色表现,遭到有关人员的妒忌与排挤,"有事则推重,事已则嫉其能,嚣然群起而挠之,或面诟手驱于稠坐。"他决意离开,回家"专治易象之学"。"于是潜心玩索,推论理气法象之奥、律吕倍半之术,皆精深要眇,卓然可观。"他制定了研究易学、数学、水利机械、自鸣钟四项研究计划,可惜未完成便去世了。

金泳既受到徐浩修重视,又与徐有本在学术上交流十几年,成为莫逆之交。他们之间的讨论直来直往,该批评时严厉批评,该表扬时也不吝其辞。从徐有本给金泳的两封讨论学术的信函中,可见他对金泳学术批评之一斑。[35,36] 金泳赴燕时,徐有本写了长诗《送金君泳赴燕》,对他大加赞扬,其中写道:"专门绝艺独倡明,白首沈潜象数秘。句弦角度指掌纹,三垣列舍罗胸次。太初四分暨授时,若思去后继者谁?亦有梅定九,积学乃参微。逊矣西士创新法,畴人绪业今在兹。割圆八线分周天,正余相求洵绝奇。"[37] 金泳去世后,徐有本"怅怅焉无用友启发之益。每读数理文字,窃不胜人琴之感也"。

金泳晚年离开观象监,没了俸禄,生活困苦,衣食无保障,与人交往"垂首丧气,涔涔如倦睡人",一旦提到数学与历法,他立刻来了精神,"张目抵掌,精采烨然动人"。人们评论说:"金公之于数学,殆若有神助然。"[34] "身抱绝艺,通国之论,皆曰金某之于历象之学,我东无两也。"[36] 他十分重视《原本》,劝说徐有本学习《原本》,说:"此非子之家学耶?之书也,九数之渊海,万象之范围,辞约而理该,其殆三代之逸典乎?子盍勉旃。"徐有本果真认真学习了《原本》,金泳赞扬道:"吾见多矣。读是书精深,罕有如子者。"金泳对几何有自己的认识,在他晚年的研究计划中有关于《数理精蕴》与《视学》的内容:

> 古人著书,上可以立世教则笔之,下可以裨民用则笔之。不尔则皆苟也。数学至西人而大备,无毫发憾,又安用赘说为哉?但区区未卒之志则有之。点、线、面、体四者,即几何之缘起,而数法终不如量法。今以《数理精蕴》线部变作面部,一以量法从事则简而易明。计盈朒、商[功]、衰分,可以不布筹而了如指掌也。西人视学之术,不传于中国。故观物度势,往往失真。今推明《视学》,使观天文察地势,与夫审立圆立方之体,绘平面、坳突之形,皆得其真象而物无遁情。百工技艺,各极其精,可裨于实用也。今人言水车专尚龙尾车制,其实龙尾远不及龙骨车之便利。今为图、为说,机牙辐毂之制,皆著尺寸,按法成车,可以兴水利、益农工也。奏时之器,如自鸣钟,时械之属,牙轮易涩,稍久则必须更改,终不如验时仪坠子之往来自然而时刻不爽也。亦具图说,详著其制,简捷完久,绝胜于钟械诸仪。而吉凶大礼,可资以考时也。凡此四条,愚之夙所耿耿者,今方不住编摩,赖天之灵,幸而卒业,则可以少裨于民生日用之需。而事钜力绵,但恐岁月不我饶也。[34]

后来李圭景对金泳也有评述:

> 正庙朝有金泳者,本以岭南晋州牧士人,后寓京师。入于日官,备观象监员,天才超出,贯通其旨,善算交食星度。尝觑视《精蕴》曰:此行数也。使我蹕成利本体比例,则当如本书深义不失其旨云。所著多发前人所未发,竟饿死慕华馆破屋中。有一子不能继述云。[11]

6 孤儿韩以亨与《原本》

韩以亨,号栗村。朴永锡(1735—1801)给他所写墓文中写道:

> 五岁而孤,家无伯叔,因而失学。驰心杂技,追逐无赖,乡党为之忧叹。至二十六岁,偶于人家见《近思录》,怃然有悟,始知有为己之学。遂折节读书,曾无师受,一以自解,日夜孜孜,理会六经,微辞奥旨,无不研究。尤精于礼学,疑晦讲辨甚多。[38]

因为自幼失怙,韩以亨早年基本上是个无赖之徒,大家都为他担忧。直到 26 岁才开始意识到读书学习,于是浪子回头,刻苦自学。他"日与同志之士,讲磨经义为事。间有从学者,教之不倦"。早年的放浪性格,决定了他对功名利禄不感兴趣的品性,粗茶淡饭即能满足自己,"终不以贫窭改其乐"。1778 年冬,他才在乡下安定下来,读书以教子孙,一时跟他学习的人不少,他干脆修筑了一所小斋,用于教学,以教书为生。"每逢春秋佳日,则携率学徒,往游于虎溪水石之间。终日吟哦,乐而忘返,"自得其乐。十年之后,他的名声传到朝鲜国王正祖那里,召他进京做事。第二年他到了京城,可惜死在了旅舍。正祖"极

加悼惜,赐以棺木,赗以钱布。"[38]在正祖的《弘斋全书·日得录》中也提到了他:

> 人才不系世类。近亦有韩以亨者,地极卑微,而多闻博识,无书不通,尤精于象数之学,而未尝自衒于人。家居加平,亦未尝出入京洛云。予稔闻其名,常欲收用而未果。才难不其然乎。[39]

韩以亨曾跟随文光道学习西方数学。按朴永锡的记述:"我东数学无闻,时有教授文光道者,倡明几何之法。公一见其书,未浃旬,尽贯其法,光道惊服其神。"他从文光道那里得到《原本》,在较短的时间内就理解了其内容,令文光道感到惊奇。他在数学上不仅在学者中有一定声望,而且得到国王的重视。

李圭景在《几何原本辨证说》中也记载了一个韩姓研究《原本》的人:

> 有市井人韩姓者,素无赖,见辱人奴,发愤学书,一览辄记,遂成博洽。闻此书在于启禧,往恳一见,启禧侮之曰:"若何能透释?"靳不借。韩屡示诚恳,始与之。归读一月,尽通奥旨,以书还。启禧与语,大奇之。[11]

李圭景对这个韩姓人的记述,与朴永锡所记韩以亨的故事不同。李圭景所说的韩姓者,早年也是个无赖,因为受到别人家奴的欺侮,开始发愤读书。他听说洪启禧有《原本》,去借阅,洪氏也瞧不起他,经不住韩氏软磨硬缠,最终借给他阅读,没想到韩氏在一个月之内便"尽通奥旨",使洪氏大为惊奇。这两个故事极其相似,朴永锡的记述是根据韩以亨的儿子提供的资料所写,李圭景是几十年后的记述。笔者高度怀疑这两个姓韩的是同一人,可能是传闻不同导致记述不同。李圭景与徐有本有联系,后者应该认识韩以亨,但没能找到他的评述。

7 结语

《原本》在西方数学史上是一部经典名著,但是,东西方数学风格迥异,旨趣不同,以《原本》为代表的西方数学以证明定理为中心,而以《九章算术》为代表的东方数学以解决问题为中心。[40]对于东方数学家来说,理解和掌握《原本》的精神不是一件容易的事情,这是由东西方文化与数学的特质不同所决定的。尽管《原本》的中国译者徐光启在《几何原本杂议》中对《原本》的重要性及其逻辑推理体系甚是推崇,但是真正开始研究时,还是回到了传统数学的老路上。史家就《原本》对中国明清数学的影响曾有专门研究[41],分析过《原本》传入后中国数学家是如何研究它和应用它。但是从整体上看,中算家的着眼点还是在具体结论上而非其逻辑推理体系上。这是在《原本》的直接影响上得出的结论,如果从间接影响的角度考察《原本》的逻辑推理思想,对明清数学还是有很大影响的,它使中国数学家的思想方法、数学观念、研究方式等都发生了转变,比如逻辑推理思想的加强、新数学概念的接受、从一般性出发考虑问题、对数学性质的重视、使用标尺作图、大量使用数学符号等等。[42]这种影响主要不是体现在数学研究的对象上,即不是对《原本》的直接研究或者问题选择上,而是体现在数学研究实践中。另一方面,《原本》对儒家思想学术[43]乃至明清文化[44]也颇有其影响。

《原本》在朝鲜的流传与影响,情况也是这样。在汉译《原本》出版后近百年,朝鲜对它才有了实质性接触,这与中朝数学交流的大趋势一致。一般来说,17世纪以来,中国数学著作在出版后几十年才在朝鲜产生影响。当然也有个别传播较快的,比如《数理精蕴》。17到18世纪之交,朝鲜学者开始接触《原本》,18世纪中叶以后,认真研读和学习《原本》的学者渐多起来,不仅数学家、历法家感兴趣,其他方面的学者也多有参与,这与朝鲜实学的迅速发展关系极为密切。对西学感兴趣,研究西学,是实学派的特点之一。当时的实学家了解过《原本》的人不在少数,但真正能够下功夫学习掌握其内容的却不多。

上文中,我们研究了徐浩修和一批研究或学习过《原本》的朝鲜数学家的工作,这些人以徐浩修为中心,都与徐浩修或他的儿子有联系,形成了一个历算学术圈。徐家处于社会最高地位;柳琴的家族背景也属于上层地位,但他本人终生没有官职,一介书生而已;而文光道出身于"中人"杂科技术职业家庭,处于社会中层地位;韩以亨和金泳是处于社会下层的平民,金泳靠着自己的学术和徐浩修的帮助一度谋得了官职,从事着相当于中人数学家的工作,但是终究不适应于官僚体系,最终还是恢复了其平民身份。这些人的社会地位悬殊,相差极大,但是能够共同研究数学与天文历法,他们全都对《原本》有浓厚的兴趣,都积极学习研究《原本》。这批朝鲜数学家对《原本》的兴趣和研究构成了《原本》在朝鲜流传历史的核心内容,在朝鲜数学史上具有重要意义。不过,上文的介绍,并没有限制在仅对《原本》的研究上,而是以他们对《原本》的研究为中心,较为全面地涉及了他们的历算工作,更多关注相关的文化史与社会史。因此本文的研究实质上是对这些学者的历算工作的一个综合报道,也是《原本》在朝鲜的一个社会文化史考察。

参考文献

[1] 郭世荣:《〈几何原本〉在朝鲜述要》,《自然辩证法通讯》2017年第2期,第30—35页。

[2] (朝鲜王朝)李德寿:《西堂私载》卷5《礼曹判书赠左赞成徐公墓碑铭》,《影印标点韩国文集丛刊》第186册,汉城:民族文化推进会,1997年,第278—281页。

[3] (朝鲜王朝)崔锡鼎:《明谷集》卷23《赠左赞成徐公墓碣铭》,《影印标点韩国文集丛刊》第154册,汉城:民族文化推进会,1995年,第341—342页。

[4] (朝鲜王朝)徐命膺:《保晚斋集》卷14《先考文敏公府君行状》,《影印标点韩国文集丛刊》第233册,汉城:民族文化推进会,1999年,第359—365页。

[5] (朝鲜王朝)徐滢修:《明皋全集》卷15《本生先考文靖公府君行状》,《影印标点韩国文集丛刊》第261册,汉城:民族文化推进会,2001年,第312—323页。

[6] (朝鲜王朝)徐命膺:《保晚斋集》卷9《新法浑天图说》,《影印标点韩国文集丛刊》第261册,汉城:民族文化推进会,1999年,第249页。

[7] (朝鲜王朝)徐有榘:《枫石全集·金华知非集》卷6《本生先考文敏公墓表》,《影印标点韩国文集丛刊》第288册,汉城:民族文化推进会,2002年,第249页。

[8] (朝鲜王朝)徐有榘:《枫石全集·金华知非集》卷7《伯氏左苏山人墓志铭》,《影印标点韩国文集丛刊》第288册,汉城:民族文化推进会,2002年,第434—436页。

[9] 郭世荣:《中国数学典籍在朝鲜半岛的流传与影响》,济南:山东教育出版社,2009年,第14—15页。

[10] (朝鲜王朝)徐有榘:《枫石全集·金华知非集》卷3《数理精蕴补解序》,《影印标点韩国文集丛刊》第288册,汉城:民族文化推进会,2002年,第350页。

[11] (朝鲜王朝)李圭景:《五洲衍文长笺散稿》卷15《〈几何原本〉辨证说》,汉城:东国文化社,1959年,上册,第478—481页。

[12] (朝鲜王朝)徐滢修:《明皋全集》卷8《几何室记》,《影印标点韩国文集丛刊》第261册,汉城:民族文化推进会,2001年,第156页。

[13] (朝鲜王朝)徐滢修:《明皋全集》卷16《义盈库主簿文君墓表》,《影印标点韩国文集丛刊》第261册,汉城:民族文化推进会,2001年,第336—337页。

[14] (朝鲜王朝)佚名:《云观先生案》,〔韩〕黄元九、李钟英编:《朝鲜后期历算家谱·索引》,汉城:韩国文化社,1991年,第697页。

[15] 黄胤锡:《颐斋全书·颐斋续稿》卷11《漫录》,汉城:景仁文化社,1976年,第546页。

[16] (朝鲜王朝)黄胤锡:《颐斋乱稿》,〔韩〕国学振兴研究事业推进委员会编辑:《韩国学资料丛书(三)》,城南:韩国精神文化研究院,1995年,第二册,第461页。

[17] (朝鲜王朝)徐命膺:《保晚斋集》卷7《新法浑天图序》,《影印标点韩国文集丛刊》第261册,汉城:民族文化推进会,1999年,第192页。

[18] (朝鲜王朝)柳得恭:《泠斋集》卷6《叔父几何先生墓志铭》,《影印标点韩国文集丛刊》第260册,汉城:民族文化推进会,2000年,第108—109页。

[19]《朝鲜正祖实录》卷 3,正祖元年(干隆四十二年,1787)二月二十四日庚申,韩国国史编纂委员会编:《朝鲜王朝实录》第 44 册,汉城:韩国国史编纂委员会,1953－1958 年版,第 653 页。

[20](朝鲜王朝)徐有榘:《枫石鼓箧集》卷 5《送远辞哭几何子(有序)》,《影印标点韩国文集丛刊》第 288 册,汉城:民族文化推进会,2002 年,第 273－274 页。

[21](朝鲜王朝)徐有榘:《枫石鼓箧集》卷 5《祭柳君弹素文(代)》,《影印标点韩国文集丛刊》第 288 册,汉城:民族文化推进会,2002 年,第 272 页。

[22](朝鲜王朝)柳得恭:《泠斋集》卷 6《叔父几何先生墓志铭》,《影印标点韩国文集丛刊》第 260 册,汉城:民族文化推进会,2000 年,第 108－109 页。

[23](朝鲜王朝)朴齐家:《贞蕤阁文集》卷 1《柳几何灵芝端研铭》,《影印标点韩国文集丛刊》第 261 册,汉城:民族文化推进会,2001 年,第 612 页。

[24](朝鲜王朝)朴齐家:《贞蕤阁初集》之《夜访柳连玉》,《影印标点韩国文集丛刊》第 261 册,汉城:民族文化推进会,2001 年,第 444－445 页。

[25](朝鲜王朝)李德懋:《青庄馆全书》卷 19《雅亭遗稿(十一)·李雨邨(调元)》,《影印标点韩国文集丛刊》第 257 册,汉城:民族文化推进会,2000 年,第 266－269 页。

[26](朝鲜王朝)徐有本:《左苏山人文集》卷 7《云龙山人小照记》,《影印标点韩国文集丛刊续编》第 106 册,首尔:古典翻译院,2010 年,第 125－126 页。

[27](朝鲜王朝)朴趾源:《燕岩集》卷 70《柳氏图书谱序》,《影印标点韩国文集丛刊》第 252 册,汉城:民族文化推进会,2000 年,第 110 页。

[28](朝鲜王朝)李德懋:《青庄馆全书》卷 11《雅亭遗稿(三)·题弹素几何室》,《影印标点韩国文集丛刊》第 257 册,汉城:民族文化推进会,2000 年,第 190 页。

[29](朝鲜王朝)徐滢修:《明皋全集》卷 8《几何室记》,《影印标点韩国文集丛刊》第 261 册,汉城:民族文化推进会,2001 年,第 156 页。

[30](朝鲜王朝)徐有榘:《枫石鼓箧集》卷 2《几何室记》,《影印标点韩国文集丛刊》第 288 册,汉城:民族文化推进会,2002 年,第 228 页。

[31](朝鲜王朝)徐有本:《左苏山人文集》卷 7《题几何蒙求》,《影印标点韩国文集丛刊续编》第 106 册,首尔:古典翻译院,2010 年,第 127 页。

[32]周振鹤:《朝鲜史料中的徐光启与〈几何原本〉》,徐汇区文化局编:《徐光启与〈几何原本〉》,上海:上海交通大学出版社,2011 年,第 99－104 页。

[33](朝鲜王朝)徐有榘:《金华知非集》卷 11《拟上经界策(上)》,《影印标点韩国文集丛刊》第 288 册,汉城:民族文化推进会,2002 年,第 506－547 页。

[34](朝鲜王朝)徐有本:《左苏山人文集》卷 8《金引仪泳家传》,《影印标点韩国文集丛刊续编》第 106 册,首尔:古典翻译院,2010 年,第 162－165 页。

[35](朝鲜王朝)徐有本:《左苏山人文集》卷 3《答金生泳书》,《影印标点韩国文集丛刊续编》第 106 册,首尔:古典翻译院,2010 年,第 57－59 页。

[36](朝鲜王朝)徐有本:《左苏山人文集》卷 3《答金生泳书》,《影印标点韩国文集丛刊续编》第 106 册,首尔:古典翻译院,2010 年,第 59－60 页。

[37](朝鲜王朝)徐有本:《左苏山人文集》卷 1《送金君泳赴燕》,《影印标点韩国文集丛刊续编》第 106 册,首尔:古典翻译院,2010 年,第 8－9 页。

[38](朝鲜王朝)朴永锡:《晚翠亭遗稿》之《韩硕士(以亨)墓文》,《影印标点韩国文集丛刊续编》第 94 册,首尔:古典翻译院,2010 年,第 326－327 页。

[39](朝鲜王朝)正祖国王李祘:《弘斋全书》卷 172《日得录十二·人物(二)》,《影印标点韩国文集丛刊》第 267 册,汉城:民族文化推进会,2001 年,第 368 页。

[40]吴文俊:《〈九章算术注释〉序》,收入白尚恕《九章算术注释》,北京:科学出版社,1983 年,序第 1 页。

[41] 梅荣照,王渝生,刘钝:《欧几里得〈原本〉的传入和对我国明清数学发展的影响》,收入席泽宗,吴德铎主编《徐光启研究论文集》,上海:学林出版社,1986年,第49—63页。

[42] 郭世荣:《论〈几何原本〉对明清数学的影响》,徐汇区文化局编:《徐光启与〈几何原本〉》,上海:上海交通大学出版社,2011年,第152—163页。

[43] 程钢:《〈几何原本〉对儒家思想学术的影响:以徐光启与焦循为例》,收入彭林主编《清代学术讲论》,桂林:广西师范大学出版社,2005年,第300—358页。

[44] 刘钝:《从徐光启到李善兰——以〈几何原本〉之完璧透视明清文化》,《自然辩证法通讯》1989年第3期,第55—63页。

An Academic Circle Studying the Euclid's *Elements* in Joseon Korea:Centered on Joseon Scholar Seo Hosu

GUO Shirong (Institute for the History of Science and Technology,
  Inner Mongolia Normal University, Huhhot, 010020)
WU Dongming (Faculty of History, Nankai University, Tianjin, 300350)

Abstract The first six books of the Chinese translation of Euclid's *Elements* translated by Mattio Ricci (1552—1610) and Xu Guangqi (1562—1633) had a great impact on the mathematics in China and then the other countries in East Asia. Since the middle of the 18th century, many Korean scholars from different fields such as mathematics, Confucianism, practical sciences, and religion were all interested in the *Elements*. They collected, read, studied, and applied the *Elements*, and wrote their writings on the subject, which formed a more enthusiastic situation. Seo Hosu(徐浩修,1736—1799) was a high official and a famous scholar whose social strata was on the highest group in Korea. As an important astronomer and mathematician, his interest in the *Elements* and his guidance on the research of the work made the *Elements* more popular in Korea which had important meaning in the history of mathematics in Korea. An academic circle was formed centered on him. The circle consisted of Seo himself, his sons Seo Yubun (徐有本,1762—1822) and Seo Yugu(徐有榘,1764—1845), his younger brother Seo Hyeongsu(徐瀅修,1749—1824), and mathematician Mun Gwangdo(文光道,1727—1775) of the middle social strata,Yu Kum(柳琴,1741—1788), Han Yihyeong(韩以亨,1742—1789) and Kim Young(金泳,1749—1817) of the civilian position, among others. Although ranging in very different social positions, they all interested greatly in the study of the *Elements*, and did research work together.

In this paper, on the basis of discovering a large number of Korean original historical materials, we introduce and discuss the mathematical researches, especially their studies in the *Elements*, of above mentioned scholars from the background of social and cultural history of mathematics.

Keywords Euclid's *Elements*, history of mathematics in Korea, Seo Hosu, Social history of mathematics

第二部分
回忆与评价

Congratulating Professor Guo Shuchun on the Occasion of His 80th Birthday

Joseph W. Dauben 道本周
Department of History
Herbert H. Lehman College and
Ph. D. Program in History, The Graduate Center
City University of New York

Any birthday is a cause for celebration, but an 80th birthday calls for a very special form of notice, and it is a pleasure on this occasion to offer my very warmest congratulations to Professor Guo Shuchun of the Institute for the History of Natural Sciences of the Chinese Academy of Sciences in Beijing. I am pleased to join the many others in applauding his career of numerous and substantial contributions to the history of Chinese mathematics. When I was asked to contribute something to present in his honor as he marks his own 80th birthday this year on August 26, 2021, it caused me to think back to when I first met Professor Guo in Beijing more than thirty years ago. In the course of the past three decades, Professor Guo has proven to be an energetic colleague, an exemplar of the best work of historical scholarship, and above all, a good friend. But as it happens, it was only by a bit of luck, a twist of fate, that we met in the spring of 1988. That happened only by chance, due to a combination of events that I can only liken to the alignment of the planets at exactly the right moment. What follows is an account of my career as it evolved from the mid-1980s, when I visited China for the first time, met Professor Guo, and became increasingly involved with the Chinese Academy of Sciences' Institute for the History of Natural Sciences. That has in turn led not only to several major projects involving Professor Guo, but to a continuing collaborative relationship that has resulted in our organizing together a number of international symposia, working on two major translation projects, and to a long and enduring friendship that has served to enrich and deepen my appreciation for the history of Chinese mathematics over the past three decades and more.

Professor 郭书春 Guo Shuchun, when I first met him in Beijing in the spring of 1988

Remarkably, I would perhaps never have met Professor Guo, never thought about diverting my research interests to the history of Chinese mathematics, and certainly not have visited Beijing and the Institute for the History of Natural Sciences in the spring of 1988 had it not been for one extraordinarily fortuitous event that could not have been predicted. This story begins not in Beijing, but in New York City, where in the mid-1980s I was teaching at both the City University of New York and at Columbia University. My home institution since 1972 has been Lehman College of the City University of New York (CUNY), named after a senior statesman and former Governor of the State of New York, Herbert H. Lehman. By 1979 I also held appointments in the Ph. D. Program in History where the CUNY doctoral programs are concentrated, and was also a Visiting Professor at Columbia University from 1979 until 1985. At that time, Columbia had no full-time historian of science in its History Department, and so I was invited to offer courses that alternated from semester to semester between "Science and Society" and "The Scientific Revolution", mirroring in fact the graduate seminars I also offered on those topics at the CUNY Graduate Center. This arrangement lasted until Columbia hired a full-time faculty member to teach the history of science in 1986. Thus, the last time I taught my Scientific Revolution course at Columbia was in 1985. It also happened that just then Columbia was hosting a Visiting Professor from China who was in New York for the academic year 1984—1985. Somehow, he heard about my course and contacted me about attending it as an auditor during the spring semester of 1985. That was Professor He Zhaowu, and of course I was delighted to welcome him to join my class of undergraduates studying the Scientific Revolution.

At the time we first met, Professor He was still a Research Fellow at the Chinese Academy of Social Sciences in Beijing. Having translated Bertrand Russell's *A History of Western Philosophy* into Chinese in 1963, and just completed a translation of Blaise Pascal's *Pensées* in 1985, he was well-acquainted with the major themes of western philosophy and had a keen interest in the roles both the Scientific Revolution and the European Enlightenment played in the evolution of western intellectual history. He especially wanted to know more about the roles both played in thinking about human rights. Later he would also translate into Chinese such works as Jean-Jacques Rousseau's *The Social Contract* (2003), Edmund Burke's *Reflections on the Revolution in France* (2010), and most recently the most difficult of all, Immanuel Kant's *Critical Essays on Historical Rationality* (2014).

Apart from the course I was teaching, we would meet from time to time on our own to discuss matters raised in class less formally but in greater detail, often over lunch. During our conversations, Professor He wanted to know more about how the cultures of England, France, and America determined their roles in and the nature of their responses to the two revolutions that figured prominently in the courses I taught in my graduate seminars at CUNY and for undergraduates at Columbia, namely the Scientific and the Industrial Revolutions.

I recall the last time I saw Professor He in New York City, just as he was about to return to Beijing, he said with the usual twinkle in his eye that made him an especially endearing person in conversation, "You should come to China, come to Beijing." Yes, indeed I thought to myself, I should do so, but I had no idea at the time how that tiny seed of an idea would eventually become a reality so soon as it did. But the following year, late in the spring of 1986, I wrote to Professor He to explain that I was planning to apply for an academic exchange under the auspices of the U. S. National Academy of Sciences and the Chinese Academy of Sciences. If successful, this would enable me to visit China as a guest lecturer. I knew about such exchanges from one in which I had participated earlier with a visit to the Soviet Union, and was aware that something similar with other countries could also be arranged. In the case of China, this depended upon securing first the sponsorship of an appropriate institution. Professor He replied on July 10 to my letter, having already taken matters in hand himself, writing as follows:

So glad to learn that you are intending to come to this country. I wrote to my friend Prof. Fu-san Zhao, Vice President of the Academy of Social Sciences (in which I had worked, for many years) and to Prof. Ji-xing Pan, Institute of History of Science, about the possibility for an arrangement of your proposed trip. ... I am writing now to Prof. Ze-zong Xi, the chairman of the Institute of History of Science and will send you his answer as soon as possible. Incidentally, I'd like to inform you that I have already left my former post in the Institute of History, Academy of Social Sciences, and taken up my new job in the Institute of Humanities, Tsing Hua University, Peking. And I think I may arrange you to give some lectures when you'll be here in Peking. Please keep contact with me about your trip.

A month later Professor He wrote again with news that he had heard back from Xi Zezong, who would send me an invitation explaining that his Institute was prepared to be my host in Beijing. After giving further thought to topics on which I could offer lectures related to the history of mathematics and science generally, ones I hoped would be of interest to audiences in China, I wrote to Professor Xi to explain in some detail what I hoped to accomplish if I could secure an invitation to visit his Institute, to which he kindly replied as follows:

Beijing, December 28, 1986
Dear Professor Joseph W. Dauben,

I acknowledge with thanks receipt of your kind letter of 15 November 1986. It is my great pleasure to tell you that my colleagues and I are very much interested in your lecture topics and research projects which are described in your detailed proposal to the U. S. Committee on Scholarly Communication with the People's Republic of China. On behalf of the Institute for the History of Natural Sciences, Academia Sinica, I have the honour to invite you to our Institute for three months in the coming year.
Xi Zezong (Director and Professor)
cc: Prof. He Zhao-Wu

With Professor Xi's invitation in hand and Professor He's backing from Tsinghua University, I submitted my application to the Committee on Scholarly Communication with the People's Republic of China, and on February 27, 1987, received provisional approval of my visit to the PRC, with the following caveat: "I am pleased to inform you that you have been selected to participate in the 1987—1988 Visiting Scholar Exchange Program (VSEP) of the CSCPRC. This year the selection panel chose nine finalists and three alternates... We must emphasize that final acceptance into the program still depends upon formal placement within a Chinese sponsoring organization and funding availability in the next fiscal year." Fortunately, the funding was in place and the necessary formalities were concluded over the next year, and by the spring of 1988 I was on my way to China.

En route, I thought about how fortunate I was to have the close connection to Tsinghua through Professor He and to the IHNS, thanks to his having contacted his friend Professor Xi on my behalf. I was looking forward to seeing Professor He again, to meeting my colleagues at the Institute, and to lecturing on a selection of topics I had agreed to offer wherever in China I might be invited to do so, including lectures on the Scientific Revolution, the sociology of science, and various topics on the history of western mathematics, specifically those dealing with the works of the German mathematician Georg Cantor, creator of transfinite set theory, the American pragmatist philosopher Charles Sanders

Peirce, and the inventor of nonstandard analysis, the mathematical logician Abraham Robinson.

The day I arrived in Beijing, I was met at the Beijing Capital Airport by Wang Linna, the Institute's liaison for foreign visitors, and she accompanied me to the Lüsongyuan binguan (Mingling Pines Garden Guesthouse), a quiet hotel within a short bicycle's ride of the Institute and not far from Wangfujing and the Forbidden City. It was, as I would later discover, a historic site in its own right, one dating back to the late Qing dynasty. Having been converted into a tourist hotel in 1980, it was laid out as a typical family courtyard dwelling, a traditional *siheyuan* (literally "four combined courtyards"), located at 22 Banchang Hutong.

Left: Courtyard of the 侣松园宾馆 *Lüsongyuan binguan* (Lüsongyuan Hotel), Dongcheng District, Beijing; Right: my first meeting with 郭书春 Guo Shuchun, with 王林娜 Wang Linna on the right

The Lüsongyuan binguan, one of the oldest courtyard hotels in Beijing, was in buildings that once belonged to a Mongolian general during the Qing dynasty, Sengge Linqin (1811—1865), a Mongolian nobleman who headed troops fighting against the Taiping and Nian Rebellions against the Qing dynasty. He later fought against Anglo-French Allied Forces in 1859 during the Dagu Naval Battle defending a battery of forts and bulwarks near Tianjin, and was involved in the Baliqiao (Eight Mile Bridge) incident in Eastern Beijing that also figured in the Second Opium War. The premises, known locally as the Sengwangfu (Seng's Princely Mansion), comprised a series of courtyards and other buildings in an enclosure whose Ancestral Hall was to become the Lüsongyuan guesthouse. With so much history with the hotel I would call my home for the next few months, I knew that this was going to be a remarkable, once-in-a-lifetime opportunity to absorb as much as I could of Chinese culture generally, and of Beijing's history in particular. As soon as I was settled and could arrange to see Professor He, I made my way to Tsinghua University where he greeted me warmly and said in a way that was typical of both his seriousness and sense of humor, "The good news is, you're here; the bad news is, you can't be at Tsinghua." He went on to explain that there were too many scholars from the US on various exchange programs with the university that semester, and consequently, it had been arranged that my official host institution, my *danwei* (my working unit), would be the IHNS. I suspected, in fact, that Professor He realized that the Institute was exactly where I needed to be in terms of my own interests as a historian of mathematics.

As we walked from the university's Old Gate, formerly the West Gate opening onto gardens of the emperors' Summer Palace and still bearing the name *Tsinghua yuan* (Qinghua Gardens), Professor He introduced me to the Tsinghua campus. As he pointed out, the *Tsinghua yuan* was constructed during the reign of the Kangxi emperor in an eastern part of the Old Summer Palace. The campus of the university, therefore, resembled a vast park, replete with lakes, islands, and beautifully planted grounds. When we came to the building that was home to the Institute of History, we paused for a photograph in front of its main entrance over which four characters were inscribed: 清华学堂 *Tsing-*

Professor 何兆武 (He Zhaowu) and Joseph W. Dauben in front of the 清华学堂 (Tsinghua xuetang), the first building constructed on the Tsinghua University campus

hua xuetang (Tsinghua College), completed in 1911 and built in part with funds from the. U. S Boxer Indemnity Program. Much later, in the summer of 2016, Liu Dun and I would co-teach a course in this same building, an "Introduction to Sociology of Science," a course we had previously offered as an IHNS graduate seminar in 1999. This was the original name of the preparatory school designed to train students in English and subjects they would need to pursue their studies in colleges throughout the United States — the result of the Boxer Indemnity Program. When the Boxer Rebellion had erupted at the end of the nineteenth century in China, eight foreign powers, including the United States, had joined forces to protect their property and other interests, and in putting an end to the rebellion, the foreign powers exacted an exorbitant amount of reparations from the Qing government. Instead of demanding its full share, the U. S. government eventually forgave much of its part of the indemnity, directing that the money be used to support the education of Chinese students in the US. The first of the new buildings that was constructed for the preparatory school, also known as Building No. 1, was the one in front of which I stood with Professor He in 1988. Then I could not have predicted that just short of thirty years later, I would also be teaching at Tsinghua, in this very building, a summer course jointly taught with Liu Dun, an "Introduction to the Sociology of Science," in 2016. This was in fact a revised version of a graduate seminar we had also taught together at the Institute for the History of Natural Sciences in 1999.

Not long after visiting Professor He at Tsinghua, several of my colleagues from the Institute for the History of Natural Sciences came to the Lüsongyuan Hotel to welcome me to Beijing, including the director and vice director of the Institute, Professor Xi Zezong, a noted historian of ancient Chinese astronomy, and Professor Li Peishan, a leading historian of modern biology. They were generous in welcoming me to the Institute, and as I came to know them over the months ahead, they were always helpful in orienting me to the fine points of Beijing's history and that of the Institute as well.

Also accompanying Professors Xi and Li were two of the Institute's leading historians of mathematics, who would soon become my mentors in teaching me as much as I could absorb over the next several months about the history of mathematics in China, namely Guo Shuchun and Liu Dun. I would later meet Professor Du Shiran at the Institute, and during the course of his seminar on the history of mathematics, I received my first introduction to the subject, one that would eventually involve the four of us in a collaborative effort which eventually would lead to another in which I am still engaged with Professor Guo. But more about that in a moment.

Soon thereafter, a delegation of historians of mathematics then in Beijing also came to the Lüsongyuan guest house to greet me, and along with Professor Guo, it included three other historians of mathematics whom I met for the first time, Wang Yusheng from the IHNS (and later director of

Professor 席泽宗 (Xi Zezong), Director of the IHNS   Professor 李佩珊 (Li Peishan), IHNS Vice Director

刘钝 Liu Dun   郭书春 Guo Shuchun   杜石然 Du Shiran

Beijing's China Science and Technology Museum, now the Beijing Science Center); Liang Zhongju, a graduate of Fudan University and Professor at Liaoning Normal University, a founding member and former Vice President of the Chinese Society for History of Mathematics, and author of *Shijie shuxue shi jianbian* (A Concise History of World Mathematics) (1980), the first of its kind in China; and Li Wenlin, at the time Deputy Director of the Institute of Mathematics of the Academy of Mathematics and Systems Science (CAS) in Beijing, later Executive Associate Editor in Chief of *Science China—Mathematics*, published by Springer Verlag, and a former President of the Chinese Society for the History of Mathematics.

王渝生 (Wang Yusheng), 梁宗巨 (Liang Zongju), JWD,
李文林 (Li Wenlin), and 郭书春 (Guo Shuchun)

Even before meeting several of the historians of mathematics affiliated with the Institute, I knew of the excellent work in this field that could be traced back to its leading pioneers, Li Yan (1892–1963) and Qian Baocong (1892–1974). Their many publications during the first half of the 20th century were both considerable and impressive. Among their students and successors were Yan Dunjie, Du Shiran, Mei Rongzhao, and He Shaogeng. Yan Dunjie was a Vice Director of the Institute, and we had corresponded for more than a year about my visiting the Institute. Unfortunately, by the time I arrived in Beijing he was seriously ill and I never met him before he died later in 1988. Du Shiran I would get to know well in the course of the next few months; he was not only the sole student of Professor Li Yan, but was especially well-known for the English translation of the book they coauthored, *Chinese Mathematics. A Concise History*, published by Oxford University Press in 1987.

Mei Rongzhao was another major figure among the historians of mathematics I met at the Institute. When I was first in Beijing in the spring of 1988, he was hard at work on the edition he would soon publish in 1990 of papers on Chinese mathematics in the Ming-Qing dynasties. It was while I was at the Institute that I also read his contribution on rod numerals and arithmetic in ancient China that had been published in English in *Ancient China's Technology and Science* a few years earlier in 1983. He Shaogeng I met during a celebration hosted by the Institute in honor of Du Shiran's forty years of scholarship, hosted by the Institute in 1994. He Shaogeng is best known for his research on such Qing dynasty figures as Ming Antu and Xiang Mingda, especially their work on infinite series. I was also interested in research he had published in 1989 on Wang Xiaotong's *Jigu suanjing* because of its importance as one of the *Ten Classics* of ancient Chinese mathematics.

Having been introduced to the leading figures at the Institute and its coterie of historians of mathematics, it was time to get down to serious business. That I did by beginning to meet with Professor Du Shiran's seminar on history of mathematics. However, life was not all work that spring, and in addition to serious study of the history of Chinese mathematics, I made a point of getting to know Beijing as best I could by bicycle, and visiting the great sites and sights of the city, from the Forbidden City and the Temple of Heaven to the small shops and hutongs of the old city. Li Wenlin took me to see the Great Wall of China, after which I could forever after say that I had proven myself to be a "hero" in the words of Mao Zedong, 不到长城非好汉 *Bu dao changcheng fei haohan* (You're not a hero until you've visited the Great Wall).

As I learned in the course of the months I spent at the Institute that spring, Professor Guo is among the world's leading experts on ancient Chinese mathematics, and the acknowledged authority on the subject of Liu Hui and the *Jiuzhang suanshu* (Nine Chapters on the Art of Mathematics). Liu Dun, when I arrived in Beijing, was a promising young historian of mathematics who would later become director of the Institute (1997—2005) and a decade or so after that, president of the Division of History of Science and Technology of the International Union of History and Philosophy of Science and Technology (DHST/IUHPST) 2009—2013, during which time he also served as president of the IUHPST for 2011—2013. He is an authority on both ancient and modern mathematics, and the history of science generally. Although we are roughly the same age, as he once remarked to me: "There's only one major difference between us (as historians of mathematics) — I spent ten years as a cowboy in Inner Mongolia during the Cultural Revolution!" I have to admit that the closest I ever got to being a cowboy was admiring the herds of buffalo on the Irvine Ranch in Southern California, where I grew up. Today, sadly, the buffalo are gone, but a part of the former Irvine property is today the campus of the University of California at Irvine.

As a result of my participation in Professor Du's mathematics seminar that spring, I was invited to give a lecture on Renaissance mathematics and the connections between the work of Galileo on projectile motion and the development of mathematical perspective as it originated in the context of Renaissance art and architecture in the works of Filippo Brunelleschi, Piero della Francesca, and Leon Battista Alberti, among others. This was something I had studied during a year spent at the American Academy in Rome thanks to an NEH Younger Humanist Fellowship in 1973－1974, and in fact was one of the topics I had listed among those I was prepared to present anywhere in China that spring where I might be invited to give lectures.

JWD: Presentation in 杜石然 (Du Shiran's) IHNS History of Mathematics seminar
Right: JWD at the Great Wall of China, April, 1988

The night before I was scheduled to leave Beijing and begin a month's tour of China, during which time I would visit many of the country's foremost historians of mathematics, I gave a thank-you party for all of my colleagues at the Institute and friends in Beijing. This was held on May 10 at 5:30 pm, at the Lüsongyuan binguan, which by then had come to feel very much like my home in Beijing. Thanks to Wang Linna, she helped arrange everything, including the menu which consisted of dozens of delicious items and ended with two kinds of soup, one hot, one cold, held in one of the hotel's guest dining rooms. Among those present were Xi Zezong, He Zhaowu, Li Peishan, Du Shiran, Mei Rongzhao, Bo Shuren, Li Wenlin, David F. Grose, Kathleen G. Dugan, Liu Dun, Wang Linna, and of course, Guo Shuchun.

In the course of the time I spent in China in the spring of 1988, I was invited to visit many institutes and universities where there was growing interest in the history of science, and I was fortunate to meet many of China's leading historians and philosophers of mathematics and science generally, including Jiang Tianji in Wuhan; Li Di in Huhhot, Inner Mongolia; Shen Kangshen in Hangzhou; and Zhang Dianzhou in Shanghai. Of these, Professor Li Di of Inner Mongolia Normal University was one of the most active promoters of the history of mathematics. Over the years he had not only amassed an impressive collection of mathematics textbooks and historic mathematical works, but created one of the country's leading programs that focused on training scholars in the history of mathematics. Subsequently, his efforts led to the establishment of advanced degree programs for the history of science at IMNU. When I was invited to visit the university in the spring of 1988, the emphasis on graduate teaching in history of mathematics had begun a decade earlier, in 1978; three years later, in 1981, the university was authorized to confer master's degrees, and two years later the Institute for the History of Science was formally established in 1983. In 2006, the Institute was among the first authorized to offer the Ph.D. degree in the History of Science and Technology as a "first-level discipline," and since 2012, the Institute has offered post-doctoral positions as well.

Left: 李迪 (Li Di) at Inner Mongolia Normal University; Right: Wuhan, Professor 江天骥 (Jiang Tianji) and his class of graduate students in the Center for American Philosophy, Wuhan University

Left: Professor 沈康身 (Shen Kangshen), in his office at home in Hangzhou
Right: JWD on the West Lake, Hangzhou

In Shanghai, with 张奠宙 (Zhang Dianzhou) (to the right of JWD) on the campus of East China Normal University

My Travels in China, Spring, 1988

By the time I returned to Beijing after having seen a good part of China, I was fully prepared to appreciate the Institute of which I had been at least briefly a visiting member. The Institute, of which Professor Guo is now an emeritus research scholar, has a long and venerable history, and is about to celebrate its 65th anniversary in 2022. The Institute traces its origins back to when it was founded as the "Research Office for the History of China's Science and Technology" by 竺可桢 Zhu Kezhen (Coching Chu), a graduate of Fudan and Harvard Universities, noted geologist, meteorologist, president for more than a decade of Zhejiang University, and former vice president of the Chinese Academy of Sciences. Zhu Kezhen was also a noted historian of science. In 1975 the Research Office was reorganized and expanded into a Research Institute of the Chinese Academy of Sciences. When I first visited the Institute in 1988, it was in a temporary location with its library in storage. Although the IHNS maintained a small official headquarters at 1 Gongyuan West Street, most members of the Institute worked elsewhere. Classes and seminars usually met in a building located at Dong Huangchenggen Beijie (Eastern Imperial City North Street), commonly referred to as the Wuli lou (Physics Building) because it had once housed the Department of Physics of the Sino-French University between 1925—1949.

As a foreigner on my own in Beijing for three months, I was lucky that a former student and now colleague among historians of science, Kathy Dugan, was also in Beijing and she proved instrumental in orienting me quickly to the ins-and-outs of life in China. Kathy had been a student in a seminar I taught while a graduate student at Harvard. She went on to obtain her Ph. D. in history of science (with honors) from the University of Kansas, and in the 1980s was teaching courses on the history of science and technology at the Graduate School of the Chinese Academy of Sciences. Her own research at the time focused on the discovery and subsequent research devoted to Peking Man, which resulted in our taking a day-trip to see the actual site at which the remains of one of the great anthropological discoveries of the last century had been made of *Homo erectus pekinensis*, discovered in 1921 at Zhoukoudian.

It was Kathy who suggested that it might be worthwhile to take advantage of my being in Beijing on an exchange from the U. S. Academy of Sciences to organize a special meeting to bring historians of science and other interested academics together to discuss the future of the history of science in China. And so, on June 7, 1988, Kathy Dugan and I hosted a symposium co-sponsored by the Committee on Scholarly Communication with the People's Republic of China and the Institute for the History of Natural Sciences, an informal symposium on "Problems and Opportunities in Professionalizing the History of Science and Technology in China." This began at 9 : 00 am at the Friendship Hotel, Beijing, with open discussion including colleagues and graduate students from a variety of universities and institutes in Beijing. Lunch was provided compliments of the CSCPRC, also at the Friendship Hotel.

Guo Shuchun and his Variorum Edition of the *Nine Chapters*

While I was at the IHNS during the spring of 1988, Guo Shuchun took the time to explain to me in some detail an ambitious project of his own to produce a meticulously collated variorum edition of the *Nine Chapters*. This interested me in particular because my mentor at Harvard, I. Bernard Cohen, had also been involved in the production of a variorum edition of Isaac Newton's *Principia*, and I therefore appreciated how valuable — but also how challenging — such a work could be.

Shortly after I left Beijing, later that year I received a letter from Professor Guo which he sent from Rome, Italy, dated October 5, 1988, asking if it might be possible to arrange for a notice of his new edition of the *Nine Chapters* to appear in *Historia Mathematica*, of which I had formerly been the editor. I hoped to do what I could in this regard to heighten awareness of the importance of this work to a wider audience, and so it was arranged that Professor Guo's own account of his project should appear in *HM* in a section of the journal devoted to "Sources." In so doing, Professor Guo pointed out that the work was hardly known during the Ming dynasty and was rescued by Dai Zhen, who edited the work for the *Siku quanshu* based upon a version in the *Yongle dadian*, although as Guo notes, Dai Zhen's version is "rather rough and his collation contains many mistakes." Furthermore, later, "Kong Jihan block-printed the text, and thereafter all editions were thrown into great confusion." Although subsequent historians of mathematics did their best to collate the text, as did Li Huang and more than a century and a half later, Qian Baocong, as Guo surmised, "For more than 200 years all of this editorial confusion has remained untouched" [Guo 1992: 201].

The noted mathematician Wu Wen-Tsun assessed the matter this way, comparing what Guo Shuchun had accomplished as similar to what the Danish philologist and historian of mathematics Johan Ludwig Heiberg did for Euclid:

> In view of the role of the *Jiu Zhang Suan Shu* in the history of mathematics and its immensurable impact upon the future, all its editions ought to be checked carefully and all the errors made in copying and printing ought to be pointed out, just as Heiberg did for Euclid's *Elements*. This work is so important that it must be done without delay. This has now been done by Guo Shuchun after years of extensive reading and considerable preparation (Wu Wen-Tsun, quoted in [Guo 1992: 201]).

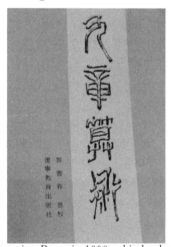

Published by Liaoning Education Press in 1990, this book went on to win First Prize
as the most outstanding collation of an ancient work in a nation-wide competition.
The announcement of the prize on the Chinese Academy of Sciences website gives further details:
https://www.cas.cn/cb/cbdt/201308/t20130823_3917458.shtml (accessed June 19, 2021)

In all, Guo drew on nearly twenty available editions of the *Nine Chapters* to provide his variorum edition. As Li Xueqin, noted paleographer and Director of the Institute of History of the Chinese Academy of Social Sciences noted: "This is now the best edition of *Jiu Zhang Suan Shu*, laying a good foundation for future research" [Guo 1992: 201]. It also had the advantage that it was published simultaneously by Liaoning Education Press in Shenyang and by the Taiwan Nine Chapters Press in Taipei, the latter making it widely available to western historians of mathematics.

A New Project Takes Shape: *Suanjing shishu* (Ten Books of Mathematical Classics)

With Professor Guo's variorum edition of the *Nine Chapters* in mind, it had already occurred to me that a similar project might be useful with respect to making the ten classic works of ancient Chinese mathematics more widely known and appreciated among western historians of mathematics — perhaps nothing quite so ambitious as a variorum edition, but a collection of excerpts from each of the ten classics, suitably translated and provided with notes and commentaries. Such an effort, in collaboration with my IHNS colleagues, would also be a way to continue my association with the Institute's historians of mathematics. I also recalled that the previous summer I had received a notice from Richard Ekman, Director of the Division of Research Programs at the National Endowment for the Humanities, announcing the Endowment's interest in "encouraging the preparation of guides to the study of the important texts in the development of science," and that it hoped to make "several awards in 1988 and 1989." This must have remained in the back of my mind, because even before I had finished my stay in Beijing in 1988, I had begun thinking about how to make the most of the experience I had had at the Institute.

Having been a part of Du Shiran's seminar and working with Liu Dun and Guo Shuchun, I was impressed not only by their seriousness as historians of mathematics, but by the care with which they went about their work. It was as if an entirely new world had opened before my eyes — although I believed myself to have been well-versed in the history of western mathematics, I am sorry to say I knew virtually nothing about mathematics in China, apart from the legendary hundred-fowls problem and the Chinese remainder theorem. But names like Liu Hui and Jia Xian were virtually unknown to me, although I would soon begin to learn more about them in considerable detail. After all, having spent the spring as a guest member of Du Shiran's seminar, and with Guo Shuchun and Liu Dun as my guides, could I have had any better introduction to the history of mathematics in China? And soon that list of my Chinese mentors would enlarge to include Lam Lay Yong in Singapore and Horng Wann-Sheng from Taiwan.

In fact, I had met Lam Lay Yong the year before my first visit to Beijing, at a meeting at the Mathematisches Forschungsinstitut in Oberwolfach, Germany (then West Germany). I was already familiar with her book, *A Critical Study of the Yang Hui suan fa* (1977), and had read her earlier paper, "On the Chinese Origin of the Galley Method of Arithmetical Division" published in *The British Journal for the History of Science* in 1966. The meeting at Oberwolfach was spearheaded by Christoph J. Scriba for the (then) annual Tagung für Geschichte der Mathematik (Conference for History of Mathematics). On that occasion Scriba has chosen to focus for a change on non-western mathematics. The meeting was scheduled for the late spring of 1987 (April 26 — May 7), where, among others, I also met Jean-Claude Martzloff for the first time.[1] It was at this meeting that Lam Lay Yong presented a preliminary version of a paper that she published the following year: "A Chinese Genesis, Rewriting the History of our Numeral System" [Lam 1988]. This paper was preceded by two others on related subjects, [Lam 1986] and [Lam 1987].

Following the spring spent in Beijing, I had arranged to visit Lam Lay Yong in Singapore towards the end of June, after several weeks spent in Hong Kong and Indonesia. I had already discussed briefly with Guo Shuchun and Liu Dun the possibility of our working together on a collaborative project that would give us an opportunity to promote a much wider appreciation of the history of Chinese mathematics internationally, and I thought Lam Lay Young would be a perfect addition to our group given her training as a mathematician and her fluency in both English and Chinese.

While in Beijing, having written to Lam Lay Yong about visiting her in Singapore, she replied in a letter dated May 19, 1988 as follows:

> I am looking forward to seeing you in Singapore... I would be most interested to dis-

---

[1] For a full report of this meeting, organized by Menso Folkerts (Munich) and Henk Bos (Utrecht), see the report by Walter Purkert, "28. Tagung zur Geschichte der Mathematik: Mathematisches Forschungsinstitut Oberwolfach, 27.4—2.5.1987" [Purkert 1988].

Jean-Claude Martzloff and JWD

蓝丽蓉 (Lam Lay Yong) and Christoph J. Scriba, Tagung für Geschichte der Mathematik, Mathematisches Forschungsinstitut, Oberwolfach, April 26—May 7, 1987

cuss with you the history of Chinese mathematics and to hear from you the latest news from China. We shall talk about this over lunch on the 14th [of June], I think that date should be alright... Your itinerary in China is very interesting... See you soon and with all good wishes...

During our meeting in Singapore I raised the possibility of working together on a project that would join forces with several members of the Institute in Beijing to produce, in English, a collection of excerpts from the *Suanjing shishu* (Ten Books of Mathematical Classics) that would offer a broad survey in English of some of the most important works of ancient mathematics in China. Lam Lay Yong was interested in joining such a project, and so I returned to Beijing in the summer of 1990 to continue discussion of such an undertaking with Du Shiran, Liu Dun, and Guo Shuchun from the IHNS. I also wanted to add Horng Wann-Sheng from National Taiwan Normal University in Taipei to our working group.

Horng Wann-Sheng and the *Ten Classics* at National Tsing Hua University, Hsinchu

I've already noted the extraordinary coincidence of my having met Professor He Zhaowu in the mid-1980s. Another unexpected event that also contributed to my decision to pursue more seriously the history of Chinese mathematics as a key focus of my own research was the fact that at virtually the same time as I met Professor He, my first graduate student with an interest in the history of Chinese mathematics, Horng Wann-Sheng, came to New York to work towards a doctoral degree in history of science at the Graduate Center of the City University of New York. This too, I later learned, was in part a matter of happenstance. The mathematics library at National Taiwan Normal University was one of only two in the entire country that had a subscription to *Historia Mathematica*, and it was there that he saw my name and decided to write in 1984, inquiring about the possibility of coming to New York to do a Ph.D. in history of mathematics at the City University of New York. Of course I wrote back, sending him all of the application materials he would need, adding that I would be delighted if he were to come to the CUNY Graduate Center, but cautioned that he would have to fulfill all of the requirements for a Ph.D. in History — a challenge he was willing to accept and, as it turned out, fulfilled admirably.

Wann-Sheng was already well-established at National Taiwan Normal University in Taipei, but took three years away from his teaching there to pursue his Ph.D. with me in New York. Between 1985 and 1988 he completed his required coursework, successfully passed his oral qualifying examination, and received final approval for his thesis project, which he devoted to the late Qing dynasty mathematician Li Shanlan. Wann-Sheng then returned to Taiwan, to resume his teaching mathematics and history of mathematics at NTNU, while he finished the research and completed writing his thesis: "Li Shanlan: The impact of Western mathematics in China during the late 19th century." Serving on his supervisory committee were Arnold Koslow, Bruce Chandler, and Zhang Dianzhou, who were also involved in the oral examination of Wann-Sheng's thesis, which he successfully defended on March 9, 1991, whereupon his Ph.D. was officially conferred by the CUNY Ph.D. Program in History.

A National Endowment for the Humanities Project

Meanwhile, in the spring of 1990 I received word from the US National Endowment for the Humanities that the collaborative project I had proposed to produce a critical edition in English of selections from the ten classics of Chinese mathematics had been approved for funding, and that the NEH grant would run for three years, from January 1, 1991—December 31, 1993. This meant there was no time to lose. I immediately wrote to my colleagues who had agreed to become involved in this project, proposing that we should begin making preparations in the course of the coming year, and then might tentatively plan a meeting where all of us could gather, possibly in Singapore, sometime in 1991 to launch the initial phase of our project.

When I returned to Beijing in 1990, the Institute had recently moved to 137 Chaoyangmen Nei Dajie (Chaonei Street), in buildings that in part comprised the Jiuye Fu (The Ninth Lord's Mansion), the former residence of Prince Fu, Yihui (1845—1877), who was in fact the ninth son of the Qing Emperor Daoguang. (Twenty years later, in April of 2010, the Institute moved to its present location, in Zhongguancun, near Peking and Tsinghua universities, and on the same campus as the Institute for Mathematics of the Chinese Academy of Mathematics and Systems Science).

Over the summer of 1990 I discussed in detail with Guo Shuchun and Liu Dun what the grant from the NEH would allow us to do, and made a point of visiting Lam Lay Yong again in Singapore, to lay the foundation for a preliminary meeting of our working group sometime the following year. I was also looking forward to spending a sabbatical year, to begin in the spring of 1991 and continue through the fall of that year, when I hoped to be back in China for an extended period of time.

I spent the first half of my sabbatical away from teaching largely at Yale University where I was determined to complete much of the research for a book I had already begun working on just prior to leaving for China in 1988, a biography of the mathematical logician, *Abraham Robinson*. Robinson had ended his career as Sterling Professor of Mathematics at Yale, and all of his papers, correspondence, and other material I needed to consult were conveniently available in the University Archives. The book would eventually be published by Princeton University Press in 1995: *Abraham Robinson: The Creation of Nonstandard Analysis. A Personal and Mathematical Odyssey*. A decade later, it appeared in a Chinese translation published by Science Press, thanks to the recommendation of Professor Wu Wen-Tsun, who kindly offered to write a preface for the Chinese version of the book. Benoit Mandelbrot, Robinson's colleague at Yale, had written a preface for the original biography which appeared in the Chinese version as well.

By mid-summer I had conferred with both Guo Shuchun and Liu Dun about our ten-classics project, and having confirmed the details of our meeting at the end of the year with Lam Lay Yong and

Horng Wann-Sheng, I then wrote to the Director of the IHNS explaining exactly what it was we had in mind:

July 22, 1991

JWD to Professor Chen Meidong, Director, IHNS 136 Chaonei Street

Dear Professor Chen Meidong,

I am pleased to extend an official invitation to three members of your Institute, Professors Du Shiran, Guo Shuchun, and Liu Dun to a meeting devoted to the "Ten Classics of Ancient Chinese Mathematics," to be held at the National University of Singapore from December 27-30, 1991. This meeting is sponsored by the U.S. National Endowment for the Humanities, and all transportation and living expenses will be paid for by a grant from the NEH, Washington D.C.

As you know, the purpose of this meeting is to organize an international collaborative effort to produce a critical English edition with notes and commentary of the "Ten Classics." I would be grateful for whatever help you and the Institute for the History of Natural Sciences may be able to give to this project, in particular to enable Professors Du, Guo, and Liu to participate in the Singapore meeting this coming December.

With all best wishes, Joe Dauben

In early September I arrived in Taiwan, where I spent the second half of my sabbatical thanks to an invitation from Fu Dawie to teach two courses in the Institute for History at Tsing Hua University in Hsinchu (the sister school of Tsinghua University in Beijing). Tsing Hua had offered me a Research Professor Award, which involved teaching one course on the Scientific Revolution and another on "Science and Society," which I co-taught as a seminar with Fu Dawie. In addition to these courses, it was arranged that Horng Wann-Sheng and I would also offer a seminar together on "The *Ten Classics* of Ancient Chinese Mathematics."

Once a week Wann-Sheng came to Hsinchu from Taipei for our ten-classics seminar at Tsinghua. This was an especially welcome opportunity for me, because it meant not only working with my former graduate student, but learning from him first-hand about the history and significance of each of the works that comprised the surviving ten mathematical classics. Our seminar on the *Ten Classics* offered students a broad survey of the contents of these works while it gave us the opportunity to map the parts of those classics we would want to feature in our NEH project. Also visiting Tsinghua that semester as guest professors were Benjamin Elman (then at UCLA) and Christopher Cullen from SOAS in London. It was in the course of that semester that I learned Cullen was hard at work on an English translation and commentary on the *Zhoubi suanjing*.

At the end of the year, with the exception of Du Shiran who was unable to join us from Japan, five of us met at the National University of Singapore from December 27—30, where Lam Lay Yong and the Department of Mathematics could not have done more to make our meeting a success. The University provided accommodations at the Visiting Faculty Guest House, and the Department of Mathematics offered us meeting space where we spent three days going over the details of how we would proceed with the work at hand.

We made a preliminary division of the *Ten Classics* into works for which we would each be responsible for generating preliminary bibliographies covering all of the existing editions constituting primary sources for each of the classics, along with the relevant secondary literature pertaining to each. Liu Dun and I agreed to concentrate at first on the *Zhoubi suanjing*. Professor Guo of course offered to take on the entire *Jiuzhang suanshu*. Lam Lay Yong was already at work on a translation of the *Sunzi suanjing* with her colleague Ang Tian Se, and so she volunteered to take on that work. Horng Wann-Sheng agreed to work on a preliminary translation of the *Wucao suanjing* (Mathematical Manual of the Five Administrative Departments).

郭书春(Guo Shuchun), JWD, 洪万生 (Horng Wann-Sheng), and
刘钝 (Liu Dun) NEH Project, Singapore, December, 1991

Following our meeting in Singapore, most of 1992 was spent in working up complete bibliographies for materials related to each of the ten classics, and in making preliminary decisions about what parts or each of the classic works would be selected for inclusion in our final reprise of these works. Then, in February of 1993, Liu Dun came to spend a year as Visiting Research Scholar at the Graduate Center of the City University of New York. By then, he was an Associate Professor in the Institute for the History of Natural Sciences and, in fact, its Vice Director. In addition to working on our translation of portions of the *Zhoubi suanjing* that were primarily concerned with mathematics, including the opening dialogue between the Duke of Zhou and the astronomer-mathematician Shang Gao about the nature of mathematics and the important matter of the *gou-gu* diagram and the purported proof that accompanied it of what amounts to a Chinese equivalent of the Pythagorean theorem, I was also concentrating additional effort on two of the other classics that I had decided to take on, Wang Xiaotong's *Jigu suanjing* (Continuation of Ancient Mathematics) and the *Shushu jiyi* (Notes on Traditions of Arithmetic Methods).

During the spring of 1993, Liu Dun and I would meet regularly at the CUNY graduate center. He also joined my seminar that semester on the Scientific Revolution and later, in the fall of 1993, on October 27, Liu Dun gave a lecture at the NY Academy of Sciences where he addressed "Recent Views on the History of Science and Technology in People's Republic of China." This provided a broad overview of the current state of the profession, including a survey of the institutions, publications, and major researchers at work on the history of science and technology throughout China, with an emphasis on the latest archaeological and archival discoveries and how they have changed our understanding of mathematics, astronomy, medicine, agriculture, and numerous technologies in ancient China.

In June of 1995 our "Ten Classics" working group, now comprised of Guo Shuchun, Liu Dun, Horng Wann-Sheng, and Lam Lay Yong, met in Beijing. In the library of the Institute for the History of Natural Sciences, Guo Shuchun went over some of the details of the complex history of the editions of the *Ten Books of Mathematical Classics*, including the *Nine Chapters*, pointing to specific

Guo Shuchun, Lam Lay Yong, JWD, Horng Wann-Sheng, and Liu Dun, NEH Project, Sheraton Great Wall Hotel, Beijing, June, 1995

JWD, Guo Shuchun, Horng Wann-Sheng, and Lam Lay Yong, NEH Project, IHNS, Beijing, June 1995

details with the help of his recently completed work, the five volumes devoted to mathematics in the *Zhongguo kexue jishu dianji tonghui* (Compendium of Classic Works of Chinese Science and Technology). This made available for the first time in facsimile form the great works of the entire sweep of Chinese mathematics from ancient times to the end of the 19th century, many of them rare works that were now available in a form that made it much easier to study and compare various editions of the major works of Chinese mathematics.

This was a major IHNS project launched in 1992 to publish a series of China's classic works of science and technology, for which Ren Jiyu served as Editor in Chief, and for which Professor Guo oversaw the five volumes devoted to mathematics in this massive undertaking covering extant works from pre-Qin times to the end of the Qing Dynasty. For the five mathematics volumes, Guo wrote an introduction that offered a general overview of the history of Chinese mathematics covering the major figures and describing their main works, offering an assessment of their economic, ideological, cultural, and political impact as they influenced the history of China and world history as well. These volumes not only drew on the rich holdings of the library of the Institute, but included copies of rare works in various libraries and repositories throughout the country. Every work in each of the volumes was accompanied by its own preface written by different experts who assessed the significance and reviewed the major versions and editions if more than one was available. In 1997 Professor Guo's effort in overseeing this project was acknowledged when the set of five volumes on mathematics was nominated for the Third National Book Awards, for which it was awarded third prize.

中国科学技术典籍通汇 数学卷 *Zhongguo kexue jishu dianji tonghui*
(Compendium of Classic Works of Chinese Science and Technology)
(Zhengzhou: Henan Education Press, 1993),
Third Prize winner in the Third National Book Awards in 1997

Meanwhile, our progress on the ten-classics project continued to develop. Liu Dun and I agreed to organize a special symposium for the 20th ICHST scheduled for Liège, Belgium, in 1997 that would focus on the *Ten Classics*. The following year, in the summer of 1998, Liu Dun was in Europe and I was spending most of the summer again at the American Academy in Rome, and so we agreed to meet in Italy and devote some time there to our project. By then he and Guo Shuchun were collaborating on a new Chinese edition of the *Ten Classics*, and at an international meeting held in Wuhan in the fall of 1998 (October 4—8), Professor Guo spoke about "A Study on the Collation of *Suan jing shi shu*." In his presentation, he stressed how collations of the *Suanjing shishu* (Ten Books of Mathematical Classics) had been an important subject since the early Qing dynasty when the *Qian-Jia xuepai* (Qian-Jia School) launched rigorous studies meant to retrieve, examine, collate, and publish ancient classic works towards the end of the 18th century.

International Colloquium on Transmission and Transformation of Mathematical Thought: A Comparative Approach, October 4—8, 1998, Central China Normal University, Wuhan, P. R. C.
Guo Shuchun is seated here in the front row, third from the right

Among the important points Professor Guo stressed was the need for a new collation of the SJSS. Although recognizing the important contributions made by Dai Zhen, his early collation of the text was not, in Guo's opinion, so serious an effort: "He made some wrong collations. And he made a lot of rhetorical correctios based on Kong Jihan's edition, which led to many confusions among different editions." Much later, the 20th-century historian of mathematics Qian Baocong (1892—1974) "contributed a lot" to his collation of the SJSS, correcting many of Dai Zhen's mistakes, but Qian Baocong also based his collation on the Kong Jihan edition, and thus did not correct all of Dai Zhen's errors. Guo thus suggested taking eight books from the editions of the Southern Song dynasty and from the Jiguge (Jigu Library 1684) edition as the basis for a new collation.

In the spring of 1999 I was back in Beijing, where I began a sabbatical leave from the City University of New York that allowed me to continue working directly with Liu Dun and Guo Shuchun on our ten-classics project. Since I was at the Institute for the History of Natural Sciences for the semester, I was invited to offer a graduate seminar, "An Introduction to the Sociology of Science," which I agreed to do jointly with Liu Dun. This was a six-week course comprised of fifteen two-hour seminar sessions conducted in English. All members of the seminar were required to participate in oral discussion and to write four essays on diverse topics related to questions of science and society from the Renaissance to the present. At the end of the course, each student was presented with a certificate confirming their successful completion of the seminar.

算经十书 *Suanjing shishu* (Ten books of mathematical classics), Guo Shuchun and Liu Dun, eds. Taipei: Jiuzhang chubanshe (Nine Chapters Press), 2001. See also [Guo and Liu 1998]

I spent the second half of my sabbatical at the Needham Research Institute in Cambridge, as a fellow at Clare Hall during the fall Michaelmas term. Fortunately, it had been arranged that I would actually be staying in an apartment on the grounds of the

JWD, Last lecture of the graduate seminar on "Science and Society," IHNS, Beijing, Spring 1999

Needham Institute, the same flat that had once been occupied by Lu Guizhen (Lu Gwei-Djen), the longtime associate of Joseph Needham and his second wife. This meant that it was no more than a short walk across the lawn to my office at the Institute, where I used the semester to work on a translation and critical commentary of the *Shushu jiyi*. Before leaving Cambridge, I was invited to present a text reading of this arcane work at one of the Institute's weekly seminars, at which very helpful comments on the work were made by Chris Cullen, Sir Geoffrey Lloyd, Michael Loewe, John Moffett, and Kim Taylor, among others who usually attended the weekly seminars. Each of these has continued to contribute in different ways to my further appreciation of the history of Chinese science

Last meeting of the seminar. Students in the course included: Sun Xiaochun, Hao Liuxiang, Han Qi, Tian Miao, Hou Gang, and Guo Jinhai, among others, and included students not only from the IHNS but from the Institute of Mathematics (CAS), Zhenzhou University, Beijing Normal University, Niaoning Normal University, and Tianjin Normal University, as well as one foreign student from Belgium (L. Oury)

Students in "The Sociology of Science," IHNS, Beijing, May 21, 1999. Liu Dun and I had occasion to teach an updated, revised version of the seminar at Tsinghua University in 2016, for which see the photograph below

"The Sociology of Science" — updated — Tsinghua University, Beijing, summer, 2016

and civilization generally.

Meetings, Meetings, Meetings

It was also while I was in Beijing that I received good news from Susan Garfield from the Rockefeller Foundation that a proposal Yvonne Dold and I had submitted to organize a conference devoted to the transmission of mathematics along the ancient silk routes had been approved, and with support from the ICHM and the NSF, that conference met at the Foundation's Study and Conference Center in Bellagio, Italy, from May 8 to 12, 2000. Eventually, a volume of proceedings from that conference, *From China to Paris: 2000 Years Transmission of Mathematical Ideas*, edited with the help of Menso Folkerts and Benno van Dalen, was published two years later thanks in part to a generous subvention from the Kurt Vogel Foundation as an issue of *Boetheus* published by Steiner Verlag [Dold-Samplonius 2002]. Liu Dun was among the participants at the Bellagio meeting, for which he presented a paper on "A Homecoming Stranger: Transmission of the Method of Double False Position and the Story of Hiero's Crown" [Liu 2002: 157—166].

In 2002 China reached another milestone when it hosted the International Congress of Mathematicians, the first time this prestigious quadrennial meeting of mathematicians from all parts of the world met in China. The opening and closing sessions were held in the Great Hall of the People, as was the closing banquet for those attending the congress. Earlier, a satellite meeting was organized at Northwest University in Xi'an devoted to History of Mathematics, for which Wu Wen-Tsun served as honorary chairman. Meeting from August 15—18, the satellite colloquium emphasized presentations devoted to "Transmission and Transformation of Mathematics: East and West," "Mathematics in China," and "Mathematical Thought of the 20th Century."

International Colloquium on the History of Mathematics, Xi'an, August 15—18, 2002.
Professor Guo is in the first row, fourth from the right

The following week, during the Beijing ICM, an International Symposium on History of Chinese Mathematics was held on Tuesday, August 27, 2002. Co-sponsored by the International Commission on History of Mathematics, the Institute of Mathematics of the Chinese Academy of Science (CAS), and the Institute for the History of Natural Sciences (CAS), I helped to organize the day-long meeting with the help of Li Wenlin and Liu Dun. This symposium was held at the China Museum of Science and Technology. During the morning session Lam Lay Yong was presented with the Kenneth O. May medal for outstanding contributions to the history of mathematics (an award she shared with Ubiratan D'Ambrosio of Brazil, who received the award in absentia). The afternoon session began with a keynote lecture delivered by Wu Wen-Tsun, President of the ICM, which drew a very large crowd to the symposium, for which the Museum had arranged a closed-circuit television broadcast which enabled the overflow audience of several hundred to watch the afternoon session in the Museum's IMAX theater. At the conclusion of the symposium, Wang Yusheng, the Museum's Director, along with Elsevier Science, hosted a reception for everyone who had participated in the day's program.

Dinner in Xi'an: Front row: Guo Shuchun, Alexei Volkov, Annie Han, Tom Archibald, Henk Bos Back row: Liu Dun, Jean-Claude Martzloff, JWD, Umberto Bottazzini, and Elena Marchisotto

Front row, left to right: 大川俊隆 Okawa Toshitaka, 陈良佐 Chen Liangzuo, 郭书春 Guo Shuchun, JWD, 刘钝 Liu Dun, 彭浩 Peng Hao; Middle row: 邹大海 Zou Dahai, 周翰光 Zhou Hanguang, 城地茂 Jochi Shigeru, 李兆华 Li Zhaohua, 武家璧 Wu Jiabi; Third row: 纪志刚 Ji Zhigang, 段耀勇 Duan Yaoyong, 田村诚 Tian Cuncheng, 王青建 Wang Qingjian, 张替俊夫 Harikae Toshio, 赵彦超 Zhao Yanchao, 郭金海 Guo Jinhai, 高红成 Gao Hongcheng

  Two years later, from August 12–14, 2004, the IHNS in Beijing hosted an international conference on the *Suanshu shu* and mathematics in China during the pre-Qin period. This included scholars from the Osaka group in Japan that had devoted considerable attention to studying this work, as well as philological and other experts, including Peng Hao, one of the first to have collated and published a transcription of the text of the *Suanshu shu* [Peng 2001].

  In the spring of 2005 I had the honor of being invited back to Beijing as the IHNS Zhu Kezhen Visiting Lecturer. This also preceded the twenty-second International Congress of History of Science and Technology, which was held in Beijing, the result of several years of elaborate preparations overseen by the Institute's then-Director, Liu Dun. For this occasion, I had also helped to organize, along with Guo Shuchun and Alexei Volkov, a symposium on the "Ten Classics of Ancient Chinese Mathematics." This meeting was again held at the China Museum of Science and Technology, with Wang Yusheng, director of the Museum, offering opening remarks, followed by Christopher Cullen from the Needham Institute who offered an "Introduction to the Symposium." This was followed by Wu Wen-Tsun, who spoke "On the Development of the Real Number System in Ancient China," with a number of subsequent presentations by Li DI, Karine Chemla, Alexei Volkov, and Jean-Claude Martzloff, among others. Guo Shuchun spoke about "Some Questions for the Ten Classics of Ancient Chinese Mathematics." Following two afternoon sessions, this symposium was followed by a general meeting of the ICHM and then a buffet dinner reception for all participants hosted by Elsevier Science, publisher of the ICHM's official journal, *Historia Mathematica*.

July 25, 2005. XXII International Congress of History of Science, Beijing, PRC. Special Symposium on the "Ten Classics of Ancient Chinese Mathematics," China Museum of Science and Technology. Here Guo Shuchun is second from the left in the first row

The Ten-Classics Project Reenvisioned

The Congress symposium helped me to reach a final decision about our ten-classics project, which originally had proposed the production of a volume edited by our team of researchers to cover, with selections, the rich history of ancient Chinese mathematics. There had been little in the way of source materials for Chinese mathematics when I had applied for the NEH grant in 1990, but in the years that followed, the *Sunzi suanjing* had been published by Lam Lay Yong and Ang Tian Se as *Fleeting Footsteps: Tracing the Conception of Arithmetic and Algebra in Ancient China* (Singapore: World Scientific Publishing Co., 1992), just as our project was getting underway. That same year Frank Swetz also published an English translation of part of the *Sea Island Mathematical Manual* (University Park, PA: Penn State University Press, 1992). Soon thereafter, Christopher Cullen published his translation and critical study of the *Zhoubi suanjing* in his *Astronomy and Mathematics in Ancient China: The Zhou Bi Suan Jing* (Cambridge University Press, 1996), and the *Jiuzhang suanshu* itself was translated by Shen Kangshen, John Crossley, and Anthony W.-C. Lun as *The Nine Chapters on the Mathematical Art: Companion and Commentary* (Oxford University Press, 1999). These were in fact the major works that were to have figured in our anthology. Then there were minor works, like the selections from the *Zhang Qiujian suanjing* that were published by Lam Lay Yong in 1997 as "*Zhang Qiujian Suanjing* (The Mathematics Classic of Zhang Qiujian): An Overview" [Lam 1997].

Meanwhile, Victor J. Katz had conceived of an anthology, namely *The Mathematics of Egypt, Mesopotamia, China, India and Islam, A Sourcebook* (Princeton, NJ: Princeton University Press,

2007). This, in essence I thought, had the potential to accomplish what the NEH grant had initially supported us to undertake, although in a somewhat different form than what I had originally envisaged. In fact, two years earlier I had just published my most recent book with Princeton University Press, the biography mentioned earlier of Abraham Robinson, the mathematical logician who had invented nonstandard analysis (PUP 2005). I was greatly indebted to Princeton for having reprinted my biography of Georg Cantor, the founder of transfinite set theory, originally published by Harvard University Press in 1979, but only in a hard-cover edition. Princeton wanted to reissue the book in both a hard-cover and a paper-back version, which it did in 1990, and the book has been in print ever since. Thus, I felt a special connection with Princeton University Press, and so I approached Princeton about whether it might be interested in publishing our ten-classics project, envisioned as a dual-language Chinese-English source book that would serve historians of mathematics and those interested in having the Chinese and English texts side-by-side. Although Princeton appreciated the intellectual merits of what we were doing, it had serious doubts about the financial viability of the project from a publisher's point of view, weighing the costs of production against the probability of sales.

This is where Victor Katz and his project entered the picture and offered what I thought was an ideal solution. His invitation to contribute a collection of excerpts from the *Ten Classics*, among other works including some masterpieces of the Song and Yuan dynasties, would mean that all of our efforts on the ten-classics project would not be lost. I was thus able to bring all of the resources we had been using to bear in providing the section on Chinese mathematics for the Katz sourcebook. In fact, the section of the sourcebook on China is the longest in the book, running to just under 200 pages, and offers a chance for readers to compare the many achievements of mathematicians in China with those from other ancient cultures. It embodies in every respect the results of our collaborative work over more than a decade to produce a collection of excerpts from the "Ten Classics of Chinese Mathematics," while placing them in the context of the larger narrative of the history of mathematics in China generally, for which the *Ten Classics* served as the culmination of the impressive traditions of ancient Chinese mathematics and provided a foundation for the further developments of mathematics in China, especially in the Song and Yuan dynasties.

Guo Shuchun and the *Nine Chapters*

Meanwhile, the collaboration that I had begun with Professor Guo, Horng Wann-Sheng, Lam Lay Yong, and Liu Dun, continued again in a new direction I had not originally anticipated. Having completed a French translation of the *Nine Chapters* with Karine Chemla published by Dunod in 2004, Professor Guo was now interested in producing an English translation as well, not just one comprised of excerpts, but of the entire work. His concept was as grand as our original aspirations for the ten-classics project had been, namely a dual-language edition of the *Nine Chapters* with Chinese and English on facing pages. This was a challenging opportunity, and the work of producing the English text for this collaboration fell to me and Xu Yibao.

This was another appealing project, given that I had already devoted considerable effort to a preliminary translation of selected portions of that work based on the collation of the text by Qian Baocong. But to work with the world's leading authority on Liu Hui, with an authoritative new collation of the text, proved irresistible. It also allowed me to collaborate with my former graduate student, Xu Yibao, who had recently received his doctorate from the City University of New York, which he earned in 2005 with a dissertation on "Concepts of Infinity in Chinese Mathematics."

Xu Yibao and the *Nine Chapters*

Xu Yibao's decision to come to New York and work with me for his Ph. D. in history of mathematics was another of those unpredictable factors that had as substantial an impact on my research as did Horng Wann-Sheng. Yibao was the second graduate student with an interest in Chinese mathematics to come to work with me for his doctorate. The third was Chang Ping-Ying, like Wann-Sheng, also from Taiwan. Ping-Ying wrote her dissertation with me on mathematical families of the Qing dynasty: "Chinese hereditary mathematician families of the Astronomical Bureau, 1620—1850," which she completed in 2015. This is now scheduled to appear shortly as a book in the Needham Research Institute's series of monographs published by Routledge under the title: *The Chinese Astronomical Bureau, 1620—1850: Lineages, Bureaucracy and Technical Expertise*.

Xu Yibao grew up in an island village of Poyang Lake in Jiangxi Province. After earning his bachelor's degree in mathematics from Shangrao Teachers College (now Shangrao Normal University), also in Jiangxi Province, he went on to study history of mathematics with Li Di at Inner Mongolia Normal University. In fact, we first met when I visited Huhhot in 1990 when I gave several lectures at IMNU as a follow-up to my first visit in 1988. I also offered a short-term seminar for graduate students, among whom in addition to Yibao were Feng Lisheng and Guo Shirong.

Yibao came to New York to begin his doctoral studies with me in 1995, after having worked for several years as an editor at the Office of Jiangxi Local History in Nanchang, China. Even before completing his dissertation, he was hired in 2003 to teach mathematics at Borough of Manhattan Community College, one of the twenty-five campuses comprising the City University of New York. Not long after completing his dissertation, he was promoted to the rank of Assistant Professor, and soon thereafter, about the time we began working with Guo Shuchun on the English translation of his new collation of the *Nine Chapters*, he was promoted to Associate Professor. By the time we completed our project in 2013, he was a Full Professor at BMCC.

As Yibao and I began working on the English translation of the *Nine Chapters* with the important commentaries by Liu Hui of the kingdom of Wei and Li Chunfeng and his associates during the Tang dynasty, we would meet more or less weekly at my office at the CUNY Graduate Center and work for several hours, discussing our translation character-by-character, word-by-word. Not only was the collaboration with Yibao especially rewarding, given the breadth of his knowledge of ancient Chinese mathematics, having been a student of Li Di at Inner Mongolia Normal University, but with Professor Guo available to respond to our questions about details of the text of his collation of the *Nine Chapters*, this proved an ideal situation in which to undertake this work.

June, 2006: Mathematical Association of America Tour to China

The following year, in June of 2006, Xu Yibao, having just recently completed his Ph. D., led a special group on a "mathematics" tour of China sponsored by the Mathematical Association of America. A group photograph in the courtyard of the Institute for the History of Natural Sciences in Beijing shows Yibao as group leader, along with members of the Institute Zhang Baichun and Han Qi among those who met with the MAA group. Professor Guo was also on hand to present his views on the *Nine Chapters* to the group, and did so with a copy of his recently published translation into French with Karine Chemla of *Les neuf chapitres: Le classique mathématique de la Chine ancienne et ses commentaires* (Paris: Dunod, 2004). It was in 2006 that their effort was rewarded with the Ikuo Hirayama Prize conferred by the Académie des Inscriptions et Belles-Lettres (Paris) of the Institut de

France for distinguished contributions to scholarship on Asia.

The MAA group visiting China in June of 2006, at the Institute for the History of Natural Sciences (CAS), Beijing. Photograph courtesy of Joel K. Haack (University of Northern Iowa)

Left: 郭书春 Guo Shuchun with Tina Straley, Executive Director at the time of the Mathematical Association of America (June 8, 2006), photograph courtesy of Joel K. Haack (University of Northern Iowa);

Right: 郭书春 Guo Shuchun and 徐义保 Xu Yibao, in the library of the IHNS, Beijing (June 8, 2006), photograph courtesy of Helmer Aslaksen (University of Oslo)

Also in the summer of 2006, Professor Guo was among those invited to participate in an international symposium organized by Horng Wann-Sheng at National Taiwan Normal University, where the symposium was held August 23—25. Nearly one hundred participants came from all parts of the world to attend this meeting, from China, France, Japan, and the US, for which Xu Yibao wrote a brief account of the meeting: "An International Symposiuum on the *Suan Shu Shu*: Appraisals and Appreciations" [Xu 2006: 3—5].

As Yibao noted in explaining the origins of this meeting: "Between December of 1983 and January of 1984, more than sixteen hundred bamboo strips were found in Han Tomb 247 at Zhangjiashan in Jiangling, Hubei Province, China. Among these, 190 are devoted to mathematics and are known collectiely as the *Suan Shu Shu* (because of three Chinese characters, *suan shu shu*, found on the verso of one of the strips)" [Xu 2006: 3]. After painstaking conservation of the strips and careful analysis of their contents, the text with commenatry was publshed in September of 2000, in the journal *Wenwu* (Cultural relics). As Yibao went on to explain, this immediately stimulated considerable interest both in China and abroad, and soon thereafter the text was translated into both English [Cullen

2004] and Japanese [2006].

Conference participants, Juming Museum, Taiwan, August 25, 2006.
Photograph courtesy of Horng Wann-Sheng

The symposium in Taipei was organized to celebrate the publication of the then most-recent study of this work, a book written by the principal organizer of the symposium, Horng Wann-Sheng, along with three other authors, Lin Cang-Yi, Su Hui-Yu, and Su Jun-Hong, namely: *Shuzhi qiyuan Zhongguo shuxueshi kaizhang Suan Shu Shu* (Origin of Numbers: The Opening Chapter in the History of Chinese Mathematics, *Suan Shu Shu* (Taipei: Taiwan Commercial Press, 2006). At this meeting, Professor Guo spoke about the relation between the *Suanshu shu* and the *Nine Chapters*, aruging that the *Suanshu shu*, although a rich compilation of early Chinese mathematics from the pre-Qin period, was not itself a direct source for the *Nine Chapers*.

Once the work of the symposium was completed, the organizers did not fail to offer considerable cultural enrichment as well. The participants were invited to visit the grounds of the Juming Museum and National Yangmingshan National park, and then, over a delicious Tang dynasty dinner served in a restaurant overlooking Taipei, participants were treated to a performance of authentic Tang dynasty courtly music and dancing [Xu 2006: 5].

Left: Xu Yibao and Guo Xuchun, August 21, 2006; Right: Xu Yibao, 郑振初 Zheng Zhenchu, Guo Shuchun, and Jian-Ping Jeff Chen, August 25, 2006

Several years later, thanks to an invitation from Thomas Lee, I was able to spend a substantial part of 2010 at National Chiao-Tung University in Taiwan. In addition to teaching a seminar with Professor Lee on the Scientific Revolution, I spent most of my time working via email with Xu Yibao on our English translation of Professor Guo's new collation of the *Nine Chapters*. By the time the year was over, I had a complete draft of our translation, one that Yibao and I would continue to revise and refine for another two years until we were satisfied that our translation, as well as our commentaries, were ready for publication, along with the newly collated version of Guo Shuchun's Chinese text of the *Nine Chapters*.

Yuelu Academy Bamboo Slips: *Shu* (Mathematics)

In December of 2007, the Yuelu Academy of Hunan University (Changsha, Hunan province) acquired a substantial number of bamboo slips, nearly 3000 in all, from an antiquities dealer in Hong Kong. Most likely looted from a tomb in Hubei province, the slips from a mathematical work simply entitled *Shu* (Mathematics) were painstakingly reassembled from seven of eight bundles of slips jumbled together and representing a diverse collection of documents received by the Academy. After undergoing rigorous scientific tests to establish their authenticity, it was possible to date the Yuelu slips to the pre-Qin Warring States period, thus making them demonstrably earlier than the *Suanshu shu*, which has been dated to the Early Han dynasty. Altogether, the *Shu* itself is comprised of a total of 254 slips.

In 2010 the Academy convened a meeting of an international group of researchers who, along with experts from the Yuelu Academy, were brought together in late September for intensive study of the text of the *Shu* itself. Thanks to Guo Shuchun, Xu Yibao and I were among those invited to participate. In addition to prominent Asian scholars from China, Japan, and Korea, two other westerners were also included in this meeting, Karine Chemla of the Centre National de Recherche Scientifique in Paris and Christopher Cullen from the Needham Research Institute in Cambridge, England. For several days this group of some thirty or so scholars spent mornings and afternoons going through the entire text of the *Shu*, giving it a slow and careful, slip-by-slip, character-by-character examination.

September 22, 2010, International Meeting to Study and Discuss the Bamboo Text of the Yuelu Academy's Recently-Acquired *Shu* (Numbers). Professor Guo is here, first row, fifth from the right

Meanwhile, that same year Professor Guo published another award-winning book, the mathematics volume that he had overseen for the series *Zhongguo kexue jishu shi — shuxue juan* (History of Chinese Science and Technology — Mathematics Volume) [Guo 2010].

This comprehensive work drew on Professor Guo's extensive knowledge of the history of Chi-

中国科学技术史—数学卷 *Zhongguo kexue jishu shi—shuxue juan* (History of Chinese Science and Technology—Mathematics Volume), edited by Guo Shuchun (2010), First Prize winner of the Guo Moruo Chinese History Award conferred in 2012

nese mathematics. His many publications, covering all periods from pre-Qin to Qing dynasty mathematics, prepared him well to assure the authoritative value of this compendium in all respects. The series as a whole was designed to surpass the account of *Science and Civilisation in China* by Joseph Needham and his collaborators. Given that the volume Needham devoted to mathematics was published in 1959, more than sixty years ago, its coverage, while groundbreaking at the time, by 2010 was sorely outdated, a matter now remedied by this volume with contributions from top experts covering all periods from pre-Qin to Qing dynasty mathematics.

Beginning with the earliest mathematics in prehistoric times, this volume provides a thorough study of the origins of mathematics in China, the creation of numbers and development of the basic arithmetic operations, including computations with fractions. The early appearance of diagrams as well as the instruments that were basic to mathematics and its applications, namely the compass, setsquare, level, and plumb-line, are all covered. This authoritative survey of the most ancient mathematics, based upon many new documents only recently available for study, lays a strong foundation for all that follows, documenting the progress mathematics made in China from solutions of basic problems of socio-economic importance, as reflected in the world-famous *Jiuzhang suanshu*, to the development of sophisticated techniques for solving higher degree equations and systems of simultaneous equations which represent the pinnacle of Chinese mathematics in the Song dynasty.

Guo's book is especially noteworthy for its detailed and expert analysis, and for bringing to light, in many cases for the first time, original documents which serve to establish Chinese mathematics as having been at the forefront of world mathematics. Another important value of what Guo accomplished here is the attention given to socio-economic, political, ideological, and cultural dimensions of mathematics, making clear, thereby, the many influences that shaped Chinese mathematics and in turn, how it was applied to solve a wide variety of problems in every-day life. In short, by including the most recent and best scholarship available devoted to history of Chinese mathematics, there is no doubt that the volume, under the editorship of Guo Shuchun, with the assistance of Li Zhaohua and the contributions of more than twenty expert collaborators, has fulfilled its aim of surpassing Needham's account of Chinese mathematics. It was certainly deserving of the honor it subsequently received in 2012, the first prize of the fourth year of the Guo Moruo Chinese History Award.

13th ICHSEA, Hefei, July 25-29, 2011

In July of 2011, Professor Guo and I co-organized a special session on ancient Chinese mathematics for the 13th International Conference on the History of Science in East Asia, which that year was held in Hefei. Prior to that meeting, I was already in Hefei, having been invited by Shi Yunli, Executive Director of the Department of History of Science and Scientific Archaeometry at the University of Science and Technology of China (CAS), to teach a summer course for graduate students on the Scientific Revolution, and to participate in the 13th International Conference on the History of Science in East Asia as well, for which he knew that Professor Guo and I had proposed a special session on ancient mathematics.

Guo Shuchun and JWD during the symposium
organized for ICHSEA 13 (Hefei), July, 2011

One highlight of the Hefei ICHSEA meeting was the opportunity it afforded to visit Huangshan. After the meeting, I returned to Beijing for another few weeks, where I was able to work with Xu Yibao and Professor Guo on various details related to our collaborative project on the *Nine Chapters*.

Summer 2012: Bamboo Slips and Liaoning Education Press

The summer of 2012 proved to be a busy one. Professor Guo, Xu Yibao, and I were nearing the completion of our *Nine Chapters* project, for which Yibao and I were putting the final touches on our introduction to the English half of the work. No sooner had we arrived in Beijing in early June than Professor Guo arranged for a group of us from the Institute, including Zou Dahai and Tian Miao, to visit Han Wei and Li Xueqin at Peking University, where a new trove of bamboo slips was being conserved and studied, including more slips constituting another early work on mathematics. Also joining us on that visit to Beida was Feng Lisheng from Tsinghua University.

Liaoning Education Press, Shenyang

As our translation of the *Nine Chapters* neared the point of publication, we felt it would be helpful to visit Liaoning Education Press, where the book would actually be produced for the prestigious Library of Chinese Classics series. Only two works devoted to mathematics had been chosen for inclusion in this official government-sponsored series of classics, Zhu Shijie's *Siyuan yujian* (Jade Mirror of the Four Unknowns) of 1303, and the *Nine Chapters*. Guo Shuchun had been invited to oversee preparation of both texts, and had already published the *Jade Mirror* in 2006. He based that work on an English translation made decades earlier by Ch'en Tsai Hsin (Chen Zaixin), who had begun his translation while studying with David Eugene Smith at Teacher's College, Columbia University, in New York City, but only finished later, sometime in 1925 after he had returned to China, where he

Left: June 14, 2012, Sackler Museum of Art and Archaeology, Peking University, Front row, 郭书春 Guo Shuchun, 韩巍 Han Wei, JWD, 冯立昇 Feng Lisheng; Second row, 杨涤非 Yang Difei, 邹大海 Zou Dahai, 田淼 Tian Miao, 张一杰 Zhang Yijie, and 徐义保 Xu Yibao; Right: Professor 李学勤 Li Xueqin (second from left), Director of the Bamboo Slips Conservation Team at Peking University, Beijing

served as Chair of the Department of Mathematics at the newly-created Yenching University when it was founded in Beijing in 1919. Guo Jinhai revised Ch'en's translation and added new material as well, working with Guo Shuchun to create the dual-language edition of the *Jade Mirror* for the Library of Chinese Classics [Guo, Ch'en, and Guo 2006].

When Professor Guo was asked to undertake a similar project for a critical Chinese-English edition of the *Nine Chapters*, he invited me and Xu Yibao to collaborate with him on that equally ambitious project. The goal of the Chinese Classics, as its editor-in-chief Yang Muzhi pointed out in a general introduction to the entire series, was to ensure that "the nation's greatest cultural achievements can be introduced to people all over the world." He went on to explain the importance of western readers being able to appreciate through sound and careful translations the great works of Chinese intellectual history. "Based on this recognition, we have edited and published the Library of Chinese Classics in a Chinese-English format as an introduction to the corpus of traditional Chinese culture in a comprehensive and systematic translation. Through the collection, our aim is to reveal to the world the aspirations and dreams of the Chinese people over the past 5,000 years and the splendour of the new historical era in China. Like a phoenix rising from the ashes, the Chinese people in unison are welcoming the cultural sunrise of the new century" (Yang Muzhi, in his Preface to [Guo, Dauben, and Xu 2013: 16]).

The actual process by which the series of classic texts and translations were chosen and produced followed a meticulous process:

> The Library of Chinese Classics includes over 100 of the most representative classic works, covering literature, history, philosophy, politics, economy, military science, and science and technology. Each selection and version was chosen after careful reasoning, comparing, and proofing. Works in classical prose were first translated into modern Chinese, and then into English. Yang Muzhi, chief editor of the series and president of the China Publishing Group, said the most important thing when preparing the Library of Chinese Classics was insuring its quality—all translations were polished by foreign experts; the fourth examination work by the work committee reinforced this, based on the third check by the publishing house [CHINA. ORG. CN].

Having invested a considerable amount of time in producing both the Chinese and English versions of the *Nine Chapters* for the Library of Chinese Classics series, we wanted to be sure that the press chosen for actually producing the book was indeed prepared to do so, fully understanding the complexity of what was ahead and having to manage what would turn out to be a three-volume published version of what we had produced. And so it was arranged that we would pay a visit to the press in Shenyang in mid-June.

Departing Beijing by train on June 17, 2012, we arrived in Shenyang in time for a late lunch with one of the editors at Liaoning Education Press, Wu Xuan (Kathy), and several members of her staff. The next day we arrived at the offices of Liaoning Education Press, and went over some of the major concerns we had, in particular about details in compositing the book that we wanted to be sure were taken into consideration in what we knew would be a complex process of laying out the Chinese and English texts on facing pages. Later in the day we visited the workshop where the text was already being compiled and formatted by a roomful of compositors at their computers, making up the pages that would constitute the final version of the book. That afternoon, Kathy wanted to be sure we had time to visit some of the historic sites of Shenyang, including the famous "Forbidden City" that was the forerunner and model for its counterpart in Beijing. This had also been home to one of the seven versions of the encyclopedic work, the *Siku quanshu* (The Complete Library of Four Treasures), from which a good part of the remaining versions of the *Ten Classics* had been initially preserved.

June 18, 2012: Our editorial team at the offices of Liaoning Education Press, from left to right: JWD, 郭书春 Guo Shuchun, 王丽君 Wang Lijun, 吴璇 Wu Xuan (Kathy), 叶北宁 Ye Beining, and 徐义保 Xu Yibao. Photographs here and below courtesy of 吴璇 Wu Xuan of Liao-ning Education Press

June 18, 2012: Left: The Forbidden City in Shenyang, from left to right: Wang Lijun, JWD, Guo Shuchun, Wu Xuan (Kathy), and Xu Yibao; Right: Visit to the Zhang Family Mansion Museum, Guo Shuchun, JWD, Wu Xuan (Kathy); Photographs courtesy of Wu Xuan

2013: Liu Hui 1750th Anniversary Meeting and the Manchester 24th ICHST

The summer of 2013 was another one full of meetings, two in particular again found me and Professor Guo collaborating as co-organizers, the first being an international conference in June to celebrate the 1750th anniversary of Liu Hui's completion of his commentary on the *Nine Chapters*. The other was the 24th International Congress of History of Science and Technology scheduled for Manchester, England, a month or so later, in July. The earlier of the two, the Liu Hui meeting, took place in Liu Hui's presumed hometown in Zouping County, Shandong Province, June 21—26, 2013. This meeting was sponsored, among others, by the Department of Culture of Shandong Province, the Institute for the History of Natural Sciences (CAS, Beijing), the Chinese Mathematical Society, the Chinese Society of History of Science and Technology, the Chinese Society for the History of Mathematics, and various committees and government agencies in Shandong Province.

I was pleased to co-chair the Academic Committee with Professor Guo, but in all honesty, in this case virtually all of the organizational work for the academic content of the symposium fell on his shoulders and those of the "Secretary Generals" of the Academic Committee, Feng Lisheng and Zou Dahai. The opening ceremony for the meeting began with welcoming remarks from the leaders of Zouping Country government, both city and provincial officials, followed by plenary lectures and section meetings over the next two days.

Participants in the meeting organized to celebrate the 1750th anniversary of Liu Hui's completion of his commentary on the *Nine Chapters*, held in Zouping County, Shandong Province, PRC, June 21-26

Following the Liu Hui meeting in Zouping, I spent several weeks in Shanghai where I taught a graduate seminar on the Scientific Revolution with Ji Zhigang at Shanghai Jiao Tong University, followed by the 24th International Congress of History of Science, Technology, and Medicine that met in Manchester, UK, from July 22 through July 28. At this congress the International Commission on History of Mathematics co-sponsored six special symposia, one of which Professor Guo and I helped to organize along with Xu Yibao and Zou Dahai. Our symposium, focusing on "Mathematical Knowledge at work in Ancient China," met on Tuesday, July 23, with three consecutive sessions running for the entire day, during which Professor Guo presented a talk on "A Discussion on the Significance of the Discovery of Mathematics Bamboo Slips from the Warring States period, Qin and Han Dynasty." This presentation reprised a talk he had given earlier at a meeting devoted to "History and Pedagogy of Mathematics" in Daejeon, Korea, July 16-20, 2012 [Guo 2012: 191-200].

Four years later, Professor Guo and I organized another symposium, along with Horng Wann-

Participants at the 25th ICHST held in Manchester, England, July of 2013.
From left, Xu Yibao (City University of New York), Horng Wann-Sheng (Taiwan Normal University),
Zou Dahai and Guo Shuchun (Institute for the History of Natural Sciences, CAS), and
José Antonio Cervera Jiménez (El Colegio de México, México)

Sheng and Zou Dahai, on ancient Chinese mathematics for the 25th International Congress of History of Science and Technology, which met in Rio de Janeiro, Brazil, at the end of July in 2017. Although the ICHM again co-sponsored the symposium, devoted to "Mathematical Methods at Work in Ancient China—Local Applications with Global Connections," in keeping with the general theme of the congress, of the twelve speakers we had invited, in the end only two were able to make the trip to Rio.

Four years later, to make up for that, with the help of Jian-Ping Jeff Chen and Zou Dahai, Guo Shuchun and I again organized a special symposium on ancient Chinese mathematics for the 26th ICHST. But instead of meeting in Prague, Czech Republic, as originally planned, that year's symposium was held virtually, online, with participants presenting their talks remotely via Zoom. Although we were not able to attend this meeting in person, technology allowed participants in different parts of the world to make their presentations in a live format that enabled questions and at least brief exchanges, despite the fact that some, like participants in the US, were literally half the world away and in totally opposite time zones from those in China. In fact, some had to make their presentations often well after midnight and some as late as 1:30 am. Despite these disadvantages and challenges, the symposium spanned two days and involved twelve participants, all of whom were able to attend the symposium and present their work. The first to open the symposium and set a high standard for those to follow was Professor Guo, whose presentation was entitled: "Concerning Classical Chinese Mathematics, We Only Know a Few Bits and Pieces." Noting that from the earliest times of the Xia Dynasty (21st-century BCE) to the compilation of the *Nine Chapters* during the Western Han Dynasty, a period of some 2000 years, although mathematics underwent a substantial evolution beginning with mathematical propositions in the *Mojing* (Mohist canon) and in various works on bamboo during the Qin and Han dynasties, their contents do not go beyond the mathematics to be found in the *Nine Chapters*. Above all, they do not include such important methods as those for finding square and cube roots, or for solving simultaneous linear equations. A millennium or so after Liu Hui, by the 13th century, Qin Jiushao introduced the general *dayan* method for solving linear systems of simultaneous congruences on a par with what was later achieved by Carl Friedrich Gauss, but no one knows how the *dayan* method was developed. Also, Qin Jiushao solved a problem involving a 10th degree equation, but only said to use "the *gu-minus-gou* rates." Even today, no one knows the precise meaning of these words. Other major achievements of the Song-Yuan period are the *tianyuan shu*, a method for solving equations in one unknown, as well as formulas for summing higher order arithmetic progressions and series using the method of "small differences." As he concluded: "Historians of mathematics must use scientific methods to examine these incomplete surviving bits and pieces in classical Chinese mathematics to reconstruct the systematic development of its procedures and methods."

Yet to come...

In conclusion, the reminiscences I've recounted here have brought back wonderful memories for me of more than thirty years of academic collaboration with Professor Guo Shuchun, ever since we first met in the courtyard of the Lüsongyuan binguan in Beijing in the spring of 1988. The first of his many and informative publications appeared in 1978, in *Zhongguo gudai keji chengjiu* (Achievements of Ancient Chinese Science and Technology), an article entitled *Gaoci fangcheng shuzhi jiefa he tianyuan shu* (Numerical solutions of higher-order equations and the *tianyuan* method) [Guo 1978]. Ever since, Professor Guo has proven to be an indefatigable researcher. An author and editor of numerous award-winning books and countless academic articles, a selection of eighty-one of his previously published works was published in two volumes in 2018 by Shandong Science and Technology Press, for which I was invited to write an introductory preface, which I was pleased to do. In that Preface, I wrote:

郭书春数学史自选集 *Guo Shuchun shuxue shi zixuan ji*
(Guo Shuchun Selected Works on History of Mathematics),
Jinan: Shandong Science and Technology Press, 2018

In his approach to the history of mathematics in China, Professor Guo has always emphasized the importance of relying on primary sources, and among these, he is internationally known for his mastery of the *Nine Chapters on the Art of Mathematics*. It is no exaggeration to say that thanks to Professor Guo and his many students who have been trained by him at the Institute for the History of Natural Sciences in Beijing, Liu Hui is no longer an obscure figure in the history of mathematics in China, but has achieved a prominence fully deserved, as Professor Guo's many studies of Liu Hui and his work have demonstrated.

Anyone wishing to survey the vast sweep of Professor Guo's work over the past five decades as he has written on so many subjects, capturing the breadth and depth of Chinese mathematics from early antiquity through such high points as those represented by the works of Liu Hui and Jia Xian, among many others, will find this a most convenient publication. By gathering together in this collection of Guo Shuchun's eighty-one most important selected papers, his own "*jiu jiu*" of the history of Chinese mathematics has been assembled in two substantial volumes. In his "Preface" to the *Nine Chapters*, Liu Hui referred to the origins of the "*jiu jiu*" in great antiquity, which provided the basics of numbers, counting, and indeed, of mathematics itself, which later made it possible, he said, to understand and follow "the subtle and profound essence of heaven and earth and everything in between." Likewise, in this collection of "*jiu jiu*," nine-nines or eighty-one of his most essential works, Guo Shuchun has provided a rich and penetrating analysis of a broad spectrum of Chinese mathematics. With masterful strokes from Professor Guo's historical brush, he paints a clear and vigorous history of Chinese mathematics through the more than fifty years of published works represented in this marvelous collection drawn from his many publications [Guo 2018: 5—6].

Not surprisingly, given this remarkable record of his publications to date, Professor Guo's research and writing continue now as vigorously as ever. And once again, we are embarked on another major project, this time a new English translation of the *Nine Chapters*. This version has been undertaken in collaboration with Jian-Ping Jeff Chen, Horng Wann-Sheng, and Zou Dahai. What sets this collation and translation apart from all others is that it not only includes the Song dynasty commentaries on the *Nine Chapters* by Jia Xian and Yang Hui, but it is based upon new variant readings of the original Chinese text based upon Professor Guo's incorporation of new collations drawing on what he now regards as the original and best of the versions to be found among the copies that survive of the *Siku quanshu*, namely the Wenjin ge edition only recently available for comparison.

As the famous American writer Mark Twain once said about turning 80, "Age is an issue of mind over matter — if you don't mind, it doesn't matter." What matters most about Professor Guo's 80th birthday is the extraordinary record of scholarship and publications he has produced in the course of his career — and so many award-winning publications at that. We have all benefitted from his committed dedication to promoting broader understanding of and appreciation for the great discoveries and methodological contributions Chinese mathematicians have made to the world's collective appreciation of mathematics internationally. It has been both a pleasure and a privilege to have worked so closely with Guo Shuchun over many productive years, and I look forward to many more in the years to come. Happy 80th birthday, Professor Guo!

Bibliography

Bu, Jingzhi (步近智), He Zhaowu (何兆武), Sun Kaitai (孙开太), and Tang Yuyuan (唐宇元). 1981. 中国思想发展史 *Zhongguo sixiang fazhan shi* (An Intellectual History of China). Beijing: China Youth Press.

_____. 1990. *An Intellectual History of China*, He Zhaowu, trans. Beijing: Foreign Languages Press.

Chang, Ping-Ying (张秉莹). 2015. "Chinese hereditary mathematician families of the Astronomical Bureau, 1620—1850." Ph. D. Dissertation, Ph. D. Program in History, The Graduate Center, City University of New York.

_____. 2022. *The Chinese Astronomical Bureau*, 1620—1850: *Lineages, Bureaucracy and Technical Expertise*. Needham Research Institute Series. London: Routledge.

CHINA. ORG. CN. 2007. "Bilingual Library of Chinese Classics Unveiled," CHINA. ORG. CN.

http://www.china.org.cn/2007-01/12/content_1195889.htm (accessed July 14, 2021).

Dold-Samplonius, Yvonne. 2002. *From China to Paris: 2000 Years Transmission of Mathematical Ideas* (*Boethius* 46). Yvonne Dold-Samplonius, Joseph W. Dauben, Menso Folkerts, and Benno van Dalen, eds. Stuttgart: Franz Steiner Verlag.

Guo, Shuchun (郭书春). 1978. 高次方程数值解法和天元术 *Gaoci fangcheng shuzhi jiefa he tianyuan shu* (Numerical solutions of higher-order equations and the *tianyuan* method), in 中国古代科技成就 *Zhongguo gudai keji chengjiu* (Achievements of Ancient Chinese Science and Technology). Beijing: China Youth Press.

_____. 1988. 贾宪《黄帝九章算经细草》初探 *Jia Xian "Huangdi jiuzhang suanjing" xicao* (Preliminary research into Jia Xian's *Detailed Solutions of the Yellow Emperor's Nine Chapters Mathematical Classic*), 自然科学史研究 *Ziran kexueshi yanjiu* (Studies in the History of Natural Sciences) 7 (4): 328-334.

_____. 1992. "Guo Shuchun's Edition of the *Jiu Zhang Suan Shu* (*Nine Chapters on the Mathematical Art*," *Historia Mathematica* 19 (2): 200-202.

_____, ed. 1993. 中国科学技术典籍通汇:数学卷 *Zhongguo kexue jishu dianji tonghui: Shuxue juan* (A Compendium of Chinese Classics of Science and Technology: Mathematics Section), 5 vols. Zhengzhou: Henan Education Press.

_____. 2009. 九章算术译注 *Jiuzhang suanshu yizhu* (A Modern Chinese Translation and Commentary on the *Nine Chapters on the Art of Mathematics*). Shanghai: Shanghai Ancient Books Press.

_____. 2010. 中国科学技术史 数学卷 *Zhongguo kexue jishu shi—shuxue juan* (History of Chinese Science and Technology—Mathematics Volume). Beijing: Science Press.

_____. 2012. "A Discussion on the Significance of the Discovery of Mathematics Bamboo Slips from the Warring States Period, Qin and Han Dynasty," *History and Pedagogy of Mathematics* 2012, Daejeon, Korea, 16 July – 20 July: 191-200. http://hpm2012.onpcs.com/Proceeding/OT2/T2-05.pdf (accessed July 3, 2021).

_____. 2018. 郭书春数学史自选集 *Guo Shuchun shuxue shi zixuan ji* (Guo Shuchun Selected Works on History of Mathematics). Shandong: Shandong Science and Technology Press, in two volumes.

Guo, Shuchun (郭书春), and Liu Dun (刘钝). 1998. 算经十书 *Suanjing shishu* (Ten Books of Mathematical Classics). Shenyang: Liaoning jiaoyu chubanshe, in two volumes; also printed in a single volume, Taipei: Jiuzhang chubanshe (Nine Chapters Press), 2001.

Guo, Shuchun (郭书春), and Karine Chemla. 2005. *Les neuf chapitres. Le classique mathématique de la Chine ancienne et ses commentaires*. Paris: Dunod.

Guo, Shuchun (郭书春), Ch'en Tsai Hsin (陈在新), and Guo Jinhai (郭金海). 2006. 四元玉鉴 *Siyuan yujian* (Jade Mirror of the Four Unknowns). Shenyang: Liaoning Education Press.

Guo, Shuchun (郭书春), Joseph W. Dauben (道本周), and Xu Yibao (徐义保). 2013. 九章算术/（魏）刘徽注；（唐）李淳风等注释；郭书春校勘并译注；道本周，徐义保英译并注 *Jiu zhang suan shu /(Wei) Liu Hui zhu ; (Tang) Li Chunfeng deng zhu shi ; Guo Shuchun jiao kan bing yi zhu ; Daoben Zhou, Xu Yibao Ying yi bing zhu* (Nine Chapters on the Art of Mathematics /with the annotations by Liu Hui (State of Wei) and notes and annotations of Li Chunfeng and associates (Tang Dynasty); a critical edition and English translation based upon a new collation of the ancient text and modern Chinese translation by Guo Shuchun; English critical edition and translation, with notes by Joseph W. Dauben and Xu Yibao). Shenyang: Liaoning Education Press, in three volumes.

Horng, Wann-Sheng (洪万生). 1991. "Li Shanlan: The Impact of Western Mathematics in China During the Late 19th Century." Ph. D. Dissertation, Ph. D. Program in History, The Graduate Center, City University of New York.

_____. (2001). 二十一世纪的《算经十书》 *Ershi yi shiji de Suanjing shishu* (Twenty-one centuries of the *Ten Books of Mathematical Classics*), introduction to [Guo and Liu 2001: iii-iv].

Lam, Lay Yong (蓝丽蓉). 1986. "The Conceptual Origins of our Numeral System and the Symbolic Form of Algebra," *Archive for History of Exact Sciences* 36: 183-195.

_____. 1987. "Linkages: Exploring the similarities between the Chinese rod numeral system and our numeral system," *Archive for History of Exact Sciences* 37: 365-392.

_____. 1994. "Jiu Zhang Suanshu 九章算术 (Nine Chapters on the Mathematical Art): An Overview," *Archive for History of Exact Sciences* 47 (1): 1-51.

_____. 1997. "*Zhang Qiujian Suanjing* (The Mathematical Classic of Zhang Qiujian): An Overview," *Archive for History of Exact Sciences* 50 (3/4): 201-224.

Lam, Lay Yong (蓝丽蓉), and Ang Tian Se (洪天赐). 1992. *Fleeting Footsteps. Tracing the Conception of Arithmetic and Algebra in Ancient China*. Singapore: World Scientific; rev. ed. 2004.

Li, Yan (李俨), and Du Shiran (杜石然). 1987. *Chinese Mathematics. A concise history*. John N. Crossley and Anthony W.-C. Lun, trans. Oxford: Clarendon/Oxford University Press.

Liu, Dun (刘钝). 2002. "A Homecoming Stranger: Transmission of the Method of Double False Position and the Story of Hiero's Crown," in [Dold-Samploinus 2002: 157-166].

Mei, Rongzhao（梅荣照）. 1983. "The Decimal Place-value Numeration and the Rod and Bead Arithmetics," in *Ancient China's Technology and Science*. Beijing: Foreign Languages Press: 57-65.

———. 1990. 明清数学史论文集 *Ming-Qing shuxue shi lunwen ji* (Collected papers on the history of mathematics under the Ming and Qing periods). Nanjing: Jiangsu jiaoyu chubanshe.

Peng, Hao（彭浩）. 2001. 张家山汉简《算数书》注释 *Zhangjiashan Hanjian Suanshu shu zhushi* (Commentary on the *Suanshu shu* Han Bamboo Slips from Zhangjiashan). Beijing: Science Press.

Purkert, Walter. 1988. "28. Tagung zur Geschichte der Mathematik: Mathematisches Forschungsinstitut Oberwolfach, 27.4—2.5.1987," *Historia Mathematica* 15 (2): 152-164.

Xu, Yibao（徐义保）. 2005. "Concepts of Infinity in Chinese Mathematics." Ph. D. Dissertation, Ph. D. Program in History, The Graduate Center, City University of New York.

———. 2006. "An International Symposiuum on the *Suan Shu Shu*: Appraisals and Appreciations," *HPM Tongxun* 9 (9): 3-5. https://math.ntnu.edu.tw/~horng/letter/909.pdf (accessed July 22, 2021).

My Gratitude to Professor Guo Shuchun, an Influential Figure in My Accidental Career

Jian-Ping Jeff Chen 陈建平

Department of Mathematics and Statistics

St. Cloud State University

St Cloud, Minnesota, 56301, USA

If I could go back in time and tell my young self in graduate school studying to be a research mathematician that I would eventually be doing research in the history of mathematics, my young self would probably have laughed, directly to my face. It is understandable. When someone is eager to learn to carry out research in "pure" mathematics, any slight variation in the projection of one's future career can be perceived as an insult or discouragement. In my experiences in graduate school, graduate students pursuing a career in mathematics do not consider the history of mathematics as a legitimate field for research in mathematics; at least, that was the case for me in the United States 30 years ago. During the course of my study of theoretical mathematics, the issues of origins of ideas were always on my mind. I was often curious about what motivated or precipitated new approaches, or how did people realize that certain things should be broadened in order to connect well-accepted theories with new perspectives. Sometimes the answers were readily available; but for many others, especially those dealing with much-less-mainstream approaches, their stories were harder to come by. Many people often dismiss such questions with a simple, "who cares." In a way, as these stories of the past are not the focus of front-end research, my young self simply agreed with others and moved on.

Fast forward to the present day, as I try to write a short piece to honor Professor Guo Shuchun's 80th birthday (or 81st, if counted in the traditional Chinese way), reflecting on how I entered into the field of the history of mathematics. In many ways, it was purely accidental. It was as if I made a random decision to turn to the right at a point in my career; but the path I followed has led me to an astonishing world that is just as fascinating as theoretical mathematics. Many people played pivotal roles in my entry and eventual modest success in this field—among them are Dr. Minghui Hu, Professor Guo Shuchun, and Professor Joseph Dauben. On this special occasion, this small piece is meant to offer my sincere gratitude to Professor Guo in particular for his influence and help in shaping me as a historian of mathematics.

In the early 2000's, I was a new assistant professor at St. Cloud State University in Minnesota, struggling with mathematics research and contemplating what to do with the future of my career. A couple of years earlier, my classmate from middle school, Minghui Hu, was a graduate student at the University of California, Los Angeles, studying history with Professor Benjamin Elman at the time. During one of my visits to California, he showed me several Chinese mathematical treatises he was studying. Their authors, Mei Wending（梅文鼎）, Dai Zhen（戴震）, and Jiao Xun（焦循）, these giants in the history of early modern Chinese mathematics, meant little to me. Nevertheless, I found their works fascinating. Minghui very quickly suggested that I should study Dai Zhen's trigonometric treatise, 勾股割圆记 *Gougu geyuan ji* (the Records of base-altitude and circle division) and perhaps consider switching to work in the history of mathematics in China. Being naïve and ignorant, I jumped at the suggestion and started to study Dai's seminal work without hesitation, not understanding what was really entailed in such an undertaking. Minghui also introduced me to Professor Joseph Dauben during a trip to New York City before attending a meeting at Princeton University. Although Minghui was a graduate student in history and I was completely unknown in the field, Professor Dauben treated us to lunch at the Harvard Club in New York City, listening to us talking about our respective works at the time. After the Princeton conference and returning to the Midwest, I continued teaching mathematics classes at my university and, when time allowed, worked on my study of Dai Zhen's trigonometrical treatise.

In 2002, the International Congress of Mathematicians was held in China, August 20-28. Before the main events in Beijing, numerous satellite conferences took place in various cities in China, including an International Colloquium for the History of Mathematics held in Xian. The topics for the conference included Transmission and Transformation of Mathematics: East and West, Mathematical Thought of the 20th Century, and Mathematics in China. During that meeting I saw Professor Dauben again and met many other leading figures in the history of Chinese mathematics for the first time. A few of these scholars left a lasting impression, including Professor Guo Shuchun. I have to admit that I do not remember much about his presentation at the conference, not even the topic; but I do remember that Professor Guo was straightforward, frank, open, and eager to help. After learning that I had recently started to study the history of mathematics in China but did not have access to material in the existing traditional Chinese mathematical treatises, he advised that I should study the works of Professors Li Yan and Qian Baocong as a starting point. Moreover, he advised me to purchase two of the most important collections for anyone interested in studying the history of Chinese mathematics: 李俨钱宝琮科学史全集 *Li Yan Qian Baocong kexueshi quanji* (Complete Collection of Li Yan and Qian Baocong's Essays on History of Science) and 中国科学技术典籍通汇数学卷 *Zhongguo kexue jishu dianji tonghui shuxue juan* (A Comprehensive Collection of Treatises in Chinese Sciences and Technology, Mathematics volumes), for both of which Professor Guo had served as editor-in-chief. Furthermore, he offered to purchase these works on my behalf at the authors' discount price. In the fall of 2002, a heavy cardboard box tied with rope and wrapped in lots of tape arrived at the office of the mathematics department at St. Cloud. In it, I found the ten volumes of Li Yan's and Qian Baocong's work and five volumes of facsimile reprints of many of the most important traditional Chinese mathematical treatises. My joy and excitement could not be contained!

The academic year 2006-2007 marked a watershed moment in my study of history of mathematics. It was my first sabbatical leave, seven years after I had started to work at St. Cloud State University. Thanks to Professor Guo's arrangement, I was able to spend that year to continue my research at the Institute for the History of Natural Sciences (IHNS, CAS) in Beijing, housed in the former residence of Prince Fu, better known as 九爷府 *Jiuye fu*. To me, the Institute's *Jiuye fu* location was purely magical. No matter how hectic life might be in the vast city of Beijing, one was transported into a Shangri-la upon stepping into the courtyard of the *Jiuye fu*. With all the hustle and bustle of Beijing melting away, one simply wanted to dive into the fantastic world of history. The IHNS put me in an office directly above the library, where I spent numerous hours browsing many important treatises and works of past scholars, thanks to colleagues there, especially those working in the library at the time.

Besides helping me with the research aspect of my stay in Beijing, Professor Guo also took care of my lodging and other related matters. He mobilized all his family to help. Guo Jian, Professor Guo's daughter, found an apartment for me in the neighborhood of an electricity company's dormitory compound, not too far away from where Professor Guo and his family lived. Professor and Mrs. Guo took me to a local branch of the Bank of China to open a bank account. He then took me to a bicycle shop in his neighborhood to purchase a bicycle, an essential tool for moving about in the neighborhood. He bargained with the owner and I got a used bike with a basket. My morning routine, usually going from my apartment to the IHNS at *Jiuyefu*, was all perfectly planned. I would leave my apartment by 7:00 am, riding my bike to Professor Guo's apartment complex, park the bicycle at a bicycle parking area in the compound, and then leisurely walk to the west gate of the complex to catch the daily "work shuttle" (班车 banche) for the Institute. Mrs. Guo even found an "hourly worker" (小时工 xiaoshi gong) to come and clean my apartment weekly. When Minghui came to Beijing to visit in the fall of 2006, he commented that Professor Guo treated me as if I were his own child.

At Professor Guo's request, towards the end of 2006 I gave a presentation on my findings of Dai Zhen's trigonometric work. Professor Guo and I often discussed Dai's work and contributions to traditional Chinese mathematics. As is well known, Dai Zhen was a scholar who found many "lost" mathematical works, including certain parts of the *Nine Chapters of Mathematical Art* (九章算术 jiuzhang suanshu) in the Great Encyclopedia Compiled during the *Yongle Reign* (永乐大典 Yongle dadian). At the time, the *Wenjin ge* (文津阁) edition of the *Complete Texts of the Four Repositories* (四库全书 Siku quanshu) was not yet available. Based on the *Nine Chapters* in the *Wenyuan ge* (文渊阁) edition of the *Siku quanshu*, Professor Guo strongly criticized Dai's collation of the *Nine Chapters*. In contrast, my findings on Dai Zhen's own work was much more positive. At the end of 2006, the only research work I had conducted was the analysis of Dai Zhen's *Records of base-altitude and circle division*, which I had studied between 2001 and 2005. Professor Dauben and Minghui were kind to help me with ways of analyzing the work and suggesting how to write research papers on historical subjects. The deeper I looked into Dai's construction of his trigonometric system, the more concerned and uneasy I became. This has everything to do with my own evaluation of Dai's work that did not conform to the established views on Dai and his works. Professor Guo's negative views on Dai's collation were thus all the more worrisome to me.

Dai Zhen has always been a controversial figure in the intellectual history of early modern China. In spite of being recognized as one of the most prominent figures in the evidential scholarship movement of the 18th century, he has been criticized by many scholars, present-day as well as his contemporaries. First, a priority dispute broke out following Dai's death regarding his collation of the *Commentaries on the Water Classic* (水经注 Shuijing zhu). The main issue is whether or not Dai Zhen, in collating this text for the Qianlong Emperor's *Siku quanshu* project, plagiarized research results from the work of *Zhao Yiqing* 赵一清 (1711-1764), namely Zhao's Explication of the Commentaries on the *Water Classic* (水经注释 Shuijing zhushi). One camp of scholars accused Dai of simply copying Zhao's work, whereas another held the view that the two scholars reached similar conclusions independently. Continuing into the 20th century, this dispute still tarnishes Dai's scholarly reputation and severely questions his moral character, regardless of the outcome.

In the field of the history of Chinese mathematics, scholars in general are in agreement about Dai's contribution to the discovery of many lost mathematical classics, thanks to the *Yongle dadian*. At the same time, many condemn him for presenting trigonometry as knowledge handed down from Chinese antiquity, which is clearly contrary to the facts and the mainstream understanding of the subject's history. The priority dispute and Dai's peculiar presentation of trigonometry led to harsh assessments of Dai's own mathematical work beginning in the late 18th century. Historians of mathematics Qian Baozong and Li Yan, both pioneers in the history of mathematics in China, have also offered rather negative evaluations of Dai's work. Qian pointed out that Dai deliberately adopted terms different from those commonly used at the time and that the level of difficulty in understanding his work far succeeds that in reading broken ancient tablets and bamboo strips. On the other hand, Li Yan concluded that Dai's mathematical practices had little or only limited influence, based on the fact that no other scholars followed Dai in adopting the new terms he coined. These views were well-established in the early 20th century and have since been widely accepted by the majority of historians of mathematics in China.

However, my studies of the Records uncovered a rather different Dai Zhen, which has been both fortunate and unfortunate for me! Dai constructed a self-contained trigonometric system to treat calculations in plane and spherical trigonometry. In the process, he showed that the entirety of trigonometry, including his choice of measure for arcs, the names for the eight trigonometric lines, the underlying principles, and the devices used for analyzing spherical problems had already existed in Chinese antiquity—or could have. While his many claims do not reflect the historical facts, they nevertheless contributed an important component as the basis for a utopia in Dai's vision of a harmonious antiquity for all things Chinese.

Looking at the diverging evaluations of Dai's works, mine as well as those of past scholars, I now realize that my 2006 findings actually complemented earlier scholars' opinions rather than contradicting them. It was however not what I was feeling at the time. Discouraged by my own work which produced conclusions that seemed to "contradict" the opinions of giants in the past, I doubted the direction in which I should be heading. But Professor Guo encouraged me, despite his own views of Dai Zhen. He used his own experience to reassure me that my analysis had value. His collations of the *Nine Chapters* have often led to conclusions and findings that do not agree with those of Qian Baocong, for example, whose collation of the classic is universally highly regarded. Professor Guo assured me that one should always argue based on evidence and analysis rather than on reputation. Encouraging words spoken at exactly the right time have a lasting impact on young scholars. For his very kind words, just when I needed to hear them, I will be forever grateful.

The years leading to 2008 were when China were preparing to showcase its economic prowess on the world stage through the spectacular events of the 2008 Olympic Games. The national aquatic center and national stadium (famously known as the Water Cube, 水立方, and the Bird's Nest, 鸟巢) were being built in 2006 and 2007. The IHNS shuttle bus drove by the site of the current Olympic Park every day. During my seven-month stay in Beijing, I witnessed the construction of the Bird's Nest, from nothing to an ultra-modern and exceedingly geometric, beautiful piece of architecture. Looking back, it became evident that my visit at the IHNS during the 2006-07 academic year paralleled the Bird's Nest evolution into a viable structure of lasting interest. My sabbatical year at the Institute laid the foundation and even provided the atlas for my continuing efforts to grow as a historian of Chinese mathematics. For someone who lacked any training in historical research and with little knowledge of traditional mathematics in China, that time at the IHNS, studying in the library, participating the presentations by experts from all around the world, and discussing new ideas with colleagues, that all served as a crash course to reorient a mathematician to learn how to conduct research as a historian. All the research that led to my subsequent visits to other research institutes, including the Needham Research Institute in Cambridge, England, in 2007; my 2012-13 year spent as a Senior Fulbright Scholar in Hohhot, Inner Mongolia China; and another sabbatical year, 2017-18, spent at the CNRS in Paris, were all based on the foundation laid during my 2006-07 visit to the IHNS. There are no words that I can say to express my gratitude not only to the Institute, but to Professor Guo in particular, for helping me to grow as a scholar.

Working with Professor Guo always offers great opportunities to learn. In 2008, Professor Guo was invited to be one of the speakers at an international conference on the history of mathematics in memory of Seki Takakazu, held in Tokyo, Japan from August 25 to 31. The organizer asked that his paper be written in English, although his presentation was given in Mandarin. When Professor Guo asked me to help him translate his paper into English for the proceedings, I felt that this was an honor and a great way to repay his kindness and tremendous help; little did I know how much it would change the direction of my future research. Professor Guo's paper, titled "*The Nine Chapters on Mathematical Procedures* and Liu Hui's Mathematical Theory," demonstrates by concrete examples the various modes utilized by Liu Hui in making arguments that validate his claims. It was an eye opening experience for me, and made me realize that the subject of reasoning in Chinese mathematical treatises is a fertile ground for further research. China's long history and its rich mathematical works at different times present many different ways of "demonstrating" the validity of various mathematical properties. I then started to examine the various modes of reasoning in Chinese mathematical treatises composed in the early-modern period in China. This research is an on-going project and hopefully, with careful examination and diligent work, meaningful results will shed more light on the matter of reasoning in traditional Chinese mathematical works.

Among the many projects in which Professor Guo has been involved recently, I am grateful to be included as part of a team working on a new English translation of the *Nine Chapters*. This project differs from previous works in two ways. First, it breaks with tradition and incorporates the commentaries of Jia Xian (贾宪) and Yang Hui (杨辉) from the Song Dynasty into the *Nine Chapters*. Their inclusion will illuminate the evolution of reasoning in this seminal classic as it advanced from the time of Liu Hui to the Song dynasty commentaries. With the publication of the *Wenjin ge* edition of the *Siku quanshu*, Professor Guo has also been able to produce a new collation of the *Nine Chapter*, and he considers this will be the most authoritative and best possible version of the *Nine Chapters*. This is the second major difference between the current project and previous versions of the text. The translation from classical Chinese into English is a joint work with Professor Joseph Dauben of the City University of New York, Professor Horng Wann-Sheng, Emeritus Professor of National Taiwan Normal University, and myself. It is a privilege to work with these well-established scholars and a rare opportunity to learn from the masters. On this special occasion, I wish Professor Guo a very happy 80th birthday, 生日快乐, and a long life full of happiness and prosperity; I also sincerely hope that our joint efforts will produce a work that can honor Professor Guo in equal measure.

跟郭老师和师母的相遇对我来说是宝物

莲沼澄子

我在 2005 年 4 月到 2006 年 3 月这一年的时间里跟郭老师学《九章算术》。那一年的美好记忆我是不会忘记的。除了学习上有郭老师的帮助之外,在我生活方面还有师母很周到的照顾。我能过得很幸福,非常感谢师母。

每周有两次我坐面包车去研究所听郭老师的课,我记得去研究所的路上李大哥一边开车一边跟大家说笑话。还有每周有一次我去老师家跟郭老师学习《九章算术》。《九章算术》、刘徽的为人、中国悠久的历史、历史中的笑话等,郭老师讲了很多内容,让我觉得很有意思,更喜欢中国了。

我跟着郭老师学《九章算术》的那一年中,他很耐心地教我。每次去老师家我问了好多问题。因为我是外国人,其中一定有很奇怪的问题会让老师觉得很为难。但老师善解人意,每次很努力地回答我的问题。有时我问问题时老师又说:"对不起,我不知道。"我听老师这样说,衷心佩服他。一般在学术方面有地位的人不会是这样,郭老师是个实事求是的人,让我很感动。我从郭老师对研究的态度学到了实事求是才是治学的正确态度。

师兄金海老师、老师夫妻、我、浩在老师家(2005 年)

我想形容郭老师的为人:温厚、温柔、善良、体贴、善解人意、非常认真、老实、热情、幽默等等。我要表达的还有很多!但是我的汉语还差得远,真遗憾想不起更多的形容词来。

我爱中国悠久的历史、文化,还有我留学的那一年照顾我的很多善良的中国人。郭老师和师母对我来说是我的中国父母。祝贺郭老师 80 岁寿辰!我、我爱人浩、儿子英明都爱您!祝郭书春老师福如东海,寿比南山!

2019 年我们再去北京时,我爱人浩、我、师母、儿子、郭老师(2019 年 10 月)

2005年我在北京时,每周有一次,我去老师家问了好几个问题

九章在台湾

孙文先 （九章出版社，台北市）

我在读台湾师范大学数学系时就涉猎一些中国数学史的古籍，对中国传统数学中最重要的经典《九章算术》特别沉迷，其中包含许多中国数学先进的思想，如：等量变换、开方术、出入相补原理、割圆术、极限概念、各种多面体求积方法与公式等等，都让我对中国数学的论证严谨、博大精深景仰不已。我在本地图书馆寻遍了相关的数据，惜知识浅薄再加上文言文的障碍，只能囫囵吞枣，无法参透其精髓。离开学校后我没有去教书而是独资设立九章出版社，社名是由台湾师范大学洪万生的前妻彭婉如女士建议的。当时台湾地区的一般民众是不能出岛的，我利用参加新加坡书展的机会随团前往新加坡，回程顺道香港旅游。在新加坡晚晴图书馆发现一本由钱宝琮著的《九章算经点校》，我请朋友协助影印一份，在香港中华书店买到一本由李俨著的《中国古代数学简史》。有了这两本书我如获至宝，对中国古代数学有了更清晰的理解，同时也对中国学者在中国数学史领域的辛勤钻研深感敬佩。

1987年，台湾方面开放台湾同胞回大陆探亲，我送一位老兵回湖南新邵老家探亲之后，我自己一个人搭火车到北京，一抵达北京火车站我即打电话给中国科学院自然科学史研究所说要去拜访杜石然教授，当时杜教授在日本访问，电话辗转给刘钝教授，我表明身份并要求要拜见研究《九章算术》的专家郭书春教授，我们约定于次日在位于九爷府的自然科学史研究所见面。这是我第一次见到郭教授，他的山东腔让我倍感亲切，因为家父是山东莱阳人。他详细介绍自然科学史研究所在中国数学史方面的研究成果并侃侃而谈他在《九章算术》中的校正工作，我也向他们汇报了台湾地区鲜有学者重视中国数学史的窘况，我们相谈甚欢，郭教授邀我次日前往府上晚餐。

次日，我依约从北京师范大学骑十几公里自行车到他位于劲松的家，当我抵达他家时，发现他们一家居住的房子非常狭小简陋，但满屋子都是书，连床铺底下都是满满的书，床铺上全是散放着的一堆一堆的书稿。郭教授兴奋地向我说明他最近发现一些刘徽注传本中的舛误与近代学者的错解，这让我深深感受到郭教授治学严谨的态度与拼搏的精神。

孙文先前往北京拜访郭书春教授

当要进餐时，郭夫人端着一脸盆的水，上面飘着一条毛巾让我洗脸洗手。当我捞起毛巾扭干展开，发现毛巾是老旧的还脱了许多支纱，我心里有点嘀咕怎么拿破毛巾待客，但是随后当我去上厕所时，看到竿子上挂着的毛巾更破旧，有的根本只剩下几支纱，原来郭夫人拿给我用的毛巾是他们家里最好的一条，我的内心顿时涌上一阵心酸。郭教授从墙边抽出一张折叠桌展开作为餐桌，他们家只有两张椅子，另一人要拨开满床的稿件腾出一个位置坐在床沿。端上的菜只有两样非常油且咸的菜，主食是马铃薯，那顿晚餐我是含着感动的泪水吃完的，从此我立志要尽己所能支持这些一箪食一瓢饮安贫乐道为学术发展而拼搏的数学家。

由于郭教授的孜孜不倦与对《九章算术》独特的论点引起国内外同行的赞赏,再加上辽宁教育出版社俞晓群先生的支持,陆续不计销量出版了郭教授的许多著作,并由郭教授领衔编写了许多中国数学史的巨著,因此也获得许多崇高的国家图书出版奖。三十几年来,郭教授著作等身,已经成为中国数学史《九章算术》研究的权威。虽然在台湾地区没什么人重视中国数学史,更少有人会读《九章算术》,但既然取名为"九章",我在台湾地区也出版了郭教授编著的《〈九章算术〉汇校本》《算经十书》等书,并同时引进辽宁教育出版社出版的一些郭教授的著作在台湾出售。

受台湾师范大学洪万生教授之邀请,郭书春教授曾于 2000 年 9 月与 2006 年 8 月两次来台湾地区访问。第一次是他在筹备好了祖冲之逝世 1500 年纪念会之后单独来台湾,在台湾师范大学、台湾清华大学做了几次报告。最令台湾地区学者耳目一新的是他在位于新竹市的台湾清华大学历史系的报告。在报告中,他讲到南宋数学家秦九韶。学术界向来都认为秦九韶成就极大,人品极坏。郭教授认为讲他坏的刘克庄、周密都是投靠投降派贾似道的,而秦九韶是追随抗战派吴潜的。秦九韶在《数书九章序》中多次表达了反对贪官污吏,主张施仁政的思想,这在数学著作是绝无仅有的。郭教授第二次来台湾是参加《算数书》研讨会,许多学者都希望聆听郭教授对于新出土《算数书》竹简的精辟见解。在陪同郭教授参观访问中国台湾各地之际,我有机会深入向郭教授请教《九章算术》内的许多疑问,郭教授倾囊相授让我获益匪浅。

每次我到北京都会去拜访郭教授,每次他都告诉我最近又出版了哪些书或又完成了什么书稿。由于拼命三郎似地查阅古籍与夜以继日地写书,长时间坐在书桌前,最近他告诉我说他罹患脊椎间盘突出,必须到医院做复健。我建议他放下"九章",升华"九章",把静态的编书工作变成动态的活动。我提议将《九章算术》内所蕴含的精辟解题思想活化,融入中小学数学课程的解题思想。可以先从培训中小学教师开始,将中国数学的"九章"发扬光大。

时值郭书春教授八十岁华诞,不揣才疏学浅谨作此文祝贺!

《郭书春数学史自选集》序

华觉明 （中国科学院自然科学史研究所）

郭书春先生和我是 20 世纪 60 年代中期大约同一时段进入中国科学院哲学社会科学部的。未几，冷板凳还没坐热，就卷入了众所周知的事件，停止了学术工作。直到 70 年代中期，我们以各自的方式开启了以科技史为安身立命之所的治学之旅[2]。如今，书春兄要出自选集，作为学友、挚友的我，当然是分外高兴的。

借作序之便，我得以先睹郭氏《自选集》的自序、目录和部分篇帙。尽管对他的业绩并不陌生，待到缀合成集，翻检一过，仍不禁为他的卓越史识，极认真、严谨的史学研探，对前辈学者敬重有加而又不讳言其缺失的史德，以及精心培育和引领年轻学者共同推动学科建设的使命感和责任心感到震撼。

书春同志治学之刻苦和认真，人所共知，毋遑多言。难得的是，他在阵阵"中国古代数学史已经做完了""没什么要做的了"的声浪中，独具慧眼，明辨其非，坚决走自己的路，从刘徽《九章算术注》再研究入手，步步着实，着着领先，开创出了中国古代数学史研究的新境界，使之提升到了一个更高的层次，从而强有力地推动了学科的持续发展。这样的远见卓识，自是值得我们赞佩和效尤的。

史学研究的一大特点，是史料占有的非全息性和历时性。为此，尊重原始文献，认真研读原著，严谨、细致地校勘历来的刊本，对古代数学史研究十分重要，也是这一领域研究者不可或缺的基本功。对此，书春兄是下了大功夫的。他遍搜所有能找到的《九章算术》刊本，诸如南宋刊本、杨辉本、《永乐大典》抄本、汲古阁本、聚珍版本、四库全书本等，一一校雠又做了汇校。经这番艰苦努力，他恢复了戴震等错改的原文 450 余条，重校前人误校近 70 条，新校前人漏校约 40 条。如此，得以厘清《九章算术》的原貌，在正本清源的基础上，对刘徽的贡献及其在数学史上的地位做出科学、准确的评价。这样的认真和严谨，贯穿于书春研究工作的全过程。仍以《九章算术注》再研究为例，"以一面乘半径，觚而裁之，每辄自倍，故以半周乘半径而为圆幂"，是刘徽论割圆术最关键的 25 个字，是证明圆面积公式"半周半径相乘得积步"的关键。但出于疏忽或没读懂，历来的注家恰恰无视这 25 字的"书眼"甚至撇而不论。通过认真阅读和研究原著，书春在这关键点取得了突破，阐明了刘徽割圆术的真谛及其价值，成为他学术成就的一大亮点。书春的数学史研究是丰富和多彩的，诸如秦汉出土简牍的解析、《算经十书》和宋元明数学，特别是贾宪、秦九韶、李冶的研究都卓有所成，在此不一一备述。需要提及的是，他对古代数学史的综合研究，突出地反映于《中国科学技术史·数学卷》这一传世之作中。中国史学界的最高奖项"郭沫若奖"一等奖颁给了这本书，有点出人意料，其实也在情理之中，它表达了史学界同仁对数学史研究成就的高度认可。

吴文俊先生称，中国的机械化算法体系和古希腊的数学公理化演绎体系各有特点，交替成为世界数学发展的主流。这一重要判语在书春同志的系列研究中得到了很好的印证。

书春兄历来对李俨、钱宝琮两位前辈极为敬重。经他提议，召开了纪念李、钱二老百年诞辰的学术研讨会。他主持了《李俨钱宝琮科学史全集》的编纂工作。1999 年修订《辞海》时，他承担了中国数学史条目的修订，发现其中有李俨先生却没有钱宝琮先生，当即致函编辑部要求加上，得到该部的首肯。与此同时，他也如实地指出钱先生当年作《九章算术》研究时限于条件，以微波榭本为底本，而这个版本缺

---

[1] 本文是郭书春著《郭书春数学史自选集》（济南：山东科学技术出版社，2008 年）的序言，现今改名，收入本书时略有修改。

[2] 我住朝内大街的家属宿舍，稍自由一些。郭住所内单身宿舍，为避军宣队的突击检查，学法语时，课本之上覆以毛选。这种治学方式，今天的年轻人是难以想象的。

失甚多,是不足为凭的,从而出现了一些误刊误判。这种未敢为长者讳的科学精神和良好学风,得到了同行们的高度评价,正如《荀子·修良》所说:"是谓是,非谓非,曰直。"直道而行,循理之正,方显学者之本真。

书春兄历来重视对年轻学者人格、治学的培养,退休之后,仍常为研究生讲课。经他的不倦努力,田淼、邹大海、郭金海、段耀勇、傅海伦、郑振初(香港)、朱一文等中青年学者都已卓然成才,使数学史研究得以持续发展,传承有序,被公认为中国科学史界及我所之强项。

书春对所从事的事业知之深而爱之切,有时溢于言表。这,我们是理解的。

我和书春同住中国科学院华严北里小区。前些年,常见他踩着三轮车接送上小学的外孙女儿。这两年,则常见他踩着三轮车带夫人去菜市场或元大都北土城公园。此情此景,或可以"执子之车,与子偕老"名之[3]。书春和他夫人王玉芝是可共患难、可同安乐的好夫妻。语云:"二人同心,利可断金。"[4] 得贤内之助,书春兄活得充实、开心,继《自选集》之后,他还会有厚重的学术建树问世是可以预期的。

是为序。

华觉明
2017 年 5 月 16 日

---

[3] 诗云:"执子之手,与子偕老。"此处套改一字,"之"用作动词,意为:牵着你的手,坐上我的车,就这样相伴,我俩慢慢变老。

[4] 语出《周易·系辞上》。

书写中国数学史研究的春天
——《郭书春数学史自选集》读后[1]

周瀚光　（华东师范大学古籍研究所）

　　望着桌上厚厚两大册共120万字的《郭书春数学史自选集》（山东科学技术出版社2018年版，以下简称《自选集》），脑子里即刻浮现出郭书春先生伏案工作、奋笔疾书、几十年如一日从事中国数学史研究的身影。据郭先生自己回忆，他真正开始从事数学史研究工作，是在20世纪70年代后期，那是一个科学研究走向春天、科学史研究走向春天的年代。四十多年来，郭先生倾注了他的全部精力投入到中国数学史的研究工作之中，呕心沥血，刻苦钻研，披星戴月，不分昼夜，终于取得了足以令他自豪和骄傲的巨大成绩。可以说，他与其他同时代的数学史工作者一起，共同书写了中国数学史研究百花齐放的春天。而他的这部《自选集》，正是这百花园中艳丽夺目、笑傲群芳的一枝奇葩。

　　《自选集》共收入郭先生在数学史研究领域最重要的81篇文章，按作者自己的编排，分为不同主题的六个部分：第一部分是"《九章算术》和刘徽研究"，共30篇论文，涉及《九章算术》的体例和编纂、刘徽的数学成就、刘徽的数学理论和逻辑思想、刘徽的思想渊源、《九章算术》的版本和校勘等各个方面。第二部分是"先秦数学及秦汉简牍研究"，共10篇论文，包括《管子》的重数思想研究、湖北张家山汉简《算数书》的校勘和研究、北京大学藏秦简《算书》及其他秦汉数学简牍研究等方面的内容。第三部分是"祖冲之和《算经十书》研究"，共5篇论文，涉及对祖冲之数学成就的再评价、对《算经十书》某些问题的澄清以及论重新校勘《算经十书》的必要性等内容。第四部分是"宋元明清数学研究"，共13篇论文，包括对宋元明清时期贾宪、秦九韶、李冶、吴敬、王文素、李善兰等数学家以及《河防通议·算法门》等数学著作的研究。第五部分是"中国古典数学综论"，共19篇论文，涉及数学与社会的关系、中国古典数学的机械化特点、对贬低中国古典数学的虚无主义态度的批评、回顾吴文俊先生的教诲以及自然科学史研究所建所50年间中国数学史研究的总结等几个不同的方面。第六部分是"研究中国数学史的体会"，共4篇文章，重点阐述了作者关于尊重原始文献并认真研读原始文献的治学宗旨和治学方法，并对当前科技古籍整理研究的现状和规划提出了自己的意见和建议。这六个部分的81篇文章虽然尚不是郭先生四十多年数学史研究工作的全部成果，他另有专著《论中国古代数学家》（海豚出版社，2017年）以及主编《中国科学技术典籍通汇·数学卷》《中国科学技术史·数学卷》《中华大典·数学典》等大型的数学史著作均没有收入《自选集》中，但仅此81篇文章，就已经涵盖了中国数学史研究的绝大多数核心区域和最新课题，并引领这一领域的探索研究达到了一个新的高度。

　　然而以上六个部分的研究成果，在作者自己的心目中，并不是轻重相当、分量相同的。郭先生本人最看重的，并且在本书中篇幅最大、所收文章最多的，其实是第一部分"《九章算术》和刘徽研究"。该部分共收入论文30篇，占了全书文章总数81篇的近四成；全书分为上、下两册，而第一部分的篇幅就占了满满的整个上册，足可见其在全书之中的分量之重。郭先生在本书的"自序"中有一个说明："之所以将《九章算术》和刘徽研究置于各专题之首，一是这是笔者40年来的主要工作，安身立命之所在；二是在《九章算术》和刘徽研究中总结出来的研究方法和结论，直接影响到其他专题的研究。"而在我看来，这一部分的工作实在是凝聚了郭先生太多太多的心血，饱含了郭先生太多太多的付出，并且确确实实令人信服地汇聚了郭先生在中国数学史研究领域所做出的众多的创造性贡献。比如在刘徽研究方面，读者可

---

[1] 本文原载于《中华读书报》，2019年2月27日。

以从《自选集》中清楚地读到郭先生关于这方面研究的诸多个独创性的"第一":第一次全面解释了刘徽的《九章算术》"圆田术"注文[2],由此揭示了刘徽关于圆面积公式的证明,并给出了刘徽求圆周率的正确程序;第一次提出并论证了刘徽的极限理论和体积理论;第一次把刘徽关于"率"的思想提到"算之纲纪"的高度来认识,并由此启发并影响了当代中小学数学教材中某些内容的改革;第一次在前人(严敦杰先生)发现宋代时刘徽曾被祀封为"淄乡男"的基础上,考证出刘徽的籍贯在今山东省邹平县;第一次深入探讨了刘徽的逻辑思想,并在此基础上提出刘徽是中国古典数学理论的奠基者……。再如,在《九章算术》的校勘方面,郭先生自 20 世纪 80 年代开始,积 30 多年之功力,孜孜不倦,持之以恒,对《九章算术》及其刘徽注进行了全面系统的研究和深入细致的校勘。他广搜版本,创见迭出,几番修订,三次出版,最终为学界提供了一部研读《九章算术》所能依据的"最佳本子"(李学勤语)。此外,郭先生的《九章算术译注》(上海古籍出版社)一书自 2009 年 12 月出版以来,广受读者欢迎,至 2017 年 2 月已重印了 6 次。现在其修订本也已完工交稿,预计很快就能看到新版。在 2015 年《广西民族大学学报》对我的一篇采访稿中,我曾经对郭先生在这方面的工作做过一个评价:"数学史界研究刘徽的专家学者很多,郭书春先生可谓是其中的佼佼者。刘徽的数学成就是通过注释《九章算术》体现出来的,而对于《九章算术》历代版本的考订和研究工作,可以说迄今为止,没有比郭书春先生做得更细、更好的。"[3] 这个评价应该是数学史界同仁们的一致公论。

我与郭书春先生相识于 20 世纪 80 年代初期,迄今已有 35 年的时间了。说起来,我们之间的相交和相知,竟也源自于对刘徽研究的缘分。那是 1984 年的初夏,《自然辩证法通讯》杂志社的樊洪业先生在重庆主持了一个小型的中国数学史研讨会,郭先生和我都参加了那次会议。会上在讨论刘徽的时候,大家一方面对刘徽的数学理论成就非常赞赏,另一方面又对这一历史现象感到困惑:为什么中国历史发展到魏晋的时候,才会出现刘徽这样一位数学家来为中国古典数学奠定理论基础呢?大家觉得这个历史现象不太好解释。我当时提了一个想法,认为这可能跟魏晋时期思想解放的社会氛围有关,跟墨家思想在秦汉 400 年间被禁而到魏晋时期重新复兴和流传有关。墨家学派在先秦时就已经具有了理论数学的萌芽和丰富的逻辑思想。刘徽读过墨子的书,他把逻辑学方法融入数学研究,用概念、命题、推理等一系列逻辑学手段来重新解读《九章算术》,这就为中国古典数学奠定了理论基础,并由此而把中国古代数学推向了一个新的高度。我的这个想法提出来之后,大家都觉得有点意思,主持会议的樊洪业先生要我回去以后就此观点写一篇论文给他。后来文章以《刘徽的思想与墨学的兴衰》为题,发表在那一年的《自然辩证法通讯》杂志上。在那次会议上,我与郭先生初次相见,并了解到他在刘徽研究方面实际上已经做了许多扎实的工作,而且他的许多观点往往与我不谋而合。正如郭先生后来在回忆这段往事时所说:

> 我们在那个会上第一次见面。我在 1979 年研究刘徽割圆术时认为刘徽的"不可割"与墨家的"不可斱"是同义语,得出"刘徽在先秦诸子中,更崇尚墨家"的结论。瀚光先生在那次会上进一步提出,中国古代数学之所以会在魏晋时期出现刘徽这样运用逻辑方法奠定古典数学理论的数学家,与当时思想解放和墨学复兴的社会思潮有关,与墨家逻辑思想在历史上的兴衰有关。这个观点在当时引起了与会代表和会议组织者的很大兴趣。我们在重庆会议上发现一些看法不谋而合,遂引为同道,经常书信往来,互相切磋学问。[4]

从那时开始,郭先生与我在刘徽研究和数学史研究方面就经常会有一些"不谋而合"的观点和主题,有时甚至达到了某种相当默契的程度。例如在 20 世纪 90 年代初期,我们两人竟然在各自独立且互不

---

[2] 与郭先生差不多同时,笔者也有一个对刘徽《九章算术》"圆田术"注文的全面解释,参见周瀚光:《刘徽评论》第 38—42 页,南京大学出版社,1994 年出版。

[3] "中国科学思想史研究的开拓和创新——周瀚光教授访谈录",《广西民族大学学报》(自然科学版)2015 年第 1 期第 3 页。

[4] 郭书春《周瀚光文集·序一》,上海社会科学院出版社 2017 年出版。

知情的情况下,几乎同时撰写了关于刘徽研究的专著:我的《刘徽评传》[5]杀青于 1991 年夏天,而郭先生则于 1992 年 3 月出版了他的专著《古代世界数学泰斗刘徽》[6]。除了研究刘徽之外,我们在数学史研究的其他方面也有许多一致的看法,比如对于原始文献的尊重、对《管子》重数思想的研究、对秦九韶人品的评价,等等。当然,我们也有一些学术观点上的分歧,例如对某种古籍底本的选择、对隋唐数学成就的评价等,有时还会争得不可开交,谁也说服不了谁。郭先生长我几岁,数学史功底也比我扎实很多,我从郭先生那里常常能得到许多有益的启示。

除了第一部分"《九章算术》和刘徽研究"之外,《自选集》的其他部分也记录了郭先生的许多独创性见解。其中笔者个人认为比较重要且需要特别指出的内容有:第二部分中关于湖北张家山出土汉简《算数书》的研究,第三部分中关于《算经十书》校勘的若干问题,第四部分中关于贾宪数学成就的评价及其思想资料来源,第五部分中关于中国古代数学发展历史如何分期以及古代数学有没有理论的讨论,第六部分中关于尊重并认真研读原始文献的观点。相信读者在阅读了全书之后,一定会赞赏郭先生的这些独创性见解,并从不同的角度得到各自的收获。

当然,《自选集》也不是完美无瑕的,也存在着一些局限和不足之处。就中国数学史研究的整体而言,隋唐数学和明清数学这两个方面,明显是作者所有研究工作中的薄弱环节。读者虽不至于过于苛求,但仍不免留下些许遗憾。

郭先生在本书的"自序"中,曾说起他小时候老家经常贴在门上的春联是:龙躔肇岁,麟笔书春。在此,笔者衷心祝愿郭先生这支书写中国数学史春天的"麟笔",能够虽老弥新,永葆青春!

---

[5] 周瀚光、孔国平《刘徽评传(附秦九韶、李冶、杨辉、朱世杰评传)》,南京大学出版社 1994 年出版。
[6] 郭书春《古代世界数学泰斗刘徽》,山东科学技术出版社 1992 年出版。

老师与老乡

王青建　（辽宁师范大学数学学院）

我与郭书春先生是正宗的山东老乡，出生地都是山东省青岛市。我本科就读的是山东师范大学，在辽宁师范大学读研究生后留在了大连，虽然一直说"普通话"，但乡音难改，常被人一语点破出生地。郭先生的乡音更重，并因此被我认作老乡。他大我十几岁，入行又早，是我的师长辈。郭先生有着典型山东人的体魄与性格：壮实、敦厚、聪明、勤奋。

第一次见到郭先生应该是在1985年内蒙古师范大学第二次全国数学史年会上。郭先生在大会上临时增加了一个"访法观感"的发言，留下深刻印象。我们之间的相熟是在第二年7月山东蓬莱举行的"首届全国青年科技史学术讨论会"上。天时、地利、人和拉近了彼此的距离，确认老乡后建立了长久的联系。"蓬莱仙境"海边的照片上我们两位"地主"笑容灿烂，不辱"山东大汉"的美誉。

1986年7月8日山东长岛月牙湾公园
左起王青建、王渝生、郭书春、席泽宗、杜瑞芝、周瀚光

此后，我与郭先生又在多个学术会议上相遇，关系逐渐熟络。比较特别的是1994年北京香山数学史年会，我们一起当选为第四届全国数学史学会常务理事，郭先生任副理事长。1998年郭先生当选为第五届数学史学会理事长，我继任常务理事。此后四年，我们一起参加中国科学技术史学会第六届代表大会（2000年8月，北京），一起筹划"20世纪数学传播与交流国际会议"（2000年10月，西安）、"2002年国际数学家大会西安卫星会议"等事项，有过共同为数学史学会服务的美好岁月。

1995年11月，我的导师梁宗巨先生去世，郭先生与时任自然科学史研究所副所长的刘钝先生一起来大连进行悼念。梁先生与郭先生都属于做学问极其认真的人，对此曾任辽宁教育出版社社长的俞晓群在《中华读书报》（2005年10月12日）上有过描述——"治学精神的严谨是绝无仅有的，甚至有些偏执"。由此，两人惺惺相惜，关系密切。郭先生和刘先生的亲临悼念对我和辽宁师范大学数学史学位点是极大的关怀与鼓励，成为此后薪火相传20多年的不竭动力。

2004年，郭先生在北京自然科学史研究所举办一个小型的"《算数书》与先秦数学国际学术研讨会"，特意邀请我参加。这既是对我等晚辈学术上的扶植，也是对我个人相关研究的肯定。会议期间郭先生和他的学生邹大海先生在资料搜集和学术研讨方面给了我很多帮助，解决了若干关键问题。我的

1994年8月30日,北京香山,第四届学会常务理事合影

左起王青建、张奠宙、郭书春、李迪、李文林、王渝生、刘钝、李兆华

前排左起:大川俊隆、陈良佐、郭书春、道本周、刘钝、彭浩

第二排左起:邹大海、周瀚光、城地茂、李兆华、武家璧

第三排左起:纪志刚、段耀勇、田村诚、王青建、张替俊夫、赵彦超、高红成、郭金海

会议论文《〈算数书〉中的记数方法》第二年发表在《自然科学史研究》上。

我与郭先生有过多次单独合影。1992年8月在北京香山植物园召开的"纪念李俨、钱宝琮诞辰100周年国际学术讨论会"期间,我们就曾拍照留念。

1995年5月,在清华大学召开的"中国数学会第七次代表大会暨60周年年会"期间,我作为列席代表旁听会议巧遇郭先生,留下在清华园的珍贵合影。

2000年10月在陕西西安交通大学召开"20世纪数学传播与交流国际会议"时,再次在法门寺合影。

2012年7月16—20日,我与郭先生都参加了"国际数学教育委员会(ICMI)在韩国大田举办的HPM 2012会议"。由于国内参会人员较少,因此"抱团"与会成为常态,与郭先生交流较多。除了学术探讨外,生活、家庭、兴趣、爱好等都是交谈的话题。期间还留下公州考察的合影。

2015年10月在广州中山大学举办的"第九届全国数学史年会暨第六届数学史与数学教育会议"上我们又一次见面,夜游广州留下了珠江边上与"小蛮腰"的合影。

2013年4月,在海南参加"第五届全国数学史与数学教育研讨会"期间,我与郭先生曾一起在三亚

北京碧云寺（1992年8月）

北京清华大学（1995年5月）

南海里畅游，回味无穷。郭先生自豪地宣称：中国的四大海（渤海、黄海、东海、南海）和世界四大洋（太平洋、印度洋、大西洋、北冰洋）中的大部分他都游过泳。"我见到海就想跳，见到山就想爬"，勇于设想，敢于实践，这就是郭先生的性格。

西安法门寺（2000年10月）

韩国公州（2012年7月）

广州珠江（2015年10月）

2017年5月"第七届数学史与数学教育学术研讨会暨全国中小学'数学文化进课堂'观摩研讨会"在大连召开。为了尽"地主之谊"，我在会后开车带郭先生和师母等人到金石滩海滨公园游玩。当时海水较凉，郭先生没留神被海浪打湿衬衫。我们都非常着急，怕先生因此感冒影响身体健康，准备返程。郭先生却大叫"没事儿"，拧干衬衫的水后穿上继续前行。这一来反映出郭先生良好的身体素质，76岁的体质让我等自叹不如；二来折射出郭先生事事为他人着想的美德，不想因为自己的变故影响大家游玩的兴致。

郭先生对我在学术合作和学会上的工作中也多有帮助。我曾参与过他主持的《中国历史大辞典·科技卷》（上海辞书出版社，2000）中科技史的条目编写。2009年我编辑《数学史通讯·第21期》时，"资料存档"栏目（从2000年开始刊登前辈名家的著述目录，当时已刊登了8位）稿源限于枯竭，为此我联系多位尚未发表著述目录的学界前辈，最先得到郭先生的响应，及时提供了他的论著目录。最终，该期刊刊登了郭先生和袁向东两位先生的论著目录，保证了该栏目的延续与质量的提升。

2017年5月22日，郭老师与师母在大连海滨公园

　　郭先生多次赠书于我，从20世纪的《中国古代数学》(1991)、《古代世界数学泰斗刘徽》(1992，让编辑胡明寄赠于我)到21世纪的《汇校九章算术》(2004)、《论中国古代数学家》(2017)、《郭书春数学史自选集》(上、下册，2018)、《九章算术·解读》(2019)等。每本书都工整地写着"青建同志雅正"或"青建教授雅正"。郭先生在做学问和做人方面都给我做出榜样。郭先生主要研究《九章算术》，为此付出大部分精力。这种"一生干好一件事"的"工匠精神"成为学术界的榜样与标杆。

　　衷心祝愿郭先生健康长寿，永葆青春！

2021年5月

郭书春先生

俞晓群 （北京草鹭文化公司）

自1982年大学毕业后，我一直从事编辑工作，至今已有将近四十年的光景。在漫长的职业经历中，因为工作需要以及个人的兴趣，我接触过许多优秀的作者。如今回忆起来，哪一位作者最让我难忘呢？总览全部所识所见，在前几位的人物中，一定包括郭书春先生。我们之间的那种友谊，不单是通常的编创关系，更有人与人之间，彼此在心灵上的尊重与认同。尤其是在学识上与人品上，我对郭先生最为敬佩，始终视他为自己做人做事的老师，心目中一生的朋友。

时值郭先生八十寿诞之际，让我们打开记忆的闸门，以郭先生的几部著作为标题，说一说彼此交往中，几段难忘的故事。

一、《九章算术汇校本》

郭书春先生是《九章算术》研究专家，堪称当今此领域中第一位的人物。前不久，还有几个出版社的编辑找我，谈到在国家为中小学推荐的阅读书目中，有郭书春先生注释的《九章算术》。他们希望我能够帮助联系到郭先生，推出新的版本。作为一个职业出版人，见到自己编的书能够成为经典著作；能够在几十年后，依然得到业界与读者的重视，实在是一件令人欣慰的事情。而更令我欣慰的，正是通过这部书稿，我有幸认识了郭书春先生。

我是在1982年初，在沈阳师范大学数学系毕业后，分配到辽宁人民出版社工作的。当时的地方出版社还不够发达，出版的学科不全，主要偏重于编辑人文类的著作，所以出版社的人员构成，大多以文、史、哲专业的编辑为主。辽宁人民出版社有文教编辑室，只是为了出版中小学教材教辅，才招来了几位理科编辑，我即是其中之一。当时有一位老编辑王常珠，她负责组织一些理科书，主要是数学方面的著作，如徐利治"运筹学小丛书"、梁宗巨《世界数学史简编》、方嘉林《拓扑学原理》等。我到任后给王常珠老师做助理，很快结识了那些大学者。其中与梁宗巨先生接触最多，一是出于我个人对于数学史的爱好，二是因为我接手梁先生的新著《世界数学通史》，还有我向梁先生组稿《数学历史典故》等。当时梁先生任《中国大百科全书·数学卷》数学史学科负责人，很有学术地位；他又是我们出版社的功勋作者，一部《世界数学史简编》名声显赫。梁先生的书稿不但文笔好，而且手稿上一字不错；写错了字，也会用刀片刮掉，重新写上正确的字，绝不肯涂抹。因此出版社对梁先生十分信任，每年研究选题，都要征求梁先生的意见，请他品评或推荐作者与作品，我们更是言听计从。梁先生历来出言谨慎，眼光又高，他肯推荐的作者很少。大约在1985年，我已经担任辽宁教育出版社理科编辑室主任，一次去大连梁先生家中，谈论书稿之余，我又请他推荐作者，他很明确地说："中国科学院科学史研究所有一位青年人郭书春，虽然只是助理研究员，但他关于《九章算术》的研究非常出色，你们如果有能力，我建议能出版他的著作。"我回到沈阳后，立即向出版社领导汇报梁先生的意见，并且安排在1986年4月去京，约见郭书春先生。

我们相约在新街口宾馆见面那天，正赶上郭先生参加申报职称的报告会。为了遵时见面，会议安排郭先生第一个做申报副研究员的报告。大约在十点钟，郭先生赶到宾馆。那时宾馆的条件很差，没有咖啡厅，客房也是多张床位，与陌生人混住。我们就坐在房间的床头柜前，一谈就是几个小时。到了下午一点钟，我们在楼下食堂吃了一点便饭，我记得只有几毛钱的馒头、咸菜。后来我在日记中，记下了这次接触的印象："我第一次见到郭先生，他在外貌上，不像梁先生那样书生气十足，谈话极其朴实、坦率，加上高高壮壮的身材，一副典型的山东大汉形象。我认真倾听郭先生关于《九章算术》研究的全部计划，包括出版《九章算术》汇校本，以及他与法国林力娜女士合作翻译出版《九章算术》法文版等等。交谈中，我渐渐被郭先生的学术水平和工作精神感染了，理解了梁先生举荐的道理。"

我记得,当时郭先生讲述他的研究计划滔滔不绝,我能够听懂的学术内容不多,但他诉说此项研究的条理清楚,尤其是他认真的工作精神,实在让我折服。他说了些什么呢?2013年,郭先生在《重视科技古籍的整理出版》一文中,详细讲述了那时候他对于《九章算术》的学术思考与研究。他写道:

> 80年代初,我遵从数学史界前辈严敦杰的指示,看了豫簪堂本《九章算术》,发现钱校本关于此本的描述有误,可见钱校本并不是没有失误。我有一个"毛病":发现问题后,喜欢穷追到底,便开始校雠不同的版本。后来又从著名珠算史家余介石夹在我所图书馆藏聚珍版《九章算术》中的一页笔记中,得知向达先生说干隆命馆臣修订过聚珍版,原藏避暑山庄,今藏南京博物院,于是在研究所当时领导、江苏省文化厅原厅长夏荣和南京博物院梁白泉院长的帮助下,三下南京,校雠了这个本子。通过对近二十个版本的校雠,发现从戴校各本到钱校本《九章算术》的版本一直非常混乱。钱校本破除对戴震的迷信,纠正了戴震的若干错校,贡献极大。然而他对南宋本、汲古阁本、大典本、聚珍版、微波榭本、李潢本等《九章算术》主要版本的使用都有严重失误。同时也发现戴震、李潢、钱宝琮等有大量错误校勘,尤其将南宋本、大典本数百条不误的刘徽注原文改错(关于《九章算术》的校勘,主要是对刘徽注的校勘),从而破除了对钱校本的迷信。我经常将自己的心得在研究所和数学史界做学术报告,许多人吃惊、赞同,然而也有人说我"反钱老",我答曰:"钱老是真正的科学家,他若知道我的结果,肯定会支持我!"但即使在这时我仍然没有全面校勘的想法。1984年秋我写了《评戴震对〈九章算术〉的整理》一文,呈吴文俊先生审阅。吴先生当即回信赞扬有加,并提出"希望能发表你关于这几种版本不同处的全部对照表"。然而怎样发表"全部对照表"?我根本不懂,就请教李学勤先生。他提出"搞汇校",鼓励我做全面校勘。我于是才有了全面校勘《九章算术》的想法。我是学数学的,文史知识先天不足。校雠各种版本,是机械性劳动,没有问题。但对校勘则是一知半解。只好边干边学,废寝忘食,"恶补"了大量关于版本、校勘的知识,我常借用恩格斯的话,把这一过程叫作"脱毛"。1986年初,我基本完成了汇校。由于《九章算术》的南宋本脱后四卷和刘徽序,而四库本和聚珍版都不宜作校勘的底本,在校勘中,我提出了通过几个子本对校恢复已失传的母本的办法,具体说来,就是通过四库本和聚珍版对校恢复已失传的戴震辑录本。这种做法,得到许多学者的支持,当然也有人认为我是在"杜撰"一个版本。我的这种方法确实不见于校勘学教程,但是,我至今认为是正确的,科学的。

见过郭先生,回到出版社后,郭先生的书稿《九章算术汇校本》立即列入重点出版计划。恰好在这一年6月,我出任辽宁教育出版社副社长兼副总编辑职务,对于这样重要的项目,操作起来有了更好的条件。比如书稿需要用繁体字排版,但辽宁找不到能够排繁体字的工厂,出版科联系到深圳的一家排版公司。那家公司不是专业书籍排版公司,更不懂古籍与科技书的排版技术,因此排出的样稿错误百出。无奈之下,在1989年9月,我只好带着出版科孙树慈主任,陪着郭先生去深圳校对书稿。那时深圳的天气很热,酒店的条件不是很好,每天只定时给几个小时的空调。我们三个人住在一个大房间里,没有桌子,郭先生从早到晚俯身在床头柜旁,一改就是一天。郭先生校对一页,工人师傅修改一页,改得不对,还要不断返改。在这个环节上,我跟孙主任帮不上忙,只能给郭先生烧水、买几元钱的盒饭,与排版公司沟通,或者上街购物。那时深圳特区与内地差异很大,可以购买的东西很多,但郭老师没有上过一次街,也没有买过一件东西。后来深圳排版公司的老板麻光先生也感动了,请我们去一家饭店吃饭,喝散啤酒。结果把我给弄醉了,但郭老师酒量巨大,一面应付,一面照顾我。后来我见到郭先生对书稿的认真态度达到近乎痴迷的状态,就劝他说:"不可能绝对没有错误,再重要的出版物,也是允许有差错率的。"郭先生正色答道:"不行啊!我们号称是汇校本,因此不同寻常,一个字也不能错。"

1990年10月,《九章算术汇校本》出版,席泽宗、梁宗巨、李学勤、李文林等先生都写了推荐信。第二年即荣获"中国教育图书一等奖"。1998年,郭先生译注《九章算术》由辽宁教育出版社出版;2004年辽宁教育出版社与中国台湾九章出版社联合出版《汇校〈九章算术〉增补版》。《九章算术汇校本》第三版改名《九章算术新校》，由中国科技大学出版社出版。2004年，《九章算术》中法对照本由巴黎Dunod出版社出版，郭先生与法国国家科研中心（CNRS）林力娜（K. Chemla）博士合作；2006年6月，此项目获法兰西学院"平山郁夫奖"。2013年，《汇校〈九章算术〉增补版》入选国家六十年来古籍出版"首届向全国推荐九十一部优秀古籍整理图书"。2015年"大中华文库"汉英对照译《九章算术》（郭书春今译，Dauben、徐义保英译）出版。2019年，《九章算术汇校本》《中法对照本九章算术》列为《中国大百科全书》第三版词条。

二、"中国古代科技名著译丛"

完成《九章算术汇校本》出版之后，我对郭先生有了更多的了解，也成为事业上的好朋友，工作中经常会向郭先生请教，不断得到他的支持。本文略举两个例子：

其一，1991年4月间，我向郭书春先生求教，请他策划一套"中国古代科技名著译丛"。最初我希望郭先生出任主编，但他说自己资历不够，建议请出李学勤先生主持这项工作，他自己可以做一些具体的事情。李学勤先生也是一位十分谦和的人，几经邀请，他才肯出任丛书主编。当时我在工作日记中记道："李、郭二位先生为人极好，宽厚通达，做事认认真真。李先生知识面宽广，书目精熟；郭先生做事踏实，任劳任怨。"4月12日，郭先生来信说："为此事我征求了几位同志的意见，褒贬不一。薄树人等认为不好做，卖不出去。潘吉星认为很有意义，肯定有销路。席泽宗也认为可以做。"

在1991年4月初，我们召开了第一次编委会，在会上发生了一点情况。当时宣布李学勤做主编，郭书春作副主编，潘吉星等作编委。潘先生参加了会议，散会后，在7月15日至19日期间，潘先生连续给我写了三封信，最长的一封达六页。他主要谈三个问题，一是对编委会的评价，言语激烈，我不复述；二是他谈到许多好题目，确实有水平，例如，他在谈首批书目时写道："我提出《天工开物》《齐民要术》《花镜》《洗冤集录》《饮膳正要》《救荒本草》。闵宗殿提出的《农书集锦》也很好，一本不成，再来一本，把讲斗鸡、斗蟋蟀、养鸟、养金鱼、栽果树、饮茶等都投放出去，看的人一定不少。"三是谈他研究《天工开物》的著作。潘先生曾在辽宁教育出版社出版过专著《肖莱马》，还为《数理化信息》组稿写稿，学术研究很有见地，与我们有着很好的业务往来。这一次他说："我可以参与搞一些东西，但退出编委会。"后来这套译丛陆续出版，其中推出许多好书，如郭书春《九章算术》、江晓原《周髀算经》、胡维佳《新仪象法要》、姜丽蓉《洗冤集录》、孙宏安《杨辉算法》、廖育群《黄帝八十一难经》、汪前进《岛夷志略》等。

其二，1995年间，我请沈昌文、杨成凯、陆灏先生策划大型丛书"新世纪万有文库"。在确定书目的过程中，沈先生对我说："这套书是追随20世纪30年代商务印书馆王云五先生主编的'万有文库'，他们出版的四千多册图书中，收有许多科技类的著作。我们几位策划人都偏重于人文学科，科学方面的书目，还要请你老兄自己开列。"我当时推荐了李醒民、郭书春等先生。郭先生编《算经十书》两册，收入"新世纪万有文库"第三辑中。后来与中国台湾九章出版社联系，出版了这个版本的繁体字修订版。直到2000年，郭先生还在为"新世纪万有文库"组织书目，他在一封信中写道："最近我搞了个科技方面的书目，数学除已出版的《算经十书》，有宋《数书九章》《详解九章算法》《杨辉算法》、元《测圆海镜》《益古演段》《算学启蒙》《四元玉鉴》。这样，中国传统数学辉煌时期的主要著作都有了。明清时期应从严掌握，珠算方面的应上一部，以《算经统宗》（明）为宜。贵社能否在'新世纪万有文库'中安排这些著作，同时在台湾九章出版社出版？请酌。《四元玉鉴》，天津李兆华与美国程贞一搞了一个校勘本，不知他是否给了陕西。"

说一点题外话，其实早在1990年，我在组织出版"国学丛书"时，已经遇到过类似的情况。当时丛书策划人有葛兆光、冯统一、王焱、陶铠、李春林、梁刚建，他们提出，中国传统文化门类，应该加上科学技术版块。葛先生说："我们这些人对自然科学方面的学者不够熟悉，我知道李俨、钱宝琮二位前辈已经过世，还有一位严敦杰先生，是否可以请他来作编委呢？"我回答说："严先生已经在两年前过世。"那还有谁呢？我推荐了杜石然先生。杜先生参加编委会后，曾经申报过一个题目。后来编委会决定，编委们每人提交一篇文章，汇成丛书第一册《国学今论》，其他著作主要由中青年学者撰写。杜先生提交的文章是《明代数学和明代社会》，他还推荐了刘钝《大哉言数》、廖育群《岐黄医道》，以及葛先生也曾提到的江晓原《天学真原》。

三、《李俨钱宝琮科学史全集》

大约在1998年,辽宁教育出版社经济形势很好,希望能做一些重点学术项目。我跟郭先生商量,提到整理出版李俨、钱宝琮二位前辈的著作。郭先生说,这件事情有难度,但非常有意义,他愿意与刘钝先生一同承担这项工作。在此后一年的时间里,郭先生废寝忘食,一鼓作气,将十卷本《李俨钱宝琮科学史全集》整理出来。交稿时郭先生对我说:"为这部书稿,把我累坏了。可是李、钱二老堪称我国科学史研究的祖师爷,他们的著作得以整理出版,是我们多年的愿望,就是累死也值得!"

1998年末,《李俨钱宝琮科学史全集》出版,第二年就荣获国家图书奖荣誉奖(实际上是最高奖)。1999年3月26日,《光明日报》用整版的篇幅采访了郭先生与我,题曰"为了学术的传承——与郭书春、俞晓群对话"。文中郭先生谈道:"我觉得李、钱二老除了给我们留下了不可估量的学术成就外,他们的研究方法和学风以及所建立起来的学术基础,对中国科技史界同样影响很大。比如对当前数学研究的影响。著名数学大师、中国科学院院士吴文俊先生近年来在机械化证明方面做出了杰出贡献,他认为他自己的机械化证明的想法就来自于中国古代数学思想。而作为现代数学家,他不可能投入大量精力去啃《九章算术》,他说正是从李、钱二老的著作中体会了中国古代数学机械化、算法化的特点,对他机械化证明的研究给予了很多启发。更为重要的一点是,数学与其他学科不同,可以说,我们今天进行的分数四则运算与《九章算术》中的方法没有什么区别。现在中小学课本受西方影响很深,而其实,有些算法中国古代比现在还高明,如果我们能很好地吸收中国古代数学思想,对改进数学教学会很有帮助。第三,研究科学史有利于我们总结科学历史发生发展的规律,总结经验教训。研究中国数学史,对于指导我们当前的数学研究很有帮助。为什么明朝之后中国数学开始落后?为什么清朝从事数学研究的人数之多在历史上是罕见的,却并没有使中国数学得以振兴。我觉得其中原因值得认真总结。钱老对此就有很多思考。我们同行碰到一块,经常谈论的话题就是李、钱二老的书能不能重印,而出全集却是我们谁都没敢想过的。学术著作卖不了几本,像辽宁教育出版社这样甘心赔本出学术著作实在难得。"

《李俨钱宝琮科学史全集》出版后,学术界更是好评如潮。江晓原博士就在一篇文章中写道:"出版《李俨钱宝琮科学史全集》,此书卷帙浩繁,凡十巨册,为科学史方面重要史料。科学史界咸称颂之,以为功德无量。我可以提供一个具体例证,我有一套此书置科学史系办公室,至今本系博士、硕士研究生频繁借阅不绝,如此嘉惠后学,诚令人感念不已。"对于这样的赞誉,郭先生也很兴奋,并且有了新的工作计划。他在2000年1月来信中写道:"上月我们开了纪念严敦杰逝世十周年学术研讨会,吴文俊、孙克定两位老先生来了,他们呼吁出版严敦杰的著作,我们感到难度较大,怎么搞,尚未有可操作的计划。不过想先出版李俨给严敦杰的信,据说有七百余封,都是学术性的,严敦杰的儿子也同意交出。我问了版权局,版权局沈仁干说著作权由李俨家属继承,严家可适当给保管费。我与刘钝商量,如出版,保管费最好由李俨子女从稿费中支付。数学史界对此呼声颇高,不知贵社是否有意于此?我想,这是李俨的信,作为二老全集的补充,你们能出版是最合适的,请酌。"

但是,时过不久,郭先生病了。2000年6月6日,郭先生来信,谈到自己此前生病的过程。他写道:"我的身体,算是虚惊一场。目前恢复到2月底发病以前的状况。只是戒酒了,另外晚上睡觉提前到11点,工作强度进一步降低。对2月底至3月下旬的病,我原有精神准备,原以为会在去年10月底交二老稿子之后,人松了劲会病。但想不到肺部会有阴影,更想不到大夫会怀疑是肺癌。4月二十几号那天,心情很难受,觉得会过早告别这个美好的世界,美好的数学史工作。后来也想通了,觉得这一生比上不足,比下有余,自己写了经得起时间考验的汇校《九章》与《刘徽》两书,又编了《汇通·数学卷》与《李俨钱宝琮科学史全集》,为本学科尽了点力,心里也就坦然了。因此住院二十天,像疗养一样,照样工作,大夫、护士都劝我休息,要养病。我说,我真把自己当病号,就糟了。后来大夫向我宣布了'好消息':他们倾向于是结核,不像癌症。试验性按结核治疗,了却了一场虚惊。当然,也不是确诊,因为痰里查不出结核病菌,也无法用气管镜或穿刺。5月下旬又做了CT,去通州区复查,阴影部分在缩小,大夫认为加强了他们的判断。"

读过这封信，我的心中一阵抽搐，在工作日志中写道："今天，郭书春先生又来了一封长信，谈的是工作，也谈到他今年以来生病的过程，读罢让我感伤不已。自从1985年，梁宗巨先生向我引荐郭书春，我在北京新街口宾馆与他第一次见面。一晃已经是15年前的事情了。那时郭老师还像一个棒小伙子，满身都透射着学术活力。……这些年，我们不断地催促郭老师写东西，希望他快交稿、快交稿。他每天都要工作到深夜，尤其是编完《李俨钱宝琮科学史全集》后，他对我说：'完稿的那一天，我出门都差一点摔倒了。'没想到，他由此得了这样一场大病。我不禁扪心自问：在学术的整体性与学者的个体性之间，我们出版人究竟充当了什么角色？你看，郭老师经历了那样的艰辛与磨难，他戒酒了，但他每天还要工作到深夜十一点。想到这些，我的眼睛变得模糊起来，已经看不清郭老师信上的文字。"

四、《论中国古代数学家》

2003年，我离开辽宁教育出版社，到辽宁出版集团工作，因此与郭先生接触少了，但遇到问题时，还会见面或书信交流。比如《九章算术汇校本》修订再版，直至第三版出版时，版权转给中国科技大学出版社，郭先生都会事先通知我，并征求我的意见，他那谦逊与温和的君子风度至今让我难以忘怀。2009年，我来到北京海豚出版社工作，依然保持着与郭先生的交往。每当有数学史界的老朋友来京，诸如道本周先生、林力娜女士等，郭先生都会事先告诉我，时而会有相见的机会。当然编创之间的交往还是存在的。那是在2014年，我给郭先生写信，希望他能抽出时间，为青少年写一本中国古代数学家的故事。此时郭先生极忙，但他还是答应了。在一年的时间里，他陆续发来几封邮件，与我们探讨这部小书的写法，邮件虽短，其中包含着许多重要的学术观点，并且郭先生的学术风格依然是那样踏实、认真。在这里，我节录几段郭先生的信件：

2015年2月17日：很感谢贵社将拙作纳入出版小开本精装书出版。考虑再三，我想将90年代发表的关于刘徽、贾宪、秦九韶的3篇文章结集，定名为《论刘徽、贾宪、秦九韶》。这三篇文章是：《刘徽——总算术之根源》《科学巨星》(9)陕西人民出版社,1998;《贾宪》《世界数学家思想方法》山东教育出版社,1994;《秦九韶——将数学进之于道》《科学巨星》(6)陕西人民出版社,1995。这三篇文章都是在我已有论文的基础上综合而成的。我关于《九章算术》和刘徽的工作，学术界比较了解，因为我的工作，人们认识到，刘徽不只是中国古代的一个重要数学家，而且是最伟大的数学家，是中国传统数学理论的奠基者。我关于贾宪、秦九韶的工作，学术界可能知之不多。自清中叶以来，人们一直认为，贾宪的著作已亡佚，只是片段被杨辉《详解九章算法·纂类》抄录，我根据对《详解九章算法》内部结构的分析及杨辉自序，发现杨辉此书不是如以往人们认为的含有《九章》本文、刘徽注、李淳风注释、杨辉详解四种内容，而是由《九章》本文、刘徽注、李淳风注释、贾宪细草、杨辉详解五种内容组成，从而认定贾宪的《黄帝九章算经细草》并未完全失传，目前尚存三分之二，得出贾宪是宋元筹算高潮的奠基者，以往人们将秦九韶、李冶、杨辉、朱世杰称作"宋元四大家"是不妥的。对秦九韶，学术界的主流看法是相信刘克庄、周密对秦九韶的诋毁，认为秦九韶成就极大，人品极坏。我将秦九韶放在南宋末年吏治黑暗，南宋统治集团内部抗战、投降两派斗争激烈的背景下考察，由于秦九韶支持吴潜为首的抗战派，刘克庄、周密都投靠投降派贾似道，因而刘克庄、周密对秦九韶的诋毁是不足信的，而秦九韶的《数书九章序》反映出秦九韶关心民间疾苦，同情底层老百姓，主张抗战，关心国计民生，有强烈的仁政思想。这三篇文章的字数可能约十至十一万字，我正在请人打字。这样做不知是否合适？请酌。

2015年3月18日：原来估计字数不对，所以只汇集关于刘徽、贾宪、秦九韶的三篇拙作。目前统计，这三篇仅约八万二千余字。因此想补充关于张苍、王孝通、李冶三篇拙作，如此统计字数约十一万五千余字，删节后可控制在十万字。关于张苍、王孝通、李冶三篇拙作的情况如下：刘徽说《九章算术》经张苍、耿寿昌删补而成书，可是自清中叶戴震整理《九章算术》，说戴震不可能删补《九章》之后，张苍就被赶出了著名数学家的队伍。我通过对《九章》内部结构的分析,并借助于日本学者关于《九章》反映的物价的分析,以及刘徽的人品,证明刘徽的看法是对的,刘徽的论述与现存任何文献都没有矛盾,相反,戴震、钱宝琮等否定张苍删补《九章》看法却与史料矛盾,由此恢复张苍著名数学家的地位,并在此基础上论述了张苍的贡献。钱宝琮认为王孝通在天文上是保守的,在数学上是了不起的革新者。我认为王孝通尽管对三次方程解法有贡献,但他指责祖冲之《缀术》全错不通,恐怕是与隋唐算学馆学官一样"莫能究其深奥"。而且他贬低前贤,吹嘘自己,不足为训。自清中叶以来,中国数学史界对李冶的误解特别多,比如说李冶是天元术的发明者,其《测圆海镜》是为阐发天元术而作。实际上,关于天元术的早期著作均已亡佚,李冶著《测圆海镜》时,天元术早已成熟,它只是现存最早的使用天元术的著作。《测圆海镜》根本不是为了阐发天元术的,而是一部阐发"洞渊九容"的著作。又如二百多年来,说天元式就是方程,由天元术建立的方程一次项旁都标"元"字。实际上,这都是以讹传讹,天元式是多项式,不是方程。两个等价的多项式相消后得出的方程,与传统方程一样,是不标"元"字的。另外,首次提出李冶在金亡之后因为长期寓居道观,受道家影响特别深。还确定了李冶被授翰林学士的确切年代(《元史》等有四五种不同说法)。

2015年4月16日:我想定名为《论中国古代数学家》,不知你们以为如何? 3月18日邮件中所说的张苍、刘徽、王孝通、贾宪、秦九韶、李冶等六篇拙作刚请打字社打好,统计字数十万九千字。因为我目前主要投入编《数学典》(今年必须出版),估计五月中旬才能将这六篇文章加工完。一加工完,即奉上。

行文及此,我还想到两件难忘的往事,附记于本文的结尾处,权作一个出版人,一个后学者,向郭先生致以真挚的敬意与感谢:

其一,我在编辑工作之余,一直从事中国古代数术研究。对此郭先生也曾经给我许多指点与帮助。比如1991年,那时我正在为三联书店撰写《数术探秘》,围绕着这个主题,曾经发表几篇论文。1990年10月写成《数在中国传统文化中的意义》一文,寄给郭先生指导。郭先生回信写道:"讨论非计算意义的'中国数'非常有意义,你的许多论点也有创见,别开生面。但文中有几处不太准确,我用铅笔勾了一下。一是哲学界到宋代仍有'周三径一'的说法,我勾掉了'哲学界',实际上,在数学与天文历法中也常使用周三径一,郭守敬制定授时历,便用周三径一。此句之前,中国人很早就认识到圆周率是一个小数,我改成了'不是整数',小数的认识应在宋金时代。历法自汉至元停止了一千多年,提法不妥。迟迟没产生小数的问题,各个民族数学史中,都是先认识分数,很久之后才认识小数,尚未见到例外情况,这可能是一个规律,与'中国数'关系不大。中国人认识并使用小数在各民族中是最早的,小数的使用在唐中叶之后已屡见,宋秦九韶《数书九章》(1247),(元)李冶《测圆海镜》(1248)已有完整的小数表示。"我的文章,后来发表在《自然辩证法研究》上。

其二,早年出版《九章算术汇校本》的经历,郭先生一直念念不忘。直到2013年8月,我参加古籍整理出版专家评审会,报到时会议组织人员见到我,纷纷指点说:"这位就是郭书春先生提到的俞晓群。"当时我一脸懵然,不知就里。一打听才知道,原来在此前召开的古籍整理学术专家评审会上,郭先生有一个大会发言,其中提到了我们合作的故事。他说道:"《九章算术》汇校本完成后,找出版社时却到处碰壁。借口是'赔本',实际上因为我当时是个助研,没有名气。正在这时,全国政协委员、辽宁师范大学梁宗巨教授向辽宁教育出版社俞晓群先生推荐了我的书。见面时我开门见山地对晓群说:'我的书赔钱。'晓群很干脆:'只要书好,我不怕赔钱。'我答云:'我是个助研,但我做到了什么程度,我心中有数,我的书肯定站得住脚。'俞晓群离开辽宁教育出版社时又嘱咐:汇校本的再版,郭老师什么时候做完,什么时候出版。这就是汇校《九章筭术》增补版。我常想:要不是严敦杰先生,我不会搞《九章筭术》的版本研究。要不是吴文俊、李学勤先生,我不会搞汇校。要不是梁宗巨、俞晓群先生,汇校本的出版要到猴年马月了。所以我特别希望当今学术界、出版界能够为从事古籍整理出版工作的年轻人创造良好的成长环境,发现人才,培养人才,大力提携人才,真诚尊重、细致关心,充分信任他们,让更多的人才快速成长,从而壮大古籍整理出版队伍。"

我和著名科学史家郭书春先生结识的岁月

杨国选 （四川省安岳县委宣传部）

2000年11月下旬，第十一届全国人大常委会副委员长、两院院士、中国科学院院长路甬祥题写"秦九韶纪念馆"馆名的六个鎏金大字，镶嵌在纪念馆正门门楣上方，金光闪闪，熠熠生辉，标志了秦九韶纪念馆修建工程已经全面竣工。郭书春先生协助祖冲之的祖籍河北省涞水县政府，召开了纪念祖冲之逝世1500周年国际学术研讨会议和祖冲之纪念馆在祖冲之中学的落成典礼，会议结束，无暇休整，又奔赴秦九韶故里四川安岳，与李迪先生一起帮助新修竣工的秦九韶纪念馆布展、策划、组织秦九韶纪念馆落成典礼暨秦九韶学术研讨国际会议。

秦九韶纪念馆与祖冲之纪念馆同时举行落成典礼，召开国际学术研讨会议，也许这是时空上的巧合，但两院院士路甬祥题写秦九韶纪念馆与祖冲之纪念馆馆名，两位数学史大师协助两座纪念馆落成典礼暨国际学术会议，这可不是巧合，应该是古今缘分吧！如果两位古代数学巨匠上天有灵，定会感知当今三位著名大师在为他们的纪念馆组织庆典，以他们的成就召开国际学术研讨会议而深感欣慰。惋惜的是，11月中旬，我带队宣传系统干部去沿海考察学习，错过了秦九韶纪念馆落成典礼暨学术研讨国际会议的召开和拜见郭先生的良机。

甲申初夏，"秦九韶学术研讨国际会议"在太湖之滨湖州召开。这座因湖而得名的历史文化名城，是中世纪伟大数学家秦九韶的经典巨著《数书九章》成书之地，也是我有幸结识先生值得留恋的美好湖滨城市。

在湖州"秦九韶学术研讨国际会议"中先生既是会议的筹备者、组织者、主持者，又是大会主题学术报告《重新品评秦九韶》的著名科学史家。其实，对于我来说唯一能沾边的，就算是与会的数学大师秦九韶故里人吧，即便在大会作了《秦九韶在四川》的学术交流，那也是十分肤浅的，不值得予以提及的。然而，先生在会议间歇对我说，他是在"炒冷饭"，我的研究是几十年来关于秦九韶史料的重大突破，并对进一步弄清秦九韶的履历十分有意义。先生是德高望重的数学史家，如此谦恭下士，如此过载之誉，我没有半点欣慰，深感的这是鞭策的艺术，唯有的就是对导师的起敬。

先生的论著《重新品评秦九韶》，那是一位科学史家以良知与胆略，以实事求是的唯物主义史学观，为秦九韶据史辩诬，沉冤昭雪，始得还真的檄文唤醒了国内外数学史界的大师们，已成为学界公共诠释的典籍。也许先生认为《重新品评秦九韶》，在2000年9月、12月分别在台湾清华大学历史系、安岳秦九韶纪念馆落成典礼暨学术研讨国际会议（四川安岳）做过学术演讲，且文献《重新品评秦九韶》又已经出版，自谦是在"炒冷饭"。无论怎样讲，可见先生的学术艺德之高尚，不愧大师风范。先生通过邮件给我发来的两个《重新品评秦九韶》电子文本，我多次拜读过，实则都是"钩沉稽古，发微抉隐"的典籍。除了展示先生实事求是的辩证唯物主义史学观之外，我想这就是先生还在不遗余力地为秦九韶据史辩诬，沉冤昭雪，进一步唤醒那些对奸臣贾似道的门人刘克庄、周密之流，对秦九韶留下的诽谤、诬陷、攻击之词不察的人们，让其了解真实的数学巨匠秦九韶及《数书九章》。先生是近代中国数学史学界为秦九韶据史辩诬，沉冤昭雪，始得还真的唯尊功臣，一点不为过。通俗地说，先生是为秦九韶洗雪、翻案第一人，功在当代，利在千秋。

湖州会议之后不久，我告诉先生，我现在已经从负责人岗位退下来了，潜心做一件事，探寻秦九韶的足迹，了解秦九韶的成谜生平。先生从邮箱给我发来他撰写的文献《尊重原始文献 避免以讹传讹》与随附的寄予。拜读之后，受益匪浅。华觉明先生曾在《郭书春数学史自选集·序》中说："不禁为他的卓越史识，极认真、严谨的史学研探，对前辈学者敬重有加而又不讳言其缺失的史德，以及精心培育和引领年轻学者共同推进学科建设的使命感和责任心感到震撼。"这是先生在半个多世纪中国数学史研究的复杂进程中,所修养而倡导的精辟学术道德准则,也是我们所有想迈进或已经从事学术研究的同仁们必须遵循的学术道德规范。随附寄予,那就是指明研究的途径与方法,无限的信任与鼓励。

湖州会议之中,我在大会做了《秦九韶在四川》的学术交流,论证了秦九韶在鄞县擢升县尉,先生建议我写一篇《秦九韶县尉考》的论文在《中国科技史杂志》上发表,我迟迟没有动笔。直到2007年,在探寻秦九韶的足迹的途中,发现了与秦季槱同年入仕、同在秘书省共事的乔行简,戊辰四月乙卯所作满月词《贺秦秘阁季槱得子》。"戊辰",即嘉定元年,"四月乙卯",即四月十六日,史证秦九韶嘉定元年三月出生普州天庆观街秦苑斋。我将史料告诉先生,他十分高兴,让我将上次没有完成的《秦九韶县尉考》合并写一篇《秦九韶生年及任县尉考》的论文,在《中国科技史杂志》上发表。我的稿件写好了,先生百忙之中帮助精心修改。继后,艾素珍教授给我发来《秦九韶生年及任县尉考》清样,并说明我加上的"致谢,本文修改过程中,得到中国科学院自然科学史研究所研究员郭书春先生的帮助,特此感谢",已被郭先生删除。我将稿件发给艾教授,请她一定要将这句常规谢语加上,《秦九韶生年及任县尉考》在《中国科技史杂志》发表才予以保留。看来不过是在一篇待发表文章之末的37字常规谢语的取舍,但它是被应该接受致谢的先生删除,意义就显然不同了。这是先生在向读者发出的这是作者独立完成的信息,以提高我这初涉跨学科门类研究者的信心与坚持。但让我深深感知的是先生"淡泊名利"的高尚精神,从先生身上又感受到中国数学史界素有的诲人不倦、有教无类的优良传统。

2009年初夏,我告诉先生,从《潼川民间故事集》查到"秦县尉巧断农夫边界与县学先生解读的故事",说的是县学先生在秦九韶《数书九章》成书之后,解读秦九韶当年在鄞县县尉任上,划分"三斜田"被洪水冲去一角变成"四不等直田"边界的公式,就是《数书九章》"漂田推积"计题雏形。先生立即回邮件说:"这一发现很重要,如果还能找到有史料能佐证更好,不过这也难,但要有信心,即使暂时没有找到也不留下遗憾。"先生十分真切的话语,是他极认真、严谨的史学研探精神,给我指明了对待学术研究的原则和方向,同时也坚定了我的信心。

2009年秋8月,我在《宋史》查阅与泸州相关的西南蛮夷之时,偶然发现卷二百四,志第一百五十七,艺文三,有杨泰之《普州志》三十卷,不过只有题目缩引。我想宋史不可能对一部地方志细化入史,能有杨泰之《普州志》三十卷入史,也说明其杨泰之《普州志》有一定影响和存在。

2010年初夏,我在四川省图书馆清康熙《四川总志》发现杨泰之撰《普州志》第二十八卷,《普州民间传说故事书录》有"秦县尉巧断农夫边界的故事",但书录,也只有题目。嘉定年间,杨泰之做过普州知府。我将这一收获告诉先生,先生说:这说明杨泰之知道"秦县尉巧断农夫边界的故事",证明了秦九韶巧断农夫边界故事的真实性。要是能找杨泰之为什么把"县学先生的解读"删除的原因就更好了。

我查阅《宋史》儒林四杨泰之传,绍定三年,主管临安府千秋鸿禧观,卒。杨泰之的《普州志》三十卷是"宝庆本",杨泰之在集纳题目"秦县尉巧断农夫边界的故事"因在绍定元年之前,杨泰之辞世时又是绍定三年,淳祐七年九月,秦九韶《数书九章》成书。因此,杨泰之《普州志》不可能有"县学先生的解读"。

我将这信息告诉先生,先生说:"你的这一发现意义重大,研究方向是对的,说明秦九韶在鄞县划分农夫边界所用计算公式至少是《数书九章》'漂田推积'计题的雏形,四川无疑是秦九韶数学研究初始之地与实践之地。"

这一问题的研究成果,完全是受益于先生的教诲和精心指导所得来的,这也是先生对待数学史研究的极认真、严谨的史学研探精神和高尚的学术美德的彰显。

2010年10月,安岳县政府决定修建"秦九韶《数书九章》艺术长廊",设计方案审定就绪,其中有一段长达近百米的《数书九章》艺术墙,墙上雕刻秦九韶《数书九章·序》全文,艺术墙中点前方是一座秦九韶像雕像。秦九韶像雕像的制作倒不难,安岳是全国著名的石刻之乡,石刻雕刻艺术工匠、大师不少,我征求石刻雕刻大师石永新的意见,他说雕刻数学大师秦九韶像是我的荣幸,全力支持。但《数书九章·序》的文本校勘,我想到的倒是非先生莫属。是年元旦刚过,先生曾告诉过我,当年是他最忙的一年。他的专著《中国古代数学》(增补修订本)(商务印书馆出版);《九章筭术译注》(上海古籍出版社出版)。受命组织全国中国数学史骨干主编的《中国科学技术史·数学卷》大型工程(科学出版社出版)。先生的工作如此繁重,敬业的精神一丝不苟,人所共知,毋遑多言。要请先生提供校勘《数书九章·序》文本,可犹豫了近半月,没办法,还是得求助先生。先生说,大好事,全力支持。不久,先生就发来《数书九章·序》校勘文本,"秦九韶《数书九章》艺术长廊"的《数书九章·序》的雕刻才顺利完成。对于先生的无私奉献精神,我唯一能做到的:就是请石刻艺术大师石永恩在"秦九韶《数书九章》艺术长廊"的《数书九章·序》末,刻上"《数书九章·序》文本,著名科学史家、中国科学院自然科学史研究所研究员郭书春先生校勘"。年末,我把"秦九韶《数书九章》艺术长廊"的《数书九章·序》雕刻照片,发给中国科学院院士、著名数学家刘应明先生,刘先生回邮件说:"感谢你们选对了《数书九章·序》校勘版本,只有郭书春先生的《数书九章·序》校勘版本是认真做了功课的,不仅校勘准确,还把人为无端删除和遗漏也补校上了。同时也感谢你们做了一件大好事,让秦九韶的《数书九章·序》像你们的石刻艺术一样,镌刻在《数书九章》艺术长廊上,千秋永存!"

2011年初夏,我发邮件告诉先生,在上海买到他主编的《中国科学技术史·数学卷》,先生回复中委婉说起去年他患了眼疾,较为严重,又遇到《中国科学技术史·数学卷》忙于交付出版社,任务之重,时间之紧,只好挂牌治疗,才算完成。读罢,深感在先生健康欠佳,工作十分繁重之际,我还给增添工作量,心情十分沉重而内疚。

2017年10月,我的《秦九韶生平考》,在中国科学院院士、数学家、四川大学副校长刘应明推荐下,在四川大学出版社出版,我将书送给先生,请求斧正。先生回邮,"全是抬爱与过载之誉,收到大作《秦九韶生平考》非常高兴,也非常震撼!您跑遍了秦九韶一生几乎所有有关的地方寻觅、考证,艰苦备尝,成效卓著,汇成巨著,不仅是对秦九韶研究事业的重大贡献,也是中国数学史研究的美好篇章,特向您表示衷心祝贺!"

先生是继李俨、钱宝琮开创中国数学史学科以来德高望重、著述颇丰的数学史巨匠,是对数学史研究的卓越贡献者。对于我来说,这么一部肤浅平淡的秦九韶生平考,如此过誉,真有些汗颜。

但我要最感谢先生的是随语后面的一段话:我先看了几个章节,特别是道古桥一节,解除了我多年的疑惑。我一直对此"道古"是不是"秦道古"存疑。当然,如将"元朝人朱世杰为纪念建桥人'道古',将'西溪桥'更名'道古桥'"作为《临安志》卷十五的引文置于引号中(第118页),说服力会更强。大作引用别人的"李冶的'天元术'"的说法是不妥的。关于李冶与天元术的关系,自清中叶以来误解很多。实际上李冶时代,天元术已经成熟。他的《测圆海镜》是现存使用天元术的最早著作,但不是为天元术而是为测圆而作的,天元术不是李冶创造的。先生不仅语重心长地给我指出不足和错误,同时,还随邮论文《关于天元术的发展的几个问题》,读后受益匪浅。

2018年11月,我拜读了先生发来的《写在中法对照〈九章算术〉入选改革开放40周年引才引智成果展览之后》,得知改革开放的第三年,中国科学院自然科学史研究所接收的第一位外国留学生林力娜(K.Chemla),也是先生教授的第一个外国留学生,再次证实了我与先生交往中的"感知"与"感受",并非只是对于我这跨学科越门类者。

林力娜(K.Chemla),初到北京时,只在从巴黎到北京两个礼拜的火车上跟别人学过几句中国话,一个中国字都不会写,其中文与汉语知识几乎是空白,却要在8个月内学习元朝李冶的数学著作《测圆海镜》,以便回国拿博士学位。先生在教授林力娜上课时的语言招数可达到了极致,法文、中文、英文甚至肢体语言一起用。对于林力娜,先生是这样评介:"林力娜真是绝顶聪明。林力娜非常敬业。林力娜常常提出一些我想不到的真知灼见。"先生如此肯定林力娜的长处,因人施教,半年之后,她便能说中国话,并借助字典看中国古代数学著作了,对《测圆海镜》的认识也开始有创见。林力娜回国不仅拿到了博士学位,还在法国国家科学研究中心工作,现在是在国际学术界非常活跃的著名中国数学史家。先生和林力娜才能合作完成"中法对照《九章算术》",2004年在巴黎出版,不到一年便脱销。2005年7月30日,中国科学院和法国国家科研中心、法国驻华大使馆在北京联合召开了该书的新闻发布会。2006年6月,该书获"法兰西学院学士院奖"("平山郁夫奖")。林力娜获法国"骑士勋章",这部书是其重要成果之一。更为重要的则是先生架起了中国数学史研究与世界数学史界研究、认识中国数学史的友谊桥梁。

先生与法国学生林力娜之间的师生情,也许有人说,导师,就是为学生传道、授业、解惑嘛,其实,远不至此。先生在文中对林力娜有过三次短语评介:林力娜真是绝顶聪明;林力娜非常敬业;林力娜常常提出一些我想不到的真知灼见。其归结:这大约是不同文化传统交融的成果吧！先生心目中对学生是启迪、是赞美之后的知识交融与诠释。其有这样的学生,归结于"不同文化传统交融的成果",唯独先生没有提到自己的功劳,哪怕是所付出的心血,先生的师德与情操是何等的高尚,已不言而喻。

或许,先生的心目中只有欣慰:李俨、钱宝琮开创的中国数学史的大旗没有在先生手里倒下,反而还在壮大。中国科学院自然科学史研究所的中国数学史学科却一直艰难而健康地发展着,几位中青年数学史研究工作者顶住压力,克服困难,取得了丰硕的成果,研究所有口皆碑,韩琦、田淼、邹大海、郭金海4位先后成为博士生导师。先生退休之后,继续从事中国数学史研究,甚至比退休前还忙,自己撰著出版了近十部著作,还受命组织全国的中国数学史研究骨干编纂了《中国科学技术史·数学卷》和《中华大典·数学典》两项大型工程。退休前撰著、编纂的几部著作在本世纪也都多次修订再版。秦九韶被评为第二批历史名人,先生又应中共四川省委宣传部和天地出版社之邀,为秦九韶立传。

今年,秦九韶纪念馆维修之后重新布展,先生依然十分关注,他是为秦九韶据史辩诬、沉冤昭雪,以还真实秦九韶的第一人,展馆的结束语,用了先生的论著《重新品评秦九韶》的结语作为引文,《重新品评秦九韶》的中心思想作为秦九韶纪念馆的结束语:

> 秦九韶是一位具有实事求是的科学精神与创新精神的伟大数学家,是一位恪守传统道德、恕道,关心国计民生,体察民间疾苦,强烈反对政府和豪强的横征暴敛,主张施行仁政,反对大商贾囤积居奇的正直官吏。在南宋朝廷腐败与国难当头之际,不避世免祸,以知识服务社会,是一位支持并积极参加抗金、抗蒙战争的爱国者。是一位把数学作为实现上述理想的有力工具的学者。

先生,您是将李、钱二老开创的中国数学史大旗接过来的旗手与著名科学史家。五十多年来,潜心数学史研究,钩沉发覆、辨伪存真、提炼精华,发表近200篇数学史研究论文,著述数学史专著数十部,完成了国家立项的《中华大典·数学典》《中国科学技术史·数学卷》等众多大型数学典籍的校勘、整理、主编、出版工作。不仅中国数学史研究的队伍在发展壮大中,而且寄予希望的中青年数学史大家已经脱颖而出,肩负起您托付他们从您手中接过而高举的中国数学史大旗,乘胜前行,发展壮大。您虽朝杖之年,却依然勤耕善耘。祝您生活之树常绿,生命之水长流。

2021年5月25日于成都

献给郭书春先生 80 岁寿诞

刘芹英　（中国财政科学研究院）

在生命的长河里，总有某些东西让我们刻骨铭心，难以忘记。人的一生中都有许许多多熟悉的人，都有值得去记忆的人，在我记忆中，郭书春先生就是占据位置最大的人之一。今年 8 月 26 日是郭书春先生 80 岁寿诞，我由此想起了与郭先生相识的过程，以及一路走来，郭先生对我工作方面的帮助和支持，以及相识 25 年来的点点滴滴，特别是一路走来，郭先生和王阿姨对我工作上的帮助和生活上的关心照顾。

一、初识郭书春先生

记得那是 1998 年 8 月的某一天，我当时还在河南财政税务高等专科学校教书，暑假期间我跟郭启庶教授一起去吉林省长春市参加"中国珠算协会算理算法专业委员会年会暨理论研讨会"。由于长春到郑州没有直达火车，需要在北京中转。会议结束返郑时在北京中转，郭启庶教授首先带我去中国珠算协会（以下简称中珠协，当时办公地点在中央财经大学内）办事儿，然后带我专程到郭书春先生家里去拜访。

郭先生热情接待了我们，聊天的过程中还讨论了一些我们感兴趣的数学问题，印象最深的是《九章算术》"率"概念的提出，以及"率"思想方法的现代应用问题等。回郑州之后，本人萌发了报考郭先生博士研究生的想法，电话咨询时郭先生做了耐心细致的答复；后来考虑到自己水平有限，最终决定还是报考了西北大学罗见今教授的博士研究生。

二、郭书春先生对我工作的支持

2002 年 11 月我曾来北京到中国科学院数学与系统所和自然科学史研究所查资料。在此期间，我再次拜访郭书春先生，这次郭先生不仅给我毕业论文的撰写提出好的建议，还赠送我一本他的专著《古代世界数学泰斗刘徽》（图 1）。

图 1

每次见面，郭书春先生总是面带微笑，感觉非常亲切。2003 年 7 月，我博士毕业被分配到财政部财政科学研究所工作，工作处室是中国珠算协会秘书处，主要从事珠算史及现代珠算珠心算理论和实践研究工作，郭先生在我工作上给予了很多帮助和很大支持。印象比较深刻的有如下几次大型学术会议和交流活动。

（一）《中华大典·数学典》编撰工作

2006年启动《中华大典·数学典》编撰工作时，郭书春先生打电话让我担任编委委员，接到电话的那一刻我非常激动，又很惶恐。激动的是大名鼎鼎的数学史家郭先生还记得我，惶恐的是怕自己不能胜任工作而辜负了先生的信任。再次感谢郭先生给我这次学习成长的机会，后来分工我负责编撰《中国传统算法概论》分典中"筹算捷算法和珠算总部"和《数学概论》分册"记数法与计算工具"总部，虽然在编撰期间本人生病耽误了些时间，但在主编及家人的帮助下，按期完成了编撰和校对工作。

（二）海峡两岸中西融合数学学术研讨会

"海峡两岸中西融合数学学术研讨会"于2006年12月在河南省济源市举办，特别邀请郭书春先生参加。众所周知，在中国传统数学代表经典《九章算术》研究方面，郭书春先生是当之无愧的学术权威，郭先生不仅对《九章算术》研究提出了理论体系，而且研究得最为透彻。特别是他探讨的"率"概念和思想方法，具有现代意义，在现代数学教育中起着非常重要的作用。

郭启庶教授创立的"优因数学"自2002年起在河南省济源市五龙口镇实验小学开始实验，经过四年的教学实践，达到了预期效果。优因数学是将中国传统数学与西方数学中优秀"基因"有机融合在一起而构建的新的数学教育教学知识体系，特别是将中国传统数学代表经典《九章算术》中"率"概念和思想方法应用在现代小学数学应用题教学中，不用再将应用题分为简单、复杂、里程、相向问题等很多类别，只是将"率"思想方法概括为"四角阵原理"，不仅使应用题解法大大简化，而且将原有分类解决的应用题统一为"率表"即可。

我记得当时邀请郭先生参加会议时，他说："我女儿早已大学毕业，孙女还没有上小学，我对小学数学教育不了解，参加这种会不合适。"我把郭启庶先生在优因数学中用"率"思想方法改革在现代小学数学教材并在济源五龙口小学卓有成效的实践讲给他听，并且说："郭先生，发现你是中国数学史界第一位以《九章算术》和刘徽的'率'为专题写论文的。"他说："这倒是。"才同意参加会。郭先生会议现场看到他研究的《九章算术》和刘徽的"率"概念和思想方法在现代小学数学教育中发挥着如此巨大作用，对小学数学教学有非常大的简化作用，当场激动得无以言表，并进行大会发言。

部分专家在河南省济源市五龙口镇实验小学合影
左起为王炳钧、杨烈全、郭书春、刘芹英、郭启庶、苑玉敏、冯立升、侯丽

（三）对中国珠算申遗成功的祝贺

我们都知道，中国珠算于2013年12月4日成功入选联合国教科文组织"人类非物质文化遗产代表作名录"。得知我在申遗现场，郭书春先生就在中国珠算申遗成功当天以电子邮件形式发来贺信，郭先生是数学史界第一个发来贺信的。原文如下：

刘芹英博士并转

中国珠算学会及中国申遗代表团

欣闻在通过联合国教科文组织的审议后,珠算正式被列入"人类非物质文化遗产名录"的喜讯,十分高兴,作为一个老数学史工作者,也对你们的努力表示感谢!

珠算是中华民族为人类文明做出的杰出贡献,至今为中国和东亚人民所乐用,也为小学数学教材改革有启迪作用。它列入"人类非物质文化遗产名录"是当之无愧的。这是中华民族的骄傲!希望做好对珠算知识的在世界范围内的推广普及工作,使之永葆青春,为世界文明的发展继续做出贡献!

中国科学院自然科学史研究所研究员　博士生导师
全国数学史学会前理事长　郭书春
2013年12月4日于北京贺

2013年12月23日,中国珠算心算协会在北京国家会计学院召开"中国珠算"入选人类非物质文化遗产代表作名录,传承、保护、弘扬珠算文化座谈会,全国人大常委会原副委员长、中国关心下一代工作委员会主任、中珠协名誉会长顾秀莲出席大会并讲话。中珠协特别邀请郭书春先生参加。邀请函如下:

邀　请　函

郭书春研究员:

2013年12月联合国教科文组织保护非物质文化遗产政府间委员会第八次会议在阿塞拜疆召开,会议通过了"中国珠算"入选联合国教科文组织"人类非物质文化遗产代表作名录"。

为进一步做好珠算文化的保护与传承、发展与弘扬,中国珠算心算协会组织珠算界及社会各界人士,在北京国家会计学院(交通图附后)举办"中国珠算"入选人类非物质文化遗产代表作名录,传承、保护、弘扬珠算文化座谈会。会议时间:2013年12月22日报到,23日上午9—12点开会。

诚邀您拨冗参会。

联系人:马继平　傅洁

联系电话:010—88191321　88191424

二〇一三年十二月十日

(四)弘扬中华珠算文化专题研讨会

由中国珠算心算协会指导,上海市珠算心算协会和华东师范大学数学教学研究所主办、台湾地区商业会珠算委员会协办的第二届"弘扬中华珠算文化"专题研讨会暨珠算申遗成功周年庆活动,于2014年10月23至24日在上海举行,郭书春应邀出席大会。郭先生在大会致辞中,特别谈到尽管珠算申遗成功,但中外数学界和数学史界对中国珠算的认识还很不到位,存在很大偏见;珠算界同仁首先要改变国内学者对珠算的偏见,更要努力改变外国学者对中国数学和珠算的认识和偏见。珠算界仍然任重而道远。

(五)中珠协学术交流活动

2016年9月27日—28日,中珠协学术研究专业委员会2016年年会暨理论研讨会在甘肃省兰州市举行,郭书春先生应邀出席。2020年12月4日,世界珠算心算联合会、中国珠算心算协会与中国财政科学研究院珠心算研究院联合举办了"首届珠心算发展高端论坛",郭书春先生应邀出席并对中国科学院数学与系统科学研究院李文林研究员以"华夏数学文化的明珠——中国古代数学算法体系与珠算"为题的主旨演讲,做了精彩点评。

郭书春先生在"首届珠心算高端论坛"大会上做精彩点评

(六)编写《中国珠算发展史》

《中国珠算发展史》编写工作于 2015 年 11 月在江苏南通中国珠算博物馆启动并成立编写组。中珠协为保证《中国珠算发展史》编写质量,特邀请郭书春、郭世荣和冯立升三位数学史界专家出席启动工作会议,并分别担任顾问、主编、副主编。编写组于 2016 年 9 月 25 日—26 日在甘肃省财会培训中心召开《中国珠算发展史》第二次编审会议;还分别于 2018 年 5 月 26 日—27 日及 7 月 17 日—18 日在内蒙古师范大学科学技术史研究院和沈阳市辽宁友谊宾馆召开《中国珠算发展史》编审会议。

《中国珠算发展史》在呼和浩特召开的编审会合影

第一排右起:卢斌、苑玉敏、郭书春、张弘力、冯立升、程北平、郭世荣、刘芳;第二排右起:赵艳艳、刘芹英、赵相翼、文志芳、张建、王海明等

郭书春先生对我工作的支持和帮助远不止上述这些,而是多方面的,全方位的。限于篇幅,在此不再一一赘述。

三、郭先生对我生活的关照

郭书春先生不仅在我工作上给予很大支持,而且在我生活上也一直给予关照。特别是在我 2014 年和 2018 年两次手术住院期间,郭先生多次打电话问候;再就是我爱人 2019 年脑出血以来,也是多次打电话问候康复情况。在此,我代表我们全家对郭先生再次表示感谢,并致以崇高的敬意。

尽管岁月轻轻滑过指尖,许多往事渐渐弥散在如沙漏般的光阴里,但永远不变的是这珍藏在记忆中的温馨点滴。

郭先生助我数学教育教学成长二三事

乔希民[1] （广州工商学院通识教育学院）

郭书春先生是我非常敬重的数学史学家与数学教育家之一，敬重他为学之道、著述丰硕与厚重笃实，我完全可以称得上是他的"金粉丝"。自我 1998 年 5 月写信请求他，怎样才能购得《中国科学技术典籍通汇·数学卷》，他很快回信告知并帮助我获得最优惠价，虽然花去了我当时三个多月的工资，但如获至宝，内心喜悦无比，时至今日仍心存感激。我是郭先生著书立说的忠实读者，收藏了他所有著、主编的学术著作与《郭书春数学史自选集》等文献，也在不同场合，向我的学生们弘扬郭先生的学术精神与成就。我在数学史研究没有任何建树，然而郭先生的数学史研究成果却促进了我数学教育教学探究的宽泛视野。

1 启发我学习与研究的源头是立学立教之本

我在"初等几何研究"教学过程中，引用郭先生主编的《中国科学技术典籍通汇·数学卷》徐光启和利玛窦合译《几何原本》（前 6 卷）所言："今详味其书，规摹次第，洵为奇矣。题论之首，先标界说；次设公论，题论所据；次乃具题，题有本解，有作法，有推论。先之所征，必后之所恃。十三卷中，五百余题，一脉贯通，卷与卷，题与题相结倚，一先不可后，一后不可先，累累交承，至终不绝矣。初言实理，至易至明，渐次积累。终竟乃发奥微之意。若暂观后来一二题旨，即其所言，人所难测，亦所难信。及以前题为据，层层印证，重重开发，则义如列眉，往往释然而失笑矣。"[1,2]，使我真正理解了徐光启察觉到了西方科学的严谨而缜密的逻辑演绎推理为国人所缺失，也感到了西方科学重基础理论探究和科学推理论证恰为"彼士立论宗旨唯尚理之所据"，俨然"独几何之学，通即全通，蔽之全蔽"的"缜密甚矣"的科学精神旨趣。我们人人能够从不同视野窥《几何原本》之一斑而见全豹，无不肃然起敬，感慨良许。经典的引用，使我有了进一步深入了解各个时期《几何原本》的兴趣，自徐光启和利玛窦合译《几何原本》[1,2]（前 6 卷）后，李善兰和伟烈亚力于 1857 年合译并完成《几何原本》（后 9 卷）（依据 15 卷版本），后再由曾国藩于 1865 年将徐光启、利玛窦版和李善兰、伟烈亚力版并为一书，重校付梓，实现了我国第一部《几何原本》足本，继而从足本刊印的有：金陵书局刊本（1878 年）、江宁藩署刊本（1882 年）、上海积山书局石印本（1896 年）、古今算术丛书本（1898 年）等，以及蒙古文（五卷）译本（内蒙古人民出版社，1987 年）。直到 1990 年 1 月，陕西科学技术出版社出版了由兰纪正、朱恩宽合译的《欧几里得·几何原本》（据希思标准英文版本《欧几里得原本 13 卷》译介），2003 年又发行第 2 版，共印 5 000 册，2011 年又作为"汉译经典"由译林出版社重新出版，该译本被称之为"真正付出过严肃认真的学术努力的"[11]当代汉语版本。之后又有众多版本：人民日报出版社（2005 年）；陕西人民出版社（2010 年）；江苏人民出版社（2011 年）；重庆出版社（2014 年）；天津人民出版社（2016 年）；北京理工大学出版社（2017 年）；台海出版社（2018 年）；四川人民出版社（2018 年）；江西人民出版社（2019 年）；福建科学技术出版社（2020 年）。此外还有上海古籍出版社出版《几何原本》（2011 年）前 6 卷单行本；地震出版社出版《几何原本》（上部，2007 年）不全版本。此外，还有世界图书出版公司出版希思英文版《欧几里得原本十三卷书》以及中华商务进口公司的英文版。在这众多的版本中首推江西人民出版社及商务印书馆由张卜天翻译的《几何原本》，其定义、定理、公设、命题均为中英文对照读本，可以说是目前继兰纪正、朱恩宽合译后更具有信、达、雅的忠实翻译佳作。无

---

[1] 乔希民，男，生于 1960 年 4 月，陕西洛南人，理学硕士，教授。主要从事数学教育和高等数学、线性代数的教学与研究，以及非经典数理逻辑与格上拓扑学的研究。

论上述版本质量如何,但在不同程度上推广和普及了纯粹数学的逻辑公理化演绎方法,实现了徐光启《几何原本杂议》的"有三至三能",即"似至晦,实至名,故能以其明明他物至晦;似至繁,实至简,故能以其简简他物至繁;似至难,实至易,故能以其易易他物至难。易生于简,简生于明,综其妙在明而已"[1,2],还有人们期待的北京大学出版社出版的《几何原本》[3]。

特别是"勾股定理研究与赏析"的教学过程中,我较为宽泛地运用了郭先生"勾股重差理论系统"对《九章算术》中公式关系、刘徽的推导关系及补充的公式关系和郭先生研究的刘徽未指出的推导公式关系,进一步提升了学生数学学习的兴趣与灵活性,丰富了学生研究数学问题的思维方式。诚如郭先生所指出的:"《九章算术》和赵爽、刘徽都是讨论勾、股、弦三事中某二者的和、差求三事中某些元素的问题。"[4]

2 促进我在数学教育教学中倡导中国消元法与中国初等变换法

"以古为镜,可以知兴替"。我在"线性代数"教学过程中,领悟了郭先生在中国传统数学《九章算术》所取得的丰硕成果[5-8],深深感悟到其初等变换思想方法贯穿于整个"线性代数"课程中。在课堂上,首先简明扼要说明(史料引入的趣味性):我国秦汉时代成书的《九章算术》是传统中国乃至古代东方极其重要的数学典籍,在西学东渐之前一直是中国与东亚国家的数学教科书,历经千年而不衰。《九章算术》的具体作者不详,而其中某些内容可上溯至先秦时期,据此或可以认为它是经历代名家(例如刘徽、祖冲之父子、李淳风等大数学家的注释)的不断增补修订而逐渐成为现今定本的"集体作品"。全书问题共分九类,故名曰《九章算术》。现今流传的大多是在三国时期魏元帝景元四年(公元263年)刘徽为《九章算术》所作的注本。其次阐述了(原文、译文、"方程术"借助多媒体课件):《九章算术》最高的数学成就为方程术,所谓方程术就是现今的线性方程组的解法。《九章算术》首次提出一般线性方程组的初等变换求解方法。例如:"方程"章中所讨论的方程,相当于高斯消元法求解线性方程组。但其思想方法是将线性方程组化为等价的简单线性方程组要用初等变换思想方法。而初等变换思想方法在计算行列式、判断向量组的线性相关性、计算矩阵的秩、求逆矩阵、求矩阵的特征值和特征向量等体现得淋漓尽致。最后,重点而又声称:我所引用《九章算术》及刘徽注今译本,首推现中国科学院自然科学研究所的古代数学史学家郭书春先生的贡献[4-10]"。我以此为切入点,设计了适合于学生的"矩阵"概念建立、"一般线性方程组的初等变换求解方法"等教学案例,再现了另一种教学设计。反思:①《九章算术》首次提出一般线性方程组的初等变换求解方法。②《九章算术》中"方程"就是方形的表达式,与现行的增广矩阵相似。"方程术"相当于现代的加减消元法或矩阵初等变换。"直除"法为开创行列式与矩阵等概念提供了基本数学思想方法。③高斯消元法是解一般线性方程组的主要方法,但由上述问题的求解过程可得到:高斯消元法应称为"中国消元法"。④本问题既可作为"矩阵"概念建立或矩阵初等变换法的引入课[11],也可作为线性方程组的引例。⑤用《九章算术卷八》问题1替代教材中的"高斯消元法",以提升学生数学学习的兴趣与好奇心。⑥《九章算术》最高的数学成就为"方程术",所谓"方程术"就是现今的线性方程组的解法,其中第一问提出的"方程术"是全章的纲[10]。上述问题的情境创设体现了数学思想方法的再创造[10-13]。

3 引导我实现数学教育教学的中国元素

郭先生对《九章算术》及刘徽注的研究,是有史以来贡献最大和最具权威的,这是有案可稽的。正因为如此,郭先生研究的学术性形态,帮助我将其转化为数学教育教学形态。我在讲授《高等数学》中,无论是"极限"概念的引入,还是"无穷级数"的深入探讨,我合情合理地运用了郭先生的《刘徽的极限理论》及文献[10]中刘徽"割圆术",既能深刻体会到刘徽"割之弥细,所失弥少,割之又割,以至于不可割,则与圆周合体而无所失矣"的无穷小分割与极限思想,又能客观地比较道家、墨家与刘徽无穷小分割的迥异,更使学生理解了圆的面积公式刘徽证明方法,本质上是步步深入探索法,明确圆的面积不会计算,但可以计算"圆面积与圆内接正$6 \cdot 2^n$边形的面积S_n之差$S-S_n$,当n无限增大时,$S-S_n$就越来越小,割之又割,割到不可再割的地步,则这个圆内接正多边形便与圆周合为一体,其面积不再小于圆面积"[4,10]。郭先生的这一释文,启发我在"极限"概念教学的直观性,学生普遍认为:该讲授易于他们理解与掌握极限过程。同时,也为积分学与无穷级数的学习埋下了伏笔。郭先生研究成果能够将学术形态转化为数学教育形态,使我受益匪浅。

我与郭先生的忘年交,虽然得益于书信、电子邮件与微信,但我更期盼郭先生学术之树常青,愿郭先生学术精神与成就永远受益于我们和年轻一代。

参考文献

[1] 郭书春. 中国科学技术典籍通汇·数学卷(五). 郑州:河南教育出版社,1993:1151－1159.

[2] 《中华大典·数学典》编纂委员会,郭书春主编.《中华大典·数学典》郭世荣主编. 数学典·会通中西算法分典(二)[M]. 济南:山东教育出版社,2018:3.

[3] 罗俊丽,乔希民,陈淑萍. 公民科学素质"数学与逻辑基准"的核心与追求[J]. 商洛学院学报,2020,34(03):84－90.

[4] 郭书春. 古代世界数学泰斗刘徽[M]. 济南:山东科学技术出版社,2013.

[5] 郭书春汇校. 九章算术新校(上下册)[M]. 合肥:中国科学技术大学出版社,2014.

[6] 刘徽注,李淳风注释,郭书春校勘并译注. 道本周,徐义保英译并注. 九章算术[M]. 沈阳:辽宁教育出版社,2013.

[7] 郭书春译注. 九章算术译注(修订版)[M]. 上海:上海古籍出版社,2020,11.

[8] 郭书春. 汇校《九章算术》(增补本)(上下册)[M]. 沈阳:辽宁教育出版社,2004.

[9] 郭书春. 中国科学技术史·数学卷[M]. 北京:科学出版社,2010.

[10] 郭书春. 郭书春数学史自选集[M]. 济南:山东科学技术出版社,2018.

[11] 乔希民. 发现教学法在线性代数课堂教学中的实施策略[J]. 贵阳学院学报(自然科学版),201611,(2):62－65.

[12] 李超,乔希民,罗俊丽. 数学思想方法视阈下线性代数课堂教学的实践与探索(Ⅰ)[J]. 渭南师范学院学报,2017,32(06):25－29.

[13] 乔希民. 数学思想方法视阈下线性代数课堂教学的中国元素(Ⅱ)[J]. 待发表.

学为师表言身教 奖掖后学为人梯

徐传胜 （临沂大学数学与统计学院）

晚生谨以此文祝贺著作等身、德高望重的郭书春先生八十寿辰。

虽然郭书春的名字早已是如雷贯耳，但我在不惑之年方走进数学史领域，考取西北大学博士研究生，故而直到 2007 年 5 月初在河北师范大学举办的"第二届数学史与数学教育会议"上，才第一次见到郭先生。当时赵继伟博士介绍我们认识，说大家都是山东老乡。能够和郭先生认识交流，实感荣幸。"老乡见老乡，笑得嘎嘎响。"由于时间关系，当时只与先生寒暄几句，并未深入交谈，然而郭老的严谨治学精神和我们山东人的醇厚淳朴性格给我留下了深刻印象。作为晚辈的我，对数学史界前辈除了尊敬和仰慕之情外，不敢奢望能和他合影留念，更不敢想能够得到其签名的宏著，然而，和郭老师的进一步交流了解，完全打消了我的这些顾虑。

1　求索不止励后生

实际上，真正和郭先生交流是 2011 年 5 月初在华东师范大学举办的"第四届数学史与数学教育会议"上。因老乡亲情关系，在会议休息时间，我鼓起勇气向先生请教了一些问题，没想到他笑脸相迎，皆一一给予详尽地诠释，破解了一些困扰我多年学习和生活的问题。先生平易近人、风趣幽默，我的胆怯和顾虑逐渐消去，与先生内心的距离也越来越近了。

当时我们学校的主要领导拟把数学专业"边缘化"，数学史更是不屑一顾。因而我想邀请一些数学史前辈前来做学术报告，展示数学史的卓越功能，力图改变一些领导的决策和管理理念。基于此，我斗胆邀请郭先生来临沂讲学，没想到先生竟然毫不迟疑地答应下来。在此次与郭先生深入接触后，我们之间的交流便多了起来。有时通过电子邮件，有时通过短信，有时通过电话交流。无论什么形式，郭先生一定会在第一时间回复，而且语气很是谦虚，这让晚辈实在有点受宠若惊。

先生对我的称谓由"传胜博士"到"传胜教授"再到"传胜"，愈发亲切了。每每读到先生的来信，皆受益匪浅，学习了科学知识的同时又给予我很大的精神鼓励。仅从 2018 年 6 月的信中，就可以看到先生对我的倍加关心，亦可看到郭先生实事求是的治学风格，虚怀若谷的高尚情操，不醉古人的进取精神和寄望后学的博大胸怀。

> 传胜：你好！
> 看到你身体在康复，安甚！我的法国学生林力娜工作起来不要命，我一直对她说，近年也常对郭金海说："延长自己的工作年龄比拼几天把身体搞垮对数学史的贡献要大得多。"切切！
> 我刚与老伴到枣庄学院参加了墨学与自然国学高端论坛会。会议主持者邀请了几次，但对是不是参加我一直犹豫。前不久在呼和浩特召开的《中国珠算发展史》审稿会上听说台儿庄有个中华珠算博物馆，才决心去。这个博物馆气魄不小，设计者曾获华东地区珠算比赛第一名，当然，中国传统数学有部分欠缺或有不准确之处。我也不客气，直率地谈了我的意见，整整半天。
> 下午博物馆安排我们游览了台儿庄，特别是台儿庄战役纪念馆。台儿庄真不错，值得一游。
> 来去匆匆，只三天，在枣庄学院实际上只一天，数学院没有人与会，我也没有与他们联系，与会者搞数学与数学史的不多。
> 我组织全国 30 余位同仁忙了十几年的《中华大典·数学典》已印出样书，即将批量印刷，

共4个分典,9册,1 450余万字,今奉上书影。今后不会像前几年那样忙了。《郭书春数学史自选集》因全力投入《数学典》推迟了几年,不久即可面世。也算先公后私吧,哈哈!

中国科学院将我和林力娜合作的中法对照《九章算术》推荐到"改革开放40周年引才引智成果展览",今奉上展览照片及我写的一篇感想,其中的一张照片你可以看到堂堂中国科学院的一个研究所当时多么破烂!

夏安!

郭书春上 2018.6.14

信中字里行间无不流露着先生对晚辈的关爱和关怀,展示着先生对数学史的执着追求,以及对科学事实一丝不苟的态度。更让我感动的是,先生年近八旬,却仍然忙碌于学术创作,丝毫没有倦怠之意,作为晚辈,实在是汗颜。

2 刘徽家乡论刘徽

《九章算术》应是郭先生一生的挚爱和珍爱之宝,在其眼中刘徽是中国古代最伟大数学家。在"学习强国"相关题目中,赞刘徽是中国的欧几里得和中国数学史上的牛顿,目前应是中国数学家的最高荣誉,能获此殊荣主要归功于刘徽对《九章算术》的注释。《九章算术》成书于公元1世纪,是古代中国乃至东方第一部自成体系的数学著述,汇集了中国先秦至汉代的数学成就,是中国数学体系确立与数学特色形成的核心标志。而刘徽的《九章算术》注释包含了许多数学创新思想,如割圆术和体积理论等,其完全可看成是独立的数学思想体系。

早在20世纪80年代,郭先生对刘徽《九章算术注》的研究就有所突破。在《九章算术》的编纂,刘徽《九章算术注》的结构、成就,刘徽的数学体系、逻辑思想渊源、时代背景等研究方面做出了突出贡献。刘徽是哪里人氏这个历史性问题自然会是学界的关注焦点之一。郭先生在查阅《宋史·礼志》《汉书·地理志》《汉书·王子侯表》《元丰·九域志》《金史·地理志》等大量原始资料的基础上,经过详尽考察和论证,考证出刘徽是山东邹平人,这是一个了不起的发现。

又鉴于此,2013年6月下旬,郭先生联合邹平县委县政府举办了纪念"刘徽注《九章算术》1750周年国际学术研讨会"。由于当时邹平县交通还不是很发达,不少学者不愿参加这个会议。郭先生就一一打电话,恳请大家克服困难前来参加会议,并解释该学术会议的重要性。早在2011年,郭先生就告知我拟举办纪念刘徽的学术会议,并邀请参加。我当然大力支持郭先生筹办这个会议,并问先生是否需要帮忙,定鼎力相助。在邹平会议召开前一周,郭先生又给我打电话落实,言语之间充满了期待。

说实话,那时临沂市到邹平县只有一班汽车,需要行程七八个小时,我的确有些畏难情绪,但无论如何不能辜负郭先生的一片盛情。同时向会议提交了一篇论文:《欧几里得》《几何原本》与刘徽注《九章算术》。拙文比较了世界数学两大思想体系:《原本》创立的逻辑演绎体系和《九章算术》创立的机械化算法体系。这篇论文的一些观点虽然过于浅薄,但郭先生还是给予了鼓励。

刚一走进会议举办地点,我就看到了郭先生忙碌的身影,他忙前跑后地接待参会人员,与会议组织者进行沟通,指挥工作人员张贴指示标志,等等。看到我的到来,郭先生立刻笑容满面地走来和我握手寒暄。我说:"您老不要太劳累了,有些事情放手让年轻人去干。"郭老回应道:"举办会议没有小事,不能有一点疏忽,力求让各方都要满意。"读书期间我曾帮着导师筹办了几次学术会议,深知其中的艰辛和繁杂。年逾七旬的郭老为之付出了多少劳动可想而知。

按照惯例,参加类似学术会议需要参会者自己缴纳会务费和住宿费,可郭先生说这些都给免了。而且住宿全是单间,这让参会学者感到了温馨和温暖,背后一定少不了郭先生的极力斡旋和辛勤努力。邹平县委县政府很是重视这个会议,选派一名领导专门负责会务工作,因而会议食宿条件让人感到非常满意。学者们在浓厚的学术气氛中,展开了学术探讨,郭先生的主旨报告更是把会议推向了高潮。这次会议邀请了一些国际权威学者和港澳台学者,足见郭先生的国际地位和学术影响。邹平会议达到或超过整个预期的效果,并给我们留下了解深刻印象。直至2021年,学者们还谈论起该会议,一致认为,其为中国古代数学史研究的一个里程碑。让我非常高兴的是,恩师曲安京教授也不辞劳苦地从西安赶来参加这次会议。曲老师当时是数学史理事会会长。

3 羲之故里唱《九章》

2015年7月下旬,临沂大学成立"刘徽应用数学研究中心",拟请郭先生前来揭牌并做主题报告,先生欣然答应前来沂蒙革命老区。我赶快给先生和师母订购好飞机票,只是临近会议举行日期郭先生身体欠佳未能成行。为了弥补缺憾,先生委派徐泽林教授连夜从上海赶来,这种责任心和担当感,实让我感动不已(徐泽林教授的报告很精彩,在当时引起不少反响。那时学校的高尔夫球场尚在使用之中,闲暇之余我们先和徐教授在训练场地练了一会打球,后又坐旅游观光小车绕球场转了一圈。据说是标准的18杆高尔夫场地,占地3 000亩。鉴于浪费土地资源,原场地现已改为中央绿地)。

转眼到了2017年春节,我庆幸自己战胜了病魔,因而再次邀请郭先生来学校讲学。一番沟通之后,先生确定4月下旬来临沂,这让我激动不已,连忙告知学校领导、订购机票和安排食宿。4月24—30日郭先生拨冗莅临沂蒙山革命老区,来临沂大学讲学。期间我和郭先生进行了解广泛的交流,先生平易近人的大家风范,高屋建瓴的科学眼光,实事求是的治学精神都给我留下了解深刻印象。

3.1 参观羲之故居

4月24日中午,郭先生和师母乘机抵达临沂市。原本我应去机场迎接,但因身体尚在恢复之中,加之23日还在发高烧,就只好委派他人去机场欢迎,我在宾馆等候。"国际交流中心"就在校园里面,距离数学学院2千米,距离我家1千米。其内设有宾馆和零点餐厅,卫生条件还不错,因此就把郭先生夫妇安排在这里住宿。

见到郭先生与师母后,看到二老身体健康、神采奕奕,我很是高兴和开心,大有他乡遇故知之感。他们见我消瘦了很多就问了个原委,我告知是由于腹部经历了一个大手术。当时体重已比原来减轻了30多斤,而且身体免疫力降低、极度羸弱,稍有不慎就会引起高烧。说来也是神奇,郭先生在临沂的那几天,我感觉心旷神怡,也没有出现发烧症状,或许这就是精神力量的效果吧!

当天下午,我本打算让二老好好休息一下,可老两口都说不累,一定让我安排一个活动。当时市区内有两个主要景点:竹简墓(孙子兵法出土)和王羲之故居。老人说那就参观市区内的王羲之故居吧!王羲之故居始建于晋代琅琊郡境内,是书圣王羲之出生并生活过的地方,内有洗砚池(传说是王羲之涮洗毛笔的水池,呈现着淡淡的墨色)、普照寺、集柳碑、晒书台、王右军祠、左公祠、四宝台、五贤祠、琅琊书院等历史古迹。其中的"普照夕阳"曾经作为古代"琅琊八景"之首名扬九州。1989年,临沂市政府对其修缮,1990年正式对外开放,2003年完成拓建。游人来此,可观美景,赏书法,思前贤。(曲安京教授2003年11月参观过,当时故居尚在修缮之中)那天下午风力还是较大,我当时几乎不敢见风,只好委派他人和郭先生一起去,并嘱咐一定要找个讲解员(这是和邓明立教授学的,一些人文景观无人讲解,游人就不知其中奥妙)。共进晚餐时,郭先生提起对"书圣"故居的一些看法,并赞誉临沂养育了"兵圣""智圣""算圣""宗圣"和"书圣"等一代风流人物。

3.2 做学术报告

4月25日早餐后,我首先陪同郭先生游览了校园,而后来到理学院办公区。学院门前的电子屏幕滚动闪现着"热烈欢迎中国科学院郭书春教授来数学与统计学院讲学"的红色大字。先生看了面带微笑,师母也很高兴,并在大门前和我留影纪念。数学与统计学院的院领导知道先生德高望重,对郭先生夫妇甚是尊重,热情接待了他们,并简要介绍了学院有关情况。

10点左右,我和郭先生移步做报告的大教室,刚一进门就响起雷鸣般的掌声。教室内座无虚席,走廊里也站满了人。听众主要是数学与应用数学专业、信息与计算科学专业和化学化工学院专业大一的学生,以及部分数学学院和历史文化的年轻教师。

报告会由江兆林院长主持,他首先介绍了郭先生的研究成果和科学成就,而后盛情邀请先生做学术报告。在热烈的掌声中,郭先生走上讲台向听众致谢,开始作题为"《九章算术》和中国古代最伟大数学家刘徽"的报告。

报告伊始,郭先生就从听众角度提出问题而导入正题"看了这个标题,大家可能会感到奇怪:中国古代最伟大的数学家不是祖冲之吗?怎么会是刘徽呢?刘徽是谁呢?"这一下就抓住了听众的注意力,大家都屏住呼吸静听诠释。

看着大家的期待目光,郭先生道:"中国科学院系统科学研究所在部分同志倡导下,于1985年10月举办了以刘徽命名的数学讨论班。原拟为祖冲之讨论班,最后确定为刘徽讨论班。中国科学院院士吴文俊先生就此做了说明,他认为,刘徽无可争议地是我国传统数学中唯一的代表人物。"

郭先生又解释道:"祖冲之确实是伟大的数学家,应该说,他的数学水平不会低于刘徽。但是他的数学著作《缀术》(一作《缀述》)由于隋唐算学馆'学官莫能究其深奥,是故废而不理',遂失传。因此,他的全部数学贡献,我们至今无法了解。我们现在仅知道他的两项确切成就:一是将圆周率精确到8位有效数字,二是与他儿子祖暅完成的球体体积公式的推导。"

紧接着郭先生点明了主题,"而这两项都是刘徽在《九章算术注》中为其提出方法或建立理论基础的。从数学的角度而言,这当然比祖冲之的贡献更重要。刘徽以演绎逻辑为主要方法全面证明了《九章算术》的算法,建立了中国传统数学的理论体系。最值得称道的是,他在世界数学史上第一次将无穷小分割方法和极限思想用于数学证明。刘徽逻辑之严谨,所达到的高度,在中国古代也无居其右者。"

看到大家都津津有味地听着,郭先生趁热打铁,展开了他报告的主要内容,其分为五大部分:《九章算术》——中国传统数学框架的确立;刘徽及其《九章算术注》《海岛算经》;算之纲纪——率;割圆术;刘徽原理和刘徽的体积理论。

五部分内容层次清晰、环环相扣,详尽介绍和分析了《九章算术》的数学贡献及其重要历史意义,探究了刘徽对中国古代数学所做卓越贡献及历史影响,其中不乏先生的一些独到见解,令人耳目一新:《九章算术》的成书,标志着中国取代古希腊成为世界数学研究的重心,也标志着世界数学从研究空间形式为主,转变为以研究数量关系为主,标志着数学机械化算法体系取代数学公理化演绎体系成为世界数学发展中的主流。这样的结论极大增加了听众的文化自信感和民族自豪感。

整场报告深入浅出,引人入胜,会场不时发出会意的笑声和掌声。郭先生最后总结道:《九章算术》是以归纳逻辑为基础的,刘徽《九章算术注》是以演绎逻辑为基础的。他的注释没有任何逻辑矛盾而不能自洽的地方,可见他的逻辑水平之高。报告首尾呼应,画龙点睛之语,把报告会推向了高潮,引发了经久不息的掌声。

虽然我曾经听过先生的报告,但这一次报告给我的印象很深刻。年逾七旬的古稀老人,两个小时的报告先生竟然一直站着讲授。由于听众主要是正在选修我课程的学生,我要求他们回去认真讨论郭先生的报告,并就《九章算术》或者刘徽科学成就写一篇小论文。"大家就是大家,站得高看得远,立意新功夫深",参会者无不赞誉郭先生的敬业精神和渊博的知识,期盼我再次邀请郭先生做报告。从小论文的写作情况来看,应是历届学生中所写内容最有见解的一次。有几个学生深受郭先生的影响,报考了数学史专业硕士研究生。而有几个学生尝试把数学史有机融入课堂教学,荣获"山东省师范技能从业大赛一等奖"或"二等奖"。

3.3 参加学术沙龙

4月26日上午是我所组建的教学团队沙龙活动,团队冠名为"魅力数学",成员多为年轻博士和骨干教师。学校宣传部曾多次采访,并在校报报道团队有关事迹和成绩。

郭先生受邀欣然参加了团队活动。他首先用自己的人生经历告诫大家,一定要珍惜时间,刻苦学习、努力拼搏,并在传承的基础上不断创新。他说,西方学术界对中国古代数学有许多偏见,这些偏见严重影响了中国学术界。郭先生认为,除少数欧洲中心论者和民族虚无主义者外,绝大多数人是因为看不到或看不懂中国古代数学著作而接受了错误的信息。而让西方人了解中国古代数学最好的办法是让他们认识《九章算术》及其刘徽注。

关于古代数学家的造像,郭先生也有着独到见解。蒋兆和先生大概是现代中国最先创作古代科学家造像的,他在20世纪50年代创作的张衡、祖冲之、僧一行、李时珍等画像已经家喻户晓,影响可谓巨

大。郭先生说,作为艺术创作,根据历史资料,为历史名人造像,是无可厚非的,甚至是应该提倡的。在一些普及读物中,在一些展览中,使用一些不与历史事实相悖的造像,给人以形象的提示,虽然印象深刻,也常会收到事半功倍的效果。事实上,蒋兆和先生画的张衡、祖冲之、僧一行、李时珍等中国古代四大科学家,对普及古代科学知识,激发人们的爱国主义感情,配合1956年向科学进军的运动,发挥了十分重大的作用。我本人20世纪50年代正在青岛一中学习,对此深有体会。

然而郭先生认为,蒋兆和的四大科学家画像年龄都偏大,大概都五六十岁。古今中外的大科学家中固然有大器晚成者,但毕竟是少数,多数科学家的最杰出的科学贡献都是在年轻时做出的,数学家尤其如此。张衡、祖冲之、僧一行的数学、天文的重大创造都是30岁前后完成的。张衡担任太史令才37岁,祖冲之完成《大明历》才33岁,僧一行去世时也不过44岁。蒋兆和创作的画像显然拔高了古代科学家的年龄,不利于鼓励青年和中小学学生少年立志,向科学高峰攀登。

艺术家创作古代科学家的造像,应该学习点历史知识,特别是科学史知识,避免画出有悖于历史常识的作品。否则谬种流传,贻害读者,特别是广大青少年。科学史工作者应该注意向社会,特别是广大教师和青少年普及准确的科学史知识。

为何西方科学家的造像却多为年轻人,是他们年轻有为还是初生牛犊不怕虎。郭先生的话让我们深思。我们的科普工作如何展开和进行,已是迫在眉睫需要研究与解决的事情。

对于古文翻译,郭先生强调翻译必须要准确,否则就会贻笑大方。他举例说明:秦九韶《数书九章·自序》中有句话是"苍姬井之,仁政攸在。"苍,苍神。《春秋元命包》:"殷时五星聚于房,房者苍神之精,周据而兴。"周人姬姓,苍姬指周代。井之,实行井田制,是儒家仁政思想的体现。有人将"苍姬井之"翻译成"一位白发苍苍的老太太在井边打水",全错不通。

榜样的力量是无限的,郭先生的谈话让参会者受益匪浅。其"知其然"又要"知其所以然",更要"知其所以必然"学术探索精神,让我们醍醐灌顶、豁然开朗;其老骥伏枥、志在千里的耕耘不辍的人生价值观,震撼着在场的每一个人,激励着我们砥砺奋进、勇往直前;先生语重心长地谆谆教诲,更是激发了我们的内动力,试做不断开拓疆域的老黄牛。2017年11月我们的"魅力数学"教学团队被评为"山东省黄大年式教学团队",是临沂大学唯一获此殊荣的教学团队。这其中也有着郭先生的一份功劳。

3.4 看望老同学

在临沂,郭先生还惦挂着两个人:张海川和靖玉树。前者是郭先生的山东大学同窗,后者原在临沂珠算学会,已退休多年。由于我的孤陋寡闻,后者我一直未能取得联系。而前者是原临沂教育学院书记,现就住在我楼下,几乎天天见面,然而似乎我也多日未见到张书记了。一问方知,张书记因病住进了疗养院。郭先生好不容易来临沂一次,一定要让他们老同学见上一面。

与张书记取得联系后,知道其身体已基本康复,告知郭先生欲看望之迫切心情,张书记内心也很激动,约定4月27日上午去疗养院。

4月27日早餐后,我购买了一束鲜花,郭先生在路上又买了一些水果,我们一同赶往汤头疗养院。其坐落在临沂市北20公里处风景秀丽的温泉古镇,这里盛产天然温泉,且历史悠久、水质极佳。经权威部门鉴定,汤头温泉内含钾、钠、钙、镁、锶、氡和硫化氢等29种矿物质与微量元素,对人体有祛痛化瘀、舒筋活络、强身健体、美容保健之奇效,素有"神水妙汤""全国四大甲级温泉之首"的美誉,相传孔子、秦始皇就来此巡游沐浴(后我也几次来这里疗养,每天泡泡温泉,有助于消化吸收,尤其适合我)。

因信息交流不方便,郭先生和张书记大学毕业后,40多年就没有见过面。当他们双手握在一起时,眼睛里都含着泪花。很快四位老人就亲切交谈起来,两位夫人谈着家长里短,儿女情长。郭先生则介绍了自己大学毕业后的人生之旅。此时张书记腿痛病症已经治疗康复,可能与泡温泉有着一定关系。他原来在临沂二中工作,被评为"特级教师",后任临沂市副市长,退休前担任临沂教育学院书记。

同郭先生一样,张书记也是工作勤奋,为人诚实,深受群众爱戴。有一次家里来电话,张书记竟亲自到我家通知。自家小院也被他打理得井井有条,栽种着一些花草树木。郭先生在我家阳台上,俯首看到了张书记的小院子。水池、凉棚、菜地、花朵和树木等都是那样和谐有序,连连赞叹不已。

郭先生和张书记聊起了他们的大学生活,回忆着每位老师和同学,虽说今日廉颇老矣,但那时恰同学少年,风华正茂,书生意气,激情燃烧。听着两位老者的人生回忆和感悟,看着他们脸上洋溢着的幸福笑容,我就像一个小孩子静静地在一旁欣赏着这一切。听君一席话,胜读十年书。两位前辈的交谈,让我进一步感悟到人生道路的艰辛和幸福。人生弯弯曲曲水,世事重重叠叠山。无论是搞科研、当教师还是管理工作;每一条通往幸福美景的大道,都充满着荆棘和坎坷;每一条通向理想之巅的途径,都充满了艰辛和汗水。

老先生们就这样聊着,笑着,很快就到了午餐时间。张书记安排我们一行在观唐宾馆用餐,这是汤头镇最好的酒店。由于其特殊的地理位置,该酒店几乎天天爆满。坐在主宾位置的郭先生很是高兴,举起酒杯感谢张书记一家的盛情款待。饭菜很是丰盛,规格也很高,大多适合老年人享用。这是张书记之子特别为老人点的菜。听说我们下午拟去竹泉村参观,他立刻拿起电话联系沂南朋友王新宇接待我们。这让我和郭先生更是感谢不已。

3.5 参观中国十大最美乡村

竹泉村是山东省第一个系统开发的古村落旅游区,具有竹林、泉水和沂蒙特色民俗文化。它背倚玉皇山,中有石龙山,左有凤凰岭,右有香山河,前有千顷田,是中国传统的风水宝地。近年成为旅游盛景,节假日简直就是游人如织。

王新宇早在沂南界等着我们。寒暄之后,他把我们带进了中国北方难得一见的桃花源式的自然生态环境。竹子是竹泉村的灵魂,为这个北国村落增添了勃勃生机和文化气韵。文人墨客喜爱竹子,沂南百姓亦爱竹之灵性。许是这片土地本就有着某种天地精华,养育了谦恭大度、宁静致远、足智多谋的智圣诸葛亮,又培育了善于天文观察、编撰《干象历》和奠定珠算理论的算圣刘洪。

村中有一清泉,泉边多竹,名曰竹泉。若竹是竹泉村的灵魂,泉则是竹泉村的生命。竹子因泉而生,泉水因竹子而妩媚灵动。泉水四季恒温,富含人体必需的十余种微量元素,经鉴定符合国家饮用天然矿泉水标准。村里百姓常年饮用此水,增强自身免疫力,延年益寿、不染恶疾。郭先生在竹泉旁边,饶有兴致地拿起长长的水舀子,品尝着这清甜的泉水。

我们沿着溪水追本溯源,泉水沿着茅屋的门前舍后流过,冷冰冰的石壁和着泉水也不那么生硬了。不论是青石小路,还是苍翠竹林,或者茅屋小舍都在顷刻间与这泉水融为一体。就这样,我和郭先生夫妇走着,看着,听着,聊着,欣赏着周围的一切自然美景。远离城市的喧嚣噪声,尽情呼吸着沁人心扉的富氧空气,静静听着泉水汩汩流淌,徜徉于滴翠的竹林间,仿佛置身于人间仙境一般,一切烦恼忧愁全消失得无影无踪。

山美不如竹美,竹美不如泉美,泉美不如村美,村美不如人美。竹泉村有着厚重的历史文化积淀,蕴含着丰富的沂蒙文化和强大的生命力,然而沂南人的淳朴好客更是给我们留下了深刻印象。我原想回临沂吃晚饭,可王新宇热情挽留,实际上在我们游玩之际,他已安排好晚餐,不是在酒楼饭店而就在竹泉村的农家小院。鱼是刚刚在泉水捞起的活鱼,鸡是在竹林吃虫长大的小公鸡,小米是刚刚碾好的(我想买一些带回家,王新宇已经准备好了,给我和郭先生各一份)。看到这样的原生态绿色有机美食,我们也就不好再推辞了,在翠绿竹林旁,听着潺潺流水和鸟儿欢快歌声,美美地享用着大自然带给我们的这一切。

3.6 参观天宇自然博物馆

大自然的遗存是人类开启自然文明的钥匙,山东省天宇自然博物馆以其丰富的馆藏,为研究、探索者提供了科研平台,为求知、求识者敞开了博大胸怀,为一切热爱自然、珍视生命的人们送上了通达自然科学知识之门。天宇自然博物馆位于平邑县城,总投资高达3亿元,陈列面积2.8万平方米,应是世界上目前最大的自然地质博物馆。

因天宇自然博物馆馆长郑晓廷被聘为临沂大学古生物研究所教授,来校讲学专家大多都去博物馆参观。我曾陪同西北大学屈长征教授、东华大学徐泽林教授参观学习,馆内藏品着实让人震撼和惊叹,难怪被誉为"一部描绘自然生命的万卷书"。因此,陪同郭先生参观该馆是我早就计划好的行程。

4月28日上午九点左右,我和夫人陪同郭先生夫妇来到了天宇自然博物馆。张国庆书记已安排好学生魏敏等待我们。他为我们购买了门票,聘请了讲解员。在讲解员的引导下,我们一行五人进入了展厅。馆藏展品主要以矿物标本和古生物化石为主。9个矿物标本展厅内,收藏有世界各地的珍奇标本上万件。

在这里,我们看到了"新疆碧玺",其集天地精华于一体,流光溢彩,堪称世界一绝,2006年被欧洲《矿物宝石标本》杂志评为"年度十佳宝石"。而产于新疆奇台的硅化木长达38米,为世界之最,2007年载入吉尼斯世界纪录(屈长征教授看到,连连称赞,因西北大学地质学院门口有一段硅化木比这个小多了)。在世界上最大石膏标本展厅内,各种透明石膏晶莹剔透,琳琅满目;而进入世界上最大钟乳石展厅,宛若走进了梦幻世界,令人遐想无限。

天宇自然博物馆因保存有1 106件较完整个体的恐龙化石,被吉尼斯世界纪录英国总部认定为"世界上最大的恐龙博物馆"。博物馆珍藏的宝贝真不少,让我们震撼的还有:产自乌拉圭的紫水晶洞高3.3米,重3.7吨,属世界之最;产于中国水晶之乡(江苏东海)重3.9吨的水晶单晶体,为亚洲之最;重达338.6克拉的金刚石,是我国有史记载的特大金刚石,比中国之最的"常林钻石"(重158.78克拉)还重179.82克拉,呈金刚光泽,宝光熠熠。一件件珍品,令人目不暇接,当时徐泽林教授拍照这些珍品都用完了手机内存。郭先生夫妇驻足观赏,不时发出啧啧赞叹声。

化石标本不仅仅是用来收藏,也是考古研究的科学依据。2014年4月14日,Plos One发表了郑晓廷研究团队的研究成果,他们发现了距今1亿2千万年的早白垩世时期的原始鸟类已经具有了先进的消化系统。该研究基于10件保存精美完整的中生代燕鸟新化石标本,其保存了燕鸟食性相关信息。研究发现,作为现代鸟类祖先的燕鸟,其消化系统在各方面都极为先进。燕鸟的食物是鱼类,燕鸟嘴里长有许多尖而弯曲的牙齿,但这些牙齿并非用来咀嚼食物,而只是用于捕捉猎物。

午餐后,我们又参观了费县奇石阵。大自然的鬼斧神工,让一块块巨石呈现着各种各样的形状,或为走兽,或为飞禽,或为人物。置身其中犹如进入了另一个世界,让人心旷神怡、思绪万千。郭先生的身体真棒,穿行于石阵之中,一点也没有感觉到累。

原来还打算去沂水大峡谷看看,可郭先生说侄子给定好了4月29日回胶东的火车票,只好作罢。

29日午餐后,我恋恋不舍地把郭先生夫妇送到临沂北站。从4月24日起至29日,我一直陪着郭先生。原来担心自己可能体力不支,但老先生的精气神深深激励着我,因而这几天既没有感到身体疲乏,更没有引发高烧症状。一日为师终身为父。郭先生比家父小两岁,我把他看作父辈一样的亲人,他对我也犹如家人一般。正是老先生对晚辈的关爱,给了我战胜病魔的勇气,给了我击败困难的意志,给了我继续前行的无尽力量。

4 余论

乡愁是一种情怀,是一种幸福。郭先生深深眷恋着齐鲁大地,深深爱着家乡人民。像刘洪、刘徽、何承天一样,追求卓越、实事求是、无私奉献,像王羲之、诸葛亮那样,淡泊名利、以勤补拙、志在千里,秉承着山东坦坦荡荡、光明磊落、诚实可靠的做人风范。郭先生八十大寿,恰逢辛丑牛年,老先生不正是我们身旁的老黄牛、拓荒牛和孺子牛吗!此乃:

春日初暖,明月夜,思绪萦绕。为师表,呕心沥血,付与芳草。四季辛劳暮与早,正本清源知多少?血和汗,看人才风貌,全知晓。爱深沉,花繁叶茂。鬓为霜,人自豪。《九章》之歌高唱,余音袅袅。滔滔长江浪推浪,芳誉留下声声好!齐努力,建神州伟业,丹心照。

铭记教诲,感念师恩

傅海伦　（山东师范大学数学与统计学院）

2021年8月26日(农历七月十九日),是恩师郭书春先生八十大寿的喜庆日。在这个特殊的日子里,真诚为恩师恭祝上寿,祝福老师,松鹤同春,福乐绵绵!同时也借此机会,追忆过去与老师相处的美好岁月,共叙师生情谊,铭记教诲,感念师恩!

一、感谢老师引领,步入中国数学史研究领域

我是1995年从湖南师范大学硕士毕业后直接考入中国科学院自然科学史研究所的。很荣幸我最终能入郭门,成为郭老师的学生。其实,当时我能到所里学习,还是费了一些周折的,这主要涉及与鲁东大学(当时是烟台师范学院)的委培事宜。考博之际,我的工作去向已定,关系档案已经转入鲁东大学。为此,郭老师和时任研究所副所长的王渝生老师专程从北京赴鲁东大学,与此同时,我也从湖南师范大学赶到鲁东大学。经三方共同商定后,我才如愿以偿。

读博后,郭老师对我的要求也极为严格。老师较早地领我进入数学史的学术领域,让我开始学习并介入中国数学史前沿问题的相关研究。从郭老师的言传身教中,我开始真正学习和研读中国数学史著作,也从那时开始真正认识李、钱二老的工作。更为重要的是,郭老师引领我认真学习、全面认识当时《九章算术》校勘与刘徽注的有关研究。我从对比研究中体会到了郭老师在此方面的卓著成果,之后越来越认识到老师对中国数学史研究的巨大贡献,特别是对《九章算术》校勘与刘徽注研究的批判、继承、发展与创新,从1990年辽宁教育出版社的汇校本到1998年的译注本,再到2004年台湾地区九章出版社的汇校增补版,近又从2009年上海古籍出版社的译注本,再到2014年中国科学技术大学出版社的新校本(上、下册),绵延不断,无人能及。其次,郭老师对《算经十书》的校点、历代版本考证及其对后世的影响,从浩瀚的历史文献中,抽丝剥茧,正本清源,可谓功夫极致,堪称楷模。再次,郭老师对中国传统数学从祖冲之到宋元五大数学家的重新认识和全面剖析,也是独树一帜,影响深远。记得我多次走进老师的家门,每次看到老师的书房、桌头、案边那一摞摞的书卷、稿件,对我就是一个极大的鼓舞!学习研究中国数学史,首先要看相当多的中国历史文献和经典,古文对我来说就是极大的挑战。特别是在我研习《九章算术》校勘与刘徽注的过程中,当时都遇到了不少古文生僻字以及古天文历算的专有名词,老师除了给我提供工具书之外,还亲自教我训诂、辨识、释义,帮我不断提高这方面的能力。

读博三年来,得到老师全面的指导、教诲和帮助。读博第一年是在中关村的中国科学院研究生院集中学习,完成学习任务后,第二年回到位于朝内大街的自然科学史研究所,郭老师给开了相关的课程,老师亲自授课,使我在听课学习过程中,学会不少研究方法。我也与别的老师和同学参与郭老师主编的《李俨钱宝琮科学史全集》的编纂工作,受益匪浅。在学习过程中,每每遇到困难,除了向老师请教之外,还时常向时任所长的刘钝老师,以及王渝生、陈久金、何绍庚、韩琦、孙小纯等老师们求教。记得曾与汪晓勤等室友专程到家里拜访过何绍庚老师、刘钝老师。三年来,尤其得到了师姐田淼、师兄邹大海的诸多指导与帮助。很难忘,当时的信息化条件还不好,电脑资源短缺,二楼研究室的电脑成了大家可以利用的最好的研究工具,师姐、师兄就把仅有的可以操作的电脑让给我使用,帮助我学习和研究文献。后来又有幸与乌云其其格、段跃勇、郭金海等师弟、师妹相识、相知,成为学友。真可谓郭门师徒,学业承继,薪火相传。

在此应特别感谢已故的吴文俊院士。1996年,在老师的科研经费捉襟见肘、我的科研经费尚无着落之时,吴先生雪中送炭,专门拨给老师2000元,用来资助我完成博士论文,使我如期完成了学业和毕业论文。为了感谢吴先生的关爱,老师也让我较早地关注数学机械化的研究,让我全面认识和挖掘中国

传统数学的机械化思想及其算法的意义,最后指导我的博士论文题目就定为"中国传统数学机械化思想"。在论文写作过程中,郭老师曾带我到吴先生家里向先生求教,吴先生给予了宝贵指导意见和建议,后来我的博士论文顺利通过答辩。在此论文的基础上,又经过几年的修改、补充、加工和提升,《传统文化与数学机械化》由科学出版社在 2003 年出版。郭老师还欣然作序,称"傅海伦将其博士论文增补为《传统文化与数学机械化》出版,是一件有意义的事"。

2016 年 4 月 13 日,师徒三人参加所里的活动(去西陵)合影

1998 年 6 月,参加我的博士毕业论文答辩的老师和部分同学合影

1998 年 6 月,郭老师与专程来参加我博士论文答辩的李迪老师合影

二、不忘恩师教诲,认真从事数学史与数学教育相结合的工作

1998 年从中国科学院科学史研究所如期毕业后,作为人才引进,入职山东师范大学数学系,从事数学教育工作,服务于山东地方教育。其实,在我读博期间,时任山东师范大学数学系的有关领导就了解到我在所里读数学史方向,即将博士毕业,而我的硕士专业研究方向是数学课程与教学论,这正好与山

东师范大学的数学教育专业十分契合,而当时系里也更亟需这方面的专业导师,所以特别希望我能回来工作。由于当时我的工作关系已属于鲁东大学(在职读博期间,我也曾于1997年回鲁东大学数学系工作了近一年时间),经过多方努力,山东师范大学领导出面,把我的档案关系从鲁东大学转入山东师范大学,我就正式入职山东师范大学,主要从事数学课程与教学论专业的建设、人才培养以及教育硕士专业学位在职研究生的培养与教学工作。繁重的工作之余,我不忘老师教诲,继续从事数学史研究,并将数学史的研究成果运用于课堂教学之中,与数学教育进行结合。先后主持并完成了全国教育科学"十五"规划课题——"数学史在数学教育中的应用研究(EHA010449,被列为教育部青年专项课题研究课题)、全国教育科学"十二五"规划课题——数学史应用于数学教育的方法论研究(DHA130274,教育部重点课题)。近年来,又主持完成了山东省高等学校人文社会科学研究重点课题——数学文化的拓展与应用研究(J17RA233)和2018年度山东省社会科学规划研究专项:齐鲁数学文化的整理、普及与应用研究(18CKPJ01)。还相继出版了《数学·科学与文化的殿堂》(陕西科学技术出版社,2004年)、《中外数学史概论》(科学出版社,2007年)。在研究论文方面,一方面致力于自己感兴趣的数学史专题进行研究,先后在《自然辩证法研究》《自然辩证法通讯》《自然杂志》《数学传播(台湾地区)》《科学技术与辩证法》等刊物上发表《数学机械化思想的产生和发展》《从民族文化传统看我国古算机械化的价值取向》《从儒学"经世致用"看我国与古算数学机械化的特征与价值》《中国传统数学的构造性思维及其现代意义》《定理机器证明思想的产生与发展》《中国传统数学机械化思想》《中国传统代数思想的文化特征》《论贾宪的数学机械化思想》《算筹、算盘与计算机》等论文。特别值得一提的是,受郭老师对《算经十书》的校点、历代版本考证研究的影响,在老师的指导下,完成了《〈算经十书〉校勘的新进展——〈算经十书〉郭书春、刘钝校点评介》(发表在《古籍整理研究学刊》2002年第4期),另外,我和老师共同合作完成了《"为数学而数学"——刘徽科学价值观探析》(发表在《自然辩证法通讯》2003年第1期)上。另一方面,致力于数学史、数学文化与数学教育相结合中的问题,在《数学教育学报》《高等数学研究》《教育史研究》《数学通报》《高等理科教育》等刊物上发表《论儒学对中国古代数学教育思想的影响》《圆周率究竟是如何推算的?》《从"贾宪三角"看数学史在数学教育中的作用与价值》《李善兰与中国数学教育的近代化》《"零""0""○"的起源与传播》《发挥数学史在实现新课程整体目标中的作用》《试析我国高校数学史教育发展与研究现状》《戴震数学教育评述》等论文。

工作期间,几次郭老师来济南,多是应邀参加一些学术活动。山东青岛胶州是老师的故土,而山东大学又是郭老师的母校,他心系家乡,牵挂母校发展,所以,老师最常到的是山东大学,多入住校内学人酒店。每一次得知老师、师母来济南,我一般会携妻子袁广玲或接站或探望。我读博期间,袁广玲也多次到北京探望,与老师、师母及邹大海、田淼等有幸结识,结下深厚情谊,她至今还时常回忆在北京的过往。记得郭老师和师母两次来到山东师范大学,第一次是我刚入职不久,当时我还住在山东师范大学校内博士院平房,老师初步了解了我在山东师范大学的工作和生活;另一次是2010年5月中下旬,趁郭老师在济南的闲暇之余,陪老师、师母走走泉城,看看泉水,邀请老师为师生做报告,给我们讲数学史。

2010年5月20日,郭老师来济南为山东师范大学师生做数学史学术报告并做专业指导

2010年5月20日,郭老师在山东师范大学做报告,师母认真聆听(我记忆中这成为师母的习惯)

郭老师与山东师范大学数学院的部分领导和老师们在一起(2010年5月20日)

与郭老师和师母在济南趵突泉合影(2010年5月20日)

三、拓展研究领域,传播数学文化,为地方文化建设服务

数学文化是人类文化的重要组成部分。我在高校工作这么多年,深刻感受到:数学文化的挖掘、整理、应用与当代传播是一个亟待解决的重要课题;"数学史、数学文化与数学教育"也不断应用于中小学教育,成为数学教育的重要组成部分。因此,我在高校从事数学教师教育的研究与教学过程中,始终不忘通过数学史来丰富发展数学文化的内涵,在此基础上,拓展研究领域,为弘扬和传播数学文化,为地方文化建设贡献自己的一份力量。

首先,多年来我一直坚持为山东师范大学的学生(从本科到硕士乃至博士)开设"数学史与数学文化"选修课,并编撰讲义讲稿,使得更多的学生通过课程学习,了解和学习数学史,感悟和体会数学文化的价值和魅力。他们毕业后,多数从事中小学数学教育教学工作,在大学里接受这方面的教育,对于胜任以后的数学教育工作具有重要的意义,因而受到学生的普遍欢迎。有不少学生还从此对数学史专业

郭老师和师母在济南李清照纪念馆(2010年5月20日)

产生了浓厚的兴趣,有的还通过自己的努力,考取了数学史方向的博士生,牛腾、曲兆华就是其中的代表,她们分别于2011年和2018年考入中国科学院自然科学史研究所,拜在师兄邹大海门下,继续深造学习。

其次,加强数学文化资源的开发、应用、拓展及其方法论研究。从齐鲁文化的发展与影响进行研究的新视角,相继完成著作《山东科学技术史》(山东人民出版社,2018年12月出版,被列入"山东地方史文库第三辑")和《山东天算史》(山东人民出版社,2000年12月出版,被列入"山东地方史文库第三辑"),进一步加强对山东古代天算史料的发掘和整理,使本研究在弘扬中国传统文化的同时,突出山东地方文化特色。在此,我要特别感谢已故的著名历史学家、山东师范大学历史与文化学院的安作璋先生。我与安先生是山东曹县老乡,是他最早把这个光荣而艰巨的任务交给了我。当时正值山东地方史文库的建设项目的关键时期,山东省老省长韩寓群亲力亲为,担任总主编。第一辑已出版,接下来要规划第二辑,需要增加选题,鉴于我在中国科学院自然科学史研究所三年科技史学习的底子,安先生建议并推荐我承担一本《山东科学技术史》的撰写任务。我深知《山东科学技术史》涉及学科门类多,自己才疏识短,诚惶诚恐,是他老人家鼓励我,使我最终克服了种种困难,完成了书稿。《山东科学技术史》虽以传统的农、医、天、算为主,但山东在纺织、桑蚕、冶炼、盐、铁、采矿、陶瓷、机械制造、建筑、雕刻、绘画、手工艺术、酿酒、军事技术等方面的传统科学技术成就也毫不逊色。基于本书篇幅所限,加上山东地方史文库还要出版第三辑,所以,我就将其中的天算部分多有删节,而将其作为后来的《山东天算史》专论内容。在此,我还要感谢山东师范大学历史文化学院前院长朱亚非教授,感谢他给我这次续写的机会。以上两本书,算是我本人铭记老师的教诲,立足山东地方,对山东地方史文库建设做了一项有益的工作,也算为弘扬齐鲁文化和古代山东人民的科学技术成就做了一份自己的努力吧!

再次,身体力行,做好数学文化的传播和普及工作。发挥数学文化创新发展研究的优势,创造条件做好数学文化的传播和科普教育活动,成为我的一项服务社会的重要工作。自2001年关注青少年的数学文化科普教育,2002年4月正式参加济南市区的科普工作,当时是响应济南市槐荫区科技协会和教育局举办的"博士进校园"和"大手拉小手"的科普教育活动,并被聘为济南第30中学学区的"名誉校长"。我为中学生编著了《数学·科学与文化的殿堂》(陕西科学技术出版社,2004年1月出版),该书是由李醒民、肖显静任主编的"中学生科学素养丛书"的数学学科部分。近20年来,一直积极响应省市区科协领导的号召,走进学区,走进校园,发挥自己在数学教育研究和面向基础教育教学的优势,坚持为中小学生做数学文化传播、科普报告和科技创新指导工作。特别是2012年12月,山东省青少年科普专家团成立以来,作为首批科普报告专家团团员,积极响应和参加山东省科学技术协会、山东省教育厅和共青团组织的"山东省青少年科普报告百校行、希望行"等系列活动,现已在全省各地市中小学校为广大青少年学生做数学科普报告60余场次,主要报告有:《数学文化漫谈》《数学让你更智慧》《数学的魅力与价值》《数学美学欣赏》《有趣的数学猜想和证明》和《智趣的数学》等.报告以揭示数学的魅力与价值为主题,以培养学生的综合科学素养为目的,内容涉及数学史、数学美学欣赏、有趣的数学猜想和证明,以及智趣的数学等数学文化内容,注重选择不同专题传播数学文化,创新工作思路和方法,通过走进学区、走进校园等方式,扩大数学文化应用的效果,受到了学校和青少年学生的普遍欢迎。通过中小学的数学文化的传播研究和数学科普教育,增进了学生对数学的感悟和理解,提高了学生的数学文化和科学素养。

其实,致力于挖掘区域科技教育资源,弘扬山东地方文化,还是受教于郭老师率先垂范。例如,郭老师不仅自己研究刘徽几十年如一日,也希望国内、国际上更多的人了解刘徽,更希望刘徽的故乡重视刘徽,弘扬刘徽。早在2012年,在纪念刘徽注《九章算术》1750周年前夕,就给我和山东大学的包芳勋教授联系,希望能联合山东当地政府和相关部门召开一次国际学术研讨会。后经多次努力,我们俩利用东道主的优势,在当地有关部门的大力支持下,"纪念刘徽注《九章算术》1750周年国际学术研讨会"于2013年6月在山东邹平县如期举行。这次研讨会的胜利召开,使得当地政府特别是邹平县科技界、教育界、文化界更加认识到刘徽作为世界古代数学泰斗对中国数学发展的巨大贡献,更加坚定了地方文化自信。

纪念刘徽注《九章算术》1750周年国际学术研讨会(2013年6月)

邹大海在纪念刘徽注《九章算术》1750周年国际学术研讨会上做报告(2013年6月)

"一位好老师,胜过万本书。"郭老师几十载躬耕陇亩,通今博古,见微知著,学富五车,为人景仰。在学生的内心深处,郭老师就是一本读不完的书。时光荏苒,岁月如梭,过去艰辛而又美好的求学时光,将永远留在我的记忆里。郭老师的谆谆教诲如清泉,如甘霖,在我的心中永远流淌。

郭老师是我们的人生楷模。值老师八十大寿之际,衷心祝愿恩师健康长寿!祝愿老师永远保持一颗年轻的心,率直本真,幸福快乐!

(傅海伦,系山东师范大学数学与统计学院教授,博士生导师)

郭书春先生指导我学习中国数学史

刘邦凡　（燕山大学文法学院(公共管理学院)）

仰慕恩师郭书春先生有三十多年之久。20 世纪 80 年代，我在四川丰都县第三中学(现重庆市丰都县第三中学)从事中学教育教学工作，工作之余一直对中国数学史有兴趣，阅读了一些数学史方面的书籍，也就想报考数学史专业的研究生，并先后给中国科学院自然科学史研究所多位先生写信求助，包括郭书春先生、王渝生先生等。在 1988 年 10 月，给郭先生写的一封信，很快就收到了郭先生的回信。他在回信中对我所提的问题一一做了回答，并指出了报考的注意事项。

郭先生当时的回信内容是：

刘邦凡同志：

您好！大札收悉。所询三事，据我所知，报告如下：(1)《中国数学史》的考试范围限于钱宝琮所著《中国数学史》，民国时期不考，但要检查古文水平，一般是取与古代数学有关的古文标点、翻译。(2)《科技史》以杜石然先生《中国科技史稿》(上、下，科学出版社)和梅森的《自然科学史》为参考书。(3)考题类型是基础知识的检查，包括顺便考查分析问题的能力，也考查文字水平(科学史成果的体现主要靠论文、论著)，但没有作文考试。(4)高等数学，我们取(c)类。(5)梅森的书找不到，可用别的参考，因国内对此无专门研究，多数同类著作以此为蓝本，然我未比较，不知优劣。(6)试题业务处不外借，对不起。以上答复不知是否满意。有问题，请来信。如可以，请告诉你的基本情况。我下午要出差，匆匆草此。

顺颂教礼！

郭书春
1988 年 10 月 28 日

郭先生的回信，对我来说非常珍贵，不仅对 1991 年报考研究生起到了重要的指导作用，而且也对我能够走向学术道路起到重要的鼓励作用。收到郭先生的回信，我再次去信汇报我的学习情况。

1991 年，我报考了中国科学院自然科学史研究所中国数学史硕士研究生，遗憾的是我的成绩没有达到复试分数线，与中国科学院自然科学史研究所失之交臂，没有能够成为郭先生的学生，没有能够直接跟随郭先生学习数学史，成为遗憾之事。

后来，我几经考试，到了西南师范大学(现西南大学)攻读逻辑学硕士生。在西南师范大学读研究生期间，我对中国数学史仍然抱有兴趣，学习之余，还撰写了几篇文章在期刊发表。这几篇文章包括：1998 年在《沈阳师范学院学报(自然科学版)》发表的《中国传统数学的逻辑思想特色》，1999 年在《青海师范大学学报(哲学社会科学版)》发表的《中国传统数学的逻辑过程》，1999 年在《南都学坛》发表的《中算名家名著的逻辑方法和思想》，2000 年在《康定民族师范高等专科学校学报》发表的《浅论"中算"逻辑与中国古代逻辑思想》等。当时撰写这几篇文章，也是对郭先生指导我学习数学史的一种汇报。

我在西南师范大学读研究生毕业后，来到燕山大学工作，于 2001 年 9 月到南开大学哲学系跟随崔清田先生攻读逻辑学专业博士研究生。初到南开大学，崔清田先生就与我谈论博士论文选题。崔清田先生是中国逻辑史学家，他对中国逻辑史有精深研究和突出贡献，善于鼓励学生开阔思路拓展研究领域。于是我就提出我的博士论文选题想围绕中国古代数学(中国传统数学)的逻辑思想史去构思。崔清田先生说他对中国古代数学知之不多，但可以请教其他中国数学史研究的专家。崔清田先生对中国古代数学的逻辑思想史早有研究，他只是没有长篇大论而已，他谦虚的表达，我也就当真了，就与他谈起与郭书春先生的交往以及郭先生的情况。崔清田先生很高兴地说："那很好啊，就去找郭老师指导，你先联系上，多与他联系，把你的情况也给他汇报一下。"于是，我就通过中国科学院自然科学史研究所联系上了郭先生，给郭先生打了电话，汇报我的一些情况以及博士论文选题的问题，郭先生热情洋溢地回答了我很多问题，对我的选题给予了肯定。2002年9月，我将选题情况写了一封信寄给了郭先生。郭先生很快回了信，再次对我的选题给予了肯定，他在回信中指出："你致力于中国传统数学与逻辑的课题，是非常好的。关于这个问题的全面研究尚未见到有见地的工作。"

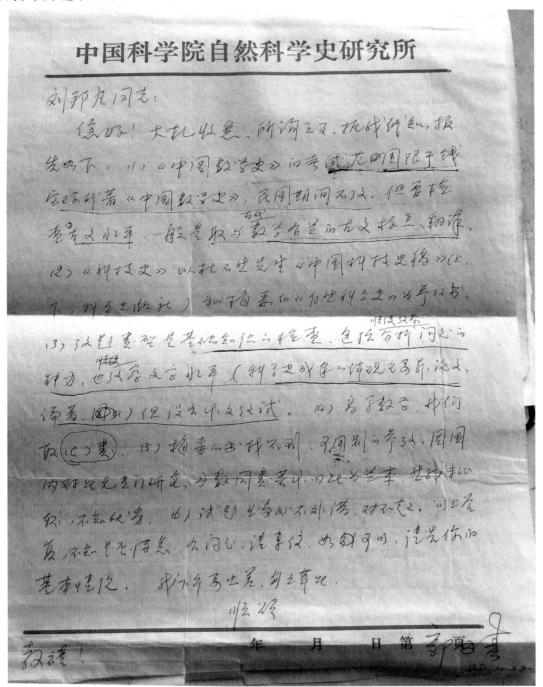

1988年10月28日郭书春先生给刘邦凡的回信

郭先生回信道：

> 邦凡同志：你好！
> 因 8 月中旬到天津、西安开数学史会，8 月 10 日来信 8 月下旬才拿到。因近日太忙，迟复为歉。今尊嘱奉上拙作《〈算数书〉校勘》，《文物》上的《〈算数书〉释文》的情况，在拙作中有全面反映，即由我的校勘记可以恢复《释文》。拙作中已发现个别错误，给你的电子邮件中已改正。《算数书》的校勘，除彭浩与我之外，还有郭世荣及中国台北洪万生的学生。另奉上拙作《试论〈算数书〉的理论贡献与编纂》。我认为，《算数书》不是《九章算术》的前身。另外，不能以《九章算术》为模式改动《算数书》的表达方式。请指正。
> 你致力于"中国传统数学与逻辑"的课题，是非常好的。关于这个问题的全面研究尚未见到有见地的工作。学术界占统治地位的观点仍然是"中国古代数学没有逻辑，没有理论"。我和巫寿康在 20 世纪 80 年代初分别做过刘徽《九章算术注》的逻辑研究，殊途同归，都得出刘徽注是以演绎逻辑为主的。我的论文发表于《自然科学史研究》1983 年第 3 期上，同年的《中国哲学年鉴》上摘录了我的观点。后来，成为拙作《古代世界数学泰斗刘徽》（山东科学技术出版社，1992 年）的重要部分。巫寿康（已故）的论文发表于《自然科学史研究》1987 年。说中国古代数学没有逻辑的人大多不懂中国数学史，或没有读懂刘徽注，李约瑟等便属于后者。帮助李约瑟写中国数学史的是王玲，他是学历史的，因此，对刘徽的评价比杨辉还低。对这个问题的研究，我认为，切忌受舆论界的影响。学术界经常引用爱因斯坦关于中国数学没有形式逻辑的话，是没有意义的，一则爱因斯坦关于中国数学的知识未必比一个高中生多；二则科学研究的出发点不是原则，而是事实。一定要从分析中国传统数学原著出发，得出自己的结论，才能有所突破。当然，读原著，必须找到好的版本。中国传统数学著作本文大都没有论证，论证多在注释中。除刘徽注外，对《九章算术》的注释，还有唐朝李淳风等（在《九章算术》中，逻辑水平低于刘徽）、北宋贾宪《黄帝九章算经细草》（约有 2/3 存杨辉书中，见发表于《自然科学史研究》1998 年第 3 期的拙作）与南宋杨辉的《详解九章算法》。另外，《杨辉算法》、明朝王文素《算学宝鉴》也含有论证。清焦循的《加减乘除释》等也应该读一下。以上看法不一定正确，仅供参考。
> 另，奉上我的论文目录。
> 顺颂研安！
>
> 郭书春上
> 2002 年 9 月 14 日

他的回信以及寄给我的材料和他的论文目录等，对我完成博士论文起到了关键性作用。有了郭先生的肯定和指导，使得我在博士论文撰写中少走了很多弯路。

我博士论文完成提纲和初稿后，寄给郭先生，他很快寄来了回信。这次郭先生的回信如下：

> 邦凡同志：
> 你好！
> 来信及贺卡收到，谢谢！并祝你新春快乐，在新的一年中顺利完成论文！
> 你的提纲我反复看了几遍，总的感觉是涉及的面太宽。既然你征求我的意见，我当然将我的看法直言相告（另页）。写出论文初稿后，如果你愿意，我可以在中国古代数学的史实方面帮你把把关。
> 我可以参加你的论文的评审或答辩。
> 目前我正在看拙作汇校《九章算术》修订版的校样，估计上半年可以出版。

祝春节好！

郭书春上
2004 年 1 月 18 日

上信用 E-mail 发给你，不知收到没有？怕耽误你用，今用信寄出。

春节过得好吧？我的春节是在看校样中度过的，汇校本修订版的尚未看完，中法对照本的中文部分的校样在年除夕递到。

要我去贵校讲学事，我这边没有问题，请命题即可。我的长项在于中国传统数学，其他方面不敢问津。又及，2004/1/30

对刘邦凡博士论文《中国逻辑与中国传统数学》提纲的意见

郭书春

选题很好，也很重要，在某种意义上说，是填补中国数学史尤其是中国逻辑史研究空白的工作。提纲非常全面，仅就提纲本身谈一些改进意见。

一、从提纲看论文铺的面太宽。比如从什么是逻辑，数学的观念、思想、方法、主题、本质等谈起，扯得太远。即使是一部专著也不见得由此谈起。不知你的论文要写多长。实际上，你的每个三级或四级标题都可以写几万字甚至十几万字。博士论文不要从猿到人。

二、一般说来，一篇论文应说明前人的研究成果及存在的问题（包括没有解决的或解决得不正确的），和前人没有触及的问题。由此引出本文所要解决的问题。我意，从中国逻辑史界对中国传统数学中的逻辑研究现状及中国数学史界关于中国古代数学的逻辑的研究现状切入。对前者我知之甚少，巫寿康先生的《刘徽〈九章算术注〉逻辑初探》（《自然科学史研究》第 6 卷第 1 期第 20—27 页，1987 年）比较好，他的工作与拙作《刘徽〈九章算术注〉中的定义及演绎逻辑试析》（《自然科学史研究》第 2 卷第 3 期第 193—203 页，1983 年）大约同时，各自独立完成的，而其结论基本一致。

三、关于中国传统数学的内容，先就提纲中提及到的谈一下。

1. 中国传统数学应该从先秦谈起。根据刘徽的记述和《九章算术》内部结构的分析，《九章算术》的主要成就是在先秦完成的，《算数书》尽管不是《九章算术》的前身，它的内容却为这一论断提供了佐证。《算数书》的绝大多数内容都是先秦完成的。《周髀算经》的内容相当大的一部分是先秦的，席泽宗、程贞一考证，陈子是公元前 5 世纪的人。保守地讲，中国数学发展的第一个高峰在先秦，西汉只是它的总结。请参看邹大海的《中国数学的兴起与先秦数学》（河北科学技术出版社，2001 年）。

2. "《九章算术》的题、答、术"，不知你怎么写。请注意，许多著作中说的"《九章算术》是一题、一答、一术"，是不符合事实的。请参考拙文《关于中国传统数学的"术"》。

3. 赵君卿与赵爽是同一人，列入《周髀算经》与《九章算术》之间不妥。

4. "率"是一个数学概念，是算之纲纪，不是推类思想。

5. 隋唐数学是中国数学的一个低潮，其水平虽高于战国、西汉，却远远落后于魏晋南北朝。所谈 6 部著作，只有《缉古算经》和赝本《夏侯阳算经》是隋唐的，《孙子算经》《张丘建算经》（注意，丘，孔刻本、钱校本误作邱，为清人避孔子讳而改）、原本《夏侯阳算经》（已佚）、《五经算术》（还有一部《五曹算经》）都是南北朝的。《数术记遗》的时代有争论，钱宝琮认为系甄鸾自撰自注，假托东汉末年徐岳，现许多学者认为是徐岳作，甄鸾注。

6. "宋元四大数学家"的提法不妥。这是一个不准确的说法，查李、钱二老没有这一提法。若说"宋元四大数学家"，则不能不包括贾宪，当然得有秦九韶、李冶、朱世杰。因为贾宪的贡献非常大，宋元数学的主要成就大都由贾宪开其先河，他的《黄帝九章算经细草》因被杨辉《详解九章算法》抄录尚存约三分之二。秦九韶、李冶、杨辉、朱世杰称为"13 世纪四大数学家"比较合适。

7.宋元数学成就中,沈括的"隙积术"是杨辉、朱世杰的"垛积术"的前身,不宜与贾宪三角列为一项。宋元数学主要成就列成7条,太碎。实际上主要是三类:(1)解方程(立成释锁法、增乘开方法、正负开方法)与列方程(天元术)、四元术(多元高次方程组的列法与解法);(2)高阶等差级数求和法(垛积术)和招差法;(3)测圆和其他几何问题。测圆方面的成就在《测圆海镜》中,被天元术掩盖了。

8."中国逻辑在宋元数学中的反映"应该有贾宪和朱世杰的内容。贾宪是宋元数学高潮的奠基者,朱世杰是中国古代计算水平最高的数学家。最伟大的数学家当然是刘徽。

仅供参考。

收到郭先生的信之后,我根据郭先生的意见对我的博士论文初稿进行全面的修改完善。在随后的博士论文撰写过程中,还多次就有关文献选用、理论建构和内容表达等多个方面请教了郭先生,郭先生总是耐心、不嫌其烦地解答我的问题、指导我的论文撰写。如果没有郭先生的指导和把关,我的博士论文很难达到毕业水平。感恩于郭先生的悉心教导和精心指导,我在博士论文的"致谢"中最先对郭先生表达了感恩之心:

> 20个世纪80年代,曾经考过中国科学院数学史的硕士,得到过郭老书春先生的谆谆教导。考入南开大学攻读博士学位以来,又幸得郭老的大力帮助和悉心指教。去年我做开题报告请教郭老,郭老寄来"热情洋溢"的信鼓励我,同时寄来他收集的许多资料以及他的鸿篇巨论,坚定了我把工作进行下去的信心;今年初,初稿完成后,再寄郭老论文提纲,郭老又寄来了十分细致的指导意见,使得我的论文得以初步完成。从未有幸面见郭老,郭老却给予我非常细致的指导与无私的帮助,在此对郭老致以深深的敬意和谢意!

2004年5月,我博士论文毕业答辩时,我遵从我恩师崔清田教授教导,邀请郭先生作为答辩主席主持我的博士论文答辩,郭先生欣然同意。在他的主持下,我顺利通过了博士论文答辩,获得了哲学博士学位。

在我攻读博士学位期间,郭先生尽管不是我名义上的指导老师,却是我博士论文撰写的主要指导老师。我的博士生导师崔清田教授也多次教导我,不要忘记郭先生的恩情,甚至在他移居加拿大之后,还问我是否还与郭老师联系,说不要忘记郭老师的恩情。郭先生和崔老师都是我一生的授业导师,我怎敢忘记,与两位恩师一直保持联系。多次邀请两位先生来燕山大学讲学和来秦皇岛北戴河度假,与两位先生及其两位师母留下很难忘的记忆。

郭书春先生主持刘邦凡博士论文答辩
(左起:李娜,郭书春,刘培育,董志铁,任晓明)

答辩后合影
(前排左起:董志铁,崔清田,郭书春,刘培育;后排左起:关兴丽,王左立,田立刚,任晓明,李娜,刘邦凡,吴克锋,刘明明,杨蕾)

刘邦凡博士论文答辩时与郭书春先生合影

从 2001 年到 2016 年，我先后担任燕山大学文法学院副院长、院长、党委书记等管理职务，一直为琐事所累。郭先生多次教导我参加有关科学技术史或数学史的会议和活动，我一直很少参加。例如，郭先生邀请我参加刘徽学术研讨会，我因故没有按时参加。郭先生来信说：

邦凡：

你好！

好久没有联系，一切都好吧？

刘徽会的第一轮通知收到了吧？欢迎你参加。

2011，2012 年秋我先后给中山大学逻辑所的研究生讲了一个月的中国数学史课，反映尚好。在那里遇到你在南开的校友周老师。

一个不坏的消息：我主编的《中国科学技术史·数学卷》获"第四届郭沫若历史奖"一等奖。中国社会科学网和我所网站报导比较准确。此书也是我在中大授课的主要参考书。

教安！

郭书春上

2013 年 3 月 2 日

但是，我最后还因为琐事拖累，没有能够参加此次会议，辜负了郭先生的教导。

没有担任管理职务以来，与郭先生的联系多了一些，我也参加了几次科学史或数学史的会议。在上海交通大学举办的"中国数学史学会换届会议"上还有幸当选为学会理事。这是郭先生教导我，使得我有了点进步才获得了这样的荣誉。

在向郭先生学习的三十多年中，不仅使自己在数学史研究中有了进步，而且为郭先生谦谦君子作风、和蔼可亲做人、精益求精地做学术的高尚情怀所感染、所吸引。从以下郭先生的来信中，我都颇受教益，感恩不已。

邦凡：

你好！

春节之后，研究所提出请所内老专家给研究生上课，今天回所，研究生处正协调研究生的课程，早则下周，晚则四月初，我可以开始上课。你希望我上半年到贵校开一次讲座，不知是一次报告，还是一个系列，请拨冗示知。

我今年上半年的安排还不少：4 月中旬海口有一个数学史与数学教育会，特邀我参加，不好不去。五一前后，石家庄有一个李冶会，他们修复了元氏县的封龙书院，李冶辞职后曾主持该书院。恢复时请我帮了点忙,所以得参加(你是否可以去?)。李冶会前后,河北师范大学邓明立先生(现任副校长)要我到师范大学几天。5月底前,我的一个学生(中国香港)要答辩。6月下旬,刘徽会。7月份曼彻斯特国际科学史大会,道本周先生(国际数学史学会前主席)要我等与他组织一个中国数学简牍的专题(除80年代的《筭数书》之外,近年又发现了几批战国秦汉数学简牍)。因此,我想,如果做一二次报告,我随时可去。如果是某种系列,可否推到下半年?请酌。

  教安!

郭书春上
2013年3月5日

邦凡院长:

  你好!

  拙作《九章筭术新校》已经由中国科学技术大学出版社出版,今天托快递奉上(请朱一文转呈),请指正。这实际上是汇校《九章筭术》的第三版。其第二版"汇校《九章筭术》增补版"去年忝列古籍整理小组首批向全国推荐的60年来出版的优秀古籍整理图书。

  我在《九章筭术新校》中重写了全部校勘记。此外,刘徽序和后四卷的底本有重大改进,即以"文津阁本"为底本,以"聚珍版"和"四库文渊阁本"参校而恢复的戴震辑录本为底本。"盖汇校本"及其"增补版"使用的"戴震辑录本"是由"聚珍版"和"四库文渊阁本"对校恢复的,我在准备"新校"时校雠了"四库文津阁本",发现"文津阁本"是戴校各版《九章》中最准确的一部。同时发现,"文渊阁本"与"聚珍版的底本"相同,而"聚珍版"是根据"戴震辑录校勘本"的副本摆印的,那么"文渊阁本"的底本也是"副本","文津阁本"的底本应该是"正本"。还发现,"副本"并不是完全照抄"正本",而是做了若干修改。

  夏安!

郭书春上
2014年7月7日

  郭先生为人为学是我一生学习的楷模,值得我永远学习。借此小文,祝福郭先生八十华诞幸福美满!祝福郭先生和师母健康长寿,万事如意。

作者简介:刘邦凡(出生于1967年),男,重庆涪陵人,博士,现任燕山大学文法学院(公共管理学院)二级教授、博士生导师,河北省重点高端智库——河北省公共政策评估研究中心首席专家。先后担任燕山大学文法学院(公共管理学院)副院长、院长和党委书记等职务。发表论文数百篇,出版著作20多部,获得各类奖项30多项,承担各类项目60多项。

郭书春先生在中山大学

张一杰　（中山大学逻辑与认知研究所）

自李俨、钱宝琮开创中国数学史研究领域后,中华人民共和国成立以来,李、钱以降,大师辈出。然而,我国大部分数学史领域的人才主要活跃在北方。较早一批数学史专家中活跃在中国南方的有沈康身,他任教于杭州大学,并开课讲授中国数学史多年;另有中国台湾的洪万生,精研数学史并推动数学教育。而在经济发达的岭南一带,虽有中山大学的何博传曾一度研究和讲授数学史,但鲜有系统研究中国数学史而有影响者。

时间来到了21世纪,时任中山大学逻辑与认知研究所所长的是逻辑学家鞠实儿。他作为恢复高考后首批大学生,曾读于杭州大学数学系。大约自1980年开始,沈康身为数学系学生开设数学史的课程,他便是这一课程的第一批学生。在数学史课程学习中,鞠实儿及其同学便被要求使用中国的传统方法来解数学问题。他一直保留当年数学史课堂笔记、习题本和考卷。求学时的训练影响了他关于文化学术史研究方法的看法。在随后的研究中,他提出了中国古代逻辑史研究的本土化原则:某种文化的论证规则和结构只能用该文化的规范来描述。因此,以本土的地方性知识作为古代人的社会文化背景,研究中国传统文化里的推理和论证,这在他眼里成为新颖而又重要的研究方向。而数学命题是用逻辑方法得到证明的;因此,从本土角度研究中国古代数学中的推理将会成为极好的比较对象,凸显出数学推理也具有文化背景的维度。鉴于以上原因,鞠实儿教授十分迫切地想要开启中国古代数学中推理与论证的本土化研究。计划在按部就班地展开,2011年,鞠实儿从逻辑学专业的研究生中顺利地招揽了一位既对中国传统文化感兴趣,同时具有物理学背景,适合进行科学史研究的博士生张一杰。故安排其进行古代汉语、版本校勘等基础知识方面的学习。然而无法忽视的问题是,他亟需中国数学史方面的专业训练。此时,鞠实儿请求当今科学史家吴国盛的帮助。后者郑重推荐郭书春先生。

郭书春,山东青岛人,1965年进入中国科学院自然科学史研究所,其时已晋升研究员,系《九章算术》和刘徽研究的著名专家。80年代起,他便和法国学者林力娜(K. Chemla)合作研究和着手翻译《九章算术》法译本。20世纪90年代出版了他的《汇校九章算术》,汇集了宋代以来的《九章》诸善本,以及清代以来直至近现代诸多训诂学者、数学家及数学史家的校勘意见,当然还有他自己原创的校勘,研究《九章算术》这部历来视为算经之首的古代数学经典文献,其《汇校》为必治之书。《九章算术》能成为经典,魏晋时期数学家刘徽的注解不可或缺。而郭书春先生对刘徽的研究也是国内首屈一指的。此外,正是他精深的文字功底和敏锐的分析,使得隐藏在南宋杨辉著作中的北宋数学家贾宪的成就重新为现代人所知。再则,过去《九章算术》也有外文译本,但是缺失刘徽注,因而外国人所能认知到的原书应有的理论高度就无疑被大大削弱了。2006年,郭书春与林力娜合作的《九章算术》及其刘徽注的法文译本正式面世,大幅度推动了全世界对中国古代数学的认识。之后,他又与前国际数学史协会主席道本周(J. W. Dauben)教授、徐义保教授合作,基于郭书春先生提供的校勘和现代汉语译文,翻译了带刘徽注的英文版《九章算术》全文。

郭先生其时已70岁高龄,邀请其南下岭南、广州进行一段较长时间的讲课,可知是一桩困难的苦差,若然遭拒亦无可奈何。抱持这一心理准备去沟通,随后得到回复,郭书春先生欣然答应此事。事情之顺利大大出乎意料,鞠实儿和张一杰喜出望外。于是,2011年11月份,郭书春先生应邀南赴中山大

---

[1] 感谢鞠实儿教授,中山大学谢耘教授和朱一文副教授对本文写作的帮助。对文中可能出现的错误,笔者文责自负。

学，开展了为期一个月的中国数学史讲习班，一周三讲，每次两个半小时。他带来了刚出版不久、由他主编的《中国科学技术史·数学卷》作为主要教材。此书是继吴文俊主编的《中国数学史大系》之后又一部集大成之作。其详细囊括汇总了当时中国数学史研究的经典结论，将自先秦到清末的中国数学史做了全面而详细的介绍，后来获得了"郭沫若中国历史学奖"一等奖。第一节课上，郭书春先生便着重讲述了校勘的几种方法和他实际运用的心得，这自然是一般阅读文献和专著所难以获得，或是获得成本很高的宝贵经验；其后，他在讲课中穿插的中国数学史研究历程中诸位名家的生平、风格、轶事等内容更是书本上难以接触到，但是对了解整个领域大有裨益的；更不用说，在短短一个月时间里，郭书春先生在中山大学逻辑与认知研究所和哲学系一连讲学十几次。他孜孜不倦地传道授业，其热忱深深地感染了参与的师生。他的讲课主题之一是刘徽的数学思想，正是受到他的影响，鞠实儿最终决定以《九章算术》刘徽注作为中国数学史论证研究的起点。

不过，这只是郭书春帮助发展中山大学数学史研究的开始。在成功的讲学之后，郭书春和鞠实儿商议，以联合培养博士生的名义派遣张一杰到中国科学院自然科学史研究所访学。2012年3月，在春寒料峭中，张一杰坐上了前往北京的火车。在三个月的访学过程中，其时还是一介研究生的张一杰，每日只知懵懂地阅读和请教，偶尔还有点思念温暖的南方。作为学生，不仅要解决吃住问题，还需要很经济地解决。但是张一杰甫至京城便无需顾虑这些问题。在住上，郭书春先生早已安排了住宿；在食上，郭先生也贴心地开具了证明，让他可以前往同院的物科饭堂，和中科大学生同等待遇地开卡打饭。在京期间，每个礼拜郭书春先生都会至少主动与他见面一次，不仅答疑释难，讨论学术，也关心其生活状况。遇到学术活动，郭书春先生也不忘捎上这位南方来的小学徒，自然史所里的博士开题、讲座，往清华大学参观清华简的复原工作等，他都积极邀请张一杰参与。虽然只是短暂的3个多月，但能在京城这一全国学术的心脏地带得到最高效的指导和最前沿的见闻，而没有一丝生活上的顾虑，张一杰得到的机会和帮助是通常情况下难以想象也难以获得的。郭老年事和辈分俱高，却在拔擢后进上亲力亲为，面面俱到，展示了一代学人的高尚品德。

其后，郭先生又于同年10月中旬，再度访问中山大学。这次讲学，他继续了去年同期的讲习班，完成了《数学卷》的讲课。2012年逗留中山大学期间，郭书春先生还明确建议中山大学发展中国数学史研究，改变该领域研究北重南轻的局面，时任哲学系主任的鞠实儿当场接受他的建议和推荐，准备建立一个中国数学史研究团队。同年，其时中山大学逻辑与认知研究所与乌得勒支大学、阿姆斯特丹大学共同筹划一个关于数学和逻辑的文化的跨学科国际会议。这次会议选在中国举行，一个重要的动机是，在一个具有有别于强势的西方文化以外的悠久文化传统的国家，以展开不同文化对比的讨论。鞠实儿邀请郭先生参与会议的组委会，得益于郭书春先生的牵头，会议邀请到了林力娜教授、郭世荣教授、邹大海研究员等海内外著名数学史专家，使得会议的数学文化单元增色不少。会议的成功举办标志着中山大学的数学史研究与主流学界进行了初步接触。郭书春先生的弟子朱一文也因为这个会议关注起中山大学的数学史研究。2013年，留法归国的朱一文在求职活动中联系了中山大学，得到郭书春和林力娜二位的推荐，最终加入中山大学哲学系，开始为本科生和研究生开设数学史和科学史相关课程。在郭先生和数学史界人士的支持下，经鞠实儿的努力，中山大学哲学系的数学史研究与教学的框架建立起来了，岭南有了粗具规模的中国数学史研究团队。

2015年，考虑到中山大学数学史研究已经起步，时任全国数学史学会理事长、西北大学的曲安京教授决定在中山大学召开"第九届全国数学史学会年会暨第六届数学史与数学教育会议"，会议由中山大学逻辑与认知研究所和中国数学会数学史分会联合主办，郭书春先生作为学术委员会主席参加，再次访穗。作为学会的年会，这次会议不仅聚集了当时国内数学史界绝大部分专家学者，林力娜教授、美国程贞一教授等国外专家也莅临交流。在这难得的盛会上，鞠实儿和张一杰报告了他们根据本土化方法对刘徽割圆术研究的新发现，中山大学逻辑与认知研究所赵希顺教授做了中国数理逻辑史的报告，朱一文则报告了对秦九韶大衍术的研究。中山大学数学史研究的研究方法论和成果首次得以与国内外学界进行正式交流，这也标志着当今中山大学数学史研究正式纳入全国数学史研究进程之中。

2016年，2018年，朱一文分别获硕导和博导资格，至今指导了三位硕士的毕业论文；2018年张一杰完成以本土化方法重新解读刘徽注论证的博士论文后毕业入站中山大学博士后，并参与朱一文的数学史课程授课。朱一文在以秦九韶为中心的宋元数学，儒家经典中的数学，以及基于课程教学的数学史方法论三个方面斩获颇丰，并于2020年获教育部"第八届高等学校科学研究优秀成果奖（人文社会科学）青年成果奖"；张一杰延续用本土化的方法解读中国古代数学，从数学实作角度来归纳中国古代数学的论证。二人的研究可概括为致力于从数学实作角度研究数学史。自2011年来访中山大学后，郭书春先生将其成果、思想乃至培养的学生带到了岭南，使此地不再是数学史的荒漠。而且，郭先生的讲课过程全程录像，保存在中山大学逻辑与认知研究所，他带来的知识和思想不会止于一时，而将是中山大学日后培养数学史学者的重要资源。目前，中山大学的中国古代数学史研究已经粗具规模。虽然，后辈学术研究的轨迹已不囿于前辈，但无论如何，前辈为后辈的发展提供了基础和机遇。"饮水不忘掘井人"，在郭书春老师80大寿之际，谨以此文记录郭书春先生在中山大学数学史研究方面的学术活动，感念他在人才培养和学术交流方面所做出的重要贡献。

第三部分
访谈录

走进中国数学史
——郭书春教授访谈录

冯立昇(清华大学科学技术史暨古文献研究所)提问
郭书春(中国科学院自然科学史研究所)作答

冯立昇(以下简称"冯"):广西民族大学学报(自然科学版)主编万辅彬先生知道我参加了您主持的两项数学史工作,我们合作著述,过从较密,相知不浅,特地委托我与您访谈。首先我很感兴趣的是您的早期求学经历,想知道您是什么时候开始对数学产生兴趣的?考大学时为什么选择了数学系?

郭书春(以下简称"郭"):我出生在山东胶州的一个偏僻农村,1953年考入青岛一中(青岛市第一中学)。尽管我的数学学得比较好,本来的兴趣却不是数学,而是历史和生物。然而,青岛一中重数理化,极力动员学习好的学生考理工科。我拗不过班主任,同意报考理工科,但大部分志愿填的是工科,只填了一个数学系,还是第十志愿。为什么被山东大学数学系录取,我也感到奇怪。可能因为我数学考得好(交卷后没有发现错误)的缘故吧!

冯:您大学毕业后是如何走上数学史的研究道路上的?

郭:1964年我大学毕业分配工作时,恰逢"文化大革命"前一个重要的文史哲经刊物、中国科学院哲学社会科学部(自1962年起归中宣部管,俗称"学部")的《新建设》杂志改刊,周扬要增加数学和自然科学的内容,办成新中国成立前《东方杂志》那样的刊物。大约我的文史功底在数学系的学生中算是比较好的,"学部"去山东大学选毕业生的同志选中了我。我到新建设杂志社报到后,不久就去参加"四清"和社会主义教育运动,回到北京已是1965年12月。因几期改刊的《新建设》在学术界反映不佳,中宣部遂决定改回原来的方向,我就调入同属"学部"的中国自然科学史研究室(所级单位,自然科学史研究所的前身),从事数学史研究。我本来就喜欢历史,搞数学史,可谓是如鱼得水,谁知真正迈入数学史的大门竟在十年之后。

冯:真是起个大早,赶个晚集!

郭:我到中国自然科学史研究室报到后,钱老(宝琮)和负责日常工作的黄炜同志因认为中国数学史已经搞得差不多了,确定我今后的研究方向是世界数学史。可是,当时处于"文化大革命"前夕,"学部"已是风雨欲来,领导布置我们学习毛主席著作,讨论历史上劳动人民创造科学的问题。"文化大革命"爆发前的四个多月,我实际上没怎么开展数学史研究。当时钱老还健在,每天上半天班,但在那种政治气氛下,他很少与我们谈业务。有时他憋不住,还会冒出一些至理名言。有一次全室会上,他说:"新中国成立初,浙江的共产党员沙文汉给我们做报告,说'共产主义道德最重要的就是实事求是',我做学问就是讲究实事求是。"钱老的话深深刻进了我的脑海。不过真正接受钱老学术上和治学方法的影响,是在十年之后从事中国数学史研究的时候。

冯:显然"文化大革命"对数学史工作和您个人的研究有很大冲击。

郭:1966年5月下旬,"学部"完全停止了科研工作。那时,除了毛主席的著作,别的书都不让看。不过这一段,我在偷偷自学法语。当时感到前途渺茫,学法语是为了多得一技,想不到后来派上了大用场。

1975年夏,国务院科教组发文件,宣布"学部"恢复业务工作。我23岁大学毕业,此时已经34岁,步入中年。恶梦醒来,非常迷茫:世界数学史是搞不了啦。但是,是不是搞中国数学史,怎么搞,心中一点数也没有。

冯:"文化大革命"结束后您又是如何重新确定科研方向和目标的?

郭:"文化大革命"结束后拨乱反正,涤荡了泼在钱老和《中国数学史》上的"污泥浊水"。可是"中国数学史没有什么可搞了""是贫矿"的舆论依然在中国数学史界和自然科学史研究所占主导地位。

正在自己苦于无出路的时候,1978年底,梅荣照先生向我建议一起研究刘徽。他说,李约瑟的《中国科学技术史·数学卷》谈到刘徽的地方比杨辉还少。我也查了美国的《世界科学家大辞典》,发现其中"刘徽"条写的完全是《九章算术》,几乎没有刘徽的东西。我同意试一试,但能得到什么结果,心中完全无数。当时根本没有想到会有什么大的成果,并且会越研究越多,成为自己后来研究数学史的主要课题,写了几部书,耗费我大半生的精力。

冯:我是1984年开始读您的论文的,当时我在内蒙古师范大学读数学史方向的研究生,那时《九章算术》及其刘徽注已成为非常引人关注的研究课题,您发表了许多关于《九章算术》和刘徽的重要文章,我差不多都看过。您的研究工作对我们年轻一代数学史学者影响很大。您能谈一谈您早期研究《九章算术》的情况吗?

郭:在梅先生提议我们一起研究刘徽的时候,恰逢全国展开关于真理标准的大讨论。这深深触动了我。我因此感到,要研究刘徽,就要从实际出发,读原著。于是,我就开始逐字逐句研读刘徽的《九章算术注》(下简称《刘徽注》)。我自认是笨人,这也是笨人的笨办法。

1979年初,我进展到刘徽的圆田术注。众所周知,中国人一直为祖冲之求圆周率的成绩感到自豪,自20世纪10年代末到1978年近60年间,有关研究一直是中国数学史学科文章涉及最多的课题。因此,读刘徽注,本来没想到会有什么新的结果。可是,当我读到"故以半周乘半径而为圆幂"时,心里豁然一亮:刘徽这不是在证明《九章算术》的圆田术"半周半径相乘得积步"吗?赶紧查钱老的《中国数学史》,却只谈刘徽怎样求圆周率,不提刘徽证明圆面积公式的问题。我回过头来再看这个注,发现它包括两个部分,第一部分是证明《九章算术》的圆田术,第二部分是求圆周率。我随后查阅了能找到的所有谈割圆术的文章,其中没有一篇涉及圆面积公式的证明,甚至一篇逐字逐句用现代汉语翻译圆田术注的文章,对其中几句画龙点睛的话,竟略而不译。我接着又发现,由于没有认识到刘徽的目的在于证明《九章算术》的圆面积公式,钱老和其他作者对刘徽求圆周率的程序也统统偏离了《刘徽注》。

在被人们研究得最多的割圆术问题上的这一突破,对于我研究《九章算术》及其《刘徽注》意义十分重大。首先,它破除了中国数学史"没有什么可搞了"、是"贫矿"的成见,克服了畏难情绪,坚定了研究《九章算术》及其《刘徽注》的信心。其次,破除了对钱老的迷信,钱老的学风严谨,功底深厚,成就极大,但他的工作也不都是尽善尽美、无懈可击。现在说来大家可能感到可笑,当时我一提出与钱老不同的看法,别人说服不了我,就说:"你反钱老!"我答曰:"毛主席的历史功过都可以评价,钱老著述中不恰当的地方,难道不可以提出不同意见?钱老是真正的学者,他如果看到我的看法,肯定也会赞同。"再次,尝到了从第一手资料出发,认真研读原著的甜头。实际上,这成为我治学的宗旨。30年来,我在《九章算术》和《刘徽注》及其他方面研究上的进展,大多得益于认真研读原著。

冯:"从第一手资料出发"对于每个做学问的人都应该效法。

郭:1979年夏末,我攻读到《九章算术》商功章阳马术的刘徽注,其中提出了一个重要原理:将堑堵分解成一个阳马和一个鳖臑,则"阳马居二,鳖臑居一,不易之率也"。1963年钱老将其证明中的极限过程作为一个未解决的问题留了下来,吴文俊先生则称其为刘徽原理。开始,我对其极限过程也弄不明白,就用土豆刻模型,可是土豆太柔软,不好用。地瓜上市后就用地瓜,刚性还是不好。妻子王玉芝从中国图书进出口总公司给我带回几块进口书箱中的泡沫塑料,好用多了。我刻出堑堵、阳马、鳖臑的模型以及其尺寸小一半的模型,不断分割拼合,几次推翻原来的理解重来……

冯:简直到了废寝忘食、绞尽脑汁的地步。

郭:有两次在梦中似乎解决问题了,醒来却发现出现逻辑错误。还有一次梦到一个穿古装的人演示分割拼合方法,但距离较远,没有看清楚。不过,经过多次分割拼合,校补了几个字,到11月份,终于明白了其极限过程。原来李潢怀疑有错误亦即钱老未解决的那段文字一个错字也没有。李潢的数学水平大概不足以理解刘徽的无穷小分割思想,钱老完全可以解决这个问题,大约受了李潢的误导,没有深究。

冯:这个问题确实应该非常值得深究!据我所知,日本数学史家三上义夫和丹麦科学史家华道安都

先后关注并深入研究过该问题。

郭：我知道华道安（Wagner）的工作是这年 12 月底。当时听李文林先生说，一位外国学者已解决了"阳马术"《刘徽注》问题，发表在《国际数学史杂志》（*Historic Mathematica*）1979 年第 6 期上。我赶紧到所图书馆查，此刊未到。查问中国图书进出口总公司，云该刊国内只订了 3 份，此期只到 2 份，按顺序先给北京图书馆和中国科学院图书馆。我赶紧到北京图书馆查阅，知道是丹麦学者华道安的文章。然而他对《刘徽注》中"令赤黑堑堵各自适当一方"的理解与我不同。三上义夫的工作发表得很早，但论文是用日文写的，很长时期也没有被翻译介绍到中国。我不懂日文，当时对日文研究文献关注不够。

冯：我注意到您早期发表的都是比较有分量的研究论文，罕见有科普文章。

郭：在我尝到研读原著的甜头，决心从事中国数学史研究之后，大约从 1981 年起，为了集中精力和时间搞研究，也为了提高自己的学术水准，我给自己立了两条规矩：

一是如果没有自己满意的论文，决不参加学术会议。这需要经得起诱惑，因为开学术会议的地方大都有风景如画的景点，而且那时没有经费的限制。有一次纪念李善兰的会，可以看钱塘大潮，许多人动员我去，我因为没有满意的论文，婉拒了。我一直恪守这个规矩。

二是十年内一般不搞科普。当时工资低，搞科普不仅可以很快出名，而且有稿费补贴家用，可谓名利双收。而中国数学史有李、钱二老的大量著述，搞科普比其他学科要容易得多。当时家庭生活也比较困难，但是我是下了狠心的。

现在检讨起来，第一个规矩到现在我还认为是对的，还在坚持。至于第二个规矩，我觉得一个科研工作者的主要精力当然要放到科研上，但科研之暇科普还是应该搞的。我当时之所以不搞，是因为快到 40 岁才入门，如果再不集中精力搞科研，那么这一辈子可能就白过了，所以实在是不得已而为之。

我根据以上成果写出《刘徽的极限理论》《刘徽的体积理论》，梅荣照也写出《刘徽的方程理论》《刘徽的勾股理论》，在 1980 年 10 月第一届全国科学史大会数学组报告后，反响较大。一位曾经主张"贫矿论"、准备改行搞桥梁史的先生离京前来所，表示收回"贫矿论"，继续中国数学史研究。

冯：您在进行《九章算术》和刘徽研究过程中，有哪些有利的条件和不利因素？

郭：中国数学史的研究基础深厚，这对后来的研究者既有有利的一面，也有不利的一面。有利的一面很明显，就是我们的研究起点比较高，可以在短时间内，很快掌握中国数学史的系统知识。记得 1992 年春我受命编纂《中国科学技术典籍通汇·数学卷》，是这套大书的开篇之作，《通汇》的编纂体例、格式等，都是《数学卷》起草的。我们很快就拿出一个版本相当精当的选编书目，用不到八个月的时间编纂完成，而且到目前为止，还是整个《通汇》中社会反映最好的卷帙之一。为什么找《数学卷》打头炮，为什么会编得又好又快？根本原因是中国数学史的研究基础比较好。这之前中国科学院就批准我 7 月份去巴黎继续中法对照本《九章算术》的翻译工作，为了编《数学卷》，我只好推迟半年多再出国。1993 年 1 月 4 号下午离京，那天上午我给王渝生博士交待工作时，绝大多数稿件都已加工完毕。

编纂中有两个插曲。一个是，我们拟定了选编书目及选定的版本之后，另一卷的主编说，《数学卷》的版本要求这么高，我们没法编了，要求我们降低版本质量。我理所当然地拒绝了。我们既然编书，当然要拿最好的版本给读者，否则既对不起读者，也对不起李、钱二老。

还有一个是，我在《数学卷》叙中写道："谨向李俨、钱宝琮、严敦杰等数学史界的前辈表示崇高敬意，他们为中国数学史学科打下的坚实基础以及他们的丰富藏书，为《数学卷》的编纂提供了得天独厚的条件。"我看校样时发现编辑把这几句话删掉了。我说你怎么给删掉了？他说你是主编，没有必要写这个。我很生气，说："这几句话必须恢复，没有二老的工作，《数学卷》不可能编得这么快。不写这几句话，我就是贪天之功据为己有，你们会陷我于不义。"三十年来的工作，我深深感到中国数学史学科基础的深厚所带来的好处。

不过另一方面，正因为中国数学史这座殿堂已经相当完备，所以也带来继续研究的困难，不像有的学科，只要耕耘，必有收获。《九章算术》和刘徽的研究，要有所突破和超越前辈们工作，有相当大的难度。

**冯：记得在"文化大革命"结束后，《九章算术》与刘徽首先成为国内数学史的研究热点，也引起了新闻媒体的关注。

郭：是的。1982年春，《人民日报》记者张继民同志来我们所了解科研成果。科研处向他推荐了我们的刘徽研究成果。他在采访我们之后，发表了《谁说中国古代数学没有理论——刘徽就是中国古代数学理论的奠基者》的报导，当天早晨就在中央人民广播电台的《新闻和报纸摘要》节目广播了，把刘徽的影响推向全国。台湾地区的洪万生先生说，他本来研究刘徽，1985年读到我的文章，感到"郭书春所认识的刘徽显然深刻多了"，遂"决定少碰刘徽，而转向19世纪清代数学史发展"。他又说："郭书春的成果连同其他史家（比方李继闵）的相关论述，共同掀起了80年代刘徽研究的高潮"。20世纪八九十年代在海峡两岸、国内外确实出现了《九章算术》和"刘徽热"，发表著述之多，为中国科学史、数学史上所仅见。不过应当指出，我们的研究只是个引子，对大陆《九章算术》和"刘徽热"起作用最大的是吴文俊先生的倡导。

冯：您整理完成的《九章算术》汇校本是关于《九章算术》校勘和整理研究的一项重大成果，国内外学术界评价都相当高，请您介绍一下您的这项重要工作。

郭：我原来没有全面校勘《九章算术》及进行版本研究的想法，1982年给中国科学院提交的与法国林力娜合作翻译《九章算术》的计划中，还说以钱宝琮校点《九章算术》为底本，做个别校勘。有一次严敦杰先生建议我看一下屈曾发刻的豫簪堂本《九章算术》。钱老提到过这个版本，说是微波榭本的翻刻本。我遵从严先生的指示看了豫簪堂本，发现其校勘记作双行夹注，与微波榭本不同，肯定不是其翻刻本。我喜欢刨根问底，于是就校雠了这两个本子，发现了很多不同，通过继续考察，判定戴震整理豫簪堂本比微波榭本早。由此举一反三，从1982到1984年，在研究所图书馆、国图和院馆支持下，在妻子和女儿帮助下，校雠了豫簪堂本、微波榭本、南宋本、汲古阁本、《四库》本、聚珍版、《永乐大典》本、杨辉本、李潢本和钱校本，先后得出戴震在豫簪堂本、微波榭本中做了大量修辞加工，戴震从《永乐大典》辑录《九章算术》的工作极为粗疏等一系列重要结论，都是钱老没有发现的；还发现钱校本的底本是他评价甚低的微波榭本在清末的一个翻刻本；根据余介石一页笔记记载的向达的提示，我三下南京，几经周折，找到了原藏承德避暑山庄的乾隆御览聚珍版《九章算术》，又陆续校雠了各版聚珍版《九章算术》，发现福建补刊本根据李潢本修改过，钱老所用的聚珍版是据补刊本翻刻的广雅本，因此将李潢的不少校勘误为聚珍版原文。总之，通过这些研究，得出了自戴震以来200余年《九章算术》的版本十分混乱的结论。

冯：可以说，您那几年的工作将《九章算术》各版本的异同及流传嬗递研究得比较彻底了。

郭：钱老对《九章算术》的校勘贡献很大，纠正了戴震、李潢大量错校，指出了校勘《九章算术》的正确方向，但是我发现钱老纠正得还不够，也有一些错校。因此我校雠的同时便一方面学习校勘学知识，一方面对戴震、李潢、钱老的校勘进行甄别，发现他们将南宋本、《永乐大典》本四百余条不误原文改错，也发现了不少原文确有舛错而他们的改动亦不恰当之处，还有若干漏校。当然，对后二者大部分校勘属于理校法的范畴，仁智各见，在所难免。

1984年秋，我完成《评戴震对〈九章算术〉的校勘与整理》一文，随即呈吴文俊、严敦杰先生审阅，吴先生于11月11日复信：十分同意"文末提出校勘工作方法的许多看法"，并"希望能发表你关于这几种版本不同处的全部对照表"。信末吴先生还写了加重点号的一句话："应当向你学习！"吴先生的信给了我很大勇气，便产生了做《九章算术》新的校勘本的想法。但是，做成什么样子才符合吴先生的要求，我不懂，遂向李学勤先生请教，他建议用"汇校本"的形式。这就是汇校本名称的由来。

准备汇校本的过程中，我找过许多出版社，都因我名微且此书肯定赔钱而被婉拒。辽宁师范大学梁宗巨先生对我的人品和学识比较欣赏，向辽宁教育出版社（以下简称"辽教"）推荐了我。1986年春，我做提副研究员报告的那天，时任理科编辑室主任的俞晓群先生来京找我谈此书出版，我说："我的书肯定赔钱，你们如果怕赔钱，就不必谈了。"俞晓群说："如果你书好，我们赔钱也出。"我说："我下的功夫，达到的深度，我有数。此书肯定站得住脚。"总算没有辜负"辽教"的期望，吴文俊、严敦杰、李学勤先生给写了序跋，出版后在海峡两岸、国内外反应不错。从此"辽教"与我，与我们所建立了比较密切的关系，我们的许多著作都在"辽教"出版。

想不到，汇校本在20世纪90年代中期就脱销，辽教要重印，我不同意重印，因为需要增补。但当时太忙,来不及做,直到 2002 年才做完,辽教与中国台湾九章出版社联合出版。本来应该出修订本,因为出现了不愿看到的情况,不得不不加修改地照录 90 年版原文而成增补版。

后来我又撰写了汇校本的姊妹篇《古代世界数学泰斗刘徽》,以及《九章算术译注》。对《九章算术》和刘徽研究成功的客观条件是当时科研条件宽松,自由选题。我对《九章算术》和刘徽研究取得进展的主观因素是坚持尊重原始文献的治学方法。数学史界对许多问题有不同看法,原因各异,不尊重原始文献,自说自话,是最重要的原因。读过我的著述的人都知道,我引原文特别多,就是为了正本清源。当然,对原始文献必须分析,比如,证明刘徽关于《九章算术》成书过程的论述是正确的,推翻一百多年的成说,证明杨辉《详解九章算法》含有《九章》本文,刘、李注,贾宪细草和杨辉详解五部分内容,贾宪的《黄帝九章算经细草》尚存 2/3,就是分别对《九章算术》和《详解九章算法》的内容、体例和结构深入分析得出的。

冯:中法文对照版《九章算术》是您和法国学者林力娜成功合作的一项重要工作,是翻译最全面、准确的一个西文版本,《刘徽注》也被完整翻译成外文,参考文献也比较详尽。该书出版后有很大反响,您是否可以谈谈相关情况。

郭:谈到中法对照本《九章算术》,得先从法国林力娜来我所留学谈起。1981 年 3 月,她利用巴黎女子高师毕业时的一笔奖学金来中国学习中国数学史,是我所第一个外国学生,研究所很重视,所内搞数学史的先生都给她讲过课,不过主要教师是梅荣照和我。为此我中断了英语学习班。林力娜来北京时只在火车上学过几句中国话,而我法语口语不行,英语只会看。她只有 8 个月的时间,还想准备关于《测圆海镜》的博士论文。怎么教她?考虑再三,我决定以钱宝琮的《中国数学史》为主要教材,边教中文、边教中国数学史。事实证明,这是一种好办法。因为师生间没有一种共通的流利语言,讲课时中文、法文混用,有时还得加手势和英文。林力娜非常聪明,进步神速,10 月底回国时,圆满完成了任务。

我感到,西方对中国古代数学的偏见,除开政治和民族、文化的因素,对许多人而言是不了解《九章算术》,更不知道刘徽。因此我建议,如果她回国取得博士学位,在法国国家科研中心(CNRS)找到工作,我们合作翻译《九章算术》及其《刘徽注》。她欣然同意。

1982 年,中国科学院和法国 CNRS 决定将合作研究翻译《九章算术》的计划纳入双方科学合作协议,为此,林力娜 3 次来所,我 2 次赴法,历时 20 余年,中法对照本《九章算术》终于在 2004 年 10 月由巴黎 Dunod 出版社出版,不久即脱销,2005 年重印,2006 年获法国学士院"平山郁夫"奖。在 2005 年 7 月 30 日由吴文俊和法国 Kahane 院士发起,中国科学院和法国驻华大使馆举办的发布会上,我说:"早知道这么难,就不干了!"引起全场大笑。这是句实话,原来真没有想到会这么难。尽管开始翻译时我基本上完成了《九章算术》的校勘,觉得自己基本上弄懂了《刘徽注》,但翻译与写论文不同,写论文对不懂的可以避开,但搞翻译则必须将每个字、每句话都得弄懂。而且这种懂不仅是"意会",还必须达到能"言传",能给林力娜讲明白。难度之大,花时间之多,不是几篇论文,甚至也不是一二本书能同日而语的。在我们的讨论中,林力娜常常提出一些深邃的看法。林力娜根据我们讨论的结果写出法译文初稿,我再看是否准确表达了原意,再讨论。一段注,有时要讨论几天才能找到我们都满意的译文。整个译文,也是几易其稿。我们认为,科技典籍的翻译应当以"信、达"为主,兼及"雅"。中法对照本《九章算术》力求做到这一点。

冯:您对中国数学典籍的整理并不限于《九章算术》及其《刘徽注》,可以介绍一下其他的整理、校勘工作吗?

郭:其他数学典籍的整理主要有《中国科学技术典籍通汇·数学卷》和重新点校的《算经十书》。前者是命题作文,我主要是选版本,组织同仁写提要。后者是鉴于钱老在校勘上贡献极大,但是他没有想到戴震会在微波榭本中做大量修辞加工,所校点的《算经十书》保留了这些修辞加工。我重新点校的《算经十书》,其中五部半以南宋本为底本,其余分别以杨辉本、汲古阁本或戴震辑录本为底本。校勘上会见仁见智,但其底本无疑是目前最好的。

此外,我还将元朱世杰《四元玉鉴》译成现代汉语,出版了中英对照《四元玉鉴》。

冯:1983 年在张家山西汉墓出土的竹简《算数书》是中国现存最早的数学著作,该书释文于 2000 年公布,很快受到海内外学者的重视,您也立即投入了研究,而且取得不少成果。

郭:首先,我对《算数书》的校勘主要纠正"释文"中的错简和错校,特别是以《九章算术》的表达方式改动《算数书》的错误。因为《算数书》表达方式的异彩纷呈,是秦及先秦数学的固有现象,是极宝贵的数学史料。其次,我得出《算数书》肯定不是《九章算术》的前身的结论,纠正了文物界的"前身"说。再次,也是我最感兴趣的,我根据对《九章算术》及其《刘徽注》的研究,得出《九章算术》的主体完成于先秦,春秋战国是中国数学的第一个高峰的看法。应该说,这很大程度上是推断,而《算数书》为这种看法和先秦数学提供了实证。

冯:数学史研究的学术传承非常重要,您还做了整理李俨、钱宝琮和严敦杰等大师的学术著作集或全集的工作,您完成这些工作后有何感受?

郭:《李俨钱宝琮科学史全集》的编纂是辽教俞晓群首先提出的,并给以资助,由我和刘钝主持。我一直为严敦杰先生没有与其学术地位相称的著作感到惋惜,自20世纪80年代初,就劝严先生缩短战线,写出自己的学术著作。待他听进我的劝告,为时已晚,不久中风卧床,留下终生遗憾。2000年纪念祖冲之诞辰1500周年之际,我整理了他的《祖冲之科学著作校释》,由辽教出版。整理前辈学术著作的过程,也是自己系统学习的好机会。

在中国数学史界,大概我是对钱老发表不同意见最多的,但是,我可以问心无愧地说,在对钱老的尊重上,我起码不亚于别人,是我提议召开了"纪念李俨钱宝琮诞辰一百周年国际学术讨论会",是我主持了《李俨钱宝琮科学史全集》的编纂。《辞海》1999年版的中国数学史条目是我修订撰写的,本来编辑部发来的辞条有李无钱,在我的坚持下,补充了钱老。我对李老、钱老和严先生一直非常景仰,在我撰著编纂的著作的前言、叙和后记中,都表达了这种感情。他们的论著博大精深,我至今受益无穷。我一直认为,我的成绩,乃至学风和治学方法是李老、钱老和严先生等前辈的著述以及他们的思想、方法长期熏陶的结果,是他们的思想、方法的继承和深化。

冯:您在中国数学通史和数学思想史方面也有重要工作,请您做些介绍。

郭:中国数学通史方面的工作,我做得不多,有一个小册子《中国古代数学》,在海峡两岸出版五六次了。这几年主编《中国科学技术史·数学卷》,我只写先秦至元的某些部分,其他部分都是同仁帮忙。数学思想史方面我有兴趣,但搞得很少,只对《九章算术》、刘徽和秦九韶、李冶做过一点,还谈不到系统。不知以后有没有机会做。

冯:目前您还在主持一项数学典籍的整理工作。

郭:由吴文俊、席泽宗推荐,我目前担任《中华大典》编委会常务编委,正主编其《数学典》,也是组织国内30几位同仁一起做。这是国家的一项重大文化工程。

冯:您是中国数学史领域的权威学者,很想了解您对中国古代数学的总体评价。对于有人认为中国古代没有数学或数学理论的观点,您有何看法?

郭:我认为,数学的发展,既有数学内部的自身因素,也必然受社会经济、政治、思想和文化背景的制约。人类进入文明社会以来,世界数学研究的中心发生了几次大的变化。约公元前3世纪至公元14世纪初,中国取代古希腊,成为世界数学研究的中心,是当时世界数学发展的主流。中国数学以算法见长,但这并不是说没有理论。《九章算术》的严谨、抽象、普适的术文就是理论,刘徽以演绎逻辑对《九章算术》及自己提出的命题的严谨证明,更是数学理论。说中国古代数学没有理论的人不是没有读过刘徽的《九章算术注》,就是读了而没有读懂。说中国古代没有数学的人最好先读读《九章算术》及其《刘徽注》再发言。

数学与物理学、化学不同。《九章算术》的运算法则,我们现在还在用。中国传统数学的某些思想、方法对现今的数学教学、数学研究仍有启迪作用。河南济源有一个五龙口小学,用中国古代"率"的思想和珠算指导小学数学教学,取得了很好的成绩。吴文俊先生受中国传统数学机械化思想的启发,创立了数学机械化理论,这是大家都知道的。可见中国传统数学还有活力。

冯:您对目前我国的数学史研究和学科发展有何看法,您认为今后应当关注哪方面的问题?

郭:许多人贬低中国古代数学,是因为不了解,不完全是偏见。因此,向国内外的学术界、教育界,尤其是大、中、小学的教师、学生传播中国数学史知识,是十分必要的。这是数学史工作者责无旁贷的使命。因此,数学史研究应当与数学教育相结合。

中国数学史的研究基础比较好,但是,还有许多工作应该做。首先是中国近现代数学史的研究一直比较薄弱,亟需大力开展。

其次,中国传统数学的研究方面,对先秦数学的研究还相对薄弱。即使是研究基础较好的汉魏至明清数学,我们以往主要关注内史的研究,内史中又着重数学成就。数学成就的研究,也多注重"过五关,斩六将",忽视"走麦城"。实际上,研究数学发展道路上的曲折,有时候则更有意义。应当开展当时社会的政治、经济、社会思潮和文化背景与数学发展的关系,即所谓外史的研究。在这种研究中,我们应该借鉴国外数学史界科学的、行之有效的研究方法,并进一步开展广泛的国际交流与合作。

再次,开展比较数学史和数学交流与传播史的研究。目前这一领域也相当薄弱。

总之,中国数学史领域还是有大量的事情要做的。一方面要克服无所作为的想法,另一方面,任何研究必须建立在踏实、深厚的内史研究基础之上。那种不搞甚至贬低内史研究,是不可能搞好其他研究的;只是变换一下名词,套用几个时髦的术语,不是真正的研究;那种空对空的东西可以哗众取宠,却经不起时间的考验。

冯:感谢您接受采访。

我的早期经历与数学史研究工作
——郭书春先生访谈录

郭书春（中国科学院自然科学史研究所）口述
郭金海（中国科学院自然科学史研究所）访问整理

摘要 郭书春是享誉国际的中国数学史家，在《九章算术》及其刘徽注的研究、《九章算术》版本校勘等方面成就卓著。在这篇访谈录中，他追忆了从少年到大学时代、参加工作后调入中国科学院中国自然科学史研究室的经历，回顾了1975年走上中国数学史研究道路，取得丰硕研究成果的历程。这篇访谈录反映了一位数学史研究者在新中国的成长历程与交织于社会变迁的曲折人生，并展现了他对数学史研究的思考和感悟。

关键词 郭书春，自然科学史研究所，数学史，政治运动

访谈时间：2016年12月11日、20日、21日
访谈地点：北京华严北里20号楼郭书春先生家；中国科学院自然科学史研究所620办公室

一、从少年到大学时代

访：郭老师，感谢您接受采访。为纪念研究所成立60周年与为撰写研究所历史准备资料，所里希望做些离退休职工的访谈。您到研究所工作较早，经历和知道的事情多，又是成就卓著的数学史家，很值得采访。我们先从您的少年时代谈起吧！

郭：我于1941年出生于山东省胶州市胶西东埠村。这是一个非常偏僻的农村，在沂蒙山区的边上。村子向南一直是丘陵，到沂蒙山区，向北是一望无际的平地，就是胶莱谷地。我们村边上有条河，是莫言的小说《红高粱》中的墨河。我父母育有6个孩子，全是男孩，我年龄最小。我父亲比较能干，有发家致富的想法。在他的努力和带领下，我们家摆脱了贫苦，变成一户殷实人家。我出生前后，包括租来的土地，家里已有田地20多亩。这也招致村里一些人的嫉妒。我在离我们村3华里的邻村上的初小，教学条件相当落后，四个年级的学生在同一个教室上学。

访：您上小学一年级时，就已经是1949年了，那时还有复式教学？

郭：我没有上过一年级，入学就插班在二年级。当时是一个老师给这个年级的学生教完了，布置好作业，再给另一个年级的学生讲。教师的水平也参差不齐。有一位老师，只上过小学四年级，认字很少。我的启蒙老师王秀峰相当好，高中毕业，一直教我们。20世纪90年代初我的住房稍有改善，便接他们夫妇来北京游玩。

上小学时，我是学习上的尖子，在当地学习是比较有名的。我哥哥是三野军官，有一次探亲回家，一块下车的有一个区里的一位干部，问我哥哥是哪个村的，我哥哥说是东埠的。那个干部说你们村有个神童，我哥说就是我小弟弟。

访：您小学学习成绩这么好，上中学是不是很顺利？

郭：不是。1953年我小学毕业。当年考入青岛第一中学（以下简称青岛一中）。当时考青岛一中非常难。这是我人生中的一个难关。另一个难关是1978年提助研。先讲考青岛一中。青岛一中是全国相当好的中学。1952年全国教育大发展，青岛一中招了16个班。但1953年全国教育大收缩，青岛一中只招4个班，计划只招200人。由于青岛一中好，门槛高，有许多学生不敢报考，但青岛一中也有1200多人报名，相当于6个人录取1个。当年招了209人，我考了201名。我哥哥是解放军，我们家是

军属。我考上可能是照顾的。

访：当时发录取通知书吗？您是怎么知道考试排名的？过了这个难关之后，您的学习情况如何？

郭：不发录取通知书，是放榜。放榜时，我特地从老家去青岛一中看榜。考上以后，我学习很吃力。这有几个原因。一是，我的学习基础差。尽管在我们当地是尖子，但到青岛一中不行。二是，有的老师讲话有口音，他们讲课，我听起来很困难。我从小没离开过我们村，别说南方口音，就是山东其他县的口音，我也听不懂。记得我的一位数学老师，是南方人。他讲排列组合时，说"男的""女的"，我就听成"蓝的""绿的"。

不过，到初中毕业时，我的学习成绩就比较靠前了。初中毕业后，我顺利考上青岛一中的高中。当时高中招了6个班，招360多名学生，我考了60几名。到高中毕业时，我的学习成绩就十分靠前了，全校表扬了10名优秀毕业生学生，其中有我。

访：当时您的学习成绩在年级排到前10名了吧！

郭：当时学校是综合学生多方面的表现来表扬的，不光看学习成绩。有的同学学习成绩不比我差，但并未获得表扬。

访：您高中毕业后，考取的是山东大学数学系。您为什么报考数学系？读数学系后的学习情况怎样？

郭：我在高中数学学得比较好，但兴趣不在数学，而是在历史和生物。1959年高考时学校极力动员学习好的学生考理工科，我拗不过班主任，同意报考理工科。当时我报的大部分志愿都是工科，只在第十志愿中填了山东大学数学系。不知道为什么，我被山东大学数学系录取了。这可能是因为我数学考得好。

访：您能否谈谈在山东大学数学系的情况？

郭：我上大学时，山东大学本科由4年改为了5年。在大学第一年，我们上课时间比较少。记得教我们高等代数的贾老师对此很有意见，在期末出的考题比较难。结果全年级有三分之二的学生成绩是"劣"（当时山东大学分优、良、中、劣四级，"劣"就是不及格）。我这次考试得的是"良"，还算是成绩不错的。系里只好决定这次考试成绩不作为升降级的根据。

访：您上大学一二年级的时候，我国正处于经济困难时期，全国各地在闹饥荒。您在大学感受到当时经济困难的形势了吗？

郭：感受到了。山东的灾荒在全国是比较突出的，当时学校的伙食很差，我们吃过粉碎的花生壳、玉米芯。一天很难吃上一顿饱饭。不过，课是照样上的。与一年级相比，课也相对正规。

访：当时山东大学数学系在全国处于什么水平？您在数学系的学习成绩如何？

郭：在全国26所重点大学中处于中等水平。我在数学系的学习成绩比较好，属于第一个团队的学生，曾被选为优秀学生。

二、从参加工作到调入中国自然科学史研究室

访：您是1965年到中国科学院中国自然科学史研究室工作的。之前，在新建设杂志社工作。您为什么到这个杂志社工作？

郭：在大学四年级时，系里内定我留校当老师，并指定尤秉礼先生指导我。到大五，高教部规定，重点大学的业务教师必须是研究生毕业。系里通知我，不留校了，参加统一分配，就分到了新建设杂志社。《新建设》是"文化大革命"前的一个重要的文史哲经刊物，隶属于中国科学院哲学社会科学部（简称"学部"，实际上自1962年起就与中国科学院脱钩，归中宣部领导）。1964年，周扬要把《新建设》杂志变成一个大型的刊物，增加数学和自然科学，甚至绘画和文艺创作的内容。我们系的分配方案中有《新建设》

杂志编辑一名。大概因为我的文史功底在数学系学生中算是比较好的,也关心时事,就被选中了[2]。

访:您为什么从新建设杂志社调到中国自然科学史研究室?

郭:《新建设》杂志改刊后,在学术界反映不好。严济慈就说,我们的文章在我们这边发都是头版头条,而到你们那边发都被当成"边角料"。这样,中宣部决定将《新建设》改为原来的方向。由此,我就调入中国自然科学史研究室。

访:当时中国自然科学史研究室跟新建设杂志社一样,也归哲学社会科学部管理。这样调动应该比较容易。您还记得到研究室报到的情景吗?

郭:1965年12月9日前后,我到研究室报到,见到的第一个人是黄炜。她是研究室的学术副秘书、党支部组织委员。黄炜见到我后,问了我的情况。当时我还不知道钱宝琮是谁,因为要在新建设杂志社当编辑,想扩大知识面,已经托人在北京买了钱宝琮主编的《中国数学史》。我对黄炜说:"我已经买了钱宝琮同志的《中国数学史》。"黄炜说:"那是钱老。"钱老的这本书出版后,中国古代数学史基本研究完了。她让我研究世界数学史。

由于黄炜要我研究世界数学史,我到研究室后就买了一套大学的法语课本《法语语法》,自学法语。当时梅荣照做数学史组的代理组长。我跟他说:"我每天晚来一个小时,在宿舍学法语。"钱老好开玩笑,见我读这本书,说书名正着读和倒着读都是"法语语法"。

访:您自学法语困难吗?

郭:我在大学学过一段法语,当时开了两个班。我们的法语老师,是南京大学法语系毕业的,但后来被开除了。我这个班就停了,当时我只学了发音。由于已经学了发音,我自学法语,还是有一定的基础。

三、数学史研究工作:从徘徊到丰收

访:1975年8月,中国自然科学史研究室改成自然科学史研究所,恢复了业务工作。当时在数学史研究方面,所里准备做哪些工作?您个人对数学史研究又是怎样考虑的?

郭:恢复工作时,梅荣照任数学史组组长。在数学史研究方面,他认为李、钱二老[3]把资料搞完了,缺点就是没有以马克思主义为指导。于是,所领导希望数学史组撰写一部新的《中国数学史》,要以马列主义、毛泽东思想为指导,以阶级斗争为纲。随后,梅荣照计划召开一次重新撰写《中国数学史》的学术讨论会。为了此事,所里给学部领导小组打了报告。学部领导小组要求撰写新的《中国数学史》要有工农兵参加,学术讨论会得有三分之一的工农兵代表。

为了顺利召开这次学术讨论会与撰写新的《中国数学史》,我和梅荣照、何绍庚、刘子央等数学史组的同事到北京774电子管厂,给工人理论小组的师傅们讲数学史。再由他们指导我们撰写《中国数学史》。在北京774电子管厂,我们还遇到了数学所的李文林、袁向东。他们也是为了撰写这部书而来。当时,梅荣照还物色到一个搞算筹的农民,找了好几个解放军。开会时,工农兵代表达到了与会人员的三分之一。

这个学术讨论会于1976年10月初在东四宾馆召开。我和梅荣照、何绍庚等所里数学史组的同事都参加了。所外的李迪、李继闵、沈康身、白尚恕、李文林、袁向东、李赞和等也参加了。会议主要讨论梅荣照起草的这部新的《中国数学史》的提纲。开会期间,粉碎了"四人帮"。尽管这次学术讨论会的指导思想是错误的,撰写这部新的《中国数学史》的计划也未能付诸实施,但会议还是讨论了一些学术问题,也是国内数学史界同仁从未有过的聚会。

恢复业务工作后,我对数学史研究一度处于徘徊期,不知道要研究什么,曾萌生调走的念头,但也不知道去哪。因为当时有人提出中国数学史研究"贫矿论",说已经没有什么可研究的了。我在大学所学

---

[2] 1964年学部从全国高校共挑选4名理科毕业生到新建设杂志社工作。除郭书春外,还有中山大学的郑锡煌、厦门大学的金秋鹏、江西大学的刘淑兰。

[3] 李、钱二老,即李俨、钱宝琮。

的和参加工作后自学的法语不足以应对世界数学史研究。1978年,研究所筹建近现代科学史研究室时,让我到这个研究室工作,我就没有去。

访:在这段徘徊期,您的心情一定很复杂,情绪也不高。

郭:对。在1978年还遇到提助研这个难关。这次评职称从3月份开始,到9月或10月份公布,历时半年。仓孝和所长做评职称的动员报告时说:"有的同志大学成绩不错,工作能力也很强,但他们所在的学科研究基础很好,研究起来特别难。我们决定等他做出一定成绩后,再给他提。"当时所里研究最好的,就是数学史这个学科。而所里没有提助研的研究数学史的,只是何绍庚和我。而何绍庚在"文化大革命"前已经写好研究生毕业论文,有了研究成果。我一听,知道这些话是针对我说的,心想这次提助研没希望了。不过,九十月份所里公布评职称结果时,仓孝和又做了一次报告,说鉴于有的同志工作能力比较强,我们考虑再三决定还是给他提。这话也是针对我说的。我一听,心里才一块石头落了地。好在我对提职称这类身外之物,历来看得很淡,否则历时半年,会把身体搞垮的。

访:虽然这道关惊险,但最终还是闯过了。

郭:提助研时,我确实没有什么成果,只写了两篇文章,收入《科学技术发明家小传》[4]《中国古代科技成就》[5]两书。当时我也没有自己独创性的东西,算是有些创新的东西,就是我对《墨经》中有一句话有一个新看法。但这种看法李约瑟(Joseph Needham,1900—1995)早讲过了,只是我不知道。不过,这关过了以后,我提副研、正研就容易了。因为那时我的研究成果已经很多,在所内研究人员中比较突出了。

访:1978年之后,您在《九章算术》及其刘徽注方面取得了突破性进展,发表了大量成果,对打破中国数学史研究"贫矿论"做出重要贡献。我听您说过是梅荣照先生建议您研究刘徽的[6]。您在这方面是如何具体做的?

郭:1978年我虽然提了助研,但不知研究什么。这年秋,梅荣照建议我和他一起研究刘徽。他说李约瑟的书中谈到刘徽的地方比杨辉还少。此后,我在所里查了美国的《世界科学家大辞典》,找到关于刘徽的条目,是何丙郁写的。我发现这个条目全是关于《九章算术》的内容,刘徽的成就一条也没提。我看到这种情况,就下决心研究。

就在这时,"真理标准"大讨论对我产生极大的影响。一开始,我很吃惊。十几年来我对"毛主席的话是检验真理的标准"始终不敢怀疑。而这次讨论提出了"实践是检验真理的唯一标准",与之针锋相对。于是,我翻出大学的哲学教材,发现里面有一节的标题是"实践是检验真理的标准"。我在大学时,哲学学得比较好,但后来却把这句话忘记了。而且,结论"实践是检验真理的唯一标准"中的"唯一"两字给我触动很大。

这一认识的飞跃,使我感到检验现在对刘徽和古代数学的看法是不是正确,唯一的标准就是刘徽《九章算术注》和古代的原始文献。因此,我决心逐字逐句地阅读和分析刘徽的《九章算术注》。起初没有大的新发现。1979年初,我开始研读《九章算术》卷一圆田术的刘徽注,也就是著名的"割圆术"。当我读到"以一面乘半径,觚而裁之,每辄自倍,故以半周乘半径而为圆幂"时,意识到刘徽这是在证明《九章算术》圆田术"半周半径相乘得积步",即圆面积公式。意识到这点以后,我赶紧查钱老的《中国数学史》,发现书中谈了刘徽的极限过程后便跳过这几句话,去谈如何求圆周率了。我再看整个圆田术刘徽注,发现它不只是求圆周率,而是明显包括两部分,第一部分是证明《九章算术》的圆面积公式,第二部分才求圆周率。而求圆周率,只是极限思想在近似计算中的应用,用不到极限过程。我到各图书馆查阅了能找到的所有谈割圆术的文章,发现没有一篇涉及圆面积公式的证明。甚至《数学教学》上刊登的一篇

---

[4] 郭书春:《解析几何的奠基者笛卡尔》,中国科学院自然科学史研究所,北京第一机床厂《小传》编写组:《科学技术发明家小传》,北京:北京人民出版社,1978年,第189—197页。

[5] 郭书春:《高次方程数值解法和天元术》,自然科学史研究所编:《中国古代科技成就》,北京:中国青年出版社,1978年,第122—140页。

[6] 郭金海:《数学史家梅荣照传略》,《自然科学史研究》,2016年第35卷第2期,第242页。

逐字逐句用现代汉语翻译圆田术注的文章,对上述画龙点睛的25个字,竟略而不译。我接着研读刘徽割圆术的第二部分,又发现钱老和所有作者由于没有认识到刘徽在证明《九章算术》圆面积公式把刘徽求圆周率的程序也统统搞错了。关于这些发现,我反复与梅荣照讨论过几次,他最终同意我是对的。

访:这些发现对您后来继续研究《九章算术》及其刘徽注一定意义重大。

郭:这些发现使我破除了中国数学史已经搞完了的成见,克服了畏难情绪,坚定了继续从事中国数学史研究的信心。其次,它们使我破除了对钱老工作的迷信。第三,它们使我尝到了从第一手资料出发,实事求是,认真研读原著,尊重原始文献的甜头。实际上,这成为我治学的宗旨。几十年来我在《九章算术》及其刘徽注和其他方面研究上的进展,纠正了清中叶以来中国数学史界流传了一二百年的若干错误看法,大多得益于认真研读原著。

访:对于科学史研究者而言,重视原始文献,认真研读原著十分重要。您除了研究刘徽,还研究《九章算术》的版本,并取得国内外瞩目的成就。您为什么研究《九章算术》的版本?

郭:我研究《九章算术》的版本是受到严敦杰先生的影响。他有一次建议我看看研究所图书馆善本部的豫簪堂本《九章算术》,是屈曾发刊刻的。钱老也提到过这个版本,说是微波榭本的翻刻本。我看了这个豫簪堂本,发现其校勘记是双行夹注,体例与微波榭本都不一样,断定不是微波榭本的翻刻本。由此,我发现钱老在《九章算术》版本研究上也不是尽善尽美。

我这个人有个毛病,发现问题就追到底。于是,我就开始校对这两个本子,发现很多不同。我校对完了,又到北京图书馆去校对《九章算术》的聚珍本,去了好几天。那时,我发现问题便记在钱老校点的《算经十书》有关《九章算术》校勘的相应页码上。后来又发现了南京博物院收藏的原藏承德避暑山庄的乾隆御览聚珍版《九章算术》。我发现这个版本很偶然。咱们所有一部清同治年间刻的聚珍版的《九章算术》,那时线装书可以借回家,可是一直没有读过。有一天我工作累了,躺在沙发上翻看此书,从书中掉落一章张纸,我发现是余介石写此书的笔记,说向达跟他讲过承德避暑山庄有一套修改过的聚珍版,新中国成立后藏南京博物院,但余介石没有找到。我按照这个线索,几经周折,最终在南京博物院找到。后来我在法国的汉学高等研究所,找到1893年的《九章算术》聚珍版补刊本。经过校对各种聚珍版的《九章算术》,我发现钱老使用的聚珍版是根据补刊本翻刻的广雅本,并非原版,将李潢的不少校勘错误误认为是聚珍版原本的内容。

后来我写过一篇文章《评戴震对〈九章算术〉的校勘与整理》,指出了《九章算术》校勘的方向,就是纠正错校,漏校不多了。以这篇文章,我做过几次报告,反响相当好。我也将这篇文章寄给过吴文俊、严敦杰、杜石然、梅荣照、李学勤、李仲均等先生。吴文俊先生评价很高,回信说同意我的校勘原则,还说希望尽快看到我关于所有《九章算术》版本不同处的对照表。吴先生信末还有一句话:"应当向你学习!"这句话下面加了圆圈,即重点号。对于做这样的对照表,我不知道该怎么做,就去请教李学勤先生。我们在劲松住同一幢楼。我以前请教过他好多问题。这时,我把吴先生信的意思告诉他。李学勤告诉我:你可以搞汇校。后来我搞汇校,是受李学勤的启发。

访:您的《汇校〈九章算术〉》很受欢迎。在国内外数学史界影响很大。您后来还出了增补版。据说,《汇校〈九章算术〉》出版并不顺利。

郭:《汇校〈九章算术〉》写出来后,起初没有地方出版。我也找过科学出版社,但被拒绝了。后来辽宁师范大学的梁宗巨先生帮了很大的忙。他对我很欣赏,跟我关系很好。他对我的工作完全持信任的态度。有一次我跟他说,我的这部书稿写完了,但没有地方出版。于是,他向辽宁教育出版社推荐了这本书,国内外反响都不错。有一次台湾地区的孙文先先生来,说我的《汇校〈九章算术〉》在台湾地区多么受欢迎,说台湾"中央研究院"数学所所长李国伟买了3本,一本放家里,一本放办公室,一本放所图书馆。

访:在上述研究之外,您还主编了《中国科学技术史·数学卷》。这是一部重要的中国数学史著作,出版后于2012年获得"郭沫若中国历史学奖"一等奖。这个奖是国内历史学界的最高奖项。您能谈谈主编这部书的情况吗?

郭:编撰多卷本《中国科学技术史》是中国科学院"八五"重点科研项目。我是1988年应数学卷主编杜石然先生约请，参加此书数学卷的编撰工作的。20世纪90年代初我完成了我承担的部分初稿。但由于各种原因，数学卷的编撰工作进展很不顺利。2004年，杜石然宣布辞去《中国科学技术史·数学卷》主编，并且是全家的"final"决定，负责《中国科学技术史》这套书的陈美东先生反复动员我做《中国科学技术史·数学卷》的主编。在他的极力劝说下，我答应出任该卷主编。我重新组建了《中国科学技术史·数学卷》的编委会，拟定了提纲，得到了数学史界许多学者的鼎力支持。当时《中国科学技术史·数学卷》没有写出，经费却已经用完，我没有在意。有一天田森打电话给我，说你自己不要经费，刚参加编写的先生复印点资料还得用钱呢！我向陈美东提出这个问题，他拨了5 000块钱，我给了院外的先生。在基本没有经费的情况下，我们完成了编撰任务。最终这部书还获得了"郭沫若中国历史学奖"一等奖，结局很圆满。颁奖后记者问我的感想，我说，我最感动的是，我们基本上是零经费运作。这在"一切向钱看"的今天，是难能可贵的。

访：近三四十年，您在中国古代数学史研究领域取得了丰硕的成果。您最得意的研究工作是什么？最满意的论文有哪些？

郭：最得意是关于《九章算术》及其刘徽注的研究。没有我的研究，20世纪八九十年代不会出现关于《九章算术》和刘徽研究的高潮。我最满意的论文，是关于这一研究的成果《刘徽的极限理论》[7]《刘徽的体积理论》[8]《〈九章算术〉和刘徽中之率的概念及其应用试析》[9]《刘徽〈九章算术注〉中的定义及演绎逻辑试析》[10]《贾宪〈黄帝九章算经细草〉初探——〈详解九章算法〉结构试析》[11]等。我对秦九韶人品的翻案工作也是满意的，发表了论文《重新品评秦九韶》[12]。

访：感谢您开诚布公地讲述了这么多的亲身经历与多年来所做的研究工作及心得、感触，令我受益匪浅。

---

7 郭书春：《刘徽的极限理论》，《科学史集刊》，1984年第11期，第37—46页。
8 郭书春：《刘徽的体积理论》，《科学史集刊》，1984年第11期，第47—62页。
9 郭书春：《〈九章算术〉和刘徽注重之率的概念及其应用试析》，《科学史集刊》，1984年第11期，第21—36页。
10 郭书春：《刘徽〈九章算术注〉中的定义及演绎逻辑试析》，《自然科学史研究》，1983年第2卷第3期，第193—203页。
11 郭书春：《贾宪〈黄帝九章算经细草〉初探——〈详解九章算法〉结构试析》，《自然科学史研究》，1988年第7卷第4期，第328—334页。
12 郭书春：《重新品评秦九韶》，姜锡东主编：《宋史研究论丛》，第10辑，保定：河北大学出版社，2009年，第191—236页。

附录　郭书春论著目录(1978年至今)

(一)所著学术著作

书名	字数(千字)	出版单位	出版时间
1. 汇校《九章算术》	350	辽宁教育出版社	1990
[1991年获全国教育图书一等奖]			
2. 汇校《九章筭术》增补版(上、下册)	500	辽宁教育出版社 台湾九章出版社	2004
[2013年入选新闻出版广电总局和全国古籍整理出版规划领导小组首届向全国推荐的60年来出版的91部优秀古籍整理图书]			
3. 九章筭术新校(上、下册)	804	中国科学技术大学出版	2014,2020
[2019年获安徽省社会科学奖(2013—2016)三等奖]			
4. 中国古代数学	75	山东教育出版社	1991
中国古代数学(繁体字本)	75	台北商务印书馆	1994,1995
5. 中国古代数学(增补本)	89	北京商务印书馆	1997,2004
6. 中国古代数学(增补修订本)	89	北京商务印书馆	2007,2009,2010
7. 古代世界数学泰斗刘徽	320	山东科学技术出版社	1992
[1993年获北方十二省科学图书奖二等奖]			
8. 古代世界数学泰斗刘徽(繁体修订本)	350	台北明文书局	1995
9. 古代世界数学泰斗刘徽(再修订本)	352	山东科学技术出版社	2013
10. 点校《九章算术》(戴震辑录本)	124	《传世藏书》海南国际新闻出版中心	1997
11. 译注《九章算术》	379	辽宁教育出版社	1998
12. 点校《算经十书》(《周髀算经》系与刘钝合作)	337	辽宁教育出版社	1998
13. 点校《算经十书》(繁体修订本,《周髀算经》系与刘钝合作)	423	台北九章出版社	2001
14. 规矩方圆——中国数学小史		辽海出版社	2001
15. 国学举要·术卷(杨文衡 陈美东 郭书春合著)		湖北教育出版社	2002
16. LES NEUF CHAPITRES : Le Classique mathématique de la Chine ancienne et ses commentaires(中法双语评注对照本《九章算术》,与法 K. Chemla 合作)		DUNOD Editeur(巴黎)	2004,2005
		Les éditions du gangourou	2013
[2006年获法兰西学士院平山郁夫奖,2018年入选中国改革开放40周年引才引智展览]			
17. 汉英对照《四元玉鉴》 Jade Mirror of the Four Unknowns [元]朱世杰著,郭书春今译,郭金海补译,陈在新英译　纳入新闻出版署《大中华文库》	500	辽宁教育出版社	2006
18. 点校《九章算术》(戴震辑录本)	64	《国学备览》首都师范大学出版社	2007

续表

书名	字数(千字)	出版单位	出版时间
19. 九章筭术译注	450	《中国古代科技名著译注丛书》上海古籍出版社	2009,2010,2013,2014,2015,2017,2018
20. 九章筭术译注(修订本)	600	《中国古代科技名著译注丛书》上海古籍出版社	2020
21. 九章筭术译注	680	《中国古代名著全本译注丛书》上海古籍出版社	2021
22. 中国传统数学史话	220	中国国际广播出版社	2012
23. 汉英对照《九章筭术》(Nine Chapters on the Art of Mathematics 郭书春校注并今译 [美]道本周,徐义保英译并注 纳入新闻出版署《大中华文库》)	820	辽宁教育出版社	2013
24. 大众数学史(杨静 潘丽云 刘献军 郭书春合作)		《大众科学技术史丛书》山东科学技术出版社	2015
25. 算经之首——《九章筭术》	150	海天出版社	2016
26. 论中国古代数学家	161	海豚出版社	2017
27. 郭书春数学史自选集(上、下册)	1200	山东科学技术出版社	2018
28. 九章算术解读	398	科学出版社	2019,2020
	[2021年获第五届中国出版政府奖图书奖]		
29.《九章算术》白话译讲(学生版)	130	北京大学出版社	2021
	《科学元典丛书·学生版》入选全国中小学生阅读指导目录		
30. 少儿彩绘版《九章算术》(上超绘图)	150	接力出版社	2022,同年修订重印 2023
	[2022年广西十佳科普读物大赛中获二等奖]		
	[入选新晨百道童书榜2022年2月知识百科榜单]		
	[入选2022年3月中华读书报月度好书榜]		
	[入选新发现·科普书单]		
	[入选《中国教育报》公布的2022年度教师喜爱的100本书和十佳童书]		

(二)主编或参编的学术著作

书名	字数(千字)	出版单位	出版时间
1. 马恩列斯论科学技术(中国科学院自然科学史研究所编)		人民出版社	1979
2. 中国历代文献精粹大典·科技卷(林文照主编 汪子春 郭书春副主编)	1100	学苑出版社	1990
3. 山东古代科学家(许义夫 张殿民 郭书春主编)	250	山东教育出版社	1992
4. 中国科学技术典籍通汇·数学卷(五册)	7000	河南教育出版社 大象出版社	1993 2002,2015
	[1997年获第三届全国图书奖提名奖]		
5. 中华科技五千年(华觉明主编 郭书春等副主编、总统稿)	733	山东教育出版社	1997
中国科技史(繁体字)		台北五南图书出版股份有限公司	2004

续表

书名	字数（千字）	出版单位	出版时间
6. 中华科技五千年（多媒体光盘 总编剧之一）		山东教育出版社 清华大学多媒体教育软件研究中心	1999
		[获第8届莫比斯多媒体光盘国际大奖赛中国赛区提名奖]	
7. 李俨钱宝琮科学史全集（10卷，主持，与杜石然、刘钝联合主编）	4478	辽宁教育出版社	1998
		[1999年获第四届全国图书奖荣誉奖即最高奖]	
8. 严敦杰《祖冲之科学著作校释》	166	辽宁教育出版社	2000
9. 严敦杰《祖冲之科学著作校释》（增补版）	231	山东科学技术出版社	2017
		[2019年获第七届中华优秀出版物奖图书奖]	
10. 严敦杰《祖冲之科学著作校释》（增补重印）	300	山东科学技术出版社	2021
		[纳入2022年丝路书香工程立项项目]	
11. 中国科学技术史·数学卷	1400	科学出版社	2010,2017
		[2012年获第四届郭沫若历史奖一等奖]	
12. 中国科学技术史·辞典卷（郭书春 李家明主编）	753	科学出版社	2011
13. 大众科学技术史丛书（12册）		山东科学技术出版社	2015
14. 中华大典·数学典（9册 主编，郭世荣 冯立升副主编）	14540	山东教育出版社	2018
15. 中华大典·数学典·中国传统算法分典（4册）	6200	山东教育出版社	2018

（三）学术论文

题目	著作、报刊、出版社	出版时间
1. 解析几何的奠基者笛卡儿	《科学技术发明家小传》 北京出版社	1978
2. 高次方程数值解法和天元术	《中国古代科技成就》 中国青年出版社	1978,1995
The Numerical Solution of Higher Equation and the Tianyuan Method *Ancient China's Technology and Science*（英译）	Foreign Languages Press	1983
DieNumerische Losung von im Gleichungen hoberen Grades And die Tianyuan methods *Wissenschaff and Thechnih alten China*（德译）	Birkhauser Verlag, Berlin	1989
3. 谈谈刘徽的数学教育思想	《人民教育》1981年第2期	1981
	《郭书春数学史自选集》上册 山东科学技术出版社	2018
4. 笛卡儿	《外国历史名人传（近代卷）》 中国社会科学出版社、重庆出版社	1981
	《世界名人谱近代卷Ⅲ》 人民出版社	1998
5.《九章算术》中的整数勾股形研究	《科学史文集》（数学史专辑） 上海科学技术出版社	1982
	《郭书春数学史自选集》上册 山东科学技术出版社	2018

续表

题目	著作、报刊、出版社	出版时间
6. 学习《数书九章》札记	《科学史文集》(数学史专辑) 上海科学技术出版社	1982
	《郭书春数学史自选集》下册 山东科学技术出版社	2018
7. 东汉墓及其出土的算筹(执笔,与李胜伍合作)	《考古》1982年第3期	1982
	《郭书春数学史自选集》下册 山东科学技术出版社	2018
8. 阿基米得	《外国历史名人传(古代卷)》 中国社会科学出版社、重庆出版社	1982
	《世界名人谱古代卷Ⅱ》 人民出版社	1998
9. 刘徽的极限理论	《科学史集刊》第11集 地质出版社	1984
	《郭书春数学史自选集》上册 山东科学技术出版社	2018
10. 刘徽的体积理论	《科学史集刊》第11集 地质出版社	1984
	《郭书春数学史自选集》上册 山东科学技术出版社	2018
11.《九章算术》和刘徽注中之率概念及其应用试析	《科学史集刊》第11集 地质出版社	1984
	《郭书春数学史自选集》上册 山东科学技术出版社	2018
12. 刘徽的面积理论	《辽宁师院学报(自)》1983第1期	1983
	《郭书春数学史自选集》上册 山东科学技术出版社	2018
13. 刘徽在数学上的伟大贡献	《数学的实践和认识》1983年第3期	1983
14. 刘徽《九章算术注》中的定义及演绎逻辑试析	《自然科学史研究》第2卷第3期	1983
	1983年《中国哲学年鉴》摘录	1983
	《郭书春数学史自选集》上册 山东科学技术出版社	2018
15. 关于刘徽研究中的几个问题	《自然科学史研究》第2卷第4期	1983
	《郭书春数学史自选集》上册 山东科学技术出版社	2018
16. 刘徽思想探源	《中国哲学史研究》1984年第2期	1984
	《郭书春数学史自选集》上册 山东科学技术出版社	2018
17.《九章算术·方程章》刘徽注新探	《自然科学史研究》第4卷第1期	1985
	《郭书春数学史自选集》上册 山东科学技术出版社	2018
18. 中国古代数学与封建社会刍议	《科学技术与辩证法》1985年第2期	1985
	《中国改革开放二十年》(下) 中央文献出版社	1999

续表

题目	著作、报刊、出版社	出版时间
	《郭书春数学史自选集》下册 山东科学技术出版社	2018
19.《九章算术》勾股章的校勘和刘徽勾股理论系统初探	《自然科学史研究》第4卷第4期	1985
	《郭书春数学史自选集》上册 山东科学技术出版社	2018
20. 略谈世界数学重心的三次大转移	《科学技术与辩证法》1986第1期	1986
	《郭书春数学史自选集》下册 山东科学技术出版社	2018
21. 关于《九章算术》的版本	《数理化信息》1986第2期 辽宁教育出版社	1986
22. 从刘徽《九章算术注》看我国对祖暅公理的认识过程	《辽宁师大学报（数学史专辑）》	1986
	《郭书春数学史自选集》上册 山东科学技术出版社	2018
23. Neuf chapitre sur l'art du calcul methode défausse position, proède（合作者林力娜）	Mathématique au fil des Ages de l'excèdent et du déficif Ganthier-villars	1987
24. 试论刘徽的数学理论体系	《自然辩证法通讯》第9卷第2期	1987
	《郭书春数学史自选集》上册 山东科学技术出版社	2018
25. 关于武英殿聚珍版《九章算术》	《自然科学史研究》第6卷第2期	1987
26. 王国维一失	《古籍整理研究学刊》1987年第2期	1987
27. 刘徽与王莽铜斛	《自然科学史研究》第7卷第1期	1988
	《郭书春数学史自选集》上册 山东科学技术出版社	2018
28. 关于中国古代数学哲学的几个问题	《自然辩证法研究》第4卷第3期	1988
	《郭书春数学史自选集》下册 山东科学技术出版社	2018
29. 贾宪《黄帝九章算经细草》初探	《自然科学史研究》第7卷第4期	1988
	《郭书春数学史自选集》下册 山东科学技术出版社	2018
30. 希腊与中国古代数学比较刍议	《自然辩证法研究》第4卷第6期	1988
	《郭书春数学史自选集》下册 山东科学技术出版社	2018
31. 贾宪的数学成就	《自然辩证法通讯》第11卷第1期	1989
	《郭书春数学史自选集》下册 山东科学技术出版社	2018
32. 关于《九章算术》的编纂	《中国科学技术史国际学术讨会》 中国科学技术出版社	1990
	《郭书春数学史自选集》上册 山东科学技术出版社	2018
33. 李籍《九章算术音义》初探	《自然科学史研究》第8卷第3期	1989
	《郭书春数学史自选集》上册 山东科学技术出版社	2018
34. 评戴震对《九章算术》的整理	梅荣照主编《明清数学史论文集》 江苏教育出版社	1990

续表

题目	著作、报刊、出版社	出版时间
	《郭书春数学史自选集》上册 山东科学技术出版社	2018
35. 刘徽	吴文俊主编《世界著名科学家传记·数学家Ⅰ》 科学出版社	1990
	吴文俊主编《世界著名数学家传记》（上） 科学出版社	1995
36.《九章筭术》版本卮言	《第二届科学史研讨会（台北1989）汇刊》	1991
	郭书春汇校《九章筭术增补版·附录三》	2004
	郭书春汇校《九章筭术新校·附录三》	2014
	《郭书春数学史自选集》上册 山东科学技术出版社	2018
37. 中国古代数学理论奠基者刘徽	许义夫 张殿民 郭书春主编《山东古代科学家》 山东教育出版社	1992
38. 数学大师秦九韶（合作者王渝生）	许义夫 张殿民 郭书春主编《山东古代科学家》 山东教育出版社	1992
39. 刘徽祖籍考	《自然辩证法通讯》第14卷第3期	1992
	《郭书春数学史自选集》上册 山东科学技术出版社	2018
40. 关于《九章筭术》的校勘	薄树人主编《中国科技史探胜》 科学出版社	1992
	郭书春汇校《九章筭术增补版·附录三》	2004
	郭书春汇校《九章筭术新校·附录三》	2014
	《郭书春数学史自选集》上册 山东科学技术出版社	2018
41. 中国古代数学哲学概述（合作者邹大海）	《辽宁教育学院学报》（增刊）	1992
42. 刘徽测望过泰山之高吗	《泰山研究论丛》（五） 青岛海洋大学出版社	1992
	《郭书春数学史自选集》上册 山东科学技术出版社	2018
43. 赵爽	杜石然主编《中国古代科学家》上册 科学出版社	1993
44. 刘徽	杜石然主编《中国古代科学家》上册 科学出版社	1993
45. 王孝通	杜石然主编《中国古代科学家》上册 科学出版社	1993
	郭书春《论中国古代数学家》 海豚出版社	2017
46. 贾宪	杜石然主编《中国古代科学家》下册 科学出版社	1993
47. 戴震	杜石然主编《中国古代科学家》下册 科学出版社	1993
48. 刘徽与先秦两汉学者	《中国哲学史》1993第2期	1993
	《郭书春数学史自选集》上册 山东科学技术出版社	2018

续表

题目	著作、报刊、出版社	出版时间
49. 中国古典数学的思维方式	苏才 武殿一主编《中国人传统思维方式新探》 辽宁教育出版社	1993
	《郭书春数学史自选集》下册 山东科学技术出版社	2018
50. 贾宪	解恩泽 徐本顺主编《世界数学家思想方法》 山东教育出版社	1993
	郭书春《论中国古代数学家》 海豚出版社	2017
51. 评宋景昌对《详解九章算法》的校勘	《自然科学史研究》第13卷第3期	1994
	《郭书春数学史自选集》下册 山东科学技术出版社	2018
52. 清代《九章算术》版本考	《文史》第40期 中华书局	1994
53. 秦九韶——将数学进之于道	李醒民主编《科学巨星》(6) 陕西人民出版社	1995
	《伟大的数学家秦九韶》(四川安岳秦九韶纪念馆)	2000
	郭书春《论中国古代数学家》 海豚出版社	2017
54. 中国古代的无穷小分割思想	《中国古代科技成就》(修订本) 中国青年出版社	1995
55. 应冷静客观地看待祖先的成就	《中国科学报》1996-01-29, 1996-01-31 第4版	1996
	《郭书春数学史自选集》下册 山东科学技术出版社	2018
56. 再论《九章筭术》的版本	李迪主编《第二届中国少数民族科技史国际学术讨论会论文集》 社会科学文献出版社	1996
	郭书春汇校《九章筭术增补版·附录三》	2004
	郭书春汇校《九章筭术新校·附录三》	2014
	《郭书春数学史自选集》上册 山东科学技术出版社	2018
57. 关于《九章算术》及其刘徽注的研究	《传统文化与现代化》1997年第1期	1997
	《郭书春数学史自选集》上册 山东科学技术出版社	2018
58. 张苍与《九章算术》	刘钝 韩琦主编《科史薪传》 辽宁教育出版社	1997
59. 《河防通议·算法门》初探	《自然科学史研究》第16卷第3期	1997
	李迪主编《第三届中国少数民族科技史国际学术讨论会论文集》 云南科学技术出版社	1998
	《郭书春数学史自选集》下册 山东科学技术出版社	2018
60. 《管子》与中国古代数学	《中国科技典籍研究——第一届中国科技典籍国际会议论文集》 大象出版社	1998
	《郭书春数学史自选集》下册 山东科学技术出版社	2018
61. 再论《九章算术》的校勘	《汉学研究》(台北)第16卷第1期	1998
	郭书春汇校《九章筭术增补版·附录三》	2004

续表

题目	著作、报刊、出版社	出版时间
	郭书春汇校《九章筭术新校·附录三》	2014
	中国科学院自然科学史研究所编《科学技术史研究六十年——中国科学院自然科学史研究所论文选》 中国科学技术出版社	2018
	《郭书春数学史自选集》上册 山东科学技术出版社	2018
62. 张苍	金秋鹏主编《中国科学技术史·人物卷》 科学出版社	1998
	郭书春《论中国古代数学家》 海豚出版社	2017
63. 刘徽	金秋鹏主编《中国科学技术史·人物卷》 科学出版社	1998
64. 李冶	金秋鹏主编《中国科学技术史·人物卷》 科学出版社	1998
	郭书春《论中国古代数学家》 海豚出版社	2017
65. 刘徽——总算术之根源	李醒民主编《科学巨星》(11) 陕西人民出版社	1998
	郭书春《论中国古代数学家》 海豚出版社	2017
66.《周髀算经》及其赵爽注选注(商高答周公问、陈子答荣方问、赵爽勾股圆方图注)	李文林主编《数学珍宝——历史文献精选·中国》 科学出版社	1998
	九章出版社	2000
67.《九章算术》及刘徽注、李淳风注选注 (分数四则运算、盈不足术、开方术、方程术与正负术、割圆术、刘徽原理、球体积公式与祖暅之原理)	李文林主编《数学珍宝——历史文献精选·中国》 科学出版社	1998
	九章出版社	2000
68.《孙子算经》选注(算筹记数法、孙子问题)	李文林主编《数学珍宝——历史文献精选·中国》 科学出版社	1998
	九章出版社	2000
69.《张丘建算经》——百鸡术注	李文林主编《数学珍宝——历史文献精选·中国》 科学出版社	1998
	九章出版社	2000
70. 贾宪:《黄帝九章算经细草》选注(贾宪三角、增乘开方法)	李文林主编《数学珍宝——历史文献精选·中国》 科学出版社	1998
	九章出版社	2000
71. 秦九韶:《数书九章》选注(大衍总数术、正负开方术)	李文林主编《数学珍宝——历史文献精选·中国》 科学出版社	1998
	九章出版社	2000
72. 李冶:《测圆海镜》——天元术注	李文林主编《数学珍宝——历史文献精选·中国》 科学出版社	1998
	九章出版社	2000
73. 朱世杰:《四元玉鉴》选注(四元术、垛积术、招差术)	李文林主编《数学珍宝——历史文献精选·中国》 科学出版社	1998
	九章出版社	2000

续表

题目	著作、报刊、出版社	出版时间
74.中国传统数学与微积分的建立	《第七届国际中国科学史会议论文集》 大象出版社	1999
	《郭书春数学史自选集》下册 山东科学技术出版社	2018
75.《算学宝鉴》面积问题试析	《珠算通讯》2000第1期（六盘水）	2000
	《王文素与〈算学宝鉴〉研究》 山西人民出版社	2002
	《郭书春数学史自选集》下册 山东科学技术出版社	2018
76.数学史研究大有作为	《自然辩证法通讯》第22卷第3期	2000
	《郭书春数学史自选集》下册 山东科学技术出版社	2018
77.从面积问题看《算学宝鉴》在中国传统数学中的地位	《汉学研究》（台北） 第18卷第2期	2000
78.关于《算经十书》的校勘	《文史》第4期 中华书局	2000
	华觉明主编《中国科技典籍研究—— 第二届中国科技典籍国际会议论文集》 大象出版社	2003
	《郭书春数学史自选集》下册 山东科学技术出版社	2018
79.祖冲之逝世1500周年国际学术研讨会闭幕辞	《郭书春数学史自选集》下册 山东科学技术出版社	2018
80.关于中国传统数学的"术"	林东岱 李文林 虞言林主编《数学与数学机械化》 山东教育出版社	2001
	《郭书春数学史自选集》下册 山东科学技术出版社	2018
On the Procedures in Traditional Chinese Mathematical Works Proceedings of the Fourth International Symposium on The History of Mathematics and Mathematical Education Using Chinese Characters	日本前桥工业大学	2001
81.《筭数书》校勘	《中国科技史料》第22卷第3期	2001
	《郭书春数学史自选集》下册 山东科学技术出版社	2018
82.是《缀术》全错不通还是王孝通莫能究其深奥	《数学史研究》第7期	2001
	《郭书春数学史自选集》下册 山东科学技术出版社	2018
83.开辟数学史研究的新天地	《中华科技史同好会会刊》（台北）	2002
84.试论《筭数书》的理论贡献与编纂	《法国汉学》第6期 中华书局	2002
	《郭书春数学史自选集》下册 山东科学技术出版社	2018
85.传统数学思想	杨文衡 陈美东 郭书春合著《国学举要·术卷》 湖北教育出版社	2002

续表

题目	著作、报刊、出版社	出版时间
86. 为数学而数学——刘徽科学价值观探析(合作者傅海伦)	《自然辩证法通讯》第25卷第1期	2003
87. 试论《筭数书》的数学表达方式	《中国历史文物》2003第2期	2003
	《中国科技典籍研究——第三届中国科技典籍国际会议论文集》大象出版社	2006
	《郭书春数学史自选集》下册 山东科学技术出版社	2018
88.《筭数书》初探	《国学研究》(北京大学)第11期	2003
	《郭书春数学史自选集》下册 山东科学技术出版社	2018
89.《算数书》中国数学パテダイム(与城地茂合作)	数学ヤミナー第42(9)期	2003
90. 中国传统数学在世界数学史上的地位	《高等数学研究》第6卷第3期	2003
91.《算数书》に関する问题点(城地茂译)	《和算研究所纪要》No 5	2004
92.《筭数书》与《算经十书》比较研究	《自然科学史研究》第23卷第2期	2004
	《郭书春数学史自选集》下册 山东科学技术出版社	2018
93. 秦九韶《数书九章·序》注释	《湖州师范学院学报》第26卷第1期	2004
	《郭书春数学史自选集》下册 山东科学技术出版社	2018
94. 对增乘开方及其相关问题的再探讨(与段耀勇合作)	《广西民族学院学报》第10卷第2期	2004
95. 中国传统数学的发展与儒学	《中国儒学年鉴》	2005
	《郭书春数学史自选集》下册 山东科学技术出版社	2018
96. 中国传统数学的机械化	《自然国学》	2006
97. 中国传统数学与数学机械化	《曲阜师大学报》(自)第32卷第3期	2006
	《郭书春数学史自选集》下册 山东科学技术出版社	2018
	纪志刚,徐泽林主编《论吴文俊的数学史业绩》上海交通大学出版社	2019
98. 关于《算经十书》的几个问题	《中华科技史学会会刊》第10期(台北)	2006
	《郭书春数学史自选集》下册 山东科学技术出版社	2018
99. 中国古代数学部分	艾素珍 宋正海主编《中国科学技术史·年表卷》科学出版社	2006
100. 关于刘徽的割圆术	《高等数学研究》第10卷第1期	2007
101. 数学在皇朝末世政治斗争漩涡中的尴尬——从南宋数学大师秦九韶的遭遇谈起	《宋代国家文化中的科学》中国科学技术出版社	2007
	《郭书春数学史自选集》下册 山东科学技术出版社	2018
102. 尊重原始文献 避免以讹传讹	《自然科学史研究》第26卷第3期	2007
	《郭书春数学史自选集》下册 山东科学技术出版社	2018
103. 五十年来自然科学史研究所的数学史研究	《中国科技史杂志》第28卷第4期	2007

续表

题目	著作、报刊、出版社	出版时间
	《郭书春数学史自选集》下册 山东科学技术出版社	2018
104. 中国古代数学部分	金秋鹏主编《中国科学技术史·图录卷》 科学出版社	2008
105. 关于《筭数书》与《九章筭术》的关系	《曲阜师范大学学报》(自)第 34 卷第 3 期	2008
	《郭书春数学史自选集》下册 山东科学技术出版社	2018
106. 王莽铜斛与刘歆圆周率刍议	《中国计量》2008 第 10 期	2008
	国家质检总局计量司:《计量史话》 中国计量出版社	2010
107. 中国科学技术史研究概况	张海鹏主编《中国历史学 30 年》 中国社会科学出版社	2008
An Overview of Recent Chinese Research on the History of Science and Technology	THIRTY YEARS OF HISTORY STUDIES Edited by ZHANG Haipeng Translated by LI Wenzhong and WU Jinshan 中国社会科学出版社 and M. C. M. Prime(USA)	2015
108. 中国传统数学分期刍议	《中华科技史学会会刊》(台北)	2008 第 12 期
109. 走进中国数学史——冯立升访郭书春	《广西民族大学学报》 (自)第 14 卷第 4 期	2008
	万辅彬、黄祖宾主编《史家心语—当代科技史名家访谈录》 科学出版社	2013
110. 关于中国数学史的几个问题刍议	《广西民族大学学报》 (自)第 14 卷第 4 期	2008
	中国人民大学书报资料中心《科学技术哲学》 2009 第 5 期转载	2009
	《郭书春数学史自选集》下册 山东科学技术出版社	2018
111. 中国传统数学发展的基本概况与特点	《走进殿堂的中国古代科技史》 上海交通大学出版社 [2010 年获第三届中华优秀出版物图书奖]	2009,2010
Overview and Features of the Developmengt of Traditional Chinese Mathematics	A History of Chinese Science and Technology vol. 1 p203－233 上海交通大学出版社	2015
112. 九章算术、刘徽与宋元数学	《走进殿堂的中国古代科技史》 上海交通大学出版社 [2010 年获第三届中华优秀出版物图书奖]	2009,2010
Nine Chapter on MathematicalArt , Liu Hui and the Mathematics in the Song and Yuan Dynasties	A History of Chinese Science and Technology vol. 1 p235－268 上海交通大学出版社	2015
113. 重温吴先生关于现代画家对古代数学家造像问题的教诲—庆祝吴文俊先生 90 华诞	《HPM 通讯》(台北)	2009
	《内蒙古师范大学学报》(数学史专辑)第 38 卷第 5 期 2009	

续表

题目	著作、报刊、出版社	出版时间
	《郭书春数学史自选集》下册 山东科学技术出版社	2018
	纪志刚　徐泽林主编《论吴文俊的数学史业绩》 上海交通大学出版社	2019
114. 九章筭术与刘徽	香港教育学院数学教育会议论文集	2009
115. 中国宋元时期重要数学发展与思想	香港教育学院数学教育会议论文集	2009
116. 重新品评秦九韶	《宋史研究论丛》(10) 河北大学出版社	2009
	《郭书春数学史自选集》下册 山东科学技术出版社	2018
117.《筭数书》"斩都"求积公式造术初探	《曲阜师范大学学报》(自)第 36 卷第 3 期	2010
	《郭书春数学史自选集》下册 山东科学技术出版社	2018
118.《九章筭术》正负术"无人"辨	《自然科学史研究》第 29 卷第 4 期	2010
	中国人民大学书报资料中心 《科学技术哲学》2011 年第 3 期转载	2011
	《郭书春数学史自选集》上册 山东科学技术出版社	2018
119. 科技古籍整理刍议	《古籍整理出版情况简报》第 479 期	2011
	《郭书春数学史自选集》下册 山东科学技术出版社	2018
120. 对经典文献的整理与注释——研治中国数学史方法的几点体会	陈久金　万辅彬编《中国科技史研究方法》 黑龙江人民出版社	2011
121. 中国传统数学与和	《青岛科技大学学报》(社)第 27 卷第 4 期	2011
	《郭书春数学史自选集》下册 山东科学技术出版社	2018
122. 中国古代数学：不仅重"实用"，而且有"理论"——郭书春先生谈《中国科学技术史·数学卷》	《中华读书报》2011 年 9 月 7 日	2011
	《郭书春数学史自选集》下册 山东科学技术出版社	2018
123. 山东古代对数学天文学的伟大贡献	《中西文化会通的先驱——全国首届薛凤祚学术思想研讨会论文集，2010》 齐鲁书社	2011
124. 关于《九章筭术》之文津阁本	《自然科学史研究》第 31 卷第 4 期	2012
	郭书春汇校《九章筭术新校·附录三》	2014
	《郭书春数学史自选集》上册 山东科学技术出版社	2018
125. 关于天元术的发展的几个问题	《高等数学研究》第 16 卷第 4 期	2013
	《郭书春数学史自选集》下册 山东科学技术出版社	2018
126. The Nine Chapter on Mathematical Procedures and Liu Hui Mathematical Theory（九章算术和刘徽的数学理论，陈建平译）	*Seki, Founder of Modern Mathematics in Japan A Commemoration on His Tercentenary* Springer Volume 39	2013

续表

题目	著作、报刊、出版社	出版时间
	《郭书春数学史自选集》上册 山东科学技术出版社	2018
127.认真研读原始文献——从事中国数学史研究的体会	《自然科学史研究》第32卷第3期	2013
	《郭书春数学史自选集》下册 山东科学技术出版社	2018
128.重视科技古籍的整理出版	《古籍整理出版情况简报》第512、513期	2013
129.中国古代最伟大的数学家刘徽——为纪念刘徽注《九章算术》1750周年而作	《数学文化》第4卷第4期	2013
130.《九章算术》、刘徽和戴震	《中国典籍与文化》（七） 国家图书馆出版社	2013
131.吴文俊与中国数学史	《吴文俊学术思想传承与创新》附录 《中国科学与工程杰出人物案例研究》第一章 科学出版社	2014
132.战国秦汉数学简牍发现之意义刍议	Research Institute for Mathematical Sciences Kyoto University *Study of the History of Mathematics* edited by Tsukane Ogawa June 2014	2014
	《郭书春数学史自选集》下册 山东科学技术出版社	2018
133.刘徽的籍贯是邹平	《滨州学院学报》第30卷第6期	2014
134.《鲁久次问数于陈起》笔谈	《自然科学史研究》第34卷第2期	2015
	《郭书春数学史自选集》下册 山东科学技术出版社	2018
135.《九章算术》与刘徽	《中国科学技术通史》Ⅰ 上海交通大学出版社	2015
136.中国古典数学的发展路径、方法论和价值取向	汝信 李惠国主编《中国古代科技文化及其现代启示》第3章 中国社会科学出版社	2016
137.吴敬《九章比类》与贾宪《九章细草》比较刍议	《自然科学史研究》第35卷第2期	2016
	《郭书春数学史自选集》下册 山东科学技术出版社	2018
138.金元数学与全真道	*Journal for History of Mathematics*, Vol29 No.6（韩国），1−9	2016
	《郭书春数学史自选集》下册 山东科学技术出版社	2018
139.十进位值制记数法和筹算	冯立昇主编《中国三十大发明》 大象出版社 ［2019年获第七届中华优秀出版物提名奖］	2017
140.宋元数学与道家和道教	吕变庭主编《科学史研究论丛》第3辑 科学出版社	2017
141.李善兰翻译的微分积分与《九章算术》	丘成桐等主编《数学与人文》第22期《数学竞赛和数学研究》 高等教育出版社	2017
142.新中国科学技术史研究70年（与郭金海合作）	中国历史研究院首届新时代史学理论论坛论文集（上册）	2019
143.关于《中华大典·数学典》	《内蒙古师范大学学报》（自汉）第48卷第六期	2019
	丘成桐等主编《数学与人文》第30辑 《数学随想》高等教育出版社	2020

续表

题目	著作、报刊、出版社	出版时间
144. 继承刘徽、祖冲之的科学精神	吕变庭主编《科学史研究论丛》第 5 辑 科学出版社	2019
145.《中华大典·数学典》编纂漫谈（与高峰合作）	自然科学史研究 2020 第 39 期增刊	2020
146. 商高、陈子与《周髀算经》	丘成桐等主编《数学与人文》第三十一集《数学与物理》 高等教育出版社	2021
147. 关于中国古典数学认识刍议	在第 26 届国际科学史大会（布拉格 2021） 中国古典数学专题组的报告 收入纪志刚 徐泽林主编《数学·历史·教育 ——三维视角下的数学史》 大连理工大学出版社	2022
148. 从"脱毛"到"入门"	吕变庭主编《科学史研究论丛》第 8 辑 科学出版社	2022
149. 宋元筹算高潮奠基者贾宪及其数学成就	吕变庭主编《科学史研究论丛》第 8 辑 科学出版社	2022

（四）中国大百科全书、辞海与其他辞典

题目	出版单位	出版时间
1. 数学词典部分中国数学史释文	上海辞书出版社	1987
2. 中国大百科全书·数学卷（第一版）·笛卡儿	中国大百科全书出版社	1988
3. 中国大百科全书·数学卷（第一版）·贾宪三角	中国大百科全书出版社	1988
4. 中国大百科全书·数学卷（第一版）·柯瓦列夫斯卡娅	中国大百科全书出版社	1988
5. 中国大百科全书·数学卷（第一版）·刘徽	中国大百科全书出版社	1988
6. 中国大百科全书·数学卷（第一版）·秦九韶	中国大百科全书出版社	1988
7. 中国大百科全书·数学卷（第一版）·增乘开方法	中国大百科全书出版社	1988
8. 中国大百科全书·数学卷（第二版）全部中国数学史类撰写修改	中国大百科全书出版社	2009
9. 辞海第五版全部中国数学史类撰写修改	上海辞书出版社	1999
10. 大辞海·数理化力学卷中国数学史类撰写	上海辞书出版社	2005
11. 辞海第六版全部中国数学史类撰写修改	上海辞书出版社	2009
12. 中学数学教师手册（部分条目）	上海教育出版社	1985
13. 中国历代文献精粹大典·科技卷·数学	学苑出版社	1990
14. 中国历代文献精粹大典·人物卷·数学家	学苑出版社	1990
15. 数学词典（部分中国数学史条目）	上海辞书出版社	1987,1992
16. 世界当代文化名人辞典（中国数学家）	北京燕山出版社	1992
17. 历史大辞典·科技卷中国数学史条目	上海辞书出版社	2000
18. 中国古代数学（84 条）多媒体文本	香港中国文化研究院	2002
19. 宋代文化史大辞典数学天文历法条目	汉语大辞典出版社	2006
20. 刘徽	数学セミナ编集部《100 人の数学者——古代キリッャから现代まご》 日本评论社	2017

续表

题目	出版单位	出版时间
21.祖冲之　祖暅之	数学セミナ编集部《100人の数学者—古代キリッャから现代まご》日本评论社	2017

(五)序跋

书名	出版单位	出版时间
1.《科技史文集·数学史专辑》编后记	上海科学技术出版社	1982
2.以刘徽的精神研究刘徽——《古代世界数学泰斗刘徽》代后记	古代世界数学家数学泰斗刘徽 山东科学技术出版社	1992
	《古代世界数学泰斗刘徽》修订本 台北明文书局	1995
	《古代世界数学泰斗刘徽》再修订本 山东科学技术出版社	2013
	《郭书春数学史自选集》上册 山东科学技术出版社	2018
3.《山东古代科学家》前言	山东教育出版社	1992
4.《中国科学技术典籍通汇·数学卷》叙	郭书春主编《中国科学技术典籍通汇·数学卷》河南教育出版社 大象出版社	1993,2002,2015
5.周瀚光《先秦数学与诸子哲学》序	上海古籍出版社	1994
6.点校《算经十书》前言	郭书春 刘钝点校《算经十书》辽宁教育出版社	1998
7.关于《算经十书》	郭书春 刘钝点校《算经十书》繁体字修订本 台北九章出版社	2001
8.《李俨钱宝琮科学史全集》前言	杜石然 郭书春 刘钝主编《李俨钱宝琮科学史全集》辽宁教育出版社	1998
	《郭书春数学史自选集》下册 山东科学技术出版社	2018
9.严敦杰《祖冲之科学著作校释》后记	辽宁教育出版社	2000
	《郭书春数学史自选集》下册 山东科学技术出版社	2018
10.傅海伦《传统文化与数学机械化》序	科学出版社	2003
11.陈仁政《说不尽的π》代前言	科学出版社	2005
12.杨江峰《蓦然回首》序	中国评论学术出版社	2006
13.刘五然等《算学宝鉴校注》序	科学出版社	2008
	《上海珠算心算》第218期	2009
14.乌云其其格《和算的发生》序	上海辞书出版社	2009
15.《中国科学技术史·数学卷》前言	科学出版社	2010,2017
16.《古代世界数学泰斗刘徽》再版前言	山东科学技术出版社	2013
17.郭金海《中国院士史》序	湖南教育出版社	2013
18.来自中科院的第一封贺信	《珠算与珠心算》2014年第1期	2014
19.董杰《大测》校释序	上海交通大学出版社	2014

续表

书名	出版单位	出版时间
20.论中国古代数学家·序	郭书春《论中国古代数学家》海豚出版社	2017
	丘成桐等主编《数学与人文》第30辑《数学随想》高等教育出版社	2020
21.周瀚光文集序	上海社会科学出版社	2017
22.严敦杰《祖冲之科学著作校释》整理弁言	山东科学技术出版社	2017
23.让科学史走出书斋	中国科学院主管中国科学报社主办《科学新闻》总第541期	2017
24.《中华大典·数学典》序	《中华大典·数学典》山东教育出版社	2018
25.《数学典·中国传统算法分典》说明	《中华大典·数学典》山东教育出版社	2018
26.关于《九章算术》——写在中法对照《九章算术》入选改革开放40周年引才引智成果展览之后	《金胶州》2018年7月6日第8版《书香》	2018
27.中法对照《九章算术》出版背后	《中国科学报》第7版	2018—08—03
28.郭书春数学史自选集·自序	山东科学技术出版社	2018
29.严敦杰《祖冲之科学著作校释》增补重印后记	山东科学技术出版社	2021
30.钱宝琮《中国数学史话》再版序	上海科学技术出版社	2023

（六）翻译

题目	出版单位	出版时间
1.公元三世纪刘徽关于锥体体积的推导	《科学史译丛》	1980第2期
英文，D. B. Wagner(华道安)：An Early Chinese Derivation of the Volume of a Pyramid: Liu Hui, Third Century A. D. Hitoria Mathematica, 1979, N6		
2.关于现代几何学研究的比较考察（埃尔朗根纲领）[法文，F. Klein(克莱因)：Le Programme d'Erlangen 与何绍庚合作 英文]	《数学史译文集》上海科学技术出版社	1981
埃尔朗根纲领（Erlangen Progam-A Comparative Review of Recent Rescarches in Geometry）[法文，与何绍庚合作 英文，(德)F. Klein(克莱因)：Le Programme d'Erlangen]	大连理工大学出版社	2021
3.关于科学史问题·微积分的诞生	《数学史译文集》上海科学技术出版社	1981
法文，J. Hadamard(阿达玛)：Oeuvres de Jacque Hadamard, vol Ⅳ pp. 267—2271		
4.关于中国数学史的新研究	《科学史译丛》	1983第4期
法文，(苏)尤什凯维奇，原载 Revue d'Histoire des sciences, vol 35, N.4(1982)		
5.亨利·邦加雷和数学	《数学史译文集续集》上海科学技术出版社	1985
法文，J. Hadamard(阿达玛)：Oeuvres de Henri Poincaré, tome Ⅺ)		
6.柯西和无穷小	《数学史译文集续集》上海科学技术出版社	1985
法文，菲希尔原著，Historia Mathematica vol 5 N3, 1978		

续表

题目	出版单位	出版时间
7. 达郎贝尔著作中偏微分方程论的创立和发展 法文,(苏)杰米多夫,原载 *Revue d'Histoire des sciences*, vol 35, N(1982)	《科学史译丛》 1987 第 2—3 期	1987
8. 数 π 在中国的历史 法文,(法)C. Jami(詹嘉玲),原载 *Archive for History of Exact Science*, vol 38, N1(1988)	《科学史译丛》 1989 第 1—2 期	1989
9. 业余学者的宗师——费马 英文,(美)T. Bell(贝尔):*Men of Mathematics*	《大数学家》 台北九章出版社	1998
10. 数学与风车——柯西 英文,(美)T. Bell(贝尔):*Men of Mathematics*	《大数学家》 台北九章出版社	1998
11. 高等数学基本教程・1 代数 与胡作弦合作,(法)J. 奎奈:*Cours élémentaires de mathématiques supérieurs*, 1 Algèbre (dunod,1976)	高等教育出版社	1983
12. 高等数学基本教程・3 积分与级数 与唐兆亮合作,(法)J. 奎奈:*Cours élémentaires de mathématiques supérieurs*, 3 Calcul integral et séries (dunod,1976)	高等教育出版社	1989

(七)古算经提要

书名	出版单位	出版时间
1.《九章算术》提要	《中国科学技术典籍通汇・数学卷》第 1 册 河南教育出版社 大象出版社	1993 2002,2015
2.《详解九章算法》提要	《中国科学技术典籍通汇・数学卷》第 1 册 河南教育出版社 大象出版社	1993 2002,2015
3.《谢察微算经》提要	《中国科学技术典籍通汇・数学卷》第 1 册 河南教育出版社 大象出版社	1993 2002,2015
4.《算学源流》提要	《中国科学技术典籍通汇・数学卷》第 1 册 河南教育出版社 大象出版社	1993 2002,2015
5.《详明算法》提要	《中国科学技术典籍通汇・数学卷》第 1 册 河南教育出版社 大象出版社	1993 2002,2015
6.《永乐大典算法》提要	《中国科学技术典籍通汇・数学卷》第 1 册 河南教育出版社 大象出版社	1993 2002,2015
7.《诸家算法及序记》提要	《中国科学技术典籍通汇・数学卷》第 1 册 河南教育出版社 大象出版社	1993 2002,2015
8.《九章算法比类大全》提要	《中国科学技术典籍通汇・数学卷》第 2 册 河南教育出版社 大象出版社	1993 2002,2015

续表

书名	出版单位	出版时间
9.《算法指南》提要	《中国科学技术典籍通汇·数学卷》第 2 册 河南教育出版社 大象出版社	1993 2002,2015
10.《九章算术细草图说》提要	《中国科学技术典籍通汇·数学卷》第 4 册 河南教育出版社 大象出版社	1993 2002,2015
11.《海岛算经细草图说》提要	《中国科学技术典籍通汇·数学卷》第 4 册 河南教育出版社 大象出版社	1993 2002,2015
12.《辑古算经考注》提要	《中国科学技术典籍通汇·数学卷》第 5 册 河南教育出版社 大象出版社	1993 2002,2015
13.《艺游录》提要	《中国科学技术典籍通汇·数学卷》第 5 册 河南教育出版社 大象出版社	1993 2002,2015
14.《四元玉鉴细草》提要	《中国科学技术典籍通汇·数学卷》第 5 册 河南教育出版社 大象出版社	1993 2002,2015
15. 中华名著要籍精诠·《九章算术》	中国广播电视出版社	1994
16. 中华名著要籍精诠·《海岛算经》	中国广播电视出版社	1994
17. 中华名著要籍精诠·《孙子算经》	中国广播电视出版社	1994
18. 中华名著要籍精诠·《夏侯阳算经》	中国广播电视出版社	1994
19. 中华名著要籍精诠·《张丘建算经》	中国广播电视出版社	1994
20. 中华名著要籍精诠·《数术记遗》	中国广播电视出版社	1994
21. 中华名著要籍精诠·《缉古算经》	中国广播电视出版社	1994
22. 中华名著要籍精诠·《算经十书》	中国广播电视出版社	1994
23. 中华名著要籍精诠·《数书九章》	中国广播电视出版社	1994
24. 中华名著要籍精诠·《测圆海镜》	中国广播电视出版社	1994
25. 中华名著要籍精诠·《益古演段》	中国广播电视出版社	1994
26. 中华名著要籍精诠·《详解九章算法》	中国广播电视出版社	1994
27. 中华名著要籍精诠·《杨辉算法》	中国广播电视出版社	1994
28. 中华名著要籍精诠·《算学启蒙》	中国广播电视出版社	1994
29. 中华名著要籍精诠·《四元玉鉴》	中国广播电视出版社	1994
30. 中华名著要籍精诠·《九章算法比类大全》	中国广播电视出版社	1994
31. 中华名著要籍精诠·《算法统宗》	中国广播电视出版社	1994

(八)评论、书评、书讯

评论、书评、书讯	出版单位	出版时间
1.《科技史文集·数学史专辑》	《数学通报》	1982 第 4 期

续表

评论、书评、书讯	出版单位	出版时间
2. 一部数学内容丰富的数学史教科书	《科学史译丛》 《山西人民出版社四十年图书评论选》	1988 第 1 期
3. 评《李冶传》（孔国平）	《自然辩证法研究》第 5 卷第 4 期	1989
4. Guo Shuchun's Edition of the Jiu Zhang Suan Shu (Nine Chapters on the Mathematical Art)	Historia Mathematica	1992,19
5. 为了学术的传承——与郭书春、俞晓群对话	《光明日报》	1999－03－26
6. 鸿篇巨制 新意迭出（评袁运开等《中国科学思想史》）	《中华读书报》2001.3.14 第 24 版	2001
7. 老课题 新视角——评查有良等《杰出数学家秦九韶》	《HPM 通讯》（台湾师大） 第 7 卷第 11 期	2004
8. 对李约瑟研究定论的一个新突破	《中华读书报·书评周刊·科学》	2014－04－02

（九）科普

题目	出版单位	出版时间
1. 电脑的起源（上）（署名戴曙明，系杜石然、郭书春、何绍庚、李文林、袁向东等合作）	《自然辩证法通讯》	1979 年第 2 期
2. 抓住数学水妖的人	《中国妇女》	1981 第 3 期
3. 怎样计算门的高和宽	《中学生数学》	1983 第 2 期
4. 我国古代的算筹	《文物天地》	1983 第 3 期
5. 女数学家柯瓦列夫斯卡娅	《百科知识》	1983 第 3 期
6. 古代的度量衡	谭家健主编《古代文史哲知识概要》（教育管理刊授中心）	1986
	谭家健主编《古代文化知识概要》（中央民院汉语系函授教材丛书）	1987
	谭家健主编《中国文化史概要》 高等教育出版社	1988,1998
	繁体字本 台北明文书局	1989
	［2010 至 2018 年重印 36 次］	
7. 我国古代杰出的数学家刘徽	《中学生数学》	1987 第 2 期
8. 我国古代数学名著《九章算术》	《科技日报》	1987－10－07
9. 莱布尼茨发明二进制与《周易》无关	《科技日报》	1987－11－17
10. 中华古算 成就辉煌	《中国教育报》第 4 版	1992－08－11
11. "算经之首"——《九章算术》	《影响中国的 100 本书》 人民出版社	1993
12. 算学	《影响中国的 100 种文化》 人民出版社	1993
13. 刘徽测望泰山之高	《欧洲时报》（巴黎）	1993
14. 开创传统数学的新纪元——贾宪三角和增乘开方法	《大科技》	1999 第 4 期
15. 世界符号代数学的诞生——中国天元术	《大科技》	1999 第 7 期
16. 江河入海口第一桥——洛阳桥	《大科技》	1999 第 8 期
17. 世界法医学第一书——《洗冤录》	《大科技》	1999 第 11 期

续表

题目	出版单位	出版时间
18. 什么叫做勾股数组	《十万个为什么·数学》 上海少年儿童出版社	1999
19. 什么是贾宪三角	《十万个为什么·数学》 上海少年儿童出版社	1999
20. 《九章算术》是怎样一部书	《十万个为什么·数学》 上海少年儿童出版社	1999
21. 田忌怎样在赛马中取胜	《十万个为什么·数学》 上海少年儿童出版社	1999
22. 为什么"一尺之捶,日取其半"会"万世不竭"	《十万个为什么·数学》 上海少年儿童出版社	1999
23. 中国古代没有演绎逻辑吗	《中华读书报》	2000-07-26
24. 中国最早的数学著作《算数书》	《中华读书报》	
25. 中国古代数学(多媒体文本)	香港中国文化研究院	2002
26. 河南省校本课程"优因数学"学术研讨会上的发言	《上海珠算心算》第221期	2009
27. "和"与中国传统数学	《中国和学年鉴》 青岛出版社	2011
28. 中国传统数学系列·算术与中国传统数学	《中学生数理化》 2012第7-8期	2012
29. 中国传统数学系列·算经之首——《九章算术》	《中学生数理化》 2012第10期	2012
30. 中国传统数学系列·《九章算术》的编纂与张苍、耿寿昌	《中学生数理化》 2012第11期	2012
31. 中国传统数学系列·祖冲之父子	《中学生数理化》 2013第7-8期	2013
32. 中国古代最伟大的数学家:刘徽	《中国社会科学报》	2013-08-05
33. 刘徽实乃中国古代最伟大的数学家	《大众日报·自然国学》	2014-02-16
34. 科技古籍整理的出版现状亟待改变	《中国新闻出版报》	2014-02-17
35. 普及中国发明创造,任重而道远	《自然辩证法通讯》第36卷第4期	2014
36. 是"毒如蛇蝎"还是"瑰奇仁人"?	《中国社会科学报》	2014-02-17
37. 对珠算知识在世界范围的推广普及工作—在上海第二届"弘扬中华珠算文化"专题研讨会暨珠算申遗成功周年庆活动(2014-10-23)上的致辞	《珠算与珠心算》总第76期	2015

(十) 回忆

书名(文章名)	出版单位	出版时间
1. 我的恩师尤秉礼先生	《山东大学》校报	2016-07
2. 慈母永在身边	《母恩难忘》 中国妇女出版社	1996
3. 我的童蒙老师王秀峰	《恩师情长》 延边大学出版社	1998
	《胶州日报》	1999
4. 我的高中数学老师曹信忱	《青岛一中校友回忆录》	1999
	《刻骨铭心的忆念》 天马图书有限公司(香港)	2000

续表

书名(文章名)	出版单位	出版时间
5. 教诲与鞭策——庆祝吴先生90华诞	姜伯驹　李邦河　高小山　李文林主编《吴文俊与中国数学》八方文化创作室(新加坡)	2010
	李邦河　高小山　李文林主编《吴文俊全集》附卷—回忆与纪念科学出版社　龙门书局	2019
	《郭书春数学史自选集》下册山东科学技术出版社	2018
6. 自学成大师　风范泽后人——严敦杰先生二三事	《中国科学院自然科学史研究所所史资料集》所庆工作组	2016年12月
7. 我的早期经历与数学史研究工作——郭书春先生访谈录　郭金海访问整理	《中国科学院自然科学史研究所所史资料集》所庆工作组	2016年12月
8. 不能忘怀的几位老同志	《中国科学院自然科学史研究所所史资料集》所庆工作组	2016年12月
9. 我是怎样在《九章算术》和刘徽的研究中取得突破	《中国科学院自然科学史研究所所史资料集》所庆工作组	2016年12月
	《定格在记忆中的光辉70年》——献给中国科学院70周年华诞》第三章《在科研道路上砥砺前行》岳爱国主编科学出版社	2019
10. 汇校《九章算术》与李学勤先生	《广西民族大学学报(自)》第25卷第3期	2019
11. 无尽的怀念——《教诲与鞭策》(续)	纪志刚　徐泽林主编《论吴文俊的数学史业绩》上海交通大学出版社	2019
12. 四十余载《九章筭术》刘徽情	《广西民族大学学报(自)》第27卷第2期	2021
13. 十部算经的研究	徐泽林主编《与改革开放同行——中国数学史事业40年》东华大学出版社	2021
14. 我与数学史学会	徐泽林主编《与改革开放同行——中国数学史事业40年》东华大学出版社	2021
15. 从"脱毛"到"入门"(《从"脱毛"到"入门"》之摘要)	《科苑金秋》,2021增刊(总第98期)。中国科学院离退休干部工作局编《百年初心——中国科学院老党员故事选》	2021

内容简介

2021年，适逢我国著名数学史家郭书春先生八十华诞，先生的同仁、挚友、学生和再传弟子共同撰文庆祝，结集而成本文集。文集分为"学术论文""回忆与评价""访谈录"3部分。"学术论文"收录论文27篇，内容涉及中国数学史、中国天文学史、数学思想与数学起源、日本数学史、朝鲜数学史等研究领域。"回忆与评价"收录文章15篇，包括对先生的回忆和为《郭书春数学史自选集》所作的序、书评等，从中可见先生指导学生、参加学术活动，与同仁、挚友交往的点点滴滴，反映了学术界对先生研究工作的认识和评价。"访谈录"收录两篇对先生的访谈，展现了先生的人生历程与学术生涯。书末附有先生的论著目录，完整地呈现了自1978年以来先生的学术成果。

本书适合数学史学者、科学史专业学者、研究生，以及数学史爱好者阅读。

图书在版编目（CIP）数据

探史求新：庆祝郭书春先生八十华诞文集./邹大海，郭金海，田淼主编.—哈尔滨：哈尔滨工业大学出版社，2023.5

ISBN 978-7-5767-0228-6

Ⅰ.①探… Ⅱ.①邹…②郭…③田… Ⅲ.①郭书春—纪念文集 Ⅳ.①K826.11-53

中国版本图书馆 CIP 数据核字（2022）第 230685 号

TANSHI QIUXIN：QINGZHU GUOSHUCHUN XIANSHENG BASHI HUADAN WENJI

策划编辑	刘培杰　张永芹
责任编辑	李广鑫　聂兆慈
封面设计	孙茵艾
出版发行	哈尔滨工业大学出版社
社　　址	哈尔滨市南岗区复华四道街10号　邮编150006
传　　真	0451-86414749
网　　址	http://hitpress.hit.edu.cn
印　　刷	黑龙江艺德印刷有限责任公司
开　　本	880 mm×1 230 mm　1/16　印张33.25　插页8　字数1 080千字
版　　次	2023年5月第1版　2023年5月第1次印刷
书　　号	ISBN 978-7-5767-0228-6
定　　价	298.00元

（如因印装质量问题影响阅读，我社负责调换）